JUST COFFEE

CAFFEINE WITH A CONSCIENCE

Mark S. Adams & Tommy Bassett III

Just Trade Center
Douglas, Arizona / Agua Prieta, Sonora

Just Coffee: Caffeine with a Conscience
ISBN: 978-0-9817976-0-1
Price: $20.00

Manuscript and publishing consultants:
    Donald A. Tubesing & Nancy Loving Tubesing
Concept and copy editing: Merrill Kempfert
Book and cover design: Joy Morgan Dey
Photography: © 2008 by Tommy Bassett III
Café Justo logo design: Cornerstone MTM, Baltimore, Maryland

1   2   3   4   5   6   7   8   9

Published by:

Just Trade Center
826 E 11th St
Douglas, Arizona 85608

Phone: 520-364-9257
http://www.fronteradecristo.org

Library of Congress PCN # 2008935718

ISBN 9780981797601

Printed in Canada by Friesens

Acknowledgements

We are grateful to God for the amazing opportunity that we have had over the last six years to work with the coffee farmers of Salvador Urbina, Chiapas, in the creation of *Café Justo*. We are indebted to the farming families for sharing their hope, trust and perseverance with us.

We are very thankful for Donald Tubesing and Merrill Kempfert, our editors. They drank countless cups of *Café Justo* over many months as they helped blend our different writing styles and perspectives into a coherent whole without losing the distinctiveness of what we each bring to the table. They have cultivated this book with the same kind of hope, trust and perseverance that we have witnessed with the growers cultivating their delicious coffee.

We are also grateful for Nancy Loving Tubesing, who generously shared her talents developed through years of work in publishing to help refine the book in its final stages. Special thanks are due to Susan Rubendall for her grammar policing and to Joy Morgan Dey, whose extraordinary graphic design vividly brings this story to life.

Finally, we want to thank all the Just Coffee partners who have dared to believe that it is more positive, effective and satisfying to build just relationships across borders over a cup of coffee than to build more walls. We would like to list all the churches, organizations and individuals who have partnered with the farmers to make *Café Justo* a reality, but attempting to recognize everyone puts us at risk of forgetting someone. So we simply say,

**"We know who you are—and so do you!
Thanks from the bottom of our coffee cups."**

Finally, we want to thank everyone who will be catalysts for the expansion of the *Café Justo* model into the future. Blessings to you.

Dedication

This book is dedicated to the growers and customers of the *Café Justo/ Just Coffee* family of cooperatives who have worked together to create an economic model that fosters the growth of mutually beneficial relationships across borders.

Most of the original members (socios) of the Café Justo Cooperative.

Contents

Preface

It is an honor for us to write a history of the *Café Justo*/Just Coffee Cooperative, a successful grower-owned, entrepreneurial, international coffee business located in Salvador Urbina, Chiapas, and Agua Prieta, Sonora, Mexico.

This is a true parable of hope trumping desperation, viable living wages replacing debilitating poverty, and warm humor emerging from utter despair. It is the story of how excellent coffee, enjoyed daily across our continent, can be a means of rebuilding the roots of community while connecting us all to a grace-filled network of mutual support.

You will read here about friends who were determined to make a difference for their communities and the communities of others. You will see evidence of what can happen when equal measures of faith, prayer and perseverance are combined in a potent, healing and life-giving mixture.

The Just Coffee miracle emerges from the efforts of a handful of residents living on the U.S./Mexico border who were committed to making a difference and the dogged determination and skill of a community of visionary southern Mexican farmers caught in the despair of local and global economic realities that had trapped them in pervasive—and seemingly permanent—poverty. Everyone you read about in these pages recognized the problem, believed that a solution could be found and worked without fail to turn the dream into reality.

Today forty families in Salvador Urbina support themselves with a living wage that allows them to remain in their home village rather than leave for the U.S. in a desperate and dangerous scramble to survive—truly a miracle, whatever your definition of the word. Two other communities in Mexico have now organized Just Coffee cooperatives, and others are forming using the model described in this book, extending the miracle further and further.

Yet it is more than this. Virtually everyone involved in Just Coffee, at every level, has been in some way personally transformed by this whole experience. Of course, everyone connected to this project has gained an enormous understanding about coffee and its production. But we have also learned more than we ever expected about family and hope and faith and dreams and patience and peace. The experience has lifted our spirits and deepened our souls.

Like many who travel to developing countries, we thought there was a lot we were going to teach the Cooperative members about business dynamics, working together for a common goal and the policies and procedures of effective management. Instead, as is so often true, we are the ones who learned so much more than we taught.

The Cooperative members and the community of Salvador Urbina changed our lives and our perspectives in immeasurable ways we never dreamed possible. Although profit has been created and economic life improved in Salvador Urbina as a direct result of the success of the *Café Justo* Cooperative, the change in our lives and perspective, from having the opportunity to work with this community and these growers, is even more startling. We have realized they don't just grow coffee in this place—they also grow character and grace, love and friendship, bravery and hope.

Although this book focuses primarily on the innovative development and ultimate success of the Just Coffee business, it is as much a story about the growers and their relationships with each other and about the customers who purchase the coffee and benefit from the labors of their love. It is truly a dream come true—and a model for bringing people together—which is far more worthy of expansion than constantly extending and strengthening the border wall that only serves to further divide us from each other.

We begin the story with a letter sent to us from the coffee-growing families of the Cooperative in Salvador Urbina. It speaks powerfully for itself. From there, we set the context for Just Coffee, looking at what's happening at the U.S./Mexico border. After several chapters telling the story of the *Café Justo* Cooperative and how it quickly evolved into a successful, sustainable project, we summarize the principles that have led to its success and share our vision for replicating and expanding the model to other locations. We close with an invitation for you to join with us in creating humane, just and lasting solutions to the current immigration challenges.

Thank you for your interest in this book. We hope that once you have read it, you will pass it along to someone you know who would benefit from the practical message of hope that it offers. Then, why not sit down with others and discuss the book together as you enjoy the taste and aroma steaming up from a good cup of freshly brewed Just Coffee.

Mark Adams and Tommy Bassett
Douglas, Arizona, and Agua Prieta, Sonora, November 2008

———————————

Note to the reader:

*Throughout this book we have used **Café Justo** (ca-FAY HOOS-toe), the official incorporated name of the Salvador Urbina **Café Justo** Cooperative, to refer to the activities and decisions of the pilot Just Coffee project in Chiapas.*

*We continue to use the familiar English translation, **Just Coffee**, for the end product as marketed in the U.S. We do this to emphasize that the coffee was produced for the U.S. consumer market in a just and fair manner—and that the coffee is 100 percent pure and certified organic.*

*The Cooperative is currently moving back to using the term **Café Justo** in the U.S. market to help distinguish their coffee from several other "Just Coffee" organizations. Watch for the new look and name.*

*When we use the pronoun **we**, it signifies that the authors were actively involved or instrumental in what's being described.*

EJIDO SALVADOR URBINA MUNICIPIO DE CACAHOATAN CHIAPAS

8 DE MARZO 2008

A NUESTROS HERMANOS DE DIFERENTES IGLESIAS DE LOS ESTADOS UNIDOS, LES ESTAMOS ENVIANDO UN CORDIAL SALUDO DE PARTE DE LOS SOCIOS DE LA COOPERATIVA CAFÉ JUSTO DESEANDOLES QUE SE ENCUENTREN MUY BIEN, GOZANDO DE LAS BENDICIONES DE NUESTRO CREADOR.

EN ENERO DE 2003, DOS DE NUESTROS SOCIOS ESTUVIERON EN AGUA PRIETA PARA LA INAUGURACION DE NUESTRO TOSTADOR. NOS LLENAMOS CON MUCHO GOZO, EN AQUEL DIA, ESTANDO PRESENTE PARA EL NACIMIENTO DE UNA NUEVA ESPERANZA PARA NUESTRA COMUNIDAD DESPUES DE TANTOS ANOS DE SUFRIMIENTO

AHORA CASI SEIS ANOS DESPUES, LA ESPERANZA SE HA VUELTO UNA REALIDAD Y AHORA ESTAMOS VENDIENDO TANTO CAFÉ QUE HEMOS COMPRADO UN NUEVO TOSTADOR Y NECESITAMOS ANADIR MAS SOCIOS PARA COMPLETAR CON EL CAFÉ QUE ESTAMOS VENDIENDO.

LES DAMOS GRACIAS A DIOS Y A CADA UNO DE UDS. QUIENES ESTAN PARTICIPANDO EN YA NO SOLAMENTE EL NACIMIENTO DE ESPERANZA Y GOZO SINO TAMBIEN EN EL CRECIMIENTO Y EXPANSION DE ESTA ESPERANZA Y GOZO.

APROVECHAMOS ESTA OPORTUNIDAD PARA INVITARLES A UDS. NUESTROS COMPANEROS EN EL NORTE QUE LO SIGAMOS TRABAJANDO JUNTOS, PARA QUE NUESTRA COOPERATIVA SIGA CRECIENDO AUMENTANDO EN SOCIOS Y BENEFICIOS PARA NUESTRA COMUNIDAD, CON MAS OPORTUNIDADES DE EMPLEO PARA NUESTRA COMUNIDAD, Y PARA OTRAS COMUNIDADES PRODUCTORES DE CAFÉ.

RESPETUOSAMENTE,

COOPERATIVA CAFÉ JUSTO Y EL COMITÉ.

C. ERI CIFUENTES PEREZ, PRESIDENTE

C. REYNALDO CIFUENTES V., SECRETARIO

C. ILDEFONSO ORTIZ M., TESORERO

A Letter from the Growers

Salvador, Urbina, Cacahoatan, Chiapas
March 8, 2008

To our sisters and brothers of different churches and organizations in the United States:

We send you a cordial greeting on behalf of the members of the *Café Justo* Cooperative wishing that you are very well, rejoicing in the blessings of our Creator.

In January of 2003, two of our members were in Agua Prieta for the inauguration of our roaster. We were filled with much joy on that day being present for the birth of a new hope for our community after so many years of suffering.

Now almost six years later, hope has become a reality, and we have sold so much coffee that we have already had to buy a larger roaster, and we have had to add more members to the Cooperative to meet the demand for our coffee.

We give thanks to God and to each one of you who are participating not only for the birth of hope and joy but also in the growth and expansion of this hope and joy.

We take this opportunity to invite you, our partners in the north, to continue working with us so that our Cooperative will keep growing, adding members and benefits for our community, with more opportunity for employment in our community and other coffee growing communities.

Respectfully,

Cooperativa Café Justo and the committee

C. Eri Cifuentes Perez, President

C. Reynaldo Cifuentes Velazquez, Vice President

C. Ildefonso Ortiz Mejia, Treasurer

Café Justo Cooperatives

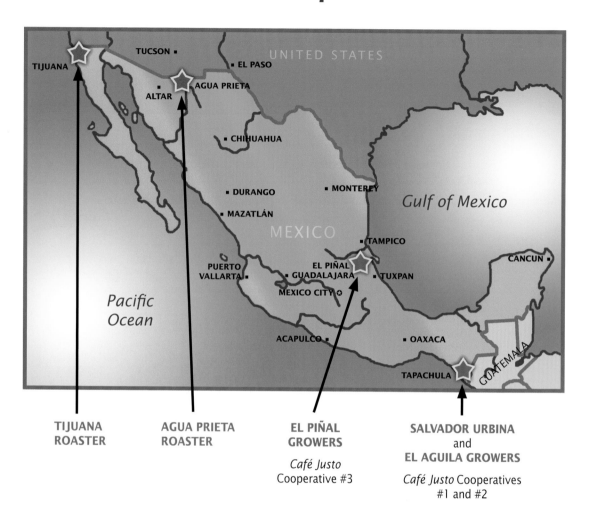

Aide Ruiz Perez

Alberto "Beto" Dominguez Sanchez

Andres Velazquez Verdugo

Coffee is our national misfortune.
—Brazilian coffee grower, 1934

The government of the United States does not always welcome the poor from other countries. In contrast to our welcoming symbol of freedom portrayed by the beacon of Lady Liberty and the famous poem by Emma Lazarus that reads, "Give me your tired, your poor, your huddled masses yearning to breathe free," our U.S. immigration policy prefers to welcome the rich, the rested and the educated who are yearning to make more money.

> **Just Coffee**—Coffee. It's only coffee. Yes . . . it's just coffee.
>
> **Just Coffee**—a great brew with world-class taste mixed with a spoon full of kindness and fairness—*Café Justo*.
>
> **Just Coffee**—a coffee with soul, filled with justice and love, fair for everyone—*Café Justo*.
>
> **Café Justo**—an instrument of grace and peace.

Young men heading north to the border past a hydration tank (marked with blue flag)

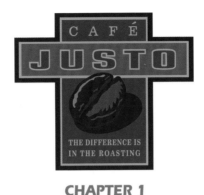

CHAPTER 1

Crisis at the U.S./Mexico Border
and One Just Response

What is really going on at the U.S./Mexico border? What's the story behind the negative headlines and alarmist talking heads on TV?

The Border Challenge

Every day thousands of healthy, mostly young people amass in Mexican towns near the U.S. border. Many have traveled up from the south in "border buses" that do a rousing business. They spend the afternoon stocking up on food and water. Then, in the evening, they slip into the darkness and begin their hide-and-seek scramble through the desert in an attempt to escape U.S. Border Patrol agents and cross into the United States.

Those caught are returned to Mexico, usually within hours. Of those not apprehended by authorities, tens of thousands have been robbed, many women raped, and more than four thousand have died attempting to make this risky trip across our southern desert.

Those who are successful fan out into towns and cities across our country and join America's

Migrant deaths by year ("4,500 and counting") as posted on the border fence between San Diego and Tijuana.

workforce, quickly blending in as invisibly as they can. In the past decade, millions of these hardworking "guest workers without papers" have settled in the United States.

The crisis and chaos of this situation has been analyzed and discussed ad nauseum at all levels of our government and news media, but to date no coherent or humane plan has emerged. While we argue about solutions, such as hiring more Border Patrol Agents and building additional border barriers, the humanitarian crisis continues to grow.

> The single most powerful reason that young male Mexicans leave the home they love . . . is that they need money to support their families.

What is creating and fueling this ongoing problem? And what, if anything, can be done about it? For years, faith-based groups and human rights organizations have been seeking humane answers to these questions.

Motivation for Crossing into the U.S.

Why do people who live south of our U.S. border leave their homes, their friends, aunts, uncles, siblings, parents—yes, even their wives and their children—and risk trekking their way into our country across the desolate and dangerous U.S./Mexico border beset with a multitude of hazards?

Why? Is it because we are such a great country with such warm and friendly people they just can't stand not to be with us? No, not really.

A few come for the adventure of the young man's quest. A few bring drugs. Most, however, come because they need work.

The single most powerful reason that young male Mexicans leave the home they love and, with great risk, cross the border into a strange land where they live in crowded apartments, work themselves to exhaustion at unenviable jobs, and spend lonely evenings thinking of home, is that they need money to support their families. When they cannot earn enough at home in Mexico to feed and clothe their children and to take care of their wives and parents, the most healthy and conscientious men come here to work.

Most of these undocumented "guest workers" save their money and send it home on a regular basis to support their extended families. One estimate from the Federal Reserve Bank of Dallas estimates that in 2003 over thirteen billion dollars was returned to the villages and towns of Mexico in this manner—approximately one-third of the entire Mexican economy.[1] Whatever the exact amount, one only

A 2003 T-shirt queries, "Would you walk across mountains and deserts for a job? 2300 migrants did and died."

has to witness the long lines at money exchanges on Friday afternoons to observe the intense energy these workers invest in completing their mission—that of forwarding their paychecks back home to their loved ones.

One Son's Story

We were once invited to be part of a Chiapas family's discussion as they struggled with the decision of whether or not to give their son permission to leave the family and find work in the U.S. The young man was determined and prepared to make this journey. Many of his immediate relatives were gathered for the discussion.

The son, stating his case, said he needed to go to the United States to help his family survive. He pointed out how the money he would earn could lift the entire family out of the poverty they had been struggling with for his entire life.

The grandparents said the people in the U.S. were cold and did not worship the same God as they do in their community.

The son responded, "But this is something I can do for the whole family."

The parents said it was too dangerous to cross the desert; many had died, and they had heard on the TV and radio about roving bands of robbers, the corrupt police and the terrible heat in the desert—a place where the son had no previous experience. His mother went on to say they had always found a way to get by, and their financial situation would certainly become better in time.

The young man assured all of them that he was stronger, smarter and more skilled than those who failed to make it, and that his leaving to find employment in the U.S. would bring honor and a brighter future to them all.

To this day we do not know how this story ends. We can only hope. We do know that this discussion takes place in thousands of village homes across Mexico every single day.

As you can imagine, it is difficult for a strong and loving, but economically disadvantaged, young person to stand by and watch the family suffer when there is no money for the basics, yet everyone on television is young, thin, happy, healthy and wealthy. Without other choices, the young or desperate go to find a better life. The possibility of earning as much in an hour as can be earned in a day, or sometimes a week, is too strong a force for many to resist, especially when work is available, and other family members are already settled and working in the U.S.

Economic Complicity North of the Border

Given the fact that such immigration is illegal, why do Americans perpetuate and even cooperate in this process? Why? Because it makes economic sense.

We save money by hiring immigrants. Our building contractors, our lumbering businesses and dairy farms, our office and hotel cleaning firms, our restaurants and landscaping operations, our agricultural enterprises and orchards enlist these workers for extremely low wages—and they pass on at least some of those savings to us.

Since an employer can go to jail for not paying income and Social Security taxes, almost all employers collect and pay these taxes. The Social Security revenue collected on these wages, however, enters our system without future repayment liability. Undocumented workers in the U.S. contribute an estimated seven billion dollars a year to our Social Security system. These workers will never receive Social Security checks from the system.[2]

Border Statistics

- 11.6 million unauthorized immigrants living in U.S. (Jan 2006)[3]

- U.S. Customs & Immigration Service is way behind on processing visa applications[4]

- Currently (July 2008) processing family-related applications filed in July 1992 through May 2002

- Currently (July 2008) processing employment-related applications filed in Oct 2001 through Dec 2003

- Funding for U.S. Border Patrol increased 519% over 16 years[5]

1986	$268 million
2002	$1.6 billion
2007?	

- Apprehension by Border Patrol of people entering the country illegally[6]

1990	1,169,939
2000	1,814,729
2003	1,046,422
2005	1,291,142
2007	1,100,000[7]

Note: According to Mexican Ambassador to the United States, Rico Ferrat, after 150 years of Mexican migration to the United States before the build-up of the wall, two million persons of Mexican descent were living in the U.S. After fifteen years of NAFTA and intense border build-up, there are now twelve million.[8]

It's not all that bad a deal for those of us who are beneficiaries of the immigrants' efforts.

For much of our country's history, the tough, boring, brutal work has been done for us on the cheap—by immigrants. Just try to get cement poured in Arizona or vegetables picked in California or fruit packed in Utah or timber cut in Oregon or your home cleaned on Long Island or harvests completed in corporate farms across the Midwest without help from a crew of our "friends" from south of the border who are hungry—hungry for work and often just plain hungry.

When good men need money to feed, clothe and house their families, they will go wherever they have to and do whatever they need to do to find a way of supporting their loved ones.

Additionally, when husbands and fathers can no longer return home easily once they have earned enough—or once the seasonal work is completed—because they will not be able to return safely to work for the next year, they end up staying long-term. Of course, when they stay permanently, their wives and children quite naturally try to follow the same dangerous path, crossing the border in whatever way they can to join their men and reunite their families. Even though this is a natural reaction, it simply adds to the difficulties and complicates the problem.

Border issues are complex. Proper registration, adequate border security and protection, and a process of legal order are needed. To be sure, at this writing in the fall of 2008, the system that manages the line in the sand between our two countries is flawed at best.

However, the single most powerful force driving the migration inward across our southern border remains economics. Until this issue is adequately resolved, hopefully humanely, we will not be able to change the realities at our border—no matter how high or how long the fence.

What if meaningful and sustainable work at a livable wage could be generated in the home village? What if there was some way for good people to support themselves among their families where they were born and raised?

What if enough people cared to ask these questions over and over again until they discovered some workable and effective solutions? But where does one start?

Mark's Story

I arrived on the border in 1998 to serve with Frontera de Cristo at Agua Prieta, Sonora, and Douglas, Arizona. Frontera de Cristo is one of six Presbyterian Bi-national Border Ministries along the U.S./Mexico border. It is a partnership between the National Presbyterian Church of Mexico and the Presbyterian Church USA.

By the time I arrived, Douglas and Agua Prieta had become the primary crossing point for persons entering the United States to work without proper papers. While the smuggling industry and growing law enforcement provided an economic boom for Douglas and Agua Prieta, these small communities on both sides of the border were nevertheless struggling.

The reality is that the thousands of persons crossing through the towns and surrounding areas were causing great stress on infrastructure and creating an increased level of fear in both communities. Neighborhoods were mushrooming in rapidly growing Agua Prieta; many homes were without drinkable water, electricity or adequate sewage. Health care services were woefully inadequate.

Seeing the suffering and experiencing the divisions that were fermenting on both sides of the border, Frontera de Cristo grappled with how we could respond more positively and faithfully to the growing crisis.

During the 1990s, Frontera de Cristo had been actively involved in offering humanitarian aid to the migrants from the south. *Lirio de los Valles* (Lily of the Valley) Presbyterian Church in Agua Prieta offered a spiritual and physical refuge for hundreds of migrants. Church families took people into their homes to live with them until the migrants could find places of their own. Frontera provided safe drinking water by truck to neighborhoods, advocated for homeless migrants sent back from the United States to Mexico and set up community health and dental screenings. All of these community service efforts were built primarily on the proverbial "give the hungry person a fish" model.

In 1998 we took a major step toward helping folks "learn how to fish" with our first ventures into economic development. We built a community center in Agua Prieta to house our education and health care outreach—and to provide a job training site for teaching salable skills. In 2000, Frontera de Cristo took another step, establishing a Micro-Credit Loan Program for small business startups that eventually funded 26 different enterprises from a beauty parlor to a printing business—thus giving these fledgling entrepreneurs a "lake of capital" in which to raise their own "fish."

Cosmetology school at the Agua Prieta Community Center.

During this period we also expanded the person-to-person aspect of our ministry, working with members of the First Presbyterian Church of Douglas and Lily of the Valley Presbyterian Church in Agua Prieta to build bridges of understanding across the border. Ranchers and Border Patrol agents, merchants and migrants, factory workers and farmers shared their perspectives as we searched for common understanding through our faith connections.

We invited groups from the U.S. to come to the border for immersion experiences, living with families in Agua Prieta, learning about the history of issues at the border, walking the path in the desert trod by hundreds of migrants every day, talking with ranchers, visiting the Border Patrol, working in one of our community service efforts and studying God's word on migration, justice, and love. Many were transformed by their experience and humbled by the complexity of the problems.

Do You Support Illegal Immigration?

One of my major jobs as a mission worker at the border was to help people reflect biblically and theologically about what it means to be a disciple of Jesus Christ—and how we are called to action—when borders divide us. In the process of building relationships and understanding across borders, I was often asked to interpret the complex issues underlying "illegal" immigration and help people understand the erratic history of U.S. border policy. A few people have expressed concern with the legality and morality of Frontera de Cristo's humanitarian aid to migrants.

> **Every time I go into the grocery store and buy fruit or vegetables, I am supporting illegal immigration. Every time I am traveling and stay in a motel, I am supporting illegal immigration.**

My response to the "illegal immigration" question came unexpectedly one evening when I was invited to speak to a group from a neighboring Presbyterian church in Arizona about the possibility of their youth engaging with our Lily of the Valley youth in some form of outreach ministry. A member of the group who was an active duty colonel in the U.S. Army, asked me a question with great intensity: "Mark, what I want to know is, do you support illegal immigration?"

To say the least, I was not prepared for that question, since I was there to talk about the joint outreach mission for our youth. However, I think my response, while not polished, captured some of the complexity of living a life of faith when borders divide:

"Colonel, I do not want to support illegal immigration, but I am afraid to say that I do almost every day."

"Every time I go into the grocery store and buy fruit or vegetables, I am supporting illegal immigration. Every time I am traveling and stay in a motel, I am supporting illegal immigration. Every time I eat brand name chicken, I am supporting illegal immigration. Every time I walk into a building that has been built in the last ten years, I am supporting illegal immigration. Every time I patronize a business that uses a landscaping service or janitorial service, and every time I play golf, I am supporting illegal immigration."

"Colonel, do you support illegal immigration?"

The question with which the colonel challenged me became the very questions that challenged her.

I could have added, every time we eat at a restaurant, we are supporting illegal immigration. Or every time we buy Store-Mart Coffee for $3 per pound, we are supporting illegal immigration. In other words, everywhere we turn we are receiving services from those who are undocumented workers and thus by default are supporting illegal immigration, whether we realize it or not.

Immigration Dilemma Provokes a Crisis of Conscience

Before the steep drop in the price paid for coffee beans in the 1980s and 1990s, there was no mass migration of people off the land in Salvador Urbina or from other coffee growing communities. In fact, coffee was such a good cash crop that the IMF and World Bank encouraged Vietnam to become a coffee exporting country through the cultivation of easy-to-grow Robusta coffee—using agro-chemicals. Vietnam's entrance into the coffee exporting world, as well as the mixing of higher quality, more expensive Arabica coffee with lower quality, cheaper Robusta, led to a sharp decline in prices paid to the coffee farmers.

> The dynamic is simple: when the coffee farming community can sustain itself on the price growers receive for their coffee, there is no mass exodus of people from the land.

Here's the injustice: as the price paid to the farmers for coffee beans fell, the profits of large coffee corporations rose. Good news for my pension investments and for the colonel's—but very bad news for the coffee growers. The dynamic is simple: when the coffee farming community can sustain itself on the price growers receive for their coffee, there is no mass exodus of people from the land. When the coffee farming community struggles to put food on the table for its families, cannot keep its children in school or provide for other basic necessities, people begin migrating elsewhere to earn their daily bread.

If people cannot find a job in Mexico that allows them to support their families, they know there are jobs in the United States for low-skilled workers without papers. The U.S. government makes available fewer than 66,000 low-skilled worker visas per year[9]—while there are an estimated twelve million low-skilled undocumented persons working illegally in the United States who support the underbelly of our economy. These hard-working individuals will risk their lives to provide for their families.

The colonel and I both realized that we had at least two things in common: neither of us wants to support illegal immigration, and we both were doing the very thing that we did not want to do.

Prior to living on the border, the reality of Paul's words in Romans 7, "I do not understand what I do. For what I want to do, I do not do—but what I hate, I do," seemed unclear. Since living on the border, Paul's words now make much more sense.

I truly do not want to support illegal immigration. Neither did the colonel. Even though we may have had a different understanding of our own participation in and connection to illegal immigration, we agreed on wanting to stop it. I do not want to cause my sisters and brothers to leave their land because of my economic practices.

In light of the above realities, what a difficult challenge we all face in dealing with the dilemma of the border. I shared with the colonel a very real challenge for people of faith and people of conscience. "How can we respond in ways other than those which support illegal immigration?"

As this story of *Café Justo* shows so clearly, the farmers of Salvador Urbina have given us a wonderful vehicle through which to respond differently. The colonel and I still do not see eye to eye on all of the options related to illegal immigration, but we can now sit down and enjoy a good cup of Just Coffee together with a clear conscience—an activity that allows both of us to support the success of the *Café Justo* Cooperative while addressing positively the root causes of immigration.

Original Just Coffee logo (2003).

Beginnings of One Just Response to the Crisis on the Border

As the 1990s ended, Frontera de Cristo's mission to build bridges instead of walls continued to unfold, but we became more and more convinced that the enormous challenges at the border required an even more creative and comprehensive response, one that moved beyond humanitarian aid, education, and micro-business incubation. We needed to find a way to respond to the fundamental impetus of migration—economic necessity.

As a mission co-worker partnering with Lily of the Valley Presbyterian Church, I noticed that an unusual number of men living in this northern border town came from the southernmost districts of Mexico. Nearly half of the families in the congregation were farmers, displaced from their home villages by the dramatic plunge of international corn and coffee prices, which meant they could no longer make an adequate living growing coffee. They had come north looking for work in the *maquiladoras* (border-town factories)—or were planning to cross the border in search of jobs in the U.S.

Over the months I learned much from these expatriate Chiapan farmers, hearing about their families and lives in the south, listening to their stories of hard times in the coffee growing communities as big corporations gained more and more control in world coffee markets and prices for coffee beans plummeted. Intrigued by our conversations and the plight of these coffee farmers, who in desperation were migrating north in increasing numbers, we began to ask ourselves, "Why are so many coffee farmers migrating when people are buying coffee for $2 and $3 per cup at Starbucks?" Where is the justice here?

Then some of the refugee farmers also began asking the "What if?" questions.

"What if?" they asked us, "What if we coffee growers in southern Mexico received a fair price for our coffee and whole villages did not have to be bused to the border to cross into the U.S. at night, leaving our hometowns empty except for the very old and the very young?"

"What if we could get a fair price for our raw coffee beans, instead of being forced to sell them to the *coyotes* (coffee brokers) at a price that leaves our families without enough money to survive for the next year?"

And later, "What if we could utilize our knowledge and energy to roast and package these beans, then import the coffee into the U.S. and sell it at an additional value-added profit? What if there were no middlemen and all coffee-generated revenue went directly to our community—the growers, roasters and packagers? What if . . . ?"

Yes, "What if . . . ?"

This is the question that led to the concept of Just Coffee and the story of the *Café Justo* Cooperative that unfolds in this book.

We listened to the refugee coffee growers from Chiapas. We researched the dynamics of the coffee industry and the supply chain. We explored possibilities for a business structure that would be more just for the coffee growers, allowing them to share fully in the entire coffee revenue stream. Eventually, in collaboration with one community of growers in Salvador Urbina, we forged a new model we came to call Fair Trade PLUS. In the *Café Justo* Fair Trade PLUS cooperative, not only do the farmers get a fair price for their harvested coffee beans, they also share in the profit of roasting, packaging and selling the end product. This new model allows people to make a decent living at home in Chiapas, thereby eliminating the underlying economic need to migrate. And you get delicious, organic, just coffee as a byproduct.

Has the *Café Justo* approach worked? Tommy's before-and-after perspectives tell the tale.

Before and After—Tommy's Story

May 2002 *(My first visit to Salvador Urbina, before the **Café Justo** Cooperative)*

It was early morning, the day after a 43-hour car trip from the U.S./Mexico border to the Mexico/Guatemala border. I have worked many years on both sides of the border but this is my first day in the coffee growing community of Salvador Urbina. As an early riser, I am walking around, taking photographs, looking for a nice place to see the sunrise in this high tropical rain forest in Chiapas.

The sun is not up yet, and the roosters are crowing loudly. I did not sleep well, having learned the hard way that roosters crow all night long, not just at or before sunrise.

Salvador Urbina is busy this morning with small buses and taxis honking for

Sunrise in Salvador Urbina.

commuters as they pass each other on the only paved road that links the coffee communities to the big city of Tapachula (down the mountain, 20 miles away).

Life gets going early here because it is the monsoon time, and it will rain hard this afternoon, just like it does every afternoon until November. If something needs to be accomplished outdoors, it needs to get done in the morning.

People like to live in Salvador Urbina, 2,600 feet above sea level, because it is so much cooler than Tapachula which is near sea level and radiates tropical heat from the concrete and pavement. Folks would prefer to work and learn here, but there are no jobs and the big schools are in the bigger city.

Salvador Urbina, a community of less than 8,000 people, lies in a valley on either side of a mountain stream. There are phone lines available, but only a few can afford the monthly charge for phone service. The closest Internet service is in Tapachula.

Salvador Urbina has always been a community of coffee growers, which means its economy rises and falls with international coffee prices. Things have not been too happy here the last twenty years because coffee prices have reached an all-time low. The last few years have been the toughest. Times are hard in Salvador Urbina, and as a result, the youth are the first to leave to find employment elsewhere.

As I walk around, I hear an announcement from the community loudspeaker. This community public address system brings paid announcements to the community, pages people when they have a phone call on the community phone and provides a few public service announcements for the local churches, schools and medical clinic. They start broadcasting around six in the morning.

The first announcement I hear is for a bus trip to Agua Prieta, Altar and Tijuana for $100 per person. It will leave when the bus is full. No one has a car. Travelers are encouraged to go to a particular home for more details. This is not a regular bus. It is a migrant bus, taking people from the southern to the northern border with the U.S. where they hope to find work, either in the Mexican border towns or across the border in the U.S.

The announcements continue, informing all who listen about who has eggs for sale and confirming that the doctor will be in town for the afternoon.

The last announcement is the same as the first; I guess the bus line owners had so much business they could afford two

Sign in Salvador Urbina advertising "Trips to Agua Prieta and Tijuana from here."

announcements per day. The PA news is repeated again in the evening. The same announcements are made every day, including the bus ticket prices, but not always about the eggs.

The normal commercial bus ticket is almost $300, but the migrant bus is old and neither heated nor air-conditioned. The driver is not in a white shirt and tie and carries no official logbook. There is no bathroom on the bus, and the seats are old, the padding thin and the windows cracked. Everything is dirty and smells like diesel, so the cost is only $100. This same transportation system will also help you find a smuggler or *coyote* to get you into the U.S.—your one stop travel agent.

I later found out that one or two buses a week go north to the popular Mexican border towns where people begin their deadly trip into the U.S. across the deserts of Arizona. This pattern has been going on for quite a while as coffee prices are at a forty-year low. As I look around, it appears that time has virtually stood still—or so it seems—for the community of Salvador Urbina, where few healthy young adult workers remain.

March 2007 *(My latest visit to Salvador Urbina, after four-plus years of Just Coffee)*

It is almost five years after my first visit to Chiapas. I get up early and go check my e-mail at the *Café Justo* warehouse and Internet café. Children fill the street, going to school in Salvador Urbina wearing their uniforms with white shirts and blouses.

Before I leave the home where I am staying, I call a neighbor to see when they are driving to Tapachula. En route to the warehouse, I stop and visit with a local leader who is adding two rooms to his home for visitors and his returning children.

When I get to the warehouse I see several people with five-gallon containers buying purified water for 2.5 pesos (U.S. equivalent of 25 cents) from the water purification system installed in the warehouse. I can smell coffee for local use roasting in the warehouse and see the employees arriving to sort and clean the Just Coffee beans before bagging and sending them to Agua Prieta for roasting and export. Cell phones still do not work here as we are in a beautiful valley, but a lot more homes now have telephone land lines.

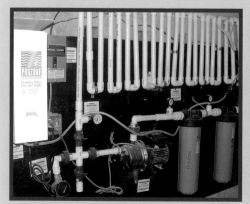

Water purification system installed in Salvador Urbina by Living Waters. (www.livingwatersfortheworld.org)

*Loading water from purification equipment in **Café Justo** warehouse.*

After checking my e-mail and making a few phone calls to the U.S., I walk uptown to grab some lunch at one of the four restaurants now open in town. Nothing fancy, just simple food served home-style in front of people's homes.

There is now even a home improvement store, an "ECONO-mat" that sells building supplies such as wiring, tile, plastic piping and other home remodeling hardware. It is the local Home Depot, opened just a year ago.

Economat building supplies store—Salvador Urbina's 2006 version of Home Depot.

During my first visit, there was no such store. There was no need for one, since no new building or home improvement projects were happening. Now, because it's the dry time of year—and because there is more money from coffee circulating locally—there are a LOT more people working on home improvements than in years past. All of this is such a contrast to my earlier visit.

I stop and buy a cold soda at one of the many little stores that have sprung up since my last visit, and I stand quietly, reflecting on the changes I see.

The city fathers are now discussing additions for the primary and secondary schools because today there are so many more students. The population of Salvador Urbina has increased to almost 10,000.

A little girl stops me and asks how my son is doing back in California. We have a nice conversation, and she asks if it is true that there will be more English classes in the Just Coffee Warehouse. The answer is yes.

My close friend picks me up, and we go into Tapachula for a few supplies and pick up his daughter from the big high school there. And I think, some day the teenagers from Tapachula may come to the big high school in Salvador Urbina. What a change!

Life is different now. The community is no longer stuck in the past but is building for the future.

What happened between Tommy's two visits? The Miracle of Just Coffee!

This book tells the remarkable story of how a very simple business concept, the *Café Justo* Cooperative, has succeeded—eventually allowing the growers to remain in their home village and live together comfortably and at peace. This small demonstration project in Chiapas has begun to reverse the migration pattern for one rural village, once depleted and despairing, but now thriving and hopeful.

The miracle of Just Coffee has emerged from an equal measure of clear thinking and hard work, with a Spirit-guided vision and a bit of serendipity thrown in. It is a simple and moving effort in which you can easily participate. This book tells the story, beginning with a Biblical vision about an ancient exiled people seeking hope in the midst of despair.

---

[1] Data from the Federal Reserve website: http/www.dallasfed.org/research/busfront/bus0401.html.

[2] Undocumented workers' contributions to the Social Security System documented at: http://news.ncmonline.com/news/view_article.html?article_id=64ba0a6571db8d23a944520f855482f6.

[3] Pew Hispanic Center.

[4] See http://www.visaportal.com/page.asp?page id=123 for a summary of the visa priority dates by country and visa type.

[5] Summarized from Secretary Chertoff's 2007 budget speech at http://www.dhs.gov/xnews/releases/pr 1170774601996.shtm.

[6] From Syracuse University website: http://trac.syr.edu/immigration/reports/141/include/rep 141table2.html.

[7] As reported on the Washington Post website: http://www.washingtonpost.com/wp-dyn-content/article/2006/10/30/AR2006103001025.html.

[8] Personal conversation with Mark Adams, March 2008.

[9] The Immigration Act of 1990 set a flexible cap for legal admissions at 675,000: 480,000 family based, 140,000 employment-based, and 55,000 "diversity immigrants." The law also set temporary immigration limits for high-skilled workers (65,000) and manual laborers (66,000). For details, see the U.S. Department of State website: http://travel .state.gov/pdf/FY05tableXVla.pdf.

Arnulfo Lopez Perez

Beltran Sanchez Rodriguez

David Cifuentes Velazquez

Salir de nuestra tierra es sufrir.
To leave our land is to suffer.
—Eduardo Perez Verdugo, 1999

For generations, the coffee farmers in Mexico worked on *fincas* (coffee plantations) owned by Germans. They were employed as *peones* (members of the landless laboring class or people held in compulsory servitude to a master in order to pay off their indebtedness). The involuntary servitude system of peonage began with the Spanish conquest of Mexico when the conquerors forced the poor, especially the indigenous peoples, to work in the fields and mines as laborers.

Even today, thousands of coffee growers are still living as *peones*, struggling to survive as raw coffee bean prices have fallen dramatically—while the retail price of a cup of brewed coffee continues to rise.

Abandoned German finca near Salvador Urbina that employed hundreds of peones in the 1800s.

Two Prophets Frame the Question
Ezekiel and Eduardo

Ezekiel, the Israelite, lived in depressing and politically volatile times, 590 years before Christ. A hundred years before he was born, his country was conquered, first by the Assyrians, later by the Babylonians. Eduardo Perez Verdugo, the coffee farmer from Chiapas driven from his home land in search of work, lives in depressing and economically volatile times, 2000 years after the birth of Christ. Both prophets in exile speak with anguish about their similar plights and both plead for justice as they search for a vision of hope amidst despair.

■ ■ ■

Ezekiel, Prophet of Israel

Exiled in Babylon, 590 BCE

The Lord set me in the middle of a valley. It was full of bones...
He asked me, "Oh Son of man, do you believe that these bones can live?"
I said, "Oh Sovereign Lord, you alone know."

—Ezekiel 37:1, 3

The prophet Ezekiel had a tough job. He was called by God to prophesy to the people of Israel, who had been living in exile for longer than they wanted to remember. These were the people who longed to be on their own land, who wrote the song that says, "We sat by the waters of Babylon and we wept . . . how can we sing the Lord's song in a strange land?"

It was a very difficult time when Ezekiel was writing his "complaints." His country was a

Sonoran "Valley of Bones" on the migrant exile route.

poor vassal state of Babylon. People did whatever necessary to keep themselves and their families alive. Most were slaves working to support the economy of their captors. Many had been forced to migrate from their homeland into Babylon in order to do the undesirable dirty work spurned by the ruling class in Babylon.

Burdened by their loneliness and their lack of ability to improve their lives, while also missing their homeland and its deep spiritual history, the people understandably felt depressed, isolated and desperate. Their lives were bleak and marginal. They wondered if there was any hope.

In the midst of this oppressive situation, the God of Israel appeared to Ezekiel. The Lord took him to a broad deserted valley filled with bones of the dead, very dry and very dead bones—symbolizing his very desperate and quite dead homeland, and asked him, "Ezekiel, do you believe these bones can live again? (Is there any hope for your country and your people?)"

Sitting in that seemingly lifeless place, trying, probably without much success, to imagine a better future for his country, he answered, perhaps politely, perhaps sarcastically, "Lord, don't ask me. You alone know. I've got no clue."

In that very moment, with very few viable options for the present and with the future totally unknown, God and Ezekiel struggled with the most important and, perhaps, the right question—the question that was on everyone's mind, "Is there any hope?"

And, in the very act of asking the question, the dream found a voice.

■ ■ ■

Eduardo Perez Verdugo, Prophet at the Border

Exiled in Agua Prieta, Mexico, 2000 CE

Salir de nuestra tierra es sufrir.
To leave our land is to suffer.

—Eduardo Perez Verdugo

Eduardo Perez Verdugo

Eduardo Perez Verdugo fled the lush mountainside of Chiapas in 1998 after Hurricane Mitch washed away much of his community. In a similar fashion, the dramatic fall in coffee and corn prices during the 1990s had already washed away much of the economic base of his community. The money he was making could barely provide for his children and wife and certainly could not be stretched to cover the costs of rebuilding.

Eduardo migrated over 2000 miles from Mexico's border with Guatemala to the northern border town of Agua Prieta. He arrived in 1999 when there was still a lot of factory work available. It didn't take long for him to find employment in a *maquiladora* (foreign-owned assembly plant) that imports materials and manufactures electronic parts for GE, Ford and Whirlpool—then re-exports the assembled products without paying any duty or tariff. Eduardo's purpose was to earn enough money to rebuild his home in Chiapas and the church building that Hurricane Mitch had destroyed. The testimony he gave to a group of visiting Presbyterians in September that year is reproduced below.

Eduardo found spiritual and material refuge with Lily of the Valley Presbyterian Church in Agua Prieta where he joined other persons from the state of Chiapas who were also living in economic exile. Corn and coffee farmers, who had seen the prices for their products drop dramatically in the early 1990s, had been drawn to the dry and dusty border town to find employment.

Located in the Sulphur Springs Valley, Agua Prieta offered people the prospect of being able to provide the basics for their families. Some brought their guitars and continued to sing the Lord's song in this new and strange land—albeit in a minor key.

Testimony given by Eduardo Perez Verdugo in Agua Prieta, Sonora, Mexico to a group of visitors from Shallowford Presbyterian Church (Atlanta, Georgia), on September 20, 1999.

My name is Eduardo Perez Verdugo and I come from Chiapas. I belong to the Christ Rock of Ages Presbyterian Church in Chiapas and I worship with the Lily of the Valley Presbyterian Church here in Agua Prieta. I am glad that you have come across the border and that we were able to worship our Lord together yesterday. Thank you for asking me to give my testimony.

I have a wife and six children. We are coffee farmers in Chiapas. It has been a struggle to survive the last couple of years. The price of coffee is going down, and many people are leaving and coming north. To leave our land is to suffer. The "gringos" and Germans who buy our coffee are giving us 260 pesos for a 70-kilo bag (about $27 for 154 pounds, 17.5 cents a pound).

Our church building was destroyed in the floods last fall. We decided that each of us would raise a certain amount of money to rebuild, but I could not both feed my family and raise the money for the church building by picking and selling my coffee.

I came to Agua Prieta with my son in June to work in the border factories. They pay more than I could make in Chiapas. I work for S.I. of Mexico. We make parts for Ford, Motorola, Toyota, Brother and many other companies. I am able to make 450 pesos a week (about $47). The work week is 48 hours, but I can work overtime and make more.

I have been offered a good job at a golf course in Phoenix. I can make more at the golf course in two months than I can make here in almost a year. If I make it across the border, I will be able to raise enough money to be home with my family in Chiapas sooner.

I have decided that I will cross the border in two weeks, on October 4th after worship. I have found a *coyote* and he will help us get across to the other side without problems. We will have to walk through the desert for three days. We know the *coyote* so he is only charging us $200 each.

I ask you to pray for the Mexican government that we will find a better way. I ask you to pray for the United States that we will find a better way.

Note: *Eduardo left for Phoenix late in the evening of October 4, 1999. Eduardo and six persons with whom he was traveling were caught by the U.S. Border Patrol. He was brought back to Agua Prieta, never having reached his new job in Phoenix.*

■ ■ ■

Just as the exiles in Babylon found a livelihood allowing them to provide for their families, so also the economic exiles who had fled their fields in the south of Mexico for the factories of Agua Prieta found a livelihood. Like the exiles in Babylon, many of the economic exiles in Agua Prieta also longed to be home.

In the 1990s, Agua Prieta experienced tremendous growth from the migration north. The economic opportunities no longer existed in the migrants' communities of origin due to global economic realities and failed economic policies. In Agua Prieta, the assembly plants facilitated by the Border Industrialization Act, a precursor to NAFTA, were still hiring.

In addition to the draw of factory jobs, Agua Prieta also saw tremendous growth during this time due to changes in the U.S. immigration policies that funneled the flow of economic migration away from Tijuana/San Diego and Juarez/El Paso and pushed the flow toward Agua Prieta/Douglas.

By 1997, the Sulphur Springs Valley had become the primary crossing point for persons without proper documents entering the United States seeking jobs. Each day, the northern Mexican border received thousands of persons from the south who were there attempting to work on the border or, more likely, risk their lives crossing into the United States. This situation was a clear witness that "justice is not flowing like a mighty stream" in areas of the world where persons can no longer support their families from the fruits of their labors.

The majority of these folks left their lands, not because they wanted to live on the border or in the United States, but because the price they received for their coffee and farm products had fallen dramatically. Daniel Cifuentes, a member of one of three Presbyterian coffee farmer families from the *ejido* (village) Salvador Urbina that were also part of the Lily of the Valley Presbyterian Church, shared with us that his family was being paid 350 *pesos* (about $33) for each 57 kilo (125.4 pounds) bag of coffee, which was down from 1300 *pesos* ($130) per bag in 1992—a 70 percent reduction!

Eduardo estimated it would take him two to three years of working 48 hours each week, at $50 a week, to earn enough money to return to the land he loved so much.

During one of his breaks from work, a friend invited him to go to Phoenix to work on a golf course where he would get paid $10 an hour. Eduardo declined the offer. The next day this friend insisted that he come, as his cousin had secured two jobs for them. Again Eduardo declined. The third day, the friend asked Eduardo how long he thought it would take for him to earn enough money in the factory to return home. His friend argued that by making $10 an hour he could be home in less than a year. Eduardo decided to go to Phoenix.

On October 4, 1999, Eduardo joined a group of Mexico's poor attempting to cross illegally into the United States. This huddled mass, longing to be economically free, went through

Nighttime at the border wall between Douglas, Arizona and Agua Prieta, Sonora.

> Why can you come and go freely into Mexico while I have to sneak into your country? Are we not both created equally?

an underground travel agency, a high-growth industry in both Mexico and the United States, in order to find jobs. If they crossed the U.S. border without detection, they would become golf course attendants in Phoenix, hospitality workers in Las Vegas, drywallers in Atlanta, dish washers in Pulaski, meat packers in Omaha, orange pickers in Orlando, landscapers in Seattle or roofers in Minneapolis.

Three days later Eduardo was back at the church building in Agua Prieta, battered and bruised both emotionally and physically. He had not achieved the "American Dream." The limp in his walk testified to the twisted ankle and the banged knee he suffered falling down an embankment during his night hike. The scrapes on his face gave witness to the tight passage through the unforgiving mesquite forests of the Sulphur Springs Valley. The look in his eyes asked the question: "Why can you come and go freely into Mexico while I have to sneak into your country? Are we not both created equally?"

Eduardo's pained expression pointed to scars deeper than the physical ones that were most apparent. As we talked, he shared more about his crossing attempt. His group had been chased by the Border Patrol. Since Eduardo was already injured, he was easily caught and promptly thrown to the ground. He tried to explain to the agent that the same blood ran through both of their veins and that both had the same need to provide for their families. While most Border Patrol agents treat migrants professionally and humanely—even empathizing with the migrants' plight—this particular agent must have had a bad night. Eduardo received a kick to his face and a boot on his neck for his efforts as the agent shouted at him, "We don't have anything in common."

Eduardo had experienced the Sulphur Springs Valley surrounding Agua Prieta and extending up into Arizona as a valley of very dry bones—a valley of despair, a valley of fear, a valley of division. After he shared his experiences with us, he reflected, *"Salir de nuestra tierra es sufrir,"* which means, "To leave our land is to suffer."

Desert grave near Eduardo's route north.

He did not say, "Not being able to enter your country legally is suffering."

He did not say, "Walking through the mesquite forests in the middle of the night and being scraped by the thorns is suffering."

He did not say, "Falling down into a ditch, twisting my ankle and banging my knee is suffering."

He did not say, "Being chased as a criminal and thrown down on the ground is suffering."

He did not say, "Being kicked and having a boot placed on my neck with my face in the desert floor is suffering."

He said, "To leave our land is to suffer."

Experiencing forced economic exile was at the core of his suffering. All the other emotional and physical suffering paled in comparison.

As we talked with Eduardo in the modern day Valley of Dry Bones, we heard the Spirit's question and could only respond with the words of Ezekiel, "O Lord, you alone know if these bones can live."

Prophet's Questions Frame the Vision

The most amazing thing about this conversation with Eduardo was that he did not stop with the phrase "To leave our land is to suffer." He continued on to say, "If only we could control the sale of our coffee, we would be able to stay on our land."

In the midst of Eduardo's pain and suffering, hope bubbled up in his being, a hope that the bones could live again, a hope that not only he but his community would be able to return to their land and provide for their families once again. Still battered and bruised, Eduardo became a voice of the Spirit of the Lord saying, "Maybe—just maybe—these bones can live!"

If only we could control the sale of our coffee, we would be able to stay on our land.

Eduardo's question was now clearly framed. "Is there any way to change this situation?" "Is there any hope?" "Will it ever be different for us?" "Can we ever return home to our families?"

For all of us, the challenge hung in the air, its echoes disturbing our innards and disquieting our minds.

In the process of asking the question, Eduardo gave voice to a dream . . . that posed a challenge . . . that framed a vision . . . that led to the miracle of Just Coffee.

David Oman Cifuentes Velazquez

Elifas Cifuentes Lopez

Emilio Navarro Barrios

I believe humans get a lot done, not because we're smart, but because we have thumbs so we can make coffee.

—Flash Rosenberg

Fair Trade

A justice-oriented movement that started in the 1940s in which more of the money for products goes to the growers, producers and artisans, rather than to the intermediaries. Beware!!! Some companies use this label, but only buy a small percentage of true Fair Trade coffee.

Fair Trade PLUS

A term coined by partners of *Café Justo* to indicate that the growers/producers of the Cooperative earn nearly all of the money the end consumer spends for the product, since they participate in the whole vertical economic chain from harvest to roasting to exporting. The Cooperative tithes 10% of the income for community improvement projects and also underwrites health care and pension benefits for its members.

A shady nursery for Fair Trade PLUS Arabica coffee trees to get a healthy start.

CHAPTER 3

Responding to the Challenge
The Search to Activate Eduardo's Dream

The New Testament offers another metaphor shedding light on Eduardo's prophetic vision at the border. In first century Palestine, times were also tough. Gospel writer Mark sets the "bad news" context for the "good news" ministry of Jesus.

> *After John was put in prison, Jesus went into Galilee proclaiming the good news of God. "The time has come. The kingdom of God is near. Repent and trust the good news."*
>
> —Mark 1:14

Precisely in the face of the bad news of John the Baptist's imprisonment, Jesus begins his ministry declaring the kingdom of God has come. Precisely in the face of Herod's squashing the messenger who prepared the way for him, Jesus calls us to repent. Precisely in the face of the government's attempting to silence the voice of one crying out in the desert, Jesus exhorts us to trust in the good news.

In a similar way, at the beginning of 2000, time was ripe for some good news to emerge amidst the bad news that had been brewing for years at the U.S./Mexico border.

Searching for Good News In The Midst of the Bad

In January, two border minister colleagues, Chuy Gallegos and Mark Adams, met with the Mountain View Presbyterian Church breakfast group in Loveland, Colorado. We had been invited to talk about the current immigration crisis. The picture we painted was pretty bleak—violence at the border had increased dramatically; more than three hundred persons

Sun of hope shines through the border fence, made from portable military aircraft landing mats.

a year were dying trying to enter the U.S.; the division in our communities had grown both physically and psychologically. We described Eduardo Verdugo's story, as well as the provocative question he had raised.

As we shared all the bad news surrounding us on the border, a member of the group raised his hand and said, "You know, it's easy to talk about how bad things are. You need to do something about it!" He challenged us to be proactive about counteracting the economic impetus for migration and help Eduardo realize his dream.

It is precisely in the face of bad news—in this case, the news that thousands of coffee farmers had been driven off their land in the last ten years and that countless numbers of them had died in our deserts—that we were called to trust in and activate the good news.

The conventional wisdom, "bad news" of the powers of the world, supports the logic that it's natural and ethically acceptable to pay a minimal amount of money to the coffee farmers so we Americans can drink cheap coffee. Meantime, the coffee companies make huge profits. The authentic "good news" suggests we can live in just and fair relationships with the farmers who grow our coffee while everyone in the coffee business—from consumer to grower to manufacturer—can cooperate in a mutually beneficial relationship allowing all to earn a living wage.

For many of us in the United States, coffee is an integral part of our lives—we might even say we couldn't live without our cups of coffee in the morning. For many people in the tropical areas of the world, coffee has been an integral part of their livelihood, as well. However, thousands of coffee growers are no longer able to provide the basic necessities for their families.

Eduardo challenged us to help start a company through which the coffee farmers in Chiapas could receive a just price for their coffee—a price that would value their work and enable them to remain on their land. He said what he and his community desired was not charity, but justice.

Eduardo had shared with us a vision of just economic relationships. Our first response was one of fear, assuming we weren't equipped to help make that vision a reality. At first we didn't know how to proceed. Then, as we slowly realized what needed to be done, we were quite sure we didn't have the know-how to accomplish this mighty task. After all, the Frontera de Cristo pastoral staff knew very little about managing any business, let alone a coffee business. But our hearts responded. We knew we could not turn our backs on this compelling challenge—we needed to trust God's promise of Good News and move forward with courage.

Our challenger in Colorado was accurate. For most of us it is easy to identify and talk about a bad situation. It is easy to be paralyzed by the bad news of increasing suffering, division and death caused by global forces that can seem so much larger than what anyone can handle. If we do decide to respond, it is easier to denounce the "evils of the global economy" than it is to countermand those evils with positive alternatives.

Eduardo did not let the suffering he had endured prevent him from envisioning an alternative for his community. By challenging us, our friend from the Colorado presentation forced us to stop talking about how bad things were. His question encouraged us to embrace Eduardo's vision and begin working toward activating the good news of hope—challenging us to make something positive happen.

> Eduardo challenged us to help start a company through which the coffee farmers in Chiapas could receive a just price for their coffee—a price that would value their work and enable them to remain on their land. He said what he and his community desired was not charity, but justice.

Looking for Fair Trade Options

Upon returning from Colorado, we met with Eduardo to explore how his dream might be fulfilled. We began by exploring ways in which the coffee growers in his home community might increase their incomes by connecting with existing Fair Trade organizations who were committed to paying farmers a fair price for their coffee beans. We first contacted representatives of Equal Exchange, a pioneer in the Fair Trade coffee industry in the United States that works with small farming cooperatives in over 13 countries bringing about more just relationships between coffee growers and consumers. During our initial explorations, we discovered two problems.

First, we learned that the company was not entering into new relationships with any additional communities. Their existing network of coffee farming cooperatives was producing more coffee than Equal Exchange could effectively market. With supply outstripping demand, they were not in a position to add new cooperatives.

While this was a daunting challenge, the second problem was even greater. Equal Exchange and other Fair Trade coffee companies in the U.S. did not buy roasted coffee from the coffee farming cooperatives. Rather, they bought—at fair prices—only the coffee beans, while still green, and then they roasted, packaged and shipped the finished product to their customers, pocketing all the additional revenues from these processes rather than allowing the farmers to benefit from these later steps. At that time, Trans-Fair,[1] the largest Fair Trade certifier in the U.S., certified only coffee that was exported in raw form from coffee growing countries and roasted in developed countries. Again cutting the farmers—and their country—out of a large portion of the coffee revenue dollar. See chart in Chapter 7 (page 88) showing where the coffee revenue goes.

> . . . the farmers would be able to participate in the whole process— from cultivation to roasting to packaging.

This meant that once the dried coffee beans were exported out of country and shipped to Fair Trade companies, the coffee farmers lost control of their product. They would never share in the revenue stream generated by the roasting, packaging and distribution functions, which produced the highest profit margins.

Eduardo's profound vision was based on his hope that the farmers would be able to participate in the whole process—from cultivation to roasting to packaging. Not only would the coffee farmers receive fair prices for their raw product, they would also retain the added value of greater profit and increased employment within their communities. Secondary jobs would also be created in the areas of business management, production, data processing and transportation. We began to talk about Eduardo's dream model as Fair Trade PLUS coffee.

Expanding the Visionary Team

In December 2000, the darkest time of the year and over a year after Eduardo had shared his challenging vision with us, the possibilities for *Café Justo* still seemed uncertain. We had spent a lot of time and energy researching options, but still had not found a way to transform dreams into reality. We were not business people and Frontera de Cristo had no one on staff who could just roll up their sleeves and help the farmers make this vertically integrated coffee business happen.

During this dark time, Dr. Cecile Lumer hosted her yearly Hanukkah party. Cecile is a botanist from New York City who "retired" to Bisbee, Arizona. Over the years, she had become very concerned about the immigration crisis and had helped found a group called Citizens for Border Solutions. Cecile and Mark had met as they both participated in a series of activities seeking to create a more humane border.

Mark recalls that pivotal evening and its importance in the Just Coffee story.

Mark Adams (right) and his wife Miriam with friends at Dr. Lumer's Hanukkah party.

Chance Meeting Leads to Unlikely Partnership

At the party, I was introduced to Arthur Thomas Bassett III. Originally from Minnesota, Tommy had migrated to Agua Prieta to manage one of the largest *maquiladoras*. These manufacturing plants in Mexico, owned by companies based in the U.S., receive special tax incentives from both countries. He met Cecile through their common interest—photography—and was not in the least concerned at the moment about "border issues."

This chance meeting seems like an amazing coincidence or else God created a moment of ironic serendipity through a Hanukkah party. This annual gathering brought together a Presbyterian pastor from South Carolina and a recovering workaholic, alcoholic, evangelical Roman Catholic with strong Protestant leanings and years of business experience—a meeting that would ultimately turn the Fair Trade PLUS concept into a successful reality! If you read this improbable sequence in a novel, you might think the author proposed it to support the plot and drive the story to a conclusion. Nevertheless, that's what happened.

I shared with Tommy Frontera de Cristo's concern about the number of people dying while migrating into the United States. As a next step, I invited Tommy to participate in the newly formed Healing Our Borders weekly prayer vigil, which an ecumenical group had begun earlier that month. This group prayed for the families of those who died seeking a better life and also prayed that our governments would find viable alternatives to the current situation that could bring peace on our border. Tommy seemed interested but was unconvinced that there was much to be done for the problem on our border. Before the evening ended, Tommy agreed to join me for lunch the following week.

Healing Our Borders Vigil remembering those who had died crossing into Cochise County.

Before that lunch at Jalisco's in Douglas, Tommy—a statistician by training—did some hard-nosed investigation. To his surprise he discovered that the number of people dying while migrating had increased by over 500 percent per year since the implementation of the "Operation Gatekeeper" Border Policy in 1994.[2] This was so startling to Tommy that he readily decided to join the Healing Our Borders prayer vigil. That was the beginning of an unlikely friendship.

As our relationship developed, it became clear that Tommy had the experiences and skills, as well as the passion, to make the vision of a grower-owned international coffee export business a reality. More importantly, Tommy himself was searching for ways to use his business skills and experience in assisting local communities rather than just increasing corporate profits.

Throughout the next year, our friendship deepened as Tommy became more involved in conceptualizing and concretizing the steps needed to move Eduardo's vision of a Fair Trade PLUS coffee cooperative toward reality. In the meantime, I continued to be in conversation with several of the Chiapas coffee farmers who were currently economic exiles in Agua Prieta, sharing Eduardo's vision with them and learning from their reactions and responses.

For a period of time, however, that initial clarity of spirit waned. As Tommy said, "We just didn't seem to be able to 'get our act together' and get moving."

Another Coffee Expert Joins the Team

Then in January 2002 we experienced another milestone. Daniel Cifuentes, an exiled coffee farmer from the community of Salvador Urbina, and one of thirteen brothers and sisters from that coffee growing community in the southern-most state in Mexico, began offering his expertise to our Fair Trade PLUS vision team. A third-generation coffee farmer, Daniel had come to the northern border to find work and possibly cross into the United States.

Daniel Cifuentes, coffee grower and visionary Café Justo founder.

From his lifetime growing up and working in the midst of a traditional coffee-growing community, Daniel understood the business of coffee. He knew that the direct cost of cultivating and bringing the dried coffee beans to market was around forty cents per pound, and he understood how the *coyotes* had conspired to keep the prices as low as possible. Leaving his family, community and home was the most painful decision Daniel had ever made, but at forty cents per pound for the coffee he raised, his options were few, and he knew the road north to the border and the U.S. was well traveled.

Daniel had come north from Chiapas and found work in one of the numerous *maquiladoras* that line the border. It was in one of these factories that Daniel met Tommy, who was director of quality control at the time.

Daniel and Mark met at Lily of the Valley Presbyterian Church in Agua Prieta and hit it off right away. Presbyterians had done a lot of missionary work in Chiapas in the 1890s and early 1900s, and Daniel had been raised Presbyterian. They had a common bond, both as Presbyterians and as migrants to the desert. Mark had migrated from the green hills of South Carolina and Daniel from the rain forest of Chiapas.

Their conversations eventually turned to the verdant mountains of Chiapas and the wonderful coffee that grows there. Something had to be done. How could it be that coffee beans were being bought at a price lower than it cost to grow them, while the cost of one plain cup of coffee in the United States alone was higher than what the growers were receiving for two pounds of coffee beans in Mexico? It just wasn't right!

Soon the discussions broadened to include Tommy and weekly calls to some of Daniel's coffee farmer relatives in Salvador Urbina. We all saw the coffee cooperative as a potential mechanism to remedy the underlying economics of immigration and create just relationships between U.S. consumers and Mexican growers. It was an opportunity to do something proactive instead of continuing our reactive Band-Aid measures that were providing support to those already in exodus on their trip crossing into the U.S.

Daniel from Chiapas could envision that this project might have the potential to procure a just and fair price for the excellent organic coffee grown for years on the ancestral lands of his forefathers. This Fair Trade PLUS coffee business, he believed, could help his community reverse the migration that was crippling both the economy and the families with whom he was raised. Tommy knew that, given the opportunity, he could help the growers make this business work. Eduardo Verdugo was finally getting to see a glimpse of an answer to his original question.

Nevertheless, the concept, the dream, and the possibility that this vision could be accomplished still needed to ferment for several months before we made the commitment to action.

In the development of any innovative project, there comes a time when the organizing visionaries have to get off dead center and just jump ahead in faith. One evening, while drinking coffee in a small room lit by a single 40-watt bulb dangling from a stark ceiling, sitting on third- or fourth-hand furniture, Daniel, Mark and Tommy committed themselves, with a handshake and a prayer, to do whatever was necessary to turn this dream into a reality. Hallelujah!

---

[1] Trans-Fair.

[2] *Border Games* and *Operation Gatekeeper* (see Resources section, page 125) provide in-depth descriptions of U.S. border policy and the human cost of its implementation.

Eri Cifuentes Perez

Fabian Ochoa

Gregorio Vazquez Perez

If you'll excuse me a minute, I'm going to have a cup of coffee.

—Broadcast from Apollo 11's LEM "Eagle" to Johnson Space Center
Houston July 20, 1969

Coffee grows on bushes or trees, normally within twenty degrees of the equator, from 2,000 to 6,000 feet above sea level, frequently on the side of a volcano. Coffee is a labor-intensive crop, planted, cultivated and picked by hand on small, almost inaccessible plots.

Shade Grown coffee is grown in the shade of other trees as it cannot tolerate strong direct sunlight. It is usually cultivated in a multicultural plant environment where the other plants are used as natural barriers to insects and provide natural fertilization. Coffee is generally good for the soil, plant life and ecosystem of the area where it is grown. All Just Coffee is shade grown.

Estate Grown coffee comes solely from a particular grower's lands, usually a small, family-run business. Just Coffee is 100% estate-grown coffee—and the *Café Justo* grower's name is on the label, so you can build a relationship with your personal coffee provider.

Pedro picks only red, ripe Arabica coffee cherries.

CHAPTER 4

Making It Up and Making It Happen
Percolating the Plan of Action

As the weeks rolled on, we sensed that this vision of a completely farmer-owned coffee growing, roasting and exporting business could become a reality. We almost felt that its success was already real. We could smell it. We were starting to taste in advance the coffee that we were preparing to brew. And my, oh my, did it wake us up and get us going! The planning got serious. We rolled up our sleeves and went to work.

Under the umbrella of Frontera de Cristo, the unlikely trio that banded together to work out the details of a Fair Trade PLUS cooperative in Salvador Urbina and get the process moving consisted of Mark, a visionary with access to capital, who knew nothing about business or coffee; Daniel, a coffee farmer with a lot of determination and selfless, hardworking commitment; and Tommy, the guy who could do whatever no one else had the time or interest to do.

Although the three of us were of very different backgrounds and dispositions, we were all totally committed to helping the coffee farmers develop a business that would bring them fair and livable incomes. We also shared a similar mindset about the things that matter most, such as the knack of not taking anything too seriously, the ability to be patient, and the willingness to be forgiving. More importantly, we all believed in prayer. We prayed a lot—and still do. We prayed so much that it felt strange whenever we participated in a meeting that did not start and end with a prayer. It still does.

Before the total business concept could be presented to the farmers in Salvador Urbina, we needed to make sure all the pieces were in place for our face-to-face discussions. First, we needed to make sure capital could be secured for purchasing a roaster. We also needed to make sure the business concept was comprehensive and realistic, which required gathering more detailed information about what's involved in starting and running a coffee business. Our ad hoc network of coffee consultants needed to help us draft tentative guidelines for the cooperative organization and a written covenant for the coffee growers of Salvador

Urbina to consider as they clarified and formalized their own commitment to becoming members of the cooperative.

Obtaining Start-Up Funding

Once our concept was clear, we needed to find initial funding for the project. The natural place to approach was Mark's employer, Frontera de Cristo Presbyterian Border Ministry, which already had a twenty-plus-year history of building relationships and understanding across the border, addressing many of the difficult immigration-related issues. Frontera de Cristo and its six sister Border Ministries stretching from the Gulf of Mexico to the Pacific Ocean invest money, people and prayer in healthcare, education, micro-economic development and improvement of bi-national relations between the two countries. Many organizations and churches talk about what can be done to diminish poverty and eliminate suffering and injustice. This organization actually does something about the problems in many different ways.

We were counting on financial assistance from this pioneering faith group to help us launch the innovative Fair Trade PLUS business we were beginning to call Just Coffee. Back in 2000, Frontera de Cristo made a commitment to address the underlying causes of immigration through a Micro-Credit Ministry whose main purpose was to develop viable employment opportunities by making loans of $500 to $5,000 available to seed startup ventures.

Since neither the coffee farmers nor we had any experience with how much money would be needed to initiate the *Café Justo* dream, as we prepared our loan application we created a whole range of possible scenarios. Finally, after much discussion we agreed that the farmers would request a $20,000 loan from Frontera de Cristo. This $20,000 loan proposal to the Micro-Credit Ministry would be the largest loan ever requested from them. As Mark was the coordinator of the Micro-Credit Ministry, we felt confident that his reputation would assist us in receiving the loan.

We prepared ourselves most diligently for the Board meeting, clarifying the business model we envisioned and working through the financial details. We also researched import/export laws, coffee packaging requirements and the selection of coffee processing equipment. The initial business plan was drafted, crafted into a PowerPoint presentation, thoroughly reviewed and then translated into Spanish.

The formal meeting with the Frontera de Cristo Board was held on Friday afternoon, March 15, 2002. We were all very anxious because so much hinged on receiving this funding, but we were believers in the farmers' vision, so we took courage.

The presentation went very well. To underscore the quality of our product, Daniel served up an initial batch of Just Coffee during the meeting. To our amazement, immediately after our presentation, the Board quickly approved a motion to lend us the full $20,000. The money was available within two weeks of that meeting. We knew in our hearts we had experienced yet another miracle!

The farmers suddenly had the capital they needed but we still had more to learn to help them realize their vision. The more we could

Daniel Cifuentes (left) and Tommy show off the $20,000 loan check from Frontera de Cristo Micro-Credit Ministry.

educate ourselves about the challenges of coffee growing and processing, the more helpful we could be in advising the coffee growers on their ultimate business plan.

Researching the Coffee Business—A Coffee Primer

The concept of Just Coffee had been simmering for two years and now we were almost ready to set off for Salvador Urbina to finalize the startup. During the years of incubation, we had been gathering information about the coffee industry from all available sources—including networking with the farmers in Chiapas through Daniel Cifuentes.

Here's some of what our on-going research taught us. Perhaps understanding a bit more about coffee and the coffee industry will raise your consciousness concerning the challenges the growers face—and make your cup of Just Coffee just a bit more tantalizing.

There are two main types of coffee: Robusta and Arabica. Arabica is the top of the line—the thoroughbred of the coffee family. It is generally known as the world's finest coffee, and it's not easy to grow.[1] Arabica grows only between 3,000 and 6,000 feet and needs at least 75 inches of rain per year.

Traditional coffee fields are small (two- to five-acre areas), often in nearly inaccessible mountainous areas (as in Chiapas), thickly covered by many types of plants which provide shade and natural herbicides, pesticides and fertilizers for the coffee. Just Coffee is 100% organically grown in the shade!

Shade grown Arabica coffee in the field.

Tending coffee plants, machete and pruning hook in hand.

Ripe red Arabica coffee cherries, ready to be picked.

Growers tend their crop with machetes, which are used for pruning, cultivating and mulching. Coffee plants bear fruit when they are three to five years old and are productive for twenty to thirty-five years, if pruned judiciously. Coffee plants flower once per season in the spring. Coffee cherries, which typically contain two seeds or beans each, are the fruit of the coffee tree. They are picked when they are bright red.

Coffee is harvested two or three times during late fall or early winter as the cherries ripen. Beans need to be processed (sorted, de-pulped, washed and dried) within twenty-four hours of harvest—otherwise they will start to ferment. The grower families in Salvador Urbina dry their coffee by spreading the beans on a concrete patio in the morning sun and then collecting it during the afternoon before the rains begin. This process is repeated daily until the coffee has dried to about 11 percent moisture content. The outer parchment of the bean is removed before roasting to improve the taste. All the discarded matter (cherries, skins, parchments) is recycled as compost in the coffee fields.

Any type of coffee bean can be decaffeinated. *Café Justo* uses the indirect natural solvent method where the coffee is soaked in water, which naturally draws out the caffeine. The beans are removed, and a natural solvent derived from fruits is added to the water. The solvent binds with the caffeine, and both are removed through a steaming process. The beans are then reunited with the decaffeinated water to reabsorb the flavor and aroma elements.

Coffee roasting is the critical process that brings out the distinctive taste of a coffee bean. Generally the coffee is roasted from ten to twenty minutes at a temperature of 400 to 480 degrees—depending on whether you want to produce a light, medium or dark roast. The final step is grinding the coffee. The Just Coffee Blends for Every Taste order form on page 122 shows the wide variety of roasts and grinds.

Spreading freshly picked and de-pulped coffee beans on the patio to dry.

Our research gained us a rudimentary knowledge base about coffee. We were determined to insure that once we got started, Just Coffee would be the very best coffee possible. The next step in our learning process would require first-hand experience in Chiapas.

Forming the *Café Justo* Cooperative— Our Road Trip To Chiapas

The time had come to go to Salvador Urbina and meet the potential members of the *Café Justo* Cooperative. In May of 2002, Tommy Bassett, Isaac Cifuentes (Daniel's brother), Mark Adams and Miriam Maldonado (Mark's wife) packed themselves into a compact 4-door Saturn with 150,000 miles on its odometer and set out for Chiapas. After forty-three hours, two thousand miles, sixty-three chimichangas and five hundred dollars in gas and tolls, we reached our destination.

Mark, Miriam and Isaac cross into Chiapas on first trip to Salvador Urbina.

47

Our goal was to meet with the coffee farmers of Salvador Urbina and plan with them how to make the vision of Just Coffee a reality. We were excited. Yes, we knew there were still some practical concerns needing to be addressed, but we were determined that we would overcome them. We knew in our hearts that one day soon the coffee farmers could own and manage a thriving, vertically integrated, international coffee roasting industry. We felt that nothing could stop us, but we did run into some unexpected roadblocks along the way.

Reynaldo Cifuentes listens intently to the Agua Prieta delegation.

In advance of our arrival, the family of Daniel Cifuentes had been talking with the various growers about the concept of a cooperative and the need for them to be open to the concept. By the time we reached the village, several meetings were already scheduled.

Reynaldo Cifuentes, Daniel's cousin, was one of the first to welcome us. We learned later he was a leader of this community. He had experienced the mass exodus of people due to the drop in prices the growers received for their coffee. He set the tone of the upcoming discussions in his greeting, "We are so glad you have come here to help us."

We responded, "We are glad you will help us enter into just economic relationships with those who provide our coffee. This project is not about people of one country helping people of another country economically. Rather it is an example of how people from both sides of the border can work together to create an economic model more in line with God's vision of the world."

Getting Down to Business

The meetings began in earnest with a small group of key growers from the community. The goal was to discuss the opportunities for a new kind of coffee business. We wanted them to understand that they could participate in a revolutionary type of coffee cooperative in which the growers would not only receive more than three times as much money for their coffee beans; they would also have control over all the revenues received from their coffee sales. They would be full owners and managers of their cooperative.

We proposed a $1.26 per pound price for the Cooperative to buy coffee from its members. The growers proposed rounding it up to $130 (U.S. dollars) per *bulto*. Since a *bulto* is a 96-pound sack of coffee, the actual price worked out to $1.33 per pound. At that time, the current price being paid by the *coyotes* was forty cents per pound.

Because the cash available for starting a cooperative was limited, we proposed to the growers that they help underwrite the start-up with a quasi-consignment arrangement. Once officially organized, the Cooperative would purchase one *bulto* for $130, and the growers would ship two additional *bultos* on consignment to their Cooperative. When these two "consignment" *bultos* were roasted, packaged and purchased by consumers, the growers would receive payment for them—and for two additional *bultos* that would be ordered by the Cooperative and paid for at the same time, cash flow permitting. Once demand and supply evened out, payments would be made monthly on a year-round basis, as the roasted Just Coffee was sold and exported.

It was a great deal for the farmers. The price the growers agreed to pay themselves through the Cooperative for one *bulto* was ten dollars more than what the local *coyotes* would

First meeting of coffee growers to consider new Cooperative proposal.

have paid them for three bags, so growers had nothing to lose. However, because of their previous experiences with Americans, there was a lot of discussion about this proposition and substantial concern among the growers. At this point, not all the growers fully believed they would also truly be the owners. Many farmers were suspicious that the Americans somehow would still be in charge and take the profits.

After these initial meetings with a handful of growers, we began a series of meetings with all the potential members of the Cooperative at which we presented an overview of the business plan.

The first large gathering was friendly. Everyone was rather patient, allowing us all the opportunity to get comfortable with one another and with the new ideas being presented. We were met with widespread support. The more we got into the details of the plan, however, the more the growers expressed concerns about the model we were suggesting. Many of their reservations came down to a matter of trust.

Challenges to Trust

Initially, most of the farmers in Salvador Urbina believed the vision of Just Coffee could not and would not ever become a reality. They had previous experience with "cooperatives." In the past, other organizations had promised them better prices and fair treatment—but had taken advantage of them and deceived them. The growers also knew of cooperatives that were not all that cooperative. One told us directly that Fair Trade was just a scheme to help the leaders of the cooperative get rich, while the rest of the farmers got about five cents more than what the *coyotes* were paying. He said we were naïve and inexperienced. Some growers expressed their skepticism clearly and forcefully, "*No va a funcionar, no sean enganados.*" That is, "It's not going to work; don't be fooled."

49

Another farmer, during a polite conversation over a cup of freshly squeezed lemonade, expanded on why this distrust was so formidable. He described a previous plan some *Americanos* had proposed to the community. This group would put down some initial money for the farmer's coffee and then pay the farmers the remaining balance throughout the rest of the year. They guaranteed at least double the price the *coyotes* paid. The *Americanos* put down 10 percent for the coffee and headed north to market the coffee—never to be heard from again. The moral: *Americanos* are not to be trusted.

Good will ambassadors Miriam and Mark visit with coffee farmers over cookies and coffee.

These challenges of trust only reinforced our conviction in the business model we were proposing—one in which the growers themselves would own equal shares and would share the profits with each other equally.

We continued to reiterate that the *Café Justo* Cooperative would need to be wholly owned and operated by the farmer-members who jointly would have full control over all economic decisions. Cooperative members would need to agree to work together as a community of equals. We also assured them that we *Americanos* were committed to helping the Cooperative make its business work—and would enthusiastically provide whatever advice and assistance might be needed in the process.

In spite of their reservations, the hesitation and resistance soon softened. Gradually everyone turned full attention to the many issues that need to be settled before *Café Justo* could formally take shape. One specific point in the business plan—the payment proposal— proved challenging.

Negotiating the Timing of Payments

The timing of the coffee payment ended up to be the key issue that we needed to resolve with the growers. The stark reality is that there would never be enough cash in the Cooperative's bank account to purchase the entire year's harvest up front like the *coyotes* did. Our hope was to help them understand that to make the *Café Justo* business work, from a cash flow perspective, the Cooperative members needed to switch from being paid a lot of cash once a year to receiving a more regular, predictable, but much smaller, paycheck. We reminded them that if the *Café Justo* business was successful, each member family would receive much more total income during the year.

Eva and Eri (left) look at family photos from Miriam and Mark (right).

This concept was so different from the pattern the growers were used

Walking to the coffee fields with Reynaldo and Eri Cifuentes between meetings.

Visiting with Señora Evarista in her kitchen.

to that it became extremely controversial. Normally coffee is purchased once each year—the growers are paid at the conclusion of each harvest, in November or December. Sometimes the growers take high interest loans from *coyotes* against the next crop to pay their expenses in August and September, when everyone is generally broke. Several elaborate price support schemes have been tried—all of which can easily lead to exploitation of the growers.

Clearly, the growers needed more time to think about the concept of payment we had outlined. We took a break and the Agua Prieta group went into the coffee fields to learn first hand about the coffee growing-business from the farming families—and to tap into their knowledge of shipping, transportation and logistics.

Building Trust

Even though the growers were very interested in the financial details, plans and projections, what they really wanted to know was whether we could be trusted. Only by talking, visiting, listening and asking questions was there a chance for them to determine this. Trusting relationships cannot be accomplished rapidly. So we were introduced to the community of Salvador Urbina one-by-one through a network of family members.

Everyone seemed very happy to meet us. The main theme of their questions to us was, "Who are you? Where do you live? Do you have family: brothers and sisters, aunts and uncles, nieces and nephews, children and cousins? Where are they? What do they do? Do you have any pictures?" This was how they determined who was trustworthy. Verbal commitment alone was not acceptable.

When we returned from our field research and joined the others for the next round of planning, everything but the payment plan had been agreed upon. The coffee growers still needed reassurance that they would not lose reimbursement for "consignment" coffee that was shipped in advance of payment. Regardless of how they were compensated for the first *bulto*, they still voiced concern, recalling their previous experience with *Americano* coffee buyers who never paid.

Cooperatives Thrive on Cooperation

After many rounds of conversation, we finally came to a sense of mutual trust and to an agreement that we would move forward together. The farmers were now ready to formally establish the Cooperative they had named *Café Justo*. The growers understood the necessity to change from receiving payments based on the timing of the harvest to payments based on the Cooperative's cash flow and sales.

*Growers discuss together the pros and cons of the **Café Justo** Cooperative idea.*

Still, the discussions continued. The growers liked the per-pound price but wanted the orders for their coffee to be stronger in the first year. Finally a democratic process prevailed and the price to be received by the farmers was agreed upon.

The good news about this intense debate was that all the growers personally experienced the hallmarks of a true cooperative in action. They clearly saw open communication, decision by consensus and a willingness to stretch their limits beyond what they thought possible. Furthermore, everyone agreed that the president and treasurer of the *Café Justo* Cooperative would receive the same share as the rest of the growers—elected positions would be volunteer and not compensated at a higher level. The growers also accepted the reality that since they owned the entire business together, they were jointly assuming the risk—the money they received would be dependent upon the amount of coffee being sold. Just as in any entrepreneurial business, payments to the growers would depend entirely on revenue received from the sold coffee.

When we left to go back home after eight days, we had the agreements we needed to get started.

The First Cups of Just Coffee!

We left Salvador Urbina having received a firm commitment from the initial group of 24 Cooperative members. The first shipment of raw coffee beans would soon be on its way. We returned with great excitement. The trip had been a success.

When we arrived in Agua Prieta, we were met with a pleasant surprise. Word about our trip's success had preceded us. Orders for roasted and packaged coffee were waiting for us when we reached home. We were face to face with a very high-class problem. We needed to produce the product we had been talking and dreaming about. And we needed to do it right now! *Café Justo* was in business.

Unfortunately, *Café Justo* had orders, but no automated roasting equipment. When the first *bultos* arrived from Chiapas, we planned to hand roast the coffee to fill the waiting orders. Hand roasting is quite an experience. To obtain the distinctive delicious flavor of great coffee, the beans need to be roasted at a temperature above 400 degrees Fahrenheit—the point at which sugars in the coffee caramelize. Throughout the roasting process, the beans must be constantly agitated to prevent burning—a daunting task over an open fire!

Initially, *Café Justo* volunteers roasted the coffee inside a small room, but that turned

Hand roasting coffee in Chiapas.

out to be too smoky and too hot. So they went outdoors and tried mesquite charcoal to give the coffee a mesquite flavor. Although the idea of mesquite-flavored coffee sounded enticing, they soon discovered the taste was not really noticeably improved. It also consumed a lot of mesquite charcoal, so they switched to LP gas.

Miriam Maldonado (Mark's wife), Carmina Sanchez and Magdalena Cifuentes (Daniel's sister) roasted the first hundred pounds of coffee. Other volunteers soon pitched in to help. We even discovered that some of the early Just Coffee customers enjoyed roasting their own coffee—even though it takes about an hour to roast a kilo (2.2 pounds).

The Cooperative was functioning. Customers were eagerly handing over their cash for bags of the coffee. Money was deposited into the bank account. The *Café Justo* Cooperative was finally up and running!

Yes, we were elated. But we were a very long way from *Café Justo* becoming a viable ongoing business. Our conversations and consultations with the growers continued for the next few months as we explored several key components of the business and the Cooperative clarified their philosophy and solidified their plan of operations.

What the Growers Taught Us—People before Profits

On reflection, our experience in Chiapas had underscored an important focus on the human dimension in the coffee growers' value system. Their determination to put relationships first in running a business was inspiring. As was their commitment to family and concern for the wider coffee growing community. During our visits to neighboring coffee farming districts, the Salvador Urbina farmers had shared their vision and hope about how the *Café Justo* model might benefit other communities. As one of them told us, "Why not say all the state of Chiapas?"

In the midst of their economic despair—and even before their own cooperative was up and running—these coffee farmers were thinking of other communities, close to them and far away. Wow! Despite their suffering, they were planning support for other people with whom they were in direct relationship—because of their shared suffering.

True American entrepreneurs that we are, we initially interpreted this approach as a mandate to envision expanding Just Coffee into a huge coffee company that could buy

*Signpost for neighboring El Aguila, Chiapas, suggested site for a second **Café Justo** Cooperative.*

millions of pounds of coffee, roast it and ship it from one central roasting facility. Having a centralized company, we imagined, would increase efficiencies and thereby increase the business profits for the farmers. We were definitely products of capitalism.

However, the farmers had a different vision—a vision that had at its core the value of relationships. In one of the meetings a farmer said, *"Si vamos a poder tostar nuestro propio café y vender directamente a nuestros clientes, porque no pueden las otras comunidades?"* Translated it means, "If we are going to roast our own coffee and sell it directly to our clients, why can't other communities do the same?"

While we were at first baffled by this mindset, the farmers were convinced that person-to-person relationships in a face-to-face manner were a necessary business value. In retrospect, keeping the business small—with relationships at the core of the business—was one of the most important lessons we learned from them. It meant they were going to keep the customer/ client relationship as direct as possible and develop a business model that would benefit the most number of families in the community, rather than being tainted by the inevitable profit-only motives of a huge cooperative. We learned that the farmers didn't much need or want the Cooperative to be maximally efficient in the wider business sense. They needed and wanted it to be productive within the community.

To support this core value, the Cooperative eventually decided to place the name of the coffee grower on each one-pound bag of Just Coffee that was sold, ensuring that the customers would at least know the name of the farmer who grew their coffee. We

First official packaging for Just Coffee, with grower's name on the top label.

Americanos never realized what an important decision this was until we began hearing from people who love knowing the name of the grower who harvested the coffee they are drinking. It adds to the personal experience—another lesson learned. This person-to-person connection also made it more likely that customers would return and buy more coffee. What a win/win situation for all!

For example, Douglass Key, pastor of Mark's home church in Clover, South Carolina, takes a bag of coffee with him to the breakfast table each morning and drinks his delicious cup of coffee. "While savoring this moment, I read the name of the farmer who made it possible for me to enjoy this coffee. I give thanks to God for the farmer and his family and I pray for them." Leone Mahoney, from the University of Arizona and Trinity Presbyterian Church in Tucson, cuts off the labels from each of her bags of coffee and puts them in her prayer book as a reminder to keep the growers in her daily prayers.

During the months after we returned from Chiapas we came to realize what the farmers taught us during out first meetings. Bigger companies are not necessarily more beneficial. Higher performance expectations and pressure to increase sales, revenues and goals by endlessly adding additional members to the Cooperative are not necessarily better for either the Cooperative owners or their customers. Small can be beautiful; personal is best! As we look back we see that this belief has now become well established as an important philosophical guideline for the Cooperative as it makes its decisions.

After much discussion that continued after we returned to Agua Prieta, the organizing farmers made another decision that facilitated more direct relationships between grower and consumer. They decided to install the roasting business at the U.S./Mexico border in Agua Prieta rather than in Salvador Urbina. At first, some had argued it would be best to have the roaster in Chiapas so the jobs created by the roasting process would remain in the coffee-growing community. Others suggested, for reasons of freshness and customer service, the roasting operation should be located at the border, staffed by Daniel Cifuentes and others who were originally from Chiapas but had now been living in Agua Prieta for some time. *Café Justo* determined that despite the benefits of having a roaster in their own community, the Agua Prieta location would extend the Cooperative's presence to the Mexico/U.S. border.

As you will discover in Chapter 6, an unexpected benefit of this decision was how it brought the Just Coffee customers closer to the Cooperative. Awareness of *Café Justo* would no longer be limited to the people who heard about it from the Website, newspapers and marketing flyers. Customers could actually go and visit Daniel just across the border. Once on site, they could experience first-hand where their coffee was being roasted, talk with the *Café Justo* staff about the coffee-making process, and better understand the migration issues.

Business on the Brink

Given the serendipitous combination of growers willing to hope and trust, the supportive startup loan from Frontera de Cristo and committed people of faith from both countries who believed in this mission, it is perhaps not all that surprising how fast everything came together at the end of 2002. The Cooperative had percolated in a few months from being just an idea to becoming a real business with the lives of 24 coffee-growing families in Salvador Urbina depending on its success.

> *As the saying goes, "Be careful what you wish for."*
> *We were suddenly faced with a joyful problem for which*
> *we had fervently prayed. Café Justo was selling coffee! Hallelujah!*
> *The problem? We couldn't produce enough coffee by hand roasting*
> *to keep up with the immediate demand. Café Justo still had*
> *to get a real roaster and figure out how to use it.*

---

[1] For more information on types of coffee see: http://www.gardfoods.com/coffee/coffee.plant.html.

Guadalupe Morales Trejo

Hernan Cifuentes Perez

Coffee should be black as Hell, strong as Death, and sweet as Love.
—Turkish Proverb

Bultos, Quintales

Burlap or plastic bags used to haul coffee beans from field to market. Full bags weigh up to 200 lbs and are carried up steep mountain slopes on the backs of the workers, using cloth head straps for support.

Coyote

In the coffee growing regions of southern Mexico, a crafty coffee buyer who tries to purchase the grower's coffee beans at the lowest possible price. Also called speculators. Many of the *coyotes* intentionally collaborate to suppress prices and misinform the growers about the quality of their product.

Coffee-picking basket in hand, worker hauls a bulto of coffee to the warehouse for sorting and weighing.

Worker "cargoing" a quintal of coffee from the fields to market via a steep mountain path.

CHAPTER 5

Setting up the Business
Are We Roasting Yet?

Café Justo chose Daniel Cifuentes to establish the Agua Prieta headquarters of the Cooperative. He was responsible for finding a suitable location for the roasting operation, purchasing and installing a roaster, figuring out the packaging/exporting/shipping processes, hiring staff, then training them to carry out all the PLUS functions of Fair Trade PLUS coffee. It was quite a daunting job description for a displaced-coffee-grower-turned-factory-worker, but Daniel enthusiastically rose to the challenge.

Finding a Location

When he began looking for a place to roast coffee in Agua Prieta, Daniel discovered that the zoning and development regulations in Mexico are not as restrictive as they are in the U.S. As long as neighbors didn't complain and nothing exploded or burned down, *Café Justo* could begin roasting nearly anywhere!

Initially, the Cooperative wanted to rent a location downtown and convert it into a U.S.-style roasting facility and a retail Just Coffee coffee shop. However, Daniel soon discovered that the rent for commercial space in downtown Agua Prieta started at $1,000 per month—much too expensive for their startup business. So we had to look for something more affordable. This was just as well, since the Cooperative also discovered that roasting and shipping the coffee was going to be more challenging than they originally thought. It would require all the energy and attention Daniel and his crew could muster. Plus the Cooperative didn't have the capital reserve to support a retail coffee shop that served customers over the counter.

The building finally selected for the Just Coffee roasting shop was originally intended to be a Laundromat, which was fortuitous because it was already partially pre-wired with lots of high voltage electricity for the dryers. The storefront was located in a triplex twenty-five

Agua Prieta Laundromat turned coffee roasting shop, at the roaster dedication (June 2006).

blocks south of the border, on the edge of a mixed commercial/residential neighborhood and very close to the main highway. The Laundromat was already a part of another Frontera de Cristo micro-loan project, so *Café Justo's* rent payment would go directly back to another Frontera de Cristo startup business—an added plus. They agreed to rent the space to *Café Justo* for $100 a month.

The composition of the neighborhood and the direction of the prevailing wind were important considerations in making this decision. While many folks love the smell of roasting coffee, it bothers some. *Café Justo* didn't want to be a bother. At the Laundromat location, the wind usually blew from the south, and there were no homes or businesses for a third of a mile to the north. Once we started roasting, when the wind did blow toward the south, Daniel got a few complaints. But the neighbors were quickly won over by the taste of the coffee that he gave them to sample. Daniel was also careful to limit roasting to the middle of the day so as not to disturb families in the evenings and on weekends. Overall the location has worked out fine for *Café Justo* and for their neighbors.

Buying and Installing the Roaster

The art of making excellent coffee is largely determined by the roasting process. *Café Justo* decided to purchase a hot air roaster rather than a barrel roaster, because its popcorn-popper-type process circulates the beans as they roast. Although hot air roasters are more expensive up front and less efficient to operate, they provide a more dependable and consistent result.

Even before they had secured a location for roasting in Agua Prieta, the Cooperative had used the bulk of its mini-loan to order a Sivetz roaster—famous for its excellent temperature controls combined with a state-of-the-art system that evacuates the chaff during the roasting process. This produces a much cleaner roast. Unfortunately, it took twelve weeks before the roaster was delivered to Douglas, Arizona. Meanwhile, Daniel and his crew of volunteers continued to roast coffee by hand.

To make it easier to handle, the roaster was brought across the border into Mexico in pieces. This transport strategy also held a few other advantages which we leave to your imagination. There was one catch—we had to assemble the thing once we got it to the new *Café Justo* headquarters.

Two days before Thanksgiving we began helping *Café Justo* assemble the roaster. They cut a hole in the roof for a humble smoke stack. The electrical boxes had been installed with up-to-date circuit breakers. Volunteer helpers gathered a random collection of tools from their car trunks, as well as a Swiss Army knife. We felt ready.

The technical specifications for the roaster were long and detailed, which was great—except for the fact that our electrician could not read English, nor did he understand electrical schematics. We all saw this as an opportunity. We now had the freedom to help the *Café Justo* staff put the roaster pieces together as they thought best.

Through a lengthy process that included reading the manual, calling Michael Sivetz himself, intermittent prayer and the use of more than a few expletives, the roaster was finally re-assembled and wired up to the electric grid. It may be true that too many cooks spoil the broth, but it seems you can never have enough help to wire and install an electric coffee roaster. At eleven p.m. the night before Thanksgiving 2002, we were drinking the first batch of coffee from *Café Justo's* new roaster.

We still vividly remember how we stood around the roaster marveling at the ten pounds of coffee that had roasted to perfection in only ten minutes. By hand, this achievement would have taken us almost four hot and sweaty hours of back-breaking work. We knew we were experiencing another element of the Just Coffee miracle.

Transportation Challenges

To roast coffee you need coffee beans—lots of them. We understood this, of course, so we helped *Café Justo* explore several ways to get the coffee beans transported the 2,100 miles from the southern border of Mexico to the northern border where the roaster is located.

Zen and the Art of Assembling a Coffee Roaster

We learned a few universal truths from our experience wrestling with the coffee roaster assembly in Agua Prieta. Perhaps these truisms will ring a bell with you.

- When all else fails, read the instructions again—after drinking a cup of coffee.

- Three guys with wrenches are better than one guy with a socket set.

- 220 volts hurts.

- Not everyone has to speak the same language when it's unclear what you are doing anyway.

- Sometimes taking everything apart because it was done backwards or because there were too many parts left over is worth the effort. At other times it's not necessary.

- There is usually more than one best solution.

- Sometimes a fun solution is better than the fast one—it's the journey and not the destination that's important.

- God is great! Throughout this experience, no one got too badly shocked; nothing burned (that we could tell); the coffee was excellent. There were only a few screws and other parts left over—and they probably were not important anyway. Better just to say a prayer of thanks and store all the leftover parts as souvenirs for the visitors.

- You quickly forget the tribulations of the task when you are gathered together in celebration drinking the results of your labor.

Mark, Tommy, Alejandro and Miriam enjoy results of the first Just Coffee roast.

The Cooperative looked at several different shipping options, including sending the coffee as luggage on the unofficial migrant bus that goes between Salvador Urbina and Agua Prieta. In the end, they arranged shipment with a large private national Mexican shipping company—selected because they had the lowest prices and they seemed to be an entirely Mexican-owned business.

When *Café Justo's* first big order of twenty 100-lb sacks of coffee from Salvador Urbina to Agua Prieta was finally shipped, they were told it would arrive in five to ten working days. How exciting for all of us! The long awaited day of roasting the first serious quantity of coffee was only days away.

Everyone waited and waited. On the eleventh day numerous phone calls were exchanged, and it was soon discovered the coffee had ended up in Nogales, Sonora, not Agua Prieta, Sonora. The distance between the two cities traverses two mountain ranges, one Mexican customs checkpoint and about a hundred miles.

No problem. The shipping invoice was clear and certainly the coffee would be forwarded. Alejandro Bahamaca, *Café Justo's* first Director of Customer Service, spoke directly with the Nogales office. They assured him that they understood clearly the coffee should have been delivered to Agua Prieta, and they apologized for the mistake. However, they also explained that *Café Justo* needed to come and pick up the coffee in Nogales because the company did not ship to Agua Prieta and had no plans to start doing so now—and any further questions should be directed to the home office in Mexico City.

The people in Mexico City were very nice and explained that it was entirely the fault of their office in Tapachula (near Salvador Urbina). They apologized profusely. They claimed that the mistake was made in the city of origin and that their people in Tapachula never should have accepted the Cooperative's money because the company does not ship to Agua Prieta. Alejandro responded how he totally understood, but they needed to get the coffee to Agua

60

Ildefonso Ortiz and Eri Cifuentes unload the first decaf coffee shipment in Agua Prieta (2006).

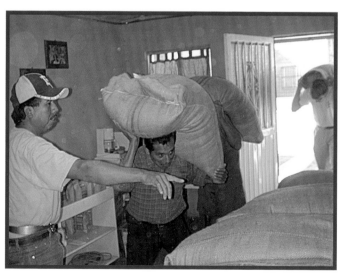

Daniel directs unloading of coffee shipment in the roasting shop.

Prieta as per the shipping contract—or they needed to refund all of the money.

The problem never did get resolved! The harder Alejandro tried, the more the company officials would apologize. Finally, Alejandro rented a truck and picked up the coffee himself. Somehow the team from Agua Prieta was able to move the coffee through the checkpoint without a bribe and without violence.

Café Justo never did get the original shipper to pay for the mistake, although everyone, including the shipper, agreed it was their mistake. We certainly learned there is no substitute for due diligence. We noted that people might be very friendly and offer to help but may not fix anything. We learned again that it is not helpful to get upset and say bad words, which was something we already knew, but due to the circumstances had forgotten several times.

Learning the Export/ Import Rules

Café Justo needed to learn how to export coffee from Mexico and import it into the United States. Coffee is a product that falls under the North American Free Trade Agreement (NAFTA) guidelines. Therefore, there are no duties required on coffee imported into the U.S. from Mexico. However, there are rules—as we learned.

At the beginning, the Cooperative pursued a policy of blissful ignorance

61

> At the beginning . . . when asked, "Are you bringing anything into the country?" the driver would truthfully answer, "Just Coffee"—and pass through the customs check without further questions.

of the guidelines. They would load up the packaged coffee in the trunk of a volunteer's car and the volunteer would drive it across the border. When asked, "Are you bringing anything into the country?" the driver would truthfully answer, "Just Coffee"—and pass through the customs check without further questions.

Eventually, however, when the U.S. Customs officials discovered that our volunteers were crossing with a hundred pounds of Just Coffee at a time, this strategy became a major issue. We were ordered to stop bringing the coffee across in the manner to which we had become accustomed.

Specifically, the Cooperative needed to import the coffee through the commercial port of entry in Douglas, Arizona. Importing is a complicated process. In the post 9/11 era, food imports require complex documentation. It took some time to learn the regulations and figure out how to accomplish all the details, as well as get all the necessary approvals.

We were "encouraged" to prepare the paperwork and ship the coffee through the commercial port of entry. This required payment of a one-time $600 fee for a USDA lab test that would verify there were no rocks, sticks or mold in the coffee. *Café Justo* also was directed to add the name and address of one of the coffee growers on the packaging—something they were happy to do, since it supported their concept of building relationships.

The U.S. government requires strict accountability and an address of origin on every coffee bag. The label which was officially approved and is recognized by Just Coffee drinkers everywhere, uses the address of the Cooperative's president, Eri Cifuentes. The English version reads, "Eri Cifuentes of the Coffee Cooperative of the unincorporated community of Salvador Urbina, which is near the city of Cacahoatan." The humorous part is the phrase, Domicilio Conocido, which could be translated as, "Everyone knows where his house is—it has no address—just ask around."

Agricultural customs officials also ordered us to place a nutritional label on the bags of roasted coffee. We were unable to convince the officials this was not needed, until finally one morning we pointed out to them a Folgers coffee can in their office that they were using as an ashtray. It had no nutritional label. They let the matter drop. Overall, the U.S. Customs officials in Douglas were and have continued to be very professional and supportive—for which we are most grateful.

Organizing the Systems and the Staff

The *Café Justo* Cooperative had hired two employees to start the roasting business—both former residents of Chiapas. Daniel Cifuentes was in charge of the roasting operation. Alejandro Bahamaca handled customer service and all incoming orders. They shared responsibility for the packaging. Most of the time, Alejandro physically processed the coffee through customs into the U.S. and made sure it got to UPS for shipping to its north –of-the-border destinations.

Just Coffee
simple,good and fair
100% pure Arabica Coffee
Shade Tree Grown,
Product of Mexico
See Our Website at:
www.justcoffee.org
Fairly priced,Hand Processed and fully Roasted in Agua Prieta,Sonora Mexico
Provided by Sr. Eri Cifuentes,
Cooperativa Cafe,Ejido Salvador Urbina,
Municipio de Cacahoatan
Domicilio Conocido
Chiapas,Mexico·Net Weight, 16oz.

Original Just Coffee bag label with the address "everyone knows!"

Like the laborious process of growing coffee, *Café Justo's* initial internal business processes were very labor intensive. Alejandro printed labels on the computer printer, then stuck them on the bags right before they were filled and weighed.

At first, *Café Justo* offered only one type of coffee—Arabica. It was packaged either as ground or whole bean coffee. Alejandro soon realized customers were interested in a variety of roasts (light, medium and dark) and grinds—percolator (coarse), drip (normal) and espresso (fine)—to supply their daily coffee fix. As successful small businesses do everywhere, *Café Justo* quickly adjusted to meet demand and expanded their product line to include a dozen or more combinations.

Later, again responding to the demand for specialty coffee, *Café Justo* added the caffeine-rich Robusta species, and eventually started supplying decaffeinated coffee along with their premium brand of Arabica called Pacamara or Margogype. All together today they package and ship almost fifty different combinations of packaged coffee. See page 122 for a complete chart of Just Coffee blends.

As *Café Justo* increased the complexity of its product line, the Cooperative also needed to further develop its organizational systems and to hire more employees who could handle the increased business and complex variety of products.

The original business plan projected a total of less than one ton of shipments in the first year. Instead, *Café Justo* produced over 6.5 tons during that first year! As Daniel often says to visiting groups, paraphrasing Isaiah the prophet, "Our plans are not God's plans . . . and God had a better plan than we did."

To facilitate this rapid and unexpected growth, everyone worked overtime—including Tommy and Mark, who volunteered many hours. As shipments increased, everyone learned how to be a little more efficient. Mark got better at taking orders, Daniel became a faster roaster and packager while Alejandro learned how to cross the border and ship the coffee more quickly. Daniel's wife, Vicki Hernandez, helped him with the packaging and shipping paperwork in the afternoons and evenings.

*Deysi taking orders in the **Café Justo** office.*

As Christmas of the first full year neared, business became stable enough that *Café Justo* was able to hire Vicki fulltime to do the packaging. The Cooperative also hired a part-time secretary, Deysi Garcia, to help with the Internet order processing. The apartment next door became available and they rented it to use for coffee storage. This expansion also provided an apartment for Daniel and Vicki so they could live next to the shop and keep an eye on everything.

As *Café Justo* grew and needed additional staff, they decided to develop a work-release program with CRREDA (*Centro de Rehabilitacion y Recuperacion de Enfermos de Drogas y Alcohol*), a drug and alcohol treatment center in Agua Prieta. The first two interns in the program, Myra and Bisael, had completed the initial three-month support program in CRREDA. They worked with *Café Justo* during the day and

Border Immersion study group visits CRREDA facility #8 in Agua Prieta.

returned to CRREDA in the evening—thus combining their rehabilitation with "real work." When needed, other participants in the CRREDA program have assisted the Cooperative with loading and unloading coffee, painting and various other tasks. In exchange, *Café Justo* provides coffee and financial support to CRREDA in this mutually beneficial exchange.

To supplement the efforts of *Café Justo* employees during busy times or on special projects, staff and friends of Frontera de Cristo Border Ministry often helped out in many aspects of the business in Agua Prieta

Blessing the Business: The Dedication Fiesta

The *Café Justo* Cooperative is always willing to celebrate or "fiesta" for just about any occasion. One of the first fiestas was the dedication for the opening of the roasting shop in Agua Prieta in January 2003. *Café Justo* decided to hold this event in Agua Prieta and bring the Cooperative officers, Eri Cifuentes, Reynaldo Cifuentes, and Ildefonso Ortiz, from Chiapas to Agua Prieta for their first visit to the northern frontier and the roasting shop.

Plans were made and guests were invited. The shop was painted and cleaned up as were the employees, who we might add cleaned up quite well! Invitations were sent to customers and supporters, food was cooked and prepared. Tickets for the bus ride from Chiapas were purchased, and preparations were made for a celebration with a hundred people.

The dedication was scheduled to start at 11:00 a.m. Saturday with refreshments and speeches from the Cooperative's president, vice president and treasurer. This was to be followed by lunch—a Chiapan-style array of tamales and mole (a chocolate jalapeño sauce that is good on everything from fingers to tacos). Following lunch we were scheduled to conduct tours of the roasting shop.

The speeches and food would take place at a home six blocks away because the roasting shop was too small to hold so many people. We would shuffle people back and forth to visit the roaster, see coffee being roasted and enjoy coffee samples—as well as try to sell a few pounds of coffee, some T-shirts and coffee cups. Yes, the entrepreneurial spirit is alive and well. We are located in a border tourist town after all!

Serving up rice and tamales at the grand dedication (Janurary 2003).

The growers from Chiapas arrived the day before the event and soon informed us that while everything here was very, very nice, they would like to leave for home as soon as possible. They did not like the desert, the dust, the heat, or the lack of rain—and they felt it was not fair that they could not cross into the U.S. without all the special papers and permits that take years to get.

We tried to calm them down. They were very gracious but they kept insisting they really didn't like the desert at all. The dryness and lack of shade and green plants made them yearn for the lush vegetation at home. There were no bananas, mangoes or papayas within reach here—something we, too, had noticed.

We understood their sincere desire to get back home as soon as possible, but it made us a little sad. We were not sad because our friends from the Cooperative didn't like the desert heat. This was predictable. We were sad because their strong feelings reminded us of all the people from the lush green rain forest of the south who were crossing the dry and dangerous desert in search of work and opportunity. We imagined how difficult it was for those frightened, isolated border-crossers to navigate the desert and know that they could not go home again soon.

After some discussion with our members from Chiapas, we all agreed they would be leaving by bus the next afternoon after the celebration ended.

The big day arrived. The tamales were ready; the dirt street in front of the roasting headquarters was swept and watered. The shade tarp was strung, and all the chairs from the Lily of the Valley had been set up in the yard where the reception would be held. The Horchata, (a popular local drink made from rice) was iced, and more than a hundred cups of coffee were brewed. Festivities were scheduled to begin around 11:00 a.m. and end by the heat of the day at 2:00 p.m. or so.

We had borrowed some vans and trucks to transport the people to and from the reception home to the roasting shop six blocks away. We also had arranged rides to and from the border to the reception for those U.S. attendees who did not want to drive in Mexico.

65

Mark addresses the crowd at the grand dedication festivities.

Finally we were all ready and waiting, standing in our "Sunday-go-to-meeting" clothes, ready for the festivities to begin.

People came from all over the state of Arizona—and several from New Mexico and California. They started arriving around 10:30 in the morning and were all pretty much there by 11:00 a.m. All, that is, except our friends from Salvador Urbina.

As we waited, we stalled. Alejandro gave out coffee. Mark made introductions. Generally we tried to hide our anxiety that the coffee gang was not there and our terror that they might not show up. Daniel and Tommy searched all over Agua Prieta for them. Eventually they arrived at the dedication around 12:15 p.m.—over an hour late, wondering what all our fuss was about.

They never really explained to us what happened other than that they needed to do some shopping. The growers had also met with the mayor of Agua Prieta and bought a carburetor for a truck.

To our relief, the celebration finally got started. The dedication was inspiring. Only one problem. By the time the growers from Chiapas began to talk, the guests were perspiring—beginning to roast like coffee beans drying on the patio under the hot sun. In the end, everything went as planned and other than the sunburn and heat, the dedication went off smoothly.

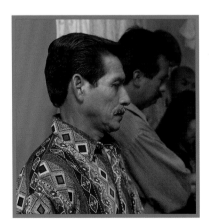

Ildefonso Ortiz meditates on the potential of Café Justo.

Afterwards, when we were sitting around discussing the fiesta, the growers told us they were very happy—amazed at how many people came to wish the Cooperative luck and success. The few guests who noticed our deviation from the schedule attributed it to "Mexican time." Some of us were frazzled, but all of us were pleased.

As a result of this celebration, *Café Justo* gained a newly enthusiastic supporter. Cooperative Treasurer Ildefonso Ortiz, from Salvador Urbina, became a true believer once he had a chance to meet the Just Coffee customers face to face. Walking down the dirt road in front of the roaster as the sun was setting Ildefonso mused, "I never believed that Presbyterians and Catholics could work together, but now I have seen it is possible." Again we learned more—being on the border is past being flexible, it's about being fluid.

Realizing the Quirky Dream

Café Justo began its official coffee processing operations in Agua Prieta with a roaster, a grinder, a scale, twenty 100-pound sacks of coffee, two tables donated from the First Presbyterian Church in Douglas and lots of one-pound, windowed paper coffee bags. The Cooperative bought some plastic tubs to hold the roasted coffee while filling and shipping orders. It was enough for a start!

The fledgling Just Coffee roasting and exporting business did have its moments. One evening we arrived at the roaster and noticed there was smoke billowing not only from the smoke stack, but out of every possible door and window in the facility. Bisael (CRREDA Intern) ran past me with a bucket of water, and Daniel and Adrian Gonzalez (Director of Customer Relations) were frantically scurrying around. Meanwhile, Myra (CRREDA Intern) was sitting calmly at her desk with her eyes tightly closed, listening to music and responding to an e-mail. Afterwards she said, "Putting out fires isn't in my job description." Fortunately, the operation sustained only minor damage.

With his sense of humor and down-to-earth viewpoint, Tommy contended that starting a coffee business seemed a lot like putting together some kind of illicit enterprise. After all, the product came in big burlap bags trucked up from the tropical jungles of Mexico. Business was often conducted in Spartan quarters under the light of a single bulb suspended from a wire coming from the ceiling. We were always buying kilos or "keys" of coffee, and it came from people with exotic names like El Gato. The product was frequently sampled to the exclamations of "That is good stuff!" and "How do you think the next crop will be?" and "Wow, that will keep you up all night!!!" And after all, the initial shipments were packaged in baggies!

Clearly, *Café Justo* is an unconventional business. From starting up without a budget or a salaried sales and marketing team, to mesquite-roasting coffee over an open fire, pouring it into zip-lock bags and crossing the coffee from Mexico into the U.S. in 75- to 100-bag batches—*Café Justo* has done things differently from the very beginning and has learned a lot in the process.

With a lot of hard work and a full measure of God's grace, *Café Justo* was finally organized and fully functioning. It took almost three years from the time Eduardo first raised his challenging question to the realization of his vision with a truly just response fashioned by the Cooperative with the assistance of Frontera de Cristo.

Without a doubt, *Café Justo* had indeed arrived.

Ildefonso Ortiz Mejia   **Ismael Juan Morales Trejo**

Coffee, according to the women of Denmark, is to the body what the Word of the Lord is to the soul.

—Isak Dinesen

To this day, we rely on word-of-mouth advertising to carry the message of the coffee and its benefits for the Cooperative to the coffee drinking public. The main advocates for coffee sales continue to be a core group of sellers who have come forth from various human rights and faith-based organizations to selflessly promote Just Coffee. These advocates have connected with *Café Justo*'s growers on a deep and purposeful level. Several have actually gone down to Salvador Urbina to meet the growers and learn more about their plight. These volunteers assume responsibility for ordering the coffee, organizing and creating promotional materials, and selling the coffee to their respective organizations and churches on a regular basis—all this for no financial benefit of their own.

A handful of red ripe coffee cherries bears witness to Café Justo's success.

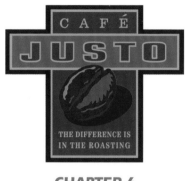

CHAPTER 6

Selling the Coffee
Word-of-Mouth Miracle Marketing

Eduardo Verdugo's vision of connecting producers and consumers in just relationships over a cup of coffee was settling into place. The coffee roaster was installed and working beautifully, producing a surprising amount of high quality coffee. The initial business plan had been written. And *Café Justo* was starting to sell many varieties of roasted coffee.

Up to this point, we had not found time to help the Cooperative develop a clearly defined outline of marketing and sales strategies. It felt so good—and frankly we were so relieved, finally, to be producing coffee—that we had not put much energy into developing a plan to sell more. While Frontera de Cristo, the Presbyterian Border Ministry organization, had committed itself to providing a bridge to the market for the coffee that *Café Justo* produced, no one in either organization had any real experience in business sales and marketing.

How was *Café Justo* going to sell all this coffee to U.S. consumers? We were not at all sure. So we did what we do best—we trusted that somehow the vision would be fulfilled. That kind of blind faith is not necessarily a commonly accepted business practice, but it's what we had to work with for the moment.

To be sure, *Café Justo* did have a lot of support for its marketing and sales efforts. We had a great story to tell and a whole host of enthusiastic volunteers who emerged from everywhere wanting to help us distribute the coffee. The business was founded on humane and sound economic principles. We were quickly developing a wide network of potential customers for Just Coffee—all by word of mouth.

Irresistible Marketing Message Draws Volunteers

Why did people respond so enthusiastically to Just Coffee? The magic is in the message. The moral of the *Café Justo* story is both simple and profound—anyone can participate in a

> ### The benefits of buying Just Coffee are nearly irresistible.
>
> - **First, the coffee is organically grown, delicious to the taste—and a good value.**
>
> - **Second, ALL the revenues go to the grower's Cooperative in Chiapas, which makes it Fair Trade PLUS.**
>
> - **Third, it allows the coffee farmers to remain in their homeland.**
>
> - **Finally, the Just Coffee drinker helps support development of new spin-off jobs and economic development south of the border.**

just solution for the current immigration crisis simply by purchasing Just Coffee.

The benefits of buying Just Coffee are nearly irresistible. First, the coffee is organically grown, delicious to the taste—and a good value. Second, ALL the revenues go to the grower's Cooperative in Chiapas, which makes it Fair Trade PLUS. Third, it allows the coffee farmers to remain in their homeland. Finally, the Just Coffee drinker helps support development of new spin-off jobs and economic development south of the border.

Regardless of the political background and beliefs of the customer, no matter where they stand on the issue of immigration—from open borders to sealed and closed borders—almost everyone can agree that the situation would be improved if potential migrants had a good solid economic reason to remain in their homeland. Who can argue against the position that it is best for everyone if the coffee growers live where they are comfortable, with their families and loved ones?

Purchasing Just Coffee has a direct impact on the negative effects surrounding migration and on the cause of migration. Buying the coffee for your home, church and workplace, giving it away as gifts and promoting it around the water cooler are relatively painless steps that have a direct and positive impact on migration patterns and on the lives of the coffee growing communities—and THE COFFEE IS GREAT!

As we told the *Café Justo* story to customers and study tours, to church groups and youth gatherings, people responded.

The Volunteers Who Emerged

We had no real experience in promoting Just Coffee beyond the exuberance of sharing a cup and letting it speak for itself, then telling the story. Nor was there enough money in the budget to hire someone to develop a marketing plan. Perhaps this was fortunate. In the midst of the organizational void, we discovered a whole network of friends and volunteers who picked up the promotional mantle for Just Coffee.

The following examples show how a spontaneous Just Coffee marketing plan unfolded through the passion and dedication of many individuals who showed up at the door and jumped in to help find customers for the coffee.

Just Coffee on Wheels

Mark tells the story of meeting Walter and Mary Danforth, who became a two-person marketing and sales tornado for Just Coffee.

On July 3, 2002, shortly after the first small coffee shipment arrived from Salvador Urbina,

Mary and Walter Danforth waltz into
Café Justo.

the phone rang in the office just as I was leaving for one of four engagements I had scheduled that day. "Frontera de Cristo, Mark speaking," I answered hurriedly.

"Mark, this is Walter Danforth," responded a strong and determined voice on the other end. "I met you in October of 1998 at a Mission Fair at University Presbyterian Church in Tempe. I have followed your ministry and would like to become more involved. I just retired and would like to come down and talk to you about the possibilities of volunteering."

"When would you like to come down?" I asked, expecting him to say a week from now.

"Today. When can I see you?" he responded.

"Well, I'm leaving for a prayer meeting right now and then have a meeting from 10:00 to 11:00. At 11:45 I have a lunch appointment and then at 1:30 I have a meeting with the Border Patrol. At 3:30 I have a meeting at the First Presbyterian Church and then a prayer vigil at 5:15." I thought it would be very clear I could not meet with him today but he immediately stated, "Sounds like you are free from 11:00 to 11:45. We'll be there."

So we met together from 11:00 to 11:45 a.m. Little did I know that Walter and Mary, his wife, would become an essential part of the sales and marketing team for Just Coffee. Walter had retired a week earlier from a career in sales. He and Mary felt a call to serve the church in a more fulltime commitment. After our initial conversation, it became evident their passions and talents matched the great need at *Café Justo*.

Walter and Mary committed themselves to be Mission Volunteers for Frontera de Cristo with the primary responsibility of promoting Just Coffee. They eventually bought an RV and traveled the country sharing the vision of *Café Justo* in churches and presbyteries in eleven different states. They invited individuals, churches and organizations to join with the Mexican coffee farmers in forming the headwaters of this unlikely, but mighty, stream of justice.

Walter and Mary began their tour on December 5, 2002—less than two weeks after *Café Justo* began roasting with its new roaster. Walter was fond of saying that he knew Mark (and not God) had arranged their northern schedule because God would not have sent him to Buffalo, New York, during the fourth week of January. But where better to sell coffee?

During their three-month RV adventure from December to February, Walter and Mary sold over a thousand pounds of coffee, serving as the main income generator for *Café Justo* in its first months. In addition, seven of the churches they visited became regular partners and are still buying Just Coffee six years later. They continue to be supporters and spiritual visionaries for the Cooperative.

Walter and Mary were the first in a series of people who became channels for connecting producers and consumers in right relationships. While each person who promoted Just Coffee used different techniques and had different political philosophies, they each shared

Father Bob Carney visits the border.

Barbara Padilla cements relationship with Café Justo employees Daniel Cifuentes and Vicki Hernandez.

a belief that Just Coffee was a much more effective response to the immigration crisis than building walls.

Immersion and a Just Coffee Cart

Father Bob Carney was pastor of St. Luke's Catholic Parish in Douglas, Arizona, before the wall between Douglas and Agua Prieta was constructed in 1997. He witnessed the increasing division and fear that had grown in the border communities. As a result, he became passionate about putting energy into building relationships across the border, rather than constructing walls on borders. He understood Just Coffee as a perfect vehicle not only for creating good economic relationships across borders but also for building human relationships that could destroy the walls of fear that separate us.

In 2002, Father Bob moved to Tucson to become the social justice gadfly of the Diocese of Tucson. He introduced Just Coffee at his new parish in Tucson and began bringing interested parishioners from Tucson down to Agua Prieta for immersion experiences on the border. He was hoping to build a wider understanding of the complex forces that were at play on our border and wanted to help individuals and parishes discover how they could become positive forces at the border.

Barbara Padilla was on one of Father Bob's first trips to Agua Prieta. She had previously gone on a diocesan trip to Altar, Sonora, a small Mexican desert village that served as a daily launching point for the nighttime border-crossing marathon. She had been deeply moved by the streams of human beings she saw crossing through such a desolate part of the border. She called her experience in Altar a transformative one that inspired her to put her faith into practice.

Father Bob led the group to visit the roasting facility in Agua Prieta and Barbara found a very specific way to make a difference.

After drinking coffee and having conversations with Daniel Cifuentes and Vicki Hernandez, she committed herself to being a Just Coffee promoter in her parish, Our Mother of Sorrows, Tucson. For Barbara, Just Coffee was no longer just about a good idea, it was about family—families on two sides of the border working together to make the world a better place.

Our Mother of Sorrows Just Coffee coffee cart.

Homer Hamby (second from left) at the Just Coffee dedication.

As she promised, Barbara formed a Just Coffee promotion group at her parish. She and others dusted off an old coffee cart and decorated it with pictures of coffee farming families from Salvador Urbina. Every other Sunday, after each mass, Barbara and her friends sell coffee to the parishioners with the support of the entire parish staff. They are not shy about sharing the story behind Just Coffee with their fellow worshippers, encouraging each person to make a difference by buying the coffee. In the first year alone, Barbara sold over a thousand pounds of coffee, which enabled at least one family to stay in Chiapas rather than leaving their land to migrate. Barbara continues to make a difference long after the coffee is sold and enjoyed.

Minute for Mission Outreach

Homer Hamby retired to Silver City, New Mexico, from a successful veterinary practice in Iowa. In the spring of 2003, he brought down some books for a community library in Agua Prieta, and we invited him to participate in our weekly Prayer Vigil for the families of those who had died in our deserts and for peace on our borders. We could tell that for Homer, the vigil was not a natural way of expressing his faith.

When we shared with him the story of Just Coffee, however, his eyes lit up and we could tell he would be a wonderful promoter. We sent him back with ten pounds of coffee to share with the First Presbyterian Church, Silver City, a congregation of about 150. We billed his pastor, Rev. Bob Reese, who at first was a bit reluctant to commit his congregation to purchasing such a large quantity of coffee.

Pastor Bob Reese (red cup) enjoying the dedication refreshments.

But during the next Sunday's church service, Homer presented the story of *Café Justo* during a "Minute for Mission" (see sample outline on page 120) and sold the entire coffee supply he had brought. One member of the congregation was so moved by Homer's simple, yet passionate, promotion of Just Coffee that he committed to selling Just Coffee at his rock shop. Homer also began taking Just Coffee to the local coffee shops and once a month offering Just Coffee after the worship services of First Presbyterian Church. By the end of the year, First Presbyterian Church was the highest per capita coffee partner in our system—selling over 540 pounds.

Just Coffee Partnerships

Hal Fray, a retired octogenarian pastor, resides in Green Valley, Arizona. In the fall of 2004, he participated in the annual Frontera de Cristo Border to Border Mission Delegation: Coffee, Migration and Faith. This trip to Chiapas allowed the participants to see the coffee harvest and interact directly with the growers and their families.

Having spent time with the coffee farmers, he returned from his week with a new found sense of purpose. Hal was convinced he could make a difference—and make a difference he has. Hal began tirelessly promoting Just Coffee in the churches of Green Valley, encouraging five of them to become *Café Justo* partners. In their first year of partnership, these churches bought hundreds of pounds of coffee.

Roy Goodman is a teacher and activist from Bisbee, Arizona. Each Saturday he takes Just Coffee and promotional material to the local farmers' market. In doing so, he has connected Just Coffee to markets beyond the church.

People just kept showing up and volunteering to help us get Just Coffee sold in their neighborhoods—too many to name in this book. What beautiful examples, each one, of how this project extends the caring community across all borders. (See pg 126 in the Resources section for information on contacting these and other *Café Justo* partners).

Rev. Hal Frey bypasses border formalities, crossing the mighty Suchiate River by boat from Guatemala into Chiapas.

In 2002, there was no clear marketing plan for Just Coffee. However, through the commitment of Walter and Mary, Bob, Barbara, Homer, Hal, Roy and countless other Just Coffee fans, word spread quickly about Just Coffee and increasing numbers of people nationwide accepted the invitation to become active participants in this innovative justice project. While over 63 percent Just Coffee sales today are in Arizona, there are *Café Justo* partners active in all fifty states. Individuals, churches, businesses and organizations across the country have decided they can make a difference by buying and promoting this delicious Just Coffee.

Without these committed folks, the vision of *Café Justo* would never have become the reality it is today. Each year the number of committed people has increased; the sales of Just Coffee have grown; and as a result, the impact on the families and community of Salvador Urbina has multiplied exponentially. The trickle of justice that began with the vision of one man is gaining strength each day and will soon transform not only one community but many communities in the south, thereby influencing a whole industry with its unique form of trickle-up economics.

Virtual Volunteers Online

Way back in 2001, when there were still nine planets, and Websites were simpler, Tommy bought a book on Website design and took a free class at the library on Website development so we could be prepared to help *Café Justo* take advantage of borderless commerce. Using this limited knowledge, Tommy eventually created a simple Just Coffee Website and posted it. What we didn't have in technical skills, we made up for with pictures, prayers and enthusiastic reviews from friends and clients.

After the Website was on line for a year or so, a generous supporter took pity on us, upgraded the site and added a shopping cart option. Websites are a lot of work to maintain—way more than we originally thought—and we are thankful for all the help that has been received throughout the years on the Just Coffee Website.

Professional PR

One of the Cooperative's major goals has been to make everything as simple as possible. The original *Café Justo* logo was a green rectangle with "Just Coffee" written in big white letters and "simple, good and fair" in smaller letters below. It was a simple concept, just like the coffee. Yet today's competitive marketplace for Fair Trade "organic" coffee requires a bit more sophisticated image. *Café Justo* has recently updated and streamlined the Just Coffee logo—once again, thanks to the generosity and skill of volunteers.

Original Just Coffee logo, 2002-2007.

New Café Justo Logo, 2007.

In October of 2006, Anne Lewis, vice president of Cornerstone MTM, a marketing firm from Baltimore, Maryland, visited *Café Justo* in Agua Prieta with a church group. During the ride back to the U.S. on the bus, Anne approached Mark while he was talking with another participant. "Do you think there is anything that Just Coffee could use in terms of marketing support? If so, let me know. I'd love to help."

Mark acknowledged that *Café Justo* could use some help with marketing and that he would talk with her later about details. The person Mark was talking with looked at him seriously and said, "Whatever you do—take her up on the offer, she's the best there is." Over the course of a year, Anne and her Cornerstone team (Patchen Mortimer, Jack Hovey) dedicated many hours, phenomenal talent and a heaping measure of passion toward helping Just Coffee develop a professional logo as well as brochures and other promotional materials—another of the myriad of "just in time" gifts that Just Coffee has received. The new logo tagline, The Difference Is in the Roasting, summarizes the key element that distinguishes Just Coffee from all other Fair Trade coffees—the *Café Justo* Cooperative not only grows the coffee, it roasts the coffee as well, and collects all the value-added revenue from the process.

Field Trips and Face-to-Face Connections

The direct link *Café Justo* establishes between growers and consumers remains the primary and most effective sales tool for Just Coffee. It is a founding principle. This is how we advance understanding and bring the critical human issues surrounding the current border

Why Buy Just Coffee? Because It's Organic, More than Fair to the Growers, and Delicious!

	Non Fair Trade Store Brand or Discount Coffees	Fair TradeCoffees	Fair Trade PLUS JUST COFFEE *Café Justo*
Quantity per package	1 lb to 3 lb packages.	Often 12 ounces packaged to look like full pound.	1 full pound (16 ounces)
Price per pound	$3.50	$4.75 to $10.00 per package equals $5.93 to $13.33 per pound.	$6.75-$8.00 ($9.00 decaf)
Grower receives	$0.60 to $0.80 per pound (based on 5-year average). No health or retirement benefits.	Fair Trade cooperatives receive $1.31-1.41 per pound. Farmers are paid $0.60-1.10 per pound. No benefits to growers or value added to community.	Growers receive $1.33 ($1.60 in 2008) per pound, plus family health insurance and retirement benefits. Cooperatives receive additional revenue from roasting and export.
Fair Trade?	No	Certified Fair Trade green coffee beans imported into U.S. and roasted by U.S. companies.	Member of the Fair Trade Federation; Fair Trade PLUS—vertical market integration keeps all money in farmers' country.
Species of beans	Cheaper, lower quality beans, unidentified proportional blends.	Varies; many flavored or mixed blends with flavor added.	100% pure Arabica, Robusto, or Marago; clearly labeled blends.
Organically grown?	No	Varies, many organic.	Yes—100% USDA Certified Organic status.
Growing locations	Anywhere in the world, purchased via spot market wherever the price is lowest.	Varies, many estate-grown.	Estate coffee—always produced by the same growers on the same lands; from Chiapas and Veracruz.
Growing method	Clear-cut, sun-grown monoculture, which requires chemicals.	Varies, mostly shade grown.	Shade grown, rain-forest friendly in an integrated plant community with no chemicals.
Insect control	Agrochemicals—typically bean beetle insecticide.	Varies, many do not use agrochemicals.	Via other nearby plants—a natural method.
Weed control & fertilizers	Herbicide and fertilizer agrochemicals applied up to 3 times per season.	Varies, many do not use agrochemicals.	Weeds are hand-removed by machete and mulched for a natural fertilizer and to retain water.
Harvesting	Hand-picked and brought to road near coffee fields. Some machine harvested.	Varies.	Hand-picked and carried out by foot or pack animal.
Drying process	Dried in gas-fired drums.	Varies, many are sun-dried.	Sun-dried slowly on patios.
Age of beans	Up to 10 years old.	Varies.	Always the most current crop.
Roasting ownership	Corporation owned—all job creation and value added through roasting is exported out of farming community.	Beans are exported to U.S.-owned Fair Trade cooperatives before roasting—no value added to original farming community.	Farmer-owned roasters—job creation and value added stays in farming community. Very positive economic impact.

issues to the forefront.

The closeness of the roasting facility to the U.S./Mexico border—the shop is only three miles south—facilitates lots of visits from customers. These personal connections are critical to the success of the Cooperative's mission and simply a lot of fun for everyone as the roasters and visitors exchange perspectives over a great cup of hot fresh Just Coffee.

On a typical visit, a group of about ten people cross the border to see our facility, hoping to better understand what we do in the business, as well as ask about the border issues that regularly face immigrants. Normally the visitors, ages eight to ninety, are part of a group, usually a school or church. The average visit lasts an hour and a half.

Daniel, the coffee roaster/production manager from Salvador Urbina, usually presents an overview of the coffee commercialization process and the history of the *Café Justo* Cooperative. Hugo Cifuentes describes how the coffee gets roasted. Vicki Hernandez demonstrates the grinding and packaging process. There is always a lot of time for questions, answers and a fresh cuppa java. The presentation is usually followed by a demonstration of the roasting equipment and discussion about the different types of coffee and roasting techniques. Of course, freshly-roasted coffee is always for sale along with Just Coffee logo souvenirs—T-shirts, coffee cups, pens, etc.

Good humor often emerges during these exchanges. One customer came to visit *Café Justo* soon after production started, when shipments were about five hundred pounds of coffee a week. The roaster shop was immaculate, and everything was organized, clean and in order, yet the visitor seemed a little reticent about the experience. After returning to Douglas she asked, "Why does Vicki use a red ALPO dog food scoop to fill the bags?" "Because it scoops up exactly a pound," we answered turning a little ALPO red. They still use the Alpo scoop for accurate measuring, but now it's usually hidden when visitors come. If you don't see the scoop when you visit, don't hesitate to ask for it!

These visits offer *Café Justo* an opportunity to act out one of their core values—offering time for the growers and the buyers of the coffee to make a personal connection. Many of the customers have never knowingly met someone from Chiapas who grows coffee. It has also been valuable for the team in the shop to meet their customers. Some customers have visited several times. There is always coffee in the pot and lively Mexican *corridos* and *cumbias* playing on the radio. So, do drop in sometime when you're in the neighborhood!

The famous Alpo scoop.

Like many businesses, the coffee roasting business goes through a seasonal cycle. Sales are slower in the hotter months and are strongest around Christmas and during the cooler months. The variation in the workload means that from June through August sales are slow and the workers have lots of time to clean and organize. Summer also happens to be the time when we receive the most visitors. November through February are the busiest months, which means the employees put in a lot of extra hours filling orders. *Café Justo* still welcomes visitors during these winter months, but only a fraction of the number who come in the summertime.

The fact that *Café Justo* encourages its customers to come and visit is a unique aspect for the business, and it is almost always meaningful both for the visitor and the staff. Since it's easier to visit Agua Prieta than it is to go all the way to Chiapas, we receive most visitors at the roasting shop.

*Immersion study group visits the **Café Justo** roasting shop.*

Border-to-Border Delegations—Coffee, Migration & Faith

In recent years the Cooperative, through Frontera de Cristo, has also organized yearly, more intensive, weeklong visits to the growers in Chiapas. Salvador Urbina is located on the border with Guatemala and is actually the southernmost point in Mexico. Each year since 2003, Frontera de Cristo has facilitated the 2,100-mile trek down to Salvador Urbina with groups of five to fifteen guests, who get a first-hand tour of the coffee cultivation region and view the actual processing of Just Coffee. Participants in these educational border-to-border delegations live with the coffee farming families, pick coffee under the shade trees of the coffee fields and visit the warehouses and drying patios. This personal connection has been more valuable to the growers and consumers than any third-party "organic" or "Fair Trade" certifications.

On the first "Coffee, Migration and Faith" trip in 2003, Cooperative member Maria Cristina invited the entire group to eat at her home with her husband Victor and their five daughters. It was the third invitation to eat the group had accepted on that day—and it was only 2:00 p.m.! Maria Cristina shared with the group how good it was to be together as family. In past years, Victor had gone north, crossing the border without proper documentation, to harvest Christmas trees in Virginia. That year (and all the years since), he would be home for Christmas.

On the same trip, coffee grower Arnulfo Lopez's daughter Maria, who was working temporarily north of the border, asked her father to open up her brand new home to the visiting strangers from the U.S. The house was so new she had never seen it or set foot in it—she was still working in the U.S. to earn enough money for furniture. How sadly ironic that Maria could be so welcoming with the fruits of her labors while at the same time she was not officially welcome as a laborer in the U.S. hospitality industry, which is fueled by undocumented workers.

Each year since, the residents of Salvador Urbina continue to generously open their homes to our group for food and shelter, offering generous hospitality, giving up their beds and sharing the stories of their life and work and faith with Border-to-Border pilgrims eager to experience more of the connection between coffee, migration and faith—and to share in the hope and joy that *Café Justo* is creating. (See page 123 for information on future delegations and experiential/educational opportunities.)

Many other Just Coffee customers have made the trip to Chiapas on their own, staying with the growers' families from several days to several weeks. The growers enjoy these visits, and the community of Salvador Urbina has seen a lot of Americans coming to look around, drink the coffee, learn about the culture and just visit. The Cooperative and its growers welcome the visitors, who have come from very diverse backgrounds.

Personal Connections Cultivate Exceptional Just Coffee Promoters

Barbara Padilla, creator of the coffee cart ministry in Tucson, is a perfect example of how a visit to the border can transform people. A mother of two teenage sons, she was living in suburban Tucson, tending to her family without much involvement in migration or social justice issues or awareness of the plight of the migrants or coffee growers. She had heard about migration and "illegals," but between golf lessons and basketball games, helping with the kid's homework and supporting her church, there was not much time or a clear path she could follow to explore the issues or have any impact on the coffee growers or desert crossers.

> Each mother who crosses the desert hopes to make a living wage so her children will have a chance to survive, avoiding the slow, suffering death brought about by poverty.

Things really changed for Barbara on her first border visit, when she met a Mexican mother of two who decided to leave her children and cross the border to find work that could pay for schooling, doctors and the clothes and books that growing children need. Barbara connected with this young migrant mother and immediately recognized a clear mission and decisive commitment to help other women and children avoid the walk along the Devil's Highway and through the desert inferno—only to face abuse, exploitation and even death. Each mother who crosses the desert hopes to make a living wage so her children will have a chance to survive, avoiding the slow, suffering death brought about by poverty.

Once she heard about the *Café Justo* Cooperative, Barbara made a deep and lasting connection with the project, seeing clearly how she could help change the lives of struggling mothers south of the border. She had always enjoyed coffee, so making the switch from corporate coffee to Just Coffee was easy. The coffee was great; the cause was even better! Soon after her border visit, Barbara initiated a Just Coffee project in her church. Before long, Our Mother of Sorrows was one of the largest Just Coffee sales outlets. And mothers in Chiapas could stay at home with their children.

Miracle Marketing Strategy

The particulars of Barbara's story are unique, but the pattern is similar in many other churches. People of conscience want to do something to eliminate suffering and injustice. Selling Just Coffee is a viable method, at the local level, of making such an impact.

Many other individuals have taken up the cause of promoting Just Coffee in their churches and communities. The resultant coffee sales—and the ways people have been touched and moved to action by the *Café Justo* story—are incredible. It is this type of energy the Cooperative has depended on from the beginning and person-to-person grass roots support continues to undergird the Cooperative's remarkable success.

The business success of *Café Justo* is based on bringing people together into a mutually beneficial relationship with a common commitment to making life better for all. The amazing personal connections and advocacy of our "volunteer" sales force are truly miraculous elements of the Just Coffee story.

**It's no exaggeration when we define our primary
sales method as the word-of-mouth Miracle Marketing
Strategy—because that's surely what it has become.**

Jorge Mario Lopez Portillo   **Juan Carlos Perez Martinez**   **Lazaro Hernandez Godinez**

Déjà Brew: "The feeling that you've had this coffee before."

—Author Unknown

The customers of *Café Justo* have made a decision to help the growers and the economy of Mexico by buying and advocating for the Cooperative's coffee. Rather than philosophizing about the merits of various immigration strategies, Just Coffee customers are doing something about the difficult situation on the U.S./Mexico border through their financial support and purchase of coffee that directly supports the growers in their desire to make a living in Chiapas.

Coffee beans patio drying in Salvador Urbina.

CHAPTER 7

Evaluating *Café Justo*
Five Years of Success, Growth and Challenge

The initial success of the *Café Justo* Cooperative was far greater than anyone had dared to hope. From the beginning, we all had felt somewhat anxious and uncertain because we were venturing into new territory. We shared the dreams, vision, goals and hopes of the farmers, but neither we nor they had been down this path before. Frankly, at the beginning, it was scary. Some of this uncertainty remained even after the Cooperative began operating and coffee sales were beginning to thrive.

Remember, the growers had heard of hustlers coming down from the U.S. and promising all sorts of great profits, then never delivering results and actually running off without paying for the coffee. We did not want that scenario repeated! We were naturally a bit nervous that insufficient sales would cause the Cooperative to run out of cash. We were also aware that a sudden jump in demand for Just Coffee could outpace the Cooperative's ability to deliver the product in a timely manner to enthusiastic customers. It was a delicate balance.

Financial Success of Café Justo

As it turned out, the first full year's production and sales (2003) were a nearly perfect match—the Cooperative delivered more than what was originally projected and the demand for Just Coffee exceeded expectations in a similar proportion. In that initial year the farmers produced eight tons of beans resulting in 13,000 pounds of roasted coffee. (Coffee loses about 15 to 18 percent of its weight during the roasting process.) The Agua Prieta roasting facility sold and shipped nearly all the inventory.

Although payments to the growers needed to be slow at first due to the tight cash flow, the Cooperative was soon able to pay the growers on a regular basis. By the end of the first year, all growers had been paid in full for the coffee they had delivered. The Cooperative's success in paying the growers fairly, consistently and completely raised their level of confidence, and they eagerly began planning for the year ahead. Trust and enthusiasm grew in the face of success. Everyone was quite happy!

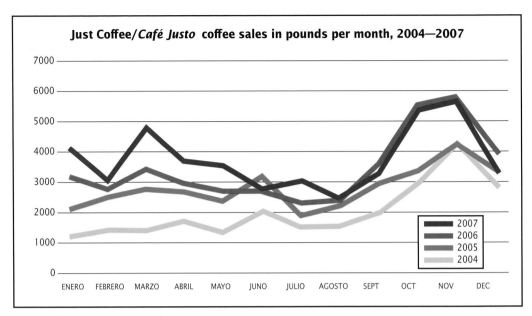

Just Coffee/*Café Justo* coffee sales in pounds per month, 2004—2007

Just Coffee sales per month by year.

Near the end of year one (October 2003), we traveled to Salvador Urbina for a business update with the Cooperative. A rise in the standard of living was already noticeable. The Cooperative members had a little extra spring in their step, for they carried with them a sense of great accomplishment. Aida Perez proudly served us cold lemonade from her new refrigerator. People were starting to install telephones in their homes. It was one of those times when we realized that by the grace of God this Cooperative had not only succeeded and survived during the first year, it had already made a positive impact on many families.

Acoustic string band entertains at a Café Justo patio celebration in Salvador Urbina.

Meetings with the growers during this trip included presentations on the revenues and spending for the year, detailed spreadsheets on sales channels and a full accounting of equipment and supplies purchased. We also discussed with the growers our estimate of potential sales for year number two. What happened next was one of the true joys for us as partners. The growers sat down together and created a plan to harvest and provide the Cooperative with an ample quantity of coffee beans to meet the anticipated demand for the second year of operation—a textbook example of the meaning of a "cooperative."

And we didn't forget to celebrate! We were treated to several parties and receptions with all families of the Cooperative.

Cooperative Venture Built Relationships

By the end of that first year, the Cooperative had begun to bring people together into new supportive relationships. We celebrated more than just having a positive financial impact through coffee sales. We took great joy in perhaps the most amazing aspect of all—the evidence of coordination and cooperation that had emerged over the year between the various growers and their families as well as the commitment and passion that was demonstrated by Just Coffee customers. This project was indeed bringing people together around a common cause, just as we all had hoped!

While most of the growers in the Cooperative were raised together in Salvador Urbina, they didn't have much history of cooperating with each other on economic development projects. In any community, there are problems and egos, disagreements and conflicts, pain and injustices. This region of Chiapas is no exception.

Although the growers were from the same community, they were nonetheless from different political parties, religions and backgrounds. Some were descendents of Guatemalan parents. Others were related to the original workers who were employed on the first German plantations that grew and shipped the coffee from this part of Mexico in the early 1800s. Many were either distantly or directly related to each other—which can make the possibility of getting along a bit more complicated.

Economic development was always the primary impetus behind *Café Justo*, but community development and cohesion has been equally important to the founders. Daniel Cifuentes said from the beginning, "I want *Café Justo* to be something that brings our community together. It doesn't matter if they are Presbyterian or Catholic, agnostic or atheist, PRI or PAN or PRD (political parties)—anyone who wants to improve our community is welcome."

The growers have always also shown a good measure of hope and patience, essential survival skills when your livelihood depends on uncontrollable forces of nature and economics. They look at situations with a practiced eye, knowing that the day is long, and family and community are more important than time. In fact, if there isn't enough time to greet one another warmly and provide generous hospitality, then something is really wrong. We learned quite clearly, that despite their differences, they share a similar hierarchy of values—people are more important than time.

As that first year ended, we could see how the coffee growers were banding together and cooperating with a new measure of faith and hope that can only be described as inspirational. Over the years since then, despite all the remaining challenges, they have persevered and overcome individual

Café Justo growers after an early socios meeting.

85

differences, uniting to provide not just excellent coffee, but also a stable and supportive environment in which to develop the Cooperative.

Clearly the Fair Trade PLUS model of vertical integration and ownership of all parts of the coffee commodity supply chain was working. The challenge *Café Justo* faced at this point was whether the success of the first year could be sustained into the second year and beyond.

Five Full Years of Growth and Success

The summary results of the first five year period answers this question with a resounding yes! Despite all the obstacles, *Café Justo* has experienced five full years of phenomenal growth and success on all financial measures—pounds of coffee sold, total Just Coffee sales revenue and income to individual Cooperative member families. Just Coffee revenues more than doubled in the second year and have increased each year since. The Cooperative members have increased their sales of coffee beans each year as well. (See chart and graphs below.)

The data speaks for itself. *Café Justo*, Salvador Urbina is now a thriving and well-managed business. The rousing economic success of the Cooperative over the five year period 2003 through 2007 has far exceeded anyone's initial dreams.

Café Justo Five Year Sales in Pounds and Dollars

YEAR	TOTAL POUNDS OF COFFEE SOLD TO COOPERATIVE BY MEMBERS	TOTAL JUST COFFEE REVENUES RECEIVED BY COOPERATIVE
2003	13,300 lbs	$72,380
2004	25,270 lbs	$185,645
2005	34,880 lbs	$253,953
2006	42,184 lbs	$315,047
2007	46,575 lbs	$366,912
TOTALS	**162,209 lbs**	**$1,193,937**

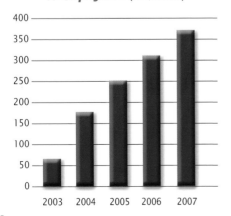

Total Just Coffee Revenue to *Café Justo* (in $1000)

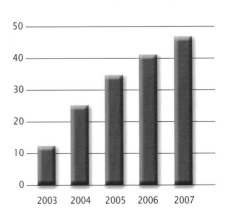

***Café Justo* 5-Year Coffee Production (in 1000 lbs)**

From the very beginning, the Cooperative has always been able to pay their direct business expenses—shipping, materials, equipment and the $1.33/pound to the growers—in a timely manner. The Cooperative has also reinvested funds into the business. After paying back the initial $20,000 loan to Frontera de Cristo, *Café Justo* has purchased and paid for a new, larger and more efficient roaster and an automatic cleaner, as well as paying for the land and the building in Salvador Urbina where the Cooperative's warehouse, coffee cleaning machines and meeting facilities are located.

What does all of this mean for individual growers and the community of Salvador Urbina? Ten percent of the Cooperative's revenue has been donated annually back to the village of Salvador Urbina for community improvement projects such as schools, water systems and parks. In 2006, the Cooperative began paying the full pension and health insurance premiums for every member family, thus bringing the average direct "wage" to the grower up to an average of $1.90 per pound ($1.33 per pound for the coffee beans, 57 cents per pound for the benefits). Additionally, the grower members reinvest part of the Cooperative's profits into land improvements and cultivation of new coffee tree stock.

All in all, the first five years demonstrate a success story that no one would have dared to predict publically ahead of time.

How do the individual grower benefits of *Café Justo* members compare to those of other coffee farmers? When we compare the revenue distribution pattern of the three main coffee production and distribution systems—Conventional, Fair Trade, and *Café Justo* Fair Trade PLUS models—the drama of the *Café Justo* success story is even more impressive. Where

Fledgling coffee plants, tenderly nurtured in growers' back yards represent their substantial investment in the economic future of Café Justo.

does the bulk of the coffee dollar end up in each of the three models? Who does it benefit? The results between the models are dramatically different.

For comparison purposes we will assume the following:

The ultimate end product retail revenue generated by each pound of coffee produced is the same in each of the three main coffee distribution models—$7.00 U.S.

The average Mexican grower family produces a harvest of 1,500 pounds of raw beans each year, which after processing results in 1,250 pounds of roasted coffee sold to U.S. consumers.

Based on these assumptions the distribution of the total retail coffee receipts from the production of one Mexican family's annual harvest is shown in the chart on page 88, which indicates where the money goes in Conventional, Organic/Fair Trade, and Fair Trade PLUS coffee market models.

Distribution of the Retail Coffee Dollar from an Average Family's Harvest

(2007 DATA)	COVENTIONAL COFFEE MARKET MODEL	ORGANIC FAIR TRADE COFFEE MARKET MODEL	*CAFÉ JUSTO* FAIR TRADE PLUS MODEL
MONEY PAID TO GROWER BY THE COOPERATIVE	$0.80 per lb	$1.10 per lb	$1.33 per pound[a]
AVERAGE PROCEEDS PER FAMILY (1,500-LB CROP)	$1,200[b]	$1,650[c]	$2,850[d] ($1.33 plus $0.57 per lb benefits)
ANNUAL REVENUE RETAINED BY COOPERATIVE FOR REINVESTMENT	$0	$465	$7,650[e]
TOTAL MONEY PAID TO COOPERATIVE THAT STAYS IN MEXICO	$1,200	$2,115	$10,500
MONEY ENDING UP IN THE UNITED STATES	**$9,300**	**$8,385**	**$0**
TOTAL RETAIL COFFEE REVENUE	$10,500	$10,500	$10,500

[a]In 2008, *Café Justo* raised the growers' payment to $1.60 per pound.

[b]$0.80 per pound average for 2007 harvest in Tapachula, Chiapas region.

[c]Assuming $1.41 per pound gross receipts to cooperative, with $1.10 going to farmer (2007).

[d]In 2008, average will be $3,255 per family ($1.60 per pound plus $0.57 per pound in benefits, assuming 1500 pound average per family).

[e]This figure represents the Cooperative's expenses for shipping, material, equipment, office, wages, the 10% contribution to community projects, plus a prudent business reserve.

> **Under the Fair Trade PLUS system 100% of the end product value of a family's yearly harvest remains in Mexico**

Note that with Conventional coffee, $1,200 (11.4%) of the end product value of a family's yearly harvest remains in Mexico and benefits the Mexican economy. With Fair Trade coffee, $2,115 (20.1%) remains in Mexico. Under the Fair Trade PLUS system of *Café Justo*, $10,500 (100%) remains in Mexico, creating new jobs, bolstering the economy of a small village, improving its infrastructure and enriching the agricultural environment.

The most obvious benefit of *Café Justo*'s Fair Trade PLUS model we have been discussing is that the growers themselves receive almost two-and-one-half times as much for their harvest as in the Conventional model, and approaching twice as much for their crop as in the Fair Trade model.

Even more impressive, however, is the fact that in the Fair Trade PLUS model the revenue remaining in Mexico to benefit the local economy is almost nine times more than in the Conventional model, and five times more than in the Fair Trade model—**a difference that is significant enough to begin strengthening the Mexican economy and to start dramatically changing the dynamics of illegal migration at the U.S./Mexico border!**

Human Side of Success

The *Café Justo* growers are successfully shedding the mindset of colonial plantation peons and are together becoming cooperative business owners, managers and developers—even

Daniel Cifuentes collects beans from the coffee cleaner at the Just Coffee Warehouse in Salvador Urbina. Retrilla (removes husks from coffee beans) and bean sorter are in the background.

to the degree of engaging in the age of the Internet and digital communications. They are a risk-taking bunch that exudes tranquility and the desire to get along and cooperate with each other. By banding together, they have been successful, even though the international coffee commodity business is rife with contention, scandal and self-serving corporate interests.

Financial success and the increased demand for coffee have provided opportunities for other farmers to join in the business. Today the *Café Justo* Salvador Urbina Cooperative has grown to forty coffee growing families, which provides enough coffee for current demand and a good economic impact for each family. Bigger is not better when people come before profits! Families now earn more that four times their previous yearly income and are able to support themselves in adequate fashion. Coffee growers can afford to stay home in Chiapas rather than migrating "illegally" to the U.S. in order to support their families. At the same time, Just Coffee drinkers in the U.S. are still paying only the same $8.00 a pound ($9.00 decaf) for the best Arabica coffee money can buy. This seems quite a powerful, commendable—and just—redistribution of at least part of the world's resources.

What's more, each bag of Just Coffee is identified with the coffee grower's name on the label. Consumers can receive their own personally packaged coffee from the grower of their choice, only a week after roasting—top quality estate-grown coffee from a person you know south of the border. Coffee that's fresh. Coffee that's delicious. Growers who are justly treated and fairly compensated. Caffeine with a conscience. And coffee drinkers who believe in the *Café Justo* motto: simple, just and fair.

Speaking of customers, the customers of Just Coffee are an integral and essential part of the *Café Justo* Cooperative success story. Not only have they been patient and generous with their support, they have also consistently savored and promoted Just Coffee in their own networks and communities. Because the Cooperative does not have a formal sales force, it has been the client partners—customers and special advocates—who have really provided the sales to keep the business growing and prospering over the years.

Many Just Coffee customers have become active advocates for the Cooperative. They give much more than opinions and consultations. They have offered their time and money to help this fledgling business get off the ground and prosper. Without the clients and client advocates, there would be little to write about the *Café Justo* Cooperative other than another failed attempt to incubate a small business in Mexico.

In its first five years of operation, thousands of people have visited the roasting shop in Agua Prieta. For many, purchasing Just Coffee was quickly transformed from being an ideological act ("I am doing this because it is a good idea") to a relational experience ("I am doing this because my sisters and brothers are making a decent living by providing me with

*Lighting the roaster in the **Café Justo** warehouse, where coffee is produced for sale locally in Salvador Urbina.*

a just cup of coffee—and a delicious one at that"). No wonder some 63 percent of the Just Coffee clients, consuming over 70 percent of the total volume, are from southern Arizona—true neighbors in the region just across the border.

In addition to creating these just relationships across the borders, Just Coffee has been a catalyst for bringing people of different theological and political backgrounds together in a common response to the phenomenon of migration along the U.S./Mexico border. Immigration is no doubt one of the most divisive issues in Arizona—and perhaps the entire United States—but Just Coffee is one response that makes sense to everyone, no matter what their preconceptions or political bias.

Initially the *Café Justo* customer base was primarily church members. Better customers cannot be found. They have not only tolerated the struggles of this small and quickly growing business, but they have also acted as part of the solution, continually offering their prayers and their marketing support. These customers have put up with mistakes and omissions with grace and patience, prayers and blessings. They have helped to revise sales materials, contributed to Website development and supported the Cooperative in the various operational struggles faced every day.

A growing number of customers have discovered Just Coffee through other channels. Recently, Arizona State Representative Kyrsten Sinema brought a delegation of nine state representatives to Agua Prieta to learn firsthand about the issues of immigration. In a letter, she thanked Aaron Boeke from Frontera de Cristo for guiding them on what she called, "The single greatest learning experience we have had about the border and the immigration issues in our country."

In particular, the group was inspired by the work of *Café Justo*. Representative Sinema said, "We are interested in setting up meetings with Whole Foods and Sprouts, two small specialty grocery stores that cater to organic, fair trade buyers, to introduce them to Just Coffee" She went on to say, "The work that Just Coffee is doing is amazing and far surpasses any efforts to stop the flow of immigration to the U.S. that government is engaged in. We are incredibly impressed with this business and the *Café Justo* members."

This type of conversion experience keeps occurring over and over again—every day, every week. The *Café Justo* Cooperative project has broadened the perspective and the lives of hundreds in the U.S. It has offered a humane perspective on the border crisis—its causes and potential solutions. It has changed the lives of those who come and see for themselves, adding a sense of compassion, as well as passion, to their commitment toward making a difference.

In his introduction to the book, Citizen Diplomacy, Carl Sagan described the process of leaving behind one's earlier perspective and beliefs and beginning to see with new eyes, as "breakthrough seeing." He said it is like the scales coming off your eyes—scales that once removed, you can never put back. For so many hundreds of our customers and visitors, once they have met a struggling economic refugee/immigrant, they never again see the national news about the border in the same way. Witnesses to the miracle of Just Coffee are usually inspired by their new understandings and drawn together into common action for justice—a major growth toward a true international faith community.

In 2007, Café Justo completed its fifth full year of operation. The community of Salvador Urbina is growing again. Residents have a realistic opportunity to earn a living and remain on their land. The transformation of Cooperative members from being isolated growers at the mercy of the coffee buyers to being active owners of an international coffee roasting and exporting business is slow, but they now have five years experience of steady growth and success. Confidence is running high. Lives have been changed, conditions and relationships improved.

Consider the story of just one grower as an example.

What Just Coffee Means to Me

At 32 years of age, Luis "Pelayo" Diaz is the youngest of the growers of *Café Justo*. Most of the persons his age from Salvador Urbina have migrated away from their community and are separated from their families and their lands. One was sent back to Chiapas from the United States in a coffin.

Pelayo was one of four coffee farmers who traveled to Agua Prieta for the dedication of the new industrial coffee roaster in May of 2006. He stood before about a hundred of *Café Justo's* clients, holding his three-year-old son, Luis, in his arms and affirmed the value of *Café Justo*.

Luis "Pelayo" Diaz supplements coffee income by selling tortillas in Salvador Urbina.

Eri Cifuentes, Pelayo and Don Gato (left to right), speaking at the roaster dedication in Agua Prieta (May 2006).

"Lo que **Café Justo** significa para mi, es que puedo mantenerme unido con mi familia, que no tengo que salir de mi comunidad para proveer para mi familia y no tengo que riesgar mi vida para que mis hijos pueden ir a la escuela. Tambien, se que Luis nunca va a tener que salir tampoco porque va a ver oportunidades aquí para el."

"What Just Coffee means to me, is that I can stay united with my family, I do not have to leave my community to provide for my family and I do not have to risk my life so my children can go to school. Also, I know that Luis will never have to leave either because there will be opportunities for him here."

Clarifying the *Café Justo* Model

What are the key factors that have led to the success of the *Café Justo* business model? Certainly not meticulous planning or MBA trained executives. Obviously not exhaustive research or sophisticated business modeling. The developers of *Café Justo* were true grass roots entrepreneurs who saw a need and had a vision.

The Cooperative, in partnership with its friends from Frontera de Cristo made the business up—and made it happen, one day at a time, one challenge at a time. Their instincts about how to organize and run a just and fair business were excellent—shaped by their perspectives from the bottom of the economic heap, from the beginning of the supply chain, from the commitment to cooperative ownership and management. Their unconventional business model has developed right alongside the business itself. And it can only be seen with the 20/20 vision of hindsight.

Looking back, several pivotal principles emerged from the way *Café Justo* decided to do business. Five underlying values have continued to guide the Cooperative as they have grown and expanded their business:

- Strive for excellence using simple and appropriate technologies. Produce top-quality coffee (Arabica, organically shade-grown), roasted and processed by the best means available.
- In every way possible, empower growers to take control of their own lives.
- Seek joyful consensus in all decision-making.
- Promote positive direct relationships between the growers and customers of Just Coffee.
- Practice financial transparency. Financial books are open to all members of the Cooperative; there are no secrets.

These principles emerged, not from a Business 101 textbook, but from the crucible of good people joining together for the economic well-being of all. They are a work in progress, constantly being refined in the marketplace and in the community of growers. How has the Cooperative implemented these cardinal principles over the first five years?

Strive for Excellence. Customer satisfaction is a testimony to the excellence of Just Coffee. Over the years *Café Justo* has consistently produced only the highest quality coffee and has responded quickly to consumer demand for blends and decaffeination. Farmers continue to use simple, holistic, environmentally-friendly practices in their cultivation, harvesting, processing and roasting.

Grower Ownership and Empowerment. *Café Justo* is totally owned by the Cooperative members, who are the ultimate decision-makers for the business. The shift from being coffee growers and wage earners to becoming international coffee business owners has been challenging but rewarding both financially and personally. Functioning as a Cooperative requires active participation by all members in planning, evaluating, considering options, making choices and taking action. Some growers are more skilled at these management tasks than others, but all participate and learn in the process.

The Cooperative is a business that needs to make a profit—not a charitable organization dependent on grants or donations. *Café Justo* generates its profits from just business practices and fair treatment of its employees and members of the Cooperative. Just dealings in all business relationships are expected, but so, too, is the requirement to provide a fair profit for all.

Joyful Consensus. What a wonderful business concept this is—but what a nightmare to manage. Learning this management style involved patience, patience and more patience.

For the most part, the growers were better at this than their "partners" from the U.S., who had been trained through their culture to review the options, make a decision and implement the plan—a task usually carried out solely by the leader or management team. North of the border, speed is valued over consensus, contention over concurrence.

For joyful consensus to work, members and consultants need to inform, teach and train each other on the issues facing the Cooperative, allowing everyone a voice in helping the group to reach a mutual decision. Members should all be learning from each other. The student and the teacher must reverse roles again and again for real learning and equality to take place.

In any group or system, there are different perspectives and conflicting beliefs to resolve. To manage by joyful consensus is a time-consuming and often tiring objective when there are more than a few members, each with distinct opinions. But, when done well, consensus-building is an extremely rewarding process with multiple mutual benefits. As in any relationship, maintaining regular and consistent communication is vital to successfully managing these dynamics.

Grower-Customer Relations. The computer is one of the key ways to maintain communication within the Cooperative and with customers. The growers in Chiapas now easily interact with the roasters in Agua Prieta via "chatting" on the Internet. Online chatting is the least expensive option for communicating across 2000 miles. This process provides

a documented record of all issues discussed and agreed upon; participants are able to exchange documents in real time; and minutes of the online meeting are automatically generated. Using a similar format every week provides consistency and is a useful training and research tool for all.

Predictably, children of the growers "excel" at spreadsheets and computer usage and have been teaching their parents the joys of technology. At this writing there are three Internet café locations in Salvador Urbina, where five years ago there were none.

Adrian Gonzalez, Customer Service Director for Café Justo captures online orders in AguaPrieta.

Financial Transparency. Financial transparency doesn't just mean that any member of the Cooperative may examine the financial data and receive answers to financial questions on how the Cooperative is spending the revenue. A significant responsibility of the Board of Directors (*Directiva*) of *Café Justo* is to present financial information to the growers in a way that clearly describes where the money comes from and where it goes. This allows the growers to make informed decisions about future expenditures. It also assures that there are no opportunities for abuses or unfair financial practices.

Near the end of each year, *Café Justo* publicly reviews both the loans the Cooperative has outstanding and the commitments to growers for the current year's coffee purchases. The growers plan together for the upcoming year(s) and decide how much coffee will be needed to meet the expected demand. With this information the growers can see how much coffee was purchased from each of the others and can fully understand what "profit" is available for community development.

*Cooperativa Directors Eri and Reynaldo review financial data with the **socios**.*

Although the growers generally do not have extensive formal education or much familiarity with financial terms and practices, they do have an excellent understanding of cash flow, debt and budgeting. Most have managed their own small farms and have seldom (or never) worked for a weekly salary. Their personal financial success hinges on their overall understanding of saving and investing for the future by postponing short term gains—the mantra of all who work the soil. They are familiar with informal strategic planning and investment as a direct result of their personal experiences with coffee farming over the years.

The families who are currently members of the Cooperative represent an accumulation of more than a thousand years of coffee growing and agricultural experience—certainly as valuable as any business degree. The same would most likely be true in any other coffee growing region. The *Café Justo* model ought to work well in any similar cultural and economic environment.

Future Challenges

Given the *Café Justo* model and the business principles that have evolved over five successful years, what challenges does the Cooperative still face as they move confidently into the future? We see three key issues that will need regular attention to insure the continued health of the business: systematic planning, leadership development, and reliance on the power of faith. And we believe that how *Café Justo* responds to these challenges will further clarify the business model for the benefit of future cooperative ventures.

Planning Processes. Cooperative members already engage in a thorough annual planning process in which they target their financial and sales goals for the next one to three years. *Café Justo* is not yet ready to make a five-year plan, but a three-year plan is realistic. This formal procedure is a new concept for the growers. They do not normally create such a plan with their own family budget. Yet, whether they realize it or not, this is the very process they follow when they plant coffee bushes that will take five years to produce—they just don't normally write it all down on paper.

Imagining and planning for the future is a skill the Cooperative will improve over time. It will take some education heavily seasoned with experience. Few businesses in Chiapas actively ask employees to join in planning for the future, so the concept is not native to the culture. But as the growers transition from being raw coffee bean sellers to becoming successful business owners, good planning is not just a nice business practice; it will be essential for long-term sustainability.

Developing New Leadership. Business consultants north of the border are fond of exhorting, "It's easier to become successful than it is to stay successful." This principle is just as likely to operate south of the border. *Café Justo* has now become successful. The new challenge for Cooperative members is to keep learning and thinking and improving operations with outside-the-box creativity and innovative hard work so that they can stay successful.

In the upcoming years, *Café Justo* will need to focus on learning and understanding more about all aspects of the coffee business, but especially on pursuing new markets and diverse marketing strategies for Just Coffee. The skills for this important work must be developed by the Cooperative member-owners themselves.

*The children of Salvador Urbina have a brighter future thanks to **Café Justo**.*

As in any emerging business, it will be important for new leaders to step forward. The growers need increasingly to mature into their identity as international business owners without losing their commitment to family and community—which has been the glue that holds the Cooperative together. It is not enough for growers simply to come to the meetings and sell their raw coffee beans to the Cooperative. Rather, all new members must identify themselves as willing participants in the total decision-making and envisioning process. As the Cooperative moves creatively into the future, current leaders must continue to expand their knowledge base and skills while encouraging others to develop and grow as well.

To maintain success, the Cooperative will need to carry on with its principles of joyful consensus and financial transparency, while never losing sight of improving customer service and coffee quality. *Café Justo* is positioned to be successful based primarily on its uniqueness as a Fair Trade PLUS business. Much of its future success will be determined by emerging new leadership.

Continued Reliance on Faith and Prayer. The Just Coffee Cooperative started as a faith-based initiative backed solely by the financial resources of the Presbyterian Church. The *Café Justo* Cooperative grew and continues to prosper through the participation and contributions of people from many different faith traditions. Representatives of many faith traditions have prayed and asked blessings during the many anniversary parties, dedications, birthdays and momentous occasions.

Although not formally aligned with any specific church, the Cooperative continues as a faith-based organization. This faith component differentiates the Cooperative from most other businesses. The clear feeling is that without prayer the Cooperative would not be enjoying the success it has achieved. The magnitude of issues and opportunities that have needed resolution is nothing short of astounding. People of faith continue to come together and discuss difficult issues as they plan carefully for success, while at the same time praying for miracles.

**The next chapter describes yet another miracle in the
Café Justo story—its replication.**

Luciano Martinez Garcia   **Luis Manuel Diaz Perez**   **Maria Cristina Gabriel Solis**

*The discovery of coffee has enlarged the realm of illusion
and given more promise to hope.*

—Isidore Bourdon

Genetically Engineered Coffee

Scientists are currently breeding coffee plants that do not need shade, grow at a lower altitude and can be planted in rows for easier machine cultivation, application of chemicals and harvesting. This "advancement" will probably put small coffee farmers at further risk for economic exploitation.

Organic Coffee

This label certifies that the coffee trees do not receive any chemical pesticides (to kill bugs/insects), herbicides (to kill unwanted plants, molds or fungus) or fertilizers (to stimulate growth). Hand weeding, mulching and pruning—combined with planting compatible plants to create a healthy growing ecosystem—is the preferred method for growing excellent coffee. Just Coffee is 100 percent organic.

Coffee bags in the Salvador Urbina warehouse, waiting for shipment to Agua Prieta.

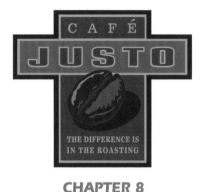

CHAPTER 8

Envisioning the Future
More Just Responses

In the preceding chapters, we've told the story of the *Café Justo* Salvador Urbina Cooperative. This innovative project has demonstrated the viability of Fair Trade PLUS coffee, incorporating all parts of the coffee supply chain into a single, integrated business that allows the growers to participate in and benefit economically from all phases of coffee production, beginning with the growing, extending to the ultimate sales to consumers—and everything in between.

Is *Café Justo* making a difference? Yes—absolutely. It's providing a living wage for a good share of the families in one small Mexican village in Chiapas. But the story of coffee, migration and faith doesn't end here.

More of this type of financial empowerment needs to occur for the crisis at the border to diminish. There is much more that can still be accomplished to shift the tide of migration at the U.S./Mexico border and empower coffee growers to provide economically for their families.

In 2006, after three successful years of the of the Fair Trade PLUS model in operation with the *Café Justo* Cooperative, Frontera

Organizing meeting for the second Café Justo Cooperative, in El Aguila, Chiapas (Jan 2006).

de Cristo began seriously to ask the question first raised by the farmers in Salvador Urbina on our initial trip—"Why not all of Chiapas?" This led us to asking a new series of "What if?" questions.

What if the *Café Justo* model could be replicated in other impoverished coffee-growing communities? What if the significant business principles that led to the success and sustenance of the *Café Justo* model could be transferred to other coffee cooperatives in Mexico?

Once again a prophetic question gave voice to a dream that posed a challenge that framed a vision that is leading Frontera de Cristo and its partners into a new concept of economic justice—the Just Trade Center.

A Broader Interfaith Vision—The Just Trade Center

After many conversations with the growers in Chiapas and our Catholic compatriots at the border who share our concern about the plight of coffee growers and our conviction that the coffee trade could be a powerful antidote to economic distress in southern Mexico, Frontera de Cristo, *Café Justo* and Catholic Relief Services-Mexico joined forces in November 2005 to create the Just Trade Center.

The Just Trade Center's expanded vision is to use the *Café Justo* Model to help launch dozens, even hundreds, of locally-owned cooperative businesses in which the local coffee growers control the most significant value-added, key income-producing steps of processing, packaging, marketing and shipping—in addition to providing the original product. We hope the multiplicity and success of the Just Trade family of Cooperatives will eventually put pressure on the major coffee buyers to re-examine both their pricing strategies and the questionable value of the antiquated intermediaries.

The separate agencies that formed the Just Trade Center brought different gifts to the collaboration. Frontera de Cristo contributed its Micro-Loan Ministry (converted into the Just Trade Revolving Fund) along with the expertise of the authors of this book and our colleagues who have been intimately involved in every step of envisioning and implementing the Fair Trade PLUS concept. *Café Justo* Salvador Urbina offered its field-tested business principles and first-hand experience creating a vertically integrated coffee business plus an extensive network of connections with other individual coffee growers and potential Fair Trade PLUS cooperatives. Catholic Relief-Mexico added its own commitment to humanitarian needs, strategies for economic justice and access to their regional Fair Trade coffee distribution centers in the U.S. In May 2006, Tommy Bassett was appointed as Director of the Just Trade Center.

Over time, we intend to test whether the *Café Justo* cooperative business model can work in other agricultural or commodity businesses, in the process formulating a self-sustaining business model for Fair Trade PLUS ventures of all sorts.

Replicating the Model—More Just Responses

The primary goal of the Just Trade Center is to identify potential grower groups and help them design and launch a sustainable business that can make a real difference in their own community. The original *Café Justo* Cooperative members have been instrumental in the process.

The success of *Café Justo* Salvador Urbina was well known throughout Chiapas by the time we started looking to initiate a second *Café Justo* project. Using our network of informal consultants and armed with ideas about whom to approach, we contacted a group of coffee

Eri Cifuentes (left) working with coffee growers near El Pinal, Veracruz.

farmers in a nearby village we had visited and who we thought might be interested in starting up their own *Café Justo* cooperative.

As expected, the growers of El Aguila were excited by the Fair Trade PLUS concept and eager to join into partnership with the Just Trade Center to form a second, independent Cooperative. After much discussion and negotiation, *Café Justo* El Aguila Cooperative was formed in October 2006 and began roasting its coffee in Tijuana the next August. In partnership with Pueblos Hermanos Presbyterian Border Ministry on the California/ Mexico border, *Café Justo* will target markets in California.

A third Cooperative, *Café Justo* Totonoca in El Piñal, Vera Cruz (established in March 2007), is currently awaiting startup financing from the Just Trade Center Revolving Fund to establish a roasting facility on the Texas border which will provide Just Coffee to customers in Texas, Oklahoma and beyond.

The Just Trade Center is currently working on *Café Justo* ventures with growers in Haiti. The Baranderes Cooperative will be partnered with Just Coffee customers in the Washington DC area. Growers with COCONO (*Cooperative Cafeiere et Cacouyere du Nord'Ouest*), from the Port-de-Paix area, will partner with customers in the Miami area.

Implementing a variation of the "each one teach one" philosophy of entrepreneurial development, under the auspices of the Just Trade Center, members of *Café Justo* Salvador Urbina have traveled to each of the new Cooperatives to provide consultation and training in all steps of the business development.

The Just Trade Center is pursuing four interrelated strategies with these new partners. As we attempt to replicate the *Café Justo* model in other coffee-growing regions, we are lending start-up capital as needed and as available through our revolving Mini-Loan Fund, offering ongoing consultation and business skill development, providing direct assistance with marketing and sales and encouraging reliance on faith-based initiatives.

Reynaldo and Eri working with an agronomist and coffee growers near Baranderes, Haiti.

Mini-Loans to Cooperatives—Not Micro-Loans to Individuals

During the initial phase of their business, entrepreneurs usually need a loan for their start-up capital. The Just Trade Center's philosophy differs significantly from the operating style of most other micro-business capital-lending organizations.

There has been much interest recently in the worldwide success of microloans to individual entrepreneurs. Such loans are clearly effective in assisting small family businesses to create some income, but seldom do they assist in generating sufficient income to develop a more substantial small business that pays taxes to the state and offers benefits to its employees.

Café Justo has demonstrated the benefits of supporting a larger, community-based model. The Just Trade Center has been gradually shifting its focus from offering multiple small micro-

Socios *Jorge, Pelayo and friends painting the remodeled* **Café Justo** *warehouse, Internet café, meeting place and coffee processing building on the main street of Salvador Urbina.*

loans to individuals ($500 to $5,000) to providing larger mini-loans (up to $20,000) to a few cooperatives with substantial up-front capital needs (like the purchase of an industrial coffee roaster) and greater long-term growth potential.

We believe that larger loans, granted over a longer period, will provide startup businesses with both the time to establish relationships and the resources needed to offer training and mentoring. Generally, the loan money will not be granted in one lump sum but rather in increments, as needed, to start up the business and forge initial industry connections and marketing relationships.

Seed money loaned to slightly larger cooperative businesses should generate more jobs and have the potential of stimulating and lifting the economy of an entire village. We believe that this kind of investment will yield longer-lasting results, especially if businesses are able to create new jobs and provide employment with health and retirement benefits for Mexican citizens working in Mexico. The Just Trade Center hopes to support the creation of cooperatives that will allow people to earn an income sufficient to let them stay in their own communities, thereby reducing economic incentives for migration.

We believe that loans, strategically placed in the right hands, become the most powerful force in economic development for the poor. When the loans are repaid, the money is available to support new ventures, reversing once more—in yet another community—the spiraling downward cycle of poverty.

Consultation and Business Skill Development. As was the case with the first *Café Justo* Cooperative, all loans made by the Just Trade Center are accompanied by ongoing technical support in the areas of business basics and marketing. The support is directed toward developing market channels, appropriately using simple technologies, maintaining financial transparency and using consensus decision making in the context of the Cooperative. Other areas of support include assistance with legal incorporation and navigating U.S. import requirements.

The Just Trade Center also provides business mentoring and technical guidance to these startup cooperative businesses. The success of ambitious, small multiple-family cooperative entrepreneurial businesses frequently requires the development of high-level business skills such as long-range planning, cash flow management and other basic business practices.

Many potential Mexican business cooperative members do not have the education or the time to learn basic skills, such as accounting, inventory control and import/export law, before starting their business. Yet the need to develop these business skills is urgent and critical for the success of any small business. For mini-loans to be productive, there must be some type of immediate business and financial assistance woven into the initial granting of the loan package. Without combining relationship-building with education in solid business practices, the probability for these loans to generate successful community businesses is diminished.

Marketing and Sales Support. The Just Trade Center provides direct assistance in generating sales for a Cooperative's product. Frontera de Cristo can tap into an extensive network of volunteers, churches and other sympathetic organizations to help new businesses identify and devise appropriate strategies for reaching target markets in the United States. Understanding U.S. marketplace dynamics and finding profitable outlets for their product is usually the most difficult and time-consuming challenge for any startup Cooperative.

We are confident that the type of empowering education and marketing assistance originally provided by the Just Trade Center to *Café Justo* Salvador Urbina will also be helpful to other new businesses that join the *Café Justo* family. With such support, Cooperatives are much more likely not only to attain initial success, but also to remain successful far into the future.

Faith-Based Initiatives. The Just Trade Center is a faith-based organization responding to the needs of the poor and vulnerable. We believe that poverty is not created by the poor. It is created by a system that has never given these individuals an equal opportunity to succeed economically. With access to small amounts of capital, two things can happen for the poor. First, grower communities can gain more control of their economic destiny. Second, by forming a cooperative, for-profit business, they can multiply the outcome of initial loans exponentially over time.

Just Coffee sales at Valley Presbyterian Church, Paradise Valley, Arizona.

Much more can and should be done—as soon as possible. According to a study completed in 2002 by Dr. Douglas S. Massey and reported by the American Immigration Law Foundation, the cost of making a single arrest along the U.S./Mexico border increased from $300 in 1992 to $1,700 in 2002. An increase of 467 percent in just a decade![1]

Let's put that $1,700 in perspective. The total initial loan to the first *Café Justo* Salvador Urbina Cooperative in 2002 was $20,000—a little less than the cost associated with twelve arrests at the border! Compare the cost-benefit ratio for the two expenditures. As a result of the $20,000 loan, forty families in Salvador Urbina are now able to support themselves. Additional jobs outside of the agricultural sector have also been created. More than fifty people have not gone to the United States seeking work—and therefore have not been arrested. The small *Café Justo* Cooperative in Salvador Urbina has already saved the U.S. over $85,000 in arrest expenses alone!

Border Fence under construction west of Douglas, Arizona (July 2004).

It makes economic sense for the U.S. to start investing money to help economically destitute Mexican farmers stay home and make a living—growing, processing and selling their crops, rather than migrating across the border. The alternative is spending more and more cash in the endlessly useless and prohibitively costly game of arresting those who cross our border in search of a way to make a life-supporting living for themselves and their families. That's the philosophy that emerges and is underscored by the success of the *Café Justo* Cooperative—one positive option for interrupting the unproductive expenditure of U.S. dollars on the symptoms rather than on the core economic issues underlying the immigration crisis.

Completed Border Fence (May 2005).

The Just Trade Center is now building on the accumulated knowledge gained in Salvador Urbina to assist other communities. To be sure, there are many discoveries yet to be made, but with the continued support of visionary people on both sides of the border, increasingly we will all—with God's grace—join in creating a more fair, just and equitable distribution of global wealth.

We believe that this goal is a Biblical mandate.

We believe that this effort is a spiritual mission.

We believe that NOW is the time for faith-based people and organizations to step forward and respond creatively to the humanitarian crisis at our shared border for which neither government has proposed satisfactory solutions.

Energy in the Wings—Even More Just Responses!

Many people have already stepped forward with just responses. There is energy in the wings to do more—and willing people lined up to help!

The Just Trade Center Advisory Board organized a celebration banquet in April 2007 to celebrate the success of the Just Coffee project and to challenge people to participate in the expansion of the *Café Justo* model. We hoped to recruit 200 people to attend this event in Tucson, Arizona, and hear the *Café Justo* story.

Making mole for the Fiesta (Vicki, Arthur, Sergio, Miriam).

On April 26, 2007, over six hundred people (four hundred was our drop-dead maximum cut-off number) squeezed into the St. Francis de Sales Catholic Church social hall for an evening of celebration for what God had done to create this new economic model. Over forty churches and organizations from seven denominations were represented at the celebration—as well as people of many political affiliations. The energy in the room was exhilarating.

The Reverend Lynne Myers, Interim Executive Presbyter of Presbytery de Cristo, testified how Just Coffee had been a unifying force in the Presbytery—bringing together churches from different theological and political

Supporters enjoying mole at the 2007 **Café Justo** *Fiesta, St Francis de Sales Catholic Church, Tucson Arizona.*

spectrums, churches from cities and rural towns, to work toward a common goal. Erica Dahl-Berdine of Catholic Relief Services Mexico commented on how Catholic Relief Services is delighted over the success of the *Café Justo* model and hopes to work to expand its impact.

As part of the celebration, the Fiesta raised more than $40,000 for the Just Trade Center Revolving Fund, which will be used to provide startup funds for future cooperatives. Already the fund provided sufficient capital for *Café Justo* El Aguila to purchase a coffee roaster and begin roasting production in Tijuana. We hope to have sufficient funds to help El Piñal start up its roasting facility on the Texas border in the fall of 2008. It's just a start. More is needed.

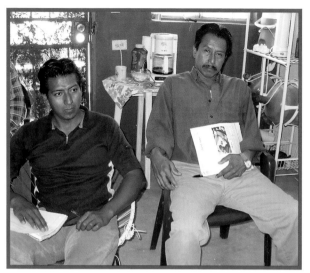

*Efren and Jorge from the El Aguila **Café Justo** Cooperative training in Agua Prieta.*

Café Justo Growers Become Teachers

We have been amazed by *Café Justo*'s active participation in helping other communities start their own value-added cooperatives. The farmers from Salvador Urbina who first took us to El Aguila in 2002 and expressed their desire for that community to experience the benefits of roasting and marketing their own coffee are now actively involved as teachers and consultants, spreading the model elsewhere and helping new cooperatives to become successful.

While many companies guard and protect their "trade secrets," the *Café Justo* members value sharing the insights of their successful model for the benefit of other communities. Efren and Jorge from the El Aguila community spent three months at the roasting facility in Agua Prieta learning from the staff about all phases of the coffee roasting and distribution process. Daniel Cifuentes educated them on the overall coffee business; Hugo Cifuentes taught them to roast coffee; Vicki Hernandez guided them through the packing process; Deysi Garcia gave them an overview of the ordering and data entry process. Pope Gonzalez explained shipping, and Adrian Gonzalez instructed them in customer service.

Eri and Reynaldo exchanging ideas with coffee growers in Baranderes, Haiti.

Some of the *Café Justo* Salvador Urbina Cooperative members have ventured far from home in their enthusiasm to spread the word about the Fair Trade PLUS coffee business. In January 2008, Eri and Reynaldo Cifuentes Perez from *Café Justo* in Salvador Urbina were invited to Baranderes, Haiti, to teach coffee farmers there about coffee cultivation techniques, the Fair Trade PLUS concept and the direct-relationship, word-of-mouth marketing model of *Café Justo*.

The President of *Café Justo* Salvador Urbina, Eri Cifuentes, and the Director of Customer Relations, Adrian Gonzalez, were keynote speakers recently at a gathering of Fair Trade coffee cooperatives from Central America. *Café Justo* is clearly making a name for itself—and providing an inspiring model for people on both sides of the border.

God has done amazing things among and through the community of faith that has gathered in support of this project! The vision of *Café Justo* and the sale of Just Coffee have dramatically transformed the community of Salvador Urbina. Families now have health care and retirement benefits, and children can stay in school. People are returning from the United States to be with their families again. The entire community has access to potable water.

The Just Trade Center is working with the *Café Justo* Salvador Urbina Cooperative to sustain its success and is also working with other communities to replicate this model for building just relationships across borders and transforming despair into hope.

Your Invitation to a Just Response

**There is so much more that can be accomplished
right now in so many communities.
The need for justice is great.
The opportunity to respond lies before us.**

**Here's where you come in.
We invite you to participate in making a very real,
personal and positive difference in the current
humanitarian crisis on the U.S./Mexico Border.**

The next chapter highlights your invitation.

---

[1]Volume 4, Issue 7, September 2005, http://www.alif.org/ipc/policy_reports_2005_beyondborders.html.

Modesto Santizo Perez   **Otilio Lopez Vazquez**   **Reynaldo Cifuentes Velazquez**

Come unto me all you who are weary . . .

—Matthew 11:28-30

The story in this book calls us to indulge in our caffeine—with a conscience.
We extend the *Café Justo* story and contribute to solving the border crisis justly whenever
we buy and drink Just Coffee—some of the most excellent coffee in the world.

Mama Yoli offers a cup of Just Coffee—grown in Chiapas,
fresh-roasted in Sonora, ready for you to savor.

CHAPTER 9

An Invitation
What You Can Do To Help

So far we haven't focused directly on the subtitle of this book—Caffeine with a Conscience—which puts the *Café Justo* story into a sharper and more personal perspective. Every day each of us makes economic decisions that affect not only our own family but families throughout the world. Each day, through both our intentional and unthinking choices, we make a difference in the lives of men, women and children, most of whom we have never met.

We live in a global economy and our economic choices—although often small and seemingly inconsequential—can have a huge accumulated global effect. The question is: will the range of economic choices you select today make a positive or negative difference in the lives of the poor?

For years, many of us drank coffee each morning without realizing that the people who grew our brew were not benefiting justly from their labor. Now we have an opportunity to participate actively with the farmers in the creation of a new economic model that strengthens communities instead of depleting them.

Using Your Purchasing Power Wisely

We all have many opportunities to make a statement with our purchases. The price of a product does not always reflect the total cost, in humanitarian terms. Buying coffee at a very low price prolongs the poverty of developing nations that depend on coffee sales. Buying low-cost coffee from the largest corporations perpetuates the economic injustice that guarantees economic migration. As stated so clearly throughout this book, many displaced coffee growers see few options other than to pursue work in countries that have a huge demand for low-skilled manual—often dangerous—labor.

It has become fashionable in our culture to watch for the best price and the best deals— whatever the product or the process that allows such deep discounts. Sometimes bargain shopping takes advantage of the most vulnerable and needy in societies around the world. Imagine telling a coffee grower that they must sell their coffee at little or no profit—or it can rot. This is what coffee growers are told when we buy the lowest price coffee we can find.

The *Café Justo* family of Cooperatives provides an opportunity for us to do something unique, direct and effective—with positive global consequences. Your coffee purchase, in support of growers who produce this coffee with labor-intensive processes, offers you a unique opportunity to make a significant impact.

Many factors—need, convenience, quality, price, value, Madison Avenue, habit—influence our most frequent purchases, Shouldn't justice be one of those items on the list of values that determine our buying decisions?

Many large corporations are trying to jump on the Fair Trade band-wagon because fairness makes good sense to consumers—and it's good marketing. Although this trend could be viewed as a threat to many of the small fair trading companies and producers, we choose to see this corporate positioning as confirmation from the Fortune 500 companies that Fair Trade is the next wave of purchasing—as well as the proper moral decision.

We believe it is time for all of us to consider the total cost when we make our buying decisions. How much are we willing to "buycott"? Buycotting is the conscious choice to buy consumer goods through a channel that helps a community or a cause—a positive market response to just and fair products.

Just Coffee—A Choice for Justice

We will seldom see the faces of those we are assisting with our informed purchases. In this one final story, Mark reminds us, however, of how much difference we can indeed make when we intentionally buycott Just Coffee.

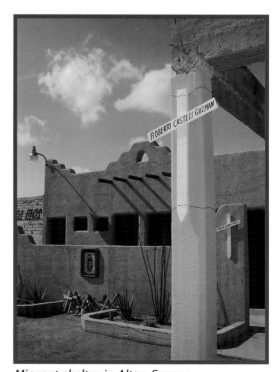

During the summer of 2002, when the *Café Justo* Cooperative was in its earliest stages , my colleague Jesus Gallegos Blanco, Tommy and I led our summer interns on a spiritual retreat to Altar, Sonora. In spite of the fact that temperatures regularly rise above 115 degrees Fahrenheit in the Altar Valley, Altar had become the primary crossing point for those in search of jobs in the United States. Increased border enforcement in more populated and less desolate areas had forced the flow of migrants to the less fortified, yet more dangerous, parts of the border. Just as putting rocks in the middle of a stream does not stop the water flow, building up the border defenses does not stop people who have few economic alternatives other than seeking the jobs that are being offered in the U.S.

Migrant shelter in Altar, Sonora.

We arrived at a migrant shelter operated by the Catholic Church. The priest, Father Rene Castaneda, invited us to participate in the weekly migrant mass. Making our way from the shelter to the sanctuary, we could feel the heat of the pavement penetrating through the soles of our shoes and the rays of sun creating little ovens between our heads and our hats. As we passed through the plaza we saw hundreds of people waiting to migrate.

We also noticed all the businesses that had sprouted up around the plaza that were catering to the needs of these migrants. There were little vending stands filled with backpacks, water bottles, hats, and sunglasses. Formerly abandoned store fronts had been turned into hostels, and a transportation center filled with old vans was ready to provide rides on the seventy-mile-long dirt "toll" road from Altar to the border.

It was difficult to hear the worship service in the cavernous sanctuary, but the gospel lesson came through very clearly, "Come to me all you who are weary and burdened and I will give you rest. Take my yoke upon you and learn from me, for I am gentle and humble in heart, and you will find rest for your souls. For my yoke is easy and my burden is light" (Matthew 11:28-30). To my surprise, after the Scripture was read, Father Renee invited me to share my reflections on the word of

Outdoor shopping mall for migrants on the square in Altar.

God to the many of those present who were weary and burdened.

It struck me that the vision of Just Coffee was a gospel vision, a vision that would give potential rest for the weary and burdened. The vision of Just Coffee required taking on the yoke of Jesus: the yoke of faith in the One who calls us to do justice, to love mercy and to walk humbly with our God; the yoke of hope for a future when farmers can plant and eat the fruits of their labors; and the yoke of love for one another across borders. Being in the presence of and worshipping with so many persons who had been so heavily burdened that they had to flee their lands confirmed in me the need for creating innovative alternatives to immigration.

Father Rene Costas saying mass with migrants before departure in Altar, Sonora.

Mark preaching at Father Rene's parish in Altar.

As we were getting into our cars for the return to Agua Prieta, three thin and tired men approached us. Their names were Epolito, Fraylon and Filadelfo. They were from the Salvador Urbina community and had heard of the creation of *Café Justo*. The previous three days they had walked through the desert in the summer heat. They shared with us the sadness and deep fear they experienced when they passed decomposing bodies in the desert. "Do you think that they will ever be returned to their families?" they queried. "No, not likely." Our unspoken response to this rhetorical question did not need to be verbalized.

Women praying for safe crossings in Altar.

The three men were heading for Atlanta where construction jobs were awaiting them—but they would rather have gone home. I did not fully realize it at the time, but soon *Café Justo* would be prepared to provide them that opportunity.

Why? Because so many along the way dared to believe.

Dare To Believe!

Eduardo Perez Verdugo dared to believe that there was another way, an alternative, to the mass exodus he saw occurring in his coffee farming community of Chiapas and to the forced economic exile.

Eri Cifuentes dared to believe that the vision of *Café Justo* could transform, not only the community of Salvador Urbina, but also the surrounding coffee growing communities of Chiapas and beyond.

Migrants waiting in front of the church in Altar.

And there are thousands of others—a few already mentioned—who have dared to believe and have influenced global economics by the totality of their daily economic decisions. Even more simply, they have dared to believe there is a way for people to be connected in just relationships across borders, even over a cup of coffee—perhaps especially over a cup of coffee.

*Barbara Padilla with **socios** Don Gato, Reynaldo, Emilio and Jorge on Border-to-Border trip to Chiapas.*

What started as a mustard seed of hope more than eight years ago has grown into a reality in which over a hundred families in three communities no longer have to migrate and be separated from one another and their farms.

Will you dare to believe with us?

Will you dare to believe what began as a dream is turning into the headwaters of a mighty stream of justice? Will you dare to believe that we can be more effective at stopping undocumented immigration by entering into just economic relationships than by building walls of division? Here is your invitation.

Your Just Response Opportunity

Dare to believe with us that YOU can make that difference!

If you want to make a difference—and if you believe you can make a difference—we offer you this personal challenge.

Throughout this book we have focused on building relationships with our customers—the visits, the grower's name on the bags, the celebrations. Now let's enlarge and personalize that connection. As *Café Justo* and the Just Trade Center move into the future, YOU can become the next vital link in expanding these relationships and allowing the vision to grow further.

How Might You Begin?

You can start by buying Just Coffee, and enjoying the great taste of our blends—while at the same time savoring the fact that you are supporting the independence of all the growers—and helping them to build a financially stable community south of our border.

> **Order now!** Check the Just Coffee Order Form on page 122, then go online at **www.justcoffee.org** and place your order.

> Or call **Adrian Gonzalez (520-364-3532)** or **Popé (poe-PAY) Gonzalez (866-545-6406)** at the *Café Justo* customer service department. You'll receive your fresh roasted coffee within the next week to ten days.

Give Just Coffee as a present. Share it with your family and friends. Take it as a hostess gift. Then tell people the *Café Justo* story and let them know how they, too, can make a difference. Package the coffee with a copy of this book to extend your influence.

Encourage your church, community organizations, and workplace to become *Café Justo* partners by making the commitment to purchase a hundred pounds of coffee over the course of a year. Urge your church to sponsor a coffee growing family for a year—*it only takes 100 U.S. families buying 12 pounds of coffee a year to support an entire Mexican family for one year.*

1 CHURCH → 100 FAMILIES → 12 POUNDS → 1 YEAR

... supports **1 FAMILY**
like Hernan's

You can also think BIG. Imagine enabling an entire community in Mexico to experience economic stability through sales of Just Coffee. It's not that difficult or overwhelming when the coffee is tasty and the cause is clear.

You could encourage your local Council of Churches to support one full *Café Justo* Cooperative of 30-40 coffee-growing families in Mexico (or Haiti or wherever!). It takes about 4,000 U.S. families drinking a pound of coffee a month to support one whole Cooperative. This would require a U.S. town of about 18,000 people or a group of 20 churches with 200 families each. No small challenge—but certainly possible!

20 CHURCHES → 200 FAMILIES → 1 POUND/MO → 1 YEAR

... supports **30-40 FAMILIES**
like Soria's

Along the way, you could initiate a Coffee Sister City relationship by starting an exchange of visits between your village and theirs. Or produce periodic personalized bulletin inserts introducing the grower families and their stories to your congregation. The relationships you can nurture are unlimited. The joys they will bring you are immeasurable.

As you participate in this commitment you are making a positive difference and developing relationships along with making prudent and just business purchases. These decisions on your part are not charity but simply a good deal for everyone. Let's call this opportunity Fair Trade with a Double PLUS!

Or you could think REALLY BIG. You could support the stability of multiple communities, by becoming a Just Coffee distributor in your region, providing high quality coffee for churches, food coops, farmers' markets and restaurants. Or start your own Just Coffee coffee shop.

Perhaps you could invite a congregation, or a group of congregations, or an individual or a group of friends to underwrite a $30,000 loan that would help launch yet one more Fair Trade PLUS business and then another and another as your grant money is recycled through start-up loans over and over again.

What if you volunteered a month or a year of your time to invest your special talents and energy in helping the Just Trade Center or *Café Justo* Cooperatives? You might work with computer systems, offer suggestions to expand marketing efforts, generate names of individuals whom we could contact to tell the Just Coffee story or offer some of your business acumen to assist in making our operation more economically successful. Maybe you'd like to take a vacation in Mexico—volunteering at one of the roasting facilities or providing tours in Agua Prieta or Tijuana. How about journeying to Salvador Urbina and El Aguila to meet directly with the growers and their families (See educational opportunities on page 123.)

Do you have a special talent for graphic design or Website development? Assistance is always welcome as we search for better ways to utilize the Internet and broadcast the message of *Café Justo*. Perhaps you know Spanish and can offer your language skills to this project.

The opportunities are endless. We know you can make a difference, and you, no doubt, have better and more creative ideas about how you can participate in this vision of Just Coffee. Please contact us at www.justcoffee.org, and let us know what intrigues you. We promise to work with you and support your vision.

Zoe assists with coffee grinding during an educational immersion trip to the border.

Although we have to admit that it is easier to describe the problem than to do something concrete to alleviate it, we have learned from the Just Coffee project that together we can indeed do something positive about the illegal immigration issue.

What will you do? As authors of this book we ask you to consider this question seriously and prayerfully. We encourage you to listen to the response that emerges from your heart at the urging of the Spirit. Be open to that still small voice and be ready to respond in ways that will spread God's grace, mercy and justice across borders and around the world—among, us, between us, and for us all!

If you feel called to join in the mission of the *Café Justo* Cooperatives, be assured you will be welcomed with open arms.

Final Thoughts from Mark and Tommy

As we looked ahead in 2000, we never foresaw the formation of the *Café Justo* Cooperative. The events of these last eight years seem mainly miraculous. Right now, as we once again look ahead, we don't know what will unfold during the upcoming years. Perhaps another miracle!

Where will these first steps, the *Café Justo* Cooperatives and the Just Trade Center, lead us next? What will emerge as we move into the future? The future is unrevealed until its season, something God alone can see.

Right now we don't know any more about the answers to these questions than we knew about the *Café Justo* Cooperative back in 2000 when Eduardo first showed up on our doorstep sharing his vision for a better way.

As we look forward today, however, we have full confidence in three assertions.

It is usually easier to describe a problem than it is to do something positive about it. The problems at the U.S./Mexico border still remain. That's easy to say. Additional creative solutions are still waiting to be imagined and implemented. That's the more difficult challenge. However, we know that wherever people of vision hear this story, new forces for possible solutions will begin to stir.

Those who are called to respond to this challenge will keep arriving. The new arrivals will bring additional energy for creating faithful forms of outreach until the problems at the border diminish. We do not yet know their names. Perhaps we have not yet met. Perhaps we are already friends. No matter. Whoever they are—the next Eduardo and Dr. Lumer and Daniel and the Danforths and Father Bob and Barbara Padilla and Homer—whoever, they will announce their presence in a manner and a timing yet unknown to us. Often they will arrive at a time and in a manner that is a surprise even to themselves.

God is still at work here. Amidst the dusty chaos, the human suffering, and the conflicting political viewpoints at the U.S./Mexico border, God is actively present.

New forms of response will continue to emerge and be given shape by the hearts and the hands of good-willed and committed people—some who consider themselves to be people of faith, and some who do not. All of us will move forward together into the unknowable future, an odd collection of unlikely compatriots, certain that here at the U.S./Mexico border God has not yet finished speaking. We look forward to living through, and eventually celebrating, the next chapter of this story.

If you are among those who may be called to respond to the challenges of this place, feel free to announce yourself.

We await your arrival,

In your good time,
In God's chosen time.

La paz de Dios sea con Ustedes!

Resources

Popé and Desi in the Café Justo office, fill orders via internet. (See order form on page 122.)

Just Coffee table set for Second Sunday Outreach at Las Placitas Presbyterian Church.

Ah, how sweet coffee tastes—Lovelier than a thousand kisses,
Sweeter far than muscatel wine.

—The Coffee Cantata, J. S. Bach

It's just coffee . . . but it packs a powerful punch!

Just Coffee is a very simple, commonsense model with a miraculous result.

What is it that drives this miracle in the mountains—the *Café Justo* Cooperative?

It offers a just response to the living wage problem.

It's a simple model without frills that's effective and successful.

It's entirely owned and managed by the people who do the work.

What a concept!

Immersion study group stops for reflection and meditation on the plight of migrants whose discarded possessions they have been collecting during clean-up patrol near the border. (See page 123.)

Chronology of the Just Coffee Miracle

Preparing the Way: Faith in Action at the Border (1990s)

1984 Frontera de Cristo bi-national Border Ministry is launched in Douglas, Arizona / Agua Prieta, Sonora, as a partnership between the Presbyterian Church USA and the National Presbyterian Church of Mexico; with the goal of building bridges and discovering God's will together. Frontera de Cristo provides the following:

- Church development.
- Economic development support and community services.
- Educational-immersion group field trips to study justice issues.
- Community Center in Agua Prieta housing health and dental screenings and job skill development programs.
- Support services for homeless migrants sent back to Mexico.
- Water in the desert.

1992 Tommy Bassett arrives in Agua Prieta to manage electronic parts plant.

1996 Coffee grower Daniel Cifuentes arrives from Chiapas in Agua Prieta after the drop in coffee prices drives him off family lands to seek work.

1998 Rev. Mark Adams joins Frontera de Cristo as Mission Co-Worker. Hurricane Mitch devastates coffee-growing areas of Chiapas.

Forming the Vision: Fair Trade PLUS Coffee (1999-2002)

1999 Eduardo Verdugo's testimony and questions challenge our thinking and plant the seed for a new business model.

2000 Healing Our Borders vigils begin. Mark Adams and Tommy Bassett meet.

2001 Concept of Just Coffee emerges.

2002 **January**—Mark and Tommy join forces with Daniel Cifuentes to develop further the vision of a Fair Trade PLUS coffee cooperative. By long distance, they discuss the cooperative idea with growers from Chiapas and propose forming a Just Coffee partnership.

March—Start-up loan of $20,000 secured from Frontera de Cristo Micro-Credit Ministry.

May—Mark and Tommy make their first trip to Chiapas. The coffee growers of Salvador Urbina embrace the Fair Trade PLUS vertical integration concept (growing, roasting, exporting) and agree to form the **Café Justo Cooperative**.

June—First *Café Justo* coffee arrives in Agua Prieta for hand roasting. Daniel Cifuentes is designated as supervisor of the roasting facility.

August—Alejandro Bahamaca is hired by *Café Justo* as first customer sales representative.

October—Cooperative purchases the first roaster with $20,000 loan from Frontera de Cristo.

November—First coffee roasted in roasting facility.

Vision in Action: The *Café Justo* Miracle Becomes a Success (2003-2004)

2003 Year One

January—Roaster is dedicated. Delegation of growers from Chiapas (including the most skeptical) visits the roasting/packaging/shipping facilities at Agua Prieta.

April—Commercial shipments of Just Coffee officially proceed through customs.

October—First Border-to-Border mission study trip to Salvador Urbina. Planning Year Two with the Cooperative. (Chapter 7)

2003 Just Coffee sales—13,300 lbs, $72,380.

2004 Year Two

May—Cooperative introduces decaffeinated Just Coffee. Third delegation of coffee growers from Salvador Urbina visits Agua Prieta.

September—New automatic coffee cleaner purchased for Salvador Urbina.

October—Second Border-to-Border mission study trip to Salvador Urbina

November—Automatic coffee sorter purchased for Salvador Urbina.

2004 Just Coffee sales—25,270 lbs, $185,645.

Just Trade Center: Multiplying the Vision, Replicating the Model (2005-2008)

2005 Year Three

October—Sixteen U.S. pilgrims visit Salvador Urbina on the third Border-to-Border mission study trip; during their stay, Hurricane Stan devastates southern Chiapas.

November—The **Just Trade Center** is established through the partnership of Frontera de Cristo, Catholic Relief Services-Mexico and *Café Justo*. Center institutes a new Revolving Loan Ministry.

December—First large donation is received for the Just Trade Center Revolving Fund.

2005 Just Coffee sales—34,880 lbs, $253,953.

2006 Year Four

March—Tommy Bassett is hired as Just Trade Center Developer

May—Cooperative purchases and dedicates a new industrial roaster.

October—A second grower's cooperative, **Café Justo El Aquila**, is established in Chiapas.

2006 Just Coffee sales—42,184 lbs, $315,047.

2007 Year Five

January—*Café Justo* is chosen as one of Catholic Relief Services' regional coffee suppliers.

February—Salvador Urbina farmers speak about *Café Justo* Cooperative model at International Conference of Central American Fair Trade Cooperatives.

March—A third growers cooperative, ***Café Justo* Totonaco** is established in Vera Cruz, Mexico.

April—*Café Justo* Fiesta in Tucson raises $40,000 for the Just Trade Center Revolving Fund which provides capital for new cooperatives.

July—Members of the Salvador Urbina cooperative train the grower members in the two newly formed cooperatives, El Aguila *Café Justo* (Chiapas) and *Café Justo* Totonaco (Vera Cruz).

August—*Café Justo* El Aguila begins roasting its coffee in Tijuana.

October—*Café Justo* repays in full original loan for the roaster. Change in Mexican export law prevents *Café Justo* from shipping coffee for six weeks.

November—Ten U.S. pilgrims visit Salvador Urbina on the fourth Border-to-Border mission study trip to Salvador Urbina.

2007 Just Coffee sales—46,575 lbs, $366,912.

2008 Year Six

January—*Café Justo* coffee growers provide consulting services to coffee farmers in Baranderes, Haiti.

January to March—Just Coffee featured as official coffee of Brian McClaren's Everything Must Change tour.

April—*Café Justo* officially certified as 100% "USDA Organic."

November—This book, ***Just Coffee: Caffeine with a Conscience***, goes to print.

. . . and the story continues.

Why Just Coffee?

Talking Points for Group Presentation, Minute for Mission, Newsletter Article

The *Café Justo* Project

1. Faith-based initiative that addresses root cause of migration—economics
2. Includes several farmer-owned coffee cooperatives
    a. Began in Salvador Urbina, Chiapas, near border with Guatemala
    b. Model replicated in El Aguila, Chiapas; Totonaco, Vera Cruz and Baranderes, Haiti
3. Vertical Integration—Cooperative consolidates all functions of coffee industry
    a. Cultivation, harvesting
    b. Roasting, packaging
    c. Marketing/Sales
    d. Exporting directly to clients/customers
4. All the revenue stays in Mexico
    a. Completely Mexican owned and operated businesses—planting to roasting to packaging to shipping
    b. No middlemen; Cooperative receives total revenue from all steps in the process
5. Value-Added: Fair Trade PLUS
    a. Cooperative pays its farmers $1.60 per pound for coffee—more than the typical Fair Trade cooperative
    b. Cooperative provides health care and retirement benefits to its members (an additional 57 cents per pound benefit)
    c. Shared profits invested in community development enterprises
        i. Installation of water purification systems
        ii. School improvements
        iii. Soil enhancement and crop management
    d. Economic trickle-up creates jobs outside of the agriculture sector
6. Delicious coffee direct to consumers
    a. High mountain Arabica, plus blends and specialty beans
    b. Shade-grown, hand-harvested, wet-processed, patio sun-dried
    c. 100% certified "USDA Organic"
        i. Natural cultivation
        ii. No chemical fertilizers, pesticides or herbicides
    d. Fresh roasted to order
    e. Estate coffee (you know who grew your brew)

One Session Adult Study Outline
Just Coffee: Caffeine with a Conscience

Gathering Together

    a. Begin by drinking coffee (*Café Justo* of course).

    b. Have various cans of coffee around (Maxwell House, Folgers and bags of coffee) and invite each person to look at the packaging.

    c. Ask each person to write down as much information about the coffee farmers that they can from their observations of the packaging: who grew the coffee, where it was grown, how much they were paid, etc.

Reflecting on the Scriptures

    a. Read Isaiah 65:17–25 once through

    b. Ask the question: What phrases or images stick in your mind from the reading of the Scripture? Then read the Scripture again.

    c. Write down the responses on a white board, butcher paper etc.

Reflecting on our Connections with Coffee Farmers

    a. Read the testimony of Eduardo Perez Verdugo beginning on page 29.

    b. Answer the following questions:

        How are we connected to Eduardo and the coffee farmers in Chiapas?

        Do our connections with the farmers reflect the vision of Isaiah 65?

Connecting Life and Faith

    a. From your reading of the book, give concrete examples of how the *Café Justo* Cooperative is seeking to live out the vision of Isaiah 65.

    b. Brainstorm all the ways in which this education class as individuals and a group can participate with *Café Justo* in living out the vision of Isaiah.

    c. Decide on three concrete actions that you will commit to.

Praying

    a. Name all the persons you remember from reading the book. If possible, identify the coffee farmer who provides your coffee. Give thanks to God for each of these hard-working people and pray for their families.

    b. Pray for wisdom and guidance as you carry out the three concrete actions that you have decided upon.

Just Coffee Order Form

Blends for Every Taste

For freshly roasted estate-grown certified organic coffee in full pound bags, order on our website (www.justcoffee.org), by email (sales@justcoffee.org) or call us toll free at: 866-545-6406. Your *Café Justo* customer service representative will be glad to help you pick the right blend and grind for your taste—or suggest a variety pack for your organization. Your delicious Just Coffee should arrive within a week to ten days. If you have a favorite grower, please identify him/her!

All coffee blends are available as whole beans or ground (specialty grinds available on request). Please specify normal or dark roast.

COFFEE BLEND	NO. OF POUNDS	GRIND (circle)	ROAST (circle)
100% Pure Arabica *The original Just Coffee—naturally sweet, light & never bitter. Our most popular. No more acid stomach!*		**B** = Whole Beans **G** = Regular Grind	**N** = Normal **D** = Dark
100% Arabica DECAF *Flavored by nature, decaffeinated in beautiful Veracruz.*		**B** = Whole Beans **G** = Regular Grind	**N** = Normal **D** = Dark
50% Pure Arabica DECAF/50% Pure Arabica *Just the right blend of high and low octane. Good all day.*		**B** = Whole Beans **G** = Regular Grind	**N** = Normal **D** = Dark
100% Pure Robusta *High octane coffee. Strongest flavors, maximum caffeine.*		**B** = Whole Beans **G** = Regular Grind	**N** = Normal **D** = Dark
50% Pure Arabica/50% Pure Robusta *Lightness of flavor with a kick of rich robust strength.*		**B** = Whole Beans **G** = Regular Grind	**N** = Normal **D** = Dark
100% Pure Marago *Premium coffee with a deep, rich chocolatey taste—extra body and character.*		**B** = Whole Beans **G** = Regular Grind	**N** = Normal **D** = Dark

New!
from the Just Trade Center

JUST COFFEE:
Caffeine with a Conscience

by Mark S Adams
& Tommy Bartlett III

4-color, 128 pages, pbk, $20.00

Immersion Learning Opportunities with Frontera de Cristo

For over 24 years, Frontera de Cristo has been dedicated to building relationships and understanding across borders. We believe that the best way to learn about the human dimension of border issues is to immerse yourself in the culture—even for a short time. We invite you to come and see with your own eyes the poverty that prompts migration and hear the stories of people of faith as they struggle to provide for their families.

One-Day, Three-Day and Week-Long Border Immersion Experiences

Frontera de Cristo's Border Immersion Experiences are tailored to the interests and time constraints of the groups that visit—church mission teams and youth groups, schools, universities and organizations. An individualized schedule is developed from experiences such as:

- Walking the desert trails where hundreds of thousands of migrants have passed looking for jobs in the US;

- Visiting *maquiladoras* (factories)

- Learning about 500 years of history, economics, and politics that have led up to our current situation;

- Visiting the *Café Justo* roaster and talking with the employees about the impact it has had on their lives;

- Visiting the US Border Patrol Station in Douglas, Arizona;

- Shopping for and eating three to six meals on a maquila salary;

- Eating and having conversations with other border groups addressing root causes of immigration;

- Serving in the Migrant Resource Center and talking with persons being returned from the United States;

- Visiting the Mexican Consulate and learning how the Mexican government is attempting to respond to immigration issues;

- Preparing a meal at the CAME migrant shelter;

- Participating in the Healing Our Borders prayer vigil in which an ecumenical group gathers to remember those who have died crossing he border, pray for their families, for our governments, and for an end to fear, division, and death on the border.

Annual Coffee, Migration and Faith Border to Border Delegation

Each fall, Frontera facilitates a delegation of 6 to 16 persons who are interested in exploring issues of migration and faith in depth, from the issues at the U.S./Mexico border to the coffee fields of Chiapas, near the Guatemala/Mexico border.

The delegation begins their journey with a three day immersion experience on the U.S./ Mexico border in and around Douglas, Arizona/Agua Prieta, Sonora:

- Walking the desert trails where hundreds of thousands of migrants have passed looking for jobs in the U.S.;
- Visiting *maquiladoras* (factories)
- Learning about 500 years of history, economics, and politics that have led up to our current situation;
- Visiting the *Café Justo* roaster and talking with the employees about the impact it has had on their lives;

The journey continues with a flight to Tapachula, Chiapas on the southern border with Guatemala where participants:

- Stay with *Café Justo* Cooperative coffee-growing families in Salvador Urbina, Chiapas;
- Pick coffee and participate in the harvest;
- Experience the long process of coffee cultivation from planting and pruning to depulping and washing to drying and threshing;
- Learn about regional coffee history at the coffee museum;
- Drink great coffee;
- Visit a Guatemala border city and learn about border issues on the Guatemala/Mexico Border;
- Eat the freshest and most varied bananas you can imagine;
- See the Water for Life water treatment plant in the *Café Justo* warehouse and other community projects made possible by Just Coffee.

Throughout the journey we cultivate growth in positive relationships across borders and reflect on the connections between coffee, migration and faith.

For more information: go to www.fronteradecristo.org and click on Immersion Opportunities; call the Frontera de Cristo office at (520) 364-9257; or e-mail mark@ fronteradecristo.org.

Where to Learn More
about Fair Trade, Immigration and Border Issues

Recommended Reading on Border Issues

Border Games: Policing the U.S./Mexican Divide, by Peter Andres (Cornell University Press, 2000).

Crossing Over: A Mexican Family on the Migrant Trail, by Ruben Martinez (Metropolitan Books, 2001).

The Devil's Highway, by Luis Alberto Urrea (Little Brown, 2004).

Hard Line: Life and Death on the U.S.-Mexican Border, by Ken Ellingwood (Pantheon, 2004).

Migration, (Church and Society, Vol 95, #6), Presbyterian Church USA, 2005.

Jonah, Jesus and Other Good Coyotes: Speaking Peace to Power in the Bible, by Daniel Smith-Christopher, (Abingdon Press, 2007).

Lives on the Line: Dispatches from the US/Mexican Divide, by Miriam Davidson (University of Arizona Press, 2000).

Operation Gatekeeper: The Rise of the "Illegal Alien" and the Remaking of the U.S.-Mexico Boundary, by Joseph Nevins (Routledge, 2001).

Books on Coffee and Fair Trade

Brewing Justice: Fair Trade Coffee, Sustainability and Survival, by Daniel Jaffee, (University of California Press, 2007)

Fair Trade Coffee: The Prospects and Pitfalls of Market-Driven Social Justice, by Gavin Fridell, (University of Toronto Press Inc, 2007).

DVDs on Border Issues

Crossing Arizona, Rainlake Productions (2006). (212) 343-0777, www.crossingaz.com. *Examines the border crisis through the eyes of those directly affected by it— frustrated ranchers picking up after migrants, humanitarian groups putting water in the desert, political activists agitating for change, employers who depend on an "illegal" work force, border guardians. As up-to-date as the nightly news, but far more in depth.*

Dying to Get In: Undocumented Immigration at the U.S./Mexican Border, by Brett Tolley. Produced by Program for Ethnographic Research and Community Studies, Elton University. 39 minutes. www.bretttolley.com. *A Border Links intern documents the harsh reality of border crossing, following men, women and children on their nightmare journeys.*

Dying to Live: A Migrant's Journey, Produced by the Center for Latino Spirituality and Culture, University of Notre Dame (2005). Contact the Center, (574) 631-3233 or latino@nd.edu for a copy ($25.00).

DVDs Featuring *Café Justo*/Just Coffee

Just Coffee: Small Solutions for Global Problems, Produced by Frontera de Cristo. Contact Tommy at (520) 249-1692 or tommy@fronteradecristo.org for a copy. *Nine-minute documentary highlights how Just Coffee is addressing root causes of migration.*

Lives for Sale, A joint production of Maryknoll and Lightfoot Films in association with Faith and Values Media, PBS. www.livesforsale.com
One-hour investigative documentary ran on PBS in 2007. Documents the tragedies of human trafficking and highlights Just Coffee as a positive way to prevent trafficking.

Faith-Based Organizations

American Friends Service Committee (AFSC) (humanitarian relief and legislative action)
www.afsc.org/immigrants-rights

Border Links (specializes in educational experiences on the border)
www.borderlinks.org

Border Working Group (Latin American political action and advocacy)
www.lawg.org

Church World Service (immigration and refugees program)
www.churchworldservice.org/immigration

Humane Borders (humanitarian aid, water in the desert)
www.humaneborders.org

Justice for Immigrants Campaign (outreach of US Conference of Catholic Bishops)
www.justiceforimmigrants.org

Lutheran Immigration and Refugee Service (advocacy)
www.lirs.org

Mennonite Central Committee (advocacy, humanitarian aid)
www.mcc.org/us/immigration

No More Deaths (humanitarian aid, desert camps, volunteers in migrant centers)
www.nomoredeaths.org

Presbyterian Church USA
http://www.binationalministry.org/

Persons Willing to Help You Become a Partner with Just Coffee

Barbara Padilla (large Catholic parish)

Sue Ellen Beatty (large Presbyterian church)

Homer Hamby (small/medium sized church)

Susan Nunn (bed and breakfast)

Vicki Willan and Roy Goodman (farmers markets)

Todd West (community food bank)

Dylan Cate (university setting)

Don Tubesing (community marketing strategies)

Contact **Tommy Bassett** at **(520) 249-1692** or **tommy@fronteradecristo.org** for information on connecting with these folks.

Socios of the Salvador Urbina *Café Justo* Cooperative

Socios pictured (page #) in *Just Coffee: Caffeine with a Conscience*

Aide Ruiz Perez 12	Hernan Cifuentes Perez 56
Alberto "Beto" Dominguez Sanchez 12	Ildefonso Ortiz Mejia 68
Andres Velazquez Verdugo 12	Ismael Juan Morales Trejo 68
Arnulfo Lopez Perez 26	Jorge Mario Lopez Portillo 82
Beltran Sanchez Rodriguez 26	Juan Carlos Perez Martinez 82
David Cifuentes Velazquez 26	Lazaro Hernandez Godinez 82
David Oman Cifuentes Velazquez 34	Luciano Martinez Garcia 96
Elifas Cifuentes Lopez 34	Luis "Pelayo" Manuel Diaz Perez 96
Emilio Navarro Barrios 34	Maria Cristina Gabriel Solis 96
Eri Cifuentes Perez 42	Modesto Santizo Perez 106
Fabian Ochoa 42	Otilio Lopez Vazquez 106
Gregorio Vazquez Perez 42	Reynaldo Cifuentes Velazquez 106
Guadalupe Morales Trejo 56	

Socios whose photos were not available

Anibal Flores	Nelson Missrain Roblero Robledo
Armando Mexa Francisco	Pedro Diaz
Concepcion Perez Ochoa	Ruben Morales
Daniel Rosales	Salstio Diaz
Edmundo Ballinas Santiago	Samuel Hidalgo Montalvo
Gregorio Vazquez	Santiago Ventura Fabian
Ignacio Jaime Escobar Castillo	Ubaldo Efren Roblero Robledo
Manuel Cifuentes Perez	

Check the website, www.fronteradecristo.org, for updated profiles of coffee growing families.

About the Authors

The Rev. Mark Adams and Tommy Bassett III wrote this book together. In real life, however, there is not much that overlaps between us because we are from the "opposites attract" clan. Mark is a genteel southerner coming from the reserved environs of Clover, South Carolina. Tommy is a Minnesotan who left for the west as soon as he learned there

Mark Adams

Tommy Bassett III

were places that were warm year-round with few mosquitoes and just as friendly people.

After graduating from Furman University (BA in History), teaching high school Spanish, and receiving his MDiv from Columbia Theological Seminary, Mark arrived at the border in 1998. An ordained Presbyterian minister, he serves as Mission Co-Worker at Frontera de Cristo, an unusual bi-national ministry centered in Agua Prieta, Sonora and Douglas, Arizona. Mark's background in history and theology—enriched by ten years of life on the border—affords him a unique and fundamental perspective on migration and our connections to and with one another across borders.

Tommy arrived at the border in 1992 to work as manager of an electronics manufacturing maquiladora in Agua Prieta. Tommy graduated from the University of Arizona with a BA in Sociology and Philosophy. His twenty-plus years in industrial manufacturing and experience in cross-border business helped forge his perspective on social justice. He serves as Developer for the Just Trade Center, which is a partnership of *Café Justo*, Frontera de Cristo and Catholic Relief Services of Mexico.

Although we arrived at the border from different origins, via different paths, we share similar experiences with respect to the disheartening ravages of migration and the difficulty of life on the border. Collaborating on this book brought us closer together and deepened an already rich and vital relationship. We hope our friendship, shared vision and similar goals are as apparent in these pages as our commitment to the cause of justice on the border.

Despite our differences—or perhaps because of them—we have collaborated on many exciting initiatives to build relationships and understanding across borders. And through these efforts, God has made a difference!

We'd love to hear from you.

Mark Adams, mark@fronteradecristo.org

Tommy Bassett III, tommy@fronteradecristo.org

This Book Comes With Lots of FREE Online Resources

Nolo's award-winning website has a page dedicated just to this book. Here you can:

KEEP UP TO DATE. When there are important changes to the information in this book, we'll post updates.

GET DISCOUNTS ON NOLO PRODUCTS. Get discounts on hundreds of books, forms, and software.

READ BLOGS. Get the latest info from Nolo authors' blogs.

LISTEN TO PODCASTS. Listen to authors discuss timely issues on topics that interest you.

WATCH VIDEOS. Get a quick introduction to a legal topic with our short videos.

And that's not all.
Nolo.com contains thousands of articles on everyday legal and business issues, plus a plain-English law dictionary, all written by Nolo experts and available for free. You'll also find more useful **books, software, online apps, downloadable forms,** plus a **lawyer directory.**

With
Downloadable FORMS

Get forms and more at
www.nolo.com/back-of-book/ELLI.html

14th Edition

Every Landlord's Legal Guide

Marcia Stewart & Attorney Janet Portman

FOURTEENTH EDITION   MAY 2018

Cover & Book Design   TERRI HEARSH

Proofreading   ROBERT WELLS

Index   JULIE SHAWVAN

Printing   BANG PRINTING

ISSN 2576-7194 (online)
ISSN 2576-7186 (print)

ISBN 978-1-4133-2517-1 (paperback)
ISBN 978-1-4133-2518-8 (ebook)

This book covers only United States law, unless it specifically states otherwise.

Please note

We believe accurate, plain-English legal information should help you solve many of your own legal problems. But this text is not a substitute for personalized advice from a knowledgeable lawyer. If you want the help of a trained professional—and we'll always point out situations in which we think that's a good idea—consult an attorney licensed to practice in your state.

About the Authors

Marcia Stewart is the coauthor of *Every Tenant's Legal Guide, Renters' Rights, Leases & Rental Agreements, First-Time Landlord,* and *Nolo's Essential Guide to Buying Your First Home.* Marcia received a Master's degree in Public Policy from the University of California at Berkeley.

Janet Portman, an attorney and Nolo's Executive Editor, received undergraduate and graduate degrees from Stanford and a law degree from Santa Clara University. She is an expert on landlord-tenant law and the coauthor of *Every Tenant's Legal Guide, Every Landlord's Guide to Finding Great Tenants, First-Time Landlord, Renters' Rights, The California Landlord's Law Book: Rights and Responsibilities, California Tenant's Rights, Leases & Rental Agreements,* and *Negotiate the Best Lease for Your Business.* As a practicing attorney, she specialized in criminal defense before joining Nolo.

Table of Contents

Appendixes

Introduction: Your Landlord Companion

Whether you own one rental property or a hundred, you want to run a profitable business, protect your investment, and avoid legal hassles. Your success depends heavily on knowing and complying with dozens of state, federal, and local laws that affect you. Fortunately, you don't need a law degree—just this book.

We'll take you step by step through all your important tasks, from accepting rental applications to returning security deposits when a tenant moves out and everything between, including preparing a lease, handling repairs, and dealing with tenants who pay rent late, make too much noise, or cause other problems. We cover straightforward procedures (such as how to legally reject a prospect) as well as more tricky situations (like what to do when a tenant threatens to withhold rent until you make certain repairs). Here's how we can help you:

State-specific legal info. This book includes all kinds of important state-specific information. Want to know about security deposit laws in your state? You can look up the deposit limit, find out whether you need to keep the deposit in a separate account or pay interest on it, and whether you're exempt from the rules based on the number of rental properties you own.

Legal forms and letters. This book includes dozens of forms, letters, notices, checklists, and agreements. From the most complicated (your lease or rental agreement) to the simplest (a time estimate for repair), we've got you covered, including forms for the collection, itemization, and return of deposits, and a landlord-tenant checklist to record the condition of the rental unit at the start and end of the tenancy. Each form is easy to customize and has complete instructions. There are filled-in samples in the text, and you'll find the forms on the companion page for this book on the Nolo website (see below for details).

Getting Expert Help

Throughout this book, we'll alert you to situations in which it's wise to get expert help beyond this book, including:

- **Preparing eviction papers.** We explain how to terminate a tenancy, but if you need to pursue an eviction lawsuit, get more help. Evictions are governed by very specific state and local laws and procedures.

- **Rentals in mobile home parks and marinas.** In most states, completely different sets of laws govern these rentals.

- **Renting out a condo or town house.** Many owners will find this book helpful, but additional rules will apply to your rental situation, courtesy of your homeowners' association's CC&Rs (covenants, conditions, and restrictions). Sometimes CC&Rs clash with, or may go beyond, federal, state, or local laws, and it's often difficult to predict, let alone determine, which approach a court would uphold.

- **Live-work units.** If you're renting out these units, you'll find this book helpful, but be aware that zoning regulations may apply.

- **Section 8 housing.** If you participate in the Section 8 rent-assistance program, you'll find most of the day-to-day recommendations of this book usable, but you'll need to use the lease addendum supplied by the housing authority that administers the program.

- **Short-term rentals.** Because many landlord-tenant laws specifically exclude short-term, hotel-like rentals, much of the advice and rules discussed here will not apply to rentals on Airbnb, VRBO, or other online services. But we can tell you this: If you intend to run such a business, first check with your local government. Many municipalities require registration, limit the number of short-stay days per year, or otherwise restrict short-term rentals. See Chapter 8 for more on the subject.

Time-tested and timely. This book, which first appeared in 1996, has been updated many times since to keep up with the constantly changing world of residential landlording. Ours is the only book on the shelf that combines current, comprehensive legal information and practical advice usable by landlords in every state. It now covers emerging issues such as how to restrict tenant use of short-term rental services such as Airbnb. And in case important laws change during the life of this edition, you'll find updates on this book's companion page (described below).

Our approach to running a residential rental business rests on recognizing that tenants are your best asset and the key element in your financial success. Our approach will guard your legal and financial interests and, at the same time, make your customers—your tenants—feel that your practices are fair and reasonable.

In a nutshell: Choose tenants carefully; keep good tenants happy; teach mediocre tenants how to improve; get rid of bad tenants by applying policies that are strict, fair, and legal; and back up everything with good records and paperwork. Follow that simple philosophy, and you can run a business that's both satisfying and profitable.

Get Legal Updates, Forms, and More on This Book's Companion Page on Nolo.com

This book includes three dozen useful forms and worksheets, including a lease, a rental application, and security deposit itemizations. You can download any of the forms and worksheets in this book at:

www.nolo.com/back-of-book/ELLI.html

When there are important changes to the information in this book, we'll post updates on this same dedicated page (what we call the book's companion page). See Appendix B, "How to Use the Downloadable Forms on the Nolo Website," for a list of forms available on Nolo.com.

Other Helpful Nolo Books and Resources for Landlords

Nolo publishes a comprehensive library of books for landlords and property managers. Besides *Every Landlord's Legal Guide,* Nolo offers:

- *Every Landlord's Guide to Finding Great Tenants,* by Janet Portman. Focuses solely on advertising and showing your rental, evaluating prospects, and choosing and rejecting tenants, with over 40 forms, including a credit report evaluation, marketing worksheets, and departing tenant's questionnaire. Especially useful for landlords who own multiunit properties or have a lot of tenant turnover.
- *Every Landlord's Guide to Managing Property*, by Michael Boyer. Provides practical and legal compliance advice for small-time landlords who manage property and tenants on the side (while holding down a day job). Includes do-it-yourself advice on handling day-to-day issues, such as nitty-gritty maintenance and conflicts with tenants regarding late rent, pets, and unauthorized occupants. Explains how to manage and grow a successful rental property business with minimal hassle and cost.
- *Every Landlord's Tax Deduction Guide,* by Stephen Fishman. Includes all the information you need to take advantage of tax deductions and write-offs available to landlords, such as depreciation, legal services, travel, and insurance. Includes instructions on filling out Schedule E.
- *Leases & Rental Agreements,* by Marcia Stewart, Ralph Warner, and Janet Portman. Includes a lease, rental agreement, and several other basic forms. If you own *Every Landlord's Legal Guide,* you don't need *Leases and Rental Agreements.*

- *The California Landlord's Law Book: Rights & Responsibilities,* by David Brown, Janet Portman, and Nils Rosenquest, and *The California Landlord's Law Book: Evictions*, by David Brown and Nils Rosenquest. Contain all the information California landlords need to run their business and handle an eviction in court by themselves. *Every Landlord's Legal Guide* covers residential landlord-tenant law in all 50 states, including California, but these books provide more details, including rent control rules in California cities and step-by-step instructions on how to file and handle an eviction lawsuit.
- *First-Time Landlord: Your Guide to Renting Out a Single-Family Home*, by Janet Portman, Ilona Bray, and Marcia Stewart. Covers the basics that first-time or "accidental" landlords need to rent and manage a single-family home or condo, including how to determine if a property will turn a profit, renting out a room in a house when owners are still living in it, and how to use a lease-option-to-buy contract.

You can order these books from Nolo's website (www.nolo.com) or by phone (800-728-3555). You can also find Nolo books at public libraries and bookstores.

In addition to these books, Nolo offers many single-copy interactive online forms of interest to landlords, such as state-specific leases and rental agreements.

Be sure to check out the Landlords section of Nolo.com for a wide variety of articles of interest to landlords, including state eviction rules. The Nolo website includes other useful resources, including legal updates on this book's companion page (described above). You can also find an experienced landlord's attorney at Nolo's Lawyer Directory (see www.nolo.com/lawyers).

Screening Tenants: Your Most Important Decision

FORMS IN THIS CHAPTER

Chapter 1 includes instructions for and samples of the following forms:

- Rental Application
- Consent to Contact References and Perform Credit Check
- Tenant References
- Notice of Denial Based on Credit Report or Other Information
- Notice of Conditional Acceptance Based on Credit Report or Other Information
- Receipt and Holding Deposit Agreement

The Nolo website includes downloadable copies of these forms. See Appendix B for the link to the forms in this book.

Choosing tenants is the most important decision any landlord makes, and to do it well you need a reliable system. Follow the steps in this chapter to maximize your chances of selecting tenants who will pay their rent on time, keep their units in good condition, and not cause you any legal or practical problems later.

How Landlord's Associations Can Help

All the rules and procedures for choosing tenants may seem overwhelming the first time around. This chapter provides all the legal and practical information and forms you need to do the job right. You can also get a lot of advice from talking with other landlords. You may want to check out local or state rental property associations, which range from small, volunteer-run groups of landlords to substantial organizations with paid staff and lobbyists, that offer a wide variety of support and services to their members. Here are some services that may be available from your landlords' association:

- legal information and updates through newsletters, publications, seminars, and other means
- tenant screening and credit check services
- training and practical advice on compliance with legal responsibilities, and
- a place to meet other rental property owners and exchange information and ideas.

If you can't find an association of rental property owners online or in your phone book, ask other landlords for references. You can also contact the National Apartment Association (NAA), a national organization whose members include many individual state associations (www.naahq.org), and the National Multifamily Housing Council (www.nmhc.org), which provides useful networking opportunities and research.

RELATED TOPIC

Before you advertise your property for rent, make a number of basic decisions—including how much rent to charge, whether to offer a fixed-term lease or a month-to-month rental agreement, how many tenants can occupy each rental unit, how big a security deposit to require, and whether you'll allow pets. Making these important decisions should dovetail with writing your lease or rental agreement (see Chapter 2.)

Avoiding Fair Housing Complaints and Lawsuits

Federal and state antidiscrimination laws limit what you can say and do in the tenant selection process. Because the topic of discrimination is so important we devote a whole chapter to it later in the book (Chapter 5), including legal reasons for refusing to rent to a tenant and how to avoid discrimination in your tenant selection process. You should read Chapter 5 before you run an ad or interview prospective tenants. For now, keep in mind four important points:

1. **You are legally free to choose among prospective tenants as long as your decisions are based on legitimate business criteria.** You are entitled to reject applicants with bad credit histories, income that you reasonably regard as insufficient to pay the rent, or past behavior—such as property damage or consistent late rent payments—that makes someone a bad risk. A valid occupancy limit that is clearly tied to health and safety or legitimate business needs can also be a legal basis for refusing tenants. It goes without saying that you may legally refuse to rent to someone who can't come up with the security deposit or meet some other condition of the tenancy.

2. **Fair housing laws specify clearly illegal reasons to refuse to rent to a tenant.** Federal law prohibits discrimination on the basis of race, religion, national origin, gender, age, familial status, or physical or mental disability (including recovering alcoholics and people with a past drug addiction). Many states and cities also prohibit discrimination based on marital status or sexual orientation.

3. **Anybody who deals with prospective tenants must follow fair housing laws.** This includes owners, landlords, managers, and real estate brokers,

and all of their employees. As the property owner, you may be held legally responsible for your employees' discriminatory statements or conduct, including sexual harassment. "Your Liability for a Manager's Acts," in Chapter 6, explains how to protect yourself from your employee's illegal acts.

4. **Consistency is crucial when dealing with prospective tenants.** If you don't treat all tenants more or less equally—for example, if you arbitrarily set tougher standards for renting to a member of a racial minority—you are violating federal laws and opening yourself up to lawsuits.

How to Advertise Rental Property

You can advertise rental property in many ways:

- posting a notice online (see "Craigslist and Online Apartment Listing Services," below, for details)
- putting an "Apartment for Rent" sign in front of the building or in one of the windows
- taking out ads in a local newspaper
- posting flyers on neighborhood bulletin boards, such as the local laundromat or coffee shop
- listing with a local real estate broker that handles rentals
- hiring a property management company that will advertise your rentals as part of the management fee, or
- posting a notice with university, alumni, or corporate housing offices.

The kind of advertising that will work best depends on a number of factors, including the characteristics of the particular property (such as rent, size, amenities), its location, your budget, and whether you are in a hurry to rent. Many smaller landlords find that instead of advertising widely and having to screen many potential tenants in an effort to sort the good from the bad, it makes better sense to market their rentals through word of mouth—telling friends, colleagues, neighbors, and current tenants, and by posting on Facebook and other social media.

Craigslist and Online Apartment Listing Services

Dozens of online services now make it easy to reach potential tenants, whether they already live in your community or are moving from out of state.

Craigslist and other online community posting boards allow you to list your rentals at no or low charge and are a good place to start. Craigslist, the most established community board, has local sites for every major metropolitan area. Check out www.craigslist.org for details. Local online services may also be available, particularly in large urban areas; examples include Apartable.com in New York City and Westside Rentals in Southern California.

National apartment listing services are also available, with the largest ones representing millions of apartment units in the United States. Some of the most established are:

- www.apartments.com
- www.hotpads.com (a Zillow company)
- www.rentals.com
- www.rent.com
- www.apartmentsearch.com
- www.apartmentguide.com,
- www.forrent.com
- www.zumper.com, and
- onradpad.com.

These national sites offer a wide range of services, from simple text-only ads that provide basic information on your rental (such as the number of bedrooms) to full-scale virtual tours and floor plans of the rental property. Services typically include mobile apps, too. Prices vary widely depending on the type of ad, how long you want it to run, and any services you purchase (some websites provide tenant-screening services).

Before you use any online apartment rental service, make sure it's reputable. Find out who owns it, how long the company has been in business and how they handle problems with apartment listings. Check for any consumer complaints, and avoid paying any hefty fee without thoroughly checking out a company and its services.

To stay out of legal hot water when you advertise, just follow these simple rules.

Describe the rental unit accurately. As a practical matter, you should avoid abbreviations and real estate jargon in your ad. Include basic details, such as:

- rent and deposit
- size—particularly number of bedrooms and baths
- location—either the general neighborhood or street address
- move-in date and term—lease or month-to-month rental agreement
- special features—such as fenced-in yard, view, washer/dryer, fireplace, remodeled kitchen, furnished, garage parking, doorman, hardwood floors, or wall-to-wall carpeting
- pets (whether you allow or not and any restrictions, such as dog breeds your insurance prohibits)
- your nonparticipation in the Section 8 program (assuming you have the choice—see Chapter 5 for details)
- phone number, website, and/or email for more details (unless you're going to show the unit only at an open house and don't want to take calls), and
- date and time of any open house.

If you have any important rules (legal and non-discriminatory), such as no smoking, put them in your ad. Letting prospective tenants know about your important policies can save you or your manager from talking to a lot of unsuitable people. For example, your ad might say you require credit checks in order to discourage applicants who have a history of paying rent late.

Be sure your ad can't be construed as discriminatory. The best way to do this is to focus only on the rental property—not on any particular type of tenant. Specifically, ads should never mention sex, race, religion, disability, or age (unless yours is really legally recognized senior citizens housing). And ads should never imply through words, photographs, or illustrations that you prefer to rent to people because of their age, sex, or race. For example, an ad in a church newsletter that contains a drawing of a recognizably white (or black or Asian) couple with no children might open you to an accusation of discrimination based on race, age, and familial status (prohibiting children).

Quote an honest price in your ad. If a tenant who is otherwise acceptable (has a good credit history and impeccable references and meets all the criteria explained below) shows up promptly and agrees to all the terms set out in your ad, you may violate false advertising laws if you arbitrarily raise the price. This doesn't mean you are always legally required to rent at your advertised price, however. If a tenant asks for more services or different lease terms that you feel require more rent, it's fine to bargain and raise your price, as long as your proposed increase doesn't violate local rent control laws.

Don't advertise something you don't have. Some large landlords, management companies, and rental services have advertised units that weren't really available in order to produce a large number of prospective tenants who could then be directed to higher-priced or inferior units. Such bait-and-switch advertising is clearly illegal under consumer fraud laws, and many property owners have been prosecuted for such practices. So if you advertise a sunny two-bedroom apartment next to a rose garden for $800 a month, make sure that the second bedroom isn't a closet, the rose garden isn't a beetle-infested bush, and the $800 isn't the first week's rent.

Keep in mind that even if you aren't prosecuted for breaking fraud laws, your advertising promises can still come back to haunt you. A tenant who is robbed or attacked in what you advertised as a "high-security building" may sue you for medical bills, lost earnings, and pain and suffering.

Finding Tenants Who Are Advertising Themselves

Tradition has it that landlords list available rentals, tenants find them. But tenants advertising themselves as ready to rent—not so much. All of that has changed with the proliferation of online sites that allow prospecting tenants to market themselves to landlords. Neighborhood Laundromat bulletin board, meet the likes of Craigslist ("Housing Wanted") and private social media networks like Next Door.

Apartment seekers who post online ads describe their property needs and their price range, hoping that a landlord in the area will see their post and contact them. The idea is similar to the practice in adoptions, where would-be adopting parents produce glossy and glowing descriptions of themselves and the family they want to raise, aimed at women who will choose the family that will get their child.

The Craigslist pages are chock-full of posts that run the gamut from sophisticated to self-defeating. If you decide to peruse these pages, keep these tips in mind:

- The ad should reveal relevant information about the tenant's needs and nature, so that you don't call someone who isn't suited for your rental. Without information that tells you that this person has "pre-screened" himself, responding to the ad is likely a waste of time.

- The ad should describe a seeker that fits every landlord's search for tenants who are stable, clean, and honest. Of course, the words on the page don't make it true, but if you encounter information that raises red flags (a history of short-term rentals), take heed.

- The ad should explain what the tenant is looking for (a quiet, secluded home, or a utilitarian studio downtown), but not spell "demanding, high maintenance tenant." Be on the lookout for requirements that, if you meet them, would involve you in a fair housing problem (such as, "Looking for a quiet, adult community").

- Look carefully at the writer's description of his job, interests, and how he spends his free time. Any activities that spell "property damage" or "party animal" may backfire. You'd be surprised at how many tenant-advertisers

describe their love of alcohol and music (without mentioning that they use earbuds).

- Beware the post that plays the sympathy card. Tenants may be down on their luck, but it's naïve to expect landlords to choose them because they feel sorry for them. It's admirable to work with in-place tenants who have hit a rough patch, in hopes that they can turn their fortunes around, but you're taking a risk to begin a landlord-tenant relationship on this basis.

Renting Property That's Still Occupied

Often, you can wait until the old tenant moves out to show a rental unit to prospective tenants. This gives you the chance to refurbish the unit and avoids problems such as promising the place to a new tenant, only to have the existing tenant not move out on time or leave the place a mess.

To eliminate any gap in rent, however, you may want to show a rental unit while its current tenants are still there. This can create a conflict; in most states, you have a right to show the still-occupied property to prospective tenants, but your current tenants are still entitled to their privacy.

To minimize disturbing your current tenant, follow these guidelines:

- Before implementing your plans to find a new tenant, discuss them with the outgoing tenant, so you can be as accommodating as possible.

- Give the current tenant as much notice as possible before entering and showing a rental unit to prospective tenants. State law usually requires at least one or two days. (See Chapter 13 for details.)

- Try to limit the number of times you show the unit in a given week, and make sure your current tenant agrees to any evening and weekend visits.

- Consider reducing the rent slightly for the existing tenant if showing the unit really will be an imposition.

- If possible, avoid putting a sign on the rental property itself, since this almost guarantees that your existing tenant will be bothered by strangers. Or, if you can't avoid putting up a sign, make sure any sign clearly warns against disturbing the occupant and includes a telephone number for information. Something on the order of "For Rent: Shown by Appointment Only. Call 555-1700. DO NOT DISTURB OCCUPANTS" should work fine.

If, despite your best efforts to protect their privacy, the current tenants are uncooperative or hostile, wait until they leave before showing the unit. Also, if the current tenants are complete slobs or have damaged the place, you'll be far better off to apply paint and elbow grease before trying to rerent it.

Dealing With Prospective Tenants and Accepting Rental Applications

It's good business, as well as a sound way to protect yourself from future legal problems, to carefully screen prospective tenants.

Tell Prospective Tenants Your Basic Requirements and Rules

Whether prospective tenants call about the rental, or just show up at an open house, it's best to describe all your general requirements—rent, deposits, pet policy, move-in date, maximum number of occupants, and the like—and any special rules and regulations up front. This helps you avoid wasting time showing the unit to someone who simply can't qualify—for example, someone who can't come up with the security deposit. Describing your general requirements and rules up front can also help avoid charges of discrimination, which can occur when a member of a racial minority or a single parent is told key facts so late in the process that she jumps to the conclusion that you've made up new requirements just to keep her out.

Also be sure to tell prospective tenants about the kind of personal information they'll be expected to supply on an application, including phone numbers of previous landlords and credit and employment references.

CAUTION

Show the property to and accept applications from everyone who's interested. Even if, after talking to someone on the phone, you doubt that a particular tenant can qualify, it's best to politely take all applications. Refusing to take an application may unnecessarily anger a prospective tenant, and may make the applicant more likely to look into the possibility of filing a discrimination complaint. And discriminating against someone simply because you don't like the sound of his or her voice on the phone (called linguistic profiling) is also illegal and may result in a discrimination claim. Show the property to and accept applications from anyone who's interested and make decisions about who will rent the property later. Be sure to keep copies of all applications. (See discussion of record keeping below.)

Ask Interested Tenants to Complete a Rental Application

To avoid legal problems and choose the best tenant, ask all prospective tenants to fill out a written rental application that includes information on the applicant's employment, income, and credit; Social Security and driver's license numbers or other identifying information; past evictions or bankruptcies; and references.

A sample Rental Application is shown below and the Nolo website includes a downloadable copy. See Appendix B for the link to the forms in this book.

Before giving prospective tenants a Rental Application, complete the box at the top, filling in the property address, rental term, first month's rent, and any deposit or credit check fee tenants must pay before moving in. Here are some basic rules for accepting rental applications:

Give an application to all adult applicants. Each prospective tenant—everyone age 18 or older who wants to live in your rental property—should completely fill out a written application. This is true whether you're renting to a married couple or to unrelated roommates, a complete stranger, or the cousin of your current tenant.

Rental Application

Separate application required from each applicant age 18 or older.

Date and time received by landlord _____

Credit check fee ___$38_____ Received _____

THIS SECTION TO BE COMPLETED BY LANDLORD

Address of Property to Be Rented: __178 West 81st St., Apt. 4F_____

Rental Term: ☐ month-to-month ☑ lease from __March 1, 20xx__ to __February 28, 20xx__

Amounts Due Prior to Occupancy

First month's rent .... $ ___3,000___

Security deposit .... $ ___3,000___

Other (specify): __Broker's fee_____ $ ___3,000___

TOTAL.. $ ___9,000___

Applicant

Full Name—include all names you use(d): ___Hannah Silver_____

Home Phone: __609-555-3789__ Work Phone: __609-555-4567__ Cell Phone: __609-987-6543__

Email: ___hannah@coldmail.com_____ Fax*:_____

Social Security Number: __123-00-4567__ Driver's License Number/State: __D123456/New Jersey__

Other Identifying Information: _____

Vehicle Make: ___Toyota_____ Model: ____Corolla___ Color: ___White_____ Year: __2015__

License Plate Number/State: __NJ1234567/New Jersey_____

Additional Occupants

List everyone, including minor children, who will live with you:

Full Name	Relationship to Applicant
Dennis Olson	Husband

Rental History

FIRST-TIME RENTERS: ATTACH A DESCRIPTION OF YOUR HOUSING SITUATION FOR THE PAST FIVE YEARS.

Current Address: __39 Maple St., Princeton, NJ 08540_____

Dates Lived at Address: __May 2011 - date_____ Rent $ __2,000__ Security Deposit $ __4,000__

Landlord/Manager: __Jane Tucker_____ Landlord/Manager's Phone: __609-555-7523__

Reason for Leaving: ___New job in NYC_____

* By providing this fax number I agree to receive facsimile advertisements from the landlord or management company.

Previous Address: _1215 Middlebrook Lane, Princeton, NJ 08540_

Dates Lived at Address: _June 2008 - May 2011_ Rent $ _1,800_ Security Deposit $ _1,000_

Landlord/Manager: _Ed Palermo_ Landlord/Manager's Phone: _609-555-3711_

Reason for Leaving: _Better apartment_

Previous Address: _1527 Highland Dr., New Brunswick, N.J. 08444_

Dates Lived at Address: _Jan. 2007 - June 2008_ Rent $ _800_ Security Deposit $ _800_

Landlord/Manager: _Millie and Joe Lewis_ Landlord/Manager's Phone: _609-555-9999_

Reason for Leaving: _Wanted to live closer to work_

Employment History

SELF-EMPLOYED APPLICANTS: ATTACH TAX RETURNS FOR THE PAST TWO YEARS

Name and Address of Current Employer: _Argonworks, 54 Nassau St., Princeton, NJ_

Phone: _609-555-2333_

Name of Supervisor: _Tom Schmidt_ Supervisor's Phone: _609-555-2333_

Dates Employed at This Job: _2008 - date_ Position or Title: _Marketing Director_

Name and Address of Previous Employer: _Princeton Times_

13 Junction Rd., Princeton, NJ Phone: _609-555-1111_

Name of Supervisor: _Dory Krossber_ Supervisor's Phone: _609-555-2366_

Dates Employed at This Job: _Jan. 2007 - June. 2008_ Position or Title: _Marketing Associate_

ATTACH PAY STUBS FOR THE PAST TWO YEARS, FROM THIS EMPLOYER OR PRIOR EMPLOYERS.

Income

1. Your gross monthly employment income (before deductions): $ _8,000_

2. Average monthly amounts of other income (specify sources): $ _____

   Note: This does not include my husband's income. $ _____

   See his application. $ _____

   TOTAL: $ _8,000_

Bank/Financial Accounts

	Account Number	Bank/Institution	Branch
Savings Account:	1222345	N.J. Federal	Trenton, NJ
Checking Account:	789101	Princeton S&L	Princeton, NJ
Money Market or Similar Account:	234789	City Bank	Princeton, NJ

Credit Card Accounts

Major Credit Card: ☑VISA ☐MC ☐Discover Card ☐Am Ex ☐Other: _____

Issuer: _City Bank_   Account No. _1234 5555 6666 7777_

Balance $_1,000_   Average Monthly Payment: $ _1,000_

Major Credit Card: ☐VISA ☐MC ☐Discover Card ☐Am Ex ☑Other: _Dept. Store_

Issuer: _City Bank_   Account No. _2345 0000 9999 8888_

Balance $ _500_   Average Monthly Payment: $ _500_

Loans

Type of Loan (mortgage, car, student loan, etc.)	Name of Creditor	Account Number	Amount Owed	Monthly Payment

Other Major Obligations

Type	Payee		Amount Owed	Monthly Payment

Miscellaneous

Describe the number and type of pets you want to have in the rental property: _None now, but we_ _might want to get a cat some time_

Describe water-filled furniture you want to have in the rental property: _None_

Do you smoke? ☐ yes ☑ no

Have you ever:

Filed for bankruptcy?	☐ yes	☑ no	How many times _____
Been sued?	☐ yes	☑ no	How many times _____
Sued someone else?	☐ yes	☑ no	How many times _____
Been evicted?	☐ yes	☑ no	How many times _____
Been convicted of a crime?	☐ yes	☑ no	How many times _____

Explain any "yes" listed above: _____

References and Emergency Contact

Personal Reference: _Joan Stanley_   Relationship: _Friend, coworker_

Address: _785 Spruce St., Princeton, NJ 08540_

    Phone: _609-555-4578_

Personal Reference: _Marnie Swatt_   Relationship: _Friend_

Address: _82 East 59th St., #12B, NYC_

    Phone: _212-555-8765_

Contact in Emergency: _Connie & Martin Silver_   Relationship: _Parents_

Address: _7852 Pierce St., Somerset, NJ 08321_

    Phone: _609-555-7878_

Source

Where did you learn of this vacancy? _Ryan Cowell, Broker_

I certify that all the information given above is true and correct and understand that my lease or rental agreement may be terminated if I have made any material false or incomplete statements in this application. I authorize verification of the information provided in this application from my credit sources, credit bureaus, current and previous landlords and employers, and personal references. This permission will survive the expiration of my tenancy.

Hannah Silver   _February 15, 20xx_
Applicant   Date

Notes (Landlord/Manager): _____

Consent to Contact References and Perform Credit Check

I authorize _____Jan Gold_____ to

obtain information about me from my credit sources, current and previous landlords, employers, and personal

references, to enable _____Jan Gold_____ to evaluate my rental application.

I give permission for the landlord or its agent to obtain a consumer report about me for the purpose of this

application, to ensure that I continue to meet the terms of the tenancy, for the collection and recovery of any

financial obligations relating to my tenancy, or for any other permissible purpose.

_Michael Clark_____
Applicant signature

_Michael Clark_____
Printed name

_123 State Street, Chicago, Illinois_____
Address

_312-555-9876_____
Phone Number

_February 2, 20xx_____
Date

Insist on a completed application. Always make sure that prospective tenants complete the entire Rental Application, including Social Security number (SSN) or Individual Taxpayer Identification Number (ITIN), explained below, driver's license number, or other identifying information (such as a passport number); current employment; and emergency contacts. You may need this information later to track down a tenant who skips town leaving unpaid rent or abandoned property. Also, you may need the Social Security number or other identifying information, such as a passport, to request an applicant's credit report.

! CAUTION

Don't ask for an applicant's date of birth. This rental application does not ask applicants for their dates of birth (DOB). Many fair housing experts believe that doing so is risky, should a disappointed applicant attempt to challenge your rejection as an instance of age discrimination—having the date on the application at least establishes that you knew of the applicant's age. Some landlords still ask for the DOB, responding to credit reporting companies' requests for this information. You should be able to order a credit report and a screening report using the applicant's Social Security number; if vendors balk, you may want to ask for the DOB.

You may encounter an applicant who does not have an SSN (only citizens or immigrants authorized to work in the United States can obtain one). For example, someone with a student visa will not normally have an SSN. If you categorically refuse to rent to applicants without SSNs, and these applicants happen to be foreign students, you're courting a fair housing complaint.

Fortunately, nonimmigrant aliens (such as people lawfully in the U.S. who don't intend to stay here permanently, and even those who are here illegally) can obtain an alternate piece of identification that will suit your needs as well as an SSN. It's called an Individual Taxpayer Identification Number (ITIN), and is issued by the IRS to people who expect to pay taxes. Most people who are here long enough to apply for an apartment will also be earning income while in the U.S. and will therefore have an ITIN. Consumer reporting agencies and tenant screening companies can use an ITIN to find the information they need to effectively screen an applicant. On the Rental Application, use the line "Other Identifying Information" for an applicant's ITIN.

Getting a Unit Ready for Prospective Tenants

It goes without saying that a clean rental unit in good repair will rent more easily than a rundown hovel. And, in the long run, it pays to keep your rental competitive. Before showing a rental unit, make sure the basics are covered:

- Clean all rooms and furnishings, floors, walls, and ceilings—it's especially important that the bathroom and kitchen are spotless.
- Remove all clutter from closets, cupboards, and surfaces.
- Take care of any insect or rodent infestations.
- Make sure that the appliances and fixtures work. Repair leaky faucets and frayed cords, replace burnt-out lights, and check the unit for anything that might cause injury or violate health and safety codes. (Chapter 9 discusses state and local health and safety laws.)
- Cut the grass, trim shrubbery, and remove all trash and debris on the grounds.
- Update old fixtures and appliances, and repaint the walls and replace the carpets if necessary.

Nolo's *Every Landlord's Guide to Managing Property* includes extensive advice on preparing your rental units for new tenants, including detailed cleaning, painting, and repair routines, how to get rid of pet odors, and other specific turnaround tasks.

If the previous tenant left the place in good shape, you may not need to do much cleaning before showing it to prospective tenants. To make this more likely, be sure to send outgoing tenants a move-out letter describing your specific cleaning requirements and conditions for returning the tenant's security deposit. (Chapter 15 discusses move-out letters.)

> ! CAUTION
> **Do not consider an ITIN number as proof of legal status in the U.S.** The IRS does not research the taxpayer's immigration status before handing out the number.

Check for a signature and consider getting a separate credit check authorization. Be sure all potential tenants sign the Rental Application, authorizing you to verify the information and references and to run a credit report. (Some employers and others require written authorization before they will talk to you.) You may also want to prepare a separate authorization, signed and dated by the applicant, so that you don't need to copy the entire application and email or fax it every time a bank or employer wants proof that the tenant authorized you to verify the information. A sample Consent to Contact References and Perform Credit Check is shown above, and the Nolo website includes a downloadable copy. See Appendix B for the link to the forms in this book.

When you talk to prospective tenants, stick to questions on the application. Avoid asking questions that may discriminate, specifically any inquiries as to the person's birthplace, age, religion, marital status or children, physical or mental condition, or arrests that did not result in conviction. (See Chapter 5 for details on antidiscrimination laws.)

Request Proof of Identity and Immigration Status

In these security-sensitive times, many landlords ask prospective tenants to show their driver's license or other photo identification as a way to verify that the applicant is using his real name.

Except in California (Cal. Civ. Code § 1940.3), and New York City (N.Y.C. Admin. Code § 8-107(5)(a)), you may also ask applicants for proof of identity and eligibility to work under U.S. immigration laws, such as a work permit, a U.S. passport, or a naturalization certificate. Do so using Form I-9 (*Employment Eligibility Verification*) from the U.S. Citizenship and Immigration Services, or USCIS (a bureau of the U.S. Department of Homeland Security). This form (and instructions

for completing it) are available at www.uscis.gov/i-9, or by phone at 800-375-5283. Remember that an Individual Taxpayer Identification Number (ITIN) is not proof of legal status in the U.S.—it is merely a way for the IRS to identify a taxpayer.

Some people who have the right to be in the United States, such as some students and other temporary visa holders, may not have the right to work, which is the focus of the I-9 form. To confirm their right to be in the U.S., ask for their I-94 or other document describing their status.

Under federal fair housing laws, you may not selectively ask for such immigration information—that is, you must ask all prospective tenants, not just those you suspect may be in the country illegally. It is illegal to discriminate on the basis of national origin, although you may reject someone on the basis of immigration status, as discussed in Chapter 5.

> RELATED TOPIC
> **For a related discussion on security issues regarding suspected terrorists,** see "Cooperating With Law Enforcement in Terrorism Investigations" in Chapter 13.

> ! CAUTION
> **Take your time to evaluate applications.** Landlords are often faced with anxious, sometimes desperate people who need a place to live immediately. On a weekend or holiday, especially when it's impossible to check references, a prospective tenant may tell you a terrific hard-luck story as to why normal credit- and reference-checking rules should be ignored in their case and why they should be allowed to move right in. Don't believe it. People who have planned so poorly that they will literally have to sleep in the street if they don't rent your place that day are likely to come up with similar emergencies when it comes time to pay the rent. Taking the time to screen out bad tenants will save you lots of problems later on.
>
> **Never, never let anyone stay in your property on a temporary basis.** Even if you haven't signed a rental agreement or accepted rent, you give someone the legally protected status of a tenant by giving that person a key or allowing him or her to move in as much as a toothbrush. Then, if the person won't leave voluntarily, you will have to file an eviction lawsuit. Chapter 8 discusses the legal rights of occupants you haven't approved.

Checking References, Credit History, and More

If an application looks good, your next step is to follow up thoroughly. The time and money you spend are some of the most cost-effective expenditures you'll ever make.

> ! **CAUTION**
>
> **Be consistent in your screening.** You risk a charge of illegal discrimination if you screen certain categories of applicants more stringently than others. Make it your policy, for example, to always require credit reports; don't just get a credit report for a single parent or older applicants.

Here are six steps of a very thorough screening process. You should always go through at least the first three to check out the applicant's previous landlords, income, and employment, and run a credit check.

Check With Current and Previous Landlords and Other References

Always call current and previous landlords or managers for references—even if you have a written letter of reference from them. (A prior landlord may be a better source of information than a current one, since a past landlord has no motive to give a falsely glowing report on a troublemaker.) Also call employers and personal references listed on the application.

To organize the information you gather from these calls, use the Tenant References form, which lists key questions to ask landlords, managers, and other references. A sample is shown below and the Nolo website includes a downloadable copy. See Appendix B for the link to the forms in this book.

> 💡 **TIP**
>
> **Check out pets, too.** If the prospective tenant has a dog or cat, be sure to ask previous landlords if the pet caused any damage or problems for other tenants or neighbors. It's also a good idea to meet the dog or cat, so you can make sure that it's well-groomed and well-behaved, before you make a final decision. You must, however, accommodate a mentally or physically disabled applicant whose pet serves as a support animal—no matter how mangy-looking the pet might be. For more information on renting to tenants with pets, see Chapter 2, Clause 14.

Be sure to take notes of all your conversations and keep them on file. You may note your reasons for refusing an individual on the Tenant References form—for example, negative credit information, insufficient income, or your inability to verify information. You'll want to record this information so that you can survive a fair housing challenge if a disappointed applicant files a discrimination complaint against you.

Occasionally, you may encounter a former landlord who is unwilling to provide key information. This reluctance may have nothing to do with the prospective tenant, but instead reflects an exaggerated fear of lawsuits. Landlords fear that their negative remarks about former tenants can be disclosed to rejected applicants if they request it, though under federal law, these conversations need not be disclosed when the landlord or landlord's employee is the one doing the calling (see "Choosing—And Rejecting—an Applicant," below). Still, most landlords do not understand this fine point of law, and many will be reluctant to be candid. But if a former landlord seems hesitant to talk, an approach that often works is to try to keep the person on the line long enough to verify the dates of the applicant's tenancy. If you get minimal cooperation, you might say something like this: "I assume your reluctance to talk about Julie has to do with one or more negative things that occurred while she was your tenant." If the former landlord doesn't say anything, you have all the answer you need. If she says instead, "No, I don't talk about any former tenants—actually, Julie was fairly decent," you have broken the ice and can probably follow up with a few general questions.

Tenant References

Name of Applicant: _____Michael Clark_____

Address of Rental Unit: _____123 State Street, Chicago, Illinois_____

Previous Landlord or Manager

Contact (name, property owner or manager, address of rental unit): _Kate Steiner, 345 Mercer St.,_

___Chicago, Illinois; (312) 555-5432_____

Date: _____February 4, 20xx_____

Questions

When did tenant rent from you (move-in and move-out dates)? _____December 2012 to date_____

What was the monthly rent? _____$1,250_____ Did tenant pay rent on time? ☐ Yes ☑ No

If rent was not paid on time, did you have to give tenant a legal notice demanding the rent? ☐ Yes ☑ No

If rent was not paid on time, provide details _____He paid rent a week late a few times_____
_____

Did you give tenant notice of any lease violation for other than nonpayment of rent? ☐ Yes ☑ No

If you gave a lease violation notice, what was the outcome? _____

Was tenant considerate of neighbors—that is, no loud parties and fair, careful use of common areas?

_____Yes, considerate_____
_____

Did tenant have any pets? ☑ Yes ☐ No If so, were there any problems? _He had a cat, contrary_

_____to rental agreement_____

Did tenant make any unreasonable demands or complaints? ☐ Yes ☑ No If so, explain: _____
_____

Why did tenant leave? _____He wants to live someplace that allows pets_____
_____

Did tenant give the proper amount of notice before leaving? ☑ Yes ☐ No

Did tenant leave the place in good condition? Did you need to use the security deposit to cover damage?

_____No problems_____

Any particular problems you'd like to mention? _____No_____
_____

Would you rent to this person again? _____Yes, but without pets_____
_____

Other comments: _____
_____
_____

Employment Verification

Contact (name, company, position): ___Brett Field, Manager, Chicago Car Company___

Date: ___February 5, 20xx___   Salary: $ _80,000 + bonus___

Dates of Employment: ___March 2011 to date___

Comments: ___No problems. Fine employee. Michael is responsible and hard-working.___

_____

_____

_____

_____

_____

_____

Personal Reference

Contact (name and relationship to applicant): ___Sandy Cameron, friend___

Date: ___February 5, 20xx___   How long have you known the applicant? _Five years___

Would you recommend this person as a prospective tenant? ___Yes___

Comments: ___Michael is very neat and responsible. He's reliable and will be a great tenant.___

_____

_____

_____

_____

_____

_____

Credit and Financial Information

___Mostly fine - see attached credit report___

_____

_____

_____

Notes, Including Reasons for Rejecting Applicant

___Applicant had a history of late rent payments and kept a cat, contrary to the rental___

___agreement.___

_____

_____

_____

_____

Verify Income and Employment

Obviously, you want to make sure that all tenants have the income to pay the rent each month. Call the prospective tenant's employer to verify income and length of employment. Make notes on the Tenant References form, discussed above.

Before providing this information, some employers require written authorization from the employee. You will need to mail or fax them a signed copy of the release included at the bottom of the Rental Application form or the separate Consent to Contact References and Perform Credit Check form shown above. If for any reason you question the income information you get by telephone—for example, you suspect a buddy of the applicant is exaggerating on his behalf—you may also ask applicants for copies of recent paycheck stubs.

It's also reasonable to require documentation of other sources of income, such as Social Security, disability, workers' compensation, public assistance, child support, or alimony. To evaluate the financial resources of a self-employed person or someone who's not employed, ask for copies of recent tax returns or bank statements.

TIP

How much income is enough? Think twice before renting to someone if the rent will take more than one-third of their income, especially if they have a lot of debts.

Obtain a Credit Report

Private credit reporting agencies collect and sell credit files and other information about consumers. Many landlords find it essential to check a prospective tenant's credit history with at least one credit reporting agency to see how responsible the person is managing money. Jot your findings down on the Tenant References form.

TIP

Get the tenant's consent to run a credit report. Because many people think that you must have their written consent before pulling a credit report to evaluate a prospective tenant, we have included it in our consent forms (at the end of the Rental Application and in the separate Consent to Contact References and Perform Credit Check form). But there's another reason for doing this: A written consent will help you if, later, when the applicant is a tenant (or an ex-tenant), you decide that you need an updated credit report. For example, you may want to consult a current report in order to help you decide whether to sue a tenant who has skipped out and owes rent. Without a broadly written consent, your use of a credit report at that time might be illegal (see the "Advisory Opinion to Long (07-06-00)," on the FTC website at www.ftc.gov.

How to Get a Credit Report

A credit report contains a gold mine of information for a prospective landlord. You can find out, for example, if a particular person has ever filed for bankruptcy or has been:

- late or delinquent in paying rent or bills, including student or car loans
- convicted of a crime, or, in many states, even arrested
- evicted (your legal right to get information on evictions, however, may vary among states)
- involved in another type of lawsuit such as a personal injury claim, or
- financially active enough to establish a credit history.

Depending on the type of report you order (the offerings vary according to the agency you deal with), you may also get an applicant's credit score, the most popular being the "FICO" score. This number, ranging from 300 to 850, purports to indicate the risk that an individual will default on payments. High credit scores indicate less risk. Generally, any score above 650 is considered a medium risk or less. Don't put too much value in a

California Law on Application Screening Fees and Credit Reports

California state law limits credit check or application screening fees you can charge prospective tenants and specifies what you must do when accepting these types of fees. (Cal. Civ. Code § 1950.6.) Here are key provisions of the law:

- You may charge a screening fee whose maximum is regulated by law (Cal. Civ. Code § 1950.6). To learn the current allowable charge, go to the city of Berkeley's Rent Stabilization website (www.ci.berkeley.ca.us) and type "tenant application screening fee" in the search box. You'll get a list of articles, one of which will give the current allowable fee for all of California.

- This screening fee may be used for "actual out-of-pocket costs" of obtaining a credit report, plus "the reasonable value of time spent" by a landlord in obtaining a consumer credit report or checking personal references and background information on a rental applicant.

- If you use the screening fee to obtain the applicant's credit report, you must give the applicant a copy of the report upon his or her request.

- If you spend less (for the credit report and your time) than the screening fee you collected, you must refund the difference. If you never get a credit report or check references on an applicant, you must refund the entire screening fee.

- Unless the applicant agrees in writing, you may not charge a screening fee if no rental unit is available. However, if a unit will be available within a reasonable period of time, you may charge the fee without obtaining the applicant's written permission.

- You must provide an itemized receipt when you collect an application screening fee. A sample receipt is shown below.

Landlords in California should also be aware that consumers may place a "freeze" on their credit reports, preventing anyone but specified parties (such as law enforcement) from getting their credit report. (Cal. Civ. Code §§ 1785.11.2 and following.) However, consumers can arrange for certain persons—such as a landlord or management company—to access their report; or the freeze itself can be suspended for a specified period of time. If an applicant has placed a freeze on his or her credit report, you'll need access so that you can receive a copy of their report. An applicant who fails to lift a freeze will have an incomplete application, which is grounds for rejecting that application. (Cal. Civ. Code § 1785.11.2(h).)

Sample California Application Screening Fee Receipt

This will acknowledge receipt of the sum of $ _____ by _____

_____ [Property Owner/Manager] from _____

[Applicant] as part of his/her application for the rental property at _____

_____ [Rental Property Address].

As provided under California Civil Code Section 1950.6, here is an itemization of how this $ _____ screening fee will be used:

☐ Actual costs of obtaining Applicant's credit/screening report $_____

☐ Administrative costs of obtaining credit/screening report and
    checking Applicant's references and background information $_____

☐ Total screening fee charged $_____

_____   _____

Applicant   Date

_____   _____

Owner/Manager   Date

high credit score, since this number does not reflect the many other good-tenant characteristics (such as ability to get along with neighbors and take good care of your property) that are very important.

Information covers the past seven to ten years. To run a credit check, you'll need a prospective tenant's name, address, and Social Security number or ITIN (Individual Taxpayer Identification Number.) Three credit bureaus have cornered the market on credit reports:

- Equifax (www.equifax.com)
- TransUnion (www.transunion.com), and
- Experian (www.experian.com).

Unless you run your business from a commercial location (that is, you're not running your business from home), and have passed the FTC's required onsite inspection (required to insure proper and secure storage of credit reports), you will not be able to order a credit report directly from the big three bureaus. Instead, you'll need to work through a credit reporting agency or tenant screening service (type "tenant screening" into your browser's search box). Look for a company that operates in your area, has been in business for a while, and provides you with a sample report that's clear and informative. You can also find tenant screening companies in the yellow pages under "Credit Reporting Agencies." Your state or local apartment association may also offer credit reporting services. With credit reporting agencies, you can often obtain a credit report the same day it's requested. Fees depend on how many reports you order each month.

If you do not rent to someone because of negative information in a credit report, or you charge someone a higher rent because of such information, you must give the prospective tenant the name and address of the agency that reported the negative information. This is a requirement of the federal Fair Credit Reporting Act. (15 U.S. Code §§ 1681 and following.) You must also tell the person that he has a right to obtain a copy of the file from the agency that reported the negative information, by requesting it within 60 days of

being told that your rejection was based on the individual's credit report.

Tenants who are applying for more than one rental are understandably dismayed at the prospect of paying each landlord to pull the same credit report. They may obtain their own report, make copies, and ask you to accept their copy. Federal law does not require you to accept an applicant's copy—that is, you may require applicants to pay a credit check fee for you to run a new report. Wisconsin and Washington are exceptions: State law in Wisconsin forbids landlords from charging for a credit report if, before the landlord asks for a report, the applicant offers one from a consumer reporting agency and the report is less than 30 days old. (Wis. Adm. Code ATCP 134.05(4)(b).) And in Washington, landlords must advise tenants whether they will accept a screening report done by a consumer reporting agency (in which case you may not charge the tenant a fee for a screening report). Landlords who maintain a website that advertises residential rentals must include this information on the home page. (Wash. Rev. Code Ann. § 59.18.257)

Credit Check Fees

It's legal in most states to charge prospective tenants a fee for the cost of the credit report itself and your time and trouble. Any credit check fee should be reasonably related to the cost of the credit check—$30 to $50 is common. California sets a maximum screening fee and requires landlords to provide an itemized receipt when accepting a credit check fee. See "California Law on Application Screening Fees and Credit Reports," above, for details.

Some landlords don't charge credit check fees, preferring to absorb the cost as they would any other cost of business. For low-end units, charging an extra fee can be a barrier to getting tenants in the first place, and a tenant who pays such a fee but is later rejected is likely to be annoyed and possibly more apt to try to concoct a discriminatory reason for the denial.

The Rental Application form in this book informs prospective tenants of your credit check fee. Be sure prospective tenants know the purpose of a credit check fee and understand that this fee is not a holding deposit and does not guarantee the rental unit. (We discuss holding deposits below.)

Also, if you expect a large number of applicants, you'd be wise not to accept fees from everyone. Instead, read over the applications first and do a credit check only on those who are genuine contenders (for example, exclude and reject those whose income doesn't reach your minimum rent-to-income ratio). That way, you won't waste your time (and prospective tenants' money) collecting fees from unqualified applicants.

> CAUTION
> **It is illegal to charge a credit check fee if you do not use it for the stated purpose and pocket it instead.** Return any credit check fees you don't use for that purpose.

Investigative or Background Reports

Some credit reporting companies and "tenant screening companies" also gather and sell background reports about a person's character, general reputation, personal characteristics, or mode of living. If you order a background check on a prospective tenant, it will be considered an "investigative consumer report" under federal law (the Fair Credit Reporting Act, 15 U.S. Code §§ 1681 and following, as amended by the Fair and Accurate Credit Transactions Act of 2003) and you must tell the applicant, within three days of requesting the report, that the report may be made and that it will concern his character, reputation, personal characteristics, and criminal history. You must also tell the applicant that more information about the nature and scope of the report will be provided upon request; and, if asked, you must provide this information within five days.

If you turn down the applicant based wholly or in part on information in the report, you must tell the applicant that the application was denied based on information in the report, and give the applicant the credit or tenant screening agency's name and address.

Using SmartMove to Get Information About Applicants

Transunion, one of the three major credit reporting companies, has come up with a creative way for landlords to obtain screening reports without having to use a credit reporting agency (SmartMove, www.mysmartmove.com). The method also protects applicants' credit scores, in that the report counts only as a "soft inquiry" to the applicant's file (multiple requests for credit reports are a negative sign). Importantly, SSNs are not revealed to the landlord. Either the landlord or the applicant can pay for the service.

Applicants whose landlords will accept the SmartMove report initiate the screening process by filling out an application to generate a report. The report contains a recommendation on whether to rent to this applicant, based on credit, criminal, and eviction history. For a bit more money, landlords can ask for a credit score, too.

Using SmartMove has its pros and cons. On the plus side, the recommendation is geared to the rental housing context (whereas a credit score was designed to predict whether the applicant would repay a loan). Transunion accesses multiple databases to compile its information, something not done by all agencies. On the negative side, five states (CO, DE, MA, SD, and WY) do not post criminal data, so landlords who are evaluating applicants who have lived in those states will be paying for a service that isn't available (not to mention that one doesn't have to live in a particular state to commit a crime there). In addition, the service requires some work on the part of the applicants (they must complete an authentication form, to deter identity theft). This step will deter some applicants (but arguably, if an applicant isn't serious enough to complete the process, arguably he's not the one for you, either).

Small landlords who operate from home and want something more thorough than a credit score should check out SmartMove.

What You're Looking For

In general, be leery of applicants with lots of debts —so that their monthly payments plus the rent obligation exceed 40% of their income. Also, look at the person's bill-paying habits, and, of course, pay attention to lawsuits and evictions.

Sometimes, your only choice is to rent to someone with poor or fair credit. If that's your situation, you might have the following requirements:

- good references from previous landlords and employers
- a creditworthy cosigner to cosign the lease (Chapter 2 includes a cosigner agreement)
- a good-sized deposit, as much as you can collect under state law (see Chapter 4), and
- proof of steps taken to improve credit—for example, enrollment in a debt counseling group.

If the person has no credit history—for example, a student or recent graduate—you may reject them or consider requiring a cosigner before agreeing to rent to them.

> **CAUTION**
>
> **Handle credit reports carefully.** Federal law requires you to keep only needed information, and to discard the rest. See "How to Handle Credit Reports," in Chapter 7 for precise information.

Verify Bank Account Information

If an individual's credit history raises questions about financial stability, you may want to double-check the bank accounts listed on the rental application. If so, you'll probably need an authorization form such as the one included at the bottom of the Rental Application, or the separate Consent to Contact References and Perform Credit Check (discussed above). Banks differ as to the type of information they will provide over the phone. Generally, banks will at most only confirm that an individual has an account there and that it is in good standing.

> **CAUTION**
>
> **Be wary of an applicant who has no checking or savings account.** Tenants who offer to pay cash or with a money order should be viewed with extreme caution. Perhaps the individual bounced so many checks that the bank dropped the account or the income comes from an illegitimate source—such as drug dealing.

Visiting the Homes of Prospective Tenants

Some landlords like to visit prospective tenants at their home to see how well they maintain a place. If you find this a valuable part of your screening process, and have the time and energy to do it, be sure you get the prospective tenants' permission first. Don't just drop by unexpectedly. Some landlords fabricate a reason for the visit ("I forgot to have you sign something"), but it's better to be honest regarding the purpose of your visit.

Review Court Records

If your prospective tenants have lived in the area, you may want to review local court records to see if collection or eviction lawsuits have ever been filed against them. Checking court records may seem like overkill, because some of this information may be available on credit reports, but it's an invaluable tool and is not a violation of antidiscrimination laws as long as you check the records of every applicant who reaches this stage of your screening process. Because court records are kept for many years, this kind of information can supplement references from recent landlords. Call the local court that handles eviction cases for details, including the cost of checking court records.

Use Megan's Law to Check State Databases of Sexual Offenders

Not surprisingly, most landlords do not want tenants with criminal records, particularly convictions for violent crimes or crimes against children. Checking a prospective tenant's credit report, as we recommend above, is one way to find out about a person's criminal history. Self-reporting is another: Rental applications, such as the one in this book, typically ask whether the prospective tenant has ever been convicted of a crime, and, if so, to provide details.

"Megan's Law" may be able to assist you in confirming that some of the information provided in the rental application and revealed in the credit report is complete and correct. Named after a young girl who was killed by a convicted child molester who lived in her neighborhood, this 1996 federal crime prevention law charged the FBI with keeping a nationwide database of persons convicted of sexual offenses against minors and violent sexual offenses against anyone. Every state has its own version of Megan's Law. These laws typically require certain convicted sexual offenders to register with local law enforcement officials, who keep a database on their whereabouts.

How Megan's Law Works

Unfortunately, the states are not consistent when it comes to using and distributing the database information. Notification procedures and the public's access rights vary widely:

- **Widespread notification/easy access.** A few states are "wide open"—they permit local law enforcement to automatically notify neighbors of the presence of sexual offenders on the database, by way of either letters, flyers, or notices published in local newspapers. Alternately, some states make the information available to anyone who chooses to access the database.
- **Selected notification/limited access.** Other states take a more restrictive approach, allowing law enforcement to release the information only if they deem it necessary. Or, states permit public access only to persons who

demonstrate a legitimate need to know the names of convicted sexual offenders.
- **Restricted notification/narrow access.** Finally, many states are quite restrictive, permitting notification only to certain individuals or officials, and allowing access only to them.

For information on your state's Megan's Law and restrictions on your use of information derived from a Megan's Law database, contact your local law enforcement agency. To find out how to access your state's sex offender registry, you can also contact the Parents for Megan's Law (PFML) Hotline at 888-ASK-PFML or check www.parentsformeganslaw.org.

The Limitations of Megan's Law Searching

The early promise of Megan's Law databases was ambitious. Landlords expected that they could quickly find accurate information on any person, and freely use it to reject an applicant with an unsavory past. Several years' experience with the databases, and legal challenges to their use, have resulted in landlords' taking a much more cautious approach to running a Megan's Law search. Here are the issues:

- **Accuracy.** Megan's Law databases are notoriously inaccurate, the result of incomplete or old data or entries that mistake one person for another. You can't assume your search will be worth much.
- **Relevance.** The criminal offense you discover on the database may not be relevant to whether this applicant is likely to be a threat to you, your tenants, or your property. For example, in some states consensual intercourse between minors (statutory rape) is an offense for which a person must register.
- **Misleading negatives.** Many convictions result from plea bargains. For example, someone charged with a registerable offense may end up with an assault conviction—perhaps because the prosecutor couldn't prove the

charge, or because a chief witness disappeared. You'll never know whether the assault conviction was originally charged as such, or began as a far more serious charge and ended up less so because the defendant lucked out. In other words, a relatively harmless-looking conviction that would not bother you may in fact mask a more serious incident.

Tenants Will Be Checking You Out, Too

While you're checking out a potential tenant (asking for references and getting a credit report), don't be surprised if the tenant is checking you out, too. Savvy applicants will ask your current tenants what it's like to rent from you (including how quickly you handle repairs) and the pluses and minuses of living in the building.

Several websites provide tenants with background information about you and your property. One of the major ones is www.apartmentratings.com. This comprehensive website has over two million reviews of individual apartments and property managers nationwide. It includes other information useful to new tenants, such as noise and safety ratings of each rental.

- **Expectations you create in other tenants.** If you do a database check, you should let applicants know that you're doing so (this will allow applicants to opt out of the application process, and may spare you a charge of invading their privacy). Residents will assume that you have not rented to anyone on a Megan's Law list. They may relax their guard—for example, a family may assume it's okay for their children to be home alone after school. Suppose you've rented to someone who should have been on the list but mistakenly wasn't, and he assaults one of the children. The family could argue in court that they relied on your implied promise that the building was safe, and that you bear some of the responsibility since you rented to someone who posed a risk of harm.

- **Loss of other tenants.** Ironically, if you decide that a past offense was not relevant, and rent to this applicant, you may have to disclose his past (to save you from the fate described just above). Other tenants won't share your complacency, and will leave. Before you know it, your only tenant will be the one you least want.

- **Lawsuit waiting to happen.** Finally, you may be the unlucky landlord who's targeted by a lawyer armed with many legal theories of why the Megan's Law registration and search structure is unconstitutional. These arguments (due process, equal protection, privacy, and the like) are not far-fetched. They've been made already, and at some point, a judge is going to agree with one of these legal theories.

- **Illegal in some states.** Finally, in some states and cities you simply cannot use information derived from a Megan's Law database to discriminate.

Many landlord associations and landlords' lawyers have concluded that the problems associated with Megan's Law searches are simply not worth the questionable results you'll get when you run them. Their advice is to stick to the tried-and-true methods of thoroughly checking references and examining the applicant's credit report for unexplained gaps (which may be due to time in prison).

If your state does not provide an accessible database that you can use when you screen, or if you decide not to screen, you may not learn of a person's past conviction for sexual offenses until after he registers his new address (yours) with the state's data collection agency. When he does so, you may get the flyer or phone call, but he'll already be a tenant. The fallout from angry neighbors and the negative publicity for your business can be dreadful. See "Criminal Convictions," in Chapter 17 for suggestions on what to do if you find out one of your current tenants is a convicted sexual offender.

Choosing—And Rejecting—An Applicant

After you've collected applications and done some screening, you can start sifting through the applicants. Start by eliminating the worst risks: people with negative references from previous landlords, a history of nonpayment of rent, or poor credit or recent and numerous evictions. Chapter 5 discusses legal reasons for refusing to rent to a tenant, including convictions for criminal offenses. You'll want to arrange and preserve your information for two reasons: so that you can survive a fair housing challenge, if a disappointed applicant files a complaint; and so that you can comply with your legal duties to divulge your reasons for rejecting an applicant.

What Information Should You Keep on Rejected Applicants?

Be sure to note your reasons for rejection—such as poor credit history, pets (if you don't accept pets), or a negative reference from a previous landlord—on the Tenant References form or other paper so that you have a paper trail if an applicant accuses you of illegal discrimination. You want to be able to back up your reason for rejecting the person. Keep organized files of applications, credit reports, and other materials and notes on prospective tenants for at least three years after you rent a particular unit. Keep in mind that if a rejected applicant files a complaint with a fair housing agency or files a lawsuit, your file will be made available to the applicant's lawyers. Knowing that, choose your words carefully, avoiding the obvious (slurs and exaggerations) and being scrupulously truthful.

CAUTION

Be careful handling credit reports. Under the federal "Disposal Rule" of the Fair and Accurate Credit Transactions Act of 2003, you must take care that credit reports are stored in a secure place where only those who "need to know" have access. For advice on handling credit reports and other personal information on applicants, see "How to Handle Credit Reports" in Chapter 7.

How to Reject an Applicant

The Fair Credit Reporting Act, as amended by the Fair and Accurate Credit Transactions Act of 2003, requires you to give certain information to applicants whom you reject as the result of a report from a credit reporting agency (credit bureau) or from a tenant screening or reference service. (15 U.S. Code §§ 1681 and following.) These notices are known as "adverse action reports." The federal requirements do not apply if your decision is based on information that the applicant furnished or that you or an employee learned on your own.

If you do not rent to someone because of negative information contained in the credit report or their credit score (even if other factors also played a part in your decision) or due to an insufficient credit report, you must give the applicant the name and address of the agency that provided the credit report. Tell applicants they have a right to obtain a copy of the file from the agency that reported the negative information, by requesting it within the next 60 days or by asking within one year of having asked for their last free report. You must also tell rejected applicants that the credit reporting agency did not make the decision to reject them and cannot explain the reason for the rejection. Finally, tell applicants that they can dispute the accuracy of their credit report and add their own consumer statement to their report.

Use the Notice of Denial Based on Credit Report or Other Information form for this purpose. A sample is shown above and the Nolo website includes a downloadable copy. See Appendix B for the link to the forms in this book.

Assuming you choose the best-qualified candidate (based on income, credit history, and references), you have no legal problem. But what if you have a number of more or less equally qualified applicants? The best response is to use an objective tie-breaker: Give the nod to the person who applied first. If you cannot determine who applied first, strive to find some aspect of one applicant's credit history or references that objectively establishes that person as the best applicant. Be extra careful not to always

Notice of Denial Based on Credit Report or Other Information

To: _Ryan Paige_____
Applicant
_1 Mariner Square_____
Street Address
_Seattle, Washington 98101_____
City, State, and Zip Code

Your rights under the Fair Credit Reporting Act and Fair and Accurate Credit Transactions (FACT) Act of 2003. (15 U.S.C. §§ 1681 and following.)

THIS NOTICE is to inform you that your application to rent the property at _75 Starbucks Lane,_____
_Seattle, WA 98108_____

has been denied because of [*check all that apply*]:

☑ Insufficient information in the credit report provided by:

Credit reporting agency: _ABC Credit Bureau_____

Address, phone number, URL: _310 Griffey Way, Seattle, WA 98140; Phone: 206-555-1212;_
_____www.abccredit.com_____

☐ Negative information in the credit report provided by:

Credit reporting agency: _____

Address, phone number, URL: _____

_____

☑ The credit score supplied on the credit report, ____511____, was used in whole or in part when making the decision.

☑ The consumer credit reporting agency noted above did not make the decision not to offer you this rental. It only provided information about your credit history. You have the right to obtain a free copy of your credit report from the consumer credit reporting agency named above, if your request is made within 60 days of this notice or if you have not requested a free copy within the past year. You also have the right to dispute the accuracy or completeness of your credit report. The agency must reinvestigate within a reasonable time, free of charge, and remove or modify inaccurate information. If the reinvestigation does not resolve the dispute to your satisfaction, you may add your own "consumer statement" (up to 100 words) to the report, which must be included (or a clear summary) in future reports.

☐ Information supplied by a third party other than a credit reporting agency or you and gathered by someone other than myself or any employee. You have the right to learn of the nature of the information if you ask me in writing within 60 days of the date of this notice.

_Jason McGuire_____   _10-01-20xx_____
Landlord/Manager   Date

Notice of Conditional Acceptance Based on Credit Report or Other Information

To: <u>William McGee</u>
Applicant
<u>1257 Bay Avenue</u>
Street Address
<u>Anytown, FL 12345</u>
City, State, and Zip Code

Your application to rent the property at <u>37 Ocean View Drive, #10-H, Anytown, FL 12345</u>

_____ [rental property address] has been accepted, conditioned on

your willingness and ability to: <u>Supply a cosigner that is acceptable to the landlord</u>

_____

Your rights under the Fair Credit Reporting Act and Fair and Accurate Credit Transactions (FACT) Act of 2003. (15 U.S.C. §§ 1681 and following.)

Source of information prompting conditional acceptance

My decision to conditionally accept your application was prompted in whole or in part by:

☑ Insufficient information in the credit report provided by:

Credit reporting agency: <u>Mountain Credit Bureau</u>

Address, phone number, URL: <u>75 Baywood Drive, Anytown, FL 12345. 800-123-4567.</u>
<u>www.mountaincredit.com</u>

☐ Negative information in the credit report provided by:

Credit reporting agency: _____

Address, phone number, URL: _____

_____

☑ The consumer credit reporting agency noted above did not make the decision to offer you this conditional acceptance. It only provided information about your credit history. You have the right to obtain a free copy of your credit report from the consumer credit reporting agency named above, if your request is made within 60 days of this notice or if you have not requested a free copy within the past year. You also have the right to dispute the accuracy or completeness of your credit report. The agency must reinvestigate within a reasonable time, free of charge, and remove or modify inaccurate information. If the reinvestigation does not resolve the dispute to your satisfaction, you may add your own "consumer statement" (up to 100 words) to the report, which must be included (or a clear summary) in future reports.

☐ Information supplied by a third party other than a credit reporting agency or you and gathered by someone other than myself or any employee. You have the right to learn of the nature of the information if you ask me in writing within 60 days of the date of this notice.

Jane Thomas .   _May 15, 20xx_
Landlord/Manager   Date

select a person of the same age, sex, or ethnicity. For example, if you are a larger landlord who is frequently faced with tough choices and who always avoids an equally qualified minority or disabled applicant, you are exposing yourself to charges of discrimination.

Conditional Acceptances

You may want to make an offer to an applicant but condition that offer on the applicant paying more rent or a higher security deposit (one that's within any legal limits, of course, as explained in Chapter 4), supplying a cosigner, or agreeing to a different rental term than you originally advertised. If your decision to impose the condition resulted from information you gained from a credit report or a report from a tenant screening service, you have to accompany the offer with an adverse action letter (described above). Use the Notice of Conditional Acceptance Based on Credit Report or Other Information, shown above. The Nolo website includes a downloadable copy. See Appendix B for the link to the forms in this book.

Finder's Fees and Holding Deposits

Almost every landlord requires tenants to give a substantial security deposit. The laws concerning how much can be charged and when deposits must be returned are discussed in Chapters 4 and 15. Here we discuss some other fees and deposits.

Finder's Fees

You may legitimately charge a prospective tenant for the cost of performing a credit check. Less legitimate, however, is the practice of some landlords, especially in cities with a tight rental market, of collecting a nonrefundable "finder's fee" or "move-in fee" just for renting the place to a tenant. Whether it's a flat fee or a percentage of the rent, we recommend against finder's fees. First, a finder's fee may be illegal in some cities and states (particularly those with rent control). Second, it's just a way of squeezing a little more money out of

the tenant—and tenants will resent it. If you think the unit is worth more, raise the price.

Holding Deposits

If you make a deal with a tenant but don't actually sign a lease or rental agreement, you may want a cash deposit to hold the rental unit while you do a credit check or call the tenant's references. Or, if the tenant needs to borrow money (or wait for a paycheck) to cover the rent and security deposit, you might want a few hundred dollars cash to hold the place. And some tenants may want to reserve a unit while continuing to look for a better one.

Is this a wise course? Accepting a deposit to hold a rental unit open for someone is legal in some states but almost always unwise. Holding deposits do you little or no good from a business point of view, and all too often result in misunderstandings or even legal fights.

Rating Applicants on a Numerical Scale

To substantiate your claim that you are fair to all applicants, you may be tempted to devise a numerical rating system—for example, ten points for an excellent credit report, 20 points for an excellent past landlord reference, and the like. While this type of rating system may simplify your task, it has two significant drawbacks:

- Every landlord is entitled to rely on gut feelings regarding a potential tenant (as long as these are not illegally discriminatory—see Chapter 5). You can decline to rent to an applicant you feel, instinctively, is a creep. You can decline to rent to him in spite of stellar recommendations or a solid financial report. Use of a numerical rating system should not limit your exercise of good sense.
- If a rejected tenant sues you, you will have to hand over your rating sheet. It will be easier to explain your decision by referring to the whole picture, rather than defending every "point" allocated in your system. You do want to be able to point to the many specific background checks you performed and used to arrive at your decision, but you do not want to lock yourself into a numerical straitjacket that you will be asked to defend.

Receipt and Holding Deposit Agreement

This will acknowledge receipt of the sum of $ ___500___ by ___Jim Chow___

_____ "Landlord" from ___Hannah Silver___

_____ "Applicant" as a holding deposit to hold vacant

the rental property at _178 West 81st St., #4F, New York City_

_____ ,

until ___February 20, 20xx___ at ___5 P.M.___ . The property will be rented to Applicant

on a ___one-year___ basis at a rent of $ ___3,000___ per month, if Applicant signs

Landlord's written ___lease___ and pays Landlord the first month's rent and a

$ ___3,000___ security deposit on or before that date, in which event the holding deposit will be

applied to the first month's rent.

Applicant's rental of the rental property depends upon Landlord receiving a satisfactory report of Applicant's references and credit history. Landlord and Applicant agree that if Applicant fails to sign the lease or rental agreement and pay the remaining rent and security deposit, Landlord may retain of this holding deposit a sum equal to the prorated daily rent of $ ___100___ per day plus a $ ___50___ charge to compensate Landlord for time and labor.

_Hannah Silver_____   _February 16, 20xx_____
Applicant   Date

_Jim Chow_____   _February 16, 20xx_____
Landlord/Manager   Date

EXAMPLE: A landlord, Jim, takes a deposit of several hundred dollars from a prospective tenant, Michael. What exactly is Jim promising Michael in return? To rent him the apartment? To rent Michael the apartment only if his credit checks out to Jim's satisfaction? To rent to Michael only if he comes up with the rest of the money before Jim rents to someone who offers the first month's rent and deposit? If Jim and Michael disagree about the answers to any of these questions, it can lead to needless anger and bitterness and result in a small claims court lawsuit alleging breach of contract.

Another prime reason to avoid holding deposits is that the laws of most states are unclear as to what portion of a holding deposit you can keep if a would-be tenant decides not to rent or doesn't come up with the remaining rent and deposit money, or if the tenant's credit doesn't check out to your satisfaction.

In California, for example, the basic rule is that a landlord can keep an amount that bears a "reasonable" relation to the landlord's costs—for example, for more advertising and for prorated rent during the time the property was held vacant. A landlord who keeps a larger amount may be sued for breach of contract. A few states require landlords to provide a receipt for any holding deposit and a written statement of the conditions under which it is refundable.

If, contrary to our advice, you decide to take a holding deposit, it is essential that both you and your prospective tenant have a clear understanding in writing, including:

- the amount of the holding deposit
- your name and that of the applicant
- the address of the rental property
- the dates you will hold the rental property vacant
- the term of the rental agreement or lease
- conditions for renting the applicant the available unit—for example, satisfactory references and credit history and full payment of first month's rent and security deposit

- what happens to the holding deposit if the applicant signs the rental agreement or lease—usually, it will be applied to the first month's rent, and
- the amount of the holding deposit you will keep if the applicant doesn't sign a rental agreement or lease—for example, an amount equal to the prorated daily rent for each day the rental unit was off the market plus a small charge to cover your inconvenience.

A sample Receipt and Holding Deposit Agreement that covers each of these items is shown above and the Nolo website includes a downloadable copy. See Appendix B for the link to the forms in this book.

What to Do If Your Apartment Is Hard to Rent

If you have a problem filling vacancies, resist the temptation to loosen up on your screening requirements. In the long run, a tenant who constantly pays rent late, disturbs other neighbors, or damages your property is not worth the price of having your rental occupied. Instead of taking a chance on a risky applicant, consider whether the rent is too high as compared to similar properties. If so, lower it. Also, make sure the condition of the rental isn't affecting its desirability. A new paint job or carpeting may make a big difference. Some landlords have great success with resident referral programs in which you pay a premium to a tenant who refers someone to you whom you approve and sign up as a tenant. If all else fails, consider incentives such as a free month's rent or free satellite or cable TV service.

If you do provide incentives, be sure to offer them in a consistent and fair way to all eligible tenants in order to avoid charges of discrimination. Also, to avoid problems, be clear as to the terms of the freebies you're providing. For example, when exactly may the tenant use the "free" month's rent—after six months or beyond? How long will free satellite service last? How long must a referred tenant stay for you to award a premium?

Preparing Leases and Rental Agreements

FORMS IN THIS CHAPTER

Chapter 2 includes instructions for and samples of the following forms.

• Month-to-Month Residential Rental Agreement

• Month-to-Month Residential Rental Agreement (Spanish Version) (companion page only)

• Fixed-Term Residential Lease (companion page only)

• Fixed-Term Residential Lease (Spanish Version) (companion page only)

• Cosigner Agreement

The Nolo website includes downloadable copies of these forms. See Appendix B for the link to the forms in this book.

Interactive Online Lease Forms

The rental forms described here, which you can download from the book's companion page on the Nolo website, are good in all 50 states. To tailor them to your state's laws, use the charts included in this book's appendix.

If you prefer an interactive lease or rental agreement form, you can purchase one at Nolo.com. A 50-state form, as well as state-specific forms for many states, are available. And there's a special discount for purchasers of this book: just use coupon code **ELLIBOB14**.

The rental agreement or lease that you and your tenant sign forms the contractual basis of your relationship. Taken together with the laws of your state—and, in a few areas, local and federal laws—it sets out almost all the legal rules you and your tenant must follow.

Your rental agreement or lease is also an immensely practical document, full of crucial business details, such as how long the tenant can occupy your property and the amount of the rent.

Given their importance, there's no question that you need to create effective and legal agreements with your tenants. This chapter shows you how to prepare clearly written, fair, and effective lease and rental agreements, and provides clear explanations of each clause.

Why use our lease or rental agreement, when you probably already use a printed form that seems adequate? There are several good reasons:

- Our agreements are based on careful research of every state's landlord-tenant laws. Many preprinted forms ignore state-by-state differences. In particular, cheap online forms are riddled with errors, typically written by attorneys who practice in one state but assume the laws are similar in all. This doesn't stop websites that offer landlord forms from advertising state-specific leases. We don't use the illegal or unenforceable clauses that pepper many preprinted agreements. Some forms still include clauses that courts threw out years ago or are so one-sided as to be unenforceable.

- Our agreements are clearly written in plain English and easy for you and your tenants to understand. We believe strongly that it's to everyone's advantage to have a written agreement that clearly informs tenants of their responsibilities and rights.

- Our lease and rental agreements are available for download on the Nolo website (see Appendix B for the link to the forms in this book). You can easily tailor them to fit your own situation. Throughout the chapter, we suggest ways to modify clauses in certain

circumstances. We also caution you about changes likely to get you into legal hot water.

RESOURCE

Tailor our lease forms to your state. The rental documents described in this chapter and included on the book's companion page on the Nolo website are good in all 50 states. You simply need to tailor the document to your state using the charts included in this book.

CAUTION

Don't use our forms if the rent is subsidized by the government. You may need to use a special government lease if you rent subsidized housing, such as Section 8.

Which Is Better, a Lease or a Rental Agreement?

One of the key decisions you need to make is whether to use a lease or a rental agreement. To decide which is better for you, read what follows and carefully evaluate your own situation.

Month-to-Month Rental Agreement

A written rental agreement provides for a tenancy for a short period of time. The law refers to these agreements as periodic, or month-to-month, although it is often legally possible to base them on other time periods—for example, if the rent were due every two weeks.

A month-to-month tenancy is automatically renewed each month unless you or your tenant gives the other the proper amount of written notice (typically 30 days) to terminate the agreement. The rental agreements in this book are month to month, although you can change them to a different interval.

Month-to-month rental agreements give landlords more flexibility than leases. You may increase the rent or change other terms of the tenancy on relatively short notice (subject to any restrictions of local rent control ordinances). You may also end the tenancy at any time (again, subject to any rent control restrictions), as long as you give the required amount of advance warning. Not surprisingly, many landlords prefer to rent from month to month, particularly in urban areas with tight rental markets where new tenants can often be found in a few days and rents are trending upward.

On the flip side, a month-to-month tenancy probably means more tenant turnover. Tenants who may legally move out with only 30 days' notice may be more inclined to do so than tenants who make a longer commitment. Some landlords base their rental business strategy on painstakingly seeking high-quality long-term renters. If you're one of those, or if you live in an area where it's difficult to fill vacancies, you will probably want tenants to commit for a longer period, such as a year. But, as discussed below, although a fixed-term lease may encourage tenants to stay longer, it is no guarantee against turnover.

Fixed-Term Lease

A lease is a contract that obligates both you and the tenant for a set period of time—usually a year. With a fixed-term lease, you can't raise the rent or change other terms of the tenancy until the lease runs out, unless the lease itself allows future changes or the tenant agrees in writing.

In addition, you usually can't ask a tenant to move out or prevail in an eviction lawsuit before the lease term expires unless the tenant fails to pay the rent or violates another significant term of the lease or the law, such as repeatedly making too much noise, damaging the rental unit, or selling drugs on your property. This restriction can sometimes be problem-atic if you end up with a tenant you would like to be rid of but don't have sufficient cause to evict.

To take but one example, if you wish to sell the property halfway into the lease, the existence of long-term tenants—especially if they are paying less than the market rate—may be a negative factor. The new owner usually purchases all the obligations of the previous owner, including the obligation to honor existing leases. Of course,

the opposite can also be true—if you have good, long-term tenants paying a fair rent, it may be very attractive to potential new owners.

At the end of the lease term, you have several options. You can:

- decline to renew the lease, except in the few areas where rent control requirements prohibit it
- sign a new lease for a set period, or
- do nothing—which means, under the law of most states, your lease will usually turn into a month-to-month tenancy if you continue to accept monthly rent from the tenant.

Chapter 14 discusses in detail how fixed-term leases end.

Although leases restrict your flexibility, there's often a big plus to having long-term tenants. Some tenants make a serious personal commitment when they enter into a long-term lease, in part because they think they'll be liable for several months' rent if they leave early. And people who plan to be with you over the long term are often more likely to respect your property and the rights of other tenants, making the management of your rental units far easier and more pleasant.

> **CAUTION**
> **A lease guarantees less income security than you think.** As experienced landlords know well, it's usually not hard for a determined tenant to break a lease and avoid paying all of the money theoretically owed for the unused portion of the lease term. A few states allow tenants to break a lease without penalty in specific circumstances, such as the need to move to a nursing home. In addition, tenants who enter military service are entitled to break a lease. And many states require landlords to "mitigate" (minimize) the loss they suffer as a result of a broken lease—meaning that if a tenant moves out early, you must try to find another suitable tenant at the same or a greater rent. If you rerent the unit immediately (or if a judge believes it could have been rerented with a reasonable effort), the lease-breaking tenant is off the hook—except, perhaps, for a small obligation to pay for the few days or weeks the unit was vacant plus (sometimes) any costs you incurred in rerenting it.

You'll probably prefer to use leases in areas where there is a high vacancy rate or it is difficult to find tenants for one season of the year. For example, if you are renting near a college that is in session for only nine months a year, or in a vacation area that is deserted for months, you are far better off with a year's lease. This is especially true if you have the market clout to charge a large deposit, so that a tenant who wants to leave early has an incentive to find someone to take over the tenancy.

> **TIP**
>
> **Always put your agreement in writing.** Oral leases or rental agreements are perfectly legal for month-to-month tenancies and, in most states, for leases of a year or less. If you have an oral lease for a term exceeding one year, it becomes an oral month-to-month agreement after the first year is up. While oral agreements are easy and informal, it is never wise to use one. As time passes, people's memories (even yours) have a funny habit of becoming unreliable. You can almost count on tenants claiming that you made, but didn't keep, certain oral promises—for example, to repaint their kitchen or not increase their rent. Tenants may also forget key agreements, such as no subletting. And other issues, like how deposits may be used, probably aren't covered at all. Oral leases are especially dangerous, because they require that both parties accurately remember one important term—the length of the lease—over a considerable time. If something goes wrong with an oral rental agreement or lease, you and your tenants are all too likely to end up in court, arguing over who said what to whom, when, and in what context.

Leases and Rental Agreements in a Nutshell

Leases	Rental Agreements
You can't raise the rent or change other terms of the tenancy until the lease ends.	You may increase rent or change other terms of the tenancy on relatively short notice (subject to any restrictions of local rent control ordinances).
You usually can't end the tenancy before the term expires, unless the tenant doesn't pay rent or violates another term of the lease.	You or the tenant may end the tenancy at any time (subject to any rent control restrictions), by giving the required amount of written notice, typically 30 days.

Clause-by-Clause Instructions for Completing the Lease or Rental Agreement Form

This section explains each clause in the lease and rental agreement forms provided in this book. The instructions explain how to fill in the blanks and also refer you to the chapter that discusses important issues that relate to your choices. Before you complete any clause for the first time, read the detailed discussion about it in the appropriate chapter. For example, before you complete Clause 5, which covers rent, be sure to read Chapter 3.

Except for the important difference in the term of the tenancy (see Clause 4 in the forms), leases and written rental agreements are so similar that they are sometimes hard to tell apart. Both cover the basic terms of the tenancy (such as amount of rent and date due). Except where indicated below, the clauses are identical for the lease and rental agreement.

A filled-in sample rental agreement is included at the end of this chapter. This book's companion page includes copies of the Month-to-Month Residential Rental Agreement and the Fixed-Term Residential Rental Lease. Both are in English and Spanish.

Tips for Landlords Taking Over Rental Property

If you've recently bought (or inherited) property, you will likely be inheriting tenants with existing rental agreements or leases. Be sure the last owner gives you copies of all tenant and property files, including leases and rental agreements, details on deposits (location and amounts), house rules, maintenance and repair records, and all other paperwork and records relevant to the property. If you want to change any of the terms of the lease or rental agreement, follow our advice in the first part of Chapter 14.

How to Modify the Lease or Rental Agreement Form

You may want to modify our lease and rental agreement forms in some situations. The instructions suggest possible modifications for some of the clauses. If you make extensive changes on your own, however, you may wish to have your work reviewed by an experienced landlords' lawyer.

Don't be tempted to try to cram too many details into the lease or rental agreement. Instead, send new tenants a "move-in letter" that dovetails with the lease or rental agreement and highlights important terms of the tenancy—for example, how and where to report maintenance problems. You may also use a move-in letter to cover issues not included in the lease or rental agreement—for example, rules for use of a pool or laundry room or procedures for returning security deposits. Chapter 7 covers move-in letters.

 RENT CONTROL
You may need to modify the forms if required by local ordinance. Local rent control ordinances may require that your lease or rental agreement include specific information—for example, the address of the local rent control board. Check your local ordinance for more information, and modify our forms accordingly.

Clause 1. Identification of Landlord and Tenant

This Agreement is entered into between _____ _____ [Tenant] and _____ [Landlord]. Each Tenant is jointly and severally liable for the payment of rent and performance of all other terms of this Agreement.

Every lease or rental agreement must identify the tenant and the landlord or the property owner—often called the "parties" to the agreement. The term "Agreement" (a synonym for contract) refers to either the lease or rental agreement.

Any competent adult—at least 18 years of age—may be a party to a lease or rental agreement. A teenager who is slightly under age 18 may also be a party to a lease in most states if he or she has achieved legal adult status through a court order (called emancipation), military service, or marriage.

The last sentence of Clause 1 states that if you have more than one tenant, they (the cotenants) are all "jointly and severally" liable for paying rent and abiding by the terms of the agreement. This essential bit of legalese simply means that each tenant is legally responsible for the whole rent and complying with the agreement. You can legally seek full compensation from any one of the tenants should the others skip out or be unable to pay, or evict all of the tenants even if just one has broken the terms of the lease—for example, by seriously damaging the property. Chapter 8 provides more detail on the concept of joint and several liability and discusses the legal obligations of cotenants.

How to Fill in Clause 1:

Fill in the names of all tenants—adults who will live in the premises, including both members of a couple. Doing this makes everyone who signs responsible for all terms, including the full amount of the rent. Chapter 8 discusses why it's crucial that everyone who lives in your rental unit sign the lease or rental agreement. Also, make sure the tenant's name matches his or her legal documents, such as a driver's license. You may set a reasonable limit on the number of people per rental unit as discussed in "Valid Occupancy Limits," in Chapter 5.

In the last blank, list the names of all landlords or property owners—that is, the names of every person who will be signing the lease or rental agreement. If you are using a business name, enter your name followed by your business name.

Clause 2. Identification of Premises

Subject to the terms and conditions in this Agreement, Landlord rents to Tenant, and Tenant rents from Landlord, for residential purposes only, the premises located at _____ _____ [the premises], together with the following furnishings and appliances: _____ . Rental of the premises also includes _____ .

Clause 2 identifies the address of the property being rented ("the premises") and provides details on furnishings and extras such as a parking space. The words "for residential purposes only" are to prevent a tenant from using the property for conducting a business that might affect your insurance or violate zoning laws, or that might burden other tenants or neighbors.

How to Fill in Clause 2:

Fill in the street address of the unit or house you are renting. If there is an apartment or building number, specify that as well as the city and state.

Add as much detail as necessary to clarify what's included in the rental premises, such as kitchen appliances. If the unit has only a few basic furnishings, list them here. If the rental unit is fully furnished, state that here and provide detailed information on the Landlord-Tenant Checklist included in Chapter 7 or in a separate room-by-room list.

In some circumstances, you may want to elaborate on exactly what the premises do or do not include. For example, if the rental unit includes a parking space, storage in the garage or basement, or other use of the property, such as a gardening shed in the backyard or the use of a barn in rural areas, specifically include this information in your description of the premises.

Possible Modifications to Clause 2:

If a particular part of the rental property that might be assumed to be included is *not* being rented, such as a garage or storage shed you wish to use yourself or rent to someone else, explicitly exclude it from your description of the premises.

Clause 3. Limits on Use and Occupancy

The premises are to be used only as a private residence for Tenant(s) listed in Clause 1 of this Agreement, and their minor children. Occupancy by guests for more than _____ is prohibited without Landlord's written consent and will be considered a breach of this Agreement.

Clause 3 states that the rental unit is the residence of the tenants and their minor children only. It lets the tenants know they may not move anyone else in as a permanent resident without your consent. The value of this clause is that a tenant who tries to move in a relative or friend for a longer period has clearly violated a defined standard, which gives you grounds for eviction. (New York landlords, however, are subject to the "Roommate Law," RPL § 235-f, which allows tenants to move in relatives and other qualified individuals. The number of total occupants is still restricted, however, by any local statutes governing overcrowding.)

Clause 3 also allows you to set a time limit for guest stays. Even if you do not plan to strictly enforce restrictions on guests, this provision will be very handy if a tenant tries to move in a friend or relative for a month or two, calling that person a guest. It will give you the leverage you need to ask the guest to leave, request that the guest apply to become a tenant with an appropriate increase in rent, or, if necessary, evict the tenant for violating this lease provision. To avoid discrimination charges, don't make restrictions on guests that are based on the age or sex of the occupant or guest. Chapter 8 discusses guests in more detail.

How to Fill in Clause 3:

Fill in the number of days you allow guests to stay over a given time period without your consent. We suggest you allow up to ten consecutive days in any six-month period, but, of course, you may want to modify this based on your own preferences.

Investigate Before Letting a Tenant Run a Home Business

Millions of Americans run a business from their house or apartment. If a tenant asks you to modify Clause 2 to allow him to operate a business, you have some checking to do—even if you are inclined to say yes.

For one, you'll need to check local zoning laws for restrictions on home-based businesses, including the type of businesses allowed (if any), the amount of car and truck traffic the business can generate, outside signs, on-street parking, the number of employees, and the percentage of floor space devoted to the business. And if your rental unit is in a planned unit or a condominium development, check the CC&Rs of the homeowners' association.

You'll also want to consult your insurance company as to whether you'll need a different policy to cover potential liability of a tenant's employees or guests. In many situations, a home office for occasional use will not be a problem. But if the tenant wants to operate a business, especially one with people and deliveries coming and going, such as a therapy practice, jewelry importer, or small business consulting firm, you should seriously consider whether to expand or add coverage.

You may also want to require that the tenant maintain certain types of liability insurance, so that you won't wind up paying if someone gets hurt on the rental property—for example, a business customer who trips and falls on the front steps.

Finally, be aware that if you allow a residence to be used as a commercial site, your property may need to meet the accessibility requirements of the federal Americans with Disabilities Act (ADA). For more information on the ADA contact the U.S. Department of Justice, 950 Pennsylvania Ave., NW, Civil Rights Division, Disability Rights Section, Washington, DC 20530, call 800-514-0301 (800-514-0383 TTY), or check the ADA website at www.ada.gov.

> **CAUTION**
>
> **You may not be able to restrict a child care home business.** A tenant who wants to do child care in the rental may be entitled to do so, despite your general prohibition against businesses. In California and New York, for example, legislators and courts have declared a strong public policy in favor of home-based child care and have limited a landlord's ability to say no. (Cal. Health & Safety Code § 1597.40; *Haberman v. Gotbaum*, 698 N.Y.S.2d 406 (N.Y. City Civ. Ct. 1999).) If you're concerned, check with your state's office of consumer protection for information on laws that cover in-home child care in residential properties.

If you allow a tenant to run a business from your rental property, you may want to provide details in Clause 22 (Additional Provisions) of your lease or rental agreement.

> **CAUTION**
>
> **Don't discriminate against families with children.** You can legally establish reasonable space-to-people ratios, but you cannot use overcrowding as an excuse for refusing to rent to tenants with children. Space rules are available in your local or state housing code. Discrimination against families with children is illegal, except in housing reserved for senior citizens only. Just as important as adopting a reasonable people-to-square-foot standard in the first place is the maintenance of a consistent occupancy policy. If you allow three adults to live in a two-bedroom apartment, you had better let a couple with a child live in the same type of unit, or you are leaving yourself open to charges that you are illegally discriminating. Chapter 5 covers discrimination and occupancy standards.

Clause 4. Term of the Tenancy (Lease)

The term of the rental will begin on _____ ,
and end on _____ .

This clause sets out the key difference between a lease and a rental agreement: how long a rent-paying tenant is entitled to stay.

The lease form sets a definite date for the beginning and expiration of the lease and obligates both you and the tenant for a specific term.

Most leases run for one year. This makes sense, because it allows you to raise the rent at reasonably frequent intervals if market conditions allow. Leases may be shorter (six months) or longer (24 months)—this, of course, is up to you and the tenants. A long period—two, three, or even five years—can be appropriate, for example, if you're renting out your own house because you're taking a two-year sabbatical or if you're renting to a tenant who will be making major repairs to or remodeling your property.

Chapter 14 discusses a tenant's liability for breaking a lease, what exactly happens at the end of a lease, monetary consequences if a tenant "holds over" or fails to leave after the lease ends, termination of fixed-term leases, and your duty to mitigate damages. It also covers notice requirements. You may want to specify some of these issues in the lease or rental agreement or in a move-in letter you send new tenants (see Chapter 7).

How to Fill in Clause 4 (Lease):

In the blanks, fill in the starting date and the expiration date. The starting date is the date the tenant has the right to move in, such as the first of the month. This date does not have to be the date that you and the tenant sign the lease. The lease signing date is simply the date that you're both bound to the terms of the lease. If the tenant moves in before the regular rental period—such as the middle of the month and you want rent due on the first of every month—you will need to prorate

the rent for the first partial month as explained in Clause 5 (Payment of Rent).

Possible Modifications to Clause 4 (Lease):

If you want to provide for a periodic rent increase, perhaps tied to a consumer price index or your operating expenses, you'll need to add language to this effect. Without this type of built-in increase, you can't increase the rent until the lease ends.

CAUTION

Avoid liquidated damages provisions.
Some preprinted forms (not ours) include what lawyers quaintly call a "liquidated damages" clause. This means that if a tenant moves out before the lease expires, he is supposed to pay you a predetermined amount of money (damages) caused by his early departure. Unless the amount of liquidated damages is close to the damages a landlord actually suffers, this approach is likely to be illegal. Under the laws of most states, a tenant who moves out before the lease expires is legally responsible to pay only for the actual losses he caused (such as rent lost). If a suitable new tenant moves in immediately, this may be little or nothing. And, in most states, you are legally obligated to minimize your losses by trying to find a new tenant as soon as possible. Chapter 14 provides details on your responsibility to mitigate damages.

Clause 4. Term of the Tenancy (Rental Agreement)

The rental will begin on _____ , and continue on a month-to-month basis. Landlord may terminate the tenancy or modify the terms of this Agreement by giving the Tenant _____ days' written notice. Tenant may terminate the tenancy by giving the Landlord _____ days' written notice.

The rental agreement provides for a month-to-month tenancy and specifies how much written notice you must give a tenant to change or end a tenancy, and how much notice the tenant must provide you before moving out. Chapter 14 discusses changing or ending a month-to-month tenancy.

How to Fill in Clause 4 (Rental Agreement):

In the first blank, fill in the date the tenancy will begin. The date the tenancy will begin is the date the tenant has the right to move in, such as the first of the month. This date does not have to be the date that you and the tenant sign the rental agreement. The agreement signing date is simply the date that you're both bound to the terms of the rental agreement. If the tenant moves in before the regular rental period—such as the middle of the month and you want rent due on the first of every month—you will need to prorate the rent for the first partial month as explained in Clause 5 (Payment of Rent).

In the next two blanks, fill in the amount of written notice you'll need to give tenants to end or change a tenancy, and the amount of notice tenants must provide to end a tenancy. In most cases, to comply with the law of your state, this will be 30 days for both landlord and tenant in a month-to-month tenancy. See "State Rules on Notice Required to Change or Terminate a Month-to-Month Tenancy" in Appendix A for details.

Possible Modifications to Clause 4 (Rental Agreement):

This rental agreement is month to month, although you can change it to a different interval as long as you don't go below the minimum notice period required by your state's law. If you do, be aware that notice requirements to change or end a tenancy may also need to differ from those required for standard month-to-month rental agreements, since state law often requires that all key notice periods be the same.

RENT CONTROL

Your right to terminate or change the terms of a tenancy, even one from month to month, can be limited by a rent control ordinance. Such ordinances not only limit rent and other terms of tenancies, but also require the landlord to have a good reason to terminate a tenancy.

Clause 5. Payment of Rent

Regular monthly rent.

Tenant will pay to Landlord a monthly rent of $_____, payable in advance on the first day of each month, except when that day falls on a weekend or legal holiday, in which case rent is due on the next business day. Rent will be paid in the following manner unless Landlord designates otherwise:

Delivery of payment.

Rent will be paid:

☐ by mail, to _____

☐ in person, at _____

Form of payment.

Landlord will accept payment in these forms:

☐ cash

☐ personal check made payable to _____

☐ certified funds or money orders

☐ credit card

☐ bank debits

☐ electronic funds transfer _____

Prorated first month's rent.

For the period from Tenant's move-in date, _____, through the end of the month, Tenant will pay to Landlord the prorated monthly rent of $_____. This amount will be paid on or before the date the Tenant moves in.

This clause provides details on the amount of rent and when, where, and how it's paid. It requires the tenant to pay rent monthly on the first day of the month, unless the first day falls on a weekend or a legal holiday, in which case rent is due on the next business day. (Extending the rent due date for holidays is legally required in some states and is a general rule in most.)

We discuss how to set a legal rent and where and how rent is due in Chapter 3. Before you fill in the blanks, please read that chapter.

How to Fill in Clause 5:

Regular monthly rent. In the first blank, state the amount of monthly rent. Unless your premises are subject to a local rent control ordinance, you can legally charge as much rent as you want (or, more practically speaking, as much as a tenant will pay).

Delivery of payment. Next, specify to whom and where the rent is to be paid—by mail (most common) or in person (if so, specify the address, such as your office or to your manager at the rental unit). Be sure to specify the hours that rent can be paid in person, such as 9 a.m. to 5 p.m. weekdays and 9 a.m. to noon on Saturdays.

Form of payment. Note all the forms of payment you'll accept.

- Cash is an option, though generally not a good one; checks are safer.
- You can also provide for certified funds (such as a cashier's check) or money orders.
- For credit card payments, follow the instructions issued by the card's issuer.
- If you choose bank debits, give tenants the information they need to set this up.
- Finally, you may want to consider electronic funds transfers. An electronic funds transfer is the computer-based exchange of money from one account to another, either within a single financial institution or across multiple institutions. The parties involved decide whether the transfers will be automatic or manual.

Electronic funds transfers require little effort when all is going well, are not that difficult to set up, and are easy to monitor online. However, there are pros and cons with every payment method, so you should consider what is best for your situation. Examples include: direct deposit, wire transfer, and PayPal.

Describe any electronic means of payment you will accept and list any specific information that the tenant will need from you in order to successfully transfer the funds.

(Note that in California, you cannot require that rent be paid only by cash or electronic funds transfer.)

Prorated first month's rent. If the tenant moves in before the regular rental period—let's say in the middle of the month, and you want rent due on the first of every month—you can specify the prorated amount due for the first partial month. To figure out prorated rent, divide the monthly rent by 30 days and multiply by the number of days in the first (partial) rental period. That will avoid confusion about what you expect to be paid. Enter the move-in date, such as "June 21, 20xx," and the amount of prorated monthly rent.

> **EXAMPLE:** Meg rents an apartment for $2,100 per month with rent due on the first of the month. She moves in on June 21, so she should pay ten days' prorated rent of $700 when she moves in. ($2,100 ÷ 30 = $70 × 10 days = $700.) Beginning with July 1, Meg's full $2,100 rent check is due.

If the tenant is moving in on the first of the month or the same day rent is due, write in "N/A" or "Not Applicable" in the section on prorated rent, or delete this section of the clause.

Possible Modifications to Clause 5:

Here are a few common ways to modify Clause 5:

Rent due date. You can establish a rent due date different from the first of the month, such as the day of the month on which the tenant moves in. For example, if the tenant moved in on July 10, rent would be due on the tenth of each month, a system that of course saves the trouble of prorating the first month's rent.

Frequency of rent payments. You are not legally required to have your tenant pay rent on a monthly basis. You can modify the clause and require that the rent be paid twice a month, each week, or by whatever schedule suits you.

Clause 6. Late Charges

> If Tenant fails to pay the rent in full before the end of the _____ day after it's due, Tenant will pay Landlord a late charge as follows: _____ .
> Landlord does not waive the right to insist on payment of the rent in full on the date it is due.

It is your legal right in most states to charge a late fee if rent is not paid on time. This clause spells out details on your policy on late fees. Charging a late fee does not mean that you give up your right to insist that rent be paid on the due date. To bring this point home, Clause 6 states that you do not waive the right to insist on full payment of the rent on the date it is due. A late fee is simply one way to motivate tenants to pay on time. A few states have statutes that put precise limits on the amount of late fees or when they can be collected. For advice on setting a late charge policy, see Chapter 3.

How to Fill in Clause 6:

In the first blank, specify when you will start charging a late fee. You can charge a late fee the first day rent is late, but many landlords don't charge a late fee until the rent is two or three days late.

Next, fill in details on your late rent fee, such as the daily charge and any maximum fee.

Possible Modifications to Clause 6:

If you decide not to charge a late fee (something we consider highly unwise), you may simply delete this clause. If you delete this clause, you'll need to renumber the remaining clauses.

Clause 7. Returned Check and Other Bank Charges

> If any check offered by Tenant to Landlord in payment of rent or any other amount due under this Agreement is returned for lack of sufficient funds, a "stop payment," or any other reason, Tenant will pay Landlord a returned check charge of $_____ .

As with late charges, any bounced-check charges you require must be reasonable. Some states regulate the amount you can charge; in the absence of such regulation, you should charge no more than the amount your bank charges you for a returned check, probably $25 to $30 per returned item, plus a few dollars for your trouble. Some states regulate the maximum amount you can charge.

Chapter 3 covers returned check charges.

How to Fill in Clause 7:

In the blank, fill in the amount of the returned check charge.

Possible Modifications to Clause 7:

If you won't accept checks, or you are not charging a returned check fee (something we consider unwise), you may delete this clause from your lease or rental agreement (in which case, you'll need to renumber the remaining clauses).

Clause 8. Security Deposit

> On signing this Agreement, Tenant will pay to Landlord the sum of $_____ as a security deposit. Tenant may not, without Landlord's prior written consent, apply this security deposit to the last month's rent or to any other sum due under this Agreement. Within _____ after Tenant has vacated the premises, returned keys, and provided Landlord with a forwarding address, Landlord will return the deposit in full or give Tenant an itemized written statement of the reasons for, and the dollar amount of, any of the security deposit retained by Landlord, along with a check for any deposit balance.

The use and return of security deposits is a frequent source of disputes between landlords and tenants. To avoid confusion and legal hassles, this clause is clear on the subject, including:

- the dollar amount of the deposit
- the fact that the deposit may not be used for the last month's rent without your prior written approval, and
- when the deposit will be returned, along with an itemized statement of deductions.

Chapters 4 and 15 (and the chart "State Security Deposit Rules" in Appendix A) cover the basic information you need to complete Clause 8, including state rules on how large a deposit you can require, when you must return it, and the type of itemization you must provide a tenant when deductions are made.

How to Fill in Clause 8:

Once you decide how much security deposit you can charge, fill in the amount in the first blank. Unless there's a lower limit, we suggest about two months as your rent deposit, assuming your potential tenants can afford that much. In no case is it wise to charge much less than one month's rent.

Next, fill in the time period when you will return the deposit. If there is no statutory deadline for returning the deposit, we recommend three to four weeks as a reasonable time to return a tenant's deposit. Establishing a fairly short period (even if the law of your state allows more time) will discourage anxious tenants from repeatedly bugging you or your manager for their deposit refund.

Possible Modifications to Clause 8:

The laws of several states require you to give tenants written information on various aspects of the security deposit, including where the security deposit is being held, interest payments, and the terms of and conditions under which the security deposit may be withheld. The "State Security Deposit Rules" chart in Appendix A gives you information on disclosures you may need to add to Clause 8. This chart also includes a list of states that require separate accounts for deposits or interest payments on deposits.

Nonrefundable Fees

We don't recommend nonrefundable fees—for one thing, they are illegal in many states. If you do collect a nonrefundable fee—for example, for cleaning or pets—be sure your lease or rental agreement is clear on the subject.

Even if it's not required, you may want to provide additional details on security deposits in your lease or rental agreement. Here are optional clauses you may add to the end of Clause 8.

The security deposit will be held at: (*name and address of financial institution*).

Landlord will pay Tenant interest on all security deposits at the prevailing bank rate.

Landlord may withhold only that portion of Tenant's security deposit necessary to: (1) remedy any default by Tenant in the payment of rent; (2) repair damage to the premises, except for ordinary wear and tear caused by Tenant; (3) clean the premises if necessary; and (4) compensate Landlord for any other losses as allowed by state law.

Clause 9. Utilities

Tenant will pay all utility charges, except for the following, which will be paid by Landlord: _____
_____
_____ .

This clause helps prevent misunderstandings as to who's responsible for paying utilities. Normally, landlords pay for garbage (and sometimes water, if there is a yard) to help make sure that the premises are well maintained. Tenants usually pay for other services, such as phone, gas, electricity, Internet access, and cable TV.

How to Fill in Clause 9:

In the blank, fill in the utilities you—not the tenants—will be responsible for paying. If you will not be paying for any utilities, simply delete the last part of the clause ("except … Landlord:").

Disclose Shared Utility Arrangements

If there are not separate gas and electric meters for each unit, or a tenant's meter measures gas or electricity used in areas outside his unit (such as a water heater that serves several apartments or lighting in a common area), you should disclose this in your lease or rental agreement. Simply add details to Clause 20, Disclosures. This type of disclosure is required by law in some states (see "Required Landlord Disclosures," in Appendix A), and is only fair in any case. The best solution is to put in a separate meter for the areas served outside the tenant's unit. If you don't do that, you should:

- pay for the utilities for the tenant's meter yourself by placing that utility in your name
- reduce the tenant's rent to compensate for payment of utility usage outside of their unit (this will probably cost you more in the long run than if you either added a new meter or simply paid for the utilities yourself), or
- sign a separate written agreement with the tenant, under which the tenant specifically agrees to pay for others' utilities, too.

Consider Water Submetering

Making tenants pay for their water usage has become a popular way for landlords to recoup their water costs and increase their profits (studies have also shown that when tenants are billed directly, a property's overall water usage drops considerably). There are three ways to go about this. The best method is to have the water company install meters for each unit, so that each household pays the utility directly. Secondly, you can contract with a submetering company to install submeters, which transmit a unit's water usage directly to the company via digital signals (no need for a meter-reader to physically check the meter). The company bills each household directly, and the landlord pays an administrative fee. Finally, you can estimate each unit's usage by using the "RUBS" method (Ratio Utility Billing System), in which you estimate each unit's usage and share of the total bill based on the unit's square footage or number of occupants. The landlord pays the utility directly, then bills each household for its share.

All of these approaches have their limitations, however. Having the water company install individual meters is feasible in new construction, but usually not practical as a retrofit. Using a submetering company involves an initial expense (installing the submeters), though you may find an aggressive company willing to front the cost. And don't count on being able to pass through this cost (or the ongoing administrative costs) to your tenants, because some states or localities forbid it. As for RUBS, many tenants will object, arguing that whatever formula you use cannot take into account individuals' habits (the careful family of three might use less water than the wasteful couple next door, for example).

Be sure to do your homework before proceeding further. Your state might disallow submetering altogether, and your local laws might have something to say, too. Start by talking with your local water company. For more information on the issue of submetering, check out the website of the Utility Management & Conservation Association, at www.utilitymca.org., a trade association promoting agency energy conservation. If you decide to use a submetering company, shop around and look for a company with a solid reputation for customer service and accurate billing.

Clause 10. Prohibition of Assignment and Subletting

> Tenants will not sublet any part of the premises or assign this Agreement without the prior written consent of Landlord.
>
> ☐ a. Tenants will not sublet or rent any part of the Premises for short-term stays of any duration, including but not limited to vacation rentals.
>
> ☐ b. Short-stay rentals are prohibited except as authorized by law. Any short-stay rental is expressly conditioned upon the tenants' following all regulations, laws, and other requirements as a condition to offering a short-stay rental. Failure to follow all laws, ordinances, regulations, and other requirements, including any registration requirement, will be deemed a material, noncurable breach of this Agreement and will furnish cause for termination.

Clause 10 is an antisubletting clause, breach of which is grounds for eviction. It prevents a tenant from subleasing during a vacation—letting someone stay in his place and pay rent while he's gone for an extended period of time—or renting out a room to someone unless you specifically agree.

Clause 10 is also designed to prevent assignments, a legal term that means your tenant transfers her entire tenancy to someone else. Practically, you need this clause to prevent your tenant from leaving in the middle of the month or lease term and moving in a replacement—maybe someone you wouldn't choose to rent to—without your consent.

By including Clause 10 in your lease or rental agreement, you have the option not to accept the person your tenant proposes to take over the lease. Under the law of most states, however, you should realize that if a tenant who wishes to leave early provides you with another suitable tenant, you can't both unreasonably refuse to rent to this person and hold the tenant financially liable for breaking the lease.

Chapter 8 discusses sublets and assignments in detail. Chapter 14 discusses what happens when a tenant breaks a lease.

Subletting and Short-Term Stays (Airbnb)

Online businesses such as Airbnb have acted as clearinghouses for short-term, or short-stay rentals (less than 30 days), for use by vacationers or visiting businesspersons. Tenants using these platforms sublet their rentals and pocket the rent, turning your property into a hotel. Landlords are universally opposed to this practice, though even they have joined the bandwagon, taking regular rental properties out of circulation in order to operate them solely as short-term rentals.

If you want to restrict tenants from running a short-term rental business, be sure your lease is clear on this. First, however, check local law: Bowing to political pressure, many municipalities are changing their laws concerning short-stay tenancies, by requiring registration and limiting the number of short-stay days per year.

How to Fill in Clause 10:

After you have determined whether any local ordinances regulate short-term rentals, choose the appropriate alternative language for Clause 10. Alternate (a) flatly prohibits such rentals, while alternate (b) advises tenants that they must follow the short-term stay law or risk termination of their tenancies.

Clause 11. Tenant's Maintenance Responsibilities

Tenant will: (1) keep the premises clean, sanitary, and in good condition and, upon termination of the tenancy, return the premises to Landlord in a condition identical to that which existed when Tenant took occupancy, except for ordinary wear and tear; (2) immediately notify Landlord of any defects or dangerous conditions in and about the premises of which Tenant becomes aware; and (3) reimburse Landlord, on demand by Landlord, for the cost of any repairs to the premises damaged by Tenant or Tenant's guests or business invitees through misuse or neglect.

Tenant has examined the premises, including appliances, fixtures, carpets, drapes, and paint, and has found them to be in good, safe, and clean condition and repair, except as noted in the Landlord-Tenant Checklist.

Clause 11 makes the tenant responsible for keeping the rental premises clean and sanitary. This clause also makes it clear that if the tenant damages the premises (for example, by breaking a window or scratching hardwood floors), it's his responsibility for the damage.

It is the law in some states (and wise in all) to notify tenants in writing of procedures for making complaints and repair requests. Clause 11 requires the tenant to alert you to defective or dangerous conditions.

Clause 11 also states that the tenant has examined the rental premises, including appliances, carpets, and paint, and found them to be safe and clean, except as noted in a separate form (the Landlord-Tenant Checklist, described in Chapter 7). Before the tenant moves in, you and the tenant should inspect the rental unit and fill out the Landlord-Tenant Checklist in Chapter 7, describing what is in the unit and noting any problems. Doing so will help you avoid disputes over security deposit deductions when the tenant moves out.

Chapter 9 provides details on landlords' and tenants' repair and maintenance responsibilities, recommends a system for tenants to request repairs, and offers practical advice on maintaining your rental property. Chapter 9 also covers tenant options (such as rent withholding) should you fail to maintain your property and keep it in good repair.

How to Fill in Clause 11:

You do not need to add anything to this clause.

Renters' Insurance

Landlords often require tenants to obtain renters' insurance, especially in high-end rentals. This covers losses to the tenant's belongings as a result of fire or theft, as well as injury to other people or property damage caused by the tenant's negligence. Besides protecting the tenant from personal liability, renters' insurance benefits you, too: If damage caused by the tenant could be covered by either the tenant's insurance policy or yours, a claim made on the tenant's policy will affect the tenant's premiums, not yours. Renters' insurance will not cover intentional damage by the tenant.

Be advised that it may not be legal for you to require your tenants to carry renters' insurance (in particular, liability insurance). Judges in some states (including Oklahoma) have held that your tenants are by implication coinsureds under your own property policy, because their rent helps pay your premiums. Making tenants buy additional insurance that will cover any destruction they might cause to your property duplicates the insurance that you (and they) already carry and shouldn't be allowed, the theory goes. But unfortunately it's very hard to get a good handle on which states adopt this approach. Only Virginia has clear, statutory law on the subject: Virginia allows a landlord to require a tenant to pay for renters' insurance that's obtained by the landlord. However, if the landlord also requires a security deposit, the combined cost of the insurance premiums and the security deposit cannot exceed two months' rent. (Va. Code Ann. §§ 55-248.2 to -248.9.) Oregon also regulates landlords' requirements for renters' insurance (Ore. Rev. Stat. § 90.222.)

Landlords subject to rent control may not be able to require renters' insurance, because a court might consider the premiums as a rent overcharge. Clearly, before requiring tenants to carry renters' insurance, you'll need to check with your agent or lawyer on the legality of such a requirement in your state or locality.

If you decide to require insurance, insert a clause like the following under Clause 22, Additional Provisions. This will help assure that the tenant carries renters' insurance throughout his tenancy. The average cost of renters' insurance is typically less than $20 or $30 per month, depending on the location and size of the rental unit and the value of the policyholder's possessions. Some carriers offer discounts if tenants already have another type of insurance with their companies, and additional discounts for tenants who do not smoke (smoking is a major cause of house fires) and who can demonstrate they have risk-reduction measures such as smoke alarms, safes, alarm systems, or double-bolt locks.

Renters' Insurance

Within ten days of the signing of this Agreement, Tenant will obtain renters' insurance, and provide proof of purchase to Landlord. Tenant further agrees to maintain the policy throughout the duration of the tenancy, and to furnish proof of insurance on a ☐ yearly ☐ semiannual basis.

CAUTION

Don't fail to maintain the property. In most states, language you stick in a lease or rental agreement saying a tenant gives up his right to habitable housing won't be effective. By law, you have to provide habitable housing, no matter what the agreement says. If your tenants or their guests suffer injury or property damage as a result of poorly maintained property, you may be held responsible for paying for the loss. See Chapters 10, 11, and 12 for liability-related issues.

Clause 12. Repairs and Alterations by Tenant

a. Except as provided by law, or as authorized by the prior written consent of Landlord, Tenant will not make any repairs or alterations to the premises, including nailing holes in the walls or painting the rental unit.

b. Tenant will not, without Landlord's prior written consent, alter, rekey, or install any locks to the premises or install or alter any security alarm system. Tenant will provide Landlord with a key or keys capable of unlocking all such rekeyed or new locks as well as instructions on how to disarm any altered or new security alarm system.

Clause 12 makes it clear that the tenant may not make alterations and repairs without your consent, including painting the unit or nailing holes in the walls.

And to make sure you can take advantage of your legal right of entry in an emergency situation, Clause 12 specifically forbids the tenant from rekeying the locks or installing a security alarm system without your consent. If you do grant permission, make sure your tenant gives you duplicate keys or the name and phone number of the alarm company or instructions on how to disarm the security system so that you can enter in case of emergency. See Chapter 12 for more information on your responsibility to provide secure premises, and Chapter 13 for information on your right to enter rental property in an emergency.

The "except as provided by law" language in Clause 12 is a reference to the fact that, in certain situations and in certain states, tenants have a narrowly defined right to alter or repair the premises, regardless of what you've said in the lease or rental agreement. Examples include:

- **Alterations by a person with a disability, such as lowering countertops for a wheelchair-bound tenant.** Under the federal Fair Housing Acts, persons with disabilities may modify their living spaces to the extent necessary to make the space safe and comfortable, as long as the modifications will not make the unit unacceptable to the next tenant, or the tenant agrees to undo the modification when the lease is over. See Chapter 5 for details.

- **Use of the "repair and deduct" procedure.** In most states, tenants have the right to repair defects or damage that make the premises uninhabitable or substantially interfere with the tenant's safe use or enjoyment of the premises. Usually, the tenant must first notify you of the problem and give you a reasonable amount of time to fix it. (See Chapter 9 for more on this topic.)

- **Installation of satellite dishes and antennas.** Federal law gives tenants limited rights to install wireless antennas and small satellite dishes. See Chapter 9 for details.

- **Specific alterations allowed by state statutes.** Some states permit tenants to install specific equipment, often when the landlord has refused to do so. Examples include energy conservation measures, burglary prevention devices, and door and window locks. Check your state statutes or call your local rental property association for more information on these types of laws.

How to Fill in Clause 12:

If you do not want the tenant to make any repairs without your permission, you do not need to add anything to this clause.

You may, however, want to go further and specifically prohibit certain repairs or alterations by adding details in Clause 12. For example, you may want to make it clear that any "fixtures"—a legal term that describes any addition that is attached to the structure, such as bolted-on bookcases or built-in dishwashers—are your property and may not be removed by the tenant without your permission.

If you do authorize the tenant to make any repairs, provide enough detail so that the tenant knows exactly what is expected, how much repairs can cost, and who will pay. For example, if you decide to allow the tenant to take over the repair of any broken windows, routine plumbing jobs, or landscaping, give specific descriptions and limits to the tasks. Chapter 9 includes a detailed discussion of delegating repair and maintenance responsibilities, a sample agreement form regarding tenant alterations and improvements, and an overview of legal issues regarding fixtures.

CAUTION
If you want the tenant to perform maintenance work for you in exchange for reduced rent, don't write it into the lease or rental agreement. Instead, use a separate employment agreement and pay the tenant for her services. That way, if she doesn't perform, you still have the full rent, and you can simply cancel the employment contract.

Clause 13. Prohibition Against Violating Laws and Causing Disturbances

Tenant is entitled to quiet enjoyment of the premises. Tenant and guests or invitees will not use the premises or adjacent areas in such a way as to: (1) violate any law or ordinance, including laws prohibiting the use, possession, or sale of illegal drugs; (2) commit waste (severe property damage); or (3) create a nuisance by annoying, disturbing, inconveniencing, or interfering with the quiet enjoyment and peace and quiet of any other tenant or nearby resident.

This type of clause is found in most form leases and rental agreements. It prohibits tenants (and their guests) from violating the law, damaging your property, or disturbing other tenants or nearby residents. Although this clause contains some legal jargon, it's probably best to leave it as is, since courts have much experience in working with terms like waste and nuisance (defined below).

Waste and Nuisance: What Are They?

In legalese, committing **waste** means causing severe damage to real estate, including a house or an apartment unit—damage that goes way beyond ordinary wear and tear. Punching holes in walls, pulling out sinks and fixtures, and knocking down doors are examples of waste.

Nuisance means behavior that prevents tenants and neighbors from fully enjoying the use of their homes and results in a substantial danger to their health and safety. Continuous loud noise and foul odors are examples of legal nuisances that may disturb nearby neighbors and affect their "quiet enjoyment" of the premises. So, too, are selling drugs or engaging in other illegal activities that greatly disturb neighbors.

This clause also refers to tenants' right to "quiet enjoyment" of the premises. As courts define it, the "covenant of quiet enjoyment" amounts to an implied promise that you will not act (or fail to act) in a way that seriously interferes with or destroys the ability of the tenant to use the rented premises—for example,

by allowing garbage to pile up, tolerating a major rodent infestation, or failing to control a tenant whose constant loud music makes it impossible for other tenants to sleep.

If you want more specific rules—for example, no loud music played after midnight—add them to Clause 18: Tenant Rules and Regulations, or to Clause 22: Additional Provisions.

Chapter 16 includes a detailed discussion of how to deal with noisy tenants.

How to Fill in Clause 13:

You do not need to add anything to this clause.

Clause 14. Pets

No animal may be kept on the premises, without Landlord's prior written consent, except animals needed by tenants who have a disability, as that term is understood by law, and _____ under the following conditions: _____

_____

_____ .

This clause prevents tenants from keeping pets without your written permission. If you want, you can have a flat "no pets" rule, though many landlords report that pet-owning tenants are more appreciative, stable, and responsible than the norm. But it does provide you with a legal mechanism that will keep your premises from being waist-deep in Irish wolfhounds. Without this sort of provision, particularly in a fixed-term lease that can't be terminated early save for a clear violation of one of its provisions, there's little to prevent your tenant from keeping multiple, dangerous, or nonhousebroken pets, except for city ordinances prohibiting tigers and animal cruelty laws.

With the exception of trained dogs and some other animals used by people who have a mental or physical disability, you have the right to prohibit all pets, or to restrict the types of pets or dog breeds you allow. Your pet policy should cover not only pets the tenant may have, but also pets of guests. When setting your pet policy, be sure to check any insurance or homeowners' association restrictions as to breeds of dog, weight, number of pets, and species allowed.

How to Fill in Clause 14:

If you do not allow pets, simply delete the words "and _____ under the following conditions:".

If you allow pets, be sure to identify the type and number of pets in the first blank—for example, "one cat" or "one dog under 20 pounds." It's also wise to spell out your pet rules in the second blank, or in an attachment—for example, you may want to specify that the tenants will keep the grounds and street free of all animal waste, and that cats and dogs be spayed or neutered, licensed, and up-to-date on vaccinations. Your Tenant Rules and Regulations may be another place to do this. See Clause 18.

Should You Require a Separate Security Deposit for Pets?

Some landlords allow pets but require the tenant to pay a separate deposit to cover any damages caused by the pet. The laws of a few states specifically allow separate, nonrefundable pet deposits. In other states, charging a designated pet deposit is legal only if the total amount you charge for deposits does not exceed the state maximum for all deposits. (See Chapter 4 for details on security deposits.)

Even where allowed, separate pet deposits can often be a bad idea because they limit how you can use that part of the security deposit. For example, if the pet is well-behaved, but the tenant trashes your unit, you can't use the pet portion of the deposit to clean up after the human. If you want to protect your property from damage done by a pet, you are probably better off charging a slightly higher rent or security deposit to start with (assuming you are not restricted by rent control or the upper security deposit limits).

It is illegal to charge an extra pet deposit for people with trained service or companion animals.

It is important to educate tenants from the start that you will not tolerate dangerous or even apparently dangerous pets; and that as soon as you learn of a worrisome situation, you have the option of insisting that the tenant get rid of the pet (or move). You may want to advise tenants that their pets must be well-trained and nonthreatening in the second blank of Clause 14; or you could set out your policy in your Rules and Regulations (if any). Your policy might look something like this:

> Tenant's pet(s) will be well-behaved and under Tenant's control at all times and will not pose a threat or apparent threat to the safety of other tenants, their guests, or other people on or near the rental premises. If, in the opinion of Landlord, tenant's pet(s) pose such a threat, Landlord will serve Tenant with the appropriate notice to terminate the tenancy.

A policy against dangerous pets is only effective if it's enforced. To limit your liability if a tenant's pet injures someone on or even near your property, be sure that you or your manager follow through with your policy—by keeping an eye on your tenants' pets and by listening to and acting on any complaints from other tenants or neighbors. For more on landlord liability for dog bites and other animal attacks, see Chapter 10.

CAUTION
Enforce no-pets clauses. When faced with tenants who violate no-pets clauses, landlords often ignore the situation for a long time, then try to enforce it later if friction develops over some other matter. This could backfire. In general, if you know a tenant has breached the lease or rental agreement (for example, by keeping a pet) and do nothing about it for a long time, you risk having legally waived your right to object. Better to adopt a policy you plan to stick to and then preserve your right to object, by promptly giving any offending tenant an informal written notice to get rid of the animal—see the warning letter in Chapter 16 for an example. Then follow through with a termination notice, subject to any rent control law requirements.

Clause 15. Landlord's Right to Access

Landlord or Landlord's agents may enter the premises in the event of an emergency, to make repairs or improvements, or to show the premises to prospective buyers or tenants. Landlord may also enter the premises to conduct an annual inspection to check for safety or maintenance problems. Except in cases of emergency, Tenant's abandonment of the premises, court order, or where it is impractical to do so, Landlord shall give Tenant _____ notice before entering.

Clause 15 makes it clear to the tenant that you have a legal right of access to the property to make repairs or to show the premises for sale or rental, provided you give the tenant reasonable notice. In most states, 24 hours is presumed to be a reasonable amount of notice. A few states require a longer notice period. Chapter 13 provides details on landlord's right to enter rental property and notice requirements.

How to Fill in Clause 15:

In the blank, indicate the amount of notice you will provide the tenant before entering, at least the minimum required in your state. If your state law simply requires "reasonable" notice or has no notice requirement, we suggest you provide at least 24 hours' notice.

Clause 16. Extended Absences by Tenant

Tenant will notify Landlord in advance if Tenant will be away from the premises for _____ or more consecutive days. During such absence, Landlord may enter the premises at times reasonably necessary to maintain the property and inspect for damage and needed repairs.

This clause requires that the tenants notify you when leaving your property for an extended time. It gives you the authority to enter the rental unit during the tenant's absence to maintain the property as necessary and to inspect for damage and needed repairs. Chapter 13 discusses your legal right to enter during a tenant's extended absence.

How to Fill in Clause 16:

In the blank, fill in the minimum amount of time the tenant will be gone that will require the tenant to notify you of an extended absence. Ten or 14 days is common.

Clause 17. Possession of the Premises

a. *Tenant's failure to take possession.*

    If, after signing this Agreement, Tenant fails to take possession of the premises, Tenant will still be responsible for paying rent and complying with all other terms of this Agreement.

b. *Landlord's failure to deliver possession.*

    If Landlord is unable to deliver possession of the premises to Tenant for any reason not within Landlord's control, including, but not limited to, partial or complete destruction of the premises, Tenant will have the right to terminate this Agreement upon proper notice as required by law. In such event, Landlord's liability to Tenant will be limited to the return of all sums previously paid by Tenant to Landlord.

The first part of this clause (part a) explains that a tenant who chooses not to move in (take possession) after signing the lease or rental agreement will still be required to pay rent and satisfy other conditions of the agreement. This does not mean, however, that you can sit back and expect to collect rent for the entire lease or rental agreement term. As we explain in Chapter 14, you generally must take reasonably prompt steps to rerent the premises, and you must credit the rent you collect against the first tenant's rent obligation.

The second part of the clause (part b) protects you if you're unable, for reasons beyond your control, to turn over possession after having signed the agreement or lease—for example, if a fire spreads from next door and destroys the premises or contracted repairs aren't done on time. It limits your financial liability to the new tenant to the return of any prepaid rent and security deposits (the "sums previously paid" in the language of the clause).

> ! **CAUTION**
>
> **Clause 17 may not limit your liability if you cannot deliver possession because the old tenant is still on the premises—even if he or she is the subject of an eviction which you ultimately win.** When a holdover tenant prevents the new tenant from moving in, landlords are often sued by the new tenant for not only the return of any prepaid rent and security deposits, but also the costs of temporary housing, storage costs, and other losses. In some states, an attempt in the lease to limit the new tenant's recovery to the return of prepaid sums alone would not hold up in court. To protect yourself, you will want to shift some of the financial liability to the holdover tenant. You'll have a stronger chance of doing this if the old tenant has given written notice of his or her intent to move out. (See Clause 4, above, which requires written notice.)

How to Fill in Clause 17:

You do not need to add anything to this clause.

> 💡 **TIP**
>
> **Don't rerent until you are positive that the unit will be available.** If you have any reason to suspect that your current tenant will not vacate when the lease or rental agreement is up, think twice before signing a new

lease or agreement or even promising the rental unit to the next tenant. If the current occupant is leaving of her own will or appears to have another dwelling lined up (perhaps you have received a query from the new landlord), chances are that she will leave as planned. On the other hand, if you declined to renew the lease or rental agreement and there are bad feelings between you, or you suspect that the tenant has fallen on hard times and has not obtained replacement housing—and certainly if she is the subject of an eviction—you are asking for trouble if you promise the unit to someone else.

Clause 18. Tenant Rules and Regulations

☐ Tenant acknowledges receipt of, and has read a copy of, tenant rules and regulations, which are attached to and incorporated into this Agreement by this reference. Tenant understands that serious or repeated violations of the rules may be grounds for termination. Landlord may change the rules and regulations without notice.

Many landlords don't worry about detailed rules and regulations, especially when they rent single-family homes or duplexes. However, in large multitenant buildings, rules are usually important to control the use of common areas and equipment—both for the convenience, safety, and welfare of the tenants and as a way to protect your property from damage. Rules and regulations also help avoid confusion and misunderstandings about day-to-day issues such as garbage disposal, use of recreation areas, and lost key charges.

Not every minor rule needs to be incorporated in your lease or rental agreement. But it is a good idea to specifically incorporate important ones (especially those that are likely to be ignored by some tenants), such as no smoking in individual units or common areas. Doing so gives you the authority to evict a tenant who persists in seriously violating your code of tenant rules and regulations. Also, to avoid charges of illegal discrimination, rules and regulations should apply equally to all tenants in your rental property. And make sure your tenants know that these rules apply to guests as well.

What's Covered in Tenant Rules and Regulations

Tenant rules and regulations typically cover issues such as:

- elevator use
- pool rules, including policies on guest use
- garbage and recycling pickups
- vehicles and parking regulations—for examples, restrictions of repairs on the premises, or types of vehicles (such as no RVs), or where guests can park
- lock-out and lost key charges
- pet rules
- security system use
- no smoking—either in common areas in multiunit building, including the hallways, lobby, garage, or walkways, or even in individual units (see Chapter 9 for more on no-smoking policies and issues regarding tenant marijuana smoking)
- specific details on what's considered excessive noise and rules to limit noise—for example, carpets or rugs required on hardwood floors (which usually aren't soundproof)
- dangerous materials—nothing flammable or explosive should be on the premises
- storage of bikes, baby strollers, and other equipment in halls, stairways, and other common areas
- specific landlord and tenant maintenance responsibilities (such as stopped-up toilets or garbage disposals, broken windows, rodent and pest control, lawn and yard maintenance)
- use of the grounds
- maintenance of balconies and decks—for instance, no drying clothes on balconies
- display of signs in windows
- laundry room rules, and
- waterbeds.

Because tenant rules and regulations are often lengthy and may be revised occasionally, we suggest you prepare a separate attachment. Be sure the rules and regulations (including any revisions) are dated on each page and signed by both you and the tenant.

You can usually change your rules and regulations without waiting until the end of the rental (for leases) or without giving proper notice (for rental agreements)—but only if the change is minor and not apt to affect the tenant's use and enjoyment of his tenancy. Shortening the pool hours in the winter months is an example of a minor change. Closing all laundry facilities in an attempt to save on water and electrical bills is a major change that should be the subject of a proper notice (for month-to-month tenants); this may be a step that you can't take at all if your building has tenants with leases. You'll have to wait until the longest lease is up for renewal.

How to Fill in Clause 18:

If you have a set of tenant rules and regulations, check the box. Do the same if your rental is in a community with homeowners' association or condo rules. If you do not have a separate set of tenant rules and regulations, simply delete this clause (in which case you will need to renumber the remaining clauses).

Clause 19. Payment of Court Costs and Attorney Fees in a Lawsuit

In any action or legal proceeding to enforce any part of this Agreement, the prevailing party ☐ shall not / ☐ shall recover reasonable attorney fees and court costs.

Many landlords assume that if they sue a tenant and win (or prevail, in legalese), the court will order the losing tenant to pay the landlord's court costs (filing fees, service of process charges, deposition costs, and so on) and attorney fees. In some states and under certain conditions, this is true. For example, an Arizona landlord who wins an eviction lawsuit is eligible to receive costs and fees even if the lease does not have a "costs and fees" clause in it. (Ariz. Rev. Stat. §§ 33-1315, 12-341.01.) But in most states, a court will order the losing tenant to pay your attorney fees and court costs only if a written agreement specifically provides for it.

If, however, you have an "attorney fees" clause in your lease, all this changes. If you hire a lawyer to bring a lawsuit concerning the lease and win, the judge will order your tenant to pay your court costs and attorney fees. (In rare instances, a court will order the loser to pay costs and fees even though there's no "attorney fees" clause in the lease, if it finds that the behavior of the losing party was particularly outrageous—for example, filing a totally frivolous lawsuit.)

But there's another important issue you may need to know about. By law in many states, an attorney fees clause in a lease or rental agreement works both ways, even if you haven't written it that way. That is, if the lease only states that you are entitled to attorney fees if you win a lawsuit, your tenants will be entitled to collect their attorney fees from you if they prevail. The amount you would be ordered to pay would be whatever the judge decides is reasonable.

So, especially if you live in a state that will read a "one-way" attorney fees clause as a two-way street, give some thought to whether you want to bind both of you to paying for the winner's costs and fees. Remember, if you can't actually collect a judgment containing attorney fees from an evicted tenant (which often happens), the clause will not help you. But if the tenant prevails, you will be stuck paying the tenant's court costs and attorney fees. In addition, the presence of a two-way clause will make it easier for a tenant to secure a willing lawyer for even a doubtful claim, because the source of the lawyer's fee (you, if you lose) will often appear more financially solid than if the client were paying the bill himself or herself.

Especially if you intend to do all or most of your own legal work in any potential eviction or other lawsuit, you will almost surely be better off not to allow for attorney fees. Why? Because if the tenant wins, you will have to pay the tenant's fees; but if you win, the tenant will owe you nothing, since you didn't hire an attorney. You can't even recover for the long hours you spent preparing for and handling the case.

How to Fill in Clause 19:

If you don't want to allow for attorney fees, check the first box before the words "shall not" and delete the word "shall."

If you want to be entitled to attorney fees and costs if you win—and you're willing to pay them if you lose—check the second box before the words "shall recover" and delete the words "shall not."

> **CAUTION**
> **If your rental property is in Ohio, do not include the attorney fees clause**—it's prohibited by law in Ohio. (Oh. Rev. Code Ann. § 5321.13(c).)

> **CAUTION**
> **Attorney fees clauses don't cover all legal disputes.** They cover fees only for lawsuits that concern the meaning or implementation of a rental agreement or lease—for example, a dispute about rent, security deposits, or your right to access (assuming that the rental document includes these subjects). An attorney fees clause would not apply in a personal injury or discrimination lawsuit.

Clause 20. Disclosures

Tenant acknowledges that Landlord has made the following disclosures regarding the premises:

☐ Disclosure of Information on Lead-Based Paint and/or Lead-Based Paint Hazards

☐ Other disclosures: _____

_____

Under federal law, you must disclose any known lead-based paint hazards in rental premises constructed prior to 1978. (Chapter 11 provides complete details on disclosing environmental health hazards such as lead, including the specific form you must use.)

State and local laws may require you to make other disclosures before a new tenant signs a lease or rental agreement or moves in. Some disclosures that may be required include:

- the name of the owner and the person authorized to receive legal papers, such as a property manager (see Clause 21)
- details on installation and maintenance of smoke detectors and alarms (this is included on the Landlord-Tenant Checklist in Chapter 7)

- hidden (not obvious) aspects of the rental property that could cause injury or substantially interfere with tenants' safe enjoyment and use of the dwelling—for example, a warning that the building walls contain asbestos insulation, which could become dangerous if disturbed (Chapters 10, 11, and 12 discuss landlord's liability for dangerous conditions)
- planned condominium conversions (discussed in Chapter 14), and
- the presence of a methamphetamine laboratory at the rental prior to the tenant's occupancy. Even if your state does not have a specific statutory disclosure requirement, you may need to disclose the information pursuant to your duty to notify tenants of nonobvious aspects of the rental that could cause injury. See Chapter 12 for information on dealing with the remains of a meth lab.

See "Required Landlord Disclosures," in Appendix A, for disclosures required by some states.

RENT CONTROL

Rent control ordinances typically include additional disclosures, such as the name and address of the government agency or elected board that administers the ordinance. (Chapter 3 discusses rent control.)

How to Fill in Clause 20:

If your rental property was built before 1978, you must meet federal lead disclosure requirements, so check the first box and follow the advice in Chapter 11.

If you are legally required to make other disclosures as described above, check the second box and provide details in the blank space, adding additional details or pages as necessary.

CAUTION

Some problems need to be fixed, not merely disclosed. Warning your tenants about a hidden defect does not absolve you of legal responsibility if the condition makes the dwelling uninhabitable or unreasonably dangerous. For example, you are courting liability if you rent an apartment with a gas heater that you know might blow up, even if you warn the tenant that the heater is faulty. Nor can you simply warn your tenants about prior crime on the premises and then fail to do anything (like installing deadbolts or an alarm system) to promote safety. Chapters 10, 11, and 12 discuss problems that are proper subjects of warnings and those that ought to be fixed.

Clause 21. Authority to Receive Legal Papers

The Landlord, any person managing the premises, and anyone designated by the Landlord are authorized to accept service of process and receive other notices and demands, which may be delivered to:

The Landlord, at the following address: _____
_____

The manager, at the following address: _____
_____

The following person, at the following address: _____
_____

It's the law in many states, and a good idea in all, to give your tenants information about everyone whom you have authorized to receive notices and legal papers, such as a tenant's notice that he or she is ending the tenancy or a tenant's court documents as part of an eviction defense. Of course, you may want to handle all of this yourself or delegate it to a manager or management company. Make sure the person you designate to receive legal papers is almost always available to receive tenant notices and legal papers. In some states, any nonresident owner must designate an agent who is a resident of or has a business office in the state.

Be sure to keep your tenants up to date on any changes in this information.

How to Fill in Clause 21:

Provide your name and street address or the name and address of someone else you authorize to receive notices and legal papers on your behalf, such as a property manager.

CAUTION

Do you trust your manager? It's unwise to have a manager you wouldn't trust to receive legal papers on your behalf. You don't, for example, want a careless apartment manager to throw away notice of a lawsuit against you without informing you. That could result in a judgment against you and a lien against your property in a lawsuit you didn't even know about. For more information on using property managers, see Chapter 6.

Clause 22. Additional Provisions

Additional provisions are as follows: _____
_____
_____
_____ .

In this clause, you may list any additional provisions or agreements that are unique to you and the particular tenant signing the lease or rental agreement, such as a provision that prohibits smoking in the tenant's apartment or in the common areas. For more information on restrictions on smoking, see Chapter 9.

If you don't have a separate Tenant Rules and Regulations clause (see Clause 18, above), you may spell out a few rules under this clause—for example, regarding lost key charges or use of a pool on the property.

How to Fill in Clause 22:

List additional provisions or rules here or in an attachment. If there are no additional provisions, delete this clause and remember to renumber the other clauses accordingly.

TIP

There is no legal or practical imperative to put every small detail you want to communicate to the tenant into your lease or rental agreement. Instead, prepare a welcoming, but no-nonsense, "move-in letter" that dovetails with the lease or rental agreement and highlights important terms of the tenancy—for example, how and where to report maintenance problems. You may

also use a move-in letter to cover issues not included in the lease or rental agreement—for example, rules for use of a laundry room. Chapter 7 covers move-in letters.

CAUTION

Do not include exculpatory clauses or hold-harmless clauses. Many form leases include provisions that attempt to absolve you in advance from responsibility for all damages, injuries, or losses, including those caused by your legal misdeeds. These clauses come in two varieties:

- Exculpatory: "If there's a problem, you won't hold me responsible," and
- Hold-harmless: "If there's a problem traceable to me, you're responsible."

Many exculpatory clauses are blatantly illegal and will not be upheld in court (Chapter 10 discusses exculpatory clauses). If a tenant is injured because of a dangerous condition you failed to fix for several months, no boilerplate lease language will protect you from civil and possibly even criminal charges.

Clause 23. Validity of Each Part

If any portion of this Agreement is held to be invalid, its invalidity will not affect the validity or enforceability of any other provision of this Agreement.

This clause is known as a "savings" clause, and it is commonly used in contracts. It means that, in the unlikely event that one of the other clauses in this lease or rental agreement is found to be invalid by a court, the remainder of the agreement will remain in force.

How to Fill in Clause 23:

You do not need to add anything to this clause.

Clause 24. Grounds for Termination of Tenancy

The failure of Tenant or Tenant's guests or invitees to comply with any term of this Agreement, or the misrepresentation of any material fact on Tenant's rental application, is grounds for termination of the tenancy, with appropriate notice to Tenant and procedures as required by law.

Month-to-Month Residential Rental Agreement

Clause 1. Identification of Landlord and Tenant

This Agreement is entered into between ___Marty Nelson_____

_____ [Tenant] and

_____Alex Stevens_____ [Landlord].

Each Tenant is jointly and severally liable for the payment of rent and performance of all other terms of this Agreement.

Clause 2. Identification of Premises

Subject to the terms and conditions in this Agreement, Landlord rents to Tenant, and Tenant rents from Landlord, for residential purposes only, the premises located at ___137 Howell St., Philadelphia,_____

___Pennsylvania_____ [the premises],

together with the following furnishings and appliances: _____

_____.

Rental of the premises also includes _____

_____.

Clause 3. Limits on Use and Occupancy

The premises are to be used only as a private residence for Tenant(s) listed in Clause 1 of this Agreement, and their minor children. Occupancy by guests for more than ___ten days every six months____ is prohibited without Landlord's written consent and will be considered a breach of this Agreement.

Clause 4. Term of the Tenancy

The rental will begin on _____September 15, 20xx_____ , and continue on a month-to-month basis. Landlord may terminate the tenancy or modify the terms of this Agreement by giving the Tenant _____30_____ days' written notice. Tenant may terminate the tenancy by giving the Landlord _____30_____ days' written notice.

Clause 5. Payment of Rent

Regular monthly rent.

Tenant will pay to Landlord a monthly rent of $____900_____ , payable in advance on the first day of each month, except when that day falls on a weekend or legal holiday, in which case rent is due on the next business day. Rent will be paid in the following manner unless Landlord designates otherwise:

Delivery of payment.

Rent will be paid:

☑ by mail, to _____Alex Stevens, 28 Franklin St., Philadelphia, Pennsylvania 19120_____

☐ in person, at _____

Form of payment.

Landlord will accept payment in the following forms:

☐ cash

☑ personal check made payable to ___Alex Stevens_____

☑ certified funds or money orders

☐ credit card

☑ bank debits

☐ electronic funds transfer _____

Prorated first month's rent.

For the period from Tenant's move-in date, ___September 15, 20xx_____, through the end of the

month, Tenant will pay to Landlord the prorated monthly rent of $__450_____ . This amount

will be paid on or before the date the Tenant moves in.

Clause 6. Late Charges

If Tenant fails to pay the rent in full before the end of the ___third_____ day after it's due, Tenant will

pay Landlord a late charge as follows: __$10, plus $5 for each additional day that the rent___

__remains unpaid. The total late charge for any one month will not exceed $45.___

Landlord does not waive the right to insist on payment of the rent in full on the date it is due.

Clause 7. Returned Check and Other Bank Charges

If any check offered by Tenant to Landlord in payment of rent or any other amount due under this

Agreement is returned for lack of sufficient funds, a "stop payment," or any other reason, Tenant will pay

Landlord a returned check charge of $__15_____ .

Clause 8. Security Deposit

On signing this Agreement, Tenant will pay to Landlord the sum of $__1,800_____ as a security

deposit. Tenant may not, without Landlord's prior written consent, apply this security deposit to the last

month's rent or to any other sum due under this Agreement. Within __30 days_____

after Tenant has vacated the premises, returned keys, and provided Landlord with a forwarding address,

Landlord will return the deposit in full or give Tenant an itemized written statement of the reasons for,

and the dollar amount of, any of the security deposit retained by Landlord, along with a check for any

deposit balance.

[optional clauses here, if any]

The security deposit of $1,800 will be held at:

Federal Bank

1 Federal Street

Philadelphia, PA 19120

Clause 9. Utilities

Tenant will pay all utility charges, except for the following, which will be paid by Landlord:

garbage and water

.

Clause 10. Prohibition of Assignment and Subletting

Tenants will not sublet any part of the premises or assign this Agreement without the prior written consent of Landlord.

☐ a. Tenants will not sublet or rent any part of the Premises for short-term stays of any duration, including but not limited to vacation rentals.

☐ b. Short-stay rentals are prohibited except as authorized by law. Any short stay-rental is expressly conditioned upon the tenants' following all regulations, laws, and other requirements as a condition to offering a short-stay rental. Failure to follow all laws, ordinances, regulations, and other requirements, including any registration requirement, will be deemed a material, noncurable breach of this Agreement and will furnish cause for termination.

Clause 11. Tenant's Maintenance Responsibilities

Tenant will: (1) keep the premises clean, sanitary, and in good condition and, upon termination of the tenancy, return the premises to Landlord in a condition identical to that which existed when Tenant took occupancy, except for ordinary wear and tear; (2) immediately notify Landlord of any defects or dangerous conditions in and about the premises of which Tenant becomes aware; and (3) reimburse Landlord, on demand by Landlord, for the cost of any repairs to the premises damaged by Tenant or Tenant's guests or business invitees through misuse or neglect.

Tenant has examined the premises, including appliances, fixtures, carpets, drapes, and paint, and has found them to be in good, safe, and clean condition and repair, except as noted in the Landlord-Tenant Checklist.

Clause 12. Repairs and Alterations by Tenant

a. Except as provided by law, or as authorized by the prior written consent of Landlord, Tenant will not make any repairs or alterations to the premises, including nailing holes in the walls or painting the rental unit.

b. Tenant will not, without Landlord's prior written consent, alter, rekey, or install any locks to the premises or install or alter any security alarm system. Tenant will provide Landlord with a key or keys capable of unlocking all such rekeyed or new locks as well as instructions on how to disarm any altered or new security alarm system.

Clause 13. Violating Laws and Causing Disturbances

Tenant is entitled to quiet enjoyment of the premises. Tenant and guests or invitees will not use the premises or adjacent areas in such a way as to: (1) violate any law or ordinance, including laws prohibiting the use, possession, or sale of illegal drugs; (2) commit waste (severe property damage); or (3) create a nuisance by annoying, disturbing, inconveniencing, or interfering with the quiet enjoyment and peace and quiet of any other tenant or nearby resident.

Clause 14. Pets

No animal may be kept on the premises without Landlord's prior written consent, except animals needed by tenants who have a disability, as that is a term is understood by law, and one dog under 20 pounds under the following conditions: _Tenant complies with Pet Rules set out in separate_ _attachment to this Agreement._ _____ .

Clause 15. Landlord's Right to Access

Landlord or Landlord's agents may enter the premises in the event of an emergency, to make repairs or improvements, or to show the premises to prospective buyers or tenants. Landlord may also enter the premises to conduct an annual inspection to check for safety or maintenance problems. Except in cases of emergency, Tenant's abandonment of the premises, court order, or where it is impractical to do so, Landlord shall give Tenant _____ 24 hours' _____ notice before entering.

Clause 16. Extended Absences by Tenant

Tenant will notify Landlord in advance if Tenant will be away from the premises for ____ seven ____ or more consecutive days. During such absence, Landlord may enter the premises at times reasonably necessary to maintain the property and inspect for damage and needed repairs.

Clause 17. Possession of the Premises

　　a.　*Tenant's failure to take possession.*

　　　　If, after signing this Agreement, Tenant fails to take possession of the premises, Tenant will still be responsible for paying rent and complying with all other terms of this Agreement.

　　b.　*Landlord's failure to deliver possession.*

　　　　If Landlord is unable to deliver possession of the premises to Tenant for any reason not within Landlord's control, including, but not limited to, partial or complete destruction of the premises, Tenant will have the right to terminate this Agreement upon proper notice as required by law. In such event, Landlord's liability to Tenant will be limited to the return of all sums previously paid by Tenant to Landlord.

Clause 18. Tenant Rules and Regulations

☑ Tenant acknowledges receipt of, and has read a copy of, tenant rules and regulations, which are attached to and incorporated into this Agreement by this reference. Tenant understands that serious or repeated violations of the rules may be grounds for termination. Landlord may change the rules and regulations without notice.

Clause 19. Payment of Court Costs and Attorney Fees in a Lawsuit

In any action or legal proceeding to enforce any part of this Agreement, the prevailing party

☐ shall not / ☑ shall recover reasonable attorney fees and court costs.

Clause 20.　Disclosures

Tenant acknowledges that Landlord has made the following disclosures regarding the premises:

☑ Disclosure of Information on Lead-Based Paint and/or Lead-Based Paint Hazards

☐ Other disclosures: _____

_____

_____

_____ .

Clause 21. Authority to Receive Legal Papers

The Landlord, any person managing the premises, and anyone designated by the Landlord are authorized to accept service of process and receive other notices and demands, which may be delivered to:

☑ The Landlord, at the following address: ___28 Franklin St., Philadelphia, Pennsylvania 19120___

_____ .

☐ The manager, at the following address: _____

_____ .

☐ The following person, at the following address: _____

_____ .

Clause 22. Additional Provisions

Additional provisions are as follows: _____

_____

_____

_____

_____

_____

_____

_____

Clause 23. Validity of Each Part

If any portion of this Agreement is held to be invalid, its invalidity will not affect the validity or enforceability of any other provision of this Agreement.

Clause 24. Grounds for Termination of Tenancy

The failure of Tenant or Tenant's guests or invitees to comply with any term of this Agreement, or the misrepresentation of any material fact on Tenant's rental application, is grounds for termination of the tenancy, with appropriate notice to Tenant and procedures as required by law.

Clause 25. Entire Agreement

This document constitutes the entire Agreement between the parties, and no promises or representations, other than those contained here and those implied by law, have been made by Landlord or Tenant. Any modifications to this Agreement must be in writing signed by Landlord and Tenant.

Sept. 1, 20xx	Alex Stevens	Landlord	
Date	Landlord or Landlord's Agent	Title	

28 Franklin Street

Street Address

Philadelphia	Pennsylvania		19120	215-555-1578
City	State	Zip Code	Phone	Email

Sept. 1, 20xx	Marty Nelson	215-555-8751
Date	Tenant	Phone

Date	Tenant	Phone

Date	Tenant	Phone

This clause states that any violation of the lease or rental agreement by the tenant, or by the tenant's business or social guests, is grounds for terminating the tenancy, according to the procedures established by your state or local laws. Making the tenant responsible for the actions of his guests can be extremely important—for example, if you discover that the tenant's family or friends are dealing illegal drugs on the premises, have damaged the property, or have brought a dog to visit a no-pets apartment. Chapter 17 discusses terminations and evictions for tenant violation of a lease or rental agreement.

This clause also tells the tenant that if he has made false statements on the rental application concerning an important fact—such as his prior criminal history—you may terminate the tenancy and evict if necessary.

How to Fill in Clause 24:

You do not need to add anything to this clause.

Clause 25. Entire Agreement

> This document constitutes the entire Agreement between the parties, and no promises or representations, other than those contained here and those implied by law, have been made by Landlord or Tenant. Any modifications to this Agreement must be in writing signed by Landlord and Tenant.

This clause establishes that the lease or rental agreement and any attachments (such as rules and regulations) constitute the entire agreement between you and your tenant. It means that oral promises (by you or the tenant) to do something different with respect to any aspect of the rental are not binding. Any changes or additions must be in writing. Chapter 14 discusses how to modify signed rental agreements and leases.

How to Fill in Clause 25:

You do not need to add anything to this clause.

Signing the Lease or Rental Agreement

Prepare two identical copies of the lease or rental agreement to sign, including all attachments. You and each tenant should sign both copies. At the end of the lease or rental agreement, there's space to include your signature, street address, phone number, and email, or that of the person you authorize as your agent, such as a property manager. There's also space for the tenants' signatures and phone numbers. Again, as stressed in Clause 1, make sure all adults living in the rental unit, including both members of a couple, sign the lease or rental agreement. And check that the tenant's name and signature match his or her driver's license or other legal document.

If the tenant has a cosigner, you'll need to add a line for the cosigner's signature or use a separate form. Cosigners are discussed below.

If you alter our form by writing or typing in changes, be sure that you and all tenants initial the changes when you sign the document, so as to forestall any possibility that a tenant will claim you unilaterally inserted changes after he or she signed.

Give one copy of the signed lease or rental agreement to the tenant(s) and keep the other one for your files. If you are renting to more than one tenant, you don't need to prepare a separate agreement for each cotenant. After the agreement is signed, cotenants may make their own copies of the signed document.

> **CAUTION**
> **Don't sign a lease until all terms are final and the tenant understands what's expected.** All of your expectations should be written into the lease or rental agreement (or any attachments, such as Tenant Rules and Regulations) before you and the tenant sign the document. Never sign an incomplete document assuming last-minute changes can be made later. And be sure your tenant clearly understands the lease or rental agreement before signing (this may mean you'll need to review it clause by clause). Chapter 7 discusses how to get your new tenancy off to the right start.

If English is not the tenant's first language, give the tenant a written translation. (We include Spanish versions of our lease and rental agreement forms on Nolo's website. See Appendix B for the link to the forms in this book.) Some states require this; California, for example, requires landlords who discuss the lease primarily in Spanish, Chinese, Tagalog, Vietnamese, or Korean, to give the applicant an unsigned, translated version of the lease before asking the applicant to sign (doesn't apply when the tenant supplies his own translator, someone who is not a minor and can fluently read and speak both languages). (Cal. Civil Code § 1632.) But even if it's not legally required, you want your tenants to know and follow the rules.

About Cosigners

Some landlords require cosigners (sometimes known as guarantors) on rental agreements and leases, especially when renting to students who depend on parents for much of their income. The cosigner signs a separate agreement or the rental agreement or lease, under which she agrees to be jointly and severally liable with the tenant for the tenant's obligations—that is, to cover any rent or damage-repair costs the tenant fails to pay (Clause 1 discusses the concept of joint and several liability). The cosigner retains responsibility regardless of whether the tenant sublets or assigns his agreement. Clause 11 discusses sublets and assignments, and Chapter 8 covers these issues in detail.

In practice, a cosigner's promise to guarantee the tenant's rent obligation may have less value than at first you might think. This is because the threat of eviction is the primary factor that motivates a tenant to pay the rent, and obviously you cannot evict a cosigner. Also, since the cosigner must be sued separately in either a regular civil lawsuit or in small claims court, actually doing so—for example, if a tenant stiffs you for a month's rent—may be more trouble than it's worth.

Clause 5 of the cosigner agreement designates the tenant as the cosigner's "agent for service of process." This bit of legal jargon will save you some time and aggravation if you decide to sue the cosigner—it means that you won't have to find the cosigner and serve him personally with notification of your lawsuit. Instead, you can serve the legal papers meant for the cosigner on the tenant (who will be easier to locate). It's then up to the tenant to get in touch with the cosigner. If the cosigner fails to show up, you will be able to win by default. Of course, you still have to collect, and that may involve hiring a lawyer (particularly if the cosigner lives in another state). You can always assign the judgment to a collection agency and resign yourself to giving the agency a cut of any recovery.

In sum, the benefits of having a lease or rental agreement cosigned by someone who won't be living on the property are largely psychological. But these benefits may still be worth something: A tenant who thinks you can (and will) sue the cosigner—who is usually a relative or close friend—may be less likely to default on the rent. Similarly, a cosigner asked to pay the tenant's debts may persuade the tenant to pay. In addition, the cosigner agreement cautions the tenant and cosigner that you can go directly to the cosigner without having to give the cosigner notice, or warning, that the tenant has failed to perform a financial obligation; and you can make this demand without first dipping into the tenant's security deposit.

Because of the practical difficulties associated with cosigners, many landlords refuse to consider them, which is legal in every situation but one: If a tenant with a disability who has insufficient income (but is otherwise suitable) asks you to accept a cosigner who will cover the rent if needed, you must relax your blanket rule at least to the extent of investigating the suitability of the proposed cosigner. If that person is solvent and stable, federal law requires you to accommodate the applicant by accepting the cosigner, in spite of your general policy. (*Giebeler v. M & B Associates*, 343 F.3d 1143 (9th Cir. 2003).)

Cosigner Agreement

1. This Cosigner Agreement [Agreement] is entered into on ___September 1___ , ___20xx___ , between ___Marty Nelson___ [Tenant], ___Alex Stevens___ [Landlord], and ___Sandy Cole___ [Cosigner].

2. Tenant has leased from Landlord the premises located at ___137 Howell Street, Philadelphia, PA___ ___[Premises]. Landlord and Tenant signed a lease or rental agreement specifying the terms and conditions of this rental on ___September 1___ , ___20xx___ . A copy of the lease or rental agreement is attached to this Agreement.

3. Cosigner agrees to be jointly and severally liable with Tenant for Tenant's obligations arising out of the lease or rental agreement described in Paragraph 2, including but not limited to unpaid rent, property damage, and cleaning and repair costs. Cosigner further agrees that Landlord will have no obligation to give notice to Cosigner should Tenant fail to abide by the terms of the lease or rental agreement. Landlord may demand that Cosigner perform as promised under this Agreement without first using Tenant's security deposit.

4. If Tenant assigns or subleases the Premises, Cosigner will remain liable under the terms of this Agreement for the performance of the assignee or sublessee, unless Landlord relieves Cosigner by written termination of this Agreement.

5. Cosigner appoints Tenant as his or her agent for service of process in the event of any lawsuit arising out of this Agreement.

6. If Landlord and Cosigner are involved in any legal proceeding arising out of this Agreement, the prevailing party will recover reasonable attorney fees, court costs, and any costs reasonably necessary to collect a judgment.

___Alex Stevens___
Landlord/Manager

___September 1, 20xx___
Date

___Marty Nelson___
Tenant

___September 1, 20xx___
Date

___Sandy Cole___
Cosigner

___September 1, 20xx___
Date

If you decide to accept a cosigner, you should have that person fill out a separate rental application and agree to a credit check—after all, a cosigner who has no resources or connection to the tenant will be completely useless. Should the tenant and her prospective cosigner object to these inquiries and costs, you may wonder how serious they are about the guarantor's willingness to stand behind the tenant. Once you are satisfied that the cosigner can genuinely back up the tenant, add a line at the end of the lease for the dated signature, phone, and address of the cosigner, or use the cosigner agreement form we provide here.

A sample Cosigner Agreement is shown above, and the Nolo website includes a downloadable copy. See Appendix B for the link to the forms in this book. Simply fill in your name and your tenant's and cosigner's names, the address of the rental unit, and the date you signed the agreement with the tenant.

CAUTION

If you later amend the rental agreement or lease (a topic discussed in Chapter 14), have the cosigner sign the new version. Generally speaking, a cosigner is bound only to the terms of the exact lease or rental agreement he cosigns.

Basic Rent Rules

 FORMS IN THIS CHAPTER

Chapter 3 includes instructions for and a sample of the following form:

- Agreement for Delayed or Partial Rent Payments

The Nolo website includes a downloadable copy of this form. See Appendix B for the link to the forms in this book.

One of your foremost concerns as a landlord is receiving your rent—on time and without hassle. It follows that you need a good grasp of the legal rules governing rent. This chapter outlines basic state and local rent laws affecting how much you can charge, as well as where, when, and how rent is due. It also covers rules regarding grace periods, late rent, returned check charges, and rent increases.

Avoiding Rent Disputes

Here are three guidelines that can help you and your tenants have a smooth relationship when it comes to an area of utmost interest to both of you: rent.

- Clearly spell out rent rules in your lease or rental agreement as well as in a move-in letter to new tenants.
- Be fair and consistent about enforcing your rent rules.
- If rent isn't paid on time, follow through with a legal notice telling the tenant to pay or move—the first legal step in a possible eviction—as soon as possible.

 RELATED TOPIC
Related topics covered in this book include:
- Lease and rental agreement provisions relating to rent: Chapter 2
- Collecting deposits and potential problems with calling a deposit "last month's rent": Chapter 4
- Compensating a manager with reduced rent: Chapter 6
- Highlighting rent rules in a move-in letter to new tenants and collecting the first month's rent: Chapter 7
- Cotenants' obligations for rent: Chapter 8
- Rent withholding and other tenant options when a landlord fails to maintain the premises in good condition: Chapter 9
- Tenants' obligation to pay rent when breaking a lease: Chapter 14
- Accepting rent after a 30-day notice is given: Chapter 14
- Evicting a tenant for nonpayment of rent: Chapter 17
- State rent rules: Appendix A.

How Much Can You Charge?

In most states, the law doesn't limit how much rent you can charge; you are free to charge what the market will bear. However, in some cities and counties, rent control ordinances do closely govern how much rent a landlord can legally charge. (Rent control is discussed below.) And in Connecticut, which does not have rent control, tenants may challenge a rent that they believe is excessive. (Conn. Gen. Stat. Ann. §§ 7-148B and following.)

If you aren't subject to rent control, it's up to you to determine how much your rental unit is worth. To do this, check rents of comparable properties in your area, and visit a few places that sound similar to yours. Local property management companies, real estate offices that handle rental property, and Craigslist can also provide useful information. In addition, local apartment associations—or other landlords you meet at association functions—are a good source of pricing information.

Many wise landlords choose to charge just slightly less than the going rate as part of a policy designed to find and keep excellent tenants. As with any business arrangement, it usually pays in the long run to have your tenants feel they are getting a good deal. In exchange, you hope the tenants will be responsive to your business needs. This doesn't always work, of course, but tenants who feel their rent is fair are less likely to complain over trifling matters and more likely to stay for an extended period.

Rent Control

 SKIP AHEAD
Unless you own property in California; the District of Columbia; Takoma Park, Maryland; Newark, New Jersey; or New York, you aren't affected by rent control and you can skip this section.

Communities in only five states—California, the District of Columbia, Maryland, New Jersey, and

New York—have laws that limit the amount of rent landlords may charge. Typically, only a few cities or counties in each state have enacted local rent control ordinances (also called rent stabilization, maximum rent regulation, or a similar term), but often these are some of the state's largest cities—for example, San Francisco, Los Angeles, New York City, and Newark all have some form of rent control.

RESOURCE

California rent control. California landlords should consult *The California Landlord's Law Book: Rights & Responsibilities*, by David Brown, Janet Portman, and Nils Rosenquest; and *The California Landlord's Law Book: Evictions*, by David Brown and Nils Rosenquest. These books are published by Nolo and are available at bookstores and public libraries. They may also be ordered directly from Nolo's website, www.nolo.com, or by calling 800-728-3555.

The Rent Control Board

In most cities, rent control rests in the hands of a rent control board of five to ten people. Board members often decide annual rent increases, fines, and other important issues. (In many areas, the law itself limits how and when the rent may be raised.)

The actual rent control ordinance is a product of the city council or county board of supervisors. But the rent control board is in charge of interpreting the provisions of the law, which can give the board significant power over landlords and tenants.

Rent control laws commonly regulate much more than rent. For example, owners of rent-controlled properties must follow specific eviction procedures. Because local ordinances are often quite complicated and vary widely, this book cannot provide details on each city's program. Instead, we provide a general description of what rent control ordinances cover.

If you own rental property in a city that has rent control, you should always have a current copy of the ordinance and any regulations interpreting it. And be sure to keep up to date; cities change their rent control laws frequently, and court decisions also affect them. It's a good idea to subscribe to publications of the local property owners' association, and pay attention to local politics to keep abreast of changes in your rent control ordinance and court decisions that may affect you.

CAUTION

Know the law or pay the price. Local governments typically levy fines—sometimes heavy ones—for rent control violations. Violation of a rent control law may also give a tenant a legal ground on which to win an eviction lawsuit. Depending on the circumstances, tenants may also be able to sue you.

Property Subject to Rent Control

Not all rental housing within a rent-controlled city is subject to rent control. Generally, new buildings as well as owner-occupied buildings with two (or sometimes even three or four) units or fewer are exempt from rent control ordinances. Some cities also exempt rentals in single-family houses and luxury units that rent for more than a certain amount.

Limits on Rent

Rent control ordinances typically set a base rent for each rental unit that takes into account several different factors, including the rent that was charged before rent control took effect, operation and upkeep expenses, inflation, and housing supply and demand. The ordinances allow the base rent to be increased under certain circumstances or at certain times.

Rent Increases for Existing Tenants

Most local ordinances build in some mechanism for rent increases. Here are just a few common examples:

Annual increases. Some ordinances automatically allow a specific percentage rent increase each year. The amount of the increase may be set by the rent control board or may be a fixed percentage or a percentage tied to a local or national consumer price index.

Increased expenses. Some rent control boards have the power to adjust rents of individual units based on certain cost factors, such as increased taxes or maintenance or capital improvements. The landlord may need to request permission from the rent control board before upping the rent.

The tenant's consent. In some cities, landlords may increase rent under certain circumstances only if the tenants voluntarily agree to the increase—or don't protest it.

A word of caution: Even if you are otherwise entitled to raise the rent under the terms of your rent control ordinance, the rent board may be able to deny you permission if you haven't adequately repaired and maintained your rental units.

Where to Get Information About Rent Control

- **Your city rent control board.** It can supply you with a copy of the current local ordinance, and possibly also with a brochure explaining the ordinance.
- **Your state or local apartment owners' association.** Virtually every city with a rent control ordinance has an active property owners' association. The New York City Rent Stabilization Association, for example, gives members information and help on rent matters and tenant screening.
- **Local attorneys who specialize in landlord-tenant law.** Check the yellow pages, search online, or ask another landlord. Chapter 18 discusses how to find and work with a lawyer.

Rent Increases When a Tenant Moves

In most rent control areas, landlords may raise rent—either as much as they want or by a specified percentage—when a tenant moves out (and a new one moves in) or when a tenant renews a lease. This feature, called "vacancy decontrol," "vacancy rent ceiling adjustment," or a similar term, is built into many local ordinances.

In practice, it means that rent control applies to a particular rental unit only as long as a particular tenant (or tenants) stays there. If that tenant voluntarily leaves or, in some cities, is evicted for a legal or "just" cause (discussed below), the rental unit is subject to rent control again after the new (and presumably higher) rent is established.

> **EXAMPLE:** Marla has lived in Edward's apartment building for seven years. During that time, Edward has been allowed to raise the rent only by the modest amount authorized by the local rent board each year. Meanwhile, the market value of the apartment has gone up significantly. When Marla finally moves out, Edward is free to charge the next tenant the market rate. But once set, that tenant's rent will also be subject to the rent control rules, and Edward will again be limited to small annual increases as approved by the rent control board.

In some cities, no rent increase is allowed at all, even when a tenant moves out. Check your ordinance.

Legal or "Just Cause" Evictions

For rent control to work—especially if the ordinance allows rents to rise when a tenant leaves—it must place some restrictions on tenancy terminations. Otherwise, landlords who wanted to create a vacancy so they could raise the rent would be free to throw out tenants, undermining the whole system. Recognizing this, many local ordinances require landlords to have a legal or just cause—that is, a good reason—to terminate and, if the tenant doesn't leave on his own, evict.

Just cause is usually limited to a few reasons provided in the ordinance. If you really need to evict a tenant, you should have no problem finding your reason on the approved list. Here are a few typical examples of a legal or just cause to evict a tenant:

- The tenant violates a significant term of the lease or rental agreement—for example, by failing to pay rent or causing substantial damage to the premises. However, in many situations, you're legally required to first give the tenant a chance to correct the problem.

- The landlord wants to move into the rental unit or give it to an immediate family member.
- The landlord wants to substantially remodel the property, which requires the tenant to move out.
- The tenant creates a nuisance—for example, by repeatedly disturbing other tenants or engaging in illegal activity, such as drug dealing, on the premises.

Rent control ordinances often affect renewals as well as terminations midway through the rental term. Unless you can point to a just cause for tossing a tenant out, you may need to renew a lease or rental agreement under the same terms and conditions.

Your Right to Go Out of Business

It's not uncommon for landlords in rent-controlled cities to decide to get out of the residential rental business entirely. To do so, however, they must evict tenants, who will protest that the eviction violates the rent control ordinance.

No rent control ordinance can force you to continue with your business against your will. However, if you withdraw rental units from the market, you must typically meet strict standards regarding the necessity of doing so. Rent control boards do not want landlords to use going out of business as a ruse for evicting long-term tenants, only to start up again with a fresh batch of tenants whose rents will invariably be substantially higher.

If you decide to go out of business and must evict tenants, check your ordinance carefully. It may require you to give tenants a lengthy notice period or offer tenants relocation assistance, and may impose a minimum time period during which you may not resume business. If you own multiple units, the rent control ordinance may prohibit you from withdrawing more than a specified number of units; and if the premises are torn down and new units constructed, the ordinance may insist that you offer former tenants a right of first refusal. State law may also address these issues. Contact your local landlords' association or rent control board for details on the specifics.

Registration of Rental Units

Some rent control ordinances require landlords to register their properties with the local rent control agency. This allows the rent board to keep track of the city's rental units, and the registration fees provide operating funds.

Deposits and Notice Requirements

Rent control ordinances may impose rules regarding security deposits or interest payments and the type of notice you must give tenants when you want to raise the rent or terminate a tenancy. The requirements of these local ordinances are in addition to any state law requirements. For example, state law may require a 30-day notice for a rent increase. A local rent control law might also require the notice to tell the tenant that the rent control board can verify that the new rental amount is legal under the ordinance.

When Rent Is Due

Most leases and rental agreements, including the ones in this book, call for rent to be paid monthly, in advance, on the first day of the month. See Clause 5 of the form agreements in Chapter 2.

First Day, Last Day, or In-Between?

The first of the month is a customary and convenient due date for rent, at least in part because many tenants get their paychecks on the last workday of the month. Also, the approach of a new month can, in itself, help remind people to pay monthly bills due on the first.

It is perfectly legal to require rent to be paid on a different day of the month, and may make sense if the tenant is paid at odd times. Some landlords make the rent payable each month on the date the tenant first moved in. Generally, it's easier to prorate rent for a short first month and then require that rent be paid on the first of the next month. But if you have only a few tenants, and don't mind having tenants paying you on different days of the month, it makes no legal difference.

Special rules for tenants who receive public assistance. Some states make special provisions for rent due dates for public assistance recipients. Public assistance recipients in Hawaii, for example, tenants who receive public assistance may change the rent due date to within three business days (excluding Saturdays, Sundays, and holidays) after the mailing date of public assistance checks. They need to make a one-time prorated payment to cover the period between the original due date in the rental agreement and a newly established due date.

Whatever rent due date you choose, be sure to put it in your lease or rental agreement. If you don't, state law may do it for you. In several states, for month-to-month rental agreements, rent is due in equal monthly installments at the beginning of each month, unless otherwise agreed.

In a few states, however, rent is not due until the end of the term unless the lease or rental agreement says otherwise. You would probably never deliberately allow a tenant who moved in on the first day of the month to wait to pay rent until the 31st. Nor would you want tenants to continue to pay at the end of the month. By specifying that rent is due on the first of the month in your lease or rental agreement, you won't have to worry.

Collecting Rent More Than Once a Month

If you wish, you and the tenant can agree that the rent be paid twice a month, each week, or on whatever schedule suits you. The most common variation on the standard monthly payment arrangement is having rent paid twice a month. This is a particularly good idea if you have tenants who have relatively low-paying jobs and get paid twice a month, because they may have difficulty saving the needed portion of their midmonth check until the first of the month.

When the Due Date Falls on a Weekend or Holiday

The lease and rental agreements in this book state that when the rent due date falls on a weekend day or legal holiday, the tenant must pay it by the next business day. See Clause 5 of the form agreements in Chapter 2.

This is legally required in some states; it is the general rule in most. If you want to insist that the tenant always get the rent check to you on the first, no matter what, you'll have to check the law in your state to make sure it's allowed. It's probably not worth the trouble.

Grace Periods for Late Rent

Lots of tenants are absolutely convinced that if rent is due on the first, but they pay by the fifth (or sometimes the seventh or even the tenth) of the month, they have legally paid their rent on time because they are within a legal grace period. This is simply not true. It is your legal right to insist that rent be paid on the day it is due, and you should use your lease or rental agreement and move-in letter to disabuse tenants of this bogus notion.

In practice, many landlords do not get upset about late rent or charge a late fee (discussed below) until the rent is a few days past due. And your state law may require you to give tenants a few days to come up with the rent before you can send a termination notice. Even so, your best approach is to consistently stress to tenants that rent must be paid on the due date.

> CAUTION
>
> **If you wait more than three or five days to collect your rent, you are running your business unwisely, and just extending the time a nonpaying tenant can stay.** Be firm, but fair. Any other policy will get you into a morass of special cases and exceptions and will cost you a bundle in the long run. If you allow exceptions only in extreme circumstances, tenants will learn not to try and sell you sob stories.

Evictions for Nonpayment of Rent

Failure to pay rent on time is by far the most common reason landlords go to court and evict tenants. First, however, a landlord must give the tenant a written notice, demanding that the tenant either pay within a few days or move out. How long the tenant is allowed to stay depends on state law; in most places, it's about three to five days.

In most instances, the tenant who receives this kind of notice pays up, and that's the end of it. But if the tenant doesn't pay the rent (or move), you can file an eviction lawsuit. Chapter 17 explains the kinds of termination notices that landlords must use when tenants are behind on the rent, and includes a brief summary of evictions. Appendix A includes details on state laws on termination for nonpayment of rent.

If you find yourself delivering too many pay-the-rent-or-leave notices to a particular tenant, you may want to end the tenancy—even if the tenant always comes up with the rent at the last minute.

Where and How Rent Is Due

You should specify in your lease or rental agreement where the tenant should pay the rent and how you want it paid—for example, by check or money order only. See Clause 5 of the form agreements in Chapter 2.

! CAUTION
Landlords should take special care to inform tenants of where and how rent is paid. Many states require landlords to notify tenants (either in a separate writing or in a written rental agreement or lease) of the name and street address of the owner or manager responsible for collection of rent, how rent is to be paid, and who is available for services of notices.

Where Rent Must Be Paid

You have several options for where the tenant pays you rent.

By mail. Allowing tenants to mail you the rent check is the most common method of payment, by a long shot. It's pretty convenient for everyone, and you can make it even easier by giving tenants pre-addressed (and stamped, if you're feeling generous) envelopes.

At home. You can send someone to each unit, every month, to pick up the rent. But this more old-fashioned way of collecting the rent isn't well-suited to modern life, when most people aren't at home during the day.

At your office. Requiring the rent to be paid personally at your place of business or manager's office is feasible (and, in some states, legal) only if you have an on-site office. Asking tenants to drive across town is both unreasonable and counter-productive, because inevitably some of them just won't get around to it. This approach does have certain advantages. It makes the tenant responsible for getting the rent to you at a certain time or place, and avoids issues such as whether or not a rent check was lost or delayed in the mail. It also guarantees at least a bit of personal contact with your tenants, and a chance to air little problems before they become big ones.

If your lease or rental agreement doesn't specify where you want tenants to pay you rent, state law may decide. Under statutes in several states rent is payable at the dwelling unit unless otherwise agreed. This is yet another reason to specify in your rental agreement or lease that your tenant may pay by check or at your on-site office.

Form of Rent Payment

You should also specify in your lease or rental agreement how rent must be paid: by cash, check, credit card, or money order. See Clause 5 of the form agreements in Chapter 2.

For most landlords, rental checks are routine. You can eliminate the time spent mailing or walking a check to the bank by sending it right to the bank electronically. If a tenant doesn't have a checking account or has bounced too many checks, you may want to require a certified check or money order.

You should never accept postdated checks. The most obvious reason is that the check may never be good. You have absolutely no assurance that necessary funds will ever be deposited in the account. In addition, a postdated check may, legally, be considered a "note" promising to pay on a certain date. In some states, if you accept such a note (check), you have no right to bring an eviction action while the note is pending. Far better to tell the tenant that rent must be paid in full on time and to give the tenant a late notice if it isn't.

Easy Ways to Pay the Rent

More and more owners, especially those with large numbers of rental units, are looking for ways to ensure that rent payments are quick and reliable. Here are two common methods.

Online banking. Tenants with bank accounts that they trust will always have enough money on deposit to be able to handle the rent, may be willing to set up an automatic transfer. On the day they specify, the rent funds are electronically transferred to your account. Every major bank offers this service, some for a small fee.

Credit card. If you have enough tenants to make it worthwhile, explore the option of accepting credit cards. You must pay a fee—a percentage of the amount charged—for the privilege, but the cost may be justified if it results in more on-time payments and less hassle for you and your tenants. Keep in mind that you'll need to have someone in your on-site office to process the credit card payments and give tenants receipts. And if your tenant population is affluent enough, consider requiring automatic credit card debits.

CAUTION
Don't accept cash unless you have no choice. You are a likely target for robbery if word gets out that you are taking in large amounts of cash once or twice a month. And if you accept cash knowing that the tenant earned it from an illegal act, such as drug dealing, the government could seize it from you under federal and state forfeiture laws. If you do accept cash, be sure to provide a written, dated receipt stating the tenant's name and rental unit and the amount of rent and time period for which rent is paid. Such a receipt is required by law in a few states, and it's a good idea everywhere.

Changing Where and How Rent Is Due

If you've been burned by bounced checks from a particular tenant, you may want to decree that, from now on, you'll accept nothing less than a certified check or money order, and that rent may be paid only during certain hours at the manager's office.

Be careful. It may be illegal to suddenly change your terms for payment of rent without proper notice to the tenant—unless you are simply enforcing an existing term. For example, if your rental agreement states that you accept only money orders, you are on solid ground when you tell a check-bouncing tenant that you'll no longer accept her checks, and that your previous practice of doing so was merely an accommodation not required under the rental agreement.

If, however, your lease or rental agreement doesn't say where and how rent is to be paid, your past practice may legally control how rent is paid until you properly notify the tenant of a change. If you want to require tenants to pay rent at your office, for example, you must formally change a month-to-month rental agreement, typically with a written 30-day notice. If you rent under a lease, you will have to wait until the lease runs out.

Late Charges and Discounts for Early Payments

If you're faced with a tenant who hasn't paid rent on the due date, you probably don't want to immediately hand out a formal notice telling the tenant to pay the rent or leave. After all, it's not going to do anything positive for your relationship with the tenant, who may have just forgotten to drop the check in a mailbox. But how else can you motivate tenants to pay rent on time?

A fairly common and sensible practice is to charge a reasonable late fee and highlight your late fee policy in your lease or rental agreement and move-in letter to new tenants. See Clause 6 of the form agreements in Chapter 2.

Some states have statutes that put precise limits on late fees (see the "Late Fees" column in the "State Rent Rules" chart in Appendix A). But even if your state doesn't have specific rules, you are still bound by general legal principles that prohibit unreasonably high fees. Courts in some states have ruled that contracts that provide for unreasonably high late charges are not enforceable—which means that if a tenant fights you in court (either in an eviction lawsuit or a separate case brought by the tenant), you could lose. And, obviously, excessive late fees generate tenant hostility, anyway.

 RENT CONTROL

Some rent control ordinances also regulate late fees. Check any rent control ordinances applicable to your properties.

Unless your state imposes more specific statutory rules on late fees, you should be on safe ground if you adhere to these principles.

The late fee should not apply until at least three to five days after the due date. Imposing a stiff late charge if the rent is only one or two days late may not be upheld in court.

The total late charge should not exceed 4%–5% of the rent. That's $30 to $38 on a $750-per-month rental. Even in states with no statutory limits, a higher late charge, such as 10%, might not be upheld in court.

If the late fee increases each day the rent is late, it should be moderate and have an upper limit. A late charge that increases without limit each day could be considered interest charged at an illegal ("usurious") rate. State laws set the maximum allowable rate of interest, typically less than 10%, that may be charged for a debt. (Ten dollars a day on a $1,000-per-month rent is 3,650% annual interest.) A more acceptable late charge would be $10 for the first day rent is late, plus $5 for each additional day, up to a maximum of 5% of the rental amount.

Don't try to disguise excessive late charges by giving a "discount" for early payment. For one thing, this kind of "discount" is illegal in some states. One landlord we know concluded he couldn't get away with charging a $100 late charge on an $850 rent payment, so, instead, he designed a rental agreement calling for a rent of $950 with a $100 discount if the rent was not more than three days late. Ingenious as this ploy sounds, it is unlikely to stand up in court, unless the discount for timely payment is very modest. Giving a relatively large discount is in effect the same as charging an excessive late fee, and a judge is likely to see it as such.

Anyway, fooling around with late charges is wasted energy. If you want more rent for your unit, raise the rent (unless you live in a rent control area). If you are concerned about tenants paying on time—and who isn't?—put your energy into choosing responsible tenants.

If you have a tenant with a month-to-month tenancy who drives you nuts with late rent payments, and a reasonable late charge doesn't resolve the situation, terminate the tenancy with the appropriate notice.

Returned Check Charges

It's legal to charge the tenant an extra fee if a rent check bounces (see Clause 7 of the form agreements in Chapter 2). If you're having a lot of trouble with bounced checks, you may want to change your policy to accept only money orders for rent.

Most states regulate the amount you can charge for a bounced check. $25 to $40 is common for the first check; some states allow escalating charges for subsequent checks. Some states allow you to charge the stated flat fee or a specific percent of the check's amount, whichever is greater. Check with your state's consumer protection bureau or agency to learn the rule that applies to you.

If your state does not impose limits on bounced check fees, be sure that you do not impose an unreasonably high fee. Like late charges, bounced check charges must be reasonable. You should charge no more than the amount your bank charges you for a returned check charge, probably $10 to $20 per returned item, plus a few dollars for your trouble.

It is a poor idea to let your bank redeposit rent checks that bounce. Instead, tell the bank to return bad checks to you immediately. Getting a bounced check back quickly alerts you to the fact that the rent is unpaid much sooner than if the check is resubmitted and returned for nonpayment a second time. You can use this time to ask the tenant to make the check good immediately. If the tenant doesn't come through, you can promptly serve the necessary paperwork to end the tenancy.

If a tenant habitually gives you bad checks, give the tenant a notice demanding that he pay the rent or move. If the tenant doesn't make the check good by the deadline, you can start eviction proceedings.

Partial or Delayed Rent Payments

On occasion, a tenant suffering a temporary financial setback will offer something less than the full month's rent, with a promise to catch up as the month proceeds, or at the first of the next month. Although generally this is a bad business practice, you may nevertheless wish to make an exception where the tenant's financial problems truly appear to be temporary and you have known the person for a long time.

If you do give a tenant a little more time to pay some or all of the rent, establish a schedule, in writing, for when the rent will be paid. Then monitor the situation carefully. Otherwise, the tenant may try to delay payment indefinitely, or make such small and infrequent payments that the account is never brought current. A signed agreement—say for a one-week extension—lets both you and the tenant know what's expected. If you give the tenant two weeks to catch up and she doesn't, the written agreement precludes any argument that you had really said "two to three weeks." A sample Agreement for Delayed or Partial Rent Payments is shown below and the Nolo website includes a downloadable copy. See Appendix B for the link to the forms in this book.

If the tenant does not pay the rest of the rent when promised, you can, and should, follow through with the appropriate steps to terminate the tenancy.

Raising the Rent

Except in cities with rent control, your freedom to raise rent depends primarily on whether the tenant has a lease or a month-to-month rental agreement.

When You Can Raise Rent

For the most part, a lease fixes the terms of tenancy for the length of the lease. You can't change the terms of the lease until the end of the lease period unless the lease itself allows it or the tenant agrees. When the lease expires, you can present the tenant with a new lease that has a higher rent or other changed terms. It's always safest to give tenants at least a month or two notice of any rent increase before negotiating a new lease.

In contrast, you can raise the rent in a periodic tenancy just by giving the tenant proper written notice, typically 30 days for a month-to-month tenancy. (If you collect rent every 15 days, you probably have to give your tenant only 15 days' notice.) State law may override these general rules, however. In a few states, landlords must provide

Agreement for Delayed or Partial Rent Payments

This Agreement is made between ___Betty Wong___

_____ [Tenant(s)]

and __John Lewis___ , [Landlord/Manager].

1. ___Betty Wong___

   _____ [Tenant(s)]

   has/have paid __one-half of her $1,000 rent for apartment #2 at 111 Billy St.,__

   ___Phoenix, Arizona___

   on ___March 1, 20xx___ . The rent due date is __March 1, 20xx__ .

2. ___John Lewis___ [Landlord/Manager]

   agrees to accept all the remainder of the rent on or before _____March 15, 20xx_____ ,

   and to hold off on any legal proceeding to evict _____Betty Wong_____

   _____ [Tenant(s)] until that date.

___John Lewis___   ___March 2, 20xx___
Landlord/Manager   Date

___Betty Wong___   ___March 2, 20xx___
Tenant   Date

_____   _____
Tenant   Date

_____   _____
Tenant   Date

45 or 60 days' notice to raise the rent for a month-to-month tenancy. See "State Rules on Notice Required to Change or Terminate a Month-to-Month Tenancy" in Appendix A and the Chapter 14 discussion of changing terms during the tenancy. You'll need to consult your state statutes for the specific information you must provide in a rent increase notice, how you must deliver it to the tenant, and any rights tenants have to dispute rent increases.

How Much Can You Raise the Rent?

In areas without rent control, there is no limit on the amount you can increase the rent of a month-to-month or other periodic tenant. Also, as noted in "How Much Can You Charge?" above, tenants in Connecticut can challenge rent increases they feel are excessive. Similarly, there is no restriction on the period of time between rent increases. You can legally raise the rent as much and as often as good business dictates. Of course, common sense should tell you that if your tenants think your increases are unfair, you may end up with vacant units or a hostile group of tenants looking for ways to make you miserable. As a courtesy, you may wish to tell your tenants of the rent increase personally, perhaps explaining the reasons—although reasons aren't legally necessary, except in areas covered by rent control.

Avoiding Tenant Charges of Retaliation or Discrimination

You can't legally raise a tenant's rent as retaliation—for example, in response to a legitimate complaint or rent-withholding action—or in a discriminatory manner. The laws in many states actually presume retaliation if you increase rent soon—typically, within three to six months—after a tenant's complaint of defective conditions. See the Chapter 16 discussion of general ways to avoid tenant charges of retaliation. "State Laws Prohibiting Landlord Retaliation" in Appendix A lists state-by-state details.

One way to protect yourself from charges that ordinary rent increases are retaliatory or discriminatory is to adopt a sensible rent increase policy and stick to it.

For example, many landlords raise rent once a year in an amount that more or less reflects the increase in the Consumer Price Index. Other landlords use a more complicated formula that takes into account other rents in the area, as well as such factors as increased costs of maintenance or rehabilitation. They make sure to inform their tenants about the rent increase in advance and apply the increase uniformly to all their tenants. Usually, this protects the landlord against any claim of a retaliatory rent increase by a tenant who has coincidentally made a legitimate complaint about the condition of the premises.

> **EXAMPLE:** Lois owns two multiunit complexes. In one of them, she raises rents uniformly, at the same time, for all tenants. In the other apartment building, where she fears tenants hit with rent increases all at once will organize and generate unrest, Lois does things differently: She raises each tenant's rent in accordance with the Consumer Price Index on the yearly anniversary of the date each tenant moved in. Either way, Lois is safe from being judged to have retaliatorily increased rents, even if a rent increase to a particular tenant follows on the heels of a complaint.

Of course, any rent increase given to a tenant who has made a complaint should be reasonable—in relation to the previous rent, what you charge other similarly situated tenants, and rents for comparable property in the area—or you are asking for legal trouble.

> **EXAMPLE:** Lonnie has no organized plan for increasing rents in his 20-unit building, but simply raises them when he needs money. On November 1, he raises the rent for one of his tenants, Teresa, without remembering her recent complaint about her heater. Teresa is the only one to receive a rent increase in November. She has a strong retaliatory rent increase case against Lonnie, simply because an increase that seemed to single her out coincided with her exercise of a legal right. If the increase made her rent higher than those for comparable units in the building, she will have an even better case.

Security Deposits

Most landlords quite sensibly ask for a security deposit before entrusting hundreds of thousands of dollars' worth of real estate to a tenant. But it's easy to get into legal trouble over deposits, because they are strictly regulated by state law, and sometimes also by city ordinance.

The law of most states dictates how large a deposit you can require, how you can use it, when you must return it, and more. Many states require you to put deposits in a separate account and pay interest on them. You cannot escape these requirements by putting different terms in a lease or rental agreement. You may face substantial financial penalties for violating state laws on security deposits.

This chapter explains how to set up a clear, fair system of setting, collecting, and holding deposits. It may exceed the minimum legal requirements affecting your property, but it will ultimately work to your advantage, resulting in easier turnovers, better tenant relations, and fewer legal hassles.

> ### Where to Get More Information on Security Deposits
>
> Start by referring to "State Security Deposit Rules" in Appendix A. If you have any questions of what's allowed in your state, you should get a current copy of your state's security deposit law (statute) or an up-to-date summary from a landlords' association.
>
> In addition, be sure to check local ordinances in all areas where you own property. Cities, particularly those with rent control, may add their own rules on security deposits, such as a limit on the amount you can charge or a requirement that you pay interest on deposits.

CAUTION

This discussion is limited to security deposit _statutes_. Some states do not have statutes on every aspect of security deposits. That doesn't mean that there is no law on the subject. Court decisions (what lawyers call "case law") in your state may set out quite specific requirements

for refundability of deposits, whether they should be held in interest-bearing accounts, and the like. This book doesn't cover all this case law, but you may need to check it out yourself. To find out whether courts in your state have made decisions you need to be aware of, contact your state or local property owners' association or do some legal research on your own.

 RELATED TOPIC
Related topics covered in this book include:
- Charging prospective tenants' credit check fees, finder's fees, or holding deposits: Chapter 1
- Writing clear lease and rental agreement provisions on security deposits: Chapter 2
- Highlighting security deposit rules and procedures in move-in and move-out letters to the tenant: Chapters 7 and 15
- Returning deposits and deducting for cleaning, damage, and unpaid rent; how to handle legal disputes involving deposits: Chapter 15
- State Security Deposit Rules: Appendix A.

Purpose and Use of Security Deposits

All states allow you to collect a security deposit when a tenant moves in and hold it until the tenant leaves. The general purpose of a security deposit is to assure that a tenant pays rent when due and keeps the rental unit in good condition. Rent you collect in advance for the first month is not considered part of the security deposit.

State laws typically control the amount you can charge and how and when you must return security deposits. When a tenant moves out, you will have a set amount of time (usually from 14 to 30 days, depending on the state) to either return the tenant's entire deposit or provide an itemized statement of deductions and refund any deposit balance.

Although state laws vary, you can generally withhold all or part of the deposit to pay for:
- unpaid rent
- repairing damage to the premises (except for "ordinary wear and tear") caused by the tenant, a family member, or a guest

- cleaning necessary to restore the rental unit to its level of cleanliness at the beginning of the tenancy (taking into consideration "ordinary wear and tear"), or
- restoring or replacing rental unit property taken by the tenant.

States typically also allow you to use a deposit to cover the tenant's obligations under the lease or rental agreement, which may include payment of utility charges.

You don't necessarily need to wait until a tenant moves out to tap into their security deposit. You may, for example, use some of the tenant's security deposit during the tenancy—for example, because the tenant broke something and didn't fix it or pay for it. In this case, you should require the tenant to replenish the security deposit.

> **EXAMPLE:** Millie pays her landlord Maury a $1,000 security deposit when she moves in. Six months later, Millie goes on vacation, leaving the water running. By the time Maury is notified, the overflow has damaged the paint on the ceiling below. Maury repaints the ceiling at a cost of $250, taking the money out of Millie's security deposit. Maury is entitled to ask Millie to replace that money, so that her deposit remains $1,000.

To protect yourself and avoid misunderstandings with tenants, make sure your lease or rental agreement is clear on the use of security deposits and the tenant's obligations. See Clause 8 of the form agreements in Chapter 2.

> **TIP**
> **A few states exempt some landlords from security deposit rules.** For details, see the "State Security Deposit Rules" chart in Appendix A.

Dollar Limits on Deposits

Many states limit the amount you can collect as a deposit to an amount equal to one or two months of rent. And the limit within each state sometimes varies depending on various factors such as:

- age of the tenant (senior citizens may have a lower deposit ceiling)
- whether the rental unit is furnished
- whether you have a month-to-month rental agreement or a long-term lease, and
- whether the tenant has a pet or waterbed.

For details, see "State Security Deposit Rules," in Appendix A.

In some states, the rent you collect in advance for the last month is not considered part of the security deposit limit, while in others it is.

> **CAUTION**
> **An inconsistent security deposit policy is an invitation to a lawsuit.** Even if your motives are good—for example, you require a smaller deposit from a student tenant—you risk a charge of illegal discrimination by other tenants who did not get the same break.

How Much Deposit Should You Charge?

Normally, the best advice is to charge as much as the market will bear, within any legal limits. The more the tenant has at stake, the better the chance your property will be respected. And, the larger the deposit, the more financial protection you will have if a tenant leaves owing you rent.

The market, however, often keeps the practical limit on deposits lower than the maximum allowed by law. Your common sense and your business sense need to work together in setting security deposits. Here are a number of considerations to keep in mind:

- **Charge the full limit in high-risk situations—** for example, where there's a lot of tenant turnover, if the tenant has a pet and you're concerned about damage, or if the tenant's credit is shaky and you're worried about unpaid rent.
- **Consider the psychological advantage of a higher rent rather than a high deposit.** Many tenants would rather pay a slightly higher rent than an enormous deposit. Also, many acceptable,

solvent tenants have a hard time coming up with a hefty deposit, especially if they are still in a rental and are awaiting the return of a previous security deposit. And remember, unlike the security deposit, the extra rent is not refundable.

> **EXAMPLE:** Lenora rents out a three-bedroom furnished house in San Francisco for $6,000 a month. Because total deposits on furnished property in California can legally be three times the monthly rent, Lenora could charge up to $18,000. This is in addition to the first month's rent of $6,000 that Lenora can (and should) insist on before turning the property over to a tenant. But, realistically, Lenora would probably have difficulty finding a tenant if she insisted on receiving an $18,000 deposit plus the first month's rent, for a total of $24,000. So she decides to charge only one month's rent for the deposit but to increase the monthly rent. That gives Lenora the protection she feels she needs without imposing an enormous initial financial burden on her tenants.

- **Single-family homes call for a bigger deposit.** Unlike multiunit residences, where close-by neighbors or a manager can spot, report, and quickly stop any destruction of the premises, the single-family home is somewhat of an island. The condition of the interior and even the exterior may be hard to assess. And, of course, the cost of repairing damage to a house is likely to be higher than for an apartment. Unless you live next door or can frequently check the condition of a single-family rental, a substantial security deposit is a good idea.
- **Gain a marketing advantage by allowing a deposit to be paid in installments.** If rentals are plentiful in your area, with comparable units renting at about the same price, you might give yourself a competitive edge by allowing the tenant to pay the deposit in several installments over a few months, rather than one lump sum.

 TIP

If allowed under state law, require renters' insurance as an alternative to a high security deposit. If you're worried about damage but don't think you can raise the deposit any higher, require renters' insurance. Chapter 2 contains an optional clause that you add to your lease or rental agreement requiring the tenant to maintain renters' insurance, and explains the legal limitations that may apply in your state or locality. While you're at it, evaluate your own insurance policy to make sure it is adequate. If the tenant's security deposit is inadequate to cover any damage and there is no renters' insurance (or it won't cover the loss), you may be able to collect from your own carrier.

Last Month's Rent

It's a common—but often unwise—practice to collect a sum of money called "last month's rent" from a tenant who's moving in. Landlords tend to treat this money as just another security deposit, and use it to cover not only the last month's rent but also other expenses such as repairs or cleaning.

Problems can arise when:

- you try to use the last month's rent to cover repairs or cleaning, or
- the rent has gone up during the tenancy— and you want to top off the last month's rent.

We'll look at these situations below.

Applying Last Month's Rent to Damage or Cleaning

If you collect a sum of money labeled last month's rent and your tenant is leaving (voluntarily or involuntarily), chances are that he will not write a rent check for the last month. After all, he's already paid for that last month, right? Surprisingly, many tenants do pay for the last month anyway, often forgetting that they have prepaid. What happens to that last month's rent?

Ideally, the tenant will leave the place clean and in good repair, enabling you to refund the entire last month's rent and all or most of the tenant's security deposit. But if the tenant leaves the place a mess, most states allow you to treat "last month's rent" as part of the security deposit and use all or part of it for cleaning or to repair or replace damaged items.

> **EXAMPLE:** Katie required her tenant Joe to pay a security deposit of one month's rent, plus last month's rent. Her state law allowed a landlord to use all advance deposits to cover a tenant's unpaid rent or damage, regardless of what the landlord called the deposit. When Joe moved out, he didn't owe any back rent, but he left his apartment a shambles. Katie was entitled to use the entire deposit, including that labeled last month's rent, to cover the damage.

A few states restrict the use of money labeled as "last month's rent" to its stated purpose: the rent for the last month of your occupancy. In these states, if you use any of the last month's rent to repair the cabinet the tenant broke, you're violating the law.

> **EXAMPLE:** Mike collected a security deposit of one month's rent, plus last month's rent, from his tenant Amy. Mike's state required that landlords use money collected for the last month as last month's rent only, not for cleaning or repairs. When Amy moved out, she didn't owe any rent but she, too, left her apartment a mess. Mike had to refund Amy's last month's rent and, when the remaining security deposit proved too little to cover the damage Amy had caused, Mike had to sue Amy in small claims court for the excess.

In general, it's a bad idea to call any part of the deposit "last month's rent." Why? Because if your state restricts your use of the money, you've unnecessarily hobbled yourself. And if your state considers last month's rent part of the security deposit, you haven't gained anything. You may have even put yourself at a disadvantage, because you've given the tenant the impression that the last month's rent is taken care of. You would be better off if the tenant paid the last month's rent when it came due, leaving the entire security deposit available to cover cleaning and repairs.

> **EXAMPLE 1:** Fernando rents out a $600-per-month apartment in a state where the security deposit limit is two months' rent. Fernando charged his tenant, Liz, a total deposit of $1,200, calling $600 a security deposit and $600 last month's rent. Liz used this last month's rent for the last month when she gave her notice to Fernando. This left Fernando with the $600 security deposit. Unfortunately, when Liz moved out, she left $700 worth of damages, sticking Fernando with a $100 loss.

> **EXAMPLE 2:** Learning something from this unhappy experience, Fernando charged his next tenant a simple $1,200 security deposit, not limiting any part of it to last month's rent. This time, when the tenant moved out, after paying his last month's rent as legally required, the whole $1,200 was available to cover the cost of any repairs or cleaning.

How a Rent Increase Affects Last Month's Rent

Avoiding the term "last month's rent" also keeps things simpler if you raise the rent, but not the deposit, before the tenant's last month of occupancy. If you have collected the last month's rent in advance, and the rent at the end of your tenancy is the same as when your tenant moved in, your tenant is paid up. However, if the rent has increased, but you have not asked your tenant to top off the last month's rent, questions arise. Does the tenant owe you for the difference? If so, can you take money from the tenant's security deposit to make it up?

Unfortunately, there are no clear answers. But because landlords in every state are allowed to ask tenants to top off the last month's rent at the time they increase the rent, judges would probably allow you to go after it at the end of the tenancy, too. Whether you get the difference from your security deposit or sue the tenant in small claims court is somewhat academic.

> **EXAMPLE:** When Rose moved in, the rent was $800 a month, and she paid this much in advance as last month's rent, plus an additional $800 security deposit. Over the years the landlord, Artie, has raised the rent

to $1,000. Rose does not pay any rent during the last month of her tenancy, figuring that the $800 she paid up front will cover it. Artie, however, thinks that Rose should pay the $200 difference. Artie and Rose may end up in small claims court fighting over who owes what. They could have avoided the problem by discussing the issue of last month's rent when Rose's tenancy began.

How to Avoid Problems With Last Month's Rent

To minimize confusion and disputes, avoid labeling any part of the security deposit last month's rent and get issues involving last month's rent straight with your tenant at the outset.

Clause 8 of the form agreements in Chapter 2 makes it clear that the tenant may not apply the security deposit to the last month's rent. Even with this type of clause, a tenant who's leaving may ask to use the security deposit for the last month's rent. Chapter 15 discusses how to handle these types of requests.

Interest and Accounts on Deposit

In most states, you don't have to pay tenants interest on deposits or put them in a separate bank account. In other words, you can simply put the money in your personal bank account and use it, as long as you have it available when the tenant moves out.

See "State Security Deposit Rules," in Appendix A, for details on which states have rules regarding interest on and separate accounts for deposits.

Separate Accounts

Several states require you to put security deposits in a separate account, sometimes called a "trust" account, rather than mixing the funds with your personal or business accounts. Some states require landlords to give tenants information on the location of this separate trust account at the start of the tenancy, usually as part of the lease or rental agreement. The

idea is that by isolating these funds, it is more likely that you will have the money available whenever the tenant moves out and becomes entitled to it. In addition, separating these deposits makes it easier to trace them if a tenant claims that they were not handled properly. You are not required to set up separate accounts for every tenant. If you keep one account, be sure to maintain careful records of each tenant's contribution.

Interest

Several states require landlords to pay tenants interest on security deposits. Of course, you may find that it helps your relationship with your tenants to pay interest on deposits even if this is not a legal requirement. It's up to you.

Even among the states that require interest, there are many variations. A few states don't require small landlords to pay interest on deposits. Others allow landlords to keep any interest earned during the early period of the tenancy.

State laws typically establish detailed requirements, including:

- **The interest rate to be paid.** Usually it's a little lower than the bank actually pays, so the landlord's costs and trouble of setting up the account are covered.
- **When interest payments must be made.** The most common laws require payments to be made annually, and also at termination of tenancy.
- **Notification landlords must give tenants as to where and how the security deposit is being held and the rate of interest.** See Clause 8 of the form agreements in Chapter 2 for details on states that require this type of notification.

Chicago, Los Angeles, San Francisco, and several other cities (typically those with rent control) require landlords to pay or credit tenants with interest on security deposits, even if the state law does not impose this duty. A few cities require that the funds be kept in separate interest-bearing accounts.

Nonrefundable Deposits and Fees

In general, state laws are often muddled on the subject of nonrefundable deposits and fees. A few states, such as California, Delaware, Hawaii, Montana, and Oregon, specifically prohibit landlords from charging any fee or deposit that is not refundable. Some states specifically allow landlords to collect a fee that is not refundable—such as for pets or cleaning (see "States That Allow Nonrefundable Fees," below). While most of these states don't require terms to be spelled out in the lease or rental agreement, it's still a good idea to do so, in order to avoid disputes with your tenant.

Generally, it's best to avoid the legal uncertainties and not try to collect any nonrefundable fees from tenants. It's much simpler just to consider the expenses these fees cover as part of your overhead, and figure them into the rent. By avoiding non-refundable fees, you'll prevent a lot of time-consuming disputes with tenants.

If you have a specific concern about a particular tenant—for example, you're afraid a tenant's pet will damage the carpets or furniture—just ask for a higher security deposit. That way, you're covered if the pet causes damage, and, if it doesn't, the tenant won't have to shell out unnecessarily.

Charging a set fee can actually backfire. If you collect $100 for cleaning, for example, but when the tenant moves out the unit needs $200 worth of cleaning, you're stuck. You've already charged for cleaning, and the tenant could make a good argument that you're not entitled to take anything more out of the security deposit for cleaning.

If, despite our advice, you want to charge a nonrefundable fee, check your state's law to find what (if any) kinds of nonrefundable fees are allowed. Then, make sure your lease or rental agreement is clear on the subject.

> **CAUTION**
> **Don't charge a "redecoration fee" if you're already collecting the maximum allowed security deposit.** A judge is likely to view the redecoration fee as an additional, and illegal, security deposit.

States That Allow Nonrefundable Fees

The following states have statutes that permit at least certain types of nonrefundable fees, such as for cleaning or pets:

Arizona	Nevada	Washington
Florida (by custom)	North Carolina	West Virginia
Georgia	Utah	Wyoming

Citations to these statutes are in "State Security Deposit Rules" in Appendix A.

In addition, most states allow landlords to charge prospective tenants a nonrefundable fee for the cost of a credit report and related screening expenses.

In states that have no statute on the subject, the legality of nonrefundable fees and deposits is determined in court. For example, courts in Texas and Michigan have ruled that a landlord and tenant may agree that certain fees will be nonrefundable. (*Holmes v. Canlen Management Corp.*, 542 S.W.2d 199 (1976); *Stutelberg v. Practical Management Co.*, 245 N.W.2d 737 (1976).)

How to Increase Deposits

Especially if you rent to a tenant for many years, you may want to increase the amount of the security deposit. The legality of doing this depends on the situation:

- **Leases.** If you have a fixed-term lease, you may not raise the security deposit during the term of the lease, unless the lease allows it. Security deposits may be increased, however, when the lease is renewed or becomes a month-to-month tenancy.

• **Written rental agreements.** With a month-to-month tenancy, you can increase a security deposit the same way you raise the rent, typically by giving the tenant a written notice 30 days in advance of the change. Of course, you can increase the security deposit without also increasing the rent as long as you don't exceed the maximum legal amount.

EXAMPLE: Jules rents out an apartment for $750 a month in a state that limits security deposits to one month's rent. If he raises the rent to $1,000, the maximum deposit he may collect goes up to $1,000. But the deposit does not go up automatically. To raise the deposit amount, Jules must give the tenant the required notice.

RENT CONTROL
Local rent control ordinances typically restrict your right to raise deposits as well as to raise rents.

Handling Deposits When You Buy or Sell Rental Property

When you sell rental property, what should you do with the deposits you've already collected? After all, when the tenant moves out, she'll be entitled to her deposit back. Who owes her the money? In most states, whoever happens to be the landlord at the time a tenancy ends is legally responsible for complying with state laws requiring the return of security deposits. That means that you may need to hand over the deposits to the new owner. Read your state's statutes carefully as to how this transfer is handled, including any requirements that tenants be notified of the new owner's name, address, and phone number.

If you buy rental property, make sure you know the total dollar amount of security deposits. For a multiunit building, it could be tens of thousands of dollars.

Discrimination

FORMS IN THIS CHAPTER

Chapter 5 includes instructions for and a sample of the following form:

- Verification of Disabled Status

The Nolo website includes a downloadable copy of this form. See Appendix B for the link to the forms in this book.

So that all Americans would have the right to live where they chose, Congress and state legislatures passed laws prohibiting housing discrimination. Most notable of these are the federal Fair Housing Acts, which outlaw discrimination based on race or color, national origin, religion, sex, familial status, or disability. Many states and cities have laws making it illegal to discriminate based on additional factors, such as marital status or sexual orientation. Courts play a role, too, by interpreting and applying antidiscrimination laws. It is safe to say that unless you have a legitimate business reason to reject a prospective tenant (for example, poor credit history), you risk a fair housing complaint and a potentially costly lawsuit.

The discussion in this chapter is intended not only to explain the law, but to steer you away from hidden discrimination traps. It explains:

- legal reasons to turn down prospective tenants, such as a bad credit history or too many people for the size of the rental unit
- protected categories (such as race and religion) identified by federal and state laws prohibiting housing discrimination
- precautions to ensure that managers don't violate housing discrimination laws
- legal penalties for housing discrimination, including tenant lawsuits in state and federal courts, and
- whether your insurance policy is likely to cover the cost of defending a discrimination claim, and the cost of the judgment if you lose the case.

 RELATED TOPIC

Chapter 1 also discusses how to avoid discrimination in advertising your property, accepting applications, and screening potential tenants, as well as how to document why you chose—or rejected—a particular tenant.

Legal Reasons for Rejecting a Rental Applicant

The most important decision you make, save possibly for deciding whether to purchase rental property in the first place, is your choice of tenants. Chapter 1 recommends a system for carefully screening potential tenants in order to select people who will pay rent on time, maintain your property, and not cause you any problems. Here we focus more closely on making sure that your screening process does not precipitate a costly charge of discrimination.

Remember that only certain kinds of discrimination in rental housing are illegal, such as selecting tenants on the basis of religion or race. You are legally free to choose among prospective tenants as long as your decisions are based on valid and objective business criteria, such as the applicant's ability to pay the rent and properly maintain the property. For example, you may legally refuse to rent to prospective tenants with bad credit histories, unsteady employment histories, or even low incomes that you reasonably regard as insufficient to pay the rent. Why? Because these criteria for tenant selection are reasonably related to your right to run your business in a competent, profitable manner (sometimes called your "legitimate business interests"). And if a person who fits one or more obvious "bad tenant risk" criteria happens to be a member of a minority group, you are still on safe legal ground as long as:

- You are consistent in your screening and treat all tenants more or less equally—for example, you always require a credit report for prospective tenants.
- You are not applying a generalization about people of a certain group to an individual.
- You can document your legal reasons for not renting to a prospective tenant.

But pay attention to the fact that judges, tenants' lawyers, and government agencies that administer and enforce fair housing laws know full well that some landlords try to make up and document legal reasons to discriminate, when the real reason is that they just don't like people with a particular racial, ethnic, or religious background. So, if you refuse to rent to a person who happens to be African-American, has children, or speaks only Spanish, be sure you document your legitimate business reason specific to that individual (such as insufficient income or a history of eviction for nonpayment of rent). Be prepared to show that your tenant advertising, screening, and selection processes have been based on objective criteria and that a more qualified applicant has always gotten the rental unit.

This section discusses some of the common legal reasons you may use to choose or reject applicants based on your business interests. A valid occupancy limitation (such as overcrowding) can also be a legal basis for a refusal, but since this issue is fairly complicated, we have devoted a separate section to the subject.

Objective Tenant Selection Criteria— What Do They Look Like?

"Objective criteria" are tenancy requirements that are established before the applicant even walks in the door, and are unaffected by the personal value judgments of the person asking the question. For example, a requirement that an applicant must never have been evicted for nonpayment of rent is "objective," because it is a matter of history and can be satisfied by a clear "yes" or "no." "Subjective criteria," on the other hand, have no preestablished correct answers, and the results of the questions will vary depending on the person who poses the question—for example, a requirement that the applicant present "a good appearance" has no predetermined "right" answer and will be answered differently by each person who asks the question. Subjective criteria are always suspicious in a housing context because their very looseness allows them to mask deliberate illegal discrimination.

So much for theory. Here are a few examples of allowable, objective criteria for choosing tenants:

- no prior bankruptcies
- two positive references from previous landlords
- sufficient income to pay the rent—for example, an income that is at least three times the rent
- signed waiver allowing you to investigate applicant's credit history, and
- satisfactory credit report.

 TIP

To protect yourself in advance, always note your reasons for rejecting a tenant on the application. An applicant you properly reject may nevertheless file a discrimination complaint with a fair housing agency. Recognizing this, you want to be able to prove that you had a valid business reason for refusing to rent to the particular person, such as negative references from a previous landlord. This means you need to routinely document your good reasons for rejecting all potential tenants before anyone files a discrimination claim.

Poor Credit Record or Income

You can legitimately refuse to rent to a prospective tenant who has a history of nonpayment of rent or you reasonably believe would be unable to pay rent in the future.

Here's some advice on how to avoid charges of discrimination when choosing tenants on the basis of income or credit history.

Do a credit check on every prospective tenant, and base your selection on the results of that credit check. Accepting or rejecting tenants based on objective criteria tied to a credit report is the best way to protect yourself against an accusation that you're using a bad credit history as an excuse to illegally discriminate against certain prospective tenants. For example, if you establish rules saying you won't rent to someone with bad credit or who is evicted by a previous landlord for nonpayment of rent (information commonly found in credit reports), be sure you apply this policy to all tenants. Chapter 1 shows you how to check a prospective tenant's credit history and find out whether an applicant has ever been evicted, gone through bankruptcy, or been convicted of a crime.

Avoid rigid point systems that rank prospective tenants on the basis of financial stability and other factors. Some landlords evaluate prospective tenants by giving each one a certain number of points at the outset, with deductions for bad credit and negative references and additional points for extremely good ones. Points are also awarded based on length of employment and income. The person with the highest score gets the nod. Point systems give the illusion of objectivity, but because the weight you give each factor is, after all, subjective, they can still leave you open to charges of discrimination.

Don't discriminate against married or unmarried couples by counting only one spouse's or partner's income. Always consider the income of persons living together, married or unmarried, in order to avoid the accusation of marital status discrimination or sex discrimination.

If your state prohibits discrimination based on personal characteristics or traits, don't give too much weight to years spent at the same job, which can arguably discriminate against certain occupations. For example, software designers and programmers commonly move from one employer to another.

Negative References From Previous Landlords

You can legally refuse to rent to someone based on what a previous landlord or manager has to say—for example, that the tenant was consistently late paying rent, broke the lease, or left the place a shambles.

Evictions and Civil Lawsuits Involving a Tenant

Credit reports typically indicate whether the applicant has been involved in civil lawsuits, such as an eviction or breach of contract suit. For many landlords, an eviction lawsuit is a red flag. Can you reject a tenant on this basis? It depends.

If a former landlord has filed—and won—an eviction lawsuit against the applicant, you have solid grounds to reject this person. Be careful, however, if the credit report indicates that the applicant, not the former landlord, won the eviction suit: A tenant who has been vindicated in a court of law has not done anything wrong, even though you may suspect that the person is a troublemaker who just got lucky. If you reject someone simply because an eviction lawsuit was

filed against them, and if you live in a state that prohibits discrimination on the basis of someone's personal characteristic or trait, you are risking a charge that you are discriminating. In most situations, however, if the applicant is truly a poor prospect, the information you get from prior landlords and employers will confirm your suspicions, and you can reject the applicant on these more solid grounds (negative references).

The credit report may also indicate that the applicant is now, or has been, involved in another type of civil lawsuit—for example, a custody fight, a personal injury claim, or a dispute with an auto repair shop. If the legal matter has nothing to do with the applicant's rental history, ability to pay the rent, or satisfy your other tenancy requirements, you may be on shaky ground if you base a rejection solely on that basis.

Criminal Records

Understandably, many landlords wish to check an applicant's criminal history, and credit reports will often include this information. Can you reject an applicant because of a conviction for drunk driving, or murder or drug use? What if there was an arrest but no conviction?

Convictions. If an applicant has been convicted for criminal offenses, you are probably entitled to reject him on that basis. After all, a conviction indicates that the applicant was not, at least in that instance, a law-abiding individual, which is a legitimate criterion for prospective tenants or managers. For example, you may reject someone with convictions for crimes against children.

There is one exception, however, and this involves convictions for past drug use: As explained below, past drug addiction is considered a disability under the Fair Housing Amendments Act, and you may not refuse to rent to someone on that basis—even if the addiction resulted in a conviction. People with convictions for the sale or manufacture of drugs or current drug users are not, however, protected under federal law.

Arrests. A more difficult problem is posed by the person who has an arrest record but no conviction. Under our legal system, a person is presumed not guilty until the prosecution proves its case or the arrestee pleads guilty. So, is it illegal to deny housing to someone whose arrest did not result in a conviction? Because "arrestees" are not, unlike members of a race or religion, protected under federal or state law, you could probably reject an applicant with an arrest history without too much fear of legal consequences. But there is an easy way to avoid even the slightest risk: Chances are that a previously arrested applicant who is *truly* a bad risk will have plenty of other facts in his or her background (like poor credit or negative references) that will clearly justify your rejection. In short, if you do a thorough check on each applicant, you'll get enough information on which to base your decision.

Incomplete or Inaccurate Rental Application

A carefully designed rental application form is a key tool in choosing tenants, and we include a rental application in Chapter 1. This (or any other) application will do its job only if the applicant provides you with all the necessary information. Obviously, if you can reject applicants on the basis of negative references or a bad credit history, you can reject them for failing to allow you to check their background, or if you catch them in a lie.

Inability to Meet Legal Terms of Lease or Rental Agreement

It goes without saying that you may legally refuse to rent to someone who can't come up with the security deposit or meet some other valid condition of the tenancy, such as the length of the lease.

Pets

You can legally refuse to rent to people with pets, and you can restrict the types or size of pets you accept. In fact, your insurance may prohibit renting to tenants with certain breeds of dogs (and if the rental is part of a homeowners' association, additional pet restrictions may apply). You can also, strictly speaking, let some tenants keep a pet and say no to others—because pet owners, unlike members of a religion or race, are not as a group protected by antidiscrimination laws. However, from a practical point of view, an inconsistent pet policy is a bad idea, because it can only result in angry, resentful tenants. Also, if the pet owner you reject is someone in a protected category and you have let someone outside of that category rent with a pet, you are courting a discrimination lawsuit.

Keep in mind that you cannot refuse to rent to someone with an animal if that animal is a service or companion animal—for example, a properly trained dog for a person with disability. (42 U.S. Code § 3604(f)(3)(B).) Clause 14 of the form lease and rental agreements in Chapter 2 discusses pet policies and legal issues.

Sources of Antidiscrimination Laws

This section reviews the sources of antidiscrimination laws: the federal Fair Housing Act of 1968 and the federal Fair Housing Amendments Act of 1988 (throughout this chapter, we refer to these laws as the federal Acts), the 1866 Civil Rights Act, and state and local antidiscrimination laws. "Types of Illegal Discrimination," which follows, discusses specific types of discrimination that will almost surely get you into trouble with a federal, state, or local housing agency.

The Federal Fair Housing Acts

The Fair Housing Act and Fair Housing Amendments Act (42 U.S. Code §§ 3601–3619, 3631), which are enforced by the U.S. Department of Housing and Urban Development (HUD), address many types of housing discrimination. They apply to all aspects of the landlord-tenant relationship throughout the U.S.

How Fair Housing Groups Uncover Discrimination

Landlords who turn away prospective tenants on the basis of race, ethnic background, or other group characteristics obviously never come out and admit what they're doing. Commonly, a landlord falsely tells a person who's a member of a racial minority that no rentals are available, or that the prospective tenant's income and credit history aren't good enough. From a legal point of view, this can be a dangerous—and potentially expensive—tactic. Here's why: Both HUD and private fair housing groups are adept at uncovering this discriminatory practice by having "testers" apply to landlords for vacant housing. Typically, a tester who is African-American or Hispanic will fill out a rental application, listing certain occupational, income, and credit information. Then, a white tester will apply for the same housing, listing information very similar to—or sometimes not as good as—that given by the minority applicant.

A landlord who offers to rent to a white tester, and rejects—without valid reason—a minority applicant who has the same (or better) qualifications, is very likely to be found to be guilty of discrimination. Such incidents have resulted in many hefty lawsuit settlements. Fortunately, it's possible to avoid the morass of legal liability for discrimination by adopting tenant screening policies that don't discriminate, and applying them evenhandedly.

Types of Discrimination Prohibited

The Fair Housing Act prohibits discrimination on the following grounds (called protected categories):
- race or color or religion
- national origin
- familial status—includes families with children under the age of 18 and pregnant women and elderly persons
- disability or handicap, and
- sex, including sexual harassment.

Although the federal Acts use certain words to describe illegal discrimination (such as "national origin"), the Department of Housing and Urban Development and the courts are not limited to the precise language of the Acts. For instance, sexual harassment is a violation of law because it qualifies as discrimination on the basis of sex—even though the term "sexual harassment" is not used in the text of the law itself.

Aspects of Landlord-Tenant Relationship Covered

The federal Acts essentially prohibit landlords from taking any of the following actions based on race, color, religion, national origin, familial status, disability, or sex:
- advertising or making any statement that indicates a limitation or preference based on race, religion, or any other protected category
- falsely denying that a rental unit is available
- setting more restrictive standards for selecting tenants
- refusing to rent to members of certain groups
- before or during the tenancy, setting different terms, conditions, or privileges for rental of a dwelling unit, such as requiring larger deposits of some tenants, or adopting an inconsistent policy of responding to late rent payments
- during the tenancy, providing different housing services or facilities, such as making a community center or other common area available only to selected tenants, or
- terminating a tenancy for a discriminatory reason.

An individual who suspects discrimination may file a complaint with HUD or a state or local fair housing agency, or sue you in federal or state court. Guests of tenants may also sue landlords for housing discrimination under the federal Acts. (*Lane v. Cole*, 88 F.Supp.2d 402 (E.D. Pa., 2000).) Landlords may always, however, impose reasonable restrictions on guest stays.

CAUTION

Failure to stop a tenant from making discriminatory or harassing comments to another tenant may also get you into legal trouble. If one tenant reports that another is making ethnic or racial slurs or threatening violence because of their race, religion, ethnicity, or other characteristic that is considered a protected category, act promptly. A simple oral warning may stop the problem, but if not, a warning letter may be in order (see Chapter 16 for advice on writing warning letters). Depending on the situation, an eviction for tenant violation of the lease clause on quiet enjoyment of the premises may be warranted. If violence is involved, you'll need to act quickly and call the police. As with all tenant complaints, keep good records of conversations to protect yourself from tenant complaints that you acted illegally by failing to stop discrimination or harassment or that an eviction was illegal.

Seniors' Housing

If you have a multifamily property and decide you'd like to rent exclusively to seniors, you can do so as long as you follow federal guidelines. You have two options:

- **80% of your residents must be 55 or older.** You must make it known to the public, through your advertising, that you offer senior housing, and must verify applicants' ages. Once you've reached the 80% mark, you can set any other age restriction as long as it does not violate any state or local bans on age discrimination. For example, you could require the remaining 20% of tenants to be over 18 years of age, as long as no state or local law forbids such a policy.

- **Housing for tenants 62 and older.** All of your residents must be 62 or older. This includes spouses and adult children, but excludes caregivers and on-site employees.

Exempt Property

The following types of property are exempt from the federal ban against discrimination in housing, as long as their rental is accomplished without the use of discriminatory advertising (42 U.S.C.A. § 3603(b) & § 3607):

- owner-occupied buildings with four or fewer units (this is called the "Mrs. Murphy" exemption)
- single-family housing, as long as the owner owns no more than three such houses at any one time
- certain types of housing operated by religious organizations and private clubs that limit occupancy to their own members, and
- with respect to age discrimination only, housing geared toward seniors. See "Seniors' Housing," above.

CAUTION

State and local laws may cover federally exempt units. Even though your property may be exempt under federal law, similar state or local anti-housing-discrimination laws may nevertheless cover your rental units. For example, owner-occupied buildings with four or fewer units are exempt under federal law, but not under California law.

More Information From HUD and State Agencies

For more information about the Fair Housing Act, free copies of federal fair housing posters, and technical assistance on accessibility requirements, contact one of HUD's many local offices. You'll find a list of state and local offices on the HUD website at www.hud.gov (click the tab "State Info"). You can also call the agency's Housing Discrimination Hotline at 800-669-9777 (or 800-927-9275 TTY).

For information on state and local housing discrimination laws, contact your state fair housing agency. You'll find a list of state and local agencies, with contact information, on the HUD website.

The 1866 Civil Rights Act

Passed at the end of the Civil War, the 1866 Civil Rights Act also bans discrimination in housing. (42 U.S.C.A. § 1981.) Its prohibition of "racial discrimination" covers African-Americans, Hispanics, and all dark-skinned persons. Importantly, unlike the federal Fair Housing Acts, the Civil Rights Act does not exempt the "Mrs. Murphy" situation, in which the owner lives on premises that consist of four or fewer units. This means that all landlords, no matter the size of their properties or whether they live in them, may not lawfully discriminate against African-Americans, Hispanics, or other dark-skinned persons.

Display Fair Housing Posters in Rental Office

Federal regulations require you to put up special fair housing posters wherever you normally conduct housing-related business. You must display a HUD-approved poster saying that you rent apartments in accordance with federal fair housing law (24 Code of Federal Regulations (CFR) §§ 110 and following). Many state laws have similar requirements.

Hang the fair housing posters in a prominent spot in the office or area where you greet prospective tenants and take applications. If you have a model apartment, it's a smart idea to hang a poster there, too. To get free posters, available in English and Spanish, contact the U.S. Department of Housing and Urban Development.

State and Local Antidiscrimination Laws

Most state and local laws prohibiting housing discrimination echo federal antidiscrimination law in that they outlaw discrimination based on race or color, national origin, religion, familial status, disability, and sex. (If your state law doesn't track federal law group by group, it makes little difference—you're still bound by the more-inclusive federal law.) But state and local laws often go in the other direction—they may provide more detail and may also forbid some kinds of discrimination—such as discrimination based on marital status—that aren't covered by federal law. For example, in states that prohibit discrimination based on marital status, it would be illegal to refuse to rent to divorced people.

Types of Illegal Discrimination

In the sections that follow, we'll look at each of the categories of illegal discrimination and explore their obvious and not-so-obvious meaning.

Race, Color, or Religion

Fortunately, the amount of overt racial and religious discrimination has lessened over the last several decades. This is not to say, however, that discrimination doesn't exist, especially in subtle forms. And, unfortunately, HUD may see "discrimination" where your intent was completely well intentioned. Below, we'll look at some of the common examples of both intentional (but subtle) discrimination and unintended discrimination.

Intentional, Subtle Discrimination

It goes without saying that you should not overtly treat tenants differently because of their race or religion—for example, renting only to members of your own religion or race is obviously illegal. Deliberate discrimination should not be cavalierly dismissed, however, as a thing of the past practiced by insensitive oafs. Unexpected situations can test your willingness to comply with equal treatment laws and can reveal subtle forms of intentional discrimination that are just as illegal as blatant discrimination. Consider the following scenario.

> EXAMPLE: Several tenants in Creekside Apartments reserved the common room for a religious occasion. Creekside management learned that the tenants were members of a white supremacist religion that believes in the inferiority of all nonwhites and non-Christians. Creekside was appalled at the thought of these ideas being discussed on its premises, and denied the group the use of the common room. The tenants who were members of this group filed a discrimination complaint with HUD on the basis of freedom of religion. HUD supported the religious group and forced Creekside to make the common room available. Creekside wisely sent all tenants a memo stating that making the common room available reflects management's intent to comply with fair housing laws and not their endorsement of the principles urged by any group that uses the room.

As the above example illustrates, religions that are outside the mainstream are protected under the federal Acts.

> **CAUTION**
>
> **Don't discriminate on the basis of how applicants sound over the phone.** Academic studies have shown that people can often identify a person's ethnic background based on short phone conversations. Researchers have tested this theory on unsuspecting landlords, some of whom rejected large numbers of African-American applicants compared to equally qualified white callers. Fair housing advocacy groups, described in "How Fair Housing Groups Uncover Discrimination," above, can be expected to use this tactic as a way to build a case against landlords whom they suspect of regular, illegal discrimination.

Unintended Discrimination

In Chapter 1, we discussed the unintended discriminatory messages that are conveyed when advertisements feature statements such as "safe Christian community" or "Sunday quiet times enforced." (Both ads may be understood as suggesting that only Christians are welcome as tenants.) The same considerations apply to your dealings with your tenants after they have moved in. Conscientious landlords should carefully review tenant rules, signs, newsletters, and all communications to make sure that they cannot be construed in any way to benefit, support, or discriminate against any racial or religious group. The examples and advice we give below may seem "politically correct" in the extreme, but take our word for it, they are based on actual fair housing complaints and deserve to be taken seriously.

- The apartment complex newsletter invites everyone to a "Christmas party" held by the management. Non-Christian tenants might feel that this event is not intended for them and therefore that they have been discriminated against. A better approach: Call it a "Holiday Party" and invite everyone.
- Management extends the use of the common room to tenants for "birthday parties, anniversaries, and Christmas and Easter parties."

A better idea: Invite your tenants to use the common room for special celebrations, rather than list specific Christian holidays.

- In an effort to accommodate your Spanish-speaking tenants, you translate your move-in letter and house rules into Spanish. Regarding the use of alcohol in the common areas, the Spanish version begins, "Unlike Mexico, where drinking is practiced in public places, alcoholic beverages may not be consumed in common areas … ." Because to many people this phrase implies an ethnic generalization, it may well become the basis for a fair housing complaint.
- The metropolitan area where you own residential rental property contains large numbers of both Spanish-speaking and Cantonese-speaking people. Advertising in only Spanish, or translating your lease into only Cantonese, will likely constitute a fair housing violation because it suggests that members of the other group are not welcome. Of course, if you advertise only in English, you are not violating fair housing laws.

National Origin

Like discrimination based on race or religion, discrimination based on national origin is illegal, whether it's practiced openly and deliberately or unintentionally.

Even if you are motivated by a valid business concern, but choose tenants in a way that singles out people of a particular nationality, it's still illegal. Say, for instance, that two Hispanic tenants recently skipped out on you, owing you unpaid rent. So you decide to make it a practice to conduct credit checks only on Hispanics. An Hispanic applicant may interpret your actions as sending a negative message to Hispanics in general: Hispanics are not welcome because you assume all of them skip out on debts. A fair housing agency or a court of law would probably agree that this sort of selective policy is illegal discrimination.

Discrimination on the Basis of Immigration Status

Landlords often ask whether they may legally require that all tenants be in the United States legally—in other words, that they be citizens, permanent residents, visa holders, or have some other right to be here. There may be legitimate and legal business reasons why some landlords impose this requirement. For example, they may believe that people without legal status may be more likely to break their leases than others who have no need to live somewhat in the shadows. However, another motivating factor may be distrust of some renters simply because they are from other countries. Not surprisingly, landlords who are in the second camp typically require documentation of only those applicants who they suspect may be here illegally—those whose skin color, accents, or other characteristics suggest that they're "not from here." And therein lies the problem.

HUD has addressed this issue with great care. Because "immigration status" is not a protected category under the federal fair housing laws, it is not illegal to require that all applicants provide "identity documents" that establish that they meet rental criteria (which, presumably, can include legal residency). However, HUD hastily adds that "a person's ability to pay rent or fitness as a tenant is not necessarily connected to his or her immigration status." ("Immigration Status and Housing Discrimination Frequently Asked Questions," are found on the National Law Income Housing Coalition website (www.NLIHC.org—search for it by name).) And HUD makes it very clear that if landlords intend to ask for residence verification, they must ask all applicants, not only those whom they suspect may be here without legal status. Requiring verification from only some applicants is almost always an instance of race, color, or national origin discrimination.

Note that in New York City and in California, however, landlords are specifically prohibited from asking applicants for immigration status.

On the other hand, if you require all prospective tenants to consent to a credit check (as well as meeting other objective criteria as discussed above),

you will get the needed information, but in a nondiscriminatory way.

Discriminatory comments as well as policies can get you in trouble, too, as one New York owner learned the hard way. The landlord told a Honduran applicant that she couldn't rent an apartment because "Spanish people … like to have loud music." The applicant sued the landlord for the discriminatory statement. A federal court ordered the landlord to pay $24,847 in damages: $7,000 to compensate her for her losses; $9,736 for attorney fees; $2,111 for court costs; and $6,000 to penalize the landlord for making the discriminatory comment. (*Gonzales v. Rakkas*, 1995 WL 451034 (E.D. N.Y., 1995).)

TIP

If you ask one person a question, ask everyone. It cannot be emphasized enough that questions on a prospective tenant's legal status must be put to all applicants, not just the ones who you suspect are illegal, and not just the ones who are applying to live in one of your buildings in a certain part of town.

Familial Status

Discrimination on the basis of familial status includes not only openly refusing to rent to families with children or to pregnant women, but also trying to accomplish the same goal by setting overly restrictive space requirements (limiting the maximum number of people permitted to occupy a rental unit), thereby preventing families with children from occupying smaller units.

We discuss how to establish reasonable occupancy standards later in this chapter. The fact that you can legally adopt occupancy standards, however, doesn't mean you can use "overcrowding" as a euphemism for refusing to rent to tenants with children, if you would rent to the same number of adults. A few landlords have adopted criteria that for all practical purposes forbid children under the guise of preventing overcrowding—for example, allowing only one person per bedroom, with a couple counting as one person. Under these criteria, a landlord would rent a two-bedroom unit to a husband and wife and their one child, but would not rent the same unit to a mother with two children. This practice, which has the effect of keeping all (or most) children out of a landlord's property, would surely be found illegal in court and would result in monetary penalties.

It would also be illegal to allow children to occupy ground floor units only, or to designate certain apartments or buildings within an apartment community as "family" units.

It is essential to maintain a consistent occupancy policy. If you allow three adults to live in a two-bedroom apartment, you had better let a couple with a child (or a single mother with two children) live in the same type of unit, or you leave yourself open to charges that you are illegally discriminating.

> **EXAMPLE:** Jackson owned and managed two identical one-bedroom units in a duplex, one of which he rented out to three flight attendants who were rarely there at the same time. When the other unit became vacant, Jackson advertised it as a one-bedroom, two-person apartment. Harry and Sue Jones and their teenage daughter were turned away because they exceeded Jackson's occupancy limit of two people. The Jones family, learning that the companion unit was rented to three people, filed a complaint with HUD, whose investigator questioned Jackson regarding the inconsistency of his occupancy policy. Jackson was convinced that he was in the wrong, and agreed to rent to the Jones family and to compensate them for the humiliation they had suffered as a result of being refused.

Finally, do not inquire as to the age and sex of any children who will be sharing the same bedroom. This is their parents' business, not yours.

Disability

The Fair Housing Amendments Act prohibits discrimination against people who:

- have a physical or mental disability that substantially limits one or more major life

activities—including, but not limited to, hearing, mobility and visual impairments, chronic alcoholism (but only if it is being addressed through a recovery program), mental illness, HIV positive, AIDS, AIDS-Related Complex, and mental retardation
- have a history or record of such a disability, or
- are regarded by others as though they have such a disability.

The law also protects those who are "associated with" someone who has a disability, such as a family member, cotenant, or caregiver who lives with the tenant or makes house visits.

You may be shocked to see what is—and what is not—considered a disability. Although it may seem odd, alcoholism is classed as a protected disability. Does this mean that you must rent to a drunk? What about past, and current, drug addiction? Let's look at each of these issues.

Recovering Alcoholics

You may encounter an applicant, let's call him Ted, who passes all your criteria for selecting tenants but whose personal history includes a disquieting note: Employers and past landlords let you know that Ted has a serious drinking problem that he is dealing with by attending AA meetings. As far as you can tell, Ted has not lost a job or a place to live due to his drinking problem. Can you refuse to rent to Ted for fear that he will drink away the rent, exhibit loud or inappropriate behavior, or damage your property? No, you cannot, unless you can point to specific acts of misbehavior or financial shakiness that would sink any applicant, regardless of the underlying cause. Your fear alone that this might happen (however well-founded) will not legally support your refusal to rent to Ted.

In a nutshell, you may not refuse to rent to what HUD calls a "recovering alcoholic" simply because of his status as an alcoholic—you must be able to point to specific facts other than his status as an alcoholic in recovery that render him unfit as a tenant.

EXAMPLE: Patsy applied for an apartment one morning and spoke with Carol, the manager. Patsy said she would have to return that afternoon to complete the application form because she was due at her regular Alcoholics Anonymous meeting. Carol decided on the spot that she did not want Patsy for a tenant, and she told Patsy that the unit "had just been rented," which was a lie. (Patsy continued to see the newspaper ad for the unit.) Patsy filed a complaint with HUD, alleging that she was an alcoholic who had been discriminated against. Because Carol could not point to any reason for turning Patsy away other than her assumption that Patsy, as a recovering alcoholic, would be a bad tenant, the judge awarded Patsy several thousand dollars in damages.

Unfortunately, HUD has not been very helpful in explaining what steps an alcoholic must take in order to qualify as "recovering." Regular attendance at AA meetings and counseling probably qualify, but an alcoholic who is less conscientious may not make the grade. In any event, you as the landlord are hardly in a position to investigate and verify an applicant's personal habits and medical history. So how can you choose tenants without risking a violation of law?

The answer lies in putting your energies into thorough reference checking that will yield information that can unquestionably support a rejection at the rental office. If the applicant, recovering or not, is truly a bad risk, you'll discover facts (like job firings, bad credit, or past rental property damage) independent of the thorny problem of whether the person has entered the "recovery" stage of his alcoholism. And if you have a current tenant whom you suspect of alcoholism, use the same approach —focus on his behavior as a tenant, regardless of his status as an alcoholic. If the tenant damages your property or interferes with your other tenants' ability to quietly enjoy their property, he is a candidate for eviction regardless of whether he is in or out of recovery, just as would be any tenant who exhibited this behavior. Consider the following scenario, which is what Carol should have done.

EXAMPLE: Same facts as above, except that Carol went ahead and took an application from Patsy later that day and checked her references. Patsy's former landlord told Carol that Patsy had refused to pay for damage from a fire she had negligently caused; Patsy's employment history showed a pattern of short-lived jobs and decreasing wages. Carol noted this information on Patsy's application form and, as she would have done for any applicant with a similar background, Carol rejected Patsy. Patsy filed a complaint with HUD, again claiming discrimination on the basis of her alcoholism. When the HUD investigator asked to see Patsy's application and questioned Carol about her application criteria for all applicants, he concluded that the rejection had been based on legally sound business reasons and was not, therefore, a fair housing violation.

Drug Users

Under the Fair Housing Amendments Act, a person who has a past drug addiction is classed as someone who has a record of a disability and, as such, is protected under the fair housing law. You may not refuse to rent to someone solely because he is an ex-addict, even if that person has felony convictions for drug use. Put another way, your fear that the person will resume his illegal drug use is not sufficient grounds to reject the applicant. If you do a thorough background check, however, and discover a rental or employment history that would defeat any applicant, you may reject the person as long as it is clear that the rejection is based on these legal reasons.

On the other hand, someone who currently and illegally uses drugs is breaking the law, and you may certainly refuse to rent to him—particularly if you reasonably suspect the person is dealing drugs. Also, if the applicant has felony convictions for dealing or manufacturing illegal drugs, as distinct from convictions for possession of drugs for personal use, you may use that history as a basis of refusal.

Mental or Emotional Impairments

Like alcoholics or past drug users, applicants and tenants who had, or have (or appear to have) mental or emotional impairments must be evaluated and treated by the landlord and manager on the basis of their financial stability and histories as tenants, not on the basis of their mental health status. Unless you can point to specific instances of past behavior that would make a prospective tenant dangerous to others, such as assaults on tenants or destruction of property, or you have other valid business criteria for rejecting the person, a refusal to rent or a special requirement such as cosigner on the lease could result in a fair housing complaint.

No "Approved List" of Disabilities

The physical and mental disabilities that are covered by the Fair Housing Acts range from the obvious (wheelchair use and sensory disabilities) to those that may not be so apparent. The law reaches to past drug users and to those who are HIV positive.

The list of groups protected by the law is not, however, set in stone. What may seem to you like an individual's hypochondria or personal quirk may become a legally accepted disability if tested in court. For example, tenants with hypertension (which may lead to more serious medical problems) have been known to ask for protection under the fair housing laws, as have tenants suffering from "building material sensitivity" (sensitivities to vapors emitted from paint, upholstery, and rugs). Similarly, tenants who have a sensitivity or problem that is widespread throughout the population, such as asthma or allergies, may also win coverage under the fair housing laws. Contact your local HUD office to find out whether the courts have extended fair housing protections in these situations.

Questions and Actions That May Be Considered to Discriminate Against the Disabled

You may not ask an applicant or tenant if she has a disability or illness, and may not ask to see medical records, inquire about the type of medication the person takes, or ask about their ability to live independently. If it is obvious that someone has a disability—for example, the person is in a wheelchair or wears a hearing aid—it is illegal to inquire how severely he is disabled. We describe how to verify a claimed disability below.

Unfortunately, even the most innocuous, well-meaning question or remark can get you into trouble, especially if you decide not to rent to the person. What you might consider polite conversation may be taken as a probing question designed to discourage an applicant.

> **EXAMPLE:** Sam, a Vietnam veteran, was the owner of Belleview Apartments. Jim, who appeared to be the same age as Sam and who used a wheelchair, applied for an apartment. Thinking that Jim might have been injured in the Vietnam War, Sam questioned Jim about the circumstances of his disability, intending only to pass the time and put Jim at ease. When Jim was not offered the apartment—he did not meet the financial criteria that Sam applied to all applicants—he filed a complaint with HUD, alleging discrimination based on his disability. Sam was unable to convince the HUD investigator that his questions were not intended to be discriminatory, and, on the advice of his attorney, Sam settled the case for several thousand dollars.

Your well-intentioned actions, as well as your words, can become the basis of a fair housing complaint. You are not allowed to "steer" applicants to units that you, however innocently, think would be more appropriate. For example, if you have two units for rent—one on the ground floor and one three stories up—do not fail to offer to show both units to the applicant who is movement-impaired, however reasonable you think it would be for the person to consider only the ground floor unit.

The Rights of Tenants With Disabilities to Enter and Live in an Accessible Place

Your legal obligations toward applicants and tenants with disabilities extend beyond the questions you may ask or conversations you may have. The physical layout of your leasing office and other areas open to the public (where applicants will go to inquire about vacancies, for example) must be wheelchair-accessible.

You must also concern yourself with the fair housing laws after you have rented a home to a person with a disability. The Fair Housing Amendments Act requires that landlords:

- **accommodate** the needs of tenants with disabilities, at the landlord's own expense (42 U.S. Code § 3604(f)(3)(B)), and
- allow tenants with disabilities to make reasonable **modifications** of their living unit or common areas at their expense if that is what is needed for the person to comfortably and safely live in the unit. (42 U.S. Code § 3604(f)(3)(A).)

We'll look briefly at each of these requirements.

Accommodations. You are expected to adjust your rules, procedures, or services in order to give a person with a disability an equal opportunity to use and enjoy a dwelling unit or a common space. Accommodations include such things as:

- parking—if you provide parking in the first place, providing a close-in, spacious parking space for a tenant who uses a wheelchair
- service or companion animals—allowing a guide dog, hearing dog, or service dog in a residence that otherwise disallows pets
- rent payment—allowing a special rent payment plan for a tenant whose finances are managed by someone else or by a government agency
- reading problems—arranging to read all communications from management to a blind tenant, and
- phobias—for example, providing a tub and clothesline for a tenant whose clinically diagnosed anxiety about machines makes her unable to use the washer and dryer.

Does your duty to accommodate tenants with disabilities mean that you must bend every rule and change every procedure at the tenant's request? Generally speaking, the answer is no. You are expected to accommodate "reasonable" requests, but need not undertake changes that would seriously impair your ability to run your business. For example, if an applicant uses a wheelchair prefers the third-story apartment in a walk-up building constructed

in 1926 to the one on the ground floor, you do not have to rip the building apart to install an elevator.

Do You Need to Accommodate Tenants With Disabilities Who Are Dangerous?

You do not have to accommodate a tenant with a disability who poses a direct threat to others' safety, or who is likely to commit serious property damage. You must rely on objective evidence, such as current conduct or a recent history of disruptive behavior, before concluding that someone poses a threat. In particular, consider the following:

- The nature, severity, and duration of the risk of injury. For example, someone whose behavior is merely annoying is not as worrisome as someone who is prone to physical confrontations.
- The probability that injury will actually occur. Here, you must take into account to what extent the person is likely to follow through with worrisome acts.
- Whether there are any reasonable accommodations that will eliminate the direct threat. For example, if you can diffuse a situation by changing a rule or procedure, you may need to.

Applying the three criteria mentioned above can be challenging. For example, suppose residents tell you about a tenant who has threatened them with a baseball bat on several occasions. In keeping with your policy to enforce your "no threats" policy, you terminate the tenant's lease. The tenant's lawyer contacts you and suggests that as soon as his client resumes appropriate medication, the behavior will stop. Must you give this a try?

The answer is yes, though you can ask for satisfactory assurance that the tenant will receive appropriate counseling and periodic medication monitoring so that he will no longer pose a direct threat. To be sure, receiving such assurances, such as periodic letters from counselors or therapists, puts you uncomfortably in the thick of your tenant's personal problems, but there is no other way to meet your obligations to other tenants (to maintain a safe environment). You'd be on solid ground to continue with the termination if the tenant refused to work with you in this way.

Modifications. Where your duty to accommodate the needs of tenants with disabilities ends, your obligation to allow the tenant to modify living space may begin. A person with disabilities has the right to modify his living space to the extent necessary to make it safe and comfortable, as long as the modifications will not make the unit unacceptable to the next tenant, or the tenant with a disability agrees to undo the modification when he leaves. Examples of modifications undertaken by a tenant with a disability include:

- lowering countertops for a wheelchair-bound tenant
- installing special faucets or door handles for persons with limited hand use
- modifying kitchen appliances to accommodate a blind tenant, and
- installing a ramp to allow a wheelchair-bound tenant to negotiate two steps up to a raised lobby or corridor.

You are not obliged to allow a tenant with a disability to modify his unit at will, without prior approval. You are entitled to ask for a reasonable description of the proposed modifications, proof that they will be done in a workmanlike manner, and evidence that the tenant is obtaining any necessary building permits.

Unless the property is located in Massachusetts, or it is federally financed, tenants must pay for their modifications. (But if your building opened for occupancy on or after March 13, 1991, and the modification is needed because the building doesn't comply with HUD's accessibility requirements (see "New Buildings and Tenants With Disabilities," below), you must pay for the modification.) If a tenant proposes to modify the unit in such a way that will require restoration when the tenant leaves (such as the repositioning of lowered kitchen counters), you may require that the tenant pay into an interest-bearing escrow account the amount estimated for the restoration. (The interest belongs to the tenant.)

CAUTION

Your duty to evaluate any request begins when you learn of it, even if it's oral or communicated through a third party, such as an applicant's friend or family member.

New Buildings and Tenants With Disabilities

The Fair Housing Amendments Act (42 U.S. Code §§ 3604(f)(3)(C) and 3604(f)(7)) imposes requirements on new buildings of four or more units that were first occupied after March 13, 1991. All ground floor units and every unit in an elevator building must be designed or constructed so that:

- there is an accessible route from the public right of way outside the building (such as the sidewalk) to all units and common areas
- the "primary entrance" of each rental unit is accessible
- any stair landing shared by more than one rental unit is handicapped accessible (*U.S. v. Edward Rose & Sons*, 384 F.3d 258 (6th Cir. 2004))
- the public and common areas are "readily accessible to and usable by" people with disabilities, including parking areas (a good rule of thumb is to reserve 2% of the spaces)
- entryway doorways have 36" of free space *plus* shoulder and elbow room; and interior doorways are at least 32" wide
- interior living spaces have wheelchair-accessible routes throughout, with changes in floor height of no more than ¼"
- light switches, outlets, thermostats, and other environmental controls are within the legal "reach range" (15" to 48" from the ground)
- bathroom walls are sufficiently reinforced to allow the safe installation of "grab bars," and
- kitchens and bathrooms are large enough to allow a wheelchair to maneuver within the room (40" turning radius minimum) and have sinks and appliances positioned to allow side or front use.

For more information on accessibility requirements, see HUD's informative website, www.hud.gov (search "fair housing accessibility guidelines").

Verification of Disabled Status

When a tenant or applicant asks for a modification or accommodation, it may be obvious that the person falls within the legal definition of a disabled person, and that the request addresses that disability. In those cases—think of a blind applicant who asks to keep a seeing eye dog—it would be pointless for you to demand proof that the person has a disability and needs the accommodation. (Indeed, doing so might result in a harassment lawsuit.) However, many times the claimed disability, and the appropriateness of the request, are not so clear. You're entitled to ask for verification that the tenant has a disability and needs the specific modification requested, but you must do so carefully.

For years, landlords asked for a doctor's letter. Now, according to a HUD and Department of Justice guidance memo, you must be willing to listen to less formal sources. (*Reasonable Accommodations Under the Fair Housing Act,* Joint Statement of the Department of Housing and Urban Development and the Department of Justice, March 5, 2008.) Sources of reliable information include:

- **The individual himself.** A person can prove that he has met the requirement for having a legal disability (and that a modification or accommodation addresses that disability) by giving you a "credible statement." Unfortunately, the guidance memo does not define this term.
- **Documents.** A person who is under 65 years of age and receives Supplemental Security Income or Social Security Disability Insurance benefits is legally disabled. Someone could establish disability by showing you relevant identification cards. Likewise, license plates showing the universal accessibility logo, or a driver's license reflecting the existence of a disability, are sufficient proof.
- **Doctors or other medical professionals, peer support groups, nonmedical service agencies.** Information from these sources might come through letters, phone calls, or personal visits.
- **Reliable third parties.** This wide-open source of information could include friends, associates, and roommates, though some fair housing experts interpret this phrase as meaning any "third-party professional who is familiar with the disability." We don't know whether this definition will become the standard used by courts.

Many prospects and tenants will turn to a third party, usually a professional, when you ask for verification. Although you can certainly leave it up to that party to provide the written documentation, you can also give the "Verification of Disabled Status" form to your tenants, asking them to give it to their doctors or other professionals. Using this form is a convenient and safe way to elicit the information you need (and keep unwanted details out of the picture). Specifically, this form:

- **Evidences your willingness to entertain the tenant's request.** When you give the form to your tenant, make a note in the prospect's or tenant's file. This note may come in handy should you later be accused of discouraging (or even outright denying) the tenant's request.
- **Educates the third party as to the legal standard for being considered to have a disability.** By placing the federal definition of "disabled" right on the form, you're reminding the signer that this is the standard he or she must keep in mind when verifying status.
- **Identifies the precise modification or accommodation.** When you give the form to your tenant, fill in the accommodation or modification that's been requested. If you leave it blank, you risk the insertion of irrelevant or extra requests that you and the tenant have not discussed. Of course, it's possible that the third party may have additional suggestions, and if so, there's room for those suggestions (which will be subject to the same "reasonableness" standard as are all modification and accommodation requests, as explained in "How to Respond to Unreasonable Requests for Accommodations or Modifications," below).

Verification of Disabled Status

Marion Welby, MD
Third-party professional's name

31 Circle Drive, Suite 2
Address

Centerville, VA 12345

555-123-4567
Phone number

September 5, 20xx
Date

Dear ___Mr. Greene_____ (Landlord or manager's name),

I am a ___medical doctor licensed to practice in Virginia_____

_____ (describe third-party professional's work or occupation).

I am familiar with ___Al Blake_____ (Tenant), who is under my care or supervision.

In my opinion, ___Al Blake_____ (Tenant) is *legally disabled*, as that term is defined by federal law (Fair Housing Amendments Act, 42 United States Code section 3602(h)):

A disabled person is someone who

(1) has a physical or mental impairment that substantially limits one or more of such person's major life activities, or

(2) has a record of having such an impairment, or

(3) is regarded as having such an impairment.

___Al Blake_____ (Tenant) has requested the following accommodation or modification to the rental premises at __1530 Park Drive, #7, Centerville, VA__ _____ (address of rental property): __lower countertops in kitchen, lower light switches in hall, kitchen, bathroom, and bedroom__ _____ (describe proposed accommodation or modification).

In my opinion, this proposed accommodation or modification is needed in order for ___Al Blake___ _____ (Tenant) to live safely and comfortably at the rental premises.

I am willing to testify under oath or sign a sworn declaration consistent with my representations in this letter, should the need arise.

___Marion Welby, MD_____   ___September 5, 20xx___
Signature   Date

___Marion Welby, MD_____
Print name

- **Eliminates the chance that the third party will give you details of the tenant's disability.** You don't need these details, and you don't want to know them, either (you never want to give a tenant the ability to accuse you of misusing this information). A third party may nevertheless think you require the full picture and may include it in a letter. There's no place on this form for these details.

- **Cautions the third party that this is a serious matter.** You'll see that the form ends with the signer's statement that he or she will be willing to testify under oath or sign a sworn declaration consistent with his or her representations on the form. A reputable professional who is truly familiar with your tenant should not be deterred by this cautionary ending. In the unlikely event that your tenant is using someone to fraudulently verify the tenant's status, that person might think twice when seeing this concluding sentence.

A sample Verification of Disabled Status form is shown above and the Nolo website includes a downloadable copy. See Appendix B for the link to the forms in this book.

How to Respond to Unreasonable Requests for Accommodations or Modifications

The law requires you to agree to "reasonable" requests for accommodations or modifications. You don't have to go along with unreasonable ones, but you can't simply say "No" and shut the door. You must engage in what HUD calls an "interactive process" with the tenant. In essence, this means you have to get together and try to reach an acceptable compromise. For example, suppose you require tenants to pay rent in person at the manager's office. A tenant with a disability asks that the manager collect the rent at her apartment. Since this would leave the office unstaffed, you suggest instead that the tenant mail the rent check. This may be a reasonable compromise.

Sex and Sexual Harassment

You may not refuse to rent to a person on the basis of gender—for example, you cannot refuse to rent to a single woman solely because she is female. Neither may you impose special rules on people because of their gender—for example, limiting upper-story apartments to single females.

Illegal sex discrimination also includes sexual harassment—refusing to rent to a person who resists your sexual advances, or making life difficult for (or evicting) a tenant who has resisted such advances.

What is sexual harassment in a rental housing context? Courts have defined it as:

- a pattern of persistent, unwanted attention of a sexual nature, including the making of sexual remarks and physical advances, or a single instance of highly egregious behavior. A manager's persistent requests for social contact, or constant remarks concerning a tenant's appearance or behavior, could constitute sexual harassment, as could a single extraordinarily offensive remark, or

- a situation in which a tenant's rights are conditioned upon the acceptance of the owner's or manager's attentions. For example, a manager who refuses to fix the plumbing until the tenant agrees to a date is guilty of sexual harassment. This type of harassment may be established on the basis of only one incident.

EXAMPLE: Oscar, the resident manager of Northside Apartments, was attracted to Martha, his tenant, and asked her repeatedly for a date. Martha always turned Oscar down and asked that he leave her alone. Oscar didn't back off, and began hanging around the pool whenever Martha used it. Oscar watched Martha intently and made suggestive remarks about her to the other tenants. Martha stopped using the pool and filed a sexual harassment complaint with HUD, claiming that Oscar's unwanted attentions made it impossible for her to use and enjoy the pool and even to comfortably live at Northside. Oscar refused to consider a settlement when the HUD investigator spoke to him and Martha about his actions. As a result, HUD pursued the case in court, where a federal judge ordered Oscar to leave Martha alone and awarded several thousand dollars in damages to Martha.

! CAUTION

Sexual harassment awards under the Civil Rights Act have no limits. Owners and managers who engage in sexual harassment risk being found liable under either the Fair Housing Act or Title VII of the 1964 Civil Rights Act, which also prohibits sexual discrimination. The Fair Housing Act limits the dollar amount of damages that can be levied against the defendant, but there are no limits to the amount of punitive damages that can be awarded in Title VII actions. Punitive damages are generally not covered by insurance, and it is far from clear whether even actual damages in a discrimination case (that is, nonpunitive damages such as pain and suffering) will be covered, either.

Age

The federal fair housing law does not expressly use the word "age," but, nevertheless, discrimination on the basis of age is definitely included within the ban against discrimination on the basis of familial status. Many states and localities, however, have laws that directly address the issue of age.

Can you, as the landlord, refuse to rent to an older person solely because you fear that her frailty or dimming memory will pose a threat to the health or safety of the rest of your tenants? Or, can you favor younger tenants over equally qualified elderly tenants because you would like your property to have a youthful appearance?

The answer to these questions is no. You may feel that your worry about elderly tenants is well-founded, but unless you can point to an actual incident or to facts that will substantiate your concern, you cannot reject an elderly applicant on the basis of your fears alone. For example, you could turn away an older applicant if you learned from a prior landlord or employer that the person regularly forgot to lock the doors, failed to manage his income so that he was often late

in paying rent, or demonstrated an inability to undertake basic housekeeping chores. In other words, if the applicant has demonstrated that he or she is unable to live alone, your regular and thorough background check should supply you with those facts, which are legally defensible reasons to refuse to rent. As for your stylistic preference for youthful tenants, this is age discrimination in its purest form, and it will never survive a fair housing complaint.

> **EXAMPLE:** Nora's 80-year-old mother Ethel decided that it was time to find a smaller place and move closer to her daughter. Ethel sold her home and applied for a one-bedroom apartment at Coral Shores. Ethel had impeccable references from neighbors and employers and an outstanding credit history. Nonetheless, Mike, the manager of Coral Shores, was concerned about Ethel's age. Fearful that Ethel might forget to turn off the stove, lose her key, or do any number of other dangerous things, Mike decided on the spot not to rent to her. Ethel filed a fair housing complaint, which she won on the basis of age discrimination.

Learning from his experience with Ethel, Mike, the manager at Coral Shores, became more conscientious in screening tenants. The following example shows how he avoided another lawsuit on age discrimination.

> **EXAMPLE:** William was an elderly gentleman who decided to sell the family home and rent an apartment after his wife passed away. He applied for an apartment at Coral Shores. Since William had no "prior rental history," Mike, the manager, drove to William's old neighborhood and spoke with several of his former neighbors. Mike also called William's personal references. From these sources, Mike learned that William had been unable to take care of himself the last few years, having been completely dependent on his wife. Mike also learned that, since his wife's death, William had made several desperate calls to neighbors and family when he had been unable to extinguish a negligently started kitchen fire, find his keys, and maintain basic levels of cleanliness in his house. Mike noted these findings on William's application and declined to rent to him on the basis of these specific facts.

Renting to Minors

You may wonder whether the prohibition against age discrimination applies to minors (in most states, people under age 18). A minor applicant who is legally "emancipated"—is legally married, or has a court order of emancipation or is in the military—has the same status as an adult. This means you will need to treat the applicant like any other adult. In short, if the applicant satisfies the rental criteria that you apply to everyone, a refusal to rent to a minor could form the basis of a fair housing complaint. On the other hand, if the applicant is not emancipated, she lacks the legal capacity to enter into a legally binding rental agreement with you.

The issue of age discrimination may also arise during a well-established tenancy. You may have a tenant who has lived alone competently for years but who, with advancing age, appears to be gradually losing the ability to live safely by himself. Determining the point when the tenant should no longer live alone is a judgment call that will vary with every situation, and we cannot provide a checklist of "failings" that will suffice for everyone. There is, however, one universal ground rule that will, by now, sound pretty familiar: You cannot take action merely on the basis of the person's age or because you fear what that person might do. You must be able to point to real, serious violations of the criteria that apply to all tenants before you can evict or take action against an elderly tenant.

CAUTION

Elderly tenants may also qualify as disabled tenants, who are entitled to accommodation under the law. An elderly tenant who, because of her age, cannot meet one of your policies may be entitled to special treatment because she also qualifies as a disabled person. In other words, you may not be able to use an elderly tenant's inability to abide by one of the terms of the tenancy as the basis of an eviction—instead, you may be expected to adjust your policy in order to accommodate her disability. For example, an elderly tenant who is chronically late with the rent because of her sporadic disorientation might be entitled to a grace period, or a friendly reminder when the rent is due; whereas a nondisabled tenant who is chronically late with the rent is not entitled to such special treatment. And if an elderly tenant can't negotiate the stairs, the legal solution is a ramp (assuming the cost is not unreasonable), not an eviction notice.

Marital Status

Federal law does not prohibit discrimination on the basis of marital status (oddly, being married isn't included within the federal concept of "familial status"). Consequently, in most states you may legally refuse to rent to applicants on the grounds that they are (or are not) married. The issue comes up when a landlord chooses a married couple over a single applicant, or when an unmarried couple applies for a rental (or a current tenant wants to move in a special friend).

Some states have addressed these situations. About 20 states plus the District of Columbia ban discrimination on the basis of marital status, but most of these extend protection to married couples only. In these states, landlords cannot legally prefer single, platonic roommates (or one-person tenancies) over married couples. What about the reverse—preferring married couples over single roommates or a single tenant? Courts in Maryland, Minnesota, New York, and Wisconsin have ruled that the term "marital status" only protects married people from being treated differently from single people, not vice versa.

Now then, what about the remaining possibility—an unmarried couple? In only a few states—Alaska, California, Massachusetts, and New Jersey—does the term "marital status" include unmarried couples. If you own rental property in these four states, can you reject unmarried couples solely because they aren't married? It depends on your reasons. If you refuse to rent to unmarried couples on the grounds that cohabitation violates your religious beliefs and you live in California, Massachusetts, Michigan, or New Jersey, the answer is no.

TIP
Unmarried tenants may be protected by a city or county ordinance prohibiting discrimination on the basis of sexual orientation. Although usually passed to protect the housing rights of gay and lesbian tenants, most local laws forbidding discrimination based on sexual orientation also protect unmarried heterosexual couples as well. In addition, unmarried people may be able to challenge a landlord's refusal to rent to them on the basis of sex discrimination, which is covered by the federal Acts.

Sexual Orientation and Gender Identity/Expression

The federal fair housing laws do not ban discrimination on the basis of sexual orientation or gender identity or expression. However, the federal ban on discrimination on the basis of sex can apply when landlords make decisions based on their notions of gender conformity, regardless of the orientation or identity of the tenant or applicant. For example, imagine a landlord who rejects a prospective tenant because she wears traditionally masculine clothes and engages in other physical expressions that are typically male. This may be an instance of discrimination on the basis of sex.

Several states do address discrimination on the basis of orientation and identity/expression, banning both or only sexual orientation. For a comprehensive list, see the "Fair Housing/LGBT Page" on the HUD website: www.hud.gov/program_offices/fair_ housing_equal_opp/LGBT_Housing_Discrimination. Many cities also forbid these practices; contact your city attorney's office for information.

Source of Income

In several states, including California, Connecticut, the District of Columbia, Maine, Massachusetts, Minnesota, New Jersey, North Dakota, Oklahoma, Oregon, Utah, Vermont, and Wisconsin, you may not refuse to rent to a person simply because he is receiving public assistance (many localities in other states have similar law). You may, however, refuse to rent to persons whose available incomes fall below a certain level, as long as you apply that standard across the board.

Understand that the prohibition against discriminating on the basis of source of income does not necessarily mean that you must participate in the Section 8 program. In the states that ban discrimination based on the source of income, tenants' lawyers have argued that the ban supports their theory that landlords should not be free to decline to participate in government-subsidized programs; but these cases have not been universally successful. As noted in "Section 8 and Low-Income Housing Programs," below, if you don't want to participate in a Section 8 program, seek legal counsel.

Arbitrary Discrimination

After reading the above material outlining the types of illegal discrimination, you may be tempted to assume that it is legal to discriminate for any reason not mentioned by name in a state or federal law. For example, because none of the civil rights laws specifically prohibit discrimination against men with beards or long hair, you might conclude that such discrimination is permissible. This is not always true.

For example, even though California's Unruh Civil Rights Act (Cal. Civ. Code §§ 51–53.7, 54.1–54.8) contains only the phrases "sex, race, color, religion, ancestry, national origin, disability, medical condition, genetic information, marital status, gender identity, citizenship, primary language, or sexual orientation" to describe types of discrimination that are illegal, the courts have ruled that these categories are just examples of illegal discrimination. The courts in California have construed the Unruh Act to forbid all discrimination on the basis of one's personal characteristic or trait.

Even if you live in a state that does not specifically outlaw arbitrary discrimination, there is a very strong practical reason why you should not engage in arbitrary discrimination—for example, based on obesity, occupation, or style of dress. Because fair housing law includes numerous protected categories —race, sex, religion, and so on—chances are that a disappointed applicant can fit himself or herself into at least one of the protected categories and

Section 8 and Low-Income Housing Programs

Many tenants with low incomes qualify for federally sub-sidized housing assistance, the most common being the tenant-based Section 8 program of the federal Department of Housing and Urban Development (HUD). ("Section 8" refers to Section 8 of the United States Housing Act of 1937, 42 U.S. Code § 1437f.) That program pays part of the rent directly to you. The local public housing agency, you, and the tenant enter into a one-year agreement, which includes a written lease addendum supplied by the local public housing agency. The tenant pays a percentage of his monthly income to you, and the housing agency pays you the difference between the tenant's contribution and what it determines is the market rent each month.

The Pros and Cons of Section 8 Participation

Section 8 is a mixed bag for landlords. It offers several advantages:

- The housing agency pays the larger part of the rent on time every month, and the tenant's portion is low enough that he shouldn't have too much trouble paying on time, either.
- If the tenant doesn't pay the rent and you have to evict him, the housing agency guarantees the tenant's unpaid portion, and also guarantees payment for damage to the property by the tenant, up to a certain limit.
- You'll have a full house if your neighborhood or area is populated by low-income tenants.

Section 8's disadvantages are legion, however. They include:

- The housing agency's determination of what is market rent is often low, and the program caps the security deposit (which may be lower than your state's maximum).
- You are locked into a tenancy agreement for one year, and can't terminate the tenancy except for nonpayment of rent or other serious breach of the lease. (Evictions based on grounds other than nonpayment of rent or other serious breaches are difficult.)
- When HUD experiences a budget crunch, it cuts the public housing agencies' budgets. As a result, the housing agencies are likely to lower the landlords' allotments. Though this practice is legally iffy, it's done anyway.

- New Section 8 landlords must often wait up to a month or longer for a qualifying, mandatory inspection—during which they see no rent. These inspections often reveal picky, minor violations that state inspectors wouldn't cite for.

Call your local public housing agency if you wish to participate in the Section 8 program. They will refer eligible applicants to you, arrange for an inspection of the rental property, and prepare the necessary documents (including the lease addendum) if you decide to rent to an eligible applicant. Be sure to get a copy from HUD of the Section 8 rules and procedures that all participating landlords must use. Often, they vary significantly from your state or local law.

Must Landlords Participate in Section 8?

Landlords have traditionally been able to choose not to participate in the Section 8 program without fear of violating the federal fair housing laws. However, as the federal government's ability to provide sufficient low-income housing diminishes, this is changing in some localities. In New Jersey, for example, if an existing tenant becomes eligible for Section 8 assistance, you may not refuse to accept the vouchers—you must participate in the program as to this tenant, at least. (*Franklin Tower One v. N.M.*, 157 N.J. 602; 725 A.2d 1104 (1999).) In Connecticut, Maryland, and Massachusetts, landlords may not refuse to rent to existing or new tenants who will be paying with Section 8 vouchers. (*Commission on Human Rights and Opportunities v. Sullivan Associates*, 250 Conn. 763; 739 A.2d 238 (1999); Mass. Gen. Laws ch. 151B, § 4(10); *Montgomery County v. Glenmont Hills Associates Privacy*, 936 A.2d 325 (2007).)

Some states have required landlord participation in Section 8 by way of their ban on discrimination on the basis of source of income ("SOI"). These states make Section 8 vouchers one of the protected sources, and include Connecticut, Maine, Massachusetts, New Jersey, North Dakota, Oklahoma, Oregon, Utah, Vermont, Wisconsin, and the District of Columbia. However, localities in other states may pass laws that include Section 8 as a protected SOI (some cities in California and New York City, for example) even though there is no statewide protection in those states.

file a discrimination claim. Even if the applicant does not ultimately win his or her claim, the time, aggravation, and expense caused by his attempt will be costly to the landlord.

> **EXAMPLE:** Jane, a lawyer, applied for an apartment and returned her application to Lee, the landlord. Lee had spent the better part of the last year fighting a frivolous lawsuit brought by a former tenant (who was also a lawyer), and the thought of renting to another lawyer was more than Lee could bear. Jane's credit, rental, and personal references were excellent, but she was turned away.
>
> One of Lee's tenants told Jane that Lee had refused her solely because she was a lawyer. This made Jane angry, and she decided to get even. Although her state did not have a law prohibiting arbitrary discrimination, that didn't stop Jane. She filed a fair housing complaint alleging that she had been turned away because she was single, female, and Jewish. The complaint was ultimately dismissed, but not before it had cost Lee a bundle of time and energy to defend.

Valid Occupancy Limits

Your ability to limit the number of people per rental unit is one of the most hotly debated issues in the rental housing industry. Like most controversial topics, it has two sides, each with a valid point. No one disputes the wisdom of enforcing building codes that specify minimum square footage per occupant for reasons of health and safety. But it is another matter altogether when even relatively small families—especially those with children—are excluded from a large segment of the rental market because landlords arbitrarily set unreasonable occupancy policies.

The law allows you to establish an occupancy policy that is truly tied to health and safety needs. In addition, you can adopt standards that are driven by a legitimate business reason or necessity, such as the capacities of your plumbing or electrical systems. Your personal preferences (such as an exaggerated desire to reduce wear and tear by limiting the number of occupants, or to ensure a quiet uncrowded environment for upscale older tenants), however, do not constitute a legitimate business reason.

If your occupancy policy limits the number of tenants for any reason other than health, safety, and legitimate business needs, you risk charges of discrimination against families, known in legalese as "familial status" discrimination. Occupancy policies that cross over the line into discrimination toward families are discussed above.

The federal government has taken the lead in establishing occupancy standards through passage of the Fair Housing Amendments Act. But states and localities may also set their own occupancy standards, and many have. And this is where things get tricky: Ordinarily, when the federal government legislates on a particular subject, states and localities are free to pass laws on the subject, too, as long as they're equally (or more) protective of the targeted group. But the federal government's guidance (a mere memo to regional HUD directors) specifically reminded its readers that Congress didn't intend to develop "a national occupancy code." ("Fair Housing Enforcement—Occupancy Standards Notice of Statement of Policy," C.F.R. Vol. 63, No. 243, Dec. 18, 1998.) The memo practically invited states and localities to set their own occupancy standards, and didn't make it clear whether those standards had to be at least as generous (to tenants) as the federal guidance. As a result, some states developed occupancy standards that, when applied, resulted in fewer people allowed in the rental. Landlords were perplexed: Which standard did they need to follow? Their policy might be legal when examined in a state court, using state occupancy standards, but illegal when tested in a federal court, using the HUD guidance. And some states, like California, developed standards that resulted in more occupants than the federal guidance.

The way out of this morass is, fortunately, rather commonsense. To avoid lawsuits, you need to adopt an occupancy policy that is at least as generous as the federal standard, which is explained just below. And just in case your state or locality has legislated more generous standards, you'll have to follow them. If they're less generous, don't take a chance, because you risk that a tenant's lawyer will choose to sue you using the federal standard.

Minimum and Maximum Numbers of Occupants

Two kinds of laws affect your occupancy standards:

- **Minimum occupancy standards.** Federal, state, and local occupancy standards establish the minimum number of occupants you must allow in a particular unit. If you set a lower occupancy limit, you may be accused of violating a fair housing law.
- **Maximum occupancy limits.** State and local health and safety codes may set maximum limits on the number of tenants, based purely on the size of the unit and number of bedrooms and bathrooms.

Finding out whether your occupancy policy is legal is not always a simple matter. You must answer three questions for each rental situation:

- How many people must you allow in that particular unit under the federal standard?
- How many people must you allow in that unit under the state standard?
- How many people must you allow in that unit under the local standard?

Once you know the answers to each of these questions, the rest is easy: To avoid a federal, state, or local fair housing complaint, simply apply the occupancy standard that is the least restrictive—that is, the one that allows the most people. If you don't follow the least restrictive standard, be prepared to show that your policy (allowing fewer people) is motivated by reasons of health or safety or a legitimate business reason.

Unfortunately, getting the answers to the three questions is often difficult. This section will attempt to guide you through the process. It covers:

- federal occupancy standards
- common state occupancy standards and local laws on the subject
- how to calculate the number of occupants that must be allowed for each rental unit, and
- "legitimate business reasons" that might support a more restrictive policy than the law allows.

The Federal Occupancy Standard

Federal law allows you to establish "reasonable" restrictions on the number of persons per dwelling. These restrictions must be motivated by legitimate business reasons or the need to preserve the health and safety of the occupants.

The Department of Housing and Urban Development, or HUD, interprets federal law by means of memos, guidelines, and regulations. Unfortunately, HUD has never been very helpful when it comes to explaining what a "reasonable" restriction on persons per dwelling might be. HUD has simply said that a policy of two persons per bedroom will, as a general rule, be considered reasonable, but that other factors will also be considered when determining whether a landlord was illegally discriminating by limiting the number of people in a rental unit. Because the number of bedrooms is not the only factor, the federal test has become known as the "two-per-bedroom-plus" standard. These other factors include:

- the size of the bedrooms and rental unit—if the unit or the bedrooms are small, you may take that into account
- age of the children—babies do not have the same space requirements as teenagers, and you may take that into account
- configuration of the rental unit—if a room could serve as a bedroom, but there is no access to a bathroom except through another bedroom, you might be able to designate that room a "nonbedroom" and limit the number of occupants accordingly
- physical limitations of the building—for example, limitation of the sewerage or electrical system
- state and local building codes that impose their own set of minimum space requirements per occupant, and
- prior discrimination complaints against the landlord—if you must respond to a fair housing complaint, you will be at a disadvantage if you are known to repeatedly violate antidiscrimination laws.

The flexibility of the federal standard helps landlords because it lets them take into account all the particulars of a given situation. But it also means that you cannot set an occupancy limit for a unit and know for certain that it will pass the federal test. The legal occupancy maximum cannot be determined until you analyze every applicant. For example, if you decide that the family with a newborn needs less space than one with a teenager, the occupancy limit for the same unit will be different for each family.

As you might imagine, a federal "standard" that changes according to the makeup of every applicant has proven very difficult and confusing to apply, but you must do your best to apply it conscientiously.

Begin by multiplying the number of bedrooms times two, and then think about the factors listed above. For example, is one of the bedrooms so small as to be unsuitable for two people? On the other hand, could a room that you might think of as a den be usable as another bedroom? Could a couple with a baby in a bassinet comfortably occupy a bedroom that would be unsuitable for three adults? As you can see, use of the two-per-bedroom-plus standard may result in an occupancy limit that might be below or above twice the number of bedrooms.

EXAMPLE: Murray owned a large, old house that had been remodeled into two apartments. The upstairs unit had large rooms, two bedrooms, and two bathrooms. The lower apartment was considerably smaller, with one bedroom and one bath.

The Upstairs. Murray was approached by a family of five: three young children and two adults. He realized that the large bedroom could safely sleep three children, so he figured that the five people in this family came within the federal standards.

The Downstairs. The first applicants for the lower apartment were three adults. Murray told them that the occupancy limit was two. Later, a couple with a newborn applied for the apartment. Realizing that a bassinet could easily fit into the bedroom, Murray adjusted his occupancy limit and rented to the couple.

Common State and Local Occupancy Standards

Even if you are okay under the federal standard, you can't relax just yet. Remember, states and localities can set their own occupancy standards, as long as they are more generous than the federal government. You must comply with any state or local standard or (if a complaint is filed) risk prosecution by the state or local agency that administers the standard.

It is crucial to check whether any state or local standard applies to you. Contact your local and state housing authority for information, or the U.S. Department of Housing and Urban Development (HUD) office.

New York landlords, for example, must comply with the "Unlawful Restrictions on Occupancy" law, commonly known as the "Roommate Law." (N.Y. RPL § 235-f.) The Roommate Law prohibits New York landlords from limiting occupancy of a rental unit to just the tenant named on the lease or rental agreement. It permits tenants to share their rental units with their immediate family members, and, in many cases, with unrelated, nontenant occupants, too, so long as a tenant (or tenant's spouse) occupies the unit as a primary residence. The number of total occupants is still restricted, however, by local laws governing overcrowding.

CAUTION
Remember, you must apply the most generous standard—federal, state, or local—in determining how many people may occupy a particular rental unit. If you are unsure of the result, it is always safer to err on the side of more, rather than fewer, occupants.

Legitimate Reasons for a More Restrictive Occupancy Policy

What if you decide that your particular rental unit ought to be occupied by fewer than the most generous number you got when you calculated the occupancy under the federal, state, and local laws? If you set an occupancy limit that is lower than the legal standard, you must be prepared to defend it with a legitimate business reason. This term is impossible to describe in the abstract, since its meaning will vary with the circumstances of every rental property. Here are some examples of legitimate business reasons that have been advanced by landlords who have established occupancy limits lower than the government standard:

- **Limitations of the infrastructure.** The plumbing or electrical systems cannot, without extensive and expensive upgrades, accommodate more than a certain amount of use. (*U.S. v. Weiss*, 847 F.Supp 819 (1994).)
- **Limitations of the facilities.** Common areas and facilities (such as laundry rooms and hallways) would be overcrowded if more occupants were allowed.
- **Dilapidation that common sense tells you would result from more people living in the structure.** The house is so small that allowing more occupants would result in unreasonable wear and tear. (*Pfaff v. U.S. Department of Housing and Urban Development*, 88 F.3d 739 (1996).)

If your occupancy policy is lower than the most generous applicable legal standard, be prepared for an uphill fight. It is very difficult to establish a "winning" legitimate business reason that justifies a lower occupancy standard. You'd be wise to hire a neutral professional, such as an engineer, to evaluate and report on the limiting factor in light of your community's needs (for example, you'll want a report that measures your boilers' limited hot water delivery against the number of residents who you think should reasonably live there). Get that report *before* imposing a restrictive occupancy policy, and make sure it really justifies your decision to use more restrictive occupancy standards.

You will need to carefully assess whether it's worth your time and money to fight a fair housing complaint. In order to establish that your lower occupancy policy is based upon legitimate business reasons and is therefore legal, you'll need to convince a fair housing judge that:

- changing the limiting factor (such as rewiring the rental unit's electrical system to accommodate more use) is impractical from a business perspective, or
- common sense, your business experience, and the practice of landlords in your area support your lower number, or
- limiting the number of occupants is the only practical way to address the limiting factor.

Here are some examples of situations in which landlords have argued that their occupancy policy, which was lower than that allowed by the most generous applicable law, should nonetheless survive a fair housing challenge. In both cases, the landlord argued that the limitations of the septic system justified a more restrictive occupancy standard. In the first example, the landlord prevailed. In the second example, the landlord failed to establish that his occupancy policy was based upon legitimate business reasons.

> **EXAMPLE 1:** John and Mary Evans advertised the small two-bedroom cottage on their property as suitable for two people only. Their occupancy limit was based on the limitations of the septic system, which could legally accommodate no more than four people (the Evanses and two tenants in the cottage). John and Mary declined to rent to a family of four, who then filed a fair housing complaint. At the conciliation meeting arranged by the housing authority, John and Mary presented an engineer's report on the limitations of the septic system. The report estimated that it would cost many thousands of dollars to expand the septic system to accommodate more than four people on the property. The hearing officer accepted the Evanses' explanation and decided not to take the complaint further.

> **EXAMPLE 2:** The occupancy policy for all the units at Westside Terrace was three persons per apartment, even for the two-bedroom units. A family of four applied for one of the two-bedrooms and was turned down. When the family filed a complaint with HUD,

the owner of Westside Terrace justified the policy on the grounds that the building's infrastructure—its sewage capacities, pipes, and common areas—could not support as many people as would result from allowing four persons in the two-bedroom apartment units. Westside also presented evidence that it would be prohibitively expensive to upgrade these facilities. The judge heard evidence from structural and sanitary engineers which indicated that these facilities were capable of handling that number of people and had done so many times in the past. HUD decided that Westside's restrictive occupancy policy was not based on legitimate business needs, and ruled against it.

Managers and Discrimination

If you hire a manager, particularly one who selects tenants, make certain that he fully understands and abides by laws against housing discrimination. On the other hand, if you use an independent management company (which is a true independent contractor, rather than an employee such as a resident manager), the possibility that you will be liable for their discriminatory acts is greatly decreased. (See Chapter 6 on landlord liability for a manager's conduct and strategies for avoiding problems in this area.)

You should always let your tenants know that you, as well as your manager, intend to abide by the law, and that you want to know about and will address any fair housing problems that may arise. While this will not shield you from liability if you are sued due to your manager's conduct, it might (if you are lucky) result in the tenant's initial complaint being made to you, not a fair housing agency. If you hear about a manager's discriminatory act and can resolve a complaint before it gets into "official channels," you will have saved yourself a lot of time, trouble, and money.

One way to alert your tenants and prospective tenants to your commitment to the fair housing laws is to write all ads, applications, and other material given to prospective tenants to include a section containing your antidiscrimination stance. Prepare a written policy statement as to the law

and your intention to abide by it. See the sample statement below.

Also, be sure to display fair housing posters on the premises, as described earlier in the chapter.

Sample Statement on Equal Opportunity in Housing

FROM: Shady Dell Apartments

TO: All Tenants and Applicants

It is the policy of the owner and manager of Shady Dell Apartments to rent our units without regard to a tenant's race, ethnic background, sex, age, religion, marital or family status, physical disability, gender identity, or sexual orientation. As part of our commitment to provide equal opportunity in housing, we comply with all federal, state, and local laws prohibiting discrimination. If you have any questions or complaints regarding our rental policy, call the owner at (phone number).

If, despite your best efforts, you even suspect your manager may use unlawful discriminatory practices to select or deal with tenants—whether on purpose or inadvertently—you should immediately resume control of the situation yourself. Alternatively, this may be the time to shield yourself from potential liability and engage the services of an independent management company, which in most cases will be responsible for its employees' actions.

CAUTION

Never give managers or rental agents the authority to offer their own rent concessions or "deals" to selected tenants or applicants. If you want to offer inducements—a discount for signing an extended lease or one free month for tenants who begin renting in the month of March—do so on a consistent basis. Make sure offers are available to all tenants who meet the requirements of the special deal. Otherwise, a tenant who gets a worse deal from your manager than his identically situated neighbor is sure to complain—and if he is a member of a group protected by fair housing laws, he's got the makings of a case against you.

Unlawful Discrimination Complaints

A landlord accused of unlawfully discriminating against a prospective or current tenant may end up before a state, federal, or local housing agency, or in state or federal court. According to HUD, the number of fair housing complaints (most involving rentals) has declined in the last few years, from around 10,000 complaints in fiscal year 2010, to a little more than 8,000 in fiscal year 2016. According to the most recent HUD data (covering fiscal year 2016), more than half involved claims concerning disability discrimination, and about one-quarter were claims involving race (this is a notable difference from earlier years, when disability and race used to account for nearly the same percentage of complaints). ("Office of Fair Housing and Equal Opportunity Annual Report to Congress, FY 2016.") This section gives you a brief description of the legal process involved in each arena and the consequences of discrimination charges.

 SEE AN EXPERT

Get expert help to defend a housing discrimination lawsuit. With the exception of a suit brought in small claims court, you should see an attorney if a tenant sues you or files an administrative complaint against you for discrimination. For advice on finding and working with an attorney or doing your own legal research, see Chapter 18.

When a Tenant Complains to a Fair Housing Agency

A prospective or current tenant may file a discrimination complaint with either HUD (by phone, mail, or online) or the state or local agency charged with overseeing fair housing complaints. A federal HUD complaint must be filed within one year of the alleged violation, but state statutes or local ordinances may set shorter time periods. If the complaint is filed with HUD, the agency should (but doesn't always) conduct an investigation within 180 days. (Time periods for state housing agencies vary.)

After HUD investigates the complaint (and this is true of most state agencies as well), it will either dismiss the complaint or attempt to reach a conciliation agreement (compromise) between you and the person filing the complaint. For example, a tenant might agree to drop his complaint in exchange for a sum of money or your written promise to rent him an apartment or, if he's a current tenant, to stop discriminatory practices.

If conciliation is unsuccessful, the fair housing agency will hold an administrative hearing (a trial before a judge but without a jury) to determine whether discrimination has occurred. If the administrative law judge decides that a fair housing violation occurred, he or she will direct that the violation be corrected in the ways described below.

HUD litigation is typically long and laborious. It is not unusual for cases to take up to ten years before they are concluded.

When a Tenant Sues in Federal or State Court

A tenant may also file suit in federal court or state court. This can be done even after filing an administrative complaint (as long as he has not signed a conciliation agreement or a HUD administrative hearing has not started). If the tenant goes to federal court, he must do so within two years of the alleged violation.

In a typical federal lawsuit, the aggrieved tenant (or would-be tenant) has gone to a private lawyer immediately after the alleged discriminatory incident. The attorney prepares a complaint and also asks the court for an expedited hearing, hoping to get an order from the court directing the landlord to cease the discriminatory practice. These orders are called "temporary restraining orders," and they are granted if the plaintiff (the tenant) can convince the judge that he has a good chance of winning and will suffer irreparable harm if immediate relief isn't granted. The order remains in place until a more formal hearing is held. Open-and-shut cases of discrimination often settle at the temporary restraining order stage.

Penalties for Discrimination

If a state or federal court or housing agency finds that discrimination has taken place, it may order you to do one or more of the following:

- rent a particular unit to the person who was discriminated against
- pay the tenant for "actual" or "compensating" damages, including any additional rent the tenant had to pay elsewhere as a result of being turned down, and damages for humiliation or emotional distress
- pay the tenant punitive damages (extra money as punishment for especially outrageous discrimination) and the tenant's attorney fees
- in the case of a disability violation, retrofit your property or set up an escrow fund to be used for retrofitting in the future, and
- pay a civil penalty to the federal government. The maximum penalty under the federal Fair Housing Acts is $19,787 for a first violation, and $98,935 for a third violation within seven years. (24 CFR § 180.671.) Many states have comparable penalties.

Even if you are ultimately vindicated, the costs of defending a discrimination claim can be devastating. Your insurance policy may cover the dollar costs, but it cannot compensate you for lost time and aggravation. Careful attention to the discrimination rules described in this chapter and Chapter 1 will, we hope, save you from this fate.

CAUTION

If you are the subject of a fair housing complaint, do not take the matter "into your own hands." It is illegal to retaliate against, threaten, coerce, intimidate, or interfere with anyone who either files a complaint with HUD, cooperates in the investigation of such a complaint, or exercises a fair housing right.

Insurance Coverage in Discrimination Claims

Even the most conscientious landlords may find themselves facing a fair housing claim or a discrimination lawsuit. If this happens to you, will your insurance policy cover the cost of defending the claim and, if you lose, the cost of the settlement or judgment? The answers to these questions depend entirely on two highly variable factors: the wording of your insurance policy and the decisions of the courts in your state in similar cases. In short, there are no answers that will apply to everyone, but we can alert you to the issues that arise in every situation. At the very least, knowing how insurance companies are likely to approve or deny defense and judgment costs in discrimination claims should help you as you evaluate your own policy.

RELATED TOPIC

Chapter 10 discusses broad types of liability insurance, coverage for managers and other employees, and coverage for injuries suffered as a result of defective conditions on the property. The advice in that chapter on choosing property insurance is also relevant to choosing liability coverage for discrimination claims.

The Insurance Company's Duty to Defend: Broader Than the Duty to Cover

When you purchase liability insurance, you buy two things: the promise of the insurance company to defend you if you are sued for an act that arguably falls within the coverage of the policy, and its promise to pay the settlement or damage award if you lose. But sometimes (as is the case in fair housing claims) it is unclear whether, assuming you lose the case, your policy covers the conduct that gave rise to the claim. When this happens, your insurance company will usually defend you, but it may reserve the right to argue about whether it is obligated to pay the damages if the case is lost. Before you purchase insurance, find out exactly what's covered, including punitive damages in discrimination cases.

Most owners of residential rental property carry a comprehensive liability insurance policy, which typically includes business liability coverage. With this type of coverage, the insurance company agrees to pay on your behalf all sums that you are legally obligated to pay as damages "for bodily injury, property damage, or personal injury caused by an occurrence to which this insurance applies." The policy will generally define the three key terms "bodily injury," "occurrence," and "personal injury." The definitions will determine whether the insurance company will help you with a discrimination claim.

⊘ CAUTION
Find out if your policy covers administrative claims (complaints to fair housing agencies such as HUD). Insurance companies in several states have successfully argued that their duties to defend and cover you extend only to lawsuits, not fair housing agency claims. Ask your agent.

Definition of "Bodily Injury"

Discrimination complaints rarely include a claim that the victim suffered a physical injury at the hands of the landlord or manager. It is far more likely that the tenant or applicant will sue for the emotional distress caused by the humiliation of the discriminatory act.

"Bodily injury" does not usually include emotional distress. Courts in a few states, however, have held that bodily injury does include emotional distress. If your state does not include emotional distress in the concept of bodily injury, an insurance company may be able to successfully argue that a discrimination complaint is not covered by the policy.

Definition of "Personal Injury"

Insurance policies also typically provide coverage for "personal injury," or an injury that arises out of the conduct of your business. Personal injuries typically include false arrest, libel, slander, and violation of privacy rights; they also include "wrongful entry or eviction or other invasions of the right of private occupancy." As you can see

from this definition, personal injuries include items that are neither bodily injuries nor accidental. And the definition includes some offenses, like libel, that seem somewhat similar to discrimination.

Nevertheless, an insurance company may argue that a discrimination claim isn't covered under a policy's definition of "personal injury."

A Policy Specifically for Discrimination Claims and Lawsuits

As you've just learned, if you're sued for discrimination, it may be difficult or impossible to get coverage under your commercial general liability (CGL) policy. Another type of policy will offer you narrow, but certain coverage. This coverage is called "Tenant Discrimination Insurance," and it works a bit differently than your CGL policy. A CGL policy supplies the defense attorney and all resources to defend against the claim, as well as any judgment, up to the limits of your policy. When using Discrimination insurance, however, you find your own lawyer and, once a lawsuit or claim is filed (with HUD or any state or local fair housing agency), you get reimbursed for legal costs from that point on, and the amount of any judgment.

The Discrimination policy does not present any of the thorny issues encountered with a CGL policy—even intentional, blatant acts of discrimination will be covered. The policy will exclude class actions, suits by employees, any legal work and settlement that occurred without the other side having filed a lawsuit or a claim; and it may exclude punitive damages or fines, depending on state law. One definite drawback is that you must initiate the request for reimbursement, and if the carrier balks, you have to take action (with your CGL, the insurance company in most instances will step up on notice of the claim and defend you at least).

Discrimination insurance is not well known. It is relatively inexpensive. If you are interested, contact your insurance agent or broker and ask for information. You may have to supply the source: "NAS Insurance Services" is the underwriter. For more information, see www.nasinsurance.com.

Very few courts have addressed this question, let alone answered it, but in those that have, the answers have been quite mixed. For example, coverage has been denied on the grounds that "discrimination" is a specific wrong and, had the insurance company intended to cover discrimination, it would have specifically mentioned it. Coverage for discrimination claims by prospective tenants (such as applicants who have been turned away) has been denied on the theory that "the right of private occupancy" is a right enjoyed only by current, not would-be, tenants. Still other courts, realizing that the language in the policy is far from clear, have been willing to resolve the question in favor of the insured, and have ordered the insurance company to at least defend the lawsuit.

In sum, there are at least three ways that insurance companies can deny coverage, if not also the defense of a fair housing claim and award: They can claim that the discriminatory act resulted in emotional distress, which is not a type of bodily injury; they can argue that an act of discrimination was intentional, and thus not an accidental occurrence to which the policy applies; and they can argue that discrimination is not one of the personal injuries that are covered by the policy. We suggest that you give the matter some thought when choosing a broker and negotiating your policy—but by far the best use of your energy is to make sure that your business practices do not expose you to these claims in the first place.

Discrimination and Public Policy

An insurance company will occasionally argue that it should not have to cover a landlord's intentional acts of discrimination because discrimination is an evil act that someone should not be able to insure against. While this argument has some persuasive aspects—discrimination is, indeed, contrary to public policy—it falls apart when you acknowledge that all sorts of other intentional bad acts (like libel and slander) are perfectly insurable. Courts have not been persuaded by the "public policy" argument. Be sure to check with your insurance broker whether your policy covers intentional acts of discrimination.

Definition of "Occurrence"

Your insurance company will defend and pay out on a claim if it is caused by an occurrence to which the policy applies. An "occurrence" is typically defined as an accident, whose results are neither expected nor intended from the standpoint of the insured (the property owner).

It doesn't take much brainwork to see how an insurance company can argue that an act of discrimination—like turning away a minority applicant—cannot be considered an "occurrence," because it is by definition intentional, not accidental. Courts in a few states have ruled in favor of insurance companies on this issue, and courts in other states have ruled similarly when the question has come up in employment discrimination cases.

Property Managers

FORMS IN THIS CHAPTER

Chapter 6 includes instructions for and a sample of the following form:

- Property Manager Agreement

The Nolo website includes a downloadable copy of this form. See Appendix B for the link to the forms in this book.

Many landlords hire a resident manager to handle all the day-to-day details of running an apartment building, including fielding tenants' routine repair requests and collecting the rent. Landlords who own several rental properties (large or small) may contract with a property management firm in addition to, or in place of, a resident manager. Hiring a manager can free you from many of the time-consuming (and tiresome) aspects of being a residential landlord. But it can also create some headaches of its own: lots of paperwork for the IRS; worries about liability for a manager's acts; and the responsibility of finding, hiring, and supervising an employee. This chapter explains how to weigh all these factors and how to minimize complications if you do decide to get some management help.

In some states, you may not have a choice—you may be required, by law, to hire a manager. California, for example, requires a resident manager on the premises of any apartment complex with 16 or more units. (Cal. Code of Regulations, Title 25, § 42.) New York City has similar requirements for buildings with nine or more units. Check with your state or local rental property owners' association to see if your state requires resident managers, or do your own research on the subject.

RESOURCE

Several other Nolo books provide useful information on hiring, managing, and firing employees:

- *The Employer's Legal Handbook*, by Fred S. Steingold, is a complete guide to the latest workplace laws and regulations. It covers everything you need to know about hiring and firing employees, drug tests of employees, personnel policies, employee benefits, discrimination, and other laws affecting small business practices.
- *The Manager's Legal Handbook*, Lisa Guerin and Sachi Barreiro, has excellent information about hiring employees.

- *The Essential Guide to Federal Employment Laws*, by Lisa Guerin and Sachi Barreiro, has extensive discussions on relevant federal laws, including the Fair Labor Standards Act, Americans with Disabilities Act, Equal Pay Act, Immigration Reform and Control Act, Fair Credit Reporting Act, and Occupational Safety and Health Act, as well as state and federal employment discrimination laws.
- *Dealing With Problem Employees: A Legal Guide*, by Lisa Guerin and Amy DelPo, includes chapters on hiring, evaluating, disciplining, and firing employees.
- *The Essential Guide to Workplace Investigations*, by Lisa Guerin, gives employers practical information on how to investigate and resolve workplace problems.

These Nolo books are available at bookstores and public libraries. They may also be ordered directly from Nolo's website, www.nolo.com, or by calling 800-728-3555.

For free general information on employment law, from discrimination to workers' compensation, see Nolo's articles in the Employment Law Center at www.nolo.com.

Property Managers and Building Supers

The focus in this chapter is on property managers, not supers (which are more common in places like New York City). While there aren't any hard and fast rules, here's the difference between a building superintendent (super) and a manager.

Property managers usually have more tenant-relations responsibilities than supers do, such as taking apartment applications, accepting rent, and responding to tenant problems and complaints. You might also authorize a trusted manager to purchase building supplies and hire outside contractors for specialized repairs—up to an agreed-upon spending limit, of course.

Building supers, on the other hand, usually concentrate on building repairs and maintenance tasks. They often possess special skills and are experienced at running complicated heating plants and air conditioning systems. Customarily, supers don't collect rent or take rental applications.

The legal issues as to hiring and compensating managers and supers are generally the same.

Hiring Your Own Resident Manager

If you put some thought into writing a job description, and some effort into recruiting and hiring a good manager, you'll avoid problems down the road. Don't hurry the process, or jump into an informal arrangement with a tenant who offers to help out if you'll take a little off the rent—you'll almost surely regret it.

Decide the Manager's Duties, Hours, and Pay

Why do you want to hire a manager? You need to answer this question in some detail as your first step in the hiring process. Here are the key issues you need to decide.

What are the manager's responsibilities? The Property Manager Agreement included in this book includes a list of duties you may want to delegate, such as selecting tenants, collecting rents, and hiring and paying repair people. Finding an on-site manager who can handle all these aspects of the job, however, is a tall order—so tall that many owners restrict the on-site manager's job to handling routine repairs and maintenance chores. Listing the job duties and skills you're looking for in a manager will make the hiring process more objective and will give you ready standards to measure which applicants are most qualified.

Is the job full or part time? How many hours do you anticipate the manager working? What hours do you expect the manager to be on the rental property or available (for example, by pager or cell phone)?

Will the manager live on the rental property or off? If you just want someone to collect the rent and handle minor repairs, they don't necessarily need to live in. Obviously, you need a vacant apartment for a resident manager.

How much do you plan to pay the manager? You may pay an hourly wage, generally ranging from $15 to $25 per hour, or a flat salary. How much you pay depends on the manager's responsibilities, the number of hours, time of day and regularity of the schedule, benefits, and the going rate in your community. You can get an idea how much managers are paid by asking other landlords or checking want ads for managers. Offering slightly above the going rate in your area should allow you to hire the best, most experienced candidates. If you do this, you might want to try and tap into the local grapevine of experienced managers to see if maybe you can snag someone who wants to move up.

Illegal Discrimination in Hiring

Federal, state, and local laws prohibit many kinds of discrimination in hiring. The Equal Pay Act applies to every employer, regardless of size; the Immigration Reform and Control Act of 1986 (IRCA) applies to employers with four or more employees. Title VII of the Civil Rights Act and the Americans with Disabilities Act apply only if you employ 15 or more people. Some state laws apply even if you have only one employee, such as California's prohibition on worker harassment.

Pay attention to these laws even if they do not specifically bind your business. Doing so will not hinder you from making a decision based on sound business reasons: skills, experience, references. The laws only forbid making a decision based on a factor that isn't reasonably related to the applicant's ability to do the job. Following them will protect you from accusations of discrimination.

Here are some of the factors on which these laws make it illegal to discriminate: race, color, gender, religious beliefs, national origin, age (if the person is 40 or older), and disability. Several states and cities also prohibit discrimination based on marital status, sexual orientation, or other factors. Contact your state fair employment office for details.

Much of the advice in Chapter 5, which deals with illegal discrimination against tenants, will also be of help when you're hiring a manager.

Should you give the manager reduced rent? Some landlords prefer giving a resident manager reduced rent in exchange for management services, rather than paying a separate salary. This isn't a good idea—for one thing, reduced rent alone won't work for a full-time manager. Reduced rent in exchange for being a manager can be a particular problem in rent control areas, since you may not be able to adjust rent easily. If you later have to fire a manager who is compensated by reduced rent, you may run into problems when you insist that the ex-manager go back to paying the full rent. But if the tenant-manager pays the full rent and receives a separate salary, there will be no question that he is still obligated to pay the full rent, as he has done all along.

Your obligations as an employer are the same whether you compensate the manager with reduced rent or a paycheck—for example, you must still pay Social Security and payroll taxes, as discussed below. However, paying the manager by reducing rent can create problems under wages and hours and overtime laws.

Advertise the Job

Some landlords find great managers via word of mouth by talking to tenants, friends, and relatives, or getting the word out through Facebook or other social media. Others run a Craigslist ad, use an employment agency, or advertise elsewhere. What will work best depends on your particular property and needs. In writing an ad, stick to the job skills needed and the basic responsibilities—for example, "Fifty-unit apartment complex seeks full-time resident manager with experience in selecting tenants, collecting rent, and apartment maintenance."

Screen Potential Managers Over the Phone

When people call about the manager's job, be ready to describe the responsibilities, pay, and hours. Then ask some questions yourself—you'll be able to quickly eliminate unlikely candidates and avoid wasting time interviewing inappropriate people. Use the phone call to get information on potential employees, including their:

- experience and qualifications

- interest in the position and type of work
- current employment, and
- ability to work at the proposed pay and schedule.

Jot notes of your conversation so you can follow up later in a personal interview.

Interview Strong Candidates

Limit your interviews to people you're really interested in hiring as manager. There's no point meeting with someone who's unqualified or unsuitable for the job. When setting interviews, ask potential managers to bring a résumé with relevant experience and names and phone numbers of four or five references.

A face-to-face meeting provides the opportunity to get in-depth information about a person's background, work experience, and ability to handle the manager's job, and allows you to assess an individual's personality and style.

Before you begin interviewing, write down questions focusing on the job duties and the applicant's skills and experience. To avoid potential charges of discrimination, ask everyone the same questions, and don't ask questions that are not clearly job-related—for example, the applicant's medical condition, religion, or plans for having children.

Here are some examples of questions that are appropriate to ask potential managers:

- "Tell me about your previous jobs managing rental properties."
- "How much experience do you have collecting rents? Doing general repairs? Keeping records of tenants' complaints of repair problems?"
- "What have you liked most about previous manager jobs? What have you liked least?"
- "What kinds of problems have you encountered as a property manager? How did you solve them?"
- "Why do you want this job?"

You might also ask some more direct questions, like:

- "What would you do if a tenant who had paid rent on time for six months asked for a ten-day extension because money was short as a result of a family problem?"
- "What would you do if a tenant called you at 11 p.m. with a complaint about a clogged sink?"

Get a Completed Application

If your manager will also be a tenant, make sure he or she (like all other tenants) completes a rental application (as discussed in Chapter 1) and that you check references and other information carefully. Be sure the applicant signs a form authorizing you to check credit history and references, such as the Consent to Contact References and Perform Credit Check form in Chapter 1.

If your manager is not also a tenant, prepare your own application (you can use the Rental Application in Chapter 1 and cross out what's not relevant) or ask prospective managers to bring a résumé with their employment and educational background.

CAUTION

When you check a prospective manager's application or résumé, be sure to look for holes—dates when the person didn't indicate an employer. The applicant may be covering up a bad reference. Insist that the applicant explain any gaps in employment history.

Check References

No matter how wonderful someone appears in person or on paper, it's essential to contact former employers. Ideally, you should talk with at least two former employers or supervisors with whom the applicant held similar positions.

Before calling any references, make a list of key questions. Ask about the applicant's previous job responsibilities, character and personality traits, strengths and weaknesses, and reasons for leaving

the job. Review your interview notes for issues you want to explore more—for example, if you sense that the potential manager really doesn't seem organized enough to handle all the details of the manager's job, ask about it. Take your time and get all the information you need to determine whether the applicant is the best person for the job.

Character Traits of a Good Manager

Look for a person who is:

- **Honest and responsible.** This is especially important if the manager will be entitled to receive legal documents and papers on your behalf.
- **Patient.** Predictably, dealing with tenants, repair people, and guests will have its share of hassles. A person with a short fuse is a definite liability.
- **Financially responsible.** This should be demonstrated by a good credit history.
- **Personable yet professional.** Good communication skills are a must, both with you and your current and prospective tenants and any other workers the manager may supervise (for example, a cleaning crew).
- **Fastidious.** One of the manager's responsibilities will be to keep the building and common areas neat, clean, and secure.
- **Meticulous about maintaining records.** This is particularly important if collecting rent will be part of the job.
- **Fair and free of biases.** This is a must if the manager will be showing apartments, taking rental applications, or selecting tenants.
- **Unafraid of minor confrontations with tenants.** This is particularly important if the manager will be collecting overdue rents and delivering eviction notices, and handling disputes between tenants (for example, complaints over noise).

Employers are often reluctant to say anything negative about a former employee for fear of being hit by a lawsuit for defamation. Many may refuse to give any information other than the dates the person worked and the position held. It may be helpful to send the former employer a copy of the applicant's signed consent to disclosure of employment information. If a former employer is not forthcoming, you'll need to learn to read between the lines. If a former employer is neutral, offers only faint praise, or overpraises a person for one aspect of a job only—"always on time"—he may be hiding negative information. Ask former employers: "Would you hire this person back if you could?" The response may be telling. If a reference isn't glowing and doesn't cover all aspects of the job, check several other references—or hire someone else.

Check Credit History and Background

Checking an individual's credit history is especially important if you want a manager to handle money. Someone with large debts may be especially tempted to skim money from your business. And a prospective manager with sloppy personal finances is not a good choice for managing rental property. Before you order a credit report, be sure you get the applicant's consent.

You may also wish to ask a credit bureau or tenant screening company to do an investigative or background report, similar to the one some landlords run on tenants (see Chapter 1 for details).

CAUTION

Handle credit reports carefully. Federal law requires you to keep only needed information, and to discard the rest. See "How to Handle Credit Reports," in Chapter 7 for precise information.

Check Criminal and Driving Records

A property manager occupies a position of trust, often having access to tenants' apartments as well as to your money. Obviously, it's essential that

the manager not present a danger to tenants. You may want to check an applicant's criminal history; credit reports often include this information. Depending on your state's laws concerning use of Megan's Law databases, you may want to use the database to check for registered sex offenders as explained in Chapter 1.

Another reason for thoroughness is your personal liability—if a manager commits a crime, you may be held responsible as discussed in "Protect Tenants From Your Employees" in Chapter 12.

Our best advice is check carefully and consider the type, seriousness, and dates of any prior convictions and how they relate to the job. *The Employer's Legal Handbook*, by Fred S. Steingold (Nolo), includes information on state laws on obtaining and using information on arrest and conviction records when making employment decisions.

If a manager will be driving your car or truck, be sure your insurance covers someone driving your vehicle as part of their employment.

Offer the Position and Put Your Agreement in Writing

Once you make your decision and offer someone the manager's job, you may need to do some negotiations. The potential employee may, for example, want a higher salary, different hours, more vacation, a different rental unit, or a later starting date than you offer. It may take some compromises to establish mutually agreeable work arrangements. When all terms and conditions of employment are mutually agreed upon, you and the manager should complete a Property Manager Agreement (discussed below) that covers manager responsibilities, hours, and pay that can be terminated at any time for any reason by either party.

We recommend that when you hire a tenant as a manager, you also sign a separate month-to-month rental agreement that can be terminated by either of you with the amount of written notice, typically 30 days, required under state law.

Why Do You Need a Written Agreement?

Landlords and resident managers often agree orally on the manager's responsibilities and compensation, never signing a written agreement.

Even though oral agreements are usually legal and binding, they are not advisable. Memories fade, and you and your employee may have different recollections of what you've agreed to. If a dispute arises between you and the manager, the exact terms of an oral agreement are difficult or impossible to prove if you end up arguing about them in court. It is a far better business practice to put your understanding in writing.

How to Reject Applicants for the Manager's Job

It used to be a matter of simple courtesy to inform unsuccessful applicants by sending a quick but civil rejection letter, which cut down on postinterview calls, too. You didn't owe them an explanation, however, and were usually better off saying as little as possible.

Is this approach still legal? It depends on why you have rejected the applicant. If your reasons come from information that the applicant has provided, or if the applicant doesn't have the qualifications for the job, you can still use the courteous-but-minimalist approach. For example, if the applicant tells you that she has never managed real estate property, or if the interview reveals that the applicant doesn't have the necessary "people skills," you can simply say that someone more qualified got the job.

However, if your rejection is based on information from a credit reporting agency that collects and sells credit files or other information about consumers, you must comply with the Fair Credit Reporting Act (15 U.S. Code §§ 1681 and following). See "How to Reject an Applicant" in Chapter 1 for more details, including a sample Notice of Denial Based on Credit Report or Other Information form.

CAUTION
Don't promise long-term job security. When you hire someone, don't give assurances that you may not be able to honor and that may give an applicant a false sense of security. Your best protection is to make sure your Property Manager Agreement emphasizes your right to fire an employee at will—and have the applicant acknowledge this in writing (see Clause 6 of the agreement shown below). This means you'll have the right to terminate the employment at any time for any reason that doesn't violate the law.

How to Prepare a Property Manager Agreement

Below is an example of a sound written agreement that spells out the manager's responsibilities, hourly wage or salary, hours, schedule, and other terms. The step-by-step instructions that follow take you through the process of completing your own agreement.

The Nolo website includes a downloadable copy of the Property Manager Agreement. See Appendix B for the link to the form in this book.

Clause 1. Parties

Here, you provide details about you and the manager and the location of the rental property, and state that the rental agreement is a separate document.

Clause 2. Beginning Date

Fill in the month, day, and year of the manager's first day of work.

Clause 3. Responsibilities

This form includes a broad checklist of managerial duties, such as rent collection, maintenance, and repair. Check all the boxes that apply to your situation. In the space provided, spell out what is required, with as much detail as possible, particularly regarding maintenance responsibilities.

To make sure your manager doesn't act illegally on the job, also prepare a more detailed set of instructions to give to the manager when he or she starts work. We show a sample below, which you can tailor to your particular situation and state laws (for example, on discrimination and notice of entry requirements).

Clause 4. Hours and Schedule

Before filling this section in, check with your state department of labor or employment for wage and hour laws that may affect the number of hours you can schedule a manager to work in a day or days in a week. Don't expect a manager to be on call 24 hours a day. In most circumstances, you must pay overtime after 40 hours per week.

Should You Pay Benefits?

No law requires you to provide paid vacation, paid holidays, or premium pay for weekend or holiday work (unless it's for overtime). While most states do not require paid sick leave either, a handful of states require employers to provide at least a few paid sick days each year. Fringe benefits are not required, although larger employers (those with 50 or more full-time employees) may need to provide health insurance under Obamacare. You may want to provide your manager with some of these extras if you can afford to do so.

Clause 5. Payment Terms

Here you state how much and when you pay your manager. Specify the interval and dates on which you will pay the manager. For example, if the payment is weekly, specify the day. If payment is once each month, state the date, such as "the first of the month." If the payment is twice each month, indicate the dates, such as *"the 15th and the 30th, or the last previous weekday if either date falls on a weekend."*

Clause 6. Ending the Manager's Employment

This clause gives you the right to fire a manager any time for any legal reason. It makes clear that you are not guaranteeing a year's, or even a month's, employment to your new hire. You can legally fire your manager any time for any or no reason—as long as it's not for an illegal reason. In return, your manager can quit at any time, for any reason—with or without notice.

Clause 7. Additional Agreements and Amendments

Here you provide details about any areas of the manager's employment that weren't covered else-where in the agreement, such as the number of vacation or sick days, or any paid holidays the manager is entitled to each year, or how you plan to reimburse managers for the cost of materials they purchase for repairs.

The last part of this section is fairly standard in written agreements. It states that this is your entire agreement about the manager's employment, and that any changes to the agreement must be in writing.

Together, these provisions prevent you or your manager from later claiming that additional oral or written promises were made, but just not included in the written agreement.

> CAUTION
> **Make changes in writing.** If you later change the terms of your agreement, write the new terms down and have each person sign.

Clause 8. Place of Execution

Here you specify the city and state in which you signed the agreement. If there's any legal problem with the agreement later, it may be resolved by the courts where it was signed. Be advised, however, that the laws where the work is to be performed may be applied instead. So if, for example, you sign the Property Manager Agreement at your office in Maryland, but your rental property and the manager's workplace is in nearby Washington, DC, the different laws of Washington, DC, may be applied by a court.

Your Legal Obligations as an Employer

Whether or not you compensate a manager with reduced rent or a regular salary, you have specific legal obligations as an employer, such as following laws governing minimum wage and overtime. If you don't pay Social Security and meet your other legal obligations as an employer, you may face substantial financial penalties.

Most Resident Managers Are Employees, Not Independent Contractors

A resident manager will probably be considered your employee by the IRS and other government agencies. Employees are guaranteed a number of workplace rights that are not guaranteed to independent contractors. To be considered an independent contractor, a person must offer services to the public at large and work under an arrangement in which he or she controls the means and methods of accomplishing a job. Most tenant-managers are legally considered to be employees because they work for only one property owner who hires them, sets the hours and responsibilities, and determines the particulars of the job. A manager might qualify for independent contractor status if he or she works for several different landlords and controls how the work is performed.

RESOURCE

Start out by getting IRS Publication 15 (Circular E), *Employer's Tax Guide,* **which provides details about your tax and record-keeping obligations.** Contact the IRS at 800-829-4933 or www.irs.gov to obtain a free copy of this and other IRS publications and forms. *Tax Savvy for Small Business,* by Frederick W. Daily and Jeffrey A. Quinn (Nolo), covers strategies that will help you minimize taxes and stay out of legal trouble, including how to deduct

business expenses, write off or depreciate long-term business assets, keep the kinds of records that will satisfy the IRS, get a tax break from business losses, and handle a small business audit.

Employer Identification Number

As an employer, you need a federal identification number for tax purposes. If you are a sole proprietor without employees, you can use your Social Security number. Otherwise, you need to get an "employer identification number" (EIN) from the IRS. To obtain an EIN, complete IRS Form SS-4, *Application for Employer Identification Number.* Use the IRS website to apply online (go to www.irs.gov, and search for "EIN."

Income Taxes

The IRS considers the manager's compensation as taxable income to the manager. For that reason, your manager must fill out IRS Form W-4, *Employee's Withholding Allowance Certificate,* when hired. You must deduct federal taxes from each paycheck (and state taxes if required), and turn over the withheld funds each quarter to the IRS and the appropriate state tax agency. You must provide the manager with IRS Form W-2, *Wage and Tax Statement,* for the previous year's earnings by January 31. The W-2 form lists the employee's gross wages and provides a breakdown of any taxes that you withheld.

Social Security and Medicare Taxes ("FICA")

Federal Insurance Contributions Act (FICA) taxes go toward the employee's future Social Security and Medicare benefits. Every employer must pay the IRS a "payroll tax," currently equal to 7.65% of the employee's gross compensation—that is, the paycheck amount before deductions (6.2% goes to Social Security, 1.45% goes to Medicare). You must also deduct an additional 7.65% from the employee's wages and turn it over (with the payroll tax) to the IRS quarterly. For updated information

Property Manager Agreement

1. Parties

This Agreement is between ___Jacqueline Marsh___ ,

Owner of residential real property at ___175 Donner Avenue, Syracuse, New York___ ,

_____ ,

and ___Bradley Finch___ ,

Manager of the property. Manager will be renting unit ___Number 5___ of the property under a separate

written rental agreement that is in no way contingent upon or related to this Agreement.

2. Beginning Date

Manager will begin work on ___April 10, 20xx___ .

3. Responsibilities

Manager's duties are set forth below:

Renting Units

- ☑ answer phone inquiries about vacancies

- ☑ show vacant units

- ☑ accept rental applications

- ☐ select tenants

- ☑ accept initial rents and deposits

- ☐ other (specify) _____

- ☐ _____

- ☐ _____

Vacant Apartments

- ☑ inspect unit when tenant moves in and document condition of rental

- ☑ inspect unit when tenant moves out and document condition of rental

- ☐ clean unit after tenant moves out, including:

  - ☐ floors, carpets, and rugs

  - ☐ walls, baseboards, ceilings, lights, and built-in shelves

  - ☐ kitchen cabinets, countertops, sinks, stove, oven, and refrigerator

  - ☐ bathtubs, showers, toilets, and plumbing fixtures

  - ☐ doors, windows, window coverings, and miniblinds

  - ☑ other (specify) ___Hire and supervise cleaning service to clean rental unit when___

  - ☐ ___a tenant moves out.___

Rent Collection

☑ collect rents when due

☑ sign rent receipts

☑ maintain rent collection records

☑ collect late rents and charges

☑ inform Owner of late rents

☑ prepare late rent notices

☑ serve late rent notices on tenants

☑ serve rent increase and tenancy termination notices

☑ deposit rent collections in bank

☐ other (specify) _____

☐ _____

Maintenance

☑ vacuum and clean hallways and entryways

☑ replace lightbulbs in common areas

☑ drain water heaters

☑ clean stairs, decks, patios, facade, and sidewalks

☐ clean garage oils on pavement

☐ mow lawns

☐ rake leaves

☑ trim bushes

☑ clean up garbage and debris on grounds

☑ shovel snow from sidewalks and driveways or arrange for snow removal

☐ other (specify) _____

☐ _____

Repairs

☑ accept tenant complaints and repair requests

☑ inform Owner of maintenance and repair needs

☑ maintain written log of tenant complaints

☑ handle routine maintenance and repairs, including:

    ☑ plumbing stoppages

    ☑ garbage disposal stoppages/repairs

    ☑ faucet leaks/washer replacement

- ☑ toilet tank repairs
- ☑ toilet seat replacement
- ☑ stove burner repair/replacement
- ☑ stove hinges/knobs replacement
- ☑ dishwasher repair
- ☑ light switch and outlet repair/replacement
- ☐ heater thermostat repair
- ☐ window repair/replacement
- ☐ painting (interior)
- ☐ painting (exterior)
- ☑ replacement of keys
- ☐ other (specify) _____
- ☐ _____

Other Responsibilities

_____

_____

_____

_____

_____

_____

_____

_____

4. Hours and Schedule

Manager will be available to tenants during the following days and times: ___Monday through Friday,___ ___1 p.m. - 6 p.m (on the property) and by phone other times___ . If the hours required to carry out any duties may reasonably be expected to exceed ___30___ hours in any week, Manager shall notify Owner and obtain Owner's consent before working such extra hours, except in the event of an emergency. Extra hours worked due to an emergency must be reported to Owner within 24 hours.

5. Payment Terms

a. Manager will be paid:

- ☐ $ _____ per hour
- ☐ $ _____ per week
- ☑ $ ___2,500___ per month
- ☐ Other: _____

b. Manager will be paid on the specified intervals and dates:

☐ Once a week on every _____

☑ Twice a month on the first and the 15th of the month

☐ Once a month on _____

☐ Other (specify) _____

6. **Ending the Manager's Employment**

Owner may terminate Manager's employment at any time, for any reason that isn't unlawful, with or without notice. Manager may quit at any time, for any reason, with or without notice.

7. **Additional Agreements and Amendments**

a. Owner and Manager additionally agree that: Manager will be available to consult with Owner's attorney as needed, and will provide sworn testimony if necessary.

_____

_____

_____

_____

_____

_____

_____

_____

_____

b. All agreements between Owner and Manager relating to the work specified in this Agreement are incorporated in this Agreement. Any modification to the Agreement must be in writing and signed by both parties.

8. **Place of Execution**

Signed at ___Syracuse___ , ___New York___
       City   State

Jacqueline Marsh   _April 3, 20xx_
Owner   Date

Bradley Finch   _April 3, 20xx_
Manager   Date

on payroll taxes, including additional Medicare taxes for employees who earn more than $200,000 in a calendar year, see the most current edition of Circular E (*IRS Employer's Tax Guide*).

If you compensate your manager with reduced rent, you must still pay the FICA payroll tax, unless you meet certain conditions, explained below. For example, an apartment owner who compensates a manager with a rent-free $500/month apartment must pay 7.65% of $500, or $38.25, in payroll taxes each month. The manager is responsible for paying another 7.65% ($38.25) to the IRS.

You do not have to pay FICA taxes on the value of the reduced rent if the following conditions are met:

- the manager's unit is on your rental property
- you provide the unit for your convenience (or to comply with state law, since some states require on-site managers for properties of a certain size)
- your manager must actually work as a manager, and
- the manager accepts the unit as a condition of employment—in other words, he must live in the unit in order to be your resident manager.

Help With Paperwork

Employers are responsible for a certain amount of paperwork and record keeping such as time and pay records. If you hate paperwork, your accountant or bookkeeper can probably handle it for you. Or, a reputable payroll tax service that offers a tax notification service will calculate the correct amount of Social Security, unemployment, workers' compensation, and other taxes due; produce the check to pay your manager; and calculate the taxes and notify you when the taxes are due.

Payroll services can be cost-effective even if you employ only one or two people. But when you look for one, it pays to shop around. To get cost quotes, check the Web or your yellow pages under Payroll Service or Bookkeeping Service. Avoid services that charge set-up fees—basically, a fee for putting your information into the computer—or extra fees to prepare W-2 forms or quarterly and annual tax returns.

CAUTION

Always pay payroll taxes on time. If you don't, the IRS will find you—and you could be forced out of business by the huge penalties and interest charges it will add to the delinquent bill. And unlike most other debts, you must pay back payroll taxes even if you go through bankruptcy.

Unemployment Taxes

A manager who is laid off, quits for good reason, or is fired for reasons other than misconduct is probably entitled to unemployment benefits. These benefits are financed by unemployment taxes paid by employers. You must pay a federal unemployment tax (FUTA) at a rate of 6% of the first $7,000 of the employee's wages for the year. (The actual FUTA tax rate will be lower if you pay state unemployment taxes for your employee.) In addition to contributing to FUTA, you may also be responsible for contributing to an unemployment insurance fund in your state.

RESOURCE

Contact the IRS for information on Form 940 (used for tax returns), FUTA, and a local office of your state department of labor or employment or the government agency that oversees your state income tax program for state tax requirements.

Minimum Wage and Overtime

However you pay your manager—by the hour, with a regular salary, or by a rent reduction—you should monitor the number of hours worked to make sure you're complying with the federal Fair Labor Standards Act (FLSA; 29 U.S. Code §§ 201 and following) and any state minimum wage laws.

The federal minimum hourly wage is $7.25 an hour.

If your state's (or city's) minimum wage is higher than the federal rate, you must pay the higher rate.

If you compensate your manager by a rent reduction, you may not be able to count the full amount of the rent reduction in complying with minimum wage laws.

Federal wage and hour laws also require employers to pay time-and-a-half if an employee works more than 40 hours a week (with a few exceptions). Some states (most notably California) require you to pay overtime if an employee works more than eight hours in a day, even if the employee works less than 40 hours in a week.

 RESOURCE
For information on minimum wage laws, overtime rules, and record-keeping requirements, see the U.S. Department of Labor's website at www.dol.gov. Also see IRS Publication 15-B, *Employer's Tax Guide to Fringe Benefits*, available at www.irs.gov. You can also contact the nearest office of the U.S. Labor Department's Wage and Hour Division or a local office of your state's department of labor or employment.

Equal Pay for Equal Work

You must provide equal pay and benefits to men and women who do the same job or jobs that require substantially equal skills, effort, and responsibility. This is required by the Equal Pay Act, an amendment to the FLSA.

Workers' Compensation Insurance

Workers' compensation provides some replacement income and pays medical expenses for employees who are injured or become ill as a result of their jobs. It's a no-fault system—an injured employee is entitled to receive benefits whether or not you provided a safe workplace and whether or not the manager's own carelessness contributed to the injury. (You are, of course, required by federal and state laws to provide a reasonably safe workplace.) But you, too, receive some protection, because the manager, in most cases, cannot sue you for

damages. In addition, the manager is limited to fixed types of compensation—basically, partial wage replacement and payment of medical bills. Employees may also receive compensation and vocational training, if they're left with a permanent impairment and unable to return to the same line of work. The manager can't get paid for pain and suffering or mental anguish.

To cover the costs of workers' compensation benefits for employees, you'll need to purchase a special insurance policy—either through a state fund or a private insurance company. Each state has its own workers' compensation statute. Many states require all employers to get coverage; however, some states set a minimum number of employees (generally between three and five) before coverage is required.

Most wise landlords obtain workers' compensation insurance, whether or not it's required. If you don't, and you're sued by a manager who is injured on the job—for example, by falling down the stairs while performing maintenance—or even by a violent tenant, you face the possibility of a lawsuit for a large amount of money.

 CAUTION
Workers' comp doesn't apply to intentional acts. Workers' compensation typically won't cover you from employee lawsuits for injuries caused by your intentional or reckless behavior—for example, if you know of a dangerous condition but refuse to fix it, resulting in an injury.

 RESOURCE
Contact your state workers' compensation office for information on coverage and costs.

Immigration Laws

When you hire someone, even someone who was born and raised in the city where your rental property is located, you must review documents such as a passport or birth certificate that prove the employee's identity and employment eligibility. You and each new employee are required to complete USCIS Form I-9, *Employment Eligibility Verification*. These rules come from the Immigration Reform and Control Act (IRCA), a federal law that prohibits hiring undocumented workers. The law, administered by the U.S. Citizenship and Immigration Services (USCIS), prohibits hiring workers who don't have government authorization to work in the U.S.

RESOURCE
For more information, contact the USCIS by phone at 800-375-5283, or check their website at www. uscis.gov.

New Hire Reporting Form

Within a short time after you hire someone—20 days or less—you must file a New Hire Reporting form with a designated state agency. The information on the form becomes part of the National Directory of New Hires, used primarily to locate parents so that child support orders can be enforced. Government agencies also use the data to prevent improper payment of workers' compensation and unemployment benefits or public assistance benefits. For more information, check out the website of the Federal Office of Child Support Enforcement, www. acf.hhs.gov/programs/css; click "Employers."

Management Companies

Property management companies are often used by owners of large apartment complexes and by absentee owners too far away from the property to be directly involved in everyday details. Property management companies generally take care of renting units, collecting rent, taking tenant complaints, arranging repairs and maintenance, and evicting troublesome tenants. Of course, some of these responsibilities may be shared with or delegated to resident managers who, in some instances, may work for the management company.

A variety of relationships between owners and management companies is possible, depending on your wishes and how the particular management company chooses to do business. For example, if you own one or more big buildings, the management company will probably recommend hiring a resident manager. But if your rental property has only a few units, or you own a number of small buildings spread over a good-sized geographical area, the management company will probably suggest simply responding to tenant requests and complaints from its central office.

Pros and Cons of Management Companies

One advantage of working with a management company is that you avoid all the legal hassles of being an employer: paying payroll taxes, buying workers' compensation insurance, withholding income tax. The management company is an independent contractor, not an employee. It hires and pays the people who do the work. Typically, you sign a contract spelling out the management company's duties and fees. Most companies charge a fixed percentage—about 5% to 10%—of the total rent collected. (This does not include the cost of any resident manager you employ.) This gives the company a good incentive to keep the building filled with rent-paying tenants.

Another advantage is that management companies are usually well-informed about the law, keep good records, and are adept at staying out of legal hot water in such areas as discrimination, invasion of privacy, and returning deposits.

The primary disadvantage of hiring a management company is the expense. For example, if you pay a management company 10% of the $14,000 you collect in rent each month from tenants in a 12-unit building, this amounts to $1,400 a month and $16,800 per year. While many companies charge less than 10%, it's still quite an expense. Also, if the management company works from a central office with no one on-site, tenants may feel that management is too distant and unconcerned with their day-to-day needs.

Management Company Contracts

Management companies have their own contracts, which you should read thoroughly and understand before signing. Be sure you understand how the company is paid and its exact responsibilities.

A management contract is not a take it or leave it deal. You should negotiate the company's fee, obviously, as well as any extra charges you can expect to pay during the length of the contract. You may also specify spending limits for ordinary repairs. And if you are picky about who works on your property, you may be able to specify that certain repairpersons or firms should be called before others are used.

Policies on screening tenants, maintenance and repairs, and letting contracts aren't usually part of the management contract itself, but should be clearly communicated, so that the management company knows what you expect.

Questions to Ask When You Hire a Management Company

- Who are its clients: owners of single-family houses, small apartment buildings, or large apartment complexes? Look for a company with experience handling property like yours. Also ask for client references, and check to see whether other landlords are satisfied with the management company. (Don't forget to ask these landlords how their tenants feel about the service they get. Unhappy tenants are bad business.)
- What services are provided?
- What are the costs? What services cost extra?
- Will the management company take tenant calls 24 hours a day, seven days a week?
- Will there be an individual property manager assigned to your property? How frequently will the property manager visit and inspect your building?
- Is the company located fairly close to your property?
- Are employees trained in landlord-tenant law? Will the company consult an attorney qualified in landlord-tenant matters if problems arise, such as disputes over rent?
- If your property is under rent control, are company personnel familiar with the rent control law?
- Can you terminate the management agreement without cause on reasonable notice?

It's a good idea to write down these understandings and attach them to the contract as an addendum or attachment.

Special Issues Involving Leases and Insurance

The contract with your management company will usually address the issues of leases and insurance.

Leases

Many management companies will insist on using their own leases. Since they are the ones who will deal with problems, management companies often want to be the ones who will set the rules. You may find that the company's lease is acceptable—but you may also find that it is not. For example, it's common to see late-fee policies that exceed a fair and legal limit. No surprise—the more money collected by the management company, the more money it earns for itself.

If the management company uses a lease that is legally amiss, it's clearly a sign to look elsewhere. Now, what about other clauses in the company lease that are legal but not to your liking, such as a prohibition against pets? Again, no surprise—most management companies assume that pets equal more work, and they prefer not to have to deal with them. If the company will not negotiate with you over changing their "standard" lease, you may want to talk to other management companies that will be more flexible.

Insurance

All landlords need comprehensive liability insurance. Special issues arise when you hire a management company. Most important, both you and the management company need to show proof that you are each insured—and you each should be added to the other's policy as an "additional insured." Here's how it works.

You should require proof that the management company is insured under a comprehensive general liability policy, with extra coverage for "errors and omissions" and employee dishonesty. When you are added as an "additional insured," you get the benefit of that policy. If you are named in a lawsuit over something that the management company allegedly did or didn't do, you will be covered by the management company's insurer. They will defend you and pay out any settlement or verdict that results against you. Your insurance broker should be able to recommend how much insurance is adequate.

The management company will demand proof that you, too, carry adequate amounts of liability insurance, and they will also want to be named as an additional insured in your policy. If you don't currently have enough insurance coverage, the management company may refuse to take your business.

Fortunately, adding a landlord or a management company as an additional insured is not a big deal. Insurance companies do it all the time, generally at no additional cost. Simply contact your broker and ask that the management company be added. Ask the broker to send a certificate of insurance to the management company. And don't forget to demand the same of the management company—you, too, want a certificate of insurance safely in your files.

Your Liability for a Manager's Acts

Depending on the circumstances, you may be legally responsible for the acts of a manager or management company. For example, you could be sued and found liable if your manager or management company:

- refuses to rent to a qualified tenant (who is a member of a minority group or has children, for example) or otherwise violates antidiscrimination laws
- sexually harasses a tenant
- makes illegal deductions from the security deposit of a tenant who has moved out, or does not return the departing tenant's deposit within the time limit set by your state law
- ignores a dangerous condition, such as sub-standard wiring that results in an electrical fire, causing injury or damage to the tenant, or security problems that result in a criminal assault on a tenant

- invades a tenant's privacy by flagrant and damaging gossip or trespass, or
- commits a crime such as assaulting a tenant.

In short, a landlord who knows the law but has a manager (or management company) who doesn't could wind up in a lawsuit brought by prospective or former tenants.

Here's how to protect your tenants and yourself.

Choose your manager carefully. Legally, you have a duty to protect your tenants from injury caused by employees you know or should know pose a risk of harm to others. If someone gets hurt or has property stolen or damaged by a manager whose background you didn't check carefully, you could be sued, so it's crucial that you be especially vigilant when hiring a manager who will have easy access to rental units.

Make sure your manager is familiar with the basics of landlord-tenant law, especially if your manager will be selecting tenants or serving eviction notices. One approach is to give your manager a copy of this book to read and refer to. In addition, you'll want to provide detailed instructions that cover likely trouble areas, such as the legal rules prohibiting discrimination in tenant selection. Below is a sample set of instructions for a manager with fairly broad authority; you can tailor them to fit your situation. You'll also need to add any requirements that are imposed by the laws in your state—for example, stricter discrimination laws or notice requirements for entering rental property than are outlined in the sample instructions. Have the manager sign a copy of the instructions and give it to you.

Keep an eye on your manager, and listen to tenants' concerns and complaints. Encourage your tenants to report problems to you. If you hear about or suspect problems—for example, poor maintenance of the building or sexual harassment—do your own investigating. For example, when you have a vacancy, have someone you suspect the manager might discriminate against apply for a vacancy. How does your manager treat the applicant? Would you want to defend a lawsuit brought by

Sample Instructions to Manager

Dear New Manager:

Welcome to your new position as resident manager. Here are important instructions to guide you as you perform your duties under our management agreement. Please read them carefully and keep them for future reference.

1. Discrimination in rental housing on the basis of race, religion, sex, familial status, age, national or ethnic origin, or disability is illegal—whether you are accepting rental applications for vacant apartments or dealing with current residents. Your duties are to advertise and accept rental applications in a nondiscriminatory manner. This includes allowing all individuals to fill out applications and offering the unit on the same terms to all applicants. After you have collected all applications, please notify me at the phone number listed below. I will sort through the applications, set up interviews, and decide whom to accept.

2. Tenants have a right to feel comfortable and relaxed in and near their homes. To be sure all do, please avoid any comments, actions, or physical contact that could be considered offensive, even by those whom you might see as being overly sensitive on the issue. Remember, harassment is against the law and will not be tolerated.

3. Do not issue any rent increase or termination notices without my prior approval.

4. Treat all tenants who complain about defects, even trivial defects or ones you believe to be nonexistent, with respect. Enter all tenant complaints into the logbook I have supplied to you on the day they are made. Respond to tenant complaints about the building or apartment units immediately in emergencies or if the complaint involves security, and respond to other complaints within 24 hours. If you cannot correct (or arrange to correct) any problem or defect yourself, please telephone me immediately.

5. Except in serious life- or property-threatening emergencies, never enter (or allow anyone else to enter) a tenant's apartment without consent or in his or her absence, unless you have given written notice at least 24 hours in advance, either delivered personally or, if that's not possible, posted on the door. If you have given the tenant 24-hour written notice, you may enter in the tenant's absence during ordinary business hours to do repairs or maintenance work, unless the tenant objects. If the tenant objects, do not enter, but instead call me.

6. When a tenant moves in, and again when he or she moves out, inspect the unit. If possible, have the tenant accompany you. On each occasion, both you and the tenant should complete and sign a Landlord-Tenant Checklist form. Take digital pictures or make a video during both walkthroughs.

7. If you think a tenant has moved out and abandoned the apartment, do not enter it. Telephone me first.

8. Once a tenant has vacated an apartment and given you the key, keep track of all costs necessary to repair damages in excess of ordinary wear and tear. Give me a copy of this list, along with a notation of the amount of any back rent, the before

Sample Instructions to Manager (continued)

and after Landlord-Tenant Checklist forms, and the departing tenant's forwarding address. Please make sure I see this material within a week after the tenant moves out, preferably sooner. I will mail the itemization and any security deposit balance to the tenant.

9. If you have any other problems or questions, please do not hesitate to call me on my cell phone or at home. Leave a message on my voicemail if I am not available.

Sincerely,

Terry Herendeen

Terry Herendeen, Owner

1111 Maiden Lane, Omaha, Nebraska 54001

402-555-1234 (cell phone)

402-555-5678 (work)

I have received a copy of this memorandum and have read and understood it.

Dated: _____ April 7, 20xx _____

Barbara Louis

Barbara Louis, Manager

the prospective tenant? Try to resolve problems and get rid of a bad manager before problems accelerate and you end up with an expensive tenants' lawsuit.

Emergency Contacts and Procedures for Your Employees

It's an excellent idea to prepare a written set of emergency procedures for the manager, including:

- owner's name and emergency phone number, so your employee can contact you in case of emergency
- names and phone numbers of nearest hospital and poison control center
- ambulance, police, and fire departments
- names and phone numbers of contractors who can respond to a building emergency on a 24-hour basis, including any licensed plumber, electrician, locksmith, boiler mechanic, elevator service company, and air conditioner maintenance company with whom you have set up an account, and
- procedures to follow in case of a fire, flood, earthquake, hurricane, tornado, or other disaster, including how to safely shut down elevators, water, electricity, and gas.

Make sure your insurance covers illegal acts of your employees. No matter how thorough your precautions, you may still be liable for your manager's illegal acts—even if your manager commits an illegal act in direct violation of your instructions. To really protect yourself, purchase a good landlord's insurance policy.

Notifying Tenants of the Manager

In many states, you are legally required to give tenants the manager's name and address and tell them that the manager is authorized to accept legal documents on your behalf, such as termination of tenancy notices or court documents in an eviction lawsuit.

We recommend that you give tenants this information in writing, whether or not your state's law requires it. It is included in our lease and rental agreements (see Clause 21 in Chapter 2), but don't forget to notify tenants who moved in before you hired the manager.

Two sample disclosure notices are shown below. You should give each tenant a copy and post another in a prominent place in the building.

Be sure your Property Manager Agreement, discussed above, notes the manager's authority in this regard. You can put details in the last section, Additional Agreements and Amendments.

Sample Disclosure Notices as to Address of Manager and Owner

Notice: Address of Manager of Premises

Muhammad Azziz, 1234 Market Street, Apartment 1, Boston, Mass., is authorized to manage the residential premises at 1234 Market Street, Boston, Mass. If you have any complaints about the condition of your unit or common areas, please notify Mr. Azziz immediately at 555-1200. He is authorized to act for and on behalf of the owner of the premises for the purpose of receiving all notices and demands from you, including legal papers (process).

Notice: Address of Owner of Premises

Rebecca Epstein, 12345 Embarcadero Road, Boston, Mass., is the owner of the premises at 1234 Market Street, Boston, Mass.

Firing a Manager

Unless you have made a commitment (oral or written contract) to employ a manager for a specific period of time, you have the right to terminate her employment at any time. But you cannot do it for an illegal reason, such as:

- race, age, gender, or other prohibited forms of discrimination, or
- retaliation against the manager for calling your illegal acts to the attention of authorities.

EXAMPLE: You order your manager to dump 20 gallons of fuel oil at the back of your property. Instead, the manager complains to a local environmental regulatory agency, which fines you. If you now fire the manager, you will be vulnerable to a lawsuit for illegal termination.

The High Cost of a Bad Manager: Sexual Harassment in Housing

If tenants complain about illegal acts by a manager, pay attention. The owners of a Fairfield, California, apartment complex learned this lesson the hard way—by paying more than a million dollars to settle a tenants' lawsuit.

The tenants, mostly single mothers, were tormented by an apartment manager who spied on them, opened their mail, and sexually harassed them. They were afraid to complain, for fear of eviction. When they did complain to the building's owners, the owners refused to take any action—and the manager stepped up his harassment in retaliation.

Finally, tenants banded together and sued, and the details of the manager's outrageous and illegal conduct were exposed. The owners settled the case before trial for $1.6 million.

To head off the possibility of a wrongful termination lawsuit, be prepared to show a good business-related reason for the firing. It's almost essential to back up a firing with written records documenting your reasons. Reasons that may support a firing include:

- performing poorly on the job—for example, not depositing rent checks promptly, or

continually failing to respond to tenant complaints

- refusing to follow instructions—for example, allowing tenants to pay rent late, despite your instructions to the contrary
- possessing a weapon at work
- being dishonest or stealing money or property from you or your tenants
- endangering the health or safety of tenants
- engaging in criminal activity, such as drug dealing
- arguing or fighting with tenants
- behaving violently at work, or
- unlawfully discriminating against or harassing prospective or current tenants.

Ideally, a firing shouldn't come suddenly or as a surprise. Give your manager ongoing feedback about job performance and impose progressive discipline, such as an oral or written warning, before termination. Do a six-month performance review (and more often, if necessary) and keep copies. Solicit comments from tenants twice a year (as mentioned earlier) and, if comments are negative, keep copies.

Handling Requests for References

One of your biggest problems after a manager quits or has been fired may be what to tell other landlords or employers who inquire about the former manager. You may be tugged in several directions:

- You want to tell the truth—good, bad, or neutral—about the former manager.
- You want to help the former manager find another job for which he is better suited.
- You don't want to be sued for libel or slander because you say something negative.

Legally, you're better off saying as little as possible, rather than saying anything negative. Just say that it's your policy not to comment on former managers. Besides, if you politely say, "I would rather not discuss Mr. Jones," the caller will get the idea.

Evicting a Manager

If you fire a manager, you may often want the ex-employee to move out of your property, particularly if there is a special manager's unit or the firing has generated (or resulted from) ill will. How easy it will be to get the fired manager out depends primarily on whether or not you have separate management and rental agreements.

SEE AN EXPERT

In many cases, you'll want the eviction lawsuit to be handled by an attorney who specializes in landlord-tenant law. See Chapter 18 for advice on finding a qualified lawyer.

If you and the tenant-manager signed separate management and rental agreements, firing the manager does not affect the tenancy. The ex-manager will have to keep paying rent but will no longer work as manager. Evicting the former manager is just like evicting any other tenant. You will have to give a normal termination notice, typically 30 days for month-to-month tenancies, subject to any applicable rent control restrictions. If the tenant has a separate fixed-term lease, you cannot terminate the tenancy until the lease expires.

If you are evicting the manager for not paying rent or for violating a lease or rental agreement term (for example, by damaging rental property), you may be able to provide less notice. See Chapter 17 for details.

We do not recommend using a single management/rental agreement. Among other reasons, it may be difficult to evict the ex-manager in this situation.

Getting the Tenant Moved In

 FORMS IN THIS CHAPTER

Chapter 7 includes instructions for and samples of the following forms:

- Landlord-Tenant Checklist
- Move-In Letter

The Nolo website includes downloadable copies of these forms. See Appendix B for the link to the forms in this book.

Legal disputes between landlords and tenants can be almost as emotional as divorce court battles. Many disputes are unnecessary and could be avoided if—right from the very beginning—tenants knew their legal rights and responsibilities. A clearly written lease or rental agreement, signed by all adult occupants, is the key to starting a tenancy. But there's more to establishing a positive attitude when new tenants move in. You should also:

- inspect the property, fill out a Landlord-Tenant Checklist with the tenant, and photograph the rental unit and
- prepare a move-in letter highlighting important terms of the tenancy and your expectations, such as how to report repair problems.

States That Require a Landlord-Tenant Checklist

Several states require landlords to give new tenants a written statement on the condition of the rental premises at move-in time, including a comprehensive list of existing damages. Tenants in these states often have the right to inspect the premises to verify the accuracy of the landlord's list and to note any problems.

The following are among the states that require initial inspections. Check the statutes for the exact requirements in your state, including the type of inspection required at the end of the tenancy. For citations, see "Required Landlord Disclosures" in Appendix A.

Arizona	Massachusetts	North Dakota
Georgia	Michigan	Utah
Hawaii	Montana	Virginia
Kansas	Nevada	Washington
Kentucky	New Hampshire	Wisconsin
Maryland		

Inspect the Rental Unit

To eliminate the possibility of all sorts of future arguments, it is absolutely essential that you (or your representative) and prospective tenants (together, if possible) check the place over for damage and obvious wear and tear before the tenant moves in. The best way to document what you find is to jointly fill out a Landlord-Tenant Checklist form.

In some states, the law requires you to give new tenants a written statement on the condition of the premises at move-in time, including a comprehensive list of existing damage, see "States That Require a Landlord-Tenant Checklist," above. Tenants in many of these states have the right to inspect the premises as to the accuracy of the landlord's list, and to note any problems. But even if this procedure is not legally required, you should follow it to avert later problems.

Use a Landlord-Tenant Checklist

A Landlord-Tenant Checklist, inventorying the condition of the rental property at the beginning and end of the tenancy, is an excellent device to protect both you and your tenant when the tenant moves out and wants the security deposit returned. Without some record as to the condition of the unit, you and the tenant are all too likely to get into arguments about things like whether the kitchen linoleum was already stained, the garbage disposal was broken, the stove was filthy, or the bathroom mirror was already cracked when the tenant moved in.

The checklist provides good evidence as to why you withheld all or part of a security deposit. And, coupled with a system to regularly keep track of the rental property's condition, the checklist will also be extremely useful to you if a tenant withholds rent, breaks the lease and moves out, or sues you outright, claiming the unit needs substantial repairs. See Chapter 9 for instructions and forms that will let you stay updated on the condition of your rental properties.

Landlord-Tenant Checklist

GENERAL CONDITION OF RENTAL UNIT AND PREMISES

572 Fourth St.   Apt. 11   Washington, D.C.
Street Address   Unit No.   City

	Condition on Arrival	Condition on Departure	Estimated Cost of Repair/ Replacement
Living Room			
Floors & Floor Coverings	OK		
Drapes & Window Coverings	Miniblinds discolored		
Walls & Ceilings	OK		
Light Fixtures	OK		
Windows, Screens, & Doors	Window rattles		
Front Door & Locks	OK		
Fireplace	OK		
Other	N/A		
Other			
Kitchen			
Floors & Floor Coverings	Cigarette burn hole		
Walls & Ceilings	OK		
Light Fixtures	OK		
Cabinets	OK		
Counters	Stained		
Stove/Oven	Burners filthy (grease)		
Refrigerator	OK		
Dishwasher	N/A		
Garbage Disposal	OK		
Sink & Plumbing	OK		
Smoke Detector	OK		
Windows, Screens, & Doors	OK		
Other			
Dining Room			
Floors & Floor Covering	OK		
Walls & Ceilings	Crack in ceiling		
Light Fixtures	OK		
Windows, Screens, & Doors	OK		
Smoke Detector	OK		
Other			

	Condition on Arrival		Condition on Departure		Estimated Cost of Repair/ Replacement
Bathroom(s)	Bath #1	Bath #2	Bath #1	Bath #2	
Floors & Floor Coverings	OK				
Walls & Ceilings	Wallpaper peeling				
Windows, Screens, & Doors	OK				
Light Fixtures	OK				
Bathtub/Shower	Tub chipped				
Sink & Counters	OK				
Toilet	Base of toilet very dirty				
Other					
Other					

	Condition on Arrival			Condition on Departure			Estimated Cost of Repair/ Replacement
Bedroom(s)	Bdrm #1	Bdrm #2	Bdrm #3	Bdrm #1	Bdrm #2	Bdrm #3	
Floors & Floor Coverings	OK	OK					
Windows, Screens, & Doors	OK	OK					
Walls & Ceilings	OK	OK					
Light Fixtures	Dented	OK					
Smoke Detector	OK	OK	OK				
Other	Water stains in closet						
Other							
Other							

Other Areas					
Heating System	OK				
Air Conditioning	OK				
Lawn/Garden	OK				
Stairs and Hallway	OK				
Patio, Terrace, Deck, etc.	N/A				
Basement	OK				
Parking Area					
Other					
Other					
Other					
Other					
Other					

☑ Tenants acknowledge that all smoke detectors were tested in their presence and found to be in working order, and that the testing procedure was explained to them. Tenants agree to promptly notify Landlord in writing should any smoke detector appear to be malfunctioning or inoperable. Tenants will not refuse Landlord access for the purpose of inspecting, maintaining, repairing, or installing legally required smoke detectors.

FURNISHED PROPERTY

	Condition on Arrival			Condition on Departure			Estimated Cost of Repair/ Replacement
Living Room							
Coffee Table	Two scratches on top						
End Tables	OK						
Lamps	OK						
Chairs	OK						
Sofa	OK						
Other							
Other							
Kitchen							
Broiler Pan	N/A						
Ice Trays	N/A						
Other							
Other							
Dining Room							
Chairs	OK						
Stools	N/A						
Table	Leg bent slightly						
Other							
Other							
Bathroom(s)	Bath #1	Bath #2		Bath #1	Bath #2		
Mirrors	OK						
Shower Curtain	Torn						
Hamper	N/A						
Other							
Bedroom(s)	Bdrm #1	Bdrm #2	Bdrm #3	Bdrm #1	Bdrm #2	Bdrm #3	
Beds (single)	OK	N/A					
Beds (double)	N/A	OK					
Chairs	OK	OK					
Chests	N/A	OK					
Dressing Tables	OK	OK					
Lamps	OK	OK					
Mirrors	OK	OK					
Night Tables	OK	N/A					
Other							

	Condition on Arrival	Condition on Departure	Estimated Cost of Repair/ Replacement
Other			
Other Areas			
Bookcases	N/A		
Desks	N/A		
Pictures	Hall picture frame chipped		
Other			
Other			

Use this space to provide any additional explanation:

_____

_____

_____

_____

_____

_____

_____

_____

_____

_____

_____

Landlord-Tenant Checklist completed on moving in on _____ May 1, 20xx _____ and approved by:

_Bernard Cohen_____ and _Maria Crouse_____
Landlord/Manager   Tenant

                                             _Sandra Martino_____
                                             Tenant

                                             _____
                                             Tenant

Landlord-Tenant Checklist completed on moving out on _____ and approved by:

_____ and _____
Landlord/Manager   Tenant

                                             _____
                                             Tenant

                                             _____
                                             Tenant

A sample Landlord-Tenant Checklist is shown above, and the Nolo website includes a downloadable copy. See Appendix B for the link to the forms in this book.

How to Fill Out the Checklist

You and the tenant should fill out the checklist together. If that's impossible, complete the form and then give it to the tenant to review. The tenant should note any disagreement and return it to you within a few days.

The checklist is in two parts. The first side covers the general condition of each room. The second side covers furnishings, such as a living room lamp or bathroom shower curtain.

You will be filling out the first column—*Condition on Arrival*—before the tenant moves in. The last two columns—*Condition on Departure* and *Estimated Cost of Repair/Replacement*—are for use when the tenant moves out and you inspect the unit again. At that time the checklist will document your need to make deductions from the security deposit for repairs or cleaning, or to replace missing items. See Chapter 15 for details on returning security deposits and using the checklist at move-out time.

When you look at the checklist included here, you'll see that we have filled out the first column (*Condition on Arrival*) with rooms and elements in these rooms. If you happen to be renting a one-bedroom, one-bath unit, our preprinted form will work just fine. However, chances are that your rental has a different number of rooms or elements in those rooms than those on the checklist form. Changes are no problem if you use the downloadable form. You can change the entries in the *Condition on Arrival* column of the checklist, and you can add or delete rows. For example, you may want to add a row for another bedroom or a service porch, or add room elements such as a trash compactor. You may also delete items, such as a dishwasher.

The following sections explain how to complete the checklist—once you've tailored it to your particular rental.

General Condition of Rental Unit and Premises

In the *Condition on Arrival* column, make a note—as specific as possible—of items that are not working or are dirty, scratched, or simply in bad condition. For example, don't simply note that the refrigerator "needs fixing" if an ice maker doesn't work—it's just as easy to write "ice maker broken, should not be used." If the tenant uses the ice maker anyway and causes water damage, he cannot claim that you failed to tell him. Be sure to note any mildew, pest, or rodent problems. (Better yet, fix these before the new tenant moves in.)

Mark "OK" next to items that are in satisfactory condition—basically, clean, safe, sanitary, and in good working order.

 CAUTION
Make repairs and clean thoroughly before showing a rental unit. To get the tenancy off to the best start and avoid all kinds of hassles over repairs, handle problems before the start of a new tenancy. You must fix certain defects—such as a broken heater or leaking roof—under state and local housing codes. You may often be able to cover your repair and cleaning costs by deducting expenses from the outgoing tenant's security deposit (assuming the tenant is responsible for the problem).

Furnishings

The second part of the checklist covers furnishings, such as lamps or shower curtains. Obviously, you can simply delete this section of the checklist if your unit is not furnished.

If your rental property has rooms or furnishings not listed on the checklist, edit the form as explained above. If you are renting out a large house or apartment or providing many furnishings, be sure to include this information.

Sign the Checklist

After you and your new tenant agree on all of the particulars of the rental unit, you each should sign and date every page of the checklist, including any attachments. Keep the original and give the tenant a copy. If the tenant filled out the checklist on his own, make sure you review his comments, note any disagreement, and return a copy to him. You should make the checklist part of your lease or rental agreement, as we recommend in Chapter 2, Clause 11.

Be sure the tenant also checks the box on the bottom of the second page of the checklist stating that the smoke detector and fire extinguisher—required for new occupancies in many states and cities—were tested in his presence and shown to be in working order. This section on the checklist also requires the tenant to notify the landlord of any malfunctioning or broken smoke detector.

Add testing of carbon monoxide detectors if your state, such as California, requires these.

> **TIP**
> **Be sure to keep the checklist up-to-date if you repair, replace, add, or remove items or furnishings after the tenant moves in.** Both you and the tenant should initial and date any changes.

Photograph the Rental Unit

Taking photos or videos of the unit before a new tenant moves in is another excellent way to avoid disputes over security deposit deductions. In addition to the checklist, you'll be able to compare "before" and "after" pictures when the tenant leaves. This should help refresh your tenant's memory, which may result in her being more reasonable. Certainly, if you end up in mediation or court for not returning the full security deposit, being able to document your point of view with photos or videos will be invaluable. In addition, photos or a video can also help if you have to sue a former

tenant for cleaning and repair costs above the deposit amount.

Whether you take a photo with your phone or use a separate camera, make two sets of the photos as soon as possible. Give one set to your tenant. Each of you should date and sign both sets of photos. If you make a video, clearly state the time and date when the video was made.

You should repeat this process when the tenant leaves, as part of your standard move-out procedure. Chapter 15 discusses inspecting the unit when a tenant leaves.

Send New Tenants a Move-In Letter

A move-in letter should dovetail with the lease or rental agreement and provide basic information such as the manager's phone numbers (day and night) and office hours. You can also use a move-in letter to explain any procedures and rules that are too detailed or numerous to include in your lease or rental agreement—for example, how and where to report maintenance problems, details on garbage disposal/recycling, parking, mail, and laundry rooms. and building quiet hours. Consider including a brief list of maintenance dos and don'ts as part of the move-in letter—for example, how to avoid overloading circuits and proper use of the garbage disposal. Alternatively, large landlords may use a set of Rules and Regulations to cover some of these issues, see Clause 18 of the form agreements in Chapter 2.

A sample move-in letter is shown below, and the Nolo website includes a downloadable copy (see Appendix B for the link to the forms in this book). You should tailor this move-in letter to your particular needs—for example, alter it if you don't employ a resident manager or if your property is subject to rent control.

We recommend that you make a copy of each tenant's move-in letter for yourself and ask him to sign the last page, indicating that he has read it.

Move-In Letter

September 1, 20xx
_____
Date
Frank O'Hara
_____
Tenant
139 Porter Street
_____
Street Address
Madison, Wisconsin 53704
_____
City and State

Dear Frank   ,
_____
                         Tenant

Welcome to Apartment 45 B at Happy Hill Apartments
_____

_____ (address of rental unit). We hope you will enjoy living here.

This letter is to explain what you can expect from the management and what we'll be looking for from you.

Rent: Rent is due on the first day of the month. There is no grace period for the payment of rent. (See Clauses 5 and 6 of your rental agreement for details, including late charges.) Also, we don't accept postdated checks.   .

New Roommates: If you want someone to move in as a roommate, please contact us first. If your rental unit is big enough to accommodate another person, we will arrange for the new person to fill out a rental application. If it's approved, all of you will need to sign a new rental agreement. Depending on the situation, there may be a rent increase to add a roommate.   .

Notice to End Tenancy: To terminate your month-to-month tenancy, you must give at least 28 days' written notice. We have a written form available for this purpose. We may also terminate the tenancy, or change its terms, on 28 days' written notice. If you give less than 28 days' notice, you will still be financially responsible for rent for the balance of the 28-day period.   .

Deposits: Your security deposit will be applied to costs of cleaning, damages, or unpaid rent after you move out. You may not apply any part of the deposit toward any part of your rent in the last month of your tenancy. (See Clause 8 of your rental agreement.)   .

Manager: Sophie Beauchamp (Apartment #15, phone 555-1234, email Sophie@sophie.com) is your resident manager. You should pay your rent to her and promptly let her know of any maintenance or repair problems (see below) and any other questions or problems. She's in her office every day from 8 a.m. to 10 a.m. and from 4 p.m. to 6 p.m. and can be reached by phone at other times.   .

Landlord-Tenant Checklist: By now, Sophie Beauchamp should have taken you on a walk-through of your apartment to check the condition of all walls, drapes, carpets, and appliances and to test the smoke alarms and fire extinguisher. These are all listed on the Landlord-Tenant Checklist, which you should have reviewed carefully and signed. When you move out, we will ask you to check each item against its original condition as described on the Checklist.   .

Maintenance/Repair Problems: ___We are determined to maintain a clean, safe building in which all systems are in good repair. To help us make repairs promptly, we will give you Maintenance/Repair Request forms to report to the manager any problems in your apartment, such as a broken garbage disposal, or on the building or grounds, such as a burned-out light in the garage. (Extra copies are available from the manager.) In an emergency, or when it's not convenient to use this form, please call the manager at 555-1234.___ .

Semiannual Safety and Maintenance Update: ___To help us keep your unit and the common areas in excellent condition, we'll ask you to fill out a form every six months updating any problems on the premises or in your rental unit. This will allow you to report any potential safety hazards or other problems that otherwise might be overlooked.___ .

Annual Safety Inspection: ___Once a year, we will ask to inspect the condition and furnishings of your rental unit and update the Landlord-Tenant Checklist. In keeping with state law, we will give you reasonable notice before the inspection, and you are encouraged to be present for it.___ .

Insurance: ___We highly recommend that you purchase renters' insurance. The building property insurance policy will not cover the replacement of your personal belongings if they are lost due to fire, theft, or accident. In addition, you could be found liable if someone is injured on the premises you rent as a result of your negligence. If you damage the building itself - for example, if you start a fire in the kitchen and it spreads - you could be responsible for large repair bills.___ .

Moving Out: ___It's a little early to bring up moving out, but please be aware that we have a list of items that should be cleaned before we conduct a move-out inspection. If you decide to move, please ask the manager for a copy of our Move-Out Letter, explaining our procedures for inspection and returning your deposit.___

Telephone Number Changes: ___Please notify us if your phone number(s) change(s), so we can reach you promptly in an emergency.___ .

Please let us know if you have any questions.

Sincerely,

Tom Guiliano _____ _September 1, 20xx_
Landlord/Manager   Date

I have read and received a copy of this statement.

Frank O'Hara _____ _September 1, 20xx_
Tenant   Date

(As an extra precaution, ask him to initial each page.) Although this step may seem paranoid now, you won't think so if you get in a dispute with a tenant who claims you never told him something important (like the need to purchase renters' insurance).

Be sure to update the move-in letter from time to time as necessary.

Cash Rent and Security Deposit Checks

Every landlord's nightmare is a new tenant whose first rent or deposit check bounces and who must be dislodged with time-consuming and expensive legal proceedings.

To avoid this, never sign a rental agreement, or let a tenant move furniture into your property or take a key, until you have the tenant's cash, certified check, or money order for the first month's rent and security deposit. An alternative is to cash the tenant's check at the bank before the move-in date. (While you have the tenant's first check, photocopy it for your records. The information on it can be helpful if you ever need to sue to collect a judgment from the tenant.) Be sure to give the tenant a signed receipt for the deposit.

Clause 5 of the form lease and rental agreements in Chapter 2 requires tenants to pay rent on the first day of each month. If the move-in date is other than the first day of the month, rent is prorated between that day and the end of that month.

Organize Your Tenant Records

A good system to record all significant tenant complaints and repair requests will provide a valuable paper trail should disputes develop later—for example, regarding your right to enter a tenant's unit to make repairs or the time it took for you to fix a problem. Without good records, the outcome of a dispute may come down to your word against your tenant's—always a precarious situation.

How to Establish a Filing System

Set up a file folder on each property with individual files for each tenant. Include the following documents:

- tenant's rental application, references, credit report, and background information, including information about any cosigners
- a signed lease or rental agreement, plus any changes made along the way
- Landlord-Tenant Checklist and photos or video made at move-in, and
- signed move-in letter.

After a tenant moves in, add these documents to the individual's file:

- your written requests for entry
- rent increase notices
- records of repair requests, and details of how and when they were handled—if you keep repair records on the computer, you should regularly print out and save files from past months; if you have a master system to record all requests and complaints in one log, you would save that log separately, not necessarily put it in every tenant's file
- safety and maintenance updates and inspection reports, and
- correspondence and other relevant information, including copies of important emails.

See "Using Email for Notices or Other Communications with Tenants," at the end of this chapter.

CAUTION
Good records are especially important if you end up suing a tenant who breaks the lease. Chapter 14 explains the kinds of records to keep, such as receipts for advertising the property.

There are several property management software programs that allow you to keep track of every aspect of your business, from the tracking of rents to the follow-up on repair requests. Especially if you own many rental properties, these programs are well worth the cost, or you can set up your own database for each tenant with spaces for the following information:

- address or unit number
- move-in date
- phone number (cell, home, work)
- name, address, and phone number of employer
- credit information, including up-to-date information as to where tenant banks
- monthly rent amount and rent due date
- amount and purpose of deposits plus any information your state requires on location of deposit and interest payments
- vehicle make, model, color, year, and license plate number
- emergency contacts, and
- whatever else is important to you.

Once you enter the information into your database, you can sort the list by address or other variables and easily print labels for rent increases or other notices.

How to Handle Credit Reports

Under federal law, you must take special care that credit reports (and any information stored elsewhere that is derived from credit reports) are stored in a secure place where only those who "need to know" have access. ("Disposal Rule" of the Fair and Accurate Credit Transactions Act of 2003, known as the FACT Act, 69 Fed. Reg. 68690.) In addition, you must dispose of such records when you're done with them, by burning them or using a shredder. This portion of the FACT Act was passed in order to combat the increasing reports of identity theft. It applies to every landlord who pulls a credit report, no matter how small your operation. The Federal Trade Commission, which interprets the Act, encourages you to similarly safeguard and dispose of *any* record that contains a tenant's or applicant's personal or financial information. This would include the rental application itself, as well as any notes you make that include such information.

Implementing the Disposal Rule will require some effort and follow-through, though it need not be a burdensome chore. Follow these suggestions:

- **Maintain applicant, tenant, and employee files in a locked cabinet.** This is a good practice for many reasons. Only you and your manager should have access to these files.
- **Determine when you no longer have a legitimate business reason to keep an applicant's credit report.** The Act requires you to dispose of credit reports or any information taken from them when you no longer need them. Unfortunately, you may need these reports long after you've rejected or accepted an applicant—they may be essential in refuting a fair housing claim. Under federal law, such claims must be filed within two years of the claimed discrimination, but some states set longer periods. Keep the records at least two years, and longer if your state gives plaintiffs extra time.
- **Establish a system for purging old credit reports.** Don't rely on haphazard file purges to keep you legal when it comes to destroying old reports. Establish a purge date for every applicant for whom you pull a report and use a tickle system.
- **Choose an effective purging method.** The Disposal Rule requires you to choose a level of document destruction that is reasonable in the context of your business. For example, a landlord with a few rentals would do just fine with an inexpensive shredder, but a multi-property operation might want to contract with a shredding service.
- **Don't forget computer files.** Reports stored on your computer or phone, or information derived from them, must also be kept secure and deleted when no longer needed. Purchase a utility that will "wipe" the data completely—that is, a program that will delete not only the directory, but the text as well.

The Disposal Rule comes with teeth for those who willfully disregard it—that is, for those who know about the law and how to comply but who deliberately refuse to do so. You could be liable for a tenant's actual damages resulting from identity theft (say, the cost of covering a portion of a credit card's unauthorized use), or damages per violation of between $100 and $1,000, plus the tenant's attorney fees and costs of suit, plus punitive damages. The FTC and state counterparts can also enforce the Act and impose fines.

How to Respond to Security Breaches

Despite your best efforts, information about your tenants may become lost or stolen. If you lose a laptop, become prey to a computer hacker, or suffer the consequences of a dishonest employee, sensitive identifying information about residents and applicants may result in their identify theft.

Almost every state (excepting Alabama and South Dakota) has laws on the books concerning security breaches. These laws cover who should comply, define the information that's at issue ("personal information"), define what constitutes a breach, provide notice requirements, and note any exemptions. To find the law in your state, go to the website of the National Conference of State Legislatures (www.ncsl.org) and enter "security breach notification laws" in the search box.

If you're in a state with no breach notification law, head to the Federal Trade Commission, which gives excellent guidance on how to alert applicants and residents if you experience a security breach. Go to www.business.ftc.gov, and look for the FTC's *Data Breach Response: A Guide for Business*; this guide includes advice for notifying individuals, such as tenants, of a data breach and a model letter for doing so. If your state has its own notification requirements, you'll need to comply with them, too. Contact your state's consumer protection office (find yours at www.usa.gov/state-consumer).

Organize Income and Expenses for Schedule E

If you've been in the landlording business for any length of time, you will be used to reporting your income and expenses on Schedule E (assuming you file IRS Form 1040 to pay your taxes). The Schedule is relatively simple. For each address (which may include multiple rental units), you report the year's rent and list enumerated expenses (the first page of Schedule E is reproduced below). You can download a fillable version of Schedule E from www.irs.gov.

Many landlords find it easiest to use *QuickBooks* or another accounting software package to track their income and expenses. There are also programs designed specifically for completing Schedule E, notably *Quicken Rental Property Manager*, which allows you to track income, expenses, and tax deductions, and converts the information into a Schedule E at tax time. You can also design your own spreadsheet using *Excel* or a similar program to keep track of rental income and expenses. Finally, there's always the old-fashioned way of making your own paper ledger of income and expenses.

Of course, the system you use to track income and expenses is only as good as the information you enter. To maximize tax deductions, keep receipts and records of all rental-property-related expenses, such as interest payments on mortgage loans, property taxes, professional fees (your accountant, attorney, property management), insurance, repairs, advertising and tenant screening, and membership fees, plus all income from rent, late fees, and the like.

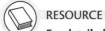 **RESOURCE**

For detailed information on completing Schedule E and valuable tax advice for landlords, see *Every Landlord's Tax Deduction Guide,* **by Stephen Fishman (Nolo).** For personalized advice, consult an accountant or tax professional (and remember, buying this book or consulting with a tax pro are both tax-deductible expenses).

SCHEDULE E (Form 1040) Department of the Treasury Internal Revenue Service (99)	**Supplemental Income and Loss** (From rental real estate, royalties, partnerships, S corporations, estates, trusts, REMICs, etc.) ▶ **Attach to Form 1040, 1040NR, or Form 1041.** ▶ **Go to** *www.irs.gov/ScheduleE* **for instructions and the latest information.**	OMB No. 1545-0074 20**17** Attachment Sequence No. **13**

Name(s) shown on return	Your social security number

Part I   **Income or Loss From Rental Real Estate and Royalties**   Note: If you are in the business of renting personal property, use **Schedule C** or **C-EZ** (see instructions). If you are an individual, report farm rental income or loss from **Form 4835** on page 2, line 40.

A Did you make any payments in 2017 that would require you to file Form(s) 1099? (see instructions) . . . . . ☐ **Yes** ☐ **No**
B If "Yes," did you or will you file required Forms 1099? . . . . ☐ **Yes** ☐ **No**

1a Physical address of each property (street, city, state, ZIP code)

A
B
C

1b	Type of Property (from list below)	2	For each rental real estate property listed above, report the number of fair rental and personal use days. Check the **QJV** box only if you meet the requirements to file as a qualified joint venture. See instructions.		Fair Rental Days	Personal Use Days	QJV
A				A			☐
B				B			☐
C				C			☐

Type of Property:
1 Single Family Residence   3 Vacation/Short-Term Rental   5 Land   7 Self-Rental
2 Multi-Family Residence   4 Commercial   6 Royalties   8 Other (describe)

Income:		Properties:		A		B		C	
3	Rents received	3							
4	Royalties received	4							
Expenses:									
5	Advertising	5							
6	Auto and travel (see instructions)	6							
7	Cleaning and maintenance	7							
8	Commissions.	8							
9	Insurance	9							
10	Legal and other professional fees	10							
11	Management fees	11							
12	Mortgage interest paid to banks, etc. (see instructions)	12							
13	Other interest.	13							
14	Repairs.	14							
15	Supplies	15							
16	Taxes	16							
17	Utilities	17							
18	Depreciation expense or depletion	18							
19	Other (list) ▶ _____	19							
20	Total expenses. Add lines 5 through 19	20							
21	Subtract line 20 from line 3 (rents) and/or 4 (royalties). If result is a (loss), see instructions to find out if you must file **Form 6198**	21							
22	Deductible rental real estate loss after limitation, if any, on **Form 8582** (see instructions)	22	(	)	(	)	(	)	

23a	Total of all amounts reported on line 3 for all rental properties	**23a**		
b	Total of all amounts reported on line 4 for all royalty properties	**23b**		
c	Total of all amounts reported on line 12 for all properties	**23c**		
d	Total of all amounts reported on line 18 for all properties	**23d**		
e	Total of all amounts reported on line 20 for all properties	**23e**		

24	**Income.** Add positive amounts shown on line 21. **Do not** include any losses	**24**	
25	**Losses.** Add royalty losses from line 21 and rental real estate losses from line 22. Enter total losses here .	**25**	( )
26	**Total rental real estate and royalty income or (loss).** Combine lines 24 and 25. Enter the result here. If Parts II, III, IV, and line 40 on page 2 do not apply to you, also enter this amount on Form 1040, line 17, or Form 1040NR, line 18. Otherwise, include this amount in the total on line 41 on page 2 . . .	**26**	

For Paperwork Reduction Act Notice, see the separate instructions.   Cat. No. 11344L   Schedule E (Form 1040) 2017

Using Email for Notices or Other Communications With Tenants

You and your tenant may often send each other messages by email rather than by post, or communicate via text messages. Will those communications serve you as well as a mailed letter, if you need evidence that the message was received at the other end?

Suppose, for example, that you want to give notice terminating a tenant's month-to-month rental agreement, and do so by sending an email that's 30 days (your state's notice period) in advance of the termination date. Or, say you need to send your tenant a request for entry so that you can show the unit to an electrician you've hired to upgrade the wiring. If you end up in a legal dispute and your tenant challenges you in court, saying that you never told him about your decision to terminate or alerted him to the electrician's visit, you'll need confirmation that the emails were received.

CAUTION

Check your lease for notice instructions! Often, the lease or rental agreement contains a clause that describes how landlords and tenants should deliver "notices and demands." Unfortunately, most of the time you'll see a generic requirement that they be delivered "in writing." But as email communications have become more and more common, some lawyers are drafting notice clauses that take email into account.

On the One Hand: Electronic Notice Is Acceptable in Most Situations

Two laws confirm the acceptability in court of electronic notices: "UETA" (the Uniform Electronic Transactions Act), adopted in some form by 47 states and the District of Columbia (not adopted in Illinois, New York, or Washington), and "ESIGN" (Electronic Signatures in Global and National Commerce Act), a federal law. Unless some other law prohibits it, UETA and ESIGN permit the use of electronic signatures and electronic notices. Put another way, under both of these laws, a legal notice cannot be denied admission in court simply because it is electronic (and not on paper).

On the Other Hand: Emails May Be Legal, But Demonstrating Their Receipt Is Not Cheap

While it may be legally permissible to introduce emails as evidence in court, first you'll have to prove that the tenant received your email. While some sophisticated services such as RPost (www.rpost.com) allow you to send tamper-proof attachments and electronic signatures, they may be expensive, depending on volume.

The Bottom Line: Stick With a Traditional Mail or Delivery Service

Currently, there is no cost-efficient way for a landlord to obtain evidence of delivery of an email message. Text messages are even harder to track, and evidence of receipt isn't available short of complex searches through users' accounts. Rarely would a landlord/tenant dispute support the expense of such a search.

If you're worried about being able to prove the receipt of your email or text, you'd be best served to also print it and mail it return receipt requested … the old fashioned way.

Cotenants, Sublets, and Assignments

 FORMS IN THIS CHAPTER

Chapter 8 includes instructions for and samples of the following forms:

- Landlord-Tenant Agreement to Terminate Lease
- Consent to Assignment of Lease
- Letter to Original Tenant and New Cotenant

The Nolo website includes downloadable copies of these forms. See Appendix B for the link to the forms in this book.

Conscientious landlords go to a lot of trouble to screen prospective tenants. However, all your sensible precautions will be of little avail if unapproved tenants simply move in at the invitation of existing tenants. Not only is it possible that you'll have difficulty getting these tenants to pay rent or maintain the rental unit, but if they fail to do so, you may have an extra tough time evicting them.

This chapter helps you analyze your options when your tenant asks questions like these:

- "Can I sublet my apartment?"
- "May I get someone else to take over the rest of my lease?"
- "Is it okay if I move in a roommate?"

We also advise you on what to do when your tenant attempts to do any of the above *without* consulting you. Because, as with so many of life's problematic situations, the best defense is a good offense, we prepare you in advance for these situations by suggesting that you protect your interests from the outset by using lease clauses that limit occupants and require your permission for subleasing or assigning. In particular, this chapter explains:

- why everyone living in a rental unit should sign a lease or rental agreement
- the legal differences between sublets and assignments
- your right (and legal and practical limitations) to prohibit sublets and assignments
- how to add a tenant to an existing tenancy, and
- how to deal with repeated overnight guests.

 RELATED TOPIC
Related topics covered in this book include:
- Limiting how long tenants' guests may stay: Chapter 2 (Clause 3)
- Requiring your written consent in advance for any sublet or assignment of the lease or rental agreement, or for any additional people to move in: Chapter 2 (Clauses 1, 3, and 10)
- Your duty to rerent the property if a tenant neither sublets nor assigns, but simply breaks the lease: Chapter 14

- Returning security deposits when one tenant leaves but the others stay: Chapter 15.

 CAUTION
New York tenants have special rights. By virtue of New York's Roommate Law (RPL § 235-f), New York tenants have the right to bring in certain additional roommates without obtaining the landlord's prior approval and subject only to any applicable local laws on overcrowding. If you own rental property in New York, be sure you understand this law before setting restrictions on tenants and roommates.

Cotenants

When two or more people rent property together, and all sign the same rental agreement or lease—or enter into the same oral rental agreement and move in at the same time—they are cotenants. Each cotenant shares the same rights and responsibilities for the rent and other terms of the lease or rental agreement. In addition, each cotenant is legally responsible to the landlord to carry out all of the terms of the lease, including being obligated to pay the entire rent and 100% of any damages to the premises if the others fail to pay their share.

Obligation for Rent

Among themselves, cotenants may split the rent equally or unequally, depending on their own personal arrangement. However, any cotenant who signs a lease or rental agreement with you is independently liable for all of the rent. Landlords often remind cotenants of this obligation by inserting into the lease a chunk of legalese which says that the tenants are "jointly and severally" liable for paying rent and adhering to terms of the agreement (see "Joint and Several Liability," below). If one tenant can't pay his share a particular month or simply moves out, the other tenant(s) must still pay the full rent during the rental period.

Joint and Several Liability

"Joint and several" refers to the sharing of obligations and liabilities among two or more people—both as a group and as individuals. When two or more tenants are "jointly and severally liable," you can choose to hold all of them, or just one of them, responsible to pay rent and to abide by the rules of the tenancy.

That means you may demand the entire rent from just one tenant should the others skip out, or evict all of the tenants even if just one has broken the terms of the lease.

Clause 1 of the form lease and rental agreements in Chapter 2 makes cotenants jointly and severally liable. Cotenants are jointly and severally liable for rent and other obligations—even if your lease or rental agreement does not include this clause. Nonetheless, we recommend you include a "jointly and severally liable" clause to alert tenants to this responsibility.

EXAMPLE: James and Helen sign a month-to-month rental agreement for a $1,200 apartment rented by Blue Oak Properties. They agree between themselves to each pay half of the rent. After three months, James moves out without notifying Helen or Blue Oak. As one of two cotenants, Helen is still legally obligated to pay Blue Oak all the rent (although she might be able to recover James's share by suing him).

Blue Oak has four options if Helen can't pay the rent:

- Blue Oak can give Helen a written notice to pay up or leave (called a Notice to Pay Rent or Quit in most states), and follow through with an eviction lawsuit if Helen fails to pay the entire rent or move within the required amount of time (usually three to five days).
- If Helen offers to pay part of the rent, Blue Oak can legally accept it, but should make it clear that Helen is still responsible for the entire rent. It's important to make this clear, since it's common for one cotenant to offer only "my portion" of the rent, when in fact each cotenant (roommate) is liable for the entire rent.

- If Helen wants to stay and finds a new cotenant with a decent credit history, Blue Oak may not be able to withhold its approval of the new person and still hold Helen to her obligation to pay 100% of the rent. If Blue Oak accepts a new person, it should, however, have him become a cotenant by signing a rental agreement (as discussed below).
- If Helen wants to stay and proposes a cotenant who proves to be unacceptable to Blue Oak (because the applicant does not meet Blue Oak's usual credit or income specifications for every new tenant), Blue Oak may say "No" and evict Helen if Helen is unable to pay the entire rent.

Violations of the Lease or Rental Agreement

In addition to paying rent, each tenant is responsible for any cotenant's action that violates any term of the lease or rental agreement—for example, each cotenant is liable if one of them seriously damages the property or moves in an extra roommate or a dog contrary to the lease or rental agreement. This means you can hold all cotenants responsible and can terminate the entire tenancy with the appropriate notice, even though some of the cotenants objected to the dog or weren't consulted by the prime offender.

If you must evict a tenant for a breach other than for nonpayment of rent (in which case you would evict all the tenants), you must decide whether to evict only the offending cotenant or all of them. Your decision will depend on the circumstances. You have no legal obligation to evict a blameless cotenant (for example, one who has no control over a dog-owning cotenant). Practically, of course, you'll want to be sure the innocent tenant can still shoulder the rent after his problem roommate is gone. On the other hand, because cotenants are "jointly and severally liable," you also have the legal right to evict all cotenants (even those who claim not to have caused the difficulty) and start over.

Special Rules for Married Couples

We strongly recommend that everyone who lives in a rental unit—including both members of a married couple—be required to sign the lease or rental agreement. This underscores your expectation that each individual is responsible ("jointly and severally liable") for the rent and the proper use of the rental property.

If, however, you neglect to have either the husband or wife sign the lease, that person may still be directly responsible to you. That's because, in some states, a spouse is financially responsible for the necessities of life of the other, including rent.

But rather than counting on your state's law for protection, just put both names on the lease or rental agreement and make them each cotenants. And, if one of your tenants gets married during the lease term, prepare a new agreement and have both spouses sign it.

Disagreements Among Cotenants

Usually, cotenants make only an oral agreement among themselves concerning how they will split the rent, occupy bedrooms, and generally share their joint living space. For all sorts of reasons, roommate arrangements may go awry. If you have been a landlord for a while, you surely know all about cotenants who play the stereo too loud, are slobs, pay their share of the rent late, have too many overnight guests or create some other problem that their roommates can't abide. If the situation gets bad enough, the tenants may start arguing about who should leave, whether one cotenant can keep another out of the apartment, or who is responsible for what part of the rent.

The best advice we can give landlords who face serious disagreements among cotenants is this: Don't get involved in spats between cotenants, as a mediator or otherwise. The reasons for our advice are both practical and legal.

On the practical side, you probably do not have the time to get to the bottom of financial or personal disputes; and, even if you do, you have no ability to enforce any decisions among your tenants. (How could you enforce a ruling that one tenant must occupy the smaller of the two bedrooms?)

On the legal side, too, you are largely helpless. For example, you cannot threaten eviction if a tenant violates an agreement with the other tenant and occupies the larger bedroom, unless you put that particular "offense" into the lease as a ground for eviction. And since it's impossible to design a lease that will predict and list every possible roommate disagreement, attempting to use a legal solution will be of little help.

If one or more cotenants approach you about a dispute, explain that they must resolve any disagreements among themselves. Remind them that they are each legally obligated to pay the entire rent, and that you are not affected by any rent-sharing agreements they have made among themselves. If one cotenant asks you to change the locks to keep another cotenant out, tell the tenant that you cannot legally do that—unless a court has issued an order that the particular tenant stay out.

The wisdom of remaining aloof during tenants' squabbles stops at the point that you fear for the physical safety of one of your tenants. Call the police immediately if you hear or witness violence between tenants, or if a reliable source tells you about it. If you have any reasonable factual basis to believe that a tenant intends to harm another tenant, you may also have a legal duty to warn the intended victim (who probably already knows) and begin proceedings to evict the aggressor. Failure to sensibly intervene where violence is threatened might result in a finding of liability if the aggressor carries through with the threat. (The fact that the parties are cotenants instead of tenants in different rental units would be immaterial to a court when determining liability.)

In the meantime, if one tenant fears violence from a cotenant, consider taking the following steps:

- Suggest mediation if you think there is a potential for a reasoned resolution.

When Couples Separate

Landlords need to be alert to the special emotional and possibly legal situations presented by a couple who rent the premises together and undergo a nasty break-up. Whether they are married or not, dealing with feuding lovers who are living together is never easy. Here are some issues to consider:

- Especially if the couple is married, one tenant may not have the legal right to deprive the other of a place to live without a court order. If violence—or even the threat of it—is involved, the fearful spouse (usually the woman) is entitled to get a quick court order restraining the other partner from coming near her, either as part of a divorce filing or, in some states, separately. To help facilitate this, you might check out how to get a restraining order (there is usually a nonlawyer procedure) and make this information available to affected tenants. For advice, call the police department, your local courthouse, a women's shelter, or an advocacy organization for women.

- If one married tenant changes the locks without your consent to keep the other out, you probably have no legal liability. (If your lease or rental agreement—like the one in this book—prohibits changing the locks without the landlord's permission, you probably have grounds for eviction.) But you should not normally participate in acts that will keep one member of a married couple out (say, by changing the locks yourself) without a court restraining order, which specifically bars the other member of the couple from coming near the remaining tenant.

- When it comes to unmarried couples, you should know if your state or municipality grants any legal status to long-term relationships between people who are not married (these can take the form of either common law marriages or domestic partner laws). If so, the law may treat people in these relationships similarly to married couples.

- When unmarried couples—whether of the same or opposite sex—separate, the law treats them as roommates. But in many states, a fearful member of an unmarried couple can qualify for a civil restraining order banning the other from the joint home, using a procedure similar to that available to married couples.

- Contact the local police department or court clerk's office on behalf of the intended victim for information on obtaining a temporary restraining order, and urge the victim to apply for one. If the judge decides that the situation merits it, he or she will issue an order forbidding the aggressor tenant from coming near the other.

- Evict the aggressor or all cotenants on the lease. If you choose to allow a blameless tenant to stay, keep in mind that the remaining tenant's ability to pay the rent may be severely curtailed by the absence of a paying cotenant.

EXAMPLE: Andy and his roommate Bill began their tenancy on friendly terms. Unfortunately, it soon became clear that their personal habits were completely at odds. Their arguments regarding housekeeping, guests, and their financial obligations to contribute to the rent escalated to a physical fight. As a result, they each asked their landlord, Anita, to evict the other.

After listening to Andy's and Bill's complaints, Anita referred them to a local mediation service, and they agreed to participate. The mediator's influence worked for a while, but Andy and Bill were soon back at loud, unpleasant shouting matches. Anita initiated eviction proceedings against both, on the grounds that their disruptive behavior interfered with the rights of the other tenants to the quiet enjoyment of their homes.

Domestic Violence Situations

States have begun to extend special protections to victims of domestic violence. If you are responding to a problematic rental situation that involves domestic violence, proceed cautiously and check first with local law enforcement or a battered women's shelter regarding special laws that may apply. Your state may have rules like the following (see "State Laws in Domestic Violence Situations," in Appendix A, for specific laws).

- **Antidiscrimination status and eviction protection.** Many states have made it illegal to discriminate against someone who is a victim of domestic violence. This means that landlords cannot refuse to rent (or terminate) solely because the person is a victim of domestic violence. (See Chapter 5 for complete information on discrimination.)

- **Early termination rights.** In several states, a tenant who is a victim of domestic violence can end a lease with 30 days' notice, upon showing the landlord proof (such as a protective order) of her status as a domestic violence victim. In a few states, tenant victims who have reported domestic violence, stalking, or sexual assaults (or who have protective orders) may terminate without giving the usual amount of notice. Similarly, some victims of domestic violence may terminate without notice and avoid liability for future rent if the victim shows the landlord a protective order or temporary injunction concerning the victim or any other occupant.

- **Changed locks.** Many states require landlords to change the locks to protect a resident tenant when shown a court order directing a perpetrator to stay away.

- **Limits on rental clauses.** In many states, landlords cannot include clauses providing for termination in the event of a tenant's call for police help in a domestic violence situation, nor can landlords make tenants pay for the cost of such calls.

- **Section 8 tenants.** Normally, Section 8 tenants may move without jeopardizing their right to continued public assistance only if they notify their public housing authority ahead of time, terminate their lease according to the lease's provisions, and locate acceptable replacement housing. Domestic violence victims, however, may circumvent these requirements if they have otherwise complied with other Section 8 requirements, have moved in order to protect someone who is or has been a domestic violence victim, and "reasonably believed" that they were imminently threatened by harm from further violence. (Violence Against Women and Department of Justice Reauthorization Act of 2005, 42 U.S. Code § 1437f (r)(5).)

In the absence of a state law giving victims of domestic violence early termination rights or other domestic violence protections, don't automatically say "No" to an early termination or other related request. First, because your policy will usually affect female, not male, tenants, it can be attacked in court as indirectly discriminating on the basis of sex (several lawsuits brought in states without statutory protections have succeeded on this theory). Aside from your vulnerability to being sued, keep in mind that it may be essential to the safety of the victim to allow her to quickly move. Finally, even your bottom line may benefit from allowing the tenancy to end immediately—what you lose in rent may pale in comparison with what your repair costs may be if your property is damaged, not to speak of the fallout from negative publicity if the situation escalates.

Although your state (and the federal law mentioned above) may give some special protections to domestic violence victims, these accommodations do not prohibit you from terminating, if necessary, for nonpayment of rent. Unfortunately, all too often the abuser will leave the property but the remaining victim struggles to pay the rent. You may legally terminate the tenancy of a domestic violence victim who falls behind in the rent, just as you would any tenant who hasn't paid.

When a Cotenant Leaves

When a cotenant leaves and someone is proposed as a substitute, you want three things to happen:

- The departing tenant should sign a Landlord-Tenant Agreement to Terminate Lease (shown below).
- You should investigate the proposed new tenant, beginning with the application process (like any new tenancy).
- The remaining tenant(s), including the replacement tenant, should sign a new lease or rental agreement.

These steps are all discussed below.

There are three reasons for formally "resetting the stage" this way: (1) to ensure that you continue to receive the entire rent, (2) to ensure that any new tenant meets your criteria for selecting tenants, and (3) to avoid the specter of the return—or attempted return—of the departed tenant who claims that he never *really* intended to leave.

Leases vs. Rental Agreements

Our discussion of subleasing and assigning assumes that there is an underlying lease for a term of one year or more. If there is a long amount of time remaining on a lease, both landlord and tenant will be very concerned about a number of issues, including a tenant's obligation for remaining rent and the landlord's duty to find a new tenant and limit (mitigate) his losses.

By contrast, a month-to-month tenancy lasts no more than 30 days. When a tenant wants to leave before the end of the 30 days (to sublet and return, say, on day 28, or to assign the rental agreement and not return at all), the short amount of time (and rent money) remaining on the rental agreement may make a landlord less willing to accept the substitute.

You should not be any less thorough in checking the background of a proposed subtenant or assignee of a rental agreement, however. In theory, the amount of money at stake may be less than that involved in a lease, since the tenancy usually can be terminated with 30 days' notice for any reason. In reality, however, other considerations (such as the health and safety of other tenants, or the possibility of accepting a tenacious bad apple who proves difficult and expensive to evict) suggest the need for the same background checking that is used in evaluating any new tenant.

Common Terms

Prime Tenant. We use this term to refer to the original tenant—someone you chose from a pool of applicants and who has signed a lease or rental agreement. This is our shortcut term—it has no legal meaning.

Here are common terms that do have accepted legal meaning.

Tenant. Someone who has signed a lease or a rental contract, or who has gained the status of a tenant because the landlord has accepted his presence on the property or has accepted rent from him. A tenant has a legal relationship with the landlord that creates various rights and responsibilities for both parties.

Cotenants. Two or more tenants who rent the same property under the same lease or rental agreement. As far as the landlord is concerned, each is 100% responsible for carrying out the agreement (in legal slang, "jointly and severally liable"), including paying all the rent.

Subtenant. Someone who subleases (rents) all or part of the premises from a tenant (not from the landlord).

Assignment. The transfer by a tenant of all his rights of tenancy to another tenant (the "assignee"). Unlike a subtenant, an assignee rents directly from landlord.

Roommates. Two or more people, usually unrelated, living under the same roof and sharing rent and expenses. A roommate is usually a cotenant, but in some situations may be a subtenant.

The rent. Although the departing tenant will still be technically liable for the rent until you formally release him from the lease or rental agreement (except where he has given timely written notice), this may not be worth much if he has left for parts unknown. And, although the remaining tenants (individually and as a group) are liable for the rent, too, they may not be able (or willing) to pay the departing tenant's share. You are almost always better off signing a lease with a new tenant if he is acceptable.

Who is entitled to live in the rental unit. As an added advantage, formally terminating a cotenant's lease or rental agreement and preparing a new one, signed by the remaining tenant(s) and any replacement tenant, will make it clear that the outgoing tenant is no longer entitled to possession of the property. Although you do not want to become entangled in your tenants' personal lives, you also want to avoid being dragged into disputes regarding who is entitled to a key and the use of your rental property.

But what happens if, despite your vigilance, a new tenant moves in without your permission who isn't acceptable to you? Assuming you see no reason to change your mind, you have a right to evict all cotenants under the terms of the clause in your lease or rental agreement that prohibits unauthorized sublets.

What to Do When a Tenant Wants to Sublet or Assign

Ideally, you want to rent to tenants who will stay a long time, or at least the entire term of the lease. But, despite your best efforts, you will encounter tenants who, for various reasons such as a job-related move, will want to leave before the expiration of their lease. Sometimes, of course, these tenants simply disappear. Other tenants, out of regard for their promise, or to recover as much as possible of their deposit, or maybe just out of concern that you will pursue them or damage their credit rating, will want to leave "legally" by supplying a stand-in for the balance of the term.

What should you do if a tenant approaches you with a request to move out, substituting another tenant in her place? Because our lease and rental agreements (Clause 10) prohibit sublets or assignments without your written consent, you have some flexibility. This section discusses your options.

Create a New Tenancy

In most situations, your best bet when confronted with a tenant who wants to sublease or assign is to simply insist that the tenancy terminate and a

new one begin—with the proposed "subtenant" or "assignee" as the new prime tenant.

Suppose a tenant wants to sublet her apartment for six months while she is out of the area, or assign the last four months of her lease because she has to move for employment reasons. If the proposed new tenant passes your standard screening process, agree to take the tenant—on the condition that the proposed new tenant sign a new lease and become a prime tenant. This gives you the most direct legal relationship with the substitute. In other words, simply treat your tenant's wish to sublet or assign as a wish to get out from under the lease early, with a candidate for the next occupant at the ready.

Comparing Subleases and Assignments		
	Sublease	**Assignment**
Rent	New tenant (subtenant) is liable to the prime tenant, not to the landlord. Prime tenant is liable to landlord.	New tenant (assignee) is liable to the landlord. Old tenant is liable if new tenant doesn't pay.
Damage to premises	Prime tenant is liable for damage caused by new tenant.	Absent an agreement to the contrary, prime tenant is not liable for damage caused by new tenant.
Violations of lease	Landlord can't sue new tenant for money losses caused by violating lease, because new tenant never signed lease. New tenant can't sue landlord for lease violations, either.	New tenant and landlord are bound by all terms in lease except those that were purely personal to the landlord or old tenant.
Eviction	Landlord can sue to evict new tenant for any reason old tenant could have been evicted. But to evict subtenant, landlord must also evict old tenant.	Landlord can sue to evict new tenant for any reason old tenant could have been evicted.

The way to accomplish this is to first release your original tenant from her obligations under the lease (see the sample Landlord-Tenant Agreement to Terminate Lease, below). Then, begin the new tenancy with the substitute in the same way that you begin any tenancy: sign a lease, present a move-in letter, and so on.

What are the pros and cons of this approach as compared to accepting a subtenancy or assignment? Here are a few:

- **Subtenancy.** If you allow a subtenancy, you have no direct legal relationship with the new tenant. Practically, this means that if you should need to sue her for damage to the property or failure to pay rent, you cannot do it directly; you must involve the original tenant.

- **Assignment.** If you allow the tenant to assign the lease, the new tenant (the assignee) steps into the original tenant's legal shoes and (unlike a subtenant) has a complete legal relationship with you. In short, you can take legal action directly against the assignee in any dispute. In addition, you get one significant advantage: If the new tenant fails to pay the rent, the old one is still legally responsible to do so. So why prefer a new tenancy? Simply because insisting on a regular tenancy will do away with any misunderstanding about who is liable. If disagreements later arise concerning liability for damages or rent, the new tenant knows exactly where she stands.

The sample Landlord-Tenant Agreement to Terminate Lease below will terminate the original tenancy so that you can rent the property to the new tenant. Then, if and when the first tenant wants to return and the second voluntarily leaves, you can again rent to the first, using a new lease. A copy of the Landlord-Tenant Agreement to Terminate Lease is available on the Nolo website. See Appendix B for the link to the forms in this book.

In most cases, tenants should be happy that you're letting them off the hook. But what if the original tenant really does want to return and is uneasy about having you rent to the new tenant directly, because he fears the second person may not honor her promise to leave? Your answer should normally be a polite version of "That's your problem." Think of it this way: Your tenant is admitting that he doesn't completely trust the new tenant to move out on demand, even though he selected her. You don't want to be in the middle of this type of situation. It's better that the original tenant bear the brunt of any problem—if there is one—than you.

Allow a Sublet or Assignment

Although you are almost always better off starting a new, independent tenancy with a proposed stand-in tenant, there are situations in which you may want to agree to a subtenancy or assignment.

You might, for example, want to accommodate —and keep—an exceptional, long-term tenant who has every intention of returning and whose judgment and integrity you have always trusted. If the proposed stand-in meets your normal tenant criteria, you may decide that it is worth the risk of a subtenancy or assignment in order to keep the prime tenant.

Another good reason is a desire to have a sure source of funds in the background. This might come up if you have a prime tenant who is financially sound and trustworthy, but a proposed stand-in who is less secure but acceptable in every other respect. By agreeing to a sublet or assignment, you have someone in the background (the prime tenant) still responsible for the rent. The risk you incur by agreeing to set up a subtenancy or assignment and the hassle that comes with dealing with more than one person may be worth what you gain in keeping a sure and reliable source of funds on the hook.

Landlord-Tenant Agreement to Terminate Lease

_____Robert Chin_____ [Landlord]

and ____Carl Mosk_____ [Tenant]

agree that the lease they entered into on _____November 1, 20xx_____ , for premises at

__56 Alpine Terrace, Hamilton, Tennessee_____ ,

will terminate on ____January 5, 20xx_____ .

_Robert Chin_____   _December 28, 20xx_____
Landlord/Manager   Date

_Carl Mosk_____   _December 28, 20xx_____
Tenant   Date

EXAMPLE: The Smith family rented a duplex for a term of two years but, after 18 months, the father's employer transferred him to another city. Mr. Smith asked Bob, the landlord, to agree to an assignment of the balance of the lease to Mr. Smith's 19-year-old son, who wanted to finish out his school year at the local college. Knowing that the son was a decent and conscientious young man, Bob agreed, but did not insist that Mr. Smith terminate his tenancy.

Bob realized that keeping Dad in the picture was insurance against the unlikely but possible event that the son would not be able to keep up with the rental payments. Another way Bob could accomplish this same goal would be to end the old lease and create a new one with Mr. Smith's son, but require that Dad also sign it as a guarantor.

If you would prefer not to allow a subtenancy or assignment, but the original tenant presses you, don't reject a proposed subtenant or assignee unless you have a good business reason. In a few states, including California and Florida, you may not unreasonably withhold your consent when asked to allow a sublet or assignment, no matter what the lease or rental agreement says. In broad terms, this requirement means that you must use the same criteria in evaluating the proposed stand-in that you used when choosing the prime tenant.

You can stay out of trouble by evaluating the proposed tenant by exactly the same standards that you use in evaluating any other new tenant: financial stability, credit history, references, and other criteria described in Chapter 1. If the would-be subtenant or assignee passes your tests, great; rent to him or her. If he fails the test that you apply to all potential tenants, you will be legally justified in saying no.

Then, if the prime tenant goes ahead and breaks the lease, leaving you with lost rents and rerental expenses, you can sue. You should be able to show a judge that you fairly considered (but objectively rejected) the proposed new tenant as part of your duty to try to limit (mitigate) your losses. But if the prime tenant convinces the judge that you unreasonably turned down an acceptable substitute tenant, chances are you'll lose.

> ! **CAUTION**
>
> **Don't discriminate illegally.** If you turn down a proposed subtenant or assignee for an illegal reason (racial discrimination, for example), you are vulnerable to a lawsuit under federal laws and some state and local laws.

Cotenants Can Sublet and Assign, Too

The legal principles that apply to tenants who want to sublet or assign also apply to a cotenant who wants to do the same thing. For example, it is not unusual for one of several roommates to want to sublet for a period of time, or assign the remainder of the lease. If you followed our advice and insisted that all roommates be official cotenants on the lease, you are well positioned to react to the cotenant's request, just as you would if the request came from a lone tenant.

Only Landlords Can Evict Tenants

A cotenant may not terminate another cotenant's tenancy. Termination and eviction are available only to landlords.

But a tenant who rents out part of his premises to another (called a subtenant) has considerably more power. If you allow this kind of subtenancy, realize that you have allowed your tenant to be a "landlord" as well (he's your tenant *and* the subtenant's landlord). And in his role as landlord to a subtenant, he *does* have the right to terminate and evict the subtenant.

Most owners want to control when and if the local police show up on their property to enforce eviction decrees. For this reason alone, you should prohibit "tenancies within tenancies" by insisting that every occupant become a full-fledged cotenant.

Sublets

A *subtenant* is someone who rents all or part of the property from a tenant and does not sign a rental agreement or lease with you. A subtenant either:

- rents (sublets) an entire dwelling from a tenant who moves out temporarily—for example, for the summer, or
- rents one or more rooms from the tenant, who continues to live in the unit.

The key to subtenant relationships is that the original tenant retains the primary relationship with you and continues to exercise some control over the rental property, either by occupying part of the unit or by reserving the right to retake possession at a later date. The prime tenant functions as the subtenant's landlord. The subtenant is responsible to the prime tenant for the rent, which is usually whatever figure they have agreed to between themselves. The prime tenant, in turn, is responsible to the landlord for the rent. The written or oral agreement by which a tenant rents to a subtenant is called a *sublease*, because it is under the primary lease.

Subtenancies are often a pain in the neck for landlords. Besides the obvious hassles of dealing with people coming and going, landlords in some states are limited by law to the kinds of lawsuits they can bring against subtenants—for example, you may be able to sue to correct behavior that is contrary to the lease, but not sue for money damages. This means, for instance, that a subtenant may go to court to force you to maintain habitable housing, but you could not sue that subtenant for money damages if he left the place a mess and the security deposit was insufficient to cover your loss (you would have to sue the original tenant). If you have an excellent long-term tenant who really wants to return after subleasing for a few months, you may want to risk it.

> **CAUTION**
>
> **Don't accept rent from a subtenant.** Repeatedly taking rent from a subtenant, plus taking other actions that indicate that you have basically forgotten about the prime tenant, might turn a subtenancy into a tenancy—and take the prime tenant off the hook for rent.

Assignments

From a landlord's point of view, assignments are usually preferable to subleases. With an assignment, you have more control over the tenant, because you have a direct legal relationship with the assignee.

An *assignee* is a person to whom the prime tenant has turned over the entire lease. In most states, this means simply that the prime tenant has moved out permanently. The assignee not only moves into the premises formerly occupied by the prime tenant, but into her legal shoes, as well. Unlike a subtenant, whose legal relationship is with the prime tenant, not you, the assignee rents directly from you. If things go wrong with respect to behavior or money matters under the lease, the assignee can sue or be sued by the landlord.

How to Assign a Lease

Typically, to accomplish an assignment the landlord and the tenant write "Assigned to John Doe" on the lease at each place where the prime tenant's name appears. The new tenant, John Doe, then signs at each place where the original tenant signed. If this is all that's done, the prime tenant remains liable for the rent, but not for damage to the property.

We suggest that a formal "Consent to Assignment of Lease" document also be used, such as the sample shown below. The Nolo website includes a downloadable copy. See Appendix B for the link to the forms in this book. Using this Consent to Assignment of Lease form protects you in two additional respects:

- It educates the prime tenant to the fact that he will remain liable for the rent if the assignee defaults.
- It obligates the prime tenant to cover damages to the property beyond normal wear and tear if the assignee refuses or is unable to do so.

Assignment doesn't, however, completely sever the legal relationship between you and the original tenant. Oddly enough, the original tenant remains responsible for the rent if the assignee fails to pay. Absent an agreement to the contrary, however,

Consent to Assignment of Lease

Carolyn Friedman   [Landlord] and

Joel Oliver   [Tenant]

and Sam Parker   [Assignee]

agree as follows:

1. Tenant has leased the premises at _____ 5 Fulton, Indianapolis, Indiana _____

   from Landlord.

2. The lease was signed on ___ April 1, 20xx ___ and will expire on ___ March 31, 20xx ___.

3. Tenant is assigning the balance of Tenant's lease to Assignee, beginning on ___ November 1, 20xx ___,
   and ending on _____ March 31, 20xx _____.

4. Tenant's financial responsibilities under the terms of the lease are not ended by virtue of this
   assignment. Specifically, Tenant understands that:

   a. If Assignee defaults and fails to pay the rent as provided in the lease, namely on ___ the first of ___
      ___ the month ___, Tenant will be obligated to do so within ___ three ___ days of being notified by
      Landlord; and

   b. If Assignee damages the property beyond normal wear and tear and fails or refuses to pay for
      repairs or replacement, Tenant will be obligated to do so.

5. As of the effective date of the assignment, Tenant permanently gives up the right to occupy the
   premises.

6. Assignee is bound by every term and condition in the lease that is the subject of this assignment.

Carolyn Friedman _____   *October 1, 20xx* _____
Landlord/Manager   Date

Joel Oliver _____   *October 1, 20xx* _____
Tenant   Date

Sam Parker _____   *October 1, 20xx* _____
Assignee   Date

the prime tenant is not liable for damage to the premises caused by the assignee. (The Consent to Assignment of Lease form, discussed above, protects you by incorporating this promise.)

Generally, the landlord and assignee are bound by promises made in the lease signed by the original tenant. For example, the lease provision in which the landlord agreed to return the security deposit in a certain manner is still in effect; it now benefits the assignee. And the assignee must honor the previous tenant's promise to abide by the lease's noise rules and use restrictions. Only in very unusual situations, where a lease provision is purely personal, is it not transferred. For example, a promise by a tenant to do a landlord's housekeeping in exchange for a rent reduction would not automatically pass to an assignee.

CAUTION

Liability for injuries remains the same. If a subtenant or assignee is injured on your property, the question of whether you are liable will be the same as if the injured person were the original tenant.

When a Tenant Brings in a Roommate

Suppose now that love (or poverty) strikes your tenant and he wants to move in a roommate. Assuming your lease or rental agreement restricts the number of people who can occupy the unit (as ours does in Clause 3), the tenant must get your written permission for additional tenants.

Giving Permission for a New Roommate

Although you may be motivated to accommodate your tenant's friend, your decision to allow a new cotenant should be based principally on whether or not you believe the new person will be a decent tenant. After all, if the original tenant moves out at some later date (maybe even because the new person is so awful), you will remain stuck with this person. So, always have the proposed new tenant complete a rental application, and follow your

normal screening procedures. If the new person meets your standards (a good credit record and references), and there is enough space in the unit, you will probably want to say yes.

CAUTION

Don't give spouses the third degree. The one exception to the rule of checking new tenants carefully has to do with spouses. If the new tenant is a spouse and there's no problem with overcrowding, be very careful before you say no. Refusal without a good, solid reason could be considered illegal discrimination based on marital status. In short, it's fine to check the person out, but say no only if you discover a real problem.

Preparing a New Rental Agreement or Lease

If you allow a new person to move in, make sure he becomes a full cotenant by preparing a new lease or rental agreement—possibly with some changed terms, such as the amount of rent—for signature by all tenants. (Chapter 14 discusses how.) Do this before the new person moves in to avoid the possibility of a legally confused situation.

We suggest that you send a letter to the original tenant and the new tenant as soon as you decide to allow the newcomer to move in. A sample Letter to Original Tenant and New Cotenant is shown below and the Nolo website includes a downloadable copy. See Appendix B for the link to the forms in this book.

Raising the Rent

When an additional tenant comes in, it is both reasonable and legal (in either a lease or a rental agreement situation) for you to raise the rent (and/or the security deposit), unless you live in an area covered by a rent control law that prohibits you from doing so. Obviously, from your point of view, more people living in a residence means more wear and tear and higher maintenance costs in the long run. Also, as long as your increase is reasonable, it should not be a big issue with existing occupants, who, after all, will now have someone else to pay part of the total rent.

Library name: GRANITEBAY

Title: Every landlord's legal guide
Author: Stewart, Marcia,
Item ID: 8697992
Date due: 9/28/2018,23:59

Please check our website for
Branch hours and contact info:

WWW.PLACER.CA.GOV/LIBRARY

Letter to Original Tenant and New Cotenant

Date _July 22, 20xx_

Dear _Abby Rivas_ and
_____New Cotenant_____

Phoebe Viorst ,
Original Tenant or Tenants

As the landlord of _239 Maple Street_
_____ [address] , I am pleased that

Abby [new cotenant]

has proved to be an acceptable applicant and will be joining _Phoebe_

_____ [original tenant or tenants] as a cotenant. Before

Abby [new cotenant]

moves in, everyone must sign a new lease that will cover your rights and responsibilities. Please contact me at

the address or phone number below at your earliest convenience so that we can arrange a time for us to meet

and sign a new lease. Do not begin the process of moving in until we have signed a lease.

Sincerely yours,

Sam Stone
Landlord

1234 Central Avenue
Street Address

Sun City, Minnesota
City and State

_612-555-4567_
Phone

Just as you may want to take this opportunity to raise the rent, you may also want to increase the amount of the security deposit. Again, however, if the property is subject to rent control, you may need to petition the local rent control board for permission to increase the rent based on an increased number of occupants.

> **TIP**
>
> **Make rent policy clear in advance.** To avoid making tenants feel that you invented a rent increase policy at the last minute to unfairly extract extra money, it's a good idea to establish in advance your rent policies for units occupied by more than one person. A move-in letter is a good place to do this. That way, your request for higher rent when an additional roommate moves in will simply be in line with what you charge everyone who occupies a unit of a certain size with a certain number of people.

Guests and New Occupants You Haven't Approved

Our form rental agreement and lease include a clause requiring your written consent for guests to stay overnight more than a reasonable amount of time. We recommend that you allow guests to stay up to ten days in any six-month period without your written permission (see Clause 3 of the form lease and rental agreements in Chapter 2). The value of this clause is that a tenant who tries to move someone in for a longer period has clearly violated a defined standard, which gives you grounds for eviction.

When deciding when and whether to enforce a clause restricting guest stays, you'll need to use a good amount of common sense. Obviously, the tenant whose boyfriend regularly spends two or three nights a week will quickly use up the ten-day allotment. However, it would be unrealistic to expect the boyfriend (assuming he has his own apartment) to become a cotenant, and you may not object to the arrangement at all. In short, you'll want to turn a blind eye.

At the same time, you may well want to keep your lease or rental agreement clause restricting guests, in the event that an occasional arrangement starts to become too permanent. But don't be surprised if a tenant claims that your prior willingness to disregard the clause limiting guests means you gave up the right to enforce it. The best way to counter this claim is to be as consistent as you can. (Don't let one tenant have a guest five nights a week and balk when another does so for two.) As long as you are reasonably consistent, a court will likely side with you if push comes to shove and you decide to evict a tenant who completely refuses to obey your rules.

Remind tenants that they are responsible for their guests' behavior and that guests must also comply with the lease or rental agreement provisions—for example, pet rules, noise limits, use of parking spaces, and the like. See Clause 24 of the form lease and rental agreements in Chapter 2.

> **CAUTION**
>
> **Avoid discrimination against guests.** In many states and cities, you cannot legally object to a tenant's frequent overnight guests based on your religious or moral views. For example, it is illegal to discriminate against unmarried couples, including gay or lesbian couples, in many states and cities. It is also illegal to discriminate against tenants' guests because of their race or other protected category.

If a tenant simply moves a roommate in on the sly—despite the fact that your lease or rental agreement prohibits it—or it appears that a "guest" has moved in clothing and furniture and begun to receive mail at your property, it's best to take decisive action right away. If you think your tenant is reasonable, send a letter telling the tenant that the new roommate or longtime guest must move out immediately. (You can use the Warning Letter for Lease or Rental Agreement Violation in Chapter 16 for this purpose.) But if you feel that the tenant will not respond to an informal notice, use a formal termination notice as explained in Chapter 17. If you allow the situation to continue, the danger is strong that the roommate will turn into a subtenant—one you obviously haven't screened or approved of. This can have significant negative consequences: While a subtenant doesn't have all the rights of a tenant, she is entitled, in an eviction proceeding, to the same legal protection as a tenant. And she may even turn into a de facto prime tenant if the original tenant suddenly moves out.

Again, your best choice is to insist that the roommate or guest fill out a formal application. Assuming he checks out, you may also increase the rent or the security deposit, unless that's prohibited by any applicable rent control ordinance.

If you do not want to rent to the guest or roommate, and if that person remains on the premises, make it immediately clear in writing that you will evict all occupants based on breach of the occupancy terms of the lease if the person doesn't leave immediately.

 SEE AN EXPERT

Get help to evict unwanted occupants. If you want to get rid of an unacceptable new occupant, initiate legal proceedings quickly. The longer you wait, the easier it will be for unauthorized occupants to claim that—if only by inaction alone—you have consented to their presence, giving them the status of a tenant. Technically, these proceedings are not an eviction (only tenants can be evicted), but are instead either a criminal complaint for trespassing or a civil suit aimed at ridding the property of a squatter. If you are faced with this situation, contact the local police and ask for assistance. If they refuse to act (which is common, since they will be worried that the trespasser may have attained the status of a tenant), you will probably need to consult a lawyer for advice.

Housesitters Are Subtenants

Many tenants, particularly with pets, have housesitters (typically unpaid) stay in their rental while they're away for a long vacation or business trip. Even if your tenant doesn't collect rent from a housesitter, that person is still legally a subtenant. Treat a housesitter the way you'd treat any proposed subtenant, and remind the tenant that your written consent is required.

Short-Term Rentals Like Airbnb

In recent years, online businesses such as Airbnb have acted as clearinghouses for short-term (less than 30-day) vacation rentals. Using residential property as a short-term rental raises concerns not only for landlords, but for city governments as a whole. Here's an overview of the key issues.

Landlords' Concerns

Especially in vacation-destination cities, tenants have begun listing their rented apartments and homes, essentially subletting their rentals, pocketing the money, and also increasing wear and tear on the premises. Landlords are universally against such use, but the issue is whether their rental agreements or leases clearly prohibit this practice.

This book is intended for landlords who engage in the traditional business of landlording—that is, renting to long-term tenants under month-to-month rental agreements or leases. Consequently, we do not address the problems faced by landlords whose traditional tenants begin to let out their homes to short-term occupants. Because of certain legal differences between regular and such short-term rentals, the law is unclear on whether standard no-sublet clauses apply so as to forbid this practice. For this reason, we advise using the following sentence at the end of a lease or rental agreement clause prohibiting subletting: "Neither shall Tenant(s) sublet or rent any part of the premises for short-term stays of any duration, including but not limited to vacation rentals." This language is included in Clause 10 of our own standard lease and month-to-month rental agreements.

Cities' Concerns

Many local governments point out that using single-family apartments and homes as hotels violates their laws that regulate hotels, which require permits, involve inspections, and include hotel taxes. Many other cities, counties, and other municipalities have legal restrictions on short-term home rentals, including New Orleans and New York City. Local rules vary greatly from place to place. The restrictions in some cities are quite severe and make most short-term rentals illegal.

! CAUTION

Be sure to check condo or homeowners' association restrictions. If your rental property is a condominium or cooperative, or is part of a planned development, your use of your property is governed by deed-like restrictions commonly called covenants, conditions, and restrictions (CC&Rs), or by bylaws duly adopted by the governing board. These may bar short-term rentals entirely, or subject them to restrictions. Unlike zoning laws or local ordinances, CC&Rs and bylaws are enforced by the homeowners' association or coop board, which may impose fines on violators and place liens on the property to collect them.

Residential property owners who decide to forgo traditional long-term renting, and instead use their property for a series of short-term rentals, should not use the forms in this book, and we do not offer any advice on whether this practice would be legal under a city's ordinance. Similarly, tenants who want to sublet their rentals to short-term occupants should not use this book or its forms.

How to Find Your Local Laws and Other Legal Restrictions on Short-Term Rentals

Airbnb's website (www.airbnb.com) has a summary of the legal requirements of more than 50 cities, with links for more information (check "Responsible Hosting" under the "Hosting" section). If your city isn't listed here, the first place to check is your local municipal or administrative code, which may be available online at your local government's website. To find yours, check out www.statelocalgov.net or www.municode.com, or call your city's zoning board or local housing authority. You might also check out the Short-Term Rental Advocacy Center (www.stradvocacy.org) created by Airbnb, HomeAway, and Trip Advisor, for information on restrictions on short-term rentals.

Landlord's Duty to Repair and Maintain the Premises

FORMS IN THIS CHAPTER

Chapter 9 includes instructions for and samples of the following forms:

- Resident's Maintenance/Repair Request
- Time Estimate for Repair
- Semiannual Safety and Maintenance Update
- Agreement Regarding Tenant Alterations to Rental Unit

The Nolo website includes downloadable copies of these forms. See Appendix B for the link to the forms in this book.

Landlords are required by law to provide rental property that meets basic structural, health, and safety standards. And if you don't meet your duties, tenants may have the legal right to:

- reduce or withhold rent
- pay for repairs themselves and deduct the cost from the rent
- sue you, or
- move out without notice and without responsibility for future rent.

Some states set more stringent requirements than others. But you will be better off in the long run if you go beyond satisfying the letter of the law. Here's why:

Happy tenants. Tenants are likely to be satisfied and easy to deal with. They will stay longer, resulting in fewer interruptions of your income stream.

Better negotiations with tenants. Knowing that your housing complies with state and local housing codes, you can respond from a position of strength if a disgruntled tenant complains without grounds about a repair or maintenance issue. You can negotiate a reasonable solution with the tenant because you know you are likely to win if the dispute ends up in court.

Lower risk of lawsuits. You will be far less likely to face the risk of tenant lawsuits based on habitability problems or injuries resulting from defective conditions.

Cheaper insurance. A good record (no lawsuits, no housing code violations) can mean lower insurance premiums.

 RELATED TOPIC
Related topics covered in this book include:

- Writing clear lease and rental agreement provisions for repair and maintenance: Chapter 2
- Setting valid occupancy limits: Chapter 5
- Delegating maintenance and repair responsibilities to a manager: Chapter 6
- Highlighting repair and maintenance procedures in a move-in letter to new tenants and using a Landlord-

Tenant Checklist to keep track of the condition of the premises: Chapter 7
- Your liability for injuries caused by defective housing conditions: Chapter 10
- Your responsibility to clean up environmental hazards: Chapter 11
- Your responsibility for crime: Chapter 12
- Your right to enter rental premises for repairs and inspections: Chapter 13
- Inspecting the rental unit before the tenant moves out: Chapter 15
- How to negotiate with tenants over legal disputes such as rent withholding: Chapter 16
- How to research state laws, local ordinances, and court cases on repair and maintenance responsibilities: Chapter 18.

Your Duty to Keep the Premises Livable

You are legally required to keep rental premises livable. In most states, the legal doctrine requiring this is called the "implied warranty of habitability." In other words, when you rent out a unit, you give the tenant an unspoken guarantee that it will be in livable condition. Arkansas is the only state that doesn't follow this rule, but landlords' responsibility there is much the same, because local laws (particularly in urban areas) usually specify health and safety requirements that amount to requiring habitable housing.

The implied warranty of habitability comes from either:

- local building codes or state statutes that specify minimum requirements for heat, water, plumbing, and other essential services, or
- widely held notions of what constitutes decent housing, derived from court opinions.

Unfortunately, in many states it's not clear which source (building codes, state statutes, court decisions, or even a mix of all of them) is the basis for the implied warranty. Why does it matter? Because the source of the warranty determines your responsibilities and the legal remedies available to tenants.

Finally, a quaint-sounding but still very powerful legal rule, the "implied covenant of quiet enjoyment," also contributes to your duty to offer and maintain fit premises. This covenant or promise, which exists by law between you and your tenants, means that you will do nothing to disturb their right to peacefully and reasonably use their rented space—and conversely, that you'll act in a way that enables peaceful use. Examples of violations of the covenant of quiet enjoyment include:

- tolerating a nuisance, such as allowing garbage to pile up or a major rodent infestation
- failing to provide sufficient working electrical outlets, so that tenants cannot use appliances, and
- failing to fix a leaky roof, which deprives a tenant of the use of the rented space.

Although the covenant of quiet enjoyment is not as far-reaching as the implied warranty of habitability, the remedies available to tenants are substantially the same in both cases.

Local or State Housing Laws

In a few states, if you comply with applicable state or local housing codes, you've satisfied the implied warranty of habitability. Landlords in these states enjoy the luxury of knowing that they can find out the exact details of their repair and maintenance responsibilities. Substantial compliance with the housing codes (rather than literal, 100% compliance) is generally sufficient.

These codes regulate structural aspects of buildings and usually set space and occupancy standards, such as the minimum size of sleeping rooms. They also establish minimum requirements for light and ventilation, sanitation and sewage disposal, heating, water supply (such as how hot the water must be), fire protection, and wiring (such as the number of electrical outlets per room). In addition, the codes typically make property owners responsible for keeping common areas (or parts of the premises which the owner controls) clean, sanitary, and safe.

Court Decisions

In many states, the implied warranty of habitability is independent of any housing code. The standard is whether the premises are "fit for human occupation" or "fit and habitable." Usually, however, a substantial housing code violation is also a breach of the warranty of habitability. But even if you comply with housing codes, a court can require more of you.

Who Pays to Fix Habitability Problems?

In most situations, landlords are responsible for paying to keep rental property habitable, whether at the beginning of the tenancy or during it, if problems arise as a result of normal wear and tear or the actions of a third party, such as a vandal. But if a tenant does something to make the property unfit—for example, by negligently breaking the water main—the financial burden of fixing it falls on the tenant. You remain responsible for seeing that the work gets done and the property is returned to a habitable state, but you could rightly bill the tenant for the repair. (Clause 11 of the form lease and rental agreements in Chapter 2 alerts the tenant to this responsibility.)

What "Fit" and "Habitable" Mean

You must always:

- Keep common areas, such as hallways and stairways, safe and clean.
- Maintain electrical, plumbing, sanitary, heating, ventilating, air-conditioning, and other facilities and systems, including elevators.
- Supply water, hot water, and heat in reasonable amounts at reasonable times.
- Provide trash receptacles and arrange for trash removal.

Additional responsibilities can depend on your circumstances. Here are some other factors to consider.

The climate. In climates that experience severe winters, storm windows or shutters may be considered basic equipment. Housing in wet, rainy areas needs to be protected from the damp. In Oregon, for example, courts have specifically made landlords responsible for waterproofing. In areas prone to insect infestations, landlords may be required to provide extermination services. Florida landlords must exterminate bedbugs, mice, roaches, and ants.

The neighborhood. In a high-crime area, good locks, security personnel, exterior lighting, and secure common areas may be seen as a necessity, as important as water and heat. (See Chapter 12.)

The environment. Lead-based paint, mold, asbestos building materials, and other environmental hazards can pose significant health problems and may make buildings unfit for habitation. (See Chapter 11.)

How to Meet Your Legal Repair and Maintenance Responsibilities

A conscientious landlord can meet repair and maintenance responsibilities by following these steps.

Comply With State and Local Housing Codes

Checking out state law and local housing ordinances, and complying with all requirements, should adequately protect you from most tenant claims of uninhabitability. State laws generally require you to make all repairs and do whatever is necessary to put and keep the premises in a fit and habitable condition. Local housing codes are often more specific, and you need to know what they call for in the way of structural requirements, facilities, and essential services such as plumbing and heat. Your local building or housing authority, and health or fire department, can provide this information.

Be sure to find out about all ordinances affecting your repair and maintenance responsibilities—for example, many cities require the installation of smoke detectors in residential units, or security items such as viewing devices in doors that open onto a hallway. Some cities also make owners responsible for the prevention of infestation and, if necessary, the extermination of insects, rodents, and other pests.

RESOURCE

Finding the laws. Appendix A includes citations for the major state laws affecting landlords. You can find these statutes online, or contact your state consumer protection agency for pamphlets or brochures that describe your repair and maintenance responsibilities in less legalistic terms. For a list of state consumer protection agencies, go to www.usa.gov/state-consumer. To find building codes for your state, search "building code" on your state government website (find yours at www.usa.gov/states-and-territories).

How Housing Code Requirements are Enforced

Local building, health, or fire department authorities may discover code violations through routine inspections or in response to a tenant complaint. When property changes hands or is used as collateral for a loan, there's usually an inspection.

Once a violation is found, you'll get a citation requiring you to remedy it within a certain amount of time, such as five business days. If you don't make the repairs within the time allowed, the city or county may sue you. Moreover, in many cities, continued failure to comply with cited violations of local housing laws is a criminal misdemeanor punishable by fines or even imprisonment. In some cases, local officials may require you to provide tenants with temporary alternative housing until the violation is corrected.

Tenants may also point out code violations if they do not pay the rent, or attempt to pay less, on the grounds that the premises are substandard. If you try to evict a tenant for not paying rent, the tenant may claim housing code violations as justification.

Complying With Changes to Housing Codes

When a housing code changes, it doesn't necessarily mean that all existing buildings are illegal because they are not "up to code." Especially when it comes to items that would involve major structural changes, lawmakers often exempt certain older buildings. They do it by writing a "grandfather clause" into the code, exempting all buildings constructed before a certain date (sometimes that date is the same as when the new code takes effect, but not always). Such exemptions often do not apply to renovations or remodeling, meaning that, over the years, you may eventually have to comply with the new rules.

Many types of code changes—for example, those involving locks, peepholes, and smoke detectors—must be made regardless of the age of the building and whether or not you do any remodeling.

Get Rid of Dangers to Children

Local ordinances prohibit "attractive nuisances." These are conditions that tend to attract children, such as abandoned vehicles; wells and shafts; basements; abandoned equipment or appliances; excavations; and unsafe fences, structures, or foliage. If children are hurt while playing in or on an attractive nuisance, you may be held liable.

Don't Allow Nuisances, Such as Excessive Noise

Besides "attractive nuisances," local housing codes prohibit nuisances in general, broadly defined as whatever is dangerous to human life or detrimental to health, as determined by the public health officer—for example, overcrowding a room with occupants, providing insufficient ventilation or illumination or inadequate sewage or plumbing facilities, or allowing drug dealing on the premises. A landlord found to have created or tolerated a nuisance will be subject to the code's enforcement and penalty provisions.

Be especially vigilant when it comes to noise, which can be a major nuisance. Landlords often hear complaints about noisy tenants—for example, an upstairs neighbor who clumps about in work boots every day at five a.m. If you ignore such complaints, you can get hit with code violations, court-ordered rent reductions, and even punitive damages. In one case, a New York City tenant complained about loud noise from a neighboring apartment in the late night and early morning hours. Neither the owner nor manager took any effective steps to stop it. A court ruled that the continuous, excessive noise violated the warranty of habitability, and entitled the tenant to a 50% rent abatement. (*Nostrand Gardens Co-Op v. Howard*, 221 A.D.2d 637, 634 N.Y.S.2d 505 (2d Dept., 1995).) For more advice on dealing with noisy tenants, including how to write an effective warning letter, see "When Warning Notices Are Appropriate" in Chapter 16.

Clause 13 of our form lease and rental agreements in Chapter 2 prohibits tenants from causing disturbances or creating a nuisance—that is, behavior (such as excessive noise) that prevents neighbors from enjoying the use of their own homes.

Consider Smoking Restrictions

There's a considerable trend among rental owners to adopt no-smoking (and no vaping) policies both in common areas, such as lobbies, and individual rental units. (The ill effects of secondhand smoke are well known, smoke damages furnishings and paint, and smoking is a fire danger.) Many owners have found that advertising a smoke-free environment gives them a distinct marketing advantage.

A smoke-free policy will also apply to marijuana: Even if your state has decriminalized the possession and use of small amounts, smokers do not have a right to light up in violation of their landlords' no-smoking policies.

Several cities have also passed no-smoking laws for multifamily buildings. For more information, visit www.smokefreemarin.com, which offers a comprehensive guide for property owners on how to introduce and implement a smoke-free policy.

If you do allow smoking in units, you may face complaints from nonsmoking tenants bothered by fumes wafting up from outside balconies, through windows, under doorjambs, or through the ventilation and heating systems.

An increasing number of frustrated neighbors have advanced creative and successful arguments based on three legal theories:

- **Nuisance.** Tenants have argued that the presence of smoke, like any noxious fume or noise, constitutes a legal nuisance in that it exposes others to a serious health risk. When courts buy this argument, the fact that the smoker did not have a no-smoking clause in his lease or rental agreement is immaterial.
- **Covenant of quiet enjoyment.** Neighbors have also claimed that their ability to use and enjoy their homes has been significantly diminished by the presence of smoke.
- **Warranty of habitability.** Some neighbors have persuaded judges that the smoke is so pervasive and noxious that it renders their rental unfit. In many states, this allows affected neighbors to break their leases.

Also, tenants with certain disabilities are protected from secondhand smoke under the Americans with Disabilities Act and the federal Fair Housing Act, as well as state and local regulations.

You may also want to consider addressing tenants' use of e-cigarettes, which are electronic heating devices that heat and vaporize a solution that typically contains nicotine. Although there's no "secondhand smoke," there *is* "secondhand aerosol" (quaintly called "vapor" by manufacturers). This by-product is a visible soup that contains nicotine, ultrafine particles, and low levels of toxins that are known to cause cancer. For more information on the effects of secondhand aerosol, search for "Electronic Smoking Devices and Secondhand Aerosol" on the website noted just below.

TIP
Consider letting a tenant who complains about smoke break the lease. In view of the increasing success that nonsmoking tenants are enjoying when they take their complaints to court, you'll probably come out ahead.

RESOURCE
Current information on nonsmoking policies and e-cigarettes. Check the American Nonsmokers' Rights Foundation website (www. no-smoke.org) for lists of state and local laws restricting smoking (search "Smokefree Lists, Maps, and Data") and e-cigarettes.

Medical Marijuana Smoking

Many states have passed "compassionate use" laws, but federal law has not followed suit—the cultivation, possession, and use of marijuana is still illegal under federal law. For this reason, landlords are free to disallow marijuana possession, use, or growing on the premises, even where the tenant has state-sanctioned, medical approval to use it. Accordingly, even tenants who have a recognizable disability under federal law cannot expect landlords to vary a no-marijuana policy pursuant to an accommodation under the federal Americans with Disabilities Act (ADA).

In practical terms, marijuana smoking can have the same effect on tenants in a multifamily building as regular tobacco smoke. But practicalities may also solve the problem for a tenant who has a legitimate need for marijuana and medical permission to use it: As more and more states allow its use for medical conditions, producers are making drops, liquids, and solid foods that contain the necessary chemical ingredients of marijuana but omit the smoke. Tenants who purchase and responsibly consume such items should not pose a problem for landlords or other tenants.

Don't Try to Evade Your Legal Responsibilities

Some landlords have attempted to get around their responsibilities for keeping premises habitable. They have tenants sign a lease saying that they understand that the landlord isn't promising to keep the premises habitable, or they argue that a tenant who moved into or stayed in substandard housing waived the right to a habitable dwelling.

In a rare showing of unanimity, courts almost everywhere have rejected both these arguments. Except for a handful of states, including Maine and Texas (and even there, in limited circumstances), neither a tenant waiver (at the beginning of the tenancy or during its life) nor a disclaimer in the lease will relieve you of the responsibility to provide fit and habitable housing.

You may, however, legally delegate some repair and maintenance responsibilities to tenants. See "Delegating Landlord's Responsibilities to Tenants," below.

CAUTION

Choose your lease or rental agreement carefully. Preprinted leases available in office supply stores or online are usually not designed for the laws of each state and could include clauses that could be illegal in your state. To be on solid ground, consult your state and local laws and use the lease or rental agreement in this book or available on Nolo.com.

Make Sure You—And Your Tenant—Know the Tenant's Obligations

State and local housing laws generally require tenants to maintain their units. If a dwelling is rendered uninhabitable due to the tenant's actions, the tenant will have a difficult, if not impossible, time fighting eviction or avoiding responsibility for the repair bill. (If the tenant won't pay up, you can deduct the expense from the security deposit.) Your lease or rental agreement should spell out these basic tenant obligations, whether or not they are required by law in your state. See Clause 11 of the form agreements in Chapter 2.

> ### Common Myths About Repairs and Maintenance
>
> Many landlords (and tenants) are under the mistaken impression that every time a rental unit turns over, certain maintenance work is legally required. In fact, the actual condition of the unit determines what repairs and maintenance are necessary.
>
> **Paint.** No state law requires you to repaint the interior every so often, but local ordinances might (New York City's does). So long as the paint isn't creating a habitability problem—for example, paint that's so thick around a window that the window can't be opened—it should comply with the law. Lead-based paint, however, may create all sorts of legal problems—for example, if a child becomes ill from eating lead-based paint chips, a court may find you liable because of your carelessness.
>
> **Drapes and carpets.** So long as drapes and carpets are not sufficiently damp or mildewy to constitute a health hazard, and so long as carpets don't have dangerous holes that could cause someone to trip and fall, you aren't legally required to replace them.
>
> **Windows.** A tenant who carelessly breaks a window is responsible for repairing it. If a burglar, vandal, or neighborhood child broke a window, however, you are responsible for fixing it.
>
> **Keys.** Many tenants think that they're entitled to fresh locks upon move-in. In some states (such as Texas) and in some cities, this is true. But even if you're not legally required to rekey, you should do so in order to reduce the chance of break-ins.

Keep the rental unit as clean and safe as the condition of the premises permits. For example, if the kitchen has a rough, unfinished wooden floor that is hard to keep clean, you should not expect it to be shiny and spotless—but a tenant with a new tile floor would be expected to do a decent job. If you have to do a major cleanup when the tenant moves out, you may legitimately deduct its cost from the security deposit.

Keep plumbing fixtures as clean as their condition permits. For example, bathtub caulking that has sprouted mold and mildew will render the tub unusable (or at least disgusting). Because it could have been prevented by proper cleaning, the tenant is responsible. On the other hand, if the bathroom has no fan and the window has been painted shut, the bathroom will be hard to air out; resulting mildew might be your responsibility.

Dispose of garbage, rubbish, and other waste. For instance, if mice or ants invaded the kitchen because a tenant forgot to take out the garbage before leaving on a two-week vacation, the tenant would be responsible for paying any necessary extermination costs.

Use electrical, plumbing, sanitary, heating, ventilating, air-conditioning, and other facilities and other systems, including elevators, properly. Examples of abuse by tenants include overloading electrical outlets and flushing large objects down the toilet.

Fix things the tenant breaks or damages. A tenant who causes a serious habitability problem on your property—for example, carelessly breaking the heater—is responsible for it. You can insist that she pay for the repair. The tenant can't just decide to live without heat for a while to save money. If necessary, you can use the security deposit to pay for it and, if that isn't enough, sue the tenant (in small claims court, if possible) besides. You can't, however, charge a tenant for problems caused by normal wear and tear—for example, a carpet that has worn out from use.

Report problems. Some states require tenants to inform the landlord, as soon as practicable, of defective conditions that the tenant believes the landlord doesn't know about and has a duty to repair.

> ⓘ **CAUTION**
> **Be sure your lease or rental agreement makes the tenant financially responsible for repairing damage caused by the tenant's negligence or misuse.** (See Clause 11 of the form agreements in Chapter 2.) That means that where the tenant or his friends or family cause damage— for example, a broken window, a toilet clogged with children's toys, or a freezer that no longer works because the tenant defrosted it with a carving knife—it's the tenant's responsibility to make the repairs or to reimburse

you for doing so. If a tenant refuses to repair or pay for the damage he caused, you can use the security deposit to cover the bill, then demand that the tenant bring the deposit up to its original level (if he refuses, he's a candidate for termination and eviction). Or you can sue, perhaps in small claims court, for the cost of the repairs.

Repair What You Provide or Promise

State and local housing laws typically deal with basic living conditions—heat, water, and plumbing, for example. They do not usually deal with amenities—features that are not essential but make living a little easier, such as drapes, washing machines, swimming pools, saunas, parking places, intercoms, and dishwashers. Although housing laws do not require you to furnish these things, if you do, you might be legally required to maintain or repair them. The law reasons that by providing amenities, you also promise to maintain them.

If the lease or rental agreement says that you will repair or maintain certain items, such as appliances, the promise is express. When you (or a manager or rental agent) say something that indicates that you will be responsible for repairing or maintaining an item or facility, the promise is implied. Implied promises are also found where you have, over time, repeatedly repaired or maintained certain aspects of the rental, establishing a practice of repair that the tenant can rely upon. Here are some typical examples of implied promises.

> **EXAMPLE 1:** Tina sees Joel's ad for an apartment, which says "heated swimming pool." After Tina moves in, utility costs rise, and Joel stops heating the pool regularly. Joel has violated his implied promise to keep the pool heated. If he wants more flexibility, he should avoid ad language that commits him to such things.

> **EXAMPLE 2:** When Joel's rental agent shows Tom around the building, she goes out of her way to show off the laundry room, saying, "Here's the terrific laundry room—it's for the use of all the tenants." Tom rents the apartment. Later, all the washing machines break down, but Joel won't fix them. Joel has violated

his implied promise to maintain the laundry room appliances in working order.

EXAMPLE 3: Tina's apartment has a built-in dishwasher. When she rented the apartment, neither the lease nor the landlord said anything about the dishwasher or who was responsible for repairing it. The dishwasher has broken down a few times, and whenever Tina asked Joel to fix it, he did. By doing so, Joel has established a usage or practice that he—not the tenant—is responsible for repairing the dishwasher.

If you violate an express or implied promise relating to the condition of the premises, the tenant may sue you (usually in small claims court) for money damages for breach of contract, and may be able to pursue other legal remedies, discussed below.

Set Up a Responsive Maintenance System—And Stick to It

If you fail to maintain the premises, you'll face various financial losses and legal problems, both from tenants—who may withhold rent and pursue other legal remedies—and from government agencies that enforce housing codes. Your best bet to avoid problems in the first place is to design a maintenance program that meets housing laws *and* satisfies the question, "Is this building safe, sound, and fit for people to live in?" In doing so, you should be mindful of a larger goal: to attract and keep reliable tenants who will stay as long as possible.

Avoiding Problems With a Good Maintenance and Repair System

Your best defense against disputes with tenants is to establish and communicate a clear, easy-to-follow procedure for tenants to ask for repairs and to document all complaints, respond quickly when complaints are made, and schedule annual safety inspections. If you employ a manager or management company, make sure they follow your guidelines as well.

Recommended Repair and Maintenance System

Follow these steps to avoid maintenance and repair problems with tenants:

1. Provide tenants with a safe, well-maintained property—for example, by installing good outdoor lighting, trimming tree limbs away from the building, and having an effective snow removal plan in cold-winter climates.
2. Clearly set out the tenant's responsibilities for repair and maintenance in your lease or rental agreement. See Clauses 11, 12, and 13 of the form agreements in Chapter 2.
3. Use the written Landlord-Tenant Checklist form (Chapter 7) to check over the premises and fix any problems before new tenants move in.
4. Don't assume tenants know how to handle routine maintenance problems such as a clogged toilet or drain. Make it a point to explain the basics when a tenant moves in and include a brief list of maintenance dos and don'ts with your move-in materials. For example, explain:
   - how to avoid overloading circuits
   - proper use of garbage disposal
   - location and use of fire extinguisher, and
   - problems tenant should definitely not try to handle, such as electrical repairs.
5. Encourage tenants to immediately report plumbing, heating, weatherproofing, or other defects or safety or security problems—whether in the tenant's unit or in common areas such as hallways and parking garages. Use the Resident's Maintenance/Repair Request form discussed below.
6. Keep a written log (or have your property manager keep one) of all complaints, including those made orally. This should include a box to indicate your immediate and any follow-up responses (and subsequent tenant communications), as well as a space to enter the date and brief details of when the problem was fixed. The Resident's Maintenance/Repair Request form, below, can serve this purpose.

7. Keep a file for each rental unit with copies of all complaints and repair requests from tenants and your response. As a general rule, you should respond in writing to every tenant repair request (even if you also do so orally or by email). In Chapter 7, "Using Email for Notices and Other Communications to Tenants" explains why it's important to communicate with tenants in writing, rather than just use email.

8. Handle repairs as soon as possible, but definitely within the time any state law requires. Notify the tenant by phone and follow up in writing if repairs will take more than 48 hours, excluding weekends. Keep the tenant informed—for example, if you have problems scheduling a plumber, let your tenant know with a phone call, note, or email.

9. Twice a year, give your tenants a checklist on which to report any potential safety hazards or maintenance problems that might have been overlooked (see the Semiannual Safety and Maintenance Update, described in "Tenant Updates and Landlord's Regular Safety and Maintenance Inspections," below). Respond promptly and in writing to all requests, keeping copies in your file.

10. Once a year, inspect all rental units, using the Landlord-Tenant Checklist as a guide as discussed in "Tenant Updates and Landlord's Regular Safety and Maintenance Inspections," below. Keep copies of the filled-in checklist in your file.

11. Especially for multiunit projects, place conspicuous notices in several places around the property about your determination to operate a safe, well-maintained building, and list phone numbers for tenants to call with maintenance requests.

12. Remind tenants of your policies and procedures for keeping the building in good repair in every written communication by printing them at the bottom of all routine notices, rent increases, and other communications. Tenants will be more likely to keep you apprised of maintenance and repair problems if you remind them that you are truly interested. A notice regarding complaint procedures such as the one below will be helpful.

13. Take care when hiring and supervising contractors for projects involving specialized skills or major repairs. Check individual references and licenses and state rules before hiring any outside workers—whether a handyperson or skilled contractor.

Sample Notice to Tenants Regarding Complaint Procedure

Fair View Apartments wants to maintain all apartment units and common areas in excellent condition so that tenants enjoy safe and comfortable housing. If you have any questions, suggestions, or requests regarding your unit or the building, please direct them to the manager between 9 a.m. and 6 p.m., Monday through Saturday, either by calling 555-9876 or by dropping off a completed Maintenance/Repair Request form at the manager's office. In case of an emergency, please call 555-1234 at any time.

Benefits of Establishing a Repair and Maintenance System

In addition to a thorough system for responding to problems, you should establish a good, nonintrusive system of periodic maintenance inspections. It will give you several advantages:

- **Prevention.** The system we recommend lets you fix little problems before they grow into big ones. For example, you would want to replace the washer in the upstairs bathtub before the washer fails, the faucet can't be turned off, and the tub overflows, ruining the floor and the ceiling of the lower unit.

- **Good tenant relations.** Communication with tenants creates a climate of cooperation and trust that can work wonders in the long run. Keeping good tenants happy is an investment in your business.

- **Rent withholding defense.** A responsive communication system gives you an excellent defense if unreasonable tenants seek to withhold or reduce rent for no good reason.

Resident's Maintenance/Repair Request

Date: _____August 29, 20xx_____

Address: _____392 Main St., #402, Houston, Texas 77002_____

Resident's name: _____Mary Griffin_____

Phone (home): _____555-4321_____   Phone (work): _____555-5679_____

Problem (be as specific as possible): _____Garbage disposal doesn't work_____

_____

_____

_____

_____

_____

Best time to make repairs: _____After 6 p.m. or Saturday morning_____

Other comments: _____

_____

_____

_____

I authorize entry into my unit to perform the maintenance or repair requested above, in my absence, unless stated otherwise above.

_____Mary Griffin_____
Resident

....

FOR MANAGEMENT USE

Work done: _____Fixed garbage disposal (removed spoon)_____

Time spent: _____1/2_____ hours

Date completed: _____August 30, 20xx_____   By: _____Paulie_____

Unable to complete on: _____ , because: _____

_____

Notes and comments: _____

_____

_____Hal Ortiz_____   _____August 30, 20xx_____
Landlord/Manager   Date

You may still have to go to court to evict the tenant, but your carefully documented procedures will provide a paper trail. If you make it your normal business practice to save all repair requests from tenants, the absence of a request is evidence that the tenant didn't complain. And if you need to establish as part of an eviction procedure that a claimed problem is phony, you may want to have the repair person who looked at the supposed defect come to court to testify as to why it was phony.

- **Limit legal liability.** An aggressive repair policy backed up by an excellent record-keeping system can help reduce your potential liability to tenants who sue for injuries suffered as a result of defective conditions on your property. There are two reasons for this: First, it is less likely that there will be injuries in the first place if your property is well maintained. Second, in many situations an injured person must prove that your negligence (carelessness) caused the problem. You may be able to defeat this claim by demonstrating that you actively sought out and quickly fixed all defects.

EXAMPLE: Geeta owns a 12-unit apartment complex and regularly encourages tenants to request repairs in writing on a form she's prepared. Several prominent signs, as well as reminders on all routine communications with tenants, urge tenants to report all problems. Most tenants do so. One month, Ravi simply doesn't pay his rent. After her phone calls are not answered, Geeta serves a Notice to Pay Rent or Quit. Still Ravi says nothing.

When Geeta files an eviction suit, Ravi claims he withheld rent because of a leaky roof and defective heater that Geeta refused to repair. At trial, Geeta testifies that she routinely saves all tenants' filled-out forms for at least a year, and that she has no record of ever receiving a complaint from Ravi, even though she gave him blank forms and sent notices twice a year asking to be informed of any problems. She also submits her complaint log, which has a space to record oral requests. The judge has reason to doubt Ravi ever complained, and rules in Geeta's favor.

Resident's Maintenance/Repair Request Form

One way to assure that defects in the premises will be reported by conscientious tenants—while helping to refute bogus tenant claims about lack of repairs—is to include a clause in your lease or rental agreement requiring that tenants notify you of repair and maintenance needs. Make the point again and describe your process for handling repairs in your move-in letter to new tenants.

Many tenants will find it easiest (and most practical) to call or email you or your manager with a repair problem or complaint, particularly in urgent cases. Make sure you have an answering machine, voicemail, or other service available at all times to accommodate tenant calls. Check your messages frequently when you're not available by phone.

We also suggest you provide all tenants with a Resident's Maintenance/Repair Request form. Give each tenant five or ten copies when they move in and explain how the form should be used to request specific repairs. (See the sample, above.) Be sure that tenants know to describe the problem in detail and to indicate the best time to make repairs. Email tenants a blank copy of the form, make sure tenants know how to get more copies. Your manager (if any) should keep an ample supply of the Resident's Maintenance/Repair Request form in her rental unit or office.

You (or your manager) should complete the entire Resident's Maintenance/Repair Request form or keep a separate log for every tenant complaint, including those made by phone. (See the discussion below.) Keep a copy of this form or your log in the tenant's file, along with any other written communication. Be sure to keep good records of how and when you handled tenant complaints, including reasons for any delays and notes on conversations with tenants. For a sample, see the bottom of the Resident's Maintenance/Repair Request form (labeled For Management Use, shown above). You might also jot down any other comments regarding repair or maintenance problems you observed while handling the tenant's

Time Estimate for Repair

Stately Manor Apartments

August 30, 20xx
Date

Mary Griffin
Tenant

392 Main St., #402
Street Address

Houston, Texas 77002
City and State

Dear Mary Griffin ,
_____Tenant_____

Thank you for promptly notifying us of the following problem with your unit: _____
Garbage disposal doesn't work

_____

_____

_____

_____

We expect to have the problem corrected on _____ September 3, 20xx _____ due to the following:
Garbage disposal part is out of stock locally, but has been ordered and will be
delivered in a day or two.

_____

_____

_____

We regret any inconvenience this delay may cause. Please do not hesitate to point out any other problems that may arise.

Sincerely,

Hal Ortiz
Landlord/Manager

complaint. The Resident's Maintenance/Repair Request form can be downloaded from the Nolo website; see Appendix B for the link to the forms in this book.

Tracking Tenant Complaints

Most tenants will simply call or email you when they have a problem or complaint, rather than fill out a Resident's Maintenance/Repair Request form. For record-keeping purposes we suggest you always fill out this form, regardless of whether the tenant does. In addition, it's also a good idea to keep a separate chronological log or calendar with similar information on tenant complaints. A faithfully kept log will qualify as a "business record," admissible as evidence in court, that you can use to establish that you normally record tenant communications when they are made. By implication, the *absence* of an entry is evidence that a complaint was *not* made. This argument can be important if your tenant has reduced or withheld rent or broken the lease on the bogus claim that requests for maintenance or repairs went unanswered.

Responding to Tenant Complaints

You should respond almost immediately to all complaints about defective conditions by talking to the tenant and following up (preferably in writing). Explain when repairs can be made or, if you don't yet know, tell the tenant that you will be back in touch promptly. Use a form such as the Time Estimate for Repair; it is shown above. The Nolo website includes a downloadable copy. See Appendix B for the link to the forms in this book. This doesn't mean you have to jump through hoops to fix things that don't need fixing or to engage in heroic efforts to make routine repairs. It does mean you should take prompt action under the circumstances—for example, immediate action should normally be taken to cope with broken door locks or security problems. Similarly, a lack of heat or hot water (especially in winter in cold areas) and safety hazards such as broken steps or exposed electrical wires should be dealt with on an emergency basis.

One way to think about how to respond to repair problems is to classify them according to their consequences. Once you consider the results of *inaction,* your response time will be clear:

- **Personal security and safety problems = injured tenants = lawsuits.** Respond and get work done immediately if the potential for harm is very serious, even if this means calling a 24-hour repair service or having you or your manager get up in the middle of the night to put a piece of plywood over a broken ground floor window.
- **Major inconvenience to tenant = seriously unhappy tenant = tenant's self-help remedies (such as rent withholding) and vacancies.** Respond and attempt to get work done as soon as possible, or within 24 hours, if the problem is a major inconvenience to tenant, such as a plumbing or heating problem.
- **Minor problem = slightly annoyed tenant = bad feelings.** Respond in 48 hours (on business days) if not too serious.

Yes, these deadlines may seem tight and, occasionally, meeting them will cost you a few dollars extra, but, in the long run, you'll be way ahead.

If you're unable to take care of a repair right away, such as a dripping faucet, and if it isn't so serious that it requires immediate action, let the tenant know when the repair will be made. It's often best to do this orally (a message on the tenant's answering machine should serve), and follow up in writing by leaving a notice under the tenant's door. If there's a delay in handling the problem (maybe the part you need to fix the oven has to be ordered), explain why you won't be able to act immediately.

CAUTION

Respect tenant's privacy. To gain access to make repairs, the landlord can enter the rental premises only with the tenant's consent, or after having given

Semiannual Safety and Maintenance Update

Please complete the following checklist and note any safety or maintenance problems in your unit or on the premises.

Please describe the specific problems and the rooms or areas involved. Here are some examples of the types of things we want to know about: garage roof leaks, excessive mildew in rear bedroom closet, fuses blow out frequently, door lock sticks, water comes out too hot in shower, exhaust fan above stove doesn't work, smoke alarm malfunctions, peeling paint, and mice in basement. Please point out any potential safety and security problems in the neighborhood and anything you consider a serious nuisance.

Please indicate the approximate date when you first noticed the problem and list any other recommendations or suggestions for improvement.

Please return this form with this month's rent check. Thank you.

—The Management

Name: _____Mary Griffin_____

Address: _____392 Main St., #402_____

_____Houston, Texas_____

Please indicate (and explain below) problems with:

☐ Floors and floor coverings _____

☐ Walls and ceilings _____

☐ Windows, screens, and doors _____

☐ Window coverings (drapes, miniblinds, etc.) _____

☐ Electrical system and light fixtures _____

☑ Plumbing (sinks, bathtub, shower, or toilet) ___Water pressure low in shower_____

☐ Heating or air conditioning system_____

☑ Major appliances (stove, oven, dishwasher, refrigerator) __Exhaust fan above stove doesn't work_

☐ Basement or attic _____

☑ Locks or security system _____Front door lock sticks_____

☐ Smoke detector _____

☐ Fireplace _____

☐ Cupboards, cabinets, and closets _____

☐ Furnishings (table, bed, mirrors, chairs) _____

☐ Laundry facilities _____

☐ Elevator _____

☐ Stairs and handrails _____

☐ Hallway, lobby, and common areas _____

☐ Garage _____

☐ Patio, terrace, or deck _____

☑ Lawn, fences, and grounds___ Shrubs near back stairway need pruning ____

☐ Pool and recreational facilities _____

☐ Roof, exterior walls, and other structural elements _____

☐ Driveway and sidewalks_____

☐ Neighborhood _____

☑ Nuisances ___ Tenant in #501 often plays music too loud _____

☐ Other _____

_____

Specifics of problems: _____

_____

_____

_____

_____

_____

Other comments: _____

_____

_____

_____

_____

_Mary Griffin_____ _February 1, 20xx_____
Tenant   Date

···

FOR MANAGEMENT USE

Action/Response: _____ Fixed kitchen exhaust fan and sticking front door lock on ____

__ February 15, and adjusted water pressure in shower. Pruned shrubs on February 21. __

__ Spoke with tenant in #501 about keeping music low on February 2. _____

_____

_____

_____

_____

_____

_Hal Ortiz_____ _February 22, 20xx_____
Landlord/Manager   Date

reasonable notice or the specific amount of notice required by state law, usually 24 hours. See Chapter 13 for rules and procedures for entering a tenant's home to make repairs and how to deal with tenants who make access inconvenient for you or your maintenance personnel.

> **TIP**
>
> **If you can't attend to a repair right away, avoid possible rent withholding.** Some landlords voluntarily offer a "rent rebate" if a problem can't be corrected in a timely fashion, especially if it's serious, such as a major heating or plumbing problem. A rebate builds goodwill and avoids rent withholding.

If, despite all your efforts to conscientiously find out about and make needed repairs on a timely basis, a tenant threatens to withhold rent, move out, or pursue another legal remedy discussed above, you should respond promptly in writing, telling him either:

- when the repair will be made and the reasons why it is being delayed—for example, a replacement part may have to be ordered to correct the running sound in a bathroom toilet, or
- why you do not feel there is a legitimate problem that justifies rent withholding or other tenant action—for example, point out that the running sound may be annoying, but the toilet still flushes and is usable.

At this point, if you feel the tenant is sincere, you might also consider suggesting that you and the tenant mediate the dispute. If you feel the tenant is trying to concoct a phony complaint to justify not paying the rent, take action to evict him.

Make Your Contractor's Insurance Policy Cover You, Too

As you go about maintaining your rental property, you'll be using outside workers to do everything from fixing minor problems to renovating entire rental units. If you hire a contractor to do extensive work, you should make sure that the contractor has insurance and that it covers you, too. Minor jobs, such as calling a plumber to install a new sink, don't require this level of attention.

Here's the problem you will avoid: Suppose your contractor does a poor job that results in an injury to a tenant or guest. The injured person may sue you, and unless your own insurance policy covers contractors' negligence, you won't be covered. Even if your policy will cover, you'll be better off if you can shift coverage onto the contractor (the fewer claims others make on your policy, the better). The way to do this is to require contractors to do the following:

- Before work begins (and ideally before you sign a contract with the contractor), have the contractor add you as an "additional insured" to the contractor's commercial general liability policy. As an additional insured, you will be covered in case someone makes a claim on the policy based on actions of the contractor at your work site.

- Require the contractor to give you a "certificate of insurance," which will prove that the contractor has the insurance and that you were added. Ask for an "ACORD 25" form, which the insurance company should supply. See www.acord.org for more information.

- Get a copy of the policy and make sure that the work you're having the contractor do is covered by the policy. Be sure that the name on the policy is the same name the contractor is using on the work contract with you.

- In your written contract with the contractor, include a clause like the following: "Contractor will have a commercial general liability insurance policy of at least [dollar amount] per occurrence and [dollar amount] aggregate in effect as of the date contractor begins work. Contractor will maintain the policy throughout the duration of the job, and will promptly notify [owner's name] of any diminution in coverage or cancellation. In the event of any claim, this policy will apply as primary insurance. Contractor will provide additional insurance for any work that requires additional insurance. Contractor will not begin work until Contractor has given [owner's name] a satisfactory certificate of insurance."

Tenant Updates and Landlord's Regular Safety and Maintenance Inspections

In addition to a thorough and prompt system for responding to problems after they have been brought to your attention, you should establish a good, nonintrusive system of frequent and periodic maintenance inspections. In short, encouraging your tenants to promptly report problems as they occur should not be your *sole* means of handling your maintenance and repair responsibilities. Here's why: If the tenant is not conscientious, or if he simply doesn't notice that something needs to be fixed, the best reporting system will not do you much good. To back it up, you need to force the tenant (and yourself) to take stock at specified intervals. In the sections below, we'll explain the tenant update system and the landlord's annual safety inspection. Make sure your lease or rental agreement and move-in letter cover these updates and inspections as well.

Tenant's Semiannual Safety and Maintenance Update

You can (nicely) insist that your tenants think about and report needed repairs by giving them a Semiannual Safety and Maintenance Update on which to list any problems in the rental unit or on the premises—whether it's low water pressure in the shower, peeling paint, poor ventilation, or noisy neighbors. Asking tenants to return this Update twice a year should also help you in court if you are up against a tenant who is raising a false implied warranty of habitability defense, particularly if the tenant did not note any problems on his most recently completed Update. As with the Resident's Maintenance/Repair Request form, be sure to note how you handled the problem on the bottom of the form. A sample Semiannual Safety and Maintenance Update is shown above and the Nolo website includes a downloadable copy. See Appendix B for the link to the forms in this book.

Landlord's Annual Safety Inspection

Sometimes, even your pointed reminder (by use of the Semiannual Update) that safety and maintenance issues need to be brought to your attention will not do the trick: If your tenant can't recognize a problem even if it stares him in the face, you'll never hear about it, either. In the end, you must get into the unit and inspect for yourself.

You should perform an annual "safety and maintenance inspection" as part of your system for repairing and maintaining the property. For example, you might make sure that items listed on the Semiannual Safety and Maintenance Update— such as smoke detectors, heating and plumbing systems, and major appliances—are in fact safe and in working order. If a problem develops with one of these items, causing injury to a tenant, you may be able to defeat a claim that you were negligent by arguing that your periodic and recent inspection of the item was all that a landlord should reasonably be expected to do.

In many states, you have the right to enter a tenant's home for the purpose of a safety inspection. This does not mean, however, that you can just let yourself in unannounced. All states that allow for inspections require advance notice; some specify 24 hours, others simply state that the landlord must give "reasonable notice." To be on the safe side, check your state's statutes and, if all that is required is "reasonable notice," allow 24 hours at least.

What should you do if your tenant objects to your safety inspection? If your state allows landlords to enter for this purpose (and if you have given adequate notice and have not otherwise abused your right of entry by needlessly scheduling repeated inspections), the tenant's refusal is grounds for eviction. If your state does not allow the landlord to enter and inspect the dwelling against the tenant's will, you have a problem. Even if your own lease or rental agreement provision allows for inspections, the provision may be considered illegal and unenforceable. Also, evicting a tenant because she refused to allow such an inspection might constitute illegal retaliatory eviction.

There may be, however, a practical way around the uncooperative tenant who bars the door. Point out that you take your responsibility to maintain the property very seriously. Remind her that you'll be checking for plumbing, heating, electrical, and structural problems that she might not notice, which could develop into bigger problems later if you're not allowed to check them out. Most tenants will not object to yearly safety inspections if you're courteous about it—giving plenty of notice and trying to conduct the inspection at a time convenient for the tenant. (You might offer to inspect at a time when she is home, so that she can see for herself that you will not be nosing about her personal items.)

Tenant Responses to Unfit Premises: Paying Less Rent

If you fail to live up to your legal duty to maintain your property, your tenants may have a variety of legal responses, each one designed to pressure you into compliance. Hopefully, you will run your business in such a way that your tenants will have no reason to take legal action. But even the most conscientious landlord may encounter a tenant who attempts to avoid his responsibility to pay the rent by claiming that the premises are unfit. If you are a victim of a scam like this, you'll need to know how to defend yourself.

Your tenants' options will probably include one or more of what we call the "big sticks" in a tenant's self-help arsenal. These include:

- withholding the rent
- repairing the problem (or having it repaired by a professional) and deducting the cost from the rent
- calling state or local building or health inspectors
- moving out, or
- paying the rent and then suing you for the difference between the rent the tenant paid and the value of the defective premises.

If you haven't fixed a serious problem that truly makes the rental unit uninhabitable—rats in the kitchen, for example—you can expect that a savvy tenant will use one or more of these options. In this section, we'll explain the two options that involve paying less rent; we'll explain the others below.

Tenants cannot use these options unless three conditions are met:

- **The problem is serious, not just annoying, and imperils the tenant's health or safety.** Not every building code violation or annoying defect in a rental home (like the water heater's ability to reach only 107 degrees F, short of the code-specified 110 degrees) justifies use of a "big stick" against the landlord.
- **The tenant told you about the problem and gave you a reasonable opportunity to get it fixed, or the minimum amount of time required by state law, but you failed to fix it.** In some states, you are given a statutorily specified amount of time (ten days to three weeks is common); in others, you must respond within a reasonable time under the circumstances.
- **The tenant (or a guest) did not cause the problem, either deliberately or through carelessness or neglect.** If they did cause it, the tenant's use of one of the self-help options won't be upheld.

Rent Withholding

If you have not met the responsibility of keeping your property livable, your tenant may be able to stop paying rent until the repairs are made. Called rent withholding or rent escrowing, most states have established this option by statute or have authorized the same by court decision; some cities also have ordinances allowing it. See "State Laws on Rent Withholding and Repair and Deduct Remedies," in Appendix A. Rent withholding can be done *only* in states or cities that have specifically embraced it.

The term "withholding" is actually a bit misleading, since in some states and cities a tenant can't simply keep the rent money until you fix the problem. Instead, tenants often have to deposit the withheld rent with a court or a neutral third party or escrow account set up by a local court or housing agency until the repairs are accomplished.

Some states that allow rent withholding do so in a roundabout way, by giving tenants an "affirmative defense" to an eviction action if they have not paid the rent due to seriously substandard conditions and have been sued for eviction. In these states, tenants can defend against the eviction by arguing that the landlord's failure to maintain a fit and habitable rental excused them from the duty to pay rent. If the judge or jury sides with the tenant, they will defeat the landlord's lawsuit.

Before a tenant can properly withhold the rent, (by using a formal escrow procedure, or by not paying the rent and expecting to defend an eviction lawsuit by mounting an affirmative defense), three requirements must be met:

- The lack of maintenance or repair has made the dwelling unlivable.
- The problems were not caused by the tenant or his guest, either deliberately or through neglect.
- You've been told about the problem and haven't fixed it within a reasonable time or the minimum amount required by state law.

In addition, under most rent withholding laws, tenants cannot withhold rent if they are behind in the rent or in violation of an important lease clause. In short, tenants who use this drastic measure need to be squeaky clean.

Typical Rent Withholding Requirements

If rent withholding is allowed in your state or city, check the law to find out:

- what circumstances justify rent withholding (normally, only significant health and safety problems justify the use of the remedy, but statutes vary as to the particulars)
- whether the tenant must give you a certain amount of notice (ten to 30 days is typical) and time to fix the defect, or whether the notice and response time simply be "reasonable" under the circumstances

- whether the tenant must ask a local court for permission to withhold rent, provide compelling reasons why the rental is not livable, and follow specific procedures, and
- whether the tenant must place the unpaid rent in a separate bank account or deposit it with a court or local housing agency, and how this is done.

> ## Illegal Lease Clauses: Don't Limit Your Tenant's Right to Withhold the Rent Under State Law
>
> Some landlords insert clauses in their leases and rental agreements purporting to prohibit a tenant from withholding the rent, even if a property is uninhabitable. In many states, the rent withholding law itself makes this practice flatly illegal. But even where a state statute or court decision does not specifically disallow this side step, these clauses may be tossed out if a tenant nevertheless withholds rent and you attempt to evict him for nonpayment of rent. Why? Because a judge will approve a tenant's waiver of his right to withhold rent only if his "waiver" has been the subject of real negotiations between him and you, and not something you have insisted upon unilaterally. If you gave your tenant a preprinted lease (with a habitability waiver) and told him to take it or leave it, a judge is likely to decide that the so-called "waiver" was in fact imposed by you and, consequently, invalid. In short, your attempt to take away the right to use this option may be worthless.

What Happens to the Rent?

While repairs are being made, the tenant may continue to pay the entire rent to the court or housing authority or may be directed to pay some rent to you and the balance to the court or housing authority. If the rent money is being held by a court or housing authority, you can sometimes ask for release of some of the withheld rent to pay for repairs. When the dwelling is certified as fit by the local housing inspectors or the court, any money in the account is returned to you, minus court costs and inspection fees.

If your state's withholding law does not require the tenant to escrow the rent and a court has not been involved, the tenant may make his own arrangements as to what to do with the money. Careful tenants (who want to prove that they are not withholding rent simply because they do not have the money) will devise their own escrow set up, by placing the rent in an attorney's trust account or a separate bank account dedicated solely for that purpose.

Rogue Rent Withholding: Without Legal Authority

In states that don't permit withholding by either statute or court decision, tenants may nevertheless attempt to reduce the rent on their own. For example, if the water heater is broken and you haven't fixed it despite repeated requests, your tenant may decide to pay a few hundred dollars less per month, figuring that a cold-water flat is only worth that much.

Can you terminate and evict a tenant who gives you a short rent check in a state that has not authorized rent withholding? In some states, the answer is yes. In others, however, a tenant's partial withholding may survive an eviction lawsuit, especially if the defects were significant and your failure to fix them flagrant and long-standing. The wise course is not to gamble—if you lose the eviction lawsuit, you may get hit with the tenant's court costs and attorney fees. Attend to maintenance problems before they escalate into rent wars.

Once you have made the repairs, you'll undoubtedly expect full payment of the withheld rent. But don't be surprised if your tenant argues that he should be compensated for having had to live in substandard conditions. He may want a retroactive reduction in rent, starting from the time that the premises became uninhabitable. (Some states limit tenants to a reduction starting from the time you were notified of the problem.)

Reducing the rent is also known in legalese as rent "abatement" or "recoupment."

Your tenant may press for a retroactive rent abatement through a court process or through negotiation with you. The following section describes how a judge will determine how much you should compensate your tenant for the inconvenience of having lived in a substandard rental unit. If a court is not involved, you and the tenant can use this same system in your own negotiations.

Determining the Value of a Defective Rental Unit

How does a judge determine the difference between the withheld rent and what a defective, unlivable unit was really worth? There are two widely used ways.

Figuring the market value. In some states, statutes or court cases say that if you've left the unit in a defective condition, all you're entitled to is the fair market value of the premises in that condition. For example, if an apartment with a heater normally rented for $1,200 per month, but was worth only $600 without operable heating, you would be entitled to only $600 a month from the escrowed funds. Of course, the difficulty with this approach—as with many things in law—is that it is staggeringly unrealistic. An apartment with no heat in winter has *no* market value, because no one would rent it. As you can see, how much a unit is worth in a defective condition is extremely hard to determine.

By percentage reduction. Another slightly more sensible approach is to start by asking what part of the unit is affected by the defect, and then to calculate the percentage of the rent attributable to that part. For example, if the roof leaked into the living room of a $1,500-a-month apartment, rendering the room unusable, a tenant might reduce the rent by the percentage of the rent attributable to the living room. If the living room were the main living space and the other rooms were too small to live in comfortably, the percentage of loss would be much greater than it would be in more spacious apartments. Obviously, this approach is far from an exact science, either.

EXAMPLE: When Henry and Sue moved into their apartment, it was neat and well maintained. Soon after, the building was sold to an out-of-state owner, who hired an off-site manager to handle repairs and maintenance. Gradually, the premises began to deteriorate. At the beginning of May, 15 months into their two-year lease, Henry and Sue could count several violations of the building code, including the landlord's failure to maintain the common areas, remove the garbage promptly, and fix a broken water heater.

Henry and Sue sent numerous requests for repairs to their landlord over a two-month period, during which they gritted their teeth and put up with the situation. Finally they had enough and checked out their state's rent withholding law. They learned a tenant could pay rent into an escrow account set up by their local court. Henry and Sue went ahead and deposited their rent into this account.

During the time that they lived in these uninhabitable conditions, Henry and Sue were not required to pay full rent. Using the "market value" approach, the court decided that their defective rental was worth half its stated rent. Accordingly, since the landlord owed them a refund for portions of their rent for May and June, Henry and Sue would be paid this amount from the escrow account.

The balance of the rent in the account would be released to the landlord (less the costs of the escrow and the tenants' attorney fees), but only when the building inspector certified to the court that the building was up to code and fit for human habitation.

Henry and Sue could continue to pay 50% of the rent until needed repairs were made and certified by the building inspector.

Repair and Deduct

If you let your rental property fall below the fit and habitable standard, tenants in many states may be able to use a legal procedure called "repair and deduct." It works like this: Under certain conditions the tenant can, without your permission and without filing a lawsuit, have the defect repaired and subtract the cost of the repairs from the following month's rent. The repair and deduct remedy is available only if state or local law has authorized it.

Like the rent withholding option described above, the repair and deduct remedy cannot be invoked at whim. Instead, most states have established specific criteria a tenant must meet before legally qualifying to use the repair and deduct procedures: The defect must either be inexpensive, involve an essential service, or both (depending on the wording of the statute); and the subject of the repair must clearly be the landlord's responsibility. Let's look more closely at these requirements.

Repairs Must Qualify

A few states allow the repair and deduct remedy for minor repairs only, such as a leaky faucet or stopped-up sink. In most states there is a dollar limit or a specific percentage of the month's rent—for example, $300 or less than one-half the monthly rent, whichever is greater.

Most states allow tenants to use the repair and deduct remedy only for essential services, such as the procuring of heat and water or for conditions that materially affect the habitability of the premises, safety of the tenant, or terms of the lease.

EXAMPLE: On a chilly November evening, the pilot light for Larry's heater failed. He called his building manager, who promised to fix it soon. After calling the manager several more times to no avail and suffering through three frigid days with no heat, Larry called a heater repair person, who came promptly and replaced the broken mechanism for $150. Since Larry lives in a state that allows the repair and deduct remedy, Larry deducted $150 from his next rent check and gave his manager the repair bill.

Repairs Must Be Your Responsibility

A tenant cannot use the rent deduction method to fix a defect or problem that was caused by the careless or intentional act of the tenant or a guest of the tenant. Thus, a tenant cannot use this remedy to replace a window he broke himself. Also, since in most states the tenant is required to keep the dwelling as clean and orderly as the premises permit, he cannot use the remedy if the problem is traceable to his carelessness or unreasonable use of the property.

You Must Be Notified of the Problem

Before using the repair and deduct remedy, the tenant must notify you of the problem. He need not, however, inform you that he intends to utilize the remedy if you fail to respond. Each state has its own procedures and timeline for notification. Generally, the tenant's notice must be in writing. However, in some states the law simply requires that the tenant give the landlord or manager "reasonable" notice of the problem (this could be orally or in writing).

You Must Be Given Time to Fix the Problem

Statutes often give you a specified amount of time to make needed repairs before a tenant can legally use the repair and deduct remedy. For nonemergency repairs, this is typically within ten to 14 days of being notified by the tenant in writing. In the case of an emergency (such as a hole in the roof or a defective heater in winter), you must respond promptly. However, in some states no time limits are given; instead, you must make the repairs in a reasonable time.

There's a Limit to How Much Rent the Tenant Can Deduct

In states that allow the repair and deduct remedy, the amount the tenant deducts is always limited to the actual and reasonable amount spent on the repair. In addition, many states impose a limit on tenants' repairs, expressed in terms of a dollar limit or a limit relative to the monthly rent (such as no more than one month's rent). States may also limit the number of times a tenant can use the remedy in one year. In most states, tenants must present an itemized accounting for the work when using this remedy and presenting less than a full month's rent.

There's a Limit to Use of the Repair and Deduct Remedy

Many states limit how often tenants may pursue this option—for example, no more than once or twice in any 12-month period. Just because a tenant has used up his ability to utilize the remedy does not mean, however, that a landlord who has refused to fix a problem can ignore it. The tenant can still invoke any of the other remedies described in this chapter: rent withholding, filing a lawsuit in small claims court, or moving out.

There Are Other Negative Effects of Repair and Deduct

A tenant's use of the repair and deduct remedy can have unpleasant consequences. The tenant may not hire a skilled, reasonably priced repair person who does the job just as you would have done. Consequently, the chances for a needlessly expensive job or a shoddy one are great. Careful adherence to the high-quality maintenance system described below should help you avoid this fate.

EXAMPLE: When Matt opened the cupboard underneath his bathroom sink, he saw that the flexible hose connecting the pipe nipple to the sink was leaking. He turned off the water and called his landlord, Lee, who promised to attend to the problem right away. After three days without a bathroom sink, Matt called a plumber, who replaced the hose for $100. Matt deducted this amount from his next rent check. Lee thought no more about this until he got a frantic call from the tenant in the apartment beneath Matt's. She described her ceiling as looking like a giant, dripping sponge. Lee called his regular plumber to check the problem out. His plumber told Lee that the repair on Matt's sink had been done negligently, resulting in a major leak into the walls. If Lee had called his own plumber, the job would have been done right in the first place, saving Lee lots of money and hassle.

Sample Letter Suggesting Compromise on Rent Withholding

May 3, 20xx

Tyrone McNab
Villa Arms, Apt. 4
123 Main Street
Cleveland, Ohio 44130

Dear Mr. McNab:

I am writing you in the hope that we can work out a fair compromise to the problems that led you to withhold rent. You have rented a unit at the Villa Arms for the last three years, and we have never had a problem before. Let's try to resolve it.

To review briefly, on May 1, Marvin, my resident manager at Villa Arms, told me that you were temporarily withholding your rent because of several defective conditions in your apartment. Marvin said you had asked him to correct these problems a week ago, but he hasn't as yet attended to them. Marvin states that you listed these defects as some peeling paint on the interior wall of your bedroom, a leaky kitchen water faucet, a running toilet, a small hole in the living room carpet, and a cracked kitchen window.

I have instructed Marvin to promptly arrange with you for a convenient time to allow him into your apartment to repair all these problems. I am sure these repairs would already have been accomplished by now except for the fact that Hank, our regular repair person, has been out sick for the last ten days.

I understand that these problems are annoying and significant to you, and I acknowledge that they should have been attended to more promptly. However, I do not believe that they justify rent withholding under state law. Rent withholding is allowed only when the defects make the premises unfit for habitation. I do not think, however, that in the long run either one of us would be well served by stubbornly standing on our rights or resorting to a court fight. My first wish is to come to an amicable understanding with you that we can live with and use to avoid problems like this in the future.

Because of the inconvenience you have suffered as a result of the problems in your apartment, I am prepared to offer you a prorated rebate on your rent for ten days, this being the estimated length of time it will have taken Marvin to remedy the problems from the day of your complaint. As your monthly rent is $900, equal to $30 per day, I am agreeable to your paying only $600 rent this month.

If this is not acceptable to you, please call me at 555-1234 during the day. If you would like to discuss any aspect of the situation in more detail, I would be pleased to meet with you at your convenience. I will expect to receive your check for $600, or a call from you, before May 10.

Sincerely,

Sandra Schmidt

Sandra Schmidt
Owner, Villa Arms

A tenant's use of repair and deduct will also complicate (or frustrate) your accounts. You should be tracking maintenance costs in order to itemize them on your Schedule E tax return. But when tenants use repair and deduct, you have no receipt (with your name on it), and no direct way to prove the expense (short of arguing that the lowered rent reflects that expense). Keep things straightforward by paying for repairs yourself.

Your Options If a Tenant Withholds, Reduces, or Repairs and Deducts Rent

When confronted with a tenant who does not pay all or part of the rent, many landlords almost reflexively turn to a lawyer to bring an eviction lawsuit. But even if you eventually get the tenant evicted (and you may not, if the judge finds the tenant's rent withholding was justified), it is usually only after considerable cost. This is appropriate in some circumstances, especially when the tenant is clearly wrong and simply throwing legal sand in the air in an effort to obscure the fact that he can't or won't pay rent. But it's important to realize that tenants can fall into at least two other categories:

- tenants who have some right on their side—that is, the needed repairs or maintenance should have been done more promptly, and
- tenants who sincerely thought they had the right to withhold or repair and deduct rent, but who overreacted to the problem or just did the wrong thing under the law.

How you react when a tenant reduces, repairs and deducts, or withholds rent should depend on which category the tenant fits into. The following sections look at your options depending on the three categories: obvious troublemakers, mistaken but sincere tenants who are worth salvaging, and tenants who had some justification for using the remedy they chose.

Obvious Troublemakers

If you keep your rental properties in good shape and properly handle repair and maintenance problems, your best bet may be to promptly and legally terminate the tenancy of any tenant who pays you less or no rent.

If you're heading for court, you may need to consult a lawyer or do some legal research first on your state's laws on evictions. If you do end up in court, be prepared to prove the following:

- The claimed defect was nonexistent, and nothing justified the tenant's failure to pay the rent.
- The tenant caused the defect himself in order to avoid paying rent.
- The claimed defect was not really serious or substantial enough to give the tenant the right to pursue a particular remedy, such as rent withholding.
- Even if the defect was substantial, you were never given adequate notice and a chance to fix it. (At this point you should present a detailed complaint procedure to the court as we recommend above. You should show, if possible, that the tenant didn't follow your complaint procedure.)
- The tenant failed to comply with some other aspect of the rent withholding law. For example, in states that require the tenant to place the withheld rent in escrow with the court, a tenant's failure to do so may defeat her attempt to use the procedure at all. A tenant who repeatedly failed to use the escrow procedure might be a candidate for eviction.

CAUTION

If in doubt, hold off on eviction. Sometimes it's hard to know if a tenant is truly a bad apple or just badly confused as to her legal rights. Until you are sure the tenant fits into the first category (had absolutely no good reason to reduce, withhold, or repair and deduct rent), don't try to evict the tenant. Under the law of virtually every state, retaliatory evictions are penalized, often severely—that is, you may not evict a tenant in retaliation for his asserting a particular right, such as the right to withhold rent or complain to governmental authorities about health or safety problems.

Mistaken But Sincere Tenants

If you think the tenant is wrong, but sincere—that is, she probably isn't trying to make up an excuse for not paying rent, but nevertheless is clearly not legally eligible to abate, withhold rent, or repair and deduct—your best course is usually to try and work things out with the tenant in a face-to-face meeting. If, for example, the tenant used the repair and deduct remedy, but you were never given adequate legal notice (and would have had the problem fixed for $50 less if you had been), it may make sense to accept the tenant's solution but make sure the tenant knows how to notify you of the problems in the future. It may be painful to make this sort of compromise, but it is not nearly as bad as trying to evict the tenant and risking that a judge might even agree with her course of action.

The chances for resolving a conflict will be greater if you have a compromise system in place when you need it. When you find yourself dealing with a tenant who is not an obvious candidate for eviction (and especially if the tenant has some right on her side, as discussed below), consider taking the following steps:

1. Meet with the tenant (or tenants) and negotiate. You should be interested in establishing a good solution to avoid problems in the future and not in determining who was "right."

2. If negotiation fails, suggest mediation by a neutral third party. Check out how this works in advance so you can move quickly should the need arise again.

3. Put your solution in writing.

4. If the process indicates a larger problem with tenant dissatisfaction, encourage the tenant or tenants to meet with you regularly to solve it.

In many cases, it may be possible for you and the tenant to come to a mutually acceptable agreement using this system. On your end, this might mean promptly having the necessary work done and better maintaining the unit in the future. You might also give the tenant a prorated reduction in rent for the period between the time the tenant notified you of the defect and the time it was corrected. In exchange, the tenant might promise to promptly notify you of problems before resorting to the same tactic in the future.

> **EXAMPLE:** A leaky roof during a rainy month deprives a tenant, Steve, of the use of one of his two bedrooms. If Steve gave his landlord, Joe, notice of the leak, and Joe did not take care of the problem quickly, Steve might be justified in deducting $300 from the $800 rent for that month. However, if Steve didn't tell Joe of the problem until the next month's rent was due, a compromise might be reached where Steve bears part of the responsibility, by agreeing to deduct only $100 from the rent.

The first step in working toward a compromise with the tenant who uses rent abatement, withholding, or repair and deduct is to call him. If you're reluctant to call, you might want to try a letter. See the sample letter above suggesting a compromise on rent withholding.

Tenants Who Are Partially Right

Sometimes, despite your best efforts to keep on top of repair and maintenance issues, a repair job falls through the cracks. It could happen while you are on vacation and your backup system doesn't work, or maybe you simply need a better manager. If, in all fairness, a tenant was justified in using rent withholding or repair and deduct, admit it and take steps to rectify the situation. For example, after getting the necessary work done, you might try to make use of the compromise procedure outlined above. Once the immediate problem is behind you, treat what happened as an opportunity to review, revise, and improve your maintenance and repair procedures:

- **Complaint procedure.** Do you have a complaint system that makes it easy for tenants to communicate their concerns? Are complaint forms readily available and easy to use?

- **Tenant education.** Do your tenants know that you intend to respond quickly to repair and maintenance problems? Do you need to remind all tenants, via a tenant notice or newsletter, of your complaint procedure?

- **Management response.** Does management respond reasonably quickly to a tenant's request for repairs?

Earlier in this chapter we provided detailed suggestions for how to set up and implement a maintenance program designed to identify repair needs before they become repair problems.

Tenant Responses to Unfit Premises: Calling Inspectors, Filing Lawsuits, and Moving Out

Tenants who are faced with unfit rentals are not limited to withholding rent or repairing the defects themselves. Other options that do not involve paying less rent include calling government inspectors, breaking the lease and moving out, and suing in small claims court.

Reporting Code Violations to Housing Inspectors

A tenant may complain to a local building, health, or fire department about problems such as inoperable plumbing, a leaky roof, or bad wiring. If an inspector comes out and discovers code violations, you will be given an order to correct the problem. Fines and penalties usually follow if you fail to comply within a certain amount of time (often five to 30 business days). If there's still no response, the city or county may sue you. In many cities, your failure to promptly fix cited violations of local housing laws is a misdemeanor (minor crime) punishable by hefty fines or even imprisonment. In rare cases, especially if tenants' health is imperiled, local officials may even require that the building be vacated.

In many areas, getting reported to a building inspector is a very big deal—an inspector who finds lots of problems can force you to clear them up immediately. But there is wide variation as to the effectiveness of building inspectors. In some cities, there are very few inspectors compared to the number of tenant complaints, and courts are largely unable to follow up on the properties that are cited. But chances are that if the complaint procedure proves ineffective, your tenant will turn to a more effective option, such as filing a lawsuit or moving out.

Severe Code Violations Will Close Your Building

If a judge decides that a building's condition substantially endangers the health and safety of its tenants, and repairs are so extensive they can't be made while tenants inhabit the building, the result may be an order to vacate the building. You usually won't have a chance to come to the court hearing to object to this dire consequence—your tenants will simply be told to get out, sometimes within hours.

In some states, you must pay for comparable temporary housing nearby. Some statutes also make you cover moving expenses and utility connection charges and give the original tenant the first chance to move back in when the repairs are completed. To find out whether you'll be liable for relocation expenses, check your state statutes (listed in "State Landlord-Tenant Statutes" in Appendix A). Look in the index to your state's codes under "Landlord-Tenant" for subheadings such as "Relocation Assistance" or "Padlock Orders."

Lawsuits by the Tenant

A consumer who purchases a defective product— be it a car, a hair dryer, or a steak dinner—is justified in expecting a minimum level of quality, and is entitled to compensation if the product is seriously flawed. Tenants are consumers, too, and may remain in possession of the premises and still sue you for the following:

- partial or total refund of rent paid while the housing conditions were substandard
- the value, or repair costs, of property lost or damaged as a result of the defect—for example, furniture ruined by water leaking through the roof

- compensation for personal injuries—including pain and suffering—caused by the defect, and

- attorney fees.

In some states, tenants may also seek a court order—similar to a rent withholding scheme—directing you to repair the defects, with rent reduced until you show proof to the court that the defects have been remedied.

CAUTION

You may not retaliate against a tenant who files a lawsuit and stays on the property. (See Chapter 16 for a discussion of retaliatory eviction.) It may seem inconsistent for a tenant to take the extreme step of suing you and expecting to remain on the property. Nevertheless, a tenant who sues and stays is exercising a legal right. Retaliation, such as delivering a rent increase or a termination notice, is illegal and will give the tenant yet another ground on which to sue.

Moving Out

If a tenant's dwelling isn't habitable and you haven't fixed it, he also has the right to move out—either temporarily or permanently. These drastic measures are justified only when there are truly serious problems, such as the lack of essential services or the total or partial destruction of the premises. Tenants may also use these options if environmental health hazards such as lead paint dust make the unit uninhabitable.

Tenant's Right to Move Out When the Unit Is Uninhabitable

The 49 states (and the District of Columbia) that require you to provide habitable housing allow tenants to move out if you don't do your job. Depending on the circumstances, tenants may move out permanently, by terminating the lease or rental agreement, or temporarily. This approach is borrowed directly from consumer protection laws. Just as the purchaser of a seriously defective car

may sue to undo the contract or return the car for a refund, tenants can consider the housing contract terminated and simply return the rental unit to you if the housing is unlivable.

The law, of course, has a convoluted phrase to describe this simple concept. It's called "constructive eviction," which means that, by supplying unlivable housing, you have for all practical purposes "evicted" the tenant. A tenant who has been constructively evicted (that is, he has a valid reason to move out) has no further responsibility for rent.

Your state statute may have specific details, such as the type of notice tenants must provide before moving out because of a major repair problem. You may have anywhere from five to 21 days to fix the problem, depending on the state and, sometimes, the seriousness of the situation. Check your state law for details.

Temporary moves. In many states, if you fail to provide heat or other essential services, tenants may procure reasonable substitute housing during the period of your noncompliance. They may recover the costs (as long as they're reasonable) of substitute housing up to an amount equal to the rent.

Permanent moves. A tenant who moves out permanently because of habitability problems may also be entitled to money from you to compensate them for out-of-pocket losses. For example, the tenant may be able to recover for moving expenses and the cost of a hotel for a few days until they find a new place. Also, if the conditions were substandard during prior months when the tenant did pay the full rent, you may be sued for the difference between the value of the defective dwelling and the rent paid. In addition, if the tenant is unable to find comparable housing for the same rent, and ends up paying more rent than they would have under the old lease, you may be on the hook for the difference.

> **EXAMPLE:** Susan signed a one-year lease for a beachfront apartment. She thought it was a great deal because the monthly rent of $700 was considerably less than similar properties in the neighborhood.

Susan's dream of an apartment began to turn into a nightmare when she discovered, soon after moving in, that the bedroom was full of mildew that attacked every surface and interfered with her breathing. After numerous complaints to the landlord, which were ignored, Susan moved out at the end of four months and rented a comparable apartment nearby for $800. She then sued the landlord for the following:

- **Compensation for the months she had endured the defective conditions.** Susan asked for the difference between the agreed-upon rent and the real value of the apartment (the apartment with its defects), times four (the number of months she paid rent).
- **The benefit of her bargain.** Susan pointed out that the rent for the first apartment was a real bargain, and that she had been unable to find a similar apartment for anything less than $800 per month. She asked for the added rent she will have to pay ($100) times eight, the number of months left on her original lease.
- **Moving costs.** Susan asked for the $250 cost of hiring a moving company to transport her belongings to her new home.

After hearing Susan's arguments and the landlord's feeble defense, the judge decided that Susan was entitled to:

- **Compensation for past problems.** The mildew problem, which had forced Susan to sleep in the living room, had essentially reduced the one-bedroom apartment to a studio apartment, which would have rented for $400 per month. Accordingly, Susan was entitled to a refund of $300 for each of the four months, or $1,200.
- **The benefit of her bargain.** The judge acknowledged that a similar apartment, such as the one she rented when she moved out, cost $100 more per month than the one she had originally rented, and awarded her that amount per month times eight, or $800.
- **Moving costs.** The judge ruled that Susan's moving costs of $250 were reasonable, and ordered the landlord to pay them.

Tenant's Right to Move Out When There Is Damage to the Premises

A tenant whose home is significantly damaged—either by natural disaster or any other reason beyond his responsibility or control—has the right to consider the lease at an end and to move out. Depending on the circumstances of the damage and the language in your lease or rental agreement, however, everyone may not be able to simply walk away from the lease or rental agreement with no financial consequences. A tenant may have the legal right to your assistance with substitute housing or living expenses. Obviously, the tenant whose rental unit is destroyed by a natural disaster has less reason to expect resettlement assistance from you than one whose home is destroyed by fire caused by your botching an electrical repair job. And the tenant whose home burns down because he left the stove on all night will probably find himself at the other end of a lawsuit.

Natural or third-party disasters. State laws vary on the extent of your responsibility depending on the cause of the damage. If a fire, flood, tornado, earthquake, or other natural disaster renders the dwelling unlivable, or if a third party is the cause of the destruction (for instance, a fire due to an arsonist), your best bet is to look to your insurance policy for help in repairing or rebuilding the unit. While waiting for the insurance coverage to kick in, give month-to-month tenants a termination notice (typically 30 days' notice is required). In some cases, you may be required by law to pay the tenant for substitute housing for 30 days. With tenants who have a lease, you may be obligated to pay for substitute housing for a longer period until the tenant finds a comparable replacement. To be prudent, raise the issue of tenant assistance with your insurance broker at the time the policy is purchased so that you know exactly where you stand if a disaster strikes.

Destruction that is traceable to the landlord. If it can be shown that you or your employees were even partially responsible for the damage, your legal responsibility to the tenant is likely to increase.

You may be expected to cover a longer period of temporary housing, and, if the substitute housing is more expensive, you may be stuck with paying the difference between the new rent and the old rent. The insurance issue will also take on a different cast: Some policies exclude coverage for natural disasters, but include (as is standard) coverage for the owner's negligent acts. The facts surrounding the property damage or destruction, applicable state law, and the wording of your insurance policy will determine how each situation is handled.

If a tenant moves out due to damage or destruction of the premises, for whatever cause, it will be important for you and the tenant to sign a written termination of the rental agreement or lease once the tenant is relocated, see the sample Landlord-Tenant Agreement to Terminate Lease in Chapter 8. This allows you to proceed with the repair or rebuilding without the pressure of tenants waiting to move in immediately. If you want to rerent to the same tenant, a new lease or rental agreement can be drawn up at that time.

Minor Repairs

You are much more likely to face tenants' minor complaints—such as leaky faucets, temperamental appliances, worn carpets, noisy heaters, hot water heaters that produce too little hot water—than major problems that make a unit unlivable. To avoid hassles with tenants over minor repairs, you may delegate responsibility to a tenant—particularly one who is especially reliable and handy. "Delegating Landlord's Responsibilities to Tenants," below, shows how to delegate minor repairs and maintenance.

You have different legal duties depending on whether a problem is major (affecting the habitability of the rental unit) or minor. Major jobs are yours, period. Minor repair and maintenance includes:

- small plumbing jobs, like replacing washers and cleaning drains
- system upkeep, like changing heating filters
- structural upkeep, like replacing excessively worn flooring

- small repair jobs, like fixing broken light fixtures or replacing the grout around bathtub tile, and
- routine repairs to and maintenance of common areas, such as pools, spas, and laundry rooms.

Most often, minor repairs are your job. But you are not required to keep the rental premises looking just like new—ordinary wear and tear does not have to be repaired during a tenancy. (When the tenant moves out, however, the cost of dealing with ordinary wear and tear will fall on you and cannot come out of the security deposit.) And if the tenant or one of his guests caused a minor repair problem, carelessly or intentionally, the tenant is responsible for repairing it—or, if your lease or rental agreement prohibits him from doing so, paying you to do it.

If the tenant had nothing to do with the repair problem, and it's not a cosmetic issue, chances go way up that you are responsible, for one of the following reasons:

- A state or local building code requires you to keep the damaged item (for example, a kitchen sink) in good repair.
- A state or local law specifically makes it your responsibility.
- Your lease or rental agreement provision or advertisement describes or lists particular items, such as hot tubs, trash compactors, and air conditioners; by implication, this makes you responsible for maintaining or repairing them.
- You made explicit promises when showing the unit—for example, regarding the security or air conditioning system.
- You made an implied promise to provide a particular feature, such as a whirlpool bathtub, because you have fixed or maintained it in the past.

Each of these reasons is discussed below. If you're not sure whether or not a minor repair or maintenance problem is your responsibility, scan the discussion to find out.

Building Codes

States (and sometimes cities) write building codes that cover structural requirements, such as roofs, flooring, and windows, and essential services, such as hot water and heat. If your tenant's repair request involves a violation of the building code, you may be facing a habitability problem, as discussed above. But building codes often cover other, less essential, details as well. For example, codes may specify a minimum number of electrical outlets per room; if a broken circuit breaker means that there are fewer working outlets, the consequence is probably not an unfit dwelling, but you are still legally required to fix the problem.

Landlord-Tenant Laws

Some state laws place responsibility for specific minor repairs and maintenance on the landlord. A common example is providing garbage receptacles and arranging for garbage pick-up. Many states have their own special rules. In Alaska, for example, the law makes landlords responsible for maintaining appliances supplied by them. (Alaska Stat. § 34.03.100.)

In many states, renters of single-family residences may agree to take on responsibilities that would otherwise belong to the landlord, such as disposing of garbage. For details, check your state's landlord-tenant codes under "State Landlord-Tenant Statutes," which are listed in Appendix A.

Promises in the Lease or Rental Agreement

When it comes to legal responsibility for repairs, your own lease or rental agreement is often just as important (or more so) than building codes or state laws. If your written agreement describes or lists items such as drapes, washing machines, swimming pools, saunas, parking places, intercoms, or dishwashers, you must provide them in decent repair. And the promise to provide them carries with it the implied promise to maintain them.

Promises in Ads

If an advertisement for your unit described or listed a feature, such as a satellite dish, especially if the feature is emphasized, you must follow through with these promises, even if your written rental agreement says nothing about the feature. Items such as dishwashers, clothes washers and dryers, microwave ovens, security gates, and Jacuzzis must be repaired by you if they break through no fault of the tenant.

Promises Made Before You Rented the Unit

It's a rare landlord or manager who refrains from even the slightest bit of puffing when showing a rental to a prospective tenant. It's hard to refrain from announcing rosy plans for amenities or services that haven't yet materialized ("We plan to redo this kitchen—you'll love the snappy way that trash compactor will work!"). Whenever you make promises like these, even if they're not in writing, your tenant can legally hold you to them.

Implied Promises

Suppose your rental agreement doesn't mention a garbage disposal, and neither did any of your advertising. And you never pointed it out when showing the unit. But there is a garbage disposal, and it was working when the tenant moved in. Now the garbage disposal is broken—do you have to fix it? Many courts will hold you legally responsible for maintaining all significant aspects of the rental unit. If you offer a unit that *already has* certain features—light fixtures that work, doors that open and close smoothly, faucets that don't leak, tile that doesn't fall off the wall—many judges reason that you have made an implied contract to keep them in workable order throughout the tenancy.

The flip side of this principle is that when your tenant has paid for a hamburger, the waiter—you—doesn't have to deliver a steak. In other words, if the rental was shabby when the tenant moved in, and you never gave the tenant reason to believe that it would be spruced up, he has no legal right to demand improvements—unless, of course, he can point to health hazards or code violations. As when you offer secondhand goods "as is" for a low price, legally your buyer/tenant is stuck with the deal.

Another factor that is evidence of an implied contract is your past conduct. If you have consistently fixed or maintained a particular feature of a rental, such as a dishwasher, you have an implied obligation to continue doing so.

Tenant Options If Landlord Refuses to Make Minor Repairs

If you have determined that the repair problem is minor and falls fairly in your lap, it's wise to attend to it promptly. Although your tenant's health and safety may not be immediately imperiled (as is true with major repairs), you don't want to court disaster. For example, the repair may be minor now but have the potential to become major and expensive; there may be a potential for injury and liability; or the problem may affect other renters, presenting the unpleasant possibility of a cadre of disgruntled tenants.

If you refuse to fix a minor problem that is your responsibility, your tenant has several options. He may:

- fix it himself
- report you to the housing inspectors, if the problem involves a code violation
- attempt to use one of the legal options designed for habitability problems, such as rent withholding or repair and deduct
- break the lease and move out, or
- sue you, usually in small claims court.

Some of these responses are appropriate, and others may not be—we'll explain why below. But keep in mind that even if a tenant improperly responds, your being in the right may be an illusory victory. Legal disputes—in court or out—are expensive and time-consuming. Unless the tenant is a whining prima donna who demands constant, unnecessary repairs, it's usually wiser to fix the problem and nip the issue in the bud.

Fixing the Problem Themselves

Your exasperated tenant might strap on his tool belt and fix the minor problem himself. If he's handy and has used the proper procedures and materials, you may come out ahead. But you have no way of gauging his expertise, and there is always the possibility that the tenant will do a slipshod job, either negligently or through spite.

> **EXAMPLE:** Colin decided to replace a window that was broken by his son's basketball. He removed the shards of glass, fitted a new pane in place and caulked the circumference. He did not, however, paint the caulk; a year later it had cracked, allowing rainwater to seep onto the windowsill and down the wall. His landlord Sarina was furious when she realized that she would have to replace the sill and the drywall, simply because Colin had not done a workmanlike job. The cost of these repairs exceeded Colin's security deposit, and Sarina had to sue him in small claims court for the balance, which she had a hard time collecting.

Reporting Code Violations

If the minor repair problem constitutes a code violation, such as inadequate electrical outlets or low water pressure, your tenant may find an ally in the building or housing agency in charge of enforcing the code. Whether the tenant will get an effective response from the agency will depend on the seriousness of the violation, the workload of the agency, and its ability to enforce its compliance orders. Since by definition the problem is minor, it's unlikely to get much action, especially if code enforcement officials are already overworked. But his complaint will remain on file, which is a public record that may come back to haunt you.

EXAMPLE: Randall was a successful landlord who owned several properties. A rotten and poorly supported deck at one of his apartment houses collapsed, killing one tenant and injuring several others. Randall was sued by the injured tenants and the family of the deceased for intentionally violating building codes when constructing the deck. Local news coverage made much of the fact that he had been cited numerous times for minor code violations; this publicity made it extremely difficult for him to get a fair trial. The jury found in favor of the plaintiffs and awarded them several million dollars. Because this tragedy was not the result of Randall's negligence, but rather an expected consequence of deliberately ignoring proper building procedures, Randall's insurance company refused to cover the award. Randall was forced to declare bankruptcy.

Using Rent Withholding or Repair and Deduct

Tenants often make the mistake of using these powerful remedies, usually reserved for major habitability problems, for minor repairs. If your tenant has done so, you should be able to terminate and evict for nonpayment of rent. Be sure to read your state's statute or other authority carefully to make sure that there's no way your tenant can justify his action under your state's withholding or repair and deduct laws.

Breaking the Lease

A disgruntled tenant may decide it's not worth putting up with your unwillingness to handle minor repairs and may simply break the lease and move out. A defect that is truly minor does not justify this extreme step. But being in the right does you little good here—in most states, you'll have to take reasonable steps to rerent and credit the new rent to the departed tenant's responsibility for the balance of the rent. The fact that he left because he didn't like the squeaky closet door does not relieve you of this duty.

Suing in Small Claims Court

Be it ever so minor, your tenant is entitled to get what he paid for—and if he doesn't, he might decide to sue in small claims court. Small claims court judges usually won't order you to paint, fix the dishwasher, or repair the intercom. The judge may, however, order that the tenant be compensated in dollars for living in a rental unit with repair problems, on the theory that the tenant is not getting the benefit of what he's paying rent for—for example, a functioning dishwasher, presentable paint, or a working air conditioner. You may be ordered to pay the tenant an amount that reflects the difference between his rent and the value of the unit with repair problems. To calculate this amount, the judge will use one of the methods described above in "Tenant Responses to Unfit Premises."

How much of a threat is a small claims suit likely to be? A judge is not going to adjust the rent because a little grout is missing from the bathroom tile. But if the dishwasher is broken, three faucets leak noisily, and the bathroom door won't close, your tenant's chances of winning go way up.

Delegating Landlord's Responsibilities to Tenants

You may want to delegate some repair and maintenance responsibilities to the tenants themselves—perhaps you live at a distance and the tenant is particularly responsible and handy. Is this legal? Courts in each state have faced this question and have come to several different conclusions. While we cannot offer a countrywide analysis of each state's position, here are the basics.

Do Not Delegate Responsibility for Major Repairs and Maintenance to the Tenant

By law, housing must be habitable, because society has decided that it is unacceptable for landlords to offer substandard dwellings. For this reason, the implied warranty of habitability and the covenant of quiet enjoyment cannot be waived by a tenant in most states. In other words, even though the tenant may be willing to live in substandard housing, society has decided that it will not tolerate such conditions.

It is a small but logical step to the next question of whether you can delegate to the tenant the responsibility of keeping the premises fit for habitation. Many courts have held that you cannot, fearing that the tenant will rarely be in the position, either practically or financially, to do the kinds of repairs that are often needed to bring a structure up to par.

Even if you do have the legal right, it is always a mistake to try and delegate to a tenant your responsibility for major maintenance of essential services, such as heat, plumbing, or electricity, or repairs involving the roof or other parts of the building structure. And remember, even inexpensive jobs can have enormous repercussions if done poorly. For instance, replacing an electrical outlet seems simple, but the results of an improper job (fire or electrocution) can be devastating. Think twice before entrusting sensitive jobs to people who are not experts.

How to Delegate Minor Repairs and Maintenance to Tenants

Delegating minor repairs is usually a different issue. Under the law of some states, and as a matter of sensible practice in all states, you may delegate minor repairs and maintenance responsibilities to the tenant—such as mowing the lawn, trimming the bushes, and sweeping the lobby—without making the tenant responsible for keeping the structure habitable. Practically speaking, however, you must be willing to check to see if the work is done properly. If you wish to delegate responsibilities to a tenant, be advised that, as far as any *other* tenants are concerned (and probably with respect to the living space of the tenant-repairperson, too), your delegation of certain maintenance and repair duties to one tenant does not relieve you of the ultimate responsibility for meeting state and local health and safety laws.

Always remember that the implied warranty of habitability makes you responsible for maintenance of common areas—for example, cleaning hallways and mowing the lawn. If you transfer this duty to someone who fails to do it, the transfer will not

shield you if you are hauled into court for failure to maintain the premises. On the other hand, if you monitor the manner in which the job is being done and step in and get it done right if the tenant does a poor job, there should be no practical problems.

Repair and maintenance arrangements between landlords and tenants often lead to dissatisfaction—typically, the landlord feels that the tenant has neglected certain tasks, or the tenant feels that there is too much work for the money. When a court is asked to step in, the validity of the arrangement will typically be judged along the following lines:

- **Was it in writing?** Any agreement as to repairs or maintenance should be written and signed, either as part of the lease or rental agreement (see Clause 12 of the form agreements in Chapter 2), or as a separate employment agreement (discussed below).

- **Was it a fair bargain?** You must adequately pay the tenant for the services provided. Often, this payment consists of a reduction in rent. A judge may look askance at a $50 reduction in monthly rent for 20 hours of work, which represents a pay scale well below the minimum wage.

- **Is it fair to other tenants?** Some courts will also inquire as to whether your agreement adversely affects your obligations to other tenants. For example, if your tenant-maintenance person does his job poorly or only now and then, the other tenants will have to live with his spotty performance.

- **Have you treated the delegation separately from your other duties as the landlord?** The agreement you have with your tenant has nothing to do with your other responsibilities. For example, if you and your tenant agree that she will do gardening work in exchange for a reduction in rent, and you feel that she is not doing a proper job, you may not respond by shutting off her water or retaliating in other ways. The proper recourse is to discuss the problem with the tenant and, if it persists, to cancel the arrangement.

(!) CAUTION

Be careful delegating repairs involving hazardous materials. The simplest repair may actually create an environmental health hazard, which may open you to liability on three fronts: You may be sued by the exposed tenant, sued by other tenants who might also be affected, and cited by the relevant regulating agency for allowing an untrained or uncertified person to work on toxic materials. For example, preparing a surface for a seemingly innocuous paint job may actually involve the creation of lead-based paint dust, and the quick installation of a smoke alarm could involve the disturbance of an asbestos-filled ceiling. Handling and disposal of toxic materials is highly regulated, and violations may subject you to significant fines.

Landlords May Be Able to Delegate More Repair Responsibilities to Single-Family Residences

In several states, the landlord and tenant of a single-family dwelling may agree in writing that the tenant is to perform some of the landlord's statutory duties—to arrange for garbage receptacles and garbage disposal, running water, hot water, and heat—in addition to making other specified repairs. States allowing this type of delegation typically require that the transaction be entered into in good faith—meaning that each side completely understands their rights and responsibilities, and neither pressures the other. In addition, the work must usually not be necessary to cure the landlord's failure to substantially comply with health and safety codes.

Although the possibility for delegation is greater in some single-family rental situations than it is in a multiunit context, we caution owners of single-family rental properties to think carefully before entering into an arrangement of this type. Unless you are very sure about the skill and integrity of your tenant, the possibilities for shoddy work and disagreements are as great as they are in any rental situation, and indeed the consequences (poor work done to an entire house) may be greater.

Compensating a Tenant for Repair and Maintenance Work

Paying an on-site tenant to do repair and maintenance tasks, such as keeping hallways, elevators, or a laundry room clean or maintaining the landscaping, is preferable to giving the tenant a reduction in rent for work performed. Why? Because if the job is not done right, you can simply cancel the employment arrangement, rather than having to amend the lease or rental agreement in order to reestablish the original rent. By paying the tenant separately, there will be no question that he is still obligated to pay the full rent as he has done all along.

You May Have to Pay Federal and State Tax on Your Tenant-Repairperson

Paying your handy tenant $300 per month, or reducing his rent by this amount, in exchange for maintenance and repair duties may have important tax consequences for you. That person may be considered your "employee" (as distinguished from an independent contractor). If you "pay" the person more than a certain amount per year, either in cash or in the form of a rent reduction, you may be obliged to pay Social Security and meet other legal obligations as an employer. These obligations are covered in the Chapter 6 discussion of compensating a tenant-manager.

Landlord Liability for Tenant Repair and Maintenance Work

The delegation of basic repair and maintenance work to a tenant may not relieve you of liability if the repair is done poorly and someone is injured or property is damaged as a result.

Of course, you could always try to recoup your losses by suing that tenant (called "seeking indemnity" in legalese), but your chances of recovery will be slim unless your tenant has sufficient monetary assets. On the other hand, a maintenance or repair service will generally carry its own insurance (you should confirm this before you engage their services).

The cruelest cut of all could be the ability of the tenant-repair person to sue you if he is injured performing the repair tasks. The tenant could argue that you had no business entrusting a dangerous job to someone whose expertise was not proven— and, in some courts and in front of some juries, he might prevail. A carefully written exculpatory clause might shield you from liability in some situations, but you can never be 100% sure that the clause will be upheld in court. Exculpatory clauses are explained in Chapter 10.

> **EXAMPLE:** Clem, the landlord, hired Tom, the teenage son of a longtime tenant, for yard work. Part of Tom's job consisted of mowing the two front lawns, which were separated by a gravel walkway. Tom cut the first lawn and, without turning off the mower, pushed it over the gravel to the second lawn. Pieces of gravel were picked up by the blades and fired to the side, where they struck and partially blinded a child playing in the next yard. Clem was sued and faced an uphill battle with his insurance company as to whether Tom's negligence was covered under Clem's policy.

Tenants' Alterations and Improvements

Your lease or rental agreement probably includes a clause prohibiting tenants from making any alterations or improvements without your express, written consent; see Clause 12 of our lease or rental agreement forms in Chapter 2. For good reason, you'll want to make sure tenants don't change the light fixtures, replace the window coverings, or install a built-in dishwasher unless you agree first.

But in spite of your wish that your tenants leave well enough alone, you're bound to encounter the tenant who goes ahead without your knowledge or consent. On the other hand, you may also hear from an upstanding tenant that she would, indeed, like your consent to her plan to install a bookshelf or closet system. To know how to deal with unauthorized alterations or straightforward requests, you'll need to understand some basic rules.

 RELATED TOPIC

Tenants with disabilities have rights to modify their living space that may override your ban against alterations without your consent. See Chapter 5 for details.

Improvements That Become Part of the Property (Fixtures)

Anything your tenant attaches to a building, fence, or deck or the ground itself (lawyers call such items "fixtures") belongs to you, absent an agreement saying it's the tenant's. This is an age-old legal principle, and, for good measure, it's wise to spell it out in your lease or rental agreement. This means when the tenant moves out, you are legally entitled to refuse her offer to remove the fixture and return the premises to its original state.

When a landlord and departing tenant haven't decided ahead of time as to who will own the fixture, the dispute often ends up in court. Judges use a variety of legal rules to determine whether an object—an appliance, flooring, shelving, or plumbing—is something that the tenant can take with her or is a permanent fixture belonging to you. Here are some of the questions judges ask when separating portable from nonportable additions:

- **Did your tenant get your permission?** If the tenant never asked you for permission to install a closet organizer, or she did and got no for an answer, a judge is likely to rule for you—particularly if your lease or rental agreement prohibits alterations or improvements.

- **Did the tenant make any structural changes that affect the use or appearance of the property?** If so, chances are that the item will be deemed yours, because removing it will often leave an unsightly area or alter use of part of the property. For example, if a tenant modifies the kitchen counter to accommodate a built-in dishwasher and then takes the dishwasher with her, you will have to install another dishwasher of the same dimensions or rebuild

Agreement Regarding Tenant Alterations to Rental Unit

_____ Iona Lott _____ [Landlord]

and _____ Doug Diep _____ [Tenant]

agree as follows:

1. Tenant may make the following alterations to the rental unit at: _____ 75A Cherry Street, Pleasantville,
   North Dakota _____

   1. Plant three rose bushes along walkway at side of residence. _____

   2. Install track lighting along west (ten-foot) kitchen wall. _____

   _____

   _____

   _____

   _____

   _____ .

2. Tenant will accomplish the work described in Paragraph 1 by using the following materials and procedures:

   1. Three bare-root roses, hybrid teas, purchased from Jackson-Perky and
      planted in March. _____

   2. "Wallbright" track lighting system purchased from "Lamps and More," plus
      necessary attachment hardware. _____

   _____

   _____

   _____ .

3. Tenant will do only the work outlined in Paragraph 1 using only the materials and procedures outlined in
   Paragraph 2.

4. The alterations carried out by Tenant:

   ☑ will become Landlord's property and are not to be removed by Tenant during or at the end of the
   tenancy, or

   ☐ will be considered Tenant's personal property, and as such may be removed by Tenant at any time up
   to the end of the tenancy. Tenant promises to return the premises to their original condition upon
   removing the improvement.

5. Landlord will reimburse Tenant only for the costs checked below:

   ☑ the cost of materials listed in Paragraph 2

   ☑ labor costs at the rate of $ _____ 25 _____ per hour for work done in a workmanlike manner
   acceptable to Landlord, up to _____ 10 _____ hours.

6. After receiving appropriate documentation of the cost of materials and labor, Landlord shall make any payment called for under Paragraph 5 by:

    ☑ lump sum payment, within _____10_____ days of receiving documentation of costs, or

    ☐ by reducing Tenant's rent by $ _____ per month for the number of months necessary to cover the total amounts under the terms of this agreement.

7. If under Paragraph 4 of this contract the alterations are Tenant's personal property, Tenant must return the premises to their original condition upon removing the alterations. If Tenant fails to do this, Landlord will deduct the cost to restore the premises to their original condition from Tenant's security deposit. If the security deposit is insufficient to cover the costs of restoration, Landlord may take legal action, if necessary, to collect the balance.

8. If Tenant fails to remove an improvement that is his or her personal property on or before the end of the tenancy, it will be considered the property of Landlord, who may choose to keep the improvement (with no financial liability to Tenant), or remove it and charge Tenant for the costs of removal and restoration. Landlord may deduct any costs of removal and restoration from Tenant's security deposit. If the security deposit is insufficient to cover the costs of removal and restoration, Landlord may take legal action, if necessary, to collect the balance.

9. If Tenant removes an item that is Landlord's property, Tenant will owe Landlord the fair market value of the item removed plus any costs incurred by Landlord to restore the premises to their original condition.

10. If Landlord and Tenant are involved in any legal proceeding arising out of this agreement, the prevailing party shall recover reasonable attorney fees, court costs, and any costs reasonably necessary to collect a judgment.

Iona Lott _____   _February 10, 20xx_ _____
Landlord   Date

Doug Diep _____   _February 10, 20xx_ _____
Tenant   Date

the space. The law doesn't impose this extra work on landlords, nor does it force you to let tenants do the return-to-original work themselves.

- **Is the object firmly attached to the property?** In general, additions and improvements that are nailed, screwed, or cemented to the building are likely to be deemed "fixtures." For example, hollow-wall screws that anchor a bookcase might convert an otherwise free-standing unit belonging to the tenant to a fixture belonging to you. Similarly, closet rods bolted to the wall become part of the structure and would usually be counted as fixtures. On the other hand, shelving systems that are secured by isometric pressure (spring-loaded rods that press against the ceiling and floor) involve no actual attachment to the wall and, for that reason, are not likely to be classified as fixtures.

Improvements That Plug or Screw In

The act of plugging in an appliance doesn't make the appliance a part of the premises. The same is true for simple connectors or fittings that join an appliance to an electrical or water source. For example, a refrigerator or freestanding stove remains the property of the tenant. Similarly, portable dishwashers that connect to the kitchen faucet by means of a coupling may be removed.

- **What did you and the tenant intend?** Courts will look at statements made by you and the tenant to determine whether there was any understanding as to her right to remove an improvement. In some circumstances, courts will even infer an agreement from your actions—for instance, if you stopped by and gave permission for your tenant to install what you referred to as a portable air conditioner, or helped her lift it into place. By contrast, if the tenant removes light fixtures and, without your knowledge, installs

a custom-made fixture that could not be used in any other space, it is unlikely that the tenant could convince a judge that she reasonably expected to take it with her at the end of her tenancy.

Responding to Improvement and Alteration Requests

If a tenant approaches you with a request to alter your property or install a new feature, chances are that your impulse will be to say no. Don't be too hasty—as you'll see below, requests for telecommunications access (cable access, satellite dishes, and antennas) are governed by special rules. As for other types of requests, perhaps the question comes from an outstanding tenant whom you would like to accommodate and would hate to lose. Instead of adopting a rigid approach, consider these alternatives.

Option One. Is the improvement or alteration one that is easily undone? For example, if your tenant has a year's lease and you plan to repaint when she leaves, you can easily fill and paint any small holes left behind when she removes the bookshelf bolted to the wall (and you can bill her for the spackling costs, as explained below). Knocking out a wall to install a wine closet is a more permanent change and not one you're likely to agree to.

Option Two. Is the improvement or alteration an enhancement to your property? For example, a wine closet might actually add value to your property. If so, depending on the terms of the agreement you reach with your tenant, you may actually come out ahead.

Before you accommodate your tenant's requests, decide which option makes sense in the circumstances and which you prefer. For example, you may have no use for an air conditioner attached to the window frame, and your tenant may want to take it with her. You'll need to make sure that she understands that she is responsible for restoring the window frame to its original condition, and that if her restoration attempts are less than acceptable, you will be justified in deducting from her security deposit the amount of money necessary to do the job right. (And if the deposit is insufficient, you can sue her in small claims court for the excess.) On the other hand, a custom-made window insulation system may enhance your property (and justify a higher rent later on) and won't do your tenant any good if she takes it with her. Be prepared to hear your tenant ask you to pay for at least some of it.

If you and the tenant reach an understanding, put it in writing. As shown in the sample Agreement Regarding Tenant Alterations to Rental Unit, above (and included as a download on the Nolo website— see Appendix B for the link), you will want to carefully describe the project and materials, including:

- whether the improvement or alteration is permanent or portable
- the terms of the reimbursement, if any, and
- how and when you'll pay the tenant, if at all, for labor and materials.

Our agreement makes it clear that the tenant's failure to properly restore the premises, or removal of an alteration that was to be permanent, will result in deductions from her security deposit or further legal action if necessary.

Cable TV Access

If your building is already wired for cable, tenants who want to sign up need only call the cable provider to activate the existing cable line to their unit. But what if you do *not* have cable access available already? And what if you have a contract with one provider, but a tenant wants another?

Congress has decreed that all Americans should have as much access as possible to information that comes through a cable or through wireless transmissions. (Federal Telecommunications Act of 1996, 47 U.S. Code §§ 151 and following.) The Act makes it very difficult for state and local governments, zoning commissions, homeowners' associations, or landlords to restrict a person's ability to take advantage of these types of communications.

Previously Unwired Buildings

If your property does not have cable, you may continue to say no to tenants who ask you for access. But don't be surprised if, in response, your tenant mounts a satellite dish on the balcony, wall, or roof. We discuss your ability to regulate these devices below.

Exclusive Contracts With Cable Providers

The FCC has ruled that in every state, exclusive contracts that you may have with cable companies are unenforceable, and exclusive clauses in existing contracts will not be enforced. So any exclusive clauses you may now have in your contracts are unenforceable, and you may not enter into any new ones. You do *not*, however, have to let any cable company that asks into your building.

Hosting Competing Cable Companies in Multiunit Buildings

Several cable companies may now be competing for your tenants' business. Until recently, adding a cable provider meant letting that company run cable from the street all the way to each rental unit that signed up for the provider's service. The initial section of that cable run, a large cable called the riser, runs from the street to a ground-level utility closet and up to the utility closets on each floor. Adding this cable is not a big deal. But the second leg, called the "home run" portion, consists of wires that run from the riser through hallway ceilings on each floor and toward each individual apartment (the last 12 inches are called "home wires"). Adding a second set of home run wires is expensive and sometimes impossible.

However, you may be able offer the home run part of existing cable to a different cable provider when a tenant asks to switch providers. A federal appellate case covering Colorado, Kansas, New Mexico, Oklahoma, Utah, and Wyoming has held that when a cable company no longer services a customer in a multiunit building, the building owner has the right to ask the provider to share the home run portion of their cable with a competitor, unless the owner's contract with the cable company gives the company the right to maintain unused cable. (*Time Warner Entertainment Co., L.P. v. Everest*, 381 F.3d 1039 (2004).)

> **CAUTION**
>
> **Don't confuse "forced access" with your rights as a landlord.** Forced access refers to the technology that lets consumers choose from among several Internet Service Providers (ISPs) when they subscribe to a cable modem-based broadband service. The argument around forced access is between cable providers and ISPs. Many state laws require cable companies to provide open access to ISPs.

If you have a contract with a cable provider and would like to invite competitors to service tenants who want alternate service, check the contract carefully for language covering maintenance of the cables the provider installed. Look for clauses that give the company the right to maintain and control cables irrespective of whether they're currently used. You may want to review the contract with your attorney. When you negotiate future contracts, keep these points in mind:

- Get rid of language that gives the provider the right to control or maintain inside wiring (including home run wiring) after the contract with you or any individual tenant expires.
- Be sure that you get control of unused home run wiring at the expiration of your contract or when a tenant decides to discontinue service. This will explicitly give you the right to offer it to a competitor. If the cable provider really wants your business, it may agree that unused home run wires will be deemed abandoned. Or, you may have to buy the wires from the provider.

> **TIP**
>
> **Require telecom companies to label their cables when they bring them into your building.** Under the National Electrical Code and FCC regulations, telecoms must remove, abandon, or sell their cables when their license with you is up. If they refuse to do so—or if they're bankrupt—you'll have to do it. To make sure you can identify the abandoned risers (the large cables that run from the street to utility closets) and don't mistakenly cut current risers, require companies to label them with permanent, weatherproof tags, and to give you an as-built diagram that will be amended if the company does any further work during the license term.

Satellite Dishes and Antennas

Wireless communications have the potential to reach more people with less hardware than any cable system. But there is one, essential piece of equipment: A satellite dish with wires connecting it to the television set or computer.

You may be familiar with the car-sized dishes often seen in backyards or on roofs of houses—the pink flamingo of the new age. Now, smaller and cheaper dishes, two feet or less in diameter, are available. Wires from the dishes can easily be run under a door or through an open window to an individual TV or computer. Predictably, tenants have bought dishes and attached them to roofs, windowsills, balconies, and railings. Landlords have reacted strongly, citing their unsightly looks and the potential for liability should a satellite dish fall and injure someone below.

Fortunately, the Federal Communications Commission (FCC) has provided considerable guidance on residential use of satellite dishes and antennas ("Over-the-Air Reception Devices Rule," 47 CFR § 1.4000, further explained in the FCC's Fact Sheet, "Over-the-Air Reception Devices Rule"). Basically, the FCC prohibits landlords from imposing restrictions that unreasonably impair your tenants' abilities to install, maintain, or use an antenna or dish that meet criteria described below. Here's a brief overview of the FCC rule.

RESOURCE
For details on the FCC's rule on satellite dishes and antennas, see www.fcc.gov/guides/installing-consumer-owned-antennas-and-satellite-dishes or call the FCC at 888-CALL-FCC (toll free; 888-TELL-FCC for TTY). The FCC's rule was upheld in *Building Owners and Managers Assn. v. FCC,* 254 F.3d 89 (D.C. Cir. 2001).

Devices Covered by the FCC Rule

The FCC's rule applies to video antennas, including direct-to-home satellite dishes that are less than one meter (39.37 inches) in diameter (or any size in Alaska); TV antennas; and wireless cable antennas. These pieces of equipment receive video programming signals from direct broadcast satellites, wireless cable providers, and television broadcast stations. Antennas up to 18 inches in diameter that transmit as well as receive fixed wireless telecom signals (not just video) are also included.

Exceptions: Antennas used for AM/FM radio, amateur ("ham") and Citizen's Band ("CB") radio, or Digital Audio Radio Services ("DARS") are excluded from the FCC's rule. You may restrict the installation of these types of antennas, in the same way that you can restrict any modification or alteration of rented space.

Permissible Installation of Satellite Dishes and Antennas

Tenants may place antennas or dishes only in their own, exclusive rented space, such as inside the rental unit or on a balcony, terrace, deck, or patio. The device must be wholly within the rented space (if it overhangs the balcony, you may prohibit that placement). Also, you may prohibit tenants from drilling through exterior walls, even if that wall is also part of their rented space.

Tenants *cannot* place their reception devices in common areas, such as roofs, hallways, walkways, or the exterior walls of the building. Exterior windows are no different from exterior walls—for

this reason, placing a dish or antenna on a window by means of a series of suction cups is impermissible under the FCC rule (obviously, such an installation is also unsafe). Tenants who rent single-family homes, however, may install devices in the home itself or on patios, yards, gardens, or similar areas.

Restrictions on Satellite Installation Techniques

Landlords are free to set restrictions on how the devices are installed, as long as the restrictions are not unreasonably expensive, or if the restrictions are imposed for safety reasons or, if your property qualifies, to preserve historic aspects of the structure. You cannot insist that your maintenance personnel (or professional installers) do the work.

Expense

Landlords may not impose a flat fee or charge additional rent to tenants who want to erect an antenna or dish. On the other hand, you may be able to insist on certain installation techniques that will add expense—as long as the cost isn't excessive and reception will not be impaired. Examples of acceptable expenses include:

- insisting that an antenna be painted green in order to blend into the landscaping, or
- requiring the use of a universal bracket that future tenants could use, saving wear and tear on your building.

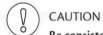

CAUTION
Be consistent in setting rules for tenant improvements. Rules for mounting satellite dishes or antennas shouldn't be more restrictive than those you establish for artwork, flags, clotheslines, or similar items. After all, attaching these telecommunications items is no more intrusive or invasive than bolting a sundial to the porch, screwing a thermometer to the wall, or nailing a rain gauge to a railing. For general guidance, see the discussion above, of "Tenants' Alterations and Improvements."

Safety Concerns

You can insist that tenants place and install devices in a way that will minimize the chances of accidents and will not violate safety or fire codes. For example, you may prohibit placement of a satellite dish on a fire escape, near a power plant, or near a walkway where passersby might accidentally hit their heads. You may also insist on proper installation techniques, such as those explained in the instructions that come with most devices. What if proper installation (attaching a dish to a wall) means that you will have to eventually patch and paint a wall? Can you use this as a reason for preventing installation? No—unless you have legitimate reasons for prohibiting the installation, such as a safety concern. You can, however, charge the tenant for the cost of repairing surfaces when the tenant moves out and removes the device.

TIP

Require tenants who install antennas or dishes to carry renters' insurance. If a device falls or otherwise causes personal injury, the policy will cover a claim. See "Renters' Insurance" in Chapter 2 for more information.

Preserving Your Building's Historical Integrity

It won't be easy to prevent installation on the grounds that doing so is needed to preserve the historical integrity of your property. You can use this argument only if your property is included in (or eligible for) the National Register of Historic Places, the nation's official list of buildings, structures, objects, sites, and districts worthy of preservation for their significance in American history, architecture, archaeology, and culture. For more information on how to qualify for the Register, see www.cr.nps.gov/nr.

Placement and Orientation of Antennas and Reception Devices

Tenants have the right to place an antenna where they'll receive an "acceptable quality" signal. As long as the tenant's chosen spot is within the exclusive rented space, not on an exterior wall or in a common area as discussed above, you may not set rules on placement—for example, you cannot require that an antenna be placed only in the rear of the rental property if this results in the tenant's receiving a "substantially degraded" signal or no signal at all.

Reception devices that need to maintain line-of-sight contact with a transmitter or view a satellite may not work if they're stuck behind a wall or below the roofline. In particular, a dish must be on a south wall, since satellites are in the southern hemisphere. Faced with a reception problem, a tenant may want to move the device to another location or mount it on a pole, so that it clears the obstructing roof or wall. Tenants who have no other workable exclusive space may want to mount their devices on a mast, in hopes of clearing the obstacle. They may do so, depending on the situation:

- **Single-family rentals.** Tenants may erect a mast that's 12 feet above the roofline or less without asking your permission first—and you must allow it if the mast is installed in a safe manner. If the mast is taller than 12 feet, you may require the tenant to obtain your permission before erecting it—but if the installation meets reasonable safety requirements, you should allow its use.

- **Multifamily rentals.** Tenants may use a mast as long as it does not extend beyond their exclusive rented space. For example, in a two-story rental a mast that is attached to the ground-floor patio and extends into the air space opposite the tenant's own second floor would be permissible. On the other hand, a mast attached to a top-story deck, which extends above the roofline or outward over the railing, would not be protected by the FCC's rule—a landlord could prohibit this installation because it extends beyond the tenant's exclusive rented space.

How to Set a Reasonable Policy on Satellite Dishes and Antennas

Although it's not entirely clear, the FCC appears to have ruled that tenants do not need your permission before installing their antennas or dishes—as long as they have placed them within their exclusive rented space and otherwise abided by the rules explained above. This means that you won't get to review a tenant's plans before the tenant installs a dish or antenna—though you can certainly react if you find that the FCC's standards have not been met.

The smart thing to do is to educate your tenants beforehand, in keeping with the FCC's guidelines, so that you don't end up ripping out an antenna or satellite dish that has been placed in the wrong spot or attached in an unsafe manner. In fact, the FCC directs landlords to give tenants written notice of safety restrictions, so that tenants will know in advance how to comply. We suggest that you include guidelines in your Rules and Regulations, or as an attachment to your lease or rental agreement. For guidance on developing sound policies, see the FCC's website at www.fcc.gov/guides/installing-consumer-owned-antennas-and-satellite-dishes.

Supplying a Central Antenna or Satellite Dish for All Tenants

Faced with the prospect of many dishes and antennas adorning an otherwise clean set of balconies, you may want to install a central antenna or dish for use by all.

You may install a central antenna, and may restrict the use of antennas by individual tenants, only if your device provides all of the following:

- **Equal access.** The tenant must be able to get the same programming or fixed wireless service that tenants could receive with their own antennas.
- **Equal quality.** The signal quality to and from the tenant's home via your antenna must be as good as or better than what they could get using their own devices.

- **Equal value.** The costs of using your device must be the same as or less than the cost of installing, maintaining, and using an individual antenna.
- **Equal readiness.** You can't prohibit individual devices if installation of a central antenna will unreasonably delay the tenant's ability to receive programming or fixed wireless services—for example, when your central antenna won't be available for months.

If you install a central antenna after tenants have installed their own, you may require removal of the individual antennas, as long as your device meets the above requirements. In addition, you must pay for the removal of the tenant's device and compensate the tenant for the value of the antenna.

How to Handle Disputes About Antennas and Satellite Dishes

In spite of the FCC's attempts to clarify tenants' rights to reception and landlords' rights to control what happens on their property, there are many possibilities for disagreements. For example, what exactly is "acceptable" reception? If you require antennas to be painted, at what point is the expense considered "unreasonable"?

Ideally, you can try to avoid disputes in the first place by setting reasonable policies. But, if all else fails, here are some tips to help you resolve the problem with a minimum of fuss and expense.

Discussion, Mediation, and Help From the FCC

First, approach the problem the way you would any dispute—talk it out and try to reach an acceptable conclusion. Follow our advice in Chapter 16 for settling disputes on your own—for example, through negotiation or mediation. You'll find the information on the FCC website very helpful. The direct broadcast satellite company, multichannel distribution service, TV broadcast station, or fixed wireless company may also be able to suggest alternatives that are safe and acceptable to both you and your tenant.

Get the FCC Involved

If your own attempts don't resolve the problem, you can call the FCC and ask for oral guidance. You may also formally ask the FCC for a written opinion, called a Declaratory Ruling. For information on obtaining oral or written guidance from the FCC, follow the directions as shown on the FCC website at www.fcc.gov/guides/installing-consumer-owned-antennas-and-satellite-dishes. Keep in mind that unless your objections concern safety or historic preservation, you must allow the device to remain pending the FCC's ruling.

Go to Court

When all else fails, you can head for court. If the antenna or satellite dish hasn't been installed yet and you and the tenant are arguing about the reasonableness of your policies or the tenant's plans, you can ask a court to rule on who's right (just as you would when seeking the FCC's opinion). You'll have to go to a regular trial court for a resolution of your dispute, where you'll ask for an order called a "Declaratory Judgment." Similarly, if the antenna or dish *has* been installed and you want a judge to order it removed, you'll have to go to a regular trial court and ask for such an order. (Unfortunately, the simpler option of small claims court will not usually be available in these situations, because most small courts handle only disputes that can be settled or decided with money, not court opinions about whether it's acceptable to do—or not do—a particular task.)

Needless to say, going to regular trial court means that the case will be drawn-out and expensive. You could handle it yourself, but be forewarned—you'll need to be adept at arguing about First Amendment law and Congressional intent and be willing to spend long hours in the library or online preparing your case. In the end, you may decide that it would have been cheaper to provide a building-wide dish (or good cable access) for all tenants to use.

Landlord's Liability for Tenant Injuries From Dangerous Conditions

As a property owner, you are responsible for keeping your premises safe for tenants and guests. If you don't meet that responsibility, you can be liable for injuries that are caused, for example, by a broken step or defective wiring. Injured tenants can seek financial compensation for medical bills, lost earnings, pain and other physical suffering, permanent physical disability and disfigurement, and emotional distress. Tenants can also look to you for the costs of property damage that results from faulty or unsafe conditions. In extreme cases, a single personal injury verdict against your business could wipe you out.

If a tenant is injured on your property, contact your insurance company the minute you hear about it (your policy probably requires it). Your agent will tell you what to do next—for example, you may need to write down details of the accident. The majority of claims against landlords are settled without trial, usually though negotiations with your insurance company. If your tenant does file a lawsuit, you'll need to hire a lawyer.

This chapter provides an overview of your liability for tenant injuries. Most important, it offers suggestions on how to avoid injuries and liability through preventive repair and maintenance.

 RELATED TOPIC
Related topics covered in this book include:

- Lease and rental agreement provisions covering landlords' and tenants' responsibilities for repairs, damage to premises, and liability-related issues, such as disclosure of hidden defects: Chapter 2

- How to minimize your liability for your property manager's mistakes or illegal acts: Chapter 6

- How to comply with state and local housing laws and avoid safety and maintenance problems and potentially dangerous situations on your rental property: Chapter 9

- Your liability for environmental health hazards: Chapter 11

- Your liability for crime on the premises, including injuries or losses to tenants by strangers or other tenants, and liability for drug dealing on rental property: Chapter 12

- Your liability for nonphysical injuries caused by intentional discrimination (Chapter 5), invasion of privacy (Chapter 13), and retaliatory conduct against the tenant (Chapter 16)

- How to choose a lawyer and pay for legal services: Chapter 18.

When Landlords Have Been Held Liable for Tenant Injuries

Just a few examples of injuries for which tenants have recovered money damages due to the landlord's negligence:

- Tenant falls down a staircase due to a defective handrail.

- Tenant trips over a hole in the carpet on a common stairway not properly maintained by the landlord.

- Tenant injured and property damaged by fire resulting from an obviously defective heater or wiring.

- Tenant gets sick from pesticide sprayed in common areas and on exterior walls without notice.

- Tenant's child is scalded by water from a water heater with a broken thermostat.

- Tenant slips and falls on a puddle of oil-slicked rainwater in the garage.

- Tenant's guest slips on ultraslick floor wax applied by the landlord's cleaning service.

- Tenant receives electrical burns when attempting to insert a stove's damaged plug into a wall outlet.

- Tenant slips and falls on wet grass cuttings left on a common walkway.

How to Prevent Injuries

Preventing an injury is a lot better than arguing about whose fault it was later. Here are steps you can take to protect yourself from lawsuits and hefty insurance settlements—and at the same time make your tenants' lives safer and happier.

Although how to protect against some types of risks may be obvious to you, how to protect against many others won't be. Get help from people who are experienced in identifying and dealing with risks. One excellent resource is your insurance company's safety inspector; your insurance agent can tell you whom to contact. Another good approach is to ask your tenants to identify all safety risks, no matter how small.

Maintain the Property Well

Our first piece of advice is the most obvious, but like a lot of obvious steps, it's often overlooked: Regularly look for dangerous conditions on the property and fix them promptly. Keep an eye out for structural problems, environmental health hazards, and any other dangerous or unsafe conditions that could contribute to an injury. For example, you can head off many trip-and-fall accidents simply by providing good lighting in hallways, parking garages, and other common areas. Keep good records on the dates and details of your property inspections and any follow-up repairs done. Ask your tenants, manager, employees, and insurance company to help you spot problems. When you become aware of a repair problem with an obvious potential for injury, put it on the top of your to-do list. Call in professional inspectors when the potential for injury or damage is great—for example, consult a structural engineer, not your handyman or even your general contractor, if you're not sure about the soundness of your fireplace or chimney.

Comply With Building Codes

Local and state health, safety, and building codes may prescribe very specific requirements for you. For example, electrical codes specify how much of a load you may place on individual circuits; building codes tell you how sturdy your deck piers must be. Once you establish basic compliance with these rules, you can't just forget about them. Because they change occasionally, stay current by reviewing them at least once a year. If your structure and the way you maintain it are up to code, you should avoid most lawsuits based on your violation of a statute.

Warn of Dangers You Can't Fix

If there are problems that you cannot control and eliminate, such as the presence of environmental hazards, educate your tenants to the dangers and their need to follow safety procedures. You have a duty to warn tenants and others about naturally occurring dangers (such as loose soil) and man-made dangers (like low doorways or steep stairs) that may not be obvious but which you know (or should know) about. Disclose hidden defects in your lease or rental agreement (see Clause 20 of the agreements in Chapter 2), or include a section in a move-in letter (Chapter 7), so that it can never be claimed that a tenant was not warned of a dangerous condition. If appropriate, also post warning signs near the hazard.

> **EXAMPLE:** Towering eucalyptus trees lined the side and back yards of the duplex Jack and Edna owned. During windy weather, the trees often dropped big strips of bark and branches. Realizing this, Jack and Edna warned their tenants to steer clear of the trees during windy spells. As an extra precaution, they included a written warning to this effect in a move-in letter to new tenants and posted signs near the trees.

Solicit and Respond Quickly to Tenants' Safety Complaints

As explained in "Responding to Tenant Complaints" in Chapter 9, make sure tenants know that you are always receptive to a legitimate concern regarding building safety. Respond appropriately—a sticky front door lock that still works might merit having the locksmith come the next day; a broken lock deserves the 24-hour locksmith.

Back your policy up with a good record-keeping system. Doing so will help you should you be challenged later. For example, suppose a tenant notifies you of a loose step. As soon as possible, you should post warning tape and signs, and arrange to have it repaired soon. Writing in your records that the loose step will be fixed tomorrow by your handyman, and noting that you placed the tape and signs, and advised your tenant to take an alternate staircase, will show that you did all that was reasonably necessary. If the tenant disregards your advice and uses the stairs anyway, you'll be able to show that you acted prudently and should not be responsible for any injuries that he suffered as a result of his decisions.

Install and Maintain Basic Safety Features

Make sure your property is well equipped with smoke detectors, fire extinguishers, good interior lighting, and ample outside lighting. Candidly appraise the security situation around your property, and improve protection if the conditions warrant it. Chapter 12 discusses liability for criminal acts on the property.

Don't Allow Dangerous Pets

It's not common, but you could be liable for the injuries caused by a tenant's pet, be it a common household companion or exotic animal.

An injured person would have to show that you:

1. actually knew (or, in view of the circumstances, must have known) of the animal's dangerous propensities, and
2. could have prevented the injury.

Fear of liability is not a reason to impose a blanket no-pets rule; cases against landlords are actually very rare. But just as you keep an eye on other dangerous conditions on the property, be aware of the potential for injury from pets. If a tenant does have a demonstrably dangerous pet, he has caused a legal nuisance, and you can require that the tenant get rid of the animal or face eviction. In Chapter 9, see "Don't Allow Nuisances."

CAUTION

Don't let tenants keep wild animals. Legally, keeping wild animals is generally considered an "ultrahazardous activity." You will be presumed to know of the dangerous aspects of a wild animal as soon as you learn that it's on the property. So if your tenant keeps a monkey and you know (or should know) about it, a court will assume

that you understood the danger, and you may be liable if the animal causes injury and you failed to take steps to prevent it.

Remove Dangers to Children

If children are drawn onto your property due to an irresistibly interesting (to children) but dangerous feature, such as a stack of building materials or an abandoned refrigerator or well (known in legal jargon as an "attractive nuisance"), you must exercise special care. If the danger can be cleaned up or removed (like a pile of junk or an abandoned refrigerator), do so. If not, place physical barriers that will keep children away from it. Warning signs aren't enough—young children can't read, and all children tend to ignore warnings.

Even if you don't create a dangerous situation yourself, but allow a tenant to do so, you may also be legally liable. For example, a tree house that your tenant builds in the backyard or a play structure that parents buy for their own children might attract other neighborhood children. If one of them falls from the tree or structure and is injured, you could be liable because you let the attractive nuisance remain on your property.

> **EXAMPLE:** An apartment building owner took great pride in the fishpond in the courtyard. The yard was accessible to the general public, and neighborhood children frequently came to watch the fish. When one child fell in and nearly drowned, the child's parents sued the landlord. The landlord was found liable for the child's accident on the grounds of negligence—the landlord should have known that the fishpond was dangerous and that unsupervised children could come onto the property and fall into the pond. The landlord should have gotten rid of the pond or fenced it off so that small children were kept out.

Laws sometimes regulate activities and conditions that are attractive and dangerous to children. For example, laws commonly require the removal of doors from unused refrigerators and the fencing or removal of abandoned cars or piles of junk.

Be sure to inform tenants of your concerns regarding anything that might be attractive and dangerous to children. For example, if the tenant of your single-family home has placed a trampoline on the property, make sure it's behind a sturdy fence so that neighborhood kids don't wander in and use it in a dangerous manner. If it can't be fenced, insist that it be removed.

Take Special Precautions With Swimming Pools

Swimming pools can mean deep trouble because they are so dangerous, and attractive, to children. Many places have laws that require fences around swimming pools and impose construction and height requirements on those fences. Landlords who fail to comply with such fencing requirements are often found liable for tragic drownings.

If your property includes a pool, you must of course comply with all safety laws. You should also take special care to make sure your tenants and their guests appreciate the dangers involved. Remind tenants that they are responsible for the proper supervision of their children. All the fencing in the world will not protect a young child who is left unattended inside a pool enclosure.

Rules requiring constant adult supervision of children and the need to walk carefully on wet, slippery surfaces should be part of any move-in letter and the rules and regulations that are part of your lease or rental agreement. The rules (including a reminder that there is no lifeguard on duty) should be repeated on signs posted near the pool. Pool supply stores are a good source of easy-to-read signs.

Supervise Contractors and Other Workers

If construction work is done on your property, make sure that the contractor and any workers (including your own) in charge of the work secure the site and remove or lock up dangerous tools or equipment whenever the site is left unattended. Remember, a pile of sand or a stack of sheet rock might look like work to an adult, but fun to a child. You might consider sending your tenants written notice of the intended project, suggesting that they take care during the construction period.

Using Exculpatory Clauses to Shield Yourself From Liability

Landlords used to be able to protect themselves from most lawsuits brought by tenants by using a lease clause that absolved the landlord of responsibility for injuries suffered by a tenant, even those caused by the landlord's negligence. Known as "exculpatory clauses," these blanket provisions are now rarely enforced by courts.

In unusual situations, you may want to include a narrowly worded "exculpatory clause" in your lease, to shield yourself from liability for injuries. For example, if you delegate appropriate repair and maintenance duties to a tenant (see Chapter 9 for tips on delegation of repairs), you might want to make it clear that the tenant is not to look to you if he injures himself in the course of his duties. An exculpatory clause, however, will *not* shield you from liability if your tenant injures a third party.

EXAMPLE: Sadie and Hal live in one half of their duplex and rent out the other. They offer Fred, their tenant, a rent reduction if he will be responsible for the upkeep of the lawn. As part of the bargain, Fred agrees to absolve Sadie and Hal of any liability if a defect in the lawn causes him an injury. Because this agreement is the result of good-faith negotiations on both sides, each party receives a benefit from the deal, and the delegated duties (gardening on a small piece of property affecting only the landlords and their one tenant) could safely and reasonably be performed by their tenant, the agreement would likely be upheld if either side challenged it later in court.

When Fred trips on a sprinkler and hurts his ankle, he is bound by the exculpatory clause and cannot sue Sadie and Hal for his injury. But when Mac, a delivery person, slips on wet grass cuttings that Fred carelessly leaves on the walkway, Fred, Sadie, and Hal find themselves at the other end of Mac's personal injury claim.

You can't use an exculpatory clause to shield yourself from all liability; if you're negligent, you're almost certainly going to be held responsible for any tenant injuries that result, no matter what your lease says.

Liability and Other Property Insurance

A well-designed insurance program can protect your rental property from losses caused by many types of perils, including damage to the property caused by fire, storms, burglary, and vandalism. A comprehensive policy will also include liability insurance, covering injuries or losses suffered by others as the result of defective conditions on the property. Equally important, liability insurance covers the cost of settling personal injury claims, including lawyers' bills for defending personal injury lawsuits.

> **RELATED TOPIC**
>
> **"How to Meet Your Legal Repair and Mainte-nance Responsibilities," in Chapter 9,** explains how to make sure you're covered by the insurance policy of any contractor you work with.

Choosing Liability Insurance Coverage

All landlords should buy liability insurance. Advice on property insurance in general and working with an insurance agent are covered below.

Get Enough Coverage!

Liability policies are designed to cover you against lawsuit settlements and judgments up to the amount of the policy limit, including both what you pay the injured person and the lawyers hired to handle the lawsuit. They provide coverage for a host of common perils, such as tenants falling and getting injured on a defective staircase. Liability policies usually state a dollar limit per occurrence and an aggregate dollar limit for the policy year. For example, your policy may say that it will pay up to $300,000 per occurrence for personal injury and a total of $1 million in any one policy year.

Depending on the value of your property and the value of the assets you are seeking to protect, buying more coverage in the form of an "umbrella policy" is a very good idea, especially in large metropolitan areas, where personal injury damage awards can be very high. Umbrella policies are not expensive, because they are rarely called upon—so the premium may be a relatively cheap way to obtain peace of mind, at the very least.

Buy Commercial General Liability Coverage

Commercial General Liability coverage is the broadest type of liability coverage, described just above, that you can purchase. Make sure your liability policy covers not only physical injury but also libel, slander, discrimination, unlawful and retaliatory eviction, and invasion of privacy suffered by tenants and guests. This kind of coverage can be very important in discrimination claims, see Chapter 5.

Buy Non-Owned Auto Liability Insurance

Be sure to carry liability insurance not only on your own vehicles but also on your manager's car or truck if it will be used for business purposes. Non-owned auto insurance will protect you from liability for accidents and injuries caused by your manager or other employee while running errands for you in their own vehicle.

Terrorism Insurance

The huge losses of September 11, 2001 produced a predictable response from insurance companies: They began writing liability and property policies that specifically excluded coverage for losses due to acts of terrorism. Congress reacted by passing the Terrorism Risk Insurance Act (15 U.S. Code §§ 6701 and following; expires Dec. 31, 2020) to help ensure that property owners have access to adequate, affordable terrorism insurance. The law requires insurance companies to offer coverage for losses due to acts of terrorism, and to void any clauses in existing policies that exclude coverage. If you want coverage under an existing policy, you are entitled to buy it. For more information, see the U.S. Department of the Treasury's website at www.treasury.gov, and type Terrorism Risk Insurance Program into the search box on the home page.

What Liability Insurance Doesn't Cover

Punitive damages are extra monetary awards, above the amount needed to compensate an injured person. They are intended to punish willful or malicious behavior.

As you might expect, insurers would like to be able to exclude punitive damages from coverage, but the industry has never adopted a standard exclusion clause. (Insurance policies are typically made up of canned, commonly used clauses that are used by virtually every insurance company.) If a policy does not specifically state whether or not punitive damages are covered (and most do not), it will be up to the courts of the state where the policyholder lives to decide whether standard policy language covers punitive awards.

States have not been consistent in their treatment of this issue. Courts in some states have ruled that punitive damages are not covered by standard comprehensive liability policies, while others have reached the opposite conclusion. Your insurance agent should be able to tell you how the courts in your state have ruled.

It's clear, however, that intentional harm or violations of criminal statutes are not covered. But it is often a matter of debate as to whether a particular act was intended. While illegal discrimination, physical assaults, harassment, or retaliation (by you or your manager) are often treated by insurers as intentional acts not covered by the policy, most liability insurers will at least pay for the defense of such lawsuits.

Choosing Property Insurance

When you go to buy property coverage, there are four main questions to consider.

What Business Property Is Insured?

Be sure your insurance covers all the property you want protected. In addition to your basic property insurance, which insures the entire building, you may need additional policies to cover:

- additions under construction

- outdoor fixtures, such as pole lights
- washing machines and other appliances
- items used to maintain the building, such as gardening equipment and tools
- boilers and heavy equipment, or
- personal business property such as computers used in managing your rental business.

 TIP
Make sure tenants know that your insurance does not cover loss or damage (caused by theft or fire) to their personal property. Tenants need to buy their own renters' insurance to cover their personal property. This does not mean, however, that you cannot be sued by a tenant (or his insurance company) if your negligence caused his loss. Your commercial general liability policy should cover you in this event.

What Perils Are Insured Against?

Be sure you know what kind of losses the property policy covers. Fire damage is covered in even the most basic policies, but damage from mud slides, windstorms, and the weight of snow may be excluded. Earthquake insurance and flood insurance are typically separate. They are often expensive and have a very high deductible, but they still are a good option if your building is highly susceptible to earthquake or flood damage. Whatever policy you decide on, read it carefully before you pay for it—not just when you've suffered a loss.

Check out "loss of rents" insurance, which covers you for the loss of rents from units that have been sidelined—for example, due to a fire or other calamity. This coverage will kick in even if you can move the tenant to another, vacant unit.

How Much Insurance Should You Buy?

Obviously, the higher the amount of coverage, the higher the premiums. You don't want to waste money on insurance, but you do want to carry enough so that a loss wouldn't jeopardize your business.

Be sure to carry enough insurance on the building to rebuild it. There's no need to insure the total value of your real property (land and structures), because land doesn't burn. Especially if you're in an area where land is very valuable, this is a big consideration. If you're in doubt as to how much it would cost you to rebuild, have an appraisal made so you know that your idea of value is realistic. (Be sure to get a rebuilding quote, not a quote on the sales value of the structure.) Because the cost of rebuilding may increase, it's wise to get a new appraisal every few years. Your insurance agent should be able to help you.

Should You Buy Coverage for Replacement Cost?

Basic fire insurance contracts cover the actual cash value of the structure, not its full replacement value. But policies are routinely available with replacement cost coverage. This is the coverage you want.

Plain "cost of replacement" coverage, however, won't be adequate if you need to bring an older building up to code after a fire or other damage. Legal requirements adopted since the building was constructed will probably require a stronger, safer, more fire-resistant building when you rebuild. Doing this can cost far more than simply replacing the old building. To cope with this possibility, you want a policy that will not only replace the building but pay for all legally required upgrades. This coverage is called "Ordinance of Law Coverage," and it is almost never included in standard policies. You must ask for it.

Working With an Insurance Agent

Here are some tips for choosing an insurance agent.

Find a knowledgeable agent who takes the time to analyze your business operations and come up with a sensible program for you. Get recommendations from people who own property similar to yours, or from real estate people with several years' experience—they will know who comes through and who doesn't. Working with an agent who knows your business is advantageous because that person is already a fair way along the learning curve when it comes to helping you select affordable and appropriate insurance.

Steer clear of an agent who whips out a package policy and claims it will solve your problems. While there are some excellent packages available, neither you nor your insurance agent will know for sure until the agent asks you a lot of questions and thoroughly understands your business. If the agent is unable or unwilling to tailor your coverage to your particular business, find someone else.

Be frank with your agent. Reveal all areas of unusual risk. If you fail to disclose all the facts, you may not get the coverage you need. Or, in some circumstances, the insurance company may later take the position that you misrepresented the nature of your operation and, for that reason, deny you coverage.

Make sure you know what your policy covers and what's excluded. Does the policy exclude damage from a leaking sprinkler system? From a boiler explosion? From an earthquake? If so, and these are risks you face, find out whether they can be covered by paying an extra premium.

Check out pet restrictions. Be sure to find out whether your insurance policy includes restrictions as to species, breeds of dog, or weight and number of pets allowed.

Insist on a highly rated carrier. Insurance companies are rated according to their financial condition and size. The most recognized rater is the A.M. Best Company, which assigns letter ratings according to financial stability (A++ is the highest) and Roman numeral ratings reflecting the size of a company's surplus (XV is the best). Given that 80% of American companies receive an A rating or higher, you don't want to choose a company rated less than that. As to surplus, you will be on solid ground to require an "X." Your local public library's business section or reference desk will likely have the *Best's Key Rating Guide.* For details, see www.ambest.com.

 RELATED TOPIC

If you have a manager or other employees, you may need workers' compensation insurance. See Chapter 6.

CAUTION
Consider insuring the cost of rubble removal and engineering surveys. Ruined buildings don't just disappear. They have to be demolished, carted away, and disposed of, and you might have to hire an engineer to oversee the whole process. A standard policy won't cover these costs, which can be astonishing—for example, you might have to comply with special disposal procedures if there is lead paint or asbestos in the debris. You can buy an endorsement for a reasonable sum that will protect you.

Saving Money on Insurance

Few landlords can really afford to adequately insure themselves against every possible risk. You need to decide what types of insurance are really essential and how much coverage to buy. Many factors affect this decision, including the condition and location of the rental property. Here are some guidelines that should help.

Set Priorities

Beyond any required coverage for your business, ask these questions: What insurance do I really need? What types of property losses would threaten the viability of my business? What kinds of liability lawsuits might wipe me out? Use your answers to tailor your coverage to protect against these potentially disastrous losses. Get enough property and liability coverage to protect yourself from common claims. Buy insurance against serious risks where the insurance is reasonably priced.

Select High Deductibles

The difference between the cost of a policy with a $250 deductible (the amount of money you must pay out of pocket before insurance coverage kicks in) and one with a $500, $1,000, or even higher deductible is significant—particularly if you add up the premium savings for five or ten years. Consider using money saved with a higher deductible to buy other types of insurance you really need. For example, the amount you save by having a higher deductible might pay for "loss of rents" coverage.

Take Preventive Measures to Avoid Losses

Good safety and security measures, such as regular property inspections, special fire prevention measures, or requiring that tenants purchase renters' insurance may eliminate the need for some types of insurance or lead to lower insurance rates. (When tenants have renters' policies, accidents that they cause will be covered by their policies; without them, your policy may end up footing the bill. When the chances of a claim go down, rates should decrease, too.) Ask your insurance agent what you can do to get a better rate.

Comparison Shop

No two companies charge exactly the same rates; you may be able to save a significant amount by shopping around. But unusually low prices may be a sign of a shaky company. Or it may be that you're comparing policies that provide very different coverage. Make sure you know what you're buying, and review your coverage and rates periodically.

RESOURCE
For more information on choosing business insurance, see the Insurance Information Institute's website at www.iii.org.

Your Liability for Tenant Injuries

If a tenant is injured on your property, are you liable? It isn't always easy to determine. Basically, you may be liable for injuries resulting from your:

- negligence or unreasonably careless conduct
- violation of a health or safety law
- failure to make certain repairs
- failure to keep the premises habitable, or
- reckless or intentional acts.

In rare instances, state law may make you automatically liable for certain kinds of injuries, even if you weren't careless.

More than one of these legal theories may apply in your situation, and a tenant can use all of them when pressing a claim. The more plausible reasons a tenant can give for your liability, the better the tenant will do when negotiating with your insurance company or making a compelling case in court.

Negligence

A tenant who files a personal injury claim will most likely charge that you acted negligently—that is, acted carelessly, in a way that wasn't reasonable under the circumstances—and that the injury was caused by your carelessness.

Negligence is always determined in light of the unique facts of each situation. For example, if you don't put adequate lights in a dark, remote stairwell, and a tenant is hurt because she couldn't see the steps and fell, your failure to install the lights might be negligence. On the other hand, extra lights in a lobby that's already well-lit would not be a reasonable expectation.

Whether or not you were negligent and are likely to be held responsible for a tenant's injury depends on answers to six questions. Your insurance adjuster (or a judge or jury, if the case goes to court) will consider these same questions when evaluating a tenant's claim.

Question 1:   Did you control the area where the tenant was hurt or the thing that hurt the tenant?

In most cases, you will be held responsible for an injury if you were legally obligated to maintain and repair the injury-causing factor. For example, you normally have control over a stairway in a common area, and if its disrepair causes a tenant to fall, you will likely be held liable. You also have control over the building's utility systems. If a malfunction causes injury (like boiling water in a tenant's sink because of a broken thermostat), you will likewise be held responsible. On the other hand, if a tenant is hurt when his own bookcase falls on him, you won't be held responsible, because you do not control how the bookcase was built, set up, or maintained.

Question 2:   Was an accident foreseeable?

You may be responsible for an injury if a tenant can show that an accident was foreseeable. For example, common sense tells anyone that loose handrails or stairs are likely to lead to accidents, but it would be unusual for injuries to result from peeling wallpaper or a thumbtack that's fallen from a bulletin board. If a freak accident does happen, chances are you will not be held liable.

Question 3:   How difficult or expensive would it have been for you to reduce the risk of injury?

The chances that you will be held responsible for an accident are greater if a reasonably priced response could have averted it. If something as simple as warning signs, a bright light, or caution tape could have prevented people from tripping over an unexpected step leading to a patio, you should have taken the step. But if there is a great risk of very serious injury, you will be expected to spend more money to avert it. For example, a high-rise deck with rotten support beams must be repaired, regardless of the cost, because there is a great risk of collapse and dreadful injuries to anyone on the deck. If you knew about the condition of the deck and failed to repair it, you would surely be held liable if an accident did occur.

Question 4:   Was a serious injury likely to result from the problem?

If a major injury was the likely result of a dangerous situation—the pool ladder was broken, making it likely a tenant would fall as he climbed out—you are expected to take the situation seriously and fix it fast.

The answers to these four questions should tell you whether or not there was a dangerous condition on your property that you had a legal duty to deal with. Lawyers call this having a "duty of due care."

> EXAMPLE 1: Mark broke his leg when he tripped on a loose step on the stairway from the lobby to the first floor. Because the step had been loose for several months, chances are his landlord's insurance company would settle a claim like this. Mark's position is strong because:

- Landlords are legally responsible for (in control of) the condition of the common stairways.
- It was highly foreseeable to any reasonable person that someone would slip on a loose step.
- Securing the step would have been simple and inexpensive.
- The probable result of leaving the stair loose—falling and injuring oneself on the stairs—is a serious matter.

EXAMPLE 2: Lee slipped on a marble that had been dropped on the public sidewalk outside his apartment by another tenant's child a few minutes earlier. Lee twisted his ankle and lost two weeks' work. Lee will have a tough time establishing that his landlord had a duty to protect him from this injury because:

- Landlords have little control over the public sidewalk.
- The likelihood of injury from something a tenant drops is fairly low.
- The burden on a landlord to eliminate all possible problems at all times by constantly inspecting or sweeping the sidewalk is unreasonable.
- Finally, the seriousness of any likely injury resulting from not checking constantly is open to great debate.

EXAMPLE 3: James suffered a concussion when he hit his head on a dull-colored overhead beam in the apartment garage. When the injury occurred, he was standing on a stool, loading items onto the roof rack of his SUV. Did his landlord have a duty to take precautions in this situation? Probably not, but it's not cut-and-dried:

- Landlords exercise control over the garage and have a responsibility to reasonably protect tenants from harm there.
- The likelihood of injury from a beam is fairly slim, because most people don't stand on stools in the garage, and those who do have the opportunity to see the beam and avoid it.
- As to eliminating the condition that led to the injury, it's highly unlikely anyone would expect a landlord to rebuild the garage. But it's possible that a judge might think it reasonable to paint the beams a bright color and post warning signs, especially if lots of people put trucks and other large vehicles in the garage.

- Injury from low beams is likely to be to the head, which is a serious matter.

In short, this situation is too close to call, but an insurance adjuster or jury might decide that James was partially at fault (for not watching out for the beams) and reduce any award accordingly.

If, based on these first four questions, you had a legal duty to deal with a condition on the premises that posed a danger to tenants, keep going. There are two more questions to consider.

Question 5: Did you fail to take reasonable steps to prevent an accident?

The law doesn't expect you to take Herculean measures to shield tenants from a condition that poses some risk. You are required to take only reasonable precautions. For example, if a stair was in a dangerous condition, was your failure to fix it unreasonable in the circumstances? Let's take the broken step that Mark (Example 1, above) tripped over. Obviously, leaving it broken for months is unreasonably careless—that is, negligent—under the circumstances.

But what if the step had torn loose only an hour earlier, when another tenant dragged a heavy footlocker up the staircase? Mark's landlord would probably concede that he had a duty to maintain the stairways, but would argue that the manager's daily sweeping and inspection of the stairs that same morning met that burden. In the absence of being notified of the problem, the landlord would probably claim that his inspection routine met his duty of keeping the stairs safe. If a jury agreed, Mark would not be able to establish that the landlord acted unreasonably under the circumstances.

Question 6: Did your failure to take reasonable steps to keep tenants safe cause an injury?

This question establishes the crucial link between your negligence and a tenant's injury. Not every dangerous situation results in an accident. A tenant has to prove that an injury was the result of your carelessness, and not some other reason. Sometimes this is self-evident: One minute a tenant is fine, and the next minute she's slipped on a freshly washed floor and has a broken arm. But it's not always so simple. For example, in the case of the loose stair, the landlord might be able to show that the tenant barely lost his balance because of the loose stair and that he had really injured his ankle during a touch football game he'd just played.

Landlord Liability for Injuries to Guests and Trespassers

If you have acted negligently and a tenant's guest or even a trespasser is injured, will you be liable? The answer varies with each state. In a few states, you're liable no matter why the injured person was on your property. As a general rule, however, you have a reduced duty of care when it comes to nontenants, especially trespassers. For example, a tenant who is injured when falling from an unfenced porch will have a fairly strong case for charging you with negligence; a trespasser, even an innocent one who has come to the wrong address, who falls off the same porch might have a harder time recovering from you.

Here's a final example, applying all six questions to a tenant's injury.

> **EXAMPLE:** Scotty's apartment complex had a pool bordered by a concrete deck. On his way to the pool, Scotty slipped and fell, breaking his arm. The concrete where he fell was slick because the landlord had spilled cleaning solution on it.
> - Did the landlord control the pool area and the cleaning solution? Absolutely. The pool was part of a common area, and the landlord had done the cleaning.
> - Was an accident like Scotty's foreseeable? Certainly. It's likely that a barefoot person heading for the pool would slip on slick cement.
> - Could the landlord have eliminated the dangerous condition without much effort or money? Of course. All that was necessary was to hose the deck down.
> - How serious was the probable injury? Falling on cement presents a high likelihood of broken bones, a serious injury.

The answers to these four questions established that the landlord owed Scotty a duty of care.
- Had his landlord also breached this duty? A jury would probably answer yes—and conclude that leaving spilled cleaning solution on the deck was an unreasonable thing to do.
- Did the spilled cleaning solution cause Scotty's fall? This one is easy, because several people saw the accident and others could describe Scotty's robust fitness before the fall. Because Scotty himself hadn't been careless, he has a good case.

Violation of a Health or Safety Law

Many state and local laws require smoke detectors, sprinklers, inside-release security bars on windows, childproof fences around swimming pools, and so on. To put real teeth in these important laws, legislators (and sometimes the courts) have decided that a landlord who doesn't take reasonable steps to comply with certain health or safety statutes is legally considered negligent. If that negligence results in an injury, the landlord is liable for it. A tenant doesn't need to prove that an accident was foreseeable or likely to be serious; nor does a tenant have to show that complying with the law would have been relatively inexpensive. The legal term for this rule is "negligence per se."

> **EXAMPLE:** A local housing code specifies that all kitchens must have grounded power plugs. There are no grounded plugs in the kitchen of one of your rental units. As a result, a tenant is injured when using an appliance in an otherwise safe manner. In many states, your violation of the law would mean you were legally negligent. If a tenant can show that the ungrounded plug caused injury, you will be held liable.

Your violation of a health or safety law may also indirectly cause an injury. For example, if you let the furnace deteriorate in violation of local law, and a tenant is injured trying to repair it, you will probably be liable, unless the tenant's repair efforts are extremely careless.

EXAMPLE: The state housing code requires landlords to provide hot water. In the middle of the winter, a tenant's hot water heater has been broken for a week, despite his repeated complaints to the landlord. Finally, to give a sick child a hot bath, a tenant carries pots of steaming water from the stove to the bathtub. Doing this, he spills the hot water and burns himself seriously.

The tenant sues the landlord for failure to provide hot water as required by state law. Many people would probably conclude that the tenant's response to the lack of hot water was a foreseeable one, and, knowing this, the landlord's insurance company would probably be willing to offer a fair settlement.

Failure to Make Certain Repairs

For perfectly sensible reasons, many landlords do not want tenants to undertake even fairly simple tasks like painting, plastering, or unclogging a drain. Many leases and rental agreements (including the ones in this book) prohibit tenants from making any repairs or alterations without the landlord's consent, or limit what a tenant can do. If you do allow tenants to perform maintenance tasks, be sure to do so with a clear, written agreement, as explained in Chapter 9.

But in exchange for reserving the right to make all these repairs yourself, the law imposes a responsibility. If, after being told about a problem, you don't maintain or repair something a tenant is not to touch—for example, an electrical switch—and the tenant is injured as a result, you could be held liable. The legal reason is that you breached the contract (the lease) by not making the repairs. (You may be negligent, as well; remember, there is nothing to stop a tenant from presenting multiple reasons why you should be held liable.)

EXAMPLE: The sash cords in the living room window in Shanna's apartment break, making it necessary to support the entire weight of the window while raising or lowering it and securing it with a block of wood. Because Shanna's lease includes a clause forbidding repairs of any nature, she reports the problem to Len, the owner. Despite his promises to repair the window, Len never gets around to it. One hot summer evening Shanna attempts to raise the heavy window, but her hands slip and the window crashes down on her arm, breaking it. Shanna threatens to sue Len, claiming that he negligently delayed the repair of the window, and further that the lease clause forbidding any repairs by the tenant contractually obligated Len to attend to the problem in a reasonably prompt manner. Mindful of the strength of Shanna's arguments, and fearful that a jury would side with Shanna and give her a large award, Len's insurance company settles the case for several thousand dollars.

Failure to Keep the Premises Habitable

One of your basic responsibilities is to keep the rental property in a "habitable" condition. Failure to maintain a habitable dwelling may make you liable for injuries caused by the substandard conditions. For example, a tenant who is bitten by a rat in a vermin-infested building may argue that your failure to maintain a rat-free building constituted a breach of your duty to keep the place habitable, which in turn led to the injury. The tenant must show that you knew of the defect and had a reasonable amount of time to fix it.

This theory applies only when the defect is so serious that the rental unit is unfit for human habitation. For example, a large, jagged broken picture window would make the premises unfit for habitation in North Dakota in winter, but a torn screen door in southern California obviously would not.

EXAMPLE: Jose notified his landlord about the mice that he had seen several times in his kitchen. Despite Jose's repeated complaints, the landlord did nothing to eliminate the problem. When Jose reached into his cupboard for a box of cereal, he was bitten by a mouse. Jose sued his landlord for the medical treatment he required, including extremely painful rabies shots. He alleged that the landlord's failure to eradicate the rodent problem constituted a breach of the implied warranty of habitability, and that this breach was responsible for his injury. The jury agreed and gave Jose a large monetary award.

(Jose might also claim that the landlord was negligent because he didn't get rid of the mice or violated a state or local statute concerning rodent control.)

Reckless or Intentional Acts

"Recklessness" usually means extreme carelessness regarding an obvious defect or problem. A landlord who is aware of a long-existing and obviously dangerous defect but neglects to correct it may be guilty of recklessness, not just ordinary carelessness.

If you or an employee acted recklessly, a tenant's monetary recovery could be significant. This is because a jury has the power to award not only actual damages (which include medical bills, loss of earnings, and pain and suffering) but also extra, "punitive" damages for outrageous or extremely careless behavior. Punitive damages, which are not covered by insurance, are awarded to punish recklessness and to send a message to others who might behave similarly. The size of the punitive award is likewise up to the jury and is often reduced later by a judge or appellate court.

> **EXAMPLE:** The handrail along the stairs in Jack's apartment house had been hanging loose for several months. Two or three times, Jack taped the supports to the wall, which did no good. One night when Hilda, one of Jack's tenants, reached for the railing, the entire thing came off in her hand, causing her to fall and break her hip.
>
> Hilda sued Jack for her injuries. In her lawsuit, she pointed to the ridiculously ineffective measures that Jack had taken to deal with a clearly dangerous situation, and charged that he had acted with reckless disregard for the safety of his tenants. (Hilda also argued that Jack was negligent because of his unreasonable behavior and because he had violated a local ordinance regarding maintenance of handrails.) The jury agreed with Hilda and awarded her punitive damages in addition to actual damages.

Intentional Harm

If you or your manager struck and injured a tenant during an argument, that would be an intentional act for which you would be liable. Less obvious, but no less serious, are emotional or psychological injuries which can also be inflicted intentionally. Intentional infliction of emotional distress may arise in these situations:

- **Sexual harassment.** Repeated, disturbing attentions of a sexual nature which leave a tenant fearful, humiliated, and upset can form the basis for a claim of intentional harm.

  EXAMPLE: Rita's landlord Mike took every opportunity to make suggestive comments about her looks and social life. When she asked him to stop, he replied that he was "just looking out for her" and stepped up his unwanted attentions. Rita finally had enough, broke the lease, and moved out. When Mike sued her for unpaid rent, she turned around and sued him for the emotional distress caused by his harassment. He was slapped with a multithousand-dollar judgment, including punitive damages.

- **Assault.** Threatening or menacing someone without actually touching them is an assault, which can be enormously frightening and lead to psychological damage.
- **Repeated invasions of privacy.** Deliberately invading a tenant's privacy—by unauthorized entries, for example—may cause extreme worry and distress.

The Law Makes You Liable

In rare circumstances, you may be responsible for a tenant's injury even though you did your best to create and maintain a safe environment and were not negligent. This legal principle is called "strict liability," or liability without fault.

In most states, strict liability is imposed only when a hidden defect poses an unreasonably dangerous risk of harm to a group of persons who can't detect or avoid it. For example, Massachusetts landlords are subject to strict liability if tenants are poisoned by lead-based paint.

If a Tenant Was at Fault, Too

If the tenant is partially to blame for an injury, your liability for the tenant's losses will be reduced accordingly.

Tenant Carelessness

If a tenant is guilty of unreasonable carelessness—for example, he was drunk and didn't watch his step when he tripped on a loose tread on a poorly maintained stairway—he may not be able to collect damages from the landlord (or may not collect as much as he would have if he hadn't been careless). It depends on the state.

- In a number of states, tenants can collect according to the percent of blame attributed to the landlord, no matter how careless the tenant was, too. For example, a tenant can collect 75% of the damages if the landlord was 75% to blame.
- Some states allow tenants to recover a portion of their damages only if their carelessness was equal to or lower than the landlord's. In these states, for example, if the tenant and landlord were equally blameworthy, the tenant could collect only half of the damages. A tenant who was 51% at fault couldn't collect at all.
- In other states, tenants can recover a portion of their damages only if their carelessness was less than the landlord's. If the tenant and landlord were equally at fault, the tenant gets nothing; a tenant who was 25% at fault gets only 75% of his damages.
- A few states don't allow a tenant to collect a dime if he was at all careless, even 1% at fault.

Tenant Risk-Taking

If a tenant deliberately chose to act in a way that caused or worsened the injury, another doctrine may apply. Called "assumption of risk," it refers to a tenant who knows the danger of a certain action and takes the chance anyway.

> **EXAMPLE:** In a hurry to get to work, a tenant takes a shortcut to the garage by using a walkway that he knows has uneven, broken pavement. The tenant disregards the sign posted by his landlord: "Use Front Walkway Only." If the tenant trips and hurts his knee, he'll have a hard time pinning blame on his landlord, because he deliberately chose a known, dangerous route to the garage.

In some states, a tenant who is injured as a result of putting himself in harm's way cannot recover anything, even if your negligence contributed to the injury. In other states, a tenant's recovery is diminished according to the extent that he appreciated the danger involved.

How Much Money an Injured Tenant May Recover

A tenant who was injured on your property and has convinced an insurance adjuster or jury that you are responsible can ask for monetary compensation, called "compensatory damages." Given the often quirky nature of American juries, these costs can be enormous. Here are things a tenant can be compensated for:

Medical care and related expenses. This includes doctors' and physical therapists' bills, including future care.

Missed work time. A tenant can sue for lost wages and income while out of work and undergoing medical treatment for injuries. He can also recover for expected losses due to continuing care.

Pain and other physical suffering. The type of injury the tenant has suffered and its expected duration affect the amount awarded for pain and suffering. Insurance adjusters require objective corroboration of a tenant's level of discomfort, such as a doctor's prescription of strong pain medication. The longer a tenant's recovery period, the greater the pain and suffering.

Permanent physical disability or disfigurement. Long-lasting or permanent effects—such as scars, back or joint stiffness, or a significant reduction in mobility—increase the amount of damages.

Loss of family, social, career, and educational experiences or opportunities. A tenant who demonstrates that the injury prevented a promotion or better job can ask for compensation for the lost income.

Emotional damages resulting from any of the above. Emotional pain, including stress, embarrassment, depression, and strains on family relationships, may be compensated. Insurance adjusters require proof, such as evaluations from a therapist, physician, or counselor.

Punitive damages. Punitive damages are awarded if a judge or jury decides that you acted outrageously, either intentionally or recklessly. As a general rule, you won't be liable for punitive damages if you refrain from extreme neglect and intentional wrongs against tenants and others.

 RESOURCE

For free information on legal issues regarding liability and insurance, see the articles and FAQs at www.nolo.com.

How to Win Your Personal Injury Claim, by Joseph Matthews, explains personal injury cases and how to work out a fair settlement without going to court.

Everybody's Guide to Small Claims Court, by Cara O'Neill, provides detailed advice on small claims court, which, in most states, allows lawsuits for about $3,000 to $10,000.

Represent Yourself in Court, by Paul Bergman and Sara Berman, will help you prepare and present your case should you end up in court.

Mediate, Don't Litigate: Strategies for Successful Mediation, by Peter Lovenheim and Lisa Guerin, gives detailed information on the mediation process. (eBook version only, available at www.nolo.com.)

These Nolo books are available at bookstores and public libraries. You can also order or download them at www.nolo.com or by calling 800-728-3555.

Landlord's Liability for Environmental Health Hazards

FORMS IN THIS CHAPTER

Chapter 11 includes samples of the following forms:

- *Protect Your Family From Lead in Your Home* Pamphlet
- *Disclosure of Information on Lead-Based Paint and/or Lead-Based Paint Hazards*

The Nolo website includes downloadable copies of these forms (in both English and Spanish). See Appendix B for the link to the forms in this book.

In 1863, an English judge could write that "Fraud apart, there is no law against letting [leasing] a tumble-down house." But in 21st century America, it's no longer legal to be a slumlord. Landlords must exercise a duty of due care toward tenants and guests alike. As discussed in Chapter 9, this duty requires you to maintain the structural integrity of the rental property. If needed repairs are not made and, as a result of defective conditions, a tenant is injured, you may be found liable.

Here we focus on an additional responsibility that has been imposed on landlords in the last few decades: the duty to divulge and remedy environmental health hazards, including some not caused by you. Put bluntly, landlords are increasingly likely to be held liable for tenant health problems resulting from exposure to environmental hazards in the rental premises. This liability is based on many of the same legal theories discussed in Chapter 10, such as negligence and negligence per se (negligence that is automatic when a statute is broken).

This chapter provides an overview of the legal and practical issues involving landlord liability for environmental health hazards, specifically asbestos, lead, radon, carbon monoxide, mold, and bedbugs.

RELATED TOPIC
Related topics covered in this book include:
- How to make legally required disclosures of environmental hazards to tenants: Chapter 2
- Maintaining habitable property by complying with housing laws and avoiding safety problems: Chapter 9
- Your liability for tenant's injuries from defective housing conditions: Chapter 10.

Asbestos

Exposure to asbestos has long and definitively been linked to an increased risk of cancer, particularly for workers in the asbestos manufacturing industry or in construction jobs. More recently, the danger of asbestos in homes has also been acknowledged.

Houses built before the mid-1970s often contain asbestos insulation around heating systems, in ceilings, and in other areas. Until 1981, asbestos was also widely used in many other building materials, such as vinyl flooring and tiles. Asbestos that begins to break down and enter the air—for example, when it is disturbed during maintenance or renovation work—can become a significant health problem to tenants.

Until the mid-1990s, however, private owners of residential rental property had no legal obligation to test for the presence of asbestos. A landlord whose tenant developed an asbestos-related disease could successfully defend himself if he could convince the judge or jury that he did not know of the presence of asbestos on his rental property.

Landlords' protection from liability for asbestos exposure all but evaporated in 1995, when the U.S. Occupational Safety and Health Administration (OSHA) issued a 200-page regulation setting strict workplace standards for the testing, maintenance, and disclosure of asbestos. Because your building will be a "workplace" for anyone working there on renovations or repairs, your building will be subject to OSHA's strict guidelines if it contains (or might contain) asbestos.

OSHA Regulations for Landlords

Regulations of the U.S. Occupational Safety and Health Administration (OSHA) require rental property owners to install warning labels, train staff, and notify people who work in areas that might contain asbestos. In certain situations, owners must actually test for asbestos.

These regulations apply to large landlords who employ maintenance staff (or managers who do maintenance work) and small-scale landlords who have no employees, but who do hire outside contractors for repair and maintenance jobs. OSHA regulations apply to any building constructed before 1981, even if you don't plan to remodel or otherwise disturb the structure. Unless you rule out the presence of asbestos by having a licensed inspector test the property, it is *presumed* that asbestos is present, and the regulations apply.

OSHA protections vary according to how much you're disturbing asbestos. For example, workers who are involved in removing asbestos receive maximum protection; those who merely perform superficial custodial tasks need less.

- **Custodial work.** Employees and contractors whose work involves direct contact with asbestos or materials that are presumed to include it—for example, certain types of floors and ceilings—or who clean in areas near asbestos are subject to OSHA regulations for "general industry." The cleaning service that washes asbestos tiles in the lobby of a pre-1981 building, or the handyman who installs smoke alarms that are embedded in acoustic-tile ceilings made with asbestos, would both fall within the custodial work category. Custodial workers must receive two hours of instruction (including appropriate cleaning techniques) and use special work procedures under the supervision of a trained superior. The general industry standard does not require testing for asbestos. Of course, if you know that high levels of asbestos are present, even custodial tasks must be performed with appropriate levels of protection, such as special masks and clothing.

- **Renovation or repairs.** Stricter procedures are triggered by removal, repair, or renovation of asbestos or asbestos-containing materials—for example, in heating systems or ceilings. At this level of activity, you must test for the presence of asbestos and assess exposure by monitoring the air. Workers must get 16 hours of training per year, oversight by a specially trained person, and respiratory protection in some situations. In addition, employers must conduct medical surveillance of certain employees and maintain specified records for many years. So, for example, your decision to replace that ugly, stained acoustic-tile ceiling would require, first, that the material be tested for asbestos, followed by worker training and

protection measures that are appropriate to the level of exposure. If you hire a contractor to do the job, the contractor will take care of these requirements, and you'll see the work reflected in the contractor's invoice.

CAUTION

There is no escaping OSHA's asbestos regulations under the theory that what you don't know about can't cause legal problems. You might think that you can escape OSHA's asbestos regulations by personally doing minor repair and maintenance and hiring independent contractors to do the major jobs. This might work for a while, until you hire a law-abiding contractor who acknowledges the independent duty to protect employees and performs asbestos testing. The results of the tests will, of course, become known to you, because you'll see the report and pay the bill.

Key Aspects of OSHA Asbestos Regulations

Which buildings are affected. The regulations apply to pre-1981 structures and newer structures found to contain asbestos.

Where asbestos is likely to be found. The regulations cover two classes of materials: those that definitely contain asbestos (such as certain kinds of flooring and ceilings) and those that the law *presumes* to contain asbestos. The second class is extremely inclusive, describing, among other things, any surfacing material that is "sprayed, troweled on, or otherwise applied." This means virtually every dwelling built before 1981 must be suspected of containing asbestos.

What work is covered. The regulations apply to custodial work and to renovation and repair work.

How to Limit Your Liability for Asbestos

If asbestos is present on your property and can be shown to be the cause of a tenant's illness, you could be found liable if you didn't disclose it, or for other reasons. Some states may consider the presence of airborne asbestos to be a breach of the implied warranty of habitability, which (depending on the state) would give the tenant the right to break the lease and move out without notice, pay less rent, withhold the entire rent, or sue to force you to bring the dwelling up to a habitable level.

Limiting your liability for asbestos-related injuries (to tenants and workers alike) begins with understanding a fundamental point: Unless you perform detailed testing to rule out the presence of asbestos, every pre-1981 structure must be treated as if it does contain asbestos. Take these steps:

- Get a copy of the OSHA regulations or the guidelines that are based on them. (See "Asbestos resources," below.)

- Realize that almost any repair or maintenance work—no matter how small—may involve asbestos materials. Test for the presence of asbestos in advance for the benefit of workers and tenants.

- If you learn of the presence of asbestos, tell your tenants. For example, if there is asbestos in the walls but it is not a health problem, point out that it is not likely to pose a danger and that you will monitor the situation.

- If possible, don't disturb asbestos. Unless the asbestos has begun to break down and enter the air, it is usually best to leave it alone and monitor it. This means that it simply may not make economic sense to do certain types of remodeling jobs. Seek an expert's opinion before taking action.

- If you must disturb asbestos—for example, when stripping floor tiles in a lobby—warn all tenants before the work starts, giving them an opportunity to avoid the area. Use written notices and place cones and caution tape around the area. You might even consider temporarily relocating your tenants. The costs of a few days or weeks in alternate housing pales compared to the expense, monetary and human, of responding to a personal injury lawsuit by an exposed tenant.

- If you learn that asbestos material is airborne (or is about to be), seek an expert's advice on how to remedy the situation. When removal is necessary, hire trained asbestos removal specialists, and make sure the debris is legally disposed of in approved hazardous waste disposal sites.

- Make sure tenants don't disturb any spaces containing asbestos, such as walls and ceilings. You might need to prohibit tenants from hanging planters from the ceiling or otherwise making holes in the ceiling. See Clause 12 of the form lease and rental agreement in Chapter 2, which prohibits tenant repairs.

- Require tenants to report any deterioration to you—for example, in sprayed-on acoustical plaster ceilings.

- Monitor asbestos as part of regular safety and maintenance procedures, discussed in Chapter 9.

RESOURCE

Asbestos resources. For information on asbestos rules, inspections, and control, contact the nearest office of the U.S. Occupational Safety and Health Administration (OSHA), go to www.osha.gov, or call 800-321-OSHA. At the website, look for asbestos in the A to Z Index. You'll find the regulations, as well as informative materials that interpret and apply the regulations.

Be sure to check into free OSHA interactive software, called *Asbestos Advisor* (on the OSHA website), that will walk you through questions designed to help identify asbestos in your property and suggest the most sensible solution.

For additional information on asbestos, including negative health effects, see the EPA website at www.epa.gov/asbestos.

Lead

As we all know, exposure to lead-based paint or lead water pipes may lead to serious health problems, particularly in children. Brain damage, attention disorders, and hyperactivity have all been associated with lead poisoning. Landlords who are found responsible for lead poisoning (even if they did not know of the presence of the lead) may face liability for a child's lifelong disability. Jury awards and settlements for lead poisoning are typically enormous, because they cover remedial treatment and education of a child for the rest of his life, and include an award for the estimated loss of earning capacity caused by the injury.

Buildings constructed before 1978 are likely to contain some source of lead, be it lead-based paint, lead pipes, or lead-based solder used on copper pipes. (In 1978, the federal government required the reduction of lead in house paint; lead pipes are generally only found in homes built before 1930, and lead-based solder in home plumbing systems was banned in 1988.) Pre-1950 housing that has been allowed to deteriorate is by far the greatest source of lead-based paint poisoning.

A federal law, the Residential Lead-Based Paint Hazard Reduction Act (commonly referred to as Title X [Ten]) is aimed at evaluating the risk of poisoning in each housing situation and taking appropriate steps to reduce the hazard. Most states have also enacted similar laws.

Is Your Property Exempt From Federal Lead Regulations?

Certain rental properties are exempt from the federal lead paint disclosure and renovation regulations, including:

- Housing for which a construction permit was obtained, or on which construction was started, after January 1, 1978. Older buildings that have been completely renovated since 1978 are not exempt, even if every painted surface was removed or replaced.
- Housing certified as lead-free by a state-accredited lead inspector. Lead-free means the absence of any lead paint, even paint that has been completely painted over and encapsulated.
- Lofts, efficiencies, studios, and other "zero-bedroom" units, including dormitory housing

and rentals in sorority and fraternity houses. University-owned apartments and married student housing are not exempt.
- Short-term vacation rentals of 100 days or less.
- A single room rented in a residential home.
- Housing designed for persons with disabilities (as explained in HUD's Fair Housing Accessibility Guidelines, 24 CFR, Ch. I, Subchapter A, App. II), unless any child less than six years old resides there or is expected to reside there.
- Retirement communities (housing designed for seniors, where one or more tenant is at least 62 years old), unless children under the age of six are present or expected to live there.

State law may still apply, even if the property isn't subject to federal rules.

Must You Have an Inspection?

Inspections are not required by federal or state law, but local law may require them. In New York City, for example, landlords must perform annual visual inspections of rental units where a child under age six resides and of any apartment that becomes vacant before it may be reoccupied. Landlords must inspect for lead-based paint hazards, defined as peeling paint or deteriorated subsurfaces such as exposed, painted wood beneath a newer coat of paint.

Even though it's not required, you might want to have an inspection done so that you can tell tenants that the property is lead-free and exempt from federal regulations. (See list of exemptions, above.) Also, if you take out a loan or buy insurance, your bank or insurance company may require a lead inspection.

Professional lead inspectors don't always inspect every unit in large, multifamily properties. Instead, they inspect a sample of the units and apply their conclusions to the property as a whole. Giving your tenants the results and conclusions of a building-wide evaluation satisfies the law, even if a particular unit was not tested. If, however, you have specific information regarding a unit that is inconsistent with the building-wide evaluation, you must disclose it to the tenant.

Disclose Lead Paint Hazards to Tenants

To comply with Title X, you must give tenants, before they sign or renew a lease or rental agreement, any information you have on lead paint hazards on the property, including individual rental units, common areas and garages, tool sheds, other outbuildings, signs, fences, and play areas. If you have had your property tested (testing must be done by state-certified inspectors; see "Lead hazard resources," below), you must show a copy of the report, or a summary written by the inspector, to tenants.

With certain exceptions (listed below), every lease and rental agreement must include a disclosure page, even if you have not tested. You can use the EPA's form, "Disclosure of Information on Lead-Based Paint and/or Lead-Based Paint Hazards." The copies are included (both Spanish and English) on Nolo's website (see Appendix B for the link to the forms in this book).

As you'll see, the disclosure form has a place for the tenant to initial, indicating that the tenant has reviewed the form. Be sure to note the time you received it, too, if you and the tenant are also signing the lease or rental agreement on the same day (and on that document enter the time you signed it, too). If you're ever challenged, you'll be able to prove that the tenant received the disclosure form before signing the rental documents.

Make a copy of the signed form and give it to the tenant; keep the original for at least three years. If a federal or state agency questions whether you're complying with the lead disclosure law (such agencies periodically do random checking), you'll have a cabinet full of signed forms as evidence. And if a tenant claims to have developed symptoms of lead poisoning from living in your rental property, you'll have proof that you disclosed what you knew.

If you have tenants who've been renting since before December 6, 1996 (the effective date of the law)—must you fill out a disclosure form for them, too? It depends on whether the tenant has a lease or is renting month to month:

- **Tenants with leases.** You need not comply until the lease ends and the tenant renews or stays on as a month-to-month tenant.
- **Month-to-month tenants.** You should have given month-to-month tenants a disclosure statement when you collected your first rent check dated on or after December 6, 1996. Do so now if you haven't yet.

Give Tenants the EPA Booklet on Lead

You must give all tenants the lead hazard information booklet *Protect Your Family From Lead in Your Home,* written by the Environmental Protection Agency (EPA), see "Lead hazard resources," below. A copy of the pamphlet (in English and Spanish) that you can print out and attach to the lease can be downloaded from the Nolo website. See Appendix B for the link to the forms in this book. The cover of this pamphlet is shown below. The pamphlet is also available in Vietnamese, Russian, Arabic, and Somali. For copies, see www.epa.gov/lead. The graphics in the original pamphlet must be included.

Some state agencies, that want to give consumers additional information about lead, have their own pamphlets, but you may not use them in place of the EPA version unless the EPA has approved them. California's pamphlet, *Residential Environmental Hazards: A Guide for Homeowners, Homebuyers, Landlords, and Tenants*, has been approved. To find out if your state has published an approved alternative, go to your state's department or agency in charge of consumer affairs, and use the search function to look for lead disclosure forms.

Enforcement and Penalties

The federal Housing and Urban Development Department (HUD) and the EPA enforce renters' rights to know about the presence of lead-based paint by using "testers," as they do when looking for illegal discrimination. Posing as applicants, testers look to see whether landlords comply with federal law.

Disclosure of Information on Lead-Based Paint and/or Lead-Based Paint Hazards

Lead Warning Statement

Housing built before 1978 may contain lead-based paint. Lead from paint, paint chips, and dust can pose health hazards if not managed properly. Lead exposure is especially harmful to young children and pregnant women. Before renting pre-1978 housing, lessors must disclose the presence of known lead-based paint and/or lead-based paint hazards in the dwelling. Lessees must also receive a federally-approved pamphlet on lead poisoning prevention.

Lessor's Disclosure

(a) Presence of lead-based paint and/or lead-based paint hazards (check (i) or (ii) below):

    (i) _____ Known lead-based paint and/or lead-based paint hazards are present in the housing (explain).

    _____

    _____

    (ii) ✓ Lessor has no knowledge of lead-based paint and/or lead-based paint hazards in the housing.

(b) Records and reports available to the lessor (check (i) or (ii) below):

    (i) _____ Lessor has provided the lessee with all available records and reports pertaining to lead-based paint and/or lead-based paint hazards in the housing (list documents below).

    _____

    _____

    (ii) _____ Lessor has no reports or records pertaining to lead-based paint and/or lead-based paint hazards in the housing.

Lessee's Acknowledgment (initial)

(c) _____ Lessee has received copies of all information listed above.

(d) _____ Lessee has received the pamphlet *Protect Your Family from Lead in Your Home.*

Agent's Acknowledgment (initial)

(e) _____ Agent has informed the lessor of the lessor's obligations under 42 U.S.C. 4852d and is aware of his/her responsibility to ensure compliance.

Certification of Accuracy

The following parties have reviewed the information above and certify, to the best of their knowledge, that the information they have provided is true and accurate.

Bill Perry	*May 9, 20xx*		
Lessor	Date	Lessor	Date
Paula Hart	*Mary 9, 20xx*		
Lessee	Date	Lessee	Date
Agent	Date	Agent	Date

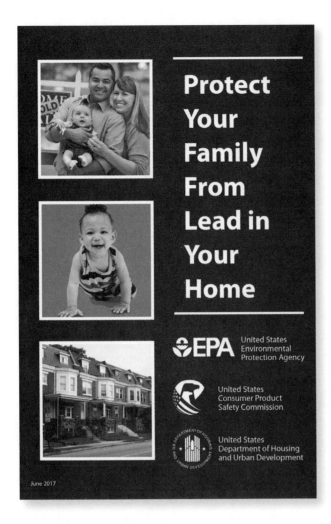

Landlords who fail to distribute the required booklet or do not give tenants the disclosure statement when the lease or rental agreement is signed can receive one or more of the following penalties:

- a notice of noncompliance—the mildest reprimand—typically, you'll be given a certain number of days in which to notify all tenants.
- a civil penalty, which can include fines of up to $16,773 per violation for willful and continuing noncompliance
- an order to pay an injured tenant up to three times his actual damages, or
- a criminal fine of many thousands of dollars per violation. (42 U.S.C. § 4852d, 15 U.S.C. § 2615(b).)

Government testers are also on the lookout for property owners who falsely claim that they don't know of lead-based paint hazards on their property. Here's how it often comes up: A tenant who becomes ill with lead poisoning complains to HUD that you said that you knew of no lead-based paint hazards on your premises. If HUD decides to investigate whether, in fact, you knew about the hazard and failed to tell tenants, their investigators get access to your records. They comb leasing, maintenance, and repair files—virtually all your business records. If HUD finds evidence that you knew or had reason to know of lead paint hazards, such as a contract from a painting firm that includes costs for lead paint removal or a loan document indicating the presence of lead paint, you will be hard-pressed to explain why you checked the box on the disclosure form stating that you had no reports or records regarding the presence of lead-based paint.

RESOURCE

The Residential Lead-Based Paint Hazard Reduction Act, or Title X [Ten] can be found at 42 U.S. Code § 4852d. The Environmental Protection Agency (EPA) has written regulations that explain how landlords should implement lead hazard reduction. (24 Code of Federal Regulations Part 35, and 40 Code of Federal Regulations Part 745.) For more information, see "Lead hazard resources," below.

Give Tenants Information When You Renovate

If you renovate occupied rental units or common areas in buildings built before 1978, you must give current tenants lead hazard information before the work begins. (40 CFR §§ 745.80–88.) Contractors must be certified and follow specific work practices to prevent lead dust contamination.

The obligation to distribute lead information rests with the renovator. If you hire an outside contractor to perform renovation work, the contractor is the renovator. But if you or your property manager, superintendent, or other employees perform the renovation work, you are the renovator and are obliged to give out the information.

The type of information depends on where the renovation is taking place. If an occupied rental unit is being worked on, you must give the tenant a copy of the EPA pamphlet *The Lead-Safe Certified Guide to Renovate Right* (or simply *Renovate Right*). If common areas will be affected, you must distribute the pamphlet to every unit.

> **TIP**
>
> **Put it in the contract.** When you hire a contractor to perform renovations, the contractor is responsible for giving out the required information. To avoid misunderstandings, make sure your renovation contract or work agreement specifically requires the contractor to provide all required lead hazard information to tenants as provided under federal law and regulations.

What Qualifies as a Renovation?

According to EPA regulations, a renovation is any change to an occupied rental unit or common area that disturbs painted surfaces. Here are some examples:

- removing or modifying a painted door, wall, baseboard, or ceiling
- scraping or sanding paint, or
- removing a large structure like a wall, partition, or window.

Repainting a rental unit in preparation for a new tenant doesn't qualify as a renovation unless it's accompanied by sanding, scraping, or other surface preparation activities that might generate paint dust.

Not every renovation triggers the federal law. There are four big exceptions.

Emergencies. If a sudden or unexpected event, such as a fire or flood, requires you to make emergency repairs to a rental unit or common area, there's no need to distribute lead hazard information to tenants before work begins.

Minor repairs or maintenance. Minor work that affects less than six square feet of a room's painted surface, or 20 square feet or less on the exterior, is also exempt. This includes routine electrical and plumbing work, so long as no more than two square feet of the wall, ceiling, or other painted surface gets disturbed by the work.

Renovations in lead-free properties. If the rental unit or building in which the renovation takes place has been certified as containing no lead paint, you're not required to give out information.

Common area renovations in buildings with three or fewer units.

Give the EPA Pamphlet When Renovating Occupied Units

Before starting a renovation to an occupied rental unit, the renovator must give the EPA pamphlet *Renovate Right* to at least one adult occupant of the unit. This requirement applies to all rental properties, including single-family homes and duplexes, unless the property has been certified lead-free by an inspector.

The renovator (whether you or an outside contractor) may mail or hand-deliver the pamphlet to the tenant. If the renovator mails it, he or she must get a "certificate of mailing" from the post office dated at least seven days before the renovation work begins. Make sure the tenant will receive the pamphlet no more than 60 days before work begins—in other words, delivering the pamphlet more than 60 days in advance won't do. The renovator should use the confirmation form at the end of the *Renovate Right* pamphlet to record the delivery method and outcomes.

Give Out Notice When Renovating Common Areas

If your building has four or more units, the renovator—you or your contractor—must notify tenants of all affected units about the renovation and tell them how to get a free copy of the EPA pamphlet *Renovate Right*. (40 CFR § 745.84(b)(2).)

In most cases, common area renovations affect all units, meaning that you must notify all tenants about the renovation. But if you're renovating a "limited use common area" in a large (at least 50 units) apartment building, such as the 16th-floor hallway, you need only notify those units serviced by, or in proximity to, the area.

To comply, the renovator must deliver a notice to every affected unit describing the nature and location of the renovation work, and the dates you expect to begin and finish work. (See a sample "Common Area Renovations Notice," below.) If you can't provide specific dates, you may use terms like "on or about," "early June," or "late July." The notices *must be delivered within 60 days before work begins.* You can slip the notices under apartment doors or give them to any adult occupant of the rental unit. You may not mail them. After the notices are delivered, keep a copy in your file, with a note describing the date and manner in which you delivered the notices.

Common Area Renovations Notice

March 1, 20xx
Dear Tenant,

Please be advised that we will begin renovating the hallways on or about March 15, 20xx. Specifically, we will be removing and replacing the baseboards, wallpaper, and trim in the 2nd, 3rd, and 4th floor corridors, and sanding and repainting the ceilings. We expect the work to be completed in early May 20xx.

You may obtain a free copy of the pamphlet *Renovate Right* from Paul Hogan, the building manager. Paul may be reached at 212-555-1212.

We will make every attempt to minimize inconvenience to tenants during the renovation process. If you have questions about the proposed renovation work, feel free to contact Mr. Hogan or me.

Very truly yours,
Lawrence Levy
Lawrence Levy, Manager

Penalties

Failing to give tenants the required information about renovation lead hazards can result in harsh penalties. Renovators who knowingly violate the regulations can get hit with a penalty of up to $37,500 per day for each violation, and can even face prison time. (40 CFR § 745.87; 15 U.S. Code § 2615.)

State and Local Laws on Lead

Most states also prohibit the use of lead-based paint in residences and require the careful maintenance of existing lead paint and lead-based building materials. If your state has its own lead hazard reduction law, you'll see that, like its federal cousin, it does not directly require you to test for lead. Does this mean that you need not conduct inspections? Not necessarily. In New York City, for example, landlords must perform annual visual inspections of rental units where a child under age six resides. Landlords must inspect for "lead-based paint hazards," defined as peeling paint or deteriorated subsurfaces. New York City landlords must also visually inspect any apartments that become vacant on or after November 12, 1999 before the unit may be reoccupied.

Check your state's consumer protection agency to find out if state laws contain additional requirements regarding lead.

Leaded Miniblinds

Some miniblinds imported from China, Taiwan, Indonesia, or Mexico that were manufactured before 1996, are likely to contain lead. If your property has leaded miniblinds, you do not have to disclose this fact unless you know that the blinds have begun to deteriorate and produce lead dust. To avoid problems, don't use these potentially dangerous miniblinds.

Why You Should Test for Lead

If you suspect that there might be lead lurking in your rental property's paint or water, you face a difficult choice. If you have the property tested and learn that lead is present, you'll know that your property has a hidden and dangerous defect. As a result, you must tell tenants and deal with the possibility that they will refuse to live on your property. If they stay, there's the potential of an expensive lead problem or risk of liability for injuries. But if you don't test, you'll live with the nagging fear that your property might be making your tenants sick and damaging the development of their children.

It may be tempting to adopt an ostrich-like approach and hope that all will work out. The odds may be with you for a while, but eventually this will prove to be a short-sighted solution. Here are six reasons why:

- Lead hazard control is much less burdensome than going through a lawsuit, let alone living with the knowledge that a child's health has been damaged.
- Ignorance of the condition of your property may not shield you from liability. At some point, some court is bound to rule that the danger of lead paint in older housing is so well known that owners of older housing are presumed to know of the danger. If that happens to you, a jury will have a difficult time believing that you were truly ignorant. Moreover, an injured tenant may be able to show the court that it was likely that you, in fact, knew of the lead problem and chose to ignore it.
- Recognizing that children are the ones most at risk for lead poisoning, you cannot simply refuse to rent to tenants with children—this is illegal discrimination in all states.
- If you include a clause in your lease or rental agreement attempting to shift responsibility for lead-based injuries from you to the tenant to protect yourself, you could effectively establish that you were aware of the lead problem. (Why else would you include it?) Many courts won't uphold this type of clause anyway.
- If you refinance or sell the property, the lender will probably require lead testing before approving a loan.
- You can expect your own insurance company to soon require lead testing as well. Lead poisoning cases are incredibly expensive— injured tenants can recover millions of dollars. It is only a matter of time before the insurance industry realizes that it cannot continue to blindly insure all properties against lead poisoning.

In sum, there is no effective way to hide a serious lead problem over the long run. Your best bet is to tackle it directly on your own terms, before you are forced to do so. The next section explains how to go about getting information on testing and reducing one of the most serious lead hazard risks: lead-based paint.

Your Insurance Policy May Not Cover Lead-Paint Poisoning Lawsuits

If you are hit with a lead poisoning lawsuit, don't presume that your insurance company will be there to defend you or compensate the victim. Depending on the terms of your policy, your insurer may be able to deny coverage for lead exposure claims—even if the suit is without merit. If you know (or presume) that your property contains lead-based paint, review your liability coverage with your insurance broker.

Because lead liability lawsuits are so expensive, some insurance companies have simply stopped writing general liability insurance on older buildings. Others exclude coverage for lead-based paint liability claims. You can still get coverage, but it might be limited or come at a higher cost.

 **RESOURCE**

Lead hazard resources. The National Lead Information Center has information on the evaluation and control of lead-based paint and other hazards, disclosure forms, copies of the *Protect Your Family From Lead in Your Home* and *Renovate Right* pamphlets, and lists of EPA-certified lead paint professionals. Call 800-424-LEAD or go to www.epa.gov/lead. The EPA also provides pamphlets, documents, forms, and information on all lead paint hazards and federal laws and regulations on its website, and offers useful advice on topics such as finding a contractor licensed to test for and remove lead. (Check out its guide for "small entities," called *Small Entity Compliance Guide to Renovate Right*.) The EPA website (www.epa.gov) also includes a map with links to state and local websites.

HUD, specifically its Office of Lead Hazard Control and Healthy Homes (see www.hud.gov/healthyhomes), has many useful resources, including guidelines for evaluating and controlling lead-based paint hazards in housing.

State housing departments have information on state laws and regulations. Start by calling your state consumer protection agency. For a list of state consumer protection agencies, go to www.usa.gov/state-consumer.

If you'd like to search for your state's legislation on your own, go to the Centers for Disease Control and Protection website at www.cdc.gov/nceh/lead. Choose the "Policy Resources" link that will take you to the database of state legislation.

Call In Expert Help to Clean Up Lead-Based Paint

Lead is relatively easy to detect—you can buy home-use kits that contain a simple swab, which turns color when drawn over a lead-based surface. Knowing how much lead is present, and how to best clean it up, however, are subjects for the experts. An environmental engineer will be able to tell you how much lead is present at floor level and above, which will alert you as to whether your property exceeds the amounts allowable by law.

In most states, you cannot legally perform lead abatement work without a special license from the state. To be on the safe side, become licensed yourself or only hire certified people.

Why not do it yourself? Because a DIY job, no matter how well-intentioned, might actually make the problem much worse. Wholesale paint removal, or sanding and repainting, often releases tremendous amounts of lead dust, the deadliest vector for poisoning. You also need special equipment to do a safe cleanup. Regular household cleaners, even TSP, do not do a very effective job of capturing lead, nor can a standard vacuum cleaner filter out microscopic lead particles.

Theoretically, some lead dust problems might be containable by frequent, lead-specific, and thorough cleaning, rather than repainting, and some cleaning companies specialize in lead dust cleaning. But painting over lead paint, if possible, is a better solution, even if it appears more costly than dust maintenance. It will certainly cost less than a lawsuit.

Radon

Radon is a naturally occurring radioactive gas that is associated with lung cancer. It can enter and contaminate a house built on soil and rock containing uranium deposits or enter through water from private wells drilled in uranium-rich soil. Radon becomes a lethal health threat when it is trapped in tightly sealed homes that have been insulated to keep in heat or have poor ventilation, when it escapes from building materials that have incorporated uranium-filled rocks and soils (like certain types of composite tiles or bricks), or when it is released into the air from aerated household water that has passed through underground concentrations of uranium. Problems occur most frequently in areas where rocky soil is relatively rich in uranium and in climates where occupants keep their windows tightly shut.

The Environmental Protection Agency estimates that millions of American homes have unacceptably high levels of radon. Fortunately, there are usually simple, inexpensive ways to measure indoor radon levels, and good ventilation will effectively disperse the gas in most situations. These measures range from the obvious (open the windows and provide cross-ventilation) to the more complex (sealing cracks in the foundation, or sucking radon out of the soil before it enters the foundation and venting it into the air above the door through a pipe). A typical household radon problem can usually be solved for $1,000 to $2,000.

If you own rental property in an area known to have radon problems but don't test, warn tenants, or take action, you could be sued for harm that tenants suffer as a result.

Whether to test for radon depends on the circumstances of each rental property; you are not legally required to test. Your city planning department or your insurance broker may know about local geology and radon dangers. Certainly, if you know radon levels are dangerously high in your area, you should test rental property. For the most professional results, hire an inspector certified by the EPA. Testing takes at least three days, and sometimes months. Do-it-yourself radon testing kits are also available. If you use one, make sure it says "Meets EPA Requirements." Kansas State University's National Radon Program Services (www.sosradon.org/purchase-kits) is a good source of discounted kits.

If testing indicates high radon levels, warn tenants and correct the problem. Start by giving them the EPA booklet *A Radon Guide for Tenants* (see "Radon resources," below).

> **RESOURCE**
>
> **Radon resources.** For information on the detection and removal of radon, contact the U.S. Environmental Protection Agency Radon Hotline Line at 800-767-7236, or visit www.epa.gov/radon. The EPA site has links to state agencies that regulate radon, gives information on finding a qualified radon reduction provider, and includes a map of radon zones by state. You can also download a copy of the booklet *A Radon Guide for Tenants* and other publications, including *A Citizen's Guide to Radon.*

Carbon Monoxide

Carbon monoxide (CO) is a colorless, odorless, lethal gas that can build up and kill within a matter of hours. Unlike any of the environmental hazards discussed so far, CO cannot be covered up or managed.

When CO is inhaled, it enters the bloodstream and replaces oxygen. Dizziness, nausea, confusion, and tiredness can result; high concentrations bring on unconsciousness, brain damage, and death. It is possible for someone to be poisoned from CO while sleeping, without waking up. Needless to say, a CO problem must be dealt with immediately.

Sources of Carbon Monoxide

Carbon monoxide is a byproduct of fuel combustion; electric appliances cannot produce it. Common home appliances, such as gas dryers, refrigerators, ranges, water heaters or space heaters; oil furnaces; fireplaces; charcoal grills; and wood stoves all produce CO. Cars and gas gardening equipment also produce CO. If appliances or fireplaces are not vented properly, CO can build up within a home and poison the occupants. In tightly sealed apartments, indoor accumulations are especially dangerous.

Preventing Carbon Monoxide Problems

If you have a regular maintenance program, you should be able to spot and fix the common malfunctions that cause CO buildup.

Here's how to avoid problems:

- Check chimneys and appliance vents for blockages.
- In your rules and regulations, prohibit the indoor use of portable gas grills or charcoal grills.
- Warn tenants never to use a gas range, clothes dryer, or oven for heating.
- Prohibit nonelectric space heaters, or specify that they must be inspected annually.

- Check the pilot lights of gas appliances as part of your regular maintenance routine. They should show a clear blue flame; a yellow or orange flame may indicate a problem.

But even the most careful service program cannot rule out unexpected problems like the blocking of a chimney by a bird's nest or the sudden failure of a machine part. You'll need a CO detector, explained below.

Carbon Monoxide Detectors

To ensure that residents are alerted immediately to the buildup of CO, you'll need to install a monitoring device, or detector, which will emit a loud shriek when CO is present. Unlike smoke detectors, which are required in every state, CO detectors are not universally mandated. But that's changing as more and more legislators recognize the need for these safety devices.

Single-family dwellings, which are more likely to have fossil-fuel-burning appliances than multifamily properties, are targeted most frequently, with laws requiring CO detectors in new construction, at renovation, and upon sale or transfer. But many states, including California, also require detectors in rentals. The National Conference of State Legislatures maintains a list of state laws at www.ncsl.org (type "carbon monoxide detectors state statutes" into the search box on the home page).

Savvy landlords will skip the research and just install the detectors. Make sure the device is "UL approved." Battery-operated models work fine, but like smoke detectors, their batteries must be changed regularly. Models that are connected to the building's interior wiring, with batteries as a back-up, are a better choice.

Responsibility for Carbon Monoxide Buildup

Most CO hazards are caused by a malfunctioning appliance or a clogged vent, flue, or chimney. It follows that the responsibility for preventing a CO buildup depends on who is responsible for the upkeep of the appliance.

Appliances. Appliances that are part of the rental, especially built-in units, are typically your responsibility, although the tenant is responsible for intentional or unreasonably careless damage. For example, if the pilot light on the gas stove that came with the rental is improperly calibrated and emits high amounts of CO, you must fix it. On the other hand, if your tenant brings in a portable oil space heater that malfunctions, that is his responsibility.

Vents. Vents, chimneys, and flues are part of the structure, and their maintenance is typically your job. In single-family houses, however, it is not unusual for landlords and tenants to agree to shift maintenance responsibility to the tenant. As always, write down any maintenance jobs that you have delegated so that it's clear. Chapter 9 discusses the pros and cons of delegating repairs to tenants.

RESOURCE

Carbon monoxide resources. The EPA offers useful instructional material, including downloadable pamphlets, at www.epa.gov/iaq/co.html. Local natural gas utility companies often have consumer information brochures available to their customers. You can also contact the American Gas Association for consumer pamphlets on carbon monoxide, at 202-824-7000 or www.aga.org.

Mold

Across the country, tenants have won multimillion-dollar cases against landlords for significant health problems—such as rashes, chronic fatigue, nausea, cognitive losses, hemorrhaging, and asthma—allegedly caused by exposure to "toxic molds" in their building.

Mold is among the most controversial of environmental hazards. There is considerable debate within the scientific and medical community about which molds, and what situations, pose serious health risks to people in their homes. (You can't tell by looking; mold comes in all colors and shapes, and while some molds look and smell disgusting, others are barely seen, hidden in walls, under floors and ceilings, or in basements and attics.) But courts have increasingly found landlords legally liable for tenant health problems associated with exposure to mold. It is crucial to identify and avoid problems with mold in your rental property before you find yourself in court.

Unsightly as it may be, not all mold is harmful to human health—for example, the mold that grows on shower tiles is not dangerous. It takes an expert to know whether a particular mold is harmful or just annoying. Your first response to discovering mold shouldn't be to call in the folks with the white suits and ventilators. Most of the time, proper clean-up and maintenance will remove mold. Better yet, focus on early detection and prevention of mold, as discussed below. This will help limit health problems of tenants as well as physical damage to structural components of your property.

Laws on Mold

No federal law sets permissible exposure limits or building tolerance standards for mold in rental properties, and only a few states have taken steps toward establishing permissible mold standards. This is bound to change as state legislators and federal regulators begin to study mold more closely. California, Indiana, Maryland, New Jersey, Texas, and Virginia are among the few that have passed legislation aimed specifically at the development of guidelines and regulations for mold in indoor air. California's law also requires landlords to disclose to current and prospective tenants the presence of any known or suspected mold. (Cal. Health & Safety Code §§ 26100 and following.)

A few cities have enacted ordinances related to mold. For example, San Francisco has added mold to its list of public health nuisances, which means tenants can sue landlords under private and public nuisance laws if they fail to clean up serious outbreaks. (San Francisco Health Code § 581.)

Your Liability for Tenant Exposure to Mold

Because there's little law on mold, you must look to your general responsibility to maintain and repair rental property for guidance. Your legal duty to provide and maintain habitable premises naturally extends to fixing leaking pipes, windows, and roofs—the causes of most mold. If you don't take care of leaks and mold grows as a result, you may be held responsible for damage to your tenant's personal belongings, such as clothes and furniture. And depending on the severity of the mold problem and your negligence in screening for or fixing it, a tenant may successfully sue you for medical bills and lost wages due to mold-caused health problems.

The picture changes when mold grows as the result of your tenant's behavior, such as keeping the apartment tightly shut, creating high humidity, and failing to keep it reasonably clean. You cannot be expected to police your tenant's lifestyle (and in many states, privacy statutes prevent you from unannounced inspections, as explained in Chapter 13). When a tenant's own negligence is the sole cause of injury, you are not liable.

CAUTION
Using a lease clause stating that you won't be liable for injuries due to mold may not do you any good. Courts are likely to see this ploy as against public policy, and won't enforce it. (*Cole v. Wyndchase Aspen Grove Acquisition Corp.*, 2006 WL 2827452, M.D. Tenn. 2006.)

Preventing Mold Problems

As we've stressed many times, the point is not who will win in court, but how to avoid getting dragged into a lawsuit, even one that you would probably win. Your efforts should be directed squarely at preventing the conditions that lead to the growth of mold. This requires maintaining the structural integrity of your property (the roof, plumbing, and windows) and adopting a thorough and prompt system for detecting and handling problems.

Here's how to proceed:

Watch the moisture. Before new tenants move in, inspect the premises and look for moisture problems (use the Landlord-Tenant Checklist form in Chapter 7). Mold often grows on water-soaked materials, such as wall paneling, paint, fabric, ceiling tiles, newspapers, or cardboard boxes. Throw in a little warmth and molds grow very quickly, sometimes spreading within 24 hours. Buildings in warm humid climates experience the most mold problems. But mold can grow whenever moisture is present; floods, leaking pipes, windows, or roofs are the leading causes. Poor ventilation makes the problem worse.

1. **Make sure every tenant understands the factors that contribute to the growth of mold.** Use your lease or house rules to educate tenants about sensible practices to reduce the chances of mold—or to fix problems should they arise. Give tenants specific advice, such as how to:
   - ventilate the rental unit
   - avoid creating areas of standing water— for example, by emptying saucers under houseplants, and
   - clean vulnerable areas, such as bathrooms, with cleaning solutions that discourage mold growth.

   The mold section of the EPA website includes lots of practical tips.

2. **Require tenants to immediately report signs of mold,** or conditions that may lead to mold such as plumbing leaks and weatherproofing problems.

3. **Check for conditions, such as leaky pipes, which could cause mold.** Do this as part of your recommended maintenance inspections (discussed in Chapter 9).

4. **Make all necessary repairs and maintenance to clean up or reduce mold.** For example:
   - Consider installing exhaust fans in rooms with high humidity (bathrooms, kitchens, and service porches), especially if window ventilation is poor.
   - Provide dehumidifiers in chronically damp climates, or rental units with poor ventilation.
   - Reduce window condensation by using storm windows or double-glazed windows.
   - Quickly respond to tenant complaints and clean up mold as discussed below.

EXAMPLE: The shower tray in Jay's bathroom begins to leak, allowing water to penetrate walls, floors, and ceilings below. Sydney, Jay's landlord, has repeatedly stressed the need for ventilation and proper housekeeping and encouraged all his tenants, including Jay, to promptly report maintenance problems. Jay ignores Sydney's recommendations, and mold grows in the bathroom. Jay develops a bad rash that he claims is a direct result of his exposure to the bathroom mold. Jay will have a tough time holding Sydney legally responsible for his health problems, simply because he failed to take advantage of Sydney's proven readiness to address the problem, which would have avoided the harm.

For useful advice on diagnosing and preventing mold, see Nolo's *Mold and Your Rental Property: A Landlord's Prevention and Liability Guide* eBook (see details in "Mold Resources," below).

Testing for Mold Toxicity

If you or your tenants discover mold on the property, should you test it to determine its harmfulness? Most of the time, no. You're better off directing your efforts to speedy cleanup. Knowing what kind of mold you have will not, in most cases, affect what you do to clean it up.

Properly testing for mold is also extremely costly. Over-the-counter test kits, which cost around $30, provide questionable results. A professional's basic investigation for a single-family home can cost $3,000 or more. And to further complicate matters, there are few competent professionals in this new field—unlike lead and asbestos inspectors, who must meet state requirements for training and competence, there are no state or federal certification programs for mold busters.

This said, it will be necessary to call in the testers if you are sued. In that event, your insurance company will hire lawyers who will be in charge of arranging for experts.

How to Clean Up Mold

Most mold is harmless, *not a threat to health* and easily dealt with. Most of the time, a weak bleach solution (one cup of bleach per gallon of water) will remove mold from nonporous materials. You and your tenants should follow these commonsense steps to clean up mold. Use gloves and avoid exposing eyes and lungs to airborne mold dust (if you disturb mold and cause it to enter the air, use masks). Allow for frequent work breaks in areas with plenty of fresh air.

- Clean or remove all infested areas, such as a bathroom or closet wall. Begin work on a small patch and watch to see if workers develop adverse health reactions, such as nausea or headaches. If so, call in a construction professional who is familiar with working with hazardous substances.
- Don't try removing mold from fabrics such as towels, linens, drapes, carpets, or clothing— just dispose of them.
- Contain the work space by using plastic sheeting and enclosing debris in plastic bags.

If the mold is extensive, consider hiring an experienced mold remediation company with excellent references, and any state-required licenses or certification. For more information, check out the sites noted in "Mold resources," below.

CAUTION

People with respiratory problems, fragile health, or compromised immune systems should not participate in clean-up activities. If your tenant raises health concerns and asks for clean-up assistance, provide it—it's a lot cheaper than responding to a lawsuit.

Insurance Coverage of Mold Problems

If structural aspects of your property have been ruined by mold and must be replaced, especially if there's a lawsuit on the horizon brought by ill tenants, contact your insurance broker immediately. Your property insurance may cover the cost of the cleanup and repairs, but only if the damage is from an unexpected and accidental event, such as a burst pipe, wind-driven rain, sewerage backup, or unanticipated roof leak. Damage due to mold in a chronically damp basement will probably not be covered under your policy. If mold grows as a result of a flood, you may also be out of luck—flooding is excluded from most insurance coverage.

Your liability policy may also cover you if you are sued by ill tenants. But watch for the insurers to try to wiggle out as the amount of claims grows. Carriers have claimed that mold falls within the "pollution exclusion" (most policies do not cover you if you commit or allow pollution—for example, if you deliberately dump solvents on the property). Unfortunately, many insurers are now simply exempting damage due to mold in new or renewed property insurance policies. Read your policy (and ask your broker) to see whether mold-related claims are allowable under your policies.

RESOURCE

Mold resources. For detailed advice on the subject of mold in residential rental properties—from mold prevention to cleanup and relevant liability and insurance issues (such as flood insurance coverage of mold problems)—see *Mold and Your Rental Property: A Landlord's Prevention and Liability Guide*, by Ron Leshnower (Nolo). This eBook, available on the Nolo website as well as on Amazon and other online retailers, includes useful sample forms, such as a mold inspection checklist. For information on the detection, removal, and prevention of mold, see www.epa.gov/mold; be sure to check out

"Mold Remediation in Schools and Commercial Buildings Guide" (which includes multifamily properties) and "A Brief Guide to Mold, Moisture, and Your Home." Publications written with the homeowner in mind are available from the California Department of Public Health at www.cdph.ca.gov. To see whether your state has enacted or is considering mold legislation that might affect residential rentals, log onto the website of the National Conference of State Legislatures (www.ncsl.org) and type "mold" into the search box on the home page. Look for the link to the "Environmental Health Legislation Databases Guide," and once there, filter by "All States" and "Indoor Air Quality—Mold." To check local mold-related rules, see your city or county website (find yours at www.statelocalgov.net).

Bedbugs

They come out at night to gorge on human blood, but can last a year between meals. A single female will lay 500 eggs in her lifetime. You'll find them in sleazy digs with slobby tenants, as well as upscale apartments with fastidious residents. They're expert hitchhikers who can catch a ride on your suitcase, furniture, or clothing. No one really knows how to kill them. What are they? They're 21st-century bedbugs, and if they show up at your rental property, you'll probably conclude that mold, asbestos, or even lead-based paint are benign by comparison. Here's how to protect your tenants and your business from this potentially devastating pest.

What's a Bedbug—And Where Does It Come From?

Bedbugs are wingless insects, about a quarter-inch in length, oval but flattened from top to bottom. They're nearly white (after molting) and range to tan or deep brown or burnt orange (after they've sipped some blood, a dark red mass appears within the insect's body). They seek crevices and dark cracks, commonly hiding during the day and finding hosts at night. Bedbugs nest in mattresses, bed frames, and adjacent furniture, though they can also infest an entire room or apartment. They easily spread from apartment to apartment via cracks in the walls, heating systems, and other openings.

Bedbug populations have resurged recently in Europe, North America, and Australia, possibly a result of the banning of effective but toxic pesticides such as DDT. Bedbugs do not carry disease-causing germs (perhaps their one saving feature). Their bites resemble those of a flea or mosquito. Secondhand furniture is a common source of infestation.

How to Deal With an Infestation

You'll learn that bedbugs have infested your property when a tenant complains of widespread, annoying bites that appear during the night. To minimize the outbreak and attempt to stop the spread of the pests to other rental units, take the following steps immediately. We can't emphasize this enough: Unless you move swiftly and aggressively, identifying infested areas and treating them thoroughly, you will be doomed to a larger and harder-to-beat infestation. You may even end up with an unrentable property.

Hiring an experienced exterminator is the only way to deal with a bedbug infestation. A can of Raid is not going to do the job and will end up costing you more money in the long run. Expect to pay from $500 to $1,500 for the initial service of a single infested unit, and more for follow-up treatments. If you find a company that offers to control bedbugs for $50 per unit, get another bid.

 TIP

Encourage tenants to promptly report pest problems. The sooner you learn about a bedbug infestation, the better you'll be able to manage it. Follow our advice in Chapter 9 for setting up a system for tenants to report problems in their rental unit, whether it's a leaky faucet or bedbugs.

Confirm the Infestation

First, make sure that you're dealing with bedbugs and not some other pest, such as fleas. Because several kinds of insects resemble bedbugs, you'll need to capture a critter or two and study them. Go to the sites mentioned above for more pictures of bedbugs than you ever wanted to see, and compare your samples. If it looks like a bedbug, call an experienced pest control operator, pronto. If you're not sure, submit your catch to a competent entomologist (insect specialist) for evaluation. To find a good entomologist, consult a reputable pest control company, look for references on your state's department of agriculture website, or look at the website of a nearby university's department of entomology.

Map the Infestation, Using a Competent Exterminator

In a multiunit building, bedbugs can travel from one unit to another. But chances are that one unit is the source, and it will have the highest concentrations of bedbugs. Hire a competent exterminator to measure the concentration of bugs in the complaining tenant's unit, and to also inspect and measure all adjoining units (on both sides, above, and below). Be sure to give all tenants proper notice of the exterminator's inspection and explain what's involved—a competent exterminator will need to look closely into drawers, closets, and shelves. Mapping the infestation (particularly if your exterminator does it more than once, over a period of time) may also help you determine when a particular unit became infested, which can help you apportion financial responsibility for the extermination. (See "Who Pays for All This?" below.)

Declutter, Move Tenants Out, Exterminate, Vacuum—And Do It Again

Bedbugs thrive in clutter, which simply gives them more hiding places. Before you can effectively deal with the bugs, tenants in infested units must remove all items from closets, shelves, and drawers, wash all bedding and clothing, and put washed items in sealed plastic bags. Then, you need to move tenants out during treatment, and allow them to return when the exterminator gives the all-clear. Most of the time, they can return the same day.

What Kills Bedbugs?

Although bedbugs are hard to kill using today's approved materials, exterminators have three ways to go after bedbugs:

- Insecticidal dusts, such as finely ground glass or silica, will scrape off the insects' waxy exterior and dry them out.
- Contact insecticides (such as chlorfenapyr, available only to licensed pest control operators) kill the bugs when they come into contact with it. For more information, search "Chlorfenapyr" at www.epa.gov.
- Insect growth regulators (IGR) interfere with the bugs' development and reproduction, and though quite effective, take a long time.

Pest control operators often use IGR in combination with other treatments. Most controllers recommend multiple treatments over a period of weeks, interspersed with near-fanatical vacuuming to capture dead and weakened bugs. Anecdotal reports claim that even with repeated applications of pesticides, it's not possible to fully eradicate heavy infestations. Honest exterminators will not certify that a building is bedbug-free.

Bedbugs will always be found in an infested room's bed. The only way to rid a mattress of bedbugs is to enclose it in a bag that will prevent bugs from chewing their way out (they will eventually die inside, but because it can take a long time, it's advisable to keep the mattress permanently sealed). Ask that tenants buy a bag guaranteed to trap bedbugs (some bags simply deter allergens). These are expensive—and you may as well resign yourself to buying them if your tenants won't or can't.

Upon return, tenants must thoroughly vacuum. Experienced exterminators will recommend a second and even a third treatment, with exhaustive cleaning and clutter-removing in between. You must insist, to the extent you're able (see "Proper Cleaning and Housekeeping: Can You Insist on It?" below), that tenants take these steps. If they don't and the infestation reappears and spreads, you could quite possibly find yourself with a building that is empty but for a thriving population of bedbugs.

Infested items that can't be treated must be destroyed. Do not allow tenants to remove infested items and simply bring them back. And use extreme care when removing infested belongings and furniture. Bag them in plastic before carting them away—otherwise, you may inadvertently distribute the bugs to the rest of the building.

Proper Cleaning and Housekeeping: Can You Insist on It?

Running a rental business involves striking a delicate balance between insisting that tenants take proper care of your property, and respecting their privacy. You can require that rental units be kept in a sanitary condition, but you can't inspect your tenants' housekeeping efforts every week.

When it comes to effectively eliminating bedbugs, however, extreme housekeeping is needed. Hopefully, your tenants will be so grateful that you're taking steps to deal with the bugs that they will cooperate voluntarily. If necessary, however, you may need to perform the vacuuming yourself (or hire someone to do it). Don't balk over the expense—compared to a widespread infestation and the potential of an empty building, the cost of a cleaning service is minimal.

CAUTION

Talk to a lawyer before deciding to evict a tenant who refuses to participate in your bedbug eradication program, or who reintroduces infested items. You may be within your rights, but you may also be courting a retaliatory eviction lawsuit, especially if the tenant was not the source of the infestation.

Who Pays for All This?

In keeping with your obligation to provide fit and habitable housing, you must pay to exterminate pests that tenants have not introduced. In Florida, this duty is explicit: since 1973, bedbugs are specified as one of the many vermin that landlords are required to get rid of, in order to maintain a fit and habitable rental. (Fla. Stat. Ann. § 83.51.) Arizona also makes landlords responsible for eradication. (Ariz. Rev. Stat. § 33-1319.) Fortunately, as explained below, your insurance may defray some of the costs.

Eradicating infestations caused by the tenant, however, can rightly be put on the tenant's tab. But determining who introduced the bedbugs is often very difficult. Even if you identify the unit where the infestation started (or the rental is a single-family home), that doesn't mean the tenants caused the problem. If they're new tenants, expect them to argue that the former occupants are responsible. Unless you discover that the new tenant came from a building that was also infested, you'll have a hard time laying responsibility on your new resident.

Another potential loss is the cost of replacing belongings that can't be salvaged. In extreme cases, bedbugs infest every nook and cranny of a rental and its contents—books, clothes, furniture, appliances. One New York landlord reported getting a phone call from a tenant who discovered bedbugs and moved out with only the clothes on his back, leaving everything—*everything*—behind. This tenant sued the owner for the cost of replacing his belongings, claiming that the landlord's ineffective eradication methods left him no choice.

Should this claim get before a judge, your liability would probably depend on the judge's view of the reasonableness of your response and the tenant's reaction. The more you can show that you took immediate and effective steps to eliminate the problem, the better you would fare. As for the tenant's response, understand that the psychological effects of living with bugs that bite you while you sleep can be very strong.

Will Your Insurance Step Up?

If you're facing a bedbug problem, you might get at least some help from your insurance policy. Here's the scoop.

Eradication. Property insurance typically does not cover instances of vermin or insect infestation.

Tenants' damaged belongings, medical expenses, and moving and living expenses. Your commercial general liability policy will probably cover you here, up to the limits of the policy.

Loss of rents. If you must leave a rental vacant while you have it treated, and you have loss of rents/ business interruption insurance, it may cover you for your loss of rental income during this period.

If your tenants have renters' insurance, it might help here. If you can confidently trace the infestation to particular tenant's actions, you could present the bills to these tenants, suggesting that they refer the matter to their insurance company. The liability portion of their renters' policy should cover them.

Disclosure to Future Tenants

The last thing you want to tell prospective tenants is that you had a bedbug problem. Knowing that a bedbug can remain alive and dormant for over a year, and that eradication attempts are often not 100%, many prospects will never consider living in a unit that has experienced a bedbug problem, even when you've done everything possible to deal with the bugs.

Whether to disclose, however, may not be an option for you. State and local legislators are beginning to address the issue of whether landlords should be required to disclose a property's bedbug history, as well as tenant and landlord duties when an infestation appears. Maine requires landlords to disclose the property's history. (14 M.R.S.A. § 6021-A). Maine's law also requires tenants to promptly report problems, and to vacate the premises if necessary. Arizona prohibits landlords from knowingly renting an infested unit (Ariz. Rev. Stat. § 33-1319), and New York City requires landlords to inform tenants of the building's and the rental unit's bedbug history for the past year

(New York City Administrative Code § 27-2018.1). Many other states have legislation; for a list, go to the National Conference of State Legislatures, www.ncsl.org and search "state bedbug laws."

The majority of tenants, however, will not have the benefit of explicit disclosure laws. But that doesn't mean that you shouldn't be forthright. First, if a prospect questions you directly about a bedbug problem, especially if it's clear that this issue is of critical importance, you must answer truthfully or risk the consequences:

- **Breaking the lease.** A tenant who learns after the fact that you didn't answer truthfully will have legal grounds for breaking the lease and leaving without responsibility for future rent.
- **Increased chances of damages.** If the bug problem reappears and this tenant sues over lost or damaged possessions, costs of moving and increased rent, and the psychological consequences of having lived with the bugs, his chances of recovering will be enhanced by your lack of candor. A lawyer will argue that your failure to disclose a dangerous situation set the tenant up for misery that could have been avoided had you been truthful.

Now, suppose you are not questioned about a rental's bedbug history, you remain silent, and a problem reappears. Will your new tenants have a strong case for breaking the lease without responsibility for future rent, or use your silence as a way to increase their chances of collecting damages from you? The answer will depend on the facts, such as how aggressively and thoroughly you attempted to rid the property of bugs.

 **RESOURCE**

Bedbugs. The Bedbugs section of the EPA website (www.epa.gov/bedbugs) has extensive information about bedbugs, including details on relevant regulations. For the definitive guide to the eradication and prevention of bedbugs, check out www.techletter.com, maintained by a pest management consulting firm. Read their articles or order the comprehensive *Bed Bug Handbook: The Complete Guide to Bed Bugs and Their Control.*

Electromagnetic Fields

Power lines, electrical wiring, and appliances emit low-level electric and magnetic fields. The farther away you are from the source of these fields, the weaker their force.

The controversy surrounding electromagnetic fields (EMFs) concerns whether or not exposure to them increases the chances of getting certain cancers—specifically, childhood leukemia. Although some early research raised the possibility of a link, later scientific studies discounted it. The same conclusion was reached in 2001 by the U.K. National Radiation Protection Board. (Scientific inquiry on EMFs has now shifted to the effects of cell phones.) The World Health Organization has exhaustively canvassed the scientific literature and has similarly concluded that "… current evidence does not confirm the existence of any health consequences from exposure to low-level electromagnetic fields." (See "About electromagnetic fields" at www.who.int/peh-emf/about/en.)

Because you cannot insist that power companies move their transmitters or block emissions, you are not responsible for EMFs or their effect—if any—on your tenants. But if a tenant complains, what should you do?

Practically speaking, a tenant's only option is to move. A tenant who has a month-to-month rental agreement or an expiring lease can simply move on. A tenant who wants to break a lease or rental agreement because of EMFs would be justified only if there were a significant threat to her health or safety. Given the debate regarding the danger from EMFs, it is unclear whether a court would decide that their presence made your property unlivable.

RESOURCE

Electromagnetic fields resources. The National Institute of Environmental Health Sciences has useful resources on EMFs. To find them, search its website, www. niehs.nih.gov.

Landlord's Liability for Criminal Activity

No one expects you to build a moat around your rental property and provide round-the-clock armed security. But in virtually every state, landlords are expected to take reasonable precautions to protect tenants from foreseeable harm. This means you must take reasonable steps to:

- protect tenants from would-be assailants, thieves, and other criminals
- protect tenants from the criminal acts of fellow tenants
- warn tenants about dangerous situations you are aware of but cannot eliminate, and
- protect the neighborhood from illegal and noxious activities, such as drug dealing, by any of your tenants.

If you don't live up to these responsibilities, you may be liable for any injuries or losses that occur as a result.

This chapter discusses your legal duties under building codes, ordinances, statutes, and, most frequently, court decisions to protect your tenants and the neighborhood. It also discusses special issues regarding terrorism that concern landlords and rental property. It is our goal to provide practical advice on how to protect your tenants and the neighborhood from crime, limit your liability, and avoid trouble before it finds you.

We can't overstate the importance of taking this subject seriously. Landlords are sued more than any other group of business owners in the country, and the legal subspecialty of "premises liability" for criminal acts (suing landlords for injuries suffered by tenants at the hands of third-party criminals) is one of the fastest-growing areas of law. Why are lawyers so eager to try to pin responsibility for the acts of criminals on landlords? The not-so-surprising answer is money: Horrific crimes such as rape and assault result in tremendous monetary awards and settlements, of which the plaintiffs' attorneys take a sizable chunk. Only liability for lead poisoning rivals premises liability for astronomical settlement and jury award costs.

If this book motivates you to do only two things, it should be to assess and address the security situation on your rental property and to make sure your insurance policy provides maximum protection against the acts of criminals.

To protect yourself, you need to:

- follow state and local laws that mandate security measures
- take reasonable steps to prevent crime
- keep promises you make to tenants about security, and
- buy enough insurance to protect yourself.

Troubled Property: Is It Time to Cut Your Losses?

If you own property in a high-crime area, you may find it impossible to raise rents enough to cover the costs of providing secure housing and purchasing comprehensive insurance. The truth is that you may be better off selling at a loss than courting an excessive risk that you will be sued for criminal acts beyond your control. If you do keep high-crime property, consider ways to legally separate it from your other assets—for example, by establishing a corporation or limited liability company.

 RELATED TOPIC

Related topics covered in this book include:

- How to choose the best tenants and avoid legal problems: Chapter 1
- Lease and rental agreement provisions prohibiting tenants' illegal activities and disturbances: Chapter 2
- How to avoid renting to convicted criminals without violating privacy and antidiscrimination laws: Chapter 5
- How to minimize danger to tenants from a manager by checking applicants' backgrounds and references: Chapter 6
- Highlighting security procedures in a move-in letter to new tenants: Chapter 7
- Responsibilities for repair and maintenance under state and local housing law: Chapter 9

- Landlord's liability for a tenant's injuries from defective housing conditions: Chapter 10
- Landlord's right of entry and tenant's privacy: Chapter 13
- Evicting a tenant for drug dealing and other illegal activity: Chapter 17.

Comply With All State and Local Laws on Security

You should find and comply with all security laws, state or local, that apply to you. For information on security regulations, contact your state or local housing agency or rental property owners' association. Here's an idea of what to expect.

Specific Rules

In many areas of the country, local building and housing codes are rich with specific rules designed to protect tenants. For example, some city ordinances require peepholes, intercom systems, deadbolt locks, and specific types of lighting on the rental property.

Only a few states have specific laws as to landlords' responsibilities to provide secure premises. For example:

- Under Florida law, landlords must provide locks and keep common areas in a "safe condition." A Florida tenant who was assaulted by someone who entered because of a broken back door lock was allowed to argue to a jury that the landlord was partially responsible. (*Paterson v. Deeb*, 472 So.2d 1210 (Fla. Dist. Ct. 1985).)
- All Texas rental units must be equipped with keyless bolts and peepholes on all exterior doors and pin locks on sliding glass doors, as well as a handle latch or security bar. (Tex. Prop. Code § 92.151-170.)

If you violate a law designed to protect tenants' safety—like a local ordinance requiring deadbolts— your tenants can complain to the agency in charge of enforcing the codes, often a local building or housing authority. The violation

may also make you automatically liable for losses that stem from the violation. (The legal term for this is "negligence per se"—see Chapter 10.) This is devastating if you're sued after a crime occurs, because you cannot argue that it was unreasonable to expect you to provide the security measure in question.

General Security Responsibilities

Even if your state and local laws offer little specific direction, you still likely have a duty to keep your premises "clean and safe" or "secure." How the courts in your state will interpret the tenant safety laws that apply to your rental property is difficult to predict. Some courts interpret tenant safety laws more strictly than others.

> **EXAMPLE 1:** The housing code in Andrew's city sets minimum standards for apartment houses, including a requirement that all areas of rental property be kept "clean and safe." The garage in Andrew's apartment house is poorly lit and accessible from the street because the automatic door works excruciatingly slowly. Andrew adds a few lights, but the garage is still far from bright. Andrew would be wise to spend the money to do the lighting job right and fix the garage door, because conditions like these could violate the "clean and safe" housing code requirement. If someone came in through the substandard garage door and assaulted a tenant, Andrew would likely be sued and found partially liable for the tenant's injuries.

> **EXAMPLE 2:** Martin is a tenant in a state that requires rental housing to be maintained in a "fit and habitable" condition. Courts in his state have interpreted this to mean, among other things, that dwellings should be reasonably secure from unwanted intrusions by strangers. One evening Martin is assaulted in the elevator by someone who got into the building through the unlocked front door. Martin sues his landlord, Jim, and is able to show that the front door lock had been broken for a long time and that Jim had failed to fix it. The jury decides that Jim's failure to provide a secure front door violated the requirement to keep the place habitable, that he was aware of the problem and had plenty of time to fix it, and that the unsecured front

door played a significant role in the assault. The jury awards Martin several thousand dollars for his injuries, lost wages, and pain and suffering.

Keep Your Promises About Security

If you promise tenants specific security features—such as a doorman, security patrols, interior cameras, or an alarm system—you must either provide them or be liable (at least partially) for any criminal act that they would have prevented.

Don't Exaggerate in Ads or Oral Descriptions

Landlords know that the promise of a safe environment is often a powerful marketing tool. In ads or during discussions with interested renters, you will naturally be inclined to point out security locks, outdoor lighting, and burglar alarms, because these features may be as important to prospective tenants as a fine view or a swimming pool.

Take care, however, not to exaggerate your written or oral description of security measures. Not only will you have begun the landlord-tenant relationship on a note of insincerity, but your descriptions of security may legally obligate you to provide what you have portrayed. If you fail to do so, or fail to conscientiously maintain promised security measures in working order (such as outdoor lighting or an electronic gate on the parking garage), a court or jury may find this lack of security to be a material factor in a crime on the premises. In this case, you may well be held liable for a tenant's losses or injuries. This is true even though you might not have been liable if you hadn't promised the specific security measures in the first place.

You won't be liable for failing to provide what was promised, however, unless this failure caused or contributed to the crime. Burned-out lightbulbs in the parking lot won't mean anything if the burglar got in through an unlocked trap door on the roof.

EXAMPLE: The manager of Jeff's apartment building gave him a thorough tour of the building before he decided to move in. Jeff was particularly impressed with the security locks on the gates of the high fences at the front and rear of the property. Confident that the interior of the property was accessible only to tenants and their guests, Jeff didn't hesitate to take his kitchen garbage to the dumpsters at the rear of the building late one evening. There he was accosted by an intruder who got in through a rear gate that had a broken lock. Jeff's landlord was held liable, because he had failed to maintain the sophisticated, effective locks that had been promised.

Ads That Invite Lawsuits

Advertisements like the following will come back to haunt you if a crime occurs on your rental property:

- "No one gets past our mega-security systems. A highly-trained guard is on duty at all times."
- "We provide highly safe, highly secure buildings."
- "You can count on us. We maintain the highest apartment security standards in the business."

Be Careful With Your Lease or Rental Agreement

The simple rule of following through with what you promise is even more crucial when it comes to written provisions in your lease or accompanying documents. Why? Your lease is a contract, and if it includes a "24-hour security" promise or a commitment to have a doorman on duty at night, your tenants have a right to expect it. If you fail to follow through, you could be sued and found liable for criminal acts that injure your tenants or their property.

EXAMPLE: The information packet given to Mai when she moved into her apartment stressed the need to keep careful track of door keys: "If you lose your keys, call the management, and the lock will be changed immediately." When Mai lost her purse containing her keys, she immediately called the management company but couldn't reach them, because it was after 5 p.m. and there was no after-hours emergency procedure. That evening, Mai was assaulted by someone who got into her apartment by using her lost key.

Mai sued the owner and management company on the grounds that they had disregarded their promise to change the locks promptly and so were partially responsible (along with the criminal) for the assailant's entry. The jury agreed and awarded Mai a large sum.

! CAUTION

Don't go overboard by specifying in your lease or rental agreement all the security measures you don't provide. Some landlords think that if they provide no security and say that tenants are completely on their own, they can eliminate liability for the acts of criminals. True, making it clear that you provide little or no security probably can reduce your potential liability for tenant injuries that result from criminal activity, but you can't excuse yourself from providing what is required by law. For example, if a local ordinance provides that exterior doors must have locks, you will increase—not decrease—your potential liability by failing to provide a front door lock.

Maintain What You Already Provide

Sometimes your actions can obligate you as much as an oral or written statement. If you provide enhanced security measures, such as security locks or a nighttime guard, without mentioning them in the lease, in advertisements, or through oral promises, you may be bound to maintain these features, even though you never explicitly promised to do so. Many landlords react with understandable frustration when their well-meaning (and expensive) efforts to protect their tenants actually *increase* their liability. But the answer is not to cut back to the bare minimum for security. Instead, be practical and keep your eye on your goal: Over time, using proven security measures will yield contented, long-term tenants and fewer legal hassles.

Prevent Criminal Acts

The best way to avoid liability for losses from crime is to prevent criminal acts in the first place.

The good news is that most successful prevention techniques—proper lighting, good locks, criminal-unfriendly landscaping, and well-trained on-site personnel—are not very expensive. Sometimes you'll have to go further, but whatever you spend on effective crime-prevention measures will pale in comparison to the costs that could result from crime on the premises.

Your Crime Prevention Checklist

- Meet or exceed requirements for safety devices, such as deadbolt locks, lighting, and window locks imposed by state and local housing codes.
- Don't hype your security measures. Keep oral and written promises regarding security measures—such as an advertisement promising garage parking or security personnel—to a truthful minimum.
- Provide and maintain adequate security measures based on an analysis of the vulnerability of your property and neighborhood. If your tenants will pay more rent if you make the building safer, you are foolish not to do it.
- Tighten up management practices to make your tenants and property safer—for example, practice strict key control.
- Educate tenants about crime problems and prevention strategies. Make it clear that they, not you, are primarily responsible for their own protection.
- Inspect the premises regularly to spot security problems, and ask tenants for their suggestions.
- Quickly respond to tenants' suggestions and complaints. If an important component of your security systems breaks, fix it on an emergency basis and provide appropriate alternative security.
- Be aware of threats to tenants' security from the manager or other tenants and handle safety and security problems pronto, especially those involving drug dealing.
- Buy adequate liability insurance to protect you from lawsuits related to crime on the property.

These costs can include increased insurance premiums, jury verdicts in excess of your insurance coverage, expensive attorney fees, and lost income due to rapid turnover of tenants. And there is no way to measure the sorrow and guilt that will come with knowing that you, as the landlord, may share responsibility for a crime because you did not take reasonable steps to prevent it. Don't pinch pennies here.

Evaluate Your Situation

The security steps you need to take depend on your circumstances: duplex or high-rise? peaceful neighborhood or high-crime area? Assess your needs and come up with a plan before you dash off to buy a security system you may not need.

Start With Your Own Inspection

Walk around your property and ask yourself two questions:

- Would I, or a member of my family, feel reasonably safe here, at night or alone?
- If I were a thief or assailant, how difficult would it be to get into the building or individual rental unit?

Schedule more than one assessment walk, at different times of the day and night. You might see something at 11 p.m. that you wouldn't notice at 11 a.m.

Consider the Neighborhood

Keep up-to-date on crime in the area of your rental property. If there have been no incidents in the neighborhood, you have less reason to equip your property with extensive security devices. (On the other hand, you certainly do not want one of your tenants to be the first to be raped or robbed on your block.) Especially if there have been criminal incidents in the neighborhood, talk to the neighbors and the police department about what measures have proven to be effective.

Get Advice From Experts

Most police departments will work with you to develop a sound security approach and educate tenants. Some will send an officer out to assess the vulnerability of your property and recommend security measures. Many will train tenants in neighborhood watch techniques, such as how to recognize and report suspicious behavior.

Another professional resource that may not immediately come to mind is your own insurance company. Some companies, having figured out that it's cheaper to offer preventive consultation services than to pay out huge awards to injured clients, consult with their clients for free on ways to deter crime. For example, drawing on its experience with claims generated by security breaches, your insurance company might be able to tell you which equipment has (and has not!) proven to be effective in preventing break-ins and assaults.

Another resource for advice is the private security industry. Listed in the phone book or online under "Security Systems," these firms typically provide an analysis of your situation before recommending specific equipment—whether it be bars on windows or an internal electronic surveillance system. Even if you do not ultimately engage their services, a professional evaluation may prove quite valuable as you design your own approach. As with other professional services, be sure to get several estimates and check references before selecting any security firm.

Security companies have a vested interest in getting you to buy products and services that may not be needed. If you own lots of rental properties, it may be worth your while to hire an independent security consultant for a disinterested evaluation. Call the International Association of Professional Security Consultants at 415-536-0288, or check their website at www.iapsc.org.

Take Basic Security Steps

At the very least, we recommend the following security measures for every rental property, from a single-family house or duplex to a multiunit building.

- **Exterior lighting.** Exterior lighting at entranceways and walkways should be activated by motion or on a timer. Do not rely on managers or tenants to turn on exterior lights. Many security experts regard the absence or failure of exterior lights as the single most common facilitator of break-ins and crime.

- **Interior lighting.** Have good, strong interior lights in hallways, stairwells, doorways, and parking garages.

- **Locks.** Sturdy dead-bolt door locks on individual rental units and solid window and patio door locks are essential, as are peepholes (with a wide-angle lens for viewing) at the front door of each unit. Lobby doors should have dead-bolt locks.

- **Landscaping.** Keep plants neat and compact. Shrubs should be no higher than three feet and trees cleared to seven feet from the ground. Trees and shrubbery should not obscure entryways or provide easy hiding places near doorways or windows. If yard maintenance is the tenants' responsibility in a single-family house, you may need to supervise the job.

You may also want to explore other measures, depending on the circumstances.

- **Security alarm.** You may want to install an alarm, hooked up to a security service.

- **Window bars.** Solid metal window bars or grills over ground floor windows are often a good idea in higher-crime neighborhoods, but local fire codes may restrict their use. All grills or bars must have a release mechanism, allowing the tenant to open them from inside. Too many people have tragically died in fires because they could not open window bars or grills that had no release mechanism.

Multiunit buildings may require additional measures:

- **Buzzers.** Intercom and buzzer systems that allow tenants to unlock the front door from their apartments are also a good idea; the front door can stay locked, and you can stress to tenants to open it only for people they know.

- **Doorman.** In some areas, a 24-hour doorman is essential and may do more to reduce

Don't Rely on "Courtesy Officers"

Some rental property owners provide on-site security by renting to police officers who, in exchange for a reduced rent, agree to be the resident "courtesy officer." The idea is to provide a professional presence on the property without paying for a regular security service. It's a poor idea, for several reasons:

- Calling the officer/tenant a courtesy officer does not change the fact that your tenants will look to him to provide consistent security protection. (In fact, because you are paying the officer by the rent reduction, he is not working as a courtesy at all.) A court would hold the police officer (and you) to the same standard of conduct expected of professional guard services.

- Because your officer/tenant can provide security only when he is home, the protection will be unpredictable. Tenants won't know when they can count on security coverage, and may do things (like coming home late at night) under the mistaken impression that the officer/tenant is on the property.

- The value of your officer/tenant's services will be as good as his wakefulness and attention. You are essentially asking him to assume a second job. But if he wants to unwind after a hard day with a few beers, how good will his judgment and response time be?

Paying a tenant for intermittent security makes you his employer, meaning you'll have to pay Social Security taxes and meet other employer obligations. (see Chapter 6 on tax issues and resident managers). And if a court finds your officer/tenant partially responsible for crime on the premises (by failing in his duties and allowing unauthorized access, for example), you will be liable as his employer.

A security service, on the other hand, is an independent contractor and takes care of these bookkeeping details. Independent contractors are generally responsible for their own lapses and should be insured (be sure you check). Of course, you could still be sued, but the chances of your being held liable will be reduced if an independent contractor provided the security service.

Signs of a Meth Lab

Landlords are increasingly encountering signs of methamphetamine (crystal meth) labs on rental properties. Meth is easily made by cooking common products such as cold remedies, salt, lighter fluid, gas, drain cleaners, and iodine on a stove or hot plate. Explosions and fires are common, and the byproducts of production pose an extreme health hazard.

According to the U.S. DEA, signs of a meth operation are:

- a large amount of cold tablet containers that list ephedrine or pseudoephedrine as ingredients
- jars containing clear liquid with a white or red colored solid on the bottom
- jars labeled as containing iodine or dark shiny metallic purple crystals inside of jars
- jars labeled as containing red phosphorus or a fine dark-red or purple powder
- coffee filters containing a white pasty substance, a dark-red sludge, or shiny white crystals
- bottles labeled as containing sulfuric, muriatic, or hydrochloric acid
- bottles or jars with rubber tubing attached
- cookware containing a powdery residue
- an unusually large number of cans of Camp Fuel, paint thinner, acetone, starter fluid, lye, and drain cleaners containing sulfuric acid or bottles containing muriatic acid
- large amounts of lithium batteries, especially ones that have been stripped
- soft silver or gray metallic ribbon (in chunk form) stored in oil or kerosene
- propane tanks with fittings that have turned blue
- strong smell of urine, or unusual chemical smells like ether, ammonia, or acetone.

If you think there's a meth lab in an occupied apartment or house, contact law enforcement immediately.

If you're left with an abandoned meth lab, here's what to do next:

- **Lock up and stay out.** Turning on lights could cause an explosion, and inhaling the fumes is very dangerous. Leave everything to the experts (see below).
- **Notify your insurance company.** Your policy may cover the cleanup costs, but some don't.
- **In case they don't know already, notify the police and fire department.** They will send a hazardous materials team to deal with the mess.
- **Cleaning.** Hire a company that specializes in meth lab cleanups to deal with the carpeting, walls, fixtures—basically, everything in the unit. Hire a licensed company if your state issues such licenses (contact the local health department to find out). Many states (either under the department of health or an environmental protection agency) include advice on cleaning up meth labs; see, for example, the Oklahoma Department of Environmental Quality (www.deq.state.ok.us) and search "guidelines for cleaning up former meth labs."
- **Test the apartment and get the official okay.** Use a different company to perform the test, and comply with any state- or local-mandated clearance requirements.
- **Find out whether you must notify future tenants.** Some states require landlords to tell applicants that the unit was a meth lab. Your state health department or health inspectors can tell you what your disclosure duties are. The Centers for Disease Control and Prevention includes of list of state departments of health at www.cdc.gov/mmwr/international/relres. html. The rental property's address may also appear on the U.S. Drug Enforcement Agency's "National Clandestine Laboratory Register" (www.dea.gov/clan-lab/clan-lab.shtml), for an indefinite time.

crime outside your building than anything else. Spread over a large number of units, a doorman may cost less than you think. If you hire a firm, insist on letters of reference and proof of insurance. You can also hire your own guard, but that gets complicated very quickly, because you will be responsible for his or her training and weapons used (if any).

- **Common areas.** Driveways, garages, and underground parking need to be well-lit and as secure (inaccessible to unauthorized entrants) as possible. Fences and automatic gates may be a virtual necessity in some areas.

- **Elevators.** Limiting access to the elevators by requiring a passkey and installing closed-circuit monitoring reduce the chances that an assailant will choose this site.

- **Security cameras.** A 24-hour internal security system with cameras and someone monitoring them is an effective crime detector. Though these systems are expensive, many reasonably affluent tenants will bear the extra costs in exchange for the added protection.

Initiate Good Management Practices

Physical safety devices and improvements aren't the only way you can improve security and decrease liability. Your business practices, including personnel policies, are crucial. They include:

Keep tenant information locked up. Keep tenant files in a locked cabinet. As an added precaution, identify residences by your own code, so that no one but you and your manager can read a tenant's file and learn where he or she lives.

Insist that employees respect tenants' privacy. Impress upon your employees the need to preserve your tenants' privacy. A tenant who wants friends, family, or bill collectors to know where she lives will tell them—you shouldn't.

Train employees to avoid dangerous situations and correct worrisome ones. Teach managers and employees to rigorously abide by your safety rules and to report areas of concern. Consider sending

employees to management courses on security offered by many landlords' associations.

Protect yourself and your employees when showing a unit. Ask for a photo ID and make a photocopy, which you should store in the office in a secure place. At the end of the tour, return the copy to the applicant or destroy it in the applicant's presence. Apply this practice to all applicants, not just those you think might pose a problem; selective practices invite discrimination claims (for example, don't ask for ID from only men, or any other protected class).

Don't undermine security measures with poor practices. Once you install security equipment, you must use it intelligently. For example, suppose you install locking gates at the property's entrance, but leave a key for the postal carrier in an unlocked box nearby. If an assailant gains entry by using that key, a jury could determine that you should be held partially responsible for the harm that ensued, because you were careless with the key.

Safeguard keys. The security of your rental property depends in large part on the locks on rental unit doors and the keys to those doors.

- Keep all duplicate keys in a locked area, identified by a code that only you and your manager know. Several types of locking key drawers and sophisticated key safes are available. Check ads in magazines that cater to the residential rental industry, or contact local locksmiths and security firms.

- Don't label keys with the rental unit number or name and address of the apartment building, and advise your tenants to take the same precaution.

- Allow only you and your manager access to master keys.

- Keep track of all keys provided to tenants and, if necessary, to your employees. Be sure all loaned keys are returned.

- Require tenants to return all keys at move-out.

- Rekey every time a new tenant moves in or loses a key.

- Give careful thought to the security problem of the front door lock: If the lock opens by an easy-to-copy key, there is no way to prevent a tenant from copying the key and giving it to others or using it after he moves out. Consider using locks that have hard-to-copy keys, or (with rental houses or small properties) rekey the front door when a tenant moves. There are also easy-to-alter card systems that allow you to change front door access on a regular basis or when a tenant moves. Again, locksmiths and security firms can advise you on options available.

- Give keys only to people you know and trust. If you have hired a contractor whom you do not know personally, open the unit for him and return to close up when he is done. Keep in mind that often even known and trusted contractors hire others you don't know.

When a Tenant Wants to Supply Additional Security

The form lease and rental agreements (Chapter 2) forbid the tenant from rekeying or adding locks or a burglar alarm without your written consent. But think carefully before you refuse permission to install extra protection. If a crime occurs that would have been foiled had the security item been in place, and you get sued, you will obviously be at a disadvantage before a judge or jury.

If you let a tenant add additional security measures, make sure the tenant gives you duplicate keys or instructions on how to disarm the alarm system and the name and phone number of the alarm company, so that you can enter in case of emergency.

Educate Tenants About Crime Prevention

After you have identified the vulnerabilities of the neighborhood—for example, by talking to the police—don't keep this information to yourself. Share it with your tenants. It's best to do this when you first show the rental unit to prospective tenants. We recommend a two-step process:

- Alert tenants to the specific risks of your neighborhood (for example, "problems are

worst Friday and Saturday night between 10 p.m. and 1 a.m.") and what they can do to minimize the chances of assault or theft (avoid being alone on the street or in outside parking lots late at night), and

- No matter how secure your building, warn tenants of the limitations of the security measures you have provided.

    EXAMPLE: Paul moves into his apartment and is told by the manager that doormen are on duty only from 6 p.m. to 6 a.m. One afternoon, someone knocks on Paul's door and identifies himself as a "building inspector" who needs to check the heating system. Realizing that the doorman is not on duty to screen visitors, Paul demands identification. When the alleged inspector refuses to show ID, Paul won't open the door. He later finds out that someone in the neighborhood has been robbed, falling for the same ruse.

This twofold approach allows you to cover your legal bases by both disclosing the risks and frankly informing tenants that you cannot ensure their safety in all possible situations. If, despite your best efforts, a crime does occur on your property, your candid disclosures regarding the safety problems of your neighborhood and the limitations of the existing security measures may help shield you from liability.

From the tenant's point of view, such disclosures highlight the need to be vigilant and assume some responsibility for safety. If you do not disclose the limitations of the security you provide (or if you exaggerate) and a crime does occur, one of the first things your tenant will say (to the police, his lawyer, and the jury) is that he was simply relying upon the protection you had assured him would be in place.

Identify Specific Concerns

Give tenants information specific to your rental property. Here are some ideas:

- If there have been incidents of crime in the area, especially in your building, inform your tenants but don't disclose the identity of the victim.

- Update your information on the security situation as necessary. For example, let tenants know if there has been an assault in or near the building by sending them a note and post a notice in the lobby, including the physical description of the assailant.

- If you hire a professional security firm to evaluate your rental property, share the results of their investigation with your tenants.

- Encourage tenants to set up a neighborhood watch program. Many local police departments will come out and meet with citizens attempting to organize such a program.

- Encourage tenants to report any suspicious activities or security problems to you, such as loitering, large numbers of late-night guests, or broken locks. (Chapter 9 recommends a system for handling tenant complaints.)

Terrorist Attacks

If you want information on preparing tenants for possible terrorist attacks, including issues for high-rise buildings, see the U.S. government website, www.ready.gov (search "terrorist hazards").

Explain the Limitations of Your Security Measures

An important component of your disclosures to tenants involves disabusing them of any notion that you are their guardian angel. Let them know where your security efforts end, and where their own good sense (and the local police force) must take over. Specifically:

- Point out each security measure—such as locking exterior gates, key locks on windows, and peepholes in every front door—and explain how each measure works. It's best to do this in writing, either as part of a move-in letter to new tenants or at the time a new security item is installed.

- Highlight particular aspects of the property that are, despite your efforts, vulnerable to

the presence of would-be assailants or thieves. Say, for example, your apartment parking garage has a self-closing door. When you explain how this door works, you might also point out that it's not instantaneous. For example, a fast-moving person could, in most situations, slip into the garage behind an entering car despite the self-closing door. Pointing this out to your tenant may result in more careful attention to the rearview mirror.

- Place signs in potentially dangerous places that will remind tenants of possible dangers and the need to be vigilant. For example, place a notice in the lobby asking tenants to securely lock the front door behind them.

- Suggest safety measures. For example, tenants arriving home after dark might call ahead and ask a neighbor to be an escort.

Giving your tenants information on how they, too, can take steps to protect themselves will also help if you are sued. If a tenant argues that you failed to inform him of a dangerous condition, you will be able to show that you have done all that could be expected of a reasonably conscientious landlord.

Inspect and Maintain Your Property

Landlords are most often found liable for crime on their property when a criminal gained access through broken doors or locks. Not only is the best security equipment in the world useless if it has deteriorated or is broken, but the very fact that it's not working can be enough to result in landlord liability. By contrast, a jury is far less likely to fault a landlord who can show that reasonable security measures were in place and working, but were unable to stop a determined criminal.

Inspect your property frequently, so that you discover and fix problems before an opportunistic criminal comes along. At the top of your list should be fixing burned-out exterior floodlights and broken locks and cutting back overgrown shrubbery that provides a lurking spot for criminals.

Protect Yourself, Too

Landlords and managers need to take precautions for their own safety as well as for that of tenants. Whether or not you live on the rental property:

- Promptly deposit rent checks and money orders. If possible, do not accept cash.
- When you show a vacant apartment, consider bringing someone with you. A would-be assailant may be deterred by the presence of another person. If you must show apartments by yourself, alert a family member or friend to the fact that you are showing a vacant unit, and when you expect to be done.
- Especially if your building is in a high-crime area, carry a small alarm device (such as beeper-sized box that emits a piercing alarm when its pin is removed), and carry a cell phone.
- Work on vacant units during the day and be alert to the fact that, although keeping the front door open (to the building or the unit) may be convenient as you go to and fro for materials and equipment, it is also an invitation to someone to walk right into the building.

Enlist your tenants to help you spot and correct security problems—both in their own rental unit and in common areas such as parking garages. The people who actually live in your rental property will generally know first about security hazards. One good approach is to post several notices in central locations, such as elevators and main lobbies, asking tenants to promptly report any security problems, such as broken locks or windows. If you rent a duplex or house, periodically meet with your tenants and discuss any changes in the neighborhood or the structure of the building.

Handle Security Complaints Immediately

Take care of complaints about a dangerous situation or a broken security item immediately, even if it's the middle of the night. A broken lock or disabled intercom system is an invitation to crime and needs to be addressed pronto.

Either fix the problem or, if that's impossible, alert tenants and take other measures. For example, you might hire a security officer and close off other entrances for a few days if your front door security system fails and a necessary part is not immediately available. Failing to do this may saddle you with a higher level of legal liability should a tenant be injured by a criminal act while the security system is out of service or a window lock broken. A few examples of quick and appropriate responses:

- The glass panel next to the front door is accidentally broken late one afternoon by a departing workman. Conscious that this creates a major security problem, you call a 24-hour glass replacement service to get it replaced immediately.
- The intercom system fails due to a power surge following an electrical storm. You hire a 24-hour guard for the two days it takes to repair the circuitry.
- Several exterior floodlights are knocked out by vandals throwing rocks at 6 p.m. A tenant, who has been encouraged by management to immediately report problems of this nature, calls you. You alert the police and ask for an extra drive-by during the night, post signs in the lobby and the elevator, close off the darkened entrance, and advise tenants to use an alternate, lighted entryway instead. The next day, you get the floodlights repaired and equipped with wire mesh protection.

 TIP
Establish good complaint procedures. Encouraging tenants to keep you informed will help you prevent crime on the property. Such procedures can also limit your liability, should you be sued, for example, by a tenant whose assailant gained access because of a broken window lock that the tenant never told you about. See Chapter 9.

Protect Tenants From Each Other

What if one of your tenants is responsible for criminal activity on the premises, or poses a danger? (Physical disputes between tenants in the same household—domestic violence—are discussed in Chapter 8.) You have a duty to take reasonable steps to protect tenants if another resident threatens harm or property damage. If you don't, and a tenant is injured or robbed by another tenant, you may be sued and pay a hefty judgment. As with your duty to protect tenants from crime at the hands of strangers, your duty to keep the peace among your tenants is limited to what is *reasonably* foreseeable and to what a *reasonable* person in your position would do.

Note that the scenarios and advice that follow assume that you are not dealing with a dangerous tenant who is also legally disabled. In that situation, you may need to work with your tenant if you can reasonably expect that the behavior will stop. See "Do You Need to Accommodate Tenants With Disabilities Who Are Dangerous" in Chapter 5.

TIP

Encourage tenants to report other tenants' suspicious or illegal activity. Establish a system to collect tenants' complaints and concerns about other tenants or the manager, just the way you handle repair complaints. This will let you respond quickly. It will serve an additional function: If you are sued for something a manager or tenant does, and if your business records show that there were no prior complaints regarding his behavior, that will bolster your claim that you acted reasonably under the circumstances (by continuing to rent to or employ the individual), because you had no inkling that trouble was likely.

When to Act

If you learn that a tenant has threatened or committed violence on your property, you may need to take action. Whether to act—by terminating the tenancy—depends on the seriousness of the behavior, and the likelihood that similar acts will

occur again on your property. Unless there's a clear history of serious problems with the offending tenant, landlords often win these cases.

> **EXAMPLE 1:** Evelyn decides to rent an apartment to David, although she knows that he was convicted of spousal abuse many years earlier. For two years David is a model tenant, until he hits another tenant, Chuck, in the laundry room over a disagreement as to who was next in line for the dryer. Chuck sues but is unable to convince a jury that Evelyn should bear some responsibility for his injuries, because he cannot show that the incident was foreseeable.

> **EXAMPLE 2:** Mary rents to Carl, who appears to be a nice young man with adequate references. On the rental application, Carl states that he has no criminal convictions. Several months later, Carl is arrested for burglary and assault of another tenant in the building. It comes out that Carl had recently been released from state prison for burglary and rape. Because Mary had no knowledge of his criminal past, she is not held liable for his actions.

On the other hand, tenants sometimes win if they can show that the landlord knew about a resident's tendency toward violence and failed to take reasonable precautions to safeguard the other tenants.

> **EXAMPLE:** Bill receives several complaints from tenants about Carol, a tenant who pushed another resident out of the elevator, slapped a child for making noise, and verbally abused a tenant's guest for parking in Carol's space. Despite these warning signs, Bill doesn't terminate Carol's tenancy or even speak with her about her behavior. When Carol picks a fight with a resident whom she accused of reading her newspaper and badly beats her up, Bill is held partly liable on the grounds that he knew of a dangerous situation but failed to address it.

What to Do

When you learn of the potential for danger from a tenant and decide to act, your response should be swift and appropriate.

Law enforcement. In an emergency—for example, one tenant brandishes a gun—of course you would just call police. Do the same if drugs are involved.

Eviction. In less dire circumstances, you'll probably want to evict the worrisome tenant, and possibly post a guard and warn other tenants until he's gone. Many states now make it relatively simple for landlords to evict troublemakers. These laws specify that harm or the threat of harm to other persons justifies a quick eviction.

Incentives. If you don't want to go through the hassle of eviction, and you want to get someone out quickly, consider offering a financial incentive to leave. Let the tenant break the lease without a penalty—it's a small price to pay to defuse a dangerous situation.

Negotiation. If the danger seems minor, you can try to talk to the troublemaker and head off future problems. For example, suppose a tenant complains about a neighbor who bangs on the walls and yells every time the tenant practices the violin during the afternoon, and the pounding is getting louder every day. The tenant can reasonably expect you to intervene and attempt to broker a solution—perhaps an adjustment of the violinist's practice schedule or some heavy-duty earplugs for the neighbor.

Protect Tenants From Your Employees

Your property manager occupies a critical position in your business. The manager interacts with every tenant and often has access to their personal files *and* their homes. If your manager commits a crime—especially if you had any warning that it might occur—you are likely to be held liable. The same goes for other employees, such as maintenance personnel. Your liability usually turns on whether or not you acted reasonably under the circumstances in hiring and supervising your employees. Let's take a closer look at what this means.

RELATED TOPIC
Chapter 6 discusses managers in detail.

Check Your Employees' Backgrounds

It is essential to thoroughly check the background of your potential manager and other on-site workers. If a manager or other worker commits a crime—for example, he robs or assaults a tenant— you are likely to be sued for negligent hiring. You may be found liable if all of the following are true:

- You failed to investigate your employee's background to the full extent allowed by the privacy laws in your state.
- A proper investigation would have revealed a past criminal conviction that would have rendered the applicant unsuitable for the job.
- The employee's offense against the tenant is reasonably related to the past conviction.

EXAMPLE: When his longtime manager suddenly leaves, Martin feels pressured to replace her fast. He hires Jack without checking his background or the information provided on the application. Martin takes Jack at his word when he says that he has no felony convictions. Several months later, Jack is arrested for stealing electronic equipment from a tenant's home that he had entered using the master key. Martin is successfully sued when the tenant learns that Jack had two prior felony convictions for burglary and grand theft.

Supervise Your Manager

As the manager's employer, you may also be held liable if your manager's negligence makes it possible for another person to commit a crime against a tenant. For example, if your manager's sloppy practices make it possible for a criminal to get a tenant's key, you will be held responsible on the grounds that you failed to properly supervise the manager.

Deal With Drug-Dealing Tenants

If you look the other way while tenants engage in illegal activity on your property—by dealing drugs, storing stolen property, engaging in prostitution, or participating in gang-related activity—you can end up paying huge fines or even losing your property altogether to government seizure. This discussion focuses on the most common problem, drug dealing, but it applies equally to other illegal activities.

It's your responsibility to know what's going on at your property. In some situations, fines are levied or property is seized even though the landlord knew almost nothing about the tenants' activities. So keep yourself well-informed, and if you even suspect that illegal drug dealing is taking place on the rental property, act quickly and decisively. If you do nothing—either out of inertia, fear of reprisals from drug dealers, or a mistaken belief that you're unlikely to get in trouble—you will almost surely regret it.

The Cost of Renting to Drug-Dealing Tenants

Increasingly, laws and court decisions have made landlords liable when a tenant engages in a continuing illegal activity such as drug dealing. If you don't quickly evict drug-dealing tenants, you'll run into some big problems:

- Good tenants may be difficult to find and keep, and the value of your property will plummet.
- Good tenants, trying to avoid drug-dealing ones, may be able to legally move out without notice and before a lease runs out. They will argue that the presence of the illegal activity has, for all practical purposes, evicted them, in that the problems associated with drug dealing prevent them from the "quiet enjoyment" of their home or violate the implied warranty of habitability. In many states, the tenant will have a very strong case to break their lease.

- Tenants injured or annoyed by drug dealers, both in the building and neighborhood, may sue you for violating nuisance laws and building codes.
- Local, state, or federal authorities may levy stiff fines against you and may even empty your building for allowing the illegal activity to continue.
- Law enforcement authorities may pursue criminal penalties against both the tenants *and* you for knowingly allowing the activity to continue.
- Your rental property might even be confiscated by the state or federal government.

Nice Properties Are Not Immune

You may think that drug crime is a problem only in seedy neighborhoods. Think again. Drug dealers often prefer smaller apartment complexes with some measure of security over large, unprotected housing units. A drug dealer, like a law-abiding tenant, wants a safe, controlled environment.

Lawsuits Against You for Harboring a Nuisance

In legal terms, a nuisance is a pervasive, continuing, and serious condition—like a pile of stinking garbage or a group of drug dealers—that threatens public health, safety, or morals. In some states, it also includes obnoxious activity that is simply offensive, like excessive noise or open sexual conduct. Property used as a drug house, which injures and interferes with the rights of neighbors to use and enjoy their property easily qualifies as a legal nuisance.

The government, and sometimes the neighbors, can sue to get a nuisance stopped (abated), often by court order and fines against the landlord. If you tolerate a nuisance on your property, you can be sued. Even though the tenant causes the nuisance, the punishment may be directed at you, as the landlord.

EXAMPLE: Alma owned a duplex in Wisconsin, which defines drug houses as nuisances. (Wisc. Stat. Ann. § 823.113.) Despite repeated complaints from the neighbors that one of her tenants was conducting a drug operation in his home (and in spite of the tenant's two arrests for dealing from that address), Alma did nothing about the problem. Responding to pressure from fed-up neighbors, the local police finally sued Alma to evict the tenant and close the duplex. The property was padlocked.

Using public nuisance abatement laws against crime-tolerant landlords is increasingly common in cities with pervasive drug problems. In extreme cases, where the conduct giving rise to the nuisance complaint is illegal (drug dealing or prostitution, for example), landlords themselves face civil fines or jail time. See "Civil and Criminal Nuisance Laws," below.

Each state has different standards for determining when a landlord may be found responsible under nuisance law. In most states, however, the landlord must have had *some* knowledge of the illegal activity before property can be seized. Generally, landlords are given a short time in which to cure the problem before the ax falls and the property is seized.

In reality, because most landlords are acutely aware of their tenants' illegal behavior—having been informed by disgusted neighbors and overwhelmed law enforcement—even in states that require that you have clear actual knowledge of the situation, this knowledge standard is usually met. Put another way, it's a rare situation in which you can credibly claim that you didn't know about drug-dealing tenants.

Know the Law

It is important to know the nuisance laws in your state. At the very least, this will alert you to the standard by which your actions (or inaction) will be judged should there be proceedings brought against you or your property. Chapter 18 gives tips on how to unearth the laws that apply to you.

Tenants and neighbors, not just the government, can sue you for knowing about the activity but failing to take steps to clean up the property. They can seek:

Civil and Criminal Nuisance Laws		
	Civil Nuisance Laws	**Criminal Nuisance Laws**
Activities the laws target	Unhealthy, immoral, or obnoxious behavior which may be, but is not necessarily, a violation of the criminal law as well	Criminal behavior
Examples of targeted activities	Excessive noise, piles of garbage and trash, and inordinate amounts of foot or car traffic	Drug dealing, prostitution, gambling, and gang activities
Who can sue	Public agencies such as city health departments, law enforcement agencies, and, in many states, affected neighbors, who may band together and sue for large sums in small claims court	Law enforcement agencies only
How landlord's liability is determined	"Preponderance of evidence" shows landlord intentionally tolerated the illegal activity, or was negligent or reckless in allowing it to occur.	Prosecutor must prove guilt "beyond a reasonable doubt" and usually must show landlord had some knowledge of illegal activity.
Possible consequences to the landlord	A court ordering the offending tenant, and sometimes the landlord, to compensate other tenants. If a health, fire, or other enforcement agency brings the nuisance action based on many violations, it can result in a court order closing down the entire building.	Liability for money damages plus fines and imprisonment. Government may also close the property.

- Monetary compensation for each of them for having put up with the situation. Each neighbor generally sues for the maximum allowed in state small claims court ($5,000 to $10,000 in most states), and the landlord often pays the maximum to *each* one. See the discussion of small claims courts in Chapter 16.
- An order from the judge directing you to evict the troublemakers, install security, and repair the premises. (Such orders are not available in all states.)

Private use of nuisance abatement laws is not as common as governmental use, but the practice will probably grow as people learn of others' successes.

Small (But Sometimes Mighty) Claims Court

The private enforcement of public nuisance laws has been creatively and successfully pursued in small claims courts in California and several other states, where groups of affected neighbors have brought multiple lawsuits targeted at drug houses.

In Berkeley, California, after failing to get the police and city council to close down a crack house, neighbors sought damages stemming from the noxious activities associated with the house. Each of the 18 plaintiffs collected the maximum amount allowed in small claims court ($3,500 at the time), avoided the expense of hiring counsel, and sent the landlord a very clear and expensive message. The problem was solved within a few weeks.

Losing Your Property: Forfeiture Laws

Federal or state forfeiture proceedings—where the government *takes* your property because of the illegal activities of one or more tenants—are the most dramatic possible consequence of owning crime-ridden rental property. Forfeitures are rare and not something you are likely to encounter if you follow the suggestions in this book for choosing decent tenants and maintaining safe and secure rental property. But they happen.

Unlike the nuisance abatement laws, which depend upon a pervasive and continuing pattern of illegal activity, forfeitures may be accomplished on the basis of a single incident. Also, unlike nuisance abatement laws, which temporarily deprive you of the use of your property, the consequence of a forfeiture is the complete and final transfer of title to the government.

You Might Forfeit the Rent Money, Too

If you know, or have reason to know, that a tenant's rent was earned in the course of an illegal act, the rent money is itself forfeitable, no matter where the act was committed. A clever dealer may live in your nice, respectable building and conduct his trade elsewhere—but if he pays the rent with the money received in drug transactions, the rent money will be forfeited if the government can show that you knew (or had reason to know) of its source.

It is harder for the government to prove that you knew of the source of the rental payments than it is to show that you knew about illegal activity on the premises—but not impossible. To protect yourself, be able to point to a careful background check (regarding the tenant's job, credit, and bank account) performed before renting to the tenant. If you can show that there appeared to be a legitimate source of income to cover the rent, it will be harder for the government to argue that it should have been obvious that the rent constituted ill-gotten gain. Your refusal to accept cash rent may help protect you from an assertion that the money was the fruit of a drug transaction.

Federal laws. The government can seize property that has "facilitated" an illegal drug transaction or that has been bought or maintained with funds, such as rent payments, gained through illegal drug dealing. (Comprehensive Drug Abuse Prevention and Control Act of 1970, 21 U.S. Code § 881.) The government's power under this law must give any landlord pause. To start forfeiture proceedings, the government need show only that it is *reasonably probable* that illegal activities are occurring on the premises, and may do so by relying on circumstantial evidence and hearsay. You must then prove either that the property did not facilitate the crime, or that the tenants' activities were done without your knowledge or consent. Your deliberate blindness will be of no avail. To prevail, you must show that you have done *all* that reasonably could be expected to prevent the illegal use of your property.

State laws. Every state has adopted the Uniform Controlled Substances Act, modifying it to suit their policy aims. The Act specifies that land involved in drug transactions is *not* forfeitable. Drug "containers," however, can be seized, and some states have interpreted that term to include property—for example, the rental property where drugs were kept. In many states, the Act has been changed to include rental or other property that "facilitated" the illegal act.

Under the Act, you must be shown to have knowledge of the illegal activity in order for forfeiture to occur, but that requirement is interpreted very differently in different states. In some states, the prosecutor need only show constructive knowledge of drug dealing—that is, what a reasonable person in the circumstances would conclude. In others, the state must prove that you actually knew of the drug problem. In a few states, landowners are accountable if they were negligent in not knowing of the drug-related activities of their tenants. In any case, it is difficult to successfully prove ignorance.

How to Prevent Drug Lawsuits and Seizures

If you follow these steps, it is unlikely that conditions will deteriorate to the point that neighbors or the government feel it is necessary to step in and take over:

- Carefully screen potential renters.
- Keep the results of your background checks that show that your tenants' rent appeared to come from legitimate sources (jobs and bank accounts).
- Don't accept cash rental payments.
- Include a clause in your lease or rental agreement prohibiting drug dealing and other illegal activity, and promptly evict tenants who violate it.
- Let tenants know you intend to keep drug dealing out of the building.
- Respond to tenant and neighbor complaints about drug dealing on the property.
- Be aware of heavy traffic in and out of the premises.
- Inspect the premises and improve lighting and security.
- Get advice from police and security professionals *immediately* if you learn of a problem.
- Consult security experts to determine whether you have done all that one could reasonably expect to discover and prevent illegal activity on your property.

If You Are Sued

If your efforts at crime prevention fail, and a tenant is injured, will you be responsible? As mentioned, if you violated a specific law requiring a safety measure, and that's what led directly to the injury or loss, you will probably be liable. But you also have a general duty to take reasonable precautions to protect tenants from foreseeable criminal assaults and property crimes. To get an idea of whether or not your precautions were reasonable under the circumstances, take a look at these six key questions. They're also discussed in Chapter 10, because they're also used if an insurance adjuster or court evaluates your negligence and assesses responsibility when a tenant suffers accidental injury.

1. Did you control the area where the crime occurred? You aren't expected to police the entire world. But a lobby, hallway, or other common area is an area of high landlord control, which heightens your responsibility. However, you exert much less control over the sidewalk outside the front door, so it may be more difficult for you to minimize the chances of a crime occurring there.

2. How likely was it that a crime would occur? You are duty-bound to respond to the foreseeable, not the improbable. Have there been prior criminal incidents at a particular spot in the building? Elsewhere in the neighborhood? If you know that an offense is likely (because of a rash of break-ins or prior crime on the property), you have a heightened legal responsibility in most states to take reasonable steps to guard against future crime.

3. How difficult or expensive would it have been to reduce the risk of crime? If cheap or simple measures could significantly lower the risk of crime, it is likely that a court would find that you had a duty to undertake them if their absence facilitated a crime, especially in an area where criminal activity is high. For instance, would inexpensive new locks and better lighting discourage thieves? How about better management practices, such as strict key control, locked tenant files, scrupulous employee screening, and trained, alert on-site personnel? However, if the only solution to the problem is costly, such as structural remodeling or hiring a full-time doorman, it is doubtful that a court would expect it of you.

4. How serious an injury was likely to result from the crime? The consequences of a criminal incident (break-in, robbery, rape, or murder) may be very serious.

5. Did you fail to take reasonable steps to prevent a crime? As ever, reasonableness is evaluated in the context of each situation. For example, if you let the bushes near a door grow high and don't replace outdoor lights, it's clearly unreasonable.

But suppose you cut the bushes back halfway and installed one light. Would that have been enough? It would be up to a jury to decide.

"Reasonable precautions" in a crime-free neighborhood are not the same as those called for when three apartments in your building have been burglarized within a month. The greater the danger, the more you must do.

6. Did your failure to take reasonable steps to keep tenants safe contribute to the crime? A tenant must be able to connect your failure to provide reasonable security with the criminal incident. It is often very difficult for tenants to convince a jury that the landlord's breach caused (or contributed to) the assault or burglary.

When an intruder enters through an unsecured front door, you are not responsible for the criminal's determination to break the law, and many juries simply won't place any responsibility on you, even if, for example, your failure to install a lock made the entry possible. To convince a jury otherwise, a tenant must emphasize that a crime of this nature was highly foreseeable and would probably have been prevented had you taken appropriate measures.

If a jury decides that you didn't meet the duty to keep tenants safe, and that this failure facilitated the crime, it will typically split the responsibility for the crime between you and the criminal. For example, jurors might decide that you were 60% at fault and the criminal 40%.

How Much Money a Tenant Is Entitled To

To get financial compensation, an injured tenant must show that he or she was harmed from the criminal incident. Tragically, this is often quite obvious, and the only issue that lawyers argue about is the worth, in dollars, of dreadful injuries. Compensation may also be awarded for mental anguish and continuing psychological effects of the encounter.

Now let's look at two realistic cases, applying the six questions.

EXAMPLE 1: Elaine was assaulted and robbed by an intruder who entered her apartment through a sliding window that was closed but could not be locked. To determine whether or not the landlord would be liable, Elaine asked herself the six questions and came up with these answers:

1. The landlord controlled the window and was responsible for its operation.
2. This burglary was foreseeable, because there had been other break-ins at the building.
3. Installing a window lock was a minor burden.
4. The seriousness of foreseeable injury was high.
5. The landlord had done nothing to secure the window or otherwise prevent an intrusion.
6. The intruder could not have entered so easily and silently had the window been locked.

Elaine concluded that the landlord owed her the duty to take reasonable steps to fix the problem. She filed a claim with the landlord's insurance company, but it didn't offer a fair settlement, and the case went to trial. The jury decided that the landlord should have installed a window lock and that because the burglar might not have entered at all through a properly secured window, the landlord was partially responsible for Elaine's injuries. The jury fixed the value of her injuries at $500,000 and decided that the landlord was 80% responsible.

EXAMPLE 2: Nick was assaulted in the underground garage of his apartment building by someone who hid in the shadows. The neighborhood had recently experienced several muggings. Nick couldn't identify the assailant, who was never caught. The automatic garage gate was broken and wouldn't close completely, allowing anyone to slip inside.

Nick decided that:

1. The landlord controlled the garage.
2. In view of the recent similar crimes in the neighborhood, an assault was foreseeable.
3. Fixing the broken gate wouldn't have been a great financial burden.
4. The likelihood of injury from an assault was high.

Nick concluded that the landlord owed him a duty of care in this situation. He then considered the last two questions. The garage door was broken, which constituted a breach of the landlord's duty. But the garage was also accessible from the interior of the building, making it possible that the assailant had been another tenant or a guest. Nick's case fell apart because the landlord's failure to provide a secure outside door hadn't necessarily contributed to the crime. If the assailant were another tenant or guest, the landlord's failure to fix the gate would have been completely unconnected to the crime. Nick probably would have had a winning case if he could have proved that the assailant got in through the broken gate.

Landlord's Right of Entry and Tenants' Privacy

FORMS IN THIS CHAPTER

Chapter 13 includes instructions for and a sample of the following form:

- Notice of Intent to Enter Dwelling Unit

The Nolo website includes a downloadable copy of this form. See Appendix B for the link to the forms in this book.

Next to disputes over rent or security deposits, one of the most common—and emotion-filled—misunderstandings between landlords and tenants involves conflicts between your right to enter the rental property and a tenant's right to be left alone at home. Fortunately many of these problems can be avoided if you adopt fair—and, of course, legal—policies to enter the tenant's unit and then clearly explain these policies to the tenant from the first day of your relationship. (And, if you employ a manager or management company, make sure they also follow your guidelines.)

This chapter recommends a practical approach that should keep you out of legal hot water.

maintenance of the premises. This means that, of necessity, you have a legal responsibility to keep fairly close tabs on the condition of the property. For this reason, and because it makes good sense to allow landlords reasonable access to their property, nearly every state has, by judicial decision or statute, clearly recognized the right of a landlord to legally enter rented premises while a tenant is still in residence under certain broad circumstances, such as to deal with an emergency and when the tenant gives permission.

For details on state rules, including allowable reasons for entry and notice requirements, see "State Laws on Landlord's Access to Rental Property" in Appendix A.

 RELATED TOPIC

Related topics covered in this book include:

- Recommended lease and rental agreement clause for landlord's access to rental property: Chapter 2
- How to make sure your manager doesn't violate tenants' right of privacy: Chapter 6
- How to highlight access procedures in a move-in letter to new tenants: Chapter 7
- Tenants' right of privacy and landlord's policy on guests: Chapter 8
- Procedures for respecting tenants' right of privacy while handling tenant complaints about safety and maintenance problems and conducting an annual safety inspection: Chapter 9
- How to protect the confidentiality of tenants' credit reports and notify tenants of any breach in your security: Chapter 9
- Tenants' right of privacy if drug dealing or terrorist activity is suspected: Chapter 12
- How to handle disputes with tenants through negotiation, mediation, and other means: Chapter 16
- State Laws on Landlord's Access to Rental Property: Appendix A.

General Rules of Entry

In most states, the tenant's duty to pay rent is conditioned on your proper repair and

How to Respect Tenants' Privacy Rights
Step 1: Know and comply with your state's law on landlord's access to rental property.
Step 2: Include a lease or rental agreement clause that complies with the law and gives you reasonable rights of entry.
Step 3: To avoid any uncertainty, highlight your policies on entry in a move-in letter to new tenants and other periodic communications.
Step 4: Notify tenants whenever you plan to enter their rental unit.
Step 5: Provide as much notice as possible before you enter, or, at a minimum, the amount of time required by state law.
Step 6: Keep written records of your requests to enter rental units.
Step 7: Protect yourself from a tenant's claim that you or your employee or independent contractor is a thief—for example, try to arrange repairs only when the tenant is home.
Step 8: Meet—and possibly mediate—with any tenants who object to your reasonable access policies to come up with a mutual agreement regarding your entry.
Step 9: Never force entry, short of a true emergency.
Step 10: Consider terminating the tenancy of any tenant who unreasonably restricts your right to enter the rental unit.

Allowable Reasons for Entry

About half the states have access laws specifying the circumstances under which landlords may legally enter rented premises. Most access laws allow landlords to enter rental units to make repairs and inspect the property and to show property to prospective tenants or buyers.

Notice Requirements

State access laws typically specify the amount of notice required for landlord entry—usually 24 hours or two days (unless it is impracticable to do so—for example, in cases of emergency). A few states simply require the landlord to provide "reasonable" notice, often presumed to be 24 hours.

Must Notice Be in Writing?

State access laws do not uniformly require that notice be in writing, but it's a good idea to give written notice. If the tenant later claims that you didn't follow legal procedures regarding right to entry, your copy of a written notice that you mailed, left in the tenant's mailbox, or posted on his door is proof that you notified him in advance of your intention to enter. It's also wise to document all oral or email requests for entry—but written notice is preferable (as explained in "Using Emails for Notices or Other Communications to Tenants" in Chapter 7). A sample letter requesting entry and a formal Notice of Intent to Enter Dwelling Unit form are included below.

Time of Day You May Enter

Most state access laws either do not specify the hours when a landlord may enter or simply allow entry at "reasonable" times, without setting specific hours and days. Weekdays between 9 a.m. and 6 p.m. would seem to be reasonable times, and perhaps Saturday mornings between 10 a.m. and 1 p.m. On the other hand, some statutes are more specific, such as Florida (between 7:30 a.m. and 8 p.m.) and Delaware (between 8 a.m. and 9 p.m.).

The Best Approach

If your state does not set specific rules regarding landlords' entry, this doesn't mean you can—or should—enter a tenant's home at any time for any reason. Once you rent residential property, you must respect it as your tenant's home. We recommend you provide as much notice as possible (in writing), try to arrange a mutually convenient time, and only enter for clearly legitimate business reasons, such as to make necessary repairs. If it's not an emergency or clearly impractical, try to give at least 24 hours' notice, especially when entering a rental unit when the tenant is likely to be home. In some circumstances, less notice (say, ten or 15 hours) might be fine—for example, if you find out Thursday evening that an electrician is available Friday morning to put extra outlets in the tenant's apartment. Except for an emergency, less than four hours' notice is not ordinarily considered reasonable. Common sense suggests that you be considerate of your tenants' privacy and do your best to accommodate their schedules. You'll go a long way toward keeping tenants and avoiding disputes and legal problems by doing so.

Entry in Case of Emergency

In all states, you can enter a rental unit without giving notice to respond to a true emergency—such as a fire or gas leak—that threatens life or property if not corrected immediately.

Here are some examples of emergency situations when it would be legal to enter without giving the tenant notice:

- Smoke is pouring out of the tenant's window. You call the fire department and use your master key—or even break in if necessary—to try to deal with the fire.
- You see water coming out of the bottom of a tenant's back door. It's okay to enter and find the water leak.
- Your on-site manager hears screams coming from the apartment next door. He knocks

on the apartment door, but no one answers. After calling the police, he uses his pass key to enter and see what's wrong.

On the other hand, your urge to repair a problem that's important but doesn't threaten life or property—say, a stopped-up drain that is not causing any damage—isn't a true emergency that would allow entry without proper notice.

If you do have to enter a tenant's apartment in an emergency, be sure to leave a note or call the tenant explaining the circumstances and the date and time you entered. Here's an example:

Sample Note to Tenant Regarding Entry in Case of Emergency

September 2, 20xx

Dear Tammy,

Due to your oven being left on, I had to enter your apartment this afternoon around 3 o'clock. Apparently, you left your apartment while bread was still in the oven, and didn't return in time to take it out. Joe, your upstairs neighbor, called me and reported smoke and a strong burning smell coming from your kitchen window, which is below his. I entered your apartment and turned the oven off and removed the bread. Please be more careful next time.

Sincerely,

Herb Layton

Herb Layton

To facilitate your right of entry in an emergency, make sure your lease or rental agreement forbids tenants from rekeying, adding additional locks, or installing a security system without your permission. (See Clause 12 of the form agreements in Chapter 2.) If you grant permission to change or add locks, make sure your tenant gives you duplicate keys. If you allow the tenant to install a security system, make sure you get the name and phone number of the alarm company or instructions on how to disarm the system in an emergency.

> **CAUTION**
> **Don't change locks.** If your tenant installs a lock without your permission, don't change the lock, even if you immediately give the tenant a key. This invites a lawsuit and false claims that you tried to lock the tenant out or stole the tenant's possessions.

Entry With the Permission of the Tenant

You can always enter rental property, even without notice, if the tenant agrees. If your need to enter is only occasional, you can probably rely on a friendly telephone call to the tenant asking for permission.

> **EXAMPLE:** Because of corrosion problems with the pipes leading to water heaters, you want to check out all apartments in your building. You call your tenants, explain the situation, and arrange a mutually convenient date and time to inspect the pipes.

If the tenant agrees to let you enter his apartment or rental unit but has been difficult and not always reliable in the past, you might even want to cover yourself by documenting the tenant's apparent co-operation. Send him a confirmatory thank-you note and keep a copy for yourself. If this note is met with unease or outright hostility, you should send the tenant a formal notice of your intent to enter.

If you have a maintenance problem that needs regular attention—for example, a fussy heater or temperamental plumbing—you might want to work out a detailed agreement with the tenant covering entry.

> **CAUTION**
> **Don't be too insistent on entry.** If you pressure a tenant for permission to enter, perhaps implying or even threatening eviction if the tenant doesn't allow immediate or virtually unrestricted access, you may face a lawsuit for invasion of privacy.

Entry to Make Repairs or Inspect the Property

Many states, either by statute or court decision, allow you and your repairperson to enter the tenant's home to make necessary or agreed-upon repairs, alterations, or improvements or to inspect the rental property.

Entry to Make Repairs

If you need to make a repair—for example, to fix a broken oven, replace the carpet, or check the point of entry of a persistent ant infestation—you generally must enter only at reasonable times, and you must give at least the required amount of notice, usually 24 hours. However, if this is impracticable—for example, a repairperson is available on a few hours' notice—you will probably be on solid ground if you explain the situation to your tenant and then give shorter notice. Of course, if your tenant agrees to a shorter notice period, you have no problem.

> EXAMPLE: Amy told her landlord Tomas that her bathroom sink was stopped up and draining very slowly. Tomas called the plumber, who said that he had several large jobs in progress but would be able to squeeze in Amy's repair at some point within the next few days. The plumber promised to call Tomas before he came over. Tomas relayed this information to Amy, telling her he would give her at least four hours' notice before the plumber came.

How to Give Tenants Notice of Entry

In many situations, the notice period will not be a problem, since your tenant will be delighted that you are making needed repairs and will cooperate with your entry requirements. However, as every experienced landlord knows, some tenants are uncooperative when it comes to providing reasonable access to make repairs, while at the same time demanding that repairs be made immediately. (Of course, if the time is really inconvenient for the tenant—you want to make a nonemergency repair the day your tenant is preparing dinner for her new in-laws—try to be accommodating and reschedule a more convenient appointment.)

Here's how to avoid having a tenant claim that you violated his legal right of privacy:

- Meet your state notice requirements; or, if there's no specified amount of notice, provide at least 24 hours' notice.
- Try to reach the tenant at home or at work to give the required amount of notice. Make sure you know how to reach the tenant during the day to give required notice.
- Provide written notice as much as possible— either a brief letter or a formal Notice of Intent to Enter Dwelling Unit (see samples below). A downloadable copy of the formal notice is on the Nolo website. See Appendix B for the link to the forms in this book.
- If you give notice orally or by email, document this fact by keeping a log of your requests for entry.
- If you can't reach the tenant personally or by phone, and if your intended date of entry is too soon to enable you to send a letter, text, or email (assuming your lease or rental agreement includes these communication methods as permissible notice methods), it's a good idea to post a note detailing your plan on the tenant's front door. If, despite all of these efforts, your tenant does not receive notice, you are probably on solid ground, in most states, to enter and do the repair, since you have done all that could reasonably be expected to comply with the notice requirements.
- Keep a copy of all requests for entry (written and oral) in your tenant's file, along with other communications, such as Resident's Maintenance/Repair Request forms (discussed in Chapter 9).

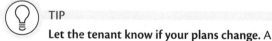

TIP

Let the tenant know if your plans change. A tenant may be justifiably annoyed if you or your repair person show up late or not at all—for example, if you're supposed to come at 2 p.m. and don't show up until 8 a.m. the next morning. If it isn't possible to come on time in the first place, call the tenant and explain the problem, and ask permission to enter later on. If the tenant denies permission, you'll have to give a second notice.

Notice of Intent to Enter Dwelling Unit

To: _Anna Rivera_
Tenant

123 East Avenue, Apt. #4
Street Address

Rochester, New York 14610
City and State

THIS NOTICE is to inform you that on _____ January 7, 20xx _____,

at approximately _____ 1:00 _____ A̶M̶/PM, the landlord, or the landlord's agent, will enter the premises

for the following reason: _____

_____

☑ To make or arrange for the following repairs or improvements:

_____ fix garbage disposal _____

_____

_____

_____

_____ .

☐ To show the premises to:

    ☐ a prospective tenant or purchaser.

    ☐ workers or contractors regarding the above repair or improvement.

☐ Other: _____

_____

_____ .

You are, of course, welcome to be present. If you have any questions or if the date or time is inconvenient,

please notify me promptly at _____ 716-555-7899 _____ .
                                                  Phone Number

Marlene Morgan   _January 5, 20xx_
Landlord/Manager   Date

Sample Informal Letter Requesting Entry

January 5, 20xx

Anna Rivera
123 East Avenue, Apartment 4
Rochester, New York 14610

Dear Ms. Rivera:

In response to your complaint regarding the garbage disposal in your apartment, I have arranged to have it repaired tomorrow, on Tuesday, January 6, at 2:00 p.m. I attempted to reach you today (at both your home and work phone numbers) and notify you of this repair appointment. Because I was unable to reach you by phone, I am leaving this note on your door.

Sincerely,

Marlene Morgan

Marlene Morgan

Entry to Inspect for Needed Repairs

It's an excellent idea to inspect your rental properties at least once or twice a year. That way you can find small problems before they become big ones, and tenants can't claim that they didn't have an opportunity to report complaints to you.

The lease and rental agreements in this book (see Clause 17 in Chapter 2) give you the right to enter a tenant's unit—after giving reasonable notice—to make this kind of regular inspection.

If you don't have a clause on access in your lease or rental agreement, state law may give you the right, anyway. Most states with privacy statutes grant this right to inspect rental property. In other states, you must determine whether the courts in your state have addressed the issue of landlord inspections.

 CAUTION

Don't use the right to inspect improperly. Don't use your right to access to harass or annoy the tenant. Repeated inspections absent a specific reason, even when proper notice is given, are an invitation to a lawsuit.

How to Avoid Tenant Theft Claims

By planning ahead, you can minimize the chances that you or your repairpersons will be accused of theft. Give plenty of notice of your entry—this gives the tenant the chance to hide valuables. Try to arrange repairs or visit the rental unit only when the tenant is home. If that's not possible, you or your manager should be present. Carefully check references of plumbers and other repair people, and only allow people whom you trust to enter alone.

Entry During Tenant's Extended Absence

Several states with privacy statutes give landlords the specific legal right to enter the rental unit during a tenant's extended absence, often defined as seven days or more. You are allowed entry to maintain the property as necessary and to inspect for damage and needed repairs. For example, if you live in a cold-weather place such as Connecticut, it makes sense to check the pipes in rental units to make sure they haven't burst when the tenant is away for winter vacation.

While many states do not address this issue either by way of statute or court decision, you should be on safe legal ground to enter rental property during a tenant's extended absence, as long as there is a genuine need to protect the property from damage. You should enter only if something really needs to be done—that is, something that the tenant would do if he were home, as part of his obligation to keep the property clean, safe, and in good repair. For example, if the tenant leaves the windows wide open just before a driving rainstorm, you would be justified in entering to close them.

 TIP

Require tenants to report extended absences. To protect yourself and make sure your tenant knows what to expect, be sure your lease or rental agreement requires the tenant to inform you when he will be gone for an extended time, such as two weeks, and alerts him of your intent to enter the premises during these times if necessary. See Clause 16 of the form agreements in Chapter 2.

Entry to Show Property to Prospective Tenants or Buyers

Most states with access laws allow landlords to enter rented property to show it to prospective tenants toward the end of a tenancy or to prospective purchasers if you wish to sell the property. Follow the same notice procedures for entry to make repairs, discussed above. As always, be sure your lease or rental agreement authorizes this type of entry. See Clause 15 of the form agreements in Chapter 2.

You can use the same Notice of Intent to Enter Dwelling Unit as the one used for entry to make repairs.

Showing Property to Prospective New Tenants

If you don't plan to renew a tenant's about-to-expire lease, or have given or received a notice terminating a month-to-month tenancy, you may show the premises to prospective new tenants during the last few weeks (or even months) of the outgoing tenant's stay. It is not a good idea, however, to show property if the current tenant is under the impression that his lease or rental agreement will be renewed, or if a dispute exists over whether the current tenant has a right to stay. If there's a chance the dispute will end up in court as an eviction lawsuit, the current tenant may be able to hang on for several weeks or even months. Insisting on showing the property in this situation only causes unnecessary friction at the same time that it's of little value, since you will be unable to tell the new tenants when they can move in.

The form lease and rental agreements in this book include a clause that may limit your liability if, for reasons beyond your control, you must delay a new tenant's move-in date after you've signed a lease or rental agreement. See Clause 17 in Chapter 2.

Showing Property to Prospective Buyers

You may also show your property—whether apartments in a multiple-unit building, a rented single-family house, or a condominium unit—to potential buyers or mortgage companies. Remember to give the required amount of notice to your tenant. It's also a good idea to tell the tenant the name and phone number of the realty company handling the property sale and the particular real estate agent or broker involved.

Problems usually occur when an overeager real estate salesperson shows up on the tenant's doorstep without warning, or calls on very short notice and asks to be let in to show the place to a possible buyer. In this situation, the tenant is within his right to say, "I'm busy right now—try again in a few days after we've set a time convenient for all of us." Naturally, this type of misunderstanding is not conducive to good landlord-tenant relations, not to mention a sale of the property. Make sure the real estate salespeople you deal with understand the law and respect your tenants' rights to advance notice.

Putting For Sale or For Rent Signs on the Property

Occasionally, friction is caused by landlords who put signs on tenants' homes, such as "For Sale" or "For Rent" signs in front of an apartment building or a rented single-family house. Even if the sign says "Don't Disturb Occupants" and you are conscientious about giving notice before showing property, prospective buyers or renters may nonetheless disturb the tenant with unwelcome inquiries.

A tenant who likes where he is living will often feel threatened and insecure about a potential sale. A new owner may mean a rent increase or eviction notice if the new owner wants to move in herself. In this situation, if your tenant's privacy is ruined by repeated inquiries the tenant may even resort to suing you for invasion of privacy, just as if you personally had made repeated illegal entries.

To head off this possibility, consider not putting a "For Sale" sign on the property. With online multiple-listing services and video house listings, signs aren't always necessary. Indeed, many real estate agents sell houses and other real estate without ever placing a "For Sale" sign on the property, except when an open house is in progress. If you or your real estate agent must put up a sign advertising sale or rental of the property, make sure it clearly warns against disturbing the occupant and includes a telephone number to call—for example, "Shown by Appointment Only" or "Inquire at 555-1357—Do Not Disturb Occupants Under Any Circumstances." If your real estate agent refuses to accommodate you, find a new one who will respect your tenants' privacy and keep you out of a lawsuit.

> ### ⓘ CAUTION
> **Don't use a lockbox.** Under no circumstances should an owner of occupied rental property that is listed for sale allow the placing of a key-holding "lockbox" on the door. This is a metal box that attaches to the front door and contains the key to that door. If the rental property is on the Multiple Listing Service (MLS), the box will likely be an electronic model, which opens when the user types in an acceptable code. Members of the MLS have their own codes, which means that any of these folks can gain entry into property. Because either type of box allows users to gain entry at any time, in disregard of notice requirements, they should not be used in an occupied rental—period. A lockbox will leave you wide open to a tenant's lawsuit for invasion of privacy, and possibly liable for any property the tenant claims to have lost.

Getting the Tenant's Cooperation

Showing a house or apartment building occupied by a tenant isn't easy on anyone. At times, you will want to show the property on short notice. And, you may even want to have an occasional open house on weekends. From your tenant's point of view, any actions you take to show the property to strangers may seem like an intolerable intrusion.

Also, if you're selling the property, your tenant may feel threatened by the change in ownership.

Obviously, the best way to achieve your ends is with the cooperation of the tenant. One good plan is to meet with the tenant in advance and offer a reasonable rent reduction in exchange for cooperation—for example, two open houses a month and showing the unit on two hour's notice, as long as it doesn't occur more than five times a week. Depending on how much the tenant will be inconvenienced, a 10% to 20% rent reduction might be reasonable. However, you should realize that this type of agreement is in force only so long as the tenant continues to go along with it. Technically, any written agreement changing the rent is really an amendment to the rental agreement, and rental agreement clauses under which tenants give up their privacy rights are typically void and unenforceable if it comes to a court fight. This may be one situation when an informal understanding that the rent be lowered so long as the tenant agrees to the frequent showings may be better than a written agreement.

Entry After the Tenant Has Moved Out

To state the obvious, you may enter the premises at any time after the tenant has completely moved out. It doesn't matter whether the tenant left voluntarily after giving back the key, or involuntarily following a successful eviction lawsuit.

In addition, if you believe a tenant has abandoned the property—that is, skipped out without giving any notice or returning the key—you may legally enter.

Entry by Others

This section describes situations when other people, such as municipal inspectors, may want entry to your rental property.

Health, Safety, or Building Inspections

While your state may set guidelines for your entry to rental property, the rules are different for entry by state or local health, safety, or building inspectors.

Neighbor's Complaints

If inspectors have credible reasons to suspect that a tenant's rental unit violates housing codes or local standards—for example, a neighbor has complained about noxious smells coming from the tenant's home or about his 20 cats—they will usually knock on the tenant's door and ask permission to enter. Except in the case of genuine emergency, your tenant has the right to say no.

Inspectors have ways to get around tenant refusals. A logical first step (maybe even before they stop by the rental unit) is to ask you to let them in. Since you can usually enter on 24 hours' notice, this is probably the simplest approach. We recommend that you cooperate with all such requests for entry.

If inspectors can't reach you (or you don't cooperate), their next step will probably be to get a search warrant based on the information from the tenant's neighbor. The inspectors must first convince a judge that the source of their information—the neighbor—is reliable, and that there is a strong likelihood that public health or safety is at risk. Inspectors who believe that a tenant will refuse entry often bring along police officers who, armed with a search warrant, have the right to do whatever it takes to overcome the tenant's objections.

Routine Inspections

Fire, health, and other municipal inspectors sometimes inspect apartment buildings even if they don't suspect noncompliance. These inspections may be allowed under state law or local ordinance. (Most ordinances exempt single-family homes and condominiums.) Your tenant has the right to say no. Then, the inspector will have to secure a warrant. A warrant will enable the inspector to enter to confirm fire or safety violations. Again, if there is any expectation that your tenant may resist, a police officer will usually accompany the inspector.

An inspector who arrives when the tenant is not home may ask you to open the door on the spot, in violation of your state's privacy laws. If the inspectors come with a warrant, you can give consent, since even the tenant couldn't prevent entry. But if the inspector is there without a warrant, you cannot speak for the tenant and say, "Come on in." Again, the inspector most show you a warrant before you can let him in.

To find out whether your city has a municipal inspection program, call your city manager's or mayor's office.

Inspection Fees

Many cities impose fees for inspections, on a per unit or building basis or a sliding scale based on the number of your holdings. Some fees are imposed only if violations are found. If your ordinance imposes fees regardless of violations, you may pass the inspection cost on to the tenant in the form of a rent hike. It's not illegal to do this, and, even in rent-controlled cities, the cost of an inspection might justify a rent increase.

If your ordinance imposes a fee only when violations are found, you should not pass the cost on to the tenant if the noncompliance is not his fault. For example, if inspectors find that you failed to install state-mandated smoke alarms, you should pay for the inspection; but if the tenant has allowed garbage to pile up in violation of city health laws, the tenant should pay the inspector's bill.

Police and Law Enforcement

Even the police may not enter a tenant's rental unit unless they can show you or your tenant a recently issued search or arrest warrant, signed by a judge. Put another way, even though you own the property, you do not have the legal right to give police permission to enter your tenant's home unless you've been shown a warrant. (*Chapman v. United States*, 365 U.S. 610 (1961).)

The police do not need a search warrant, however, if they need to enter to prevent a catastrophe such as an explosion, to retrieve or preserve evidence of a serious crime, which may otherwise be lost or destroyed, or if they are in hot pursuit of a fleeing criminal.

Also, different rules apply if law enforcement suspects terrorist activity by one of your tenants. See "Cooperating With Law Enforcement in Terrorism Investigations," just below.

Cooperating With Law Enforcement in Terrorism Investigations

The U.S.A. PATRIOT Act (PL 107-56) authorizes the FBI to obtain "tangible things," including books, records, or other documents, for use in terrorism investigations. The FBI must, however, have an order issued by a U.S. magistrate. You cannot be sued if you cooperate in good faith pursuant to this section. However, you may not disclose to anyone else that the FBI has gathered this information.

Landlords have even broader immunity against suits by tenants when they cooperate with law enforcement's antiterrorism efforts. You cannot be sued by tenants if you "[furnish] any information, facilities, or technical assistance in accordance with a court order or request for emergency assistance under this Act." (U.S.A. PATRIOT Act, Title II, § 225.) You should ask for a subpoena or warrant before you turn over tenant records or otherwise make your rental property or tenant belongings available to law enforcement.

For more information on terrorism and rental properties, contact the local office of the FBI; a list is at www.fbi.gov.

Your Right to Let Others In

You should not give others permission to enter a tenant's home. (Municipal inspections, however, may pose an exception.)

Occasionally, you or your resident manager will be faced with a very convincing stranger who will tell a heart-rending story:

- "I'm Nancy's boyfriend, and I need to get my clothes out of her closet now that I'm moving to New York."
- "If I don't get my heart medicine that I left in this apartment, I'll die on the spot."
- "I'm John's father, and I just got in from the North Pole, where a polar bear ate my wallet, and I have no other place to stay."

The problem arises when you can't contact the tenant at work or elsewhere to ask whether it's okay to let the desperate individual in. This is one reason why you should always know how to reach your tenants during the day.

The story the desperate person tells you may be the truth, and chances are that if your tenant could be contacted, she would say, "Yes, let Uncle Harry in immediately." But you can't know this, and it doesn't make sense to expose yourself to the potential liability involved should you get taken in by a clever con artist. There is always the chance that the person is really a smooth talker whom your tenant has a dozen good reasons to want kept out. You risk being legally responsible should your tenant's property be stolen or damaged. If you do let a stranger in without your tenant's permission, you may be sued for invasion of privacy for any loss your tenant suffers as a result.

In short, never let a stranger into your tenant's home without your tenant's permission. Even if you have been authorized to allow a certain person to enter, it is wise to ask for identification. Although this no-entry-without-authorization policy may sometimes be difficult to adhere to in the face of a convincing story, stick to it. You have much more to lose in admitting the wrong person to the tenant's home than you would have to gain by letting in someone who's "probably okay."

Other Types of Invasions of Privacy

Entering a tenant's home without his knowledge or consent isn't the only way you can interfere with the tenant's privacy. Here are a few other common situations, with advice on how to handle them.

Giving Information About the Tenant to Strangers

As a landlord, you may be asked by strangers, including creditors, banks, and prospective landlords, to provide credit or other information about your tenant. Did she pay the rent on time? Did she maintain the rental property? Cause any problems?

Basically, you have a legal right to give out normal business information about your tenant to people and businesses who ask and have a legitimate reason to know—for example, the tenant's bank when she applies for a loan or a prospective landlord who wants a reference. Resist your natural urge to be helpful, unless the tenant has given you written permission to release this sort of information. (We discuss release forms in Chapter 1.) You have nothing to gain, and possibly a lot to lose, if you give out information that your tenant feels constitutes a serious violation of her privacy.

And if you give out incorrect information—even if you believe it to be accurate—you can really be in a legal mess if the person to whom you disclose it relies on it to take some action that negatively affects your tenant.

> **EXAMPLE:** If you tell others that a tenant has filed for bankruptcy (and this isn't true), the tenant has grounds to sue you for defamation (libel or slander) if he is damaged as a result—for example, if he doesn't get a job.

Some landlords feel that they should communicate information to prospective landlords, especially if the tenant has failed to pay rent or maintain the premises or has created other serious problems. If you do give out this information, make sure you are absolutely factual and that the information you provide has been requested. If you go out of your way to give out negative information—for example, you try to blackball the tenant with other landlords in your area—you definitely risk legal liability for libeling your tenant.

Posting Information About Tenants Online

Online sites such as Yelp enable consumers to post reviews of everything from restaurants to car repair shops to doctors. Naturally, reviews of residential rentals are right up there in popularity, and many landlords have squirmed when encountering reviews of their buildings and management practices. It wasn't long before landlords got their own online outlets, using public and free sites designed to warn other property owners about problem tenants.

We urge you to think twice before posting information to one of these sites. In a recent case, a California court ruled that such Internet postings are not immune from libel suits, and that if the posting contains provably false statements, the poster could end up liable for damages. (*Bently Reserve L.P. v. Andreas G. Papaliolios*, 218 Cal. App.4th 418 (2013).) The same reasoning would apply to negative remarks about a tenant posted by a landlord. While you may ultimately prevail if you are challenged by a tenant who is the subject of your review, this is a headache you do not need.

> **CAUTION**
> **Beware of gossipy managers.** Many landlords have had serious problems with on-site managers who have gossiped about tenants who, for example, paid rent late, were served with an eviction notice, had overnight visitors, or drank too much. This sort of gossip may seem innocent but, if flagrant and damaging, can be an invasion of privacy for which you can be liable. Impress on your managers their duty to keep confidential all sensitive information about tenants.

Calling or Visiting Tenants at Work

Should you need to call your tenants at work (say, to schedule a time to make repairs), try to be sensitive to whether it's permissible for them to receive personal calls. While some people have bosses who don't get upset about occasional personal calls, others have jobs that are greatly disrupted by any phone call.

Under no circumstances should you continue to call a tenant at work who asks you not to do so. This is especially true when calling about late rent payments or other problems.

Never leave specific messages with your tenant's employer, especially those that could reflect negatively on her. A landlord who leaves a message like "Tell your deadbeat employee I'll evict her if she doesn't pay the rent" can expect at least a lot of bad feeling on the part of the tenant and, at worst, a lawsuit, especially if your conduct results in the tenant losing her job or a promotion.

As for visiting the tenant at work—say, to collect late rent—this is something you should avoid unless invited. What it boils down to is that no matter what you think of your tenant, you should respect the sensitive nature of the tenant's relationship with her employer.

There may, however, be times you'll need to contact the tenant at work if you can't find the tenant at home after repeated tries—for example, to serve notice of a rent increase or an eviction notice.

Undue Restrictions on Guests

A few landlords, overly concerned about tenants moving new occupants into the property, go a little overboard in keeping tabs on the tenants' legitimate guests who stay overnight or for a few days. Often their leases, rental agreements, or rules and regulations require a tenant to "register" any overnight guest.

Clause 3 of the form agreements (Chapter 2) limits guests' visits to no more than ten days in any six-month period, to avoid having a guest turn into an illegal subtenant. While you should be concerned about persons who begin as guests becoming permanent unauthorized residents, it is overkill to require a tenant to inform you of a guest whose stay is only for a day or two. Keep in mind

that just because you rent your tenant her home, you don't have the right to restrict her social life or pass judgment upon the propriety of her visitors' stays. Extreme behavior in this area—whether by you or a management employee—can be considered an invasion of privacy for which you may be held liable.

Send Only Business-Related Faxes and Texts to Residents

Since 1991, the Telephone Consumer Protection Act has prohibited businesses from sending "unsolicited" faxes (texts are also covered). Businesses that have an "established business relationship" with the recipient are exempted from this ban (Junk Fax Prevention Act of 2005). You may send faxes and texts to current, prospective, and prior tenants without worry, as long as the message concerns some aspect of the tenancy. You can also contact vendors and suppliers with faxes and texts that concern your contracts or business dealings with them. But be aware of the following requirements:

- The first page of a fax must have a conspicuous notice telling the recipient how to opt out of future faxes, giving the sender's phone number and fax number.
- The opt-out step must be free and available seven days a week, 24 hours a day.
- You may use only those fax numbers that you get from the recipients themselves or that they gave to a website or public directory for publication.

Sometime in the future, the Federal Communications Commission may issue regulations that will spell out the rules in more detail. These hopefully will guide landlords in how closely related the fax's or text's subject matter must be to landlord/tenant matters to fit within the "established business relationship" exemption. In the meantime, play it safe and do not send faxes that are unrelated to your business. For example, resist the temptation to invite residents by fax to participate in your son's baseball team fundraiser.

Spying on a Tenant

As a result of worrying too much about a tenant's visitors, a few landlords have attempted to interrogate tenants' visitors, knock on their tenants' doors at odd hours or too frequently in order to see who answers, or even peek through windows. Needless to say, this sort of conduct can render you liable for punitive damages in an invasion of privacy lawsuit. As far as talking to tenants' guests is concerned, keep your conversations to pleasant hellos or nonthreatening small talk.

Watch Out for Drug Dealing on Your Property

It's crucial that you keep a careful eye on your tenants if you suspect they're engaging in drug dealing or other illegal behavior. Landlords have a responsibility to keep their properties safe—that includes keeping dealers out by carefully screening prospective tenants (see Chapter 1) and kicking them out pronto when they are discovered. Other tenants and neighbors, as well as government agencies, may bring costly lawsuits against landlords who allow drug dealing on their properties. Chapter 12 discusses your liability for drug-dealing tenants and how to avoid problems, while at the same time respecting your tenants' legitimate expectations of privacy.

"Self-Help" Evictions

It is generally illegal for you to come on the rental property and do such things as take off windows and doors, turn off the utilities, or change the locks. For details, see "Illegal 'Self-Help' Evictions" in Chapter 17.

What to Do When Tenants Unreasonably Deny Entry

Occasionally, even if you give a generous amount of notice and have a legitimate reason, a tenant may refuse to let you in. If you repeatedly encounter unreasonable refusals to let you or your employees enter the premise, you can probably legally enter anyway, provided you do so in a peaceful manner.

Never push or force your way in. Even if you have the right to be there, you can face liability for anything that goes wrong.

For practical reasons, don't enter alone. If you really need entry and the tenant isn't home, it's just common sense to bring someone along who can later act as a witness in case the tenant claims some of her property is missing.

Another problem landlords face is that some tenants have their locks changed. This is probably illegal, because it restricts your right of access in a true emergency or when you have given proper notice. Your lease or rental agreement should require landlord key access, as well as notice of any change of locks or the installation of any burglar alarms. See Clause 12, Chapter 2.

If you have a serious conflict over access with an otherwise satisfactory tenant, a sensible first step is to meet with the tenant to see if the problem can be resolved. If you come to an understanding, follow up with a note to confirm your agreement. Here's an example:

Sample Note Confirming Agreement Regarding Entry

January 5, 20xx

Dear Anna,

This will confirm our conversation of January 5, 20xx regarding access to your apartment at 123 East Avenue, Apt. 4, for the purpose of making repairs. The management will give you 24 hours' advance written notice, and will enter only during business hours or weekdays. The person inspecting will knock first, then enter with a pass key if no one answers.

Thank you,

Marlene Morgan

If this doesn't work, you may wish to try mediation by a neutral third party. It's an especially good way to resolve disputes when you want the tenant to stay.

If attempts at compromise fail, you can terminate the tenancy. Unless your tenant has a long-term lease or lives in a rent control city that requires just cause for eviction, you can simply give the tenant a 30-day notice and terminate the tenancy, rather than put up with a problem tenant.

And, in every state, you can usually evict the tenant, including those with long-term leases, for violating a term of the lease or rental agreement. To do this, you must comply with your state law as to reasons for entry and notice periods. And your lease or rental agreement must contain an appropriate right-of-entry provision. The cause justifying eviction is the tenant's breach of that provision (see Clause 15 in the form lease and rental agreements, Chapter 2). Keep copies of any correspondence and notes of your conversations with the tenant.

If you're heading for court, you may need to consult a lawyer or do some legal research on your state's laws on evictions. If you do end up in court, be prepared to prove your entry was legal—as to purpose and amount of notice required. A good record-keeping system is crucial in this regard.

Tenants' Remedies If a Landlord Acts Illegally

Conscientious landlords should be receptive to a tenant's complaint that her privacy is being violated and work out an acceptable compromise. If you violate a tenant's right to privacy and you can't work out a compromise, the tenant may bring a lawsuit and ask for money damages. You may be held liable for your property manager's disrespect of the tenant's right of privacy, even if you never knew about the manager's conduct. A tenant who can show a repeated pattern of illegal activity, or even one clear example of outrageous conduct, may be able to get a substantial recovery.

In most states, it's easy for a tenant to press her claim in small claims court without a lawyer. For details on small claims court procedures and the maximum amount for which someone can sue, see Chapter 16.

Depending on the circumstances, the tenant may be able sue you for:

- trespass: entry without consent or proper authority
- invasion of privacy: interfering with a tenant's right to be left alone
- breach of the implied covenant of quiet enjoyment: interfering with a tenant's right to undisturbed use of his home, or
- infliction of emotional distress: doing any illegal act that you intend to cause serious emotional consequences to the tenant.

These types of lawsuits are beyond the scope of this book and require expert legal advice.

Finally, you should know that repeated abuses by a landlord of a tenant's right of privacy may give a tenant under a lease a legal excuse to break it by moving out, without liability for further rent.

Ending a Tenancy

 FORMS IN THIS CHAPTER

Chapter 14 includes instructions for and samples of the following forms:

• Amendment to Lease or Rental Agreement
• Tenant's Notice of Intent to Move Out
• Indemnification of Landlord

The Nolo website includes downloadable copies of these forms. See Appendix B for the link to the forms in this book.

Most tenancies end because the tenant leaves voluntarily. But little else is so uniform. Some tenants give proper legal notice and leave at the end of a lease term; others aren't so thoughtful and give inadequate notice, break the lease, or just move out in the middle of the night. And, of course, some tenants fail to live up to their obligations for reasons they can't control—for example, a tenant dies during the tenancy.

Whether your rentals turn over a lot or your tenants tend to stay put for years, you should understand the important legal issues that arise at the end of a tenancy, including:

- the type of notice a landlord or tenant must provide to end a month-to-month tenancy
- your legal options if a tenant doesn't leave after receiving (or giving) a termination notice or after the lease has expired
- what happens if a tenant leaves without giving required notice, and
- the effect of a condominium conversion on a tenant's lease.

This chapter starts with a brief discussion of a related topic—how you may change a lease or rental agreement during a tenancy.

RELATED TOPIC

Related topics covered in this book include:

- How to advertise and rent property before a current tenant leaves: Chapter 1
- Writing clear lease and rental agreement provisions on notice required to end a tenancy: Chapter 2
- Raising the rent: Chapter 3
- Highlighting notice requirements in a move-in letter to the tenant: Chapter 7
- Handling tenant requests to sublet or assign the lease, and what to do when one cotenant leaves: Chapter 8
- Tenant's right to move out if the rental unit is damaged or destroyed: Chapter 9
- Preparing a move-out letter and returning security deposits when a tenant leaves, and how to deal with any abandoned property: Chapter 15
- How and when to prepare a warning letter before terminating a tenancy: Chapter 16

- Terminating a tenancy when a tenant fails to leave after receiving a 30-day notice or violates the lease or rental agreement—for example, by not paying rent: Chapter 17
- State Rules on Notice Required to Change or End a Tenancy: Appendix A.

Changing Lease or Rental Agreement Terms

Once you sign a lease or rental agreement, it's a legal contract between you and your tenant. All changes should be in writing and signed by both of you.

If you use a lease, you cannot unilaterally change the terms of the tenancy for the length of the lease. For example, you can't raise the rent unless the lease allows it or the tenant agrees. If the tenant agrees to changes, however, simply follow the directions below for amending a rental agreement.

Amending a Month-to-Month Rental Agreement

You don't need a tenant's consent to change something in a month-to-month rental agreement. Legally, you need simply send the tenant a notice of the change. The most common reason landlords amend a rental agreement is to increase the rent.

To change a month-to-month tenancy, most states require 30 days' notice, subject to any local rent control ordinances (see "State Rules on Notice Required to Change or Terminate a Month-to-Month Tenancy" in Appendix A for a list of each state's notice requirements). You'll need to consult your state statutes for the specific information on how you must deliver a 30-day notice to the tenant. Most states allow you to deliver the notice by first-class mail.

TIP

Contact the tenant and explain the changes. It makes good personal and business sense for you or your manager to contact the tenant personally and tell him about a rent increase or other changes before you follow up with a written notice. If the tenant is opposed to your plan, your personal efforts will allow you to explain your reasons.

You don't generally need to redo the entire rental agreement in order to make a change or two. It's just as legal and effective to attach a copy of the notice making the change to the rental agreement. However, you may want the change to appear on the written rental agreement itself.

If the change is small and simply alters part of an existing clause—such as increasing the rent or making the rent payable every 14 days instead of every 30 days—you can cross out the old language in the rental agreement, write in the new, and sign in the margin next to the new words. Make sure the tenant also signs next to the change. Be sure to add the date, in case there is a dispute later as to when the change became effective.

If the changes are lengthy, you may either add an amendment page to the original document or prepare a new rental agreement, as discussed below. If an amendment is used, it should clearly refer to the agreement it's changing and be signed by the same people who signed the original agreement. A sample Amendment to Lease or Rental Agreement form is shown below and the Nolo website includes a downloadable copy. See Appendix B for the link to the forms in this book.

Preparing a New Rental Agreement

If you want to add a new clause or make several changes to your rental agreement, you will probably find it easiest to substitute a whole new agreement for the old one. This is simple to do if you use the lease or rental agreement shown in this book (Chapter 2) and included on this book's companion page on Nolo's website. If you prepare an entire new agreement, be sure that you and the tenant both write "Canceled by mutual consent, effective _(date)_ " on the old one, and sign it. All tenants (and any cosigner or guarantors) should sign the new agreement. The new agreement should take effect on the date the old one is canceled. To avoid problems, be sure there is no time overlap between

the old and new agreements, and do not allow any gap between the cancellation date of the old agreement and the effective date of the new one.

 TIP

A new tenant should mean a new agreement. Even if a new tenant is filling out the rest of a former tenant's lease term under the same conditions, it is never wise to allow her to operate under the same lease or rental agreement. Start over and prepare a new agreement in the new tenant's name. See Chapter 8 for details on signing a new agreement when a new tenant moves in.

How Month-to-Month Tenancies End

This section discusses how you or the tenant can end a month-to-month tenancy.

Giving Notice to the Tenant

If you want a tenant to move out, you can end a month-to-month tenancy simply by giving the proper amount of notice. No reasons are required in most states. (New Hampshire and New Jersey are exceptions, because landlords in these states must have a just or legally recognized reason to end a tenancy.) In most places, all you need to do is give the tenant a simple written notice to move, allowing the tenant the minimum number of days required by state law (typically 30) and stating the date on which the tenancy will end (see "State Rules on Notice Required to Change or Terminate a Month-to-Month Tenancy" in Appendix A). After that date, the tenant no longer has the legal right to occupy the premises.

In most states, a landlord who wants to terminate a month-to-month tenancy must provide the same amount of notice as a tenant—typically 30 days. But this is not true everywhere. For example, in Georgia, landlords must give 60 days' notice to terminate a month-to-month tenancy, while tenants need only give 30 days' notice. State and local rent control laws can also impose notice

Amendment to Lease or Rental Agreement

This is an Amendment to the lease or rental agreement dated _____March 1, 20xx_____ [the Agreement]

between _____Olivia Matthew_____ [Landlord]

and _____Steve Phillips_____ [Tenant]

regarding property located at _____1578 Maple St., Seattle, WA_____ [the premises].

Landlord and Tenant agree to the following changes and/or additions to the Agreement:

1. Beginning on June 1, 20xx, Tenant shall rent a one-car garage, adjacent to the main premises, from Landlord for the sum of $75 per month.

2. Tenant may keep one German shepherd dog on the premises. The dog shall be kept in the backyard and not in the side yard. Tenant shall clean up all animal waste from the yard on a daily basis. Tenant agrees to repair any damages to the yard or premises caused by his dog, at Tenant's expense.

_____

_____

_____

_____

_____

_____

_____

_____

_____

_____

_____

_____

Olivia Matthew   _May 20, 20xx_
Landlord/Manager   Date

Steve Phillips   _May 20, 20xx_
Tenant   Date

_____   _____
Tenant   Date

_____   _____
Tenant   Date

requirements on landlords. Things are different if you want a tenant to move because he or she has violated a term of the rental agreement—for example, by failing to pay rent. If so, notice requirements are commonly greatly shortened, sometimes to as little as three days.

Each state, and even some cities, has its own very detailed rules and procedures for preparing and serving termination notices. For example, some states specify that the notice be printed in a certain size or style of typeface. If you don't follow these procedures, the notice terminating the tenancy may be invalid. It is impossible for this book to provide all specific forms and instructions. Consult a landlords' association or local rent control board and your state statutes for more information and sample forms (Chapter 18 shows how to do your own legal research). Your state consumer protection agency may also have useful advice. Once you understand how much notice you must give, how the notice must be delivered, and any other requirements, you'll be in good shape to handle this work yourself—usually with no lawyer needed.

 RESOURCE
California resource for terminating tenancies. If you are a California landlord, see *The California Landlord's Law Book: Evictions*, by David Brown and Nils Rosenquest. It covers rules and procedures and contains forms for serving termination notices in California. This book is available at bookstores and public libraries. You may also order it directly from Nolo's website (www.nolo.com), or by phone (800-728-3555).

How Much Notice the Tenant Must Give You

In most states, the tenant who decides to move out must give you at least 30 days' notice. Some states allow less than 30 days' notice in certain situations—for example, because a tenant must leave early because of military orders. And, in some states, tenants who pay rent more frequently than once a month can give notice to terminate that matches

their rent payment interval—for example, tenants who pay rent every two weeks would have to give 14 days' notice. If your tenant joins the military and wants to terminate a rental agreement, federal law specifies the maximum amount of notice you may require (but if state law requires less notice, you must follow state rules). See "Special Rules for Tenants Who Enter Military Service," below.

Must Tenants Give Notice on the First of the Month?

In most states, a tenant can give notice at any time—in other words, they don't have to give notice so that the tenancy will end on the last day of the month or the last day of the rental cycle. For example, a tenant who pays rent on the first of the month, but gives notice on the tenth, will be obliged to pay for ten days' rent for the next month, even if the tenant moves out earlier.

Some landlords insist that tenants give notice only on the day rent is due, possibly to avoid having to prorate the rent as described above. But a rule like this may violate your state's law on the proper use of security deposits, and may not be legal. Here's how: Suppose a tenant pays rent on the first, but gives you his 30-day notice on the tenth, because he intends to move out on the tenth day of the following month. If you stick to your rule, you'll expect him to pay for an additional 20 days (the balance of the next month), and if he doesn't, you'll probably use the security deposit to cover that debt. But that may not be a proper use of the deposit in your state, especially if your statute does not allow you or the tenant to modify the conditions under which the landlord may retain the deposit. If the rule applies to tenants only (that is, *you* remain free to deliver a 30-day notice at any time, and the 30 days begins as of the day of delivery), the chances that your rule will hold up will be even slimmer.

As tempting as it may be to deal with tenant turnover on the day rent is due and avoid having to prorate rent (and though the prospect of requiring that rent be paid over an extended period is attractive), we urge you to resist this ploy and accept notice at any time during the rent term.

To educate your tenants as to what they can expect, make sure your rental agreement includes your state's notice requirements for ending a tenancy (see Clause 4 of the form agreements in Chapter 2). It is also wise to list termination notice requirements in the move-in letter you send to new tenants.

For details on your state's rules, see "State Rules on Notice Required to Change or Terminate a Month-to-Month Tenancy" in Appendix A.

Restrictions to Ending a Tenancy

The general rules for terminating a tenancy described in this chapter don't apply in all situations:

- **Rent control ordinances.** Many rent control cities require "just cause" (a good reason) to end a tenancy, such as moving in a close relative. You will likely have to state your reason in the termination notice you give the tenant.
- **Discrimination.** It is illegal to end a tenancy because of a tenant's race, religion, or other reason constituting illegal discrimination.
- **Retaliation.** You cannot legally terminate a tenancy to retaliate against a tenant for exercising any right under the law, such as the tenant's right to complain to governmental authorities about defective housing conditions.

Insist on a Tenant's Written Notice of Intent to Move

In many states, a tenant's notice must be in writing and give the exact date the tenant plans to move out. Even if it is not required by law, it's a good idea to insist that the tenant give you notice in writing (as does Clause 4 of the form agreements in Chapter 2). Why bother?

Insisting on written notice will prove useful should the tenant not move as planned after you have signed a lease or rental agreement with a new tenant. The new tenant may sue you to recover the costs of temporary housing or storage fees for her belongings because you could not deliver possession of the unit. In turn, you will want to sue the old (holdover) tenant for causing the problem by failing to move out. You will have a much stronger case against the holdover tenant if you can produce a written promise to move on a specific date instead of your version of a conversation (which will undoubtedly be disputed by the tenant).

A sample Tenant's Notice of Intent to Move Out form is shown below and the Nolo website includes a downloadable copy (see Appendix B for the link to the forms in this book). Give a copy of this form to any tenant who tells you he or she plans to move.

Accepting Rent After a 30-Day Notice Is Given

If you accept rent for any period beyond the date the tenant told you he is moving out, this cancels the termination notice and creates a new month-to-month tenancy. This means you must give the tenant another 30-day notice to start the termination process again.

EXAMPLE: On April 15, George sends his landlord Yuri a 30-day notice of his intent to move out. A few weeks later, however, George changes his mind and decides to stay. He simply pays the usual $800 monthly rent on May 1. Without thinking, Yuri cashes the $800 check. Even though she's already rerented to a new tenant who plans to move in on May 16th, Yuri is powerless to evict George unless she first gives him a legal (usually 30-day) notice to move. Unless the lease Yuri signed with the new tenant limits her liability, she will be liable to the new tenant for failing to put her in possession of the property as promised.

CAUTION

If you collected "last month's rent" when the tenant moved in, do not accept rent for the last month of the tenancy. You are legally obligated to use this money for the last month's rent. Accepting an additional month's rent may extend the tenant's tenancy.

Tenant's Notice of Intent to Move Out

April 3, 20xx
Date

Anne Sakamoto
Landlord

888 Mill Avenue
Street Address

Nashville, Tennessee 37126
City and State

Dear   Ms. Sakamoto   ,
                    Landlord

This is to notify you that the undersigned tenants,   Patti and Joe Ellis

_____ , will be moving from

999 Brook Lane, Apartment Number 11, Nashville, Tenn.   ,

on   May 3, 20xx   ,   30 days   from today.

This provides at least   30 days'   written notice as required in our rental agreement.

Sincerely,

Patti Ellis
Tenant

Joe Ellis
Tenant

_____
Tenant

If the tenant asks for more time but you don't want to continue the tenancy as before, you may want to give the tenant a few days or weeks more, at prorated rent. Prepare a written agreement to that effect and have the tenant sign it. See the sample letter extending the tenant's move-out date.

Sample Letter Extending Tenant's Move-Out Date

Hannah Lewis
777 Broadway Terrace, Apartment #3
Richmond, Virginia 23233

Dear Hannah:

On June 1, you gave me a 30-day notice of your intent to move out on July 1. You have since requested to extend your move-out to July 18 because of last-minute problems with closing escrow on your new house. This letter is to verify our understanding that you will move out on July 18, instead of July 1, and that you will pay prorated rent for 18 days (July 1 through July 18). Prorated rent for 18 days, based on your monthly rent of $900 or $30 per day, is $540.

Please sign below to indicate your agreement to these terms.

Sincerely,

Fran Moore

Fran Moore, Landlord

Agreed to by Hannah Lewis, Tenant:
Signature *Hannah Lewis*
Date *June 20, 20xx*

When the Tenant Doesn't Give the Required Notice

All too often, a tenant will send or give you a "too short" notice of intent to move. And it's not unheard of for a tenant to move out with no notice or with a wave as he hands you the keys.

A tenant who leaves without giving enough notice has lost the right to occupy the premises, but is still obligated to pay rent through the end of the required notice period. For example, if the notice period is 30 days, but the tenant moves out after telling you 20 days ago that he intended to move, he still owes you for the remaining ten days.

In most states, you have a legal duty to try to rerent the property before you can charge the tenant for giving you too little notice, but few courts expect a landlord to accomplish this in less than a month. This rule, called the landlord's duty to mitigate damages, is discussed in "If the Tenant Breaks the Lease," below.

When You or Your Tenant Violates the Rental Agreement

If you seriously violate the rental agreement and fail to fulfill your legal responsibilities—for example, by not correcting serious health or safety problems—a tenant may be able to legally move out with no written notice or by giving less notice than is otherwise required. Called a "constructive eviction," this doctrine typically applies only when living conditions are intolerable—for example, if the tenant has had no heat for an extended period in the winter, or if a tenant's use and enjoyment of the property has been substantially impaired because of drug dealing in the building.

What exactly constitutes a constructive eviction varies slightly under the laws of different states. Generally, if a rental unit has serious habitability problems for anything but a very short time, the tenant may be entitled to move out without giving notice.

Along the same lines, a landlord may terminate a tenancy (and evict, if necessary) if the tenant violates a lease or rental agreement—for example, by failing to pay rent or seriously damaging the property—by giving less notice than is otherwise required to end a tenancy. Chapter 17 explains the situations in which landlords can quickly terminate for tenant misbehavior, and gives an overview of evictions.

Special Rules for Tenants Who Enter Military Service

Tenants who enter active military service after signing a lease or rental agreement have a federally legislated right to get out of their rental obligations. (War and National Defense Servicemembers Civil Relief Act, 50 U.S.C. §§ 3901 and following.) The Act protects tenants who are part of the "uniformed services," which includes the armed forces, commissioned corps of the National Oceanic and Atmospheric Administration (NOAA), commissioned corps of the Public Health Service, and the activated National Guard.

Tenants must mail written notice of their intent to terminate their tenancy for military reasons to the landlord or manager. The notice terminates the tenancy of the servicemember and any dependents listed on the lease or rental agreement.

The term "dependent" is defined more broadly than under the U.S. tax code (as explained in Table 5, "Overview of the Rules for Claiming an Exemption for a Dependent," in IRS Publication 501, *Exemptions, Standard Deduction, and Filing Information*). A dependent for purposes of the Servicemembers Act includes a child, spouse, or anyone whom the servicemember has supported within the preceding 180 days, by paying for more than half that person's living expenses. (50 U.S.C.A. § 3911(4).)

Rental agreements. Once the notice is mailed or delivered, the tenancy will terminate 30 days after the day that rent is next due. For example, if rent is due on the first of June and the tenant mails a notice on May 28, the tenancy will terminate on July 1. This rule takes precedence over any longer notice periods that might be specified in your rental agreement or by state law. If state law or your agreement provides for shorter notice periods, however, the shorter notice will control. Recently, many states have passed laws that offer the same or greater protections to members of the state militia or National Guard.

Leases. A tenant who enters military service after signing a lease may terminate the lease by following the procedure for rental agreements, above. For example, suppose a tenant signs a one-year lease in April, agreeing to pay rent on the first of the month. The tenant enlists October 10 and mails you a termination notice on October 11. In this case, you must terminate the tenancy on December 1, 30 days after the first time that rent is due (November 1) following the mailing of the notice. This tenant will have no continuing obligation for rent past December 1, even though this is several months before the lease expires. Removing a prior owner involves different procedures however.

How Leases End

A lease lasts for a fixed term, typically one year. As a general rule, neither you nor the tenant may unilaterally end the tenancy, unless the other party has violated the terms of the lease. There's an exception for tenants who join the military and want to terminate a lease, as explained in "Special Rules for Tenants Who Enter Military Service," above.

If you and the tenant both live up to your promises, however, the lease simply ends of its own accord at the end of the lease term. At this point, the tenant must either:

- move
- sign a new lease (with the same or different terms), or
- stay on as a month-to-month tenant with your approval.

As every landlord knows, however, life is not always so simple. Sooner or later, a tenant will stay beyond the end of the term or leave before it without any legal right to do so.

Giving Notice to the Tenant

Because a lease clearly states when it will expire, you may not think it's necessary to notify tenants before the expiration date. But doing so is a very good practice. And some states or cities (especially those with rent control) actually require reasonable notice before the lease expiration date if you want the tenant to leave.

We suggest giving the tenant at least 60 days' written notice that the lease is going to expire. This reminder has several advantages:

- **Getting the tenant out on time.** Two months' notice allows plenty of time for the tenant to look for another place if he doesn't—or you don't—want to renew the lease.
- **Giving you time to renegotiate the lease.** If you would like to continue renting to your present tenant but also change some lease terms or increase the rent, your notice reminds the tenant that the terms of the old lease will not automatically continue. Encourage the tenant to stay, but mention that you need to make some changes to the lease.
- **Getting a new tenant in quickly.** If you know a tenant is going to move, you can show the unit to prospective tenants ahead of time and minimize the time the space is vacant.

RENT CONTROL

Your options may be limited in a rent control area. If your property is subject to rent control, you may be required to renew a tenant's lease unless there is a legally approved reason (just cause) not to. Reasons such as your tenant's failure to pay rent or your desire to move in a close relative commonly justify nonrenewal. If you do not have a reason for nonrenewal that meets the city's test, you may be stuck with a perpetual month-to-month tenant. Check your city's rent control ordinance carefully.

If the Tenant Continues to Pay Rent After the Lease Expires

It's fairly common for landlords and tenants not to care, or not even to notice, that a lease has expired. The tenant keeps paying the rent, and the landlord keeps cashing the checks. Is everything just the same as it was before the lease expired? The answer depends on where you live.

Creating a month-to-month tenancy. In most states, you will have created a new, oral month-to-month tenancy on the terms that appeared in the old lease. In other words, you'll be stuck with the terms and rent in the old lease, at least for the first 30 days. If

you want to change the terms in a new lease, you must abide by the law regarding giving notice for a month-to-month tenancy (discussed above). It will usually take you at least a month, while you go about giving notice to your now month-to-month tenant.

> **EXAMPLE 1:** Zev had a one-year lease and paid rent on the first of every month. When the lease expired, Zev stayed on and his landlord, Maria, accepted another month's rent check from him. Under the laws of their state, this made Zev a month-to-month tenant, subject to the terms and conditions in his now-expired lease.
>
> Maria wanted to institute a "no pets" rule and to raise the rent. But since Zev was now a month-to-month tenant, she had to give him 30 days' notice (as required by her state's law) to change the terms of the tenancy. She lost a full month of the higher rent while she complied with the 30-day requirement.
>
> **EXAMPLE 2:** Learning from her experience with Zev, Maria gave her tenant Alice a 60-day notice before Alice's lease expired. In that notice, Maria also told Alice about the new "no pets" rule and the rent increase. Alice, who wanted to get a cat, decided to move when the lease expired. Meanwhile, Maria was able to show Alice's apartment to prospective tenants and chose one who moved in—and started paying the higher rent—shortly after Alice's lease expired.

Of course, you can belatedly present the tenant with a new lease. If your tenant decides not to sign it, she can stay on as a month-to-month tenant, under the terms of the old lease, until you give her proper written notice to move on. As discussed above, this is usually 30 days.

Automatically renewing the lease. However, in a few states, the rule is quite different. If your lease expires and you continue to accept rent, the two of you have created a new lease for the same length (such as one year) and terms (such as the amount of rent) as in the old lease. In other words, you have automatically renewed the lease. The effects are dramatic: You and the tenant are now legally obligated for a new lease with the same term as the old one.

To avoid problems of tenants staying longer than you want, be sure to notify the tenant well before the lease expiration date, and don't accept rent after this date. If a tenant just wants to stay an extra few days after a lease expires, and you agree, it is wise to put your understanding on this arrangement in a letter. See the sample letter extending the tenant's move-out date above.

Retaliation and Other Illegal Tenancy Terminations

You can terminate a tenancy for a variety of reasons, such as nonpayment of rent, serious violations of the lease, and illegal activity such as drug dealing on the rental property. And, unless state or local laws require a reason, you can, with proper notice, terminate a month-to-month rental agreement or decline to renew a lease without giving any reason at all. But you can't terminate a tenancy for the *wrong* reason—in retaliation against a tenant for exercising her legal rights or in a way that discriminates illegally.

Just as you can't engage in illegal discrimination when you rent a unit in the first place, you can't unlawfully discriminate when it comes to terminating a month-to-month tenancy or deciding not to renew a lease—for example, by deciding not to continue to rent to persons of a certain ethnicity because of your political beliefs.

The second major landlord "no-no" when it comes to tenancy nonrenewals is retaliation. In most states, you may not end a tenancy in retaliation for a tenant's legally protected activities, such as complaining to a building inspector that a rental unit is uninhabitable. If you do, and the tenant stays on despite your wishes, the tenant can defend herself against a lawsuit to evict her by proving retaliation. Chapter 16 discusses laws prohibiting retaliation.

When a Lease Ends and You Want the Tenant Out

Once the lease expires, you don't have to keep renting to the tenant. If the tenant stays on after the lease ends and offers rent that you *do not accept*, the tenant is a "holdover" tenant. In some states, you must still give notice, telling the tenant to leave within a few days; if the tenant doesn't leave at the end of this period, you can start an eviction lawsuit. A few states allow landlords to file for eviction immediately, as soon as the lease expires.

CAUTION

Avoid lease and rental agreement clauses that make holdover tenants pay a higher rent. Some landlords attempt to discourage tenants from staying past the end of their tenancy by making the tenant agree, in advance, to pay as much as three times the rent if they do. Clauses like this may not be legal—they are a form of "liquidated damages" (damages that are set in advance, without regard to the actual harm suffered by the landlord), which are illegal in residential rentals in many states, including California. (However, they have been upheld in Texas.) The clause would probably not hold up in a rent control city, nor would it survive a challenge if the clause describes the rent hike as a "penalty."

Evicting Tenants in Properties Purchased Following Foreclosure

The federal "Protecting Tenants at Foreclosure Act of 2009" (PTAFA) provided that when a "federally related" mortgage loan was foreclosed upon (almost every loan), and when the bank or mortgage holder bought at the sale and took over as owner, most residential leases would survive a foreclosure—meaning the tenants could stay until the end of the lease. Under the PTAFA, month-to-month tenants (with some important qualifications) were also entitled to 90 days' notice before having to move out.

Effective on December 31, 2014, the PTAFA expired. Even without this federal law, most states (and some cities) give tenants some protection from eviction in default and foreclosure situations (although the new owner of the property must still follow state eviction procedures in order to remove a tenant from the rental unit). For example, some state and local laws require a foreclosing bank to give tenants notice about an impending foreclosure, require a new owner to give tenants a certain number of days' notice to vacate before starting an eviction after a foreclosure, or require a new owner to honor existing leases under specific circumstances. For details on state and local protections for tenants in property purchased at foreclosure, check the website of the National Housing Law Project (www.nhlp.org).

If the Tenant Breaks the Lease

A tenant who leaves (with or without notifying you beforehand) before a lease expires and refuses to pay the remainder of the rent due under the lease is said to have "broken the lease."

Once the tenant leaves for good, you have the legal right to retake possession of the premises and rerent to another tenant. A key question that arises is, how much does a tenant with a lease owe if she walks out early? Let's start with the general legal rule. A tenant who signs a lease agrees at the outset to pay a fixed amount of rent: the monthly rent multiplied by the number of months of the lease. The tenant pays this amount in monthly installments over the term of the lease. In short, the tenant has obligated himself for the entire rent for the entire lease term. The fact that payments are made monthly doesn't change the tenant's responsibility to pay rent for the entire lease term. As discussed below, depending on the situation, you may use the tenant's security deposit to cover part of the shortfall, or sue the tenant for the rent owed.

Is the Tenant Really Gone?

Sometimes, it's hard to tell whether or not a tenant has left permanently. People do sometimes disappear for weeks at a time, for a vacation or family emergency. And, even a tenant who doesn't intend to come back may leave behind enough discarded clothing or furniture to make it unclear.

Often, your first hint that a tenant has abandoned the premises will be the fact that you haven't received the rent. Or you may simply walk by a window and notice the lack of furniture. Ordinarily, the mere appearance that the rental unit is no longer occupied doesn't give you the legal right to immediately retake possession. It does, however, often give you legal justification to inspect the place for signs of abandonment.

Here are some tips for inspecting property you suspect has been abandoned:

- Is the refrigerator empty, or is most of the food spoiled?
- Have electricity and telephone service been canceled?
- Are closets and kitchen cupboards empty?

If you conclude, under your state's rules, that the property is abandoned, you have the right to retake possession of it. Each state has its own definition of abandonment and its own rules for regaining possession of rental property. See the Chapter 15 discussion of abandoned property.

Rather than trying to figure out if the situation satisfies your state's legal rules for abandonment, it may be easier to find the tenant and ask her whether or not she's coming back. If the tenant indicates that she's gone for good, get it in writing. You can write up a simple statement, along these lines: "I, Terri Tenant, have permanently moved out of my rental unit at [address] and have no intention of resuming my tenancy"—and ask the tenant to sign and date it. Or, use our Tenant's Notice of Intent to Move Out form (shown above), modified as needed. The Nolo website includes a downloadable copy of the form. See Appendix B for the link to the forms in this book.

(Also, if you try unsuccessfully to locate the tenant and then the original tenant shows up after you have rerented the unit, evidence of your efforts will be some protection if the original tenant complains.) Start by phoning each personal and business reference on the tenant's rental application. If that doesn't work, ask neighbors and, finally, check with the police.

Another way to find a tenant who has left a forwarding address with the Post Office but not with you is to send the tenant a "return receipt requested" letter, and check the box on the form that asks the postal service to note the address where the letter was delivered. You'll get the tenant's new address when you receive the return receipt.

Consider a Buyout Agreement With a Tenant Who Wants to Leave Early

A tenant who wants to get out of a lease may offer to sweeten the deal by paying a little bit extra. In the world of big business, this is known as a "buyout." For example, a tenant who wants to leave three months early might offer to pay half a month's extra rent and promise to be extra accommodating when you want to show the unit to prospective tenants. A sample Buyout Agreement is shown below.

Sample Buyout Agreement Between Landlord and Tenant

This Agreement is entered into on January 3, 20xx between Colin Crest, Tenant, who leases the premises at 123 Shady Lane, Capitol City, California, and Marie Peterson, Landlord.

1. Under the attached lease, Tenant agreed to pay Landlord monthly rent of $1,000. Tenant has paid rent for the month of January 20xx.

2. Tenant's lease expires on June 30, 20xx, but Tenant needs to break the lease and move out on January 15, 20xx.

3. Landlord agrees to release Tenant on January 15, 20xx from any further obligation to pay rent in exchange for Tenant's promise to pay January's rent plus one and one-half months' rent ($1,500) by January 15, 20xx.

4. Tenant agrees to allow Landlord to show his apartment to prospective new tenants on four hours' notice, seven days a week. If Tenant cannot be reached after Landlord has made a good-faith effort to do so, Landlord may enter and show the apartment.

5. If Tenant does not fulfill his promises as described in paragraphs 3 and 4 above, the attached lease, entered into on January 3, 20xx, will remain in effect.

Colin Crest _____   *January 3, 20xx* _____
Colin Crest, Tenant   Date

Marie Peterson _____   *January 3, 20xx* _____
Marie Peterson, Landlord   Date

TIP

Require tenants to notify you of extended absences. Clause 16 of the form lease and rental agreements (Chapter 2) requires tenants to inform you when they will be gone for an extended time, such as two or more weeks.

By requiring tenants to notify you of long absences, you'll know whether property has been abandoned or the tenant is simply on vacation. In addition, if you have such a clause and, under its authority, enter an apparently abandoned unit only to be confronted later by an indignant tenant, you can defend yourself by pointing out that the tenant violated the lease.

When Breaking a Lease Is Justified

There are some important exceptions to the blanket rule that a tenant who breaks a lease owes the rent for the entire lease term. A tenant may be able to legally move out without providing the proper notice in the following situations:

- **You violated an important lease provision.** If you don't live up to your obligations under the lease—for example, if you fail to maintain the unit in accordance with health and safety codes—a court will conclude that you have "constructively evicted" the tenant. That releases the tenant from further obligations under the lease.

- **State law allows the tenant to leave early.** A few states' laws list reasons that allow a tenant to break a lease.

  - **Job relocation or need to move because of health or age.** In Delaware, a tenant need only give 30 days' notice to end a long-term lease if he needs to move because his present employer relocated or because health problems (of the tenant or a family member) require a permanent move. In New Jersey, a tenant who has suffered a disabling illness or accident can break a lease and leave after 40 days' notice upon presenting proper proof of disability. In Rhode Island, a tenant who is 65 years of age or older (or who will turn 65 during the term of a rental agreement) may terminate

the rental agreement in order to enter a residential care and assisted living facility, a nursing facility, or a unit in a private or public housing complex designated by the federal government as housing for the elderly.

  - **Domestic violence.** In Oregon, a victim of domestic violence, sexual assault, or stalking may terminate the lease with 14 days' notice; Washington allows no-notice termination. (Ore. Rev. Stat. Ann. §§ 90.453 and following; Wash. Rev. Code Ann. §§ 59.18.575 and following.) For other states that give domestic violence victims early termination rights, see "State Laws in Domestic Violence Situations," in Appendix A.

  - **Military Service.** In all states, tenants who enter active military duty after signing a lease must be released after delivering proper notice. (See "Special Rules for Tenants Who Enter Military Service," above.) If your tenant has a good reason for a sudden move, you may want to research your state's law to see whether or not he's still on the hook for rent.

- **The rental unit is damaged or destroyed.** If the rental is significantly damaged—either by natural disaster or any other reason beyond the tenant's control—the tenant may consider the lease terminated and move out.

- **You seriously interfere with the tenant's ability to enjoy his or her tenancy**—for example, by sexually harassing the tenant or violating the tenant's privacy rights.

Your Duty to Mitigate Your Loss If the Tenant Leaves Early

If a tenant breaks the lease and moves out without legal justification, you normally can't just sit back and wait until the end of the term of the lease, and then sue the departed tenant for the total lost rent. In most states, you must try to rerent the property reasonably quickly and keep your losses to a minimum—in legalese, to "mitigate damages." Each state's rule is listed in "Landlord's Duty to Rerent" in Appendix A.

Even if this isn't the legal rule in your state, trying to rerent is obviously a sound business strategy. It's much better to have rent coming in every month than to wait, leaving a rental unit vacant for months, and then try to sue (and collect from) a tenant who's long gone.

If your state requires you to mitigate damages but you don't make an attempt (or make an inadequate one) to rerent, and instead sue the former tenant for the whole rent, you will collect only what the judge thinks is the difference between the fair rental value of the property and the original tenant's promised rent. This can depend on how easy it is to rerent in your area. Also, a judge is sure to give you some time (probably at least 30 days) to find a new tenant.

CAUTION

No double-dipping is allowed. Even if your state doesn't strictly enforce the mitigation-of-damages rules, if you rerent the property, you cannot also collect from the former tenant. Courts do not allow you to unjustly enrich yourself this way.

How to Mitigate Your Damages

When you're sure that a tenant has left permanently, then you can turn your attention to rerenting the unit.

You do not need to lower your standards for acceptable tenants—for example, you are entitled to reject applicants with poor credit or rental histories. Also, you need not give the suddenly available property priority over other rental units that you would normally attend to first.

You are not required to rent the premises at a rate below its fair market value. Keep in mind, however, that refusing to rent at less than the original rate may be foolish. If you are unable to ultimately collect from the former tenant, you will get *no* income from the property instead of less. You will have ended up hurting no one but yourself.

Keep Good Records

If you end up suing a former tenant, you will want to be able to show the judge that you acted reasonably in your attempts to rerent the property. Don't rely on your memory and powers of persuasion to convince the judge. Keep detailed records, including:

- the original lease
- receipts for cleaning and painting, with photos of the unit showing the need for repairs, if any
- your expenses for storing or properly disposing of any belongings the tenant left
- receipts for advertising the property and bills from credit reporting agencies investigating potential renters
- a log of the time you spent showing the property, and a value for that time
- a log of any people who offered to rent and, if you rejected them, documentation as to why, and
- if the current rent is less than the original tenant paid, a copy of the new lease.

EXAMPLE: When the mail began to pile up and the rent went unpaid, Jack suspected that Lorna, his tenant, had broken the lease and moved out. When his suspicions were confirmed, he added her apartment to the list of vacant units that needed his attention. In the same way that he prepared every unit, Jack cleaned the apartment and advertised it. Three months after Lorna left, Jack succeeded in rerenting the apartment.

Jack sued Lorna in small claims court and won a judgment that included the costs of advertising and cleaning and the three months' rent that he lost before the unit was rerented.

The Tenant's Right to Find a Replacement Tenant

A tenant who wishes to leave before the lease expires may offer to find a suitable new tenant, so that the flow of rent will remain uninterrupted. Unless you have a new tenant waiting, you have nothing to lose by cooperating. Refusing to cooperate could even hurt you. If you refuse to accept an excellent new tenant and then withhold the lease-breaking tenant's deposit or sue for unpaid rent, you may wind up losing in court, because you turned down the chance to reduce your losses (mitigate your damages).

Of course, if the rental market is really tight in your area, you may be able to lease the unit easily at a higher rent, or you may already have an even better prospective tenant on your waiting list. In that case, you won't care if a tenant breaks the lease, and you may not be interested in any new tenant he provides.

If you and the outgoing tenant agree on a replacement tenant, you and the new tenant should sign a new lease, and the outgoing tenant should sign a termination of lease form (discussed in Chapter 8). Since this is a new lease—not a sublease or assignment of the existing lease—you can raise the rent if you wish, unless local rent control ordinances prohibit it.

When You Can Sue

If a tenant leaves prematurely, you may need to go to court and sue for rerental costs and the difference between the original and the replacement rent. Obviously, you should first use the tenant's security deposit to cover these costs.

Deciding *where* to sue is usually easy: Small claims court (discussed in Chapter 16) is usually the court of choice because it's fast, is affordable, and doesn't require a lawyer. If you're seeking an amount that's substantially above your state's limit, you may file in regular court—but if the excess is small, you may wisely decide to forgo it and use the fast, cheap small claims court. If your lease contains an attorney fees clause (as does the form agreement in Chapter 2), you may be able to recover your attorney fees.

> **EXAMPLE:** Cree has a year's lease at $800 per month. She moves out with six months ($4,800 of rent) left on the lease. Cree's landlord, Robin, cannot find a new tenant for six weeks, and when she finally does, the new tenant will pay only $600 per month.
>
> Unless Cree can show Robin acted unreasonably, Cree would be liable for the $200 per month difference between what she paid and what the new tenant pays, multiplied by the number of months left in the

lease at the time she moved out. Cree would also be responsible for $1,200 for the time the unit was vacant, plus Robin's costs to find a new tenant. Cree would thus owe Robin $2,400 plus advertising and applicant screening costs. If Robin sues Cree for this money and uses a lawyer, and if there is an attorney fees clause in her lease, Cree will also owe Robin these costs, which can be upwards of a few thousand dollars.

Knowing *when* to sue is trickier. You may be eager to start legal proceedings as soon as the original tenant leaves, but, if you do, you won't know the extent of your losses, because you might find another tenant who will make up part of the lost rent. Must you wait until the end of the original tenant's lease? Or can you bring suit when you rerent the property?

The standard approach, and one that all states allow, is to go to court after you rerent the property. At this point, your losses—your expenses and the rent differential, if any—are known and final. The disadvantage is that you have had no income from that property since the original tenant left, and the original tenant may be long gone and not, practically speaking, worth chasing down.

> ![caution icon] **CAUTION**
> **Give accurate and updated information to credit bureaus about former tenants.** The Fair Debt Collection Practices Act [FDCPA] (15 U.S. Code §§ 1692 and following) also applies when you give information to a credit reporting agency about a current or former tenant. The Act makes it illegal to give false information, and, if the tenant disputes the debt, you must mention the fact that the sum is disputed when you report it. You must notify the credit bureau if the tenant pays all or part of the debt.
>
> The FDCPA even makes it illegal to give falsely *positive* information which you know to be untrue. When a credit bureau calls to ask about your least-favorite tenant who's applied for a home loan, don't describe him in falsely glowing terms, no matter how much you'd like to see him leave!

Termination Fees

A termination fee is a preset fee that landlords impose when tenants break a lease. They're often called cancellation fees, reletting fees, rerenting fees, or decorating fees. They're intended to compensate the landlord for the inconvenience and extra work caused by a broken lease, which include costs of cleaning, readying the unit for rerental, rekeying, advertising, showing the unit, and so on. Landlords who have to mitigate damages often add this fee to whatever loss of rent the landlord suffered before rerenting the unit. Landlords who do not have to mitigate damages may define the fee to cover both the inconvenience of the broken lease plus any lost rents.

If you've followed us through this section, you already know what the problem is with termination fees: They are preset damage amounts and, as such, are liquidated damages, which ought to run smack up against the ban on such damages in states that disallow them for lost rents. Quite so, but even in states that don't ban liquidated damages, they are ripe for attack under consumer protection statutes, which offer other ways to go after liquidated damages. Recently, they've appeared on plaintiffs' attorneys' radar, and have been disallowed in several states. The advice given to landlords by their attorneys and trade associations is uniform: Don't use them.

In response to aggressive legal challenges from tenants, one state has passed legislation that allows termination fees, as long as specific steps are followed. In Florida, before the lease is signed, landlords may offer the applicant the option of agreeing to a preset two-month's fee for breaking the lease, as long as the tenant gives the landlord two months' notice. If the applicant decides to take the offer, the lease must contain an addendum that further explains the fee. Tenants cannot be turned down if they refuse this option. (Fla. Stat. Ann. § 83.595.)

If you're determined to use a termination fee, understand that it must accurately reflect the financial losses you suffer when a tenant takes off unexpectedly, such as staff time spent securing the apartment or trying to locate the departed tenant.

To accurately and fairly charge lease-breaking tenants for the cost of rerenting, do a "time and motion" analysis of your actual costs to rerent, and add in how much your advertising costs, too. Since you'll be spending that money earlier than you'd planned, thanks to the tenant's early departure, figure out how much interest you'll be losing when you remove that money from your interest-bearing bank account. For example, if you typically spend $1,500 every time you rerent, and your tenant left six months early, your damages would be six months' of interest on $1,500.

> **CAUTION**
> **Don't ask for the return of "rent concessions."** If you've offered a free month's rent as a concession for new tenants, demanding its return when that tenant breaks a lease is risky. A court is likely to see your concession as simply a roundabout way to charge a lower, market rent spread over the period of the lease, and will not allow you to recoup it.

A Tenant's Death: Consequences for Cotenants and the Landlord's Duties

When a tenant dies, landlords, family members, and cotenants will naturally be concerned about what happens to the lease or rental agreement: Is it still in effect? When does it terminate? What happens to the security deposit and the tenant's belongings in the rental? And, if the deceased tenant had a cotenant or subtenant, those people will also wonder about their status. If the tenant had time remaining on a lease, can the next of kin take over? As the landlord, you're likely to encounter some of these questions, addressed below.

Death of a Single Tenant: Requests for the Tenant's Property

You are legally required to take reasonable precautions to preserve a deceased tenant's property. When a tenant who lives alone passes away, your first response should be to secure the premises after the body has been removed. The best way to do this is to change the locks, so that people with copies of existing keys cannot get in.

It's very common for landlords to be approached by a friend or relative of a recently deceased tenant, asking for items such as the tenant's address book (to notify friends and family of the death), or clothing needed for the funeral. These are reasonable requests, but when landlords allow a visitor to enter the rental, they run the risk that the person will take valuable items, and that the executor or administrator of the tenant's estate or next of kin will sue the landlord for allowing it to happen. On the other hand, most landlords won't want to supervise a grieving family member's visit to the rental. In practice, landlords and would-be visitors work it out, ideally when the visitor has a provable, close relationship to the tenant and lives locally. (For some protection, you may want to ask the visitor to sign an indemnification agreement, explained below.)

Family members or others may also want access to the rental in the weeks after the tenant's death. At this point, careful landlords will not allow access unless the visitor can prove that they have a legal right to have it. The proof that visitors can bring with them when approaching you depends on how the estate will be settled. Here are the possibilities.

Estates That Are in Probate

If the deceased tenant's estate has begun the probate process in court (a proceeding that divvies up the assets and pays bills), the judge will have appointed a personal representative of the estate. This person is called the executor if the deceased person named one in a will; if there was no will, the court appoints an administrator. The personal representative is not necessarily the next of kin or the person who will eventually inherit the tenant's property.

The personal representative is the only person who has the right to take possession of the deceased tenant's property. The personal representative's authority comes from documents called Letters Testamentary (for executors) or Letters of Administration (for administrators), which are signed by a judge (states use these or similar-sounding names for these documents). These papers look official and have a court seal, and any personal representative should have a set of originals. The representative seeking access should make an appointment to see you and bring the originals plus a copy to leave with you.

Small Estates That Will Avoid Formal Probate

Estates that are worth less than a certain amount (for example, $150,000 in California, excluding certain assets) will not go through probate, nor will probate be involved if the tenant used a probate-avoiding living trust (see below). Because there's no court proceeding for a small estate, the visitor won't have any official letters to show you.

If the deceased had a will, the named executor will distribute the assets according to the will's terms. If the deceased died without a will, the person or persons who are entitled to the property, as determined by the laws of intestate succession of the state in which the deceased resided, are entitled to the property. In either situation, the claimants must fill out and have notarized an affidavit that attests to their right to obtain the property. The claimants show this affidavit to banks, storage unit owners, and so on—and to landlords. Importantly, claimants must typically wait a period of time after the person dies before claiming the personal property.

As explained, the most official-looking document that a small estate claimant has will be his own sworn statement that he is entitled to the property. The claimant should show you an original affidavit and leave you with a copy. But because the affidavit was prepared without court oversight, you might worry that you have no way of verifying that the visitor is entitled to the property inside the tenant's unit.

You can address that worry to some extent by asking the claimant to sign an agreement, promising to reimburse you for any monetary losses you might suffer as a result of the claimant's actions. For example, if the tenant's estate later claimed that the visitor removed cash and jewelry, and a court held you partially responsible because you allowed the claimant to enter, the claimant would be legally bound to pay any damages that you were ordered to pay to the estate.

The indemnification agreement shown below accomplishes this task. The indemnification agreement asks the visitor to state why he or she is entitled to access. You should ask for identification, and to see a copy of the tenant's will if the visitor claims to be the executor. The form you present to the visitor will hopefully have a deterring effect on anyone who thinks they can enter and take what they see. Below, you'll see a filled-out sample of the Indemnification of Landlord form.

> **CAUTION**
>
> **The indemnification agreement isn't a total shield.** Keep in mind that the tenant's estate is not bound by the claimant's agreement with you, which means that the estate can still look to you to make good on any losses caused by the visitor's removal of property. In theory, you can then look to the visitor for reimbursement, relying on the agreement he signed and suing if necessary. But the indemnification agreement is only as good as the visitor's ability to pay off any judgment you obtain. So if someone takes valuables and disappears, or has few assets (is "judgment proof," in legalese), you will have a hard time collecting. Understanding this, you may not find the indemnification agreement very comforting.

> **FORM**
>
> You'll find a downloadable copy of the **Indemnification of Landlord** form on the Nolo website. See Appendix B for the link to the forms in this book.

Estates That Avoid Probate Through the Use of Living Trusts

A living trust is a probate-avoiding tool that allows a deceased's property to be distributed without going to probate court. The trust names a "successor trustee," who assumes control of the deceased's property when the deceased dies. The successor trustee gathers all of the property, both tangible and intangible, and distributes it to the beneficiaries as specified in the trust.

Although the successor trustee doesn't have to go to court and obtain official letters, he or she will have the next best thing: A copy of the trust document itself, which was prepared by the deceased and usually signed in the presence of a notary. The trustee should bring this to the property and show it to you, directing your attention to the clause that names the successor trustee. For added assurance, you might require the indemnification agreement, described above. You could also ask for a copy of the "Certification of Trust," a short document that accompanies a trust (it may also be called an "abstract of trust" or a "memorandum of trust"). It establishes the existence of the trust without revealing any of the details, as to who gets what, and it's the document that the trustee shows to banks and so on.

Keep in mind that even if the named beneficiary for a particular item under the terms of the trust shows up and asks for that item, you do not have the right to turn it over—that task belongs solely to the successor trustee, who should distribute it to the beneficiary as directed by the terms of the trust.

> **CAUTION**
>
> **Do not use the indemnification agreement for people who want to take property that they claim belongs to them.** It's one thing for an executor, trustee, or personal representative to ask to remove the tenant's property; it's another matter altogether when people ask to take property that they claim belongs to them. Your state law may provide a method that such persons can use, but it's typically not available until some weeks after the tenant's death, and the claimant must show up with a signed affidavit (sworn statement) attesting, among other things, to the claimant's right to the property. So, if your deceased tenant's friend wants the return of his tools that he loaned to your tenant, he'll have to wait and do a bit of paperwork.

Indemnification of Landlord

This indemnification agreement is between _____Walter Lee_____, Landlord/Manager of the rental property at __75 B St. Oakhurst, CA__ and __Sophie Jones__ [*Visitor*]. This agreement concerns Visitor's access to the Rental Premises rented by ___Barbara Jones___ [*Deceased Tenant*].

No executor or administrator has been appointed to represent the estate of Deceased Tenant. Visitor is Deceased Tenant's _____ (for example, daughter, friend), and is taking responsibility, in the absence of a court-appointed personal representative, to gather and dispose of Deceased Tenant's property according to California law.

[*Check if applicable*]
☑ Visitor is Deceased Tenant's executor.

Visitor accepts responsibility for any liability to Deceased Tenant's estate or third parties resulting from Visitor's removal of property from the Rental Premises.

In the event of any third-party claim, demand, suit, action, or proceeding [Claim] against Landlord based upon Visitor's removal or use of property, Landlord will have the right to select counsel to defend itself. If the third-party claim results in an enforceable judgment or is settled, Visitor will indemnify and hold harmless Landlord and any successors or assigns. Visitor will cooperate fully in the defense of any such Claim. Landlord may settle any such Claim against it or waive any appeal of any judgment of a trial court or arbitrator against it. If a Claim is successfully defended, Visitor's indemnity will be limited to fifty percent (50%) of the cost of defense.

__Sophie Jones__	__April 10, 20xx__
Visitor's signature	Date
Sophie Jones	
Print name	

__Walter Lee__	__April 10, 20xx__
Landlord or Manager's signature	Date
Walter Lee	
Print name	

Visitor's contact information: Home

__1707 20th Avenue__	__San Rafael, CA 91234__
Street	City, state, zip
Ø	__415-123-4567__
Phone	Cell

Visitor's contact information: Work

__505 Folsom Street__	__San Francisco, CA 94102__
Street	City, state, zip
__415-987-6543__	__415-123-4567__
Phone	Cell

Other ID (such as a driver's license): __Calif. Driver's License #R0261345__

Death of a Tenant With Cotentants or Subtenants: Requests for the Tenant's Property

The deceased tenant may have had a cotenant (each signed the same lease or rental agreement), or a resident subtenant (who rented directly from the tenant). In either case, these residents are now living among the deceased's tenant's belongings, and may face the same requests from family or kin that you would encounter if the tenant had lived alone (see above). Understandably, those residents may look to you for guidance.

Begin by understanding that relatives and friends of the deceased roommate have no immediate right to his or her belongings. And, the remaining residents do not have to admit anyone to their home unless they want to (law enforcement situations excepted, of course).

Although remaining tenants have no specific responsibility for preserving the tenant's belongings, they could face civil liability to the estate if they let someone in who removes the deceased's property and absconds with it. But remaining tenants should use common sense: If the deceased's brother asks for clothing for the funeral, and they feel comfortable monitoring his activity while in the rental, they're unlikely to encounter problems.

If the people approaching the remaining tenants are, instead, the executor, administrator, successor trustee, or beneficiary in a small estate situation, remaining cotenants and subtenants should ask for the documents explained in sections above.

CAUTION

Remaining residents should protect themselves from claims that they have taken the deceased's property. The last thing they want is a claim by the estate that the roommates helped themselves to your deceased tenant's valuables. If remaining roommates are concerned about this eventuality, consider offering to do an inventory of the tenant's belongings as soon as possible.

What Happens to the Lease or Rental Agreement?

The landlord and the tenant's estate (or next of kin), and possibly any cotenants or subtenants, will need to confront the question of what happens to the tenant's rental agreement or lease now that the tenant is dead—and in particular, whether you are entitled to rent past the date of the tenant's death; and in a cotenancy situation, whether remaining cotenants can demand rent from the estate (if so, for how long). Occasionally, relatives or friends may want to take over the tenant's unit. Do they have the right to do so? The answers depend on whether the tenant lived alone or with cotenants, and rented under a rental agreement or a lease.

Single Tenants With Month-to-Month Rental Agreements

State laws determine when a month-to-month, deceased tenant's responsibility for rent ends. For example, in California the obligation ends 30 days after the date the rent was last paid. So, if rent was last paid for the period October 1 to 31, then the tenancy expires on October 31st. It does not matter whether the tenant died on the 2nd of the month or the 30th of the month—as of 12:01 am on November 1, the rental agreement is over and so is any obligation to pay rent. Not all states follow this method; you'll need to learn the procedure in your state. (See "Doing Your Own Legal Research," in Chapter 18.)

This rule will not prevent the landlord, however, from being compensated by the estate if the tenant's belongings remain on the property after the rent obligation ends. This often happens while the legalities of who is entitled to what are being sorted out. When the tenant's belongings remain in the unit, the landlord is dealing with a "holdover tenant" situation, and is entitled to rent for those days. Landlords can deduct this amount from the security deposit, or (when the deposit is insufficient) make a claim to the estate for prorated rent through the date the property remained on the premises (this is how the landlord would ask for unpaid back rent, too).

If the security deposit cannot cover the holdover rent and there's a probate proceeding, you can file a creditor's claim form (available from the court clerk) with the probate clerk of the court. You will have a specified amount of time in which to file the claim, usually beginning when the court officially appoints the estate's executor. If the estate doesn't go through probate (many small estates do not), you can bill the next of kin.

In practice, landlords will avoid keeping a deceased tenant's belongings in a rental, expecting to bill the estate for rent. Instead, they will want to get the rental on the market as soon as possible, and that means emptying the unit of the tenant's property. But you can't just throw the property away or sell it. You must follow the procedures required under any specific statutes in your state dealing with a deceased tenant's property; or in the absence of these, as if the tenant had moved out and abandoned the property. Any proceeds and claims should be directed to the estate. (State laws on handling abandoned property are covered in Appendix A.)

Because the tenancy will legally end as of the date specified by state law, you are not obliged to accept a substitute tenant proposed by the deceased tenant's family or friends. If someone would like to move in, you should treat that person just as you would any other applicant, by evaluating the applicant's creditworthiness and rental history with the same care you use with any applicant.

Cotenants and Subtenants With Month-to-Month Rental Agreements

When a cotenant dies, the remaining tenants retain their monthly rental agreement—it is generally not automatically terminated by law, as it is when a sole tenant dies. But the remaining cotenants must come up with the full rent as soon as the deceased's obligations end (see above), and in practice, this means quickly finding a new roommate whom you will accept as a new tenant.

Until a new cotenant joins the tenancy as a cotenant, the remaining cotenants must cover the entire rent. Because the deceased's obligation to pay rent will have ended on a certain date, the remaining tenants cannot look to the estate to pay the deceased's share after that date while they look for a new roommate.

If there is a subtenant who paid rent to the deceased (as opposed to the landlord), the subtenant's rights will end at the same time as the deceased tenant's monthly agreement ends. Unless the subtenant makes a new arrangement with you, or you accept rent from the subtenant, the subtenant will have to move at the end of the period for which rent was paid. An exception may exist if a rent control ordinance addresses the situation.

Single Tenants With Leases

Unlike the result described above for month-to-month tenants, when a tenant with a lease dies, the lease might not be terminated, depending on state law. Instead, you may be able to treat the situation as you would if the tenant had broken the lease by moving away midterm, without a legal justification. In other words, the tenant (now, the estate or next of kin) remains responsible for the rent through the end of the lease term, but the landlord must use reasonable efforts to find a replacement tenant (the landlord's duty to mitigate damages is explained in detail earlier in this chapter). When the landlord begins receiving rent from the next tenant (or when the landlord could have received rent, had the landlord used reasonable efforts to find a replacement), the estate's responsibility for rent ends. Not all states handle the situation this way; again, you'll need to learn the rule in your state.

Cotenants With Leases

Finally, when one member of a cotenancy dies, the remaining tenants are not treated as if they have moved out mid-lease. Instead, as happens when a cotenant moves out without dying, those who remain must shoulder the entire rent themselves if they hope to avoid termination for nonpayment of rent. Typically, they find a replacement whom they present to the landlord. Once you accept that replacement, by adding the new person to the lease or otherwise treating the newcomer as a tenant (by accepting rent from the new resident, for example), the new assortment of cotenants can work out among themselves how they will divide up responsibility for the rent.

What Happens to the Deceased Tenant's Security Deposit?

Security deposits can involve hefty sums. In these days of high rents, many thousands of dollars may be sitting in the landlord's bank account. What happens to the deceased tenant's deposit? It depends on whether the tenant was renting solo, or was in a cotenancy situation. These situations are covered below.

Solo Tenants With Rental Agreements or Leases

As explained above, state law will determine when the tenancy will terminate—for deceased tenants who rented month to month or for lease-holding tenants. At that time, landlords must handle the deposit as they would normally, deducting for damage and unpaid rent, and sending the balance, if any, to the estate.

If the deposit is inadequate to cover deductions for unpaid rent and damage, you can make a claim to the deceased tenant's estate for any unpaid rent through the date the property remained on the premises. If the estate is in probate, you will need to submit a filled-out creditor's claim form (available from the court clerk) to the probate clerk of the court. You'll have a specified amount of time in which to file the claim, beginning when the court officially appoints the estate's executor. If the estate doesn't go through probate (many small estates do not), you can bill the next of kin.

Cotenants With Rental Agreements or Leases

By contrast to the result just above, the fate of the deposit of a deceased cotenant is quite murky. The estate, of course, would like the landlord to return the deceased tenant's share of the deposit as of the date the rental agreement terminated or when responsibility for the rent under a lease ended. The remaining cotenants, on the other hand, may want the deposit to stay put, ready to cover any damage that you charge for when the last of them move out (particularly if they believe that existing damage was caused by their deceased roommate). And you would probably just as soon do nothing—your interest is in keeping the deposit topped-off and firmly in your bank account, returning it to whatever tenants are on the scene when the entire tenancy ends. Remember, you generally don't care how cotenants divided up the deposit (or how they allocated the rent). As long as the sums are paid in full, you're happy and it's up to the roommates to share the responsibilities in a way that they can agree upon.

Despite all of this, although it involves considerable work on your behalf, the fairest and safest course for both the remaining tenants and the estate (and any new roommate) would be for you to conduct an inspection when the estate's obligation for rent ends, as if the entire tenancy were ending. But understand that you are under no legal obligation to do so—that's because the tenancy is not ending, and final inspections are required only when, in fact, the tenancy is about to end. So if you are asked to perform an interim inspection, it's your call as to whether to do so.

With an interim inspection held soon after the deceased tenant's death, you can assess any damage, deduct from the deposit as needed, "return" the balance to the remaining cotenants, and demand that the entire deposit be immediately topped-off again. The remaining cotenants can sort out among themselves who was responsible for the deductions. In theory, if the deceased tenant did not contribute to the deductions, the estate would be entitled to his or her full share of the deposit and the remaining cotenants should forward that amount. But if you deduct only for damage caused by the deceased tenant, for example, that amount would be subtracted from the deceased tenant's share and the remaining tenants would return only the balance to the estate.

> **EXAMPLE:** Tom, Dick, and Harry were cotenants who each contributed $1,000 toward the $3,000 security deposit. Tom died suddenly and Dick and Harry decided to remain in the rental. They asked their landlord, Len, to conduct a "final inspection," as if they were vacating. Len decided to deduct for repairing holes in the wall of Tom's bedroom, which would require $500 worth of work. Len sent a check for $2,500 to Dick (who had written the original check, having collected shares from Tom and Harry), who sent $500 to Tom's estate.
>
> Because they were remaining, Dick and Harry had to immediately pay the $3,000 deposit themselves (essentially, they and Len simply traded checks). When they found Rex, a new roommate whom the landlord accepted as a tenant, Rex contributed his $1,000 to the $3,000 deposit, by writing $500 checks to Dick and Harry.

The advantage to the remaining residents of the process just described is that when the deceased tenant's share of the deposit is insufficient to cover that tenant's damage, the other cotenants can protect their shares by making a claim on the estate right away. For example, suppose the damage caused by Tom required $1,500 worth of repairs. You're entitled to deduct that amount, without regard to whether it exceeds Tom's portion of the deposit. With proper documentation, Dick and Harry could make a claim on Tom's estate for the $500 not covered by Tom's share. This system is also fair for any new roommate—Rex, who took over Tom's bedroom, will not end up being charged with damage that occurred before he moved in.

Condominium Conversions

Converting a rental property into condominiums usually means the end of a tenant's tenancy. But condo conversions are not always simple.

Many states regulate the conversion of rental property into condominiums—that is, they limit the number of conversions and give existing tenants considerable rights. Here are some of the basic issues that your state's condo conversion law may address:

- **Government approval.** Converting rental property to condos usually requires plan approval (often called a "subdivision map approval") from a local planning agency. If the property is subject to rent control, there are probably additional requirements.
- **Public input.** In most situations, the public— including current tenants—can speak out at planning agency hearings regarding the proposed condominium conversion and its impact on the rental housing market. You are usually required to give tenants notice of the time and place of these hearings.
- **Tenants' right of first refusal.** Most condominium conversion laws demand that you offer the units for sale first to the existing tenants, at prices that are the same as or lower than the intended public offering. To keep tenant opposition to a minimum, you may decide to voluntarily offer existing tenants a chance to buy at a significantly lower price.
- **Tenancy terminations.** Month-to-month tenants who don't buy their units should receive notice to move at some point during the sales process. Tenants with leases usually have a right to remain through the end of the lease. The entire condo conversion approval process typically takes many months—time enough for current leases to expire before the final okay has been given.

- **Renting after the conversion has been approved.** If you offer a lease or rental agreement *after* the condo conversion has been approved, many states require you to give the tenant plenty of clear written warnings (in large, bold-faced type) that the unit may be sold and the tenancy terminated on short notice. But, if you continue to rent units after you've gotten subdivision approval, you'll usually do so on a month-to-month basis, so the short notice really won't be any different from what any month-to-month tenant would receive.

- **Relocation assistance and special protections.** Some statutes require owners to pay current tenants a flat fee to help with relocation. Some also require owners to provide more notice or additional relocation assistance for elderly tenants or those with small children.

RELATED TOPIC

For advice on researching your state's statutes and court cases on condominium conversions, see the discussion of legal research in Chapter 18.

Returning Security Deposits and Other Move-Out Issues

FORMS IN THIS CHAPTER

Chapter 15 includes instructions for and samples of the following forms:

- Move-Out Letter
- Letter for Returning Entire Security Deposit
- Security Deposit Itemization (Deductions for Repairs and Cleaning)
- Security Deposit Itemization (Deductions for Repairs, Cleaning, and Unpaid Rent)

The Nolo website includes downloadable copies of these forms. See Appendix B for the link to the forms in this book.

As any small claims court judge will tell you, fights over security deposits account for a large percentage of the landlord-tenant disputes. Failure to return security deposits as legally required can result in substantial financial penalties if a tenant files suit.

Fortunately, you can take some simple steps to minimize the possibility that you'll spend hours haggling in court over back rent, cleaning costs, and damage to your property. First, of course, you must follow the law scrupulously when you return security deposits. But it's also wise to send the tenant, before he or she moves out, a letter setting out your expectations for how the unit should be left.

This chapter shows you how to itemize deductions and refund security deposits as state laws require, and how to protect yourself both at the time of move-in and at termination. It describes the penalties you face for violating security deposit laws. This chapter also covers how to defend yourself against a tenant's lawsuit as well as the occasional necessity of taking a tenant to small claims court if the deposit doesn't cover unpaid rent, damage, or cleaning bills. Finally, it discusses what to do when a tenant moves out and leaves personal property behind.

We cover key aspects of state deposit law in this chapter and in Chapter 4. In addition, be sure to check local ordinances in all areas where you own property. Cities, particularly those with rent control, may add their own rules on security deposits.

RELATED TOPIC

Related topics covered in this book include:

- How to avoid deposit disputes by using clear lease and rental agreement provisions: Chapter 2
- Deposit limits; requirements for keeping deposits in a separate account or paying interest; last month's rent and deposits: Chapter 4
- Highlighting security deposit rules in a move-in letter to new tenants; taking photographs and using a Landlord-Tenant Checklist to keep track of the condition of the premises before and after the tenant moves in: Chapter 7

- Notice requirements for terminating a tenancy: Chapter 14
- State Security Deposit Rules: Appendix A.

Preparing a Move-Out Letter

Chapter 7 explains how a move-in letter can help get a tenancy off to a good start. Similarly, a move-out letter can also help reduce the possibility of disputes, especially over the return of security deposits.

Your move-out letter should tell the tenant how you expect the unit to be left, explain your inspection procedures, list the kinds of deposit deductions you may legally make, and tell the tenant when and how you will send any refund that is due.

A sample Move-Out Letter is shown below and the Nolo website includes a downloadable copy. See Appendix B for the link to the forms in this book. You may want to add or delete items depending on your own needs and how specific you wish to be.

Here are a few points you may want to include in a move-out letter:

- specific cleaning requirements, such as what to do about dirty walls, or how to fix holes left from picture hooks
- instructions regarding recycling and disposing of paint and household hazardous wastes
- a reminder that fixtures (items that the tenant attaches more or less permanently to the wall, such as built-in bookshelves) must be left in place (see the discussion of fixtures in Chapter 9 and Clause 12 of the form agreements in Chapter 2)
- details of how and when the final inspection will be conducted
- a request for a forwarding address where you can mail the tenant's deposits
- information on state laws (if any) that allow a landlord to keep a tenant's security deposit if the tenant's forwarding address is not provided within a certain amount of time ("Mailing the Security Deposit Itemization," below), and
- information on state laws regarding abandoned property (discussed at the end of this chapter).

Move-Out Letter

<u>July 5, 20xx</u>
Date

<u>Jane Wasserman</u>
Tenant

<u>123 North Street, Apartment #23</u>
Street Address

<u>Atlanta, Georgia 30360</u>
City and State

Dear <u>Jane</u>,

Tenant

We hope you have enjoyed living here. In order that we may mutually end our relationship on a positive note, this move-out letter describes how we expect your unit to be left and what our procedures are for returning your security deposit.

Basically, we expect you to leave your rental unit in the same condition it was when you moved in, except for normal wear and tear. To refresh your memory on the condition of the unit when you moved in, I've attached a copy of the Landlord-Tenant Checklist you signed at the beginning of your tenancy. I'll be using this same form to inspect your unit when you leave.

Specifically, here's a list of items you should thoroughly clean before vacating:

- ☑ Floors
    - ☑ sweep wood floors
    - ☑ vacuum carpets and rugs (shampoo if necessary)
    - ☑ mop kitchen and bathroom floors
- ☑ Walls, baseboards, ceilings, and built-in shelves
- ☑ Kitchen cabinets, countertops and sink, stove and oven—inside and out
- ☑ Refrigerator—clean inside and out, empty it of food, and turn it off, with the door left open
- ☑ Bathtubs, showers, toilets, and plumbing fixtures
- ☑ Doors, windows, and window coverings
- ☑ Other

<u>Microwave oven-clean inside and out</u>

_____

_____

_____

_____

_____

_____

_____

If you have any questions as to the type of cleaning we expect, please let me know.

Please don't leave anything behind—that includes bags of garbage, clothes, food, newspapers, furniture, appliances, dishes, plants, cleaning supplies, or other items that belong to you.

Please be sure you have disconnected phone and utility services, canceled all newspaper subscriptions, and sent the post office a change of address form.

Once you have cleaned your unit and removed all your belongings, please call me at ___555-1234___ to arrange for a walk-through inspection and to return all keys. Please be prepared to give me your forwarding address where we may mail your security deposit.

It's our policy to return all deposits either in person or at an address you provide within ___one month___ _____ after you move out. If any deductions are made—for past-due rent or because the unit is damaged or not sufficiently clean—they will be explained in writing.

If you have any questions, please contact me at ___555-1234_____ .

Sincerely,
Denise Parsons
Landlord/Manager

Inspecting the Unit When a Tenant Leaves

After the tenant leaves, you will need to inspect the unit to assess what cleaning and damage repair is necessary. At the final inspection, check each item—for example, refrigerator or bathroom walls—on the Landlord-Tenant Checklist you and the tenant (hopefully) signed when the tenant moved in. (An excerpt is shown below. See Chapter 7 for a complete Checklist.) Note any item that needs cleaning, repair, or replacement in the middle column, *Condition on Departure.* Where possible, note the estimated cost of repair or replacement in the third column; you can subtract those costs from the security deposit.

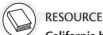

RESOURCE

California has special rules and procedures for move-out inspections. California tenants are entitled to a pre-move-out inspection, when you tell the tenant what defects, if any, need to be corrected in order for the tenant to optimize the security deposit refund. California landlords must notify the tenant in writing of the right to request an initial inspection, at which the tenant has a right to be present. (Cal. Civ. Code § 1950.5(f).) For details, see *The California Landlord's Law Book: Rights & Responsibilities*, by David Brown, Janet Portman, and Nils Rosenquest (Nolo). This book is available at bookstores and public libraries, or may be ordered directly from Nolo (online at www.nolo.com or by phone, 800-728-3555).

Many landlords do this final inspection on their own and simply send the tenant an itemized statement with any remaining balance of the deposit. If at all possible, we recommend that you make the inspection with the tenant who's moving out, rather than by yourself. A few states actually require this. Doing the final inspection with the tenant present (in a conciliatory, nonthreatening way) should alleviate any of the tenant's uncertainty concerning what deductions (if any) you propose to make from the deposit. It also gives the tenant a chance to present her point of view. But, best of all, this approach avoids the risk that a tenant who feels unpleasantly surprised by the amount you withhold from the deposit will promptly take the matter to small claims court.

Landlord-Tenant Checklist

GENERAL CONDITION OF RENTAL UNIT AND PREMISES

572 Fourth St.
Street Address

Apt. 11   Washington, D.C
Unit No.   City

	Condition on Arrival	Condition on Departure	Estimated Cost of Repair/ Replacement
Living Room			
Floors & Floor Coverings	OK	OK	Ø
Drapes & Window Coverings	Miniblinds discolored	Miniblinds missing	$75
Walls & Ceilings	OK	Several holes in wall	$100
Light Fixtures	OK	OK	Ø
Windows, Screens, & Doors	Window rattles		Ø
& Locks	OK		

If you have any reason to expect a tenant to take you to court over deductions you plan to make from a security deposit, have the unit examined by another, more neutral person, such as another tenant in the same building. This person should be available to testify in court on your behalf, if necessary, should you end up in small claims court.

> **TIP**
>
> **Photograph "before" and "after."** In Chapter 7, we recommend that you take photos or videos of the unit before the tenant moves in. You should do the same when the tenant leaves, so that you can make comparisons and have visual proof in case you are challenged later in court.

Should You Let the Tenant Clean or Fix the Damage?

Many tenants, faced with losing a large chunk of their security deposit, may want the chance to do some more cleaning or repair any damage you've identified in the final inspection. A few states require you to offer the tenant a second chance at cleaning before you deduct cleaning charges from the security deposit. Even if your state does not require it, you may wish to offer a second chance anyway if the tenant seems sincere and capable of doing the work. This may help avoid arguments and maybe even a small claims action. But, if you need to get the apartment ready quickly for another tenant or doubt the tenant's ability to do the work, just say no. And think twice if repairs are required, not just cleaning. If a tenant does a repair poorly—for example, improperly tacking down a carpet that later causes another tenant to trip and injure herself—you will be liable for the injury.

To be on the safe side, keep your inspection notes, photos, videos, and related records for at least two years. Technically speaking, in most states tenants have up to four years to sue you over security deposit agreements, but few will do so after a year or so.

Applying the Security Deposit to the Last Month's Rent

If no portion of the tenant's deposit was called last month's rent, you are not legally obliged to apply it in this way. When giving notice, a tenant may ask you to apply the security deposit toward the last month's rent.

Why should you object if a tenant asks to use a deposit you are already holding as payment for the last month's rent? The problem is that you can't know in advance what the property will look like when the tenant leaves. If the tenant leaves the property a mess, but the whole security deposit has gone to pay the last month's rent, obviously you will have nothing left to use to repair or clean the property. You will have to absorb the loss or sue the tenant.

You have two choices if you are faced with a tenant who wants to use a security deposit for last month's rent. The first alternative is to grant the tenant's request. Tell the tenant that you'll need to make a quick inspection first, and then, if you have good reason to believe that the tenant will leave the property clean and undamaged, don't worry about the last month's rent. But don't forget to send the tenant a written statement setting out what happened to the deposit. You can prepare a brief letter, similar to the one we show in "Preparing an Itemized Statement of Deductions," below, for returning the tenant's entire security deposit.

Your second choice is to treat the tenant's non-payment (or partial payment) of the last month's rent as an ordinary case of rent nonpayment. This means preparing and serving the notice necessary to terminate the tenancy, and, if the tenant doesn't pay, following up with an eviction lawsuit. But because it typically takes at least several weeks to evict a tenant, this probably won't get the tenant out much sooner than he would leave anyway. However, it will provide you with a court judgment for the unpaid last month's rent. This means that you may use the security deposit to pay for cleaning and repair costs, and apply any remainder to the judgment for nonpayment of rent. You then take your judgment and attempt to enforce it, as discussed below ("If the Deposit Doesn't Cover Damage and Unpaid Rent").

> **EXAMPLE:** Ari paid his landlord Jack a $1,000 deposit when he rented his $900-per-month apartment on a month-to-month basis. The rental agreement required Ari to give 30 days' notice before terminating the tenancy.
>
> Ari told Jack on November 1 that he would be leaving at the end of the month, but he did not pay his rent for November. When he left on December 1, he also left $500 worth of damages. Jack followed his state's procedures for itemizing and returning security deposits, and applied the $1,000 deposit to cover the damage. This left Jack with only $500 for the $900 rent due, so he sued in small claims court for the $400 still owing. Jack was awarded a judgment for $400 plus the filing fee.

Basic Rules for Returning Deposits

You are generally entitled to deduct from a tenant's security deposit whatever amount you need to fix damaged or dirty property (outside of "ordinary wear and tear") or to make up unpaid rent (see "Purpose and Use of Security Deposits" in Chapter 4). But you must do it correctly, following your state's procedures. While the specific rules vary from state to state, you usually have between 14 and 30 days after the tenant leaves to return the tenant's deposit. See the column "Deadline for Landlord to Itemize and Return Deposit" in the "State Security Deposit Rules" chart in Appendix A. A few states require landlords to give tenants advance notice of intended deductions; see "Advance notice of deduction" in the same chart.

State security deposit statutes typically require you to mail, within the time limit, the following to the tenant's last known address (or forwarding address if you have one):

- The tenant's entire deposit, with interest if required, or

- A written, itemized accounting as to how the deposit has been applied toward back rent and costs of cleaning and damage repair, together with payment for any deposit balance, including any interest that is required. We show you below how to prepare an itemized statement, including how to handle situations when you're not sure of the exact deductions.

Even if there is no specific time limit in your state or law requiring itemization, promptly presenting the tenant with a written itemization of all deductions and a clear reason why each was made is an essential part of a savvy landlord's overall plan to avoid disputes with tenants. In general, we recommend 30 days as a reasonable time to return deposits.

 TIP

Send an itemization even if you don't send money. Quite a few landlords mistakenly believe that they don't have to account for the deposit to a tenant who's been evicted by court order or who breaks the lease. But a tenant's misconduct does not entitle a landlord to pocket the entire deposit without further formality. In general, even if the tenant leaves owing several months' rent—more than the amount of the deposit—you still must notify the tenant in writing, within the time limit, as to how the deposit has been applied toward cleaning or repair charges and unpaid rent. You may then need to sue the tenant if the deposit doesn't cover damage and unpaid rent.

Deductions for Cleaning and Damage

As you can imagine, many disputes over security deposits revolve around whether or not it was reasonable for the landlord to deduct the cost of cleaning or repairing the premises after the tenant moved. Unfortunately, standards in this area are often vague. Typically, you may charge for any cleaning or repairs necessary to restore the rental unit to its condition at the beginning the tenancy, but not deduct for the cost of ordinary wear and tear.

Reasonable Deductions

In general, you may charge only for cleaning and repairs that are actually necessary. Items for which cleaning is often necessary—and costly—include replacing stained or ripped carpets or curtains (particularly smoke-contaminated ones) fixing damaged furniture, and cleaning dirty stoves, refrigerators, and kitchen and bathroom fixtures. You may also need to take care of such things as flea infestations left behind by the tenant's dog or mildew in the bathroom caused by the tenant's failure to clean properly. That's why we recommend highlighting these types of trouble spots in a move-out letter. See "Preparing a Move-Out Letter," above, for a sample move-out letter.

That said, every move-out is different in its details, and there are simply no hard and fast rules on what is wear and tear and what is your tenant's responsibility. But here are some basic guidelines:

- You should not charge the tenant for filth or damage that was present when the tenant moved in.
- You should not charge the tenant for replacing an item when a repair would be sufficient. For example, a tenant who damaged the kitchen counter by placing a hot pan on it shouldn't be charged for replacing the entire counter if an expertly done patch will do the job. Of course, you have to evaluate the overall condition of the unit—if it is a luxury property that looks like an ad in *Architectural Digest*, you don't need to make do with a patch.
- The longer a tenant has lived in a place, the more wear and tear can be expected. In practical terms, this means that you can't always charge a tenant for cleaning carpets, drapes, or walls, or repainting.

- You should not charge for cleaning if the tenant paid a nonrefundable cleaning fee. Landlords in some states are allowed to charge a cleaning fee, which is separate from the security deposit and is specifically labeled as nonrefundable.
- You should charge a fair price for repairs and replacements.

You can deduct a reasonable hourly charge if you or your employees do any necessary cleaning. If you have cleaning done by an outside service, be sure to keep your canceled checks or credit card receipts, and have the service itemize the work. It's wise to patronize only those cleaning services whose employees are willing to testify for you, or at least send a letter describing what they did in detail, if the tenant sues you in small claims court contesting your deposit deductions. See "If a Tenant Sues You," below.

TIP

Don't overdo deductions from security deposits. When you make deductions for cleaning or damage, it's often a mistake to be too aggressive. Tenants who believe they've been wronged (even if it isn't true) are likely to go to small claims court. The result will be that you or an employee will spend hours preparing your defense, waiting around the courthouse, and presenting your side of the case. Even if you prevail (or, as is most likely, the judge makes a compromise ruling), the value of the time involved will have been considerable. In the long run, it may be wiser to withhold a smaller portion of the deposit in the first place.

See "What Can You Charge For?" below, for some examples of what a court will consider to be ordinary wear and tear, and what crosses the line and is considered damage that the tenant must pay for.

Common Disagreements

Common areas of disagreement between landlords and tenants concern repainting, carpets, and fixtures.

What Can You Charge For?	
Ordinary Wear and Tear: Landlord's Responsibility	**Damage or Excessive Filth: Tenant's Responsibility**
Curtains faded by the sun	Cigarette burns in curtains or carpets
Water-stained linoleum by shower	Broken tiles in bathroom
Minor marks on or nicks in wall	Large marks on or holes in wall
Dents in the wall where a door handle bumped it	Door off its hinges
Moderate dirt or spotting on carpet	Rips in carpet or urine stains from pets
A few small tack or nail holes in wall	Lots of picture holes or gouges in walls that require patching as well as repainting
A rug worn thin by normal use	Stains in rug caused by leaking fish tank
Worn gaskets on refrigerator doors	Broken refrigerator shelf
Faded paint on bedroom wall	Water damage on wall from hanging plants
Dark patches of ingrained soil on hardwood floors that have lost their finish and have been worn down to bare wood	Water stains on wood floors and windowsills caused by windows being left open during rainstorms
Warped cabinet doors that won't close	Sticky cabinets and interiors
Stains on old porcelain fixtures that have lost their protective coating	Grime-coated bathtub and toilet
Moderately dirty miniblinds	Missing miniblinds
Bathroom mirror beginning to "de-silver" (black spots)	Mirrors caked with lipstick and makeup
Toilet flushes inadequately because mineral deposits have clogged the jets	Toilet won't flush properly because it's stopped up with a diaper

Painting

Although most state and local laws (with the exception of New York City) provide no firm guidelines as to who is responsible for repainting when a rental unit needs it, courts usually rule that if a tenant has lived in your unit for many years, repainting should be done at your expense, not the tenant's. On the other hand, if a tenant has lived in a unit for less than a year, and the walls were freshly painted when she moved in but are now a mess, you are entitled to charge the tenant for all costs of cleaning the walls. If repainting badly smudged walls is cheaper and more effective than cleaning, however, you can charge for repainting.

When to Charge the Tenant for Repainting

One landlord we know uses the following approach, with excellent success, when a tenant moves out and repainting is necessary:

- If the tenant has occupied the premises for six months or less, the full cost of repainting (labor and materials) is subtracted from the deposit.
- If the tenant lived in the unit between six months and a year, and the walls are dirty, two-thirds of the painting cost is subtracted from the deposit.
- Tenants who occupy a unit for between one and two years and leave dirty walls are charged one-third of the repainting cost.
- No one who stays for two years or more is ever charged a painting fee. No matter how dirty the walls become, the landlord would always repaint as a matter of course if more than two years had passed since the previous painting.

Obviously, these general rules must be modified occasionally to fit particular circumstances.

Rugs and Carpets

If the living room rug was already threadbare when the tenant moved in a few months ago and looks even worse now, it's pretty obvious that the tenant's footsteps have simply contributed to the inevitable, and that this wear and tear is not the tenant's responsibility. On the other hand, a brand-new, good quality rug that becomes stained and full of bare spots within months has probably been subjected to the type of abuse the tenant will have to pay for. In between, it's anyone's guess. But clearly, the longer a tenant has lived in a unit, and the cheaper or older the carpet was when the tenant moved in, the less likely the tenant is to be held responsible for its deterioration.

> **EXAMPLE:** A tenant has ruined an eight-year-old rug that had a life expectancy of ten years. If a replacement rug would cost $1,000, you would charge the tenant $200 for the two years of life that would have remained in the rug had their dog not ruined it.

Fixtures

The law generally considers pieces of furniture or equipment that are physically attached to the rental property, such as bolted-on bookshelves, to be your property, even if the tenant (not you) paid for them. Disputes often arise when tenants, unaware of this rule, install a fixture and then attempt to remove it and take it with them when they leave. To avoid this kind of dispute, the lease and rental agreements in this book forbid tenants from altering the premises without your consent. That includes the installation of fixtures. See Clause 12 of the form agreements in Chapter 2.

If the tenant leaves behind built-in bookshelves, you can remove the shelves, restore the property to the same condition as before they were installed, and subtract the cost from the tenant's security deposit. Unless your lease or rental agreement says otherwise, you do not have to return the bookshelves to the tenant. Legally, you've only removed something that has become part of the premises and, hence, your property. Chapter 9 offers suggestions on how to avoid disputes with tenants over fixtures.

Deductions for Unpaid Rent

In most states you can deduct any unpaid rent from a tenant's security deposit, including any unpaid utility charges or other financial obligations required under your lease or rental agreement.

 CAUTION
Even if the tenant's debt far exceeds the amount of the security deposit, do not ignore your statutory duties to itemize and notify the former tenant of your use of the security deposit. It may seem like a waste of time, but some courts will penalize you for ignoring the statute, even if you later obtain a judgment that puts the stamp of approval on your use of the deposit.

Month-to-Month Tenancies

If you rent on a month-to-month basis, ideally your tenant will give the right amount of notice and pay for the last month's rent. Usually, the notice period is the same as the rental period: 30 days. Then, when the tenant leaves as planned, the only issue with respect to the security deposit is whether the tenant has caused any damage or left the place dirty. But there are three common variations on this ideal scenario, and they all allow you to deduct from the tenant's security deposit for unpaid rent:

- The tenant leaves as announced, but with unpaid rent behind.
- The tenant leaves later than planned, and hasn't paid for the extra days.
- The tenant leaves as announced, but hasn't given you the right amount of notice.

Let's look at each situation.

The Tenant Leaves With Rent Unpaid

If the tenant has been behind on the rent for months, you are entitled to deduct what is owed from the security deposit—either during the tenancy or when the tenant leaves. If you deduct during the tenancy, be sure to follow your state's law on itemization.

The Tenant Stays After the Announced Departure Date

A tenant who fails to leave when planned (or when requested, if you have terminated the rental agreement) obviously isn't entitled to stay on rent-free. When the tenant eventually does leave, you can figure the exact amount owed by prorating the monthly rent for the number of days the tenant has failed to pay.

> **EXAMPLE:** Your tenant Erin gives notice on March 1 of her intent to move out. She pays you the rent of $1,200 for March. But because she can't get into her new place on time, Erin stays until April 5 without paying anything more for the extra five days. You are entitled to deduct 5/30 (one-sixth) of the total month's rent, or $200, from Erin's security deposit.

The Tenant Gives Inadequate Notice

A tenant who gives less than the legally required amount of notice before leaving (typically 30 days) must pay rent for that entire period. If the tenant gave less than the legally required amount of notice and moved out, you are entitled to rent money for the balance of the notice period unless the place is rerented within the 30 days.

> **EXAMPLE 1:** Your tenant Tom moves out on the fifth day of the month, without giving you any notice or paying any rent for the month. The rental market is flooded, and you are unable to rerent the property for two months. You are entitled to deduct an entire month's rent (for the missing 30 days' notice) plus one-sixth of one month (for the five holdover days for which Tom failed to pay rent).

> **EXAMPLE 2:** Sheila pays her $900 monthly rent on October 1. State law requires 30 days' notice to terminate a tenancy. On October 15, Sheila informs you that she's leaving on the 25th. This gives you only ten days' notice, when you're entitled to 30. You're entitled to rent through the 30th day, counting from October 15, or November 14, unless you find a new tenant in the meantime. Because the rent is paid through October 31, Sheila owes you the prorated rent for 14 days in November. At $900 per month or $30 a day, this works out to $420, which you can deduct from Sheila's security deposit.

Fixed-Term Leases

If a tenant leaves before a fixed-term lease expires, you are usually entitled to the balance of the rent due under the lease, less any rent you receive from new tenants or could have received if you had made a diligent effort to rerent the property.

If a tenant leaves less than a month before the lease is scheduled to end, you can be almost positive that, if the case goes to court, a judge will conclude that the tenant owes rent for the entire lease term. It would be unreasonable to expect you to immediately find a new tenant to take over the few days left of the lease. But if the tenant leaves more than 30 days before the end of a lease, your duty to look for a new tenant will be taken more seriously by the courts. See Chapter 14 for more on your duty to try to rerent the property promptly.

> **EXAMPLE:** On January 1, Anthony rents a house from Will for $1,200 a month and signs a one-year lease. Anthony moves out on June 30, even though six months remain on the lease, making him responsible for a total rent of $7,200. Will rerents the property on July 10, this time for $1,250 a month (the new tenants pay $833 for the last 20 days in July), which means that he'll receive a total rent of $7,083 through December 31. That's $117 less than the $7,200 he would have received from Anthony had he lived up to the lease, so Will may deduct $117 from Anthony's deposit. In addition, if Will has spent a reasonable amount of money to find a new tenant (for newspaper ads, rental agency commissions, and credit checks), he may also deduct this sum from the deposit.

Deducting Rent After You've Evicted a Tenant

In most states, if you successfully sue to evict a holdover tenant, you will obtain a court order telling the tenant to leave (which you give to a law enforcement agency to enforce) and a money judgment ordering the tenant to pay you rent through the date of the judgment. Armed with these court orders, you can subtract from the security deposit:

- the amount of the judgment, and
- prorated rent for the period between the date of the judgment and the date the tenant actually leaves.

EXAMPLE: Marilyn sues to evict a tenant who fails to pay May's rent of $900. She gets an eviction judgment from the court on June 10 for rent prorated through that date. The tenant doesn't leave until the 17th, when the sheriff comes and puts him out. Marilyn can deduct the following items from the deposit:

- costs of necessary cleaning and repair, as allowed by state law
- the amount of the judgment (for rent through June 10)
- rent for the week between judgment and eviction (seven days at $30/day, or $210).

Before you subtract the amount of a court judgment for unpaid rent from a deposit, deduct any cleaning and repair costs and any unpaid rent not included in the judgment. The reason is simple: A judgment can be collected in all sorts of ways—for example, you can go after the former tenant's wages or bank account—if the security deposit is not large enough to cover everything owed you. However, you are much more limited when it comes to collecting money the tenant owes you for damage and cleaning if you don't have a judgment for the amount. If you don't subtract these items from the deposit, you'll have to file suit in small claims court as discussed below. But if you subtract the amount for cleaning, damage, and any unpaid rent not covered in the judgment first, you will still have the judgment if the deposit isn't large enough to cover everything.

EXAMPLE 1: Amelia collected a security deposit of $1,200 from Timothy, whom she ultimately had to sue to evict for failure to pay rent. Amelia got a judgment for $160 court costs plus $1,000 unpaid rent through the date of the judgment. Timothy didn't leave until the sheriff came, about five days later, thus running up an additional prorated rent of $100. Timothy also left dirt and damage that cost $1,000 to clean and repair.

Amelia (who hadn't read this book) first applied the $1,200 security deposit to the $1,160 judgment, leaving only $40 to apply toward the rent of $100 which was not reflected in the judgment, as well as the cleaning and repair charges, all of which totaled $1,100. Amelia must now sue Timothy for the $1,060 he still owes her.

EXAMPLE 2: Now, assume that Monique was Timothy's landlord in the same situation. But Monique applied Timothy's $1,200 deposit first to the cleaning and damage charges of $1,000, and then to the $100 rent not reflected in the judgment. This left $100 to apply to the $1,160 judgment, the balance of which she can collect by garnishing Timothy's wages or bank account.

Preparing an Itemized Statement of Deductions

Once you've inspected the premises and decided what you need to deduct for cleaning, repair, back rent, or other purposes allowed by your state statute, you're ready to prepare a statement for the tenant. The statement should simply list each deduction and briefly explain what it's for.

This section includes samples of three security deposit itemization forms, which you can use for different types of deductions. Copies of all three forms can be downloaded from the Nolo website. (See Appendix B for the link to the forms in this book.) Whatever form you use, be sure to keep a copy in your tenant records and receipts for repairs or cleaning in case the tenant ends up suing you at a later date. See "If a Tenant Sues You," below.

> **CAUTION**
> **If your city or state requires you to pay interest on a tenant's entire deposit, you must also refund this amount.** For details, see Chapter 4.

Returning the Entire Deposit

If you are returning a tenant's entire security deposit (including interest, if required), simply send a brief letter like the one below.

Letter for Returning Entire Security Deposit

<u>October 11, 20xx</u>
Date

<u>Gerry Fraser</u>
Tenant

<u>976 Park Place</u>
Street Address

<u>Sacramento, CA 95840</u>
City and State

Dear <u>Gerry</u>,
            Tenant

Here is an itemization of your $ <u>$1,500</u> security deposit on the property at <u>976 Park Place</u>

which you rented from me on a <u>month-to-month</u> basis on
<u>March 1, 20xx</u> and vacated on <u>September 30, 20xx</u>.

As you left the rental property in satisfactory condition, I am returning the entire amount of the security

deposit of <u>$1,500, plus $150 in interest, for a total of $1,650</u>.

Sincerely,

Tom Stein

Landlord/Manager

Security Deposit Itemization
(Deductions for Repairs and Cleaning)

Date   November 8, 20xx

From: Rachel Tolan

123 Larchmont Lane

St. Louis, Missouri 63119

To: Lena Coleman

456 Penny Lane, #101

St. Louis, Missouri 63119

Property Address: 789 Cora Court, St. Louis, Missouri

Rental Period: January 1, 20xx to October 31, 20xx

1. Security Deposit Received: $ 1,000

2. Interest on Deposit (if required by lease or law): $ N/A

3. Total Credit (sum of lines 1 and 2): $ 1,000

4. Itemized Repairs and Related Losses:

    Repainting of living room walls, required

    by crayon and chalk marks

                                                             $ 300

5. Necessary Cleaning:

    Sum paid to resident manager for 5 hours

    cleaning at $20/hour: debris-filled

    garage, dirty stove, and refrigerator $ 100

6. Total Cleaning & Repair (sum of lines 4 and 5): $ 400

7. Amount Owed (line 3 minus line 6):

    ☐ Total Amount Tenant Owes Landlord: $

    ☑ Total Amount Landlord Owes Tenant: $ 600

Comments: A check for $600 is enclosed.

Itemizing Deductions for Repairs, Cleaning, and Related Losses

If you are making deductions from the tenant's security deposit only for cleaning and repair, use the Security Deposit Itemization (Deductions for Repairs and Cleaning). A sample is shown above.

For each deduction, list the item and the dollar amount. If you've already had the work done, attach receipts to the itemization. If your receipts are not very detailed, add more information on labor and supplies, for example:

- "Carpet cleaning by ABC Carpet Cleaners, $160, required because of several large grease stains and candle wax embedded in living room rug."
- "Plaster repair, $400, of several fist-sized holes in bedroom wall."
- "$250 to replace curtains in living room, damaged by cigarette smoke and holes."

"Deductions for Cleaning and Damage," above, will help you determine proper amounts to deduct for repairs and cleaning.

If you can't get necessary repairs made or cleaning done within the time required to return the security deposit, make a reasonable estimate of the cost. But keep in mind that if the tenant subsequently sues you, you will need to produce receipts for at least as much as the amount you deducted.

When you're trying to put a dollar amount on damages, the basic approach is to determine whether the tenant has damaged or substantially shortened the useful life of an item that does wear out. If the answer is yes, you may charge the tenant the prorated cost of the item, based on the age of the item, how long it might have lasted otherwise, and the cost of replacement.

Itemizing Deductions for Repairs, Cleaning, and Unpaid Rent

If you have to deduct for unpaid rent as well as cleaning and repairs, use the form Security Deposit Itemization (Deductions for Repairs, Cleaning, and Unpaid Rent). A sample is shown below.

Handling Deposits When a Tenant Files for Bankruptcy

Landlords often see a tenant's bankruptcy filing as the ultimate monkey wrench in what may already be a less-than-perfect landlord-tenant relationship. Indeed, unless you've completed your eviction case and have received a judgment for possession before the tenant files for bankruptcy, you'll have to go to the bankruptcy court and ask for permission to begin (or continue) your eviction case. (Evictions and bankruptcy are explained in Chapter 17.) Fortunately, the effect of the bankruptcy on your use of the security deposit is not so drastic.

Your course of action all depends on timing: When did the tenant file his petition, and when did you use the deposit to cover unpaid rent or damage? Here are three common scenarios and the rules for each:

- **Tenant hasn't paid the rent and/or has caused damage. You assess your total losses and deduct from (or use up) the deposit, and then tenant files for bankruptcy.** No problem here, since you used the money before the tenant filed. You're also on solid ground if you've gone to court and obtained a money judgment that can be satisfied fully, or at least partially, by the security deposit. The key is to use the funds, or get the judgment, before the tenant files.

TIP

Take care of business quickly. You probably won't know about your tenant's plans to file for bankruptcy. It's wise to assess your losses soon after the tenant vacates and to leave a paper trail that will establish that the deposit was used before the filing date. If you keep deposits in a separate bank account and move these funds to another account as you use them, you'll have good proof.

- **Tenant causes damage that would normally be covered by the security deposit, or fails to pay the rent.** Before you have the chance to use the money to pay for the damage or rent, you receive a notice from the bankruptcy

Security Deposit Itemization
(Deductions for Repairs, Cleaning, and Unpaid Rent)

Date _December 19, 20xx_

From: _Timothy Gottman_

8910 Pine Avenue

Philadelphia, Pennsylvania 19106

To: _Monique Todd_

999 Laurel Drive

Philadelphia, Pennsylvania 19106

Property Address: _456 Pine Avenue #7, Philadelphia, Pennsylvania 19106_

Rental Period: _January 1, 20xx to October 31, 20xx_

1. Security Deposit Received: $ _1,200_

2. Interest on Deposit (if required by lease or law): $ _N/A_

3. Total Credit (sum of lines 1 and 2): $ _1,200_

4. Itemized Repairs and Related Losses:

   Carpet repair $160, curtain cleaning $140, plaster

   repair $200, painting of living room $300

   (receipts attached) $ _800_

5. Necessary Cleaning:

   Sum paid to resident manager for 10 hours

   cleaning at $20/hour: debris-filled garage,

   dirty stove and refrigerator $ _200_

6. Defaults in Rent Not Covered by Any Court Judgment
   (list dates and rates):

   5 days at $20/day from November 6 to

   November 11 (date of court judgment or

   date of physical eviction) $ _100_

7. Amount of Court Judgment for Rent, Costs, Attorney Fees: $ _1,160_

8. Other Deductions:

Specify: _____

_____

_____ $ _____

9. Total Amount Owed Landlord (sum of lines 3 through 8): $ _____2,260_____

10. Amount Owed (line 3 minus line 9):

☑ Total Amount Tenant Owes Landlord: $ _____1,060_____

☐ Total Amount Landlord Owes Tenant: $ _____

Comments: _The security deposit has been applied as follows: $1,000 for damage and_
cleaning charges, $100 for defaults in rent (not covered by any court judgment),
and the remaining $100 toward payment of the $1,160 court judgment. This leaves
$1,060 still owed on the judgment. Please send that amount to me at once or I shall
take appropriate legal action to collect it.

court stating that the tenant has filed. Once you receive this notice, you are prohibited from taking any action against the tenant, including using the security deposit, without an okay from the court (this is called a "Relief from Stay"). Instead of going to court, you can just sit tight and wait until the bankruptcy proceeding is over. Then, you can use the money to cover the tenant's debt. However, be aware that the amount a landlord can recover from a tenant's assets, including a deposit, is limited to the greater of either one year's worth of rent or 15% of the remaining lease term, not to exceed three years. (11 U.S.C. § 502.)

- **Tenant files for bankruptcy, then causes damage that would normally be covered by the security deposit.** Follow the same advice as above.

⊘ CAUTION

Use "last month's rent" and "security deposit" correctly. Some states do not allow you to use a deposit you have labeled "last month's rent" to cover damage or cleaning. If you live in a state that has adopted this approach, make sure that your security deposit itemization form complies with the law and that you use the available deposits correctly.

This Security Deposit Itemization (Deductions for Repairs, Cleaning, and Unpaid Rent) form includes spaces for you to include unpaid rent not covered by a court judgment (line 6) and, if you have won an eviction lawsuit against the tenant, the amount of the court judgment you won (line 7). ("Deductions for Unpaid Rent," above, shows you how to figure these amounts, and explains why it's better to deduct cleaning and damage costs from the security deposit before deducting any of a court judgment.) If the tenant has left without paying utility charges or another financial obligation required under your lease or rental agreement, provide details on line 6 (Defaults in Rent Not Covered by Any Court Judgment).

If there's a court judgment involved, explain how you applied the deposit in the Comments section at the bottom of the itemization form. This makes it clear that you are demanding the balance owed and that you can still collect any part of the judgment not covered by the security deposit.

Mailing the Security Deposit Itemization

Some tenants will want to personally pick up any deposit as soon as possible. If that isn't feasible, mail your security deposit itemization to the tenant's last known address or forwarding address as soon as is reasonably possible, along with payment for any balance you owe. Don't wait until the end of the legally specified period if you have all the information necessary to act sooner, as it almost guarantees that a large number of anxious tenants will contact you. And, if you miss the deadline, you may be liable for hefty financial penalties, as discussed in "If a Tenant Sues You," below. Some states require landlords to use certified mail; check your state's statutes for any special mailing requirements. If the tenant hasn't left you a forwarding address, mail the itemization and any balance to the address of the rental property itself. That, after all, is the tenant's last address known to you. If your former tenant has left a forwarding address with the Post Office, it will forward the mail.

It will be useful for you to know the tenant's new address if the tenant's deposit doesn't cover all proper deductions and you want to sue in small claims court. (See the discussion below.) It will also help you collect any judgment you have against the tenant.

There are two ways that you can learn the new address:

- **Set up an account with the Postal Service.** You can pay the Post Office in advance to tell you whenever one of your letters is forwarded. Because of the cost involved, this procedure makes sense for landlords with many rental units.
- **Use "Return Receipt Requested."** For smaller landlords or people who rarely face this situation, it may not be worth your while to prepay. Instead, you can send the letter "Return Receipt Requested" and, on the Postal Service form, check the box that tells the carrier to note the address where the letter was delivered. This address will be on the receipt that is sent back to you.

If the tenant has left no forwarding address, the letter will come back to you. The postmarked envelope is your proof of your good-faith attempt to notify the tenant, in case the tenant ever accuses you of not returning the money properly. Some states specifically allow the landlord to retain the deposit if he cannot locate the tenant after a reasonable effort or a certain amount of time has passed, such as 60 or 90 days. If your state laws do not specify what happens to the deposit if you cannot locate the tenant, you'll need to seek legal advice on what to do with the deposit.

Security Deposits From Cotenants

When you rent to two or more cotenants (they all sign the same written lease or rental agreement), you do not usually have to return or account for any of the deposit until they all leave. In other words, you're entitled to the benefit of the entire deposit until the entire tenancy ends. Legally, any question as to whether a departing cotenant is entitled to any share of the deposit should be worked out among the cotenants.

From a practical point of view, however, you may want to work out an agreement with a departing cotenant who wants part of the deposit back. For instance, you may be willing to refund his share of the deposit if the new cotenant gives you a check for that amount. The drawback of this approach is that the new cotenant will not want to get stuck paying for damage that was caused by the departing tenant. If you accommodate this request, too, you may have to do an extra inspection in the middle of the lease term. (On the other hand, you may welcome an opportunity to discover and correct problems before they grow.)

> **EXAMPLE:** Bill and Mark were cotenants who had each contributed $500 toward the $1,000 security deposit. Bill needed to move before the lease was up and asked Len, their landlord, if he would accept Tom as a new cotenant. Len agreed.
>
> Bill wanted his $500 back, and, although Tom was willing to contribute his share of the deposit, he did not want to end up paying for damage that had been caused before he moved in. To take care of this, Len agreed to inspect if Tom would first give him a check for $500. When he got the check, Len inspected and found $200 worth of damage. He deducted this amount from Bill's share of the deposit and wrote Bill a check for $300. Len left it up to Bill and Mark to fairly apportion the responsibility for the damage. With Tom's $500 check, the security deposit was once again topped off.

If a Tenant Sues You

No matter how meticulous you are about properly accounting to your tenants for their deposits, sooner or later you may be sued by a tenant who disagrees with your assessment of the cost of cleaning or repairs. Tenants may also sue if you fail to return the deposit when and how required or violate other provisions of state or local law, such as a requirement that you pay interest on deposits.

Tenants usually sue in small claims court, where it's cheap to file, lawyers aren't necessary, and disputes typically go before a judge (there are no juries) within 30 to 60 days, without formal rules of evidence. (We use the term small claims court here, but the exact name may vary depending upon the state. The courts are called "Justice of the Peace," "Conciliation," "District," "Justice," "City," or "County" in different places.)

The maximum amount for which someone can sue in small claims court varies among the states, but in most states it's about $5,000 to $10,000. For details, see "State Small Claims Court Limits" in Appendix A.

 CAUTION

Penalties for violating security deposit statutes can turn a minor squabble into an expensive affair. While it is rarely worth your while to go to court over a matter of $50 or even a couple of hundred dollars, the same is not true for the tenant. Why? Because many statutes allow a victorious tenant to collect not only actual damages (the amount improperly deducted from the deposit), but penalties as well. Small claims courts are empowered to award these penalties.

This section suggests several strategies for dealing with small claims suits over security deposits, including how to prepare and present a case in small claims court.

RESOURCE

For more information on small claims court procedures, see *Everybody's Guide to Small Claims Court* (National Edition), by Cara O'Neill (Nolo).

When a Tenant May Sue

Before going to court, the tenant will most likely express dissatisfaction by way of a letter or phone call demanding that you refund more than you did or fix some other problem involving the deposit. In some states, this sort of demand must be made before the tenant can begin a small claims suit. After making a demand, the tenant can bring suit immediately.

A tenant who is going to sue will probably do it fairly promptly but may have up to a few years to do so, depending on the state. Don't throw out cleaning bills, receipts for repairs, or photographs showing dirt and damages after only a few months, lest you be caught defenseless.

Who Goes to Small Claims Court?

If your business is incorporated, you can send an employee such as a property manager, as long as the person is authorized to represent you in legal proceedings. If you are not incorporated, you'll probably have to go yourself, but a few states allow managers to go in your place. In most states you can be represented by a lawyer in small claims court, but it's rarely worth the cost. Procedures are simple and designed for nonlawyers.

Settling a Potential Lawsuit

If you receive a demand letter or phone call from a tenant, your best bet is almost always to try to work out a reasonable compromise. Be open to the idea of returning more of the deposit to the

tenant, even if you believe your original assessment of the cost of repairs and cleaning was more than fair and you feel you will surely win in court. For practical reasons, it usually doesn't make sense for you or an employee to prepare a small claims case and spend time in court to argue over $50, $100, or even $200. This is especially true because, fair or not, some judges are prone to split the difference between the landlord's and the tenant's claims.

If you and the tenant can't reach a reasonable compromise, you may wish to get help from a local landlord-tenant mediation service.

Sample Settlement Agreement Regarding Return of Security Deposit

Lionel Washington, "Landlord," and LaToya Jones, "Tenant," agree as follows:

1. Landlord rented the premises at 1234 State Avenue, Apartment 5, Santa Fe, New Mexico, to Tenant on July 1, 20xx, pursuant to a written rental agreement for a tenancy from month to month.

2. Under the Agreement, Tenant paid Landlord $1,000 as a security deposit.

3. On October 31, 20xx Tenant vacated the premises.

4. Within 30 days (the time required by New Mexico law) after Tenant vacated the premises, Landlord itemized various deductions from the security deposit totaling $380 and refunded the balance of $620 to Tenant.

5. Tenant asserts that she is entitled to the additional sum of $300, only $80 of the deductions being proper. Landlord asserts that all the deductions were proper and that he owes Tenant nothing.

6. To settle the parties' entire dispute, and to compromise on Tenant's claim for return of her security deposit, Landlord pays to Tenant the sum of $150, receipt of which is hereby acknowledged by Tenant as full satisfaction of her claim.

Lionel Washington   *12/1/xx*

Lionel Washington, Landlord   Date

LaToya Jones   *12/1/xx*

LaToya Jones, Tenant   Date

If you arrive at a compromise settlement with your former tenant, you should insist that your payment be accepted as full and final satisfaction of your obligation to return the deposit. The best way to do this is to prepare and have the tenant sign a brief settlement agreement, like the sample shown above.

Splitting the Difference With Tenants

One landlord we know with thousands of units experiences about 250 move-outs each month. In about one-third, he receives a complaint from a tenant who claims too much of the deposit was withheld.

This landlord's general policy is to offer to settle for 70% of the disputed amount. Since the average amount withheld is $175, this means the landlord is willing to reduce this amount by $52.50. If a tenant refuses to accept this compromise, the landlord will often make a second offer of a 50% reduction.

He does this not because he thinks his original assessment was wrong, but because he finds that coming to a settlement with a tenant costs a lot less than fighting in court. However, if the settlement offer isn't accepted promptly by the tenant, he fights to win—and almost always does.

Preparing for a Small Claims Court Hearing

If no compromise is possible and the tenant sues you, the court will officially notify you of the date, time, and place of the small claims court hearing.

It's still not too late at this stage to try to work out a settlement by paying part of what the tenant's suing for. However, if you compromise at this stage, make sure the tenant has correctly dismissed the small claims courts suit. Be sure your settlement is in writing.

Before your court hearing, gather tangible evidence showing the premises needed cleaning or were damaged when the tenant left. It is essential to take to court as many of the following items of evidence as you can:

- Copies of the lease or rental agreement, signed by both you and the tenant.
- Copies of move-in and move-out letters clarifying rules and policies on cleaning, damage repair, and security deposits.
- A copy of the Landlord-Tenant Checklist that you should have filled out with the tenant when the tenant moved in and when she moved out, signed by both you and the tenant. This is particularly important if the tenant admitted, on the Checklist, to damaged or dirty conditions when she moved out.
- Photos or a video of the premises before the tenant moved in that show how clean and undamaged the place was.
- Photos or a video after the tenant left that show a mess or damage.
- An itemization of hours spent by you or your repair or cleaning people on the unit, complete with the hourly costs for the work, plus copies of receipts for cleaning materials or credit card itemizations or canceled checks.
- Damaged items small enough to bring into the courtroom (a curtain with a cigarette hole would be effective).
- Receipts or a canceled check for professional cleaning (particularly of carpets and drapes) and repair.
- One, or preferably two, witnesses who were familiar with the property, who saw it just after the tenant left, and who will testify that the place was a mess or that certain items were damaged. People who helped in the cleaning or repair are particularly effective witnesses. There is no rule that says you can't have a close friend or relative testify for you, but, given a choice, it's better to have a witness who's neither a friend nor kin.
- If it's difficult for a witness to come to court, a written statement (a signed letter) or a declaration under penalty of perjury can be used in most states. Documents, however, usually aren't as effective as live testimony. If you do present a written statement from a

witness, make sure the statement includes the date of the event, exactly what the witness saw in terms of damage, any credentials that make the person qualified to testify on the subject, and any other facts that have a bearing on the dispute. A sample statement is shown below.

Sample Declaration of Cleaning Service

I, Paul Stallone, declare:

1. I am employed at A & B Maintenance Company, a contract cleaning and maintenance service located at 123 Abrego Street, Central City, Iowa. Gina Cabarga, the owner of an apartment complex at 456 Seventh Street, Central City, Iowa, is one of our accounts.

2. On May 1, 20xx I was requested to go to the premises at 456 Seventh Street, Apartment 8, Central City, Iowa, to shampoo the carpets. When I entered the premises, I noticed a strong odor, part of what seemed like stale cigarette smoke. An odor also seemed to come from the carpet.

3. When I began using a steam carpet cleaner on the living room carpet, I noticed a strong smell of urine. I stopped the steam cleaner, moved to a dry corner of the carpet and pulled it from the floor. I then saw a yellow color on the normally white foam-rubber pad beneath the carpet, as well as smelled a strong urine odor, apparently caused by a pet (probably a cat) having urinated on the carpet. On further examination of the parts of the carpet, I noticed similar stains and odors throughout the carpet and pad.

4. In my opinion, the living room carpet and foam-rubber pad underneath need to be removed and replaced, and the floor should be sanded and sealed.

I declare under penalty of perjury under the laws of the State of Iowa that the foregoing is true and correct.

Paul Stallone   6/15/xx
Paul Stallone, Cleaner   Date

Small Claims Suits Don't Affect Other Lawsuits

Nothing that happens in small claims court affects the validity of any judgment you already have—for example, from an earlier eviction suit—against the tenant. So, if you got a judgment against a tenant for $1,200 for unpaid rent as part of an eviction action, this judgment is still good, even though a tenant wins $200 against you in small claims court based on your failure to return the deposit.

Penalties for Violating Security Deposit Laws

If you don't follow state security deposit laws to the letter, you may pay a heavy price if a tenant sues you and wins. In addition to whatever amount you wrongfully withheld, you may have to pay the tenant extra or punitive damages (penalties imposed when the judge feels that the defendant has acted especially outrageously) and court costs. In many states, if you "willfully" (deliberately and not through inadvertence) violate the security deposit statute, you may forfeit your right to retain any part of the deposit and may be liable for two or three times the amount wrongfully withheld, plus attorney fees and costs.

If the Deposit Doesn't Cover Damage and Unpaid Rent

Tenants aren't the only ones who can use small claims court. If the security deposit doesn't cover what a tenant owes you for back rent, cleaning, or repairs (or if your state prohibits the use of the security deposit for unpaid rent), you may wish to file a small claims lawsuit against the former tenant.

Be sure your claim doesn't exceed your state's small claims court limit or, if it does, decide whether it make sense to scale it back to the limit. Given the costs of going to formal court, this can sometimes make sense.

RESOURCE
For detailed advice, see *Everybody's Guide to Small Claims Court* (National Edition), by Cara O'Neill (Nolo).

The Demand Letter

If you decide that it is worthwhile to go after your tenant for money owed, your first step is to write a letter asking for the amount of your claim. Although this may seem like an exercise in futility, the law in many states requires that you make a demand for the amount sued for before filing in small claims court. But, even if there is no such requirement, it is almost essential that you send some sort of demand letter. It is not only useful in trying to settle your dispute, it's also an excellent opportunity to carefully organize the case you will present in court.

Your demand can consist of a brief cover letter along with a copy of your earlier written itemization of how you applied the tenant's security deposit to the charges (in which you also requested payment of the balance). The tone of your cover letter should be polite, yet firm. Ask for exactly what you want, and be sure to set a deadline. Conclude by stating that you will promptly file a lawsuit in small claims court if you don't reach an understanding by the deadline.

Should You Sue?

If your demand letter does not produce results, think carefully before you rush off to your local small claims court. Ask yourself three questions:

- Do I have a strong case?
- Can I locate the former tenant?
- Can I collect a judgment if I win?

If the answer to any of these questions is no, think twice about initiating a suit.

Do You Have a Strong Case?

Review the items of evidence listed above in "Preparing an Itemized Statement of Deductions."

If you lack a substantial number of these pieces of ammunition you may end up losing, even if you are in the right. Small claims court is rarely about justice, but always about preparation and skill.

Can You Locate the Former Tenant?

To begin your small claims court case, legal papers must be sent to the tenant. So, you'll need an address where the tenant lives or works. If the tenant left a forwarding address, locating the tenant won't be an issue. But if you don't have a home or work address for the tenant, you'll need to do a little detective work if you want to sue.

Start by filing a "skip-trace" form at the Post Office using the tenant's name and last known address. If the tenant asked the Post Office to forward mail to a new address, you'll be supplied with the forwarding address. Or, use an Internet search engine's "people finder" to check for a new address or phone number. You can also use a commercial service, known as a judgment recovery agency, to find your ex-tenant. Typically, these outfits not only find the tenant, but collect any judgment that the landlord has against the tenant. If you don't yet have a judgment, you'll simply pay for the service, which may not be cost-efficient if the amount of money at stake is modest.

Can You Collect a Judgment If You Win?

Winning a small claims court case won't do you any good if you can't collect a judgment. Suing a person you know to be bankrupt, insolvent, or just plain broke may not be worth the effort, since you'll have little chance of transforming your court judgment into cash. When you evaluate the solvency of the tenant, keep in mind that small claims judgments are good for ten years in many states. So, if you have a spat with a student or someone who may get a job soon, it might be worthwhile to get a judgment with the hope of collecting later.

Using Collection Agencies

If you don't want to sue in small claims court, consider hiring a licensed local collection agency to try to collect from the tenant. The agency will probably want to keep as its fee anywhere from one-third to one-half of what it collects for you. (The older the debt or the more difficult it is to locate the tenant, the more the agency will want.) If the agency can't collect, you can authorize it to hire a lawyer to sue the ex-tenant, usually in a formal (non-small-claims) court. Many collection agencies pay all court costs, hoping to recover them if and when they collect the resulting judgment. In exchange for taking the risk of paying costs and losing the case, however, collection agency commissions often rise an additional 15%–20% when they hire a lawyer to sue.

Of course, turning a matter over to a collection agency doesn't necessarily mean you wash your hands of the matter. The collection agency still takes direction from you. If the tenant defends against a lawsuit filed by a collection agency's lawyer, you must be involved in the litigation. The only way to walk away from it completely is to sell the debt to the collection agency, which may pay you only a fraction of the amount owed.

Pay particular attention to the issue of how you will collect a judgment. The best way to collect any judgment against your ex-tenant is to garnish wages. If she's working, there is an excellent chance of collecting if payment is not made voluntarily. Another way is to find out the name and address of the defendant's employer. If you sued an employed person, you may be able to collect your judgment out of his or her salary. You can't, however, garnish a welfare, Social Security, unemployment, pension, or disability check. So, if the person sued gets income from one of these sources, you may be wasting your time unless you can identify some other asset that you can efficiently get your hands on.

Bank accounts, motor vehicles, and real estate are other common collection sources. But people who run out on their debts don't always have much in a bank account (or they may have moved the account to make it difficult to locate), and much of their personal property may be exempt under state debt protection laws.

CAUTION

Take care of your reputation. If you are a landlord with many rental units and regularly use a local small claims court, make particularly sure that every case you bring is a good one. You do not want to lose your credibility with the court in future cases by ever appearing to be unfair or poorly prepared.

What to Do With Property Abandoned by a Tenant

Whether a tenant moves out voluntarily or with the aid of a sheriff or marshal after you win an eviction lawsuit, you may find yourself not only cleaning up and repairing damage, but also dealing with personal property left behind. Usually, this will just be trash that the tenant obviously doesn't want, such as old wine bottles, food, and newspapers. When it's clear that you're dealing with garbage, you're perfectly within your rights to dispose of it.

Getting rid of things clearly of some value—such as a bicycle, jewelry, clothes, or furniture—is another story. In some states, you can face serious liability for disposing of the tenant's personal property (other than obvious trash) unless you follow specific state rules. Typically, the more valuable the property left behind by a tenant, the more formalities you must comply with when disposing of it. Not surprisingly, states that heavily regulate other aspects of landlords' dealings with tenants also impose complicated requirements on how you handle abandoned property. States with fewer laws governing the landlord-tenant relationship tend to pay scant attention to this subject.

This section provides an overview of how to handle abandoned property. It covers the general legal issues that should be understood by all landlords: whether your state allows you to deal with the property as you see fit or requires you to follow detailed (and often onerous) procedures. Because state laws vary so much, we cannot give you detailed state-by-state instructions on how to comply. For this reason, it is critical that you read your own state statute for details on issues such as how to notify tenants and how much time you must give them to reclaim property before you may dispose of or sell it. In addition, you would be wise to check with your local landlords' association or state consumer protection agency to make sure that the process set out in your statute is all you need to know. In some states, courts have modified the procedures in the statutes, often imposing additional requirements—and, unfortunately, legislatures don't always revisit their statutes to bring them into line with court-ordered changes. "State Laws on Handling Abandoned Property" in Appendix A gives you citations to your state's statutes.

SEE AN EXPERT

If you're dealing with property of obvious significant value or have good reason to suspect that a tenant may cause problems later, consult a lawyer before you dispose of, donate, or sell the tenant's possessions. Obviously, you want to protect yourself from claims by the departing tenant that you have destroyed or stolen her property. In legal jargon, this is known as "unlawful conversion." Conversion occurs when you take someone else's property and convert it to your own use or benefit, either by selling it or otherwise disposing of it or using it yourself.

Why Has the Tenant Left?

In many states, your options when dealing with tenants' property will differ depending on the circumstances of the tenant's departure. To understand the issue, let's look at the reasons tenants leave. Here are typical scenarios, covered at length below:

- The tenant decides to move at the end of a lease or after giving you a termination notice. In this situation, many states give you maximum flexibility to dispose of leftover belongings.
- The tenant decides to move after receiving a termination notice (even one for cause, such

as nonpayment of rent) from you. Many states give you maximum flexibility to dispose of leftover belongings in this situation.

- The tenant is physically evicted, along with his or her personal belongings that may be dumped on the street or sidewalk by the sheriff. Some states require landlords to take more pains with the property of a tenant who has been evicted—though some require less effort.
- The tenant simply disappears. In a few states, property belonging to tenants who simply move out unexpectedly must be treated differently from property that's left after a clearly deliberate move.

When you read your state's law, be on the lookout for different rules based on the reason for the tenant's departure.

Planned Moves

Often, if the tenant has left voluntarily but has inconsiderately left you with a pile of stuff, you will have more latitude when it comes to discarding abandoned property than you will if the tenant has been evicted. The reasoning here is that tenants who decide upon and plan their own departure—even the ones who leave after receiving a three-day notice— have time to pack or dispose of their belongings themselves. Tenants who fail to take care of business are in no position to demand that you, the landlord, handle their property with kid gloves—and many state laws don't require that you do so.

Evicted Tenants

Law enforcement officials who physically evict tenants will also remove property from the rental unit. In these situations, tenants arguably have less opportunity to arrange for proper packing, storing, or moving than they would if they were moving voluntarily (even though most states give tenants a few days' warning of the sheriff's impending visit). For this reason, landlords in some states must make more of an effort to preserve the property, locate the tenant, and wait before selling or disposing of items left behind. Typically, law enforcement officials are permitted to place the tenant's possessions on the sidewalk or street; then the landlord may be required to step in and store the possessions.

Paradoxically, some states take the opposite approach, reasoning that a tenant who has lost an eviction lawsuit isn't entitled to special treatment when it comes to reclaiming items left in the rental unit.

Unannounced Departures

Odd as it seems, it's not unusual for tenants to simply disappear with no notice, leaving considerable belongings behind. Sometimes, the tenant is behind on the rent and figures that abandoning his possessions will be cheaper, in the long run, than paying the rent. Here again, your state may impose special procedures, which may require you to store the property for a significant time or make extra efforts to locate the tenant. One reason for this extra concern is to protect tenants who have *not* abandoned the tenancy or their possessions, but have gone on a trip or vacation and simply didn't bother to tell you. The idea is that by taking special pains to determine that the tenant is gone for good and giving tenants ample time to claim their things, landlords can avoid problems down the road. State rules requiring landlords to store property and locate tenants reduce a tenant's ability to sue you for prematurely disposing of property—that is, before the tenant reappears and demands his belongings. "If the Tenant Breaks the Lease" in Chapter 14 discusses how to tell whether tenants have really abandoned the premises, and how to locate them.

When the Tenant Owes You Money

It's annoying enough to have to deal with a tenant's abandoned belongings—but worse yet is when that tenant also owes you money. When a tenant who has moved voluntarily, been evicted, or simply disappeared also owes you back rent or money for damages, you may be inclined to first take or sell whatever property of value that's left behind, and worry about finding the tenant later. As tempting as this course appears, it's a risky one in many states—even if you have a court judgment for money damages.

Some states do allow you to keep or sell abandoned property if the tenant owes you money, even if there is no court judgment directing the tenant to pay. In legal parlance, you have an "automatic lien" on your tenants' belongings. This differs from the normal lien process—which involves formally recording your claim (your lien) against the tenant's property, then "getting in line" in case others have filed ahead of you.

> ### Distress and Distraint: What Are They?
>
> A few states still have statutes on the books that provide for "distress" or "distraint." These were medieval procedures that allowed a landlord who was owed money, after or even during the tenancy, to simply grab his tenant's possessions. In the words of one judge, it "allowed a man to be his own avenger." In America, the practice of requiring security deposits was developed in states that did not allow a landlord to use distress and distraint.
>
> This crude, quick, and drastic remedy was the ultimate in self-help. It won't surprise you to learn that in states that still have laws providing for distress or distraint, courts have stepped in and ruled it unconstitutional, or have added so many safeguards (notice, a hearing, and so on) that the original process is unrecognizable. If you encounter a distress or distraint statute when reading your state's laws, resist the temptation to follow it without first learning—through legal research or talking to your landlords' association or lawyer—how modern landlords comply.

If your state statute gives you a lien on your tenant's property, we advise you to use it very carefully. In particular:

- **Use restraint when seizing consumer or other goods that may not be paid for.** If your tenant has financed his TV, sofa, or computer and is paying in installments, the merchant has a lien that's ahead of yours. This is called a "superior" lien—meaning that the merchant, not you, has first claim to the item when the tenant stops paying. (Not surprisingly, the tenant will typically stop payments after abandoning the item.) You cannot simply seize and sell an abandoned item, such as a computer, that is not paid off. Instead, you will have to turn the item over if the merchant comes to collect it. If you have already sold the item, you may have to pay the merchant the balance due or the value of the item. You can try to avoid this eventuality by publicizing your intent to seize and sell the item, as explained below.

- **Follow your state's rules for publicizing your lien.** Many states require a landlord to post notices in newspapers announcing your intent to sell an item abandoned by a tenant. This is to make sure that others—like the merchants mentioned above—who have superior liens on a tenant's property don't lose out when you jump ahead of them and take or sell the item. Merchants are presumed to read the legal notices; failure to do so may result in the merchants' losing their right to assert the superiority of their lien. It's a good idea to publicize the sale of a tenant's valuable abandoned property even if your statute doesn't require it.

- **Don't seize items that are necessary for basic living.** Many states that give landlords an automatic lien will exempt certain items, such as season-appropriate clothing, blankets, tools, and things needed for a minor child's education, from your grasp. If you're not sure whether an item is a tool of your ex-tenant's trade or simply supports his hobby, don't take it.

 CAUTION

Check out court cases—don't rely on your lien statutes alone. In most states with lien statutes on the books, courts have stepped in with additional requirements, such as providing for notice and an opportunity for the tenant (and other creditors) to be heard. Read any cases that have interpreted your lien law (see Chapter 18 for help in doing legal research), or ask your landlords' association or lawyer for assistance.

Legal Notice Requirements

Many states require landlords to provide tenants written notice that they are dealing with abandoned property. California requires landlords to provide specific information regarding abandoned property on a variety of termination forms (Cal. Civ. Code §§ 1946, 1946.1). A few states even provide a form, which you'll see printed right in the statute. The notice must typically give the tenant a set amount of time to reclaim the property, after which the landlord can take specific steps. Some state rules require specific information in the notice, such as:

- **A detailed description of the property left behind.** It's a good idea to have an objective person (such as another tenant in the building or a neighbor) witness your inventory of the abandoned property to protect yourself against charges that you have taken or destroyed any of the tenant's property. Don't open locked trunks or suitcases; just list the unopened containers. You might consider photographing or videotaping the property.

- **The estimated value of the abandoned property.** Here, you're asked to guess what you could get for it at a well-attended flea market or garage sale.

- **Where the property may be claimed.** Many states sensibly require you to provide the address of the rental premises or an outside storage place.

- **The deadline for the tenant to reclaim property, such as seven or ten days.** This is usually set by state law.

- **What will happen if property is not reclaimed.**
This also may be set by state law.

Even if your state law doesn't explicitly require it, it's a good idea to send tenants this kind of detailed notice and allow a reasonable amount of time for the tenant to pick up his belongings. Mail your notice "return receipt requested" so that you will have proof that the tenant received it—this will be useful should an ex-tenant show up months later looking for belongings left behind.

How to Handle Abandoned Property if the Tenant Doesn't Respond

If the ex-tenant doesn't contact you within the time specified in the notice, follow your state rules regarding what to do with property. In some states, landlords are pretty much free to do what they want if the tenant does not respond within the specified amount of time, such as 30 days— that is, you may throw the property out, sell it, or donate it to a nonprofit organization that operates secondhand stores. In some states, as explained above, landlords can use the property to satisfy unpaid rent or damages, or may even be allowed to keep it when there's no debt. Other states require you to give the property to the state. Depending on how thoroughly your state has legislated in this area, you'll encounter rules on the following issues:

- **Procedures based on the value of the property.** Several states allow landlords to keep or dispose of property only if the expense of storing or selling it exceeds a specified figure (such as a few hundred dollars) or the property's value.
- **Sale of abandoned property.** Some states require landlords to inventory, store, and sell tenants' property. A few require landlords to sell the property at a public sale (supervised by a licensed and bonded public auctioneer) after first publishing a notice in the newspaper.
- **Proceeds of sale of property.** States that require you to store and sell the property on behalf of the tenant also allow you to use any money

you make from the sale to cover the costs of advertising and holding the sale and storing the property. For example, you may be able to charge the tenant the prorated daily rental value for keeping the property on your premises or any out-of-pocket costs you incur for renting storage space (including moving the property to the storage space). As explained above, some states allow you to use the proceeds to pay for any money owed to you by the tenant—for example, for unpaid rent or damage to the premises. In many states, the excess proceeds of selling the tenant's property belong to the tenant, or you may be required to pay the balance to a government agency, such as the State Treasurer. State rules are often very specific on this issue, so don't just keep sale proceeds without a clear understanding of your state law.

Exceptions to State Rules on Abandoned Property

Your state's rules on abandoned property don't apply to obvious garbage—nor do they apply in the following situations:

Fixtures. If a tenant attaches something more or less permanently to the wall, such as built-in bookshelves, it is called a "fixture." As described in "Tenants' Alterations and Improvements" in Chapter 9, absent a specific written agreement such as a lease provision, fixtures installed by the tenant become a part of the premises. Fixtures belong to the landlord and do not have to be returned to the tenant.

Motor vehicles. Occasionally, a departing tenant will leave an inoperable or "junker" automobile in the parking lot or garage. Motor vehicles are often a special category of personal property to which state rules on abandoned property don't apply. If the tenant has left a car or other vehicle behind, call the local police, giving the vehicle's license plate number, make, and model, and indicate where it's parked. The police will probably arrange to have it towed after determining that it is abandoned after tagging it.

TIP

Don't hassle the tenant over a little amount of money. In most situations, where there is not a lot of property involved, you're probably better off giving the tenant his belongings and forgetting about any storage charges, particularly if you didn't incur any out-of-pocket expenses. It's just not worth it to get into fights over $100 worth of old dishes, books, and clothes.

Landlord Liability for Damage to Tenant's Property

A landlord will not generally be held liable for damage to property, unless this occurs through his or her willful destruction or negligent care of the tenant's property. To avoid problems, be sure you take care in moving and storing the tenant's belongings until they are returned to the tenant, disposed of, or sold.

Problems With Tenants: How to Resolve Disputes Without a Lawyer

FORMS IN THIS CHAPTER

Chapter 16 includes instructions for and a sample of the following form:

• Warning Letter for Lease or Rental Agreement Violation

The Nolo website includes a downloadable copy of this form. See Appendix B for the link to the forms in this book.

Legal disputes—actual and potential—come in all shapes and sizes when you're a landlord. Here are some of the more common ones:

- **Rent.** You and your tenant disagree about the validity, timing, or methods of a rent increase.

- **Habitability.** Your tenant threatens to withhold rent because he claims a leaky roof or some other defect has made the living room unusable.

- **Access to the premises.** Your tenant won't let you show her apartment to prospective new tenants or enter for some other good reason. You feel it's your legal right to do so, and your tenant claims that your legal reason for invading her privacy is bogus.

- **Security deposits.** You and a departing tenant disagree about how much security deposit you owe the tenant based on your claim that the unit is dirty or damaged or both.

- **Lease or rental agreement violation.** Your tenant (or former tenant) has failed to pay rent, moved in a new roommate (or a pet) without your permission, hosted a series of loud parties, or in some other way violated your lease or rental agreement.

How you handle such disputes can have a profound effect on your bottom line, not to mention your mental health. In some cases, such as a tenant's nonpayment of rent, your only option may be to terminate the tenancy. Rarely should lawyers and litigation be your first choice. Instead, you will usually want to consider alternatives that can give you better control over the time, energy, and money you spend.

This chapter discusses four commonly available options to resolve a legal dispute without a lawyer:

- negotiation
- mediation
- arbitration, and
- small claims court.

While we focus here on disputes with tenants, you should also find much of the advice useful for resolving all types of business disputes—for example, with your manager, insurance company, or repairperson.

This chapter also explains how to avoid charges of retaliation in your dealings with tenants.

RELATED TOPIC

How to terminate a tenancy based on non-payment of rent and other illegal acts is discussed in Chapter 17.

Put It in Writing

To help avoid legal problems in the first place, and minimize those that can't be avoided, it makes sense to adopt efficient, easy-to-follow systems to document important facts of your relationship with your tenants. Throughout this book, we recommend many forms and record-keeping systems that will help you do this, including move-in and move-out letters, a landlord-tenant checklist, and a maintenance/repair request form. The key is to establish a good paper trail for each tenancy, beginning with the rental application and lease or rental agreement through a termination notice and security deposit itemization. Such documentation will be extremely valuable if attempts at resolving your dispute fail and you end up evicting or suing a tenant, or being sued by a tenant. Also, you'll obviously want to keep copies of any correspondence and notes of your conversations with tenants. Chapter 7 recommends a system for organizing tenant information, including records of repair requests.

Negotiating a Settlement: Start by Talking

If you have a conflict with your tenant over rent, repairs, your access to the rental unit, noise, or some other issue that doesn't immediately warrant an eviction, a sensible first step is to meet with the tenant—even one you consider to be a hopeless troublemaker—to see if the problem can be resolved. This advice is based on the simple premise that unless you have the legal grounds (and the determination) to evict a tenant, it's almost always better to try and negotiate a settlement rather than let the dispute escalate into a court fight. This is doubly true if you are convinced your case is just. Given the cost and delays built into the arthritic American legal system, the more you rely on it, the more you are likely to regret going to court.

So forget about suing, except possibly in small claims court (discussed below), and try to evaluate the legal and financial realities objectively. Your goal should be to achieve the best result at the lowest cost. If instead you act on the conviction (whether it's right or wrong makes no difference) that your rights are being trampled by the other side, chances are you'll end up spending far too much time and money fighting for "the principle" involved. Over time, a landlord who allows himself to be controlled by this sort of emotional reaction is almost sure to fare emotionally and financially poorer than a person who keeps an eye on the overall objective: to make a good living and enjoy doing it.

Your first step in working toward a compromise with an unhappy or problem tenant is to call the tenant and arrange a time to meet. Dropping over unannounced to talk may work in some circumstances but is generally not a good idea, since it may emotionally threaten the tenant and put him in a defensive position. It may be appropriate to write a letter first, offering to meet with the tenant to work something out. (See, for example, the sample letter in Chapter 9 in which the landlord suggests a compromise with a tenant who withholds rent because of defective conditions in his apartment.)

Here are some helpful pointers for negotiating with tenants:

- **Solicit the tenant's point of view.** Once the tenant starts talking, listen closely and don't interrupt, even if some of his points are not true or some of his opinions are inflammatory.
- **When the tenant has wound down, acknowledge that you have heard his key points, even if you disagree with them.** Sometimes it's even a good idea to repeat the tenant's concerns so he will realize you know what they are and will stop repeating them.
- **Avoid personal attacks.** This only raises the level of hostility and makes settlement more difficult. Equally important, don't react impulsively to the emotional outbursts of the tenant.
- **Be courteous, but don't be weak.** If you have a good case, let the tenant know you have the resources and evidence to fight and win if you can't reach a reasonable settlement.
- **Before the negotiation goes too far, try and determine if the tenant is a truly an unbearable jerk whom you really want to be rid of or just another slightly annoying person.** If a tenant falls into the first category, your strategy should be to terminate the tenancy as soon as legally and practically possible.
- **If possible, try to structure the negotiation as a mutual attempt to solve a problem.** For example, if a tenant's guests have been disturbing the neighbors, jointly seek solutions that recognize the interests of both parties.
- **Try to figure out the tenant's priorities.** Maybe dollars are less important than pride, in which case a formula for future relations that meets the needs of a thin-skinned tenant to be treated with respect might solve the problem.
- **Put yourself in the tenant's shoes.** What would you want to settle? Sometimes your answer may be something like "a sense that I've won." Fine—the best settlements are often those in which both sides feel they've won (or at least not given up anything fundamental). So, your job is to let the tenant have at least a partial sense of victory on one or more of the issues in dispute.
- **When you propose a specific settlement, make it clear that you're attempting to compromise.** Offers of settlement (clearly labeled as such) can't be introduced against you if you ever end up in court.

- **Money is a powerful incentive to settlement.** If you are going to have to pay something eventually, or spend a lot of time and money on a costly eviction lawsuit or preparing a small claims case, it makes overall financial sense to come to the negotiating table willing to pay—perhaps by reducing rent for a short period of time, cutting in half the money owed for damages to the premises, or offering an outright cash settlement for the tenant to leave (with payment made only as the tenant leaves and hands you the keys). Savvy landlords know that many financially strapped tenants may settle at a surprisingly low figure if they can walk away from the bargaining table with payment in hand. If this saves the costs and delays inherent in a long eviction battle, and allows you to rerent the unit to a paying tenant, it can be well worth the money.

- **If you reach an understanding with your tenant, promptly write it down and have all parties sign it.** You or your lawyer should volunteer to prepare the first draft. If you're paying the tenant some money as part of your agreement, make sure the tenant acknowledges in writing that your payment fully satisfies her claim. Chapter 15 includes an example of a settlement agreement for a security deposit dispute that you can use as a model for settling disputes.

- **If the negotiation process indicates a larger problem with tenant dissatisfaction, think carefully how to avoid similar disputes in the future**—for example, you may need to revise your systems for handling repair complaints or returning security deposits.

RESOURCE
Recommended reading on negotiation.
Getting to Yes: Negotiating Agreement Without Giving In, by Roger Fisher, William Ury, and Bruce M. Patton (Penguin Books). This classic offers a strategy for coming to mutually acceptable agreements in all kinds of situations, including landlord-tenant disputes.

The Power of a Positive No: Save the Deal, Save the Relationship and Still Say No, by William Ury (Bantam Books). This sequel to *Getting to Yes* discusses techniques for negotiating with obnoxious, stubborn, and otherwise difficult people.

When Warning Notices Are Appropriate

In some situations, it may be appropriate to give a tenant a written notice to cease the problem or disruptive activity, particularly if the tenant has not created other problems and you feel that he's apt to respond to your polite but firm reproof. You may also want to send a warning notice if your oral warning or attempts to negotiate have been unsuccessful.

A sample Warning Letter for Lease or Rental Agreement Violation is shown below, and the Nolo website includes a downloadable copy (see Appendix B for the link to the forms in this book). You can use this warning letter for many purposes, such as warning the tenant to stop having loud parties, repair damage to your property, or get rid of a long-term guest.

Be sure your letter includes the following information:

- Details of the problem behavior, including dates and times of the occurrence.
- What exactly you want the tenant to do (such as stop having noisy parties, pay for damage to the rental unit, or get rid of a long-term guest).
- The specific lease or rental agreement provision that prohibits this behavior, such as a clause on tenant's right to quiet enjoyment (Clause 13 of our form lease and rental agreements in Chapter 2), a clause requiring tenants to repair damaged property (Clause 11 of our form agreements), or a lease restriction on guests (Clause 3 of our form agreements).
- The consequences for the tenant's failure to comply (such as termination or eviction proceedings).

Warning Letter for Lease or Rental Agreement Violation

November 4, 20xx
Date

Jerry Brooks
Tenant

179 Lynwood Drive
Street Address

Tampa, Florida 33611
City and State

Dear __Jerry__ ,
　　　　　　Tenant

This is a reminder that your lease prohibits __annoying, disturbing, or interfering with the quiet__
__enjoyment and peace and quiet of any other tenant or nearby resident (Clause 13)__
[violation]. It has come to my attention that, starting __on November 2, 20xx__ , [date
of violation] and continuing to the present, you have broken this condition of your tenancy by _____
__holding several noisy parties that lasted until 2 a.m., disturbing other tenants__

_____ .

It is our desire that you and all other tenants enjoy living in your rental unit. To make sure this occurs, we
enforce all terms and conditions of our leases. So please immediately __keep noise within reasonable__
__limits and no loud parties after midnight on weekends or 10 p.m. on weekdays__

_____ .

If it proves impossible to promptly resolve this matter, we will exercise our legal right to begin eviction
proceedings.

Please contact me if you would like to discuss this matter further and clear up any possible misunderstandings.

Yours truly,

Clark Johnson
Landlord/Manager

Belle Epoque, 387 Golf Road
Street Address

Tampa, Florida 33611
City and State

813-555-1234
Phone

CAUTION
Don't waste your time sending a warning letter to someone unlikely to respond—for example, a tenant who is always late in paying rent or whose behavior (such as drug dealing or violence) justifies immediate action. Instead, start termination proceedings right away.

What happens if the tenant does not reform, despite your reminder? If the misbehavior is grounds for terminating the tenancy and you want him out, in a sense you'll have to start over: You'll have to give him a formal termination notice that meets your state's requirements. (Termination notices are explained in Chapter 17.)

CAUTION
Your warning note will not qualify as a termination notice. For example, if your tenant has kept a dog in violation of the lease, and he keeps the pet despite your polite note asking him to remove the dog, in most states you'll have to give the tenant a formal notice telling him to get rid of the dog within a certain number of days or move. (If he does neither, you can file for eviction.) In short, an informal warning may simply allow a wrongdoing tenant to delay the inevitable.

Understanding Mediation

If you're unsuccessful negotiating a settlement, but still want to work something out with the tenant, you may wish to try mediation by a neutral third party, often available at little or no cost from a publicly funded program. (See "How to Find a Mediation Group," below.)

Mediation can make good sense, especially if any of the following are true:

- You are dealing with someone who has proven to be a good tenant in the past and you think the tenant is worth dealing with in the future.
- The tenant agrees to split the cost (if any) of mediation.
- The tenant is as receptive as you are to some method of avoiding the expense and delay of litigation, or the possibility of being evicted.

- The tenant is up to date on rent (or the rent money is put in some type of escrow account).
- You are trying to avoid the risk of one influential tenant poisoning your relationship with others.

If mediation doesn't make sense, make clear your intention (and legal right) to sue or evict the tenant. See "Representing Yourself in Small Claims Court," below, and Chapter 17.

Many people confuse mediation with arbitration. While both are nonjudicial ways to resolve disputes, there's a huge difference: Arbitration results in a binding decision, while mediation doesn't, since the mediator has no power to impose a decision but is there simply to help the parties work out a mutually acceptable solution to their dispute.

Mediation in landlord-tenant disputes is usually fairly informal. More likely than not, the mediator will have everyone sit down together from the very beginning and allow both parties to express all their issues—even emotional ones. This often cools people off considerably and frequently results in a fairly quick compromise. If the dispute is not resolved easily, however, the mediator may suggest ways to resolve the problem, or may even keep everyone talking long enough to realize that the real problem goes deeper than the one being mediated. Typically this is done through a caucus process—each side is put in a separate room. The mediator talks to each person sequentially to try and determine his or her bottom line. Then, shuttling back and forth, the mediator helps the parties structure an acceptable solution. At some point, everyone has to get back together to sign off.

For example, if a tenant has threatened rent withholding because of a defect in the premises, the mediator may discover that the tenant's real grievance is that your manager is slow to make repairs. This may lead to the further finding that the manager is angry at the tenant for letting her kids pull up his tulips. So, the final solution may fall into place only when the tenant agrees to provide better supervision for the kids in exchange for the manager getting the repairs done pronto.

How to Deal With Noisy Tenants

Tenants often cite noise as one of their biggest complaints about apartment living. Many types of noise, including street traffic, garbage trucks, or rowdy bars, are out of the landlord's control. If tenants complain about noises outside the building, your best bet is to steer them to the city manager or mayor's office for help. Most cities have local ordinances that prohibit excessive, unnecessary, and unreasonable noise, and police enforce these laws. If the problem is a neighbor's barking dog, the local animal control agency is responsible. Most local noise ordinances designate certain "quiet hours"—for example, from 10 p.m. to 7 a.m. on weekdays. Some universally disturbing noises, such as honking car horns, are commonly banned or restricted. Many communities also prohibit sustained noise that exceeds a certain decibel level (set according to the time of day and the neighborhood zoning).

Noise caused by other tenants, however, is your responsibility. Anyone who lives in an apartment building must expect to hear the sounds of their neighbor's daily lives. But when the occasional annoying sound turns into an ongoing din—whether a blasting stereo, loud TV, or barking dog—expect to hear complaints from other residents in your property. You should take these complaints seriously. As discussed in Chapter 9, tenants are entitled to quiet enjoyment of the premises, the right to occupy their apartments in peace, free of excessive noise. You may face legal problems if you fail to stop disturbances that are of a regular and ongoing nature—for example, electronic dance music blaring from a tenant's apartment each and every weekend. Landlords who tolerate excessive and unreasonable noise that interferes with other tenants' normal activities (such as sleeping at night) despite repeated tenant complaints may get hit with code violations or a small claims lawsuit (for tolerating a nuisance) or court-ordered rent reductions. Good tenants may move out.

Here are some specific tips to avoid problems with noisy tenants:

- Include a clause in your lease or rental agreement prohibiting tenants from causing disturbances or creating a nuisance that interferes with other tenants' peace and quiet and prevents neighbors from enjoying the use of their own homes. (See Clause 13 of the form agreements in Chapter 2.)

- Include specific noise guidelines in your tenant rules and regulations, such as the hours that loud music, dance parties, and barking dogs will not be tolerated. Look at your local noise ordinance for guidance and remind tenants of noise laws that may apply in your community, such as prohibitions against honking car alarms, firecrackers, or disorderly conduct. You might make the same points in a move-in letter to new tenants.
- Consider requiring rugs or carpets on wood floors to muffle the noise heard by tenants downstairs.
- Check out inexpensive ideas to soundproof paper-thin walls.
- Respond quickly to noise complaints. Start with an oral request to keep the noise down. Then, move on to a warning letter (such as the sample shown above) if necessary. Terminate the tenancy if necessary.
- Keep records of all tenant complaints about a neighbor's noise (with details on the date, time, and location of the noise), so that you have solid documentation to back up a termination or eviction case. If the noise is really bad, make a tape recording as additional evidence.
- If violence is involved, such as a domestic disturbance, call the police immediately.

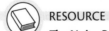

RESOURCE

The Noise Pollution Clearinghouse (www.nonoise.org) is an excellent source of information on state and local noise laws. If you can't find your local ordinance there, do some online legal research (Chapter 18 explains how).

For a general overview of noise involving neighbors, see *Neighbor Law,* by Emily Doskow and Lina Guillen. If barking dogs is the problem, see *Every Dog's Legal Guide*, by Mary Randolph. Both books are published by Nolo and available online at www.nolo.com or by phone at 800-728-3555.

Does mediation really work? Surprisingly, yes, given the fact that there's no one to impose a solution. One reason is the basic cooperative spirit that goes into mediation. By agreeing to mediate a dispute in the first place, you and the tenant must jointly establish the rules, which, in turn, sets the stage for cooperating to solve your dispute. Also, the fact that no judge or arbitrator has the power to impose what may be an unacceptable solution reduces the fear factor on both sides. This, in turn, often means both landlord and tenant take less extreme—and more conciliatory—positions.

RESOURCE

Recommended reading on mediation. *Mediate, Don't Litigate*, by Peter Lovenheim and Lisa Guerin (Nolo), available as a downloadable electronic book at www.nolo.com. This book explains the mediation process from start to finish, including how to prepare for mediation and draft a legally enforceable agreement.

How to Find a Mediation Group

For information on local mediation programs, call your mayor's or city manager's office, and ask for the staff member who handles "landlord-tenant mediation matters" or "housing disputes." That person should refer you to the public office or business or community group that attempts to informally—and at little or no cost—resolve landlord-tenant disputes before they reach the court stage. Most local courts also provide referrals to community mediation services. For lists of professional mediators and extensive information on mediation, see www.mediate.com.

Using Arbitration

Many organizations that offer mediation also conduct arbitration if the parties can't reach an agreement. Almost any dispute with a tenant or other party that can be litigated can be arbitrated. With arbitration, you get a relatively quick, relatively inexpensive solution to a dispute without going to court. Like a judge, the arbitrator—a neutral third party—has power to hear the dispute and make a final, binding decision. Where does this power come from? From you and the other party. In binding arbitration, you agree in advance in writing to submit to arbitration and to be bound by the arbitrator's decision.

You can include a clause in your lease or rental agreement that requires that arbitration be used for any contractual dispute, although this usually makes sense more for longer-term leases of expensive properties. Otherwise, you and the tenant can also decide to use arbitration after a dispute arises. If you and the tenant agree to binding arbitration, an informal hearing is held. Each person tells his or her side of the story, and an arbitrator reaches a decision, which is enforceable in court.

If the losing party doesn't pay the money required by an arbitration award, the winner can easily convert the award to a court judgment, which can be enforced like any other court judgment. Unlike a judgment based on litigation, however, you generally can't take an appeal from an arbitration-based judgment. (An exception is when there was some element of fraud in the procedures leading to the arbitration award.)

How to Find an Arbitrator

To find an arbitrator or learn more about arbitration, contact the American Arbitration Association, the oldest and largest organization of its kind, with offices throughout the country. For more information, check your local phone book or see www.adr.org.

Keep in mind that you are not required to use an organization for arbitration. You and the other party are free to choose your own arbitrator or arbitration panel and to set your own procedural rules. Just remember that for arbitration to be binding and legally enforceable, you need to follow the simple guidelines set down in your state's arbitration statute. You can usually find the statute by looking in the statutory index under "Arbitration" or checking the table of contents for the civil procedure sections. See Chapter 18 for advice on doing this kind of legal research.

Representing Yourself in Small Claims Court

If your attempts at settling a dispute involving money fail, you may end up in a lawsuit. Fortunately, there are many instances when you can competently and cost-efficiently represent yourself in court. This is almost always true when your case is at the small claims level.

A few states use names other than small claims court, but traditionally the purpose has been the same: to provide a speedy, inexpensive resolution of disputes that involve relatively small amounts of money (generally less than $10,000). "State Small Claims Court Limits," in Appendix A, lists each state's small claims court limit.

Most people who go to small claims court handle their own cases. In fact, in some states, lawyers aren't allowed to represent clients in small claims court. In any event, representing yourself is almost always the best choice—after all, the main reason to use the small claims court is because the size of the case doesn't justify the cost of hiring a lawyer.

A landlord can use small claims court for many purposes—for example, to collect unpaid rent or to seek money for property damage after a tenant moves out and her deposit is exhausted. Small claims court offers a great opportunity to collect money that would otherwise be lost because it would be too expensive to sue in regular court. And, in a few states, eviction suits can be filed in small claims court.

Landlords can also be sued in small claims court—for example, by a tenant who claims that you failed to return a security deposit. Chapter 15 discusses small claims suits over security deposits.

TIP

Don't waste your time suing total deadbeats. As a general rule, if you suspect you cannot collect the money—from a paycheck, bank account, or other financial resource—don't waste your time in small claims court. A judgment you can't collect is worthless.

RESOURCE

Recommended reading on small claims court. *Everybody's Guide to Small Claims Court* (National Edition), by Cara O'Neill (Nolo), provides detailed advice on bringing or defending a small claims court case, preparing evidence and witnesses for court, and collecting your money judgment when you win. *Everybody's Guide to Small Claims Court* will also be useful in defending yourself against a tenant who sues you in small claims court—for example, claiming that you failed to return a cleaning or security deposit. Your state's small claims court website (listed in the chart in Appendix A) will also have useful information on specific state rules and procedures.

Learning the Rules

Small claims court procedures are relatively simple and easy to master. Basically, you pay a small fee, file your lawsuit with the court clerk, see to it that the papers are served on your opponent, show up on the appointed day, tell the judge your story, and present any witnesses and other evidence. The key to winning is usually to present evidence to back up your story. For example, a photograph of a dirty or damaged apartment and the convincing testimony of someone who helped you clean up are usually all you need to prevail if you are trying to recover money over and above the tenant's deposit or defending against a tenant's suit for the return of a deposit.

Court rules—dealing with such things as where you file your lawsuit, how papers can be served on your opponent (service of process), and the deadline (statute of limitations) for filing a small claims suit—are usually published on small claims court websites. In addition, clerks in small claims court are expected to explain procedures to you. In some states, they may even help you fill out the necessary forms, which are quite simple, anyhow. If necessary, be persistent: If you ask enough questions, you'll get the answers you need to handle your own case comfortably. Also, in some states such as California, you can consult a small claims court adviser for free.

Meeting the Jurisdictional Limits

How much can you sue for in small claims court? The maximum amount varies from state to state. Generally, the limit is $5,000 to $10,000. But, more recently, recognizing that formal courts have become prohibitively expensive for all but large disputes, many states have begun to increase the monetary size of the cases their small claims courts can consider. Check your state's small claims court limit on the chart in Appendix A, but also ask the court clerk for the most current limit; state legislatures regularly increase these limits.

TIP
You can scale your case down to fit small claims court limits. Don't assume that your case can't be brought in small claims court if it's for slightly more than the limit. Rather than hiring a lawyer or trying to go it alone in formal court, your most cost-effective option may be to sue for the small claims maximum and forget the rest.

How to Avoid Charges of Retaliation

As we've discussed throughout this book, residential tenants have a number of legal rights and remedies. While the specifics vary by state, here are a few rights tenants typically have:

- the right to complain to governmental authorities about health or safety problems, and, in many states, the right to withhold rent from, or even to file a lawsuit against, a landlord who fails to keep the premises in proper repair
- the right to be free from discriminatory conduct based on factors such as race, religion, children, sex, and disability, and to complain to administrative agencies, or even courts, when she (the tenant) feels her rights are being violated
- privacy rights limiting landlord's access, and
- the right to engage in political activity; for example, a tenant who actively campaigns for local candidates whom you find obnoxious,

organizes a tenant union, or campaigns for a rent control ordinance, has an absolute right to do so without fear of intimidation.

Because tenant protection laws would be meaningless if you could legally retaliate against a tenant who asserts her legal rights, the laws or court decisions in most states forbid such retaliation. For example, the right of a tenant to complain to the local fire department about a defective heater would be worth little if you, angry about the complaint, could retaliate against her with an immediate termination notice or by doing anything else that works to the tenant's disadvantage, such as increasing rent. The general idea is that tenants should not be punished by landlords just because they are invoking their legal rights or remedies.

Unfortunately, tenants sometimes unfairly accuse landlords of retaliatory misconduct—for example, a tenant who can't or won't pay a legitimate rent increase may claim you are guilty of retaliation. The same sort of unreasonable reliance on tenant protection laws can occur when you seek to terminate the tenancy for a perfectly legitimate reason and the tenant doesn't want to move. How do you cope with this sort of cynical misuse of the law? As with most things legal, there is no single answer. However, if you plan ahead and consider how one tenant might misuse the law and how you can counter this misuse, you should be able to minimize any legal problems.

You start with one great advantage when faced with a tenant who attempts to defeat your legitimate rent increase or tenancy termination with phony retaliation claims. As a businessperson, you have the organizational ability and mind-set to plan ahead—anticipate that some tenants will adopt these tactics, and prepare to meet them. The tenant, on the other hand, will probably be dealing with the situation on a first-time, ad hoc basis, and often will have a superficial, or just plain wrong, knowledge of the law.

Here are some tips on how to anticipate what tenants might do, so you're prepared to avoid or counter false retaliation claims.

Establish a good paper trail to document important facts of your relationship with your tenants. For example, set up clear, easy-to-follow procedures for tenants to ask for repairs, and respond quickly when complaints are made, coupled with annual safety inspections. (We show you how in Chapter 9.) This sort of policy will go a long way toward demonstrating that a complaint is phony—for example, if a tenant faced with a rent increase or tenancy termination suddenly complains to an outside agency about some defect in the premises they rent, without talking to you first. Also, if your periodic inquiries result in complaints from several tenants, but you only end one tenancy, you can show you don't have a policy of retaliating against tenants who do complain.

Be prepared to demonstrate that you have a good reason to end the tenancy—even though the law in your area may say that a landlord doesn't need a reason to terminate a tenancy. In other words, in anticipation of the possibility that a tenant may claim that you are terminating her tenancy for retaliatory reasons, you should be prepared to prove that your reasons were valid and not retaliatory. When you think of it, this burden isn't as onerous as it might first appear. From a business point of view, few landlords will ever want to evict an excellent tenant. And, assuming there is a good reason why you want the tenant out—for example, the tenant repeatedly pays his rent late in violation of the rental agreement—you only need document it.

Have legitimate business reasons for any rent increase or other change in the conditions of the tenancy, and make the changes reasonable. The best answer to a charge of retaliation is proof that your act was based on legitimate business reasons and was wholly independent of any exercise by tenants of their rights.

If a tenant makes a complaint for even an arguably legitimate reason at about the time you were going to raise the rent or give the month-to-month tenant a termination notice anyway, wait. First take care of the complaint. Next, let some time pass. Then, do what you planned to do anyway (assuming you can document a legitimate reason for your action). Be sure to check "State Laws Prohibiting Landlord Retaliation" in Appendix A to see whether your state has any law as to the time period when retaliation is presumed.

The delay may cost you a few bucks, or result in some inconvenience, or even cause you to lose some sleep while you gnash your teeth, but all of these are preferable to being involved in litigation over whether or not your conduct was in retaliation for the tenant's complaint.

EXAMPLE: A tenant, Fanny, makes a legitimate complaint to the health department about a defective heater in an apartment she rents from Abe. Even though Fanny does so without having had the courtesy to tell her landlord Abe first, Fanny is still within her legal rights to make the complaint. About the same time Fanny files the complaint, neighboring tenants complain to Abe, not for the first time, about Fanny's loud parties that last into the wee hours of the morning. Other tenants threaten to move out if Fanny doesn't. In response to the neighboring tenants' complaints, Abe gives Fanny a 30-day notice. She refuses to move, and Abe must file an eviction lawsuit. Fanny responds that the eviction was in retaliation for her complaint to the health department. A contested trial results. Perhaps Abe will win in court, but, in this situation, there is a good chance he won't.

Now, let's look at how you might better handle this problem:

Step 1. Fix the heater.

Step 2. Write the tenant, reminding her of your established complaint procedures. Tell her very politely that you consider this sort of repair a routine matter which, in the future, can be handled more quickly and easily by telling you instead of the public agency. A sample letter is shown below.

Step 3. Carefully document the noise complaints of the neighbors. If possible, get them in writing. Feel out the neighbors about whether they would testify in court if necessary. Also, consider whether an informal meeting between all affected parties or a formal mediation procedure might solve the problem.

**Sample Letter Reminding Tenant
of Complaint Procedure**

February 1, 20xx

Fanny Hayes
Sunny Dell Apartments
123 State Street, Apt. 15
Newark, NJ 07114

Dear Ms. Hayes:

As you know, Ms. Sharon Donovan, my resident manager at Sunny Dell Apartments, repaired the heater in your unit yesterday, on January 31.

Ms. Donovan informs me that you never complained about the heater or requested its repair. In fact, she learned about the problem for the first time when she received a telephone call to that effect from Cal Mifune of the County Health Department. Apparently, you notified the Health Department of the problem without first attempting to resolve it with Ms. Donovan.

While you certainly do have a legal right to complain to a governmental agency about any problem, you should be aware that the management of Sunny Dell Apartments takes pride in its quick and efficient response to residents' complaints and requests for repairs.

In the future, we hope that you'll follow our complaint procedure and contact the manager if you have a problem with any aspect of your apartment.

Sincerely,

Abe Horowitz
Abe Horowitz, Owner

Step 4. Write the tenant about the neighbors' complaints. The first letter should be conciliatory. Offer to meet with the tenant to resolve the problem, but also remind the tenant of the rental agreement (or lease) provision prohibiting nuisances (such as excessive noise) that disturb the quiet enjoyment of other tenants (see Clause 13 of the form lease and rental agreements in Chapter 2). If the first letter doesn't work, follow up with another letter, even if you don't think this will do any good, either. These letters will help you greatly should a court fight develop later.

Step 5. If possible, wait a few months, during which you should carefully document any more complaints before giving the tenant a 30-day notice. As a general rule, the longer you can reasonably delay court action, the less likely a claim of retaliation by the tenant will stick.

This sort of preparatory work may influence the tenant not to claim you are guilty of retaliatory conduct. However, even if it does not, and you do end up in court, you should win easily.

Defending yourself against charges of retaliation is well beyond the scope of this book, and a lawyer is strongly advisable. A good insurance policy which protects you from so-called "illegal acts" may cover you if your act is not deliberate and intentional and you can turn your legal defense over to the insurance company.

Late Rent, Terminations, and Evictions

Unfortunately, even the most sincere and professional attempts at conscientious landlording sometimes fail, and you need to get rid of a troublesome tenant—someone who pays the rent late, keeps a dog in violation of a no-pets clause in the lease, repeatedly disturbs other tenants and neighbors by throwing loud parties or selling drugs, or otherwise violates your agreement or the law.

Termination is the first step toward an eventual eviction. You'll need to send the tenant a notice announcing that the tenancy is over, and that, if he doesn't leave, you'll file an eviction lawsuit. Or the notice may give the tenant a few days to clean up his act (pay the rent, find a new home for the dog). If the tenant leaves (or reforms) as directed, no one goes to court.

Eviction itself—that is, physically removing the tenant and his possessions from your property—generally can't be done until you have gone to court and proved that the tenant did something wrong that justifies ending the tenancy. If you win the eviction lawsuit, you can't just move the tenant and his things out onto the sidewalk. In most states, you must hire the sheriff or marshal to perform that task.

This chapter explains when and how you can terminate a tenancy based on nonpayment of rent and other illegal acts. It also provides an overview of the eviction procedure that follows a termination notice, and tells you what you can—and cannot—do under the law.

RELATED TOPIC

Related topics covered in this book include:

- Rent control laws that require a legally recognized reason, or "just cause," to evict: Chapter 3
- Evicting a resident manager: Chapter 6
- Substantially failing to maintain rental property so that tenants cannot use it (constructive eviction): Chapter 9
- Ending a month-to-month tenancy with a 30-day notice: Chapter 14
- How to end a tenancy at a property that you have purchased at foreclosure: Chapter 14

- Using a security deposit to cover unpaid rent after you've evicted a tenant: Chapter 15
- How to use a warning letter, negotiation, or mediation to resolve a dispute with a tenant: Chapter 16
- How to get legal help for an eviction lawsuit: Chapter 18.

CAUTION

Watch out for charges of retaliation. Landlords in most states may not end a tenancy in response to a tenant's legitimate exercise of a legal right, such as rent withholding, or in response to a complaint to a housing inspector or after a tenant has organized other tenants. What if your tenant has exercised a legal right (such as using a repair and deduct option) but is also late with the rent? Naturally, the tenant will claim that the real motive behind your eviction is retaliation.

In some states, the burden will be on you to prove that your motive is legitimate if you evict within a certain time (typically six months) of a tenant's use of a legal remedy or right. In others, it's up to the tenant to prove your motive. Chapter 16 includes advice on how to avoid charges of retaliation, and Appendix A gives details on state laws prohibiting landlord retaliation.

RESOURCE

California landlords should consult *The California Landlord's Law Book: Evictions,* **by David Brown and Nils Rosenquest (Nolo).** It contains eviction information and tear-out court forms.

The Landlord's Role in Evictions

The linchpin of an eviction lawsuit (sometimes called an unlawful detainer, or UD, lawsuit) is properly terminating the tenancy before you go to court. You can't proceed with your lawsuit, let alone get a judgment for possession of your property or for unpaid rent, without terminating the tenancy first. This usually means giving your tenant adequate written notice, in a specified way and form. If the tenant doesn't move (or reform), you can file a lawsuit to evict.

State laws set out very detailed requirements for landlords who want to end a tenancy. Each state has its own procedures as to how termination notices and eviction papers must be written and delivered ("served"). Different types of notices are often required for different types of situations. You must follow state rules and procedures exactly. Otherwise, you will experience delays in evicting a tenant—and maybe even lose your lawsuit—even if your tenant has bounced rent checks from here to Mandalay.

Because an eviction judgment means the tenant won't have a roof over his head (and his children's heads), state laws are usually very demanding of landlords. In addition, many rent control cities go beyond state laws (which typically allow the termination of a month-to-month tenant at the will of the landlord) and require the landlord to prove a legally recognized reason, or just cause, for eviction.

Alternatives to Eviction

Before you proceed with an eviction lawsuit, consider whether it might be cheaper in the long run to pay the tenant a few hundred dollars to leave right away. A potentially lengthy lawsuit—during which you can't accept rent that you may be unable to collect even after winning a judgment—may be more expensive and frustrating than buying out the tenant and quickly starting over with a better one. Especially if there's a possibility that your tenant might win the lawsuit (as well as a judgment against you for court costs and attorney fees), you may well be better off compromising—perhaps letting the tenant stay a few more weeks at reduced or no rent.

Chapter 16 provides tips on avoiding an eviction lawsuit by negotiating a settlement with a tenant.

Even if you properly bring and conduct an eviction lawsuit for a valid reason, you are not assured of winning and having the tenant evicted if the tenant decides to mount a defense. You always run the risk of encountering a judge who, despite the merits of your position, will hold you to every technicality and bend over backwards to sustain the tenant's position. The way that you have conducted business with the tenant may also affect the outcome: A tenant can point to behavior on your part, such as retaliation, that will shift attention away from the tenant's wrongdoing and sour your chances of victory. Simply put, unless you thoroughly know your legal rights and duties as a landlord before you go to court, and unless you dot every "i" and cross every "t," you may end up on the losing side. Our advice, especially if your action is contested, is to be meticulous in your business practices and lawsuit preparation.

It is beyond the scope of this book to provide all the step-by-step instructions and forms necessary to terminate a tenancy or evict a tenant. This chapter will get you started, and Chapter 18 shows how to research termination and eviction rules and procedures in your state. Many are clearly set out in state statutes. Other useful resources for eviction procedures and forms include:

- the website of the court that handles evictions in your area (see, for example, the Michigan Courts' Self Help Center at www.courts.mi.gov/self-help/center)
- your state consumer protection or attorney general's office (find yours at www.usa.gov/state-consumer)
- your state bar association (for example, the Florida State Bar website, www.floridabar.org, includes sample eviction forms), and
- your state or local apartment association.

California landlords should use the Nolo book described above.

Termination Notices

You may terminate a month-to-month tenancy simply by giving the proper amount of notice (30 days in most states). Reasons are usually not required. Leases expire on their own at the end of their term, and you generally aren't required to renew them.

If your tenant has done something wrong, you'll usually want him out sooner. State laws allow you to do this by serving the tenant with one of three different types of termination notices, depending on the reason why you want the tenant to leave. Although terminology varies somewhat from state to state, the substance of the three types of notices is remarkably the same.

- **Pay Rent or Quit** notices are typically used when the tenant has not paid the rent. They give the tenant a few days (three to five in most states) to pay or move out ("quit").
- **Cure or Quit** notices are typically given after a violation of a term or condition of the lease or rental agreement, such as a no-pets clause or the promise to refrain from making excessive noise. Typically, the tenant has a set amount of time in which to correct, or "cure," the violation; a tenant who fails to do so must move or face an eviction lawsuit.
- **Unconditional Quit** notices are the harshest of all. They order the tenant to vacate the premises with no chance to pay the rent or correct the lease or rental agreement violation. In most states, Unconditional Quit notices are allowed only when the tenant has repeatedly:
  - violated a lease or rental agreement clause
  - been late with the rent
  - seriously damaged the premises, or
  - engaged in illegal activity.

Many states have all three types of notices on the books. But, in some states, Unconditional Quit notices are the *only* notice statutes, as noted below. Landlords in these states may extend second chances if they wish, but no law requires them to do so.

Many states have standards for the content and look of a termination notice, requiring certain language and specifying size and appearance of type (consult your state's statute, as noted in Appendix A, before writing your notice). When you're sure that the notice complies with state law, resist any temptation to add threatening graphics or language. The Fair Debt Collection Practices Act, cited below, and its counterparts written by many states, forbids you from threatening unlawful actions or implying that you are affiliated with the government. Threats (or implications) that you will resort to a self-help eviction (covered below) or even using a picture of a policeman may constitute a deceptive collection practice.

You may have a choice among these three notices, depending on the situation. For example, a Wisconsin landlord may give month-to-month tenants an Unconditional Quit *or* a Pay Rent or Quit notice for late payment of rent. The tenant cannot insist on the more lenient notice.

For the details and citations to your state's statutes on termination notices, see the following charts in Appendix A:

- "State Rules on Notice Required to Change or Terminate a Month-to-Month Tenancy"
- "State Laws on Termination for Nonpayment of Rent"
- "State Laws on Termination for Violation of Lease," and
- "State Laws on Unconditional Quit Terminations."

Late Rent

Not surprisingly, the number one reason landlords terminate a tenancy is nonpayment of rent. If a tenant is late with the rent, in most states you can immediately send a termination notice, giving the tenant a few days—usually three to five—in which to pay up. The exact number of days varies from state to state. But not every state requires you to give a tenant a second chance to pay the rent; in a few states, if the tenant fails to pay rent on time, you can simply demand that he leave by sending an Unconditional Quit notice.

Legal Late Periods

In most states, you can send a Pay Rent or Quit notice as soon as the tenant is even one day late with the rent. A handful of states will not let you send a

Involving Your Lawyer May Trigger the Fair Debt Collection Practices Act

The Fair Debt Collection Practices Act (15 U.S. Code §§ 1692 and following) governs debt collectors and requires, among other things, that debtors be given 30 days in which to respond to a demand for payment (even if your pay-or-quit notice specifies fewer days). If you prepare and send your own pay-or-quit notices, you aren't a "debt collector," and you won't have to comply with this Act. However, if your lawyer sends the notice, the Act may apply. This can result if your lawyer regularly handles your termination work and genuinely gets involved in each case; ironically, you may also be subject to the Act if you're simply using the lawyer's name or stationery and he has no real connection with the case.

When your lawyer regularly sends notices for you and is genuinely involved in each case. Odd as it may sound, a lawyer who regularly handles rent demand notices on behalf of landlord-clients is considered a "debt collector" under the law in some cases—at least in Connecticut, New York, and Vermont (states covered by the federal Second Court of Appeals; *Romea v. Heiberger & Associates*, 163 F.3d 111 (2d Cir. 1998)). Consequently, the tenant must have 30 days to pay or quit, no matter what your statute says. However, if your lawyer does not regularly engage in debt collection, it's likely that the lawyer will not be considered a regular debt collector. (*Goldstein v. Hutton*, 374 F.3d 56 (2004).) A pay-or-quit rent demand notice that's signed or sent by a manager in these states, however, won't violate federal law, so long as it was the manager's job to collect rent before the tenant defaulted in the payment of rent. (*Franceschi v. Mautner-Glick Corp.*, 22 F.Supp.2d 250 (S.D. N.Y. 1998).)

When your lawyer rubber-stamps your notices. Under the Fair Debt Collection Practices Act, it's illegal for someone to lend his name to a creditor for its intimidation value. (15 U.S. Code § 1692j(a).) If your attorney simply sends out termination notices at your bidding (or lends you stationery or a signature stamp), and if the lawyer does not consider the facts of each case, it's likely that you'll come under this stricture. The consequence is that *you* will be held to the letter of the Act—and your pay-or-quit notice will, among other things, become a 30-day notice. (*Nielsen v. Dickerson*, 307 F.3d 623 (7th Cir. 2002).)

The lesson to be learned here is to handle your notices yourself!

---

termination notice (either a Pay Rent or Quit notice or an Unconditional Quit notice) until the rent is a certain number of days late. In these states, tenants enjoy a statutory "grace period," plus the time specified in the Pay Rent or Quit notice, in which to come up with the rent. See "State Rent Rules," in Appendix A, for states that impose a grace period.

> **EXAMPLE:** Lara, a Maine tenant, couldn't pay her rent on time. State law required her landlord Luke to wait until the rent was seven days late before he could send a termination notice. Luke did so on the eighth, giving Lara notice that she must pay or move within seven days. In all, Lara had fourteen days in which to pay the rent before Luke could file for eviction.

 TIP

Late rent fees are unaffected by Pay Rent or Quit time periods or legal late periods. If your lease or rental agreement specifies late fees, they'll kick in as soon as your lease or rental agreement (or in some states, state law) says they can. The number of days specified in your Pay Rent or Quit notice will not affect them, nor will a legally required grace period.

Accepting Rent After You Deliver a Termination Notice

If the tenant is late with the rent and you deliver a termination notice—whether or not it gives the tenant a few days to pay the rent—you can expect a phone call, email, or a visit from your tenant, hoping to work something out. Chapter 16 offers some pointers on negotiating and dealing with these requests. Here are the legal rules.

If the Tenant Pays the Whole Rent

If you have sent a Pay Rent or Quit notice but then accept rent for the entire rental term, you have canceled the termination notice for that period. In most states, it's as if the tenant had paid on time in the first place.

> **EXAMPLE:** Zoe's rent was due on the first of the month. She didn't pay on time, and her landlord sent her a three-day pay rent or quit notice. Zoe borrowed money from her parents and paid on the third day, saving her tenancy and avoiding an eviction lawsuit.

If the Tenant Is Chronically Late Paying Rent

In several states, you don't have to give tenants a second chance to pay the rent if they are habitually late. Typically, you're legally required to give the tenant a chance to pay and stay only once or twice within a certain period. If your state gives you a "no second chances" option for repeated late rent episodes, you'll see the rule reflected on the chart, "State Laws on Unconditional Quit Terminations" in Appendix A.

Some states insist that you give the tenant a *written* Pay Rent or Quit notice for the first late payment, so that there is proof that rent was late. Other statutes allow you to use the Unconditional Quit notice merely for "repeated lateness." In that case, you need not have given the tenant a notice to pay or quit for the first tardiness, but it's good business practice to do so, anyway. If your tenant claims that he has always paid the rent on time, you'll have prior Pay Rent or Quit notices to show otherwise.

Special Rules for Tenants in Military Service

If your tenant is in the military or the activated reserves, your ability to evict for nonpayment of rent is subject to the War and National Defense Servicemembers Civil Relief Act, 50 U.S.C. §§ 3951. The Act does not prevent you from serving a termination notice for nonpayment of rent. Instead, it requires the court to stay (postpone) an eviction for up to three months unless the judge decides that military service does not materially affect the tenant's ability to pay the rent.

The Act only applies to evictions for nonpayment of rent. It does not apply to evictions for other reasons, such as keeping pets in violation of the lease or failing to move when a lease is up. Nor does it apply if you've terminated a rental agreement with a 30-day notice.

- **Tenants affected.** The War and National Defense Servicemembers Civil Relief Act applies if your tenant's spouse, children, or other dependents occupy the rental unit. Courts give a broader meaning to the term "dependent" than the one used by the IRS.
- **Rental amount.** The Act's protections apply when the rent is $2,400 per month or less (adjusted annually for inflation). To learn the current rent ceiling, go to www.federalregister.gov and type "housing price inflation adjustment" in the query box. At press time, the available figure was for 2015 ($3,329.84).
- **The effect on an eviction lawsuit.** Once you have filed your lawsuit, you must tell the court that the tenant is an active service person. The judge will decide whether the service person's status in the military affects his or her ability to pay the rent. If the judge decides that it does, the case may be stayed for up to three months.
- **Requisitioned pay.** The Secretary of Defense or the Secretary of Transportation may order that part of the service person's pay be allotted to pay the rent. Ask the judge in your case to write a letter to the service branch, asking that a reasonable amount be sent to you to pay the rent. Be advised, however, that current Defense Finance and Accounting Service regulations make no provision for such allotments.

TIP

You can always use a 30-day notice for month-to-month tenants who are chronically late. You need not worry about the complexities of your state's Unconditional Quit procedure for month-to-month tenants who repeatedly pay late. Simply terminate the tenancy with a 30-day notice, which may be quicker, in the long run, if the tenant challenges your use of the Unconditional Quit notice. Even if you live in a rent control area that requires landlords to have good reason to evict, repeatedly paying late is ample legal reason to end a tenancy.

If You Accept a Partial Rent Payment

By accepting even a partial amount of rent a tenant owes—whether for past months or even just the current month—you will, in most states, cancel the effect of a Pay Rent or Quit notice. But you can still go ahead with your attempts to get the tenant out—just pocket your tenant's payment with one hand and simultaneously hand him a new termination notice with the other, demanding that he pay the new balance or leave.

> **EXAMPLE:** Danny's rent of $900 was due on the first of the month. Danny didn't pay January's rent and didn't have enough for February, either. On February 2, Danny's landlord, Ali, sent him a three-day notice to pay $1,800 or leave. Danny paid $900 on February 3 and thought that he'd saved his tenancy. He was amazed when, later that day, Ali handed him a new notice to pay $900 or leave. Ali properly filed for eviction on February 7 when Danny failed to pay.

CAUTION

If you sign a written agreement with the tenant setting up a payment schedule for delayed or partial rent, you must comply with this agreement. If the tenant does not end up honoring this agreement, you may then take steps to terminate the tenancy.

Other Tenant Violations of the Lease or Rental Agreement

In addition to nonpayment of rent, you may terminate a tenancy if a tenant violates other terms of the lease or rental agreement, such as:

- keeping a pet in violation of a no-pets rule
- bringing in an unauthorized tenant
- subleasing or assigning without your permission
- repeatedly violating "house rules" that are part of the lease or rental agreement, such as using common areas improperly, making too much noise, having unruly guests, or abusing recreation facilities, or
- giving false information concerning an important matter on the rental application or lease.

Giving Tenants Another Chance

The laws in most states insist that you give the tenant a few days (anywhere from three to 30 days, depending on the state) to correct, or "cure," the violation before the tenancy can end. However, there are two important "but ifs" that allow you to use an Unconditional Quit notice instead of the more generous Cure or Quit notice:

- **Repeated violations.** If the tenant has violated the same lease clause two or more times within a certain period of time, he may lose the right to a second chance. You may give him an Unconditional Quit notice instead.
- **The violation cannot be corrected.** Some lease violations cannot be corrected because the effect of the violation is permanent. For instance, suppose your lease prohibits tenant alterations or improvements without your consent (see Clause 12 of the form agreements in Chapter 2). If, without asking, your tenant removes and discards the living room wallpaper, you can hardly demand that the tenant cease violating the lease clause, because it is simply too late to save the wallpaper. If a lease violation cannot be cured, you may use an Unconditional Quit notice.

Criminal Convictions

You are generally free to reject prospective tenants with criminal records. Sometimes, however, you won't know about these convictions until you have already rented the unit. Maybe you never checked the applicant's background, or you didn't have access to reliable information. Regardless of why you didn't know beforehand, if you learn that a tenant has a record—and particularly if he is a convicted sex offender—your first impulse will probably be to look for a way to get him out of your building. Here's what to do:

- **Month-to-month tenants.** In most states, you may terminate any month-to-month tenancy with a 30-day notice, and you need not give a reason, as long as you do not have discriminatory or retaliatory motives. Note, however, that tenants in rent control cities with "just cause" eviction protection, and all tenants in New Hampshire and New Jersey (where there are statewide just cause protections) may be able to resist a termination on this basis.
- **Tenants with leases.** You will not be able to terminate an otherwise law- and rule-abiding tenant purely because you now know that he has a criminal past, no matter how unsavory or alarming. However, if your lease or rental agreement states that false and material information on the rental application will be grounds for termination (as does the one in this book), you can terminate and evict on this basis. In some states, your right to do so is established by state law, even if your rental agreement or lease is silent on the matter.

Violations of a Tenant's Legal Responsibilities

Virtually every state allows you to terminate the tenancy of a tenant who has violated basic responsibilities imposed by law, including:

- grossly deficient housekeeping practices that cause an unhealthy situation, such as allowing garbage to pile up
- seriously misusing appliances, like damaging the freezer while attempting to defrost it with an icepick
- repeatedly interfering with other tenants' ability to peacefully enjoy their homes, such as hosting late parties, playing incessant loud music, or running a noisy small business (repairing cars in the driveway of a rental duplex, for example)
- substantially damaging the property—for instance, knocking holes in the walls or doors, and
- allowing or participating in illegal activities on or near the premises, such as drug dealing or gambling.

Many careful landlords incorporate these obligations into their leases or rental agreements— (something we recommend in Chapter 2, Clause 13, "Violating Laws and Causing Disturbances"). But, even if these obligations are not mentioned in your rental documents, tenants are still legally bound to observe them.

Tips on Dealing With a Tenant During an Eviction

- Avoid all unnecessary one-on-one personal contact with the tenant during the eviction process unless it occurs in a structured setting—for example, at a neighborhood dispute resolution center or in the presence of a neutral third party.
- Keep your written communications to the point and as neutral as you can, even if you are boiling inside. Remember, any manifestations of anger on your part can come back to legally haunt you somewhere down the line.
- Treat the tenant like she has a right to remain on the premises, even though it is your position that she doesn't. Until the day the sheriff or marshal shows up to evict the tenant, the tenant's home is legally her castle, and you may come to regret any actions on your part that don't recognize that fact.

If a tenant or guest substantially damages the premises, you'll be within your rights to use an Unconditional Quit notice. The law does not require you to give tenants accused of serious misbehavior a second chance. Tenants who have earned this type of termination notice generally get only five to ten days to move out.

Tenant's Illegal Activity on the Premises

In recent years, many states have responded aggressively to widespread drug dealing in residential neighborhoods by making it easier for landlords to evict based on these activities. Indeed, in some states you must evict known drug dealers or risk having authorities close down or even confiscate your entire property. To say the least, the threat of losing rental property is strong motivation to quickly evict tenants suspected of engaging in illegal acts.

You usually don't have to wait until the tenant is convicted of a crime or even arrested. In some states, for example, a judge will order a tenant's eviction if the landlord has a "reasonable suspicion" that criminal activity has taken place and that the tenant or tenant's guests are involved. (That burden of proof is easier to establish than "beyond a reasonable doubt.") By contrast, in other states, you may not begin an eviction for illegal activity unless there's been a criminal conviction for criminal acts on the rented premises.

Evictions based on criminal activity are often called "expedited evictions," because they take less time than a normal eviction. Expedited evictions are preceded by an Unconditional Quit notice that tells the tenant to move out (and do it quickly). If the tenant stays, you can go to court and file for eviction. The court hearing on the eviction is typically held within a few days, and, if you win, the tenant is given very little time to move.

How Eviction Lawsuits Work

When the deadline in the termination notice passes, your tenant will not be automatically evicted. In almost every state, you must file and win an eviction lawsuit before the sheriff or marshal can physically evict a tenant who refuses to leave after receiving the termination notice. The whole process may take weeks—or months—depending on whether or not the tenant contests the eviction in court.

What Court Hears Evictions?

Eviction lawsuits are filed in a formal trial court (called "municipal," "county," or "justice") or in small claims court. A few states, including Illinois, Massachusetts, and New York, have separate landlord-tenant courts in larger cities, similar to small claims courts, specifically set up to handle evictions. Some states give landlords the choice; others confine eviction lawsuits to one court or the other. Call the clerk of your local small claims court to find out whether it handles evictions.

If you have a choice between regular trial court and small claims court, you'll want to consider:

- **Amount of unpaid rent.** If you're also suing for unpaid rent that is higher than the small claims court's jurisdictional amount, you must use a higher court. States' small claims court limits are listed on the chart in Appendix A.
- **Attorney fees clause.** If your lease or rental agreement contains an attorney fees clause, and you have a strong case and a reasonable chance of collecting from your tenant, you may want to hire an attorney and go to formal court, figuring that the fee will come from the tenant's pocket when you win. On the other hand, if the tenant has little or no funds, your chances of collection are dim, and you may realistically choose small claims instead.

There are important differences between regular trial courts and small claims (or landlord-tenant) court:

- In small claims court, the regular rules of evidence are greatly relaxed, and you can show or tell the court your side of the story without adhering to the "foundation" requirements that apply in higher courts. ("Laying a foundation" is explained in "Rules of Evidence in Formal Court," below.)

- In regular court, you and the tenant may engage in a pretrial process called "discovery," in which you ask each other about the evidence that supports your positions. Information gathered during discovery can be used at trial. Discovery includes depositions (where witnesses are questioned under oath), interrogatories (sets of preprinted questions that cover information normally involved in a landlord-tenant dispute), and "requests for admissions," (specific statements of fact that the other side is asked, under oath, to admit or deny). The discovery process is normally available in formal court, but not in small claims or landlord-tenant courts.

- In regular court, you and the tenant may each attempt to wash the case out of court quickly by filing pretrial requests to the court to dismiss or limit the case. In small claims and landlord-tenant court, the idea is to decide the entire case after one efficient court hearing, and these motions are not used.

RESOURCE

***Everybody's Guide to Small Claims Court*, by Cara O'Neill (Nolo),** describes the workings of your small claims court in detail.

Represent Yourself in Court: How to Prepare & Try a Winning Case, by Paul Bergman and Sara Berman (Nolo), explains how to present evidence and arguments in formal court.

First Steps: The Complaint and Summons

An eviction lawsuit begins when you file a legal document called a "Complaint" or a similar term. The Complaint lists the facts that you think justify the eviction. It also asks the court to order the tenant to leave and pay back rent, damages directly caused by his unlawfully remaining on the property, court costs, and sometimes attorney fees.

Fortunately, your Complaint need not be a lengthy or complicated legal document. In some states, landlords use a preprinted Complaint form, prepared by the court, that allows you to simply check an appropriate box, depending on what you intend to argue. Courts are increasingly putting official forms online; typically, you can download the PDF file and complete it by hand, or complete it online and then print it (but not save it). To learn whether your court offers these downloads, type the court's name in your browser, then look for links to forms.

Even in states that still follow an old-fashioned approach of requiring that documents be typed up on numbered legal paper, you can find the information you need from legal form books available at law libraries. These books contain "canned" forms that fit many different situations. When you sign your Complaint, be sure to note under your typed name that you are appearing "Pro per" or "Pro se" if you have not hired a lawyer.

Normally, you cannot sue a tenant for anything but back rent and damages. Because an eviction procedure is so quick, most states do not allow you to add other legal beefs to an eviction Complaint. For example, if you claim that the tenants have damaged the sofa, and their security deposit won't cover the cost of replacement, you must sue the tenants in small claims court in a separate lawsuit.

When you file a Complaint, the clerk will assign a date on which the case will be heard by the court. That date is entered on the Summons, a piece of paper that tells the tenant he's been sued and must

Rules of Evidence in Formal Court

It's important to back up your eviction lawsuit with as much hard evidence as possible. For example, if the basis of the termination is that the tenant has violated a rental rule (by keeping a pet), be sure that you have a copy of the lease and rules that your tenant signed when he moved in.

In small claims court, you can present practically any evidence you want to the judge. But, if you are in a formal court, the judge will not examine documentary evidence until you have established that it is likely to be trustworthy. Presenting the legal background of evidence is called "laying a foundation." Here are a few hints on how to prepare evidence for formal court:

- **Photographs.** If your termination notice is based on your tenant knocking a hole in the kitchen wall, show the judge a photograph of the gaping hole. To get the picture into evidence, someone will have to testify that the picture is an accurate depiction of how the wall looked. Ask a neutral witness to look at the wall and come to court ready to testify that the photo is an accurate portrayal. Your witness need not have taken the photo.
- **Letters.** You may have sent a termination notice for nonpayment of rent because your tenant

improperly used the repair and deduct remedy by failing to give you a reasonable amount of time to fix the problem yourself. You'll want to show the judge a copy of the letter you sent to the tenant promising to fix the defect within the week (the tenant didn't wait). In court, this means you'll need to introduce your letter into evidence. To do this, you can simply testify that the letter is a true copy, that the signature is your own, and that you mailed or handed it to your tenant.

- **Government documents.** If your tenant has withheld rent because of what she claims are uninhabitable conditions, you may decide to evict for nonpayment of rent. If the tenant filed a complaint with a local health department and they issued a report giving your property a clean bill of health, you'll want the report considered by the court (admitted into evidence). Ask the health department inspector to testify that he wrote the report as part of his normal duties when investigating possible health violations. To get the inspector to court, you'll need to ask the judge for an order, called a "subpoena," that you can serve on the inspector.

answer your charges in writing and appear in court within a specified number of days or lose the lawsuit. You must then arrange for the tenant to be given the Complaint and the Summons. In legal jargon, this is called "service of process."

State laws are quite detailed as to the proper way to deliver, or "serve," court papers. Most critically, neither you (including anyone who has an ownership interest in your business) nor your employees can serve these papers. (In some states, any adult not involved in the lawsuit can serve papers.) The method of delivery is specified, as well: Typically, the preferred way is "personal" service, which means that a law enforcement officer or professional process server personally hands the tenant the papers.

If, despite repeated attempts, the process server cannot locate the tenant, most states allow

something called "substituted service." This means the process server leaves a copy of the papers with a competent adult at the tenant's home, or mails the papers first-class and also leaves a copy in a place where the tenant will likely see it, such as posted on his front door.

Failure to properly serve the tenant is one of the most common errors landlords make, and may result in court dismissal of your lawsuit even before trial. Even a seemingly minor mistake—such as forgetting to check a box, checking one you shouldn't, or filling in contradictory information—will increase the chances that your tenant can successfully contest the lawsuit. Again, it is vital that you pay close attention to your state rules and procedures on evictions.

The Tenant's Answer to the Complaint

The next step in a typical eviction lawsuit involves the tenant's response to your claims that something he's done (or not done) justifies his eviction. At this point, the lawsuit has gone beyond the technicalities of the way you filed the lawsuit, and you and the tenant are meeting the reasons for the eviction head-on.

In some states, tenants who have been served with an eviction lawsuit can just show up at the hearing and present their defenses in person. In other states, the tenant must file a document called an Answer on or before the date printed on the Summons. Like your Complaint, it need not be a complex document. Your tenant will probably consult the same set of legal form books that you used in writing your Complaint.

In general, the Answer may contain two kinds of responses:

- **Denials.** The tenant may dispute that what you say is true. For example, if you are evicting for nonpayment of rent and your tenant claims that he paid his rent to the manager, he will simply deny that the rent is unpaid. Or, if you've filed an eviction lawsuit because the tenant has a dog, but the tenant claims that the animal actually belongs to the tenants in the next unit, he'll also simply check the "denials" box. If there is no Answer form, you'll see a typed paragraph that looks something like this: "Defendant denies the allegations in Paragraph X of Plaintiff's Complaint." (You are the plaintiff in the lawsuit; the tenant is the defendant.)

- **Affirmative defenses.** The Answer is also the place where your tenant can state what the law calls "affirmative defenses"—good legal reasons (such as discrimination or retaliation) that he hopes will excuse what would otherwise be grounds for eviction. For example, a tenant who's being evicted for not paying the rent might use a habitability defense to justify his actions—in this case, the tenant would claim that he used some of the rent money to pay for repairing a serious problem you had ignored.

Complete Your Lawsuit, Even If You Think You've Won Already

It's very common for tenants to move out after receiving a Summons and Complaint. Especially if the security deposit will cover your losses, or you know that attempting to collect any excess won't be worth your time and trouble, you might be tempted to forget about the lawsuit and turn your attentions to rerenting quickly.

Never walk away from a lawsuit without formally ending it. Usually, this will involve appearing in court and asking the judge to dismiss the case. Doing so preserves your reputation as someone who uses the courts with respect—if you are simply a no-show, expect a chilly reception the next time you appear in court. In addition, if you don't appear for trial but the tenant does, *the tenant* may win and be entitled to move back in and collect court costs and attorney fees.

If you and the tenant have reached a settlement that involves the tenant paying you money but the tenant hasn't paid you yet, it's a good idea to take that written settlement with you to court and ask the judge to make it part of his ruling while dismissing the case. Depending on the rules in your state, you will then have a court order (sometimes called a "stipulated settlement") that you can immediately use if the tenant fails to pay voluntarily. (You can take it to a collection agency or use it to garnish wages.) Otherwise, you'll have to take the written agreement to small claims court to get a judgment.

Finally, don't overlook the possibility that the tenant may not have actually moved out (or may move back in). You'll be on safe ground if you get a judgment before retaking possession.

The Trial

Many eviction cases never end up in trial—for example, because the tenant moves out or negotiates a settlement with the landlord. But each case that does go to trial will have its own unpredictable twists and turns that can greatly affect trial preparation and tactics. For this reason, you will probably need to hire a lawyer, if you haven't done so already, to help you prepare for and conduct the trial.

What you must prove at trial obviously depends on the issues raised in your Complaint and the tenant's Answer. For example, the testimony in a case based on nonpayment of rent where the tenant's defense is that you failed to keep the premises habitable will be very different from that in a case based on termination of a month-to-month tenancy by 30-day notice where the tenant denies receiving the notice.

All contested evictions are similar, however, in that you have to establish the basic elements of your case through solid evidence that proves your case (and refutes your tenant's defense). In formal court, you'll have to abide by your state's rules of evidence. But in an informal court, you may be able to introduce letters and secondhand testimony ("I heard her say that … "). Also, you can introduce evidence without elaborate "foundations." (See "Rules of Evidence in Formal Court," above.)

The Judgment

Eviction lawsuits are typically decided either on the spot or very soon thereafter, after the judge has heard the witnesses and consulted any relevant statutes, ordinances, and higher court opinions.

If You Win

If you win the eviction case, you get an order from the judge declaring that you are entitled to possession of the property (you may get a money judgment for back rent and court costs and attorney fees, too). You'll need to take the order, called a judgment, to the local law enforcement official who will carry out the eviction.

Unfortunately, having a judgment for the payment of money is not the same as having the money itself. Your tenant may be unable (or unwilling) to pay you—despite the fact that you have converted your legal right to be paid into a formal court order. Unless the tenant voluntarily pays up, you will have to collect the debt—for example, by using the tenant's security deposit or hiring a collection agency.

If You Lose

If you lose the eviction case, your tenant can stay, and you'll likely end up paying for your tenant's court costs and fees. You may also be hit with money damages if the judge decides you acted illegally, as in the case of discrimination or retaliation.

If your tenant wins by asserting a habitability defense, the court may hold on to the case even after the trial is over. That's because the court doesn't want to simply return the tenant to an unfit dwelling. In some states, a judge may order you to make repairs while the rent is paid into a court account; when an inspector certifies that the dwelling is habitable, the judge will release the funds.

How Tenants May Stop or Postpone an Eviction

If you win the eviction lawsuit, you'll want to move quickly to physically remove the tenant from the property. In rare instances, a tenant may be able to get the trial judge to stop the eviction, but only if he can convince the court of two things:

- Eviction would cause a severe hardship for the tenant or his family. For example, the tenant may be able to persuade the judge that alternate housing is unavailable and his job will be in jeopardy if he is forced to move.
- The tenant is willing and able to pay any back rent owed (and your costs to bring the lawsuit) and future rent, as well.

It's very unusual for a judge to stop an eviction, for the simple reason that if the tenant's sympathetic predicament (and sufficient monetary reserves) weren't persuasive enough to win the case for him in the first place, it's unlikely that these arguments can prevail after the trial.

The tenant may, however, ask for a postponement of the eviction. Typically, evictions are postponed in three situations:

- **Pending an appeal.** If the tenant files an appeal, he may ask the trial judge to postpone ("stay") the eviction until a higher court decides the case. A tenant who has been evicted in small claims court may, in a few states, enjoy an automatic postponement during the appeal. Of course, this is one reason why smart landlords in these states never use small claims court.
- **Until the tenant's circumstances improve.** A tenant may be able to persuade a judge to give him a little more time to find a new home.
- **Until the weather improves.** Contrary to popular belief, judges in many cold-climate states (including Alaska, Minnesota, and North Dakota) are not required to postpone an eviction on frigid days. But there's nothing to stop tenants from asking the judge, anyway. In the District of Columbia, however, a landlord may not evict on a day when the National Weather Service predicts at 8:00 a.m. that the temperature at the National Airport will fall below freezing within the next 24 hours. (D.C. Code § 42-3505.01(k).)

Eviction

In most states, you cannot move a tenant's belongings out on the street, even after winning an eviction lawsuit. Typically, you must give the judgment to a local law enforcement officer, along with a fee which the tenant has been charged as part of your costs. The sheriff or marshal gives the tenant a notice telling him that he'll be back, sometimes within just a few days, to physically remove him if the tenant isn't gone.

Illegal "Self-Help" Evictions

As any experienced landlord will attest, there are occasional tenants who do things so outrageous that the landlord is tempted to bypass normal legal protections and take direct and immediate action to protect his property. For example, after a tenant's numerous promises to pay rent, a landlord may consider changing the locks and putting the tenant's property out in the street. Or, a landlord who is responsible for paying the utility charges may be tempted to simply not pay the bill in the hopes that the resulting lack of water, gas, or electricity will hasten a particularly outrageous tenant's departure. When you realize how long a legal eviction can sometimes take, these actions can almost seem sensible.

If you are tempted to take the law into your own hands to force or scare a troublesome tenant out of your property, heed the following advice: *Don't do it!* Shortcuts such as threats, intimidation, utility shutoffs, or attempts to physically remove a tenant are illegal and dangerous, and if you resort to them you may well find yourself on the wrong end of a lawsuit for trespass, assault, battery, slander and libel, intentional infliction of emotional distress, and wrongful eviction. So, although the eviction process can often entail some trouble, expense, and delay, it's important to understand that it is the only game in town.

If you are sued by a tenant whom you forcibly evicted or tried to evict, the fact that the tenant didn't pay rent, left your property a mess, verbally abused you, or otherwise acted outrageously will not be a valid defense. You will very likely lose the lawsuit, and it will cost you far more than evicting the tenant using normal court procedures.

Today, virtually every state forbids "self-help" evictions—their eviction statutes warn landlords that their procedures are the *only* way to retake possession of rental property. And, in many states the penalties for violating these laws are steep. Tenants who have been locked out, frozen out by having the heat cut off, or denied electricity or water can sue not only for their actual money losses (such as the need for temporary housing, the value of food that spoiled when the refrigerator stopped running, or the cost of an electric heater when the gas was shut off), but also for penalties, as well. In some states, the tenant can collect and still remain in the premises; in others, he is entitled to monetary compensation only. See "Consequences of Self-Help Evictions" in Appendix A.

Even if your state has not legislated against self-help evictions, throwing your tenant out on your own is highly risky and likely to land you in more legal entanglements than had you gone to court for an eviction judgment in the first place.

The potential for nastiness and violence is great; the last thing you want is a patrol car at the curb while you and your tenant wrestle over the sofa on the lawn. And you can almost count on a lawsuit over the "disappearance" of your tenant's valuable possessions, which she'll claim were lost or taken when you removed her belongings. Using a neutral law enforcement officer to enforce a judge's eviction order will avoid these unpleasantries.

> **CAUTION**
>
> **Don't seize tenants' property under the guise of handling "abandoned" property.** A few states allow you to freely dispose of a tenant's leftover property when he has moved out. Do so only if it is quite clear that the tenant has left permanently, intending to turn the place over to you. Seizing property under a bogus claim that the tenant had abandoned it will expose you to significant monetary penalties.

Stopping Eviction by Filing for Bankruptcy

Tenants with significant financial burdens may decide to declare bankruptcy. There are several kinds of bankruptcy; the most common are "Chapter 7," in which most debts are wiped out after as many creditors as possible have been paid; or "Chapter 13," in which some debts—but not necessarily all—are paid off over time according to a court-approved plan.

If your tenant has filed for either Chapter 7 or 13 bankruptcy and is behind in the rent, becomes unable to pay the rent, or violates another term of his tenancy (such as keeping a pet in violation of a no-pets clause), you can't deliver a termination notice or proceed with an eviction. This prohibition is known as the "automatic stay," and it means that you need to go to the federal bankruptcy court and ask the judge to "lift," or remove the stay. (11 U.S. Code § 365(e).) In most cases, you'll get the stay lifted within a matter of days and can proceed with your termination and eviction. (You won't have to go to court if your tenant is using illegal drugs or endangering the property, as explained below in "Bankrupt Tenants, Drugs, and Damage.")

The automatic stay does not apply, however if you completed your eviction proceeding and got a judgment for possession *before* the tenant filed for bankruptcy. Under the Bankruptcy Abuse Prevention and Consumer Protection Act of 2005, landlords can proceed with the eviction without having to go to court and ask for the stay to be lifted.

In very narrow circumstances, and only for evictions based on rent nonpayment, a tenant can stop the eviction even if you got a judgment before the tenant filed for bankruptcy. Here are the specifics:

- Along with his or her bankruptcy petition, the tenant must go to court and file a paper certifying that state law allows the tenant to avoid eviction by paying the unpaid rent, even after the landlord has won a judgment for possession. Very few states extend this option to tenants. The certification must be served on the landlord.
- At the same time, the tenant must deposit with the clerk of the bankruptcy court any rent that would be due 30 days from the date the petition was filed.
- The tenant then has 30 days after filing the petition to actually pay the back rent. He or she must file another certification with the bankruptcy court (and serve it on the landlord), stating that he or she has paid the amount due.

At any point during these 30 days, you can file an objection to the tenant's certification, and you'll get a hearing in the bankruptcy court within ten days. If you convince the judge that the tenant's certifications are not true, the court will lift the stay and you can proceed to recover possession of the property.

A Tenant's Lease After Bankruptcy

You might find yourself with a new tenant if your existing tenant files for Chapter 7 bankruptcy. How could this happen? The bankruptcy trustee appointed to the case has the right to take over a valuable lease and rent the space to a new tenant at a profit (as long as the lease doesn't contain a clause prohibiting subletting). The upside? Because the trustee steps into the tenant's shoes, the trustee must pay any past-due rent. By contrast, in a Chapter 13 case a trustee won't take over a lease, and a tenant who's behind on the rent but would like to stay must propose a plan to bring the rent current within a reasonable period. (11 U.S. Code §§ 365(b)(1)(A), (B), & (C).)

Bankrupt Tenants, Drugs, and Damage

You may find yourself needing to evict a tenant who is using illegal drugs on the property or endangering your property. If the tenant files for bankruptcy before you win a judgment for possession, you'll be able to proceed with the eviction without asking the bankruptcy judge to lift the stay. Here are the steps to take:

- **When you've begun an eviction case but don't have a judgment.** Prepare a certification, or sworn statement, that you have begun an unlawful detainer case based on the tenant's endangerment of the property or use of illegal drugs on the property (or such use by the tenant's guests).
- **When you haven't yet filed your eviction lawsuit.** Prepare a certification, or sworn statement, that the activity described above has happened within the past 30 days.
- **File the certification with the bankruptcy court and serve the tenant as you would serve any legal notice.**

A tenant who objects must file with the court, and serve on you, a certification challenging the truth of your certification. The bankruptcy court will likely hold a hearing within ten days, at which the tenant must convince the court that the situation you describe did not exist or has been remedied. If the court rules for you, you may proceed with the eviction without asking that the stay be lifted; but if the tenant wins, you may not proceed.

Lawyers and Legal Research

Landlords should be prepared to deal with most routine legal questions and problems without a lawyer. If you bought all the needed information at the rates lawyers charge—$150 to $400 an hour—it should go without saying that you'd quickly empty your bank account. Just the same, there are times when good advice from a specialist in landlord-tenant law will be helpful, if not essential—for example, in lawsuits by tenants alleging housing discrimination or claiming that dangerous conditions or wrongful acts caused injury, or in complicated eviction lawsuits. Throughout this book, we point out specific instances when an attorney's advice or services may be useful.

Fortunately, for an intelligent landlord there are a number of other ways to acquire a good working knowledge of the legal principles and procedures necessary to handle problems with tenants and managers. Of course, that's the main purpose of this book. But in addition to the information we provide, this chapter specifically recommends a strategy to most efficiently and effectively use legal services and keep up to date on landlord-tenant law, so that you can anticipate and avoid many legal problems.

As a sensible landlord, it doesn't make sense to try and run your business without ever consulting a lawyer. When legal problems are potentially serious and expensive, it makes sense to get expert help. But since you almost surely can't afford all the services a lawyer might offer, you obviously need to set priorities. When thinking about a legal problem, ask yourself: "Can I do this myself?"; "Can I do this myself with some help from a lawyer?"; "Should I simply put this in my lawyer's hands?"

Or, put another way, your challenge isn't to avoid lawyers altogether, but rather to use them on a cost-effective basis. Ideally, this means finding a lawyer who's willing to serve as a kind of self-help law coach, to help you educate yourself. Then, you can often do routine or preliminary legal work on your own, turning to your lawyer only occasionally for advice and fine-tuning.

How Lawyers Can Help Landlords

Here are some important things lawyers can do to help landlords:

- prepare (or review your drafts of) key documents, such as your lease or manager agreement
- confirm that you have a good claim or defense vis-à-vis an individual tenant—whether it's a dispute over how much security deposit you must return or your right to raise the rent
- make a quick phone call or write a letter to the tenant and get a problem resolved quickly
- summarize and point you to the law that applies in a given situation
- provide any needed assistance with evictions, including preparing notices and forms
- answer questions along the way if you're representing yourself in court or in a mediation proceeding, and
- handle legal problems that are—or are threatening to become—serious, such as a tenant's personal injury lawsuit or discrimination charge.

Finding a Lawyer

How frequently you'll need a lawyer's help will depend on many factors, including the type, number, and location of rental units you own; the kinds of problems you run into with tenants; the number of property managers and other employees you hire; and your willingness to do some of the legal work yourself.

In looking for a lawyer you can work with, and to manage your subsequent relationship with that person, always remember one key thing: You're the boss. Just because your lawyer has specialized training, knowledge, skills, and experience in dealing with legal matters is no reason for you to abdicate control over legal decision making and how much time and money should be spent on a particular legal problem. We say this because, despite the fact that you have an intimate knowledge of your business and are in the best position to call the shots, some lawyers will be willing or even eager to try and run your business for you while overcharging you for the privilege. The key is to find a lawyer who can provide the amount and type of legal services you need.

Compile a List of Prospects

Finding a good, reasonably priced lawyer expert in landlord-tenant legal issues is not always an easy task. If you just pick a name out of the telephone book or you find one online—even someone who advertises as a landlord law expert—you may get an unsympathetic lawyer, or one who will charge too much, or one who's not qualified to deal with your particular problem. If you use an attorney you or a friend or relative has relied on for other legal needs, you will very likely end up with someone who doesn't know enough about landlord-tenant law.

This sorry result is not inevitable—there are competent landlords' lawyers who charge fairly for their services. As a general rule, deep experience in landlord-tenant law is most important. As with so many other areas of the law, the information needed to practice effectively in this field has become increasingly specialized in the past two decades—so much so that a general practitioner simply won't do.

The best way to find a suitable attorney is through some trusted person who has had a satisfactory experience with one. Your best referral sources are other landlords in your area. Ask the names of their lawyers and a little bit about their experiences. Also ask rental property owners about other lawyers they've worked with, and what led them to make a change. If you talk to a few landlords, chances are you'll come away with several leads on good lawyers experienced in landlord-tenant law.

Your local landlords' association will also likely know of lawyers who have experience in landlord-tenant law.

RESOURCE

Looking for a lawyer? Asking for a referral to an attorney from someone you trust can be a good way to find legal help. Someone looking to hire a lawyer, even if only for consultation, can also try these excellent and free resources:

Nolo's Lawyer Directory. Nolo has an easy-to-use online directory of lawyers, organized by location and area of expertise. You can find the directory and its comprehensive profiles at www.nolo.com/lawyers.

Lawyers.com. At Lawyers.com you'll find a user-friendly search tool that allows you to tailor results by area of law and geography. You can also search for attorneys by name. Attorney profiles prominently display contact information, list topics of expertise, and show ratings—by both clients and other legal professionals.

Martindale.com. Martindale.com allows you to search not only by practice area and location, but also by criteria like law school. Whether you look for lawyers by name or expertise, you'll find listings with detailed background information, peer and client ratings, and even profile visibility.

Keep in mind that these online resources are simply modern versions of the yellow pages: The listed lawyers have paid to have their names show up on the relevant pages.

Shop Around

Once you have the names of hopefully top-notch prospects, your job has just begun. You need to meet with each attorney and make your own evaluation. If you explain that, as a local landlord, you have a continuing need for legal help, many lawyers will be willing to speak to you for a half-hour or so at no charge or at a reduced rate so that you can size them up and make an informed selection. Briefly explain your business and legal needs and how much work you plan to do yourself.

Look for experience, personal rapport, and accessibility. Some of these traits will be apparent almost immediately; others may take longer to discover. In addition to the person making the original recommendation, you may want to talk with some of the lawyer's other landlord clients about their satisfaction with the lawyer's work. A lawyer should be able to provide you with such a list.

Here are some things to look for in your first meeting.

Will the lawyer answer all your questions about fees, his experience in landlord-tenant matters, and your specific legal problems? Stay away from lawyers who make you feel uncomfortable asking questions. Pay particular attention to the rapport between you and your lawyer. No matter how experienced and well-recommended a lawyer is, if you feel uncomfortable with that person during your first meeting or two, you may never achieve an ideal lawyer-client relationship. Trust your instincts and seek a lawyer whose personality is compatible with your own. Be sure you understand how the lawyer charges for services.

Will the lawyer provide the kind of legal help you want? If you plan to be actively involved in dealing with your legal business, look for a lawyer who doesn't resent your participation and control. By reading this book all the way through and consulting other resources, such as those available online or at a nearby law library, you can answer many of your questions on your own. For example, you might do the initial legal work in evictions and similar procedures yourself, but turn over to a lawyer cases which become hotly contested or complicated.

Unfortunately, some lawyers are uncomfortable with the very idea of helping people help themselves. They see themselves as all-knowing experts and expect their clients to accept and follow their advice without question. Obviously, this is not the type of lawyer a self-helper will want.

Is the lawyer willing to assist you when you have specific questions, billing you on an hourly basis when you handle your own legal work—such as evictions? One key to figuring out if a lawyer is really willing to help you help yourself is to ask: Is he willing to answer your questions over the phone and charge only for the brief amount of time the conversation lasted? If, instead, he indicates that he prefers to provide advice

in more time-consuming (and therefore profitable) office appointments, you'll want to keep looking. There are plenty of lawyers who will be very happy to bill you hourly to help you help yourself. By providing helpful consultations on problems that are routine or involve small dollar amounts, a lawyer can generate referrals for full-service representation on bigger, more complex matters that you (or your friends or family) face in the future. And if, despite his initial assurances, the lawyer later tries to dissuade you from representing yourself or won't give any advice over the phone despite your invitation to bill you for it, find someone else.

Will the lawyer clearly lay out all your options for handling a particular legal problem, including alternate dispute resolution methods such as mediation?

Will the lawyer be accessible when you need legal services? Unfortunately, the complaint logs of all law regulatory groups indicate that many lawyers are not reasonably available to their clients in times of need. If every time you have a problem there's a delay of several days before you can talk to your lawyer on the phone or get an appointment, you'll lose precious time, not to mention sleep. And almost nothing is more aggravating than to leave a legal question or project in a lawyer's hands and then have weeks or even months go by without anything happening. So be sure to discuss with any lawyer whether she will really commit herself to returning your phone calls promptly, work hard on your behalf, and follow through on all assignments.

If your property is in a rent-controlled city, does the lawyer practice in or near that city and know its rent control laws and practices?

Does the lawyer represent tenants, too? Chances are that a lawyer who represents both landlords and tenants can advise you well on how to avoid many legal pitfalls of being a landlord. On the other hand, you'll want to steer clear of lawyers who represent mostly tenants, since their sympathies (world view) are likely to be different from yours.

Types of Fee Arrangements With Lawyers

How you pay your lawyer depends on the type of legal services you need and the amount of legal work you have. Once an agreement is reached, it's a good idea to ask for a written fee agreement—basically an explanation of how the fees and costs will be billed and paid. As part of this, negotiate an overall cap on what you can be billed absent your specific agreement.

If a lawyer will be delegating some of the work on your case to a less-experienced associate, paralegal, or secretary, that work should be billed at a lower hourly rate. Be sure to get this information recorded in your initial written fee agreement.

There are four basic ways that lawyers charge for their services.

Hourly fees. In most parts of the United States, you can get competent services for your rental business for $150 to $350 an hour, with most lawyers billing in ten- or 15-minute increments. Comparison shopping among lawyers will help you avoid overpaying. But the cheapest hourly rate isn't necessarily the best. You can often benefit by hiring a more experienced landlord's attorney, even if her hourly rates are high, since she will be further along the learning curve than a general practitioner and should take less time to review and advise you on the particulars of your job.

Flat fees. Sometimes, a lawyer will quote you a flat fee for a specific job. For example, a lawyer may offer to represent you in court for routine eviction cases (such as for nonpayment of rent) that present little trouble, even when they are contested by the tenant (which is actually fairly rare). In a flat fee agreement, you pay the same amount regardless of how much time the lawyer spends on a particular job. If you own many rental units and anticipate providing a fair amount of business over the years, you have a golden opportunity to negotiate flat fees that are substantially below the lawyer's normal hourly rate. After all, the lawyer will see you as a very desirable client, since you'll generate continuing business for many years to come.

Retainer fees. In some circumstances, it can also make sense to hire a lawyer for a flat annual fee, or retainer, to handle all of your routine legal questions and business, such as noncontested eviction cases. You'll usually pay in equal monthly installments and, normally, the lawyer will bill you an additional amount for extraordinary services—such as representing you in a complicated eviction lawsuit. Since the lawyer can count on a reliable source of income, you can expect lower overall fees. Obviously, the key to making a retainer fee arrangement work is to have a written agreement clearly defining what's routine and what's extraordinary. This type of fee arrangement is more economically feasible for larger landlords (a dozen or more rental units) with regular legal needs. Also, retainer fee agreements are usually best negotiated after you and your lawyer have worked together long enough to have established a pattern—you know and trust each other well enough to work out a mutually beneficial arrangement.

Contingency fees. This is a percentage (such as one-third) of the amount the lawyer obtains for you in a negotiated settlement or through a trial. If the lawyer recovers nothing for you, there's no fee. Contingency fees are common in personal injury cases, but relatively unusual for the kinds of legal advice and representation landlords need.

Saving on Legal Fees

There are many ways to hold down the cost of legal services. Here is a short list of some of the key ways to save on legal fees.

Be organized. Especially when you are paying by the hour, it's important to gather important documents, write a short chronology of events, and concisely explain a problem to your lawyer. Since papers can get lost in a lawyer's office, keep a copy of everything that's important, such as your lease or rental agreement, move-in letter to new tenants, correspondence with tenants, repair logs, and other records.

Be prepared before you meet. Whenever possible, put your questions in writing and email, fax, or deliver them to your lawyer before meetings, even phone meetings. That way, the lawyer can find answers if he doesn't know them off the top of his head without having to call you back and charge for a separate phone conference. Early preparation also helps focus the meeting, so there is less of a chance of digressing into (and having to pay to discuss) unrelated topics.

Read trade journals in your field, such as publications of your local or state apartment association. Law changes continuously, so you'll want to keep up with specific legal developments affecting your business. Send pertinent articles to your lawyer—and encourage your lawyer to do the same for you. This can dramatically reduce legal research time.

Show that you're an important client. Mutual respect is key in an attorney-client relationship. The single most important way to show your lawyer how much you value the relationship is to pay your bills on time. Beyond that, let your lawyer know about plans for expansion and your business's possible future legal needs. And drop your lawyer a line when you've recommended him or her to your landlord colleagues.

Bundle your legal matters. You'll save money if you consult with your lawyer on several matters at one time. For example, in a one-hour conference, you may be able to review with your lawyer several items—such as a new lease or rental agreement clause, anti-age-discrimination policy, or advertisement for your apartment complex. Significant savings are possible, because lawyers commonly divide their billable hours into parts of an hour. For example, if your lawyer bills in 15-minute intervals and you only talk for five minutes, you are likely to be charged for the whole 15. So it usually pays to gather your questions and ask them all at once, rather than calling every time you have a question.

 TIP

Carefully review lawyer bills. Always read your bill. Like everyone else, lawyers make mistakes, and your charges may be wrong. For example, a "0.1" of an hour (six minutes) may be transposed into a "1.0" (one hour) when the data are entered into the billing system. That's $200 instead of $20 if your lawyer charges $200 per hour. If you have any questions about your bill, feel free to ask your lawyer. You hired him to provide a service, and you have the right to expect a clear explanation of your bill.

Use nonlawyer professionals for evictions. Look to "unlawful detainer assistants," "legal typing services," or "independent paralegals" for help with evictions in large metropolitan areas. For a flat fee that is usually much lower than what lawyers charge, and often at a faster pace, non-lawyer eviction services take the basic information from you, provide the appropriate eviction forms, and fill them out according to your instructions. This normally involves typing your eviction papers so they'll be accepted by the court, arranging for filing, and then serving the papers on the tenant.

Unlawful detainer assistants, paralegals, and typing services aren't lawyers, and most handle only routine cases. They can't give legal advice about the requirements of your specific case and can't represent you in court if the tenant contests the eviction suit. You must decide what steps to take in your case, and the information to put in the needed forms.

To find a nonlawyer eviction service, check with a landlords' association, or look online or in the telephone book under "Eviction Services," "Paralegals," or "Unlawful Detainer Assistant." Be sure the eviction service or typing service is reputable and experienced, as well as reasonably priced. Typically they charge by the page or by the document. Ask for references and check them. As a general matter, the longer a nonlawyer eviction service has been in business, the better.

 RESOURCE
Recommended reading on lawsuits. California landlords can handle eviction lawsuits themselves by using *The California Landlord's Law Book: Evictions*, by David Brown and Nils Rosenquest (Nolo). Contact your state or local apartment association for information on any step-by-step guides to evictions in your state.

Represent Yourself in Court: How to Prepare & Try a Winning Case, by Paul Bergman and Sara Berman (Nolo), offers more general advice on handling any civil lawsuit on your own or with a lawyer-coach's help.

Costs Can Mount Up

In addition to the fees they charge for their time, lawyers often bill for some costs as well—and these costs can add up quickly. When you receive a lawyer's bill, you may be surprised at both the amount of the costs and the variety of the services for which the lawyer expects reimbursement. These can include charges for:

- overnight mail
- messenger service
- expert witness fees
- court filing fees
- process servers
- work by investigators
- work by legal assistants or paralegals
- deposition transcripts
- online legal research, and
- travel.

Many lawyers absorb the cost of photocopying, faxes, phone calls, and the like as normal office overhead—part of the cost of doing business—but that's not always the case. So in working out the fee arrangements, discuss the costs you'll be expected to pay. If a lawyer is intent on nickel-and-diming you to death, look elsewhere. For example, if you learn the law office charges $3 or more for each page it faxes, red flags should go up. On the other hand, it is reasonable for a lawyer to pass along costs of things like court costs, process server fees, and any work by investigators.

 TIP
Lawyer fees are a tax-deductible business expense. If you visit your lawyer on a personal legal matter (such as reviewing a contract for the purchase of a house) and you also discuss a business problem (such as a new policy for hiring managers), ask your lawyer to allocate the time spent and send you separate bills. At tax time, you can easily list the business portion as a tax-deductible business expense.

Resolving Problems With Your Lawyer

If you see a problem emerging with your lawyer, nip it in the bud. Don't just sit back and fume; call or write your lawyer. Whatever it is that rankles, have an honest discussion about your feelings. Maybe you're upset because your lawyer hasn't kept you informed about what's going on in your lawsuit against your tenant for property damage, or maybe your lawyer has missed a promised deadline for reviewing your new system for handling maintenance and repair problems. Or maybe last month's bill was shockingly high or you question the breakdown of how your lawyer's time was spent.

Your Rights as a Client

As a client, you have the following rights:

- courteous treatment by your lawyer and staff members
- an itemized statement of services rendered and a full advance explanation of billing practices
- charges for agreed-upon fees and no more
- prompt responses to phone calls, emails, and letters
- confidential legal conferences, free from unwarranted interruptions
- up-to-date information on the status of your case
- diligent and competent legal representation, and
- clear answers to all questions.

Here's one way to test whether a lawyer-client relationship is a good one: Ask yourself if you feel able to talk freely with your lawyer about your degree of participation in any legal matter and your control over how the lawyer carries out a legal assignment. If you can't frankly discuss these sometimes-sensitive matters with your lawyer, fire that lawyer and hire another one. If you don't, you'll surely waste money on unnecessary legal fees and risk having legal matters turn out badly.

Remember that you're always free to change lawyers. If you do, be sure to fire your old lawyer before you hire a new one. Otherwise, you could find yourself being billed by both lawyers at the same time. Also, be sure to get all important legal documents back from a lawyer you no longer employ. Tell your new lawyer what your old one has done to date and pass on the file.

But firing a lawyer may not be enough. Here are some tips on resolving specific problems:

- If you have a dispute over fees, the local bar association may be able to mediate it for you.
- If a lawyer has violated legal ethics—for example, conflict of interest, overbilling, or not representing you zealously—the state agency that licenses lawyers may discipline or even disbar the lawyer. Although lawyer oversight groups are typically biased in favor of the legal profession, they will often take action if your lawyer has done something seriously wrong.
- Where a major mistake has been made—for example, a lawyer has missed the deadline for filing a case—you can sue for malpractice. Many lawyers carry malpractice insurance, and your dispute may be settled out of court.

Attorney Fees in a Lawsuit

If your lease or written rental agreement has an attorney fees provision (see Clause 19 of the form agreements in Chapter 2), you are entitled to recover your attorney fees if you win a lawsuit concerning the meaning and implementation of that agreement. There's no guarantee, however, that a judge will award attorney fees equal to your attorney's actual bill, or that you will ultimately be able to collect the money from the tenant or former tenant. Also, as discussed in Chapter 2, an attorney fees clause in your lease or rental agreement usually works both ways. Even if the clause doesn't say so, you're liable for the tenant's attorney fees if you lose. (Landlord's insurance does not cover such liability where the lawsuit is unrelated to items covered by the policy, such as eviction lawsuits by the landlord and security deposit refund suits by the tenant.)

Doing Your Own Legal Research

Using this book is a good way to educate yourself about the laws that affect your business—but one book is not enough by itself. Some landlord associations publish legal updates in their newsletters and on their websites to keep members abreast of new laws and regulations that affect their property.

While we recommend that you stay up to date on state, local, and federal laws that affect your landlording business (see the section just below), at one time or another you'll probably need to do some further research. For example, you may want to read a specific court case or research a more open-ended question about landlord-tenant law—for instance, your liability for an assault that took place on your rental property.

Lawyers aren't the only source for legal help. There's a lot you can do on your own. Every state has placed its statutes online (go to your state's main page, which will be at www.[postal code abbreviation].gov, and look for links to laws or statutes). Rules put out by federal and state regulatory agencies are often available online, too.

In addition to the Internet, law libraries are full of valuable information, such as state statutes that regulate the landlord-tenant relationship. Your first step is to find a law library that's open to the public. You may find such a library in your county courthouse or at your state capitol. Publicly funded law schools generally permit the public to use their libraries, and some private law schools grant access to their libraries—sometimes for a modest fee.

Don't overlook the reference department of the public library if you're in a large city. Many large public libraries have a fairly decent legal research collection. Also, ask about using the law library in your own lawyer's office. Some lawyers, on request, will share their books with their clients.

RESOURCE

Recommended reading on legal research. We don't have space here to show you how to do your own legal research in anything approaching a comprehensive fashion. To get started, see Nolo's Laws and Legal Research page at www.nolo.com/legal-research. Here you can learn about researching and understanding statutes, and get advice on finding local ordinances and court cases. To go further, we recommend *Legal Research: How to Find & Understand the Law,* by Stephen Elias and the Editors of Nolo (Nolo). This nontechnical book gives easy-to-use, step-by-step instructions on how find legal information.

Where to Find State, Local, and Federal Laws

Every landlord is governed by state, local, and federal law. In some areas, like antidiscrimination standards, laws overlap. When they do overlap, the stricter laws will apply. In practical terms, this usually means that the laws that give tenants the most protection (rights and remedies) will prevail over less-protective laws.

State Laws

If you're a typical landlord, you'll be primarily concerned with state law. State statutes regulate many aspects of the landlord-tenant relationship, including deposits, landlord's right of entry, discrimination, housing standards, rent rules,

repair and maintenance responsibilities, and eviction procedures.

The website of your state consumer protection agency or attorney general's office may provide a guide to state laws that affect landlords, and copies of the state statutes themselves. Also, representatives of state agencies can often help explain how the landlord-tenant laws they administer are interpreted. For a list of state consumer protection agencies, go to www.usa.gov/state-consumer.

We refer to many of the state laws affecting landlords throughout this book and include citations so that you can do additional research. State laws or codes are collected in volumes and are available online (discussed below) in many public libraries and in most law libraries. Depending on the state, statutes may be organized by subject matter or by title number ("chapter"), with each title covering a particular subject matter, or simply numbered sequentially, without regard to subject matter.

"Annotated codes" contain not only all the text of the laws (as do the regular codes), but also a brief summary of some of the court decisions (discussed below) interpreting each law and often references to treatises and articles that discuss the law. Annotated codes have comprehensive indexes by topic, and are kept up to date with paperback supplements ("pocket parts") stuck in a pocket inside the back cover of each volume.

Most states have made their statutes available online. You can find these on the website maintained by the Cornell Legal Information Institute (www.law.cornell.edu).

If you know the statute's number or citation (available in the charts in Appendix A of this book), you can go directly there. If you don't know the statute number, you can enter a keyword that is likely to be in it, such as "deposit" or "security deposit." If you just want to browse through the statutes, you can search the table of contents for your state's laws. With a little trial and error, you should have no trouble finding a particular landlord-tenant statute.

RESOURCE

For a complete discussion of landlord-tenant laws in California, see *The California Landlord's Law Book: Rights & Responsibilities*, by David Brown, Janet Portman, and Nils Rosenquest, and *The California Landlord's Law Book: Evictions*, by David Brown and Nils Rosenquest. These books are published by Nolo and are available at bookstores and public libraries. They may also be ordered directly from Nolo's website at www.nolo.com or by calling 800-728-3555.

Local Ordinances

Local ordinances, such as rent control rules, health and safety standards, and requirements that you pay interest on tenants' security deposits, will also affect your business. Many municipalities have websites—just search for the name of a particular city. Sometimes the site is nothing more than a not-so-slick public relations page, but sometimes it includes a large body of information, including local ordinances available for searching and downloading. Check out State & Local Government on the Net (www.statelocalgov.net) and Municode.com, good sources for finding local governments online.

Finally, your local public library or office of the city attorney, mayor, or city manager can provide information on local ordinances that affect landlords. If you own rental property in a city with rent control, be sure to get a copy of the ordinance, as well as all rules issued by the rent board covering rent increases and hearings.

Federal Statutes and Regulations

Congress has enacted laws, and federal agencies such as the U.S. Department of Housing and Urban Development (HUD) have adopted regulations, covering discrimination, wage and hour laws affecting employment of managers, and landlord responsibilities to disclose environmental health hazards. We refer to relevant federal agencies throughout this book and suggest you contact them for publications that explain federal laws affecting landlords, or copies of the federal statutes and regulations themselves.

We include citations for many of the federal laws affecting landlords throughout this book. The U.S. Code is the starting place for most federal statutory research. It consists of 50 separate numbered titles. Each title covers a specific subject matter.

Most federal regulations are published in the Code of Federal Regulations ("CFR"), organized by subject into 50 separate titles.

To access the U.S. Code online, visit the Cornell Legal Information Institute (www.law.cornell.edu). This site provides the entire U.S. Code as well as the Code of Federal Regulations. Finally, check www.usa.gov, the official U.S. website for government information.

How to Research Court Decisions

Sometimes the answer to a legal question cannot be found in a statute. This happens when:

- Court cases and opinions have greatly expanded or explained the statute, taking it beyond its obvious or literal meaning.
- The law that applies to your question has been made by judges, not legislators.

Court Decisions That Explain Statutes

Statutes and ordinances do not explain themselves. For example, a state law may require you to offer housing that is weatherproofed, but it may not tell you whether you must provide both storm windows and window screens. But others before you have had the same questions, and they may have come up in the context of a lawsuit. If a judge interpreted the statute and wrote an opinion on the matter, that written opinion, once published, will become "the law" as much as the statute itself. If a higher court (an appellate court) has also examined the question, then its opinion will rule.

To find out if there are written court decisions that interpret a particular statute or ordinance, look in an "annotated code" (discussed in "Where to Find State, Local, and Federal Laws," above). If you find a case that seems to answer your question, it's crucial to make sure that the decision you're reading is still "good law"—that a more recent opinion from a higher court has not reached a different conclusion. To make sure that you are relying on the latest and highest judicial pronouncement, you must use the library research tool known as *Shepard's*. Nolo's *Legal Research: How to Find & Understand the Law,* by Stephen Elias and the Editors of Nolo, has a good, easy-to-follow explanation of how to use the *Shepard's* system to expand and update your research.

Court Decisions That Make Law

Many laws that govern the way you must conduct your business do not even have an initial starting point in a statute or ordinance. These laws are entirely court-made, and are known as "common" law. An example is the implied warranty of habitability, which is court-made in many states.

Researching common law is more difficult than statutory law, because you do not have the launching pad of a statute or ordinance. With a little perseverance, however, you can certainly find your way to the cases that have developed and explained the legal concept you wish to understand. A good beginning is to ask the librarian for any "practice guides" written in the field of landlord-tenant law. These are outlines of the law, written for lawyers, that are kept up to date and are designed to get you quickly to key information. Because they are so popular and easy to use, they are usually kept behind the reference counter and cannot be checked out. More sophisticated research techniques, such as using a set of books called "Words and Phrases" (which sends you to cases based on keywords), are explained in the book *Legal Research,* mentioned above.

How to Read a Case Citation

If a case you have found in an annotated code (or through a practice guide or keyword search) looks important, you may want to read the opinion. You'll need the title of the case and its "citation," which is like an address for the set of books, volume, and page where the case can be found. Ask the law librarian for help.

Although it may look about as decipherable as hieroglyphics, once understood, a case citation gives lots of useful information in a small space. It tells you the names of the people or companies involved, the volume of the reporter (series of books) in which the case is published, the page number on which it begins, and the year in which the case was decided.

> **EXAMPLE:** *Smith Realty Co. v. Jones*, 123 N.Y.S.2d 456 (1994). Smith and Jones are the names of the parties having the legal dispute. The case is reported in volume 123 of the New York Supplement, Second Series, beginning on page 456; the court issued the decision in 1994.

Most states publish their own official state reports. All published state court decisions are also included in seven regional reporters. There are also special reports for U.S. Supreme Court and other federal court decisions.

State Landlord-Tenant Law Charts

How to Use the State Landlord-Tenant Law Charts

The State Landlord-Tenant Law Charts are comprehensive, 50-state charts that give you two kinds of information:

- citations for key statutes and cases, which you can use if you want to read the law yourself or look for more information (see the legal research discussion in Chapter 18), and
- the state rules themselves, such as notice periods and deposit limits—in other words, what the statutes and cases say.

When you're looking for information for your state, simply find your state along the left-hand list on the chart, and read to the right—you'll see the statute or case, and the rule.

A few subjects, such as the legality of nonrefundable fees, are addressed by only a handful of states. For these issues, we've put minicharts in chapters throughout the book. These charts, which list only the states that address the issue, include the following:

- States That Allow Nonrefundable Fees (Chapter 4)
- States That Require a Landlord-Tenant Checklist (Chapter 7)

State Landlord-Tenant Statutes

Here are some of the key statutes pertaining to landlord-tenant law in each state. In some states, important legal principles are contained in court opinions, not codes or statutes. Court-made law and rent stabilization—rent control—laws and regulations are not reflected in this chart.

State	Statute	State	Statute
Alabama	Ala. Code §§ 35-9-1 to 35-9-100; 35-9A-101 to 35-9A-603	Mississippi	Miss. Code Ann. §§ 89-7-1 to 89-8-29
Alaska	Alaska Stat. §§ 34.03.010 to 34.03.380	Missouri	Mo. Rev. Stat. §§ 441.005 to 441.880; §§ 535.010 to 535.300
Arizona	Ariz. Rev. Stat. Ann. §§ 12-1171 to 12-1183; 33-1301 to 33-1381; 33-301 to 33-381	Montana	Mont. Code Ann. §§ 70-24-101 to 70-27-117
Arkansas	Ark. Code Ann. §§ 18-16-101 to 18-16-306; 18-16-501 to 18-16-509; 18-17-101 to 18-17-913	Nebraska	Neb. Rev. Stat. §§ 76-1401 to 76-1449
		Nevada	Nev. Rev. Stat. Ann. §§ 118A.010 to 118A.530; 40.215 to 40.425
California	Cal. Civ. Code §§ 1925 to 1954.05; 1954.50 to 1954.605; 1961 to 1995.340	New Hampshire	N.H. Rev. Stat. Ann. §§ 540:1 to 540:29; 540-A:1 to 540-A:8; 540-B:1 to 540-B:10
Colorado	Colo. Rev. Stat. §§ 38-12-101 to 38-12-104; 38-12-301 to 38-12-302; 38-12-401 to 38-12-402; 38-12-501 to 38-12-511; 38-12-701; 13-40-101 to 13-40-123	New Jersey	N.J. Stat. Ann. §§ 46:8-1 to 46:8-50; 2A:42-1 to 42-96
		New Mexico	N.M. Stat. Ann. §§ 47-8-1 to 47-8-51
Connecticut	Conn. Gen. Stat. Ann. §§ 47a-1 to 47a-74	New York	N.Y. Real Prop. Law §§ 220 to 238; Real Prop. Acts §§ 701 to 853; Mult. Dwell. Law (all); Mult. Res. Law (all); Gen. Oblig. Law §§ 7-101 to 7-109
Delaware	Del. Code Ann. tit. 25, §§ 5101 to 5907		
Dist. of Columbia	D.C. Code Ann. §§ 42-3201 to 42-3610; D.C. Mun. Regs., tit. 14, §§ 300 to 311	North Carolina	N.C. Gen. Stat. §§ 42-1 to 42-14.2; 42-25.6 to 42-76
Florida	Fla. Stat. Ann. §§ 83.40 to 83.683	North Dakota	N.D. Cent. Code §§ 47-16-01 to 47-16-41
Georgia	Ga. Code Ann. §§ 44-7-1 to 44-7-81	Ohio	Ohio Rev. Code Ann. §§ 5321.01 to 5321.19
Hawaii	Haw. Rev. Stat. §§ 521-1 to 521-82	Oklahoma	Okla. Stat. Ann. tit. 41, §§ 101 to 136
Idaho	Idaho Code §§ 6-301 to 6-324; §§ 55-208 to 55-308	Oregon	Or. Rev. Stat. §§ 90.100 to 91.225
Illinois	735 Ill. Comp. Stat. §§ 5/9-201 to 321; 765 Ill. Comp. Stat. §§ 705/0.01 to 742/30; 765 Ill. Comp. Stat. §§ 750/1 to 750/35	Pennsylvania	68 Pa. Cons. Stat. Ann. §§ 250.101 to 399.18
		Rhode Island	R.I. Gen. Laws §§ 34-18-1 to 34-18-57
Indiana	Ind. Code Ann. §§ 32-31-1-1 to 32-31-9-15; 36-1-24.2-1 to 36-1-24.2-4	South Carolina	S.C. Code Ann. §§ 27-40-10 to 27-40-940
Iowa	Iowa Code Ann. §§ 562A.1 to 562A.37	South Dakota	S.D. Codified Laws Ann. §§ 43-32-1 to 43-32-32
Kansas	Kan. Stat. Ann. §§ 58-2501 to 58-2573	Tennessee	Tenn. Code Ann. §§ 66-28-101 to 66-28-521
Kentucky	Ky. Rev. Stat. Ann. §§ 383.010 to 383.715	Texas	Tex. Prop. Code Ann. §§ 91.001 to 92.355
Louisiana	La. Rev. Stat. Ann. §§ 9:3251 to 9:3261; La. Civ. Code Ann. art. 2668 to 2729	Utah	Utah Code Ann. §§ 57-17-1 to 57-17-5, 57-22-1 to 57-22-7
Maine	Me. Rev. Stat. Ann. tit. 14, §§ 6000 to 6046	Vermont	Vt. Stat. Ann. tit. 9, §§ 4451 to 4469a
Maryland	Md. Code Ann. [Real Prop.] §§ 8-101 to 8-604	Virginia	Va. Code Ann. §§ 55-217 to 55-248.40
Massachusetts	Mass. Gen. Laws Ann. ch. 186, §§ 1A to 29; ch. 186a, §§ 1 to 6	Washington	Wash. Rev. Code Ann. §§ 59.04.010 to 59.18.912
		West Virginia	W.Va. Code §§ 37-6-1 to 37-6A-6
Michigan	Mich. Comp. Laws §§ 554.131 to 554.201; 554.601 to 554.641	Wisconsin	Wis. Stat. Ann. §§ 704.01 to 704.95; Wis. Admin. Code ATCP §§ 134.01 to 134.10
Minnesota	Minn. Stat. Ann. §§ 504B.001 to 504B.471	Wyoming	Wyo. Stat. §§ 1-21-1201 to 1-21-1211; 34-2-128 to 34-2-129

State Rent Rules

Here are citations for statutes that set out rent rules in each state. When a state has no statute, the space is left blank. See the "Notice Required to Change or Terminate a Month-to-Month Tenancy" chart in this appendix for citations to raising rent.

State	When Rent Is Due	Grace Period	Where Rent Is Due	Late Fees
Alabama	Ala. Code § 35-9A-161 (c)		Ala. Code § 35-9A-161 (c)	
Alaska	Alaska Stat. § 34.03.020(c)		Alaska Stat. § 34.03.020(c)	
Arizona	Ariz. Rev. Stat. Ann. §§ 33-1314(C), 33-1368(B)		Ariz. Rev. Stat. Ann. § 33-1314(C)	Ariz. Rev. Stat. Ann. § 33-1368(B) [1]
Arkansas	Ark. Code Ann. § 18-17-401	Ark. Code Ann. §§ 18-17-701, 18-17-901	Ark. Code Ann. § 18-17-401	
California	Cal. Civ. Code § 1947		Cal. Civ. Code § 1962	*Orozco v. Casimiro*, 121 Cal. App.4th Supp. 7 (2004) [2]
Colorado				
Connecticut	Conn. Gen. Stat. Ann. § 47a-3a	Conn. Gen. Stat. Ann. § 47a-15a	Conn. Gen. Stat. Ann. § 47a-3a	Conn. Gen. Stat. Ann. §§ 47a-4(a)(8), 47a-15a [3]
Delaware	Del. Code Ann. tit. 25, § 5501(b)		Del. Code Ann. title 25, § 5501(b)	Del. Code Ann. tit. 25, § 5501(d) [4]
D.C.		D.C. Code Ann. § 42-3505.31		D.C. Code Ann. § 42-3505.31 [5]
Florida	Fla. Stat. Ann. § 83.46(1)			
Georgia				
Hawaii	Haw. Rev. Stat. § 521-21(b)		Haw. Rev. Stat. § 521-21(b)	Late charge cannot exceed 8% of the amount of rent due.
Idaho				
Illinois	735 Ill. Comp. Stat. Ann. § 5/9-218		735 Ill. Comp. Stat. Ann. § 5/9-218	
Indiana	*Watson v. Penn*, 108 Ind. 21 (1886), 8 N.E. 636 (1886)			
Iowa	Iowa Code Ann. § 562A.9(3)		Iowa Code Ann. § 562A.9(3)	Iowa Code Ann. § 562A.9 [6]
Kansas	Kan. Stat. Ann. § 58-2545(c)		Kan. Stat. Ann. § 58-2545(c)	
Kentucky	Ky. Rev. Stat. Ann. § 383.565(2)		Ky. Rev. Stat. Ann. § 383.565(2)	
Louisiana	La. Civ. Code Ann. art. 2703		La. Civ. Code Ann. art. 2703	
Maine		Me. Rev. Stat. Ann. tit. 14, § 6028		Me. Rev. Stat. Ann. tit. 14, § 6028 [7]
Maryland				Md. Code Ann. [Real Prop.] § 8-208(d)(3) [8]
Massachusetts		Mass. Gen. Laws Ann. ch. 186, § 15B(1)(c); ch. 239, § 8A		Mass. Gen. Laws Ann. ch. 186, § 15B(1)(c) [9]
Michigan	*Hilsendegen v. Scheich*, 21 N.W.2d 894 (1885)			

[1] Late fees must be set forth in a written rental agreement and be reasonable. (Arizona)

[2] Late fees will be enforced only if specified language is included in a written lease or rental agreement. (California)

[3] Landlords may not charge a late fee until 9 days after rent is due. (Connecticut)

[4] To charge a late fee, landlord must maintain an office in the county where the rental unit is located at which tenants can pay rent. If a landlord doesn't have a local office for this purpose, tenant has 3 extra days (beyond the due date) to pay rent before the landlord can charge a late fee. Late fee cannot exceed 5% of rent and cannot be imposed until the rent is more than 5 days late. (Delaware)

[5] Fee policy must be stated in the lease, and cannot exceed 5% of rent due, nor be imposed until rent is five days late (or later, if lease so provides). Landlord cannot evict for failure to pay late fee (may deduct unpaid fees from security deposit at end of tenancy). (D.C.)

[6] When rent is $700 per month or less, late fees cannot exceed $12 per day, or a total amount of $60 per month; when rent is more than $700 per month, fees cannot exceed $20 per day or a total amount of $100 per month. (Iowa)

[7] Late fees cannot exceed 4% of the amount due for 30 days. Landlord must notify tenants, in writing, of any late fee at the start of the tenancy, and cannot impose it until rent is 15 days late. (Maine)

[8] Late fees cannot exceed 5% of the rent due. (Maryland)

[9] Late fees, including interest on late rent, may not be imposed until the rent is 30 days late. (Massachusetts)

State Rent Rules (continued)

State	When Rent Is Due	Grace Period	Where Rent Is Due	Late Fees
Minnesota				Minn. Stat. Ann. § 504B.177 [10]
Mississippi				
Missouri	Mo. Rev. Stat. § 535.060			
Montana	Mont. Code Ann. § 70-24-201(2)(c)		Mont. Code Ann. § 70-24-201(2)(b)	
Nebraska	Neb. Rev. Stat. § 76-1414(3)		Neb. Rev. Stat. § 76-1414(3)	
Nevada	Nev. Rev. Stat. Ann. § 118A.210		Nev. Rev. Stat. Ann. § 118A	Nev. Rev. Stat. Ann. § 118A.200(3)(g), (210/5)(c) [11]
New Hampshire				
New Jersey		N.J. Stat. Ann. § 2A:42-6.1	N.J. Stat. Ann. § 2A:42-6.1	N.J. Stat. Ann. § 2A:42-6.1 [12]
New Mexico	N.M. Stat. Ann. § 47-8-15(B)		N.M. Stat. Ann. § 47-8-15(B)	N.M. Stat. Ann. § 47-8-15(D) [13]
New York				
North Carolina		N.C. Gen Stat. § 42-46		N.C. Gen. Stat. § 42-46 [14]
North Dakota	N.D. Cent. Code § 47-16-20			
Ohio				
Oklahoma	Okla. Stat. Ann. tit. 41, § 109	Okla. Stat. Ann. tit. 41, § 132(B)	Okla. Stat. Ann. tit. 41, § 109	*Sun Ridge Investors, Ltd. v. Parker*, 956 P.2d 876 (1998) [15]
Oregon	Or. Rev. Stat. § 90.220	Or. Rev. Stat. § 90.260	Or. Rev. Stat. § 90.220	Or. Rev. Stat. § 90.260 [16]
Pennsylvania				
Rhode Island	R.I. Gen. Laws § 34-18-15(c)	R.I. Gen. Laws § 34-18-35	R.I. Gen. Laws § 34-18-15(c)	
South Carolina	S.C. Code Ann. § 27-40-310(c)		S.C. Code Ann. § 27-40-310(c)	
South Dakota	S.D. Codified Laws Ann. § 43-32-12			
Tennessee	Tenn. Code Ann. § 66-28-201(c)	Tenn. Code Ann. § 66-28-201(d)	Tenn. Code Ann. § 66-28-201(c)	Tenn. Code Ann. § 66-28-201(d) [17]
Texas		Tex. Prop. Code Ann. § 92.019 [18]		
Utah				
Vermont	Vt. Stat. Ann. tit. 9, § 4455			
Virginia	Va. Code Ann. § 55-248.7(C)		Va. Code Ann. § 55-248.7(C)	
Washington				
West Virginia				
Wisconsin				
Wyoming				

[10] Late fee policy must be agreed to in writing, and may not exceed 8% of the overdue rent payment. The "due date" for late fee purposes does not include a date earlier than the usual rent due date, by which date a tenant earns a discount. (Minnesota)

[11] A court will presume that there is no late fee provision unless it is included in a written rental agreement, but the landlord can offer evidence to overcome that presumption. (Nevada)

[12] Landlord must wait 5 days before charging a late fee, but only when the premises are rented or leased by senior citizens receiving Social Security Old Age Pensions, Railroad Retirement Pensions, or other governmental pensions in lieu of Social Security Old Age Pensions; or when rented by recipients of Social Security Disability Benefits, Supplemental Security Income, or benefits under Work First New Jersey. (New Jersey)

[13] Late fee policy must be in the lease or rental agreement and may not exceed 10% of the rent specified per rental period. Landlord must notify the tenant of the landlord's intent to impose the charge no later than the last day of the next rental period immediately following the period in which the default occurred. (New Mexico)

[14] Late fee when rent is due monthly cannot be higher than $15 or 5% of the rental payment, whichever is greater (when rent is due weekly, may not be higher than $4.00 or 5% of the rent, whichever is greater); and may not be imposed until the rent is 5 days late. A late fee may be imposed only one time for each late rental payment. A late fee for a specific late rental payment may not be deducted from a subsequent rental payment so as to cause the subsequent rental payment to be in default. (North Carolina)

[15] Preset late fees are invalid. (Oklahoma)

[16] Landlord must wait 4 days after the rent due date before imposing a late fee, and must disclose the late fee policy in the rental agreement. A flat fee must be "reasonable." A daily late fee may not be more than 6% of a reasonable flat fee, and cannot add up to more than 5% of the monthly rent. (Oregon)

[17] Landlord can't charge a late fee until the rent is 5 days late (the day rent is due is counted as the first day). If day five is a Sunday or legal holiday, landlord cannot impose a fee if the rent is paid on the next business day. Fee can't exceed 10% of the amount past due. (Tennessee)

[18] Late fee provision must be included in a written lease and cannot be imposed until the rent remains unpaid one full day after the date it is due. The fee is valid only if it is a reasonable estimate of uncertain damages to the landlord that are incapable of precise calculation. Landlord may charge an initial fee and a daily fee for each day the rent is late. (Texas)

State Rules on Notice Required to Change or Terminate a Month-to-Month Tenancy

Except where noted, the amount of notice a landlord must give to increase rent or change another term of the rental agreement in a month-to-month tenancy is the same as that required to end a month-to-month tenancy. Be sure to check state and local rent control laws, which may have different notice requirements.

State	Tenant	Landlord	Statute	Comments
Alabama	30 days	30 days	Ala. Code § 35-9A-441	No state statute on the amount of notice required to change rent or other terms
Alaska	30 days	30 days	Alaska Stat. § 34.03.290(b)	
Arizona	30 days	30 days	Ariz. Rev. Stat. Ann. § 33-1375	
Arkansas	30 days	30 days	Ark. Code Ann. § 18-17-704	No state statute on the amount of notice required to change rent or other terms
California	30 days	30 or 60 days	Cal. Civ. Code § 1946; Cal. Civ. Code § 827a	30 days to change rental terms, but if landlord is raising the rent, tenant gets 60 days' notice if the sum of this and all prior rent increases during the previous 12 months is more than 10% of the lowest rent charged during that time. 60 days to terminate (landlord), 30 days (tenant).
Colorado	21 days	21 days	Colo. Rev. Stat. § 13-40-107	
Connecticut		3 days	Conn. Gen. Stat. Ann. § 47a-23	Landlord must provide 3 days' notice to terminate tenancy. Landlord is not required to give a particular amount of notice of a proposed rent increase unless prior notice was previously agreed upon.
Delaware	60 days	60 days	Del. Code Ann. tit. 25, §§ 5106, 5107	After receiving notice of landlord's proposed change of terms, tenant has 15 days to terminate tenancy. Otherwise, changes will take effect as announced.
District of Columbia	30 days	30 days	D.C. Code Ann. § 42-3202	No state statute on the amount of notice required to change rent or other terms
Florida	15 days	15 days	Fla. Stat. Ann. § 83.57	No state statute on the amount of notice required to change rent or other terms
Georgia	30 days	60 days	Ga. Code Ann. §§ 44-7-6, 44-7-7	No state statute on the amount of notice required to change rent or other terms
Hawaii	28 days	45 days	Haw. Rev. Stat. §§ 521-71, 521-21(d)	
Idaho	One month	One month	Idaho Code §§ 55-208, 55-307	Landlords must provide 15 days' notice to increase rent or change tenancy.
Illinois	30 days	30 days	735 Ill. Comp. Stat. § 5/9-207	
Indiana	One month	One month	Ind. Code Ann. §§ 32-31-1-1, 32-31-5-4	Unless agreement states otherwise, landlord must give 30 days' written notice to modify written rental agreement.
Iowa	30 days	30 days	Iowa Code Ann. §§ 562A.34, 562A.13(5)	To end or change a month-to-month agreement, landlord must give written notice at least 30 days before the next time rent is due (not including any grace period).
Kansas	30 days	30 days	Kan. Stat. Ann. § 58-2570	No state statute on the amount of notice required to change rent or other terms
Kentucky	30 days	30 days	Ky. Rev. Stat. Ann. § 383.695	

State Rules on Notice Required to Change or Terminate a Month-to-Month Tenancy (continued)

State	Tenant	Landlord	Statute	Comments
Louisiana	10 days	10 days	La. Civ. Code Art. 2728	No state statute on the amount of notice required to change rent or other terms
Maine	30 days	30 days	Me. Rev. Stat. Ann. tit. 14 §§ 6002, 6015	Landlord must provide 45 days' notice to increase rent.
Maryland	One month	One month	Md. Code Ann. [Real Prop.] § 8-402(b)(3), (b)(4)	Two months' notice required in Montgomery County (single-family rentals excepted) and Baltimore City.
Massachusetts	See comments	See comments	Mass. Gen. Laws Ann. ch. 186, § 12	Interval between days of payment or 30 days, whichever is longer.
Michigan	One month	One month	Mich. Comp. Laws § 554.134	
Minnesota	See comments	See comments	Minn. Stat. Ann. § 504B.135	For terminations, interval between time rent is due or three months, whichever is less; no state statute on the amount of notice required to change rent or other terms
Mississippi	30 days	30 days	Miss. Code Ann. § 89-8-19	No state statute on the amount of notice required to change rent or other terms
Missouri	One month	One month	Mo. Rev. Stat. § 441.060	No state statute on the amount of notice required to change rent or other terms
Montana	30 days	30 days	Mont. Code Ann. §§ 70-24-441, 70-26-109	Landlord may change terms of tenancy with 15 days' notice.
Nebraska	30 days	30 days	Neb. Rev. Stat. § 76-1437	No state statute on the amount of notice required to change rent or other terms
Nevada	30 days	30 days	Nev. Rev. Stat. Ann. §§ 40.251, 118A.300	Landlords must provide 45 days' notice to increase rent. Tenants 60 years old or older, or physically or mentally disabled, may request an additional 30 days' possession, but only if they have complied with basic tenant obligations as set forth in Nev. Rev. Stat. Chapter 118A (termination notices must include this information).
New Hampshire	30 days	30 days	N.H. Rev. Stat. Ann. §§ 540:2, 540:3	Landlord may terminate only for just cause.
New Jersey	One month	One month	N.J. Stat. Ann. §§ 2A:18-56, 2A:18-61.1	Landlord may terminate only for just cause.
New Mexico	30 days	30 days	N.M. Stat. Ann. §§ 47-8-37, 47-8-15(F)	Landlord must deliver rent increase notice at least 30 days before rent due date.
New York	One month	One month	N.Y. Real Prop. Law § 232-b	No state statute on the amount of notice required to change rent or other terms
North Carolina	7 days	7 days	N.C. Gen. Stat. § 42-14	No state statute on the amount of notice required to change rent or other terms
North Dakota	30 days	30 days	N.D. Cent. Code §§ 47-16-15, 47-16-07	Tenant may terminate with 25 days' notice if landlord has changed the terms of the lease.
Ohio	30 days	30 days	Ohio Rev. Code Ann. § 5321.17	No state statute on the amount of notice required to change rent or other terms
Oklahoma	30 days	30 days	Okla. Stat. Ann. tit. 41, § 111	No state statute on the amount of notice required to change rent or other terms

State Rules on Notice Required to Change or Terminate a Month-to-Month Tenancy (continued)

State	Tenant	Landlord	Statute	Comments
Oregon	30 days or 72 hours (lack of bedroom exit only)	Landlord may not increase the rent during the first year, and must give 90 days' notice for any rent increases thereafter.	Or. Rev. Stat. §§ 91.070, 90.427, 90.460	To terminate, 30 days for occupancies of one year or less; 60 days for occupancies of more than one year (but only 30 days if the property is sold and other conditions are met). Tenant may terminate on 72 hours' notice if landlord's failure to provide proper bedroom emergency exit, properly noticed, has not been corrected. Temporary occupants are not entitled to notice. (Or. Rev. Stat. § 90.275.)
Pennsylvania			No statute	
Rhode Island	30 days	30 days	R.I. Gen. Laws §§ 34-18-16.1, 34-18-37	Landlord must provide 30 days' notice to increase rent.
South Carolina	30 days	30 days	S.C. Code Ann. § 27-40-770	No state statute on the amount of notice required to change rent or other terms
South Dakota	One month	One month	S.D. Codified Laws Ann. §§ 43-32-13, 43-8-8	If tenant (or spouse or minor child) is in the active duty in the military, landlord must give two months' notice, in the absence of tenant misconduct, sale of the property, or passing of the property into the landlord's estate.
Tennessee	30 days	30 days	Tenn. Code Ann. § 66-28-512	No state statute on the amount of notice required to change rent or other terms
Texas	One month	One month	Tex. Prop. Code Ann. § 91.001	Landlord and tenant may agree in writing to different notice periods, or none at all. No state statute on the amount of notice required to change rent or other terms
Utah		15 days	Utah Code Ann. § 78B-6-802	No state statute on the amount of notice required to change rent or other terms
Vermont	One rental period, unless written lease says otherwise	30 days	Vt. Code Ann. tit. 9, §§ 4467, 4456(d)	If there is no written rental agreement, for tenants who have continuously resided in the unit for two years or less, 60 days' notice to terminate; for those who have resided longer than two years, 90 days. If there is a written rental agreement, for tenants who have lived continuously in the unit for two years or less, 30 days; for those who have lived there longer than two years, 60 days.
Virginia	30 days	30 days	Va. Code Ann. §§ 55-248.37, 55-248.7, 55-225.32	Rental agreement may provide for a different notice period. No state statute on the amount of notice required to change rent or other terms, but landlord must abide by notice provisions in the rental agreement, if any.
Washington	20 days	20 days	Wash. Rev. Code Ann. §§ 59.18.200, 59.18.140	Landlord must give 30 days' notice to change rent or other lease terms.
West Virginia	One month	One month	W.Va. Code § 37-6-5	No state statute on the amount of notice required to change rent or other terms
Wisconsin	28 days	28 days	Wis. Stat. Ann. § 704.19	No state statute on the amount of notice required to change rent or other terms
Wyoming			No statute	

State Security Deposit Rules

Here are the statutes and rules that govern a landlord's collection and retention of security deposits. Many states require landlords to disclose, at or near the time they collect the deposit, information about how deposits may be used, as noted in the Disclosure or Requirement section. Required disclosures of other issues, such as a property's history of flooding, are in the chart, "Required Landlord Disclosures."

Alabama

Ala. Code § 35-9A-201

Exemption: Security deposit rules do not apply to a resident purchaser under a contract of sale (but do apply to a resident who has an option to buy), nor to the continuation of occupancy by the seller or a member of the seller's family for a period of not more than 36 months after the sale of a dwelling unit or the property of which it is a part.

Limit: One month's rent, except for pet deposits, deposits to cover undoing tenant's alterations, deposits to cover tenant activities that pose increased liability risks.

Deadline for Landlord to Itemize and Return Deposit: 60 days after termination of tenancy and delivery of possession.

Alaska

Alaska Stat. § 34.03.070

Limit: Two months' rent, unless rent exceeds $2,000 per month. Landlord may ask for an additional month's rent as deposit for a pet that is not a service animal, but may use it only to remedy pet damage.

Disclosure or Requirement: Orally or in writing, landlord must disclose the conditions under which landlord may withhold all or part of the deposit.

Separate Account: Required.

Advance notice of deduction: Not required.

Deadline for Landlord to Itemize and Return Deposit: 14 days if the tenant gives proper notice to terminate tenancy; 30 days if the tenant does not give proper notice or if landlord has deducted amounts needed to remedy damage caused by tenant's failure to maintain the property (Alaska Stat. § 34.03.120).

Arizona

Ariz. Rev. Stat. Ann. § 33-1321

Exemption: Excludes, among others, occupancy under a contract of sale of a dwelling unit or the property of which it is a part, if the occupant is the purchaser or a person who succeeds to his interest; occupancy by an employee of a landlord as a manager or custodian whose right to occupancy is conditional upon employment in and about the premises.

Limit: One and one-half months' rent.

Disclosure or Requirement: If landlord collects a nonrefundable fee, its purpose must be stated in writing. All fees not designated as nonrefundable are refundable.

Advance notice of deduction: Not required.

Deadline for Landlord to Itemize and Return Deposit: 14 days; tenant has the right to be present at final inspection.

Arkansas

Ark. Code Ann. §§ 18-16-303 to 18-16-305

Exemption: Excludes, among others, occupancy under a contract of sale of a dwelling unit or the property of which it is a part, if the occupant is the purchaser or a person who succeeds to his or her interest; occupancy by an employee of a landlord whose right to occupancy is conditional upon employment in and about the premises; and landlord who owns five or fewer rental units, unless these units are managed by a third party for a fee.

Limit: Two months' rent.

Advance notice of deduction: Not required.

Deadline for Landlord to Itemize and Return Deposit: 60 days.

California

Cal. Civ. Code §§ 1950.5, 1940.5(g)

Limit: Two months' rent (unfurnished); 3 months' rent (furnished). Add extra one-half month's rent for waterbed.

Advance notice of deduction: Required.

Deadline for Landlord to Itemize and Return Deposit: 21 days.

Colorado

Colo. Rev. Stat. §§ 38-12-102 to 38-12-104

Limit: No statutory limit.

Advance notice of deduction: Not required.

Deadline for Landlord to Itemize and Return Deposit: One month, unless lease agreement specifies longer period of time (which may be no more than 60 days); 72 hours (not

State Security Deposit Rules (continued)

counting weekends or holidays) if a hazardous condition involving gas equipment requires tenant to vacate.

Connecticut

Conn. Gen. Stat. Ann. § 47a-21

Exemption: Excludes, among others, occupancy under a contract of sale of a dwelling unit or the property of which the unit is a part, if the occupant is the purchaser or a person who succeeds to his interest; and occupancy by a personal care assistant or other person who is employed by a person with a disability to assist and support such disabled person with daily living activities or housekeeping chores and is provided dwelling space in the personal residence of such disabled person as a benefit or condition of employment.

Limit: Two months' rent (tenant under 62 years of age); one month's rent (tenant 62 years of age or older). Tenants who paid a deposit in excess of one month's rent, who then turn 62 years old, are entitled, upon request, to a refund of the amount that exceeds one month's rent.

Separate Account: Required.

Interest Payment: Interest payments must be made annually (or credited toward rent, at the landlord's option) and no later than 30 days after termination of tenancy. The interest rate must be equal to the average rate paid on savings deposits by insured commercial banks, rounded to the nearest 0.1%, as published by the Federal Reserve Board Bulletin.

Advance notice of deduction: Not required.

Deadline for Landlord to Itemize and Return Deposit: 30 days, or within 15 days of receiving tenant's forwarding address, whichever is later.

Delaware

Del. Code Ann. tit. 25, §§ 5514, 5311

Limit: One month's rent on leases for one year or more. For month to month tenancies, no limit for the first year, but after that, the limit is one month's rent (at the expiration of one year, landlord must give tenant a credit for any deposit held by the landlord that is in excess of one month's rent). No limit for furnished units. Tenant may offer to supply a surety bond in lieu of or in conjunction with a deposit, which landlord may elect to receive.

Separate Account: Required. Orally or in writing, the landlord must disclose to the tenant the location of the security deposit account.

Advance notice of deduction: Not required.

Deadline for Landlord to Itemize and Return Deposit: 20 days.

District of Columbia

D.C. Code Ann § 42-3502.17; D.C. Mun. Regs. tit. 14, §§ 308 to 310

Exemption: Tenants in rent-stabilized units as of July 17, 1985 cannot be asked to pay a deposit.

Limit: One month's rent.

Disclosure or Requirement: In the lease, rental agreement, or receipt, landlord must state the terms and conditions under which the security deposit was collected (to secure tenant's obligations under the lease or rental agreement).

Separate Account: Required.

Interest Payment: Interest payments at the prevailing statement savings rate must be made at termination of tenancy.

Advance notice of deduction: Not required.

Deadline for Landlord to Itemize and Return Deposit: 45 days.

Florida

Fla. Stat. Ann. §§ 83.49, 83.43 (12)

Exemption: Occupancy under a contract of sale of a dwelling unit or the property of which it is a part in which the buyer has paid at least 12 months' rent or in which the buyer has paid at least 1 month's rent and a deposit of at least 5 percent of the purchase price of the property; cooperative properties, condominiums, and transient residencies.

Limit: No statutory limit.

Disclosure or Requirement: Within 30 days of receiving the security deposit, the landlord must disclose in writing whether it will be held in an interest- or non-interest-bearing account; the name of the account depository; and the rate and time of interest payments. Landlord who collects a deposit must include in the lease the disclosure statement contained in Florida Statutes § 83.49.

Separate Account: Landlord may post a security bond securing all tenants' deposits instead.

State Security Deposit Rules (continued)

Interest Payment: Interest payments, if any (account need not be interest-bearing) must be made annually and at termination of tenancy. However, no interest is due a tenant who wrongfully terminates the tenancy before the end of the rental term.

Advance notice of deduction: Required.

Deadline for Landlord to Itemize and Return Deposit: 15 to 60 days depending on whether tenant disputes deductions.

Georgia

Ga. Code Ann. §§ 44-7-30 to 44-7-37

Exemption: Landlord who owns ten or fewer rental units, unless these units are managed by an outside party, need not supply written list of preexisting damage, nor place deposit in an escrow account. Rules for returning the deposit still apply.

Limit: No statutory limit.

Disclosure or Requirement: Landlord must give tenant a written list of preexisting damage to the rental before collecting a security deposit.

Separate Account: Required. Landlord must place the deposit in an escrow account in a state or federally regulated depository, and must inform the tenant of the location of this account. Landlord may post a security bond securing all tenants' deposits instead.

Advance notice of deduction: Required.

Deadline for Landlord to Itemize and Return Deposit: One month.

Hawaii

Haw. Rev. Stat. § 521-44

Limit: One month's rent. Landlord may require an additional one month's rent as security deposit for tenants who keep a pet.

Advance notice of deduction: Not required.

Deadline for Landlord to Itemize and Return Deposit: 14 days.

Idaho

Idaho Code § 6-321

Limit: No statutory limit.

Advance notice of deduction: Not required.

Deadline for Landlord to Itemize and Return Deposit: 21 days, or up to 30 days if landlord and tenant agree.

Illinois

765 Ill. Comp. Stat. 710/1; 715/1 to 715/3

Limit: No statutory limit.

Disclosure or Requirement: If a lease specifies the cost for repair, cleaning, or replacement of any part of the leased premises; or the cleaning or repair of any component of the building or common area that will not be replaced, the landlord may withhold the dollar amount specified in the lease. Landlord's itemized statement must reference the specified dollar amount(s) and include a copy of the lease clause.

Interest Payment: Landlords who rent 25 or more units in either a single building or a complex located on contiguous properties must pay interest on deposits held for more than six months. The interest rate is the rate paid for minimum deposit savings accounts by the largest commercial bank in the state, as of December 31 of the calendar year immediately preceding the start of the tenancy.

Advance notice of deduction: Not required.

Deadline for Landlord to Itemize and Return Deposit: For properties with 5 or more units, 30 to 45 days, depending on whether tenant disputes deductions or if statement and receipts are furnished.

Indiana

Ind. Code Ann. §§ 32-31-3-9 to 32-31-3-19

Exemption: Does not apply to, among others, occupancy under a contract of sale of a rental unit or the property of which the rental unit is a part if the occupant is the purchaser or a person who succeeds to the purchaser's interest; and occupancy by an employee of a landlord whose right to occupancy is conditional upon employment in or about the premises. Does apply to leases signed after July 1, 2008, that contain an option to purchase.

Limit: No statutory limit.

Advance notice of deduction: Not required.

Deadline for Landlord to Itemize and Return Deposit: 45 days.

State Security Deposit Rules (continued)

Iowa

Iowa Code Ann. § 562A.12

Limit: Two months' rent.

Separate Account: Required.

Interest Payment: Interest payment, if any (account need not be interest-bearing) must be made at termination of tenancy. Interest earned during first five years of tenancy belongs to landlord.

Advance notice of deduction: Not required.

Deadline for Landlord to Itemize and Return Deposit: 30 days.

Kansas

Kan. Stat. Ann. §§ 58-2550, 58-2548

Exemption: Excludes, among others, occupancy under a contract of sale of a dwelling unit or the property of which it is a part, if the occupant is the purchaser or a person who succeeds to the purchaser's interest; and occupancy by an employee of a landlord whose right to occupancy is conditional upon employment in and about the premises.

Limit: One month's rent (unfurnished); one and one-half months' rent (furnished); for pets, add extra one-half month's rent.

Advance notice of deduction: Not required.

Deadline for Landlord to Itemize and Return Deposit: 30 days.

Kentucky

Ky. Rev. Stat. Ann. § 383.580

Limit: No statutory limit.

Disclosure or Requirement: Orally or in writing, landlord must disclose where the security deposit is being held and the account number.

Separate Account: Required.

Advance notice of deduction: Required.

Deadline for Landlord to Itemize and Return Deposit: 30 to 60 days depending on whether tenant disputes deductions.

Louisiana

La. Rev. Stat. Ann. § 9:3251

Limit: No statutory limit.

Advance notice of deduction: Not required.

Deadline for Landlord to Itemize and Return Deposit: One month.

Maine

Me. Rev. Stat. Ann. tit. 14, §§ 6031 to 6038

Exemption: Entire security deposit law does not apply to rental unit that is part of structure with five or fewer units, one of which is occupied by landlord.

Limit: Two months' rent.

Disclosure or Requirement: Upon request by the tenant, landlord must disclose orally or in writing the account number and the name of the institution where the security deposit is being held.

Separate Account: Required.

Advance notice of deduction: Not required.

Deadline for Landlord to Itemize and Return Deposit: 30 days (if written rental agreement) or 21 days (if tenancy at will).

Maryland

Md. Code Ann. [Real Prop.] § 8-203, § 8-203.1, § 8-208

Limit: Two months' rent.

Disclosure or Requirement: Landlord must provide a receipt that describes tenant's rights to move-in and move-out inspections (and to be present at each), and right to receive itemization of deposit deductions and balance, if any; and penalties for landlord's failure to comply. Landlord must include this information in the lease.

Separate Account: Required. Landlord may hold all tenants' deposits in secured certificates of deposit, or in securities issued by the federal government or the State of Maryland.

Interest Payment: For security deposits of $50 or more, when landlord has held the deposit for at least six months: Within 45 days of termination of tenancy, interest must be paid at the daily U.S. Treasury yield curve rate for 1 year, as of the first business day of each year, or 1.5% a year, whichever is greater, less any damages rightfully withheld. Interest accrues monthly but is not compounded, and no interest is due for any period less than one month. (See the Department of Housing and Community Development website for a calculator.) Deposit must be held in a Maryland banking institution.

Advance notice of deduction: Required.

State Security Deposit Rules (continued)

Deadline for Landlord to Itemize and Return Deposit: 45 days.

Massachusetts

Mass. Gen. Laws Ann. ch. 186, § 15B

Limit: One month's rent.

Disclosure or Requirement: At the time of receiving a security deposit, landlord must furnish a receipt indicating the amount of the deposit; the name of the person receiving it, and, if received by a property manager, the name of the lessor for whom the security deposit is received; the date on which it is received; and a description of the premises leased or rented. The receipt must be signed by the person receiving the security deposit.

Separate Account: Required. Within 30 days of receiving security deposit, landlord must disclose the name and location of the bank in which the security deposit has been deposited, and the amount and account number of the deposit.

Interest Payment: Landlord must pay tenant 5% interest per year or the amount received from the bank (which must be in Massachusetts) that holds the deposit. Interest should be paid yearly, and within 30 days of termination date. Interest will not accrue for the last month for which rent was paid in advance.

Advance notice of deduction: Not required.

Deadline for Landlord to Itemize and Return Deposit: 30 days.

Michigan

Mich. Comp. Laws §§ 554.602 to 554.616

Limit: One and one-half months' rent.

Disclosure or Requirement: Within 14 days of tenant's taking possession of the rental, landlord must furnish in writing the landlord's name and address for receipt of communications, the name and address of the financial institution or surety where the deposit will be held, and the tenant's obligation to provide in writing a forwarding mailing address to the landlord within 4 days after termination of occupancy. The notice shall include the following statement in 12-point boldface type that is at least 4 points larger than the body of the notice or lease agreement: "You must notify your landlord in writing within 4 days after you move of a forwarding address where you can be reached and where you will receive mail; otherwise your landlord shall be relieved of sending you an itemized list of damages and the penalties adherent to that failure."

Separate Account: Required. Landlord must place deposits in a regulated financial institution, and may use the deposits as long as the landlord deposits with the secretary of state a cash or surety bond.

Advance notice of deduction: Required. Not a typical advance notice provision: Tenants must dispute the landlord's stated deductions within 7 days of receiving the itemized list and balance, if any, or give up any right to dispute them.

Deadline for Landlord to Itemize and Return Deposit: 30 days.

Minnesota

Minn. Stat. Ann. §§ 504B.175, 504B.178, 504B.195

Limit: No statutory limit. If landlord collects a "prelease deposit" and subsequently rents to tenant, landlord must apply the prelease deposit to the security deposit.

Disclosure or Requirement: Before collecting rent or a security deposit, landlord must provide a copy of all outstanding inspection orders for which a citation has been issued, pertaining to a rental unit or common area, specifying code violations that threaten the health or safety of the tenant, and all outstanding condemnation orders and declarations that the premises are unfit for human habitation. Citations for violations that do not involve threats to tenant health or safety must be summarized and posted in an obvious place. With some exceptions, landlord who has received notice of a contract for deed cancellation or notice of a mortgage foreclosure sale must so disclose before entering a lease, accepting rent, or accepting a security deposit; and must furnish the date on which the contract cancellation period or the mortgagor's redemption period ends.

Interest Payment: Landlord must pay 1% simple, noncompounded interest per year. (Deposits collected before 8/1/03 earn interest at 3%, up to 8/1/03, then begin earning at 1%.) Any interest amount less than $1 is excluded.

Advance notice of deduction: Not required.

Deadline for Landlord to Itemize and Return Deposit: Three weeks after tenant leaves and landlord receives

State Security Deposit Rules (continued)

forwarding address; five days if tenant must leave due to building condemnation.

Mississippi

Miss. Code Ann. § 89-8-21

Limit: No statutory limit.

Advance notice of deduction: Not required.

Deadline for Landlord to Itemize and Return Deposit: 45 days.

Missouri

Mo. Ann. Stat. § 535.300

Limit: Two months' rent.

Advance notice of deduction: Not required.

Deadline for Landlord to Itemize and Return Deposit: 30 days.

Montana

Mont. Code Ann. §§ 70-25-101 to 70-25-206

Limit: No statutory limit.

Advance notice of deduction: Required. Tenant is entitled to advance notice of cleaning charges, but only if such cleaning is required as a result of tenant's negligence and is not part of the landlord's cyclical cleaning program.

Deadline for Landlord to Itemize and Return Deposit: 30 days; 10 days if no deductions.

Nebraska

Neb. Rev. Stat. § 76-1416

Limit: One month's rent (no pets); one and one-quarter months' rent (pets).

Advance notice of deduction: Not required.

Deadline for Landlord to Itemize and Return Deposit: 14 days.

Nevada

Nev. Rev. Stat. Ann. §§ 118A.240 to 118A.250

Limit: Three months' rent; if both landlord and tenant agree, tenant may use a surety bond for all or part of the deposit.

Disclosure or Requirement: Lease or rental agreement must explain the conditions under which the landlord will refund the deposit.

Advance notice of deduction: Not required.

Deadline for Landlord to Itemize and Return Deposit: 30 days.

New Hampshire

N.H. Rev. Stat. Ann. §§ 540-A:5 to 540-A:8; 540-B:10

Exemption: Entire security deposit law does not apply to landlord who leases a single-family residence and owns no other rental property, or landlord who leases rental units in an owner-occupied building of five units or fewer (exemption does not apply to any individual unit in owner-occupied building that is occupied by a person 60 years of age or older).

Limit: One month's rent or $100, whichever is greater; when landlord and tenant share facilities, no statutory limit.

Disclosure or Requirement: Unless tenant has paid the deposit by personal or bank check, or by a check issued by a government agency, landlord must provide a receipt stating the amount of the deposit and the institution where it will be held. Regardless of whether a receipt is required, landlord must inform tenant that if tenant finds any conditions in the rental in need of repair, tenant may note them on the receipt or other written instrument, and return either within five days.

Separate Account: Required. Upon request, landlord must disclose the account number, the amount on deposit, and the interest rate. Landlord may post a bond covering all deposits instead of putting deposits in a separate account.

Interest Payment: Landlord who holds a security deposit for a year or longer must pay interest at a rate equal to the rate paid on regular savings accounts in the New Hampshire bank, savings & loan, or credit union where it's deposited. If a landlord mingles security deposits in a single account, the landlord must pay the actual interest earned proportionately to each tenant. A tenant may request the interest accrued every three years, 30 days before that year's tenancy expires. The landlord must comply with the request within 15 days of the expiration of that year's tenancy.

Advance notice of deduction: Not required.

Deadline for Landlord to Itemize and Return Deposit: 30 days; for shared facilities, if the deposit is more than 30 days' rent, landlord must provide written agreement acknowledging receipt and specifying when deposit will be returned—if no written agreement, 20 days after tenant vacates.

State Security Deposit Rules (continued)

New Jersey

N.J. Stat. Ann. §§ 46:8-19, 44:8-21.1, 44:8-21.2, 44:8-26

Exemption: Security deposit law does not apply to owner-occupied buildings with three or fewer units unless tenant gives 30 days' written notice to the landlord of the tenant's wish to invoke the law.

Limit: One and one-half months' rent. Any additional security deposit, collected annually, may be no greater than 10% of the current security deposit.

Separate Account: Required. Within 30 days of receiving the deposit and every time the landlord pays the tenant interest, landlord must disclose the name and address of the banking organization where the deposit is being held, the type of account, current rate of interest, and the amount of the deposit.

Interest Payment: Landlord with 10 or more units must invest deposits as specified by statute or place deposit in an insured money market fund account, or in another account that pays quarterly interest at a rate comparable to the money market fund. Landlords with fewer than 10 units may place deposit in an interest-bearing account in any New Jersey financial institution insured by the FDIC. All landlords may pay tenants interest earned on account annually or credit toward payment of rent due.

Advance notice of deduction: Not required.

Deadline for Landlord to Itemize and Return Deposit: 30 days; five days in case of fire, flood, condemnation, or evacuation.

New Mexico

N.M. Stat. Ann. § 47-8-18

Limit: One month's rent (for rental agreement of less than one year); no limit for leases of one year or more.

Interest Payment: Landlord who collects a deposit larger than than one month's rent on a year's lease must pay interest, on an annual basis, equal to the passbook interest.

Advance notice of deduction: Not required.

Deadline for Landlord to Itemize and Return Deposit: 30 days.

New York

N.Y. Gen. Oblig. Law §§ 7-103 to 7-108

Limit: No statutory limit for nonregulated units.

Disclosure or Requirement: If deposit is placed in a bank, landlord must disclose the name and address of the banking organization where the deposit is being held, and the amount of such deposit.

Separate Account: Statute requires that deposits not be co-mingled with landlord's personal assets, but does not explicitly require placement in a banking institution (however, deposits collected in buildings of six or more units must be placed in New York bank accounts).

Interest Payment: Landlord who rents out nonregulated units in buildings with five or fewer units need not pay interest. Interest must be paid at the "prevailing rate" on deposits received from tenants who rent units in buildings containing six or more units. The landlord in every rental situation may retain an administrative fee of 1% per year on the sum deposited. Interest can be subtracted from the rent, paid at the end of the year, or paid at the end of the tenancy according to the tenant's choice.

Advance notice of deduction: Not required.

Deadline for Landlord to Itemize and Return Deposit: A "reasonable time."

North Carolina

N.C. Gen. Stat. §§ 42-50 to 42-56

Exemption: Not applicable to single rooms rented on a weekly, monthly, or annual basis.

Limit: One and one-half months' rent for month-to-month rental agreements; two months' rent if term is longer than two months; may add an additional "reasonable" nonrefundable pet deposit.

Disclosure or Requirement: Within 30 days of the beginning of the lease term, landlord must disclose the name and address of the banking institution where the deposit is located.

Separate Account: Required. The landlord may, at his option, furnish a bond from an insurance company licensed to do business in the state.

Advance notice of deduction: Not required.

Deadline for Landlord to Itemize and Return Deposit: 30 days; if landlord's claim against the deposit cannot be finalized within that time, landlord may send an interim accounting and a final accounting within 60 days of the tenancy's termination.

State Security Deposit Rules (continued)

North Dakota

N.D. Cent. Code § 47-16-07.1

Limit: One month's rent. If tenant has a pet that is not a service or companion animal that tenant keeps as a reasonable accommodation under fair housing laws, an additional pet deposit of up to $2,500 or two months' rent, whichever is greater. To encourage renting to persons with felony convictions, landlords may charge up to two months' rent as security.

Separate Account: Required.

Interest Payment: Landlord must pay interest if the period of occupancy is at least nine months. Money must be held in a federally insured interest-bearing savings or checking account for benefit of the tenant. Interest must be paid upon termination of the lease.

Advance notice of deduction: Not required.

Deadline for Landlord to Itemize and Return Deposit: 30 days.

Ohio

Ohio Rev. Code Ann. § 5321.16

Limit: No statutory limit.

Interest Payment: Any deposit in excess of $50 or one month's rent, whichever is greater, must bear interest on the excess at the rate of 5% per annum if the tenant stays for six months or more. Interest must be paid annually and upon termination of tenancy.

Advance notice of deduction: Not required.

Deadline for Landlord to Itemize and Return Deposit: 30 days.

Oklahoma

Okla. Stat. Ann. tit. 41, § 115

Limit: No statutory limit.

Separate Account: Required.

Advance notice of deduction: Not required.

Deadline for Landlord to Itemize and Return Deposit: 45 days.

Oregon

Or. Rev. Stat. § 90.300

Limit: No statutory limit. Landlord may not impose or increase deposit within first year unless parties agree to modify the rental agreement to allow for a pet or other cause, and the imposition or increase relates to that modification.

Advance notice of deduction: Not required.

Deadline for Landlord to Itemize and Return Deposit: 31 days.

Pennsylvania

68 Pa. Cons. Stat. Ann. §§ 250.511a to 250.512

Limit: Two months' rent for first year of renting; one month's rent during second and subsequent years of renting.

Disclosure or Requirement: For deposits over $100, landlord must deposit them in a federally or state-regulated institution, and give tenant the name and address of the banking institution and the amount of the deposit.

Separate Account: Required. Instead of placing deposits in a separate account, landlord may purchase a bond issued by a bonding company authorized to do business in the state.

Interest Payment: Tenant who occupies rental unit for two or more years is entitled to interest beginning with the 25th month of occupancy. Landlord must pay tenant interest (minus 1% fee) at the end of the third and subsequent years of the tenancy.

Advance notice of deduction: Not required.

Deadline for Landlord to Itemize and Return Deposit: 30 days.

Rhode Island

R.I. Gen. Laws § 34-18-19

Limit: One month's rent.

Advance notice of deduction: Not required.

Deadline for Landlord to Itemize and Return Deposit: 20 days.

South Carolina

S.C. Code Ann. § 27-40-410

Limit: No statutory limit.

Advance notice of deduction: Not required.

Deadline for Landlord to Itemize and Return Deposit: 30 days.

South Dakota

S.D. Codified Laws Ann. § 43.32-6.1, § 43-32-24

State Security Deposit Rules (continued)

Limit: One month's rent (higher deposit may be charged if special conditions pose a danger to maintenance of the premises).

Advance notice of deduction: Not required.

Deadline for Landlord to Itemize and Return Deposit: Two weeks and must supply reasons if withholding any portion; 45 days for a written, itemized accounting, if tenant requests it.

Tennessee

Tenn. Code Ann. § 66-28-301

Limit: No statutory limit.

Exemption: Does not apply in counties having a population of less than 75,000, according to the 2010 federal census or any subsequent federal census.

Separate Account: Required. Orally or in writing, landlord must disclose the location of the separate account (but not the account number) used by landlord for the deposit.

Advance notice of deduction: Required.

Texas

Tex. Prop. Code Ann. §§ 92.101 to 92.109

Limit: No statutory limit.

Advance notice of deduction: Not required.

Deadline for Landlord to Itemize and Return Deposit: 30 days. Landlord need not refund deposit if lease requires tenant to give written notice of tenant's intention to surrender the premises.

Utah

Utah Code Ann. §§ 57-17-1 to 57-17-5

Limit: No statutory limit.

Disclosure or Requirement: For written leases or rental agreements only, if part of the deposit is nonrefundable, landlord must disclose this feature.

Advance notice of deduction: Not required.

Deadline for Landlord to Itemize and Return Deposit: 30 days.

Vermont

Vt. Stat. Ann. tit. 9, § 4461

Limit: No statutory limit.

Advance notice of deduction: Not required.

Deadline for Landlord to Itemize and Return Deposit: 14 days; 60 days if the rental is seasonal and not intended as the tenant's primary residence.

Virginia

Va. Code Ann. § 55-248.15:1

Exemption: Single-family residences are exempt where the owner(s) are natural persons or their estates who own in their own name no more than two single-family residences subject to a rental agreement. Exemption applies to the entire Virginia Residential Landlord and Tenant Act.

Limit: Two months' rent.

Advance notice of deduction: Not required.

Deadline for Landlord to Itemize and Return Deposit: 45 days. Lease can provide for expedited processing and specify an administrative fee for such processing, which will apply only if tenant requests it with a separate written document. Landlord must give tenant written notice of tenant's right to be present at a final inspection.

Washington

Wash. Rev. Code Ann. §§ 59.18.260 to 59.18.285

Exemption: Security deposit rules do not apply to a lease of a single-family dwelling for a year or more, or to any lease of a single-family dwelling containing a bona fide option to purchase by the tenant, provided that an attorney for the tenant has approved on the face of the agreement any lease so exempted. Rules also do not apply to occupancy by an employee of a landlord whose right to occupy is conditioned upon employment in or about the premises; or the lease of single-family rental in connection with a lease of land to be used primarily for agricultural purposes; or rental agreements for seasonal agricultural employees.

Limit: No statutory limit.

Disclosure or Requirement: In the lease, landlord must disclose the circumstances under which all or part of the deposit may be withheld, and must provide a receipt with the name and location of the banking institution where the deposit is being held. No deposit may be collected unless the rental agreement is in writing and a written checklist or statement specifically describing the condition and cleanliness of or existing damages to the premises and furnishings is provided to the tenant at the start of the tenancy.

State Security Deposit Rules (continued)

Separate Account: Not required.

Advance notice of deduction: Not required.

Deadline for Landlord to Itemize and Return Deposit: 21 days.

West Virginia

W.Va. Code § 37-6A-1 et seq.

Deadline for Landlord to Itemize and Return Deposit: 60 days from the date the tenancy has terminated, or within 45 days of the occupancy of a subsequent tenant, whichever is shorter. If the damage exceeds the amount of the security deposit and the landlord has to hire a contractor to fix it, the notice period is extended 15 days.

Wisconsin

Wis. Admin. Code ATCP 134.04, 134.06; Wis. Stat. § 704.28

Exemption: Security deposit rules do not apply to a dwelling unit occupied, under a contract of sale, by the purchaser of the dwelling unit or the purchaser's successor in interest; or to a dwelling unit that the landlord provides free to any person, or that the landlord provides as consideration to a person whom the landlord currently employs to operate or maintain the premises.

Limit: No statutory limit.

Disclosure or Requirement: Before accepting the deposit, landlord must inform tenant of tenant's inspection rights, disclose all habitability defects, and show tenant any outstanding building and housing code violations, inform tenant of the means by which shared utilities will be billed, and inform tenant if utilities are not paid for by landlord.

Advance notice of deduction: Not required.

Deadline for Landlord to Itemize and Return Deposit: 21 days.

Wyoming

Wyo. Stat. §§ 1-21-1207, 1-21-1208

Limit: No statutory limit.

Disclosure or Requirement: Lease or rental agreement must state whether any portion of a deposit is non-refundable, and landlord must give tenant written notice of this fact when collecting the deposit.

Advance notice of deduction: Not required.

Deadline for Landlord to Itemize and Return Deposit: 30 days, when applying it to unpaid rent (or within 15 days of receiving tenant's forwarding address, whichever is later); additional 30 days allowed for deductions due to damage.

Required Landlord Disclosures

Many states require landlords to inform tenants of important state laws or individual landlord policies, either in the lease or rental agreement or in another writing. Common disclosures include a landlord's imposition of nonrefundable fees (where permitted), tenants' rights to move-in checklists, and the identity of the landlord or landlord's agent or manager. Disclosures concerning the security deposit are in the chart, "State Security Deposit Rules."

Alabama

Owner or agent identity: Landlord must disclose to the tenant in writing at or before the commencement of the tenancy the name and address of the person authorized to manage the premises, and an owner of the premises or a person authorized to act for and on behalf of the owner for the purpose of service of process and for the purpose of receiving notices and demands. (Exception: does not apply to resident purchaser under a contract of sale (but does apply to a resident who has an option to buy), nor to the continuation of occupancy by the seller or a member of the seller's family for a period of not more than 36 months after the sale of a dwelling unit or the property of which it is a part.) (Ala. Code § 35-9A-202)

Alaska

Owner or agent identity: Landlord must disclose to the tenant in writing at or before the commencement of the tenancy the name and address of the person authorized to manage the premises, and an owner of the premises or a person authorized to act for and on behalf of the owner for the purpose of service of process and for the purpose of receiving notices and demands. (Alaska Stat. § 34.03.080)

Extended absence: The rental agreement must require that the tenant notify the landlord of an anticipated extended absence from the premises in excess of seven days; however, the notice may be given as soon as reasonably possible after the tenant knows the absence will exceed seven days. (Alaska Stat. § 34.03.150)

Arizona

Nonrefundable fees permitted? Yes. The purpose of all nonrefundable fees or deposits must be stated in writing. Any fee or deposit not designated as nonrefundable is refundable. (Ariz. Rev. Stat. § 33-1321)

Move-in checklist required? Yes. Tenants also have the right to be present at a move-out inspection. (Ariz. Rev. Stat. § 33-1321)

Separate utility charges: If landlord charges separately for gas, water, wastewater, solid waste removal, or electricity by installing a submetering system, landlord may recover the charges imposed on the landlord by the utility provider, plus an administrative fee for the landlord for actual administrative costs only, and must disclose separate billing and fee in the rental agreement. If landlord uses a ratio utility billing system, the rental agreement must contain a specific description of the ratio utility billing method used to allocate utility costs. (Ariz. Rev. Stat. § 33-1314.01)

Owner or agent identity: Landlord must disclose to the tenant in writing at or before the commencement of the tenancy the name and address of the person authorized to manage the premises, and an owner of the premises or a person authorized to act for and on behalf of the owner for the purpose of service of process and for the purpose of receiving notices and demands. (Ariz. Rev. Stat. § 33-1322)

Business tax pass-through: If the landlord pays a local tax based on rent and that tax increases, landlord may pass through the increase by increasing the rent upon 30 days' notice (but not before the new tax is effective), but only if the landlord's right to adjust the rent is disclosed in the rental agreement. (Ariz. Rev. Stat. § 33-1314)

Availability of Landlord and Tenant Act: Landlord must inform tenant in writing that the residential Landlord and Tenant Act is available on the Arizona department of housing's website. (Ariz. Rev. Stat. § 33-1322)

Bedbug information: Landlords must provide existing and new tenants with educational materials on bedbugs, including information and physical descriptions, prevention and control measures, behavioral attraction risk factors, information from federal, state, and local centers for disease control and prevention, health or housing agencies, nonprofit housing organizations, or information developed by the landlord. (Ariz. Rev. Stat. § 33-1319)

Arkansas

No disclosure statutes.

Required Landlord Disclosures (continued)

California

Nonrefundable fees permitted? No. (Cal. Civ. Code § 1950.5(m))

Move-in checklist required? No

Must fee policy be stated in the rental agreement? N/A

Registered sexual offender database: Landlords must include the following language in their rental agreements: "Notice: Pursuant to Section 290.46 of the Penal Code, information about specified registered sex offenders is made available to the public via an Internet Web site maintained by the Department of Justice at www.meganslaw.ca.gov. Depending on an offender's criminal history, this information will include either the address at which the offender resides or the community of residence and ZIP Code in which he or she resides." (Cal. Civ. Code § 2079.10a)

Tenant paying for others' utilities: Prior to signing a rental agreement, landlord must disclose whether gas or electric service to tenant's unit also serves other areas, and must disclose the manner by which costs will be fairly allocated. (Cal. Civ. Code § 1940.9)

Ordnance locations: Prior to signing a lease, landlord must disclose known locations of former federal or state ordnance in the neighborhood (within one mile of rental). (Cal. Civ. Code § 1940.7)

Toxic mold: Prior to signing a rental agreement, landlord must provide written disclosure when landlord knows, or has reason to know, that mold exceeds permissible exposure limits or poses a health threat. Landlords must distribute a consumer handbook, developed by the State Department of Health Services, describing the potential health risks from mold. (Cal. Health & Safety Code §§ 26147, 26148)

Pest control service: When the rental agreement is signed, landlord must provide tenant with any pest control company disclosure landlord has received, which describes the pest to be controlled, pesticides used and their active ingredients, a warning that pesticides are toxic, and the frequency of treatment under any contract for periodic service. (Cal. Civ. Code § 1940.8, Cal. Bus. & Prof. Code § 8538)

Intention to demolish rental unit: Landlords or their agents who have applied for a permit to demolish a rental unit must give written notice of this fact to prospective tenants, before accepting any deposits or screening fees. (Cal. Civ. Code § 1940.6)

No-smoking policy: For leases and rental agreements signed after January 1, 2012: If the landlord prohibits or limits the smoking of tobacco products on the rental property, the lease or rental agreement must include a clause describing the areas where smoking is limited or prohibited (does not apply if the tenant has previously occupied the dwelling unit). For leases and rental agreements signed before January 1, 2012: A newly adopted policy limiting or prohibiting smoking is a change in the terms of the tenancy (will not apply to lease-holding tenants until they renew their leases; tenants renting month-to-month must be given 30 days' written notice). Does not preempt any local ordinances prohibiting smoking in effect on January 1, 2012. (Cal. Civ. Code § 1947.5)

Notice of default: Lessors of single-family homes and multifamily properties of four units or less, who have received a notice of default for the rental property that has not been rescinded, must disclose this fact to potential renters before they sign a lease. The notice must be in English or in Spanish, Chinese, Tagalog, Vietnamese, or Korean (if the lease was negotiated in one of these languages), and must follow the language specified in Cal. Civ. Code § 2924.85(d).

Flooding: In leases or rental agreements signed after July 1, 2018, landlord must disclose, in at least eight-point type, that the property is in a special flood hazard area of an area of potential flooding if the landlord has actual knowledge of this fact. Actual knowledge includes receipt from a public agency so identifying the property; the fact that the owner carries flood insurance; or that the property is in an area in which the owner's mortgage holder requires the owner to carry flood insurance. Disclosure must advise tenant that additional information can be had at the Office of Emergency Services' website, and must include the web address for the MYHazards tool maintained by the Office. Disclosure must advise tenant that owner's insurance will not cover loss to tenant's property, and must recommend that tenant consider purchasing renters' insurance that will cover loss due to fire, flood, or other risk of loss. Disclosure must

Required Landlord Disclosures (continued)

note that the owner is not required to provide additional information. (Cal. Govt. Code § 8589.45)

Colorado

No disclosure statutes.

Connecticut

Miscellaneous disclosures:

Common interest community: When rental is in a common interest community, landlord must give tenant written notice before signing a lease. (Conn. Gen. Stat. Ann. § 47a-3e)

Owner or agent identity: Before the beginning of the tenancy, landlord must disclose the name and address of the person authorized to manage the premises and the person who is authorized to receive all notices, demands, and service of process. (Conn. Gen. Stat. Ann. § 47a-6)

Summary of Landlord-Tenant Code: A summary of the code, as prepared by the Consumer Protection Unit of the Attorney General's office, must be given to tenants at the beginning of the rental term. Failure to do so enables the tenant to plead ignorance of the law as a defense.

Delaware

Nonrefundable fees permitted? No, except for an optional service fee for actual services rendered, such as a pool fee or tennis court fee. Tenant may elect, subject to the landlord's acceptance, to purchase an optional surety bond instead of or in combination with a security deposit. (*Stoltz Management Co. v. Phillip*, 593 A.2d 583 (1990); Del. Code Ann. tit. 25, § 5311)

Owner or agent identity: On each written rental agreement, the landlord must prominently disclose the names and usual business addresses of all persons who are owners of the rental unit or the property of which the rental unit is a part, or the names and business addresses of their appointed resident agents. (25 Del. Code Ann. § 5105)

Summary of Landlord-Tenant Law: A summary of the Landlord-Tenant Code, as prepared by the Consumer Protection Unit of the Attorney General's Office or its successor agency, must be given to the new tenant at the beginning of the rental term. If the landlord fails to provide the summary, the tenant may plead ignorance of the law as a defense. (25 Del. Code Ann. § 5118)

District of Columbia

Rental regulations: At the start of every new tenancy, landlord must give tenant a copy of the District of Columbia Municipal Regulations, CDCR Title 14, Housing, Chapter 3, Landlord and Tenant; and a copy of Title 14, Housing, Chapter 1, § 101 (Civil Enforcement Policy) and Chapter 1, § 106 (Notification of Tenants Concerning Violations).

Florida

Nonrefundable fees permitted? Yes, allowed by custom, although there is no statute.

Owner or agent identity: The landlord, or a person authorized to enter into a rental agreement on the landlord's behalf, must disclose in writing to the tenant, at or before the commencement of the tenancy, the name and address of the landlord or a person authorized to receive notices and demands on the landlord's behalf. (Fla. Stat. Ann. § 83.50)

Radon: In all leases, landlord must include this warning: "RADON GAS: Radon is a naturally occurring radioactive gas that, when it has accumulated in a building in sufficient quantities, may present health risks to persons who are exposed to it over time. Levels of radon that exceed federal and state guidelines have been found in buildings in Florida. Additional information regarding radon and radon testing may be obtained from your county health department." (Fla. Stat. Ann. § 404.056)

Georgia

Nonrefundable fees permitted? Yes, nonrefundable fees, such as pet fees, are allowed by custom, although there is no statute.

Move-in checklist required? Landlord cannot collect a security deposit until he has given tenant a list of preexisting damage, but this isn't an interactive checklist. (Ga. Code Ann. § 44-7-33)

Flooding: Before signing a lease, if the living space or attachments have been damaged by flooding three or more times within the past five years, landlord must so disclose in writing. (Ga. Code Ann. § 44-7-20)

Owner or agent identity: When or before a tenancy begins, landlord must disclose in writing the names and addresses of the owner of record or a person authorized to act for the owner for purposes of service of process

Required Landlord Disclosures (continued)

and receiving and receipting demands and notices; and the person authorized to manage the premises. If such information changes during the tenancy, landlord must advise tenant within 30 days in writing or by posting a notice in a conspicuous place. (Ga. Code Ann. § 44-7-3)

Former residents, crimes: If asked by a prospective tenant, landlord must answer truthfully when questioned about whether the rental was the site of a homicide or other felony, or a suicide or a death by accidental or natural causes; or whether it was occupied by a person who was infected with a virus or any other disease that has been determined by medical evidence as being highly unlikely to be transmitted through the occupancy of a dwelling place presently or previously occupied by such an infected person. (Ga. Code Ann. § 44-1-16)

Hawaii

Nonrefundable fees permitted? No.

Other fees: The landlord may not require or receive from or on behalf of a tenant at the beginning of a rental agreement any money other than the money for the first month's rent and a security deposit as provided in this section. (Haw. Rev. Stat. § 521-43)

Owner or agent identity: Landlord must disclose name of owner or agent; if owner lives in another state or on another island, landlord must disclose name of agent on the island. (Haw. Rev. Stat. § 521-43)

Move-in checklist required? Yes. (Haw. Rev. Stat. § 541-42)

Tax excise number: Landlord must furnish its tax excise number so that tenant can file for a low-income tax credit. (Haw. Rev. Stat. § 521-43)

Idaho

No disclosure statutes.

Illinois

Utilities: Where tenant pays a portion of a master metered utility, landlord must give tenant a copy in writing either as part of the lease or another written agreement of the formula used by the landlord for allocating the public utility payments among the tenants. (765 Ill. Comp. Stat. § 740/5)

Rent concessions: Any rent concessions must be described in the lease, in letters not less than one-half inch in height consisting of the words "Concession Granted," including a memorandum on the margin or across the face of the lease stating the amount or extent and nature of each such concession. Failure to comply is a misdemeanor. (765 Ill. Comp. Stat. §§ 730/0 to 730/6.)

Radon: Landlords are not required to test for radon, but if the landlord tests and learns that a radon hazard is present in the dwelling unit, landlord must disclose this information to current and prospective tenants. If a tenant notifies a landlord that a radon test indicates the existence of a radon hazard in the rental unit, landlord must disclose that risk to any prospective tenant of that unit, unless a subsequent test by the landlord shows that a radon hazard does not exist. Requirements do not apply if the dwelling unit is on the third or higher story above ground level, or when the landlord has undertaken mitigation work and a subsequent test shows that a radon hazard does not exist. (420 Ill. Comp. Stat. §§ 46/15, 46/25)

Indiana

Owner or agent identity: Landlord's agent must disclose in writing the name and address of a person living in Indiana who is authorized to manage the property and to act as the owner's agent. (Ind. Code Ann. § 32-31-3-18)

Iowa

Owner or agent identity: Landlord must disclose to the tenant in writing at or before the commencement of the tenancy the name and address of the person authorized to manage the premises, and an owner of the premises or a person authorized to act for and on behalf of the owner for the purpose of service of process and for the purpose of receiving notices and demands. (Iowa Code § 562A.13)

Utilities: For shared utilities, landlord must fully explain utility rates, charges, and services to the prospective tenant before the rental agreement is signed. (Iowa Code § 562A.13)

Contamination: The landlord or a person authorized to enter into a rental agreement on behalf of the landlord must disclose to each tenant, in writing before the commencement of the tenancy, whether the property is listed in the comprehensive environmental response compensation and liability information system maintained by the federal Environmental Protection Agency. (Iowa Code § 562A.13)

Required Landlord Disclosures (continued)

Kansas

Move-in checklist required? Yes. Within 5 days of move-in, landlord and tenant must jointly inventory the rental. (Kan. Stat. Ann. § 58-2548)

Owner or agent identity: Landlord must disclose to the tenant in writing at or before the commencement of the tenancy the name and address of the person authorized to manage the premises, and an owner of the premises or a person authorized to act for and on behalf of the owner for the purpose of service of process and for the purpose of receiving notices and demands. (Kan. Stat. Ann. § 58-2551)

Kentucky

Move-in checklist required? Yes. Landlord and tenant must complete a checklist before landlord can collect a security deposit. (Ky. Rev. Stat. Ann. § 383.580)

Owner or agent identity: Landlord must disclose to the tenant in writing at or before the commencement of the tenancy the name and address of the person authorized to manage the premises, and an owner of the premises or a person authorized to act for and on behalf of the owner for the purpose of service of process and for the purpose of receiving notices and demands. (Ky. Rev. Stat. Ann. § 383.585)

Louisiana

Foreclosure: Before entering into a lease or rental agreement, landlord must disclose to potential tenants their right to receive notification of any future foreclosure action. If the premises are currently subject to a foreclosure action, landlord must also disclose this in writing. (La. Stat. Ann. § 9:3260.1)

Maine

Utilities: No landlord may lease or offer to lease a dwelling unit in a multiunit residential building where the expense of furnishing electricity to the common areas or other area not within the unit is the sole responsibility of the tenant in that unit, unless both parties to the lease have agreed in writing that the tenant will pay for such costs in return for a stated reduction in rent or other specified fair consideration that approximates the actual cost of electricity to the common areas. (14 Me. Rev. Stat. Ann. § 6024)

Energy efficiency: Landlord must provide to potential tenants who will pay for energy costs (or upon request from others) a residential energy efficiency disclosure statement in accordance with Title 35-A, section 10006, subsection 1 that includes, but is not limited to, information about the energy efficiency of the property. Before a tenant enters into a contract or pays a deposit to rent or lease a property, the landlord must provide the statement to the tenant, obtain the tenant's signature on the statement, and sign the statement. The landlord must retain the signed statement for at least 3 years. Alternatively, the landlord may include in the application for the residential property the name of each supplier of energy that previously supplied the unit, if known, and the following statement: "You have the right to obtain a 12-month history of energy consumption and the cost of that consumption from the energy supplier." (14 Me. Rev. Stat. Ann. § 6030-C)

Radon: By 2012 and every ten years thereafter, landlord must test for radon and disclose to prospective and existing tenants the date and results of the test and the risks of radon, using a disclosure form prepared by the Department of Health and Human Services (tenant must sign acknowledgment of receipt). (14 Me. Rev. Stat. Ann. § 6030-D)

Bedbugs: Before renting a dwelling unit, landlord must disclose to a prospective tenant if an adjacent unit or units are currently infested with or are being treated for bedbugs. Upon request from a tenant or prospective tenant, landlord must disclose the last date that the dwelling unit the landlord seeks to rent or an adjacent unit or units were inspected for a bedbug infestation and found to be free of a bedbug infestation. (Me. Rev. Stat. Ann. § 6021-A)

Smoking policy: Landlord must give tenant written disclosure stating whether smoking is prohibited on the premises, allowed on the entire premises, or allowed in limited areas of the premises. If the landlord allows smoking in limited areas on the premises, the notice must identify the areas on the premises where smoking is allowed. Disclosure must be in the lease or separate written notice, landlord must disclose before tenant signs a lease or pays a deposit, and must obtain a written acknowledgment of notification from the tenant. (14 Me. Rev. Stat. Ann. § 6030-E)

Required Landlord Disclosures (continued)

Maryland

Move-in checklist required? Yes. Before collecting a deposit, landlord must supply a receipt with details on move-in and move-out inspections, and the receipt must be part of the lease. (Md. Code Ann. [Real Prop.] § 8-203.1)

Habitation: A lease must include a statement that the premises will be made available in a condition permitting habitation, with reasonable safety, if that is the agreement, or if that is not the agreement, a statement of the agreement concerning the condition of the premises; and the landlord's and the tenant's specific obligations as to heat, gas, electricity, water, and repair of the premises. (Md. Code Ann. [Real Prop.] § 8-208)

Owner or agent identity: The landlord must include in a lease or post the name and address of the landlord; or the person, if any, authorized to accept notice or service of process on behalf of the landlord. (Md. Code Ann. [Real Prop.] § 8-210)

Massachusetts

Move-in checklist required? Yes, if landlord collects a security deposit. (186 Mass. Gen. Laws § 15B(2)(c))

Insurance: Upon tenant's request and w/in 15 days, landlord must furnish the name of the company insuring the property against loss or damage by fire and the amount of insurance provided by each such company and the name of any person who would receive payment for a loss covered by such insurance. (Mass. Gen. Laws Ann. 186 § 21)

Tax Escalation: If real estate taxes increase, landlord may pass on a proportionate share of the increase to the tenant only if the lease discloses that in the event of an increase, the tenant will be required to pay only the proportion of the increase as the tenant's leased unit bears to the property being taxed (that proportion must be disclosed in the lease). In addition, the lease must state that if the landlord receives a tax abatement, landlord will refund a proportionate share of the abatement, minus reasonable attorneys' fees. (186 Mass. Gen. Laws § 15C)

Utilities: Landlord may not charge for water unless the lease specifies the charge and the details of the water sub-metering and billing arrangement. (186 Mass. Gen. Laws § 22(f))

Michigan

Move-in checklist required? Yes. However, the requirement does not need to be stated in the lease. (Mich. Comp. Laws § 554.608)

May landlord charge nonrefundable fees? Yes. (*Stutelberg v. Practical Management Co.*, 245 N.W.2d 737 (1976))

Owner or agent identity: A rental agreement must include the name and address at which notice can be given to the landlord. (Mich. Comp. Laws § 554.634)

Truth in Renting Act: A rental agreement must also state in a prominent place in type not smaller than the size of 12-point type, or in legible print with letters not smaller than 1/8 inch, a notice in substantially the following form: "NOTICE: Michigan law establishes rights and obligations for parties to rental agreements. This agreement is required to comply with the Truth in Renting Act. If you have a question about the interpretation or legality of a provision of this agreement, you may want to seek assistance from a lawyer or other qualified person." (Mich. Comp. Laws § 554.634)

Rights of domestic violence victims: A rental agreement or lease may contain a provision stating, "A tenant who has a reasonable apprehension of present danger to him or her or his or her child from domestic violence, sexual assault, or stalking may have special statutory rights to seek a release of rental obligation under MCL 554.601b." If the rental agreement or lease does not contain such a provision, the landlord must post an identical written notice visible to a reasonable person in the landlord's property management office, or deliver written notice to the tenant when the lease or rental agreement is signed. (Mich. Comp. Laws § 554.601b)

Minnesota

Owner or agent identity: Landlord must disclose to the tenant in writing at or before the commencement of the tenancy the name and address of the person authorized to manage the premises, and an owner of the premises or a person authorized to act for and on behalf of the owner for the purpose of service of process and for the purpose of receiving notices and demands. (Minn. Stat. Ann. § 504B.181)

Required Landlord Disclosures (continued)

Outstanding inspection orders, condemnation orders, or declarations that the property is unfit: The landlord must disclose the existence of any such orders or declarations before the tenant signs a lease or pays a security deposit. (Minn. Stat. Ann. § 504B.195)

Buildings in financial distress: Once a landlord has received notice of a deed cancellation or notice of foreclosure, landlord may not enter into a periodic tenancy where the tenancy term is more than two months, or a lease where the lease extends beyond the redemption period (other restrictions may apply). (Minn. Stat. Ann. § 504B.151)

Landlord and tenant mutual promises: This mutual promise must appear in every lease or rental agreement: "Landlord and tenant promise that neither will unlawfully allow within the premises, common areas, or curtilage of the premises (property boundaries): controlled substances, prostitution or prostitution-related activity; stolen property or property obtained by robbery; or an act of domestic violence, as defined by MN Statute Section 504B.206 (1)(e), against a tenant, licensee, or any authorized occupant. They further promise that the aforementioned areas will not be used by themselves or anyone acting under their control to manufacture, sell, give away, barter, deliver, exchange, distribute, purchase, or possess a controlled substance in violation of any criminal provision of chapter 152."

Mississippi

No disclosure statutes.

Missouri

Meth Labs: Landlord who knows that the premises were used to produce methamphetamine must disclose this fact to prospective tenants, irrespective of whether the people involved in the production were convicted for such production. (Mo. Rev. Stat. § 441.236)

Owner or Agent Identity: Landlord must disclose to the tenant in writing at or before the commencement of the tenancy the name and address of the person authorized to manage the premises, and an owner of the premises or a person authorized to act for and on behalf of the owner for the purpose of service of process and for the purpose of receiving notices and demands. (Mo. Rev. Stat. § 535.185)

Montana

Nonrefundable fees permitted? No. A fee or charge for cleaning and damages, no matter how designated, is presumed to be a security deposit. (Not a clear statement that such a fee isn't nonrefundable, but by implication it must be.) (Mont. Code Ann. § 70-25-101(4))

Move-in checklists required? Yes, checklists are required when landlords collect a security deposit. (Mont. Code Ann. § 70-25-206)

Owner or agent identity: A landlord or a person authorized to enter into a rental agreement on his behalf must disclose to the tenant in writing at or before the commencement of the tenancy the name and address of the person authorized to manage the premises; and the owner of the premises or a person authorized to act for the owner for the purpose of service of process and receiving notices and demands. (Mont. Code Ann. § 70-24-301)

Nebraska

Owner or agent identity: The landlord or any person authorized to enter into a rental agreement on his or her behalf shall disclose to the tenant in writing at or before the commencement of the tenancy the name and address of the person authorized to manage the premises; and an owner of the premises or a person authorized to act for and on behalf of the owner for the purpose of service of process receiving notices and demands. (Neb. Rev. Stat. § 76-1417)

Nevada

Nonrefundable fees permitted? Yes. Lease must explain fees that are required and the purposes for which they are required. (Nev. Rev. Stat. Ann. § 118A.200)

Move-in checklist required? Yes. Lease must include tenants' rights to a checklist and a signed record of the inventory and condition of the premises under the exclusive custody and control of the tenant. (Nev. Rev. Stat. Ann. § 118A.200)

Nuisance and flying the flag: Lease must include a summary of the provisions of NRS 202.470 (penalties for permitting or maintaining a nuisance); information regarding the procedure a tenant may use to report to the appropriate authorities a nuisance, a violation of a building, safety, or health code or regulation; and

Required Landlord Disclosures (continued)

information regarding the right of the tenant to engage in the display of the flag of the United States, as set forth in NRS 118A.325. (Nev. Rev. Stat. Ann. § 118A.200)

Foreclosure proceedings: Landlord must disclose to any prospective tenant, in writing, whether the premises to be rented is the subject of a foreclosure proceeding (disclosure need not be in the lease). (Nev. Rev. Stat. Ann. § 118A.275)

Lease Signed By an Agent of the Landlord Who Does Not Hold a Property Management Permit: In single-family rentals only, unless the lease is signed by an authorized agent of the landlord who holds a current property management permit, the top of the first page of the lease must state, in font that is at least twice the size of any other size in the agreement, that the tenant might not have valid occupancy unless the lease is notarized or signed by an authorized agent of the owner who holds a management permit. The notice must give the current address and phone number of the landlord. In addition, it must state that even if the foregoing has not been provided, the agreement is enforceable against the landlord. (Nev. Rev. Stat. Ann. § 118A.200)

New Hampshire

Move-in checklist required? Yes. Landlord must inform tenant that if tenant finds any conditions in the rental in need of repair, tenant may note them on the security deposit receipt or other writing (not a true checklist). (N.H. Rev. Stat. Ann. § 540-A:6)

New Jersey

Flood zone: Prior to move-in, landlord must inform tenant if rental is in a flood zone or area (does not apply to properties containing two or fewer dwelling units, or to owner-occupied properties of three or fewer units). (N.J. Stat. Ann. § 46:8-50)

Truth in Renting Act: Except in buildings of 2 or fewer units, and owner-occupied premises of 3 or fewer units, landlord must distribute to new tenants at or prior to move-in the Department of Community Affairs' statement of legal rights and responsibilities of tenants and landlords of rental dwelling units (Spanish also). (N.J.S.A. §§ 46:8-44, 46:8-45, 46:8-46)

Child Protection Windowguards: Landlords of multi-family properties must include information in the lease about tenants' rights to request windowguards. The Legislature's Model Lease and Notice clause reads as follows: "The owner (landlord) is required by law to provide, install and maintain window guards in the apartment if a child or children 10 years of age or younger is, or will be, living in the apartment or is, or will be, regularly present there for a substantial period of time if the tenant gives the owner (landlord) a written request that the window guards be installed. The owner (landlord) is also required, upon the written request of the tenant, to provide, install and maintain window guards in the hallways to which persons in the tenant's unit have access without having to go out of the building. If the building is a condominium, cooperative or mutual housing building, the owner (landlord) of the apartment is responsible for installing and maintaining window guards in the apartment and the association is responsible for installing and maintaining window guards in hallway windows. Window guards are only required to be provided in first floor windows where the window sill is more than six feet above grade or there are other hazardous conditions that make installation of window guards necessary to protect the safety of children." The notice must be conspicuous and in boldface type. (N.J. Admin. Code § 5:10-27.1)

New Mexico

Owner or agent identity: Landlord must disclose to the tenant in writing at or before the commencement of the tenancy the name and address of the person authorized to manage the premises, and an owner of the premises or a person authorized to act for and on behalf of the owner for the purpose of service of process and for the purpose of receiving notices and demands. (N.M. Stat. Ann. § 47-8-19)

New York

Air Contamination: Landlord who receives a government report showing that the air in the building has, or may have, concentrations of volatile organic compounds (VOCs) that exceed government guidelines must give written notice to prospective tenants and current tenants. The notice must appear in at least 12-point type bold face type on the first page of the lease or rental agreement. It must read as follows: "NOTIFICATION OF TEST RESULTS The property has been tested for contamination of indoor air: test results and additional information are available upon request." (N.Y. ECL § 27-2405).

Required Landlord Disclosures (continued)

North Carolina

Going to court fees: Yes, Landlord may collect only one of the following, when specific conditions are met: Complaint filing fee, court appearance fee, and second trial fee. Failure to pay the fees cannot support a termination notice. (N.C. Gen. Stat. § 42-46)

North Dakota

Move-in checklist required? Yes. Landlord must give tenant a statement describing the condition of the premises when tenant signs the rental agreement. Both parties must sign the statement. (N.D. Cent. Code § 47-16-07.2)

Ohio

Owner or agent identity: Every written rental agreement must contain the name and address of the owner and the name and address of the owner's agent, if any. If the owner or the owner's agent is a corporation, partnership, limited partnership, association, trust, or other entity, the address must be the principal place of business in the county in which the residential property is situated. If there is no place of business in such county, then its principal place of business in this state must be disclosed, including the name of the person in charge thereof. (Ohio Rev. Code Ann. § 5321.18)

Oklahoma

Flooding: If the premises to be rented has been flooded within the past five (5) years and such fact is known to the landlord, the landlord shall include such information prominently and in writing as part of any written rental agreements. (41 Okla. Stat. Ann. § 113a)

Owner information: As a part of any rental agreement the lessor shall prominently and in writing identify what person at what address is entitled to accept service or notice under this act. Landlord must disclose to the tenant in writing at or before the commencement of the tenancy the name and address of the person authorized to manage the premises, and an owner of the premises or a person authorized to act for and on behalf of the owner for the purpose of service of process and receiving notices and demands. (41 Okla. Stat. Ann § 116)

Oregon

Nonrefundable fees permitted? No. (Or. Rev. Stat. § 90.302)

Other fees? Landlords' written rules may not provide for tenant fees, except for specified events as they arise, including a late rent payment; tenant's late payment of a utility or service charge; a dishonored check, pursuant to Or. Rev. Stat. § 30.701(5); failure to clean up pet waste in areas other than tenant's unit; failure to clean up garbage and rubbish (outside tenant's dwelling unit); failure to clean pet waste of a service or companion animal from areas other than the dwelling unit; parking violations and improper use of vehicles within the premises; smoking in a designated nonsmoking area; keeping an unauthorized pet capable of inflicting damage on persons or property; and tampering or disabling a smoke detector.)

Owner or agent identity: Landlord must disclose to the tenant in writing at or before the commencement of the tenancy the name and address of the person authorized to manage the premises, and an owner of the premises or a person authorized to act for and on behalf of the owner for the purpose of service of process and for the purpose of receiving notices and demands. (Or. Rev. Stat. § 90.305)

Legal proceedings: If at the time of the execution of a rental agreement for a dwelling unit in premises containing no more than four dwelling units the premises are subject to any of the following circumstances, the landlord must disclose that circumstance to the tenant in writing before the execution of the rental agreement:

a. Any outstanding notice of default under a trust deed, mortgage, or contract of sale, or notice of trustee's sale under a trust deed;

b. Any pending suit to foreclose a mortgage, trust deed, or vendor's lien under a contract of sale;

c. Any pending declaration of forfeiture or suit for specific performance of a contract of sale; or

d. Any pending proceeding to foreclose a tax lien.

(Or. Rev. Stat. § 90.310)

Utilities: The landlord must disclose to the tenant in writing at or before the commencement of the tenancy any utility or service that the tenant pays directly to a utility or service provider that directly benefits the landlord or other tenants. A tenant's payment for a given utility or service benefits the landlord or other tenants if the utility or service is delivered to any area other than the tenant's dwelling unit.

Required Landlord Disclosures (continued)

A landlord may require a tenant to pay to the landlord a utility or service charge that has been billed by a utility or service provider to the landlord for utility or service provided directly to the tenant's dwelling unit or to a common area available to the tenant as part of the tenancy. A utility or service charge that shall be assessed to a tenant for a common area must be described in the written rental agreement separately and distinctly from such a charge for the tenant's dwelling unit. Unless the method of allocating the charges to the tenant is described in the tenant's written rental agreement, the tenant may require that the landlord give the tenant a copy of the provider's bill as a condition of paying the charges. (Or. Rev. Stat. § 90.315)

Recycling: In a city or the county within the urban growth boundary of a city that has implemented multifamily re-cycling service, a landlord who has five or more residential dwelling units on a single premises must notify new tenants at the time of entering into a rental agreement of the opportunity to recycle. (Or. Rev. Stat. § 90.318)

Smoking policy: Landlord must disclose the smoking policy for the premises, by stating whether smoking is prohibited on the premises, allowed on the entire premises, or allowed in limited areas. If landlord allows smoking in limited areas, the disclosure must identify those areas. (Or. Rev. Stat. § 90.220)

Carbon monoxide alarm instructions: If rental contains a CO source (a heater, fireplace, appliance, or cooking source that uses coal, kerosene, petroleum products, wood, or other fuels that emit carbon monoxide as a by-product of combustion; or an attached garage with an opening that communicates directly with a living space), landlord must install one or more CO monitors and give tenant written instructions for testing the alarm(s), before tenant takes possession. (Or. Rev. Stat. § 90.316, 90.317)

Flood zone: If a dwelling unit is located in a 100-year flood plain, the landlord must provide notice in the dwelling unit rental agreement that the dwelling unit is located within the flood plain. If a landlord fails to provide a notice as required under this section, and the tenant of the dwelling unit suffers an uninsured loss due to flooding, the tenant may recover from the landlord the lesser of the actual damages for the uninsured loss or two months' rent. (Or. Rev. Stat. § 90.228)

Renters' insurance: Landlord may require tenants to maintain liability insurance (certain low-income and subsidized tenancies excepted), but only if the landlord obtains and maintains comparable liability insurance and provides documentation to any tenant who requests the documentation, orally or in writing. The landlord may provide documentation to a tenant in person, by mail, or by posting in a common area or office. The documentation may consist of a current certificate of coverage. Any landlord who requires tenants to obtain renters' insurance must disclose the requirement and amount in writing prior to entering into a new tenancy, and may require the tenant to provide documentation before the tenancy begins. (Or. Rev. Stat. § 90.367)

Homeowner Assessments: If landlord wants to pass on homeowners' association assessments that are imposed on anyone moving into or out of the unit, the written rental agreement must include this requirement. Landlord must give tenants a copy of each assessment before charging the tenant. (Or. Rev. Stat. § 90.302)

Pennsylvania

No disclosure statutes.

Rhode Island

Owner disclosure: Landlord must disclose to the tenant in writing at or before the commencement of the tenancy the name and address of the person authorized to manage the premises, and an owner of the premises or a person authorized to act for and on behalf of the owner for the purpose of service of process and for the purpose of receiving notices and demands. (R.I. Gen. Laws § 34-18-20)

Code violations: Before entering into any residential rental agreement, landlord must inform a prospective tenant of any outstanding minimum housing code violations that exist on the building that is the subject of the rental agreement. (R.I. Gen. Laws § 34-18-22.1)

Notice of Foreclosure: A landlord who becomes delinquent on a mortgage securing real estate upon which the rental is located for a period of 120 days must notify the tenant that the property may be subject to foreclosure; and until the foreclosure occurs, the tenant must continue to pay rent to the landlord as provided under the rental agreement. (R.I. Gen. Laws § 34-18-20)

Required Landlord Disclosures (continued)

South Carolina

Owner or agent identity: Landlord must disclose to the tenant in writing at or before the commencement of the tenancy the name and address of the person authorized to manage the premises, and an owner of the premises or a person authorized to act for and on behalf of the owner for the purpose of service of process and for the purpose of receiving notices and demands. (S.C. Code Ann. § 27-40-420)

Unequal security deposits: If landlord rents five or more adjoining units on the premises, and imposes different standards for calculating deposits required of tenants, landlord must, before a tenancy begins, post in a conspicuous place a statement explaining the standards by which the various deposits are calculated (or, landlord may give the tenant the written statement). (S.C. Code Ann. § 27-40-410)

South Dakota

Meth labs: Landlord who has actual knowledge of the existence of any prior manufacturing of methamphetamines on the premises must disclose that information to any lessee or any person who may become a lessee. If the residential premises consists of two or more housing units, the disclosure requirements apply only to the unit where there is knowledge of the existence of any prior manufacturing of methamphetamines. (S.D. Codified Laws Ann. § 43-32-30)

Tennessee

Owner or agent identity: The landlord or any person authorized to enter into a rental agreement on the landlord's behalf must disclose to the tenant in writing at or before the commencement of the tenancy the name and address of the agent authorized to manage the premises, and an owner of the premises or a person or agent authorized to act for and on behalf of the owner for the acceptance of service of process and for receipt of notices and demands. (Tenn. Code Ann. § 66-28-302)

Showing rental to prospective tenants: Landlord may enter to show the premises to prospective renters during the final 30 days of a tenancy (with 24 hours' notice), but only if this right of access is set forth in the rental agreement or lease. (Tenn. Code Ann. § 66-28-403)

Texas

Nonrefundable fees permitted? Yes. (*Holmes v. Canlen Management Corp.*, 542 S.W.2d 199 (1976))

Owner or agent identity: In the lease, other writing, or posted on the property, landlord must disclose the name and address of the property's owner and, if an entity located off-site from the dwelling is primarily responsible for managing the dwelling, the name and street address of the management company. (Tex. Prop. Code Ann. § 92.201)

Security device requests: If landlord wants tenant requests concerning security devices to be in writing, this requirement must be in the lease in boldface type or underlined. (Tex. Prop. Code Ann. § 92.159)

Return of security deposit: A requirement that a tenant give advance notice of moving out as a condition for refunding the security deposit is effective only if the requirement is in the lease, underlined or printed in conspicuous bold print. (Tex. Prop. Code Ann. § 92.103)

Domestic violence victims' rights: Victims of sexual abuse or assault on the premises may break a lease, after complying with specified procedures, without responsibility for future rent. Tenants will be responsible for any unpaid back rent, but only if the lease includes the following statement, or one substantially like it: "Tenants may have special statutory rights to terminate the lease early in certain situations involving family violence or a military deployment or transfer." (Tex. Prop. Code Ann. § 92.016)

Tenant's rights when landlord fails to repair: A lease must contain language in underlined or bold print that informs the tenant of the remedies available when the landlord fails to repair a problem that materially affects the physical health or safety of an ordinary tenant. These rights include the right to repair and deduct; terminate the lease; and obtain a judicial order that the landlord make the repair, reduce the rent, pay the tenant damages (including a civil penalty), and pay the tenant's court and attorneys' fees. (Tex. Prop. Code Ann. § 92.056)

Landlord's towing or parking rules and policies: For tenants in multiunit properties, if the landlord has vehicle towing or parking rules or policies that apply to the tenant, the landlord must give the tenant a copy of the rules or policies before the lease agreement is signed.

Required Landlord Disclosures (continued)

The copy must be signed by the tenant, included in the lease or rental agreement, or be made an attachment to either. If included, the clause must be titled " Parking" or "Parking Rules" and be capitalized, underlined, or printed in bold print.) (Tex. Prop. Code Ann. § 92.0131.)

Electric service interruption: Landlord who submeters electric service, or who allocates master metered electricity according to a prorated system, may interrupt tenant's electricity service if tenant fails to pay the bill, but only after specific notice and according to a complex procedure. Exceptions for ill tenants and during extreme weather. (Tex. Prop. Code Ann. § 92.008(h))

Utah

Nonrefundable fees permitted? Yes. By custom, if there is a written agreement and if any part of the deposit is nonrefundable, it must be so stated in writing to the renter at the time the deposit is taken.

Move-in checklists required? Yes. Landlords must give prospective renters a written inventory of the condition of the residential rental unit, excluding ordinary wear and tear; give the renter a form to document the condition of the residential rental and allow the resident a reasonable time after the renter's occupancy of the unit to complete and return the form; or provide the prospective renter an opportunity to conduct a walk-through inspection of the rental. (Utah Code. Ann. § 57-22-4)

Applicant Disclosures: Before accepting an application or collecting an application fee, landlord must disclose whether the rental unit is expected to be available, and the criteria landlord will use in evaluating potential renter's application. Failure to comply will not invalidate the lease or provide tenant with a legal cause of action. (Utah Code Ann. § 57-22-4)

Vermont

No disclosure statutes.

Virginia

Move-in checklist required? Yes. Within 5 days of move-in, landlord or tenant or both together must prepare a written report detailing the condition of the premises. Landlord must disclose within this report the known presence of mold. (Va. Code Ann. § 55-248.11:1)

Owner or agent identity: Landlord must disclose to the tenant in writing at or before the commencement of the tenancy the name and address of the person authorized to manage the premises, and an owner of the premises or a person authorized to act for and on behalf of the owner for the purpose of service of process and for the purpose of receiving notices and demands. (Va. Code Ann. § 55-248.12)

Military zone: The landlord of property in any locality in which a military air installation is located, or any person authorized to enter into a rental agreement on his behalf, must provide to a prospective tenant a written disclosure that the property is located in a noise zone or accident potential zone, or both, as designated by the locality on its official zoning map. (Va. Code Ann. § 55-248.12:1)

Mold: Move-in inspection report must include whether there is any visible evidence of mold (deemed correct unless tenant objects within five days); if evidence is present, tenant may terminate or not move in. If tenant stays, landlord must remediate the mold condition within five business days, reinspect, and issue a new report indicating that there is no evidence of mold. (Va. Code Ann. § 55-248.11:2) If evidence of mold appears during the tenancy, landlord must promptly remediate, reinspect, and make available to the tenant copies of any available written information on how to get rid of mold. (Va. Code Ann. § 55-248.16)

Ratio utility billing: Landlord who uses a ratio utility billing service, who intends to collect monthly billing and other administrative and late fees, must disclose these fees in a written rental agreement. (Va. Code Ann. § 55-226.2)

Condominium plans: If an application for registration as a condominium or cooperative has been filed with the Real Estate Board, or if there is within six months an existing plan for tenant displacement resulting from demolition or substantial rehabilitation of the property, or conversion of the rental property to office, hotel, or motel use or planned unit development, the landlord or any person authorized to enter into a rental agreement on his behalf must disclose that information in writing to any prospective tenant. (Va. Code Ann. § 55-248.12(C).)

Defective drywall: Landlords who know of the presence of unrepaired defective drywall in the rental must disclose this before the tenant signs a lease or rental agreement. (Va. Code Ann. § 55-248.12:2.)

Required Landlord Disclosures (continued)

Washington

Move-in checklists required? Yes. Checklists are required when landlords collect a security deposit. If landlord fails to provide checklist, landlord is liable to the tenant for the amount of the deposit. (Wash. Rev. Code Ann. § 59.18.260)

Nonrefundable fees permitted? Yes. If landlord collects a nonrefundable fee, the rental document must clearly specify that it is nonrefundable. (Wash. Rev. Code Ann. § 59.18.285)

Fire protection: At the time the lease is signed, landlord must provide fire protection and safety information, including whether the building has a smoking policy, an emergency notification plan, or an evacuation plan. (Wash. Rev. Code Ann. § 59.18.060)

Owner or agent identity: In the rental document or posted conspicuously on the premises, landlord must designate to the tenant the name and address of the person who is the landlord by a statement on the rental agreement or by a notice conspicuously posted on the premises. If the person designated does not reside in Washington, landlord must also designate a person who resides in the county to act as an agent for the purposes of service of notices and process. (Wash. Rev. Code Ann. § 59.18.060)

Mold: At the time the lease is signed, landlord must provide tenant with information provided or approved by the department of health about the health hazards associated with exposure to indoor mold. (Wash. Rev. Code Ann. § 59.18.060)

Screening criteria: Before obtaining any information about an applicant, landlord must provide (in writing or by posting) the type of information to be accessed, criteria to be used to evaluate the application, and (for consumer reports) the name and address of the consumer reporting agency to be used, including the applicant's rights to obtain a free copy of the report and dispute its accuracy. Landlord must advise tenants whether landlord will accept a comprehensive reusable tenant screening report done by a consumer reporting agency (in which case the landlord may not charge the tenant a fee for a screening report). If landlord maintains a website that advertises residential rentals, the home page must include this information. (Wash. Rev. Code Ann. § 59.18.257)

Tenant screening fee: Landlords who do their own screening may charge a fee for time and costs to obtain background information, but only if they provide the information explained in "Screening Criteria," above. (Wash. Rev. Code Ann. § 59.18.257.)

West Virginia

Nonrefundable fees permitted? Yes. Nonrefundable fee must be expressly agreed to in writing. (W.Va. Code § 37-6A-1(14))

Wisconsin

Move-in checklist required? Yes. Tenant has a right to inspect the rental and give landlord a list of defects, and to receive a list of damages charged to the prior tenant. Tenant has 7 days after start of the tenancy to return the list to the landlord. (Wis. Admin. Code § 134.06; Wis. Stat. Ann. § 704.08)

Owner or agent identity: Landlord must disclose to the tenant in writing, at or before the time a rental agreement is signed, the name and address of: the person or persons authorized to collect or receive rent and manage and maintain the premises, and who can readily be contacted by the tenant; and the owner of the premises or other person authorized to accept service of legal process and other notices and demands on behalf of the owner. The address must be an address within the state at which service of process can be made in person. (Wis. Admin. Code § 134.04)

Nonstandard rental provisions: If landlord wants to enter premises for reasons not specified by law, landlord must disclose the provision in a separate written document entitled "NONSTANDARD RENTAL PROVISIONS" before the rental agreement is signed. (Wis. Admin. Code § 134.09)

Uncorrected code violations: Before signing a rental contract or accepting a security deposit, the landlord must disclose to the tenant any uncorrected code violation of which the landlord is actually aware, which affects the dwelling unit or a common area and poses a significant threat to the tenant's health or safety. "Disclosure" consists of showing prospective tenants the portion of the building affected, as well as the notices themselves. (Wis. Stat. §§ 134.04, 704.07(2)(bm))

Required Landlord Disclosures (continued)

Habitability deficiencies: Landlord must disclose serious problems that affect the rental unit's habitability. (Wis. Admin. Code § 134.04)

Utility charges: If charges for water, heat, or electricity are not included in the rent, the landlord must disclose this fact to the tenant before entering into a rental agreement or accepting any earnest money or security deposit from the prospective tenant. If individual dwelling units and common areas are not separately metered, and if the charges are not included in the rent, the landlord must disclose the basis on which charges for utility services will be allocated among individual dwelling units. (Wis. Admin. Code § 134.04)

Disposing of abandoned property: If landlord intends to immediately dispose of any tenant property left behind after move-out, landlord must notify tenant at the time lease is signed. (But landlord must hold prescription medications and medical equipment for seven days, and must give notice before disposing of vehicles or manufactured homes to owner and any known secured party.) (Wis. Stat. § 704.05(5))

Wyoming

Nonrefundable fees permitted? Yes. If any portion of the deposit is not refundable, rental agreement must include this information and tenant must be told before paying a deposit. (Wyo. Stat. § 1-21-1207)

State Laws in Domestic Violence Situations

Many states extend special protections, such as early termination rights, to victims of domestic violence. Here is a summary of state laws. For more information, check with local law enforcement or a battered women's shelter.

Alabama

No statute

Alaska

Alaska Stat. § 29.35.125(a)

Miscellaneous provisions: A city may impose a fee on the owner of residential property if the police go to the property an excessive number of times during a calendar year when called for assistance or to handle a complaint, an emergency, or a potential emergency. This fee may not be imposed for responses to calls that involve potential child neglect, domestic violence, or stalking.

Arizona

Ariz. Rev. Stat. §§ 33-1315, 33-1318, 33-1414

- Lease cannot include a waiver of some or all DV rights
- Landlord entitled to proof of DV status
- Early termination right for DV victim
- Lease cannot prohibit calling the police in a DV situation or otherwise penalize DV victim
- DV victim has the right to have the locks changed
- Penalty for falsely reporting domestic violence (including obtaining early termination)
- Perpetrator of DV liable to landlord for resulting damages

Arkansas

Ark. Code Ann. § 18-16-112

- Landlord entitled to proof of DV status
- Landlord cannot refuse to rent to victim of DV
- Landlord cannot terminate a victim of DV
- Lease cannot prohibit calling the police in a DV situation or otherwise penalize DV victim
- DV victim has the right to have the locks changed
- Perpetrator of DV liable to landlord for resulting damages
- Landlord or court may bifurcate the lease

California

Cal. Civ. Code §§ 1941.5, 1941.6, 1946.7; Cal. Code Civ. Proc. §§ 1161, 1161.3

- Landlord entitled to proof of DV status
- Landlord cannot refuse to rent to victim of DV
- Landlord cannot terminate a victim of DV
- Early termination right for DV victim
- DV is an affirmative defense to an eviction lawsuit
- DV victim has the right to have the locks changed
- Landlord or court may bifurcate the lease
- Landlord has limited right to evict the DV victim

Miscellaneous provisions: Protection against termination has been expanded to include elder or dependent adults.

Colorado

Colo. Rev. Stat. §§ 13-40-104(4), 13-40-107.5(5), 38-12-401, 38-12-402, 38-12-503

- Lease cannot include a waiver of some or all DV rights
- Landlord entitled to proof of DV status
- Landlord cannot terminate a victim of DV
- Early termination right for DV victim
- Lease cannot prohibit calling the police in a DV situation or otherwise penalize DV victim

Miscellaneous provisions: Legal protections extend to victims of unlawful sexual behavior and stalking, as well as domestic violence. Landlords may not disclose that tenants were victims of such acts, except with permission or as required by law. Landlord may not disclose such facts to tenant's new address if tenant terminates as permitted by law.

Connecticut

Conn. Gen. Stat. Ann. § 47a-11e

- Landlord entitled to proof of DV status
- Early termination right for DV victim

Delaware

Del. Code Ann. tit. 25, §§ 5141(7), 5314(b), 5316

- Landlord entitled to proof of DV status
- Landlord cannot terminate a victim of DV
- Early termination right for DV victim

State Laws in Domestic Violence Situations (continued)

District of Columbia

D.C. Code Ann. §§ 2-1402.21, 42-3505.07, 42-3505.08

- Lease cannot include a waiver of some or all DV rights
- Landlord entitled to proof of DV status
- Landlord cannot refuse to rent to victim of DV
- Early termination right for DV victim
- DV is an affirmative defense to an eviction lawsuit
- Lease cannot prohibit calling the police in a DV situation or otherwise penalize DV victim
- DV victim has the right to have the locks changed
- Landlord or court may bifurcate the lease

Miscellaneous provisions: Landlord must make reasonable accommodation in restoring or improving security and safety measures that are beyond the landlord's duty of ordinary care and diligence, when such accommodation is necessary to ensure the tenant's security and safety (tenant may be billed for the cost).

Florida

No statute

Georgia

No statute

Hawaii

Haw. Rev. Stat. §§ 521-80 to 521-82

- Landlord entitled to proof of DV status
- Early termination right for DV victim
- DV victim has the right to have the locks changed
- Penalty for falsely reporting domestic violence (including obtaining early termination)
- Landlord or court may bifurcate the lease

Miscellaneous provisions: Landlord may not disclose information gathered with respect to tenant's exercise of rights under these laws, unless the tenant consents in writing, the information is required or relevant in a lawsuit, or the disclosure is required by law.

Idaho

No statute

Illinois

735 Ill. Comp. Stat. 5/9-106.2; 765 Ill. Comp. Stat. 750/1 through 750/35

- Landlord entitled to proof of DV status
- Early termination right for DV victim

- DV is an affirmative defense to an eviction lawsuit
- DV victim has the right to have the locks changed
- Landlord or court may bifurcate the lease

Miscellaneous provisions: Landlord may not disclose to others that a tenant has exercised a right under the law; violations expose landlord to damages that result, or $2,000.

Indiana

Ind. Code Ann. §§ 32-31-9-1 through 32-31-9-15

- Landlord entitled to proof of DV status
- Landlord cannot refuse to rent to victim of DV
- Landlord cannot terminate a victim of DV
- Early termination right for DV victim
- Lease cannot prohibit calling the police in a DV situation or otherwise penalize DV victim
- DV victim has the right to have the locks changed

Iowa

Iowa Code §§ 562A.27A, 562A.27B, 562B.25A(3)

- Lease cannot include a waiver of some or all DV rights
- Landlord entitled to proof of DV status
- Landlord cannot terminate a victim of DV
- Lease cannot prohibit calling the police in a DV situation or otherwise penalize DV victim
- Landlord has limited right to evict the DV victim

Miscellaneous provisions: Landlord can recover from the tenant the cost to repair damage caused by emergency responders called by tenant. Cities cannot impose penalties against residents or landlords, including fines, permit or license revocations, and evictions, when they had a reasonable belief that emergency assistance was necessary, and it was in fact needed.

Kansas

No statute

Kentucky

Ky. Rev. Stat. §§ 383.300, 383.302

- Lease cannot include a waiver of some or all DV rights
- Landlord entitled to proof of DV status
- Landlord cannot refuse to rent to victim of DV
- Landlord cannot terminate a victim of DV
- Early termination right for DV victim
- DV is an affirmative defense to an eviction lawsuit
- DV victim has the right to have the locks changed

State Laws in Domestic Violence Situations (continued)

- Perpetrator of DV liable to landlord for resulting damages
- Landlord or court may bifurcate the lease

Louisiana

La. Rev. Stat. Ann. § 9:3261.1

- Lease cannot include a waiver of some or all DV rights
- Landlord entitled to proof of DV status
- Landlord cannot refuse to rent to victim of DV
- Landlord cannot terminate a victim of DV
- Early termination right for DV victim
- Lease cannot prohibit calling the police in a DV situation or otherwise penalize DV victim

Miscellaneous provisions: Statute applies only to multifamily housing of six or more units; does not apply if building has ten or fewer units and one is occupied by the owner.

Maine

Me. Rev. Stat. Ann. tit. 14, §§ 6000, 6001, 6002, 6025

- Landlord entitled to proof of DV status
- Landlord cannot terminate a victim of DV
- Early termination right for DV victim
- DV victim has the right to have the locks changed
- Perpetrator of DV liable to landlord for resulting damages
- Landlord or court may bifurcate the lease

Miscellaneous provisions: Landlord may terminate and/or bifurcate the lease with 7 days' notice when a tenant perpetrates domestic violence, sexual assault, or stalking (against another tenant, a tenant's guest, or the landlord or landlord's employee or agent), and the victim is also a tenant.

Maryland

Md. Real Prop. Law §§ 8-5A-01 through 8-5A-06

- Landlord entitled to proof of DV status
- Early termination right for DV victim

Massachusetts

186 Mass Gen. Laws §§ 24, 25, 26, and 28

- Lease cannot include a waiver of some or all DV rights
- Landlord entitled to proof of DV status
- Landlord cannot refuse to rent to victim of DV
- Early termination right for DV victim

- DV victim has the right to have the locks changed

Michigan

Mich. Comp. Laws § 554.601b

- Landlord entitled to proof of DV status
- Early termination right for DV victim
- Landlord or court may bifurcate the lease

Minnesota

Minn. Stat. Ann. §§ 504B.205, 206

- Lease cannot include a waiver of some or all DV rights
- Landlord entitled to proof of DV status
- Landlord cannot terminate a victim of DV
- Early termination right for DV victim
- DV is an affirmative defense to an eviction lawsuit
- Lease cannot prohibit calling the police in a DV situation or otherwise penalize DV victim

Miscellaneous provisions: Landlord must keep information about the domestic violence confidential. In a multitenant situation, termination by one tenant terminates the lease of all, though other tenants may reapply to enter into a new lease. All security deposit is forfeited.

Mississippi

No statute

Missouri

No statute

Montana

No statute

Nebraska

No statute

Nevada

Nev. Rev. Stat. Ann. §§ 118A.345, 118A.347, 118A.510

- Lease cannot include a waiver of some or all DV rights
- Landlord entitled to proof of DV status
- Landlord cannot terminate a victim of DV
- Early termination right for DV victim
- DV victim has the right to have the locks changed
- Perpetrator of DV liable to landlord for resulting damages

Miscellaneous provisions: Protections extend to victims of harassment, sexual assault, and stalking, as well as domestic

State Laws in Domestic Violence Situations (continued)

violence. Landlord may not disclose the fact of a tenant's early termination to a prospective landlord; nor may a prospective landlord require an applicant to disclose any prior early terminations. Antiretaliation protection extended to tenants who are domestic violence victims or who have terminated a rental agreement pursuant to law.

New Hampshire

N.H. Rev. Stat. Ann. § 540:2.VII

- Landlord entitled to proof of DV status
- Landlord cannot terminate a victim of DV
- DV victim has the right to have the locks changed
- Landlord or court may bifurcate the lease

New Jersey

N.J. Stat. Ann. §§ 46:8-9.5 through 46:8-9.12

- Lease cannot include a waiver of some or all DV rights
- Landlord entitled to proof of DV status
- Early termination right for DV victim

New Mexico

N.M. Stat. Ann. § 47-8-33(J)

- DV is an affirmative defense to an eviction lawsuit
- Landlord or court may bifurcate the lease

New York

N.Y. Real Prop. Law §§ 227-c(2) and 227–d; N.Y. Real Prop. Acts. Law § 744; N.Y. Crim. Proc. Law § 530.13(1); N.Y. Dom. Rel. Law § 240(3)

- Landlord cannot refuse to rent to victim of DV
- Landlord cannot terminate a victim of DV. Early termination right for DV victim
- Penalty for falsely reporting domestic violence (including obtaining early termination)
- Landlord or court may bifurcate the lease

Miscellaneous provisions: Anti-discrimination protection and eviction protection do not apply to owner-occupied buildings with two or fewer units.

North Carolina

N.C. Gen. Stat. §§ 42-40, 42-42.2, 42-42.3, 42-45.1

- Landlord entitled to proof of DV status
- Landlord cannot refuse to rent to victim of DV
- Early termination right for DV victim
- DV victim has the right to have the locks changed

North Dakota

N.D. Cent. Code § 47-16-17.1

- Landlord entitled to proof of DV status
- Landlord cannot refuse to rent to victim of DV
- Landlord cannot terminate a victim of DV
- Early termination right for DV victim

Miscellaneous provisions: Landlord may not disclose information provided by a tenant that documents domestic violence. Landlords who violate the provisions providing early termination are subject to damages including actual damages, $1,000, reasonable attorneys' fees, costs, and disbursements.

Ohio

No statute

Oklahoma

No statute

Oregon

Or. Rev. Stat. §§ 90.449, 90.453, 90.456, 90.459

- Landlord entitled to proof of DV status
- Landlord cannot refuse to rent to victim of DV
- Landlord cannot terminate a victim of DV
- Early termination right for DV victim
- Lease cannot prohibit calling the police in a DV situation or otherwise penalize DV victim
- DV victim has the right to have the locks changed
- Landlord or court may bifurcate the lease
- Landlord has limited right to evict the DV victim

Pennsylvania

No statute

Rhode Island

R.I. Gen. Laws §§ 34-37-1 through 34-37-4

- Landlord cannot refuse to rent to victim of DV
- Landlord cannot terminate a victim of DV
- Landlord or court may bifurcate the lease

South Carolina

No statute

South Dakota

No statute

State Laws in Domestic Violence Situations (continued)

Tennessee

Tenn. Code Ann. §§ 66-7-109(e), 66-28-517(g)

- Landlord entitled to proof of DV status
- Landlord cannot terminate a victim of DV
- Landlord or court may bifurcate the lease
- Landlord has limited right to evict the DV victim

Miscellaneous provisions: The rights granted under this law do not apply when the perpetrator is a child or dependent of any tenant. Landlord may evict a victim who allows an ousted perpetrator to return to the premises.

Texas

Tex. Prop. Code Ann. §§ 92.015, 92.016, 92.0161

- Lease cannot include a waiver of some or all DV rights
- Landlord entitled to proof of DV status
- Early termination right for DV victim
- Lease cannot prohibit calling the police in a DV situation or otherwise penalize DV victim

Miscellaneous provisions: Tenant who exercises termination rights will be released from any delinquent rent unless the lease includes a clause that specifically describes tenants' rights in domestic violence situations. Landlord may not prohibit or limit a tenant's right to call police or other emergency assistance, based on the tenant's reasonable belief that such help is necesssary.

Utah

Utah Code Ann. § 57-22-5.1

- Landlord entitled to proof of DV status
- Early termination right for DV victim
- Lease cannot prohibit calling the police in a DV situation or otherwise penalize DV victim
- DV victim has the right to have the locks changed

Vermont

15 Vt. Stat. Ann. § 1103(c)(2)(B)

- Landlord or court may bifurcate the lease

Virginia

Va. Code Ann. §§ 55-225.5, 55-225.16, 55-248.18:1, 55-248.21:2, 55-248.31(D)

- Landlord entitled to proof of DV status
- Landlord cannot terminate a victim of DV
- Early termination right for DV victim
- DV victim has the right to have the locks changed
- Landlord or court may bifurcate the lease

Miscellaneous provisions: Right to change locks extends to "authorized occupants" (someone entitled to occupy a dwelling unit with the consent of the landlord, but who has not signed the rental agreement and does not have the financial obligations as a tenant under the rental agreement). Tenant/victim's right to continued possession when perpetrator is ousted does not apply if perpetrator returns to the premises and tenant fails to notify landlord.

Washington

Wash. Rev. Code Ann. §§ 59.18.570, 59.18.575, 59.18.580, 59.18.585, 59.18.352, 59.18.130(8)(b)(ii)

- Landlord cannot terminate a victim of DV
- Early termination right for DV victim
- DV is an affirmative defense to an eviction lawsuit

West Virginia

No statute

Wisconsin

Wis. Stat. Ann. § 106.50(5m)(d)

- Landlord cannot refuse to rent to victim of DV
- Landlord cannot terminate a victim of DV
- DV is an affirmative defense to an eviction lawsuit
- Landlord has limited right to evict the DV victim

Wyoming

Wyo. Stat. §§ 1-21-1301 to 1-21-1304

- Lease cannot include a waiver of some or all DV rights
- Landlord entitled to proof of DV status
- Landlord cannot terminate a victim of DV
- Early termination right for DV victim
- Landlord has limited right to evict the DV victim

State Laws on Rent Withholding and Repair and Deduct Remedies		
State	**Statute or case on rent withholding**	**Statute or case on repair and deduct**
Alabama	Ala. Code § 35-9A-405	No statute
Alaska	Alaska Stat. §§ 34.03.190, 34.03.100(b)	Alaska Stat. §§ 34.03.180, 34.03.100(b)
Arizona	Ariz. Rev. Stat. Ann. § 33-1365	Ariz. Rev. Stat. Ann. §§ 33-1363 to -1364
Arkansas	No statute	No statute
California	*Green v. Superior Court*, 10 Cal.3d 616 (1974)	Cal. Civ. Code § 1942
Colorado	Colo. Rev. Stat. § 38-12-507	No statute
Connecticut	Conn. Gen. Stat. Ann. §§ 47a-14a to -14h	Conn. Gen. Stat. Ann. § 47a-13
Delaware	Del. Code Ann. tit. 25, § 5308(b)(3)	Del. Code Ann. tit. 25, §§ 5307, 5308
District of Columbia	*Javins v. First Nat'l Realty Corp.*, 428 F.2d 1071 (D.C. Cir. 1970)	No statute
Florida	Fla. Stat. Ann. § 83.60	Fla. Stat. Ann. § 83.60
Georgia	No statute	Not addressed by statute, but Georgia courts recognize a tenant's right to this remedy. See Georgia Landlord Tenant Handbook, 2012, Georgia Department of Community Affairs (http://www.dca.state.ga.us/ housing/housingdevelopment/programs/downloads/ Georgia_Landlord_Tenant_Handbook.pdf) and see *Abrams v. Joel*, 108 Ga. App. 662, 134 S.E.2d 480 (1963)
Hawaii	Haw. Rev. Stat. § 521-78	Haw. Rev. Stat. § 521-64
Idaho	No statute	No statute
Illinois	765 Ill. Comp. Stat. §§ 735/2, 735/2.2 (applies only when a court has appointed a receiver to collect rents, following landlord's failure to pay for utilities)	765 Ill. Comp. Stat. § 742/5
Indiana	No statute	No statute
Iowa	Iowa Code Ann. § 562A.24	Iowa Code Ann. § 562A.23
Kansas	Kan. Stat. Ann. § 58-2561	No statute
Kentucky	Ky. Rev. Stat. Ann. § 383.645	Ky. Rev. Stat. Ann. §§ 383.635, 383.640
Louisiana	No statute	La. Civ. Code Ann. art. 2694
Maine	Me. Rev. Stat. Ann. tit. 14, § 6021	Me. Rev. Stat. Ann. tit. 14, § 6026
Maryland	Md. Code Ann. [Real Prop.] §§ 8-211, 8-211.1	No statute
Massachusetts	Mass. Gen. Laws Ann. ch. 239, § 8A	Mass. Gen. Laws Ann. ch. 111, § 127L
Michigan	Mich. Comp. Laws § 125.530	*Rome v. Walker*, 198 N.W.2d 850 (1972); Mich. Comp. Laws § 554.139
Minnesota	Minn. Stat. Ann. §§ 504B.215(3)(d), 504B.385	Minn. Stat. Ann. § 504B.425

State Laws on Rent Withholding and Repair and Deduct Remedies (continued)		
State	Statute or case on rent withholding	Statute or case on repair and deduct
Mississippi	No statute	Miss. Code Ann. § 89-8-15
Missouri	Mo. Ann. Stat. §§ 441.570, 441.580	Mo. Ann. Stat. § 441.234
Montana	Mont. Code Ann. § 70-24-421	Mont. Code Ann. §§ 70-24-406 to -408
Nebraska	Neb. Rev. Stat. § 76-1428	Neb. Rev. Stat. § 76-1427
Nevada	Nev. Rev. Stat. Ann. § 118A.490	Nev. Rev. Stat. Ann. §§ 118A.360, 118A.380
New Hampshire	N.H. Rev. Stat. Ann. § 540:13-d	No statute
New Jersey	*Berzito v. Gambino*, 63 N.J. 460 (1973)	*Marini v. Ireland*, 265 A.2d 526 (1970)
New Mexico	N.M. Stat. Ann. § 47-8-27.2	No statute
New York	N.Y. Real Prop. Law § 235-b, *Semans Family Ltd. Partnership v. Kennedy*, 675 N.Y.S.2d 489 (N.Y. City Civ. Ct.,1998)	For emergency repairs (such as broken door lock) only: N.Y. Real Prop. Law § 235-b; *Jangla Realty Co. v. Gravagna*, 447 N.Y.S. 2d 338 (Civ. Ct., Queens County, 1981)
North Carolina	No statute	No statute
North Dakota	No statute	N.D. Cent. Code §§ 47-16-13, 47-16-13.1
Ohio	Ohio Rev. Code Ann. § 5321.07 (does not apply to student tenants; or when landlord owns three or fewer rental units, as long as landlord has given written notice to tenant)	No statute
Oklahoma	Okla. Stat. Ann. tit. 41, § 121	Okla. Stat. Ann. tit. 41, § 121
Oregon	Or. Rev. Stat. § 90.365	Or. Rev. Stat. § 90.365
Pennsylvania	68 Pa. Cons. Stat. Ann. § 250.206; 35 Pa. Cons. Stat. Ann. § 1700-1	*Pugh v. Holmes*, 405 A.2d 897 (1979)
Rhode Island	R.I. Gen. Laws § 34-18-32	R.I. Gen. Laws §§ 34-18-30 to -31
South Carolina	S.C. Code Ann. § 27-40-640	S.C. Code Ann. § 27-40-630
South Dakota	S.D. Codified Laws Ann. § 43-32-9	S.D. Codified Laws Ann. § 43-32-9
Tennessee	Tenn. Code Ann. § 68-111-104	Tenn. Code Ann. § 66-28-502
Texas	No statute	Tex. Prop. Code Ann. §§ 92.056, 92.0561
Utah	No statute	Utah Code Ann. § 57-22-6
Vermont	Vt. Stat. Ann. tit. 9, § 4458	Vt. Stat. Ann. tit. 9, § 4459
Virginia	Va. Code Ann. §§ 54-248.25, 54-248.25.1, 54-248-27	No statute
Washington	Wash. Rev. Code Ann. §§ 59.18.110, 59.18.115	Wash. Rev. Code Ann. §§ 59.18.100, 59.18.110
West Virginia	No statute	No statute
Wisconsin	Wis. Stat. Ann. § 704.07(4)	No statute
Wyoming	Wyo. Stat. § 1-21-1206	No statute

State Laws on Landlord's Access to Rental Property

This is a synopsis of state laws that specify circumstances when a landlord may enter rental premises and the amount of notice required for such entry.

State	State Law Citation	Amount of Notice Required in Nonemergency Situations	To Deal With an Emergency	To Inspect the Premises	To Make Repairs, Alterations, or Improvements	To Show Property to Prospective Tenants or Purchasers	During Tenant's Extended Absence
Alabama	Ala. Code §§ 35-9A-303, 35-9A-423	Two days	✓	✓	✓	✓	✓
Alaska	Alaska Stat. §§ 34.03.140, 34.03.230	24 hours	✓	✓	✓	✓	✓
Arizona	Ariz. Rev. Stat. Ann. § 33-1343	Two days (written or oral notice); notice period does not apply, and tenant's consent is assumed, if entry is pursuant to tenant's request for maintenance as prescribed in Ariz. Rev. Stat. § 33-1341, paragraph 8	✓	✓	✓	✓	
Arkansas	Ark. Code Ann. § 18-17-602	No notice specified		✓	✓	✓	
California	Cal. Civ. Code § 1954	24 hours (48 hours for initial move-out inspection)	✓	✓	✓	✓	
Colorado	No statute						
Connecticut	Conn. Gen. Stat. Ann. §§ 47a-16 to 47a-16a	Reasonable notice	✓	✓	✓	✓	
Delaware	Del. Code Ann. tit. 25, §§ 5509, 5510	Two days	✓	✓	✓	✓	
D.C.	D.C. Code Ann. § 42-3505.51	48 hours	✓	✓	✓	✓	✓
Florida	Fla. Stat. Ann. § 83.53	12 hours	✓	✓	✓	✓	✓
Georgia	No statute						
Hawaii	Haw. Rev. Stat. §§ 521-53, 521-70(b)	Two days	✓	✓	✓	✓	✓
Idaho	No statute						
Illinois	No statute						
Indiana	Ind. Code Ann. § 32-31-5-6	Reasonable notice	✓	✓	✓	✓	
Iowa	Iowa Code Ann. §§ 562A.19, 562A.28, 562A.29	24 hours	✓	✓	✓	✓	✓
Kansas	Kan. Stat. Ann. §§ 58-2557, 58-2565	Reasonable notice	✓	✓	✓	✓	✓
Kentucky	Ky. Rev. Stat. Ann. §§ 383.615, 383.670	Two days	✓	✓	✓	✓	✓
Louisiana	La. Civ. Code art. 2693	No notice specified			✓		
Maine	Me. Rev. Stat. Ann. tit. 14, § 6025	24 hours	✓	✓	✓	✓	
Maryland	No statute						
Massachusetts	Mass. Gen. Laws Ann. ch. 186, § 15B(1)(a)	No notice specified	✓	✓	✓	✓	
Michigan	No statute						
Minnesota	Minn. Stat. Ann. § 504B.211	Reasonable notice	✓	✓	✓	✓	
Mississippi	No statute						
Missouri	No statute						

State Laws on Landlord's Access to Rental Property (continued)

State	State Law Citation	Amount of Notice Required in Nonemergency Situations	To Deal With an Emergency	To Inspect the Premises	To Make Repairs, Alterations, or Improvements	To Show Property to Prospective Tenants or Purchasers	During Tenant's Extended Absence
Montana	Mont. Code Ann. §§ 70-24-312, 70-24-426	24 hours	✓	✓	✓	✓	✓
Nebraska	Neb. Rev. Stat. §§ 76-1423, 76-1432	One day	✓	✓	✓	✓	✓
Nevada	Nev. Rev. Stat. Ann. § 118A.330	24 hours	✓	✓	✓	✓	
New Hampshire	N.H. Rev. Stat. Ann. § 540-A:3	Notice that is adequate under the circumstances	✓	✓	✓	✓	
New Jersey	N.J.A.C. 5:10-5.1	One day, by custom; in buildings with three or more units, one day (by regulation)	✓	✓	✓	✓	
New Mexico	N.M. Stat. Ann. §§ 47-8-24, 47-8-34	24 hours	✓	✓	✓	✓	✓
New York	No statute						
North Carolina	No statute						
North Dakota	N.D. Cent. Code § 47-16-07.3	Reasonable notice	✓	✓	✓	✓	
Ohio	Ohio Rev. Code Ann. §§ 5321.04(A)(8), 5321.05(B)	24 hours	✓	✓	✓	✓	
Oklahoma	Okla. Stat. Ann. tit. 41, § 128	One day	✓	✓	✓	✓	
Oregon	Or. Rev. Stat. §§ 90.322, 90.410	24 hours	✓	✓	✓	✓	✓
Pennsylvania	No statute						
Rhode Island	R.I. Gen. Laws § 34-18-26	Two days	✓	✓	✓	✓	✓
South Carolina	S.C. Code Ann. §§ 27-40-530, 27-40-730	24 hours	✓	✓	✓	✓	✓
South Dakota	No statute						
Tennessee	Tenn. Code Ann. §§ 66-28-403, 66-28-507	24 hours (applies only within the final 30 days of the rental agreement term, when landlord intends to show the premises to prospective renters and this right of access is set forth in the rental agreement)	✓	✓	✓	✓	✓
Texas	No statute						
Utah	Utah Code Ann. §§ 57-22-4, 57-22-5(2)(c)	24 hours, unless rental agreement specifies otherwise	✓		✓		
Vermont	Vt. Stat. Ann. tit. 9, § 4460	48 hours	✓	✓	✓	✓	
Virginia	Va. Code Ann. §§ 55-248.18, 55-248.33	For routine maintenance only: 24 hours, but no notice needed if entry follows tenant's request for maintenance.	✓	✓	✓	✓	✓
Washington	Wash. Rev. Code Ann. § 59.18.150	Two days; one day to show property to actual or prospective tenants or buyers	✓	✓	✓	✓	
West Virginia	No statute						
Wisconsin	Wis. Stat. Ann. § 704.05(2)	Advance notice	✓	✓	✓	✓	
Wyoming	No statute						

State Laws on Handling Abandoned Property

Most states regulate the way landlords must handle property left behind by departed tenants. Many set notice requirements as to how landlords must contact tenants regarding abandoned property. States may also regulate how landlords must store abandoned property and dispose of it if the tenant doesn't claim his or her belongings. For details, check your state statute, listed in this chart. Keep in mind that court cases not mentioned here may further describe proper procedures in your state.

State	Statute	State	Statute
Alabama	Ala. Code 1975 § 35-9A-423	Missouri	Mo. Rev. Stat. § 441.065
Alaska	Alaska Stat. § 34.03.260	Montana	Mont. Code Ann. § 70-24-430
Arizona	Ariz. Rev. Stat. Ann. § 33-1370	Nebraska	Neb. Rev. Stat. §§ 69-2303 to 69-2314
Arkansas	Ark. Code Ann. § 18-16-108	Nevada	Nev. Rev. Stat. Ann. §§ 118A.450, 118A.460
California	Cal. Civ. Code §§ 1965, 1980 to 1991	New Hampshire	N.H. Rev. Stat. Ann. § 540-A:3(VII)
Colorado	Colo. Rev. Stat. §§ 38-20-116, 13-40-122	New Jersey	N.J. Stat. Ann. §§ 2A:18-72 to 2A:18-84
Connecticut	Conn. Gen. Stat. Ann. §§ 47a-11b, 47a-42	New Mexico	N.M. Stat. Ann. § 47-8-34.1
Delaware	Del. Code Ann. tit. 25, §§ 5507, 5715	New York	No statute
D.C.	No statute	North Carolina	N.C. Gen. Stat. §§ 42-25.9, 42-36.2
Florida	Fla. Stat. Ann. §§ 715.104 to 715.111	North Dakota	N.D. Cent. Code § 47-16-30.1
Georgia	Ga. Code Ann. § 44-7-55	Ohio	*Ringler v. Sias*, 428 N.E.2d 869 (Ohio Ct. App. 1980)
Hawaii	Haw. Rev. Stat. § 521-56	Oklahoma	Okla. Stat. Ann. tit. 41, § 130
Idaho	Idaho Code § 6-311C	Oregon	Ore. Rev. Stat. §§ 90.425, 105.165
Illinois	735 Ill. Comp. Stat. § 5/9-318	Pennsylvania	68 P.S. § 250.505a
Indiana	Ind. Code Ann. §§ 32-31-4-1 to 32-31-4-5, 32-31-5-5	Rhode Island	R.I. Gen. Laws § 34-18-50
		South Carolina	S.C. Code Ann. §§ 27-40-710(D), 27-40-730
Iowa	*Khan v. Heritage Prop. Mgmt.*, 584 N.W.2d 725, 730 (Iowa Ct. App. 1998)	South Dakota	S.D. Codified Laws Ann. §§ 43-32-25, 43-32-26
Kansas	Kan. Stat. Ann. § 58-2565	Tennessee	Tenn. Code Ann. § 66-28-405
Kentucky	No statute	Texas	Tex. Prop. Code § 92.014
Louisiana	La. Civ. Code § 2707, La. Civ. Proc. § 4705	Utah	Utah Code Ann. § 78B-6-816
Maine	Me. Rev. Stat. Ann. tit. 14, §§ 6005, 6013	Vermont	Vt. Stat. Ann. tit. 9, § 4462; Vt. Stat. Ann. tit. 12, § 4854a
Maryland	Md. Code, Real Property, § 8-208	Virginia	Va. Code Ann. §§ 55-225.40 to 55-225.42; 55-248.38:1 to 55-248.38:2
Massachusetts	M.G.L.A. 239 § 4	Washington	Wash. Rev. Code Ann. § 59.18.310
Michigan	No statute	West Virginia	W.Va. Code §§ 37-6-6, 55-3A-3
Minnesota	Minn. Stat. Ann. § 504B.271	Wisconsin	Wis. Stat. Ann. § 704.05(5)
Mississippi	Miss. Code Ann. §§ 89-7-31, 89-7-35, 89-8-13	Wyoming	Wyo. Stat. § 1-21-1210

State Laws Prohibiting Landlord Retaliation

State	Statute	Tenant's Complaint to Landlord or Government Agency	Tenant's Involvement in Tenants' Organization	Tenant's Exercise of Legal Right	Retaliation Is Presumed If Negative Reaction by Landlord Within Specified Time of Tenant's Act
Alabama	Ala. Code § 35-9A-501	✓	✓		
Alaska	Alaska Stat. § 34.03.310	✓	✓	✓	
Arizona	Ariz. Rev. Stat. Ann. § 33-1381	✓	✓		6 months
Arkansas [1]	Ark. Code Ann. § 20-27-608	✓			
California [2]	Cal. Civ. Code § 1942.5	✓	✓	✓	180 days
Colorado [3]	Colo. Rev. Stat. § 38-12-509	✓			
Connecticut	Conn. Gen. Stat. §§ 47a-20, 47a-33	✓	✓	✓	6 months
Delaware	Del. Code Ann. tit. 25, § 5516	✓	✓	✓	90 days
D.C.	D.C. Code § 42-3505.02	✓	✓	✓	6 months
Florida [4]	Fla. Stat. Ann. § 83.64	✓	✓	✓	
Georgia	No statute				
Hawaii	Haw. Rev. Stat. § 521-74	✓		✓	
Idaho	No statute				
Illinois	765 Ill. Comp. Stat. § 720/1	✓			
Indiana	No statute				
Iowa	Iowa Code Ann. § 562A.36	✓	✓		1 year
Kansas	Kan. Stat. Ann. § 58-2572	✓	✓		
Kentucky	Ky. Rev. Stat. Ann. § 383.705	✓	✓		1 year
Louisiana	No statute				
Maine [5]	4 Me. Rev. Stat. Ann. tit. 14, §§ 6001(3)(4), 6021-A	✓	✓	✓	6 months
Maryland	Md. Code Ann. [Real Prop.] § 8-208.1	✓	✓	✓	
Massachusetts [2]	Mass. Ann. Laws ch. 239, § 2A; ch. 186, § 18	✓	✓	✓	6 months
Michigan	Mich. Comp. Laws § 600.5720	✓	✓	✓	90 days
Minnesota	Minn. Stat. Ann. §§ 504B.285, 504B.441	✓		✓	90 days
Mississippi	Miss. Code Ann. § 89-8-17			✓	
Missouri	No statute				

[1] Only prohibits retaliation by landlord who has received notice of lead hazards. (Arkansas)

[2] Applies when a retaliatory eviction follows a court case or administrative hearing concerning the tenant's underlying complaint, membership in a tenant organization, or exercise of a legal right. In this situation, a tenant may claim the benefit of the antiretaliation presumption only if the eviction falls within six months of the final determination of the court case or administrative hearing. (California and Massachusetts) Landlord cannot terminate based on tenants' (or their associates') immigration or citizenship status. (California)

[3] Tenant is protected against retaliation only for complaints of violations of the warranty of habitability. Tenant must prove actual violation in order to prevail. Any termination, rent increase, or service decrease that follows a complaint is presumed to be not retaliatory (timing alone of such actions will not make them retaliatory.) (Colorado)

[4] Statute lists retaliatory acts as illustrative, not exhaustive, and includes retaliation after the tenant has paid rent to a condominium, cooperative, or homeowners' association after demand from the association in order to pay the landlord's obligation to the association; and when the tenant has exercised his or her rights under state, local, or federal fair housing laws. (Florida)

[5] Allows tenant to raise his complaint to a fair housing agency as an affirmative defense to an eviction; retaliation presumed if tenant is served with an eviction notice within 6 months of tenant's exercise of rights regarding bedbug infestations (does not apply to eviction for nonpayment or for causing substantial damage). (Maine)

State Laws Prohibiting Landlord Retaliation (continued)

State	Statute	Tenant's Complaint to Landlord or Government Agency	Tenant's Involvement in Tenants' Organization	Tenant's Exercise of Legal Right	Retaliation Is Presumed If Negative Reaction by Landlord Within Specified Time of Tenant's Act
Montana	Mont. Code Ann. § 70-24-431	✓	✓		6 months
Nebraska	Neb. Rev. Stat. § 76-1439	✓	✓		
Nevada [6]	Nev. Rev. Stat. Ann. § 118A.510	✓	✓	✓	
New Hampshire	N.H. Rev. Stat. Ann. §§ 540:13-a, 540:13-b	✓	✓	✓	6 months
New Jersey [7]	N.J. Stat. Ann. §§ 2A:42-10.10, 2A: 42-10.12	✓	✓	✓	
New Mexico	N.M. Stat. Ann. § 47-8-39	✓	✓		6 months
New York	N.Y. Real Prop. Law § 223-b	✓	✓	✓	6 months
North Carolina	N.C. Gen. Stat. § 42-37.1	✓	✓	✓	12 months
North Dakota	No statute				
Ohio	Ohio Rev. Code Ann. § 5321.02	✓	✓		
Oklahoma	No statute				
Oregon	Or. Rev. Stat. § 90.385	✓	✓		
Pennsylvania	68 Pa. Cons. Stat. Ann. §§ 250.205, 399.11		✓	✓	6 months (for exercise of legal rights connected with utility service)
Rhode Island	R.I. Gen. Laws Ann. §§ 34-20-10, 34-20-11	✓		✓	
South Carolina	S.C. Code Ann. § 27-40-910	✓			
South Dakota	S.D. Code Laws Ann. §§ 43-32-27, 43-32-28	✓	✓		180 days
Tennessee	Tenn. Code Ann. §§ 66-28-514, 68-111-105	✓		✓	
Texas	Tex. Prop. Code § 92.331	✓	✓	✓	6 months
Utah	*Building Monitoring Sys. v. Paxton*, 905 P.2d 1215 (Utah 1995)	✓			
Vermont [8]	Vt. Stat. Ann. tit. 9, § 4465	✓	✓	✓	90 days
Virginia	Va. Code Ann. §§ 55-225.18, 55-248.39	✓	✓		
Washington	Wash. Rev. Code §§ 59.18.240, 59.18.250	✓		✓	90 days
West Virginia	*Imperial Colliery Co. v. Fout*, 373 S.E.2d 489 (1988)	✓		✓	
Wisconsin	Wis. Stat. § 704.45	✓		✓	
Wyoming	No statute				

[6] Statute protects tenants or tenants' guests who reasonably request emergency assistance. Local government cannot deem the request itself to be a "nuisance." Landlord may, however, take appropriate adverse actions based on information supplied by emergency responders, as can local governments with regard to declaring a nuisance. (Nevada)

[7] If a tenant fails to request a renewal of a lease or tenancy within 90 days of the tenancy's expiration (or by the renewal date specified in the lease if longer than 90 days), a landlord may terminate or not renew without a presumption of retaliation. (New Jersey)

[8] Retaliation presumed only when landlord terminates for reasons other than rent nonpayment, after tenant has filed complaint with a governmental entity alleging noncompliance with health or safety regulations. (Vermont)

State Laws on Termination for Nonpayment of Rent

If the tenant is late with the rent, in most states the landlord cannot immediately file for eviction. Instead, the landlord must give the tenant written notice that the tenant has a specified number of days in which to pay up or move. If the tenant does neither, the landlord can file for eviction. In some states, the landlord must wait a few days after the rent is due before giving the tenant the notice; other states allow the landlord to file for eviction immediately. The following rules may be tempered in domestic violence situations, depending on state law (see "State Laws in Domestic Violence Situations" in this appendix).

State	Statute	Time Tenant Has to Pay Rent or Move Before Landlord Can File for Eviction	Legal Late Period: How Long Landlord Must Wait Before Giving Notice to Pay or Quit
Alabama	Ala. Code § 35-9A-421	7 days	
Alaska	Alaska Stat. §§ 09.45.090, 34.03.220	7 days	
Arizona	Ariz. Rev. Stat. § 33-1368	5 days	
Arkansas [1]	Ark. Stat. §§ 18-17-701, 18-16-101	5 days	
California	Cal. Civ. Proc. Code § 1161(2)	3 days	
Colorado	Colo. Rev. Stat. § 13-40-104(1)(d)	3 days	
Connecticut	Conn. Gen. Stat. §§ 47a-23, 47a-15a	9 days	Unconditional Quit notice cannot be delivered until the rent is 9 days late.
Delaware	Del. Code Ann. tit. 25, §§ 5501(d), 5502	5 days	If rental agreement provides for a late charge, but landlord does not maintain an office in the county in which the rental unit is located, due date for the rent is extended 3 days; thereafter, landlord can serve a 5-day notice.
District of Columbia	D.C. Code § 42-3505.01	30 days (nonpayment of a late fee cannot be the basis of an eviction)	
Florida	Fla. Stat. Ann. § 83.56(3)	3 days	
Georgia	Ga. Code Ann. §§ 44-7-50, 44-7-52	Landlord can demand the rent as soon as it is due and, if not paid, can file for eviction. Tenant then has 7 days to pay to avoid eviction.	
Hawaii	Haw. Rev. Stat. § 521-68	5 days	
Idaho	Idaho Code § 6-303(2)	3 days	
Illinois	735 Ill. Comp. Stat. § 5/9-209	5 days	
Indiana	Ind. Code Ann. § 32-31-1-6	10 days	
Iowa	Iowa Code § 562A.27(2)	3 days	
Kansas	Kan. Rev. Stat. §§ 58-2507, 58-2508, 58-2564(b)	10 days (tenancies over 3 months) 3 days (tenancies less than 3 months)	
Kentucky	Ky. Rev. Stat. Ann. § 383.660(2)	7 days	
Louisiana	La. Civ. Proc. art. 4701	Landlord can terminate with an Unconditional Quit notice.	
Maine	Me. Rev. Stat. tit. 14, § 6002	7 days	Notice cannot be delivered until the rent is 7 days late, and must tell tenant that tenant can contest the termination in court (failure to so advise prohibits entry of a default judgment).

[1] Willful failure to move within ten days is a misdemeanor that subjects the tenant to a misdemeanor (fine only).

State Laws on Termination for Nonpayment of Rent (continued)

State	Statute	Time Tenant Has to Pay Rent or Move Before Landlord Can File for Eviction	Legal Late Period: How Long Landlord Must Wait Before Giving Notice to Pay or Quit
Maryland	Md. Code Ann. [Real Prop.] § 8-401	Can file immediately; must give 5 days' notice to appear in court; if tenant doesn't pay and landlord wins, tenant has 4 days to vacate. If tenant pays all back rent and court costs before end if trial, tenant can stay.	
Massachusetts[2]	Mass. Ann. Laws ch. 186, §§ 11 to 12	Tenants with rental agreements or leases, in accordance with agreement, or if not addressed in the agreement, 14 days' notice (but tenant can avoid by paying rent and costs before answer); holdover tenants: landlord can file for eviction immediately.	
Michigan	Mich. Comp. Laws § 554.134(2)	Landlord may terminate immediately with 7-day notice	
Minnesota	Minn. Stat. Ann. §§ 504B.135, 504B.291	14 days' notice required if tenancy at will (no lease); 30 days' or more notice for a lease with a term of more than 20 years	
Mississippi	Miss. Code Ann. §§ 89-7-27, 89-7-45	3 days. Tenant may stay if rent and costs are paid prior to removal.	
Missouri	Mo. Rev. Stat. § 535.010	Landlord can terminate with an Unconditional Quit notice.	
Montana	Mont. Code Ann. § 70-24-422(2)	3 days	
Nebraska	Neb. Rev. Stat. § 76-1431(2)	3 days	
Nevada	Nev. Rev. Stat. Ann. § 40.251	5 days	
New Hampshire	N.H. Rev. Stat. Ann. §§ 540:2, 540:3, 540:9	7 days. Tenant also owes $15 in liquidated damages, but use of this remedy is limited to three times within twelve months.	
New Jersey	N.J. Stat. Ann. §§ 2A:18-53, 2A:18-61.1, 2A:18-61.2, 2A:42-9	30 days. Landlord must accept rent and costs any time up to the day of trial.	
New Mexico	N.M. Stat. Ann. § 47-8-33(D)	3 days	
New York State	N.Y. Real Prop. Acts Law § 711(2)	3 days	
North Carolina	N.C. Gen. Stat. § 42-3	10 days	
North Dakota	N.D. Cent. Code 47-32-01	Landlord can file for eviction when rent is 3 days overdue and can terminate with an Unconditional Quit notice.	
Ohio	Ohio Rev. Code Ann. § 1923.02(A)(9)	Landlord can terminate with an Unconditional Quit notice.	
Oklahoma	Okla. Stat. Ann. tit. 41, § 131	5 days	
Oregon[3]	Or. Rev. Stat. § 90.394(2)(a)	72 hours (3 days)	Notice cannot be delivered until the rent is 8 days late.
	Or. Rev. Stat. § 90.394(2)(b)	144 hours (6 days)	Notice cannot be delivered until the rent is 5 days late.
Pennsylvania	68 Pa. Cons. Stat. Ann. § 250.501(b)	10 days	

2   For tenants at will who have not received notices in the preceding 12 months, 10 days to pay, 4 more to quit (unless notice is insufficient, then 14 days to pay). (Massachusetts)

3   Landlord has a choice: Serve pay or quit notice after rent is 8 days late (tenant has 72 hours to pay or quit), or serve the notice earlier, after rent is overdue 5 days (tenant has longer, 144 hours, to pay or quit). (Oregon)

State Laws on Termination for Nonpayment of Rent (continued)

State	Statute	Time Tenant Has to Pay Rent or Move Before Landlord Can File for Eviction	Legal Late Period: How Long Landlord Must Wait Before Giving Notice to Pay or Quit
Rhode Island	R.I. Gen. Laws § 34-18-35	5 days. Tenant can stay if rent paid back prior to commencement of suit. If tenant has not received a Pay or Quit notice for nonpayment of rent within past 6 months, tenant can stay if rent and costs paid back prior to eviction hearing.	15 days.
South Carolina	S.C. Code Ann. § 27-40-710(B), § 27-37-10(B)	5 days. If there is a written lease or rental agreement that specifies in bold, conspicuous type that landlord may file for eviction as soon as tenant is 5 days late (or if there is a month-to-month tenancy following such an agreement), landlord may do so without further notice to tenant. If there is no such written agreement, landlord must give tenant 5 days' written notice before filing for eviction.	
South Dakota	S.D. Codified Laws Ann. §§ 21-16-1(4), 21-16-2	3 days, and landlord can terminate with an Unconditional Quit notice.	
Tennessee	Tenn. Code Ann. § 66-28-505	14 days to pay; additional 16 days to vacate.	
Texas	Tex. Prop. Code Ann. § 24.005	3 days' notice to move (lease may specify a shorter or longer time).	
Utah	Utah Code Ann. § 78B-6-802	3 days	
Vermont	Vt. Stat. Ann. tit. 9, § 4467(a)	14 days	
Virginia[4]	Va. Code Ann. §§ 55-225, 55-225.38(C), 55-243, 55-248.31	5 days. Tenant who pays rent, costs, interest, and reasonable attorneys' fees can stay, but may invoke this right only once in any 12-month period.	If tenant does not pay and does not move within the time alotted, for each day that the tenant remains, tenant will owe rent of up to 150% of the per diem of the monthly rent, but only if the rental agreement includes a clause specifying this result.
Washington	Wash. Rev. Code Ann. § 59.12.030(3)	3 days	
West Virginia	W.Va. Code § 55-3A-1	Landlord can file for eviction immediately, no notice required, no opportunity to cure.	
Wisconsin	Wis. Stat. Ann. § 704.17	Month-to-month tenants: 5 days; landlord can use an Unconditional Quit notice with 14 days' notice. Tenants with a lease less than one year, and year-to-year tenants: 5 days (cannot use Unconditional Quit notice). Tenants with a lease longer than one year: 30 days (cannot use Unconditional Quit notice).	
Wyoming	Wyo. Stat. §§ 1-21-1002 to 1-21-1003	Landlord can file for eviction when rent is 3 days or more late and tenant has been given at least 3 days' notice. Landlord can also terminate with an Unconditional Quit notice.	

[4] If tenant does not pay and does not move within the time allotted, for each day that the tenant remains, tenant will owe rent of up 150% of the per diem of the monthly rent, but only if the rental agreement includes a clause specifying this result.

State Laws on Termination for Violation of Lease

Many states give the tenant a specified amount of time to cure or cease the lease or rental agreement violation or move before the landlord can file for eviction. In some states, if the tenant has not ceased or cured the violation at the end of that period, the tenant gets additional time to move before the landlord can file; in others, the tenant must move as soon as the cure period expires. And some states allow the landlord to terminate with an Unconditional Quit notice, without giving the tenant a chance to cure or cease the violation. The following rules may be tempered in domestic violence situations, depending on state law (see "State Laws in Domestic Violence Situations" in this appendix).

State	Statute	Time Tenant Has to Cure the Violation or Move Before Landlord Can File for Eviction
Alabama	Ala. Code § 35-9A-421	14 calendar days
Alaska	Alaska Stat. §§ 09.45.090, 34.03.220	10 days for violators of agreement materially affecting health and safety; 3 days to cure for failing to pay utility bills, resulting in shut-off, additional 2 to vacate.
Arizona	Ariz. Rev. Stat. § 33-1368	5 days for violations materially affecting health and safety; 10 days for other violations of the lease terms.
Arkansas	Ark. Stat. §§ 18-17-701, 18-17-702	Tenant has 14 days to cure a remediable violation. If violation materially affects tenant's health and safety, tenant must remedy as promptly as conditions require in case of emergency (or within 14 days after written notice by the landlord if it is not an emergency); failure entitles landlord to terminate the tenancy.
California	Cal. Civ. Proc. Code § 1161(3)	3 days
Colorado	Colo. Rev. Stat. § 13-40-104(1)(d.5),(e)	3 days (no cure for certain substantial violations).
Connecticut	Conn. Gen. Stat. Ann. § 47a-15	15 days; no right to cure for nonpayment of rent or serious nuisance.
Delaware	Del. Code Ann. tit. 25, § 5513(a)	7 days
District of Columbia	D.C. Code § 42-3505.01	30 days
Florida	Fla. Stat. Ann. § 83.56(2)	7 days (no cure for certain substantial violations).
Georgia	No statute	Landlord can terminate with an Unconditional Quit notice.
Hawaii	Haw. Rev. Stat. §§ 521-72, 666-3	10 days notice to cure: if it has not ceased, must wait another 20 to file for eviction; 24 hours to cease a nuisance: if it has not ceased in 24 hours, 5 days to cure before filing for eviction.
Idaho	Idaho Code § 6-303	3 days
Illinois	735 Ill. Comp. Stat. 5/9-210	10 days
Indiana	No statute	Landlord can terminate with an Unconditional Quit notice.
Iowa	Iowa Code § 562A.27(1)	7 days
Kansas	Kan. Stat. Ann. § 58-2564(a)	14 days to cure and an additional 16 to vacate.
Kentucky	Ky. Rev. Stat. Ann. § 383.660(1)	15 days
Louisiana	La. Civ. Proc. art. 4701	5 days
Maine	Me. Rev. Stat. Ann. tit. 14 § 6002	7 days
Maryland	Md. Real Prop. Code Ann. § 8-402.1	30 days unless breach poses clear and imminent danger, then 14 days (no cure).
Massachusetts	No statute	Landlord can terminate with an Unconditional Quit notice.
Michigan	Mich. Comp. Laws § 600.5714	For causing serious, continuous health hazards or damage to the premises: 7 days after receiving notice to restore or repair or quit (domestic violence victims excepted).

State Laws on Termination for Violation of Lease (continued)

State	Statute	Time Tenant Has to Cure the Violation or Move Before Landlord Can File for Eviction
Minnesota	Minn. Stat. Ann. § 504B.285 (Subd.4)	Landlord can immediately file for eviction.
Mississippi	Miss. Code Ann. § 89-8-13	30 days
Missouri	No statute	Landlord can terminate with an Unconditional Quit notice.
Montana	Mont. Code Ann. § 70-24-422	14 days; 3 days if unauthorized pet or person on premises.
Nebraska	Neb. Rev. Stat. § 76-1431	14 days to cure, 16 additional days to vacate.
Nevada	Nev. Rev. Stat. Ann. § 40.2516	5 days to cure
New Hampshire	N.H. Rev. Stat. Ann. § 540:3	30 days
New Jersey	N.J. Stat. Ann. §§ 2A:18-53(c), 2A:18-61.1(e)(1)	3 days; lease must specify which violations will result in eviction. (Some courts have ruled that the tenant be given an opportunity to cure the violation or condition any time up to the entry of judgment in favor of the landlord.)
New Mexico	N.M. Stat. Ann. § 47-8-33(A)	7 days
New York	N.Y. Real Prop. Acts Law §§ 711, 753(4)[NYC]	Regulated units: 10 days or as set by applicable rent regulation. Nonregulated units: No statute. Lease sets applicable cure and/or termination notice periods.
North Carolina	No statute	Landlord can terminate with an Unconditional Quit notice if lease specifies termination for violation.
North Dakota	No statute	
Ohio	Ohio Revised Code §§ 1923.02(A)(9) and 1923.04	3 days
Oklahoma	Okla. Stat. Ann. tit. 41, § 132(A), (B)	10 days to cure, additional 5 days to vacate.
Oregon	Or. Rev. Stat. §§ 90.392, 90.405	14 days to cure, additional 16 days to vacate; 10 days to remove an illegal pet.
Pennsylvania	No statute	Landlord can terminate with an Unconditional Quit notice.
Rhode Island	R.I. Gen. Laws § 34-18-36	20 days for material noncompliance.
South Carolina	S.C. Code Ann. § 27-40-710(A)	14 days
South Dakota	S.D. Codified Laws Ann. §§ 21-16-1(7), 21-16-2	Landlord must give tenant 3 days' notice to quit (no opportunity to cure) before filing for eviction, in specified situations. Other situations require no notice.
Tennessee	Tenn. Code Ann. § 66-28-505(d)	14 days
Texas	Tex. Prop. Code § 24.005	3 days
Utah	Utah Code Ann. § 78B-6-802	3 days
Vermont	Vt. Stat. Ann. tit.9 § 4467(b)(1)	30 days
Virginia	Va. Code. Ann. § 55-248.31	21 days to cure, additional 9 to quit. If tenant does not cure and does not move within the time allotted, for each day that the tenant remains, tenant will owe rent of up 150% of the per diem of the monthly rent, but only if the rental agreement includes a clause specifying this result.
Washington	Wash. Rev. Code Ann. § 59.12.030(4)	10 days
West Virginia	W.Va. Code § 55-3A-1	Landlord can immediately file for eviction; no notice is required.
Wisconsin	Wis. Stat. Ann. § 704.17	5 days, no opportunity to cure for public housing tenants who have committed drug-related violations.
Wyoming	Wyo. Stat. §§1-21-1002, 1-21-1003	3 days

State Laws on Unconditional Quit Terminations

The following rules may be tempered in domestic violence situations, depending on state law (see "State Laws in Domestic Violence Situations" in this appendix).

State	Statute	Time to Move Out Before Landlord Can File For Eviction	When Unconditional Quit Notice Can Be Used
Alabama	Ala. Code § 35-9A-421	7 days	Intentional misrepresentation of a material fact in a rental application or rental agreement, possession or use of illegal drugs in the rental or common areas, discharge of a firearm (some exceptions), criminal assault of a tenant or guest on the premises (some exceptions).
Alaska	Alaska Stat. § 34.03.220(a)(1)	24 hours	Tenant or guest intentionally causing more than $400 of damage to landlord's property or same violation of lease within 6 months
	§ 9.45.090(a)(2)(G)	24 hours to 5 days	Tenant or guest intentionally causing more than $400 of damage to landlord's property and specified illegal activity on the premises, including allowing prostitution
	§ 34.03.220(e)	3 days	Failure to pay utility bills twice within six months
	§ 34.03.300(a)	10 days	Refusal to allow the landlord to enter
Arizona	Ariz. Rev. Stat. Ann. § 33-1368	10 days	Material misrepresentation of criminal record, current criminal activity, or prior eviction record
		Immediately	Discharging a weapon, homicide, prostitution, criminal street gang activity, use or sale of illegal drugs, assaults, acts constituting a nuisance or breach of the rental agreement that threaten harm to others
Arkansas	Ark. Stat. Ann. §§ 81-17-701, 18-16-101	5 days	Noncompliance by the tenant with the rental agreement when the violation is not remediable; using (or allowing another person to use) the premises in a way constituting a common nuisance, or permitting/conducting specified criminal offenses; rent unpaid within five days of rent due date. If rent is unpaid within ten days of due date, tenant may be charged with a misdemeanor (fine only).
California	Cal. Civ. Proc. Code § 1161(4)	3 days	Assigning or subletting without permission, committing waste or a nuisance, illegal activity on the premises
Colorado	Colo. Rev. Stat. § 13-40-104(1)(e.5)	3 days	Any repeated violation of a lease clause
Connecticut	Conn. Gen. Stat. Ann. §§ 47a-23, 47a-15, 47a-15a	3 days	Nonpayment of rent, serious nuisance, violation of the rental agreement, same violation within 6 months relating to health and safety or materially affecting physical premises, rental agreement has terminated (by lapse of time, stipulation, violation of lease, nonpayment of rent after grace period, serious nuisance, occupancy by someone who never had the right to occupy), when summary eviction is justified (refusal to a fair and equitable increase, intent of the landlord to use as a principal residence, removal of the unit from the housing market), domestic or farm worker who does not vacate upon cessation of employment and tenancy
	Conn. Gen. Stat. Ann. § 47a-31	Immediately	Conviction for prostitution or gambling

State Laws on Unconditional Quit Terminations (continued)

State	Statute	Time to Move Out Before Landlord Can File For Eviction	When Unconditional Quit Notice Can Be Used
Delaware	Del. Code Ann. tit. 25, §§ 5513, 5514	7 days	Violation of a lease provision that also constitutes violation of municipal, county, or state code or statute, or same violation of a material lease provision repeated within 12 months
		Immediately	Violation of law or breach of the rental agreement that causes or threatens to cause irreparable harm to the landlord's property or to other tenants
District of Columbia	D.C. Code § 42-3505.01(c)	30 days	Court determination that an illegal act was performed within the rental unit
Florida	Fla. Stat. Ann. § 83.56(2)(a)	7 days	Intentional destruction of the rental property or other tenants' property or unreasonable disturbances; for destruction, damage, or misuse of the landlord's or other tenants' property by intentional act or a subsequent or continued unreasonable disturbance (after written warning within previous 12 months); a subsequent or continuing noncompliance within 12 months of a written warning by the landlord of a similar violation
Georgia	Ga. Code Ann. §§ 44-7-50, 44-7-52	Immediately	Nonpayment of rent more than once within 12 months, holding over
Hawaii	Haw. Rev. Stat. §§ 521-70(c), 521-69, 666-3	Immediately	Causing or threatening to cause irremediable damage to any person or property
		5 days	Second failure to abate a nuisance within 24 hours of receiving notice
Idaho	Idaho Code § 6-303	Immediately	Using, delivering, or producing a controlled substance on the property at any time during the lease term
		3 days	Assigning or subletting without the consent of the landlord or causing serious damage to the property
Illinois	735 Ill. Comp. Stat. § 5/9-210	10 days	Failure to abide by any term of the lease
	740 Ill. Comp. Stat. § 40/11	5 days	Unlawful use or sale of any controlled substance
Indiana	Ind. Code Ann. § 32-31-1-8	Immediately	Tenants with lease: holding over. Tenants without lease: committing waste
Iowa	Iowa Code Ann. § 562A.27	7 days	Repeating same violation of lease within 6 months that affects health and safety
	Iowa Code Ann. § 562A.27A	3 days	Creating a clear and present danger to the health or safety of the landlord, tenants, or neighbors within 1,000 feet of the property boundaries
Kansas	Kan. Stat. Ann. § 58-2564(a)	30 days	Second similar material violation of the lease after first violation was corrected
Kentucky	Ky. Rev. Stat. Ann. § 383.660(1)	14 days	Repeating the same material violation of the lease within 6 months of being given a first cure or quit notice
Louisiana	La. Civ. Code art. 2686, La. Code Civ. Proc. art. 4701	5 days	Failure to pay rent, using dwelling for purpose other than the intended purpose (lease may specify shorter or longer notice, or eliminate requirement of notice), or upon termination of the lease for any reason

State Laws on Unconditional Quit Terminations (continued)

State	Statute	Time to Move Out Before Landlord Can File For Eviction	When Unconditional Quit Notice Can Be Used
Maine	Me. Rev. Stat. Ann. tit. 14, § 6002	7 days	Tenants at will: Violations of law relating to the tenancy, substantial and unrepaired damage to the premises; causing, permitting, or maintaining a nuisance; causing the dwelling to be unfit for human habitation; tenant is a perpetrator of domestic violence, sexual assault, or stalking and the victim is also a tenant
Maryland	Md. Code Ann. [Real Prop.] § 8-402.1(a)	14 days	Breaching lease by behaving in a manner that presents a clear and imminent danger to the tenant himself, other tenants, guests, the landlord, or the landlord's property, lease provides for termination for violation of lease clause, and landlord has given 14 days' notice
	Md. Code Ann. [Real Prop.] § 8-401(e)(1)	30 days	Any lease violation if the lease states that tenancy can terminate for violation of the lease; and, when tenant is late with the rent three times within the past 12 months, but landlord must have won an eviction lawsuit for each prior nonpayment of rent episode (tenants may reinstate their tenancy by paying rent and court costs after the landlord has won an eviction lawsuit, but before physical eviction)
Massachusetts	Mass. Ann. Laws ch. 186, § 12	14 days	Tenant at will receiving second notice to pay rent or quit within 12 months
Michigan	Mich. Comp. Laws § 600.5714(d) and (e)	7 days	Failure to pay rent, causing or threatening physical injury to an individual (landlord must have filed a police report)
	Mich. Comp. Laws § 554.134	24 hours	Manufacture, dealing, or possession of illegal drugs on leased premises (landlord must first file a police report)
Minnesota	Minn. Stat. Ann. § 504B.135	14 days	Tenant at will who fails to pay rent when due
Mississippi	Miss. Code Ann. § 89-8-13	14 days	Repeating the same act, which constituted a lease violation and for which notice was given, within 6 months
		30 days	Nonremediable violation of lease or obligations imposed by statute
Missouri	Mo. Ann. Stat. §§ 441.020, 441.030, 441.040	10 days	Using the premises for gambling, prostitution, or possession, sale, or distribution of controlled substances; assigning or subletting without consent; seriously damaging the premises or violating the lease
Montana	Mont. Code Ann. § 70-24-422(1)(e)	5 days	Repeating the same act—that constituted a lease violation and for which notice was given—within 6 months
	Mont. Code Ann. § 70-24-422	3 days	Unauthorized pet or person living on premises; destroying or removing any part of the premises; creating a reasonable potential that the premises may be damaged or destroyed, or that neighboring tenants may be injured, due to tenant's drug, or gang-related, or other illegal activity
		14 days	Any other noncompliance with rental agreement that can't be remedied or repaired
Nebraska	Neb. Rev. Stat. § 76-1431(1)	14 days	Repeating the same act, that constituted a lease violation and for which notice was given, within 6 months
	Neb. Rev. Stat. § 76-1431(4)	5 days	When tenant or guest engages in violent criminal activity or sells a controlled substance on the premises, or acts in a way that threatens the health or safety of other tenants, landlord, landlord's employees or agents (does not apply if tenant has sought a protective order or alerted the police)

State Laws on Unconditional Quit Terminations (continued)

State	Statute	Time to Move Out Before Landlord Can File For Eviction	When Unconditional Quit Notice Can Be Used
Nevada	Nev. Rev. Stat. Ann. § 40.2514	3 days	Assigning or subletting in violation of the lease; substantial damage to the property; conducting an unlawful business; permitting or creating a nuisance; causing injury and damage to other tenants or occupants of the property or adjacent buildings or structures; unlawful possession for sale, manufacture, or distribution of illegal drugs
	§ 40.2516	Immediately	Violation of lease term that can't be cured
New Hampshire	N.H. Rev. Stat. Ann. § 540:1-a		Different rules apply depending on whether the property is "restricted" (most residential property) or "nonrestricted" (single-family houses, if the owner of such a house does not own more than 3 single-family houses at any one time; rental units in an owner-occupied building containing a total of 4 dwelling units or fewer; and single-family houses acquired by banks or other mortgagees through foreclosure).
	§ 540:2, 540:3	7 days	Restricted property: Neglect or refusal to pay rent due and in arrears, upon demand; substantial damage to the premises; failure to comply with a material term of the lease; behavior of the tenant or members of his family that adversely affects the health or safety of the other tenants or the landlord or his representatives; failure of the tenant to accept suitable temporary relocation required by lead-based paint hazard abatement; other good cause. Nonrestricted: Neglect or refusal to pay rent due and in arrears, upon demand; substantial damage to the premises; behavior of the tenant or members of his family that adversely affects the health or safety of the other tenants or the landlord or his representatives; failure of the tenant to accept suitable temporary relocation required by lead-based paint hazard abatement; failure to prepare unit for insect (including bedbug) remediation
		30 days	Nonrestricted only: For any legal reason other than those specified just above (for which 7 days' notice is required)
New Jersey	N.J. Stat. Ann. §§ 2A:18-53(c), 2A:18-61.2(a), 2A:19-61.1	3 days	Disorderly conduct; willful or grossly negligent destruction of landlord's property; assaults upon or threats against the landlord; termination of tenant's employment as a building manager, janitor, or other employee of the landlord; conviction for use, possession, or manufacture of an illegal drug either on the property or adjacent to it within the last two years, unless the tenant has entered a rehabilitation program (includes harboring anyone so convicted); conviction or civil liability for assault or terroristic threats against the landlord, landlord's family, or landlord's employee within the last two years (includes harboring); liability in a civil action for theft from landlord, landlord's family, landlord's employee, or another tenant; committing or harboring human trafficking
	N.J. Stat. Ann. §§ 2A:18-61.2(b), 2A:18-61.1	One month	Habitual failure to pay rent after written notice; continued violations, despite repeated warnings, of the landlord's reasonable rules and regulations; at the termination of a lease, refusal to accept reasonable changes of substance in the terms and conditions of the lease, including specifically any change in the term thereof

State Laws on Unconditional Quit Terminations (continued)

State	Statute	Time to Move Out Before Landlord Can File For Eviction	When Unconditional Quit Notice Can Be Used
New Mexico	N.M. Stat. Ann. § 47-8-33(I)	3 days	Substantial violation of the lease
	N.M. Stat. Ann. § 47-8-33(B) & (C)	7 days	Repeated violation of a term of the rental agreement within 6 months
New York	N.Y. Real Prop. Law § 232-a	30 days	In New York City, holdover of month-to-month tenancy
North Carolina	N.C. Gen. Stat. § 42-26(a)	Immediately	Violation of a lease term that specifies that eviction will result from noncompliance or holdover of tenancy
North Dakota	N.D. Cent. Code § 47-32-02	3 days	Holding over after the lease has expired; holding over after a sale or any judicial process ending the tenancy; violating a material term of the lease; using the property in a manner contrary to the agreement of the parties, using the property in a manner that unreasonably disturbs othe tenants' peaceful enjoyment
	N.D. Cent. Code § 47-16-07.6	Not specified	Making a false claim of a legal disability, in an attempt to obtain an accommodation (waiver of landlord's no pets rule); or knowingly providing fraudulent documentation in connection with such a claim. Each violation is an infraction and entitles the landlord to evict and demand a damage fee of up to $1,000.
Ohio	Ohio Rev. Code Ann. §§ 1923.02 to 1923.04, 5321.17	3 days	Nonpayment of rent; violation of a written lease or rental agreement; when the landlord has "reasonable cause to believe" that the tenant has used, sold, or manufactured an illegal drug on the premises (conviction or arrest not required)
Oklahoma	Okla. Stat. Ann. tit. 41, § 132	Immediately	Criminal or drug-related activity or repeated violation of the lease
Oregon	Or. Rev. Stat. §§ 90.396, 90.403	24 hours	Violence or threats of violence by tenant or a guest; intentionally causing substantial property damage; giving false information on an application within the past year regarding a criminal conviction (landlord must terminate within 30 days of discovering the falsity); committing any act "outrageous in the extreme" (see statute); intentionally or recklessly injuring someone (or placing them in fear of imminent danger) because of the tenant's perception of the person's race, color, religion, national origin, or sexual orientation; second failure to remove a pet that has caused substantial damage
Pennsylvania	68 Pa. Cons. Stat. Ann., § 250.501(b) and (d)	10 days	Nonpayment of rent
		15 days (lease 1 year or less or lease of unspecified time)	Violations of the terms of the lease
		30 days (lease more than 1 year)	Violations of the terms of the lease
	68 Pa. Cons. Stat. Ann., § 250.505-A	10 days (any tenancy)	First conviction for illegal sale, manufacture, or distribution of an illegal drug; repeated use of an illegal drug; seizure by law enforcement of an illegal drug within the leased premises

State Laws on Unconditional Quit Terminations (continued)

State	Statute	Time to Move Out Before Landlord Can File For Eviction	When Unconditional Quit Notice Can Be Used
Rhode Island	R.I. Gen. Laws § 34-18-36(e)	20 days	Repeating an act which violates the lease or rental agreement or affects health or safety twice within 6 months (notice must have been given for the first violation)
	R.I. Gen. Laws §§ 34-18-24, 34-18-36(f)	Immediately	Any tenant who possesses, uses, or sells illegal drugs or who commits or attempts to commit any crime of violence on the premises or in any public space adjacent. "Seasonal tenant" whose lease runs from May 1 to October 15 or from September 1 to June 1 of the next year, with no right of extension or renewal, who has been charged with violating a local occupancy ordinance, making excessive noise, or disturbing the peace
South Carolina	S.C. Code Ann. § 27-40-710	Immediately	Nonpayment of rent after receiving one notification during the tenancy or allowing illegal activities on the property
South Dakota	S.D. Cod. Laws §§ 21-16-1, 21-16-2	3 days	Nonpayment of rent, substantial damage to the property, or holdover
Tennessee	Tenn. Code Ann. § 66-28-505(a)	7 days (applies only in counties having a population of more than seventy-five thousand (75,000), according to the 2010 federal census or any subsequent federal census)	Repeating an act that violates the lease or rental agreement or affects health or safety twice within 6 months (notice must have been given for the first violation)
	Tenn. Code Ann. § 66-7-109	3 days (applies only in counties of less than 75,000 residents, according to the 2010 federal census or any subsequent federal census; residential tenants in a housing authority; and tenants who are not mentally or physically disabled)	Committing a violent act; engaging in drug-related criminal activity; or behaving in a manner that constitutes or threatens to be a real and present danger to the health, safety, or welfare of the life or property of other tenants, the landlord, the landlord's representatives, or other persons on the premises. (If the underlying act of violence was also domestic abuse, as defined, only the perpetrator may be evicted.)
Texas	Tex. Prop. Code § 24.005	3 days (lease may specify a shorter or longer time)	Nonpayment of rent or holdover
Utah	Utah Code Ann. § 78B-6-802	3 days	Holdover, assigning or subletting without permission, substantial damage to the property, carrying on an unlawful business on the premises, maintaining a nuisance, committing a criminal act on the premises
Vermont	Vt. Stat. Ann. tit. 9, § 4467	30 days	Three notices for nonpayment or late rent within a 12-month period or any violation of the lease or landlord-tenant law

State Laws on Unconditional Quit Terminations (continued)			
State	**Statute**	**Time to Move Out Before Landlord Can File For Eviction**	**When Unconditional Quit Notice Can Be Used**
Virginia	Va. Stat. Ann. § 55-248.31	30 days	Repeated violation of lease (after earlier violation was cured or nonremediable lease violation materially affecting health and safety). If tenant does not move within the time allotted, for each day that the tenant remains, tenant will owe rent of up 150% of the per diem of the monthly rent, but only if the rental agreement includes a clause specifying this result.
	Va. Stat. Ann. § 55-248.32	Immediately	A breach of the lease or rental agreement that is willful or a criminal act, is not remediable, and is a threat to the health or safety of others. If tenant does not move within the time allotted, for each day that the tenant remains, tenant will owe rent of up 150% of the per diem of the monthly rent, but only if the rental agreement includes a clause specifying this result.
Washington	Wash. Rev. Code Ann. § 59.12.030	3 days	Holdover, serious damage to the property, carrying on an unlawful business, maintaining a nuisance, or gang-related activity
West Virginia	W.Va. Code § 55-3A-1	Immediately	Failure to pay rent, violation of any lease provision, or damage to the property
Wisconsin	Wis. Stat. Ann. § 704.17	14 days (month-to-month tenants)	Failure to pay rent, violation of the rental agreement, or substantial damage to the property
		14 days (tenants with a lease of less than one year, or year-to-year tenants)	Failing to pay the rent on time, causing substantial property damage, or violating any lease provision more than once within one year (must have received proper notice for the first violation)
		5 days (all tenants)	Causing a nuisance on the property (landlord must have written notice from a law enforcement agency regarding the nuisance)
Wyoming	Wyo. Stat. §§ 1-21-1002, 1003	3 days	Nonpayment of rent, holdover, damage to premises, interference with another's enjoyment, denying access to landlord, or violating duties defined by statute (such as maintaining unit, complying with lease, disposing of garbage, etc.)

State Small Claims Court Limits

State	Statutes	Dollar limit	Evictions	Court Website
Alabama	Ala. Code §§ 6-3-2; 6-3-7; 12-12-31; 12-12-70; 12-12-71	$6,000	No.	www.alabamalegalhelp.org (click "Consumer Issues/ Small Claims Actions")
Alaska	Alaska Stat. §§ 22.15.040; 22.15.050	$10,000	No. (See www.courts. alaska.gov/webdocs/ forms/sc-100.pdf)	www.courts.alaska.gov/ forms/#sc (see "Small Claims" heading)
Arizona [1]	Ariz. Rev. Stat. Ann. §§ 22-501 to 22-524	$3,500	No. (www.mohave courts.com/Justice/ JCSS_SmallClaims.html)	www.azcourts.gov/self servicecenter/Self-Service-Forms#SmallClaims
Arkansas	Ark. Const. amend. 80, § 7	$5,000	No.	https://courts.arkansas. gov/sites/default/files/tree/ small_claims_info_0.pdf www.arlegalservices.org/ smallclaimspacket
California	Cal. Civ. Proc. Code §§ 116.110 to 116.950	$10,00 for individuals, except that a plaintiff may not file a claim over $2,500 more than twice a year. Limit for local public entity or for businesses is $5,000. $6,500 is the limit in suits by an individual against a guarantor that charges for its guarantor or surety services.	No.	www.courtinfo.ca.gov/ selfhelp/smallclaims www.dca.ca.gov/ publications/small_claims/ index.shtml
Colorado	Colo. Rev. Stat. §§ 13-6-401 to 13-6-417	$7,500	No.	www.courts.state.co.us/ userfiles/file/Self_Help/ smallclaimshandbook%20 finaltocourt%204-11.pdf www.courts.state.co.us/ Forms/SubCategory. cfm?Category=Small
Connecticut	Conn. Gen. Stat. Ann. §§ 47a-34 to 47a-42; 51-15; 51-345; 52-259	$5,000 (except in landlord-tenant security deposit claims)	No.	www.jud.state.ct.us/faq/ smallclaims.html
Delaware	Del. Code Ann. tit. 10, §§ 9301 to 9640	$15,000	Yes.	http://courts.delaware.gov/ JPCourt https://courts.delaware. gov/help/proceedings/ jp_startcivil.aspx
District of Columbia	D.C. Code Ann. §§ 11-1301 to 11-1323; 16-3901 to 16-3910; 17-301 to 17-307	$10,000	No.	www.dccourts.gov/services/ civil-matters/requesting-10k-or-less www.dccourts.gov/ sites/default/files/Small ClaimsHandbook.pdf

[1] Justice Courts, similar to small claims court but with more procedures, have a limit of $10,000. Rules can be found at Ariz. Rev. Stat. Ann. §§ 22-201 to 22-284. (Arizona)

State Small Claims Court Limits (continued)

State	Statutes	Dollar limit	Evictions	Court Website
Florida		$5,000	Yes.	www.flcourts.org/resources-and-services/family-courts/family-law-self-help-information/small-claims.stml www.flcourts.org/gen_public/family/self_help/smallclaims.shtml
Georgia	Ga. Code Ann. §§ 15-10-1; 15-10-2; 15-10-40 to 15-10-54; 15-10-80; 15-10-87	$15,000 (no limit in eviction cases)	Yes.	http://consumer.georgia.gov/consumer-topics/magistrate-court
Hawaii [2]	Haw. Rev. Stat. §§ 604-5; 633-27 to 633-36.	$5,000; no limit in landlord-tenant residential security deposit cases. For return of leased or rented personal property, the property must not be worth more than $5,000.	No.	www.courts.state.hi.us/self-help/small_claims/small_claims
Idaho	Idaho Code §§ 1-2301 to 1-2315	$5,000	No.	www.courtselfhelp.idaho.gov/small-claims
Illinois [3]	735 Ill. Comp. Stat. §§ 5/2-101 to 5/2-208; 705 Ill. Comp. Stat. § 205/11	$10,000	Yes.	www.ag.state.il.us/consumers/smlclaims.html
Indiana	Ind. Code Ann. §§ 33-28-3-2 to 33-28-3-10 (circuit court); 33-29-2-1 to 33-29-2-10 (superior court); 33-34-3-1 to 33-34-3-15 (Marion County Small Claims Court)	$6,000 ($8,000 in Marion County)	Yes, if total rent due does not exceed $6,000 ($8,000 in Marion County).	www.in.gov/judiciary/ 2710.htm
Iowa	Iowa Code §§ 631.1 to 631.17	$5,000	Yes.	www.iowacourts.gov/Court_Rules__Forms/Small_Claims_Forms
Kansas	Kan. Stat. Ann. §§ 61-2701 to 61-2714	$4,000	No.	www.kscourts.org/rules-procedures-forms/small-claims-information
Kentucky [4]	Ky. Rev. Stat. Ann. §§ 24A.200 to 24A.360	$2,500	Yes.	http://courts.ky.gov/courts/jefferson/small claims/Pages/default.aspx http://courts.ky.gov/resources/publications resources/Publications/P6SmallClaims Handbookweb.pdf

[2] Professional moneylenders and collection agents cannot sue in small claims court. (Hawaii)

[3] An alternative procedure exists for claims of $1,500 or less in Cook County's Pro Se Court. Plaintiffs represent themselves, and lawyers are allowed for defendants. See www.cookcountyclerkofcourt.org/includes/pages/community_resources/pro_se_faqs.asp. (Illinois)

[4] Professional moneylenders and collection agents cannot sue in small claims court. (Kentucky)

State Small Claims Court Limits (continued)

State	Statutes	Dollar limit	Evictions	Court Website
Louisiana	La. Rev. Stat. Ann. §§ 13:5200 to 13:5211 (city court); La. Code Civ. Proc., Art. 4831, 4832, 4845, 4901 to 4925, and Art. 42 (justice of the peace court)	$5,000 (city court); $5,000 (justice of the peace, but no limit in eviction cases)	Available in Justice of the Peace courts only.	www.lsba.org/Public/CourtStructure.aspx http://brgov.com/dept/citycourt/civilfaqs.htm (Baton Rouge)
Maine	Me. Rev. Stat. Ann. tit. 14, §§ 7481 to 7487	$6,000	No.	www.courts.state.me.us/maine_courts/small_claims/index.shtml
Maryland	Md. Code Ann. [Cts. & Jud. Proc.] §§ 4-405; 6-403	$5,000	Yes, as long as the rent claimed does not exceed $5,000.	www.courts.state.md.us/legalhelp/smallclaims.html
Massachusetts 5	Mass. Gen. Laws ch. 218, §§ 21 to 25; ch. 223, § 6; ch. 93A, § 9 (consumer complaints)	$7,000; no limit for property damage caused by motor vehicle	No.	www.mass.gov/ago/consumer-resources/consumer-assistance/small-claims-court.html
Michigan	Mich. Comp. Laws §§ 600.8401 to 600.8427	$6,000	No.	http://courts.mi.gov/administration/scao/forms/pages/small-claims.aspx https://michiganlegalhelp.org/self-help-tools/money-and-debt/i-have-small-claims-case
Minnesota 6	Minn. Stat. Ann. §§ 491A.01 to 491A.03	$15,000 ($4,000 for claims involving consumer credit transactions)	No.	www.mncourts.gov/Help-Topics/Conciliation-Court.aspx
Mississippi	Miss. Code Ann. §§ 9-11-9 to 9-11-33; 11-9-101 to 11-9-147; 11-25-1; 11-51-85	$3,500	Yes.	http://courts.ms.gov/trialcourts/justicecourt/justicecourt.html
Missouri	Mo. Rev. Stat. §§ 482.300 to 482.365	$5,000	No.	www.courts.mo.gov/page.jsp?id=704 www.mobar.org/uploadedFiles/Home/Publications/Legal_Resources/Brochures_and_Booklets/small%20claims.pdf
Montana	Mont. Code Ann. §§ 25-2-118; 3-12-101 to 3-12-107 (district court); 25-33-101 to 25-33-306 (appeals); 25-35-501 to 25-35-807; 3-10-1001 to 3-10-1004 (justice court)	$7,000	No.	https://dojmt.gov/consumer/guide-to-small-claims-court
Nebraska	Neb. Rev. Stat. §§ 25-505.1; 25-2801 to 25-2807	$3,600 from July 1, 2015, through June 30, 2020 (adjusted every five years based on the Consumer Price Index)	No.	https://supremecourt.nebraska.gov/self-help/small-claims

5 Consumer complaint small claims: (1) plaintiff must make written demand for relief at least 30 days before filing suit; (2) attorneys' fees available; (3) triple damages available. (Massachusetts)

6 Educational institution may bring actions to recover student loans, if loans were originally awarded in the county in which it has administrative offices, even though the defendant is not county resident. (Minnesota)

State Small Claims Court Limits (continued)

State	Statutes	Dollar limit	Evictions	Court Website
Nevada	Nev. Rev. Stat. Ann. §§ 73.010 to 73.060	$10,000	No.	www.lasvegasjustice court.us/divisions/small_claims/ [Las Vegas] www.washoecounty.us/rjc/divisions/civil/small-claims-civil.php [Reno]
New Hampshire	N.H. Rev. Stat. Ann. §§ 503:1 to 503:11	$10,000	No.	www.courts.state.nh.us/district/eclaims/index.htm http://doj.nh.gov/consumer/complaints/small-claims.htm
New Jersey [7]	NJ R LAW DIV CIV PT Rule 6:1-2	$3,000 ($5,000 for claims relating to security deposits); certain landlord-tenant suits cannot be brought	No.	www.judiciary.state.nj.us/forms/10290_small_claims.pdf
New Mexico	N.M. Stat. Ann. §§ 34-8A-1 to 34-8A-10 (metropolitan court); 35-3-3, 35-3-5, 35-8-1 and 35-8-2 (magistrate court); 35-11-2, 35-13-1 to 35-13-3 (appeals)	$10,000	Yes.	https://metro.nmcourts.gov/uploads/files/Metro%20Self%20Help/Pamphlets/SH101%20-%20How%20to%20File%20a%20Lawsuit%20Rev%201-17.pdf www.nmcourts.gov/about-the-courts.aspx www2.nmcourts.gov/othercourts/magistrate_brochure.pdf
New York [8]	New York Unif. City Ct. Act §§ 1801 to 1815, 1801-A to 1814-A (commercial claims); N.Y. Unif. Dist. Ct. Act §§ 1801 to 1815, 1801-A to 1814-A (commercial claims); N.Y. Unif. Just. Ct. Act §§ 1801 to 1815; N.Y. City Civ. Ct. Act §§ 1801 to 1815; 1801-A to 1814-A (commercial claims)	$5,000 (town and village justice courts, $3,000)	No.	www.courts.state.ny.us/courthelp/smallClaims/index.shtml
North Carolina	N. C. Gen. Stat. §§ 7A-210 to 7A-232; 42-29	$10,000	Yes.	www.nccourts.org/Courts/Trial/SClaims www.legalaidnc.org/get-help/Documents/small-claims-guide/guide-to-small-claims-court.pdf

[7] The Special Civil Part, like the small claims court but with more procedures, has a limit of $15,000. See www.judiciary.state.nj.us/civil/civ-03.htm. (New Jersey)

[8] Corporations and partnerships cannot sue in small claims court, but may appear as defendants. (Does not apply to municipal and public benefit corporations and school districts.) Instead, they can bring commercial claims, which have similar rules to small claims courts but are subject to these additional restrictions: (1) Same limits and procedures as regular small claims except claim is brought by corporation, partnership, or association; (2) Business must have principal office in N.Y. state; (3) Defendant must reside, be employed, or have a business office in the county where suit is brought. (New York)

State Small Claims Court Limits (continued)

State	Statutes	Dollar limit	Evictions	Court Website
North Dakota [9]	N. D. Cent. Code §§ 27-08.1-01 to 27-08.1-08	$15,000	No.	www.ndcourts.gov/ndlshc/SmallClaims/SmallClaims.aspx
Ohio	Ohio Rev. Code Ann. §§ 1925.01 to 1925.18	$6,000	No.	www.supremecourt.ohio.gov/jcs/interpretersvcs/forms/english/5.pdf https://lasclev.org/smallclaimscourtbrochure
Oklahoma [10]	Okla. Stat. Ann. tit. 12, §§ 131 to 141; 1751 to 1773	$10,000	Yes.	www.oklahomacounty.org/158/Small-Claims www.okbar.org/public/brochures/smallclaimscourt.aspx
Oregon	Or. Rev. Stat. §§ 46.405 to 46.570; 55.011 to 55.140	$10,000	No.	www.osbar.org/public/legalinfo/1061_SmallClaims.htm
Pennsylvania [11]	42 Pa. Cons. Stat. Ann. §§ 1123; 1515	$12,000	Yes.	http://fjd.phila.gov/municipal/civil/ [Philadelphia] www.pabar.org/clips/bringingsuitBeforeDJ.pdf
Rhode Island	R.I. Gen. Laws §§ 10-16-1 to 10-16-16; 9-4-3; 9-4-4; 9-12-10 (appeals)	$2,500	No.	www.courts.ri.gov/Courts/districtcourt/Pages/Small%20Claims%20Court.aspx [currently under construction] www.ribar.com/for%20the%20public/findingandchoosingalawyer.aspx
South Carolina	S.C. Code Ann. §§ 22-3-10 to 22-3-320; 15-7-30; 18-7-10 to 18-7-30	$7,500	Yes.	www.sccourts.org/selfHelp/FAQMagistrate.pdf
South Dakota	S.D. Codified Laws Ann. §§ 15-39-45 to 15-39-78; 16-12B-6; 16-12B-12; 16-12B-16; 16-12C-8; 16-12C-13 to 16-12C-15	$12,000	No.	http://ujs.sd.gov/Small_Claims
Tennessee [12]	Tenn. Code Ann. §§ 16-15-501 to 16-15-505; 16-15-710 to 16-15-735; 16-15-901 to 16-15-905; 20-4-101; 20-4-103	$25,000. No limit in eviction suits or suits to recover personal property.	Yes.	http://tncourts.gov/programs/self-help-center http://gs4.shelbycountytn.gov/gscvinq/gscv_civildivision [Shelby]

[9] Plaintiff may not discontinue once small claims process is begun; if plaintiff seeks to discontinue, claim will be dismissed with prejudice (plaintiff cannot refile claim). (North Dakota)

[10] Collection agencies may not sue in small claims court. (Oklahoma)

[11] If claiming more than $2,000 personal injury or property damage, must submit statement of claim signed under oath (Philadelphia Municipal Court). (Pennsylvania)

[12] Tennessee has no actual small claims system, but trials in general sessions court are normally conducted with informal rules. (Tennessee)

State Small Claims Court Limits (continued)

State	Statutes	Dollar limit	Evictions	Court Website
Texas [13]	Tex. Gov't. Code Ann. § 27.060	$10,000	Separate small claims courts have been abolished as of August 2013; both small claims cases and evictions are heard in Justice Court. Evictions cases are governed by Rules 500-507 and 510 of Part V of the Rules of Civil Procedure.	www.txcourts.gov/courts/overview/about-texas-courts/trial-courts.aspx
Utah	Utah Code Ann. §§ 78A-8-101 to 78A-8-109	$11,000	No.	www.utcourts.gov/howto/smallclaims/index.asp
Vermont	Vt. Stat. Ann. tit. 12, §§ 5531 to 5541; 402	$5,000	No.	www.vermontjudiciary.org/self-help/debt-collection-small-claims
Virginia [14]	Va. Code Ann. §§ 8.01-262; 16.1-76; 16.1-77; 16.1-106; 16.1-113; 16.1-122.1 to 16.1-122.7	$5,000	No.	www.courts.state.va.us/resources/small_claims_court_procedures.pdf www.courts.state.va.us/courts/gd/home.html
Washington	Wash. Rev. Code Ann. §§ 12.36.010 to 12.40.120; 3.66.040	$5,000	No.	www.courts.wa.gov/newsinfo/resources/?fa=newsinfo_jury.scc&altMenu=smal www.atg.wa.gov/small-claims-court-0
West Virginia	W.Va. Code §§ 50-2-1 to 50-6-3; 56-1-1	$10,000	Yes.	www.courtswv.gov/lower-courts
Wisconsin	Wis. Stat. §§ 799.01 to 799.445; 421.401; 801.50; 808.03	$10,000. No limit in eviction suits.	Yes.	www.wicourts.gov/services/public/selfhelp/smallclaims.htm
Wyoming	Wyo. Stat. Ann. §§ 1-21-201 to 1-21-205; 5-9-128; 5-9-136	$6,000	No.	www.courts.state.wy.us/court_rule/rules-and-forms-governing-small-claims-cases

[13] Separate small claims courts have been abolished as of August 2013; both small claims cases and evictions are heard in Justice Court. Evictions cases are governed by Rules 500-507 and 510 of Part V of the Rules of Civil Procedure. (Texas)

[14] General district courts, similar to small claims court but with more procedures, can hear claims up to $25,000. (See Va. Code Ann. §§ 16.1-77 to 16.1-80.) (Virginia)

		Landlord's Duty to Rerent		
State	Legal authority	Must make reasonable efforts to rerent	Has no duty to look for or rent to a new tenant	Law is unclear or courts are divided on the issue
Alabama	Ala. Code §§ 35-9A-105, 35-9A-423	✓		
Alaska	Alaska Stat. § 34.03.230(c)	✓		
Arizona	Ariz. Rev. Stat. § 33-1370	✓		
Arkansas	*Weingarten/Arkansas, Inc. v. ABC Interstate Theatres, Inc.*, 811 S.W.2d 295 (Ark. 1991)		✓	
California	Cal. Civ. Code § 1951.2	✓		
Colorado	*Schneiker v. Gordon*, 732 P.2d 603 (Colo. 1987)	✓ [1]		
Connecticut	Conn. Gen. Stat. Ann. § 47a-11a	✓		
Delaware	25 Del. Code Ann. § 5507(d)(2)	✓		
District of Columbia	*Int'l Comm'n on English Liturgy v. Schwartz*, 573 A.2d 1303 (D.C. 1990)		✓ [2]	
Florida	Fla. Stat. Ann. § 83.595		✓ [3]	
Georgia	*Peterson v. Midas Realty Corp.*, 287 S.E.2d 61 (Ga. Ct. App. 1981)		✓	
Hawaii	Haw. Rev. Stat. § 521-70 (d)	✓		
Idaho	*Consol. Ag v. Rangen, Inc.*, 128 Idaho 228 (Idaho 1996)	✓		
Illinois	735 Ill. Comp. Stat. § 5/9-213.1	✓		
Indiana	*Nylen v. Park Doral Apartments*, 535 N.E.2d 178 (Ind. Ct. App. 1989)	✓		
Iowa	Iowa Code § 562A.29 (3)	✓		
Kansas	Kan. Stat. Ann. § 58-2565(c)	✓		
Kentucky	Ky. Rev. Stat. Ann. § 383.670	✓		
Louisiana	La. Civ. Code § 2002, *Gray v. Kanavel*, 508 So.2d 970 (La. Ct. App. 1987)	✓ [4]		✓
Maine	14 Me. Rev. Stat. Ann. § 6010-A	✓		
Maryland	Md. Code Ann., [Real Prop.] § 8-207			✓
Massachusetts	*Edmands v. Rust & Richardson Drug Co.*, 191 Mass. 123, 128 (1906) and assorted other cases Booklet from MA.gov says LL has a duty to mitigate: www.mass.gov/ocabr/docs/landlordrights.pdf. Ditto from MassLegal Help: www.mass.gov/ocabr/docs/landlordrights.pdf. But the Supreme Court has not yet ruled definitively.	✓	✓	
Michigan	*Fox v. Roethlisberger*, 85 N.W.2d 73 (Mich. 1957)	✓		
Minnesota	*Control Data Corp. v. Metro Office Parks Co.*, 296 Minn. 302 (Minn. 1973)		✓	

[1] Case law is not dispositive, but state practice seems to require mitigation. See ColoradoLegalServices.org ("Breaking a Lease—What You Need to Know").

[2] Despite this legal authority, DC attorneys report that judges take failure to mitigate into consideration when ascertaining the landlord's damages. (District of Columbia)

[3] Landlord has the option of rerenting, standing by and doing nothing (tenant remains liable for rent as it comes due), or invoking its right to a liquidated damages, or early termination, provision. Latter remedy is available only if the lease includes a liquidated damages addendum, or addition, that provides for no more than two months' damages and requires tenant to give no more than 60 days' notice. Liquidated damages provision must substantially include specified language in Fl. Stat. Ann. § 83.595. (Florida)

[4] Court decisions are uniform although more recent decisions appear to require mitigation. (Louisiana)

	Landlord's Duty to Rerent (continued)			
State	Legal authority	Must make reasonable efforts to rerent	Has no duty to look for or rent to a new tenant	Law is unclear or courts are divided on the issue
Mississippi	*Alsup v. Banks*, 9 So. 895 (Miss. 1891)		✓ [5]	
Missouri	*Rhoden Inv. Co. v. Sears, Roebuck & Co.*, 499 S.W.2d 375 (Mo. 1973), Mo. Rev. Stat. § 535.300	✓ [6]		
Montana	Mont. Code Ann. § 70-24-426	✓		
Nebraska	Neb. Rev. Stat. § 76-1432	✓		
Nevada	Nev. Rev. Stat. Ann. § 118.175	✓		
New Hampshire	*Wen v. Arlen's, Inc.*, 103 A.2d 86 (N.H. 1954), *Modular Mfg., Inc. v. Dernham Co.*, 65 B.R. 856 (Bankr. D. N.H. 1986)			✓
New Jersey	*Sommer v. Kridel*, 378 A.2d 767 (N.J. 1977)	✓		
New Mexico	N.M. Stat. Ann. § 47-8-6	✓		
New York	*Rios v. Carrillo*, 53 AD3d 111, 115 (2nd Dept., 2008); *Gordon v. Raymond Eshaghoff*, 60 AD3d 807, 2009 WL 711546 (2nd Dept., decided March 17, 2009) and *Smith v. James*, 22 Misc. 3d 128 (A) (Supreme Court, Appellate Term, 9th & 10th Dist., 2009)		✓	
North Carolina	*Isbey v. Crews*, 284 S.E.2d 534 (N.C. Ct. App. 1981)	✓		
North Dakota	N.D. Cent. Code § 47-16-13.5	✓		
Ohio	*Stern v. Taft*, 361 N.E.2d 279 (Ct. App. 1976)	✓ [7]		
Oklahoma	41 Okla. Stat. Ann. § 129	✓		
Oregon	Or. Rev. Stat. § 90.410	✓		
Pennsylvania	*Stonehedge Square Ltd. P'ship v. Movie Merchs.*, 715 A.2d 1082 (Pa. 1998)		✓	
Rhode Island	R.I. Gen. Laws § 34-18-40	✓		
South Carolina	S.C. Code Ann. § 27-40-730 (c)	✓		
South Dakota	No cases or statutes in South Dakota discuss this issue.			✓
Tennessee	Tenn. Code Ann. § 66-28-507 (c)	✓ [8]		
Texas	Tex. Prop. Code Ann. § 91.006	✓		
Utah	Utah Code Ann. § 78B-6-816, *Reid v. Mutual of Omaha Ins. Co.*, 776 P.2d 896 (Utah 1989)	✓		
Vermont	9 Vt. Stat. Ann. § 4462		✓	
Virginia	Va. Code Ann. §§ 55-248.33, 55-248.35	✓		
Washington	Wash. Rev. Code Ann. § 59.18.310	✓ [9]		
West Virginia	W.Va. Code § 37-6-7, *Teller v. McCoy*, 253 S.E.2d 114 (W.Va. 1978)	✓		
Wisconsin	Wis. Stat. Ann. § 704.29	✓		
Wyoming	*Goodwin v. Upper Crust, Inc.*, 624 P.2d 1192 (1981)	✓		

[5] Many Miss. attorneys believe this old case is not sound authority, and that a trial judge would find a duty to mitigate in spite of it. (Mississippi)

[6] Landlord must mitigate only if intending to use tenant's security deposit to cover future unpaid rent. (Missouri)

[7] Duty to mitigate applies in absence of any clause that purports to relieve the landlord of this duty (courts must enforce this clause). (Ohio)

[8] Applies only to counties having a population of more than 75,000, according to the 2010 federal census or any subsequent federal census. (See Tenn. Code Ann. § 66-28-102). (Tennessee)

[9] Detailed procedures must be followed when premises are vacant due to tenant's death. (See Wash. Rev. Code Ann. § 59.18.595.) (Washington)

Consequences of Self-Help Evictions

State	Amount Tenant Can Sue For	Statute Provides for Tenant's Court Costs & Attorneys' Fees	Statute Gives Tenant the Right to Stay	Statute or Legal Authority
Alabama	Self-help evictions are not allowed, but no specific penalties are provided (judge decides on consequences).	N/A	N/A	Ala. Code § 35-9A-427
Alaska	One and one-half times the actual damages. If tenant elects to terminate the lease, landlord must return entire security deposit.	No	Yes	Alaska Stat. § 34.03.210
Arizona	Two months' rent or twice the actual damages, whichever is greater. If tenant elects to terminate the lease, landlord must return entire security deposit.	No	Yes	Ariz. Rev. Stat. § 33-1367
Arkansas	Self-help evictions are not allowed, but it's up to the court to determine damages.	N/A	N/A	*Gorman v. Ratliff*, 712 S.W. 2d 888 (1986)
California	Actual damages plus $100 per day of violation ($250 minimum). Tenant may ask for an injunction prohibiting any further violation during the court action.	Yes	Yes	Cal. Civ. Code § 789.3
Colorado	Tenant may sue for any damages.	N/A	N/A	Colo. Rev. Stat. § 38-12-510
Connecticut	Double actual damages. Landlord may also be prosecuted for a misdemeanor.	Yes	Yes	Conn. Gen. Stat. Ann. §§ 47a-43, 47a-46, 53a-214
Delaware	Triple damages or three times per diem rent for time excluded, whichever is greater. Tenant may recover court costs, but not attorneys' fees.	Yes	Yes	Del. Code Ann. tit. 25, § 5313
District of Columbia	Actual and punitive damages.	No	No	*Mendes v. Johnson*, 389 A.2d 781 (D.C. 1978)
Florida	Actual damages or three months' rent, whichever is greater.	Yes	No	Fla. Stat. Ann. § 83.67
Georgia	Landlord may not resort to self-help evictions. Damages are determined by the court.	N/A	N/A	*Forrest v. Peacock*, 363 S.E. 2d 581 (1987), reversed on other grounds, 368 S.E.2d 519 (1988)
Hawaii	Two months' rent or free occupancy for two months (tenant must have been excluded "overnight"). Court may order landlord to stop illegal conduct.	Yes	Yes	Haw. Rev. Stat. § 521-63(c)
Idaho				
Illinois				
Indiana	Statute doesn't specify damages.	N/A	N/A	Ind. Code Ann. § 32-31-5-6
Iowa	Actual damages, plus punitive damages up to twice the monthly rent and attorneys' fees. If tenant elects to terminate the lease, landlord must return entire security deposit.	Yes	Yes	Iowa Code § 562A.26
Kansas	Actual damages or one and one-half months' rent, whichever is greater.	No	Yes	Kan. Stat. Ann. § 58-2563

Consequences of Self-Help Evictions (continued)

State	Amount Tenant Can Sue For	Statute Provides for Tenant's Court Costs & Attorneys' Fees	Statute Gives Tenant the Right to Stay	Statute or Legal Authority
Kentucky	Three months' rent.	Yes	Yes	Ky. Rev. Stat. Ann. § 383.655
Louisiana	Landlord may not resort to self-help evictions. Damages are determined by the court.	N/A	N/A	*Weber v. McMillan*, 285 So.2d 349 (1973)
Maine	Actual damages or $250, whichever is greater. The court may award costs and fees to landlord if it finds that the tenant brought a frivolous court lawsuit or one intended to harass.	Yes	No	Me. Rev. Stat. Ann. tit. 14, § 6014
Maryland	Landlord may not resort to self-help evictions. Damages are determined by the court.	N/A	N/A	*In re Promower, Inc., v. Scuderi, et al.*, 56 B.R. 619 (U.S. Bankruptcy Court, D. Maryland, 1986)
Massachusetts	Three months' rent or three times the actual damages.	Yes	Yes	Mass. Gen. Laws ch. 186, § 15F
Michigan	Up to three times actual damages or $200, whichever is greater.	No	Yes	Mich. Comp. Laws § 600.2918
Minnesota	Statute doesn't specify damages.	Yes	Yes	Minn. Stat. § 504B.375
Mississippi				
Missouri	Landlord may not resort to self-help evictions. Damages are determined by the court.	N/A	N/A	*Steinke v. Leight*, 235 S.W.2d 115 (1950), Mo. Stat. Ann § 441.233
Montana	Three months' rent or three times the actual damages, whichever is greater.	Yes	Yes	Mont. Code Ann. § 70-24-411
Nebraska	Up to three months' rent.	Yes	Yes	Neb. Rev. Stat. § 76-1430
Nevada	Up to $2,500 or actual damages, whichever is greater, or both. If tenant elects to terminate rental agreement or lease, landlord must return entire security deposit and any prepaid rent.	No	Yes	Nev. Rev. Stat. Ann. § 118A.390
New Hampshire	Actual damages or $1,000, whichever is greater; if court finds that landlord knowingly or willingly broke the law, two to three times this amount. Each day that a violation continues is a separate violation. Court may order a tenant who brings a frivolous suit or one intended to harass to pay landlord's costs and fees.	Yes	Yes	N.H. Rev. Stat. Ann. §§ 540-A:3, 540-A:4, 358-A:10
New Jersey	Self-help in prohibited, and landlord who engages in self-help is a "disorderly person," a criminal offense that subjects the landlord to up to six months in jail.	N/A	N/A	N.J. Stat. Ann. §§ 2A:39-1, 2C:43-8
New Mexico	A prorated share of the rent for each day of violation, actual damages, and civil penalty of twice the monthly rent.	Yes	Yes	N.M. Stat. Ann. § 47-8-36
New York	Three times the actual damages.	No	No	N.Y. Real Prop. Acts Law § 853

Consequences of Self-Help Evictions (continued)

State	Amount Tenant Can Sue For	Statute Provides for Tenant's Court Costs & Attorneys' Fees	Statute Gives Tenant the Right to Stay	Statute or Legal Authority
North Carolina	Actual damages.	No	Yes	N.C. Gen. Stat. § 42-25.9
North Dakota	Triple damages.	No	No	N.D. Cent. Code § 32-03-29
Ohio	Actual damages.	Yes	No	Ohio Rev. Code Ann. § 5321.15
Oklahoma	Twice the average monthly rental or twice the actual damages, whichever is greater.	No	Yes	Okla. Stat. tit. 41, § 123
Oregon	Two months' rent or twice the actual damages, whichever is greater.	No	Yes	Or. Rev. Stat. § 90.375
Pennsylvania	Self-help evictions are not allowed, but no specific penalties are provided (it's up to the court to determine damages).	N/A	N/A	*Wofford v. Vavreck*, 22 Pa. D. & C.3d 444 (1981); *Kuriger v. Cramer*, 498 A.2d 1331 (1985)
Rhode Island	Three months' rent or three times the actual damages, whichever is greater.	Yes	Yes	R.I. Gen. Laws § 34-18-34
South Carolina	Three months' rent or twice the actual damages, whichever is greater.	Yes	Yes	S.C. Code Ann. § 27-40-660
South Dakota	Two months' rent. If tenant elects to terminate the lease, landlord must return entire security deposit.	No	Yes	S.D. Codified Laws Ann. § 43-32-6
Tennessee	Actual and punitive damages. If tenant elects to terminate the lease, landlord must return entire security deposit.	Yes	Yes	Tenn. Code Ann. § 66-28-504
Texas	A civil penalty of one month's rent plus $1,000, actual damages, court costs, and reasonable attorney's fees.	Yes	Yes	Tex. Prop. Code §§ 92.008, 92.009, 92.0081,
Utah	Self-help evictions are not allowed, but no specific penalties are provided.	No	No	Utah Code Ann. § 78B-6-814
Vermont	Unspecified damages. Court may award costs and fees to landlord if the court finds that the tenant brought a frivolous lawsuit or one intended to harass.	Yes	Yes	Vt. Stat. Ann. tit. 9, §§ 4463, 4464
Virginia	Actual damages.	Yes	Yes	Va. Code Ann. §§ 55-248.26, 55-225.2
Washington	Actual damages. For utility shut-offs only, actual damages and up to $100 per day of no service. Court may award costs and fees to the prevailing party.	Yes	Yes	Wash. Rev. Code Ann. § 59.18.300
West Virginia				
Wisconsin	Self-help evictions are prohibited. The court will determine damages.	N/A	N/A	Wis. Adm. Code ATCP § 134.09(7)
Wyoming				

How to Use the Downloadable Forms on the Nolo Website

This book comes with downloadable files that you can access online at **www.nolo.com/back-of-book/ELLI.html** To use the files, your computer must have specific software programs installed. Here is a list of types of files provided by this book, as well as the software programs you'll need to access them:

- **RTF.** You can open, edit, print, and save these form files with most word processing programs such as Microsoft *Word*, Windows *WordPad*, and recent versions of *WordPerfect*.

- **PDF.** You can view these files with Adobe *Reader*, free software from www.adobe.com. Government PDFs are sometimes fillable using your computer, but most PDFs are designed to be printed out and completed by hand.

Editing RTFs

Here are some general instructions about editing RTF forms in your word processing program. Refer to the form instructions in this book for help about what should go in each blank.

- **Underlines.** Underlines indicate where to enter information. After filling in the needed text, delete the underline. In most word processing programs you can do this by highlighting the underlined portion and typing CTRL-U.

- **Bracketed and italicized text.** Bracketed and italicized text indicates instructions. Be sure to remove all instructional text before you finalize your document.

- **Optional text.** Optional text gives you the choice to include or exclude text. Delete any optional text you don't want to use. Renumber numbered items, if necessary.

- **Alternative text.** Alternative text gives you the choice between two or more text options. Delete those options you don't want to use. Renumber numbered items, if necessary.

- **Signature lines.** Signature lines should appear on a page with at least some text from the document itself.

Every word processing program uses different commands to open, format, save, and print documents, so refer to your software's help documents for help using your program. Nolo cannot provide technical support for questions about how to use your computer or your software.

CAUTION
In accordance with U.S. copyright laws, the forms provided by this book are for your personal use only.

List of Forms Available on the Nolo Website

Go to: www.nolo.com/back-of-book/ELLI.html

Forms in RTF Format

File Title	File Name
Agreement for Delayed or Partial Rent Payments	Delay.rtf
Agreement Regarding Tenant Alterations to Rental Unit	Alteration.rtf
Amendment to Lease or Rental Agreement	Amendment.rtf
Consent to Assignment of Lease	AssignConsent.rtf
Consent to Contact References and Perform Credit Check	CheckConsent.rtf
Cosigner Agreement	Cosigner.rtf
Fixed-Term Residential Lease	FixedLease.rtf
Fixed-Term Residential Lease (Spanish Version)	PlazoFijo.rtf
Indemnification of Landlord	Indemnification.rtf
Landlord/Tenant Checklist	Checklist.rtf
Landlord-Tenant Agreement to Terminate Lease	Terminate.rtf
Letter for Returning Entire Security Deposit	DepositReturn.rtf
Letter to Original Tenant and New Cotenant	TenantLetter.rtf
Month-to-Month Residential Rental Agreement	MonthToMonth.rtf
Month-to-Month Residential Rental Agreement (Spanish version)	Mensual.rtf
Move-In Letter	MoveIn.rtf
Move-Out Letter	MoveOut.rtf
Notice of Conditional Acceptance Based on Credit Report or Other Information	Acceptance.rtf
Notice of Denial Based on Credit Report or Other Information	Denial.rtf
Notice of Intent to Enter Dwelling Unit	EntryNotice.rtf
Property Manager Agreement	Manager.rtf

Forms in RTF Format

File Title	File Name
Receipt and Holding Deposit Agreement	Receipt.rtf
Rental Application	Application.rtf
Resident's Maintenance/Repair Request	RepairRequest.rtf
Security Deposit Itemization (Deductions for Repairs and Cleaning)	Itemization1.rtf
Security Deposit Itemization (Deductions for Repairs, Cleaning, and Unpaid Rent)	Itemization2.rtf
Semiannual Safety and Maintenance Update	SafetyUpdate.rtf
Tenant's Notice of Intent to Move Out	MoveNotice.rtf
Tenant References	References.rtf
Time Estimate for Repair	Repair.rtf
Verification of Disabled Status	StatusVerification.rtf
Warning Letter for Lease or Rental Agreement Violation	Warning.rtf

Forms in Adobe Acrobat PDF Format

File Title	File Name
Disclosure of Information on Lead-Based Paint or Lead-Based Paint Hazards (English version)	lesr_eng.pdf
Disclosure of Information on Lead-Based Paint or Lead-Based Paint Hazards (Spanish version)	spanless.pdf
Protect Your Family From Lead in Your Home	leadpdfe.pdf
Protect Your Family From Lead in Your Home (Spanish version)	leadpdfs.pdf
Rental Application	Application.pdf
Resident's Maintenance/Repair Request	RepairRequest.pdf
Tenant's Notice of Intent to Move Out	MoveNotice.pdf

Index

THIRD
EDITION

CONCEPTS AND EXPERIENCES IN ELEMENTARY SCHOOL SCIENCE

Peter C. Gega

Professor Emeritus
San Diego State University

Joseph M. Peters

Professor
The University of West Florida

Merrill

an imprint of Prentice Hall

Upper Saddle River, New Jersey   Columbus, Ohio

Cover photo: © Mugshots/The Stock Market
Editor: Bradley J. Potthoff
Production Editor: Louise N. Sette
Copy Editor: Margaret C. Gluntz
Photo Coordinator: Anthony Magnacca
Design Coordinator: Julia Zonneveld Van Hook
Text Designer: John Edeen
Cover Designer: Brian Deep
Production Manager: Deidra M. Schwartz
Director of Marketing: Kevin Flanagan
Marketing Manager: Suzanne Stanton
Advertising/Marketing Coordinator: Julie Shough

This book was set in Galliard and Helvetica by The
Clarinda Company and was printed and bound by
R.R. Donnelley & Sons Company. The cover was
printed by Phoenix Color Corp.

© 1998 by Prentice-Hall, Inc.
Upper Saddle River, New Jersey 07458

Earlier editions © 1994, 1991 by Macmillan
Publishing Company

Printed in the United States of America

10 9 8 7 6 5 4 3

ISBN: 0-13-716417-3

Prentice-Hall International (UK) Limited, *London*
Prentice-Hall of Australia Pty. Limited, *Sydney*
Prentice-Hall of Canada, Inc., *Toronto*
Prentice-Hall Hispanoamericana, S. A., *Mexico*
Prentice-Hall of India Private Limited, *New Delhi*
Prentice-Hall of Japan, Inc., *Tokyo*
Prentice-Hall Asia Pte. Ltd., *Singapore*
Editora Prentice-Hall do Brasil, Ltda., *Rio de Janeiro*

**Library of Congress Cataloging-in-
Publication Data**
Gega, Peter C.
  Concepts and experiences in elementary school
science / Peter C. Gega, Joseph M. Peters.—3rd ed.
    p.   cm.
  Includes bibliographical references (p.   ) and
index.
  ISBN 0-13-716417-3 (pbk.)
  1. Science—Study and teaching (Elementary)
I. Peters, Joseph M.   II. Title.
LB1585.G38   1998
372.3'5'044—dc21   97-12064
                                                          CIP

Photo Credits

This book is dedicated to Willard Korth, Science Education, The University of Pittsburgh, who has been an inspiration and mentor for countless students and colleagues.

PREFACE

This text is a science content and experience resource book for teachers of elementary and early middle-level learners. It identifies important traditional and contemporary concepts in science and related activities and investigations which are used to develop children's knowledge and skills.

Organization of the Text

This text consists of 12 chapters of subject matter, broad investigations, and activities that provide numerous active and interesting concrete experiences to use with children in the elementary and middle-level classroom. These are in two forms: activities and investigations. The *activities* offer first-hand experiences through which children may learn concepts and procedures. The *investigations* offer chances for you and your students to inquire, as co-investigators if you wish, into open-ended problems and topics. Both kinds of learning experiences use everyday, easy-to-get materials and can also enrich school science programs.

This text will provide explanations of subject matter that can help with developing students' background knowledge. These are tied to the learning experiences and give useful, everyday examples of science concepts and principles at work. The explanations are provided in an effort to assist you in guiding children confidently and creatively.

The companion text, *How to Teach Elementary School Science* (Third Edition, 1998, Upper Saddle River, NJ: Merrill/Prentice Hall), focuses on the methods of teaching elementary science. A comprehensive volume titled *Science in Elementary Education* (Eighth Edition, 1998, Upper Saddle River, NJ: Merrill/Prentice Hall) contains the content from both books.

Acknowledgments

I personally wish to thank all of the many people who helped with this edition of *Concepts and Experiences in Elementary School Science*. I especially wish to thank Carol Briscoe, The University of West Florida; George O'Brien, Florida International University; and Cynthia Ledbetter, University of Texas—Dallas, who reviewed the manuscripts and provided suggestions for the third edition. I would also like to extend my gratitude to other colleagues at The University of West Florida who reviewed applicable sections of the text, including Lisbeth Dixon-Krauss, Russell Lee, and Keith Whinnery. Additionally, I am grateful to Brad Potthoff from Merrill/Prentice Hall for his encouragement and constructive comments.

I would also like to acknowledge the reviewers of this text: S. Wali Abdi, The University of Memphis; Leonard J. Garigliano, Salisbury State; Marlene Nachbar Hapai, University of Hawaii at Hilo; Charlotte Iiams, Moorhead State University; Robert J. Miller, Eastern Kentucky University; Michael Odell, University of Idaho; and David Pepi, University of Wisconsin–River Falls.

Most importantly, I would like to show my heartfelt appreciation to my wife, Darlene, for her daily editorial assistance and to my children, Joe and Brenda, for their patience during the revision.

—*Joseph M. Peters*

CONTENTS

SUMMARY OF INVESTIGATIONS

SUMMARY OF ACTIVITIES

Concepts
and Experiences
in Elementary
School Science

ᴡ **Tʜɪs Tᴇxᴛ Cᴀɴ Hᴇʟᴘ Yᴏᴜ**

This text can help you to apply and learn more deeply the teaching strategies developed in *How to Teach Elementary School Science,* Third Edition. It reflects the typical subject matter areas found in children's textbooks, school district science guides, the National Research Council's National Science Education *Standards,* and the American Association for the Advancement of Science's *Benchmarks.* To help bolster your science background, concepts are developed within several major topics in the first section of each chapter. These are followed by sample *Standards* and *Benchmarks* and then *investigations* and *activities* clustered according to the same topics. The investigations offer opportunities to inquire into a broad topic in open-ended ways.

Method of Instruction
out line of events

Iɴᴠᴇsᴛɪɢᴀᴛɪᴏɴs

Each investigation is organized as follows:

Title. The learning topic is stated briefly for quick reference.

Introduction. Several questions or statements are given to arouse children's interest, tie in their former experiences, and sometimes introduce a needed term. This sets the stage for exploring a problem.

Exploratory Problem. A broad problem is posed to follow up the introduction. It is stated in a way that requires children to explore concrete materials. Think of the introduction and exploratory problem as a transition into your bridge.

Needed. Materials needed are listed next. These are the kind easily available at school and home.

Try This. Suggestions are made about how to explore the materials or learn some procedure. This is to help students build readiness for discoveries. If it is not needed, move directly to the discovery problems.

Discovery Problems. Both broad and narrow questions guide discoveries within several related activities. Marginal notes identify the science processes used in the activities.

Each investigation has a *Teaching Comments* section with these parts:

Preparation and Background. Comments tell how to get or prepare needed materials. Some additional information about the topic also is given.

Generalization. This is a statement of the science principle that explains the activities.

Sample Performance Objectives. Examples of a possible process objective and a knowledge objective are given to help you assess student performance. The investigations are mostly wide-ranging and open-ended, allowing for additional state, school district, or other objectives to fit your exact situation.

For Younger Children or *For Older Children.* One of these headings is found in most of the investigations. Suggestions are made about which activities are developmentally appropriate for the children.

Some Ways to Use the Investigations

What teaching style best suits your needs and those of your students?

Some teachers say they succeed with a loose, relatively unstructured way of working with their students. They pose mainly broad questions with their students; narrow questions or helpful hints are supplied only as a last resort.

Frequent side excursions by students into newly aroused problems or interests are commonplace and welcome. Other teachers believe they have more success with a tightly structured, planned progression of activities. They believe their students learn more when specific objectives are pursued and carefully appraised. They do not ignore new problems and interests, but they view them as less important than helping students achieve main concepts.

The investigations of this text have been planned to suit either teaching style. Here are a few suggestions about how you might use them.

When planning *units,* choose investigations that fit the unit topic or generalizations. Besides giving students suitable hands-on experiences, the open-ended nature of the investigations can help you provide for individual differences.

When using *learning centers,* remember to verbally preview the activities which will take place. List on the first activity card the remaining material to be learned, including the discovery problems. Then write each discovery problem on a separate activity card, or photocopy the problems and tape them to a card.

For *individual projects* or *small group work,* you might furnish the entire investigation without the "Teaching Comments" section. Children can decide which activities to stress after consulting with you.

For *whole class* work, it is easy to present each investigation as written, or to select parts that seem suited to your situation.

Grade Placement

Since all the investigations have open-ended opportunities, they are suitable for a broad range of learning levels. The activities within each typically range from simple or observa-tional at the beginning to more complex toward the end.

Most of the investigations include some activities appropriate for children of varying abilities and ages, usually 5 to 12 years. You'll find suggestions for working with students at either extreme of the age-ability range in the Teaching Comments. In the simpler investigations, suggestions for older children are added. In the more complex ones, suggestions are added for younger children.

Some of the investigations do not include such suggestions. These investigations will probably be too abstract or otherwise unsuitable for primary-age children.

ACTIVITIES

The activities are usually narrower in scope than the investigations. They are mainly to help children learn concepts and procedures through direct experiences. They may be used independently or they may complement investigations and contribute to additional projects.

Each activity begins with a question to focus children's attention on some interesting event or procedure. Directions are then given to help students observe the event or develop the procedure. Occasionally, some information is given within the directions to help clarify the students' experience. Narrow questions are used to focus observations or help children think about what is happening. Broad questions may also be used to help extend the experience or stimulate thinking. A parenthetical Teaching Comment in many of the activities presents needed information for you, the teacher.

LIGHT ENERGY AND COLOR

LIGHT ENERGY
AND COLOR

Pathways of
Light

Reflections
and Mirrors

Shadows

Perception and
the Eye

Lens and
Retina

Rods and
Cones

Light Energy
and Color
Benchmarks and
Standards

Light Refraction

Light Speed

Lenses

Color

Prisms

Mixing Colors

Why does something look larger under a magnifying glass? What makes a rainbow? Why does writing appear backwards in a mirror? Children want to know many things about the behavior of light. These and other phenomena become understandable when we learn how light travels; how it can be "bent," or refracted; the nature of color; and how we see.

Pathways of Light Concepts

(Experiences begin p. 16)

Imagine reaching for something that is visible in front of you and not finding it there, or shining a flashlight in the darkness and having it illuminate only something in *back* of you. This, of course, is not likely to happen because light travels in straight lines.

It is true that a beam of light can "bend" under certain conditions, such as when going from air into water or glass, or the reverse (we will explore this more deeply in the next section). Scientists also know that light passing through space is attracted and curved by the gravitational fields of massive objects in space. Other than these exceptions, though, light does appear to travel in straight lines.

This property makes many interesting things take place. For example, look at the pinhole "camera" in Figure 1-1. Light from the candle flame shines through a narrow pinhole in the cereal box end. At the other end, an *inverted* image appears on waxed paper taped over the opening. Why? The numerals in the figure suggest an answer. If light travels in straight lines, the light going from spot one on the left can only go to spot one on the right, and vice versa.

Shadows

Because light travels in straight lines, it is easy to block it with objects. This is why we can identify an object from its shadow.

Only objects we cannot see through, such as metal and wood, cast true shadows. These are called *opaque* objects. *Transparent* objects, such as clear glass and cellophane, do not cast a shadow because very little light is blocked by them. *Translucent* objects, such as frosted glass and waxed paper, allow only some light to pass through; not enough light is blocked to produce a true shadow.

Children can learn to make large or small shadows and clear or fuzzy shadows. They can do this by varying the distance from the light source to the opaque object and the place where the shadow falls. Shadow exploration is interesting to children of all ages. It can lay the foundation for understanding some important principles of physics in later grades.

Reflections

There are several ways in which we can alter the pathways of light, and some are surprising. For instance, why do people powder their noses?

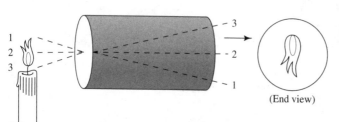

Figure 1-1
A pinhole "camera."

Psychological reasons aside, they do it to scatter light reflections.

You know that a ball thrown straight down on smooth, level pavement bounces back up. Try it on rough gravel, however, and its return path is unpredictable. A smooth, shiny surface reflects light rays with very little scattering. But a rough or uneven surface may scatter the rays so thoroughly that reflections may be scarcely visible. What makes makeup powder so effective? Put some under a microscope. Greatly magnified, it resembles gravel!

Of course, even better reflections are possible with mirrors than with noses. Try sprinkling some powder or chalk dust over half of a mirror, leaving the remainder clear. Shine a flashlight on both sections of the mirror. Does the powder help to reduce glare? Scattered light rays are called *diffused reflections*. Light rays that are not scattered are *regular reflections*.

The only time we can see something that doesn't glow by itself is when light reflects off it and travels to our eyes, such as light reflecting off of the moon. Children generally do not think of light as reflecting off objects. Rather, there is the misconception that all objects are seen directly instead of the reflection of light which is cast from an object.

Mirrors

When you deal with flat, or *plane* reflectors, a special kind of regular reflection becomes possible. If you stand by a mirror and can see the eyes of another person, that person can also see your eyes. No matter from what position or angle you try it, the same results happen if you are close enough to the mirror to see a reflection. The angle at which light strikes a plane reflector (called the angle of incidence) always equals the angle at which it is reflected.

Some explanations of convex and concave mirrors can be discussed at the elementary level. Convex mirrors are those with a bulging center that reduces a wide field to a small area. This is why they are used for rearview mirrors on some automobiles. Concave mirrors are those with a scooped-out center enabling them to magnify images. They are useful for cosmetic work or shaving. Observing images with flexible plastic mirrors is a way to demonstrate how bending a mirror to change its plane will change an image.

If we could not look at our photographs, or double reflections in two mirrors, we would never know how we appear to others. A mirror always produces a reversed image of the observer.

To learn why this is so, study Figure 1-2. In a sense, a mirror image is an optical illusion. Light rays reflect off the mirror into the boy's eyes. He stares outward along the lines of the incoming rays. To him, his image appears to be just as far in back of the mirror as he is in front of it.

Symmetry

Working with mirrors will enable you to introduce the concept of symmetry or the idea of balanced proportions in objects and geometric

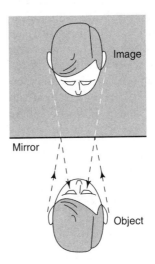

Figure 1-2
Why a mirror image is reversed.

Figure 1-3
Symmetry in letters of the alphabet. Dotted
lines show how to hold a mirror to reconstruct
the original letters.

forms. The concept is of value in many fields, including biology, mathematics, and the arts.

A butterfly, for example, has symmetry. If you draw an imaginary line down the middle of its body, the left half is a near duplicate of its right half. A starfish has another kind of symmetry. If you turn its body around on an imaginary axis, a rotational balance is evident.

Children will be surprised at the ways a mirror can reveal balanced proportions. They can learn to predict which letter shapes will reveal the property of symmetry. Notice that each of the letters in Figure 1-3 is symmetrical. The left and right sides of A are opposite, but alike. The remaining letters are different in that the symmetry is vertical—that is, found in the tops and bottoms, but not laterally. A few letters like X, O, I, and H have both lateral and vertical balance. Some, such as L, F, and J, have none at all.

LIGHT REFRACTION CONCEPTS
(Experiences p. 29)

Have you ever jumped into the shallow part of a swimming pool only to discover it was deeper than it seemed? Light travels slower in water than it does in air. This results in an optical illusion, even though we may be looking straight down into the water.

The topic of reflection and refraction lends itself to misconceptions. Illustrations in textbooks are often inadequate and explanations are sometimes poor (Iona & Beaty, 1988). What is important is to allow children plenty of time to discuss their constructions regarding these concepts.

Density and Light Speeds

The speed of light changes when it travels into or out of media of different densities. The event is especially curious if the light beam enters or leaves a different medium at a slant. A change in speed may cause the beam to change direction of travel, or to *refract*.

Examples of refraction are all around us. A pencil placed partway into water looks bent. Distant images shimmer through unevenly heated air as we drive along a hot road. The scenery looks distorted through a cheap glass window because its thickness is uneven. Interestingly, the function of an automobile windshield wiper is to restore the rainy outside surface of a windshield to a plane surface. As water is wiped away, the light rays enter the glass at a uniform angle, rather than unevenly.

What happens when light enters or leaves water? Why does it bend? Let's look for a moment into the concept of *density* as it relates to this event. You know that anything in motion will slow down or stop when something is in the way. It is easy to dash across an empty room at top speed. Scatter some people around the room and the runner will slow down, bumping head-on into some people and deflecting off others.

A similar thing happens with light as it travels through air, water, and glass. Water is denser than air. It has more matter in the same space. Therefore glass is denser than water. When light enters a denser medium, it slows down. The reverse is also true. What makes light "bend" can be understood through an analogy.

Notice Figure 1-4. Sketch A explains why the coin in Sketch B appears to be in front of its true location. In the first sketch, the two wheels are rolling freely in the direction shown. But what happens when the leading wheel strikes the sand? The device moves on, but at a slightly different angle. To reverse this, if the device travels upward from the sand along the broken line, one wheel will hit the paved portion sooner. The direction will again change, but in an opposite way.

In Sketch B, light bends in a similar direction. As it leaves the water, the light bends slightly toward the horizontal. The observer sights along a stick toward where the coin seems to be. The line of sight seems to be a straight line from eye to coin, but it is not. If the stick is pushed into the water at the same angle at which it is poised (sliding it in the groove formed by a closed book cover may ensure this) it will overshoot the target.

Lenses

People have learned to control light refractions with lenses. Eyeglasses can correct certain vision problems. Magnifying glasses and optical instruments extend the power of sight far beyond that available to the naked eye.

Figure 1-5 shows how light refracts when passing through a convex lens. In Drawing A, the light rays enter the eye from two opposite slants. (It may help to think of the wheels–axle analogy again.) As the eye follows these slanted rays to the lens, they seem to continue outward, and so they form an enlarged image of the object.

How can we make the object appear even larger? Compare Drawings B and C. Notice that the two lenses differ in thickness, although their diameters are the same. Each will bring the sun's rays to a point or focus at a different distance. The distance from the point of focus to the lens is the *focal length*. Notice that the thicker lens has the shorter focal length. By extending the slanted rays outward, you can see why it magnifies more than the lens in Drawing C.

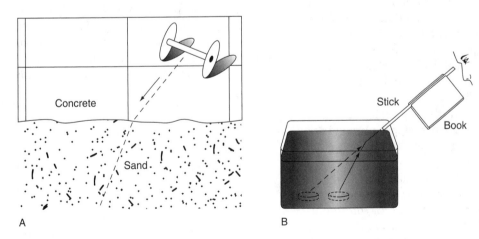

A

B

Figure 1-4
Light "bends" and changes direction (B) in the same way the wheels change direction (A) when they hit a different surface.

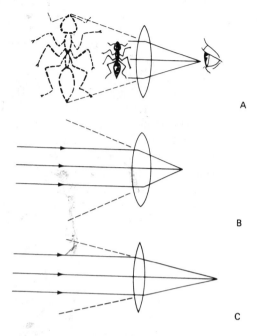

Figure 1-5
The shape of a convex lens is what determines how an image is magnified.

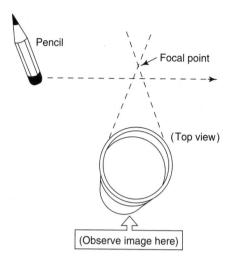

Figure 1-6
When an object that is inside the focal length of a convex lens is moved right, its image also moves right. But if the object is *outside* the focal length when moved right, its image moves left.

A curious thing may happen when we observe a moving object through a convex lens. Figure 1-6 shows the focal point of a small jar of water as light passes through it. (Though the jar is really a cylindrical lens, it acts as a convex lens in this example.) If a pencil is moved to the right *inside* the focal length of the lens, its image will also move to the right. But if it is moved to the right *outside* the focal length, its image will move to the left. The reason is apparent if we notice what happens beyond the focal point. The light rays cross and go to opposite sides.

Convex lenses *converge* light rays, or bring them together, as you have seen. Concave lenses cause light rays to *diverge*, or spread out. This causes objects viewed through them to appear smaller. You can see why in Figure 1-7. The light from the object slants outward toward X and Y as it goes through the lens

(remember the wheels–axle analogy). As the eye follows these slanted rays back to the lens, the rays seem to continue inward at a slant and form a smaller image of the object.

Thick drinking glasses and glass eye cups often have concave-shaped bases. Students can check if images are smaller by looking through them. Perhaps the easiest concave lens to make is simply to leave an air bubble in a small, capped jar of water. An object viewed through

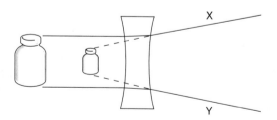

Figure 1-7
A concave lens makes objects appear smaller because the light rays diverge.

the bubble will look smaller, but if viewed through the convex part of the jar, it will appear larger.

Commercial lenses can teach a great deal. Children may learn even more, though, by fashioning their own lenses from a variety of transparent objects, containers, and fluids. A plastic soda bottle works well to "bend" light (Wilson, 1990). A clear glass marble will also magnify objects. So does a water drop or drops of other fluids. A small drinking glass with vertical sides (not tapered) magnifies things well when it is filled with water or other fluids. Narrow olive jars make especially powerful magnifiers. However, the best possibilities for controlled study of homemade lenses will happen if you use clear, small plastic pill vials.

COLOR CONCEPTS
(Experiences p. 32)

When our ancestors saw a rainbow, they were probably inclined to give a magical or supernatural explanation to account for it. Later, people thought that the colors came from the rain droplets through which sunlight passes. It was not until Isaac Newton (1642–1727) performed experiments with prisms that it was realized these colors were the parts of visible sunlight itself.

There are six universally recognized colors in the visible spectrum of sunlight: red, orange, yellow, green, blue, and violet.

A prism separates light because each color has a different wavelength and rate of vibration. Red light has the longest wavelength, with about 1,200 waves per millimeter, or 30,000 waves to 1 inch. Violet light has the shortest wavelength, with about twice that number of waves per unit. As a light beam passes through a prism, the longer waves are refracted least and the shorter waves most (Figure 1-8).

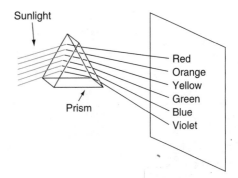

Figure 1-8
A prism separates white light into a spectrum of six colors.

Differences in colors are often compared with pitch differences in sound. A low sound is a result of relatively slow vibrations. Its visual counterpart is the color red. A high sound results from fast vibrations. Its counterpart is violet.

Mixing Colors

There are two basic ways we can mix colors: one with colored beams of light and the other with paints or dyes. When light beams of only three primary colors (red, blue, and green) are added together in the right proportions on a white screen, different color combinations occur. These are shown in the overlapping sections of Figure 1-9. When red, blue, and green are used as colored light beams, they are called the additive colors.

Scientists have found that three certain colored pigments can *absorb* these additive colors. That is, if you shine a red or blue or green light on the right pigment, there is almost no color reflection at all. The pigment looks black. Blue light is absorbed by a yellow pigment, and red light by a blue–green pigment called cyan. Green light is absorbed by a purple–red pigment called magenta.

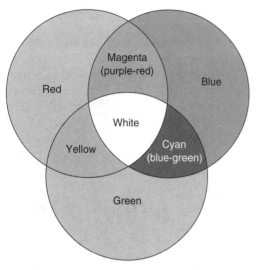

Figure 1-9
The additive colors. When beams of red, blue, and green light are added together in the right proportions, the overlapping colors result. Color television is produced by an additive process.

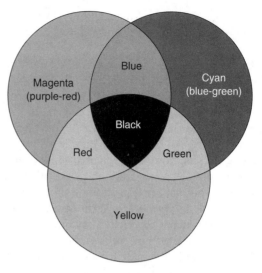

Figure 1-10
The subtractive colors. Paints and dyes absorb, or "subtract," some colors from white light and reflect what is left. Note the overlapping colors when the three primary pigments are mixed in the right proportions.

If a *white* light beam shines on these colored pigments, each will absorb, or "subtract," the specific color mentioned above and reflect to our eyes what is not absorbed. We can mix these pigments to get various colors, but the results we get from mixing all three are the *opposite* from mixing the three light beams. This is shown in Figure 1-10. In summary, when viewing an object, the color we see depends on (1) the color of light shining on the object and (2) the color reflected by the object to our eyes. Children can do some experiments with colored construction paper and colored light beams to help them understand these ideas and their practical effects. With ordinary materials, it is hard to predict the exact hues that will result from the many possible combinations. Another interesting activity is to use colored slides, a prism, and a slide projector to experiment with color (Dalby, 1991).

Don't be surprised if you find several boys in your class who are at least partly color blind.

One male in 12 has the deficiency, contrasted with only 1 in 200 females. Most commonly, reds and greens are seen in shades of gray; other colors are perceived normally. Rarely do color blind people see all colors in black and white and shades of gray.

PERCEPTION AND THE EYE CONCEPTS
(Experiences p. 37)

In this section, we will examine how the eye works and apply some ideas discussed previously. Although the eye has many parts, we'll concentrate on three parts directly involved in sight: the *iris, retina,* and *lens* (see Figure 1-11).

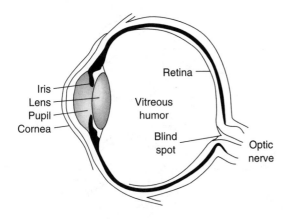

Figure 1-11
An eye illustration.

are distributed in other parts of the retina and are sensitive to dim light.

Chemical changes sensitize either rods or cones under certain conditions. For example, when we walk into a dark theater on a sunny day, it takes several minutes before the rods work well. To achieve optimum sensitivity, up to a half hour may be required. It is thought that cones are most sensitive to three basic colors: red, green, and blue. According to this idea, we see many colors because the basic colors are seen in various combinations.

Lens

An eye lens is convex in shape and works like any other convex lens, with one important difference. A muscle permits it to change shape. If a large, close object appears before you, the lens thickens. This refracts light rays entering the eye sharply enough for a focus to occur on the retina. However, light rays from a small or distant object enter the lens in a near parallel fashion. Only a small refraction is needed to bring the rays to a focus on the retina.

To experience this action, look at a distant object, then suddenly look at something a foot away. Do you feel the tug of your lens muscles pulling the lens? Do you find the near object is fuzzy for the brief instant it takes for the muscles to adjust lens thickness? In a camera, of course, focusing is achieved by moving the lens back and forth.

Iris

The iris contains pigment that absorbs some colors and reflects others. It is because the kind and amount of this coloring matter varies in individuals that eyes appear to be brown, hazel, or blue. Two sets of tiny muscles control the size of a small hole (pupil) in the iris. This regulates the amount of light entering the eye.

Cats' pupils can dilate far more than ours. This is one reason they see better than humans in near darkness. A dramatic example of this capacity appears when the headlights of an automobile suddenly shine into the eyes of a cat on a dark night. The two shiny round spots we see are the headlight reflections from *inside* the cat's eyes.

Retina

Why is it hard to see when we first walk into a darkened movie theater? Our eyes make a second important adjustment when light varies in brightness. The retina contains two kinds of light-sensitive cells: *rods* and *cones*. Cones are less sensitive than rods and are clustered near the back of the eyeball. They work best in strong light and enable us to see color. Rods

Eyeglasses

Two of the main vision problems corrected by eyeglasses concern image focus. In *near-sightedness,* the cornea or the lens may be thicker, or the eyeball longer, than normal. This causes an image to focus in front of the retina rather than on it. Notice in Figure 1-12 how the problem is corrected. Sketch A shows a normal eyeball. Sketch B shows a longer-than-normal eyeball and a focal point in front of, rather than on, the

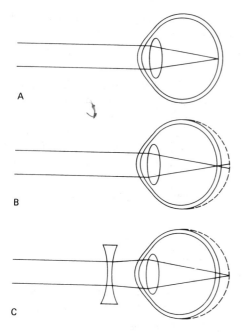

A

B

C

Figure 1-12
In near-sightedness an abnormally shaped cornea or eyeball causes an image to focus in front of the retina rather than on it. A concave lens can correct the problem.

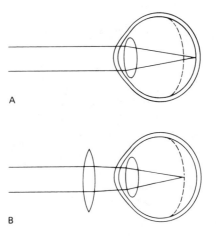

A

B

Figure 1-13
In farsightedness, the image focuses at some imaginary point beyond the retina. A convex lens corrects this.

retina. In C, a concave eyeglass lens spreads out the incoming light rays. This lengthens the focal point just enough to fall on the retina.

In *farsightedness,* the cornea or the lens may be thinner, or the eyeball shorter, than normal. So the focal point is at some imaginary distance beyond the retina. Sketch A of Figure 1-13 shows this happening with a shorter-than-normal eyeball. In Sketch B, a convex eyeglass lens corrects the defect by forcing the light rays to converge at a shorter focal point, which is on the retina.

Perception

An excellent example of how the brain and eyes work together takes place when we judge distance. Each eye sees an object from a different angle. The closer the object, the greater the difference between what the two eyes perceive. We actually see a tiny bit *around* the object. At the same time, we feel our eyes turn inward. With greater distances, the angle gets smaller. The brain interprets this accordingly.

Beyond about 50 yards, we rely mainly on size to judge distance. A small telegraph pole looks far away mostly because we know that telephone poles are large. We also use other clues such as increased haze and the surrounding scene.

A movie film flashes only *still* pictures on a screen. The apparent motion of a motion-picture projection results from *persistence of vision.* It takes about one-sixteenth of a second for an image to fade from our vision after it is withdrawn. By flashing 24 images a second on a screen, a projector creates the illusion of motion.

It took some experience before the present speed of projecting individual motion-picture frames was adopted. Early motion pictures were photographed and projected at much slower speeds. The short, unlighted pause between frames was noticeable. This is how the term *flickers* came about.

It is easy to experience the persistence-of-vision effect with a pencil and a small pad of paper. For example, children can be guided to draw a pole that falls over. First, an upright pole is drawn on the bottom and center of the first page. On succeeding pages, in the same spot, they draw the pole at successively lower angles, until it is horizontal. A total of about 20 pages is more than adequate. When the pad pages are rapidly flipped over, an animated sequence of a falling pole appears. Children enjoy making flip books.

LIGHT ENERGY AND COLOR BENCHMARKS AND STANDARDS

Examples of standards in the area of light energy and color are guidelines related to: how sunlight is made up of many colors; how light reflecting off objects allows us to see;

and how light travels. Specific examples are as follows:

SAMPLE BENCHMARKS (AAAS, 1993).

■ Light from the sun is made up of a mixture of many different colors of light, even though to the eye the light looks almost white. Other things that give off or reflect light have a different mix of colors (By grades 6–8, p. 90).

■ Something can be "seen" when light waves emitted or reflected by it enter the eye (By grades 6–8, p. 90).

SAMPLE STANDARDS (NRC, 1996).

■ Light travels in a straight line until it strikes an object. Light can be reflected by a mirror, refracted by a lens, or absorbed by an object (by Grades K–4, p. 127).

■ Light interacts with matter by transmission (including refraction), absorption, or scattering (including reflection). To see an object, light from that object—emitted by or scattered from it—must enter the eye (by Grades 5–8, p. 155).

INVESTIGATIONS AND ACTIVITIES

PATHWAYS OF LIGHT EXPERIENCES
(Concepts p. 6)

INVESTIGATION: *A PINHOLE CAMERA*

Have you ever used a pinhole camera (Figure 1-14)? Light from an object shines through a tiny pinhole at one end. It travels to a waxed-paper screen at the other end. What you see is called an *image* of the object. What you see may surprise you.

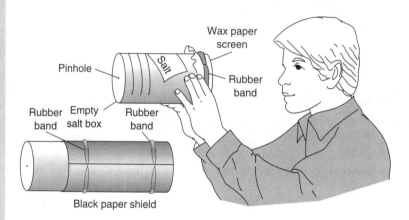

Figure 1-14

EXPLORATORY PROBLEM

How can you make and use a pinhole camera?

NEEDED

salt or cereal box	sticky tape	pin	black paper
three rubber bands	waxed paper	scissors	

TRY THIS

1. Punch a hole in the center of the box bottom. Use a pin.
2. Remove the box top. Put waxed paper over the box's open end to make the screen. Use a rubber band to hold it.
3. Point the camera at brightly lit objects in or outside a *dark* room. What do you see on the waxed paper screen?

To use the camera in a *lighted* place, you must shield the screen from the light. Roll black paper into a large tube and fit it around the screen end of the box. Secure with two rubber bands. Press your face against the paper shield's open end to see images on the screen.

DISCOVERY PROBLEMS

experimenting **A.** How must you move the camera to do these things? To make the image move right? left? up? down? To make the image get smaller? larger? What happens if the camera is still and the image moves? (For example, have person walk from right to left.)

experimenting **B.** How can you make a brighter, sharper image appear on the screen? What will happen to the image if you change the pinhole size? line the inside of the box with black paper? white paper? use a longer or larger box or a shoe box? use paper other than waxed paper for the screen?

experimenting **C.** How can you make a pinhole camera with a larger paper cup? How can a second cup be used as a light shield?

hypothesizing **D.** What other ideas can you think of to try?

TEACHING COMMENT

PREPARATION AND BACKGROUND

Several kinds of boxes will serve for this activity, including milk cartons. If a black paper shield is used, it should be large. The observer's eyes will need to be about 30 centimeters (1 foot) away from the screen to see a sharp image.

Most children will be surprised to find that an upside-down image appears on the screen. You might sketch Figure 1-1 on the chalkboard and invite students to think through what happens.

GENERALIZATION

Light travels in straight lines.

SAMPLE PERFORMANCE OBJECTIVES

Process: The child can construct a pinhole camera and show how it works.

Knowledge: The child can explain how the flame image becomes inverted in Figure 1-1.

FOR YOUNGER CHILDREN

With teacher guidance, many primary children will be able to do the exploratory problem and discovery Problem A.

INVESTIGATION: *SHADOWS*

What is a shadow? How can you make a shadow?

EXPLORATORY PROBLEM A

How can you change the length and direction of a shadow?

NEEDED

white sheet of paper	flashlight
pencil	small nail
partner	

TRY THIS

1. Put a nail, head down, on some white paper (Figure 1-15).

2. Shine the flashlight on the nail. What kind of a shadow do you see?

Figure 1-15

DISCOVERY PROBLEMS

experimenting **A.** How can you make a long shadow? a short shadow?

experimenting **B.** How can you shine the light on the nail so there is no shadow?

experimenting **C.** How can you make a shadow that points left? right?

predicting **D.** Let your partner turn off the flashlight and point it at the nail. Where will the shadow be when your partner turns on the flashlight again? (The flashlight must be held still.) Draw a line on the paper where you think the shadow will be.

predicting **E.** Can you tell how long a shadow will be?

EXPLORATORY PROBLEM B

What kinds of shadows can you make and see outdoors?

NEEDED

outdoor area   sunshine   partner

TRY THIS

1. Go outdoors into the sunshine.
2. Make some shadows on the ground (Figure 1-16).

Figure 1-16

DISCOVERY PROBLEMS

experimenting **A.** Can you and a partner make your shadows shake hands without really touching each other's hands?

experimenting **B.** How can you make your shadow seem to stand on your partner's shadow's shoulders?

experimenting **C.** How can you make a pale, fuzzy shadow darker and sharper?

experimenting **D.** How should you stand so your shadow is in front of you? in back of you? to your left? to your right?

predicting **E.** Draw a line where the shadow of some object is now. Where do you think the shadow will be in an hour? Draw a second line, then check to see later.

hypothesizing **F.** What are some other things you can try with shadows?

TEACHING COMMENT

PREPARATION AND BACKGROUND

In this investigation, children discover how to predict the lengths and directions of shadows. They learn how to make shadows dark and sharp and pale or fuzzy by changing the distance between an object and the light source. They also learn that this affects the shadow's size.

GENERALIZATION

A shadow may be made when an object blocks some light; a shadow may be changed by moving the object or the light source in different ways.

SAMPLE PERFORMANCE OBJECTIVES

Process: The child can manipulate a light source and object to vary a shadow's length and direction.

Knowledge: The child can state how a shadow's darkness and sharpness may be changed.

FOR OLDER CHILDREN

Try determining the sizes of objects by their shadows.

ACTIVITY: *HOW MANY PENNIES CAN YOU "MAKE" WITH TWO MIRRORS?*

NEEDED

two small mirrors   penny

TRY THIS

1. Fit two mirrors together like two walls joined to make a corner.
2. Place the penny between the mirrors. How many pennies do you see?
3. Change the mirror angle. Move the mirrors in other ways. Move the penny, too. What is the largest number of pennies you can make? the fewest number?

INVESTIGATION: *MIRROR REFLECTIONS*

What are some of the things you can do with a mirror?

EXPLORATORY PROBLEM A

Can you see someone's eyes in a mirror without the other person seeing your eyes in the mirror? (Say the other person is also looking into the mirror.) How can you find out?

NEEDED

small mirror   sticky tape   partner

TRY THIS

1. Tape a mirror flat against a wall at your eye level.
2. Have your partner stand in back and to the right of the mirror.
3. Now you stand in back and to the left of the mirror (Figure 1-17).

Figure 1-17

4. Move around slowly until you see your partner's eyes in the mirror. Can your partner now see your eyes in the mirror?

DISCOVERY PROBLEMS

predicting **A.** What will happen if you or your partner move farther to the side?

predicting **B.** What will happen if you or your partner move farther back?

inferring **C.** Is there any spot where you can see your partner's eyes without him seeing your eyes?

EXPLORATORY PROBLEM B

How can you use two mirrors to see over objects taller than you?

NEEDED

two small mirrors   soft clay   meter stick or yardstick

TRY THIS

1. Push a piece of clay into the meter stick near each end.

2. Push a mirror sideways into each lump of clay. Have the mirror surfaces face each other.

3. Fix the mirrors so they look like those in Figure 1-18. When done, you will have a *periscope*.

4. Hold the periscope upright. Look in the bottom mirror. What can you see? You may have to move the mirrors a little to see clearly.

5. Over what tall objects can you see with your periscope?

Figure 1-18

DISCOVERY PROBLEMS

experimenting   **A.** How can you use your periscope to see around a corner?

experimenting   **B.** How can you see around a corner with just one mirror on the stick?

EXPLORATORY PROBLEM C

What is the shortest mirror in which you can see your feet and head at the same time?

NEEDED

two small mirrors   meter stick or yardstick
sticky tape   partner

TRY THIS

1. You can use two small mirrors instead of a large, full-length mirror. Have your partner stand at arm's length from the wall.

2. Tape one mirror flat against the wall at your partner's eye level.

3. Hold the second mirror flat against the wall below the first mirror.

4. Move it slowly down the wall. Have your partner say stop when she can see her shoes in the bottom mirror.

5. Tape the bottom mirror flat against the wall.

6. Now your partner should be able to see her head and feet. The top and bottom mirrors are like the top and bottom of a large, full-length mirror (Figure 1-19).

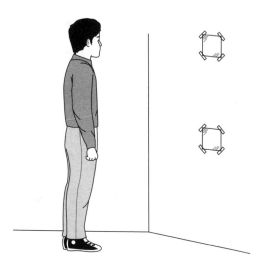

Figure 1-19

DISCOVERY PROBLEMS

measuring **A.** How long is it from the top of one mirror to the bottom of the other mirror compared to your partner's height? Half as long? three-fourths as long? just as long as your partner is tall? Measure and find out.

observing **B.** Does moving back from the mirror make a difference in the size needed?

experimenting **C.** Does the mirror size needed depend on a person's height? How could you find out?

predicting **D.** Can you predict the size of the shortest full-length mirr~ need to see yourself? Switch with your partner and find

TEACHING COMMENT

PREPARATION AND BACKGROUND

When light strikes a mirror at an angle, it is reflected at the same angle in a different direction. That is why if you see someone's image in a mirror, it is possible for that person to see yours. This also explains how periscopes work. Notice in Figure 1-18 that the two mirror angles are identical. For the same reason, a full-length mirror needs to be only about half as long as you are tall.

Check that the mirror is taped *flat* against the wall in the last investigations. If it is not, an error in measurement is likely.

GENERALIZATION

When light travels to a mirror at a slant, it is reflected at the same slant in another direction.

SAMPLE PERFORMANCE OBJECTIVES

Process: The child can construct a workable periscope.

Knowledge: The child can demonstrate positions where two persons should be able to see, at one time, each other's image in a mirror.

FOR YOUNGER CHILDREN

Most primary children should be able to do the exploratory sections of Investigations A and B.

ACTIVITY: *HOW CAN TWO MIRRORS SHOW WHAT YOU REALLY LOOK LIKE?*

NEEDED

two mirrors

TRY THIS

1. Look into one mirror. Think of your image as another person facing you.
2. Wink your left eye, then your right. Which eye does the image blink each time?
3. Get two mirrors. Fit them together in the way that two walls are joined. Move them slightly so half of your face is seen in each mirror (Figure 1-20).
4. Wink each eye. Touch your left ear. Tilt your head to the right. What happens each time? Study Figure 1-20. How can you explain why your right eye appears on the left, like that of a real person facing you?

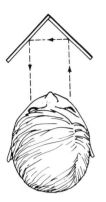

Figure 1-20

TEACHING COMMENT

Each mirror reflects half of the image onto the adjoining mirror. This puts it back to normal. A single mirror can only reflect an object backwards. This is why our one-mirror image is not how we look to others.

ACTIVITY: HOW CAN YOU RELAY LIGHT WITH MIRRORS?

NEEDED

three to four small mirrors
sunshine or bright flashlight

TRY THIS

1. Hold a mirror in the light. Reflect the light onto a wall.

2. Pick a target on the wall. Reflect the light so it shines on the target.

3. Reflect your light onto another mirror held by a partner. Have your partner try to hit the target.

   a. With how many mirrors can you and some partners relay the light and hit a target? How will you tell if light is being passed from every mirror? Make a drawing that shows how the mirrors were held to hit the target (Figure 1-21).

   b. Have a contest between two or more teams. Which team can hit a target fastest with light passed along from several mirrors? How can you make the contest fair?

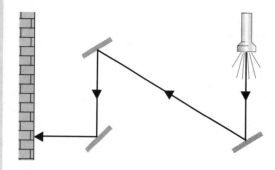

Figure 1-21

TEACHING COMMENT

Caution: If using a laser, caution children *not* to look directly into the laser. A fair contest will prevent one team from observing and profiting from the mistakes of the other. You can tell if every mirror in a relay is being used by shading each mirror in turn with your hand. The light shining on the target in each instance will disappear. Strong light is needed if more than two mirrors are used.

INVESTIGATION: *MIRROR BALANCE*

Suppose you made a small, simple drawing. Then you erased half of it. Could you hold a mirror on the drawing so it would seem whole again? Would it depend on the drawing? In what way? Drawings that allow you to do this are said to have *mirror* balance, or symmetry.

EXPLORATORY PROBLEM

How can you find out which things have mirror balance?

NEEDED

paper	pencil
small mirror	ruler

TRY THIS

1. Put the edge of your mirror on Line 1 of the butterfly in Figure 1-22. Can you see what seems like the whole butterfly? You can, because the butterfly has side-by-side balance.

2. Now put the mirror on Line 2. Can you see a whole butterfly now? You cannot, because a butterfly's body is balanced only one way.

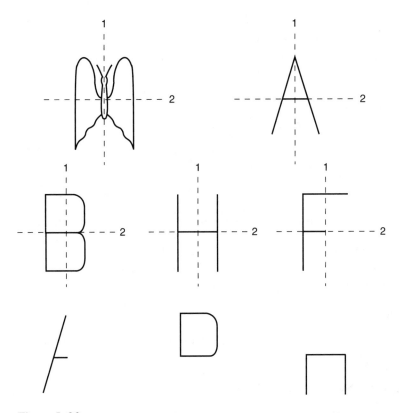

Figure 1-22

3. Some letters of the alphabet have balance, too. Put your mirror on Line 1 of the capital letter *A*. Can you see what seems like a whole letter *A*? You can, because capital letter *A* has side-by-side balance.

4. Now, put the mirror on Line 2. Can you see a whole letter *A*? You cannot, because this capital letter is balanced only one way.

5. Try your mirror both ways on capital *B*. Notice that you cannot see a whole letter on Line 1. But you can on Line 2. That is because a capital *B* only has up-and-down balance.

6. Try your mirror both ways on capital *H*. Notice that you see a whole letter both ways. A capital *H* has both side-by-side and up-and-down balance.

7. Try your mirror both ways on capital *F*. Notice that you cannot see a whole letter either way. A capital *F* has no balance.

DISCOVERY PROBLEMS

classifying **A.** Which capital letters of the alphabet do you think have side-by-side balance? up-and-down balance? both kinds? no balance? Arrange the letters into four groups. Then check each letter with your mirror to see if you put it into the right group.

inferring **B.** Some words may be made up of only letters from one group. How many words can you think of whose letters have only side-by-side balance? only up-and-down balance? only letters with both kinds of balance?

experimenting **C.** Use what you know to write secret code words.

TEACHING COMMENT

PREPARATION AND BACKGROUND

This is an introduction to mirror symmetry. Symmetry is the idea of balanced proportions in the shapes of objects.

Try to have available small rectangular mirrors with the trim removed from the edges. The trim may obscure part of the reflected drawing or letter. *Caution:* If the mirror edges are sharp, cover them with a strip of cellophane tape.

GENERALIZATION

Some objects have evenly balanced or symmetrical shapes; a mirror may be used to explore an object's symmetry.

SAMPLE PERFORMANCE OBJECTIVES

Process: The child can classify the letters of the alphabet by their symmetry.

Knowledge: The child can draw or identify an object that is symmetrical.

FOR YOUNGER CHILDREN

Find and mount mirror-sized magazine pictures of objects and patterns. Some should, and some should not, be symmetrical. On what place or places in each picture can children put a small mirror to see the whole object?

Have them classify the pictures into two groups such as those they can make whole again and those they cannot. Challenge children to use their mirrors to change each picture or pattern. Colored pictures, particularly, are fascinating for young children to explore.

LIGHT REFRACTION EXPERIENCES
(Concepts p. 8)

INVESTIGATION: *SOME EVERYDAY MAGNIFIERS*

How can you make something seem larger? That is, how can you magnify it?

EXPLORATORY PROBLEM

What everyday objects can you use to magnify things?

NEEDED

two pencils
two jars of water (two sizes)
two clear-glass marbles (two sizes)
book
waxed paper
newspaper

TRY THIS

1. Place a piece of waxed paper on a printed page.
2. Dip a pencil tip into some water. Let a drop run off onto the waxed paper.
3. How does the print look through the water drop?

DISCOVERY PROBLEMS

observing A. Make water drops of different sizes. Which drops magnify the print more?

observing B. Put the waxed paper on a book. Make a row of drops, each drop bigger than the next. Hold up the book and paper to eye level. Look at the outline of the drops. Which are smaller and rounder? Which are larger and flatter? Which will magnify more?

predicting C. Get two different-sized clear marbles. Which one do you think will magnify more? How much more? How will you find out?

observing D. Get a narrow jar of water. Put your pencil inside. Does your pencil look larger? Move your pencil to different places, inside and outside the jar. Where does it look the thickest (Figure 1-23)?

observing E. Get another, wider jar of water. Will it magnify more or less than the first jar?

inferring F. What other everyday things can you use as magnifiers?

Figure 1-23

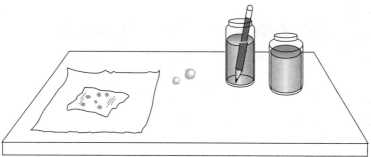

TEACHING COMMENT

PREPARATION AND BACKGROUND

Any clear, curved, transparent material acts like a lens. That is, light rays that pass through the material are bent. This may cause objects viewed through the lens to appear magnified. Children will enjoy and learn from trials with additional examples of clear glass and plastic materials. Clear, narrow plastic pill vials become especially good magnifiers when filled with water and capped.

The magnifying power of a glass marble may be measured by placing it on narrow-lined paper. The student counts the number of lines seen inside the clear marble. The marble with the fewest visible lines has the greatest magnification.

GENERALIZATION

A clear, curved object may appear to magnify things; a narrow, curved object magnifies more than one of greater diameter.

SAMPLE PERFORMANCE OBJECTIVES

Process: The student can measure the difference in magnifying power of two different improvised lenses.

Knowledge: When shown two water-filled containers of different diameters, the student can predict which will have the greater magnifying power.

FOR YOUNGER CHILDREN

Most young students should be able to do all but Discovery Problems C and E.

ACTIVITY: HOW CAN YOU MEASURE THE MAGNIFYING POWER OF A HAND LENS?

NEEDED

hand magnifying lens   sheet of lined paper   ruler   pencil

TRY THIS

1. Draw two or three evenly spaced lines between the printed lines on your paper. A half sheet of extra lines should be enough.
2. Pencil a small x in the middle of the paper where you have drawn lines.
3. Center the x in the lens. Move the lens up and down until the x looks most clear.
4. Count all the lines you see inside the lens (Figure 1-24).

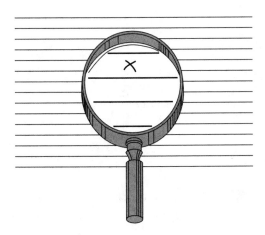

Figure 1-24

5. Count all the lines *outside* the lens that are between the first and last lines seen inside the lens.
6. Divide the larger figure by the smaller one. This gives the power of the lens. For example, if the answer is two, your lens makes things appear about twice as large as they are.
   a. What is the power of your lens?
   b. What is the power of other lenses you can try?
   c. How does the power of thicker lenses compare with thinner lenses?
   d. How far above the x must you hold different lenses to see it clearly?

TEACHING COMMENT

Thicker lenses usually magnify more than thinner lenses of the same diameter. The distance from the point of focus to the lens is the focal length. Because they have shorter focal lengths, thicker or curvier lenses must be held closer to the x to see it clearly.

COLOR EXPERIENCES
(Concepts p. 11)

INVESTIGATION: *HOW TO MIX COLORS*

Suppose you have two different-colored crayons. How can you use the crayons to make *three* different colors?

EXPLORATORY PROBLEM A

How can you make more than three colors with three different crayons?

NEEDED

white paper   crayons (red, yellow, and blue)   crayons of other colors

TRY THIS

1. Rub three short, thick lines *lightly* across the white paper. Make one red, one yellow, and one blue.
2. Rub three thick up-and-down lines *lightly* on the white paper, so they cross the first three. Use the same three colors (Figure 1-25).

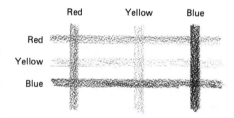

Figure 1-25

3. What colors do you see where the lines cross?

DISCOVERY PROBLEMS

observing   **A.** How many colors did you make?

experimenting **B.** How many new colors can you make with crayons of other colors? Draw pictures and color them.

EXPLORATORY PROBLEM B

How can you make many colors by mixing water samples of several colors?

NEEDED

four baby food jars   paper towel
water   three drinking straws
food coloring (red, yellow, and blue)

TRY THIS

1. Fill three small jars half full with water.
2. Put two drops of different food coloring in each jar.
3. Put a different straw in each jar and stir the colored water.
4. Mix a little colored water from two jars into a fourth jar. Use a straw to lift out the liquid from each jar. (See Figure 1-26.)

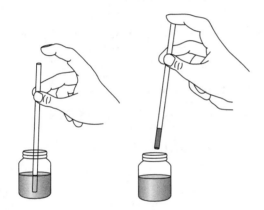

Figure 1-26

DISCOVERY PROBLEMS

experimenting and measuring **A.** How many new colors can you make by mixing two different colors each time? Use the same volume of each color when mixing colors. Keep a record.

observing **B.** What happens when you mix more of one color than another?

inferring **C.** Mix a mystery color made from two colors. Use more of one color than another. Can someone else figure out how to match exactly your mystery color? Can you match someone else's mystery color? Try many different colors.

TEACHING COMMENT

PREPARATION AND BACKGROUND

Children will get the best results when combining crayon colors if they rub lightly. When red, yellow, and blue paints or dyes are paired and mixed in the right proportions, we see green, orange, and purple.

GENERALIZATION

When red, yellow, and blue dyes are paired and mixed, they produce green, orange, and purple. Different shades are produced by mixing different proportions of the colors.

SAMPLE PERFORMANCE OBJECTIVES

Process: The child can infer what combinations of colored liquids produced a new color and the general proportions used.

Knowledge: The child can state how to produce varying shades of mixed colors.

FOR OLDER CHILDREN

You might begin with Discovery Problem B and move quickly to C.

ACTIVITY: *HOW ARE THE COLORS MADE IN COMIC STRIPS?*

NEEDED

colored comic strips from different newspapers   strong hand lens

TRY THIS

1. Study different comic strip pictures with a hand lens.
2. Notice how many colors are made from only a few colors.
3. Notice that some dots may be printed side by side. Or one colored dot may be printed partly over a dot of another color.
4. Observe how different shades are made by changing the distance between dots.
   a. What side-by-side colored dots do you see? What colors do they make?
   b. What overprinted colors do you see? What colors do they make?
   c. In what ways are cartoon colors from different newspapers alike? different?

TEACHING COMMENT

A dissecting microscope is ideal for analyzing colored comics.

INVESTIGATION: *THE MAKEUP OF COLORED LIQUIDS*

You know that a colored liquid can be made by mixing two or more colors. Most inks and dyes are made in that way. Some of the colors mixed to make another color are surprising.

EXPLORATORY PROBLEM

How can you find out the colors that make up a colored dye or ink?

NEEDED

food coloring (red, blue, green, yellow)   baby food jar half full of water
scissors   waxed paper
four toothpicks   white paper towel or coffee filters

TRY THIS

1. Cut some strips from a white paper towel. Make them about 10 by 2 centimeters (4 by ¾ inches).
2. Put one drop of red food coloring and one of blue on waxed paper. Mix them.
3. Touch the toothpick to the coloring. Make a sizable dot on the middle of one strip.
4. Hold the strip in a small jar that is about half full of water. The colored dot should be just above the water level (Figure 1-27).

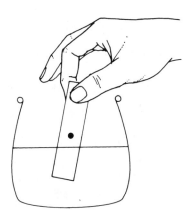

Figure 1-27

5. What happens to the coloring as water is soaked up past the colored dot? (This may take a minute or longer.) How many colors appear as the colored dot spreads out?

DISCOVERY PROBLEMS

observing **A.** What colors are in other food coloring samples? How are different brands of the same colors alike or different?

inferring **B.** Try a game with a partner. Mix drops from several food colors, then test them on strips. Keep a record. Remove the tested strips from the jar and let them dry. Can your partner tell which food colors were mixed for each strip? Switch places with your partner. Can you tell what mixed colors were used for your partner's strips?

observing **C.** What colors make up some inks?

observing **D.** What other paper or filters can be used? How do they change the color separation?

TEACHING COMMENT

PREPARATION AND BACKGROUND

The basic process of this investigation is called paper chromatography. The separate pigments that make up the color of a dye are absorbed at slightly different rates by the paper. This has the effect of spreading out the pigments, which makes them visible. Only washable (nonpermanent) dyes will work.

GENERALIZATION

The colors that make up a dye may be discovered through paper chromatography. Most dyes contain several blended colors.

SAMPLE PERFORMANCE OBJECTIVES

Process: Given the materials, the child can demonstrate how to use paper chromatography to analyze the colored pigments in a dye.

Knowledge: The child can predict the colors blended in several common dyes.

ACTIVITY: *WHAT COLORS MAKE UP SUNLIGHT?*

NEEDED

cake pan about half-filled with water   mirror
sunshine   white paper

TRY THIS

1. Place the pan in the sun. Have the mirror face the sun.

2. Hold the mirror upright against the pan's inside rim.

3. Slowly tip back the mirror. Light must strike the mirror below the water's surface.

4. Point the mirror toward a white wall or large sheet of white paper (Figure 1-28).

   a. What colors do you see on the wall?

   b. What happens to the colors if you stir the water lightly?

   c. Try using the light from a filmstrip projector inside the classroom. How will these colors compare with those of sunlight?

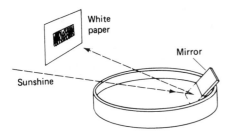

Figure 1-28

Teaching Comment

This crude prism does an excellent job of refracting sunlight into its full spectrum of colors. Stirring the water mildly mixes the colors into white light again. The projector light's spectrum will be similar but not identical to that of sunlight.

PERCEPTION AND EYE EXPERIENCES
(Concepts p. 12)

INVESTIGATION: *How You See Distance*

Suppose you had to see for a while with just one eye. How might this make a difference in telling how far something is from you?

EXPLORATORY PROBLEM

How can you test if two eyes let you tell distance better than one eye?

NEEDED

two pencils   ball
empty soda bottle   partner

TRY THIS

1. Have a partner hold up a thumb at your eye level.
2. Hold a pencil upright, eraser end down, about 6 inches above the thumb. Using both eyes, try to touch the top of your partner's thumb with the eraser. Move the pencil down fairly quickly but gently (Figure 1-29).

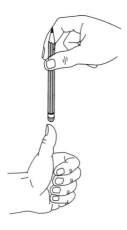

Figure 1-29

3. Have your partner slightly change the distance his or her thumb is from you.
4. Using one eye, try again to touch your partner's thumb. Move the pencil down fairly quickly but gently.

DISCOVERY PROBLEMS

observing **A.** In which trial was it easier to touch your partner's thumb?

observing **B.** Does which eye you close make any difference? How does using two eyes compare with using one? (Be sure your partner slightly changes his thumb position for each trial.)

observing **C.** Does which hand you use make any difference?

experimenting **D.** How else can you test if two eyes are better than one for telling distance?

TEACHING COMMENT

PREPARATION AND BACKGROUND

When we see an object with two eyes, each eye views it from a slightly different angle. So our perception of the object's distance is usually more accurate than if only one eye is used. With distant objects, the advantage decreases. We tend to use size, background, and other clues to estimate distance.

In this investigation, it is important for an object's position to be moved for each trial. Otherwise, muscle memory alone from a preceding trial may allow the child to touch the object. For the test to be valid, the child should not benefit from experience. Also, the pencil should be moved down with some speed, although gently. If done slowly, self-correction becomes too easy.

GENERALIZATION

Two eyes are usually better than one for judging distance.

SAMPLE PERFORMANCE OBJECTIVES

Process: The child can demonstrate a test for distance perception with two eyes and one eye.

Knowledge: The child can predict situations in which distance perception is more difficult with one eye than with two eyes.

FOR YOUNGER CHILDREN

Younger students should be able to do most of the investigation with some teacher guidance.

INVESTIGATION: *YOUR SIDE VISION AND COLOR*

Suppose you notice an object from the corner of your eye while staring straight ahead. Can you notice it is there *before* you can tell its color? Or can you also tell the color at the same time?

EXPLORATORY PROBLEM

How far to the side can you tell different colors?

NEEDED

four small (5-centimeter, or 2-inch) paper squares of different colors
four larger (10-centimeter, or 4-inch) paper squares of different colors
partner

TRY THIS

1. Keep your eyes on some object across the room during this experiment.
2. Have a partner stand at your right side, about a step away.
3. Ask your partner to hold up a small colored square opposite your ear. (You should not know the color.)
4. Have your partner slowly move the square forward in a big circle (Figure 1-30).

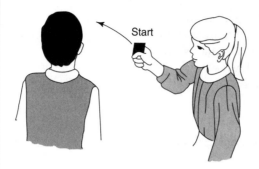

Figure 1-30

5. Say "stop" when you first notice the square at your side.

6. Then tell your partner the square's color if you can.

7. If you cannot, have your partner move the square forward until you can tell.

DISCOVERY PROBLEMS

observing **A.** Was it as easy to notice the color as the object itself?

observing **B.** Will it make any difference if you try the test from your left side?

observing **C.** Will it make any difference if you try different colors? Can you identify some colors farther to the side than others?

observing **D.** Will it make any difference if you try the larger squares?

experimenting **E.** What results will you get if you test other people?

Teaching Comment

PREPARATION AND BACKGROUND

The eye's inside lining, or retina, contains millions of cells sensitive to light intensity and color. Most of the eye's color-sensitive cells are clustered at the back of the eyeball near the optic nerve. To see color, some colored light must reach there. When light enters the eye at an angle, this area may not be stimulated. So we can usually detect the presence of an object at our side before we can distinguish its color.

Be sure the children keep their eyes fixed on some far object as they do this investigation, so they can properly test their side (peripheral) vision.

GENERALIZATION

An object at one's side can be noticed before its color can be identified.

SAMPLE PERFORMANCE OBJECTIVES

Process: The child can test different colors to determine the limits of side vision in identifying each.

Knowledge: The child can demonstrate that a colored object will be detected from the side before its color can be identified.

ACTIVITY: *WHAT HAPPENS WHEN YOUR EYES TIRE FROM SEEING ONE COLOR?*

NEEDED

construction paper (blue, yellow, red)   watch with second hand
scissors   pencil
white paper

TRY THIS

1. Pencil an **x** in the center of the white paper.

2. Cut out one small (5-centimeter, or 2-inch) square each of blue, yellow, and red paper.

3. Put the blue square on the **x**. Look at it steadily for 30 seconds.

4. Remove the square and look at the **x**.

   a. What color appears at the **x**?

5. Rest your eyes for a minute or so. Then try the yellow and red squares in the same way.

   b. What color appears after the yellow square? red square?

REFERENCES

American Association for the Advancement of Science. (1993). *Benchmarks for science literacy.* New York: Oxford University Press.

Dalby, D. K. (1991). Fine tune your sense of color. *Science and Children, 29* (3), 24–26.

Iona, M., & Beaty, W. (1988). Reflections on refraction. *Science and Children, 25* (8), 18–20.

National Research Council. (1996). *National science education standards.* Washington, DC: National Academy Press.

Wilson, J. E. (1990). Bent on teaching refraction. *Science and Children, 28* (3), 28–30.

SELECTED TRADE BOOKS: LIGHT ENERGY AND COLOR

For Younger Children

Baines, R. (1985). *Light.* Troll Associates.

Brockel, R. (1986). *Experiments with light.* Children's Press.

Carle, E. (1991). *My very first book of colors.* Harper Collins.

Carroll, J. (1991). *The complete color book.* Good Apple.

Collins, D. (1983). *My big fun thinker book of colors and shapes.* Education Insights.

Crews, D. (1981). *Light*. Greenwillow.

Goor, R., & Goor, N. (1981). *Shadows: Here, there, everywhere*. Crowell.

Livingston, M. (1992). *Light and shadow*. Holiday House.

Smith, K. B., & Crenson, V. (1987). *Seeing*. Troll Associates.

Suess, Dr. (1996). *My many colored days*. Alfred Knopf.

Taylor, B. (1990). *Bouncing and bending light*. Watts.

Taylor, B. (1991). *Color and light*. Watts.

Taylor, K. (1992). *Flying start science series: Water; light; action; structure*. Wiley.

For Older Children

Ardley, N. (1991a). *Science book of color*. HarBrace.

Ardley, N. (1991b). *Science book of light*. HarBrace.

Asimov, I. (1986). *How did we find out about the speed of light?* Walker, 1986.

Berger, M. (1987). *Lights, lenses, and lasers*. G. P. Putnam's Sons.

Catherall, E. (1982). *Sight*. Silver Burdett.

Cooper, M. (1981). *Snap! Photography*. Messner.

De Bruin, J. (1986). *Light and color*. Good Apple.

Dunham, M. (1987). *Colors: How do you say it?* Lothrop.

Hecht, J. (1987). *Optics: Light for a new age*. Macmillan.

Hill, J., & Hill, J. (1986). *Looking at light and color*. David & Charles.

Jennings, T. (1992). *Sound and light*. Smithmark.

Murata, M. (1993). *Science is all around you: water and light*. Lerner.

Simon, H. (1981). *The magic of color*. Lothrop.

Simon, S. (1985). *Shadow magic*. Lothrop.

Simon, S. (1991). *Mirror magic*. Lothrop.

Walpole, B. (1987). *Light*. Garrard.

Ward, A. (1991). *Experimenting with light and illusions*. Chelsea House.

Wilkins, M.J. (1991). *Air, light, and water*. Random House.

Whyman, K. (1986). *Light and lasers*. Watts.

Whyman, K. (1989). *Rainbows to lasers*. Watts.

Resource Books

Butzow, C. M., & Butzow, J. W. (1989). *Science through children's literature: An integrated approach* (eye, vision, optics topics pp. 169–173; shadows and light topics pp. 174–177). Teacher Ideas Press.

Shaw, D. G., & Dybdahl, C. S. (1996). *Integrating science and language arts* (color topics pp. 1–52). Allyn and Bacon.

HEAT ENERGY

Conduction, Convection, and Radiation	HEAT ENERGY	Heat Energy Benchmarks and Standards

Changing States of Matter

Temperature and Heat Energy

Temperature and Pressure

Heat Quantity and Capacity

Expansion and Contraction

Calorie and BTU

Molecules

Cohesion

The rising cost of fuels has made more people realize that knowing about heat energy has economic as well as scientific value. Energy affects many aspects of our lives. This chapter considers what happens when materials are heated and cooled, how materials change state, the difference between heat and temperature, and how heat travels.

EXPANSION AND CONTRACTION CONCEPTS
(Experiences p. 53)

Question: How tall is the tallest building in the United States?

Answer: I don't know; it keeps changing.

Although answers like this seldom come up in normal conversation, it is a good one. The height of a tall structure may vary a half foot or more, depending on temperature differences when the measurements are taken. Likewise, a steel bridge may change more than a foot in length, and a ship captain may stride a slightly longer deck in southern waters than in northern waters.

Molecules

The molecular theory of matter offers an interesting explanation for these and many other events. To understand molecules, let's look for a moment at a drop of water. If we could subdivide it with an imaginary eyedropper for years on end, eventually we would get to a point where one more subdivision would produce two atoms of hydrogen and one of oxygen. Both are gases and, of course, look nothing like water. From this, we can say that a molecule is the smallest particle of a substance that can exist by itself and have the properties of that substance when interacting with other molecules.

Strictly speaking, only some gases are exclusively made up of molecules. Some liquids and many solids are composed of electrically charged atoms or groups of atoms called *ions*. But as nearly all ionic particles have physical properties very similar to molecules, it is convenient to treat them as such.

Is there any direct proof that molecules exist? Recently, yes. Pictures of some large molecules have been taken through powerful electron microscopes. But for the most part, scientists have had to rely on indirect evidence. It is a remarkable tribute to the brainpower of earlier scientists that they were able to forge so powerful a theory from their secondhand observations.

Many early experiments may be duplicated today. A unit of alcohol added to a unit of water results in slightly less than two units of liquid. When gold and lead bars are clamped together for a long period, there is a slight intermingling of these elements. Solid sugar crystals disappear when stirred into a liquid.

Matter is composed of tiny particles that have an attractive force (cohesion) between them. There is space between molecules. In a solid material, molecules are very close together and are relatively fixed in place because their cohesion is greater than that of gases or liquids. Molecules of most liquids are slightly farther apart; their weaker cohesion permits them to slide about and take the shape of a container. Gas molecules are widest apart and have almost no cohesive attraction. Therefore, they can conform to a container's shape or escape from an uncovered container.

Molecules are always in motion, but they come almost to a standstill at absolute zero (−460°F or −273°C). Above this temperature, molecules of solids vibrate in place, whereas liquid and gas molecules move faster and more freely. With increased temperature, motion increases and the molecules move farther apart. The reverse happens when temperature is decreased. This is why most matter expands when heated and contracts when cooled.

Water

If liquids *contract* when cooled, why do some water pipes burst in freezing weather? Although molecular theory states that liquids contract when cooled, we note an interesting exception when water temperature drops toward freezing. Water does contract in volume with decreased temperature until about 39°F (4°C). Then its molecules begin to assemble into a crystalline form that becomes ice at 32°F (0°C). The latticelike arrangement of these crystals takes up more space, about 4 percent more, than an equal number of free-moving water molecules. This is why water pipes and engine blocks of water-cooled automobiles may burst in winter.

It also explains why a lake freezes from the top down, rather than the reverse. At 39°F (4°C), water is densest and sinks to the bottom of the lake. Colder water, being less dense, floats to the surface. It freezes into surface ice and traps the heat energy in the slightly warmer water below. Unless the air temperature is extremely cold, this trapped energy is enough to keep the pond from freezing completely.

The importance of this phenomenon to living things can hardly be overestimated. Though it is clear that aquatic life is saved, consider what would happen to the world's climate if bodies of water froze from the bottom up. Because the heat trapped by ice would escape, ice formation would increase. Gradually, the earth's climate would become colder and would eventually become fatal to most life forms.

Differences in Cohesion

Different materials vary in their rates of expansion and contraction because their cohesive forces vary. It is easier to tear a paper sheet apart than an equally thin steel sheet because steel molecules attract one another with much greater force. A cohesive disparity is likewise true of alcohol and water. Notice in Figure 2-1 how water bulges above the glass rim when it is overfilled.

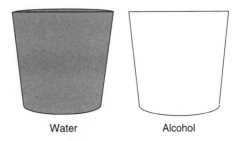

Water   Alcohol

Figure 2-1
Surface tension in alcohol and water.

The cohesive force of water molecules is greater than that of alcohol. This explains why equal amounts of heat energy cause alcohol to expand more than water. It is easier to overcome the weaker cohesive force. It also tells us why alcohol evaporates faster than water.

Expansion, contraction, and changes of state from solids to liquids and gases are the results of a constant tug of war between heat energy and cohesive force. Which side wins depends on which force is more powerful.

Safety

Some experiences will require use of a lighted candle. *Caution:* Supervise these occasions closely. Probably it will be advisable to handle any burning candle yourself. Never allow a child with long hair or loose, trailing apparel to work by an open flame. Always use a metal tray or other fireproof material to contain a burning or hot substance. Develop standards about not touching a hot plate or other materials at random.

CHANGING STATES
OF MATTER CONCEPTS
(Experiences p. 57)

Sometimes we get so used to our environment it is hard to think of the things around us in new ways. Most everyone knows that air is a mixture of gases. Yet a favorite stunt of science demonstrators at high school assemblies is to grandly pour liquid air from one container to another. Many persons know that carbon dioxide is a gas. Yet it is possible to trip over some or drop it on your toe when it is in the form of dry ice. Steel is certainly a durable solid. But high-temperature tests for possible spaceship uses turn it into vapor.

Temperature

The state of matter at any given moment depends on its temperature. Temperature is a measure of the average speed of molecular movements. When increased heat energy is applied to a solid, its molecules vibrate faster. If the motion is powerful enough to overcome the molecules' cohesive forces, the molecules move farther away, and the solid becomes a liquid. If further energy is applied, the molecules move even faster and farther apart to become a gas. With loss of heat energy, the opposite occurs. The decreased speed of molecules enables cohesive force to be reasserted, thus forming a liquid, then a solid when enough heat is lost.

Does a solid become a liquid before it becomes a gas? Or a gas, liquid before it becomes a solid? Usually, but a mothball changes to a gas directly, as does dry ice. Frost is an example of vapor freezing directly into a solid state. These phenomena are examples of *sublimation.*

Different substances change state at different temperatures. Adding salt to fresh water lowers its freezing point. Sea water, for example, freezes at 28.5°F (–2°C) instead of 32°F (0°C). Unless the temperature is very low, sprinkling rock salt on an icy sidewalk melts the ice. We add an antifreeze liquid (ethylene glycol) to our automobile radiators to prevent freezing. A heavy salt solution would be even more effective, except for its unfortunate tendency to corrode metal.

What Pressure Does

Pressure also has an interesting effect on changes of state. As a liquid warms, some of its molecules move so fast they bounce off into the air. We recognize this as evaporation. The same thing happens with boiling, except the process is faster. To leave the surface of a liquid, though, molecules must overcome not only the cohesive pull of nearby molecules but also the pressure of air molecules immediately above.

At sea level, a square-inch column of air extending to outer space weighs 14.7 pounds (6.6 kilograms). At the top of a tall mountain there is much less air, therefore, less weight pressing down. With less pressure, it is easier for liquid molecules to escape into vapor form. So at 90,000 feet (27,000 meters), water boils at room temperature. Astronauts or pilots of high-altitude airplanes wear pressure suits, or are enclosed in a pressurized cabin, to keep their blood from boiling.

Since we normally associate boiling with a temperature of about 212°F, it is important to realize another practical effect of decreased pressure. Boiling-point temperature decreases about 1°F for each 550-foot increase in altitude. At a high location, it is hard to cook foods satisfactorily in an open container because of the low temperature at which boiling happens. A pressure cooker is almost a necessity.

The effect of a different kind of pressure is readily observable with ice. Why is it possible to skate on ice, when we cannot on other smooth surfaces? The answer is that we do not skate directly on the ice. Our body weight exerts enough pressure through the ice skate blades to liquefy the ice. This furnishes a water-lubricated surface on which we slide. As the temperature drops, however, it takes increasing pressure to melt the ice. It may be difficult to skate at all.

Heat Loss and Gain

Does an iced drink start warming up after the ice has half melted? A change of state always results in the absorption or release of heat energy. It requires energy for the fixed, jiggling molecules of a solid, like ice, to acquire a more freely moving liquid state. Interestingly, until an ice cube melts completely in a container of water, there is no appreciable increase in water temperature. The heat energy absorbed first changes the state of the frozen water, then raises the water temperature once the cube has melted. The next time you have an iced drink, try stirring the liquid until the last bit of ice has melted. You should sense no rise in temperature until after the frozen cubes have completely changed state.

Additional energy is required for liquid molecules to move fast enough and far enough apart to become a gas. Heat is absorbed from whatever accessible substance is warmer than the changing material.

So if you hold an ice cube in your hand, it removes heat from your body. More heat is required as the liquid evaporates. This is why evaporation has a cooling effect. As the speed of evaporation increases, so does cooling. This is why rubbing alcohol cools your skin more effectively than water. Ethyl chloride evaporates so quickly that it is used by physicians to numb flesh for painless surgery.

Conversely, heat energy is released when a gas condenses to a liquid or a liquid freezes to a solid state. That is because molecular motion continually decreases with each event. It used to be common in rural homes to place tubs of water near vegetable bins in the basement. As the water freezes, enough heat is given off to prevent the vegetables from freezing.

Heat is absorbed in evaporation and released through condensation. This principle applied in electric refrigeration. A liquid refrigerant moves at low pressure into the freezing unit. There it flashes into a vaporous state, cools rapidly, and absorbs heat. As the now slightly warmed vapor leaves the unit, a motor-driven pump compresses the vapor until it has changed to a hot liquid under high pressure. The liquid next circulates in tubes attached to the back of the refrigerator that radiate the heat into the air. The cycle then repeats itself.

TEMPERATURE AND HEAT ENERGY CONCEPTS
(Experiences p. 60)

You have seen before that the temperature of a material depends on the speed of its molecules. So molecules of a cold substance move slower than those of a hotter substance.

Heat Quantity

Although the concept of temperature is understood by many children, quantity of heat is a subtler idea. Consider a white-hot horseshoe just removed from a blacksmith's forge and a large bathtub of warm water. Which contains more heat? Very probably the water. The amount of heat a material contains depends on *how many* molecules it has, as well as how fast they are moving. This is why the owner of a large house pays larger winter heating bills than someone who owns a small house, although the same air temperature may be maintained. It also explains why it takes about half as long to bring one liter of water to a boil as two. There are half as many molecules to move.

Heat Capacity

Different materials have different capacities for heat energy. For example, it takes more heat for iron to reach a given temperature than an equal weight of lead. More energy is required to heat water to a given temperature than any other common material, liquid or solid, and water retains this heat longer.

The most important effect of water's high heat capacity is found in weather and climate. Because the earth's oceans and lakes gain and lose heat more slowly than the land, they moderate changes in air temperature throughout the world. The most noticeable effects are found in coastal regions. Summers are cooler and winters warmer there than they are inland.

The Calorie and the BTU

Two measures are commonly used to tell heat capacity: the calorie and the British Thermal Unit (BTU). A calorie is the quantity of heat needed to raise the temperature of a gram (about ounce) of water 1° Celsius. The caloric value of a food is found simply by burning a dry sample of known weight in a special chamber of a carefully insulated container of pure water. The temperature rise is multiplied by the weight of water in the container. For example, assume 50 grams of water rises 20°C. $50 \times 20 = 1,000$ calories.

To make calculations less cumbersome, a "large calorie" is used in finding heat value of foods. Equivalent to 1,000 small calories, the large calorie is what you see published in diet lists.

The British Thermal Unit, or the quantity of heat needed to raise 1 pound of water 1° Fahrenheit, is used widely by engineers. It is found by multiplying the mass of water by the temperature increase. So to raise the temperature of 5 pounds of water 30°F requires 150 BTU.

Of course, this information is more for you than for the students at this level. Yet it is not too early for many children to grasp the general idea of heat quantity. For this reason, we have included an activity in which children heat different-sized nails, put them in water, and measure the increases in water temperature.

Heat Conservation

Heat energy is *conserved* when liquids are mixed, that is, not lost but transferred in proportion to the original amount. One liter of warm water has half the heat energy of two liters at the same temperature. Also, if two equal volumes of water at different temperatures are mixed, the resulting temperature is halfway between that of the two samples.

Thermal Equilibrium

In some elementary science curricula, the concept of *equilibrium* is introduced. For example, when water is brought to a boil, its temperature stays at 212°F or 100°C (at sea level) until all the water has evaporated. Because it loses heat energy as fast as it gains the energy, we see a state of dynamic equilibrium or a stable condition that remains until the water disappears.

A second example is seen when something cools. You know that when a jar of hot water is left standing long enough, it loses heat energy to the surrounding air and surface on which it rests. Eventually, the water temperature becomes stable when it reaches *thermal equilibrium* with these interacting objects. The air, of course, is the chief interacting object that influences the water's final temperature.

CONDUCTION, CONVECTION, AND RADIATION CONCEPTS
(Experiences p. 64)

Until the nineteenth century, it was generally thought that heat was a fluidlike substance (caloric) that could be poured from one material to another. Scientists now realize that heat is a form of energy, with *energy* being defined as the capacity to do work.

Changing Forms of Energy

Many experiments have shown that energy can be changed from one form to another. Our practical experience also shows that this is so. Electrical energy changes to heat in toasters and hot plates; chemical energy yields heat through fires and explosives; mechanical energy (motion) provides the force needed to overcome friction and, in the process, heat is released.

Heat, in turn, changes to other forms of energy. Hot fuel turns a generator to produce electricity, or gasoline is burned in automobile engines to produce mechanical energy.

If you put a pan of hot water in a cool room, after a while the water cools to room temperature. But place a pan of cool water in a hot oven, and the water warms to oven temperature. In moving toward thermal equilibrium, as we saw before, heat energy always travels from a place of higher temperature to one of lower temperature.

A misconception of what heat is may interfere with understanding how it travels. Instead of viewing cold as a lesser degree of heat, many students think that cold is distinctly different and the opposite of heat. So it's logical for them to think that "cold" leaves the ice cube in a drink and goes into the liquid, rather than that heat goes from the liquid into the cube, making it melt (Erickson, 1979).

Since heat is felt rather than seen, it may also affect children's understanding of how it travels. By about age eight, they begin to think of heat as something that travels from a source to another place. But before then, for example, they are more likely to view a hot stove or fire as something that instantly makes them warm (Albert, 1978).

In moving from one location to another, heat energy may travel in one or more of three ways: by *conduction, convection,* and *radiation.* Let's consider these ways one at a time.

Conduction

If you grasp the metal handle of a hot frying pan, you quickly let go. How is it possible for the heat energy to go from the hot stove grid to the handle? Molecular conduction is responsible. As heat energy enters the pan bottom, its molecules begin to vibrate faster. This motion is passed along, molecule by molecule, up the pan's sides to its handle. Eventually, all the particles are vibrating faster, and you feel the heat.

Of all solids, metals are the best conductors. Their molecules are very close together and transmit heat energy quickly. But each type of metal varies somewhat in conductivity. Copper is the best common conductor, followed by aluminum, steel, and iron. Other solids are comparatively poor conductors, including ceramic materials. This is one reason we use ceramic cups to hold hot coffee and microwave food.

Because molecules of liquids are farther apart than solids, it is reasonable to expect that they conduct heat less efficiently than solids. Our ordinary experiences with bathwater help confirm this thought. When hot water is added to cooler water, it takes a long time for the heat to reach all portions of the tub. For this reason, we stir the water a bit to hasten the process.

Gases are the poorest conductors of all. Their molecules are spread so far apart they do not collide often and regularly enough to pass on increased energy to any appreciable extent. This is why it is possible for frozen-food sections in supermarkets to have open counters. Very little heat energy is conducted downward from the warmer air above the counter.

Convection

Although liquids and gases conduct poorly, it is easy to heat a pan of water quickly to boiling temperature or quickly roast a frankfurter in the hot air over a fire. This means that there must be another, more efficient method of heat transfer in liquids and gases than conduction. To identify it, examine what happens when air is warmed.

Watch the smoke from burning material. Why does it rise? Is it unaffected by gravity? A clue to its behavior is found when smoke is pumped into an airless vacuum chamber. The smoke particles fall like lead weights. Therefore, smoke does not just "rise"; something must push it up.

When the glowing part of burning material warms the adjacent air, the increased energy agitates air molecules to increased speeds and they spread farther apart. Because fewer molecules take up a given volume of space, they are lighter than an equal volume of the surrounding air. The lighter air is pushed up with the smoke particles as it is replaced by heavier, colder air. As the mass of lighter air rises, it carries increased energy with it. This is why air near the ceiling is warmer than air near the floor.

When there is an opening for warm air to escape and cool air to flow into a room, a *convection current* is set up. This is what happens when we open a window at top and bottom to freshen the air in a room. It is also the primary cause of winds in the atmosphere.

Similar convection currents are set up in heated liquids. Warmed, expanded water in a pan rises as it is continually replaced by cooler, heavier water until the same temperature is reached in the entire container. Adding color to the liquid will help children to see this effect (Rubino & Duerling).

Because of the way convective currents move, a heating unit is usually located at the bottom of a hot-water tank and a cooling unit at the top of a refrigerator. Convection also helps to set up ocean currents. Warm water at the equator is continually being replaced by cold water flowing from the polar regions. Air convection currents form winds that contribute to the distribution of these giant water currents. A third important factor is the earth's rotation. Because water has a high heat capacity, ocean currents are responsible for altering the climates of many countries.

Radiation

A common example of the third method of heat transfer, radiation, is found in the fireplace of a house. This is especially noticeable when the air temperature is low. As you warm yourself in front of the fire, only the portion of your body that faces the fire feels warm. Conduction is poor, because air is the conducting medium. Convection is negligible, because most of the hot air escapes up the chimney. Heat reaches you primarily by radiation.

All vibrating molecules release a certain amount of energy through invisible heat rays called *infrared waves*. These waves largely pass through transparent materials like air and glass but are absorbed by opaque objects, which become warmer as a result. We are aware of radiant energy only when the emitting source is warmer than body temperature. The sun is by far our most important source of radiant energy. In its rays are found visible light, invisible infrared waves, and other forms of radiant energy.

From Solar to Heat Energy

An air traveler who goes from a cold to a tropical climate quickly notices many differences in the new surroundings. Among the most impressive are house colors, which are largely light pastels and dazzling white. Similar differences can be noted in clothing colors. Dark-colored materials absorb more sunlight than light-colored materials.

Figure 2-2 reveals why persons in tropical countries find a greater need for lighter colors than those who live farther away from the equator. Light is most intense when it is received from directly overhead. If the same amount of light is spread out over a larger area, any part of that area receives less light and so less heat.

The changing of solar energy to heat energy is most noticeable when there is an effective way of preventing the heat from escaping. A common example is the temperature rise within a tightly closed automobile parked in sunlight. The rapidly vibrating short waves of sunlight can pass through the windows. When they strike the upholstery they are absorbed, then

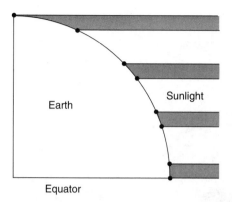

Figure 2-2
Light is most intense when received from exactly overhead. This explains why people in tropical climates find a greater need for light-colored clothing and buildings than others do.

reradiated as longer, slower-vibrating heat waves. The longer waves are largely unable to penetrate glass, so most of the heat stays inside, building up in intensity as sunlight continues to stream in. Because the same thing happens in greenhouses, this phenomenon is aptly called the *greenhouse effect*.

Our atmosphere is also warmed largely by reradiated heat waves. The atmosphere is like a giant glass cover that traps the longer, reradiated heat waves. However, this analogy is not perfect. Fortunately for us, the atmosphere is far less efficient than glass. A substantial amount of reradiated heat escapes into space. Were this not so, the earth's air temperature would become so hot it would be intolerable to life.

Because of the greenhouse effect, air temperatures get warmest in the afternoon rather than at midday. Although the sun is most nearly overhead at midday, the buildup of heat continues for several hours afterward.

Solar Heating for Homes

Solar energy is becoming a popular way to heat water and even entire homes, especially in the sunbelt regions of the south and southwest. Let's examine one way this is done.

A *flat-plate collector* is attached to, or built into, the house roof. Its purpose is to collect as much solar energy as possible. The collector, made of metal and glass, is positioned to face the sun. The glass is mounted just over a blackened metal plate. Water pipes, also painted black, are attached to the plate. Sunlight is absorbed by the plate and pipes. Water inside the pipes is heated by conduction. The glass cover contributes to the buildup of heat by trapping the absorbed light energy (Figure 2-3).

The heated water is stored in a large tank. Pipes circulate it throughout the house as needed. Other pipes are connected to hot water faucets in the house.

Notice the three conditions that affect the efficiency of the solar collector. The collector plate and pipes are painted black to absorb sunlight. A clear glass cover admits sunlight but prevents most of the absorbed energy from escaping. Finally, the collector is mounted on a slope that faces the sun.

Controlling Heat Loss

Knowing how heat travels permits us to control it. We use *insulation* to prevent or retard heat energy transfer. For example, to retard conduction we use poor conductors. Since air is a poor conductor, materials with air spaces, such as wood and wool, make excellent insulators.

In homes, convection and conduction are reduced by using hollow walls designed to trap the air. Because some convection takes place anyway, many homeowners fill the walls with a light, fluffy material, such as fiberglass or cellulose insulation.

An excellent way to insulate for radiation is to reflect it away, because it behaves like light as it travels. This is why insulating materials in the home may use a shiny foil exterior, particularly in the attic. It also explains why silver-colored paint is used on large gasoline storage tanks.

Figure 2-3
A flat-plate solar energy collector.

HEAT ENERGY BENCHMARKS AND STANDARDS

Students in early grades should develop an understanding that materials can exist in liquid, gas, or solid form. Experimentation with water can be effective in introducing them to the states of matter and how heat affects the movement of molecules and the state of a substance. Specific Benchmarks and Standards are as follows:

SAMPLE BENCHMARKS (AAAS, 1993).

■ Heating and cooling cause changes in the properties of materials. Many kinds of changes occur faster under hotter conditions (by Grades 3–5, p. 77).

■ Some materials conduct heat much better than others. Poor conductors can reduce heat loss (by Grades 3–5, p. 84).

SAMPLE STANDARDS (NRC, 1996).

■ Materials can exist in different states—solid, liquid, and gas. Some common materials, such as water, can be changed from one state to another by heating and cooling (by Grades K–4, p. 127).

■ Heat moves in predictable ways, flowing from warmer objects to cooler ones, until both reach the same temperature (by Grades 5–8, p. 155).

INVESTIGATIONS AND ACTIVITIES

EXPANSION AND CONTRACTION EXPERIENCES
(Concepts p. 44)

ACTIVITY: *HOW DOES HEAT AFFECT A SOLID?*

NEEDED

brass screw and screw eye (each screwed into the eraser end of a separate pencil, see Figure 2-4),
small dish and candle
matches

TRY THIS

1. Light the candle and fix it to the dish.
2. Try to pass the screw through the screw eye as in Figure 2-4. This should not be possible.

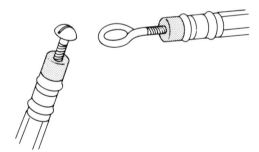

Figure 2-4

3. Heat the screw eye in the flame for a minute or so.
4. Try Step 2 again.
   a. Does the screw head pass through the heated screw eye? If so, keep passing the screw head through the eye. How many seconds go by before you cannot do it?
   b. What will happen if you heat the screw but not the screw eye? If you heat both screw and screw eye? How can you explain what happened in a and b?

TEACHING COMMENT

The screw eye should be slightly smaller than the screw head. Pliers can be used to slightly close or open the screw eye as needed. ***Caution:*** Supervise burning the candle closely.

INVESTIGATION: *MEASURING TEMPERATURE WITH A WATER THERMOMETER*

Many thermometers use red-colored alcohol or mercury in a closed tube. What happens to these liquids when they get warmer? cooler? You can make a water thermometer that works in much the same way.

EXPLORATORY PROBLEM

How can you make a water thermometer?

NEEDED

small soda bottle
soft clay
small card
plastic straw
sticky tape
crayon
red food coloring
pencil
thermometer
ruler

TRY THIS

1. Fill the bottle almost full with water.
2. Add some food coloring to the water so it is easy to see.
3. Dry the bottle opening with a paper towel. Then put the straw about halfway into the bottle opening.
4. Use clay to stop up the bottle opening and around the straw. Try to get a tight fit without getting the clay wet.
5. The water should rise about halfway up the straw beyond the clay. If not, move the straw up or down. Then press the clay down tightly again.

6. Put the bottle in the sun. After an hour, lightly mark the water level on the straw with crayon. Then put the bottle in a refrigerator for an hour and mark the level.

7. Measure the distance between the two marks. On a card, mark two dots the same distance and draw evenly spaced lines between. Give each line a number, with the highest on top. Put the column of numbers on the right side of the card.

8. Tape the card to the straw so the top and bottom numbers are even with the two marks on the straw (Figure 2-5).

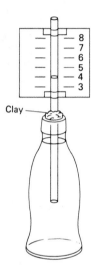

Figure 2-5

9. Use your water thermometer to record daily temperatures for a week. You might use a table like this:

Table 2-1
Daily Temperature Record

	Water Thermometer Readings				
Time	M	T	W	TH	F
9:30 A.M.	4	5			
Noon	6	7			
2:30 P.M.	7	7			

DISCOVERY PROBLEMS

measuring   **A.** At what time of day is it coolest? warmest?

inferring   **B.** During the week, what was the coolest morning? noon? afternoon?

predicting   **C.** How closely can you predict the noon temperature from the 9:30 a.m. temperature? the 2:30 p.m. temperature from the noon temperature? Try this for a few days.

communicating   **D.** Ask a partner to make another water thermometer. Keep two separate records. How closely do your readings agree with your partner's? If they do not agree, can you figure out why?

measuring   **E.** Get a regular thermometer. Measure the temperature with it and your water thermometer. Write the actual temperatures on the left side of the straw card. After a few days, use only your water thermometer to predict the real temperature. Then check the regular thermometer each time. How accurate is your water thermometer? How could you make it more accurate?

TEACHING COMMENT

PREPARATION AND BACKGROUND

A one-hole rubber stopper and glass tube are more reliable than clay and a straw. Wet the tube and stopper before inserting the tube. Hold the tube with a thickly folded paper towel to guard against breakage and use a twisting motion.

Water, especially with this large volume, takes considerable time to gain and lose heat, so readings should be hours apart. Rubbing alcohol responds more quickly to heat and may be substituted.

GENERALIZATION

Liquids expand when heated and contract when cooled.

SAMPLE PERFORMANCE OBJECTIVE

Process: The child can construct, calibrate, and read a water thermometer.

Knowledge: The child can explain how a liquid thermometer works.

ACTIVITY: *HOW DOES HEAT AFFECT AIR?*

NEEDED

empty soda bottle (cool)
round balloon
partner

TRY THIS

1. Snap the balloon opening over the bottle opening.
2. Wrap both hands around the bottle to warm it. Let a partner help, also.
   a. What happens to the balloon? What seems to be happening to the air inside the bottle?
   b. What will happen to the balloon when the bottle cools? Why?
   c. How else can you warm the bottle air? cool the bottle air?
   d. How could you find out if heated air expands by using only a balloon and string?

TEACHING COMMENT

A partly filled balloon may be placed in sunlight. A string may be wrapped around it to compare before and after sizes. A round, moderately sized balloon inflates more easily than the small tubular kind.

CHANGING STATES OF MATTER EXPERIENCES
(Concepts p. 45)

INVESTIGATION: THE MELTING OF ICE CUBES

Suppose you have a glass of water. It has the same temperature as the air. Would an ice cube melt faster in the water or air?

EXPLORATORY PROBLEM

How can you find out if water or air will melt an ice cube faster?

NEEDED

thermometer
small plastic bag
water
salt
ice cubes
spoon
two glasses (same)

TRY THIS

1. Measure the air temperature inside one glass with a thermometer.
2. Also measure the temperature inside a glass of water. It should be about the same as the air temperature. If not, let the water stand a while.
3. Find two ice cubes that are the same size.
4. Put one ice cube into the empty glass. Put the other into the glass of water.
5. Compare how fast the ice cubes melt (Figure 2-6).

Figure 2-6

DISCOVERY PROBLEMS

experimenting   **A.** How can you make an ice cube melt faster in water? Will stirring the water make a difference? Will an ice cube melt faster in warmer water? Does breaking or crushing the cube make a difference? Does changing the volume of water make a difference?

experimenting   **B.** How fast will ice cubes melt in other liquids? Will an ice cube melt faster in salt water? Does the amount of salt make a difference? What other liquids can you try? Can you predict the melting order of ice cubes in them?

TEACHING COMMENT

PREPARATION AND BACKGROUND

The first activity of this investigation requires water of room temperature. Blend warm and cold tap water. Or simply let a glass of water stand for a while.

If you believe your students are capable, try asking only the leading, broad question in Discovery Problems A and B. Probably the students will suggest testing most of the variables posed in the narrow questions that follow.

GENERALIZATION

The melting time of an ice cube changes with different conditions.

PERFORMANCE OBJECTIVES

Process: When asked to test a specific variable, the child can set up an experiment in which other variables are controlled.

Knowledge: The child can predict several conditions that will affect the melting times of ice cubes.

FOR YOUNGER CHILDREN

Younger students can do the exploratory problem, if they are given water that is at room temperature, and respond to the narrow questions in A and B. But they typically will not control variables unless shown how.

ACTIVITY: *WHAT HAPPENS TO THE TEMPERATURE OF AN ICED DRINK AS THE ICE MELTS?*

NEEDED

two ice cubes
cup of water
thermometer

TRY THIS

1. Put the ice cubes in the water.
2. Take the water temperature once a minute throughout this activity. Stir the water a bit each time.
3. Repeat Step 2 until you get the same reading twice. Then answer these questions:
   a. What will happen to the temperature as the ice keeps melting?
   b. When does the water temperature rise again? (A graph can help you keep track.)

TEACHING COMMENT

The ice melting process can be speeded up by heating a metal cup on a hot plate turned to low. Similar results should happen.

TEMPERATURE AND HEAT ENERGY EXPERIENCES

(Concepts p. 47)

INVESTIGATION: *HEAT ENERGY*

Suppose you have two iron nails, one large and one small. Both are heated to the same temperature over a candle flame. Which nail do you think would have more heat energy in it? Or, would both nails have the same heat energy?

EXPLORATORY PROBLEM

How can you compare the amount of heat energy in heated nails?

NEEDED

pie pan
soft clay
candle and match
large and small nail
two small empty juice cans
water
pliers or tongs
clock
two small thermometers

TRY THIS

1. Stick the candle upright in the middle of the pan with clay (Figure 2-7).
2. Fill both cans with enough water to cover the nails when they are dropped in later. Check to be sure the water level and temperature are the same in the cans.
3. Light the candle. Use pliers to hold both nails in the flame for three minutes.
4. Drop one nail into each can. Wait one minute. Then stir the water in each can lightly with a thermometer and check the temperatures.

DISCOVERY PROBLEMS

measuring　　**A.** Which can of water is warmer? Which nail had more heat energy in it?

observing　　**B.** Maybe one nail was just cooler than the other. Suppose you heated both nails longer to be sure they are the same temperature. Would you still get uneven results?

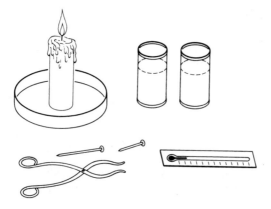

Figure 2-7

experimenting **C.** How can you give the *small* nail more heat energy than the larger one?

predicting **D.** Suppose you heated together a large aluminum nail and a large iron nail. Which, if either, do you think would have more energy?

communicating **E.** How can you see what happens to the water temperature for each minute you heat a nail? Make a graph to help.

Table 2-2
Minutes Nail Is Heated Versus Water Temperature

Water Temperature (°C)

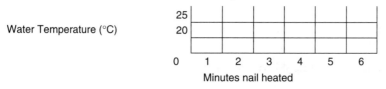

Minutes nail heated

TEACHING COMMENT

PREPARATION AND BACKGROUND

Be sure to supervise this investigation closely for safety. *Caution:* Children should handle heated material only with tongs or pliers. Also, you might prefer to light and extinguish the candle. A hot plate can be used to heat more objects at a time than is possible with a candle.

GENERALIZATION

The amount of heat energy in the same materials depends on their mass as well as temperature.

SAMPLE PERFORMANCE OBJECTIVES

Process: The child can graph and interpret data.

Knowledge: The child can predict that the larger of two heated identical materials will contain more heat energy.

INVESTIGATION: *THE MIXING OF HOT AND COLD WATER*

Have you ever added cold water to cool down hot bath water? Have you added hot water to heat up cool bath water? You can learn to predict the temperatures of a water mixture.

EXPLORATORY PROBLEM

How can you predict the temperature of two mixed samples of water?

NEEDED

large container of hot water
large container of cold water
two small styrofoam cups
half-gallon milk carton with top cut off
two thermometers
paper and pencil

TRY THIS

1. Fill one small cup with hot water. Take the temperature of the water and record it.

2. Fill another small cup with cold water. Take the temperature and record it (Figure 2-8).

3. Pour both cups of water into the large carton. Take the temperature of the mixed water and record it.

4. Study your records. Let's say your recorded temperatures are like the ones in Table 2-3:

   Notice that the temperature of the mixture is halfway between the hot and cold temperatures (60 + 20 = 80, 40 is half of 80). Look at the temperature of your mixture. Is it about halfway between the hot and cold temperatures?

DISCOVERY PROBLEMS

predicting   **A.** Suppose you mix *two* cups of hot and *two* cups of cold water. How hot do you predict the mixture will be?

predicting   **B.** Suppose you mix two cups of only hot water. How hot do you predict the mixture will be?

Figure 2-8

Table 2-3
Temperature Recordings

Hot Water	Cold Water	Mixture
60°C	20°C	40°C

predicting **C.** Suppose you mix two cups of cold water with one of hot water. Will the mixture be hotter or colder than halfway between the two temperatures? How closely can you predict the temperature of the mixture?

TEACHING COMMENT

PREPARATION AND BACKGROUND

The temperature of mixed water depends on the temperature and the volume of each water sample mixed. When the volumes of water samples are equal, the mixture temperature is the average of the sample temperatures. But if the volumes are different, this has to be considered when figuring the average. For example, if one water sample is twice the volume of another, it will have twice the influence on the mixture temperature. *Caution:* Never heat the water beyond the point that someone can comfortably touch it.

GENERALIZATION

The temperature of mixed water samples depends on the temperature and volume of each sample. The mixture temperature is always somewhere between the high and low sample temperatures.

SAMPLE PERFORMANCE OBJECTIVES

Process: The child can measure water sample temperatures and calculate the average of several samples.

Knowledge: The child can purposefully vary the direction of temperature change (cold or hot) in a mixture by controlling the volume or temperature of added water.

CONDUCTION, CONVECTION, AND RADIATION EXPERIENCES
(Concepts p. 48)

ACTIVITY: *WHAT MAKES SOME THINGS FEEL COLDER EVEN WHEN THEY HAVE THE SAME TEMPERATURE?*

NEEDED

metal object
newspaper
piece of wood
thermometer

TRY THIS

1. Hold the bulb of a thermometer against any metal object, such as scissors. Find its temperature. Do the same with a piece of wood and a folded newspaper. They should all be the same temperature. If not, keep them together and wait an hour or so.

2. Touch a metal object with one hand and some wood with the other. Compare the metal and newspaper, also.

   a. Which one felt coolest? warmest? Some materials conduct heat well and some poorly. Good conductors take away heat quickly from our warm skin, so they feel cool. Poor conductors take away heat slowly. This makes them seem warm because less heat is lost from our skin.

   b. What other materials can you compare at school and home? Make a record of what you find. Share your record with others who test heat conductors.

TEACHING COMMENT

It is assumed in this activity that the temperature of tested materials will be lower than body temperature. If your students seem capable, you might invite them to attempt an explanation after Problem 2a and withhold, for a time, the explanation given.

ACTIVITY: *HOW DO WARM AND COLD WATER FORM A CURRENT?*

NEEDED

two matched clear soda bottles
red food coloring
small card
white paper
cake pan or tray
hot and cold tap water

TRY THIS

1. Fill one bottle with cold and the other with hot tap water.
2. Add red coloring to the hot water bottle. Put this bottle on the pan.

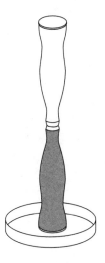

Figure 2-9

3. Hold a card tightly over the opening of the cold water bottle. Turn the bottle upside down and place it carefully on top of the hot water bottle (Figure 2-9).

    a. What do you think will happen if you remove the card? Try it and see. Be careful not to tip over the bottle. Hold white paper behind the bottle to see better.

4. Empty the bottles and do Steps 1 and 2 again, but now put the hot water bottle on top.

    b. What do you think will happen now when you remove the card? How can you explain the results?

ACTIVITY: *WHERE DOES WARMED AIR GO?*

NEEDED

yardstick or substitute
string
two thumbtacks
two matched paper bags
bit of clay
sticky tape
hot plate

TRY THIS

1. Stick a thumbtack into the middle of the stick near the edge. Tie string to the tack.
2. Hang the stick from the top of a wide table. Use another tack to fasten the loose string end there.
3. Fasten a string to each bag bottom with sticky tape.
4. Hang the bags upside down from the stick ends. Use a tiny bit of clay to balance the stick if needed (Figure 2-10).

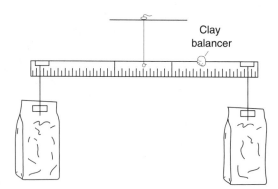

Figure 2-10

5. Place a cold, unplugged hot plate under a bag. (*Caution:* The bag should be at least 30 centimeters or 1 foot above the hot plate since it is flammable.)
6. Plug in the hot plate.
   a. What do you think will happen to the bag when you turn on the hot plate?
   b. What will happen to the bag when you turn off the hot plate?

TEACHING COMMENT

For safety, it's best for you to demonstrate this activity, and to turn off the hot plate as soon as the bag rises.

INVESTIGATION: SOLAR ENERGY AND COLORS

Have you ever felt extra warm when wearing a colored shirt in sunlight? When a colored shirt soaks up sunlight, it does get warmer. But how does the kind of color affect how warm it gets?

EXPLORATORY PROBLEM

How can you compare how warm different colors get in sunlight?

NEEDED

sheets of different-colored construction paper (such as blue, red, green, white)
four thermometers
four paper clips
sunshine
partner

TRY THIS

1. Fold the four colored sheets in half. Clip together the open side.
2. Push a thermometer all the way into each folded, clipped sheet (Figure 2-11).
3. Place the sheets in a row where it is sunny.
4. Wait five minutes. Then check the thermometer temperatures.

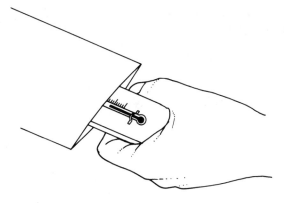

Figure 2-11

DISCOVERY PROBLEMS

predicting **A.** Before you check, what do you think the warmest to coolest colors will be?

classifying **B.** Suppose you also tried colored sheets such as orange, yellow, and black. Where would they fit in the order found in A?

observing **C.** How well can you feel the difference in heat among the colors? Close your eyes. Let a partner help you place your hands on the sheets. Can you feel the hottest and coolest sheets?

measuring **D.** Will a large colored sheet get warmer than a small one?

measuring **E.** Suppose you placed *all* the colored sheets in the shade. Would some colors still get warmer than others?

TEACHING COMMENT

PREPARATION AND BACKGROUND

It is possible on extra-bright, hot days for the temperature inside the paper folders to rise quickly. On such days, leave the thermometer tops exposed. Have someone observe and remove any thermometer before it rises near the breaking point.

GENERALIZATION

Absorbed sunlight changes to heat energy; darker colors get warmer than lighter colors.

SAMPLE PERFORMANCE OBJECTIVES

Process: The child can read a thermometer accurately to within one degree.

Knowledge: The child can select which colors are likely to be relatively warmer or cooler in sunlight.

FOR YOUNGER CHILDREN

With some help, younger students can detect by touch alone which colors become warmest or stay coolest in sunshine (Problem C).

ACTIVITY: *HOW DO GREENHOUSES AND CLOSED AUTOMOBILES GET WARM?*

NEEDED

two matched glass jars and cap
two thermometers

two pieces of dark cloth
sunshine

TRY THIS

1. Place each jar on its side. Put a piece of cloth into each. Place a thermometer on each cloth. Cap only one jar.
2. Turn the jars so their tops face away from the sun.
3. Watch the thermometers. Keep a record of any changes each minute. Remove a thermometer before it gets close to its highest temperature, because it can break.

   a. In which jar does the temperature climb faster? How much faster? A graph will help to answer these questions.

   b. How much, if any, difference in jar temperature will there be on a cloudy day?

ACTIVITY: *WHERE IS IT HOTTEST AROUND A LIGHTED LAMP?*

NEEDED

table or gooseneck lamp (shade removed)
ruler
small pane of glass
thermometer
watch

TRY THIS

1. Check the room temperature with your thermometer. Then switch on the lamp.
2. Hold the bulb end of the thermometer toward the lamp light. Try the three places shown in the picture (Figure 2-12). Keep the thermometer the same distance from the light each time. Wait for the thermometer to reach room temperature before trying a new place.

   a. How hot does the thermometer get in each place?
3. Turn the lamp upside down. Again, hold the thermometer bulb toward the light.

   b. How hot does the thermometer get? How can you explain your results?
4. Set the lamp upright again. Hold a piece of glass between the light and the thermometer. Hold the thermometer in all four places again.

   c. What are your findings now? How can you explain them?

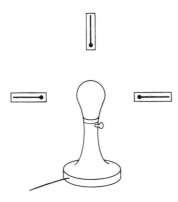

Figure 2-12

TEACHING COMMENT

Tape the edges of the glass shield with masking tape to avoid a nicked finger. A transparent shield of plastic kitchen wrap will also work. The temperature above an unshielded bulb should be highest because both convection and radiation occur. But convected heat is blocked by a transparent shield, so the temperature above a shielded bulb should be like that found in other positions around the bulb.

INVESTIGATION: *How to Keep Heat In or Out*

Most houses have an inside and outside wall. Packed between the double walls of many houses is *insulation*. This is a light, fluffy material that helps to keep heat in or out. You can work with cans of water and different materials to learn about insulation.

EXPLORATORY PROBLEM

What can you do to see how insulation works?

NEEDED

two small tin cans
hot water
two large tin cans with lids
piece of cloth
kitchen foil
different insulation materials
rubber band
ice cubes
thermometer

TRY THIS

1. Pour the same amount of hot water into each small can.
2. Cover each small can with the same size of foil. Use a rubber band to hold each cover tight (Figure 2-13).

Figure 2-13

3. Wrap one small can with cloth.
4. Put this can into one large can and cap it.
5. Put the other small can into a second large can and cap it.
6. After 20 minutes, remove the four can covers. Dip a finger into each small can of water. Which is warmer?

DISCOVERY PROBLEMS

measuring
A. How much warmer is one can of water than the other? How can you use a thermometer to find out?

experimenting
B. How hot can you keep a small can of water? Have a contest with a friend. Try different materials, such as sawdust, cotton, wool, puffed rice, or torn paper. Or try your own secret mix of materials. Put the materials between the larger and smaller can walls. Whoever has the warmer can of water after 30 minutes (or longer) wins.

inferring
C. Can you figure out which single material is the best insulator? worst insulator? Does how tightly it is packed make a difference?

experimenting
D. In summer, you want your house to stay cool. Does insulation keep heat out as well as in? Find out. How cool can you keep a

small can with an ice cube inside? Have a contest with a friend. Whoever has the larger ice cube after one hour (or longer) wins.

inferring   **E.** Are the best materials for keeping the can warm also best for keeping the can cold? If not, which are best?

TEACHING COMMENT

PREPARATION AND BACKGROUND

Use matched one-pound coffee cans with lids for the larger cans. Small, identical juice cans will fit nicely into the coffee cans. Identical pieces of foil may be used to cap the small cans, so insulating materials do not fall inside. Either hot or warm water from the tap will do for this activity.

GENERALIZATION

Insulating materials may be used to slow the movement of heat energy

PERFORMANCE OBJECTIVES

Process: The child can test which of several heat insulating materials is most efficient.

Knowledge: The child can describe (explain) the contrasting properties of efficient and inefficient heat insulating materials.

REFERENCES

Albert, E. (1978). Development of the concept of heat in children. *Science Education, 62*(3), 389–399.

American Association for the Advancement of Science. (1993). *Benchmarks for science literacy.* New York: Oxford University Press.

Erickson, G. L. (1979). Children's conceptions of heat and temperature. *Science Education, 63*(1), 83–93.

National Research Council. (1996). *National science education standards.* Washington, DC: National Academy Press.

Rubino, A. M., & Duerling, C. K. (1991). Around the world in science class. *Science and Children, 28*(7), 37–39.

SELECTED TRADE BOOKS: HEAT ENERGY

For Younger Children

Ardley, N. (1983). *Hot and cold.* Watts.

Hillerman, A. (1983). *Done in the sun.* Sunstone Press.

Llewellyn, C. (1991). *First look at keeping warm.* Gareth Stevens.

Maestro, B., & Maestro, G. (1990). *Temperature and you.* Lodestar Books.

Oleksy, W. (1986). *Experiments with heat.* Children's Press.

Petersen, D. (1985). *Solar energy at work.* Children's Press.

Santrey, L. (1985). *Heat.* Troll Associates.

Stille, D. R. (1990). *The greenhouse effect*. Children's Press.

Wade, H. (1979). *Heat*. Raintree.

For Older Children

Adler, I., & Adler, R. (1973). *Heat and its uses*. John Day.

Bendick, J. (1974). *Heat and temperature*. Watts.

Cobb, V. (1973). *Heat*. Watts.

George, J. C. (1983). *One day in the desert*. Thomas Crowell.

Kaplan, S. (1983). *Solar energy*. Raintree.

Knapp, B. (1990). *Fire*. Steck-Vaughn.

Langley, A. (1986). *Energy*. Watts.

Mebane, R. C., & Rybolt, T. R. (1987). *Adventures with atoms and molecules*. Enslow.

Scott, J. M. (1973). *Heat and fire*. Enslow.

Whyman, K. (1987). *Heat and energy*. Watts.

Yount, L. (1981). *Too hot, too cold, or just right*. Walker.

Resource Book

Butzow, C. M., & Butzow, J. W. (1989). *Science through children's literature: an integrated approach* (states of matter topics pp. 200–205). Teacher Ideas Press.

SOUND ENERGY

Molecules and
Sound

Waves and
Vibrations

Loudness

Sound Vibrations

Sound Energy
Benchmarks and
Standards

Echoes

Sonar

Reflected and
Absorbed Sounds

Hearing and
Locating Sounds

SOUND
ENERGY

How Pitch
Changes

Hearing Ranges

How Sounds
Travel

Musical
Instruments

The Human Ear

Sonic Booms

Mass and
Noise

Speed of Sound

Play a radio loudly and the windows rattle. Watch a parade at a distance and the marchers seem to be out of time with the music. Sing in the shower and suddenly your voice takes on new dimensions. There are few topics that present so many accessible materials and interesting things to explore as sound energy.

In this chapter, we'll consider how sound vibrations are made; how sounds travel in air, water, and solids; how sounds are reflected and absorbed; how the pitch of sounds may change; and how we hear.

SOUND VIBRATIONS CONCEPTS
(Experiences p. 85)

Every so often in science fiction a sinister scientist invents a machine that can collect and play back all the sounds that have ever been made. At first the scientist uses the machine to help historians find out what King John *really* said at Runnymede, but soon after he offers the enemy military secrets discussed at the Pentagon.

Molecules and Sounds

Of course, all signs show that such a machine could never be invented. Sounds are simply waves of compressed molecules pulsating outward in all directions and planes from a vibrating source.

Consider the air around you. It is composed of tiny, individual molecules of different gases mixed similarly throughout the lower atmosphere. These molecules are rapidly and randomly moving about. A fast-vibrating source like the hummingbird's wings, a bell, a guitar string, and a "twanged" ruler held on the edge of a desk compress billions of these molecules with each back-and-forth movement because the molecules are in the way. Since air molecules are elastic, they quickly assume their original

shape after moving out of the vibrating object's path. But before this happens, they transfer energy to other molecules over a distance.

Please note that it is the *wave of energy* rather than the molecules that may travel a great distance. Each molecule may move less than a millionth of a hair's width, but this is enough to bump the next randomly moving molecule and pass on the outward movement. Figure 3-1 shows a wave motion resulting from a compression and rarefaction effect on molecules pushed by a vibrating ruler.

A sound fades away when energy behind the original vibrations is used in the transmitting process. As one molecule bumps another, it

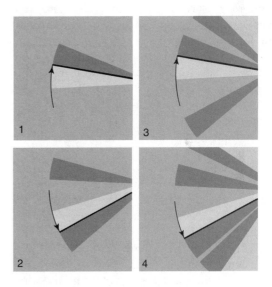

Figure 3-1
A vibrating ruler producing sound waves. In 1, the ruler is pushing the air molecules together (compression). Notice the thinned-out space below it (rarefaction). Picture 2 shows the opposite happening, with the first part of the sound wave now moving away. Picture 3 and 4 show another sound wave being produced. The wave moves outward as the molecules push others in the way, which in turn squeeze other molecules.

uses a tiny amount of energy. As more molecules are bumped, there is less energy available. The sound stops when energy of the randomly moving molecules exceeds the wave's energy. The molecules simply resume their normal helter-skelter movements.

Loudness

How is loudness explained? First, for the moment, let's call it *intensity;* "loudness" is what we actually hear. If our ears are working poorly, a very intense sound may be barely heard. So loudness is a matter of individual perception. Intensity, on the other hand, can be consistently and accurately recorded by a sensitive sound detector in terms of the *decibel,* a unit of measurement in sound. The distinction between loudness and intensity may be too subtle for most children.

You know that shouting requires more energy than whispering. A boost in energy forces any vibrating medium to vibrate to and fro more widely than usual, but in the same amount of time. This compresses molecules more forcefully, so the greater energy is able to move more molecules.

Of course, distance is also a factor in sound intensity. The farther away we are from the source, the weaker the sound. Molecules are pushed less because there is progressively less energy available.

Interestingly, the same mathematical relationship is found in sound loss as in other forms of energy such as light, magnetism, and electricity. Intensity fades with the square of the distance between any sound source and listener. At 20 feet (6 meters), a sound has only one-fourth the intensity it exhibits at 10 feet (3 meters) from the source.

Waves

Sometimes the analogy of a water wave is used to teach how sound travels. A pebble is dropped into water, and a circular series of ripples spreads out on the water's surface. This example may be useful to show to your class, but it contains two main defects. Water waves are up-and-down motions that travel at right angles to the line of the waves. These are called *transverse waves.* Sound waves come from back-and-forth motions that make longitudinal waves. This is the kind of wave you see when a row of dominoes falls, each one striking the next in order. Also, water waves move only horizontally, while sound waves travel outward in all planes. Many science teachers ask students to imagine sound waves as they would a series of rapidly blown soap bubbles, each enveloped within another that is slightly larger, all quickly expanding.

The wave idea is useful to distinguish between sounds and noises. A sound consists of regularly pulsating vibrations; the time interval between each compression and rarefaction is the same. Noise is heard when irregular vibrations are passed on.

Forced Vibrations

If you place the handle of a vibrating tuning fork against a table top, the sound suddenly gets louder. The vibrating fork forces the table top to vibrate with equal speed. This sets in motion many more air molecules than would the fork alone. Try putting a vibrating tuning fork against other objects. Almost any hard object can be forced to vibrate at the fork's natural frequency.

A peculiar example of forced vibrations can occur when a group of soldiers marches over a bridge. If there are enough persons marching in step, the entire structure can be forced to vibrate in time to the step, and the bridge may weaken or collapse. For this reason, soldiers do not stay in step when crossing a bridge.

Thomas Edison used his knowledge of forced vibrations when inventing the phonograph. He attached a sharp needle to a thin diaphragm that vibrated when sound waves struck it. The needle was placed against a cylinder wrapped with soft tinfoil. As he spoke, he slowly cranked the cylinder around and around. The vibrating needle cut a series of impressions into the metal. To play back his sounds, he placed the needle in the impression first scratched and cranked the cylinder. As it followed the impressions, the needle was forced to vibrate, thus causing the diaphragm to vibrate. Edison could hear his recorded voice!

Sympathetic Vibrations

Have you ever heard windows vibrate in their frames as a low-flying airplane passes overhead? Or noticed dishes faintly rattle occasionally as a loud radio is played? To see why this happens, consider two identical tuning forks. If one vibrates and is held near the other, the second one also begins to vibrate. But with two tuning forks of different pitches, only the struck one vibrates.

When forks are of identical pitch, sound waves arrive at the proper time to set the still fork in motion. Each additional air compression pushes a prong as it starts to bend in from a previous one. Each rarefaction arrives as the prong starts to bend back out. The steady, timed, push-pause-push-pause rhythm sets the fork vibrating in almost the same way as you would push someone on a swing.

When forks are of different pitch, the timing is wrong for this to happen. For example, a prong may bend inward properly with a compression, but as it starts to bend back, another air compression may strike it prematurely and slow or stop it. The same thing would happen with a moving swing that is pushed while only partway back on a downswing.

Every solid object has a natural frequency of vibration. If sound waves of that frequency push against an object, it may start resonating—vibrating sympathetically.

Remember that objects vibrate sympathetically only when they have the same natural pitch as the initial sound maker. On the other hand, objects *forced* to vibrate always do so at the frequency of the vibrating object placed against them, regardless of their own natural frequency.

You may have learned that a very loud note sung or played into a thin drinking glass can shatter it through violent sympathetic vibrations; such vibrations have the natural pitch of the glass. However, it is not true that seashore sounds may be detected in shell souvenirs unless someone is listening at the beach. What is heard are only sympathetic reflections of nearby sounds.

Properties of Objects and Vibrations

Suppose someone hands you two closed shoe boxes. Inside one is a marble. The other contains a small ruler. Could you tell which box contains which object by tipping them back and forth and listening to the sounds? Of course, you may say. But what allows you to do this?

Every object has certain physical properties that produce "appropriate" vibrations. We expect a round (cylindrical) pencil to roll smoothly and a six-sided pencil to roll roughly. We assume that a short pencil lying crosswise in a box takes longer to slide and bump against the side than a longer pencil, if the box is tipped from side to side.

How Sounds Travel
Concepts
(Experiences p. 88)

Watch a parade from afar and band members seem to be out of step with the music they are playing. See a carpenter hammering a nail on a distant rooftop, and you hear the sound as the hammer is lifted instead of when the nail is struck. Note the increasing speed of aircraft, and be assured that protests to the Federal Aviation Administration about sonic booms continue to mount.

Speeds of Sound

The speeds at which sound waves travel lie behind each of the events mentioned. Light travels so fast (about 186,000 miles or 297,000 kilometers per second) that it seems instantaneous to our eyes. But sound is another matter. At sea level and 42°F (6.5°C), sound waves move about 1,100 feet (330 meters) per second in the air, only as fast as a low-powered rifle bullet. Sound also travels in liquids and solids. It moves about 5 times faster in water than it does in air; in steel, sound may travel 15 times faster than it does in air. Three conditions affect the speed of sound: temperature, density, and the elasticity, or "springiness," of the molecules conducting the sound.

Density by itself does not increase the speed of sound. In fact, the speed of sound may decrease with density. But often associated with density is greatly increased elasticity of molecules. When highly elastic, close-together molecules of a solid transmit sound, it travels much faster than in either air or water.

Sounds travel faster when the temperature goes up. In fact, it is about one foot per second faster in air for every one degree Fahrenheit. Have you ever wondered why sounds carry such large distances on certain days? On a cold winter day with snow on the ground, for example, air next to the ground is often colder than the air far above the ground. Instead of a sound wave spreading out uniformly and rapidly dying out, the temperature difference causes parts of the wave to travel at different speeds.

Given the same medium and temperature, all sounds travel at the same speed. If this were not so, it would be hard or impossible to conduct concerts in large auditoriums. The reedy sound of an oboe and the brassy timbre of a trombone always reach your ears at the same time, if they are begun at the same time.

Sonic Booms

When children live where sonic booms often occur, someone may ask what happens when an airplane "breaks the sound barrier." We know that a sound-producing object sends out sound waves in all directions. When the object is set in motion, it continues to send out waves in all directions. But let's continue to increase this object's velocity. As it goes faster, it is harder for waves to travel outward in front of it. When an airplane reaches a certain speed (about 750 miles, or 1,200 kilometers, per hour; this varies greatly with altitude and temperature), air compressions of these sound waves pile up into a dense area of compressed air. This can subject the airplane to severe stresses.

A powerful engine and proper design enable an airplane to wedge through the dense air. But what happens to the compressed air? The tremendous energy is passed on, molecule to molecule, until it hits the earth as a booming shock wave. The shock wave continues on the ground in a wide strip that traces the airplane's flight path. It stops only when the pilot slows the aircraft to less than the speed of sound. Sonic booms that cause the least damage start at very high altitudes. By the time energy in the original area of compressed air is passed on to the ground, much of it has dissipated.

Similar shock waves are formed by an explosion, except they may move out equidistantly in all directions. Very rapid expansion of gases in an explosion compresses the surrounding air. As the shock wave of compressed air moves outward, it may flatten almost anything in its path until the pressure finally dissipates over a distance.

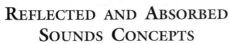

REFLECTED AND ABSORBED SOUNDS CONCEPTS
(Experiences p. 95)

Sound Reflection

One reason why singing in the shower is so popular has to do with the nature of sound reflections. As a sound hits the smooth walls, it bounces back and forth, seeming louder and prolonging the notes a little. This is pleasing to the ear. The smoother the reflecting surface, the better sound reflects. On a very smooth wall, sound reflections bounce off like light reflections from a mirror. The angle of reflection equals the angle of incidence.

Because sound can be reflected, we can direct or channel it in certain directions by using different devices. Open-air theaters often have a large shell-like structure surrounding the stage. (See Figure 3-2.) This enables sounds to be directed toward an audience with reduced energy loss. The same principle is used with cheerleaders' megaphones.

An even more efficient way to conserve sound energy is to enclose it in a tube. Because the sound is kept from spreading out by continual reflections within the encircling wall, such concentrated sound loses energy slowly

Figure 3-2
Open-air theaters often have a shell-like structure to reflect sounds to the audience.

and may travel a long way. Sometimes children use garden hoses as speaking tubes because these work well at surprising distances.

A reverse application of this reflection principle is found in the old-fashioned ear trumpet and in the ears of animals such as rabbits and donkeys. In these cases, sounds are "gathered," or reflected inward. Besides large ears, many animals have the additional advantage of being able to cock them separately in different directions.

Echoes

Since sound takes time to travel and can be reflected, it stands to reason that at a certain distance you should be able to hear a distinctly separate reflection of an original sound, an echo. Most persons need an interval of at least one-tenth of a second to distinguish between two sounds. If the interval is shorter than this, you hear one sound, much like the way your brain interprets separate frames of a motion picture as continuous motion.

If we assume that a sound wave travels at a speed of 1,100 feet (330 meters) per second, in one-tenth of a second it travels 110 feet (33 meters). To hear an echo, or a distinguishable, separate sound, we must stand far enough away from a reflecting surface for the sound wave to travel a total distance of 110 feet (33 meters). Since the sound travels *to* the reflecting surface and *back* to our ears, a distance of 55 feet (16.5 meters) from the surface is adequate to hear an echo. Remember, this distance varies a bit with temperature variations.

Sometimes the combination of a loud sound and many distant reflecting surfaces produces multiple echoes, or *reverberations*. A common example is thunder, which may reverberate back and forth from cloud to earth and among air layers of varying densities.

An interesting application of echo detection is found in a United States Navy device called *sonar*. (The term is coined from the words SOund NAvigation and Ranging.) This appa-

ratus sends a sound wave through the water and detects reflections from any direction. The time between an initial sound and its received echo enables a sonar operator to know the distance of a reflector, whether it is a submarine or an underwater obstruction. Similar devices are used on fishing vessels to detect schools of fish.

A strange use of sound reflections is found in the bat. By listening to reflections of its cries, a bat flying in total darkness avoids collisions and may even catch insects in midair. (See Figure 3-3.)

Absorbed Sounds

Have you ever noticed how different sounds seem in a room before and after furnishings are installed? Rugs, drapes, and cloth-covered furniture absorb more sound waves than we commonly realize. But even a furnished room may have a "hollow" sound if the walls and ceilings are hard and smooth.

Porous acoustical tile on ceilings cuts down sound reflections. So does the use of rough, porous plaster blown on with a compressed-air applicator. Besides absorbing some sound

Figure 3-3
A bat's ears are well suited for echo ranging.

waves, a rough surface interferes with the wave reflection, just as light is diffused when it hits an irregular surface.

Sometimes older children ask, "What happens to a sound when it goes into a porous material?" It appears that sound energy is changed to heat energy. The regular pulsating movements of a wave are broken up into the normal, irregular motions of individual molecules. As this happens, any energy passed into the porous substance is transmitted to other air molecules, slightly raising the temperature.

How Pitch Changes
Concepts
(Experiences p. 101)

Many pilots of crop-dusting airplanes actually rely on sound to gauge the safeness of their air speed. While flying low, it is hard to watch both an air-speed indicator in the cockpit and ground obstructions. Flying speed is therefore estimated by listening to the pitch of sound made by the vibration of the airplane's struts and wires as the wind rushes past. Some seasoned pilots can judge their margin of safety to within narrow limits by this method.

Sometimes children fasten small cards against the spokes of their bicycle wheels to simulate a motor sound while riding. As the spokes go around and hit the card, it vibrates and makes a sound. The pitch rises with increased speed of vibrations and lowers with decreased speed of vibrations.

Stringed Instruments

In a stringed instrument, pitch depends on the length, tightness, and thickness of the strings. Shortening a string causes faster vibrations, raising pitch. Lengthening it has an opposite effect.

Tightening a string also increases pitch, whereas lessening tension decreases it. A thick string vibrates more slowly than a thin one, and so produces a lower sound.

Why do different instruments, a violin and a cello, for instance, play a note at the same pitch and yet sound different? This is because of the *quality* of tone (timbre) produced by these instruments. Most vibrations include more than just simple, back-and-forth movements along a string's entire length. Although there is a fundamental vibration that governs the basic pitch, other parts of the string vibrate at faster frequencies. The combinations of vibrations are different with each string and with various stringed instruments. Together they produce tones of distinctly recognizable qualities.

Wind Instruments

In wind instruments, sound is made by a vibrating column of air. The vibrations may be started by a player's lips, as with trumpets and tubas, or by blowing past a reed, as with the saxophone and clarinet.

Pitch is regulated by changing the length of the air column vibrating within the instrument. In a wind instrument, such as the saxophone, air-column length is changed by opening and closing valves with the fingers. In a trombone, air-column length is regulated by pulling or pushing a long, closed double tube, called the slide.

The property of timbre is also present in wind instruments. In this case, it is caused by the combinations of additional air vibrations set up within each instrument. Quality of voices is produced in much the same way. This is regulated by the size and shape of air cavities in the mouth and nose.

Homemade Instruments

An interesting way for children to learn about pitch and tonal quality is for them to make their own stringed and wind instruments. Rubber bands of different sizes make pleasant sounds when placed around topless cigar boxes or sturdy shoe box lids. Strong nylon fishing line, fastened on pieces of wood with nails and screw eyes, also works well (see Figure 3-4). When the line is fastened to a screw eye, its tension is adjusted by turning the eye in the appropriate direction. Tuned properly, nylon fishing line sounds somewhat like the string on a regular instrument. Simple tunes can be composed and played on the stringed instruments that children fashion.

Soda straws and bottles make acceptable wind instruments. Interestingly, opposite results in pitch occur with partly filled soda bottles, depending on whether they are used as wind or percussion instruments. That is, if you blow over the tops of soda bottles containing varying volumes of water, the scale may go from low to high, left to right. However, if you *strike* the bottles sharply with a pencil, the opposite happens. The scale will go from high to low, left to right. With blowing, the bottle's *air* mainly vibrates; when striking the bottle, the *water* and glass mainly vibrate.

Mass and Noise

When a noise is made, the amount of mass in the vibrating object usually determines its pitch. A large, dropped wood block sounds lower than a smaller one. When thick paper is torn, it sounds lower than thin paper. A dropped nickel sounds lower than a dime. Both young and older children show interest in this phenomenon.

HEARING AND LOCATING SOUNDS CONCEPTS
(Experiences p. 107)

The ear must be ranked among the body's most remarkable organs. In our hearing, sound waves are channeled into the ear canal by the outer ear, which acts as a megaphone in reverse. As sound waves collide with the eardrum, this thin membrane of stretched skin begins vibrating at the same frequency as the waves.

Just inside the eardrum are three tiny, connected bones: the hammer, anvil, and stirrup

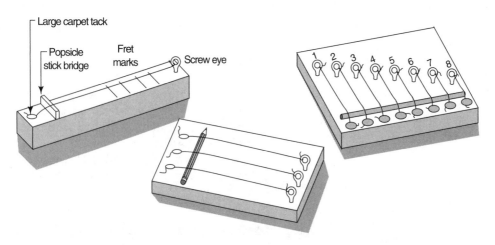

Figure 3-4
Children can experiment with pitch and tone by making their own instruments.

(see Figure 3-5). A vibrating eardrum starts the attached hammer shaking, and this movement is transmitted through the connected bones to the cochlea, or inner ear. This snail-shaped apparatus is filled with a watery fluid and lined with sensitive nerve endings that trail off to the auditory nerve and brain. The transmitted vibrations pass through the fluid and excite the nerve endings. These excitations are converted into electrical impulses that zip to the brain.

Children should learn some reasonable rules for ear care and safety. A sharp object jabbed into the ear may cause a punctured eardrum. This greatly impairs or prevents eardrum vibrations and results in hearing loss in the affected ear. They should also beware of a sharp blow against the outer ear. This compresses air within the air canal and may cause a ruptured eardrum. Blowing the nose forces air up through the eustachian tube. If a person is suffering from a cold, hard blowing may force germs up the tube and infect the middle ear.

Hearing Ranges

Although our ears are sensitive to a wide range of pitches, there are limits to what we can hear. Almost no one can detect a sound that vibrates less than about 16 times per second, or more than 20,000 times per second. As we grow older, this range is gradually narrowed.

Hearing ranges in animals often exceed those of humans. A bat may detect sounds that vary between 10 vibrations to 100,000 vibrations per second. A dog's hearing begins at only several vibrations and goes to 40,000 vibrations per second. This is why it is possible to use a "silent" whistle for calling a dog: The sound is simply too high for humans to hear. A cat's hearing is even more remarkable; it can detect sounds up to 50,000 cycles. Sounds that are inaudible to us are called _infrasonic_ when they vibrate <u>too slowly</u> and _ultrasonic_ when they vibrate <u>too fast.</u>

Locating Sounds

Most people can tell the direction from which a sound comes, even when blindfolded. With two ears, a sound usually reaches one ear just before the other. The slight difference is enough to let the brain interpret the information.

Persons with only one functioning ear can receive similar signals by quickly turning the head slightly on hearing the first sound. When the sound is very short, this may not be possible.

Sound Energy Benchmarks and Standards

Children in the early grades have trouble associating the characteristics of sounds with the properties of the sound's source. Experiences with activities involving the making and hearing of sounds will allow students opportunities to make these associations. Additionally, children will begin to understand that sounds are vibrations and travel in waves.

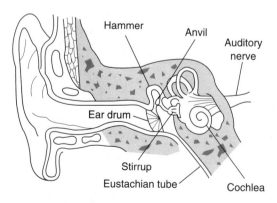

Figure 3-5
The human ear.

Some specific Benchmarks and Standards are as follows:

SAMPLE BENCHMARKS (AAAS, 1993).

■ Things that make sound vibrate (By Grades K–2, p. 89).

■ Vibrations in materials set up wavelike disturbances that spread away from the source. Sound and earthquake waves are examples.

These and other waves move at different speeds in different materials (By Grades 6–8, p. 90).

SAMPLE STANDARDS (NRC, 1996).

■ Sound is produced by vibrating objects. The pitch of the sound can be varied by changing the rate of vibration (By Grades K–4, p. 127).

INVESTIGATIONS AND ACTIVITIES

SOUND VIBRATIONS EXPERIENCES
(Concepts p. 75)

ACTIVITY: *WHAT MAKES YOUR VOCAL CORDS WORK?*

NEEDED

vocal cords

TRY THIS

1. Hum softly and feel your throat. Feel your voice box vibrate.
2. Hum with tightly closed lips. Then pinch your nose.
   a. What happens? Why?
3. Breathe out as much air as you can from your lungs. Try to say something *without* taking in air.
   b. What happens? Why?
4. Try to say your name the way a cat or cow makes sounds—while breathing air *in*.
   c. What happens? Why is this hard to do?

TEACHING COMMENT

Air is needed in all these cases to make the vocal cords vibrate. It is hard to speak while breathing in because the normal way humans make sounds is by breathing out.

ACTIVITY: *HOW CAN ONE VIBRATING OBJECT MAKE ANOTHER VIBRATE?*

A. NEEDED

tuning fork

TRY THIS

1. Strike a tuning fork against a rubber heel. (Never against something hard.)
2. As the sound dies, place the handle end against a table top. Notice how the sound gets louder as the table top is also made to vibrate.

3. Try holding the vibrating tuning fork against many different objects.

   a. From which object can you get the loudest sound?

   b. Which object allows you to hear the tuning fork when it has almost stopped vibrating?

B. NEEDED

two matched large soda bottles
one small soda bottle

TRY THIS

1. Blow over the top of one large bottle to make a sound. Blow short, strong tones.

2. Hold the opening of a second large bottle close to your ear, but not touching. Blow short sounds again with the first large bottle.

   a. Do you hear the same note from the second bottle? If you are not sure, have someone else blow short notes on one bottle while you listen with the second bottle.

3. Do Steps 1 and 2 again, but this time listen with the small bottle.

   b. Do you hear the same note from the small bottle? Any note?

TEACHING COMMENT

Activity A is an example of forced vibrations. If a tuning fork is unavailable, a sturdy, stiff rubber comb may be used instead. Run a finger down the teeth ends while holding the comb against a surface. B is an example of sympathetic vibrations. If you vibrate one object, a second object may also vibrate if it has the same natural rate of vibrations as the first. No actual touching is necessary. The transfer of energy occurs in the air.

INVESTIGATION: *MYSTERY SOUNDS*

Can you hear something make a sound and tell what it is without looking?

EXPLORATORY PROBLEM

How can you find out if you can identify something by sound?

NEEDED

pairs of small objects that roll (crayons, ping-pong balls, marbles, pencils, BBs, small pill vials)
pairs of small objects that slide (buttons, paper clips, checkers, dominoes, bottle

caps, safety pins)
shoe box with lid
partner

TRY THIS

1. Place one object from each pair of rolling objects on your desk.
2. Give the other rolling objects to your partner. He should put these where you cannot see them.
3. Have your partner put one of his objects in the shoe box. You should not know which one it is.
4. Slowly tip the shoe box back and forth. Listen to the sound (Figure 3-6).

Figure 3-6

5. Look at the objects on your desk. Which one may be the same as the one in the box? Point to a desk object so your partner knows which one you picked.
6. Look inside the shoe box. Does the object inside match the desk object you picked?

DISCOVERY PROBLEMS

inferring **A.** How many of the *rolling* objects can you identify? Which object is easiest to tell? hardest to tell?

inferring **B.** Suppose your partner holds and tips the box. Can you tell each rolling object just as easily?

inferring **C.** How many of the *sliding* objects can you identify? Which object is easiest to tell? hardest to tell?

TEACHING COMMENT

PREPARATION AND BACKGROUND

This investigation mainly calls for children to make inferences by interpreting data. Try to use objects of about the same weight. This will eliminate weight as a clue. Children will focus on the sounds they hear or vibrations they feel in their fingers as they handle the shoe box.

GENERALIZATION

An object may be identified by the sounds it makes when interacting with another object.

SAMPLE PERFORMANCE OBJECTIVES

Process: After some practice, the child can infer the identity of several objects from the sounds they make.

Knowledge: The child can describe how the properties of an object are related to the sounds it makes.

FOR OLDER CHILDREN

Older students can be challenged by increasing the number and similarity of paired objects to select from.

HOW SOUNDS TRAVEL EXPERIENCES
(Concepts p. 77)

ACTIVITY: *HOW FAST DOES SOUND TRAVEL?*

NEEDED

large outdoor space   partner
hammer   piece of wood

TRY THIS

1. Go outdoors to a large, open space.
2. Place a thick piece of wood on the ground. Walk a few steps away.
3. Watch a partner sharply hit the wood once with a hammer.
   a. Do you hear the sound at about the same time the hammer hits?
4. Move farther away. Have your partner hit the wood again. Repeat this pattern several times until you are far away.

b. When do you hear each sound now? At the same time the hammer hits? Or does each sound appear later and later, *after* each hit?

TEACHING COMMENT

To ensure enough space for this activity, you might suggest two widely separated, familiar reference points at least the length of a football field.

ACTIVITY: *DOES SOUND TRAVEL FARTHER IN AIR OR IN WOOD?*

NEEDED

meter stick or yardstick
partner
wristwatch (one that ticks)

TRY THIS

1. Hold a wristwatch tightly against the end of a meter stick.
2. Touch the other end of the stick to a partner's ear. Only you should hold the stick (Figure 3-7).

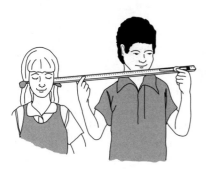

Figure 3-7

    a. Can your partner hear the ticking through the wood? If not, move the watch forward on the stick until the ticking is heard.

3. Measure the distance between watch and ear when the ticking is heard.
4. Next, do not use the stick. Hold the watch in the air at ear level the same distance you found in Step 3.

b. Can your partner hear the ticking now? (If you think your partner is just guessing, remove and then return the watch a few times. Each time, ask if the watch can be heard.)

c. From how far away can you hear a ticking watch through wood? Try a broomstick, window pole, long narrow board, and other wood things around you.

INVESTIGATION: *THE VIBRATIONS OF METAL OBJECTS*

Many everyday objects made of metal make beautiful sounds when they vibrate. A metal coat hanger is one example. These things sound much better when you hear them through a solid material than through the air. String is one such solid material.

EXPLORATORY PROBLEM

How can you hear the sounds of a metal hanger through a string?

NEEDED

two matched metal hangers	scissors
yarn	different metal objects
several kinds of string	partner

TRY THIS

1. Cut a piece of string about 60 centimeters (2 feet) long.

2. Loop the middle of the string once around the hanger hook.

3. Wrap several turns of string end around the tip of each forefinger.

4. Gently put the tip of each wrapped finger into an ear (Figure 3-8).

5. Bend from the waist so the hanger hangs free. Ask your partner to strike a pencil and other objects gently against the metal. You can also make the hanger vibrate by yourself. Sway back and forth until the hanger swings. Then have it hit something that is hard.

DISCOVERY PROBLEMS

communicating **A.** How can you describe the sounds you hear?

observing **B.** What happens to the sound if your partner holds one of the strings? both strings?

experimenting **C.** What kind of string will give the clearest, loudest sound? Cut off equal lengths of different kinds of string and yarn. Test them in pairs. Tie one string end to the hook of one hanger. Tie another

Figure 3-8

to a second matched hanger. Put one string end into each ear. Have a partner first strike one hanger, then the other. When you find the best string, try it with both ears.

inferring   **D.** Does the length of a string affect the loudness? If so, in which kind of string do you notice it most? (You can test pairs of strings as in C.)

observing   **E.** What sounds do other metal objects make? Test things such as old spoons, forks, cooling racks, oven racks, and different-sized cans.

TEACHING COMMENT

PREPARATION AND BACKGROUND

Oven cooling racks, barbecue griddles, and other gridlike objects of metal make particularly strange, even eerie, sounds. These sounds come from the overtones produced when the many parts of the object vibrate differently.

GENERALIZATION

The sounds of a vibrating object may be heard more loudly and clearly through a solid than through air.

SAMPLE PERFORMANCE OBJECTIVES

Process: The child can describe a sound an object makes well enough for another person to recognize the sound when it is made.

Knowledge: The child can select a string, from several different strings, that conducts sounds most efficiently.

FOR YOUNGER CHILDREN

Use the "Try This" sequence and Problem E as general experience activities.

INVESTIGATION: *A STRING TELEPHONE*

Have you ever used a "string telephone"? It's a handy way to talk to someone far across a large room without shouting.

EXPLORATORY PROBLEM

How can you make a string telephone?

NEEDED

two sturdy paper cups
two paper clips
strong string (about 8 meters or 26 feet long)
partner
nail

TRY THIS

1. Punch a hole into the bottom center of each cup using a nail.
2. Put a string end into each hole.
3. Tie each string end to a paper clip. This will keep the string from slipping out of each hole.
4. Stretch the string tightly between you and your partner.
5. Speak into one cup while your partner listens with the other cup (Figure 3-9).

DISCOVERY PROBLEMS

observing   **A.** Can you hear better through the string telephone than through the air? Whisper softly through the phone. Do it a little louder until your partner hears you. Then whisper to her at the same loudness without the telephone.

experimenting   **B.** How can you stop a sound from reaching you on the string telephone?

experimenting   **C.** Suppose two other children have a string telephone. How can you make a party line?

experimenting   **D.** What can you do to make your phone work better? Try containers of different sizes and materials. Try different kinds of string and waxing the string with candle wax.

Figure 3-9

TEACHING COMMENT

PREPARATION AND BACKGROUND

Holding the string or letting it sag will dampen or stop sounds. So will touching the vibrating cup bottom. For a party line, cross and loop around once the lines of two sets of phones.

Cylindrical cereal boxes (for example, oatmeal boxes) and salt boxes work well for string telephones. Metal can bottoms are too thick and rigid to vibrate well. Hard string or waxed string is superior to softly woven string.

GENERALIZATION

Sound vibrations can travel through string and other solid materials.

SAMPLE PERFORMANCE OBJECTIVES

Process: The child can discover through experimenting at least one way to improve the performance of a string telephone.

Knowledge: The child can explain how sound travels from one string telephone to another.

FOR YOUNGER CHILDREN

Younger students can construct and explore how to operate a string telephone but may not be able to find ways to improve the telephone's performance.

ACTIVITY: *WHAT ARE UNDERWATER SOUNDS LIKE?*

NEEDED

half-filled aquarium tank or large glass bowl
partner
two spoons

TRY THIS

1. Press an ear against the tank *above* the water level. Listen.
2. Have someone repeatedly hit two spoons together inside the tank, but *above* the water.
3. Again, press your ear against the tank but *below* the water level. Listen.
4. Now have the spoons hit together *below* the water level (Figure 3-10).

   a. How can you describe the difference between the two sets of sounds?

   b. Does sound seem to travel better in water or in air?

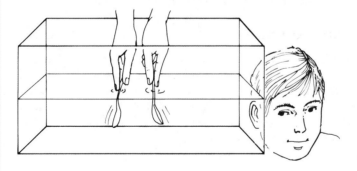

Figure 3-10

REFLECTED AND ABSORBED SOUNDS EXPERIENCES

(Concepts p. 79)

INVESTIGATION: *SOUNDS AND MEGAPHONES*

What do you do when you want your voice to go far? Do you cup your hands to your mouth? This helps to keep the sound from spreading out, so it travels farther. There's another way to do this. You can make a megaphone.

EXPLORATORY PROBLEM A

How can you make and use a megaphone?

NEEDED

sheet of heavy paper   sticky tape   two partners

TRY THIS

1. Roll up the paper from one corner to make a cone. The small opening should be large enough to speak into.
2. Fasten the two ends and middle with sticky tape (Figure 3-11).

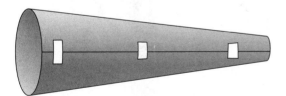

Figure 3-11

3. Have a partner stand across the room from you.
4. Point the megaphone toward your partner. Whisper some numbers.
5. Have your partner walk toward you until he hears you, then stop walking.

DISCOVERY PROBLEMS

inferring   **A.** Can your partner hear you without the megaphone? Have him stay where he stopped. Whisper numbers just as before. How can you tell if your partner hears you?

inferring   **B.** Can you send a message to someone without another person hearing? Have a second partner stand to one side of you. She should be as far from you as your first partner. Point the megaphone toward your first partner and whisper numbers. How can you tell if only your first partner hears you?

observing   **C.** How close must someone be to your first partner to hear you whisper?

EXPLORATORY PROBLEM B

How can a megaphone help us to hear better?

NEEDED

two megaphones   windup clock
sticky tape   meter stick or yardstick

TRY THIS

1. Put the clock on a table.

2. Stand where you cannot hear the clock.

3. Put the megaphone to your ear. Point it toward the clock (Figure 3-12).

Figure 3-12

4. Slowly move toward the clock until you hear it. Then stop.

DISCOVERY PROBLEMS

observing   **A.** Can you hear the clock without the megaphone at that distance?

predicting **B.** How much closer will you need to be to hear it?

experimenting   **C.** Will different-sized megaphones make a difference in how far the sound travels? How can you find out?

TEACHING COMMENT

PREPARATION AND BACKGROUND

A megaphone tends to conserve sound energy by reflecting it in a specific direction. This allows sound to travel farther than when it spreads out in all directions. The effect also happens in reverse. The large end of a megaphone can gather sound and reflect it inward. If we listen at the small end, the sound is louder than without the megaphone. More sound energy reaches the ear.

GENERALIZATION

A megaphone reflects sounds in one direction. It may be used to increase our speaking or hearing range.

SAMPLE PERFORMANCE OBJECTIVES

Process: The child can test how a megaphone's size affects its efficiency.

Knowledge: The child can explain in everyday terms how a megaphone works.

INVESTIGATION: *ECHOES*

You probably know that smooth, hard walls reflect sounds well. A reflected sound that you hear is called an echo. Sound vibrations take time to travel to a wall and then back to you. When you are at the right distance, you hear the returning sound as a separate sound.

EXPLORATORY PROBLEM

How can you make an echo happen?

NEEDED

meter stick or yardstick	scissors
string	piece of wood
large outside wall	hammer

TRY THIS

1. Find a big wall outdoors in a large area. Try to locate a wall that has no buildings opposite it.

2. Measure a distance of about 25 meters (82 feet) from the wall. (You might cut a 5-meter string to speed up measuring.)

3. Hit a piece of wood once sharply with a hammer. Listen for an echo. If you hear more than one echo, try to find another place (Figure 3-13).

Figure 3-13

DISCOVERY PROBLEMS

measuring   **A.** How close can you be to the wall and still hear an echo?

measuring   **B.** How far away from the wall can you hear an echo? As you move farther away, does it take less or more time to hear the echo?

observing   **C.** Try another wall. How do the results compare with A and B?

observing   **D.** How many echoes will there be with two reflecting walls? Try to find two facing, widely separated walls. Stand at different distances between them and bang the hammer. How do these results compare with those from a single wall?

TEACHING COMMENT

PREPARATION AND BACKGROUND

A trundle wheel is even more efficient than a 5-meter string for quick measurements. This device is a wheel with an attached, broomlike handle. The wheel's size is such that when rolled once around on a surface, it travels one meter (or yard, as the case may be).

In B, students will probably run out of space before they can fully answer the question. However, they should become aware that increasing the distance also increases the time it takes to hear an echo.

In D, the clearest results should occur with two widely separated, opposing walls.

GENERALIZATION

Echoes may be heard when sounds are reflected over a distance.

SAMPLE PERFORMANCE OBJECTIVES

Knowledge: The child can predict that an echo will be heard later if the distance between the reflecting wall and the observer is increased.

Process: The child can reliably measure the shortest distance at which an echo may usually be heard.

FOR YOUNGER CHILDREN

Use the "Try This" suggestion and Problems A through C as large-group experiences without the measurements.

INVESTIGATION: *MATERIALS THAT QUIET SOUND*

Many people today are trying to cut down unwanted noise. They are putting materials around them that soak up sounds. These materials are called sound insulators. Some materials are better insulators than others.

EXPLORATORY PROBLEM

How can you find out which materials are good sound insulators?

NEEDED

shoe box	newspaper
pencil and paper	aluminum foil
windup alarm clock	different kinds of cloth
meter stick or yardstick	insulation materials of your choice

TRY THIS

1. Wind up an alarm clock. Set the clock to ring within a few minutes.

2. Put the clock inside a shoe box and put on the lid.

3. Wait until the alarm rings. Measure how far away you can hear the ringing (Figure 3-14).

4. Record the distance.

Figure 3-14

DISCOVERY PROBLEMS

observing and measuring **A.** Suppose you wrap a sheet of newspaper around the clock. From how far away can you hear the sound now? Record and compare this distance with the first one.

predicting and measuring **B.** What will happen if you wrap the clock in cloth? Record and compare this distance with the other distances.

experimenting **C.** What insulation materials will work best? Is it possible not to hear any ringing at all? Arrange your materials any way you want. All should fit inside the shoe box. How will you know whether the alarm has gone off?

TEACHING COMMENT

PREPARATION AND BACKGROUND

Loosely woven, soft, fluffy materials absorb sounds well. Hard surfaces reflect sounds. This is why a formerly empty room seems quieter after carpeting, drapes, and upholstered furniture are put in.

GENERALIZATION

Loosely woven, fluffy materials are good sound insulators.

PERFORMANCE OBJECTIVES

Process: The child can measure and compare the relative effectiveness of several sound insulating materials.

Knowledge: When shown several new materials, the child can predict which will be a more effective sound insulator.

FOR YOUNGER CHILDREN

Many younger students will be unable to measure the hearing distance with a meter stick. Let them measure with different lengths of string or the number of footsteps between them and the clock.

HOW PITCH CHANGES EXPERIENCES
(Concepts p. 81)

ACTIVITY: *WHAT HAPPENS TO PITCH AS SPEED OF VIBRATIONS CHANGES?*

A. NEEDED

comb
small card

TRY THIS

1. Hold a comb in one hand and a card in the other.
2. Pull the card tip across the teeth of the comb slowly and steadily. Listen to the pitch of the sound (how high or low it is).
3. Do Step 2 again, but faster this time. Listen again.
4. Try many different speeds. Listen each time.
   a. What is the pitch like when the vibrations are slow?
   b. What happens to the pitch as the vibrations move faster?

B. NEEDED

bicycle
small card

TRY THIS

1. Turn a bicycle upside down.
2. Crank a pedal around slowly to move the rear wheel.
3. Hold the tip of a card against the spokes as the wheel slowly turns. Listen to the pitch as the card vibrates.
4. Crank the wheel faster and faster. Listen again to the pitch as the card vibrates faster and faster.
   a. What is the pitch like when the vibrations are slow?
   b. What happens to the pitch as the vibrations move faster?

TEACHING COMMENT

Caution: For safety, be sure that fingers holding the card are well away from the spinning wheel.

INVESTIGATION: *HOW TO MAKE A RUBBER-BAND BANJO*

What kinds of stringed instruments have you seen? How are they played?

EXPLORATORY PROBLEM

How can you make a rubber-band banjo?

NEEDED

topless cigar box or stiff shoe box lid
ruler
eight rubber bands (four thick, four thinner)
pencil and paper

TRY THIS

1. Write the numbers *1* through *8* on the inside of the lid. Use a ruler to space them evenly across the whole lid.
2. Put four thick rubber bands around half of the lid. Space them from numbers *1* through *4*.
3. Put four thinner bands around the other half of the lid. Space them from numbers *5* through *8* (Figure 3-15).

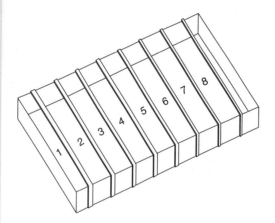

Figure 3-15

DISCOVERY PROBLEMS

observing   A. Pluck one of the rubber bands. How can you make a soft sound? A louder sound?

observing   **B.** Which bands—thick or thin—make the higher sounds? (The highness or lowness of a sound is its *pitch*.)

observing   **C.** What happens to the pitch when a band is shortened? Press down a rubber band halfway across the lid. Pluck the band half nearest you.

observing   **D.** How does tightening a band on the lid affect the pitch? loosening the band? (Pull the band up or down at the side of the lid.)

classifying   **E.** Can you make an eight-note scale? Tighten or loosen each band in order as needed. Pluck the bands *lightly* so each stays tuned.

observing   **F.** What songs can you play on your banjo? Try some simple songs first: "Mary Had a Little Lamb," "Merrily We Roll Along," "Three Blind Mice," and "Twinkle, Twinkle, Little Star."

communicating   **G.** Can you write songs well enough for other people to play?

Teaching Comment

PREPARATION AND BACKGROUND

The tightness, thickness, and length of a rubber band (or string) all affect its pitch. Sounds are higher with taut, thin, short strings; they are lower with looser, thicker, or longer strings on any stringed instrument.

The tension of each rubber band may be adjusted by pulling up or down at the side of the lid. Friction between the band and lid will hold the band in place for a while. However, the band will need to be strummed or plucked gently. A sturdy lid is preferable to a flimsy one that bows in the middle.

GENERALIZATION

Length, tension, and thickness affect the pitch of a vibrating string.

SAMPLE PERFORMANCE OBJECTIVES

Process: The child can communicate to another child a familiar song by using written symbols, such as numbers.

Knowledge: When shown a stringed instrument, the child can predict the relative pitches of sounds the strings make.

FOR YOUNGER CHILDREN.

Many younger students can discover the factors that affect the pitch of a string. But they will do so less systematically and completely than older children. Many will be able to do Problems A–D.

INVESTIGATION: *A Soda-Straw Oboe*

Have you ever seen an oboe? It is a reed instrument. When the player blows on the mouthpiece, two flat, thin reeds vibrate. This makes the air inside the oboe vibrate. By opening and closing holes, the player makes different amounts of air vibrate. This changes the pitch of the notes played. You can make an instrument like this from a soda straw.

EXPLORATORY PROBLEM

How can you make a soda-straw oboe?

NEEDED

paper or plastic straws (one smaller to fit inside the larger one)
straight pin
cellophane tape
scissors
small paper cup

TRY THIS

1. Pinch the straw end between your thumb and forefinger to flatten it.
2. Snip off the flattened corners with scissors, as in the picture (Figure 3-16). If you have a plastic straw, cut to make a point.

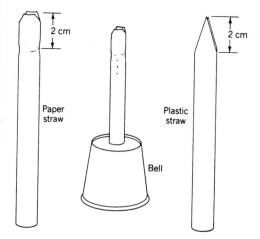

Figure 3-16

3. Put about 3 centimeters (1 inch) of the cut straw end into your mouth. Keep your lips closed but a little loose. Blow hard into the straw. If there is no sound, blow less hard until a sound is made.

DISCOVERY PROBLEMS

observing
A. What happens if you change the length of the straw? Join another straw of the same size to the first straw. To do so, slightly pinch the end of the second straw. Then gently push the pinched end into the first straw. Try adding a third straw in the same way.

observing
B. What happens if you change the length another way? Try to fit a smaller straw into the larger one. If it is too loose, wrap some cellophane tape around the end of the smaller straw. Slide the second straw up and down as you blow.

predicting
C. What do you think will happen if you snip off pieces of a single straw while blowing? Try it and see.

experimenting
D. How can eight people with different-sized straws play a song?

TEACHING COMMENT

PREPARATION AND BACKGROUND

Paper straws typically work more easily than plastic straws in this activity. If students find it hard or impossible to produce a sound, often the cut "reed" is to blame. It may help to press down gently with the lips on the straw just below the flattened part. This will open up the reed slightly and let it vibrate more easily when blown. A plastic-straw reed should be pointed for best results.

A "bell" for the instrument can be made by punching a small hole in the bottom of a paper cup and inserting the straw end into it. It should noticeably increase the loudness of the instrument.

GENERALIZATION

The pitch of a wind instrument is changed by changing the length of the vibrating air column inside.

SAMPLE PERFORMANCE OBJECTIVES

Knowledge: The child can show at least two ways to change the pitch of a soda-straw oboe.

Process: The child can improve the performance of a soda-straw oboe by testing, observing results, and making changes.

INVESTIGATION: *A BOTTLE XYLOPHONE*

Do you know what a xylophone looks like? This instrument has a row of different-sized blocks of wood. The player makes sounds by striking the blocks with two special sticks. You can easily make an instrument that works like a xylophone. But instead of wood, you can use bottles of water.

EXPLORATORY PROBLEM

How can you make a bottle xylophone?

NEEDED

eight matched soda bottles   pencil and paper   water

TRY THIS

1. Put different levels of water in each bottle.
2. Line the bottles in a row (Figure 3-17), in any order.

Figure 3-17

3. Tap each of the bottles lightly with a pencil. Notice how high or low each sound is. This is called *pitch*.

DISCOVERY PROBLEMS

observing   **A.** How much water is there in the bottle of highest pitch? lowest pitch?

classifying   **B.** Can you put the bottles in order from lowest to highest pitch?

experimenting   **C.** What must you do with the bottles to make an eight-note scale?

observing   **D.** Can you play a simple song? Put paper slips in front of the bottles. Number them from 1 to 8, for an eight-note scale. Notice the numbers of the notes you play.

communicating   **E.** Can you write a song so someone else can play it correctly? Write on paper the numbers of the notes to be played. Use your own made-up song or a known song. Observe how well the song is played.

hypothesizing   **F.** How can you improve the way you wrote your song?

predicting   **G.** Suppose you blew over each bottle top. Now the air inside would vibrate rather than the water. How do you think that would affect each pitch? Try it and see.

TEACHING COMMENT

PREPARATION AND BACKGROUND

Bottles made of plain glass make clearer, purer sounds than those made of rippled glass. If you or a child can play the piano, children may enjoy playing this eight-note xylophone either as an accompanying or as a leading instrument. Children may also enjoy singing with the instrument.

GENERALIZATION

An instrument's pitch depends on how much mass vibrates. As mass increases, pitch lowers. With less mass, the pitch gets higher.

SAMPLE PERFORMANCE OBJECTIVES

Knowledge: The child can predict which of two unevenly filled bottles will sound lower when struck.

Process: The child can correctly order an eight-note scale with proportionately filled bottles of water.

HEARING AND LOCATING SOUNDS EXPERIENCES
(Concepts p. 82)

ACTIVITY: *HOW DO YOU LOCATE SOUNDS WITH YOUR EARS?*

NEEDED

eight partners
quiet room
16 pencils

TRY THIS

1. Have your partners sit in a large circle about half the width of the classroom.

2. Sit in the center of the circle. Keep your eyes tightly closed. Listen with both ears.

3. Let each partner, in some mixed order, lightly tap two pencils together once.

   a. Can you tell from which direction the sound comes? Point to the spot each time. Have someone record how often you are right or wrong.

4. Now try Step 3 again, but this time listen with only one ear. Hold a hand tightly over the other ear.

   b. Can you locate the sounds as well as before?

   c. Will you get the same results with your other ear?

REFERENCES

American Association for the Advancement of Science. (1993). *Benchmarks for science literacy.* New York: Oxford University Press.

National Research Council. (1996). *National science education standards.* Washington, DC: National Academy Press.

SELECTED TRADE BOOKS: SOUND ENERGY

For Younger Children

Allington, R. L., & Cowles, K. (1980). *Hearing.* Raintree.

Barrett, S. (1980). *The sound of the week.* Good Apple.

Broekel, R. (1983). *Sound experiments.* Children's Press.

Friedman, J. T. (1981). *Sounds all around.* Putnam.

Hughes, Anne, E. (1979). *A book of sounds.* Raintree.

Jennings, T. (1990). *Making sounds.* Watts.

Lee, J. D. (1985). *Sounds!* Stevens.

Moncure, J. B. (1982). *Sounds all around.* Children's Press.

Oliver, S. (1991). *Noises.* Random House.

Richardson, J. (1986). *What happens when we listen?* Gareth Stevens.

Spier, P. (1990). *Crash! Bang! Boom!* Doubleday, 1990.

Wade, H. (1979). *Sound.* Raintree.

Webb, A. (1988). *Sound.* Watts.

Wyler, R. (1987). *Science fun with drums, bells and whistles.* Messner.

For Older Children

Ardley, N. (1991). *Sound waves to music: Projects with sound.* Watts.

Brandt, K. (1985). *Sounds.* Troll Associates.

Catherall, E. (1982). *Hearing.* Silver Burdett.

Kettlekamp, L. (1982). *The magic of sound.* Morrow.

Knight, D. C. (1983). *All about sound.* Troll Associates.

Knight, D. C. (1980). *Silent sound: the world of ultrasonics.* Morrow.

Kohn, B. (1979). *Echoes.* Dandelion.

Newman, F. R. (1983). *Zounds! The kid's guide to sound making.* Random House.

Pettigrew, M. (1987). *Music and sound.* Watts.

Riley, P. (1987). *Light and sound.* David & Charles.

Taylor, B. (1991). *Sound and music.* Watts.

Ward, A. (1991). *Experimenting with sound.* Chelsea House.

Ward, B. (1981). *The ear and hearing.* Watts.

Resource Books

Butzow, C. M., & Butzow, J. W. (1989). *Science through children's literature: an integrated approach* (sound and hearing topics, pp. 112–118). Teacher Ideas Press.

LeCroy, B., & Holder, B. (1994). *Bookwebs: a brainstorm of ideas for the primary classroom* (sound activities, pp. 57–63). Teacher Ideas Press.

Sullivan, E. P. (1990). *Starting with books: an activities approach to children's literature* (hearing impairment, pp. 23–25). Teacher Ideas Press.

MAGNETIC INTERACTIONS

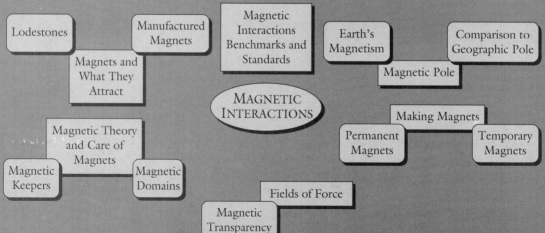

Lodestones

Manufactured Magnets

Magnetic Interactions Benchmarks and Standards

Earth's Magnetism

Comparison to Geographic Pole

Magnets and What They Attract

Magnetic Pole

MAGNETIC INTERACTIONS

Magnetic Theory and Care of Magnets

Making Magnets

Permanent Magnets

Temporary Magnets

Magnetic Keepers

Magnetic Domains

Fields of Force

Magnetic Transparency

At the primary level, magnets may be studied more than any other science topic. It is common for young children to have their own magnets and magnetic toys. This chapter considers several kinds of magnets and what they attract, how to make magnets, the field of force that surrounds a magnet, magnetic poles, and the theory and care of magnets.

MAGNETS AND WHAT THEY ATTRACT CONCEPTS
(Experiences p. 117)

There are many magnets around the home and classroom for us to use as examples in teaching. In kitchens, cloth pot holders containing magnets are placed on the sides of stoves. Automatic can openers have magnets to hold opened can lids. Cabinet doors remain closed because of magnets. Some people wear magnetic earrings. Toy stores have many toys that in some way use magnetism. At school, speakers, magnetic paper holders, and some games also have magnetics.

What Magnets Attract

In nearly all these cases, *the metals attracted to a magnet are iron and steel.* Less well known magnetic metals are cobalt and nickel. Among the more common metals *not* attracted by magnets are brass, aluminum, tin, silver, stainless steel, copper, bronze, and gold.

It will help you to know several facts that can clear up some common misunderstandings. For example, a question may arise about the attractable property of so-called tin cans. These are made of thin sheet steel and coated lightly with tin. Although tin is not attractable, steel is. Confusion may also result if some straight pins are attracted by a magnet and other identical-appearing pins are not because they are made of brass. Also, the U.S. five-cent piece is largely composed of copper and so should not be used as an example.

Lodestones

Natural magnets are sometimes called "lodestones," or "leading stones," because ancient mariners used them as crude compasses. Lodestones are made of magnetite, an iron ore found in different locations on the earth's crust.

Only some of these deposits are magnetized and theories have been developed to explain this phenomenon. One such theory holds that lightning may have been responsible. It is thought that electricity discharged into the ore may have arranged many atoms within the ore in a manner like that found in magnets.

Traces of magnetite are common in soils. A magnet dragged along the ground or in a playground sandbox may attract many particles. These particles can be an effective substitute in activities in which iron filings are used.

Manufactured Magnets

Artificial magnets are often made of steel and magnetized by electricity. Named for their shape, there are bar, V, U, horseshoe, and cylindrical magnets, to name the more familiar varieties (Figure 4-1). Each of these magnets attracts substances most strongly at the ends, or poles. The U, V, and horseshoe magnets are more powerful than the others when all factors are equal; they are bent so two poles attract instead of one.

Powerful alnico magnets are available at scientific supply houses and in commercial kits. These are made from aluminum, cobalt, nickel, and iron. Alnico magnets are used for home and commercial purposes.

Figure 4-1
Magnets (A) bar; (B) V; (C) U-shaped; (D) horseshoe; (E) cylindrical; and (F) lodestone.

MAKING MAGNETS CONCEPTS
(Experiences p. 121)

Magnets made from a relatively soft material, such as iron, usually hold their magnetism only a short time. So they are called *temporary* magnets. Those made from a harder material, such as steel, retain their magnetism far longer. They are called *permanent* magnets. You can make either kind from common materials. Let's see how.

Temporary Magnets

A magnet can be made from an iron nail by stroking it in one direction with one pole of a permanent magnet. Its power increases with the number of strokes you apply. Be sure to lift the magnet clear at the end of each stroke before beginning another. Merely rubbing it back and forth will usually bring poor results. Within a few minutes after making this magnet, you will notice a marked loss in its power, regardless of how many strokes it has received.

A second way to make a temporary magnet is by holding a magnet very close to any attractable object. For example, if you hold a magnet near the head of a small nail, you may be able to pick up a few tacks or a paper clip with the nail. Move the magnet farther away from the nail head, and the objects typically will fall off the nail. This is called *induced* magnetism.

You can also make a temporary magnet by wrapping an insulated wire around a nail and connecting the two wire ends to a battery. This is an *electromagnet*. Any wire that carries an electric current generates a weak magnetic field around it. Wrapping the wire around the nail core concentrates the field into the core. Disconnect the wire from the battery and the nail is no longer an effective magnet.

Permanent Magnets

It takes longer to magnetize a steel object by stroking it with a magnet than it does an iron one. However, steel may hold its magnetism for years.

A more efficient way to make permanent magnets is by electricity. The steel object is placed into a tube wrapped in wire and attached to a battery or other electrical source. Current is applied for a few seconds to magnetize the object. An upcoming activity shows this method.

FIELDS OF FORCE CONCEPTS
(Experiences p. 124)

As children explore with magnets, they can observe that a magnet will attract from a distance. For example, a small nail or paper clip will "jump" to a nearby magnet. They will also see that the attractive force is strongest at the poles. This gives us the chance to introduce the field of force surrounding a magnet.

Inferring the Field

While we cannot see the field directly, its presence may be inferred. Sprinkle iron filings on a sheet of stiff white paper placed over a magnet, and you will see the filings distribute in an orderly way. Their greatest concentration will be at the poles. (See Figure 4-10.) Theoretically, a magnetic field extends outward to an indefinite distance. For practical purposes, the field ends when we can no longer detect it.

Magnetic Transparency

If you hold a powerful magnet against the *back* of your hand, it can attract and move a paper clip in the *palm* of your hand. A magnetic field can also go through many other materials without any apparent loss of power. It seems as if these materials are "transparent" to the field's lines of force. This makes it possible for people to wear magnetic earrings and plumbers to locate iron pipes in closed walls. *Caution:* Please note that computer disks and other media, televisions, and wristwatches may be affected by magnets. Materials of iron or steel are considered "opaque" to this force. When they are touched by a magnet, the force passes inside them and back into the magnet.

MAGNETIC POLE CONCEPTS
(Experiences p. 128)

Suspend a bar magnet from a string in North America and a curious thing happens: It points toward the north magnetic pole. Do the same in South America and it points toward the south magnetic pole. (This assumes no interfer-

ence from nearby metals.) A magnetized needle placed horizontally on a floating foam plastic chip or slice of cork also points toward a magnetic pole.

To see why this is so, consider the poles of a magnet. When another magnet or magnetized object is held near a suspended or floating magnet, the like poles (north–north or south–south) repel each other. The opposite poles attract each other.

Earth's Magnetism

The earth itself acts like a giant magnet. No one knows why, but there are some theories. One explanation holds that several parts of the earth's interior rotate at different speeds. The resulting friction strips electric particles from atoms. This causes an electric current to be generated that creates a magnetic field. Because the earth's core is supposedly made of nickel–iron, the effect is that of a huge electromagnet buried within the earth.

Recall the discussion before that dealt with magnetic fields of force. When iron filings are sprinkled on paper placed over a bar magnet, they reveal lines of force looping from one pole to another and concentrating at both poles. On a gigantic scale, a similar kind of magnetic field happens with the earth's magnetism. (See Figure 4-2.)

Lines of force from the earth's magnetism run roughly north and south far into space and then loop down to concentrate at the north and south magnetic poles. Therefore, a freely swinging magnet—bar, horseshoe, or any other type with dominant poles—aligns itself parallel to these lines of force. Since lines of force end at the magnetic poles, properly following a compass in the northern hemisphere eventually results in one's arrival at the north magnetic pole. This is located above the upper Hudson Bay region of Canada. If one follows a compass south, the trip ends near Wilkes Land, a part of Antarctica.

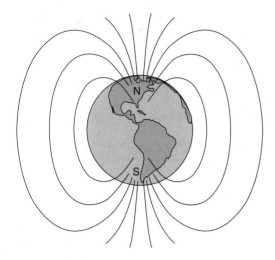

Figure 4-2
The earth has a magnetic field that is concentrated at both poles.

Geographic Poles

The north and south *magnetic* poles should not be confused with the north and south *geographic* poles. The geographic and magnetic poles are about 1,600 kilometers (1,000 miles) apart in the north and 2,400 kilometers (1,500 miles) apart in the south. In other words, when a compass points north it does *not* point true north, or toward the north star. Charts must be made for navigators that show the angular variation between true north and the direction toward which a compass points. These charts must be periodically changed, as the magnetic poles are slowly but continually shifting. (See Figure 4-3.)

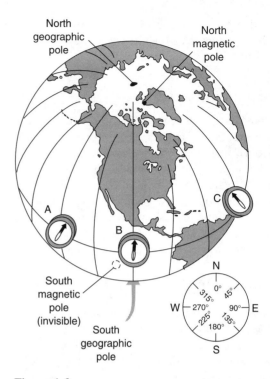

Figure 4-3
Note in A, B, and C an angle between the meridian on which the compass is located and the direction toward which the needle points. These differences must be added or subtracted from a compass heading to determine true north. For example, true headings for A, B, and C should all be 0°, or north. Actual readings are 35°, 5°, and 315°. A chart would show the need to subtract 35° from A, 5° from B, and the need to add 45° to C.

MAGNETIC THEORY AND CARE OF MAGNETS CONCEPTS
(Experiences p. 130)

Although magnetism has been known and used for many centuries, science cannot fully explain it. One theory, when simply explained, can be understood by children. It is based on observations they can make for themselves: Heating or repeatedly dropping a magnet will cause it to lose its magnetic properties. And, although a magnet may be broken into smaller and smaller pieces, each fragment continues to have a north and south pole. To find out why, you need to understand domains.

Magnetic Domains

Scientists believe that there are many tiny clusters of atoms, called *domains,* within potentially magnetic objects. The clusters are normally randomly arranged. But when an object is stroked in one direction, or otherwise magnetized, the domains line up in a single direction. See Figure 4-4. Notice that in Drawing A, the bar magnet could be broken into many pieces, yet each piece would continue to have opposite poles. Heating a magnet forces the domains into violent motion, and so they are likely to be disarranged, as in Drawing B. Repeatedly dropping a magnet jars the domains out of line, with the same result.

Caring for Magnets

Magnets can keep much of their power for years when properly cared for. Storing magnets improperly in the classroom is probably the chief reason why they quickly become weak. A small metal bar, called a *keeper,* should be placed across the poles of a magnet before it is

stored. If the regular keeper has been lost, a nail can be substituted. Placing opposite poles of magnets together is another effective way to store them. Children can also learn not to drop magnets, which is another common reason why magnets become weaker.

Figure 4-5 shows two charts which provide guidance to help children remember some rules when handling magnets. The first chart is for primary children. The second is suitable for older children.

MAGNETIC INTERACTIONS BENCHMARKS AND STANDARDS

Magnets are commonly studied in the primary grades. Children should complete activities designed to observe and classify magnetic and nonmagnetic objects. Early activities will also lay the groundwork for future study of forces. Specific examples of Benchmarks and Standards are as follows:

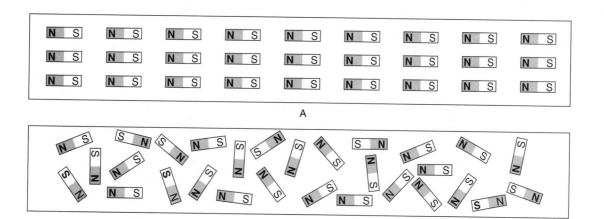

Figure 4-4
A magnetized (A) and unmagnetized (B) steel bar.

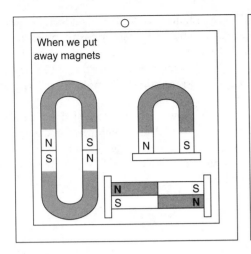

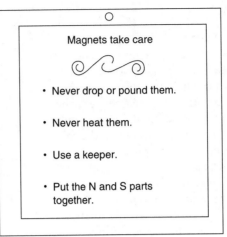

A   B

Figure 4-5
Sample charts to help children remember how to handle magnets.

SAMPLE BENCHMARKS (AAAS, 1993).

■ Magnets can be used to make some things move without being touched (by Grades K–2, p. 94).

■ Without touching them, a magnet pulls on all things made of iron and either pushes or pulls on other magnets (by Grades 3–5, p. 94).

SAMPLE STANDARD (NRC, 1996).

■ Magnets attract and repel each other and certain kinds of other materials (by Grades K–4, p. 127).

INVESTIGATIONS AND ACTIVITIES

MAGNETS AND WHAT THEY ATTRACT
EXPERIENCES
(Concepts p. 111)

INVESTIGATION: *OBJECTS MAGNETS CAN PULL*

Have you ever played with a magnet? If so, what were you able to do with it?

EXPLORATORY PROBLEM

How can you find out which objects magnets can pull?

NEEDED

two bags of small objects   magnet

TRY THIS

1. Take out the objects from only *one* bag now.
2. Touch your magnet to each object.
3. Which objects are pulled by the magnet? Put these in a group.
4. Which objects are not pulled by the magnet? Put those in another group (Figure 4-6).

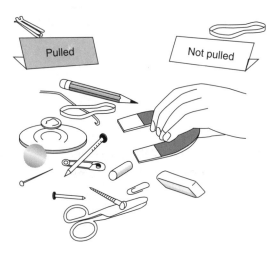

Figure 4-6

DISCOVERY PROBLEMS

observing
A. How are the objects in the pulled group alike?

inferring
B. Can you make a rule about which objects your magnet pulls? Put the objects back into the bag. Put the bag away.

predicting and classifying and inferring
C. Take out the objects from the *second* bag. Which do you think your magnet will pull? Will not pull? Put the objects into two groups. Now use your magnet on the objects in each group. Was every object in the right group?

predicting
D. Which objects around the room will your magnet pull? Record your prediction and verify.

observing
E. What other magnets can you try? Will they pull the same objects your first magnet pulled?

TEACHING COMMENT

Try to get a variety of attractable and nonattractable small objects for both bags of test materials. Here are some common objects and the chief metals or metal alloys that make them up:

nail ⟶ iron
wire ⟶ copper
pins ⟶ steel (or brass)
screws ⟶ brass (or iron or aluminum)
hair curler ⟶ aluminum
penny ⟶ bronze

Give children the names of metals as needed to help them generalize about their experience.

GENERALIZATION

A magnet pulls objects made of iron or steel.

SAMPLE PERFORMANCE OBJECTIVES

Process: The child can infer a rule about which objects magnets pick up.

Knowledge: The child can apply the rule to new objects by predicting which will be attracted to a magnet.

ACTIVITY: *HOW CAN A MAGNET SEPARATE MIXED MATERIALS?*

NEEDED

magnet	plastic spoon
salt	small jar with lid
kitchen plastic wrap	white paper with turned-up edges
iron filings	sandbox or loose soil

TRY THIS

1. Put two spoonfuls each of filings and salt into the jar.
2. Cap the jar and shake it to mix the two materials.
3. Pour the mixture onto a white paper "tray."
4. Try using the spoon to separate the filings and salt.
5. Now use the magnet, but first cover the poles with kitchen plastic wrap.
6. To remove the filings from the magnet, remove the kitchen wrap.
   a. Which was easier, Step 4 or 5?
   b. Many bits of iron may be found in sand and soils. Cover the magnet's poles again with wrap. Poke the magnet around in a sandbox or loose soil. How many iron bits do you find?

INVESTIGATION: *THE POWER OF MAGNETS*

Some people say you can tell how strong a magnet is just by looking at it. What do you think?

EXPLORATORY PROBLEM

How can you find out the power of a magnet?

NEEDED

several different magnets	two small pieces cut from a straw
pencil	sheet of lined paper
paper clips	

TRY THIS

1. Put a paper clip on two pieces of soda straw, placed on a sheet of lined paper.
2. Make a pencil mark at the front of the clip.
3. Line up an end (pole) of a magnet with the clip. (See Figure 4-7.)

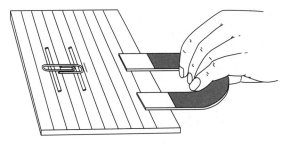

Figure 4-7

4. Slowly bring the magnet near the paper clip.
5. Stop moving the magnet when the clip moves.
6. Count the lines between the pencil mark and magnet.

DISCOVERY PROBLEMS

measuring and classifying   **A.** Test several magnets. Which is the most powerful? Can you put them in order from weakest to strongest?

measuring   **B.** Are both ends (poles) of magnets equally powerful? How can you find out?

observing   **C.** Do all parts of a magnet pull the clip? Which part of a magnet is strongest? weakest?

experimenting   **D.** What are some other ways to test a magnet's power? Do you get the same results?

TEACHING COMMENT

PREPARATION AND BACKGROUND

A magnet attracts objects most strongly at the ends or poles. The attractive power gradually weakens as you go toward the center of the magnet. The center has very little or no magnetic attraction.

GENERALIZATION

Magnets vary in power; magnets attract objects most strongly at their poles.

SAMPLE PERFORMANCE OBJECTIVES

Process: The child can measure the relative power of several magnets and arrange them in order from least to most powerful.

Knowledge: The child can describe the parts of a magnet that are likely to be most and least powerful.

MAKING MAGNETS EXPERIENCES
(Concepts p. 112)

INVESTIGATION: *HOW TO MAKE MAGNETS*

Suppose you have an iron nail and a magnet. With these materials, you can make another magnet.

EXPLORATORY PROBLEM

How can you make a magnet?

NEEDED

strong magnet
two matched iron nails
steel straight pins
two screwdrivers (large and small)

TRY THIS

1. Get a large iron nail. Touch it to some steel pins to see if it attracts them.
2. Put one end of the magnet on the nail near the head.
3. Stroke the whole nail with the magnet 20 times. Stroke in one direction only (Figure 4-8).
4. Touch the nail again to some pins. How many pins does the nail attract? Record this number.

DISCOVERY PROBLEMS

observing   **A.** How much stronger can you make your nail magnet? How many pins does it attract after 30 strokes? 40 strokes? Record how many pins are attracted each time.

observing   **B.** How strong is the nail magnet after 10 minutes? Compare.

observing   **C.** Test the other nail, to see if it attracts pins. If not, stroke this nail *back and forth,* instead of just one way. How strong is the magnet after 20 strokes? 30 strokes? 40 strokes?

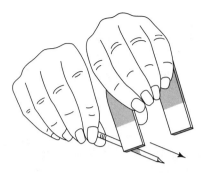

Figure 4-8

predicting   **D.** Suppose you stroke a *small* steel screwdriver one way with a magnet. How many pins will it attract after 20 strokes? 30 strokes? 40 strokes? Record and compare your findings with those for the nail.

predicting   **E.** Suppose you stroke a *large* steel screwdriver one way with a magnet. Will you get the same results?

predicting   **F.** How strong do you think both screwdrivers will be after 10 minutes?

hypothesizing **G.** What other objects can you make into magnets? How strong can you make each one?

TEACHING COMMENT

PREPARATION AND BACKGROUND

An iron or steel object may be magnetized by stroking it with a magnet. A soft iron object that is magnetized, such as a nail, weakens after several minutes. A steel object, such as the shank of a screwdriver, retains its magnetism. However, steel is harder to magnetize. Only a strong magnet is likely to produce significant results. Stroking an object both ways with a magnet is less effective than stroking it in one direction. Use steel straight pins to test the strength of whatever magnets are made.

    In Problems D and E, observe whether students test *each* screwdriver for magnetism *before* they proceed.

GENERALIZATION

Iron and steel may be magnetized by a magnet; steel holds its magnetism longer than iron.

SAMPLE PERFORMANCE OBJECTIVES

Process: The child can infer by comparing data that there is a connection between the number of strokes used to magnetize an object and the object's magnetic power.

Knowledge: The child will say that a steel object should be used if a permanent magnet is to be made.

ACTIVITY: *HOW CAN YOU MAKE LONG-LASTING MAGNETS WITH ELECTRICITY?*

NEEDED

thin (number 26 or 28) insulated copper wire
magnet
three D-size flashlight cells
pencil
3-by-5-inch file card
scissors
two steel bobby pins
tacks
sticky tape

TRY THIS

1. Tightly roll a small file card around a pencil. Fasten it with sticky tape.
2. Tightly wind about 80 turns of thin copper wire in one direction around the tube. Leave 30 centimeters (1 foot) of wire free at each end. Tape the coil ends so the wires stay tightly wound.
3. Strip the insulation from the wire ends with scissors.
4. Remove the pencil from the tube. Put a straightened bobby pin inside.
5. Put three flashlight batteries together as in the picture. (See Figure 4-9.)

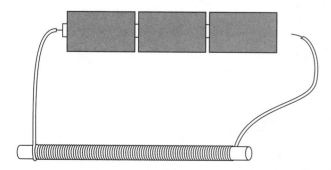

Figure 4-9

6. Touch the stripped ends of the wire to opposite ends of the batteries. Do this for no more than 5 seconds.

7. Remove the bobby pin and touch it to some tacks.

   a. How many tacks does the bobby pin pick up?

   b. Suppose you made a second bobby-pin magnet by stroking it with a regular magnet. Could you make it as strong as or stronger than the "electrocuted" bobby pin? If so, how many times would it need to be stroked? Find out.

   c. Magnetize with electricity other things that will fit into the tube. Which objects can be magnetized? Which will hold most of their magnetism over a week or more? Which will not?

FIELDS OF FORCE EXPERIENCES
(Concepts p. 112)

INVESTIGATION: *MAGNETIC FIELDS*

Have you found that some objects can be attracted to a magnet even when the magnet doesn't touch them? That's because around every magnet there is an invisible *field of force*. The magnet pulls on any attractable object within its field. Although the field is invisible, there are ways to tell where it is.

EXPLORATORY PROBLEM

How can you find out about a magnet's field of force?

NEEDED

container of iron filings
four matched bar magnets
four matched horseshoe or U magnets
two sheets of stiff white paper with turned-up edges
partner

TRY THIS

1. Place a bar magnet on a table. Lay a sheet of white paper with turned-up edges over it.

2. Sprinkle some iron filings on this paper tray. Do this over and around where you think the magnet is (Figure 4-10).

3. Observe closely how the filings line up and where they are thick and thin.

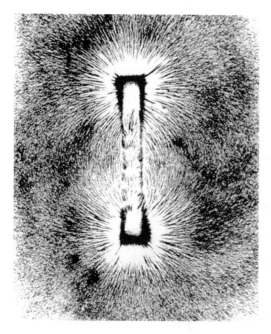

Figure 4-10

DISCOVERY PROBLEMS

inferring   **A.** Ask your partner to observe your magnetic field, but don't tell how you arranged your magnet or what kind it is. Can your partner make one just like it?

inferring   **B.** Have your partner make a magnetic field for you. Can you match it?

predicting   **C.** Here are more fields for you and your partner to try: How will two bar magnets look with like poles close together? unlike poles close together? How will horseshoe or U magnets look with like and unlike poles close together? First, draw what you predict.

experimenting   **D.** What fields can you make with different combinations of magnets, positions, and distances apart?

inferring   **E.** What were the easiest fields of force for you and your partner to figure out? the hardest fields to figure out?

TEACHING COMMENT

PREPARATION AND BACKGROUND

Students should learn that iron filings only crudely show a magnet's field of force. The field extends much beyond where the filings stop.

Permanent inference sheets of magnetic fields can be easily made. These will allow individual students to do the activity by trying to match the sheets. To make a permanent record of a field, use plastic spray to fix the filings on a stiff sheet of paper. Hold the spray can far enough away from the sheet that filings are not blown away. For best results, be sure to use fine, powderlike filings and sprinkle lightly. Let the spray dry before removing the sheet from the underlying magnets.

You may also use a magnetic field detector available from scientific supply companies. These show the lines of force more accurately and work very well with refrigerator magnets.

GENERALIZATION

A field of force surrounds a magnet; it is most powerful near the ends or poles.

SAMPLE PERFORMANCE OBJECTIVES

Knowledge: The child can point out the most and least powerful areas in a magnetic field.

Process: When shown a record of a magnetic field, the child can infer the positions and distances apart of several magnets.

INVESTIGATION: *DOES MAGNETISM GO THROUGH OBJECTS?*

Do you think magnetism can be blocked by some materials? If so, which ones? Do you think it can pass through other materials? If so, which ones?

EXPLORATORY PROBLEM

How can you find out if magnetism can go through materials?

NEEDED

ruler
strong magnet
books
small paper clip
thread
small thin materials to test

TRY THIS

1. Set up your objects as in Figure 4-11. Be sure that the clip does *not* touch the magnet.
2. Make the space between the clip and magnet as big as possible, but do not let the clip fall. Slowly pull the thread end to widen the space.

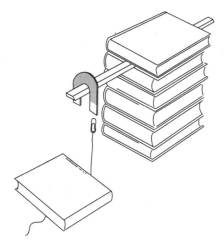

Figure 4-11

3. Test one of your thin, flat materials. Put it in the space between the clip and magnet without touching them.

4. Does the clip stay up? Then magnetism can go through the material. Does the clip fall? Then magnetism cannot go through the material.

DISCOVERY PROBLEMS

predicting **A.** Which of your materials do you think magnetism will go through? Which will magnetism not go through? Put the materials in two piles, then test them to find out.

predicting **B.** Will magnetism go through *two* materials put together? Test the materials to find out. (Be sure the two materials can fit between the magnet and clip.)

experimenting **C.** Do you think magnetism will go through water? How can you find out?

experimenting **D.** What are other ways to test if magnetism can go through your objects?

TEACHING COMMENT

PREPARATION AND BACKGROUND

In the Exploratory Problem, try to provide materials thin enough to pass between the paper clip and magnet.

GENERALIZATION

Magnetism goes through many objects, but not those made from iron or steel.

SAMPLE PERFORMANCE OBJECTIVES

Process: The child can infer the location of a hidden iron object by using a magnet.

Knowledge: Given a magnet and several objects, the child can show that magnetism passes through objects unless they are made of iron or steel.

FOR YOUNGER CHILDREN

Younger children should be able to do most of the activities in this investigation.

MAGNETIC POLE EXPERIENCES
(Concepts p. 113)

ACTIVITY: *HOW CAN YOU MAKE A NEEDLE COMPASS?*

NEEDED

two sewing needles
magnet
cork top (thin slice or styrofoam chip)
water
drinking glass
paper towel

TRY THIS

1. Place a glass on a paper towel. Fill it to the brim with water.
2. Magnetize a needle. Stroke it 10 times, from thick end to point, with the magnet's *S* pole.
3. Scratch a narrow groove in the sliced cork top. Lay the needle in the groove. (This will keep it from rolling off.)
4. Carefully place the cork and needle on the water surface (Figure 4-12).
   a. In which direction does the needle point?
   b. Move the needle gently so it points somewhere else. Wait a few seconds. What happens?
   c. Use your magnet. How can you *push* away either end of the needle with it?
   d. How can you *pull* either end of the needle with the magnet?
5. Replace the magnetized needle with one that has not been magnetized. Float the cork and needle on the water as before.
   e. What do you think will happen if you try steps 4a through 4d again? Find out.

Figure 4-12

TEACHING COMMENT

A glass filled to the brim with water keeps a floating cork centered. With less water, the cork will drift against the glass's sides.

ACTIVITY: *HOW CAN YOU USE A COMPASS TO TELL DIRECTIONS?*

NEEDED

topless cardboard box (large)
partner
large open area
magnetic compass

TRY THIS

1. Go to a large, open space outdoors. Study the compass. Notice how the needle points. Turn the compass so that the part marked "north" is under the pointing needle.

2. Walk 20 steps toward the north and observe the needle. While walking, try to keep the needle exactly on north.

3. Stop, then turn completely around. Look at the compass. Now "north" is behind you and "south" is straight ahead. The other end of the needle should point south. Walk 20 steps toward the south while watching the needle. Keep it exactly on south. If you do so, you should return to where you started.

a. Can you use only your compass well enough to walk somewhere and find your way back? How close will you get? Mark where you are. Put a box over your head so you cannot see around you. Looking at only your compass, walk 300 steps north and then 300 steps south. Have a partner watch out for you.

b. How well can you do Step 3a *without* a compass?

c. How can you use your compass to walk east or west? Practice these directions as in Steps 1 through 3, and then try the box test again.

TEACHING COMMENT

"North" as shown on a compass may vary slightly from true north because of regional magnetic variation. For the purpose of this activity, such variation may be ignored.

MAGNETIC THEORY AND CARE OF MAGNETS EXPERIENCES
(Concepts p. 114)

ACTIVITY: *WHAT ARE SOME WAYS A MAGNET CAN LOSE ITS MAGNETISM?*

A. NEEDED

magnet
concrete sidewalk
two large matched nails
tacks or paper clips

INTRODUCTION

Test to see how *dropping* a magnet affects its magnetism. (Use magnetized nails so that regular magnets will not be destroyed.)

TRY THIS

1. Magnetize two nails. Stroke each nail its whole length 30 times with one pole of a magnet.

2. Test to see if each nail magnet attracts the same number of tacks. If not, stroke the weaker magnet until it is equally strong.

3. Hold one nail high and drop it on a hard surface. Do this 20 times.

4. Test each nail again. You might record what you find in this way:

	Dropped Magnet	Other Magnet
Before	6 tacks	6 tacks
After	2 tacks	5 tacks

    a. How did dropping the nail magnet affect it?

    b. What will happen if you drop the second nail magnet?

B. NEEDED

magnet
candle and match
two large matched nails
cake pan (to hold candle)
tacks or paper clips
glass of water
pliers or tongs

INTRODUCTION

Test to see how *heating* affects magnetism.

TRY THIS

1. Again, do Steps 1 and 2 in Section A.

2. Use pliers to hold one magnetized nail upright in a candle flame for three minutes.

3. Before testing, dip the nail in water to cool it.

4. Test the two nails. Record your findings as in Section A.

    a. How did heating the nail magnet affect it?

    b. What will happen if you heat the second nail magnet?

TEACHING COMMENT

Iron nails do not retain magnetism very long. So it is possible that the second magnet, too, will be weaker during the post-test. But this change should be slight. *Caution:* Supervise the candle activity closely for safety.

REFERENCES

American Association for the Advancement of Science. (1993). *Benchmarks for science literacy.* New York: Oxford University Press.

National Research Council. (1996). *National science education standards.* Washington, DC: National Academy Press.

SELECTED TRADE BOOKS: MAGNETIC INTERACTIONS

For Younger Children

Freeman, M. (1980). *The real magnet books.* Scholastic.

Jennings, T. (1990). *Magnets.* Watts.

Kirkpatrick, R. K. (1985). *Look at magnets.* Raintree.

Knight, D. C. (1967). *Let's find out about magnets.* Watts.

Podendorf, I. (1971). *Magnets.* Children's Press.

Schneider, H., & Schneider, N. (1979). *Secret magnets.* Scholastic.

Wade, H. (1979). *The magnet.* Raintree.

For Older Children

Adler, D. (1983). *Amazing magnets.* Troll Associates.

Adler, I., & Adler, R. (1966). *Magnets.* Day.

Catherall, E. A., & Holt, P. N. (1969). *Working with Magnets.* Whitman.

Fitzpatrick, J. (1987). *Magnets.* Silver Burdett.

Freeman, M. B. (1968). *The book of magnets.* Four Winds.

Santrey, L. (1985). *Magnets.* Troll Associates.

Sootin, H. (1968). *Experiments with magnetism.* Norton.

Victor, E. (1967). *Exploring and understanding magnets and electromagnets.* Benefic.

Ward, A. (1991). *Experimenting with magnetism.* Chelsea House.

Resource Book

Shaw, D. G., & Dybdahl, C. S. (1996). *Integrating science and language arts: a sourcebook for K–6 teachers* (physical cycles including magnetism pp. 93–110). Allyn and Bacon.

CHAPTER 5

ELECTRICAL ENERGY

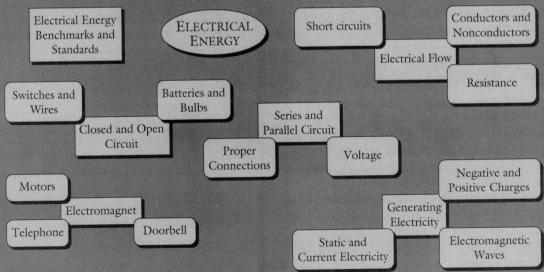

Can children learn to appreciate the advantages of a ready source of electricity? One good beginning is for them to count the number of electrical devices we use and then try to devise nonelectrical substitutes for them. By doing activities like those in this chapter, children should also begin to appreciate some of the things that make electrical energy available and the principles that make them work.

We'll consider how electrical circuits are closed and opened, some conditions that affect the flow of electricity, electromagnets, and ways to produce electricity.

CLOSED AND OPEN CIRCUIT CONCEPTS
(Experiences page 146)

Each time we push a button or flip a switch that "turns on" electricity, there is a continuous flow of electrical energy in wires connected from the generating plant to our appliance and back again to the plant. On a smaller scale, much the same thing happens when a battery is connected to a miniature bulb. If there is a continuous connection between the source of electricity and the appliance or device using it, lights go on, bells ring, or motors spin. This continuous connection is called a *closed circuit*. Anytime there is a break or gap in the circuit, the electric flow stops. This condition is called an *open circuit*.

Switches

Regardless of their shape, size, or method of operation, electric switches serve only to open or close a circuit. They offer a safe and convenient way of supplying the flow of electricity when we want it by providing a linkage through which the energy can flow to the connecting wires.

Batteries

Much of the work in this chapter calls for the use of dry cells, copper wire, and flashlight bulbs. Size D flashlight cells or number 6 dry cells should be used because they are safe, fairly long lasting, and relatively inexpensive. When fresh, they deliver 1½ volts of electricity, as contrasted with 110 to 120 volts or so supplied in the home.

In other words, it would take as many as 80 of these cells connected together to have a force usually supplied by the current found in the home. *Caution:* House current is dangerous for electrical investigations and children should be reminded never to use household electrical currents for investigations.

Bulbs

Because the chapter calls for experiments with miniature bulbs (flashlight-type bulbs), it will be helpful to understand how to use them properly. Miniature bulbs are designed to be used with a loosely specified number of 1½ volt dry cells. Therefore, there are one-cell, two-cell, or multi-cell bulbs. One-cell bulbs are sometimes marked "1.2v," 2-cell bulbs "2.5v," and so forth.

If three dry cells are connected to a one-cell bulb, it is likely that the thin tungsten filament inside will burn out quickly. Be careful to match the bulb with the number of cells used. Too many cells will cause the bulb to burn out quickly; too few will cause it to glow feebly, if at all.

Fahnestock Clips

Many unit activities call for the use of commercial-type miniature bulbs and sockets. While several substitutes are possible, these are usually cumbersome and less useful. For maximum ease in using miniature sockets, Fahnestock clips should be fastened to each side of the socket with the screws found there. (See Figure 5-1

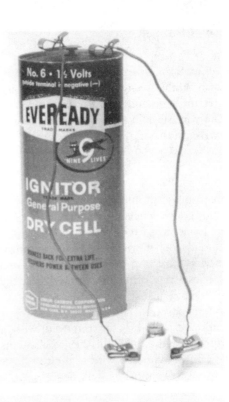

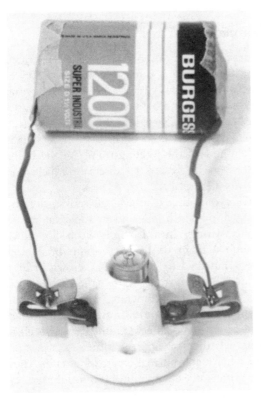

Figure 5-1
A number 6 dry cell and two D cells connected in complete circuits.

for an example.) To connect a wire, simply press down on the springy, open end of the clip and insert the wire end into the exposed half-loop. The wire stays in place when you release the pressure on the clip.

Wire

The wire you use should also be selected with an eye to convenience. Number 22 wire is excellent for almost every activity. Get plastic-covered solid copper wire, rather than cotton-covered wire consisting of many small, twisted strands. These strands become unraveled at the ends, and cotton insulation is harder to strip off than a plastic covering.

Insulation can quickly be removed with a wire-stripper (Figure 5-2); this device also cuts wires efficiently. With the wire suggested here, scissors may serve almost as well.

Connections

There are several easy ways to connect cells and bulbs, depending on the kinds of materials you have. Figure 5-1 shows how a D-size cell and a number 6 cell can be connected to form a closed or complete circuit. Tape or a wide rubber band will hold the stripped wire ends snugly against the D-cell terminals. The center terminal (positive), recognizable by the bump, corresponds to the center terminal on a large cell. The opposite terminal (negative) is equivalent

Figure 5-2
A wire stripper.

to the rim-mounted terminal on the large cell. The third arrangement needs only a single wire, with one end touching the negative terminal and the other wrapped around the bulb base. The base touches the positive terminal to complete the circuit. Notice that the wire end wrapped around the bulb base also serves as a bulb holder.

SERIES AND PARALLEL CIRCUIT CONCEPTS
(Experiences page 149)

There are only two basic ways to connect electrical devices in a circuit: through series or parallel wiring (Figure 5-3).

Connecting Wires

In series wiring, all of the usable electricity flows through each bulb or appliance. A chief disadvantage of this circuit is obvious to anyone who has had a bulb burn out in an old-fashioned, series-type string of Christmas-tree lights. When one bulb burns out, the circuit is broken and all the lights go out. All the bulbs must then be tested to discover which one needs to be replaced.

To avoid the troubles of series circuits, most wiring for home and commercial use is parallel wiring. In this kind, electricity flows through a main wire and through branching wires connected to it as well, as shown in Figure 5-3(B). (In this figure, the Fahnestock clips represent the branching wires.) If a light or other fixture should burn out, no other light or fixture is affected. Bulbs receive electricity whether or not the others are in use. And when children make parallel circuits, they will notice no change in bulb brightness as bulbs are added.

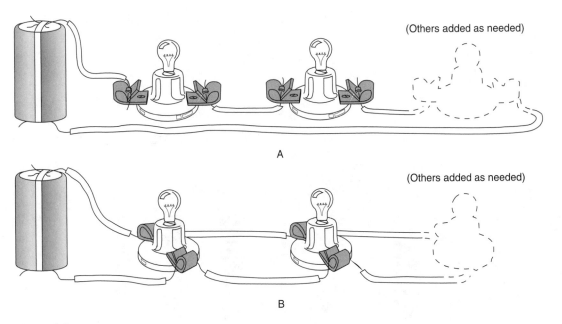

(Others added as needed)

A

(Others added as needed)

B

Figure 5-3
Two contrasting circuits: (A) Lights in series, and (B) lights in parallel.

Connecting Cells

Cells can also be arranged in series and parallel as shown in Figure 5-4. A wide rubber band can serve to affix wires to flashlight cells, but the cells will buckle where they join unless they are enclosed. A sheet of rolled, stiff paper can be used for this purpose. If children work in pairs, these holders may not be required, as four hands should be able to hold everything together.

Note that in the series examples, negative terminals (–) are joined to positive (+) terminals. In the parallel examples, positives are joined to positives and negatives are joined to negatives.

Voltage

Hooking up cells in series increases the *voltage,* or pressure, behind the flow of electricity. In contrast, arranging several or more cells in par-

allel makes available a longer-lasting supply of current without increasing the voltage. For example, a bulb connected to two cells in series will burn about twice as brightly as when the cells are connected in parallel. However, the bulb will burn about two times longer with the parallel arrangement.

An analogy, as shown in Figure 5-5, can clarify why these differences take place. Cells in series are like connected tanks of water with one mounted higher than the other. The force of the flow is directly related to how many higher tanks are used. In contrast, cells in parallel are like water tanks mounted on the same level. The water flows at about the same rate as it would with one tank. So in this case, the water supply lasts about twice as long as in the other setup.

In studying circuits, children have many interesting chances to make predictions about which bulbs will light and to make inferences about hidden wires.

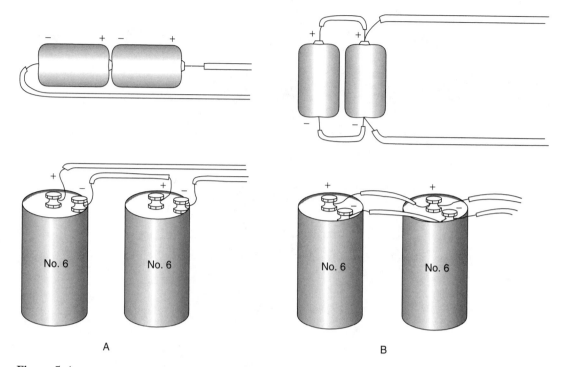

Figure 5-4
Batteries arranged in series (A) and parallel (B).

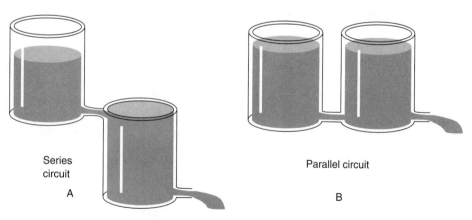

Figure 5-5
(A) is twice as forceful as (B), but (B) will flow twice as long.

ELECTRICAL FLOW CONCEPTS
(Experiences 158)

Conductors

The term *conductor* is usually given to any substance that permits an easy flow of electricity. Metals are by far the best conductors of electricity, and so they are commonly used for wires. Although several of the precious metals are better conductors, copper is most often used, as it is comparable in efficiency and yet cheap enough to produce in quantity.

We often hear the term *nonconductor* for materials such as rubber, glass, plastic, cloth, and other nonmetallic substances. This is misleading, as almost anything will conduct electricity if given enough voltage. These materials are better called poor conductors, or *insulators*.

This is why electricians may wear rubber gloves, and electric wires are covered with cloth, plastic, or rubber. It also explains why appliance plugs are covered with rubber or plastic, and glass separators are used on power line poles to keep apart high voltage lines.

Some poor conductors become good conductors when wet. Pure, or distilled, water is a poor conductor, but when dissolved minerals are added to it, it becomes a fairly good one. Wet human skin is a far better conductor than dry skin. For this reason, it is safer to turn appliances on and off with dry hands.

Resistance

Although metals conduct electricity much better than nonmetals, there is still some resistance in metal wire to the flow of electrons. Of course, the longer the wire, the greater will be the resistance.

You may have experienced the gradual dimming of lights in a theater or adjusted the brightness of dashboard lights in an automobile. The change in both cases may have been caused by a *rheostat,* or dimmer switch. One kind of rheostat increases or decreases the length of wire through which electric current flows, thereby increasing or decreasing the wire's resistance. A simple model is shown in Figure 5-6. Some metals have so much resistance to the flow of electricity that they glow brightly when there is enough electrical pressure or voltage to force relatively large quantities of electricity to flow in them. Unfortunately, most metals melt or evaporate within a short period of time when hot enough to give off light.

This necessitated a long search by Thomas Edison for materials to be used as bulb filaments before he was able to find reasonable success. Some of the materials he tried reveal the exhaustive character of the search. Bamboo slivers, sewing thread, even human hair, were carbonized and tested!

Tungsten, sometimes called wolfram, is the metal used in *incandescent bulbs* today. (Any bulb that gives light from a very hot filament is called an incandescent bulb.) With a melting point of almost 3,400°C (6,200°F), tungsten is well able to withstand the temperature caused by the movement of electricity through its highly resistant structure. An inactive gas, such as argon, is pumped into the bulbs to help pre-

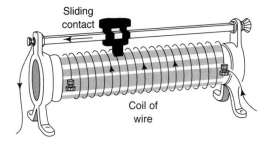

Figure 5-6
A simple rheostat, or dimmer switch.

vent the burning away of the filament. Still, some of the tungsten evaporates eventually, and the filament separates, breaking the circuit. The ever-darkening appearance of the portion of the bulb next to the filament shows the deposition of the evaporating tungsten. Electric heaters also have wires of highly resistant metal. Most heaters today use nichrome wire, a combination of nickel and chromium.

So far, you have seen that length and composition of wire affect resistance to the flow of electricity. Another factor is the diameter of the wire. An analogy here will help explain why size of wire affects resistance. Imagine part of a large crowd in a sports stadium converging into a narrow passageway. As some of the people begin to enter the passageway, the forward speed of the crowd slackens. At the end of the passageway, the forward pace again picks up.

A thick wire presents a broad pathway for the flow of electricity. A narrow wire constricts the flow. In the "effort" to crowd through the narrow pathway, much friction is created, and the wire grows hot. If the wire is thin enough and made of material like tungsten, it can also produce much light as it heats.

Circuit Hazards

You have seen that when bulbs or appliances are wired into a circuit, they show resistance to the flow of electrical energy. At the place where the energy enters these resistors, a change of energy takes place. Some of the electrical energy changes into heat (heater) or light (bulb) or sound (radio) or motion (motor). In other words, a significant amount of electrical energy is "used up," or changed.

Suppose, though, there is no resistor connected in the circuit. Because the copper wire has relatively low resistance, a great surge of electricity flows through the wire. The wire now heats up rapidly, even though it normally offers little resistance to a current.

Short Circuits

In residential and commercial circuits, intense heating of the wires may come from a "short circuit." This may happen when two bare wires touch each other, preventing the main supply of current from flowing through the resistor. Since the resistor is largely bypassed, a huge amount of electricity flows.

A common cause of short circuits happens when an appliance cord is placed under a heavily traveled rug. If the insulation between the two internal wires wears away, they may touch and a short may develop. A circuit is not necessarily shortened in length for a "short" circuit to occur. The essential thing is that the resistor is bypassed.

Overloaded Circuits

Overloading a circuit is perhaps an even more frequent cause of wires overheating. Many older houses, for example, were wired when only a few of today's common appliances were widely used. Small-diameter, lightly insulated wires were adequate then. But as more and more of today's appliances are added to circuits, intense heating occurs and poses a potential threat of fire.

Fuses and Circuit Breakers

Fuses and circuit breakers protect us from the fire hazard. In some older houses, a screw-in-type fuse contains a narrow metal strip that melts at a fairly low temperature. When a fuse is placed in a circuit, the electricity must travel through the strip. Should the wire heat up dangerously, the strip melts and the circuit opens, thereby shutting off the current.

A bimetallic strip circuit breaker is used instead of a fuse in many houses. This consists of two thin, metal ribbons fused together. The ribbons are made of two different metals. When placed in a circuit and heated, the bimetallic strip bends away from one of the contact points, opening the circuit. The bending is the result of different expansion rates of the metals.

Another modern type of circuit breaker works because any wire containing current electricity generates some magnetism. Increasing the supply of current has the effect of increasing the magnetism. When a movable steel rod is enclosed in a coil of wire placed in a circuit, it may be pulled upward as the current (and so magnetism) increases. If the rod is connected to a contact point, its upward movement will result in the circuit being opened. A spring catch that can be reset by hand prevents the rod from dropping down again. An electromagnetic device that operates this way is called a *solenoid*.

ELECTROMAGNET CONCEPTS
(Experiences page 163)

In 1820, a professor of physics at Copenhagen made a discovery that opened up for development one of the most useful devices ever conceived, the electromagnet. *Hans Christian Oersted* had believed for years that there was a relationship between magnetism and electricity. Despite much research, Oersted had not succeeded in discovering a useful connection between these two phenomena. One day, while lecturing to a class, he noticed that a wire carrying electric current was deflecting a nearby compass needle. Oersted realized immediately that the wire was generating a magnetic field. His later experiments, writings, and lectures helped spread the new concept of electromagnetism to the world.

The telephone, electric motor, and many other tools of modern living had their origin in Oersted's work and related discoveries. Consider some of these devices now.

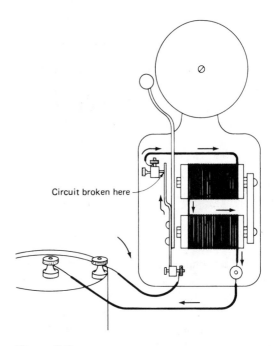

Figure 5-7
An electric bell or buzzer.

Electric Bell

An electric bell or a buzzer operates because its electric current is "interrupted," or continually turned off and on. Figure 5-7 shows how this happens. Follow the current as it moves from the battery into the bell. When the current flows around into the two electromagnets, they pull the metal clapper, which rings the bell. The act of moving the clapper breaks the circuit at the contact point, and the electricity stops flowing. The clapper then springs back into place and current flows again to repeat the cycle.

The Telephone

Figure 5-8 shows how the telephone works. Notice the complete, or closed, circuit between the transmitter and receiver. When we speak into the transmitter, a very thin metal

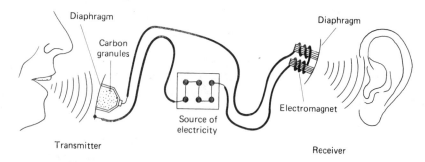

Figure 5-8
A telephone circuit.

diaphragm vibrates from sounds we make. The diaphragm variably squeezes the carbon granules behind it. Loud sounds, for example, squeeze the granules more tightly than soft sounds. This makes the granules conduct variable electrical pulses rather than a steady current.

The electrical impulses rather than the voice itself are transmitted in the wire. So they are able to travel to the other telephone's receiver almost instantly rather than at the much slower speed of sound. As the variable electric current reaches the receiver, it also causes the electromagnets to pull the diaphragm in a variable way. This sets the diaphragm vibrating in the same manner as the first one, and sounds are created.

To summarize, sound energy is used to vary electric energy at one end, which is then used to make sound energy at the other end. Students can experiment with old telephones and batteries to see how this works.

Electric Motor

You may know it is possible to rotate a suspended bar magnet with a second bar magnet. This is because unlike poles attract each other, and like poles repel each other. The suspended magnet is rotated by alternately attracting and repelling each pole. To do this, you twist the bar magnet you are holding so the poles are attracted at first and then repelled. If timed properly, the suspended magnet will rotate smoothly.

You can demonstrate a similar technique with an electromagnet. However, you will not need to twist it to make the suspended magnet rotate.

Figure 5-9 shows how to proceed. First, find the pole on the electromagnet that is the opposite of the bar magnet's nearer pole. It will attract the bar magnet. Next, reverse the way you touch the terminals on the battery. This will also reverse the poles on the electromagnet. The nearer pole of the bar magnet will now be repelled. Rotate the suspended magnet smoothly by touching the battery terminals first one way, then the opposite way. A child can hold the electromagnet in one fixed position while you do this.

In an electric motor, the electromagnet spins. A device reverses the current automatically, which continually reverses the poles of the electromagnet. The electromagnet spins because it is first attracted to, and then repelled from, another magnet inside. An electric motor is really a spinning electromagnet.

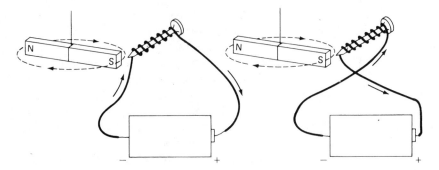

Figure 5-9
You can get a bar magnet to spin by alternately reversing the way you touch
the wire ends of an electromagnet to a battery's terminals.

GENERATING ELECTRICITY
CONCEPTS
(Experiences 165)

Electricity can be generated in several ways. First we will consider how to produce static electricity, then current electricity, and last, electromagnetic waves that can be sent to various places without wires.

Static Electricity

Not all electricity is useful. Almost everyone has experienced some form of *static electricity:* the crackling sound of hair when it is combed after having been washed and dried; the slight shock felt when a metal door knob is touched after scuffing across a rug; the flash of lightning that briefly illuminates a darkened sky. In each case, an electric charge appears to build up on an object and then stay there (hence, the name *static*) until a conductor provides a route through which the charge can escape. Although forms of static electricity vary considerably, their causes are similar. To understand these

causes, it will be helpful for us to peer briefly into the makeup of molecules and atoms.

We know that most matter is made up of *molecules.* A molecule is the smallest bit of any substance that retains the chemical properties of that substance. If we subdivide the molecule further, it no longer resembles the original substance; we have arrived at the atomic level.

Only two of the particles of which an atom is composed need concern us here: *electrons* and *protons.* Each of these particles has a tiny electric charge. The electron's charge is a *negative charge* and the proton's charge is a *positive charge.*

In their "normal" state, atoms have as many electrons as protons. Because these particles attract each other with equal force, they balance or neutralize each other. The atom is said to be *neutral,* or uncharged. But electrons are easily dislodged or torn away from atoms by rubbing and other means.

When neutral, unlike materials are rubbed together, one tends to lose electrons to the other. For example, when a hard rubber rod is rubbed with a wool cloth, the cloth loses some of its electrons to the rod. This gives the cloth a positive charge and the rod a negative charge. When a glass rod is rubbed with silk, however, some electrons leave the glass and go onto the silk cloth. This gives the silk a negative charge and the glass a positive charge.

The basic law of static electricity is *like charges repel and unlike charges attract each other.* Children may discover that identical objects rubbed with the same material will repel each other. If the objects are rubbed with different materials, they will usually attract each other.

What causes lightning? It is produced by friction. A cloud contains varying amounts of dust particles, rain drops, air (gas) molecules, and sometimes ice crystals. When violent currents occur in clouds, these substances rub together in various combinations. If a huge electric charge is built up, it may be attracted by an oppositely charged cloud or the ground. When this happens, we see lightning. (Thunder results when the air through which lightning passes quickly heats up and cools. The rapid expansion and contraction of the air forces air molecules to smash together, which causes loud sounds.)

Current Electricity

Static electricity is both unreliable and hard to manage, so we use current electricity to meet our needs. This generally comes from two sources: batteries and huge power plants.

Children are curious about how a battery can "make" electricity. Some think it is stored, like water is stored in a tank. What really happens is that chemical energy changes into electrical energy.

This is how an automobile battery works. When two different metal strips (zinc and copper, for example) are placed in an acid, both strips begin to slowly dissolve. However, the zinc dissolves faster than the copper. A surplus of electrons from the dissolving parts of the zinc strip builds up on the rest of the strip, giving it a strong negative charge. Some electrons are also released at the slower-dissolving copper

strip, but these go into the acid, leaving the copper strip with a positive charge. If we connect the end of the zinc strip to the end of the copper strip with a wire, a continuous circuit is set up. Electrons flow from the zinc strip through the wire to the copper strip. If we connect a bulb in this circuit, it lights; a connected starter starts an automobile engine.

Many pairs of dissimilar metal strips, or *electrodes,* can be used to get this effect, and other liquids besides acid can work to release and hold electrons. Such liquids are called *electrolytes.*

A "dry" cell or flashlight battery works in a way similar to the "wet" cell just described. A moist, paste-like electrolyte is used in place of a liquid. The electrodes are most commonly a carbon rod (found in the center of the cell), and a zinc cylinder (which surrounds the paste and rod).

Dry cells are convenient, but they are too weak and expensive for widespread residential or commercial use. *Mechanical energy,* the energy of motion, is by far the main method for generating electricity. Today, most electricity is produced by changing the energy in fuels and falling water.

In hydroelectric power plants, water falls on the blades of huge wheels, causing them to revolve. Other power plants may use oil, coal, natural gas, or atomic energy to heat water into steam. The steam forces giant turbines to whirl. Either large magnets are spun rapidly inside a wire coil, or a wire coil is spun inside of magnets. Both options cause electrons to flow into the wire.

Producing Electromagnetic Waves

You know that a steady electric current produces a weak magnetic field around a wire. This is why we can make an electromagnet. Long ago, scientists learned that by rapidly varying the electric current in a wire they could change the magnetic field. Instead of a steady field, rapidly vibrating energy waves were given off by the wire. These are called *radio waves*.

At a radio station, music or voice vibrations are changed into a variable electric current. The method is like that used in a telephone transmitter. The vibrating current is strengthened until strong radio waves are given off by the wire carrying the current. The waves are beamed off in all directions from a tall tower. Some of the waves strike a radio antenna. A weak current begins vibrating in the antenna, and the current is picked up and strengthened in the radio. A connected loudspeaker vibrates and produces sound energy much like a telephone receiver.

ELECTRICAL ENERGY BENCHMARKS AND STANDARDS

The idea of a complete circuit is complex for most students. They have difficulty conceptualizing that the electrons not only flow *from* the source, but that there must be a complete circuit back *to* the source. It is important to use hands-on activities to develop this understanding. Further recommendations for electrical principles include:

SAMPLE BENCHMARKS (AAAS, 1993)

■ Electric currents and magnets can exert a force on each other (by Grades 6–8, p. 95).

■ Make safe electrical connections with various plugs, sockets, and terminals (by Grades 3–5, p. 293).

SAMPLE STANDARDS (NRC, 1996)

■ Electricity in circuits can produce light, heat, sound, and magnetic effects. Electrical circuits require a complete loop through which an electrical current can pass (by Grades K–4, p. 127).

■ Electrical circuits provide a means of transferring electrical energy when heat, light, sound, and chemical changes are produced (by Grades 5–8, p. 155).

INVESTIGATIONS AND ACTIVITIES

CLOSED AND OPEN CIRCUIT EXPERIENCES
(Concepts p. 134)

INVESTIGATION: *HOW TO MAKE A BULB LIGHT*[1]

Have you ever used a flashlight? The electricity to light the bulb comes from one or more batteries. You don't need a flashlight to make the bulb light. You can do it with a single wire and a battery.

EXPLORATORY PROBLEM

How can you light a flashlight bulb with a wire and a battery?

NEEDED

D-size battery
2 wires (6 inches or 15 centimeters long)
two flashlight bulbs
paper and pencil

TRY THIS

1. Remove the insulation from both ends of the wire.
2. Put the bulb bottom on the raised button end of the battery. (See Figure 5-10.)
3. Touch one wire end to the metal side of the bulb.
4. Touch the other wire end to the battery bottom.

Figure 5-10

---

[1] Also see the sample lesson plan in *How to Teach Elementary School Science*, Third Edition, page 60.

DISCOVERY PROBLEMS

experimenting

A. How many other ways can you light the bulb? Keep a record of what you do. Make drawings of the circuits.

predicting

B. Study each of the drawings in Figure 5-11. Which ways will light the bulb? Which will not? Record your predictions and then test them.

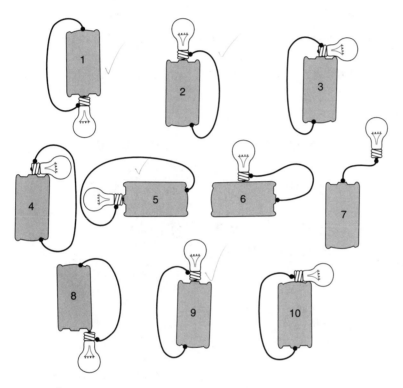

Figure 5-11

experimenting

C. How many ways can you light a bulb with two wires? (Use one battery.) Record your observations.

experimenting

D. How many ways can you light two bulbs with two wires? (Use one battery.) Record your observations.

TEACHING COMMENT

Use number 22 or 24 bell wire, available at most hardware or electrical supply stores. Be sure that the plastic covering is stripped from both ends of the wire to ensure good contact. *Caution:* Advise students to quickly notice, and discontinue trying a connection, if the wire they use to connect the bulb and battery begins to get warm. This happens when the bulb (resistor) is bypassed and the wire ends touch only the battery terminals—a type of short circuit.

GENERALIZATION

Electricity flows when there is a complete circuit; there are several ways to light a bulb.

SAMPLE PERFORMANCE OBJECTIVES

Process: The child can connect a battery and bulb with wire in several different ways to light the bulb.

Knowledge: The child can describe the bulb and battery parts that must be connected for a bulb to light.

FOR YOUNGER CHILDREN

Many younger students can do the exploratory activity, especially when plastic battery and bulb holders are used.

ACTIVITY: *HOW CAN YOU MAKE SOME PAPER-CLIP SWITCHES?*

NEEDED

flashlight bulb	two paper clips
sticky tape	cardboard
bulb holder	six paper fasteners
scissors	five small wires
D-size battery	

TRY THIS

1. Cut a small piece of cardboard. Punch two holes in it and put in two paper fasteners as in Figure 5-12.

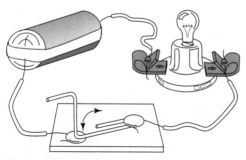

Figure 5-12

2. Strip bare the ends of the wires with scissors. Assemble the rest of the materials as shown. Bend a paper clip for the switch.

   a. What happens when you move the switch on and off the paper fastener? How does this switch work in the circuit?

3. Suppose you have a stairway light. You need to control it from both upstairs and downstairs. Make a pair of switches to control a single light. Do it as in Figure 5-13.

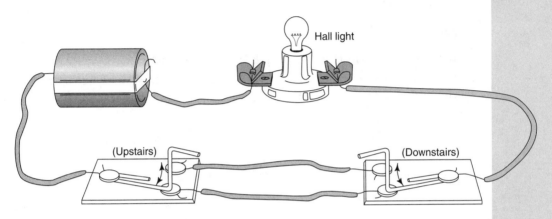

Figure 5-13

   b. What happens when you move each switch from one paper fastener head to another? What would happen if there was only a single wire between the two switches? How do these switches work?

TEACHING COMMENT

For the light to work properly, all connections need to be tight. Be sure the paper fasteners are securely seated and the wires are stripped of insulation where contact is made.

SERIES AND PARALLEL CIRCUIT EXPERIENCES
(Concepts p. 136)

INVESTIGATION: *SERIES CIRCUITS*

What does the word *series* mean to you? Here, it means placing electric bulbs in order, with one ahead or behind the next one.

EXPLORATORY PROBLEM

How can you set up a series circuit?

NEEDED

three flashlight bulbs
four wires
three bulb holders
two D-size batteries

TRY THIS

1. Remove the insulation from the ends of each wire with scissors.
2. Use two bulbs and bulb holders, two batteries, and three wires. Set up the circuit as shown in Figure 5-14.

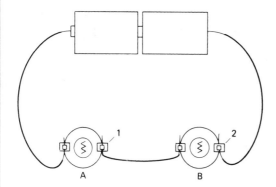

Figure 5-14

DISCOVERY PROBLEMS

predicting **A.** Suppose you remove Light A. What will happen to Light B? If you remove Light B, what will happen to Light A?

predicting **B.** Suppose you disconnect the wire at Place 1. What do you think will happen to Light A? Light B?

predicting **C.** Suppose you disconnect the wire at Place 2. What will happen to Light A? Light B?

observing **D.** Add another bulb to the series. Use one more wire, bulb, and bulb holder. What, if anything, happens to the lights?

inferring **E.** How can you explain the results in A through D? That is, how does electricity seem to flow in a series circuit?

TEACHING COMMENT

PREPARATION AND BACKGROUND

If any wire or bulb is disconnected, all the bulbs go out. This is because all of the electricity flows through each connected part in a series circuit. For the same reason, adding more bulbs to the circuit causes all the lighted bulbs to get dimmer. Each resistor cuts down the available flow of electricity.

GENERALIZATION

In a series circuit, all the electricity flows through each connected part.

SAMPLE PERFORMANCE OBJECTIVES

Knowledge: The child can set up a working series circuit with two or more bulbs.

Process: The child can predict the effect on other parts of a series circuit when one or more parts are disconnected.

INVESTIGATION: *PARALLEL CIRCUITS*

What does the word *parallel* mean to you? Here, it means placing electric wires side by side in a parallel circuit.

EXPLORATORY PROBLEM

How can you set up a parallel circuit?

NEEDED

three flashlight bulbs
six wires
three bulb holders
two D-size batteries

TRY THIS

1. Remove the insulation from the ends of each wire with scissors.
2. Use two batteries, two bulbs and bulb holders, and four wires. Set up the circuit as shown in Figure 5-15.

DISCOVERY PROBLEMS

predicting **A.** Suppose you remove Light A. What will happen to Light B? If you remove Light B, what will happen to Light A?

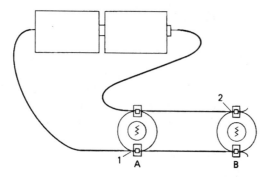

Figure 5-15

predicting   **B.** Suppose you disconnect the wire at Place 1. What do you think will happen to Light A? Light B?

predicting   **C.** Suppose you disconnect the wire at Place 2. What will happen to Light A? Light B?

observing   **D.** Add another bulb to the circuit. Use two more wires, a bulb, and bulb holder. What, if anything, happens to the brightness of the lights?

inferring   **E.** How can you explain the results in A through D? That is, how does electricity seem to flow in a parallel circuit?

TEACHING COMMENT

PREPARATION AND BACKGROUND

In a parallel circuit, the wires are arranged to bypass a burned-out or missing light. Therefore, adding more bulbs to the circuit does not noticeably affect bulb brightness. Each bulb beyond receives the same flow of electricity (but all bulbs must have the same resistance in order to burn equally bright).

GENERALIZATION

In a parallel circuit, the electricity flows both to and around each connected bulb.

SAMPLE PERFORMANCE OBJECTIVES

Knowledge: The child can set up a working parallel circuit with two or more bulbs.

Process: The child can predict the effect on other parts of a parallel circuit when one or more parts are disconnected.

INVESTIGATION: *HIDDEN PARTS OF ELECTRIC CIRCUITS*

Suppose you have a folder like that shown in Figure 5-16. Notice the four holes on the front cover. Each hole has aluminum foil underneath, so each looks the same. Now, look at the back of the front cover. A foil strip goes from Hole 1 to Hole 3. It conducts electricity like a wire. However, only small pieces cover Holes 2 and 4. Suppose you do not know where the strip is, and you cannot open the folder.

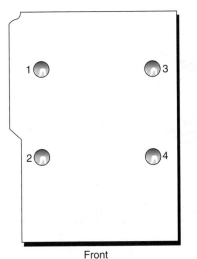
Front

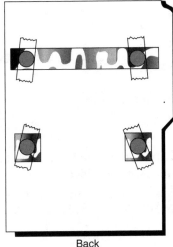
Back

Figure 5-16

EXPLORATORY PROBLEM

How can you test for and find the hidden strip?

NEEDED

paper punch	ruler
D-size battery	pencil
manila folder	scissors
aluminum foil	two wires (30-centimeter or 12-inch)
sticky tape	flashlight bulb

TRY THIS

1. First prepare your own folder. Cut a regular-size folder in half, the shorter way. (Save half for later use.)

2. Punch four holes and cover them with foil as in Figure 5-16. Fasten the foil with sticky tape. Number the holes on the cover.

3. Now prepare your tester as in Figure 5-17. Bare the ends of two wires. Tape the ends to a battery. Bend one of the opposite wire ends into a loop. Wrap the other end around the bulb base and twist it to hold it fast.

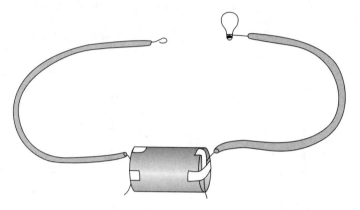

Figure 5-17

4. Touch the bulb bottom to the looped end of the other wire. If the bulb lights, you are ready to test your folder.

5. Press the bulb bottom into one hole. Press the wire loop into another hole. Test these pairs of holes; see which completes the circuit and lights the bulb:

   1—2   2—3   3—4
   1—3   2—4
   1—4

DISCOVERY PROBLEMS

inferring and experimenting **A.** Suppose you have tested another folder. Here are the results:

Paired Holes	Bulb Lights
1—2	yes
1—3	no
1—4	yes
2—3	no
2—4	yes
3—4	no

Let's say there are two strips connecting holes. How do you think they are arranged? Is more than one way possible? Make drawings of your ideas. Then prepare a folder and test your ideas.

inferring

B. Can you test and find out how different folders are "wired"? Have others prepare hidden circuits for you. (You can do the same for them.) Keep a record of your results and what you observe. Then open each folder to check your observations.

Teaching Comment

PREPARATION AND BACKGROUND

In this case, the foil strip conductor is hidden and stretches between two holes. Touching the bulb bottom and the free wire end to the strip completes the circuit, allowing electricity to flow. The free wire end is bent into a loop to avoid gouging the foil.

GENERALIZATION

Parts of an electric circuit may be inferred from tests if the wires are hidden.

SAMPLE PERFORMANCE OBJECTIVES

Process: The child can use a circuit tester to connect hidden wires and infer the location of the wires.

Knowledge: The child can explain that a bulb lights when an electric circuit is completed in any of several combinations of connections.

ACTIVITY: *How Can You Make an Electric "Nerve Tester" Game?*

NEEDED

bare copper bell wire (60 centimeters or 2 feet)
number 22 or 24 insulated wire
clay
flashlight bulb

sticky tape
bulb holder
heavy cardboard
scissors

TRY THIS

1. Put two lumps of clay on some cardboard, as shown in Figure 5-18.
2. Bend the heavy bare copper wire as shown and stick each end into a clay lump.
3. Cut three pieces of the lighter, insulated wire as shown. Bare the ends.
4. Attach the three wires to the bulb holder and battery. Attach the free end of the battery wire to the end of the heavy wire. Twist it around and push the twisted wires slightly into the clay.

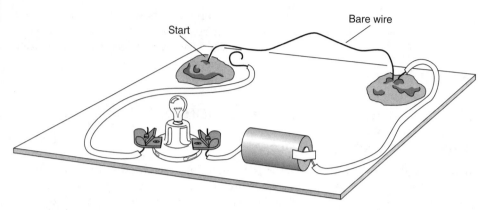

Figure 5-18

5. Bend the free end of the light bulb wire around a pencil to make a slightly open loop. Touch the loop end to the heavy wire. See if the light goes on.

6. To play the game, carefully place the open loop over the heavy wire so the wire is inside the loop. Move the loop from one end to the other and back without touching the heavy wire. If it touches, the light will go on. The person who lights the bulb least often wins. Predict and observe the following:

   a. Who has the steadiest nerves in the class?

   b. How does practice help?

   c. Is your left hand shakier than your right hand?

   d. Are people shakier before or after lunch? What other things might affect how shaky people are?

TEACHING COMMENT

Any single-strand, somewhat stiff wire will serve for the heavier wire. Even a piece cut from a wire coat hanger will work if the paint is sanded off. To make the bulb light more brightly when the wire is touched, use two batteries in series.

ACTIVITY: HOW CAN YOU MAKE A TWO-WAY BLINKER SYSTEM?

NEEDED

two flashlight bulbs and holders
four large tacks
two small wooden blocks
hammer
thin aluminum pie pan

scissors
sticky tape
wire (6 meters or 7 yards long)
D-size battery
partner

TRY THIS

1. Cut three short pieces of wire and two equally long wires, as shown in Figure 5-19. Bare the ends of all five wires.

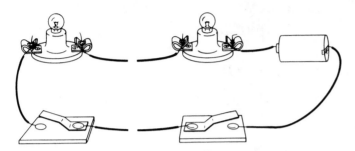

Figure 5-19

2. Cut 2 strips 10 centimeters (4 inches) long from the pie pan. Attach the strips, wires, and battery. Use tape to fasten wires to the battery. Use a hammer to pound in the tacks.

3. To send dot–dash signals, press the key a short or longer time. The second key must be held down by your partner while you are sending a message. Both lights will flash on and off as signals are sent.

4. Try using the International Morse Code to send signals:

A	B	C	D
. —	— . . .	— . — .	— . .
E	**F**	**G**	**H**
.	. . — .	— — .	. . . .
I	**J**	**K**	**L**
. .	. — — —	— . —	. — . .
M	**N**	**O**	**P**
— —	— .	— — —	. — — .
Q	**R**	**S**	**T**
— — . —	. — .	. . .	—
U	**V**	**W**	**X**
. . —	. . . —	. — —	— . . —
Y	**Z**		
— . — —	— — . .		

a. What messages can you send and receive?

b. How can you send clearer messages?

Teaching Comment

If both lights are dim, add a second battery in series; if only one bulb is dim, replace it with another that matches the bright bulb.

ELECTRIC FLOW EXPERIENCES
(Concepts page 139)

INVESTIGATION: *Materials That Conduct Electricity*

You know electricity can travel through a wire, but how about other materials?

EXPLORATORY PROBLEM

How can you find out which materials conduct electricity?

NEEDED

small wooden objects	sticky tape
pencil	small plastic objects
small glass objects	flashlight bulb
flashlight (D-size) battery	small rubber objects
small metal objects	two wires (30 centimeters or 12 inches long)

TRY THIS

1. Arrange your materials as shown in Figure 5-20, except for the key. Bare both ends of each wire. Be sure the wire is wrapped tightly around the bulb base by twisting the end.

2. Touch the bulb bottom to the end of the other wire. If the bulb lights, you are ready to test materials.

Figure 5-20

3. Get some objects to test, such as a key. Touch the bulb bottom to one part. Touch the end of the other wire to another part. If the bulb lights, the object is a conductor of electricity. If it does not light, the object is a nonconductor.

DISCOVERY PROBLEMS

observing and communicating **A.** What, if any, rubber objects are conductors? plastic objects? metal objects? wooden objects? glass objects? Make a chart like this one to record your findings:

Object	Made From	Conductor	Nonconductor
Key	metal	X	
Others			

observing **B.** Some objects are made of several materials. With a pencil you can test wood, paint, metal, rubber, and graphite. Which of these will conduct electricity?

observing **C.** Look around the room. What other objects can you test that are made of several materials?

inferring **D.** Make your conductor tester more powerful. Use two batteries end to end. Test some materials again. How do these results compare with your first results?

TEACHING COMMENT

PREPARATION AND BACKGROUND

If the bulb is to operate properly, the wire wrapped around the bulb base should be twisted tightly for good contact.

GENERALIZATION

Metals are usually good conductors of electricity; most other solid materials are nonconductors or poor conductors.

SAMPLE PERFORMANCE OBJECTIVES

Process: The child can classify materials as electrical conductors or nonconductors after testing them with an electrical circuit.

Knowledge: Shown new materials, the child can predict which will, or will not, conduct electricity.

INVESTIGATION: *HOW TO MEASURE BULB BRIGHTNESS*

Have you noticed that a bulb burns less brightly as a battery wears down? A bulb's brightness can help you know how fresh a battery is.

EXPLORATORY PROBLEM

How can you measure the brightness of a lit flashlight bulb?

NEEDED

two sheets of paper   partner
flashlight bulbs   several batteries of the same size (D)
wire (30 centimeters or 12 inches long)   pencil

TRY THIS

1. Have a partner light a bulb with one battery and wire.
2. Tear a small piece from a paper sheet.
3. Hold it tightly against the bulb. Can you see the glow through the paper? (See Figure 5-21.)
4. Tear off another piece of paper. Hold both pieces together tightly against the bulb. Can you still see the glow through the double thickness?

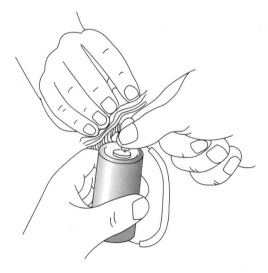

Figure 5-21

5. Keep adding pieces until you cannot see the bulb's glow.

6. Record the largest number of pieces through which you saw a glow.

DISCOVERY PROBLEMS

measuring and classifying

A. Get some batteries of the same size. How can you compare how strong each is? Can you put them in order from weakest to strongest? Record your findings.

predicting and communicating

B. How many times brighter will the bulb be with two batteries? three batteries? Add batteries end to end. The raised button end of each battery should face the same way. Record your findings.

measuring and classifying

C. Get different flashlight bulbs. How can you compare how brightly each burns? Can you put them in order from dimmest to brightest? Record findings. Will someone else get the same results?

TEACHING COMMENT

PREPARATION AND BACKGROUND

Most fresh D-size flashlight batteries can be interchanged and a given bulb will glow with no noticeable difference in brightness. However, as batteries wear down unevenly, the brightness is affected.

GENERALIZATION

The brightness of a flashlight bulb may vary because of its resistance to electricity and the power of the battery.

SAMPLE PERFORMANCE OBJECTIVES

Process: The child can measure the relative brightness of lighted flashlight bulbs.

Knowledge: When shown a lighted bulb that glows dimly, the child can explain that one reason for the dimness may be the weakness of the battery.

ACTIVITY: *HOW CAN YOU MAKE A DIMMER SWITCH?*

NEEDED

graphite (pencil "lead" about 7 centimeters or 3 inches)
circuit tester
sticky tape

TRY THIS

1. Tape each end of the graphite to a table top.
2. Touch the bulb base of the tester to the graphite. Touch the wire end just next to it. The bulb should light.
3. Slowly, move the wire end of the tester along the graphite. Move it first away from the bulb, then back again, as in Figure 5-22.

   a. What happens to the bulb brightness as the graphite connection gets longer? shorter?

   b. Where have you used dimmer switches at home or elsewhere?

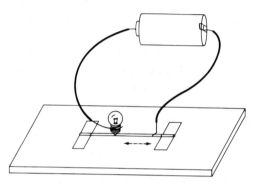

Figure 5-22

TEACHING COMMENT

Graphite from either a mechanical or a cut-apart wooden pencil may be used. Graphite is resistant to electricity. If the tester bulb does not light, try adding one or two more batteries in series.

ACTIVITY: HOW DOES A FUSE WORK?

NEEDED

three D-size batteries
small piece of heavy cardboard
three short wires
two all-metal tacks
flashlight bulb and holder
foil from a gum wrapper
scissors

TRY THIS

1. Prepare the fuse. Cut a piece from the gum wrapper about 4 centimeters (1.6 inch) long and 0.5 centimeter (.2 inch) wide. Leave the paper attached to the foil. Cut a V-shaped nick in the middle of the piece, so there is barely any foil left.

2. Bare the ends of the wires. Also, bare a small section in the middle of two wires.

3. Set up the materials as shown in Figure 5-23.

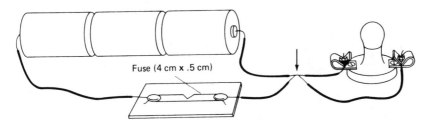

Fuse (4 cm x .5 cm)

Figure 5-23

4. Holding the insulated part of the wire, touch one bare wire part with the other. This makes a short circuit.

   a. What happens to the fuse? to the wires? to the light?

   b. Why do you think it is important to have a fuse in a house current?

ELECTROMAGNET EXPERIENCES
(Concepts page 141)

INVESTIGATION: ELECTROMAGNETS

Suppose you have some wire, a large nail, and a flashlight battery. With these materials you can make a magnet or an electromagnet.

EXPLORATORY PROBLEM

How can you make an electromagnet?

NEEDED

pencil	partner
box of paper clips	large iron nail
wire (2 meters or about 6 feet)	two flashlight batteries

TRY THIS

1. Get a large nail. Touch it to a paper clip to test the nail for magnetism. The nail should be free of magnetism to start.

2. Bare the wire ends. Wrap the wire tightly around the nail. Leave about ½ meter (1½ feet) of wire free at both ends.

3. Have your partner touch the bare wire ends to a battery. (See Figure 5-24.) Touch the nail end to some paper clips. How many paper clips does your electromagnet pick up?

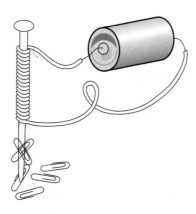

Figure 5-24

4. Have your partner move one wire away from the battery. What happens? *Note:* Do not leave the battery connected for more than 10 seconds each time.

DISCOVERY PROBLEMS

observing

A. Which end of your electromagnet will pick up more clips?

experimenting, communicating and predicting

B. How can you change the strength of your electromagnet? Make a record of what you try and the results. What will happen if you wrap more wire around the nail? What will happen if you take away the iron nail? What will happen if you switch a pencil for the nail? What will happen if you use an aluminum rod instead of the nail? What will happen if you use two batteries end to end?

observing

C. Can an electromagnet attract anything a regular magnet cannot attract?

TEACHING COMMENT

PREPARATION AND BACKGROUND

Use number 22 or 24 bell wire insulated with plastic. Strip off some insulation at both ends so good contact can be made with the battery. A regular D-size flashlight battery works well. Be sure to advise children that the wires should be held to the battery no more than about 10 seconds without interruption. Otherwise, its power will be drained quickly. A 3- to 4-inch iron nail should be adequate for the core of the electromagnet. If possible, get a similar-sized rod of aluminum. It will present an interesting contrast if used in place of the nail.

Most of the materials attracted to an electromagnet fall when the electromagnet is disconnected from the battery. One paper clip or other light item may remain. This shows that there is some magnetism left in the nail.

GENERALIZATION

Electricity flowing through a wire acts like a magnet; its magnetic power can be increased in several ways.

SAMPLE PERFORMANCE OBJECTIVES

Process: The child can state at least one hypothesis about how an electromagnet's strength may be increased.

Knowledge: The child can demonstrate how an electromagnet works.

FOR YOUNGER CHILDREN

Some primary students may have trouble manipulating the materials.

GENERATING ELECTRICITY EXPERIENCES
(Concepts page 143)

INVESTIGATION: *STATIC ELECTRICITY*

When you comb your hair on a dry day, does it crackle and stick to the comb? Have you felt a shock when you touched something after crossing a carpet? These are examples of static electricity. You can get static electricity by rubbing different objects together.

EXPLORATORY PROBLEM

What objects can you rub together to produce static electricity?

NEEDED

plastic spoon and fork   piece of wool and nylon
paper and pencil   sticky tape
heavy string   plastic bag
rubber comb

TRY THIS

1. Attach string to the spoon with sticky tape. Attach it where the spoon balances. Hang the spoon from a table edge. Tape the string end to the table.

2. Hold the fork backward. Bring the fork handle near the hanging spoon handle, but don't touch it (Figure 5-25). Notice that probably nothing happens. So far, there is no static electricity.

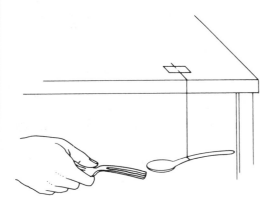

Figure 5-25

3. Rub each handle with some wool. Bring the fork handle near the spoon again. Watch what happens.

4. Rub one handle again with wool but the other with nylon. Watch what happens. (Static electricity may have either a positive [+] or a negative [−] charge. When two objects have the same charge, positive or negative, they *repel* or push each other away. When each has a different charge, they attract each other.)

DISCOVERY PROBLEMS

inferring

A. Did each object in Step 3 have the same charge or did they have different charges? How about in Step 4?

observing and communicating

B. What happens when you rub the handles with different materials? Which combinations make the handles repel? attract? Keep a careful record. To do so, you might set up a chart like this:

Fork Rubbed With	Spoon Rubbed With		
	Wool	Plastic	Nylon
Wool	Repel		
Plastic			
Nylon			

predicting

After you complete the first column, can you predict the remaining results?

experimenting

C. What results will you get if you substitute other objects for the plastic fork? For example, what happens if you rub a rubber comb with each material?

TEACHING COMMENT

BACKGROUND AND PREPARATION

Almost any plastic items may be substituted for the fork and spoon. The use of a heavy string will keep the suspended object from spinning too freely. Students will find that using an unlike material in Problem C will change their findings. Postpone this activity on rainy or especially humid days, as results will be less noticeable.

GENERALIZATION

Rubbing different materials together may produce static electricity. Like charges repel, and unlike charges attract each other.

SAMPLE PERFORMANCE OBJECTIVES

Knowledge: The child can demonstrate that identical objects rubbed with different materials will develop unlike static charges.

Process: The child can use data on a simple chart to predict new data.

INVESTIGATION: *A WAY TO GENERATE ELECTRICITY*

Have you ever seen an electric generator in a power plant? Usually, a huge magnet spins and produces an electric current in a coil of wire. You can even produce a current by moving a small magnet in and out of a small coil of wire. But the current will not be enough to light a bulb. To tell that there is a current, you need a current detector, or *galvanometer.*

EXPLORATORY PROBLEM

How can you generate electricity and tell it is being produced?

NEEDED

insulated wire (12 meters or 13 yards)
magnetic compass
two strong magnets (one stronger)
scissors
sticky tape

TRY THIS

1. Bare the wire ends with scissors.
2. Coil 50 turns of wire around your hand. Slip off the coil and fasten it in three places with sticky tape. This will keep the coil tight.
3. Wrap 20 turns of wire narrowly around the compass. This will be your galvanometer (Figure 5-26).
4. Twist the bare ends of the wire together to close the circuit.
5. Push a magnet end into the coil. See how the compass needle moves. Pull the magnet out of the coil. Watch again how the needle moves. This shows you have

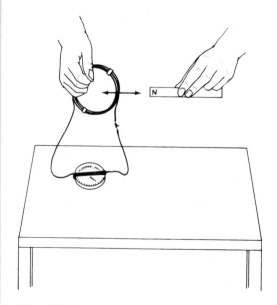

Figure 5-26

generated a current each time. The farther the needle moves, the stronger the current. (However, be sure the magnet is far enough from the compass so it does not *directly* affect it. You want the electricity in the *wires* to move the needle.)

DISCOVERY PROBLEMS

observing   **A.** Does it make any difference if the coil or magnet moves?

observing   **B.** What happens to the needle if you move the magnet faster? slower?

observing   **C.** What difference does it make if you move the magnet's other end?

observing   **D.** How does using a stronger or weaker magnet affect the compass needle?

observing   **E.** How does changing the number of turns in the coil affect the needle?

experimenting   **F.** What is the strongest current you can generate? That is, how far can you make the compass needle move?

TEACHING COMMENT

PREPARATION AND BACKGROUND

By moving the magnet alternately in two directions, the current that is produced also alternates directions. This is shown by the compass needle moving first one way, then the other. The mechanical energy used to move the magnet comes, in this case, from the students. The teaching strategy of the discovery sequence is to give enough experience for students to experiment on their own in F.

GENERALIZATION

An electric current may be generated when a magnet and a wire coil interact. A galvanometer may be used to detect the current.

SAMPLE PERFORMANCE OBJECTIVES

Knowledge: The child can construct a crude galvanometer and use it to detect small differences in electric currents.

Process: The child can generate a stronger electric current by experimenting with several variables.

REFERENCES

American Association for the Advancement of Science. (1993). *Benchmarks for science literacy.* New York: Oxford University Press.

National Research Council. (1996). *National science education standards.* Washington, DC: National Academy Press.

SELECTED TRADE BOOKS: ELECTRICAL ENERGY

For Younger Children

Bailey, M. W. (1978). *Electricity.* Raintree.

Berger, M. (1990). *Switch on, switch off.* Harper Collins.

Bains, R. (1981). *Discovering electricity.* Troll Associates.

Challand, H. (1986). *Experiments with electricity.* Children's Press.

Curren, P. (1977). *I know an electrician.* Putnam.

Lillegard, D., & Stoker, W. (1986). *I can be an electrician.* Children's Press.

Taylor, B. (1991). *Batteries and magnets.* Watts.

Wade, H. (1979). *Electricity.* Raintree.

For Older Children

Ardley, N. (1984). *Discovering electricity.* Watts.

Brandt, K. (1985). *Electricity.* Troll Associates.

Cobb, V. (1986). *More power to you!* Little, Brown.

De Bruin, J. (1985). *Young scientist explores electricity and magnetism.* Good Apple.

Gutnik, M. J. (1986). *Electricity: from Faraday to solar generators.* Watts.

Mackie, D. (1986). *Electricity.* Penworthy.

Math, I. (1981). *Wires and watts.* Scribners.

Provenzo, E. F., & Provenzo, A. B. (1982). *Rediscovering electricity.* Oak Tree.

Stanley, L. R. (1980). *Easy to make electric gadgets.* Harvey.

Taylor, B. (1990). *Electricity and magnets.* Watts.

Vogt, G. (1985). *Electricity and magnetism.* Watts.

Vogt, G. (1986). *Generating electricity.* Watts.

Ward, A. (1986). *Experimenting with batteries, bulbs, and wires.* David & Charles.

Whyman, K. (1986). *Electricity and magnetism.* Watts.

Zubrowski, B. (1991). *Blinkers and buzzers.* Morrow.

Resource Books

Butzow, C. M., & Butzow, J. W. (1989). *Science through children's literature. An integrated approach* (batteries and electric circuit topics, pp. 226–231). Teacher Ideas Press.

Shaw, D. G., & Dybdahl, C. S. (1996). *Integrating science and language arts. A sourcebook for K–6 teachers* (electric circuit topics, pp. 102–103). Allyn and Bacon.

SIMPLE MACHINES AND HOW THEY WORK

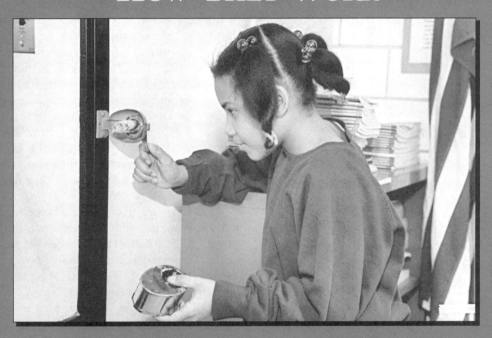

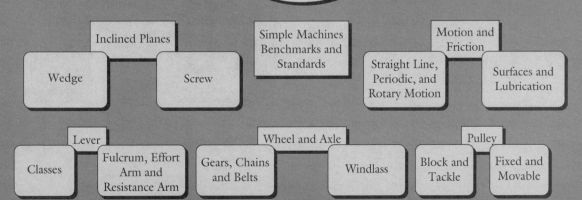

SIMPLE MACHINES AND HOW THEY WORK

Inclined Planes

Simple Machines Benchmarks and Standards

Motion and Friction

Wedge

Screw

Straight Line, Periodic, and Rotary Motion

Surfaces and Lubrication

Lever

Wheel and Axle

Pulley

Classes

Fulcrum, Effort Arm and Resistance Arm

Gears, Chains and Belts

Windlass

Block and Tackle

Fixed and Movable

Imagine a parade of the world's machines including airplanes, tweezers, bulldozers, baby carriages, computers, and egg beaters—almost endless line of inventions without which we would fare far less well. But perhaps the most remarkable thing about these inventions lies in their construction. All machines, no matter how complex, are variations of just six simple machines. These are the inclined plane (ramp), wedge, screw, lever, wheel and axle (windlass), and pulley. We'll consider these machines and the effects of motion and friction on them in this chapter.

Screws and Inclined Planes Concepts
(Experiences p. 181)

For any machine to do work, force must overcome gravity, inertia, molecular cohesion (the binding force that holds materials together), and friction. Machines may be used to reduce the force needed to do work, speed up work, or change the direction of a force.

Inclined Planes

Although they may not have thought about it, even small children have had experiences with inclined planes, such as climbing stairs, walking up a hill, or coasting down a slanted driveway on roller skates. They know from these experiences that it is harder to climb a steep hill than a gradual hill. Children may even unknowingly use the idea that distance may be increased to decrease force, as when a bicycle rider rides diagonally back and forth up a hill. This background of common experiences lets us focus on force/distance relationships fairly quickly when working with inclined planes.

Does an inclined plane or other simple machine make work "easier"? No, if we mean that some part of the total effort is saved. In terms of *work,* or force moving a resistance over a distance, it is impossible to get out of a machine any more than is put into a machine. Another way of saying this is:

Effort times distance equals resistance times distance, or ED = RD.

Let's apply this idea to the inclined plane in Figure 6-1. Suppose we want to push a 50-pound barrel to a height of 5 feet and the inclined plane is 10 feet long. If we were to push the barrel up the incline, it would take less force (25 pounds of force) than if we were to pick it straight up (50 pounds of force.) The total amount of force to move the barrel up the incline would be the distance of the incline, which is 10 feet, times the effort required, which is 25 pounds. This is a total of 250 foot-pounds. Notice that this equals the 250 foot-pounds of work which would be required to lift the barrel straight up a distance of 5 feet times an effort of 50 pounds.

This assumes that we are physically able to do the work in both cases. Yet it *is* easier for us to apply less force for a longer distance and time. Muscles get tired quickly from concentrated, heavy work. It is in that sense, then, that a simple machine makes work "easier."

The reduction of force provided by a simple machine is called its *mechanical advantage.* This is found by *dividing the force of the resistance by*

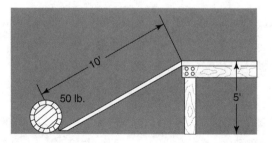

Figure 6-1
An inclined plane.

the force of the effort. In the foregoing example, the mechanical advantage is

$$\frac{R\,(50\ pounds)}{E\,(25\ pounds)} = 2$$

In other words, it is twice as easy to lift the barrel with the inclined plane as without it. Or we can say it takes half as much effort.

Students can make crude measurements to grasp the force/distance relationship. For instance, a string can be used to compare the length of an inclined plane with the height to which it rises. A rubber band attached to an object may have a ruler held beside it to measure different degrees of applied force in terms of "stretch." A spring scale, if available, will be even more effective than a rubber band.

Wedges

A wedge can be thought of as two inclined planes placed back to back. Although the classic use of this machine has waned along with professional rail-splitters and wood-choppers, the wedge principle is employed in many other ways. For example, "streamlining" is a way of better enabling objects to pierce air and water. More speed can be achieved with the same amount of applied force. Paper cutters, knives, pencil sharpeners, nails, and needles are all wedges we use every day for cutting or piercing functions.

Screws

"The screw is just an inclined plane wrapped around a nail." This is what one child said, and it is a fairly accurate description. We usually think of the screw as a nail-like object with a spiral thread that holds together pieces of wood or metal. But other applications of this machine are all around us.

There are spiral staircases, roads that wind around a steep hill or mountain, vises for workbenches, clamps to hold things together,

adjustable piano stools, and the adjustable parts of wrenches, to name just a few. Sometimes a screw is not so obvious, like propellers for ships and airplanes.

When used to lift things, the mechanical advantage of the screw is the greatest of any simple machine. It is relatively easy for a small person to lift up the front of an automobile with a screw-type jack, and jackscrews employed by house movers actually lift entire houses off their foundations. As with an inclined plane, though, the price paid for such a gain in force is increased distance.

Each time a screw is given a complete turn, it advances into a piece of wood or lifts an object only as far as the distance between its threads. This distance is called *pitch* and is illustrated in Figure 6-2. The paired drawings show that two screws of similar size, but different pitches, would vary in the number of times turned if screwed into some wood or used to lift something. We expect a steep spiral staircase to take more effort than a longer, gradual one when walking up to the same height. Likewise, the steeper the pitch of a screw, the more force is needed to make it rotate. However, it advances farther and faster than one with a narrower, more gradual pitch.

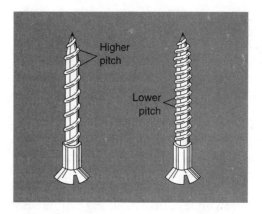

Figure 6-2
The pitch of a screw is the distance between its threads.

The mathematical relationships here are identical to those of other simple machines. Mechanical advantage is again found by dividing resistance by effort.

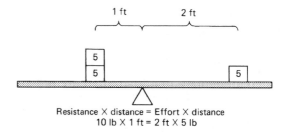

Resistance × distance = Effort × distance
10 lb × 1 ft = 2 ft × 5 lb

Figure 6-3
To find the mechanical advantage of a lever, divide the effort-arm length by the resistance-arm length.

LEVER CONCEPTS
(Experiences page 183)

No one knows who actually first contrived the lever, but it has been known and used for a very long time. The ancient Greek scientist Archimedes is supposed to have said he could move the world if given a long enough lever, a fulcrum, and place to stand. It is widely assumed that primitive people also had knowledge of levers, but probably only in a practical way.

The principles of this simple machine are used in so many ways that a moment's reflection produces surprising examples: The ancient Japanese sport of judo is based on knowledge that the human skeleton is comprised of lever systems. Also, a golfer with long arms may swing the club head faster than a golfer with shorter arms.

Three Parts

The seesaw is a lever familiar to most children. It has three parts: (1) *fulcrum,* or point on which it pivots; (2) *effort arm,* the part on which the force is exerted; and (3) *the resistance,* or load, arm, that part which bears the load to be raised. When the seesaw is perfectly balanced on the fulcrum, the resistance and effort arms will alternate if two equally heavy riders alternately push against the ground to make the seesaw go up and down.

As with other machines, effort times distance (from the fulcrum) equals resistance times distance (from the fulcrum). This is shown in Fig-

ure 6-3. The mechanical advantage in this example is 2. Another way to calculate the mechanical advantage is simply to divide the effort-arm length by the resistance-arm length. Friction is usually so minor in the lever that it does not need to be taken into account.

Primary children can arrive at an intuitive understanding of the "law of levers" if they are given experience with balancing objects.

Three Classes

Levers are found with parts arranged in three different combinations called *classes*. Children do not need to memorize these combinations or even their examples. But analyzing how everyday levers work can sharpen their observation and classification skills. Notice the three arrangements in Figure 6-4. Seesaws, crowbars, and can openers are first-class levers. Two levers of this kind are placed together in tools such as scissors and pliers. By varying the effort-arm length, you change the amount of required force or gain in speed and distance. This type also changes direction of movement. You exert force in a direction opposite to which the load moves. If both effort and resistance arms are equal, however, a first-class lever can change only the direction of a force. Neither

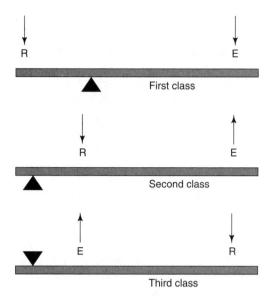

Figure 6-4
Three classes of levers; *R* is resistance, E effort.

reduced force nor gain in speed and distance takes place.

Second-class levers are illustrated by the wheelbarrow and post puller. A nutcracker illustrates joined, double levers of this type. Speed or distance are not as likely to be considerations when using a second-class lever as in the previous case.

Should you forget third-class levers, just think of your arm. Your elbow is the fulcrum, your bicep provides the effort at a point just below and opposite the elbow, and your fist represents the load or resistance. Other common applications are found in the broom, baseball bat, fly swatter, and fishing pole, to name just a few. Sugar or ice cube tongs represent double levers of the class. Analysis of this lever reveals that force is traded to get added speed or distance. With a fishing pole, for example, you want to increase the speed of your hands to hook a nibbling fish securely before it can react and get away.

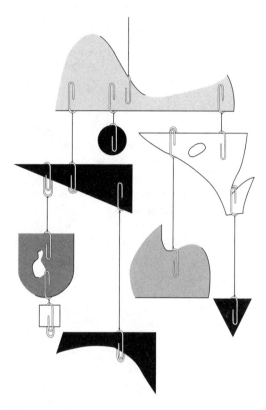

Figure 6-5
A tagboard and paper clip mobile.

Mobiles

A mobile is a combination of several suspended levers with attached figures. In some mobiles, even the figures may function as levers (Figure 6-5).

When children work on mobiles, they may have problems balancing the figures and keeping them from touching. For solutions, they need to think about variables such as figure size and shape, string length, best position for figures, and where to fasten them. This sharpens their thinking skills. Mobiles are also an interesting way to combine artwork with science.

WHEEL AND AXLE CONCEPTS
(Experiences p. 189)

The windlass, or wheel and axle, is a commonly misunderstood simple machine. Although a windlass looks like a wagon wheel and axle, it is different. We put wheels on a wagon to reduce friction by lessening the surface area that comes in contact with the road. Its axles are stationary. Greater "leverage" is indeed present in a large wheel compared to a small wheel. This is why a large wheel can roll over uneven ground more easily than a small wheel. Still, a wagon wheel and axle combination is not regarded as a simple machine.

In a windlass, the axle and wheel are firmly fixed together. Spinning the axle causes the wheel to rotate; force at the axle is traded off to gain an advantage in speed and distance on the outside of the wheel. By turning the wheel, though, an advantage in force can be gained; speed and distance are then reduced or sacrificed at the axle.

A windlass is really a continuous lever on a continuous fulcrum. Therefore, when a handle is placed anywhere on the wheel, it becomes the end of the force arm. The axle's radius is the load arm. Figure 6-6 illustrates this idea.

The theoretical mechanical advantage in a windlass is calculated like that of a lever. If the effort-arm length is 18 inches and resistance arm length is 2 inches, mechanical advantage equals 9. Because friction is so great with a windlass, however, actual mechanical advantage is found only through dividing resistance by effort.

Placing the windlass handle (effort) ever farther away from the axle (fulcrum) decreases needed effort, just as it did with the lever. At the same time, it increases the distance through which the effort is applied.

Understanding the force/distance relationship makes it easy for children to see why a meat grinder needs a longer crank than a pencil sharpener (Figure 6-7), for example, and why a

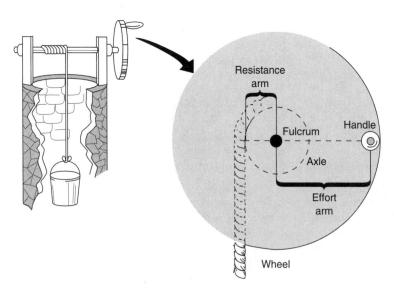

Resistance arm

Fulcrum

Handle

Axle

Effort arm

Wheel

Figure 6-6
A windlass is a lever.

Figure 6-7
A pencil sharpener can be used as a wheel and axle.

large steering wheel is easier to turn than a smaller one.

Gears, Chains, and Belts

Wheel and axle combinations may be modified to interact with one another by using belts, chains, and wheels with toothlike projections (gears). The bicycle is a common example of two modified wheels and axles joined by a chain. Because the front gear, or sprocket, is larger than the rear sprocket, one turn of the larger sprocket forces several or more turns of the smaller rear one. Older students can find the theoretical mechanical advantage of the larger sprocket by counting and comparing the number of teeth on each sprocket.

PULLEY CONCEPTS
(Experiences page 194)

Pulleys for teaching can be bought through science supply houses. Yet in elementary school activities, two clothesline pulleys or two smaller single pulleys, found in most hardware stores, should work just as well. "Single" pulleys have but one grooved wheel or sheave. Some pulleys have two or more sheaves for combined use with other pulleys in heavy lifting.

Fixed and Movable Pulleys

As its name implies, a *fixed pulley* is securely fastened to some object. A *movable pulley* moves vertically—or laterally, as the case may be—with the load (Figure 6-8).

The pulley's similarity to a lever and windlass is diagrammed in Figure 6-8. As with a windlass, the wheel-like arrangement is really a continuous lever.

Observe why a fixed pulley can do no more than change the direction of a force. Like a seesaw whose fulcrum is centered, the effort arm and resistance arm are of equal length. There is no useful mechanical advantage. If one foot of rope is pulled downward, the resistance moves upward one foot. This happens, for example, when a flag is raised on a flagpole.

Notice why a movable pulley offers a theoretical mechanical advantage of two. The resistance arm is only half the effort-arm length. Like a wheelbarrow, this is a variation of a second-class lever. Distance is traded for decreased effort. We must pull the rope two feet for each foot the load is lifted.

Block and Tackle

By placing a fixed and movable pulley in combination, we are able not only to change the direction of a force but also to decrease the force necessary to lift a load. Such an arrangement is called a *block and tackle* (Figure 6-9). By adding more movable pulleys (or pulleys with two or more sheaves), effort can be reduced even further.

Friction finally limits how far we can go in adding pulleys to reduce effort. It can be partly overcome by greasing or oiling the axle.

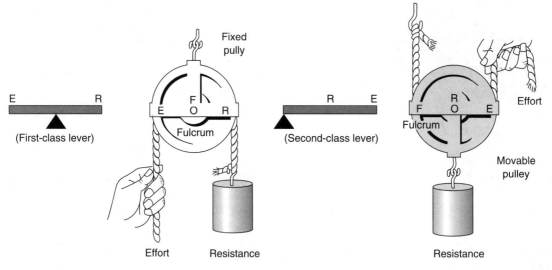

Figure 6-8
A fixed pulley offers no mechanical advantage because its effort and resistance arms are equally long. A movable pulley, however, does make work easier because its resistance arm is only half the length of the effort arm.

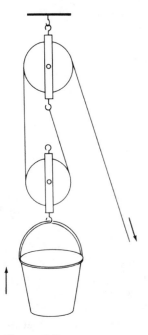

Figure 6-9
Block and tackle.

Since each rope in a block-and-tackle setup supports an equal fraction of a load, it is easy to know the theoretical mechanical advantage. Two supporting ropes have a mechanical advantage of two, three ropes three, and so on. Because of friction, though, actual mechanical advantage must be calculated through dividing resistance by effort, as with all simple machines.

Students may use a rubber band (or spring scale) in the activities to measure differences in the force needed to lift things with pulleys. To attach a rubber band, first fashion a paper-clip hook. Simply pierce or loop the pulley cord at the place where you wish to measure needed force, insert the hook, and then attach a rubber band to it. As before, a ruler can measure the amount of stretch.

MOTION AND FRICTION CONCEPTS
(Experiences p. 196)

Most machines we use are *complex;* that is, they are combinations of simple machines. It is interesting to see how these machines and their parts move and interact.

Three Basic Motions

Some machines have mainly a *straight-line motion.* A few examples are toy or real trains, bicycle (turning requires some leaning), roller skates, and steamrollers.

Some machines or their parts make a repeated forward and backward movement called *periodic motion.* The pendulum in a grandfather clock is one example. Others are a swing, a mechanical walking doll, a metronome, and some lawn sprinklers.

A number of machines or their parts make a continuous spinning motion in one direction as they work. This is *rotary motion.* A few examples are the merry-go-round, the turntable on a record player, a rotary lawn sprinkler, and clock hands.

It can be fascinating to examine mechanical toys and other machines. Their parts are designed to produce a particular motion and, in some cases, to change it.

Any moving machine or part continues to produce its designed motion unless another force is applied to alter, reverse, or stop it. When we rotate a telephone dial, for instance, a metal stop prevents us from going beyond one rotation. A spring then returns the dial to its original position. Also, the front wheel of a moving bicycle may be turned by applying a force to the handlebars. But what happens if the force is applied too strongly? Perhaps painful experience has taught you that bicycle

and rider will continue in a straight line until road friction finally stops both.

Friction

Accompanying all motion is *friction,* the resistance produced when two surfaces rub together. No surface is perfectly smooth. The tiny ridges in a "smooth" surface, or the larger bumps and hollows in a rough one, catch and resist when the surfaces rub together. The mutual attraction of molecules on the opposing surfaces also adds to the resistance we call friction. Surface pressure is another condition that affects friction. A heavy object has more friction than a lighter one.

Lubricating a surface is effective because the oil or grease fills in the spaces between ridges and bumps. Opposing surfaces mostly slide against the lubricant rather than rubbing against each other.

In many machines, ball bearings or roller bearings are used to change sliding friction to rolling friction. Rolling friction is less than sliding friction because a load-bearing rolling object rolls over tiny surface ridges or bumps rather than catching against them.

Friction reduces a machine's efficiency by robbing some of its power (and so its energy). It also creates heat as surfaces rub and wears out parts. But not all of its effects are bad. Friction also allows us to brake a car or bicycle, walk or run, or write on paper. A frictionless world would create far more problems than it would solve.

SIMPLE MACHINES BENCHMARKS AND STANDARDS

Practical examples of the uses of simple machines will help reinforce the types of simple machines and how they can be used in combination with each other. Forces and motion related to the use of simple machines are common themes, as evidenced in the following sample Benchmarks and Standards:

SAMPLE BENCHMARKS (AAAS, 1993).

■ The way to change how something is moving is to give it a push or a pull (by Grades K–2, p. 89).

■ Something that is moving may move steadily or change its direction. The greater the force is, the greater the change in motion will be.

The more massive an object is, the less effect a given force will have (by Grades 3–5, p. 89).

SAMPLE STANDARDS (NRC, 1996).

■ The position and motion of objects can be changed by pushing or pulling. The size of the change is related to the strength of the push or pull (by Grades K–4, p. 127).

■ The motion of an object can be described by its position, direction of motion, and speed. That motion can be measured and represented on a graph (by Grades 5–8, p. 154).

INVESTIGATIONS AND ACTIVITIES

SCREWS AND INCLINED PLANES
EXPERIENCES

(Concepts p. 172)

INVESTIGATION: *INCLINED PLANES*

It is easier to walk up a steep hill or a low hill? Suppose both hills were the same height, but one was twice as long. Which would be easier then? A hill is a kind of *inclined plane.*

EXPLORATORY PROBLEM

How can you measure the force needed to use an inclined plane?

NEEDED

flat board (60 centimeters or 2 feet)   seven same-sized books
flat board (120 centimeters or 4 feet)   paper clip
rubber band (or spring scale)   roller skate
ruler

TRY THIS

1. Lay an end of the smaller board on one book (Figure 6-10).

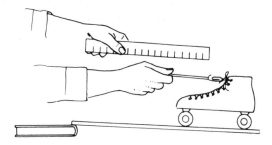

Figure 6-10

2. Place a roller skate on the board. Hook a bent paper clip around the tied shoelace. Attach a rubber band.

3. Pull the skate slowly up the board. Measure with a ruler how much the rubber band stretches. (Or measure the pull with a spring scale.)

4. Now make the inclined plane or "hill" three books high. Do Steps 2 and 3 again.

DISCOVERY PROBLEMS

measuring   **A.** What was the difference in rubber band stretch in the two trials?

measuring   **B.** How much stretch will there be with "hills" of different heights? Measure also a height of two books, then five and six books. (Do not measure four books now.) Record what you find on a graph such as this:

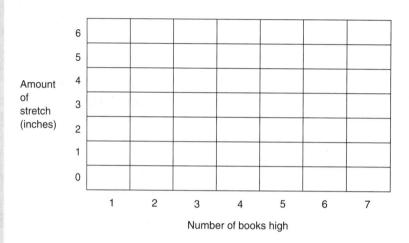

predicting   **C.** Examine your graph data for heights of one, two, three, five, and six books. Can you predict the stretch for four books? Write this down and then test your prediction.

predicting   **D.** Examine your data again. Can you predict the stretch for seven books?

predicting   **E.** Switch this board for one twice as long. Suppose you used one through seven books again. What do you think your results would be? Write down your ideas and then test them.

inferring   **F.** What pictures of different inclined planes can you bring to school?

TEACHING COMMENT

BACKGROUND AND PREPARATION

One long board, rather than two different-sized boards, can be used to demonstrate how changing board lengths affects the force needed to go up a given height. The books may first be placed under the midpoint of the board, and the board tilted. The tilted part beyond the books may be ignored. However, this can confuse some students, especially the younger ones. Pairs of boards of almost any lengths may be used, but the larger one should be twice as long as the smaller one.

A spring scale is likely to yield more accurate measurements than a rubber band. A rubber band may not stretch uniformly and, of course, does not indicate force in standard units. Try several rubber bands to select one that stretches easily for heights of one to seven books. If needed, snip and use a single strand.

Two kinds of predicting occur in this investigation. In Problem C, the child predicts *within* the data (interpolating); in D, the child predicts *beyond* the data (extrapolating).

GENERALIZATION

The force needed to go up an inclined plane increases with height and decreases with distance.

SAMPLE PERFORMANCE OBJECTIVES

Knowledge: The child can state that doubling the length of an inclined board halves the force needed to go up a given height.

Process: The child can accurately predict needed force within and beyond graphed data for an inclined plane.

FOR YOUNGER CHILDREN

Try the activity without the graphing of data. Younger students generally notice and understand why there are differences in rubber band stretch.

LEVER EXPERIENCES
(Concepts p. 174)

INVESTIGATION: *SOME COMMON LEVERS*

Have you used a baseball bat? a seesaw? a house broom? These and many other things we use are examples of *levers*. How levers work can be surprising. Some that look almost alike work differently. Some that look different work the same way.

EXPLORATORY PROBLEM

How can you tell in which ways levers are alike and different?

NEEDED

Real or picture examples of levers in everyday things (canoe paddle, crowbar, paper cutter, baseball bat, seesaw, post puller, house broom, can opener, wheelbarrow, tennis racket, golf club, boat oar)

TRY THIS

1. Figure 6-11 shows a fishing pole in action. Notice how this lever is used. The tip carries the load or resistance (R). The opposite end, which is held, moves very

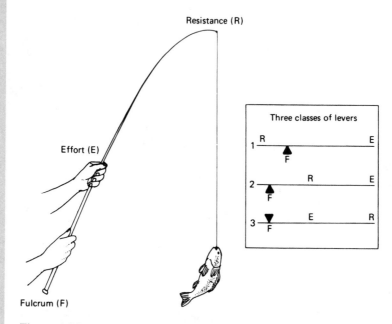

Figure 6-11

little. This is the fulcrum (F). To pull up the resistance takes effort (E). This happens *between* the fulcrum and resistance.

2. Study the three smaller drawings in Figure 6-11. Levers can be grouped into three classes, depending on how they are used. Each group has a place for the fulcrum, resistance, and effort. But notice that, in each group, the placement of these points is different. This is a good way to tell them apart.

DISCOVERY PROBLEMS

classifying **A.** In which group does the fishing pole belong?

classifying **B.** Examine real or picture examples of many levers. Use them, or think of how they are used. In which group does each belong? Here's a way to record what you find:

Lever	1. RFE	2. FRE	3. FER
Fishing pole			✓
Paper cutter			
Others			

inferring   **C.** Which of these levers are really alike?

classifying   **D.** Examine the bottom half of your arm. It is a lever, also. In which group does it belong?

inferring   **E.** Play a game with some friends. Think of a common lever. Can they find out what it is by asking questions? You can answer only yes or no. If they get stuck, act out the way it is used. (A good way for them to begin is to find out the load–fulcrum–effort order.)

classifying   **F.** What other real or picture examples can you find? In which group does each belong?

TEACHING COMMENT

BACKGROUND AND PREPARATION

It is the *internal* order of resistance–fulcrum–effort that counts in classifying levers. So there is no difference between R–F–E or E–F–R, for example (this may be a difficult concept for a few students).

It is not important for children to memorize the internal order of each class. But it is worthwhile for them to develop skill in observing and classifying likenesses and differences in objects.

In Problem D, the part played by the upper arm muscle (bicep) in moving the forearm may be confusing. The actual pull on the *forearm* is just below and opposite the elbow on the inside.

GENERALIZATION

Levers may be grouped by where places on each are used for the resistance, fulcrum, and effort.

SAMPLE PERFORMANCE OBJECTIVES

Knowledge: The child can demonstrate where to place a lever on a fulcrum to reduce effort.

Process: The child can classify examples of levers into three groups by how they work.

INVESTIGATION: *SOME COMMON DOUBLE LEVERS*

Scissors are an example of a double lever that has cutting parts. We use many tools that are double levers. How many can you name or describe? Some that look almost alike work differently. Some that look different work about the same way.

EXPLORATORY PROBLEM

How can you tell in which ways double levers are alike and different?

NEEDED

pliers	tweezers
lemon squeezer	nutcracker
sugar tongs	tin snips

TRY THIS

1. Figure 6-12 shows a pair of scissors. Notice how the parts are used, especially the cutting parts. When you cut something, it resists being cut. So each part that does this work is called the *resistance* (R).

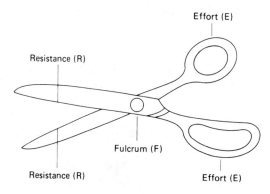

Figure 6-12

2. Notice where the two parts of the scissors join and pivot. This is the *fulcrum* (F).

3. Observe the handles in action. To cut something requires force or effort, so each of these parts is called the *effort* (E).

DISCOVERY PROBLEMS

observing **A.** All tools that are double levers have parts for the resistance (R), fulcrum (F), and effort (E). But they are not always in that order. Examine some real or picture examples of double-lever tools. Which tools are arranged differently? How many different arrangements do you find?

classifying **B.** You can classify these and other double levers by how the three parts are arranged. In which group will each fit? Here's a way to record what you find:

Double Lever	1. RFE	2. FRE	3. FER
Scissors	✓		
Pliers			
Others			

inferring   **C.** Can you name parts of your body that work like a double lever?

classifying   **D.** What other real or picture examples of double levers can you find? In which group does each belong?

TEACHING COMMENT

BACKGROUND AND PREPARATION

In classifying double levers, it is the *internal* order of the resistance–fulcrum–effort that counts, just as it did with single levers. There is no difference between R–F–E and E–F–R, for example.

GENERALIZATION

Double levers may be grouped by how places on each are used for the resistance, fulcrum, and effort.

SAMPLE PERFORMANCE OBJECTIVES

Knowledge: The child can explain where the places are on double levers for the resistance, fulcrum, and effort.

Process: The child can classify examples of double levers into three groups by how they work.

INVESTIGATION: *THE MAKING OF A MOBILE*

Notice the balanced group of objects in Figure 6-13. This is a *mobile*. The word means "something that moves." Even a tiny breeze can move the objects. They may almost seem to be alive!

What kind of mobile objects would you like to make? Fishes, birds, butterflies, balloons, and airplanes are all fun to do. You can even use cutout letters of your name.

EXPLORATORY PROBLEM

How can you make a mobile?

NEEDED

plastic soda straws
tagboard
thin knitting yarn
sticky tape
paper clips
ruler
scissors
crayons or paints and brushes

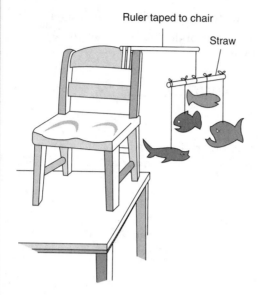

Ruler taped to chair

Straw

Figure 6-13

TRY THIS

1. Cut some strings of yarn 20 to 30 centimeters (8 to 12 inches) long.

2. Tie one end of each string to a paper clip.

3. Decide what kind of objects to hang. Then cut three or four objects from tagboard.

4. Set up a place to hang your mobile. Tape a ruler to a chair. Put the chair on a table.

5. Hang the objects from a straw with yarn. Loop the yarn once around the straw. Make half a knot. Then, pull the yarn tight. Clip the paper clip to each object in the usual way.

6. Try to balance the objects. Slide the yarn on the straw. Change where each object is clipped if necessary.

DISCOVERY PROBLEMS

experimenting and hypothesizing

A. How can you make a mobile with more straws and objects? It will help to draw your mobile on paper first. Start with a few materials. Add more later. Think about these things:

What can you do to balance your objects?

How can you keep the objects from touching?

How big should each object be? What shape? Where should each be placed?

How long should each string be? Where is it best to clip the string on each object?

hypothesizing

B. How can you color your objects with crayons or paints?

TEACHING COMMENT

PREPARATION AND BACKGROUND

Making mobiles is an interesting way to combine artwork with valuable concepts about balance.

GENERALIZATION

For mobile objects to balance, we consider variables such as object size and shape, weight, string length, best positions for the objects, and where to fasten them.

SAMPLE PERFORMANCE OBJECTIVES

Process: When shown a simple unbalanced mobile, the child can infer which variable or variables need attention.

Knowledge: The child can explain how to make a mobile.

FOR OLDER CHILDREN

Invite older children to use common, but light, three-dimensional objects for mobiles (bottle caps, empty milk cartons, wire hangers) in multiple tiers.

WHEEL AND AXLE EXPERIENCES
(Concepts p. 176)

ACTIVITY: *HOW DOES A SCREWDRIVER HANDLE MAKE WORK EASIER?*

NEEDED

screwdriver with round handle
masking tape
piece of soft wood
screw
hammer

TRY THIS

1. Tap in the screw so it sticks into the wood.

2. Hold the screwdriver below the handle at the steel shank. Try to turn the screw.

3. Now hold the handle. Again, try to turn the screw.

   a. Which was easier?

   b. Maybe your hand slipped on the smooth steel shank. Probably it did not slip on the handle. What will happen if you wrap tape around both parts and try again?

   c. Which is easier this time?

4. Look at the screwdriver on end from the steel tip toward the handle. Notice the difference in width between the steel shank and the handle.

   d. Why do you think it is easier to turn a screw using the handle rather than using the shank?

INVESTIGATION: *WHEEL–BELT SYSTEMS*

Have you ever noticed how bicycle gears turn? The two gears are connected by a chain. When you push one gear around, the other moves too.

A gear is just a wheel with teeth. There are many ways to connect wheels. Often, they are connected with belts. Several connected wheels are called a *wheel–belt system*. You can make your own wheel–belt system with spools and rubber bands.

EXPLORATORY PROBLEM

How can you make a wheel–belt system?

NEEDED

four empty sewing spools
four finishing nails
crayon

board (about the size of this page)
our rubber bands
hammer

TRY THIS

1. Pound four nails into the board as shown in Figure 6-14.

2. Make one crayon dot on the rim of each spool.

3. Put a spool on each of two nails.

4. Place a rubber band around the two spools.

5. Turn one spool. Watch the other spool turn too.

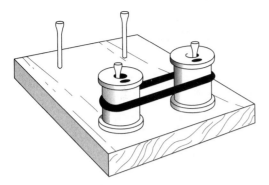

Figure 6-14

DISCOVERY PROBLEMS

predicting **A.** How will the spools turn when connected in different ways? Notice the drawings in Figure 6-15. Each set of spools starts with the left spool. An arrow shows how each is turning. Another spool in the set has a question mark. It is next to a dot on the spool rim. See how the spools are connected.

Will the dot on the rim turn left or right? Make a record of what you think. Then use your wheel–belt board to find out.

predicting **B.** Notice the Figure 6-16 drawings. How should the spools be connected to turn in these ways? How many different connections can you think of? Make drawings of what you think. Then, use your wheel–belt board to find out if they work.

experimenting **C.** What wheel–belt systems can you invent? Make up and trade some problems with friends. Fix your board so you can use more spools.

Teaching Comment

PREPARATION AND BACKGROUND

Part of an end piece from a discarded vegetable crate is ideal for the wheel–belt system base. Be sure that only finishing nails are pounded into the wood. These nails have small heads, allowing the spools to slip easily over them.

Note that this investigation deals only with the direction the spools turn. By using different-sized spools, children also can study how size governs the speed of turning. Because much slipping will happen with the rubber bands, the size–speed relationship cannot be determined accurately. Children can get the idea better by inverting a bicycle and studying the relative turnings of the large gear and the small gear.

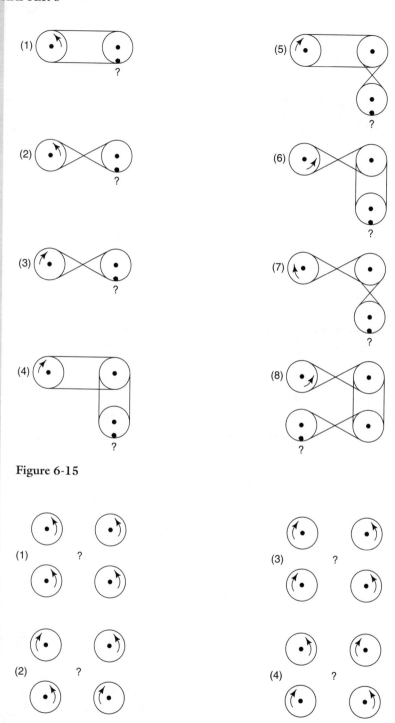

Figure 6-15

Figure 6-16

GENERALIZATION

A wheel–belt system can be used to change the direction of a force.

SAMPLE PERFORMANCE OBJECTIVES

Process: When shown a two-, three-, or four-wheel–belt system, the child can predict the direction each wheel will turn.

Knowledge: The child can point out some everyday examples of wheel–belt systems or their equivalents.

FOR YOUNGER CHILDREN

Many primary students work well with wheel–belt systems. But use fewer spools than with older children.

ACTIVITY: *HOW DO BICYCLE GEARS AFFECT SPEED?*

NEEDED

10-speed bicycle   chalk

TRY THIS

1. Observe the different-sized gears or sprockets on the rear wheel. Notice that all are smaller than the large pedal sprocket. See how a chain connects the large sprocket with a smaller one.
2. Adjust the chain so it is on the largest of the small gears.
3. Turn the bicycle upside down. Face the chain side.
4. Move the near pedal around. Notice how the rear wheel turns.
   a. How many times does the wheel turn compared to the pedal? Chalk a spot on the rear tire. Crank the pedal around one full turn. Count the turns made by the chalked wheel.
5. Adjust the chain so it is on the smallest rear gear. (You may have to set the bicycle upright to do so.)
   b. Crank the pedal one full turn. How many times does the rear wheel turn now?
   c. How does changing the rear gear size affect how fast you can go?

TEACHING COMMENT

Ten-speed bicycles have two different-sized front sprockets. When the smaller one is used, it causes the pedals to revolve faster. This decreases the forward speed, but allows less force to be used. For simplicity, use only one front sprocket in this activity.

PULLEY EXPERIENCES
(Concepts p. 177)

INVESTIGATION: *HOW PULLEYS WORK*

Many people use *pulleys* to help them work. Have you used a pulley to raise and lower a flag on a flagpole? Painters and roofers use pulleys to haul supplies up and down. Sometimes people work with only a single pulley, but often two or more are used together.

EXPLORATORY PROBLEM

How can you set up one or more pulleys to lift a load?

NEEDED

two single-wheel pulleys
sticky tape
rubber band or spring scale
book
strong cord
ruler
broom handle or stick
scissors
paper clip

TRY THIS

1. Make a place to hang the pulley. Lay a stick over the backs of two separated chairs. Use tape to keep it from sliding. Loop and tie cord around the stick. Hang a pulley from the loop.
2. Set up a single pulley as shown in Figure 6-17(A). This is a fixed pulley. Use a book for the load. Pull the cord *down* to lift the load. Practice a few times.
3. Now set up the pulley differently, as shown in Figure 6-17(B). This is a *movable* pulley. Pull the cord *up* to lift the load. Practice a few times.

DISCOVERY PROBLEMS

observing

A. What differences do you notice in using both pulleys?

measuring

B. Which takes less force to lift the load, the fixed or movable pulley? How much less? To measure, hook a rubber band to the pull cord with a paper clip. Measure the stretch with a ruler, or use a spring scale.

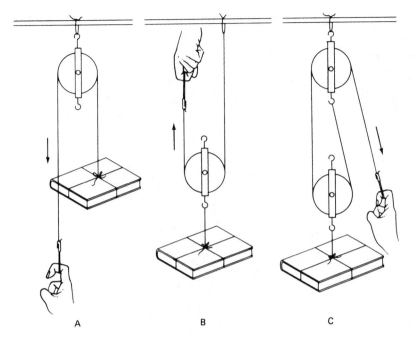

A   B   C

Figure 6-17

measuring

C. How far must you pull the cord to lift the load 1 meter (3 feet) with each pulley? Measure length of pull from where the cord leaves the pulley.

predicting

D. See Figure 6-17(C). It shows a fixed and a movable pulley working together. This is a *block and tackle*. Which do you think takes less force to lift a load: a single fixed pulley or a block and tackle? How far must you pull the cord with each to lift the book 1 meter (3 feet)? Predict and then measure to answer each question.

predicting and measuring

E. Compare the block and tackle with the single movable pulley. Which do you think takes less force to lift a load? How far must you pull the cord with each to lift the book 1 meter (3 feet)? Predict and then measure to answer each question.

observing

F. What examples of pulleys can you find in the classroom? school? How do they work?

observing

G. What other pulleys can you collect and try? How do they compare with the three pulleys of this investigation?

TEACHING COMMENT

BACKGROUND AND PREPARATION

If a spring scale is used, be sure the load does not exceed its capacity.

If you plan to do this investigation in a whole-group setting, consider placing the broomstick holder and supporting chairs on a table. This will help students to get a clearer view.

GENERALIZATION

A fixed pulley changes the direction of a force. A movable pulley reduces force needed to lift a load.

SAMPLE PERFORMANCE OBJECTIVES

Knowledge: The pupil can set up a block and tackle to lift a load.

Process: The child can measure the difference in force applied, and the distance a rope is pulled, with a single and fixed pulley.

FOR YOUNGER CHILDREN

Let younger students experience the basic activity and manipulate the block and tackle.

MOTION AND FRICTION EXPERIENCES
(Concepts page 179)

ACTIVITY: *HOW DO MACHINES AND THEIR PARTS MOVE?*

NEEDED

magazine pictures of different machines
toy machines

INTRODUCTION

Some machines move mostly in a straight line when they work, such as a locomotive and roller skates. Some machines or their parts go back and forth, such as a grandfather clock and swing. Some machines or their parts go around, such as a merry-go-round and bicycle wheel.

TRY THIS

1. Find pictures of machines and machine parts in magazines.
2. Cut out and group the pictures by how the machines or their parts seem to move.

    a. Which machines or parts move mostly in a straight line?

    b. Which go back and forth?

    c. Which spin or go around as they work?

    d. Which machines do all of these things? some of these things?

    e. How do some toy machines and their parts move?

3. Look for real examples of machines working. Watch how they and their parts move. Make a record of what you find out.

    f. What machine can you make up and draw? How will your machine or its parts move? What work will it do?

INVESTIGATION: *PENDULUMS*

Have you ever seen an old-fashioned grandfather clock? One kind has a long weighted rod underneath that swings back and forth. The swinging part is called a *pendulum.* You can keep time with your own pendulum made with a string.

EXPLORATORY PROBLEM

How can you make a string pendulum?

NEEDED

thin string (about 1 meter or 1 yard long)
meter stick or yardstick
pencil
three heavy washers
paper clip
clock or watch with second hand
sticky tape
graph paper

TRY THIS

1. Tape a pencil to a table edge so it sticks out.

2. Bend a paper clip into a hook shape. Tie one string end to the hook.

3. Loop the free end of the string once around the pencil. Tape the string end to the table top.

4. Put two washers on the hook (Figure 6-18).

5. Move the washers to one side and then let go. Each time the washers swing back to that side, count one swing. Be sure the string does not rub against the table edge.

DISCOVERY PROBLEMS

measuring

          A. How many swings does the pendulum make in one minute? Have someone

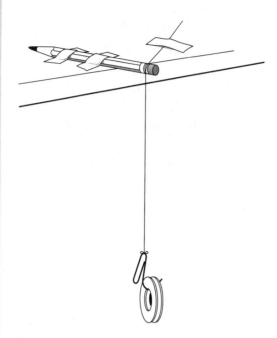

Figure 6-18

help by observing the second hand on a clock. Then you can count the swings.

hypothesizing

B. Do wide swings take more time than narrow swings? Suppose you let go of your pendulum far to one side. What difference might that make in the number of swings it takes in one minute?

hypothesizing

C. Does the amount of weight used change the swing time? What might happen if you use a one-washer weight? a three-washer weight?

hypothesizing

D. Does the length of string used make a difference in swing time? (Measure length from the pencil to the end of the washers.) What might happen if you use a short string? longer string?

experimenting

E. How can you get your pendulum to swing 60 times in 1 minute?

inferring

F. Suppose you had a grandfather clock that was running slow. What could you do to its pendulum to correct it? What if it was running fast?

communicating, predicting, and experimenting

G. How well can you predict with your pendulum? Make a graph such as the one shown in Figure 6-19. Try several string lengths for your pendulum. Count the swings for each length. Let's say you find that a 20-centimeter string swings 65 times in 1 minute. Make a mark on your graph where lines running from these two numbers meet. (See Figure 6-19.) Make marks for three or four other string lengths and their swings. Then draw a straight line between the marks. Suppose you know the length of a pendulum, but you have not yet tried it. How can you use your graph to predict its number of swings? Suppose you know the number of swings of a pendulum, but you have not yet measured its length. How can you use your graph to predict the pendulum's length? How can you make your predictions more accurate?

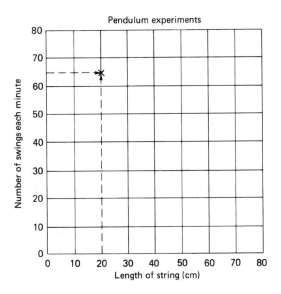

Figure 6-19

TEACHING COMMENT

PREPARATION AND BACKGROUND

The timing of events is possible with a pendulum because its to-and-fro motion recurs with near-perfect regularity. Through manipulating variables, children can discover that the *length* of the weighted string affects the swing rate, or period, of a pendulum. Be sure your students realize that one complete swing consists of the swing out *and* return movement.

GENERALIZATION

A pendulum is any object that swings regularly back and forth; its length affects its swing rate.

SAMPLE PERFORMANCE OBJECTIVES

Process: The child can accurately predict the swing rate of a pendulum for one minute by using graph data.

Knowledge: The child can state how to increase and decrease the swing rate of a pendulum.

FOR YOUNGER CHILDREN

An easy way for younger students to see the effect of manipulating a variable is to set up two identical pendulums. When both are set to swinging, they should perform in the same way. Thereafter, change only one variable at a time with one pendulum—weight or width of swing or length—so its performance may be contrasted with the unchanged pendulum. This strategy can keep the investigation concrete and understandable from the beginning through Problem D or E.

INVESTIGATION: *FRICTION*

Suppose someone asks you to slide a wooden box across the floor. On what kind of floor surface would it be easiest to start the box sliding? hardest? When an object catches or drags on a surface, we say much *friction* is present. If it slides or moves easily, little friction is present.

EXPLORATORY PROBLEM

How can you find out about the friction of different surfaces?

NEEDED

two same-sized wooden blocks
ruler
thumb tack
sticky tape
thin rubber band
three wide rubber bands

paper clip
two round pencils
sheets of sandpaper
waxed paper
kitchen foil
construction paper

TRY THIS

1. Place a wood block on a wood table. Fasten a rubber band to it with a thumb tack.
2. Hook the rubber band with an opened paper clip. Hold the rubber band end over the end of a ruler. (See Figure 6-20.)

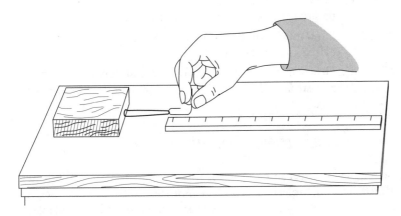

Figure 6-20

3. Pull the rubber band very slowly. Observe where the rubber band end is over the ruler. How far does the band stretch before the block moves? Read the ruler to the nearest whole number. Always make the reading *before* the block starts to slide.

DISCOVERY PROBLEMS

measuring

A. How much will the rubber band stretch if you pull the block a second time? a third time? Record the results and the average for the three trials as shown below:

Surface Tested	Stretch for Each Trial (cm)	Average Stretch (cm)	Predicted Stretch
Wood	11 15 13	13	
Others			

measuring and predicting **B.** How much will the band stretch if the block is placed on other surfaces? Tape a small piece of kitchen foil to the table and place the block on it. Test this and other surfaces such as sandpaper, waxed paper, or construction paper. (To prepare a rubber surface, wrap three wide rubber bands around the block.) Try to predict first how far the band will stretch each time. Record the results.

measuring **C.** How much will the band stretch if the block is placed on its side? if a second block is put on top?

measuring **D.** How much will the band stretch if two round pencils are placed under the block?

experimenting **E.** How can you make the most friction between the block and surface? least friction? (Use more materials if necessary.)

TEACHING COMMENT

Two identical wooden play blocks can be used for this investigation, or cut 2 4-inch squares from a 2-inch by 4-inch piece of wood. A *thin* rubber band works best to pull with. To make it even stretchier, cut and use it as a single strand. If available, a spring scale may be used to compare results. There should be little relative difference, although the spring scale may be calibrated in ounces or grams. *Caution:* Make sure the tack that holds the rubber band to the block is secure before the band is pulled.

GENERALIZATION

Friction between two surfaces depends on the force that presses the surfaces together and the materials that make up the surfaces; some surfaces have more friction than others.

SAMPLE PERFORMANCE OBJECTIVES

Process: The child can measure with a ruler how much a rubber band stretches to test the friction between a wooden block and the surface on which it rests.

Knowledge: The child can predict that a smooth surface will have less friction than a rougher one.

FOR YOUNGER CHILDREN

Younger students may not be ready to use a ruler for measurements. Instead, they may mark a piece of paper, in place of a ruler, to show the rubber band's relative amounts of stretch. Before this is done, allow time for them to play with and become familiar with the different materials.

REFERENCES

American Association for the Advancement of Science. (1993). *Benchmarks for science literacy.* New York: Oxford University Press.

National Research Council. (1996). *National science education standards.* Washington, DC: National Academy Press.

SELECTED TRADE BOOKS: SIMPLE MACHINES AND HOW THEY WORK

For Younger Children

Barton, B. (1987). *Machines at work.* Harper & Row.

Gibbons, G. (1982). *Tool book.* Holiday House.

Kiley, D. (1980). *Biggest machines.* Raintree.

Lampton, C. (1991). *Sailboats, flag poles, cranes: using pulleys as simple machines.* Millbrook Press.

Lauber, P. (1987). *Get ready for robots.* Scholastic.

Rockwell, A., & Rockwell, H. (1985). *Machines.* Harper & Row.

Robbins, K. (1983). *Tools.* Macmillan.

Wade, H. (1979a). *Gears.* Raintree.

Wade, H. (1979b). *The lever.* Raintree.

Weiss, H. (1983). *The world of machines.* Raintree.

Wilkin, F. (1986). *Machines.* Children's Press.

Wyler, R. (1988). *Science fun with toy cars and trucks.* Messner.

For Older Children

Adkins, J. (1980). *Moving heavy things.* Houghton.

Baines, R. (1985). *Simple machines.* Troll Associates.

Barrett, N. S. (1985). *Robots.* Watts.

Brown, W. F., & Brown, M. G. (1984). *Experiments with common wood and tools.* Macmillan.

Fleisher, P., & Keeler, P. (1991). *Looking inside: Machines and constructions.* Macmillan.

Gardner, R. (1980). *This is the way it works.* Doubleday.

Hellman, H. (1971). *The lever and the pulley.* Lippincott.

James, E., & Barkin, C. (1975). *The simple facts of simple machines.* Lothrop.

Jupo, F. (1972). *The story of things (tools).* Prentice-Hall.

Lefkowitz, R. J. (1975). *Push, pull, stop, go: A book about forces and motion.* Parents.

Taylor, B. (1990). *Force and movement.* Watts.

Weiss, H. (1983). *Machines and how they work.* Harper & Row.

Resource Books

Butzow, C. M., & Butzow, J. W. (1989). *Science through children's literature. An integrated approach* (force and movement topics, pp. 197–199). Teacher Ideas Press.

Shaw, D. G., & Dybdahl, C. S. (1996). *Integrating science and language arts. A sourcebook for K–6 teachers* (wheel and gear topics, pp. 96–100). Allyn and Bacon.

CHAPTER 7

PLANT LIFE AND ENVIRONMENT

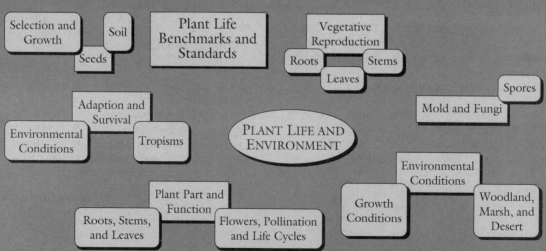

"Chances for open-ended experiments are greater with plants than with any other area of elementary school science." That is what one longtime teacher said, and we agree. At the same time, there is more need for planning ahead and keeping track of activities so that they may be interrelated. Living things take time to grow, and growth rates can seldom be exactly predicted.

The most complex and familiar plants we see are those that produce seeds, of which there are two basic groups. One group is the *gymnosperms*. These plants are flowerless; they develop seeds attached to open scales or cones. Evergreens such as pine, hemlock, spruce, juniper, fir, and redwood are examples of gymnosperms. There are about 600 species.

The second and far larger group (about 250,000 species) is the *angiosperms*, or flowering plants. These form their seeds in closed compartments or cases within the flower.

In this chapter, we'll consider seeds and ways they grow, how new plants can be started from plant parts, how environmental conditions affect plants, how plant parts work, and how plants respond to their environment. A brief, final section takes up the tiny plantlike organisms called *molds*.

SEED-RELATED CONCEPTS
(Experiences p. 216)

"Where do seeds come from?" is a question curious children may ask when they study flowering plants. Seeds are produced in a central part of the flower called the *ovary*. As the ovary ripens, its seeds become enveloped either by a fruity pulp, a pod, or a shell, depending on the kind of plant.

Pears and peaches are fruits whose pulp we eat. Beans, peas, and peanuts are examples of seeds enclosed in pods. When we "shell" string beans, lima beans, peas, or peanuts, we are removing these seeds from their pods. Walnuts, pecans, and coconuts have hard outer shells.

Seed Parts

Seeds come in many different shapes, colors, and sizes. Still, they have three things in common: a protective seed cover, a baby plant (embryo), and a food supply that nourishes the seed as it pushes up through the soil and grows into a young plant. In some plants, such as the bean and sweet pea, the food supply is in two seed "leaves," or cotyledons (Figure 7-1). In other seeds, such as corn and rice, there is only a single cotyledon.

Growth Stages

What happens when a seed grows into a young plant or seedling? For an example, look at Figure 7-2. In A, the seed swells from moisture in the soil. The coat softens and splits. A tiny root and stem emerge. In B, the upper part of the stem penetrates the soil surface and lifts the folded cotyledons out of the seed cover. In C, the cotyledons and tiny plant leaves unfold. Roots deepen and spread. In D, roots become more extensive. The cotyledons are smaller and shriveled. Nearly all the food supply is con-

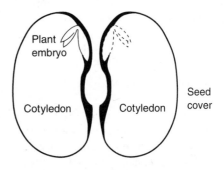

Figure 7-1
Parts of a bean seed.

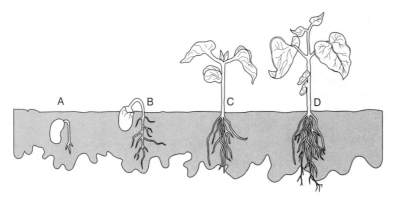

Figure 7-2
From seed to seedling.

sumed. The plant begins to make its own food through photosynthesis within its maturing leaves. In a short while, the shriveled cotyledons, now useless, will drop off the growing plant. This growth process, from seed to seedling, is called *germination*.

Survival Conditions

Some flowering plants produce thousands of seeds a year. If they all grew into plants, before long there would scarcely be room on earth for anything else. Fortunately, a variety of factors enable only a small percentage of wild seeds to grow. Seeds are destroyed by birds, insects, bacteria, and other organisms. And unless proper conditions of moisture, temperature, and oxygen are present, seeds remain dormant. After several years in a dormant state, all but a few kinds of seeds lose their potential ability to germinate. These few, however, may not lose this ability for hundreds or even thousands of years.

Weeds are everywhere about us. What makes them so prolific? Perhaps you have noticed that weeds appear at different times during a growing season. This is because growth requirements of moisture, temperature, and oxygen vary greatly among different kinds of seeds. Of course, this has great survival value.

How Seeds Travel

We know that people plant seeds in gardens. But they do not plant weeds in fields and vacant lots. Nor do they plant seeds in many other places where plants grow. Where do these seeds come from?

Students can learn that seeds travel in several ways. Some are scattered through the actions of animals and people. The sharp hooks or barbs on the cocklebur, burdock, and beggar tick cling to clothing or animal fur (Figure 7-3). Birds eat fleshy fruits but may not digest the hard seeds. The seeds pass out of their bodies some distance away. People throw away fruit pits or watermelon seeds. The wind blows many seeds. Some, such as the goldenrod, milkweed, and dandelion, have "parachutes." The maple tree seed has "wings." Water can carry seeds from place to place because many seeds float. The capacity of seeds to disperse widely and in different ways is another survival feature.

Sprouting Seeds

It is much cheaper to buy seeds (the kind you eat) at a grocery store than at a seed store, even though a smaller percentage will grow. Some easy-to-grow seeds are kidney beans, lima beans, pinto beans, whole green peas, and yellow peas.

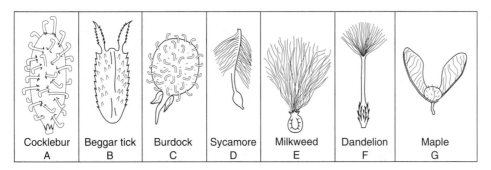

| Cocklebur A | Beggar tick B | Burdock C | Sycamore D | Milkweed E | Dandelion F | Maple G |

Figure 7-3
Some common seeds.

To ensure that only live, healthy seeds are planted, treat them as follows:

Soak the seeds in water for several hours to soften them.

Remove the seeds and drop them into a mixture of one part liquid bleach to eight parts water.

Take out the seeds immediately after immersing them.

To sprout the treated seeds, first soak several paper towels in water. Fold and place them in an aluminum pie pan or dish. Place the treated seeds on top of the wet towels. Then cover the pan with clear plastic wrap to prevent the water from evaporating.

Inspect the seeds every day. Within several days to a week, many bean or pea seeds will have parts sticking out of the seed cover. These sprouted seeds are alive. They are likely to grow into plants if planted while moist and cared for properly.

Soil

All containers may be filled with garden soil, sand, sawdust, or vermiculite, an inexpensive insulating material made up of fluffy bits of mica. Only the garden soil will have minerals needed for healthy growth of plants beyond the seedling stage.

The other "soil" materials let more air circulate around the seed cover and plant roots. They are also more porous and so they are harder to overwater. Plants rooted in these materials may be more easily removed, examined, and replanted without serious root damage.

Small holes punched in containers will aid good drainage. Any water runoff can be caught in a saucer placed below. If holes cannot easily be made, as with a glass jar, include an inch of gravel in the jar bottom before adding soil. Water only when the soil surface feels slightly dry.

Instruct students to plant seeds only slightly deeper than their length. But always follow instructions on the seed package for seed store varieties. Since it takes energy to push through the soil, a small seed planted too deeply runs out of food before it reaches the surface. Also, keep the soil somewhat loose so air can get to the roots.

VEGETATIVE
REPRODUCTION CONCEPTS
(Experiences p. 221)

Many people think that only seeds produce new flowering plants. Yet some of the most useful and interesting ways to grow new plants are through the propagation of roots, stems, and even leaves. This is called vegetative reproduction.

Roots

Consider the orange-colored tap root of the carrot plant (the part we eat). A carrot plant is usually grown from seed in the spring and harvested some months later. If left in the ground, however, all parts above the soil surface die as the weather becomes cold. No growth occurs during this time. As warmer weather approaches, tender shoots grow from the tap root and emerge into sunlight. These grow into stems and leaves. Some time thereafter, flowers and seeds are produced. Like a seed, a tap root provides the food energy needed for shoots to emerge and grow. Parsnips and beets are other examples of tap roots that grow in this way (Figure 7-4).

New plants may be grown from tap roots in the classroom by embedding them in moist

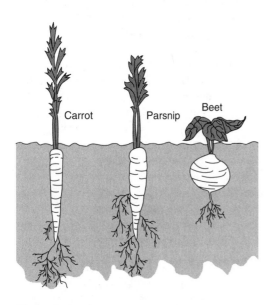

Figure 7-4
Carrots, parsnips, and beets have tap roots.

sand or garden soil. A favorite method of many teachers is to cut off all but the top quarter of a tap root and imbed it in a small bowl containing a layer of pebbles and some water. At least half of the root cutting is above water to assure a sufficient oxygen supply. When sufficient foliage and roots have emerged, cuttings are planted in garden soil for full growth.

Stems

Most ground-cover plants, such as grass, strawberry, and ivy, spread quickly after planting. These plants send out stems or runners that take root, push up shoots, and develop into new plants. These lateral stems may spread above ground, like the strawberry plant and Bermuda grass do, or below ground, like quack grass. The most persistent weed grasses are of the underground-stem variety, as frustrated lawn growers will testify.

New plants may be propagated from stem cuttings of the geranium and begonia. Other common plants whose stems grow independently are the coleus, oleander, philodendron, and English ivy. Dipping the ends of stem cuttings in a commercial hormone preparation may start root growth in half the usual time.

Sometimes on opening a bag of white potatoes, we find some of them beginning to sprout. Usually, this happens when the potatoes are left undisturbed for a time in a dark, warm place. White potatoes are swollen parts of underground stems, called *tubers*. The dark spots, or "eyes," are buds, from which shoots grow.

Farmers today seldom, if ever, use potato seeds in growing crops. Instead, they cut potatoes into several bud-bearing parts and plant these. Each bud grows into a new plant that produces more potatoes.

Occasionally, we see shoots growing from onion bulbs stored in the home pantry. Bulbs, too, are modified stems. All contain thick, fleshy leaves wrapped tightly around a small, immature stem. Tulips and gladioli are typical flowers that may be grown from both bulbs and seeds.

Leaves

Even some *leaves* may develop into whole plants. Suggestions follow for using an African violet, echeveria, and bryophyllum plant.

Use a fresh African violet leaf with attached petiole (leaf stalk). Put the stalk into an inch of water in a drinking glass. For better support of the leaf, use a card with a hole punched in it placed across the glass rim. Insert the leaf petiole through the hole and into the water. After roots begin to grow, plant the leaf in rich soil.

The bryophyllum leaf is sometimes sold in variety stores under the name "magic leaf." To propagate, pin it down flat on damp sand with several toothpicks or straight pins. Tiny plants should grow from several of the notches around the leaf rim.

Why Vegetative Reproduction?

Sometimes children ask, "If plants can grow from seeds, why are the other ways used?" There are several reasons. All of these methods result in whole plants in far less time. Also, some things cannot be grown from seed (such as seedless oranges). In this case, branches of seedless oranges are grafted onto an orange tree grown from seed.

But the most important reason is quality control. We can never be sure of the results when we plant seeds of some plants. Vegetative reproduction carries the assurance that the new plants will be very much like the parent plant. If large, healthy potatoes are cut up and planted, for instance, we probably can harvest near-identical specimens.

All the foregoing methods of vegetative reproduction are asexual. In other words, reproduction does not require involvement of plant sex organs. Certain lower animal-like forms also can reproduce themselves asexually. In another section, we will discuss sexual reproduction in flowering plants; that is, how fertile seeds are produced.

ENVIRONMENTAL CONDITIONS CONCEPTS
(Experiences p. 223)

Plants grow and flourish only when the environment provides proper amounts of minerals, water, light, temperature, and—more indirectly—space. Because the classroom is an artificial habitat, or home, for plants, students will need to furnish the conditions the plants need to survive.

Growth Conditions

Children will find that soil-watering requirements for plants are like those for germinating seeds. Overwatering causes the plant to die of oxygen deprivation or disease. Underwatering usually results in a droopy, malnourished plant. The absence of vital soil minerals and extremes in temperature also have a weakening, or even fatal, effect on plants.

Crowding of plants is harmful to growth largely because competition deprives individual plants of enough of what they need for good growth. Even the hardiest plants develop to less than normal size under crowded conditions.

Green plants need light energy to manufacture their own food, but not necessarily sunshine. Electric lights may be substituted.

Many commercial flower growers take advantage of this fact to regulate the growth rates or blooming times of their flowers to coincide with different holidays. Plants generally grow faster when exposed to light for increased time periods. But overexposure retards growth and delays normal blooming times.

Three Habitats

Even the casual observer can notice that different kinds of plants live in different habitats. Cacti are unlikely to be found in woodlands, and ferns do not ordinarily live in deserts. It may be hard for us to take students directly to different habitats. It is possible, though, to bring several habitats to the classroom in miniature form.

The *terrarium* is a managed habitat for small land plants and, if desired, small animals likely to be found with the plants. Three basic kinds are the woodland, marsh, and desert terrariums. Almost any large glass or plastic container will do for the basic structure. An old aquarium tank is usually best, but a large jar turned on its side will also do. The container should be thoroughly cleaned before use.

To make a *woodland terrarium,* cover the bottom of the container with a 2.5-centimeter (1-inch) layer of pebbles, sand, and bits of charcoal mixed together. This layer will allow drainage, and the charcoal will absorb gases and keep the soil from turning sour. Add to the bottom layer a second layer about twice as thick, consisting of equal parts of rich garden soil and sand mixed together with a bit of charcoal. Sprinkle the ground until moist, but do not leave it wet, as molds may develop.

Dwarf ivy, ferns, liverworts, and lichens are ideal plants. Partridge berry and mosses provide a nice ground cover, if desired.

After a week or so, the plants should take hold, and a few small animals can be introduced. A land snail, earthworms, a small land turtle, a salamander, or a small frog are suitable for a miniature woodland habitat. A little lettuce will feed the snail or turtle; earthworms get nutrition from the soil. Food for frogs and salamanders might include small live insects, such as mealworms, flies, sow bugs, ants, and the like. A small, shallow dish pressed into the soil can serve as a water source.

Keep the terrarium covered and out of the sunlight to avoid the buildup of heat. A glass sheet loosely fitted to permit air circulation will help keep high humidity inside, reducing the need to water the soil. Here, too, water will evaporate from the soil, condense on the underside of the glass cover, and fall as "rain" in a miniature water cycle.

To make a *marsh terrarium,* the soil must be more acidic and damper than in the previous terrarium. Cover the container bottom with pebbles. Add to that a 6-centimeter (3-inch) layer of acid soil and peat moss mixed in about equal parts. These materials can be bought at a plant nursery.

Suitable plants are the Venus's-flytrap, sundew, pitcher plant, mosses, and sedges.

Some appropriate animals include frogs, toads, small turtles, and salamanders. Again, press a small, shallow dish of water flush with the soil surface for the animals. Keep this terrarium covered and in a cool part of the room.

To make a *desert terrarium,* cover the container bottom with about 3 centimeters (1 inch) of coarse sand. Sprinkle this lightly with water and an equally thick layer of fine sand on top. Get a few small potted cacti or other desert succulents. Bury these so the pot tops are flush with the sand surface. Sprinkle plants lightly with water about once a week.

Suitable animals are lizards, including the horned toad. Push a partly buried dish into the sand for their water source. Mealworms and live insects will do for food. Place a stick and a few stones in the sand on which the animals may climb or rest. This terrarium may be left uncovered and in the sun.

PLANT PART AND FUNCTION CONCEPTS
(Experiences p. 227)

Children are usually surprised to learn that, besides fruits and vegetables, all the meat they eat has originally been derived from green plants. Flesh-eating animals depend on plant-eating animals. This is true in the ocean as well as on land. Everything alive basically depends on food synthesized from raw materials in the leaves of green plants.

The plant itself depends on the proper working of its several parts to produce this food. In this section, we'll examine how these parts work. Let's begin with plant roots.

Roots

The experience of weeding a garden makes us very conscious of one function of roots: They anchor the plant. We also know that food storage in roots enables the plant to survive when food making cannot occur. Another function of roots is the absorption of soil water.

Plants that are transplanted sometimes grow poorly for a while, or even die. This is usually due to damage done to tiny, very delicate root hairs that grow from the older root tissue (Figure 7-5). It is the root hairs that absorb nearly all the water, rather than the older fibrous material.

There may be billions of root hairs on a single plant, enough to stretch hundreds of miles if laid end to end. If laid side by side in rows, they would take up the floor area of an average-sized home. Root hairs are so small they are able to grow in the tiny spaces between soil particles and make direct contact with water and air trapped therein.

Growth takes place largely at the tip of a root. A tough root cap protects the sensitive

Figure 7-5
A seedling has many root hairs.

growing portion as it punches through the soil. Because the soil is abrasive, the root cap tissue is continually worn off and replaced by new tissue.

Stems

Water absorbed by the roots goes into the stems, through which it is transported by narrow tubes to all parts of the plant. Dissolved minerals in the water are deposited within the cells of these parts. When water reaches the leaves, some of it evaporates into the air.

Exactly how does this continual movement of water happen in the plant? This has been a mystery until recent times. Modern molecular theory gives an answer.

As you know, molecules that are alike have an attractive force which binds them together (cohesion). These molecules may also be attracted to unlike molecules (adhesion). The thin tubes that transport water in a plant run from root to stem to leaf. Adhesion of water molecules to the tube walls helps to support the tiny water column. Cohesion causes the water molecules to stick together. As water molecules evaporate into the air, they "tug" slightly at the molecules below because of cohesive attraction. Because of cohesion, all the other molecules rise in a kind of chain reaction unless an air bubble separates some molecules to a distance beyond their effective cohesive attraction.

Leaves

A leaf seems thin and simple in structure from the outside. Yet the intricate mechanisms within it, which produce the world's food supply, have never been fully duplicated by scientists.

Inside the leaf cells is a green-pigmented chemical, *chlorophyll*. Chlorophyll enables a leaf to chemically combine carbon dioxide from air with water to form a simple sugar. The energy needed to power this chemical synthesis in the leaf comes from sunlight, which is absorbed by the chlorophyll. *Photosynthesis*, as the process is called, literally means "to put together with light."

From the sugar leaves manufacture, the plant cells make starch, which may be stored in all parts of the plant. With additional compounds received from the soil and through soil bacteria, plant cells can manufacture proteins and vitamins.

Carbon dioxide is taken up in photosynthesis and oxygen is released as a waste product. But when a plant consumes the food stored in its cells, it takes up oxygen and gives off carbon dioxide as a waste product. Fortunately for us, much more oxygen is released to the air through photosynthesis than is used by plants in oxidizing their stored food. In fact, green plants are the chief source of the world's present oxygen supply.

How do these gases enter and leave the leaf? Thousands of microscopic openings, called *stomates*, may be found in a green leaf. In land plants, these are largely, but not exclusively, located in the leaf's underneath surface. Each *stomate* is surrounded by special cells that regulate the size of the opening (Figure 7-6). Water in the leaf evaporates into the air through the stomates, a process called *transpiration*. Regulation of these openings has great survival value. In dry spells and at night, the stomates stay closed, thereby preventing any appreciable loss of water.

Interestingly, most of the photosynthesis on earth happens in the ocean within uncountable numbers of microscopic algae that float on and near the water surface. We have not yet learned how to use the tremendous food supply this source potentially affords to a hungry world.

Flowers

Many people value flowers because of their beauty. But for flowering plants, flowers have a more vital function. They are the only means by

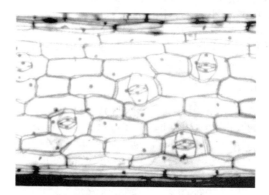

Figure 7-6
Guard cells (stomates) in a leaf.

which species can naturally survive. The flower is the reproductive system of a flowering plant. Its two principal organs are the *pistil,* which contains unfertilized egg cells, and *stamens,* which produce dustlike *pollen* cells. (See Figure 7-7.)

When a pollen grain lands on the sticky end of a pistil, a tube begins to grow that "eats" its way down to the pistil base, or *ovary.* There, it joins onto an egg cell, or *ovule.* A sperm cell released from the pollen grain travels down the tube and unites with the ovule. Other ovules in the ovary may be fertilized by additional pollen in the same way.

The ovules, now fertilized, begin growing into seeds. The entire ovary begins to swell as a fleshy fruit begins to grow around the seeds. As the ovary becomes larger, parts of the flower drop off. Finally, a whole fruit forms. In the apple, the ovary is enveloped by a stem part that swells up around it. The next time you eat an apple, look at the core end opposite the fruit stem. Quite likely the tiny dried-up remains of the pistil and stamens will be visible.

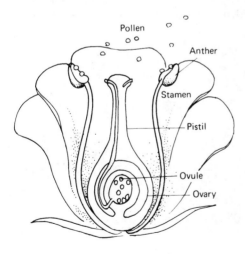

Figure 7-7
Parts of a flower.

When examining flowers with children, use single flowers, such as tulips and sweet peas, rather than composite flowers, such as daisies and sunflowers. The centers of these composite types consist of many tiny flowers, each complete with pistil and stamens. They are too small to be readily observed and may be confusing to the children.

Pollination

Self-pollination happens when pollen from a flower's own stamens fertilize the ovules. *Cross-pollination* occurs when pollen from another flower perform this function. However, pollen must be from the same type of flower for fertilization to take place.

Much pollination happens through gravity, as when pollen simply falls from tall stamens onto a shorter pistil. Or pollen may fall from a flower high up on a stem to one lower down. Insects are also primary distributors of pollen. As they sip nectar from flowers, pollen grains rub off onto their bodies. When the insects visit other flowers, these grains may become dislodged. It is interesting to note that bright colored and fragrant flowers are visited by the most insects. Wind is also an important distributor of pollen. In spring, the air contains billions of pollen grains, bringing pollination to plants and hay fever to many people.

Life Cycles

Many garden flowers and vegetables grow from seed, then blossom, produce seeds, and die in one growing season. These are known as *annuals.* Examples are petunias, zinnias, beans, and tomatoes. Those that live two seasons are *biennials.* Examples are hollyhocks, forget-me-nots, carrots, and turnips. Plants that live more than two growing seasons are *perennials.* Trees and most shrubs fit into this classification.

ADAPTION AND SURVIVAL CONCEPTS
(Experiences p. 236)

Adaptation

If you were asked to invent a plant, what adaptive properties would you want it to have for survival value? Whatever your design, it would be wise to have your plant regulate itself to some extent according to its needs.

Assume it has the same needs as other plants. Because it requires water, and water soaks down into the soil, you would want the plant roots to grow downward. But what if there were no water below the roots? You would want roots that could overcome the pull of gravity and grow toward a water source, even if the source were to one side or above the roots.

Because the plant needs light, you would want the stem to be able to grow toward a light source if light became blocked or dimmed. At the same time, it would be desirable to design the leaf stalk to give maximum exposure of the leaf to sunlight. An efficient stalk should be able to grow longer if another leaf blocks its light. It might also turn the leaf perpendicular to the sun's rays as the sun appears at different positions in the sky.

Most green plants respond to gravity, water, light, and touch. These responses to environmental stimuli are called plant *tropisms*. Let's see why they happen.

Tropisms

Figure 7-8 shows a radish seedling growing on wet blotting paper inside a water glass. The glass has been placed on its side for 24 hours. Notice that the seedling shoot, or stem, is beginning to curve upward, although the root is starting to grow downward. *Both* reactions are responses to gravity.

Why the opposite directions? Check the magnified sections of the seedling. Gravity concentrates plant hormones *(auxins)* all along the bottom cells from the beginning of the stem to the root tip. The cells along the bottom of the stem are stimulated by the hormones to grow faster than cells above. Growth of these cells is fastest by the stem tip (left inset). As these bottom cells become elongated, the stem begins to curve upward. Root cells, however, are much more sensitive than stem cells. So the concentration of hormones along the bottom root cells has the opposite effect; it inhibits cell growth. Top cells are least affected and elongate faster, so that the root tip begins to curve downward. Cell growth is fastest by the tip (right inset).

Tropistic responses seem to be the result of plant hormones that concentrate in various parts of the plant. As we have seen, this causes some cells to grow faster than others. Such responses can happen only in growing tissue.

Survival and Environment

The survival of plant (and animal) species is more than a matter of properties the organism

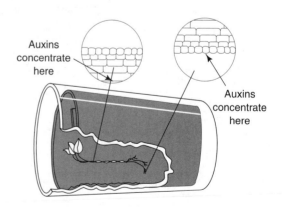

Figure 7-8
Seedling shoots curve upward and roots grow down almost as soon as sprouting occurs.

inherits by chance. The environment also plays a part because it is continually changing.

For example, a long dry spell will favor plants with small bad-tasting leaves and deep roots. Why? Large-leafed plants will lose too much water to survive. Shallow-rooted plants will not be able to tap moisture deep down. Plants with tasty leaves will be eaten first by hungry, thirsty animals.

MOLD AND FUNGI CONCEPTS
(Experiences p. 237)

In recent years, growing molds has become popular in elementary science programs. It offers students many chances to experiment with variables at several levels.

Molds are a subgroup of a broader group of organisms called fungi. Some common examples of other fungi are mushrooms, mildews, puffballs, and yeasts. Molds will grow on a wide variety of animal and plant materials and some synthetic materials.

Tiny, seedlike spores from molds are found in the air almost anywhere. When the spores settle on a substance, they may grow. Molds get the nutrients they need to live from the material they grow on. Unlike the green plants, molds and other fungi cannot manufacture their own food.

Molds may grow under a wide variety of conditions. But those found commonly in classrooms are most likely to thrive when it is dark, moist, and warm.

PLANT LIFE BENCHMARKS AND STANDARDS

Throughout the elementary years, it is important that children build an understanding of biological concepts through direct experiences with living things. Plants are excellent sources for observational activities, classification tasks, and experimentation. A sampling of Benchmarks and Standards related to the study of plants in the elementary classroom is as follows:

SAMPLE BENCHMARKS (AAAS, 1993).

■ Plants and animals have features that help them live in different environments (by Grades K–2, p. 102).

■ Plants and animals both need to take in water, and animals need to take in food. In addition, plants need light (by Grades K–2, p. 119).

SAMPLE STANDARDS (NRC, 1996).

■ Each plant or animal has different structures that serve different functions in growth, survival, and reproduction (by Grades K–4, p. 129).

■ Plants and some microorganisms are producers—they make their own food (by Grades 5–8, pp. 157–158).

INVESTIGATIONS AND ACTIVITIES

SEED-RELATED EXPERIENCES

(Concepts p. 205)

INVESTIGATION: *SEED PARTS*

What is inside a bean seed? Can you draw a picture of how it might look inside?

EXPLORATORY PROBLEM

How can you find out about the parts of seeds?

NEEDED

bean seeds
paper towel
corn seeds
glass of water

TRY THIS

1. Soak some bean and corn seeds in water overnight.
2. Open a soaked bean seed with your thumbnails (Figure 7-9).

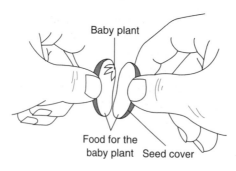

Figure 7-9

DISCOVERY PROBLEMS

observing   **A.** What do you notice about your seed?

How many different parts do you find?

How does the seed feel to you without its cover?

What does the seed smell like?

observing **B.** Open the corn seed. How is it like the bean seed? How is it different?

observing **C.** Soak and open other kinds of seeds. In what ways are they alike and different?

communicating **D.** How well can you describe a seed? Put a seed among three different kinds of seeds. Describe it. Will someone be able to pick it out?

TEACHING COMMENT

PREPARATION AND BACKGROUND

Seeds from flowering plants have three things in common: a protective seed cover, a baby plant (embryo), and a food supply. The food nourishes the sprouted embryo as it pushes up through the soil and grows into a young plant. When its food supply is gone, a green plant can make (photosynthesize) its own food from substances in air, water, and soil if light shines on it. In some plants, such as the bean and sweet pea, the food supply is located in two seed halves, or cotyledons. In other seeds, such as corn and rice, there is only a single cotyledon.

GENERALIZATION

Most seeds have a baby plant, food supply, and cover.

SAMPLE PERFORMANCE OBJECTIVES

Process: The child can state several likenesses and differences she has observed among different seeds.

Knowledge: When shown a seed he has not already examined, the child can predict that it consists of an embryo, food supply, and cover.

FOR OLDER CHILDREN

If possible, let older students gather and examine some seeds from evergreen plants such as the pine, hemlock, spruce, fir, juniper, and redwood. They may observe how the seeds are attached to open scales or cones. Have them look up information about the reproductive process of such plants.

INVESTIGATION: *THE GROWTH OF SEEDS*

Where do green plants come from? Have you planted seeds? What did you do?

EXPLORATORY PROBLEM

How can you plant seeds so they may grow?

NEEDED

soil
bean seeds soaked overnight in water
water
paper towel
pencil
topless milk carton or paper cup
pie pan

TRY THIS

1. Poke holes into the carton bottom with a pencil or nail.
2. Put the carton on a pie pan.
3. Fill the carton almost full with soil.
4. Water the soil slowly until water leaks into the pie pan.
5. Poke a hole in the soil. Make it about as deep as the seed you plant is long (Figure 7-10).

Figure 7-10

6. Put the seed into the hole. Cover it with wet soil. Tap the soil down lightly.
7. Water the soil when it feels dry to your touch, but not more than once a day.
8. Measure your growing plant three times a week. Put a strip of paper alongside. Tear off some to match the plant's height. Date the strips and paste them on a large sheet of paper. What can you tell from this plant record?

DISCOVERY PROBLEMS

experimenting **A.** Try some experiments with more materials. In what kind of soil will a seed grow best? Try sand, sawdust, or soil from different places. Or mix your own soil from some of these.

experimenting **B.** Will a seed live and grow if you water it with salt water? How much salt can you use? What else might you use to "water" a growing seed?

experimenting **C.** Will a broken or damaged seed grow? Will a seed that was frozen or boiled grow? Will a seed grow if the seed cover is taken off?

experimenting **D.** Does the position of a seed make a difference? For example, what will happen if you plant a seed upside down?

Teaching Comment

PREPARATION AND BACKGROUND

A seed that is soaked before it is planted will sprout faster than one planted dry. But don't leave a seed in water longer than overnight. It may die from insufficient air.

GENERALIZATION

Some plants grow from seeds; proper conditions are needed for seeds to sprout and grow.

SAMPLE PERFORMANCE OBJECTIVES

Process: The child sets up an experiment to test a condition that may affect seed growth.

Knowledge: The child describes how seeds may be properly grown into plants.

FOR YOUNGER CHILDREN

Be sure that these children learn right away how to properly plant and care for a growing seed.

ACTIVITY: *How Deep Can You Plant a Seed and Still Have It Grow?*

NEEDED

six sprouted bean seeds
sticky tape
tall, clear jar with straight sides
black paper

TRY THIS

1. Plant two seeds in soil at the bottom of the jar. Place the seeds next to the glass, so they can be seen.

2. Add more soil. Plant two seeds in the middle of the jar the same way.

3. Add more soil. Plant two seeds near the top of the jar.

4. Wrap black paper around the jar. Remove the paper for a short time to observe the seeds each day. Water the seeds as needed.

   a. Which seeds will have enough food energy to grow to the surface?

   b. What would happen if you planted smaller seeds, like radish seeds?

ACTIVITY: *IN WHAT PLACES ARE SEEDS IN THE SOIL?*

NEEDED

shoe boxes
outdoor places
clear kitchen wrap
small shovel
plastic bags

TRY THIS

1. Line some shoe boxes with plastic bags.

2. Half-fill each shoe box with bare soil from a different place. Record where each place is on the box. Try garden soil, soil where weeds grow, and other bare soils.

3. Water the soil so it is damp. Cover each box with clear kitchen wrap.

4. Leave each box in a warm, well-lighted place for several weeks or more.

   a. In which box do you expect seeds to grow?

   b. In which box, if any, did seeds grow?

   c. Will wild plants grow in the exact places from which you took soil? Observe these places from time to time.

VEGETATIVE REPRODUCTION EXPERIENCES

(Concepts p. 207)

ACTIVITY: *HOW CAN YOU GROW NEW PLANTS FROM CUT STEMS?*

NEEDED

three clear plastic drinking glasses
soil
sand
water
knife
healthy geranium plant

TRY THIS

1. Cut a strong stem about 13 centimeters (5 inches) long from the plant. Cut just below where leaves join the stem. Trim away all but two or three leaves on top.

2. Stick the cutting into a half-glass of water. Watch for roots to appear.

3. Some cuttings grow roots faster when placed in sand or soil. Make two more cuttings. Plant one at a slant in a glass containing sand. Plant the other the same way in soil. The stem end should be against the glass. In this way, you will be able to see roots start. Keep the soil or sand damp.

   a. In which container does the cutting grow roots fastest?

   b. Does the thickness of a cutting affect root growth? Does the length of a cutting? Plan ways to answer these questions.

TEACHING COMMENT

Caution: Handle the knife yourself or closely supervise its use.

ACTIVITY: *HOW CAN YOU GROW SWEET POTATO VINES?*

NEEDED

sweet potato
wide-mouth plastic drinking glass
three toothpicks
water

INTRODUCTION

Sweet potatoes are the swollen root ends of the sweet potato plant. You can grow beautiful, trailing vines from them indoors.

TRY THIS

1. Place the sweet potato in a glass of water, stem end up. (This end has a small scar where it was attached to the plant.) Stick toothpicks in the sides to support it, if needed. Only about one-third of the sweet potato should be in the water. Keep the water level the same during this activity (Figure 7-11).

Figure 7-11

2. Leave the glass in a warm, dark place until buds and roots grow. Then put it in a sunny or well-lighted place.

   a. How long does it take before you see the first growth?

   b. What changes do you notice as the buds and roots grow?

   c. What happens to the sweet potato as vines grow?

ACTIVITY: *HOW CAN YOU GET NEW GROWTH FROM TAP ROOTS?*

NEEDED

two fresh carrots (one small and one large)
knife
two low glass jars
gravel

TRY THIS

1. Cut off the top 5 centimeters (2 inches) of each carrot. (You can eat the rest.) Trim away any stems and leaves growing from the top.

2. Put gravel into each jar. Stick each carrot top about halfway into the gravel.

3. Fill each jar with just enough water to cover the bottom. Leave each jar in a warm, well-lighted place. Observe each day.

   a. How long does it take for stems and leaves to grow?

   b. What happens to the tap root part as stems and leaves grow?

   c. Which, if either, carrot top shows more growth?

   d. What will happen if you plant the carrot tops in soil?

   e. Can you get new growth from other tap roots? Try a beet, turnip, and parsnip.

TEACHING COMMENT

Caution: For safety you may wish to cut the carrots.

ENVIRONMENTAL CONDITIONS EXPERIENCES
(Concepts p. 209)

INVESTIGATION: *HOW COLORED LIGHT AFFECTS PLANT GROWTH*

Plants need light to grow. But must it be white sunlight? Perhaps plants will grow just as well or better in colored light.

EXPLORATORY PROBLEM

What can you do to find out how plants grow in colored light?

NEEDED

four cellophane or plastic sheets (red, green, blue, and clear)
four topless shoe boxes
scissors
lawn area
sticky tape

TRY THIS

1. Cut out the bottoms of four shoe boxes. Leave a 2.5-centimeter (1-inch) border on all sides.

2. Cover each cutout bottom with a different-colored cellophane sheet. Fasten the sheets with sticky tape.

3. Place the shoe boxes close together, with cellophane sheets facing up, on a healthy patch of lawn. Lift the boxes once each day for two weeks to observe the grass. Water the grass as needed but do not mow it (Figure 7-12).

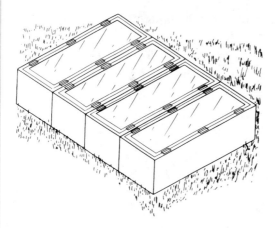

Figure 7-12

DISCOVERY PROBLEMS

observing   **A.** What differences, if any, do you notice each day in the grass under the boxes?

observing   **B.** How do the grass samples compare in height and color?

communicating   **C.** What kind of a record can you make to keep track of what happens?

inferring   **D.** What color seems best for grass growth? worst?

hypothesizing   **E.** What other colors can you test? How will the grass be affected?

experimenting   **F.** How can you test other plants? How will they be affected?

TEACHING COMMENT

PREPARATION AND BACKGROUND

Other kinds of plants may be tested with shoe boxes as shown in Figure 7-13. Punch holes in the sides of the box for adequate air circulation. Boxes may be slipped off quickly for observing, measuring, and watering the plants.

Some children may also like to try growing plants under artificial light. A goose-neck lamp with a 50-watt bulb works well as a light source. If the bulb is left on 24 hours a day, students may discover that plant growth slows down.

GENERALIZATION

Plants grow better in natural light than in colored light.

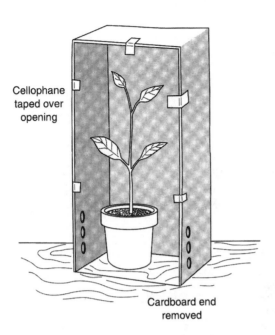

Cellophane taped over opening

Cardboard end removed

Figure 7-13

SAMPLE PERFORMANCE OBJECTIVES

Knowledge: The child can name the light colors that are most likely and least likely to help plants grow.

Process: The child can make a record from daily observations of plants and correctly infer from it.

FOR YOUNGER CHILDREN

Try the basic activity and Problems A and B.

INVESTIGATION: *HOW SALT WATER AND OTHER LIQUIDS AFFECT PLANTS*

Many places have too little fresh water to grow plants. So some people want to use ocean water. How do you think salt water would affect land plants?

EXPLORATORY PROBLEM

How can you find out what salt water does to plants?

NEEDED

six containers of healthy young radish plants
measuring cup
iodine-free salt
other liquids
teaspoon

TRY THIS

1. Mix a teaspoonful of salt into a half liter (or pint) of water.
2. Water one container of plants with only this salt water. Water a matched container of plants with only fresh water. Observe both sets of plants each day (Figure 7-14).

Figure 7-14

DISCOVERY PROBLEMS

observing **A.** What changes do you notice from day to day? Keep a record of what you observe.

experimenting **B.** Will the plants live if *any* salt is in the water? How much can you use?

experimenting **C.** How will other plants be affected by salt water?

experimenting **D.** What other liquids can be used to water plants? How do you think the plants will be affected?

TEACHING COMMENT

PREPARATION AND BACKGROUND

If ocean water is available, it may be used in place of the salt water mixture. For Problem B, the ocean water may be diluted with fresh water.

GENERALIZATION

When watered with salt water, land plants die or grow poorly.

SAMPLE PERFORMANCE OBJECTIVES

Knowledge: The child predicts plant destruction or poor growth when certain land plants are watered with ocean water.

Process: The child finds through experimenting how much salt water, if any, sample radish plants can tolerate.

FOR YOUNGER CHILDREN

Most younger students will be able to do the activities if help is given in matching plants and otherwise controlling variables.

PLANT PART AND FUNCTION EXPERIENCES
(Concepts p. 211)

ACTIVITY: *WHAT ARE PLANT ROOTS LIKE?*

NEEDED

places where weeds grow
newspaper
small shovel
magnifying glass
pail of water
notebook

TRY THIS

1. Dig up some small weeds from both dry and wet places if possible. Try not to damage the roots. Dig deeply and loosen the soil around the weed. Then slip the shovel under it.
2. Soak the roots in water to remove the soil.
3. Carefully place each plant inside a folded newspaper. Observe the plant roots in class.

a. Which plants have a single, large tap root with smaller branching roots?

b. Which plants have branching roots?

c. Can you see tiny root hairs with a magnifying glass? On what parts of the roots do most appear?

d. What other differences among the roots do you notice?

INVESTIGATION: *HOW WATER RISES IN PLANT STEMS*

We usually water the *roots* of a plant. How, then, does water in the roots get to the leaves?

EXPLORATORY PROBLEM

How can you use a celery stalk to study how water travels in plant stems?

NEEDED

white celery stalk (fresh, with many leaves)
red food coloring or water-soluble ink
glass of water
knife
ruler

TRY THIS

1. Put a few drops of red coloring into the glass of water. This will help you to see how the water moves through the stalk.

2. Cut off the lower end of the stalk at a slant.

3. Put the stalk into the colored water right away (Figure 7-15).

4. Leave the stalk where it will get bright light.

DISCOVERY PROBLEMS

observing and communicating   **A.** Check the stalk every hour. How far does water rise in one hour? in more than one hour? Make a record of what you see each time.

observing   **B.** After a few hours, or the next day, remove the stalk. Cut it across near the bottom. What do you notice about this cutoff part?

observing   **C.** Cut the stalk the long way. What do you notice? Can you find any long colored tubes?

experimenting   **D.** Use other stalks for experiments. What can you do to change how fast the water rises? For example: Does

Figure 7-15

the number of leaves on the stalk make a difference? Does the amount of light make a difference? Does wind make a difference? Will using liquids other than water make a difference? Have a race with someone to see whose celery stalk wins.

experimenting

E. How can you *prevent* water from rising in the stalk if it stands in water?

experimenting

F. Get a white carnation with a long stem, or some other white flower. How can you make it a colored flower?

predicting

G. Suppose you split the flower stem partway up and stand each half in different-colored water. What do you think will happen to the flower?

TEACHING COMMENT

PREPARATION AND BACKGROUND

Sometimes the water-conducting tubes in a celery stalk or flower stem become clogged. To open the tubes, make a fresh diagonal cut across the stalk or stem base. Immerse *quickly* to keep air bubbles from forming in the tubes.

GENERALIZATION

Stems conduct liquids from one part of a plant to another; light, wind, and the condition and number of attached leaves affect the conduction rate.

SAMPLE PERFORMANCE OBJECTIVES

Process: The child can change the rate at which water rises in a stem by manipulating one variable.

Knowledge: The child can state how to color a carnation after experimenting with celery stalks.

FOR YOUNGER CHILDREN

Caution: You will want to do whatever cutting of stalks is necessary.

INVESTIGATION: *THE PROPERTIES OF LEAVES*

Have you ever collected different kinds of leaves? There are more than 300,000 different kinds! How can you tell one leaf from another? What do you look for?

EXPLORATORY PROBLEM

How can you describe the properties of leaves?

NEEDED

six or more different leaves
partner
pencil and paper

TRY THIS

1. *Size:* How large is the leaf? Compare their sizes with other things in the classroom.

2. *Shape:* What is the shape of the leaf? Some are oval; some are almost round. Others are shaped like a heart, star, or other figure.

3. *Color:* What is the color of the leaf? Most fresh leaves are green, but some are darker or lighter than others. Some leaves have other colors.

4. *Veins:* These are the small tubes that carry liquid throughout the leaf. How do the veins look? In some leaves, they are side by side. In others, the veins look like many Vs in a row with a main center vein. Some leaves have several long veins with Vs. In a few leaves, veins cannot be seen.

5. *Edges:* What do the leaf edges look like? Some are smooth. Some edges are wavy. Other leaf edges look like saw teeth (Figure 7-16).

6. *Feel:* How does the leaf feel to you? Is it rough? smooth? waxy? hairy? slippery? sticky?

7. *Smell:* What does the leaf smell like? Some leaves may not have a noticeable smell.

Figure 7-16

DISCOVERY PROBLEMS

classifying and inferring

A. Play a game with a partner. Sort your leaves into two groups according to one property (shape, veins, and so forth). Let your partner study your groups. Can he tell which property you used to sort your leaves? Try other properties. Take turns with your partner in this sorting game.

communicating

B. How well can you describe your leaves? Can you make a chart that someone else can use to identify them? Make a chart of all the properties you observe about your leaves. Label your leaves in A, B, C order. Try to remember which is which.

Leaf	Shape	Veins	Edges	Size	Feel
A					
B					
C					
D					

inferring and communicating

C. Give your completed chart and your leaves to your partner. They should be out of order, so your partner must study your chart to tell which leaf is A, B, C, and so on. Which chart descriptions were helpful? Which confused your partner? How could these be made clearer?

TEACHING COMMENT

PREPARATION AND BACKGROUND

Important: To further the processes of careful observing and communicating, use only leaves that are roughly similar in this investigation. You want different kinds of leaves, but if each is grossly and obviously different from others this will defeat the purpose of the investigation. It is best to do this investigation with fresh, unblemished leaves, such as weed leaves. Copy leaves on a copy machine and have students cut them out to use in class if needed.

GENERALIZATION

Leaves vary in size, shape, color, texture, vein pattern, and other properties; no two leaves are identical.

SAMPLE PERFORMANCE OBJECTIVES

Process: The child can communicate leaf descriptions that enable other persons to identify the leaves.

Knowledge: The child can state at least five of the general properties that can be used to describe leaves.

FOR YOUNGER CHILDREN

Most primary-level children should be able to do Discovery Problem A, and some should be able to do B.

INVESTIGATIONS: *HOW LEAVES LOSE WATER*

A plant usually takes in more water than it can use. What do you think happens to the extra water?

EXPLORATORY PROBLEM

How can you find out if water is lost from leaves?

NEEDED

fresh leaf with stalk
water

plastic water glasses (four matched)
petroleum jelly
knife
paper towel
two cardboard squares
scissors

TRY THIS

1. Fill one glass almost full with water.
2. Make a small hole in the center of a piece of cardboard.
3. Cover the glass with the cardboard.
4. Take a fresh leaf. Cut off at a slant the tip of its stalk.
5. Quickly put the stalk into the hole in the cardboard.
6. Seal around the hole with petroleum jelly.
7. Put another glass upside down on top of the cardboard.
8. Leave the glass in sunlight for several hours (Figure 7-17).

DISCOVERY PROBLEMS

hypothesizing   **A.** Do water drops form inside the top glass? Where do you think they come from?

experimenting   **B.** Maybe water drops would appear in the glass without the leaf. How could you find out?

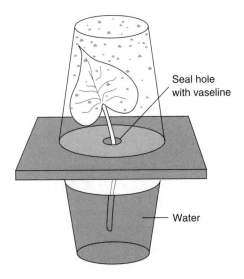

Seal hole
with vaseline

Water

Figure 7-17

experimenting **C.** What affects how many water drops appear? Leaf size? the kind of leaf? the freshness of the leaf? Does the amount of light affect how many drops appear? How can you find out?

experimenting **D.** From which side does the leaf give off water? Top? bottom? both sides? How can you use petroleum jelly to find out?

communicating **E.** Keep a record of your results. Compare your record with others.

TEACHING COMMENT

PREPARATION AND BACKGROUND

Many tiny openings, called *stomates,* are found in a green leaf. Gases are taken in and released through them during the leaf's food-making process. Water, in the form of water vapor, is also released through the stomates. In this activity, the released water vapor is trapped by the plastic cover. It then condenses into visible water drops on the plastic. In land plants, stomates are usually found in the bottom leaf surface. Water loss varies with weather conditions and the size and kind of leaf.

GENERALIZATION

Plants lose water through tiny openings in their leaves; the amount of water lost depends on several conditions.

SAMPLE PERFORMANCE OBJECTIVES

Process: The child will arrange a second (control) setup when needed, as in B.

Knowledge: The child can state at least one condition that influences the rate of water loss in leaves.

ACTIVITY: *HOW CAN YOU MAKE LEAF RUBBINGS?*

NEEDED

different leaves with thick veins
tissue paper
crayons

TRY THIS

1. Place tissue paper over a fresh leaf.
2. Rub a crayon back and forth. A beautiful vein pattern will appear.
3. Try different colors and leaves.

4. Play a matching game with someone.
   a. Can your partner match each of your patterns with the right leaf? Can you match your partner's patterns and leaves?
   b. How can you use your patterns to make holiday or greeting cards?

ACTIVITY: *HOW CAN YOU LEARN ABOUT PLANT BUDS?*

NEEDED

small branches and twigs from plants
nail
pruning shears or knife
jar of water

TRY THIS

1. Find a low tree or bush with fallen leaves.
2. Look for small branches or twigs that have buds. Observe just above where each leaf was attached to the twig or stem.
3. Cut off a few twigs that have buds. (Ask permission first.)
   a. How are the buds arranged? What patterns, if any, do you notice?
4. Pick apart one or two buds with a thin nail.
   b. How can you describe the buds?
   c. Which of the remaining buds will grow leaves? To see, stick the twig into a jar of water. Change the water every two or three days.

TEACHING COMMENT

The beginning of spring is a good time to collect twigs for budding.

ACTIVITY: *WHAT IS INSIDE FLOWERS?*

NEEDED

several flowers
straight pin
newspaper
magnifying glass

TRY THIS

1. Bend back a few flower petals to see inside, as shown in Figure 7-7.
2. Remove one of the stamens. Pick apart the anther, the part on the end.
   a. Can you see any dustlike pollen? What color is it? How does the pollen look under a magnifying glass?
3. Examine the pistil end.
   b. What does it look like? Is it sticky when touched?
4. Use a pin to carefully slit open the pistil's thicker end.
   c. Can you see any baby seeds inside? What do they look like?
5. Examine other flowers in the same way.
   d. How are other flowers alike? different?

Teaching Comment

Florists are usually willing to donate unsalable flowers to schools.

Adaption and Survival Experiences
(Concepts p. 214)

Activity: *How Does Gravity Affect a Growing Plant?*

NEEDED

paper towels
soaked radish seed
plastic drinking glass
plastic kitchen wrap

TRY THIS

1. Line the inside of a glass with a wet, folded paper towel.
2. Crumple and stuff some towels inside the lined glass. This will hold the first towel in place.
3. Put a soaked radish seed between the glass and the first towel. The seed should be in the middle of the glass.
4. Pour about 2.5 centimeters (1 inch) of water into the glass.
5. Wait until the seed sprouts, grows leaves, and roots.
6. Pour out what water is left. Cover the glass with kitchen wrap to keep the towel lining moist.

7. Tip over the glass onto one side.

    a. What happens to the upper stem of the plant over the next few days?

    b. What happens to the roots?

    c. What will happen if you tip over the glass onto the opposite side?

ACTIVITY: *How Can You Make a Plant Grow Toward the Light?*

NEEDED

small and large paper cups
bean seeds
soil

TRY THIS

1. Plant one or two bean seeds in a small paper cup of soil. Water as needed.

2. Wait until leaves appear.

3. Punch a hole into the side of the large paper cup with a pencil.

4. Cover the small cup with the large cup. Uncover briefly when you need to water.

5. Leave the cups in a well-lighted place. Be sure the cup hole faces the light.

    a. What do you notice after a few days?

    b. What do you think would happen if you turned the plant around? (Be sure the cup hole faces the light.)

MOLD AND FUNGI EXPERIENCES
(Concepts p. 215)

INVESTIGATION: *How Molds Grow*

On what things have you seen molds? How did the molds look?

EXPLORATORY PROBLEM

How can you make a mold garden?

NEEDED

aluminum foil
large pickle jar with lid

sand
baby food jars with lids
water
bread slice
magnifying glass
small pieces of different foods
tissue paper
clay
spoon
medicine dropper

TRY THIS

1. Fill a large glass jar about one-third full with sand.
2. Put the jar down on its side. Shake the jar so the sand settles evenly.
3. Sprinkle some water on the sand to make it damp. Use a spoon.
4. Put different objects that might mold on the sand.
5. Screw the lid on the jar (Figure 7-18). Do not remove it.
6. Leave the jar where you can observe it each day.

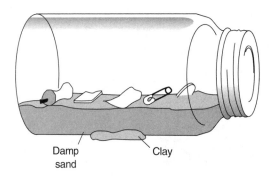

Damp   Clay
sand

Figure 7-18

DISCOVERY PROBLEMS

hypothesizing and communicating
A. On which objects do you think molds will grow? Which will not mold? Which do you think will be covered by molds first? last? Keep a record of your results.

experimenting
B. Try some experiments. How can you get a fresh piece of bread to mold? Keep the bread inside a baby food jar (or plastic bag). Keep the lid on each jar after starting each experiment, B through F.

experimenting	**C.** Is water needed for molds to grow on bread? If so, how much? Fresh bread may contain some moisture. How can you start with dry bread?
experimenting	**D.** Will bread molds grow better in the dark or light? How about dim light?
experimenting	**E.** How can you *prevent* mold from growing on a piece of bread?
experimenting	**F.** What other experiments would you like to try?

Teaching Comment

PREPARATION AND BACKGROUND

For bread experiments, try to get the white home-baked kind or store bread without preservatives. Commercial bread often contains a mold-inhibiting chemical called sodium propionate. *Caution:* The molds or other organisms in this investigation are typically harmless. However, play it safe by having children (1) keep all moldy materials covered, (2) wash their hands if a mold is touched, (3) avoid sniffing molds, (4) avoid growing molds in soil samples, and (5) dispose of all used, still-closed containers in a tightly sealed bag.

GENERALIZATION

Some molds grow well under dark, moist, and warm conditions.

SAMPLE PERFORMANCE OBJECTIVES

Process: The child can set up an experiment to test one condition that may affect mold growth.

Knowledge: The child can state one or more conditions that influence the growth of molds.

FOR YOUNGER CHILDREN

Most primary children can profit from setting up the mold garden and observing and recording results.

REFERENCES

American Association for the Advancement of Science. (1993). *Benchmarks for science literacy*. New York: Oxford University Press.

National Research Council. (1996). *National science education standards*. Washington, DC: National Academy Press.

SELECTED TRADE BOOKS: PLANT LIFE AND ENVIRONMENT

For Younger Children

Busch, P. (1979). *Cactus in the desert*. Crowell.

Challand, H. (1986). *Plants without seeds*. Children's Press.

Gibbins, G. (1991). *From seed to plant*. Holiday.

Kirkpatrick, R. K. (1985). *Look at seeds and weeds*. Raintree.

Kuchalla, S. (1982). *All about seeds*. Troll Associates.

Lauber, P. (1981). *Seeds: pop, stick, glide*. Crown.

Miner, O. I. (1981). *Plants we know*. Children's Press.

Moncure, J. B. (1990). *What plants need*. Child's World.

Penn, L. (1986). *Wild plants and animals*. Good Apple.

Selsam, M. E., & Hunt, J. (1977). *A first look at flowers*. Walker.

Taylor, B. (1991). *Growing plants*. Watts.

Tresselt, A. (1992). *The gift of a tree*. Lothrop, Lee & Shepard.

Webster, V. (1982). *Plant experiments*. Children's Press.

For Older Children

Bates, J. (1991). *Seeds to plants: Projects with botany*. Watts.

Cochrane, J. (1987). *Plant ecology*. Watts.

Coldrey, J. (1987). *Discovering flowering plants*. Watts.

Conway, L. (1980). *Plants*. Good Apple.

Conway, L. (1986). *Plants and animals in nature*. Good Apple.

Gallant, R. A. (1991). *Earth's vanishing forests*. Macmillan.

Holley, B. (1986). *Plants and flowers*. Penworthy.

Hogner, D. C. (1977). *Endangered plants*. Crowell.

Lambert, M. (1983). *Plant life*. Watts.

Leutscher, A. (1984). *Flowering plants*. Watts.

Marcus, E. (1984). *Amazing world of plants*. Troll Associates.

Penn, L. (1987). *Plant ecology*. Watts.

Sabin, L. (1985). *Plants, seeds, and flowers*. Troll Associates.

Taylor, K., & Burton, J. (1993). *Forest Life*. Dorling Kindersley.

Resource Books

Butzow, C. M., & Butzow, J. W. (1989). *Science through children's literature. An integrated approach* (tree topics, pp. 49–54; seed topics, pp. 55–60). Teachers Ideas Press.

Fredericks, A. D., Meinbach, A. M., & Rothlein, L. (1993). *Thematic units: An integrated approach to teaching science and social studies* (plant topics, pp. 123–131). HarperCollins.

LeCroy, B., & Holder, B. (1994). *Bookwebs: a brainstorm of ideas for the primary classroom* (seed activity, p. 69). Teachers Ideas Press.

Shaw, D. G., & Dybdahl, C. S. (1996). *Integrating science and language arts. A sourcebook for K–6 teachers* (plant topics, pp. 60–62). Allyn and Bacon.

ANIMAL LIFE AND ENVIRONMENT

Animal Life
and
Environment

Animals with Backbones	Animals Without Backbones	Ecology	Classification of Animals
Mammals	Insects	Biotic Potential	Two-group System
Birds	Crayfish and Brine Shrimp	Habitats	Modern System
Reptiles and Amphibians	Earthworms	Food Chains and Webs	Animal Life Benchmarks and Standards
Fish	Snails	Material Cycles	

Can a gnat have *anything* in common with an elephant?

Despite their enormous diversity, all animals share certain common needs and physical properties. By carefully observing how animals are formed, we can place them into groups with common properties. These groups enable us to learn many of the interesting adaptations of animals without having to study each group member.

This chapter discusses animals with backbones, animals without backbones, and interactions of living things with each other and their environment, or ecology. But right now, let's briefly consider some ways to classify animals.

CLASSIFICATION OF ANIMALS CONCEPTS
(Experiences p. 265)

Of some 1,250,000 different forms of living things, animals make up almost 1,000,000. They run, walk, crawl, fly, slither, and swim. They range in size from microscopic organisms to the blue whale, which may be up to about 30 meters (100 feet) long. Their colors embrace all shades of the spectrum. The diversity of animals is truly amazing.

How do scientists keep track of them? A system developed by the great Swedish naturalist Carolus Linnaeus (1707–78) provided the foundation for modern classification. Its basis is the physical structure of the living thing. Six main categories are used, which range from the general to the particular description of group properties.

For example, let's classify a dog. Parenthetical remarks refer to the general meaning of each category.

Kingdom Animalia (the subject belongs to the animal, not the plant, kingdom).[1]

Phylum Chordata (it has a backbone or a notochord).

Class Mammalia (it is a mammal).

Order Carnivora (it eats meat).

Family Canidae (it belongs to a group with doglike characteristics).

Genus Canis (it is a coyote, wolf, or dog).

Species Canis familiaris (it is a common dog).

Such a system has important advantages to biologists. It is possible to pinpoint most living things and to note relationships that otherwise might be easy to miss. Because the system is accepted by scientists the world over, accuracy of communication is realized.

For elementary school science, however, you will want to work with a simpler classification scheme. The following one should be useful and will fit nicely into any more formal structure the child may develop later in high school and college. Although in this chapter we will not study all the subgroups described, seeing the overall classification scheme should be helpful to you.

We can divide the entire animal kingdom into two huge groups, each with a manageably small number of subgroups.

ANIMALS WITH BACKBONES (VERTEBRATES)

Mammals (human, dog, etc.).

Birds (sparrow, penguin, etc.).

Reptiles (turtle, lizard, etc.).

---

[1] Some scientists have named a third kingdom called protists, which includes single-celled plant-like and animal-like organisms. Other scientists have classified living things into five kingdoms: monera (for example, bacteria), protists, fungi, plants, and animals.

Amphibians (frog, toad, etc.).

Fishes (carp, bass, etc.).

ANIMALS WITHOUT
BACKBONES (INVERTEBRATES)

Echinoderms Animals with spiny skins (sand dollar, starfish, etc.).

Arthropods Animals with jointed legs: insects (fly, moth, etc.); arachnids (spider, scorpion, etc.); crustaceans (crab, lobster, etc.); myriapods (millipede and centipede).

Mollusks Animals with soft bodies (clam, snail, etc.).

Worms (flatworm, segmented worm, etc.).

Corals and relatives (sea anemone, coral, etc.).

Sponges (The natural sponges we use are the fibrous skeletons of these animals.)

When young children use the term *animal,* they are inclined to mean mammal, or at best, another animal with a backbone. Yet the five classes of vertebrates—mammals, birds, reptiles, amphibians, and fishes—make up a scant 5% of the animal species in existence.

Animals without backbones make up the rest. Insects, which make up 70% of all animals, represent by far the largest class of invertebrates. There are more than 800,000 species. (A species is a group whose members can generally reproduce only among themselves.)

ANIMALS WITH
BACKBONES CONCEPTS
(Experiences page 265)

Despite their fewer numbers, the five classes of vertebrates represent the highest forms of life on this planet. We'll begin with the most advanced form, mammals.

Mammals

Look around long enough and you will find animals everywhere: below the ground (mole, gopher, woodchuck); on the ground (humans, giraffe, elephant); in trees above the ground (monkey, sloth, tree squirrel); in the air (bat); and in the water (whale, seal, dolphin). What can such a diverse collection of creatures have in common? All of them are mammals. That is, all have some fur or hair, and all have milk glands. To be sure, you will not find much hair on a whale, only a few bristles on the snout. And sometimes fur or hair is greatly modified, as with the porcupine's quills. But look closely enough, and if it is a mammal, it has hair.

Both male and female mammals have mammary, or milk, glands. (You can see how the term *mammals* originated.) Ordinarily, of course, only the female produces the milk used in suckling the young.

Another distinction of mammals is their intelligence, the highest of all animal groups. But other unique properties are few and subtle.

INTERNAL DEVELOPMENT. Mammals are usually born wholly formed, although growth continues to the adult stage of the life cycle. The embryo develops within the mother from a tiny egg fertilized by a sperm cell from a male of the same species.

During its development, the embryo is attached to the mother by a placenta, or membranous tissue. Water, oxygen, and food pass from mother to embryo through this tissue. In turn, liquefied waste materials flow the other way. These are absorbed into the mother's bloodstream, sent to the kidneys, and eliminated. The navel pit in the abdomen of humans, or "belly button," is a reminder of this early state of our development.

The two known exceptions to this developmental pattern are the spiny anteater and duck-billed platypus, both of Australia. Each lays eggs. The hatched young, though, are cared for and suckled by the mother just like other mammals.

WARM-BLOODED. Mammals are warm-blooded and have efficient hearts with four definite chambers. Their blood temperatures stay at relatively the same level, whether the air warms or cools. Animals of lesser complexity are cold-blooded. That is, their blood temperature changes as their environmental temperature changes.

It is both an advantage and a disadvantage to be warm-blooded. Vigorous activity is possible within most air temperature ranges. But the body heat of mammals must be conserved, or death occurs.

In cold climates, thick blubber or fur performs this function, as does hibernation, and, in some cases, migration. In warm climates, humans perspire. Some animals estivate, or become relatively inactive for a period in whatever suitably cool refuge can be found.

Some cold-blooded animals can withstand great cold or heat, but most depend on a narrow temperature range for normal activity or survival. We will go into more detail later with several specific animals.

Although the terms are still relative, it is more accurate to say, "constant-temperatured" and "variable-temperatured" rather than "warm-blooded" and "cold-blooded" when we refer to animals. In hot weather, for example, a "cold-blooded" animal might have a higher body temperature than a "warm-blooded" one.

TEETH. The teeth of mammals are particularly interesting to observe since they seem adapted to specific uses. We can see the four main kinds of teeth by examining our own in a mirror. In front are the chisel-like incisors. On both sides of these teeth are the cone-like canines. Farther back are the front molars, and last, the back molars. Now note how these teeth are used by several kinds of mammals.

Prominent, sharp incisors are characteristic of gnawing mammals such as rats, mice, gerbils, guinea pigs, hamsters, muskrats, beavers, and rabbits. The incisors of these rodents grow continuously at the root and are worn down at the opposite end by gnawing. When prevented from gnawing, incisors may grow so long that the animal cannot close its mouth, and so starves to death.

The flesh eaters have small incisors and prominent canines, sometimes called "fangs." Their molars have curved, sharp edges. The canines are useful for tearing meat. The molars are suited for chopping it into parts small enough to swallow.

Plant eaters have wide, closely spaced incisors and large, flat-surfaced molars. Canines do not appear. The incisors work well in clipping off grasses and plant stems. The molars grind this material before swallowing.

You and I are omnivores; in other words, we are capable of eating both plants and animals. Human teeth include all four types.

Classroom Mammals

The classroom is likely to be a restrictive place for mammals, so it is wise to select those that will fare reasonably well there. It is also important to get an animal that can be used to fulfill some lasting educational purposes. (Most school districts have policies as to what animals, if any, are permitted in classrooms.)

Experienced teachers often recommend use of white rats and gerbils (Figure 8-1) over common classroom animals such as white mice, hamsters, and guinea pigs.

Although simple cages for rodents can be homemade from strong screening material, a commercial cage is usually more secure and better suited to the animals' needs. A commercial cage, like that shown in Figure 8-2, should serve well and last indefinitely.

Following are some suggestions for housing and caring for a female and male white rat or gerbil.

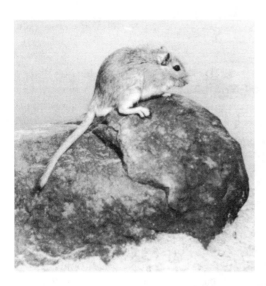

Figure 8-1
A gerbil.

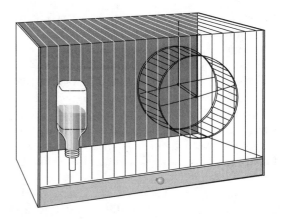

Figure 8-2
A commercially produced cage such as this is
well suited for housing white rats.

CAGE. Use a commercially produced cage with exercise wheel and inverted water bottle as recommended. Cover the floor with a four-page thickness of newspaper. Scatter a generous covering of sawdust, wood shavings, peat moss, or shredded newspaper over the paper. Remove the floor covering and replace with fresh materials twice a week or more often if odor develops.

The cage should be in a draft-free location, as rodents are quite susceptible to colds. Ideally, the temperature should not fall below 15°C (60°F). However, a deep floor covering usually provides some insulation against the loss of heat energy, since the animals will burrow into it.

FOOD.[2] Dry pellets for small laboratory animals, including rats, are sold at most pet and feed stores. In addition, provide bits of carrots, lettuce, cheese, and bread for the animal to eat. A constant supply of pellets and other nonper-
ishable food may be left in a small, flat container in the cage. However, remove any perishable food within an hour after it has been offered. A fresh bottle of water and tray of pellets should last over weekends, but provisions for feeding will need to be made for longer periods.

HANDLING. White rats are typically very gentle, likable creatures. They should be handled daily for a short period. This tames them and accustoms them to being around children.

Caution: Although there is little chance that a white rat will bite if treated gently, remind children to keep their fingers away from the animal's mouth when handling it. Notify the school nurse immediately if *any* classroom animal bites a child. Although the bite itself is usually minor, germs the animal may harbor in its mouth may cause infection unless the wound is promptly treated.

BREEDING. Rats usually breed within a few days. Provide some loose cotton or shredded newspaper that the female can use in preparing a nest. Remove the male from the cage after it appears obvious that the female is pregnant.

---

[2] For food and other requirements of animals often kept in classrooms, please see Appendix D.

Return the male to the pet store, or give it to the Humane Society.

About three to four weeks after mating, the female will give birth to eight or more young in the nest. Do not disturb the female for ten days after this event. The newborn young will be blind and hairless. They may be weaned gradually to a regular diet after they are about two weeks old. Feed them milk that contains soft bread crumbs for a week and adult food thereafter.

All rats should be given to a responsible party after completion of this activity. Abandoned rodents become wild and add quickly to the local pest population.

During the eight weeks or so of working with these animals, try to have time for frequent, short class discussions about the behavior and habits of the caged rats. Emphasize the birth, appearance, care, feeding, and physical development of the young. You may note rapid day-to-day improvement in children's verbal reporting skills as they tell the latest news about their rats. It is also an excellent journal-writing activity.

Use a chart with rotating names for assigning tasks such as replacement of water, paper, and food. Most children are delighted to serve. This may be an excellent opportunity to motivate students and help them achieve a greater sense of responsibility.

Birds

"A bird is an animal with feathers." This is a primary child's definition, but it really cannot be much improved. Almost all other properties we see in birds may be found here and there among other animal groups, although not in the same combinations. The coloring and construction of birds' feathers vary tremendously, from the luxuriant plumage of a peacock to the scruffy covering of a New Zealand kiwi.

Although we ordinarily think of birds as fliers, chickens and road runners seldom fly, and some birds, like the ostrich, penguin, and kiwi, cannot fly at all.

FOOD AND HEAT LOSS. "He eats like a bird." How often we have heard a person who eats sparingly described this way. It is hardly fitting. Few other animals possess such voracious appetites for their size. Many birds must eat their weight in food each day just to stay alive.

To see why this is so, examine a small, flying bird closely. Notice that its body volume is relatively small when compared to the large surface area of its skin. As body volume decreases, the relative size of skin surface increases. If this seems unclear, inspect a pint and a quart milk carton. The small carton holds only half as much but clearly has more than one-half the surface area of the larger carton.

A large skin surface area causes heat energy to radiate rapidly away from the body. This is bad when the body volume is small, because the heat generating capacity is also small. To generate enough heat energy for normal functioning when heat energy is quickly being radiated away, a high metabolic rate (the rate at which food is oxidized and assimilated) must be maintained. The rapid burning of fuel causes body temperatures in birds of 39° to 43°C (102° to 110°F), the highest of any animal group.

The same principle of volume relative to surface area applies to mammals, too. Smaller mammals usually eat more for their size than larger ones. As we travel toward the earth's polar regions, we can observe a general increase in mammals' body size. As body volume increases, the relative size of skin surface decreases. Comparatively less heat energy is radiated away. This has great survival value.

FLIGHT ADAPTATIONS. The bodies of most birds are well suited for flight. Inside are several air sacs connected to the lungs. Many bones are hollow, or nearly so, and further reduce body weight. Even a chicken has relatively little marrow in its longer bones. It is said that the evolutionist Charles Darwin had a pipe stem made from a wing bone of an albatross.

The body of a bird is streamlined and closely fitted with three kinds of feathers. Next to the skin are fluffy, soft down feathers. These contain numerous "dead-air" pockets that help conserve body heat. Contour feathers hug the body closely, and large flight feathers help to propel and steer the bird as it flies.

Most birds continually preen their feathers. This is done by using the bill to press a drop of oil from a gland located just above the tail and then spreading the oil over the feathers. A shiny, waterproof coating results. It is so effective that a duck can float for many hours without becoming waterlogged. If the oil were suddenly removed, a swimming duck would disappear into the water like a slowly submerging submarine.

If you can locate a large, recently molted feather, dip it in water before and after washing it in soap or detergent. Notice how water soaks in after the washing.

The thick white meat or breast section on poultry is partly the result of selective breeding by humans. However, nearly all birds have their largest and strongest muscles in this section because these muscles control the major wing movements.

SENSES. The remarkably keen eyesight of birds has been well advertised. Less known is that they have three eyelids. Two shut the eye, and the third, which is transparent, sweeps back and forth, cleaning away dust or other foreign matter without need for blinking. Eyes of most birds are located on the sides of the head. So they must continually cock the head to one side to see directly forward. Their hearing is also acute despite the lack of outer ears. Two small earholes suffice. On the other hand, birds do not appear to discriminate well among various odors or tastes.

BEAKS AND FEET. Most birds have horny beaks; their various shapes show great diversity of function. Although all known modern birds are toothless, fossil records indicate that a variety of toothed birds lived in ancient times. The feet of birds are equally diverse in form. On the legs we find scales, which reveal their evolutionary connection to the reptiles.

Figure 8-3 shows some common structures and functions of birds' bills and feet. The duck's bill is useful for scooping up small fish and plants in water because it is shaped like a shovel. The scooped-up water spills out through the uneven sides of the bill, but the food remains inside. The duck's webbed feet are useful for paddling in water.

The woodpecker's bill is like a large, pointed nail, useful for digging insects out of tough tree bark. (The bills of most other insect catchers

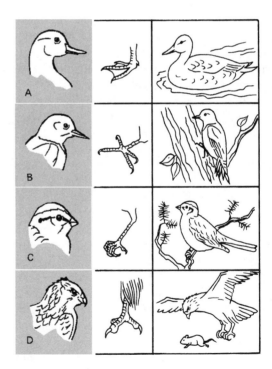

Figure 8-3
(A) Duck, (B) woodpecker, (C) sparrow, (D) hawk.

are more slender.) Its feet can dig securely into a vertical tree trunk.

The sparrow's bill is small, but strong enough to crack open seeds and some nuts, like a pet canary's does. Its feet are useful for perching because they automatically close around a tree limb. It requires no effort, and the bird may sleep in this position without danger of falling.

The hawk's bill is like a sharp hook, useful for tearing the flesh from bones of field mice and other small animals it preys on. Its feet are useful for grasping and holding its prey.

REPRODUCTION. As in mammals, sexual reproduction begins with an egg cell fertilized within the female by a sperm cell. However, fertilization is not necessary for an egg to be laid. Many chickens lay an egg every day. We eat these unfertilized eggs.

An egg acquires its hard shell in the lower part of the hen's oviduct, or egg-conducting tube. Glands produce a limy secretion that gradually hardens over a period of hours before the egg is laid. The shell is porous and permits both oxygen to enter and carbon dioxide to leave. In a fertilized egg, this is essential for life in the developing chick embryo.

CHICK HATCHING. It is fairly easy to hatch chicks in the classroom. To do so, you will need fertilized eggs and an incubator. Get the eggs from a hatchery or farmer. Buy a small incubator from a pet shop or scientific supply house. It is essential to success that a near-constant temperature of 38° to 39°C (101° to 103°F) be maintained for the 21-day incubation period. Fertilized eggs should be turned over twice a day. This keeps the growing embryo from sticking to the shell. A mark placed on the egg will allow you to keep track of egg positions.

In 21 days, or sooner if the eggs have not been freshly laid, the hatching will take place. This process may take several or more hours. Since some hatching may happen at night, it is good to have several eggs. This will increase the chance that a few chicks will hatch during school hours.

Children can observe how a chick breaks out of its shell using a tiny "egg tooth" on top of its beak. This drops off shortly after the chick emerges. (See Figure 8-4.) The chick will look wet and scraggly until its downy feathers dry. No food is necessary for at least 24 hours, as it will have digested the egg yolk and some egg white before breaking out of the shell. (It is a common misconception that an egg yolk *is* the undeveloped embryo, rather than the chick's principal food.)

CARING FOR CHICKS. Chicks need constant warmth. This is furnished by a brooder, or warm box. An incubator can be used temporarily if the lid is raised, but it may be too confining after a few days. If the chicks are to be kept for more than several days, use a cardboard box with a shielded, goose-neck lamp shining into it.

Chick feed may be bought at a pet store. Leave some feed and clean water in dishes within the brooder at all times. A fresh newspa-

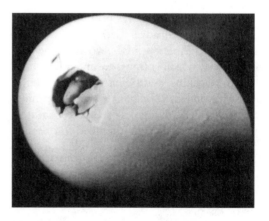

Figure 8-4
A chick starts to peck itself out of the egg. Note the egg tooth.

per floor cover each day will keep the brooder clean.

Reptiles

Many children know that snakes are reptiles but are unaware that the term also includes turtles, lizards, alligators, and crocodiles. What do these animals have in common? Typically they have dry, scaly skin. Those with feet have five toes which bear claws. All are lung breathers, which means that even an aquatic turtle will drown if placed underwater for an extended time period.

COLD-BLOODED. Reptiles have well developed hearts with three chambers (some have almost four). Unlike mammals and birds, reptiles are cold-blooded. In winter, reptiles in relatively cold climates hibernate below ground; they become unable to move when the temperature drops very low. It is no accident that reptiles are rare in regions beyond the temperate zones and proliferate in the tropics.

REPRODUCTION. In reptiles, reproduction begins with the internal fertilization of an egg, similar to mammals and birds. But the process thereafter is different enough to warrant our attention. All of the turtles and most of the lizards and snakes lay eggs in secluded areas on land. The eggs have tough, leathery covers, and for the most part depend on the sun's warmth for incubation.

Some snakes and lizards retain the egg internally until the incubation period is complete. The young are then born alive. However, the process differs from the development of mammalian young.

In mammals, as was noted, the embryo is attached to the female and nourished directly through a placental membrane. In reptiles, there is no internal attachment. The egg incubates until the growing embryo inside is sufficiently developed to hatch and so leave the female.

EYES. Turtles and most lizards have three eyelids, as do birds. Snakes have no eyelids. A transparent, horny cover over the eye protects it from injury as the animal moves among sticks and vegetation. Just before a snake sheds its skin, up to several times a year, the transparent eye cover becomes milky in color. Interestingly, the only easy way to tell the several species of legless lizards from snakes is to note whether the eyes blink.

COMMON LIZARDS. Children may bring lizards, often swifts, to class. (See Figure 8-5.) In the southwestern United States, it is common for children to bring the gentle and easily tamed horned toad. Nearly all lizards may be housed satisfactorily in a terrarium containing some sand and placed where it is sunny. The anole (American chameleon), the kind often bought at fairs and pet shops, is more suited to a woodland terrarium. (See page 210 for descriptions of terrariums.)

Chameleons are interesting for children to observe. Like many lizards, they change body

Figure 8-5
A typical small lizard, the Eastern Fence Swift.

color under different conditions of light, temperature, and excitation. However, the color change is greater in chameleons than in most other lizards. It is brought about by dilation and contraction of blood vessels in the skin.

Many lizards have fragile tails that break off easily when seized. In some species, the broken-off tail part wriggles about animatedly, thereby often distracting the attention of a would-be captor until the lizard escapes. Lizards can grow back (regenerate) new tails.

CLASSROOM SNAKE. If possible, try to get a small, tame snake for the children to examine. Let the children touch it and learn that it has dry, cool skin, rather than a slimy coating. Children can learn that nearly all snakes in this country are highly beneficial to humans, and that snakes consume many thousands of destructive rodent and insect pests each year.

At the same time, students should learn an intelligent respect for snakes. If poisonous snakes appear locally, show pictures of what they look like. *Caution:* Instruct children never to hunt for snakes unless accompanied by a responsible and informed older person. In the continental United States, the rattlesnake, copperhead, water moccasin, and coral snake are dangerous to humans.

Amphibians

These are animals that typically spend part of their lives in water and part on land. The main kinds are frogs, toads, and salamanders. Amphibians represent an interesting evolutionary link between fishes and reptiles and have many properties of both groups. If animal life originally began and evolved in the sea, as is generally supposed, it is probable that early amphibians were the first vertebrates to emerge from the water and live successfully on land.

COLD-BLOODED. Amphibians are cold-blooded and have hearts with three chambers.

Like other cold-blooded animals, they hibernate in cold weather, usually by burrowing in the ground or mud. The adults breathe through lungs, but are also able to absorb some oxygen through the skin. The latter method of breathing is especially useful in hibernation. Still, skin breathing is inadequate for sustained activity, and even a frog will drown eventually if forced to remain underwater.

Frogs and salamanders usually have moist, smooth skins that must remain moist if they are to survive. For this reason, a bowl of water is needed in a terrarium that houses these creatures.

FROGS AND TOADS. One day a child may show you a small amphibian and ask, "Is this a toad or a frog?" Although it is hard to distinguish between them all the time, a toad usually has dry, rough skin. Its body is broad and fat, and the eyelids are more prominent than those of frogs. Another indicator is where it was caught. Frogs are likelier to live by water, whereas toads are mostly land dwellers (Figure 8-6).

Can toads cause warts? Many children think they can. The toad's warty-looking tubercles are glands that secrete a fluid that can sicken attacking animals. But the substance cannot cause warts. It may irritate the eyes, though, if they are rubbed after handling a toad. Advise students to wash their hands after playing with a toad.

SALAMANDERS. Less common than frogs and toads are salamanders; chances are that few students will have these as pets. Most salamanders have four legs of the same size and long, tubular bodies with tails. Superficially, they resemble lizards and are often mistaken for them. They differ from lizards in several ways: The forelegs of salamanders have four toes instead of five; they have no claws; and typically the skin is smooth rather than rough. *Caution:* A salamander's skin may secrete a mild poison,

Figure 8-6
Toad (left) and frog. Notice the external eardrum, just behind and below the eye.

so hands should be thoroughly washed after handling it.

REPRODUCTION. Perhaps the most striking difference between amphibians and the other groups we have examined is in their means of reproduction. Female amphibians lay their eggs in water or in very moist places on land. Immediately after the eggs are laid, the males fertilize them by shedding sperm over them. Therefore, fertilization is external, unlike that in higher-order animals.

A single female frog or toad may lay several thousand eggs at one time. The eggs are coated with a thick, jellylike substance that quickly absorbs water and swells in size. This substance protects the developing embryo and serves as a first source of food. Eggs may often be found in ponds in spring. Look for gelatinous clumps (frog) or strings (toad) near grassy edges or where cattails grow.

After one or two weeks, the embryo hatches as a tadpole, or "polliwog," which looks completely unlike the adult. It is only after several months to several years, depending on the species, that tadpoles acquire the adult form. (See Figure 8-7.) This process of changing forms, called metamorphosis, is another distinct departure from the growth and development pattern of higher animals.

In their initial growth stages, tadpoles breathe like fishes; that is, they obtain oxygen from water through tiny gills. Be sure to "age" tap water for at least 24 hours to rid it of chlorine before adding it to the container in which

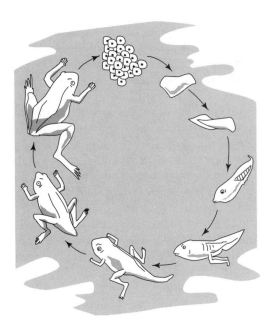

Figure 8-7
Metamorphosis of the frog.

the tadpoles are kept. Use tap water only if pond water is not available.

Fishes

Next to mammals, fishes are the vertebrates that present the greatest diversity in appearance, adaptations, and habits. Certainly, fishes are most numerous, both as individuals and in numbers of species. (When only one species is referred to, *fish* is both singular and plural. *Fishes* means those of several species.) Fossil records show that these creatures were the first animals with true backbones.

BREATHING. Fishes are cold-blooded and have hearts with only two chambers. They breathe through gills instead of lungs. Gills are composed of thousands of blood vessels contained in hair-like filaments located in back of the head on both sides. We cannot easily see these filaments on a live fish, as gill covers conceal them.

A fish breathes by opening and closing its mouth. In the process, water is taken in and then forced out of the gill openings. As water passes over the gills, oxygen dissolved in the water filters into the filaments and blood vessels and then circulates throughout the body. At the same time, carbon dioxide passes out of the filaments and is swept away.

One of the advantages in carefully classifying living things by structure is that it enables us to see relationships we might otherwise miss. In fishes, for example, an organ called the "air bladder" appears to be a forerunner of the lung. The bladder is an air-filled sac usually located in the middle of a fish between its kidney and stomach. By compressing and expanding its air bladder, a fish can rise and descend in the water.

In the lungfish, this organ has been modified into a crude lung, enabling it to breathe air directly in addition to breathing through the gills. A lungfish typically lives in a muddy pond or marsh, which may dry up in summer. It survives by burrowing into the mud and breathing air supplied through a hole in the mud cover. When its pond fills again with seasonal rainfall, the lungfish resumes the normal gill-breathing behavior of fishes. The lungfish appears to be a clear link between fishes and amphibians in the long evolutionary march of vertebrates from the sea.

BODY. The body of a fish is well suited for its environment. Its streamlined contours offer a minimum of resistance to the water. A slimy, mucous-like secretion that exudes between the overlapping body scales further reduces friction and insulates the skin from attack by microorganisms. A large tail fin, wagged from side to side, propels it through the water. Vertical fins on top and bottom keep the fish on an even keel while it is moving. Two pairs of side fins, one pair near the gills (pectoral fins), and the other pair farther back (pelvic fins), balance the fish when it is stationary. These fins are also used to assist turning, in the manner of oars, and for swimming backward. When held out laterally, they brake the swimming fish to a stop. Pectoral fins correspond to forelegs, and pelvic fins correlate to hind legs, in other animals.

SENSES. The eyes of a fish are always open, since it has no eyelids. Focusing is done by shifting the pupil forward and back, rather than by changing the lens shape, as in humans.

So-called flatfish, such as the flounder and halibut, lie on one side. Both eyes are arranged on one side of the head. Because these fish are typically bottom dwellers, this eye arrangement permits greater vision.

Although there are no external ears, fish hear with auditory capsules deep within the head. In many fishes, a lateral line of sensory scales extends along both sides of the body from head to tail. These scales are particularly sensitive to sounds of low pitch. Some expert anglers claim that a fish can hear heavy footsteps (always of other, inexpert anglers, of course) on a nearby bank.

The taste sense appears to be mostly lacking, but a fish is sensitive to smells. Nostril pits on the snout lead to organs of smell just below. The whole body, and especially the lips, seems to be sensitive to touch. In species like the catfish, extra touch organs are found in the form of "whiskers."

REPRODUCTION.   In fishes, reproduction is accomplished by either external or internal fertilization of the egg, depending on the species. The female goldfish, for example, lays eggs on aquatic plants. The male fertilizes the eggs by shedding sperm cells over them. Goldfish usually reproduce only in large tanks or ponds.

Guppies and many other tropical varieties use internal fertilization. The male has a modified anal fin that carries sperm. The fin is inserted into a small opening below the female's abdomen, and sperm cells are released. Fertilized eggs remain in the female's body until the embryos hatch and are "born." Many of the young guppies are eaten by the adult fish, unless sufficient plant growth makes it difficult to detect them.

To raise as many guppies as possible, place the pregnant female (its underside will look swollen) and some plants in a separate container. After the young are born, remove the mother. The young may join the adult guppies safely in about one month.

Try not to be too efficient at breeding guppies, however. Someone good at arithmetic has calculated that a single pair will become three million guppies in a year, assuming all generations and offspring stay alive. A female guppy may produce several dozen young every 4 to 6 weeks at a water temperature of 21° to 27°C (70° to 80°F).

Male guppies differ from the females in several ways. They are about half the size (exclusive of the tails), much narrower in body, and more brilliantly colored (Figure 8-8).

Figure 8-8
Male (right) and female guppy.

Setting Up an Aquarium

An aquarium is an excellent source to observe ecological principles firsthand. In this watery habitat, plants and animals interact with each other and their environment, and reproduction takes place in several ways. It is possible to see a near balance of nature through the interactions, and the consequences when there is an imbalance.

CHILDREN'S AQUARIA.   It is easy for children to set up a number of small aquaria for short-range observations of a week or two. For the containers, they may use large, wide-mouth jars or plastic shoe boxes. One or two goldfish and a few sprigs of water plants per container should do nicely. Tap water can be put into the containers and aged for at least 24 hours before the fish are introduced. A tiny amount of fish food, no more than the fish can eat in a few minutes, should be sprinkled on the water once a day. A more elaborate, long-range habitat for aquatic animals and plants is described next.

TANK.   The materials needed are a tank, some clean sand (not the seashore variety), a few aquatic snails and plants, and several small fish. A rectangular tank of 19- to 23-liter (5- to 6-gallon) capacity serves best for a classroom aquarium. The rectangular shape has less viewing distortion than a bowl. It also permits more oxygen from the air to dissolve in the water because of the relatively greater surface area exposed at the top.

The tank must be clean. Dirt, grease, or caked lime can be removed by scrubbing thoroughly with salt and water. The salt is abrasive enough to have a scouring effect. Should detergent or soaps be needed, repeated rinsing of the tank is essential. Any residue may be harmful to future inhabitants. About two inches of clean sand may then be placed and spread evenly on the bottom of the tank.

PLANTS. A pet store can supply several varieties of inexpensive plants, any of which will serve well. *Sagittaria* and *vallisneria* will produce more oxygen than others and are rooted plants. Anchor the plants firmly in the sand. If necessary, also anchor with several clean stones. Placing the plants toward the back of the tank will permit easier viewing of the fish.

WATER. Put a large piece of paper or cardboard over the plants before pouring or siphoning water into the tank. This prevents the plants from becoming dislodged and helps to keep the sand in place. The paper should be removed immediately thereafter. Should tap water be used, it must stand for at least 24 hours to permit the chlorine to escape and the water to reach room temperature. The water level should be about an inch lower than the tank top.

Moving the tank after it is filled may warp the tank seams and start a leak. (If a leak does occur, apply epoxy glue to the inside joints and seams after thoroughly drying out the tank.)

ANIMALS. Goldfish and guppies are among the best fishes to use, as they can withstand a broad temperature change. But do not mix the two, because goldfish prey on guppies. Small catfish, sunfish, minnows, zebras, and bullheads are also easy to keep and interesting to observe.

If several water snails are bought at the pet store along with the plants and fish, they will add interest and value. Snails keep the aquarium clean by scavenging excess fish food and eating the green slime (algae) that may form on the glass. Only a few are needed, as they multiply rapidly and can become a problem. Children delight in examining snails' eggs, laid on the glass sides, and seeing the snails scrape off and eat the algae. A few hand lenses placed around the aquarium make the viewing easier.

A properly set-up aquarium needs little attention. Plants give off some of the oxygen needed by the animals and absorb some of their waste materials. The animals also provide carbon dioxide needed by the plants to photosynthesize. What if the aquarium is *not* properly set up? Here, we can look for clues that may indicate improper light, temperature, oxygen, and feeding.

LIGHT. If algae grow rapidly on the sides, there is too much light. A northeast corner location or other place of good but indirect light should work best. Adding more snails and wrapping black paper around the tank for a while can retard growth of algae. But it may also be necessary to clean the tank. Algae will not hurt the fish unless there is so much that some decays. However, visibility may be hampered.

TEMPERATURE. If the temperature is too low, reproduction will slow down noticeably or stop. Some fish may die. The best temperature range for fish recommended here is 10° to 21°C (50° to 70°F). An exception is the guppy, which requires 21° to 29.5°C (70° to 85°F) water if you want it to reproduce.

When most kinds of tropical fish are used, a heater is a necessity. This can be in the form of a light bulb mounted in the cover of the tank, although an immersible heater works better.

OXYGEN SUPPLY. Insufficient oxygen is indicated when fish stay very close to the surface of the water. This is where the greatest amount of oxygen dissolved directly from the air is located. Occasionally, some fish might be seen to break the surface and gulp air directly. Insufficient surface area or overcrowding can cause this condition.

About an inch of goldfish (not including the tail) per gallon is proper. If guppies are used, about six per gallon are satisfactory. Having too many snails will also add to an oxygen-poor condition. Increase the number of *sagittaria* and *vallisneria* for more oxygen.

CLOUDY WATER. A cloudy water condition occurs from overfeeding the fish or not removing dead plants and animals. Bacterial action on uneaten food and other organic matter poisons the water and promotes the growth of other microorganisms. The most practical solution is to discard everything but the fish, filter, and gravel, carefully clean the tank, and begin again.

FEEDING. Only a small sprinkling of packaged fish food every other day (enough to be completely eaten in five minutes) is required for feeding. Tiny bits of chopped beef and earthworm can also be used. Feeding is not needed over weekends, but some means for feeding during vacations is necessary.

COVER. A glass top or piece of kitchen plastic wrap may be used to cover the aquarium. For better air circulation, leave some space open or punch a few holes in the plastic-wrap cover.

A top helps to keep the water clean and cuts down on loss of water through evaporation or loss of an overly athletic fish. It also shows condensation and precipitation in a small water cycle, because water droplets form on the bottom surface and fall back into the tank.

ANIMALS WITHOUT BACKBONES CONCEPTS
(Experiences p. 272)

As mentioned at the beginning of this chapter, the invertebrates make up most of the animals on earth. Of these, insects are by far the largest group. We'll begin this section with insects and why they have done so well, and then consider four more animals you might have for many classroom activities: crayfish, brine shrimp, snails, and earthworms.

Insects and Life Cycles

If we were to eliminate all insects, some very undesirable consequences would take place. Here are only a few: Probably half of all the flowering plants on earth would disappear since bees, flies, moths, and butterflies help to pollinate them. Most of the land birds would vanish because their main source of food is insects. Biological research would be hampered because the short life cycles of insects are ideal for quick results in medical and hereditary studies.

As mentioned, insects make up an astounding 70% of all animal species. Hundreds of new species are discovered each year. They are found almost everywhere on earth. What makes them so successful?

LEGS AND SKELETON. The first thing we might note about insects is that they have jointed legs. Instead of an internal skeleton, such as we find in vertebrates, they have an external skeleton made of a crusty substance called *chitin*. Muscles and other body parts are attached inside to this semirigid exterior. To continue growing, an immature insect must *molt*, or shed its outside covering from time to time. We can see that the need for molting greatly limits insect size. A heavy body would collapse before the soft, new covering hardened. Jointed legs and an external skeleton are also typical of the several other classes that make up the arthropods.

THE ADULT INSECT. The easiest way to recognize an adult insect is to look for six legs and three body parts: head, thorax (chest), and abdomen (Figure 8-9). Notice that this leaves out spiders, which have eight legs, and many other arthropods such as sow bugs, centipedes, or scorpions.

The head contains a primitive "brain" and mouth parts that vary considerably among insect orders. Most insects have two compound eyes, which are aggregates of many lenses, and several simple eyes as well, each of which has only one lens. The eyes are always open since there are no eyelids. Two hairlike feelers or antennae, sensitive to touch and sometimes smell, are also found on most insect heads.

The middle section, or thorax, is where the six legs and wings are attached. Some insects have two wings, and others have four; a few have none.

The abdomen contains the organs of digestion, excretion, and reproduction. Tiny holes (spiracles) in the thorax and abdomen furnish air for breathing. The air is piped into the internal organs by a network of connected tubes.

Crickets and katydids hear through a tiny eardrum located on each foreleg just below the "knee" joint. Look for an oval spot of slightly different color. Grasshoppers also have visible eardrums. These are located on each side of the abdomen's first section. Lift up the insect's wings and look for a disk-like membrane just above where the rear legs are attached.

SURVIVAL FEATURES. There are several reasons why insects have survived so successfully. Most can fly. This provides a great range for potential food. Insects typically have very sensitive nervous systems; they are particularly sensitive to odors related to their food. The thorax of an insect may be packed with striated muscles that can contract immediately on signal. This makes many insects difficult to catch. The compound eyes increase this advantage because they cover a wide-angle view.

Although insects are cold-blooded, as are all known invertebrates, their small size often permits them to secure adequate shelter when the weather becomes cold. Many pass through the winter months in a resting or inactive stage. Perhaps most important for their survival as a group is how quickly they produce new generations.

LIFE CYCLES. The life cycles of insects are most interesting. Eggs are fertilized internally and hatched externally. In most species, the insect goes through a complete metamorphosis of four stages as it matures: egg, larva, pupa, and adult. The hatched larva (caterpillar) eats continually and sheds its skin several times as it grows. Then it either spins a cocoon (moth larva, for example) or encases itself in a chrysalis (a butterfly larva, for example) and enters the pupa stage. The body tissues change during this "resting" period. Sometime later an adult insect emerges.

Some insects, such as the grasshopper, cricket, termite, and aphid, go through an incomplete

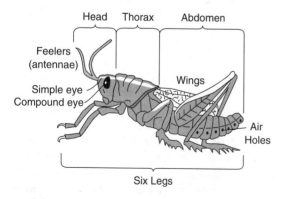

Figure 8-9
Insects have three distinct body parts and six legs.

metamorphosis of three stages: egg, nymph, and adult. The hatched young, or nymphs, resemble the adult except that they appear out of proportion and lack wings. As they grow, molting takes place at least several times. There is no pupa stage. (See Figure 8-10).

Students will relish observing some insects go through several stages of their life cycles, and they will learn from this procedure. Suggestions for doing so with crickets and mealworms are included in upcoming activities.

COMMON TYPES OF INSECTS. There are insects distributed throughout the world, from the polar regions to the tropics. They range in size from microscopic to more than 60 centimeters (24 inches). With 800,000 species already found, scientists believe more than 800,000 could be on the Earth. Some common insects are the butterfly, moth, and mealworm.

Butterflies and Moths. Some teachers like to show stages in the life cycles of butterflies and moths. Students will not be able to locate eggs, as these are usually too small to see. Even so, they should be able to find and bring in caterpillars, cocoons, and chrysalises. Remind them to take several leaves from the plant on which the caterpillar was feeding when captured. A fresh supply may be needed every few days.

Use a glass jar or similar container to house each of these specimens (Figure 8-11). Place inside some soil and an upright twig from which the larva might suspend its chrysalis. Either a cheesecloth lid secured with an elastic band or a perforated jar top should provide enough air. Moisten the soil occasionally for cocoons and chrysalises, as they may dry up without sufficient humidity.

For a larger, more elaborate insect terrarium, see Figure 8-12. You will need two cake pans, a section of wire screen, paper fasteners, an upturned jar lid (for water), several twigs and leaves, and some soil. Roll the screen into a cylinder to fit inside the cake pans. Secure the screen seam with several paper fasteners. Put soil in the base. To make the base heavier and firmly implant a small branch, you may want to pour some mixed plaster of paris into the bottom cake pan before adding the soil.

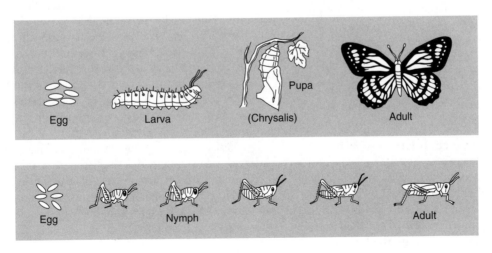

Figure 8-10
Grasshopper and butterfly metamorphoses.

Figure 8-11
A transparent jar may permit students to observe the life cycles of some insects.

Cake pan

Paper fastener

Figure 8-12
A homemade terrarium for butterflies and moths.

To show the entire life cycle of an insect from egg to adult, raise some silkworm moths in class. Within about eight weeks, children will see larvae hatch from the eggs, feed busily for a time, spin cocoons and pupate, emerge from the cocoons as adult moths, mate, lay eggs, and die. Eggs and specific instructions can be purchased inexpensively from a biological supply house (Appendix C). The mulberry leaves on which the larvae feed are found in most parts of the continental United States.

Another insect with a short (six to eight weeks) life cycle is the greater wax moth. It also may be bought from several supply companies.

Mealworms. The grain beetle *(Tenebrio molitor)* is one of the easiest insects to keep and observe. It, too, undergoes a complete four-stage metamorphosis. This insect has a particularly interesting larval stage, during which time it is called a mealworm. Mealworms shed their skin from 10 to 20 times during the four or five months they remain in the larval stage. The entire metamorphosis takes six to nine months.

Cultures of this insect can be bought cheaply at pet stores.

Crayfish and Brine Shrimp

Crayfish, shrimp, lobsters, crabs, water fleas, and sow bugs make up a group of animals called *crustaceans*. Like the insects and other animals with jointed legs, crustaceans have an external skeleton made of chitin. Muscles and other body parts are attached inside to this semirigid exterior. Like insects, crustaceans need to shed their outside covering or molt several times in order to grow.

Unlike insects, which have three body parts, crustaceans have only two: a fused-together head and thorax, and an abdomen. All crustaceans but the sow bug and its relatives live in water. All breathe through gills and have two main pairs of feelers or antennae.

CRAYFISH. With its hard shell and five pairs of legs, the crayfish looks much like a lobster

(Figure 8-13). They are widely found in the United States, living in and along the banks of muddy freshwater streams, marshes, and ponds.

Crayfish are caught with minnow traps, scooped up with small nets, or simply pulled up when they grasp a chunk of fish dangling at the end of a string. Biological supply houses (see Appendix C) also furnish them.

Crayfish are found more easily at night, when they emerge from burrows or from between stones to prey on small fish and insects. During the day or night, they may also be caught by flipping over flat stones and quickly grasping them by hand from the rear. They can be safely brought back to the classroom in a plastic bucket loosely filled with wet grass and pond weeds and just enough water to cover the bucket bottom.

Crayfish need a roomy, shallow water habitat. A child's plastic wading pool is suitable for keeping them in a classroom. Their behaviors there give many chances for observing, reporting, and other language activities. Their interactions are particularly interesting to observe, as a recognizable "pecking order" soon emerges.

BRINE SHRIMP. Adult brine shrimp are no more than 12 millimeters (½ inch) long (Figure 8-14). However, these animals are crustaceans,

Figure 8-14
Brine shrimp.

just like their distant cousins, the shrimp, which we eat. Their tiny eggs are found around the shores of salt lakes and salt flats.

Brine shrimp eggs may be hatched in salt water within a wide range of salt concentrations. The eggs are produced in a curious way. The first group of eggs produced by the female hatch inside its body. What emerges are tiny, almost transparent brine shrimp. Any further eggs produced by the same female are released directly into the water. These eggs will hatch only if they are first dried. They may survive for years in a dry condition before being hatched.

Snails

Snails belong to one of the largest animal groups, the soft-bodied *mollusks*. Most live in the ocean; they include the squid, octopus, oyster, clam, and many other less familiar animals. Mollusks are divided into three subgroups according to how the foot is attached.

Snails are among the *belly-footed* mollusks (gastropods). They have a single shell and travel on what seems to be their abdomen, but what is really a soft, muscular foot. The foot secretes a mucus, or slime, that reduces friction and

Figure 8-13
A crayfish.

protects it from being irritated as the snail moves over different surfaces. The mucus is so effective that a snail may travel over a row of upturned razor blades without injury (although children should not try this).

Water, or pond, snails have two stalks, or tentacles, each with a tiny eye at the base. Most are smaller than the land snails, and many breathe through gills.

Land, or garden, snails are lung breathers and have four tentacles. The upper two have primitive eyes at the tips. The lower two carry organs of smell. When threatened, land snails retract their tentacles; water snails do not.

Like the water snail, the land snail has both male and female sex organs. It lays tiny, single eggs, up to about 100 at a time. These may be found in small depressions in the soil, often by the base of a plant. The tiny snails that hatch from the eggs eat leaves, as do the adults. The adults live for about five years.

Land snails need a humid environment to be active. When its habitat begins to dry out, a land snail usually attaches itself to some object. A mucous secretion forms and dries over its shell opening. This seal greatly reduces water loss. The snail may remain in this inactive state for months until its habitat becomes humid again.

Snails have file-like tongues that shred vegetation into bits small enough to be swallowed. In an aquarium, the tongue of a snail may be observed with a hand lens as it scrapes green algae off the sides of the tank.

Earthworms

The earthworm is a segmented worm, the most developed of three broad groups of worms. Its body may have more than 100 segments. The earthworm's peculiar way of eating is what makes it so valuable to farmers and gardeners: It literally eats its way through the soil. The decaying plant and animal matter in the soil is digested as it passes through the earthworm's body.

The eliminated soil is improved in fertility, but the side effects are even more important. The soil is loosened and aerated. Also, mineral-rich soil below the surface is brought up and mixed with mineral-depleted surface soil. The earthworm moves through and on the soil by alternately stretching and contracting its body.

Earthworms are skin breathers. That is, they take in oxygen and release carbon dioxide directly through the skin. For this to happen, the skin must be moist. Handling dries out their skin, so it is important to have wet hands or use a wet file card and spoon if much handling is necessary.

ECOLOGICAL CONCEPTS
(Experiences page 281)

In previous sections, you have seen some ways that animal bodies are adapted to the requirements of their physical environments. In this section, we take up some of the factors that influence the numbers and quality of animal populations. To do so, we will first need to examine some concepts from *ecology,* or the study of interactions of living things with each other and their physical environment.

Habitats and Their Dwellers

A *habitat* is the specific environment or place where an animal or plant lives. There are many different kinds of habitats. On land, we see desert, woodland, frozen tundra, farm, vacant lot, and garden habitats, to name just a few. Each contains animals and plants equipped to live in these locations. There are also many freshwater and saltwater habitats with their diverse living things. Some habitats fluctuate between a semidry and a watery condition, like seashores. Here, too, we see creatures equipped to live and continue their kind.

POPULATIONS. Within a habitat, we usually can find a number of organisms of the same kind that live and reproduce there. This is a *population*. A habitat is likely to have more than one population. For example, a "vacant" lot may contain a half-dozen different animal populations: worms, snails, spiders, or various insects. It most likely will contain different plant populations as well: dandelions, alfalfa, clover, various grasses, or various weeds.

COMMUNITIES. A human community is made up of people with different skills and needs. When groups of these persons interact properly, the community sustains itself. Likewise, a natural community is made up of interacting plant and animal populations. Plants grow when their needs for raw materials are met. Plant eaters eat some of the plants, and animal eaters eat some of the plant eaters.

FOOD CHAINS AND WEBS. The connection between plants, plant eaters, and animal eaters is called a *food chain*. For example, in a freshwater habitat, tiny fish called minnows eat water plants, and they in turn are eaten by frogs.

We can diagram the relationship like this:

water plants → minnows → frogs

The arrows show the direction of food transfer.

Real-life food chains are seldom so simple. Usually more animals are involved, and they eat more than one kind of plant or other animals. For example, we may see something like Figure 8-15.

We can classify the organisms in this *food web* into three groups: producers (plants), consumers (animals), and decomposers (bacteria and molds). All three types are usually present in a food web. Consumers are further grouped as *predators* (animal eaters) and *prey* (those eaten by the animal eaters). Most preyed-upon animals are plant eaters.

A large percentage of plants and animals do not complete their life cycles because they are

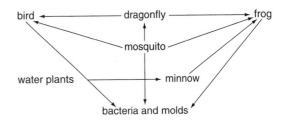

Figure 8-15
Food chain.

consumed. Those that do complete their cycle finally become food for the decomposers. These organisms are essential to new life because through decay they break down animal and plant matter into minerals, water, and gases. The minerals become part of the soil. The water and gases go back into the air. These elements are used again by growing plants.

AN ECOSYSTEM AND ITS ENERGY. To survive, animal and plant communities depend on interactions with the physical environment and with each other. Air, water, soil, temperature, and light all play a part in sustaining life. This web of relationships between a community and its physical environment is called an *ecosystem*. There is no strict agreement as to its size. Some scientists regard the whole earth as one ecosystem. To others, the term may refer to the interactions within a small habitat.

All life in any ecosystem depends on the transfer of energy. You saw how this happens with food webs. But there must be a source to start the energy transfer. That source is the sun. The process that makes the energy usable, of course, is photosynthesis. Even our fossil fuels hold the sun's energy, locked up millions of years ago in buried plant and animal forms.

Biotic Potential

A while back, we jokingly suggested that you not be too efficient at breeding guppies. A single pair might result in three million guppies in a year. A huge reproductive capacity is found in many other living things as well. The greatest increase possible in a population without deaths is called its *biotic potential*. For many reasons, no population achieves this potential. Let's look at some of these reasons.

LIMITING FACTORS. Every known organism needs certain environmental conditions to survive. Without certain supplies of air, chemicals, water, light, or proper temperature, for example, living things typically die. If only a certain amount of these factors is present, organisms may barely survive, but not reproduce. Every organism seems to have an optimum range of conditions in which it flourishes. Knowing these conditions is the key to successfully cultivating plants and raising animals.

Physical barriers, disease, and predators also limit populations. Sea plant growth stops at the shores, animals suffer from diseases just as humans do, and predators must eat to stay alive.

ADAPTATIONS. Both animals and plants (as we saw in the preceding chapter) have some adaptations that allow many to survive when limiting factors come into play. When winter comes, some birds migrate and some mammals hibernate or grow thicker coats of fur. At other times, many insects go undetected by predators because their body color blends into their surroundings. Grasshoppers may literally fly on to greener pastures when they run low on food. In a huge population sheer numbers allow some members to survive even with a combination of bad conditions.

With less prolific animals, such as birds and mammals, fewer offspring would seem to pose a greater risk to population survival. But the lack of numbers is compensated for by an increased capacity to care for their young.

For example, a bird may build a nest for its eggs and feed its young until they are ready to fly. It has the capacity to pick the proper materials from its environment and assemble them in a way that suits the function. The bird does not have to learn this task from older birds: It does the intricate job properly the first time.

So-called instinctive behavior is a common property of animals. A spider does not have to learn how to make its complex web. Nor does an ant have to learn to choose between a solution of high-energy sugar water and an artificial sweetener of little caloric value. There are many such examples in nature.

Such adaptations bring about a dynamic balance in population sizes. Limiting factors reduce populations, but adaptive behaviors counter these factors enough so that sizes stabilize.

The significant exception to the rule, of course, is the human animal. By eradicating most diseases and predators, the human population has grown at a fantastic pace. In the long run, however, limiting factors will exact their toll unless we, too, live in ways that make ecological sense.

POLLUTION. The problem of environmental pollution is that it introduces another limiting factor into ecosystems. Pollution usually happens faster than organisms can adapt to the changes introduced. The result is a decline in at least some of the populations subjected to the pollution. The populations most likely to decline are the more complex forms of plant and animal life, including humans. Those less likely to decline are the primitive plants and animals, the decomposers, and their kin.

Material Cycles

Scientists refer to the earth as a closed ecosystem. That is, almost no new raw materials enter or leave the system. Because an ecosystem ultimately depends on its raw materials, it is essential to life that these materials are never used up. Fortunately, they never are. The materials basic to life are used over and over in a kind of cycle. Next, we will consider three important cycles.

CARBON DIOXIDE–OXYGEN CYCLE. Living things need oxygen to convert stored food into energy. As a by-product, they give off carbon dioxide. This is true of plants as well as animals. Decomposers also release carbon dioxide as they work. Fortunately, plants need carbon dioxide to photosynthesize. During this process, the plants take in carbon dioxide and give off much oxygen.

Decomposers and animals give plants carbon dioxide, and plants give living things oxygen. The process is continual and may be diagrammed like Figure 8-16.

There is another side to this gas exchange that is important to realize. An essential part of living cells is the element carbon. Plants get the carbon they need from the food they make during photosynthesis. Animals get carbon from the plants they eat or from animals that eat plants.

NITROGEN CYCLE. Another cycle occurs with the element nitrogen. It, too, is an essential part of living cells. There is plenty of nitrogen in the air, but neither plants nor animals can use it in a gaseous form. How can it be converted into a form living things can use?

The basic way this is done in nature is through bacteria attached to the roots of plants such as clover, beans, alfalfa, and peas. The bacteria combine nitrogen with other elements to make chemical compounds called nitrates.

Plants absorb the nitrates as they grow. Animals eat the plants and therefore get the nitrogen they need. When the animals die, decomposers convert the nitrogen into a gaseous form again as part of the decay process.

This process is continual and may be diagrammed as illustrated in Figure 8-17.

WATER CYCLE. As you may know, water on the earth's surface continually evaporates, condenses at some altitude in the sky, and falls again as rain, hail, or snow. Living things need water to transport chemicals to cells and remove waste materials from cells. Plants release water through transpiration, a process whereby water vapor passes out mainly through leaves into the air. Animals release water through exhalation, perspiration, and in waste products. The released water goes into the air and becomes part of the water cycle.

Seen in this way, it is possible that a trace of the water that sustains you today may once have fallen on a dinosaur or on Julius Caesar's Rome.

ANIMAL LIFE BENCHMARKS AND STANDARDS

Elementary students place animals high on their list of topics which they are most curious about

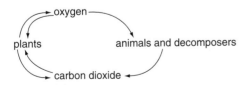

Figure 8-16
Carbon dioxide–oxygen cycle.

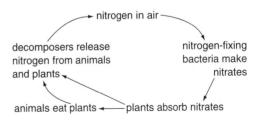

Figure 8-17
Nitrogen cycle.

and want to further explore. Animals provide basic understandings of interrelationships, habitat, cycles, structure, and function. There are many concepts related to animals, the following of which are provided as examples of basic Benchmarks and Standards:

SAMPLE BENCHMARKS (AAAS, 1993).

■ A lot can be learned about plants and animals by observing them closely, but care must be taken to know the needs of living things and how to provide for them in the classroom (by Grades K–2, p. 15).

■ All living things are composed of cells, from just one to many millions, whose details usually are visible only through a microscope. Different body tissues and organs are made up of different kinds of cells (by Grades 6–8, p. 112).

SAMPLE STANDARDS (NRC, 1996).

■ Organisms have basic needs. For example, animals need air, water, and food (by Grades K–4, p. 129).

■ Millions of species of animals, plants, and microorganisms are alive today (by Grades 5–8, p. 158).

INVESTIGATIONS AND ACTIVITIES

CLASSIFICATION OF ANIMALS EXPERIENCES
(Concepts p. 242)

ACTIVITY: *HOW CAN YOU CLASSIFY ANIMALS?*

NEEDED

Computer with Internet access
scissors
tape
newsprint end rolls (available from newspaper publishers)

TRY THIS

1. Search the Internet for pictures of animals and print pictures of various animals.
2. Cut out the pictures and arrange them on the newsprint according to your own classification system.
3. Compare your classification system with other students.
   a. How is your system the same or different?
   b. How do you think it would compare with the scientific system?

TEACHING COMMENT

Older children can look up scientific classifications of the animals and compare systems after they have developed their own classification system. Pictures from magazines can also be substituted for Internet pictures. As an extension activity, students can search the Internet for sites that show live animals, such as viewable ant farms.

ANIMALS WITH BACKBONES EXPERIENCES
(Concepts page 243)

ACTIVITY: *WHAT BONES MAKE UP A CHICKEN SKELETON?*

NEEDED

chicken bones (boiled and stripped clean)
tray or newspaper

TRY THIS

1. See the drawing of a chicken skeleton in Figure 8-18. Notice the different kinds of bones for each of its parts.

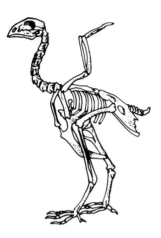

Figure 8-18

2. Examine the chicken bones brought from home.
   a. Can you find the leg bones?
   b. Which are the large back and breast bones?
   c. Which are the rib bones?
   d. Which are the wing bones?
3. What other bones can you find? Can you tell what they are?
   e. Which bones seem to be missing?

TEACHING COMMENT

The head bones and feet are usually not provided with store-bought chickens.

ACTIVITY: HOW CAN YOU RAISE AND OBSERVE TADPOLES?

NEEDED

pond water with some water plants and algae
plastic shoe box or aquarium tank

sloping rock for tank
hand lens
frog or toad eggs
fish food
small net

TRY THIS

1. Put the tadpole eggs and pond water into the tank. The water should have a few plants and algae for the tadpoles to eat.

2. Place a large, sloping rock into the tank. It should rise out of the water at one end. When the tadpoles grow legs, they can crawl onto the rock.

3. When the tadpoles grow legs, sprinkle some dry fish food into the tank twice a week.

4. Every two weeks replace the old pond water with fresh pond water. Use a small dip net to transfer the tadpoles.

   a. Use a hand lens to observe the tadpoles. When can you see these things happening:

   Tiny tadpoles with gills hatching from the eggs?

   Tiny tadpoles sticking closely to the water plants?

   Bodies and tails getting longer?

   Hind legs starting to grow?

   Gills disappearing?

   Front legs developing?

   Tails shrinking?

   b. What else can you notice about tadpoles?

TEACHING COMMENT

It is likely that the school semester will end before the tadpoles grow into adults. If so, let some children take the tadpoles home or release them where the eggs were found.

INVESTIGATION: HOW TO TRAIN GOLDFISH

Have you trained a dog or other pet to do something? Many animals can learn to respond to some signal. You can even train goldfish.

EXPLORATORY PROBLEM

How can you get goldfish to respond to a lit flashlight?

NEEDED

two goldfish in tank
fish food
flashlight

TRY THIS

1. Shine the flashlight into a corner of the tank. The fish should not swim toward the light.

2. Each day, sprinkle a little food near the same corner of the tank. At the same time, shine the flashlight on the food (Figure 8-19). Watch the fish swim toward the lighted food.

Figure 8-19

3. Do this for at least four days in a row.

4. At the next feeding time, just shine the light.

DISCOVERY PROBLEMS

observing   **A.** How do the fish act now when only the light is used?

observing   **B.** How many times will the fish respond if only the light is used? (Do not skip more than two feeding days.)

experimenting   **C.** How can you train the fish to respond to an *unlit* flashlight?

experimenting   **D.** How can you train the fish to respond to a sound?

observing   **E.** What differences, if any, are there in the behavior of the two fish?

experimenting   **F.** How will other fish, such as guppies, respond to training?

experimenting   **G.** Are some fish "smarter" (more quickly trained) than others? How could you find out?

TEACHING COMMENT

PREPARATION AND BACKGROUND

If the fish do not respond, try extending the training period. Also, make sure the fish are fed only sparingly. Should more fish and containers be available (plastic shoe boxes will serve), small groups can pursue different discovery problems.

Children enjoy telling others about training animals. Reporting their attempts and successes allows many chances for verbal and written language development (science journals).

GENERALIZATION

Animals can be conditioned to respond to signals.

SAMPLE PERFORMANCE OBJECTIVES

Knowledge: The child can describe how to condition a fish to respond to a signal.

Process: The child can determine through experimenting whether some fish learn more quickly than others.

FOR YOUNGER CHILDREN

Try the basic activity and Problems A and B.

ACTIVITY: *HOW DO TEMPERATURE CHANGES AFFECT A FISH?*

NEEDED

goldfish in small bowl of water
pitcher of ice water
watch with second hand
thermometer

TRY THIS

1. Notice how the fish's gills open and close. This is called a gill beat.

   a. How many gill beats does it make in one minute? Take the water temperature and record it.

2. Slowly pour ice water into the bowl. Do not lower the temperature more than about 10°C (15°F) below the starting temperature. Observe the gill beats again.

   b. How many beats does the fish make in one minute now?

3. Wait long enough for the water temperature to rise again to the first reading.

   c. About how many gill beats a minute do you think the fish will make? Watch and find out.

INVESTIGATION: *MAKING CASTS OF ANIMAL TRACKS*

When animals walk in mud or on damp ground, they leave tracks. By examining these tracks closely, we may be able to tell many things about an animal. A large, heavy animal may leave deep, large tracks. A track of a running animal may be pushed up a little at one end. Each kind of animal leaves a different track.

Animal tracks are interesting to study and keep, but rain can wash them away. There is a way you can save them. You can make a cast of an animal track.

EXPLORATORY PROBLEM

How can you make a cast of an animal track?

NEEDED

place with damp dirt
paper towel
thin cardboard
scissors
old plastic bowl
sticky tape
plaster of paris
newspaper
stick for mixing
water
petroleum jelly
flat-bladed, dull knife

TRY THIS

1. Have someone in your class make a shoe print in the damp ground. (It will be more fun if you don't know who that person is.)

2. Make a low wall around the shoe track with cardboard. Tape it closed.

3. Spread petroleum jelly thinly on the inside surface of the wall. This will keep the plaster from sticking to it.

4. Mix plaster of paris and water in a bowl. Go easy on the water. Make the mixture like a thick milkshake. Pour about 2.5 centimeters (1 inch) of the mixture into the wall (Figure 8-20).

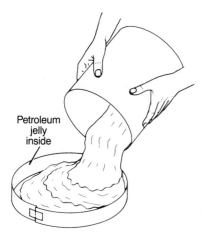

Petroleum
jelly
inside

Figure 8-20

5. Wait about an hour for it to harden. Remove the cast from the shoe print and take off the cardboard. Notice that the cast is an opposite or raised model of the shoe print. To make a model that looks like the real shoe print, you must make a second cast, or *mold*.

6. Spread petroleum jelly thinly over the top of the first cast. Place it on newspaper. Put a cardboard wall, also coated thinly with petroleum jelly, around the cast. Tape it closed.

7. Pour about 2.5 centimeters (1 inch) of plaster mix into the wall. Wait again an hour for it to set.

8. Remove the wall. Carefully slip a knife between the two casts to separate them. Clean off the petroleum jelly with a paper towel. The second cast should now look like the original shoe print.

DISCOVERY PROBLEMS

inferring   **A.** What can you tell from the cast of the shoe print? Was it made by a girl or boy? How large or heavy might the person be? What kind of shoe was worn? Check by looking at different persons' shoes. Last, you can see if anyone's shoe fits the mold.

inferring **B.** Make a cast of a track from an animal that does not wear shoes. What bird or other animal do you think it might be? How large or heavy might it be? Was it walking or running?

observing **C.** Where can you find the most animal tracks around your school? home?

classifying **D.** What kind of a collection of animal track casts can you make?

Teaching Comment

PREPARATION AND BACKGROUND

If plaster of paris is in short supply, you might have students begin with a small animal track rather than a human footprint. Caution children not to spill plaster on their clothing. However, small spills may be brushed off after drying.

Almost any large discardable container will serve to mix the plaster and water. A plastic container can be bent to pour the mixture more neatly into a narrow form.

GENERALIZATION

We can infer some things about an animal from its tracks.

SAMPLE PERFORMANCE OBJECTIVES

Knowledge: The child can make a negative and positive cast of an animal track.

Process: The child can infer several properties of an animal from its tracks.

ANIMALS WITHOUT BACKBONES EXPERIENCES
(Concepts p. 255)

INVESTIGATION: *MEALWORMS AND WHAT THEY DO*

Have you ever seen a mealworm? You can buy them at a pet store to feed to lizards and fish. It's fun to observe mealworms and what they do.

EXPLORATORY PROBLEM

How can you find out about mealworms and what they do?

NEEDED

mealworms
spoon
three rulers
small card

shoe box lid
small jar of bran
magnifier
cotton swab
rough paper towel
ice cube
straw
black sheet of paper

TRY THIS

1. Put a mealworm in an upturned shoe box lid (Figure 8-21).

2. Use a spoon and card to move it to where you want.

3. Use a hand magnifier to see it more clearly.

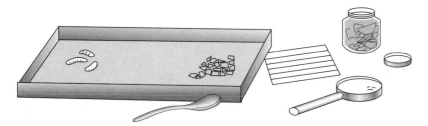

Figure 8-21

DISCOVERY PROBLEMS

observing | **A.** What do you notice about the mealworm? How many legs does it have? How many feelers on its head? What is on its tail end? How many body segments, or parts, does it have?

inferring | **B.** Put it on a rough paper towel, then on a smooth surface. On which does it seem to travel easier?

observing | **C.** Put a few more mealworms in the shoe box lid. Observe how they look and act. In what ways can you tell different mealworms apart?

experimenting | **D.** In what ways can you get a mealworm to back up? Which way is best?

observing | **E.** Suppose you place the mealworms on a slant. Will they go up or down? Does the amount of slant make a difference?

measuring | **F.** How far can a mealworm go in half a minute?

observing | **G.** Which food do they seem to like best? Try cornflakes, flour, bread, crackers, and other foods.

hypothesizing **H.** Suppose you put two mealworms into a narrow straw, one at each end. What do you think will happen when they meet?

experimenting **I.** Do mealworms like moisture? How could a cotton swab be used to find out? How else might you find out?

experimenting **J.** Will a mealworm move to or away from a cold place? How could an ice cube be used to find out?

experimenting **K.** Will a mealworm move to a dark or light place? How can black paper be used to find out?

predicting **L.** Which way will a mealworm go each time (Figure 8-22)?

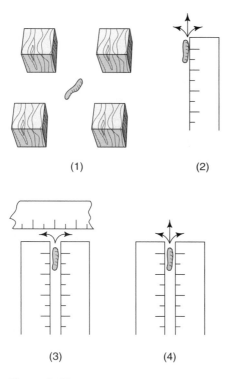

Figure 8-22

experimenting **M.** How can you get a mealworm to go in a straight line for at least 10 centimeters (4 inches)? No fair touching it!

hypothesizing **N.** What are some more questions about mealworms you would like to investigate?

observing **O.** Watch the mealworm go through its life cycle. What do you notice at the different stages of life?

TEACHING COMMENT

PREPARATION AND BACKGROUND

Mealworms are the larval stage of the grain beetle, an insect often found in rotting grain or flour supplies. They may be bought cheaply at pet stores and are fed to a variety of small animals, including some fishes.

Mealworms can be kept in a closed glass jar containing bran or other cereal flakes. Punch small holes in the jar lid for air. A potato or apple slice can be added to provide extra moisture. When the old bran looks powdery, dump out everything, then wash and dry the jar. Put fresh bran and the live, healthy-looking mealworms back into the jar.

GENERALIZATION

Some behaviors of an animal are inborn, and some are influenced by its environment.

SAMPLE PERFORMANCE OBJECTIVES

Process: The child can test the preferences of mealworms as to temperature, light, food, and moisture.

Knowledge: The child can state the apparent preferences of mealworms as to temperature, light, food, and moisture.

FOR YOUNGER CHILDREN

Younger students should be able to do most of the activities in the investigation.

ACTIVITY: *HOW CAN YOU RAISE CRICKETS?*

NEEDED

several male and female crickets
plastic shoe box
custard cup or small dish
screen top for shoe box
paper towel
dry soil
dry oatmeal or bran
raisins
hand lens

TRY THIS

1. Put about 5 centimeters (2 inches) of dry soil into the container.

2. Fill the custard cup with soil. Sprinkle water on it until it is all damp. Bury it in the dry soil so the damp soil is even with the dry soil. (This is where the female can lay eggs.)

3. Scatter some pieces of torn paper towel around the container. (The crickets can hide underneath when they need to.)

4. Scatter some dry oatmeal and a few raisins at one end.

5. Put no more than three or four crickets inside the container. Cover it with a screen large enough to bend down at the sides.

   a. How do the crickets act? How do they use the pieces of toweling? How do the females lay eggs? How do the crickets eat? move about?

   b. What happens when cricket eggs hatch? What do the young (nymphs) look like? What do they look like as they get older? Use a hand lens to help you see.

   c. What else can you observe about the crickets?

TEACHING COMMENT

If children are unable to catch crickets in fields, they may often be bought at fish-bait stores. The female may be recognized by a long slender "tail," or *ovipositor,* through which it deposits eggs in damp soil. Note that from egg to adult takes about six months, with adults living about three months.

INVESTIGATION: *BRINE SHRIMP*

Have you ever visited a salt lake? If so, maybe you have seen *brine shrimp.* These small animals lay tiny eggs. You can find out many interesting things about brine shrimp, but first you will need to hatch the eggs.

EXPLORATORY PROBLEM

How can you hatch brine shrimp eggs?

NEEDED

vial of brine shrimp eggs
tap water
noniodized salt
magnifier
plastic teaspoon
small babyfood jars
measuring cup
small package of brewer's yeast

TRY THIS

1. Let a cup of tap water stand overnight. Then mix four teaspoons of salt into it.
2. Pour the water into several babyfood jars. Use one jar now (Figure 8-23). Cap and save the other jars for later use.
3. Take just a tiny pinch of eggs from the vial. Sprinkle them on top of the water.
4. Observe the eggs closely a few times each day. Use a magnifier to see better.

DISCOVERY PROBLEMS

observing	**A.** When do you first notice changes in the eggs? What changes do you see?
observing	**B.** When do you first notice tiny brine shrimp? How do they look to you? Can you describe what they are doing?
observing	**C.** What changes do you notice as the brine shrimp grow? Observe them each day.
observing	**D.** Do brine shrimp ever seem to rest or sleep? How can you find out?
observing	**E.** How long does it take for a shrimp to start growing?
experimenting	**F.** How long can you keep a brine shrimp alive?
experimenting	**G.** Do newly hatched shrimp go where it is light or dark? How about month-old shrimp? How can you find out?
observing	**H.** How can you tell which brine shrimp are female?
experimenting	**I.** Will brine shrimp eggs hatch in fresh water? in water with twice as much or more salt than you first used?
hypothesizing	**J.** Suppose you hatch many shrimp eggs in one jar and only a few in another. What do you think will happen as the shrimp grow?
hypothesizing	**K.** What else would you like to investigate about brine shrimp?

Figure 8-23

TEACHING COMMENT

PREPARATION AND BACKGROUND

Brine shrimp are sold at pet stores for fish food. The eggs may be hatched in salt water. About four teaspoons of salt per cup of water work well for both hatching and growth. But the shrimp may hatch within a wide range of salt concentrations. Be sure to use either noniodized or marine salt.

About six weeks are needed for the shrimp to reach maturity under the best conditions. A water temperature of about 27°C (80°F) is ideal. Children will be able to distinguish female from male adults most easily by the females' egg pouches.

It is harder to keep brine shrimp alive for a lengthy period than it is to hatch them. Some precautions will help. Have students make a crayon mark on their jars at the beginning water level. Be sure any evaporated water is replaced by aged tap water containing the proper salt concentration. The water should stand for at least 24 hours to allow the chlorine to escape. Put a tiny pinch of baking soda in each shrimp container once a week to neutralize the acid that builds up. Above all, do not overfeed the shrimp. A tiny pinch of yeast once a week is adequate to grow the bacteria on which they feed.

As with other long-range observational activities, this one is ideal for motivating artwork and language experiences.

GENERALIZATION

Brine shrimp will hatch and grow from eggs, stay alive, and reproduce when conditions are like those of their natural habitat.

SAMPLE PERFORMANCE OBJECTIVES

Process: The child can observe and describe several developmental changes in newly hatched brine shrimp over a two-week period.

Knowledge: The child can state several environmental conditions that are favorable for maintaining live brine shrimp.

FOR YOUNGER CHILDREN

Younger students should be able to do this investigation through Problem C.

INVESTIGATION: *SNAILS AND WHAT THEY DO*

Have you ever seen a snail? If so, where? Many water snails live in and around the edges of ponds. Land snails can be found in gardens, lawns, and around damp soil. They are easiest to find early in the morning or at night. Land snails are usually larger than water snails, so they are easier to observe. What they do is surprising.

EXPLORATORY PROBLEM

How can you find out about land snails and what they do?

NEEDED

live land snail
small stiff card
wide-mouth glass jar containing some damp soil
magnifier
spoon
aluminum pie plate
ruler
sheet of black paper
piece of lettuce
paper towel
small paper cup of water

TRY THIS

1. Put a snail on a pie plate.
2. Use a spoon and card to move it where you want.
3. Use a magnifier to see it more clearly (Figure 8-24).

Figure 8-24

DISCOVERY PROBLEMS

observing **A.** What do you notice about the snail? How does it move? How can you describe its head? shell? other parts?

observing **B.** How many stalks (feelers) do you observe on its head? Which seem to have eyes? Which seem to be used for feeling?

observing **C.** What happens when you gently touch the two longer stalks? the two shorter stalks? How close can you get before the stalks move?

experimenting **D.** How can you get the two longer stalks to move in different directions?

observing **E.** What happens when you tap the snail's shell gently?

observing **F.** Try to put the snail upside down on its shell. Can the snail right itself? If so, how?

observing **G.** Put the snail on a piece of black paper. Observe the silver trail it makes. How far does the snail go in one minute?

communicating **H.** How well can you draw an animal? Make a drawing of your snail. Show it to someone who does not know you are studying snails. Can that person tell it is a snail?

communicating **I.** How well can you describe an animal? Write a description of your snail without saying what it is. Show the description to someone who does not know you are studying snails. Can that person tell it is a snail?

observing **J.** Give the snail some lettuce to eat. Observe its mouth parts with a magnifier. How does it eat?

experimenting **K.** What foods does your snail seem to like best? Circle your snail with bits of different foods. Which does the snail go to first? What happens when you try this several times? How long should you wait between each trial? Why?

experimenting **L.** Will a snail go to the dark or light? Put your snail in the pie pan. How can you use a sheet of black paper to find out?

experimenting **M.** Will a snail go where it is dry or wet? How can you use a paper towel to find out?

hypothesizing **N.** What other experiments would you like to try with snails? What other kinds of snails can you find to try?

TEACHING COMMENT

PREPARATION AND BACKGROUND

Land snails can be found where there is plenty of vegetation and moisture. They seem to prefer cool, shady places, especially under leaves, logs, and rocks. Early morning is probably the easiest time to collect snails, when leaves are heavy with dew. If collected in a dry "resting" condition, place them on a water-soaked paper towel to reactivate them.

Several collected snails may be kept in one glass jar. The jar top should have some holes punched into it for air. Place an inch or two of soil inside and keep it damp. For extra moisture, sink a bottle cap flush with the soil surface and fill it with water. Leave a small piece of lettuce inside for food. Keep the jar in a shady place. After several days, the jar will need to be cleaned.

Try to have a number of snails available for observation and experiments. Even when treated gently, this animal needs a rest period between activities.

GENERALIZATION

Some behaviors of an animal are inborn, and some are influenced by its environment.

SAMPLE PERFORMANCE OBJECTIVES

Process: The child can test the preferences of a snail as to light, food, and moisture.
Knowledge: The child can predict places where land snails are likely to be found.

FOR YOUNGER CHILDREN.

Younger children should be able to do most of the observational activities.

ECOLOGICAL EXPERIENCES
(Concepts p. 260)

ACTIVITY: *WHAT IS A FOOD CHAIN?*

NEEDED

six cards with one of these words or pictures on each (sun, plant, insect, toad, snake, hawk)
six persons
six pins

INTRODUCTION

Plants need the sun to grow. Many insects eat plants, many toads eat insects, many snakes eat toads, and many hawks eat snakes. This is one example of a food chain. See what happens when a food chain is broken.

TRY THIS

1. Each person should pin a card to his clothes.
2. Stand in line and hold hands in this order: sun, plant, insect, toad, snake, hawk.

a. What animal would die if there were no snakes to eat? (The snake person should drop hands now.)

b. What animals would die if there were no toads to eat? (The toad person drops hands.)

c. What animals would die if there were no insects to eat? (Insect person drops hands.)

d. What animals would die if there were no plants to eat? (Plant person drops hands.)

e. What would happen if there were no sun to let plants grow?

TEACHING COMMENT

Be sure to point out that these animals might eat a wider variety of food than is shown in this simple chain. However, the basic idea of interdependence is valid. This can be clarified further by making more food chains. Older children can connect two or more food chains to make a more complicated food web. Run strings between and among individuals in the web to show the intricate interrelationships involved.

INVESTIGATION: *HOW COLOR PROTECTS ANIMALS*

If you were an insect that lived in the grass, what enemies might you have? How might having the right color protect you from being eaten by birds and other animals?

EXPLORATORY PROBLEM

How can you test whether color affects the chances to survive?

NEEDED

brown and green construction paper
lawn area
scissors
bare dirt area
½ cup of bird seed
set of food colors
jar

TRY THIS

1. Cut out 100 same-sized pieces of green paper and 100 of brown paper. Make each piece about the size of your thumbnail.

2. Have someone scatter 50 pieces of each color on a lawn area.

3. Pretend the paper pieces are insects and you are a bird. Try to find as many pieces as you can in one minute. Let some partners help you (Figure 8-25).

Figure 8-25

DISCOVERY PROBLEMS

inferring **A.** How many pieces of each color paper did you find? Which color would be better if you were a lawn insect?

experimenting **B.** Suppose you were an insect that lived in a bare dirt area. Which color would be better? What could you do to find out?

experimenting **C.** How could colored seeds be tested with real birds? Mix a few drops of food coloring with water in a jar. Drop in the seeds to color them.

observing **D.** Observe closely insects on different plants. How are their colors like those of the plant? different?

observing **E.** How are other animals protected by their skin colors? Look in books and magazines for colored pictures of animals in their natural habitats.

TEACHING COMMENT

PREPARATION AND BACKGROUND

Try to have the colors of the construction paper match as closely as possible the lawn and bare dirt areas.

For the bird-seed activity, allow several hours between scattering the seeds and locating the surviving seeds. Make sure students realize that they may not be able to locate all the surviving seeds. How can they increase their chances of locating survivors? They may decide to enclose groups of seeds with string or to try other methods.

GENERALIZATION

Survival chances increase when an animal's color matches its surroundings.

SAMPLE PERFORMANCE OBJECTIVES

Process: The child can design a test of survival for colored seeds in different locations with real birds.

Knowledge: The child predicts smaller survival chances when an animal's color is unlike its surroundings and greater chances when its color is similar.

FOR YOUNGER CHILDREN

Try the basic activity. Be sure children understand the analogy of people representing birds and bits of colored paper representing insects.

INVESTIGATION: *ANT RESPONSES TO SWEETENERS*

Some people do not use regular sugar because it has high-energy value. Instead, they may use an artificial sweetener, which has very little energy value. Many people cannot tell the difference between the two. You probably know that ants and some other insects are attracted to sugar. But what attracts them? Is is the taste or something else?

EXPLORATORY PROBLEM

How can you test ant responses to real and artificial sugar?

NEEDED

one or more artificial sweeteners
sugar
two small matched bottle caps
water
two paper cups
teaspoon

TRY THIS

1. Mix one bottle cap each of sugar and water in a cup. Use a spoon to stir. Pour the mixture into one cap until it is full (Figure 8-26).

2. Do the same with sweetener and water. Use a second cap and cup. Remember to rinse the spoon clean before you stir again.

3. Place both caps close together where there are ants. Mark which cap contains the sugar. Watch what happens.

Figure 8-26

DISCOVERY PROBLEMS

observing	**A.**	What do you notice? Which mixture attracts more ants?
observing	**B.**	What will happen if you test the sweetener by itself?
observing	**C.**	What will happen if you test it with different kinds of ants?
observing	**D.**	What will happen if you test different sweeteners?
experimenting	**E.**	How can you find out how other insects will act toward artificial sweeteners?
inferring	**F.**	Keep a record of your findings. Look it over. How do the responses of these animals help them to stay alive?

TEACHING COMMENT

PREPARATION AND BACKGROUND

You may want to check where students put the caps. They should be equally accessible to the ants.

GENERALIZATION

The ability to respond to a high-energy food can help an animal to survive.

SAMPLE PERFORMANCE OBJECTIVES

Knowledge: The child states that insects are more likely to be attracted to sugar than to low-energy sweeteners.

Process: The child designs ways to test responses of several different insects toward sweeteners.

FOR YOUNGER CHILDREN

You might have younger students first try themselves to discriminate between light solutions of sugar water and sweetener water. Afterward, they can try to fool some ants or other insects.

INVESTIGATION: *THE FRIGHT DISTANCES OF WILD ANIMALS*

One difference between wild and tame animals is how easily they are frightened. How close have you come to a wild bird before it flew off? How about other wild animals?

EXPLORATORY PROBLEM

What are the fright distances of some wild birds?

NEEDED

wild birds
different kinds of bird food (bread crumbs, seeds, bacon bits)
handkerchief
meter stick or yardstick

TRY THIS

1. Go where there are some wild birds.
2. Sprinkle some bread crumbs on the ground at different distances from you.
3. Watch where the birds pick up the crumbs each time. Measure the closest distance the birds dare to come near you.

DISCOVERY PROBLEMS

measuring

A. What is the fright distance of these birds? Is every bird in this group frightened at the same distance? Are other kinds of birds frightened at another distance?

hypothesizing

B. What would be the fright distance if you tried other foods?

hypothesizing

C. Suppose you go to the same place and drop crumbs each day for a week. What do you think the fright distance of the same birds would be then?

measuring

D. How close can you get to different birds without food? Slowly walk toward each perched bird until

it flies away. Measure the distance between you
and the perch place each time.

experimenting

E. How do different sounds and noises affect fright
distance? Different movements?

experimenting and communicating

F. What are the fright distances of other wild animals? Find squirrels, chipmunks, and other animals. Make a record of what happens.

TEACHING COMMENT

PREPARATION AND BACKGROUND

Pupils can usually notice differences in bird species, but they often have trouble
communicating what they see. A simple bird identification book can help.

If possible, let children repeat this activity over several days. They will discover
that birds and other wild animals typically decrease their fright distances if the same
harmless stimulus is presented each time.

Caution: Children should never touch wild animals that approach humans and
never feed them by hand. Such animals are abnormal and may be ill.

GENERALIZATION

Fright behavior is an inborn property of wild animals that helps them to survive.
Fright distance may decrease when animals become used to objects or events.

SAMPLE PERFORMANCE OBJECTIVES

Knowledge: The child can state that fright distances vary with different species of
wild animals.

Process: The child can measure fright distances of animals under several conditions
and draw proper inferences from the data.

INVESTIGATION: *BIRD NESTS*

Have you ever seen a bird nest close up? Birds do not have to learn how to make
nests. This is an inborn behavior. A nest is used to lay and hatch eggs in. The
hatched chicks stay there until they grow up enough to fly. The materials used for
the nest may come from many different things. Sometimes the materials birds use
are quite surprising.

EXPLORATORY PROBLEM A

How can you find out more about how some birds make nests?

NEEDED

several abandoned bird nests
pencil
tweezers

TRY THIS

1. Look for abandoned bird nests in trees and large bushes. The best time for this is in winter.
2. Collect several nests. Ask a responsible adult to help you.
3. Bring the nests to class.

DISCOVERY PROBLEMS

observing   **A.** What is the size and shape of each nest? How is each made?

observing   **B.** How are the nests alike? different?

observing   **C.** What materials were used to make the nests? Use tweezers and a pencil to help you pick apart the nests.

inferring   **D.** Make a list of the materials. Which seem to come from where the birds live? Which, if any, seem to come from far away? (Keep this list for use next spring.)

inferring   **E.** What kind of bird probably made each kind of nest? Get some bird books from the library. See if they can help you find out.

EXPLORATORY PROBLEM B

Given choices, what materials will some birds pick to make nests?

NEEDED

60-centimeter (2-foot) cardboard square
thread
aluminum foil
large nail
different strings
scissors
different cloth pieces
different-colored yarn
paper strips

TRY THIS

1. Do this activity in early spring, when many birds build nests.
2. Punch many holes in the cardboard with a large nail. Wiggle the nail in each hole to make it larger.

3. Cut narrow pieces of cloth, paper, and foil.

4. Cut small pieces of string and yarn.

5. Thread these materials partway through the cardboard's holes. Label under each hole what is there.

6. Tack the cardboard to a tree where other trees and bushes grow.

7. Check the board each day to see what is missing.

DISCOVERY PROBLEMS

observing   **A.** Which materials were taken first? Replace these materials right away. Will they be taken again before other materials? Check again to see.

experimenting   **B.** How can you change the picked materials to make them less attractive? You might cut longer pieces of yarn, for example, or cut wider cloth strips. How can you make the unpicked materials more attractive?

observing   **C.** What will happen if you move the board to another place? How will your findings compare with those before?

observing   **D.** Make a list of the materials selected. How does it compare with the list of nest materials you made in the winter?

TEACHING COMMENT

PREPARATION AND BACKGROUND

Bird's nests are usually abandoned by winter and are rarely used again. So winter is a good time to collect nests. In the unlikely event that eggs are found, the nest should be left undisturbed. The materials-selection board is best placed off the ground on a tree trunk or low limb away from traffic. However, it should be visible and accessible to the children.

GENERALIZATION

Birds use materials from the environment to build their nests; the ability to build nests has survival value.

SAMPLE PERFORMANCE OBJECTIVES

Knowledge: The child can describe the kinds of materials local birds are likely to use in nest building.

Process: The child can compose two listings of findings and compare them for similarities and differences.

REFERENCES

American Association for the Advancement of Science. (1993). *Benchmarks for science literacy*. New York: Oxford University Press.

National Research Council. (1996). *National science education standards*. Washington, DC: National Academy Press.

SELECTED TRADE BOOKS: ANIMAL LIFE AND ENVIRONMENT

For Younger Children

Aaseng, N. (1987a). *Meat-eating animals*. Lerner.

Aaseng, N. (1987b). *Prey animals*. Lerner.

Breeden, R. (Ed.). (1974). *Creepy crawley things*. National Geographic Society.

Bruchac, J. (1992). *Native American animal stories*. Fulcrum.

Carle, E. (1987). *The very hungry caterpillar*. Philomel.

Carle, E. (1995). *The very lonely firefly*. Philomel.

Cousins, L. (1991). *Country animals*. Morrow.

Crump, D. (1983). *Creatures small and furry*. National Geographic Society.

Day, J. (1986). *What is a mammal?* Golden Books.

Dreyer, E. (1991). *Wild animals*. Troll Associates.

Fleming, D. (1993). *In the small, small pond*. Henry Holt.

Fowler, A. (1992). *It's best to leave a snake alone*. Children's Press.

Freedman, R. (1980). *Tooth and claw: A look at animal weapons*. Holiday.

Palotta, J. (1992). *The icky bug counting book*. Charlesbridge.

Penn, L. (1983). *Young scientists explore animal friends*. Good Apple.

Pfloog, J. (1987). *Wild animals and their babies*. Western.

Priestly, A. (1987). *Big animals*. Random House.

Savage, S. (1992). *Making tracks*. Lodestar.

Stone, L. M. (1983). *Marshes and swamps*. Children's Press.

Sutton, F. (1983). *The big book of wild animals*. Putman.

Urquhart, J. C. (1982). *Animals that travel*. National Geographic.

Wildsmith, B. (1991). *Animal homes*. Oxford.

Wozmek, F. (1982). *The ABC of ecology*. Davenport.

For Older Children

Bright, M. (1987). *Pollution and wildlife*. Watts.

Dean, A. (1977). *How animals communicate*. Messner.

Dean, A. (1978). *Animal defenses*. Messner.

Earthbooks Staff. (1991). *National Wildlife Federation's book of endangered species*. Author.

Fichter, G. S. (1991). *Poisonous animals*. Watts.

Flegg, J. (1991). *Animal builders*. Newington.

Gallent, R. A. (1986). *The rise of mammals*. Watts.

Grossman, S., & Grossman, M. L. (1981). *Ecology*. Wonder.

Leon, D. (1982). *The secret world of underground creatures*. Messner.

Maynard, T. (1991). *Animal inventors*. Watts.

Penny, M. (1987). *Animal evolution*. Watts.

Pringle, L. (1987). *Home: How animals find comfort and safety*. Macmillan.

Sabin, F. (1985). *Ecosystems and food chains*. Troll Associates.

Sanders, J. (1984). *All about animal migrations*. Troll Associates.

Yamashita, K. (1993). *Paws, wings, and hooves*. Lerner.

Resource Books

Butzow, C. M., & Butzow, J. W. (1989). *Science through children's literature. An integrated approach* (animal reproduction and development topics, pp. 61–65; ducks, ants, spiders, ladybugs, fish, pp. 66–94; animal adaption topics, pp. 102–106). Teacher Ideas Press.

Fredericks, A. D., Meinbach, A. M., & Rothlein, L. (1993). *Thematic units: An integrated approach to teaching science and social studies* (animals and how they grow topics, pp. 111–122). HarperCollins.

LeCroy, B., & Holder, B. (1994). *Bookwebs: a brainstorm of ideas for the primary classroom* (animal activities pp. 30–31). Teachers Ideas Press.

Shaw, D. G., & Dybdahl, C. S. (1996). *Integrating science and language arts. A sourcebook for K–6 teachers* (animal life topics, pp. 57–59). Allyn and Bacon.

CHAPTER 9

HUMAN BODY AND NUTRITION

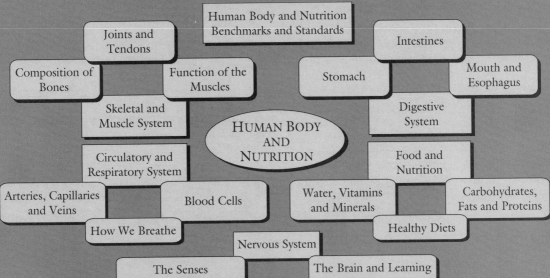

Human Body and Nutrition
Benchmarks and Standards

Joints and
Tendons

Intestines

Composition of
Bones

Function of the
Muscles

Stomach

Mouth and
Esophagus

Skeletal and
Muscle System

Digestive
System

HUMAN BODY
AND
NUTRITION

Circulatory and
Respiratory System

Food and
Nutrition

Arteries, Capillaries
and Veins

Blood Cells

Water, Vitamins
and Minerals

Carbohydrates,
Fats and Proteins

How We Breathe

Healthy Diets

Nervous System

The Senses

The Brain and Learning

By any measure, the human body is a masterpiece of organization. It is composed of millions of tiny cells, many of them differing in shape, size, and internal makeup according to the work they do.

Groups of cells that work together are tissues. Examples are the connective tissue that holds the body together, muscle tissue, nerve tissue, blood tissue, and epithelial (skin) tissue. When tissues work together, they are called *organs.* Examples are the lungs, heart, stomach, and eyes. Organs that work together are *systems.*

We will consider several body systems in this chapter, including the skeletal and muscle systems, which support and move the body; the nervous system, which controls the body; the circulatory and respiratory systems, which move the blood and permit breathing; and the digestive system, which fuels the body by breaking down foods into simpler forms. A final section examines *nutrition:* the makeup of foods and how they affect the body.

Skeletal and Muscle System Concepts
(Experiences p. 303)

It is hard to imagine how the human body would look without bones. It has more than 200 bones joined into a skeletal framework that gives the body its overall shape and support. The bones are not all individual, unique pieces that fit together. Rather, there are groups of bones, all well fitted for their specialized work.

Groups of Bones

The main part of the skull consists of eight relatively flat bones joined together into the characteristic helmet-like shape. In children, the joints between the bones are movable. This allows the bones to grow as children get older.

In adults, the skull bones will have grown together into a solid, curved surface with immovable joints. The only head bone we can ever move voluntarily is the jawbone. Chewing and normal conversation depend on this movement.

The skull is joined to a stack of oval and irregular small bones called the *vertebrae,* or spine. The vertebrae permit bending and twisting motions. In between each small bone is a pad of tough, elastic tissue called *cartilage.* The cartilage pads keep the spinal bones from grinding or hitting together as we move. As we age during adulthood, the pads continue to compress, making us shorter. Between 40 and 70, for example, we may lose an inch or more in height.

The spinal bones also have holes in them. This allows the bundle of nerves that make up the spinal cord to run through the length of the protective vertebrae. Side holes in the vertebrae permit nerve branches from the spinal cord to go out to other parts of the body.

Many children think that "standing up straight" means having a straight backbone. This is not so. Although the vertebrae are stacked in a column, the column is curved in a shallow *S* form. This permits better balance than a vertical backbone.

Attached to the backbone are 12 pairs of ribs. The top 10 pairs curve around and join the breastbone in front. But if you feel your two pairs of bottom ribs, you may notice that they are not joined in front. For this reason, they are called "floating ribs."

The ribs form a flexible cage that protects the heart, lungs, and other organs. The cartilage that fastens the ribs is somewhat elastic, and the ribs are bendable. This is why the chest can expand and contract as we breathe.

The *hipbones* are fastened at the other end of the backbone. With the bottom of the backbone, they form a large and open shallow bowl in front. The bowl helps to support the body and protects some of the organs below the waist. The lowest parts of the hipbones are used for sitting.

The *long bones* of the arms and legs are the levers that allow us to walk, run, and throw. These bones are strong but also light for their size, because they are mostly hollow inside. If they were solid, the increased weight would slow us down considerably. Long bones are thicker at the ends than in the center section and fit the ends of adjoining bones.

Composition of Bones

A soft material called *marrow* is found inside many bones, particularly the long bones. There are two kinds of marrow. *Red* marrow is found at the ends of the bones; these are the sites where red blood cells are manufactured. *Yellow* marrow is stored inside the middle of the bones and is mainly composed of fat.

A newborn baby's skeleton is composed mostly of soft cartilage. As the baby grows, its body continually replaces the cartilage with calcium and other minerals from digested food, so the skeleton continually hardens. Children's bones typically are softer than those of adults because they contain more cartilage. This makes their bones less likely to break under stress. Some cartilage never changes to bone, like the ears, tip of the nose, and several other places.

Movable Joints

A rigid skeletal framework would be of little use. The reason we can move is because many bones are held together by movable joints. Tough, thick cords of elastic tissue, called *ligaments,* make up the material that joins bone to bone. We have several different kinds of movable joints, and each allows different movements. Hinged joints allow us to bend the elbow, knee, and fingers. Notice that the movement is in only one direction.

The thumb is particularly interesting. It has only two hinged joints, yet we can move the thumb so it opposes any finger. A third joint up near the wrist makes this movement possible.

A ball-and-socket joint at the shoulder allows rotary motion of the arm. A similar socket connects the upper leg bone at the hip, but movement in this case is more restricted. Other kinds of joints allow wrist, head, foot, and other motions. In all, we have six different kinds of movable joints.

Muscles

Under the skin, and inside the body, are about 600 muscles, two-thirds of which are *voluntary* muscles. These muscles are connected to bones, and we can move them on command. Some muscles, such as those that move food through the intestines and those that make the heart beat, cannot ordinarily be controlled. These are the *involuntary* muscles.

Muscles can only pull; they work in opposite pairs. This is easiest to see with the jointed leg bones. If you swing a leg forward, muscles in the front part of the thigh and hip contract and pull the leg forward. If you swing the leg back, muscles in the back part of the thigh and hip contract and pull the leg back.

Tendons

Muscles are attached to bone and cartilage by the *tendons.* These are tough, white, twisted fibers of different lengths. Some are cordlike; others are wider and flat. Tendons are enclosed in sleeves of thin tissue that contain a slippery liquid. This permits them to slide back and forth without rubbing.

Tendons are strong and unstretchable. Some that are easy to observe are found inside the elbow and back of the knee. One of the strongest and thickest tendons in the body is the Achilles tendon. It is located just above the heel of the foot. Also easy to observe are the tendons that pull the finger bones as you wiggle your fingers. If you try this and touch the forearm with the opposite hand, you will notice that muscles in the forearm, not muscles in the hand, mainly move the fingers. Children are usually surprised by this.

Makeup of Muscles

How do muscles work? Why do they get tired? Why does exercise make us warm?

A microscope reveals that voluntary muscles are made up of bundles of fibers, each about the size of a human hair, but far stronger. Like the entire muscle, each fiber shortens as it pulls and lengthens as it relaxes. The number of fibers that work depends on how heavily the muscle is strained. Also, not all the fibers work simultaneously. Each is rapidly and continually switched on and off by the nervous system as the muscle works. This allows each fiber some rest and greater overall endurance for the muscle.

The energy to move a muscle comes from a form of sugar called *glycogen*. It is found inside the muscles' cells. About a fourth of the energy released by this sugar goes into moving the muscle. The rest is released as heat. The faster a muscle is used, the more heat is produced. This is why heavy exercise makes us warm.

Sooner or later, heavy exercise fatigues the muscle. Not only is the supply of glycogen consumed, but waste products build up in the cell faster than they can be removed. As the waste products build up, the muscle fibers work more and more slowly.

NERVOUS SYSTEM CONCEPTS
(Experiences p. 305)

Nerves

What happens inside the nervous system when we sense an object and react to it? The central part of the nervous system is composed of the brain and spinal cord. Nerves connected to the brain and spinal cord branch out in ever-smaller tendrils to all parts of the body.

When nerve endings are stimulated in some sense organs, ordinarily an electrical message is zipped through sensory nerves from the receptor to the spinal cord and then to the brain. In turn, the brain flashes back a message along motor nerves, which control muscles. The time between when the brain receives a signal and when it returns a command to the muscles is called one's *reaction time*.

Quick Reflexes

A curious thing happens, however, when a quick reflexive action is required. The brain is bypassed until the reflex action happens. For example, if you should touch a finger to a hot stove, the electrical impulses travel from the finger to the spinal cord. But instead of the signal going to the brain, the spinal cord itself flashes a signal along the motor nerves, which immediately activate muscles to jerk the hand away. Meanwhile, the spinal cord also sends impulses to the brain that cause you to feel pain. The sensation, though, is felt *after* you have already reacted to the danger. This, of course, has survival value.

Brain

The brain is the control center of the body. Instead of a single mass, it is made up of three parts: the *cerebrum,* the *cerebellum,* and the *medulla.* Each has a different job.

The cerebrum is the brain's largest part. It consists of two halves that occupy the top portion of the skull. This is the part that governs the conscious, rational processes and receives signals from the senses. The cerebrum also controls the body's voluntary muscles.

The cerebellum is a far smaller part and is located below and behind the cerebrum. It governs perception of balance and coordinates the voluntary muscles.

The medulla adjoins the top of the spinal column at the base of the skull. It governs the involuntary muscles used for digesting food, coughing or sneezing, breathing, pumping blood, and the like.

Learning

How successfully we adapt to the environment often depends on our ability to learn. We learn in several different ways. At the lowest level is trial-and-error learning. This is how we learn to do handwriting or hit a golf ball. The brain works in combination with the senses and muscles to provide corrective feedback.

Learning increases when we organize the data we deal with. Recognizing patterns, outlining, and drawing diagrams are some ways we improve learning. Learning also increases when we associate something we do not know with something we do know. Using memory devices to learn names or to remember spelling words are examples. Reasoning and problem solving are at the highest levels of learning.

The Senses

We receive most of the sensations our brains turn into perceptions through five organs: the eye, ear, nose, tongue, and skin. How do they work? Let's look at each in turn.

THE EYE. In the eye, as in the other sense organs, are the tiny nerve endings of neurons, or nerve cells. The retina, or back section of the eyeball, contains two kinds of light-sensitive neurons: rods and cones. The cones are clustered in and around the center of the retina and are sensitive to color. The rods are distributed outside the cones and are sensitive to light, but not color. The nerve endings of both rods and cones join into a bundle called the optic nerve, which leads to the brain.

THE EAR. The ear has three parts: outer, middle, and inner. The first two parts pass on sound vibrations to the inner ear, located deep inside the skull. The inner ear contains the cochlea, a spiral passage shaped like a snail's shell. Inside are sound-sensitive nerve endings and a liquid. When vibrations move into the inner ear, the cochlea's liquid vibrates and stimulates the nerve endings. This instantly transmits electric impulses to the auditory nerve, which then zips them to the brain. At that point, we hear.

If you have ever been seasick, you can probably blame your inner ear. It has an intricate part that controls our sense of balance. The part consists of three tubes, formed in half circles, called the semicircular canals. The tubes contain a thin liquid and are arranged in three different positions relative to each other. These positions correspond to the three ways we move our heads: up and down, sideways tilt, and the turning motion. Each motion of the head sloshes the liquid in one of the canals, stimulating nerve endings inside. The impulses are flashed along a branch of the auditory nerve that leads to the cerebellum rather than to the large cerebrum.

One seasickness theory states that the several motions felt in the inner ear conflict with what we see. This is especially so below deck. The sensory conflict triggers the body reaction.

THE NOSE. The nose has nerve endings in the nasal cavity that are sensitive to chemicals. When breathed into the nose, the chemicals dissolve in the moist film of mucous that covers a membrane in the nasal cavity. There nerve endings are stimulated to send signals to the sensory nerves and brain. Continual exposure to one odor causes the nerve cells to become insensitive to that odor. Yet other odors may be detected very well at the same time.

Nerve cells of the nose seem to sense only four primary odors: burnt, rancid, acid, and fragrant odors. Some scientists think that every other odor may simply be some combination of two or more of the four primary odors.

THE TONGUE. Exactly what we taste is an individual matter, even though our tongues are similarly constructed. The tongue contains clusters of nerve cells in the tiny bumps we call taste buds. Taste buds are sensitive to four flavors:

sweet, sour, salty, and bitter. Most buds are clustered in the tip, on the edges, and in the back of the tongue. The tip tends to be sensitive to sweet and salty flavors, the sides to sour flavors, and the back to bitter flavors. However, the exact places vary with people. The taste buds clump into small mounds called *papillae*. These are connected to a sensory nerve that leads to the brain.

Do you remember how tasteless food is when a head cold causes a stuffy nose? It is easy to confuse the sense of taste with that of smell. As we eat, the odors given off by the food stimulate the sense of smell. So both organs work together.

Sometimes the sense of smell dominates. For example, if you chew a tiny piece of radish while you hold a small fresh piece of apple or onion under your nose, you will believe that you are eating the apple or onion.

THE SKIN. Our skin contains no fewer than five different kinds of nerve endings, which are sensitive to pressure, touch, pain, heat, and cold. These nerve endings are positioned at various depths in the skin. Pressure, for example, is felt much deeper in the skin than touch.

Our nerve endings are also scattered unevenly. The lips and finger tips have many more endings clustered together than other places such as the back of the neck or arm. This is why they are so sensitive.

CIRCULATORY AND RESPIRATORY SYSTEM CONCEPTS
(Experiences p. 317)

Circulatory System

It would be difficult to design a better system than the human blood system for the same function. Blood is the vehicle that transports food, chemicals, and oxygen to all parts of the body. It picks up wastes from the cells and moves them through organs whose job is to remove them. Blood also protects the body.

The liquid part of blood is a clear, yellowish substance called *plasma*. In the plasma are three kinds of solid materials: *red cells, white cells,* and *platelets*. The red cells are most numerous and give the blood its characteristic color. They carry oxygen from the lungs to the body's cells and carbon dioxide from the cells back to the lungs. White cells are larger and move about freely among the body's cells, attacking and consuming disease germs. Platelets also have an important function. They help to make the blood clot wherever the body is injured and bleeding.

Blood moves in the body because it is pumped by the heart, a powerful muscle about the size of one's fist. It pumps blood by alternately contracting and relaxing. Oxygen-poor blood flows into one side of the heart. Squeezing motions pump this blood into the lungs, where it receives oxygen. The oxygen-rich blood then flows back into the opposite side of the heart from where it is pumped to the rest of the body.

In a sense, the circulatory system is really a combination of two interconnected networks of tubes of various sizes. One network sends the blood from the heart to the lungs and back again to the heart. The other sends blood from the heart to the rest of the body and returns it to the heart.

Oxygen-rich blood flows from the heart to the body through thick tubes called *arteries*. Arteries branch out all over the body, getting progressively narrower until they become extremely fine *capillaries*. Capillaries may be as narrow as one-fiftieth the diameter of a human hair and are threaded throughout the cells. Digested food and oxygen pass through the capillaries into the adjacent cells. Capillaries also take up carbon dioxide and other waste products from the cells. The waste-carrying capillaries join into progressively larger tubes called *veins,* which carry blood back to the heart. The entire trip takes about 15 seconds. Note that the veins do not carry "blue" blood as most children's science text illustrations would indicate. Those of us who have donated blood realize that it is a dark red as opposed to the bright red of oxygenated blood found in arteries.

Respiratory System

Body cells use oxygen to oxidize, or "burn," food. This process releases energy. Carbon dioxide and water vapor are by-products of this process, just as they are when a candle burns inside an inverted jar. A candle goes out when the oxygen supply is diminished. Likewise, oxidation of food requires a steady supply of enough oxygen. The job of the respiratory system is to replace the carbon dioxide and water vapor in our blood with oxygen. Let's see how this is done.

As we breathe in air through the nose, it passes through hollow nasal passages above the mouth where it is warmed and filtered. Hairlike, moving cilia inside the passages catch dust and airborne particles. These particles are swept to the mouth and coughed up or swallowed. The membrane lining the passages is coated with mucous, which also traps airborne materials.

The air then moves through the voice box or larynx and down into the throat. Two tubes are found there. One tube channels food into the stomach and is called the gullet, or *esophagus.* A second tube, the *windpipe,* or trachea, is located in front of the esophagus. It goes to the lungs. A flap of tissue, the epiglottis, covers the windpipe automatically when we eat or drink. This usually prevents food or liquids from entering the windpipe.

The windpipe shortly divides into two tubes called *bronchi.* One bronchus is attached to each lung. In the lungs, the bronchi split into progressively smaller branches of tubes. Each of the tiniest tubes ends in a tiny air sac. Since there are many thousands of these sacs, the lungs have a soft, spongy appearance.

Each sac swells like a tiny balloon when we breathe air into the lungs. Surrounding each sac are many capillaries. Oxygen from breathed-in air in the sac passes through the sac's thin wall into the capillaries. Carbon dioxide and water vapor in the capillaries pass the opposite way into the air sacs. These gases then move up through the branched tubes and are exhaled.

Your students may read that body cells use oxygen to "burn" digested food and that carbon dioxide is one by-product of the process. But don't be surprised if most still assume that the air they breathe out is the same as the air they breathe in (Mintzes, 1984).

To show them the difference, you might get some limewater from a drugstore, two identical balloons and small glass jars, and a bicycle tire pump. (Limewater is an indicator for carbon dioxide.) Pour limewater into each of the two jars until half full. Have a child fill one balloon with the pump and the other using lung power. Release the air from one balloon under the limewater surface of one jar, then do this with the second balloon and jar. The limewater exposed to the lung air should turn milky; the other should stay about the same.

Breathing

Children typically believe that the act of breathing in forces the lungs to draw in air and expand. This is not what happens. Breathing in occurs because of unequal air pressure. Examine the process yourself.

Notice what happens when you take a deep breath: The chest cavity enlarges. It enlarges because rib muscles contract and pull the ribs up and outward. At the same time the *diaphragm,* a thin sheet of muscle between the chest and the abdomen, pulls downward. This further enlarges the chest cavity. Enlarging the chest cavity reduces the air pressure inside the lungs. So the stronger outside air pressure forces air into the air passages and lungs.

When we breathe out, the diaphragm relaxes and moves upward. At the same time, the rib muscles relax, and the ribs move down and inward. This reduces the size of the chest cavity, which forces air out of the lungs.

DIGESTIVE SYSTEM CONCEPTS
(Experiences p. 324)

We can eat food, but when is it inside the body? The answer to this seemingly simple question depends on whose point of view we take.

Most people would say that food is inside the body once it is swallowed. To biochemists, however, any food still within the 9-meter (30-foot) digestive tube they call the *alimentary canal* is considered outside the body. This underlines the uselessness of foods we eat until they are digested, or chemically broken down and dissolved into a form that can be used in the cells. The digestive system (Figure 9-1) is marvelously suited to this function. Let's see how it works.

The Mouth

The digestive process begins when we start chewing food. Our front teeth (incisors and canines) cut and tear the food. Back teeth (molars) crush it into small particles. At the same time, saliva pours into the food from six salivary glands in and near the mouth. Saliva softens the food and begins the chemical breakdown of starches. A gradual, sweetening flavor is experienced when we chew starchy foods such as cooked potato, soda cracker, or bread. The saliva contains an enzyme called ptyalin that reduces large starch molecules into simple sugar molecules. (An enzyme is a catalyst, or chemical that brings about or speeds up chemi-

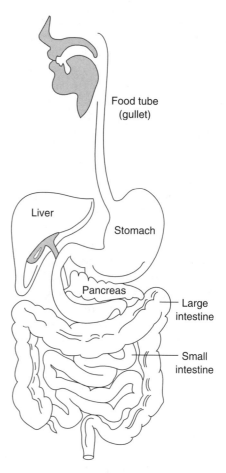

Figure 9-1
The digestive system.

cal reactions without being changed itself.) Besides ptyalin, several other enzymes in the body's digestive system help break down food into usable form.

The Food Tube

Swallowed food passes into the esophagus, or food tube. It is squeezed down into the stomach by regular, wavelike contractions of smooth muscles that surround the esophagus. Similar muscles are located all along the alimentary canal. Because it is muscle action (peristalsis), not gravity, that moves the food inside the canal, it is possible to eat and swallow while standing on our heads.

The Stomach

Peristaltic motions continue in the stomach. The food is churned slowly in gastric juices secreted from the stomach lining. Several enzymes and diluted hydrochloric acid break down most of the proteins. Digestion of starch stops because acid prevents ptyalin from working. Some fats are broken down, but for the most part, fats go through the stomach undigested.

If the stomach's hydrochloric acid is so powerful, why doesn't this corrosive liquid digest the stomach itself? Only in recent years have researchers pinpointed the reason. A small amount of ammonia (this is an alkali or base) is secreted in the lining of the stomach. It effectively neutralizes acid next to the lining without interfering with the acid's digestive action elsewhere in the stomach. We use the same principle of neutralizing an acid when we drink seltzer or soda water to settle a "sour" stomach.

The Intestines

After about two to six hours in the stomach, depending on what and how much has been eaten, the partially digested food materials are pushed into the small intestine. Here, glands within intestinal walls produce digestive juices with enzymes that begin working on the food. Additional digestive juices are secreted into the intestine from small tubes connected to the liver and pancreas.

Throughout the small intestine, peristaltic motion continues as digestive juices complete the breakdown of carbohydrates into simple sugars, proteins into amino acids, and fats into fatty acids and glycerine. At various portions of the small intestine, the sugars and amino acids are absorbed into blood vessels within its lining. Digested fats are first absorbed into the lymph system and then later transported into the blood stream.

Nondigestible material or waste, composed chiefly of cellulose, passes into the large intestine. Much of the water contained in waste material is absorbed into the intestinal walls. The remaining substance is eliminated from the body.

Food products dissolved in the blood are distributed to cells after they are processed by the liver. In the cells, these products are oxidized, changed into protoplasm, or stored as fat.

FOOD AND NUTRITION CONCEPTS
(Experiences p. 325)

We may eat hundreds of foods combined in thousands of ways. But nutritionally speaking, there are four kinds: sugars, starches, fats, and proteins. Some persons would add three more: vitamins, minerals, and water. These seven nutrients may be combined into three groups:

1. Foods for energy—sugars, starches, and fats.
2. Foods for growth and repair of cells—proteins.
3. Food for regulation of body processes—vitamins, minerals, and water.

Carbohydrates

If we heat table sugar in a test tube, the sugar gradually turns black, and water vapor is given off. The black material is carbon. The water is formed as hydrogen and oxygen atoms given off by individual sugar molecules combine. Heat some starch, and again carbon and water appear. Both sugar and starch are *carbohydrates*, a name that means "carbon and water."

Although sugar and starches are composed of the same elements, these elements may appear in various combinations and form relatively small or large molecules. "Simple" sugar molecules, for example, are the smallest carbohydrate molecules. They may be found in grapes and many other fruits. When two simple sugar molecules become attached, a complex sugar, such as table sugar, is formed. A starch molecule is nothing more than a long chain of sugar molecules tightly attached to one another.

In digestion, carbohydrates are broken down into simple sugars. Only in this form are these molecules small enough to pass through cell membranes into the cells, where they "burn" and release energy. The "burning" is a result of *oxidation,* a process in which oxygen chemically combines with fuel—in this case, sugar—and releases heat energy. (Rusting is a form of slow oxidation; fire is very fast oxidation.) The oxygen comes from the air we breathe.

Fats

Analysis shows that fats are also composed of carbon, hydrogen, and oxygen. However, fat molecules have relatively fewer oxygen atoms than carbohydrates. Because they are oxygen "poor," fat molecules can combine with more oxygen atoms and yield about twice as much energy as carbohydrates.

Foods rich in carbohydrates and fats provide our principal source of energy. But when we eat more than we need of these materials, the cells store any excess in the form of fat. Fat storage does not occur uniformly throughout all body cells, as every figure-conscious person knows.

Proteins

The proteins are extremely complex, large molecules. A single molecule may contain thousands of atoms. Like the preceding nutrients, proteins are made up of carbon, hydrogen, and oxygen. But proteins also contain nitrogen and, typically, sulfur. Proteins are the main source of materials (amino acids) needed for growth and repair of body cells. Excess proteins can be oxidized in cells and so provide energy.

Although all animal and some plant foods (mainly beans, peas, nuts) are rich in proteins, no single plant source contains sufficient amino acids for complete growth and repair of body cells. However, a *combination* of legumes and grains (beans and rice) can furnish all the needed amino acids.

Vitamins

Vitamins are essential to health because they regulate cell activities. These substances permit biochemical processes to take place. Without proper vitamins, the body may suffer from several deficiency diseases, such as scurvy, rickets, and anemia. A balanced diet is usually all that is needed to prevent the disease. But, particularly in the last decade, scientists have found clues that vitamins may play a larger role than previously thought in achieving optimal health and preventing some chronic diseases, such as cancer, decline of the immune system in the aged, heart disease, eye degeneration, and others. This is why some nutritionists recommend a daily multivitamin as "insurance." However, most researchers see the need for more evidence before they can recommend large doses of vitamins aimed at specific diseases or conditions.

Minerals

Several minerals are essential because they help to regulate cell activities. In addition, some minerals are incorporated into body tissue. Calcium and phosphorus form the hard portions of our bones and teeth. Milk is especially rich in these two minerals. Iron and copper help form red blood cells. A proper amount of iodine is needed in the thyroid gland for normal oxidation to take place in cells. Salt is often iodized to prevent goiter, an iodine deficiency. Some minerals cannot be used by cells unless specific vitamins are present. Most fruits and vegetables are rich in vitamins and minerals.

Water

There are many reasons why water is essential to life and good nutrition. It changes chemically to form part of protoplasm. Water is the chief part of blood. It cools the body and carries away accumulated poisons. It is important to digestion and excretion. About two-thirds of the body itself is composed of water.

Besides drinking water directly, we take in much water in the food we eat. For example, celery is about 95 percent water, and fresh bread is about 35 percent water.

Choosing a Healthful Diet

A century ago many Americans were likely to suffer from undernutrition, but today the problem is often the opposite. Most of us eat too much, particularly of foods rich in fat, such as meat and dairy products. This increases the risk of heart disease, stroke, and diabetes, and may also increase the incidence of certain types of cancer. Nutritionists today recommend that we eat far more grains, fruits, and vegetables than has been customary in the American diet.

Many children and adults realize that they must eat a variety of foods to have a proper or "balanced" diet, but are unsure of its makeup. To help us select a healthful combination of nutrients, the U.S. Department of Agriculture has published a food pyramid, with guidelines for five groups of foods (Figure 9-2).

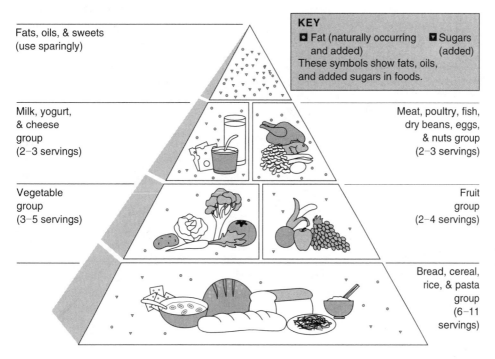

Fats, oils, & sweets
(use sparingly)

KEY
◨ Fat (naturally occurring and added)   ◪ Sugars (added)
These symbols show fats, oils, and added sugars in foods.

Milk, yogurt, & cheese group
(2–3 servings)

Meat, poultry, fish, dry beans, eggs, & nuts group
(2–3 servings)

Vegetable group
(3–5 servings)

Fruit group
(2–4 servings)

Bread, cereal, rice, & pasta group
(6–11 servings)

Figure 9-2
Food guide pyramid.

Notice that grains, at the base, get the most servings, while fats, oils, and sweets are to be used only sparingly. In the dairy group, many nutritionists recommend that only nonfat or low-fat products be served. In the meat group, they suggest lean rather than well-marbled meat, skinless poultry, and egg whites rather than whole eggs.

Of course, the pyramid is only a general guide. Size of servings and the number of calories we need to eat depend on our size, age, health, and lifestyle.

HUMAN BODY AND NUTRITION BENCHMARKS AND STANDARDS

As students progress through the elementary years, they gain a more comprehensive understanding of the complexity of the human body and the need to care for it through proper nutrition and exercise. Some examples of specific standards related to the human organism are as follows:

SAMPLE BENCHMARKS (AAAS, 1993).

- People need water, food, air, and waste removal, and a particular range of temperatures in their environment (by Grades K–2, p. 128).
- Food provides energy and materials for growth and repair of body parts. Vitamins and minerals, present in small amounts in foods, are essential to keep everything working well (by Grades 3–5, p. 144).

SAMPLE STANDARDS (NRC, 1996).

- Humans have distinct body structures for walking, holding, seeing, and talking (by Grades K–4, p. 129).
- The human organism has systems for digestion, respiration, reproduction, circulation, excretion, movement, control, and coordination, and for protection from disease. These systems interact with one another (by Grades 5–8, p. 156–175).

INVESTIGATIONS AND ACTIVITIES

SKELETAL AND MUSCLE SYSTEM EXPERIENCES
(Concepts p. 292)

ACTIVITY: *WHAT HAPPENS WHEN MINERALS ARE REMOVED FROM A BONE?*

NEEDED

narrow jar and cap
vinegar
two clean matched chicken bones

TRY THIS

1. Put one bone in the jar. Leave the other one outside.
2. Fill the jar with enough vinegar to cover the bone.
3. Cap the jar and wait five days.
4. Remove the bone from the jar and rinse it with water.
   a. Compare the bones. In what ways are the two bones different? How easily does each bone bend? How are the bones still alike?
   b. What difference would it make if your bones had no hard minerals? What foods are rich in minerals?

ACTIVITY: *HOW USEFUL ARE YOUR THUMBS?*

NEEDED

paper clip
pencil and paper
tape

TRY THIS

1. Make a list of some things you can do now with one or two hands. Which do you think you cannot do without thumbs? Which might you do less well? Which might you do as well?
2. You might record what you think on a chart. You can make a check mark first for what you think, and then an *X* for what you find out.

Can Do with Thumbs	Without Thumbs		
	Can't Do	Do Less Well	Do as Well
Pick up paper clip	✓	X	
Tie shoelace			
Write my name			
Shake hands			
Button a shirt			

3. Ask someone to tape your thumbs to your hands.

4. Try doing the things on the list without using your thumbs. What surprises, if any, did you find? How do your thumbs help you?

ACTIVITY: *WHAT HAPPENS WHEN YOU OVERWORK YOUR MUSCLES?*

NEEDED

pencil and paper
watch with second hand

TRY THIS

1. Open one hand all the way, then quickly close it to make a tight fist.

2. Open and close it just like that for one minute without stopping. Do it as fast as you can.

3. Count and record what you are able to do during the first and last 30 seconds.

   a. How do the first half and the last half figures compare?

   b. What difference might it make if you change hands?

   c. If you went slower, would you be able to make more fists in one minute?

   d. Can you make as many fists in a second trial? If not, how long must you rest in between to do so?

NERVOUS SYSTEM EXPERIENCES
(Concepts p. 294)

INVESTIGATION: *EYE BLINKING*

When do your eyes blink? Do they blink when something suddenly comes near them? Eye blinking can protect your eyes. Have you also found that your eyes blink at other times? Regular eye blinking wipes your eyes clean and keeps your eyes soft and moist.

EXPLORATORY PROBLEM

How much can you control your protective eye blinking?

NEEDED

clear kitchen wrap
sticky tape
tissue paper
scissors
large file card
partner

TRY THIS

1. You will need to make an eye shield. Cut out the center of a large file card. Leave at least a 2-centimeter (or 1-inch) border.
2. Stick a double layer of clear kitchen wrap to the border with tape.
3. Hold up the shield to your eyes. Look at your partner through the clear wrap (Figure 9-3). Let him *gently* toss a tiny wad of tissue toward it. ***Caution:*** Closely monitor this activity.

DISCOVERY PROBLEMS

observing	**A.** Do your eyes blink each time the wad hits the shield? Can you stop your eyes from blinking?
communicating	**B.** Are you able to control your eye blinking with practice? If so, how much practice? Keep a record.
observing	**C.** Trade places with some other people. How does their protective eye blinking compare to yours?
observing and inferring	**D.** How often do a person's eyes blink the regular way? Secretly observe the number of times someone blinks for one minute. Compare the blinking rates of different people. Do their blinking rates change when they know you are observing them?

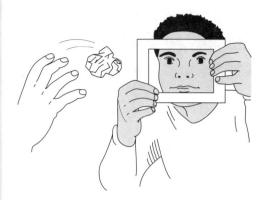

Figure 9-3

observing   **E.** How often do some animals blink their eyes? Which animals can you observe?

TEACHING COMMENT

PREPARATION AND BACKGROUND

Blinking is an automatic reflex that children like to investigate. Many children find it hard to prevent the protective blinking reaction when the wad is tossed at the shield. This is good, because the reaction has survival value. Regular blinking, of course, is easily controllable when we are conscious of the act. The rate varies widely among persons and is influenced by a variety of factors.

GENERALIZATION

Eye blinking is a protective reflex action that is partly controllable. The rate of blinking varies among different people.

SAMPLE PERFORMANCE OBJECTIVES

Process: The child can make an accurate record of the blinking rates of different people and order them according to frequency.

Knowledge: The child can explain why automatic eye blinking has greater survival value than conscious blinking.

INVESTIGATION: *YOUR REACTION TIME*

Have you ever had to stop fast when riding your bike? The time between when we sense something and when we act is called our *reaction time*. What people would you expect to have fast reaction times? slower reaction times?

EXPLORATORY PROBLEM

How can you find out about your reaction time?

NEEDED

ruler
paper
partner
pencil

TRY THIS

1. Have your partner hold up a ruler just above your open thumb and forefinger. The ruler's lowest marked number should be facing down. Keep your eye on this ruler end.

2. Have your partner drop the ruler without warning. When you see it drop, close your fingers quickly and catch the ruler (Figure 9-4).

Figure 9-4

3. At what number did you catch the ruler? Read the closest whole number just above your two closed fingers. This is your reaction time number.

DISCOVERY PROBLEMS

hypothesizing and communicating **A.** What persons in your class may have faster reaction times than yours? slower reaction times? Test these people and your partner. Keep a record.

inferring

B. Will you react to a sound faster than to what you see? Have your partner make a sound just as she drops the ruler. Your eyes should be closed. Catch the ruler when you hear the sound. Compare this reaction time number with the one made when you saw the ruler drop.

inferring

C. Will you react to a touch faster than to sound or sight? Your eyes should be closed. Your partner can touch your head lightly when she drops the ruler. Catch the ruler when you feel her touch. Compare this reaction time with the other times.

experimenting

D. Does the time of day affect your reaction time? Does practice make a difference? Does which hand you use make a difference? How can you find out? What other ideas would you like to try?

TEACHING COMMENT

PREPARATION AND BACKGROUND

For meaningful comparisons, it is important that students do the test in the same way. *Caution:* It is important that the ruler be turned before it is dropped. You want the flat part of the ruler, *not* the ruler edges, to be pinched by the two fingers.

GENERALIZATION

People have different reaction times. The sense signal people react to also makes a difference in their reaction times.

SAMPLE PERFORMANCE OBJECTIVES

Process: The child can measure relative differences in reaction time of people by using a dropped ruler.

Knowledge: The child can state several variables that may influence a person's reaction time.

INVESTIGATION: *HOW PRACTICE IMPROVES LEARNING*

Suppose you learn to do something one way, and then someone says you must learn to do it another way. Why might this be hard to do? How might learning to draw or write backward be a problem? How might practice help?

EXPLORATORY PROBLEM

How can you learn to do mirror drawing or writing?

NEEDED

small mirror
paper
clay
pencil
book
ruler
watch or clock with second hand
graph paper

TRY THIS

1. Draw a triangle on paper, no larger than the one in Figure 9-5.

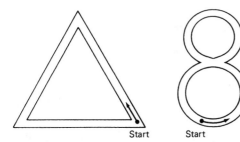

Figure 9-5

2. Arrange the paper, a mirror, and a book as in Figure 9-6. Use two pieces of clay to hold up the mirror.
3. Sit so you must look into the mirror to see the triangle.
4. Place your pencil point on the triangle corner at "start."
5. Observe a watch and notice the time.
6. Draw a line inside and around the whole triangle. Look at the mirror to see what you are doing. Keep the line between the triangle's inside and outside borders. If you go beyond the borders, stop drawing. Start again from the place where you left the border.
7. When you complete the drawing, check the time again. Record in seconds how long it took for this first trial.

Figure 9-6

DISCOVERY PROBLEMS

measuring **A.** How will practice affect the time needed to draw around the triangle? How much faster will your second trial be? third trial? fourth trial? Make a record like this of what you find out:

NUMBER OF TRIALS	TIME TO FINISH (SECONDS)
1	160
2	140
3	100
4	70

communicating **B.** Make a graph of your findings. Notice how to do this on the graph in Figure 9-7. Suppose it took 160 seconds to finish the first trial.

Put your finger on 1 at the bottom. Follow the line up to and opposite 160. A dot is placed where the two lines cross. Check to see how the other figures are recorded. See how a line has been drawn from one dot to the next. This line is called a *curve*. The graph tells about learning, so the line may be called a *learning curve*.

predicting **C.** Study your own learning curve. How fast do you think you can draw the triangle after six trials? seven trials? eight trials? nine trials? ten trials? Record your findings on your graph and complete your learning curve.

inferring **D.** How does your learning curve compare to those of others? Do some people learn mirror drawing faster than others?

predicting **E.** Try a mirror drawing of another figure, such as a large 8 (Figure 9-5). What shape will your learning curve be for this figure? Will people who learned fast before learn fast again?

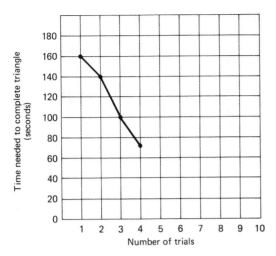

Figure 9-7

hypothesizing   **F.** What other problems about learning mirror drawing can you investigate?

TEACHING COMMENT

PREPARATION AND BACKGROUND

You may have to help some students with the line graphs if they lack experience. Also, expect some students to have trouble deciding how many seconds it takes to draw completely around each figure.

GENERALIZATION

An earlier learning may interfere with a later learning. Proper practice can improve one's performance.

SAMPLE PERFORMANCE OBJECTIVES

Process: The child can record data accurately on a graph.

Knowledge: The child can predict when an earlier learning is likely to interfere with later learning.

FOR YOUNGER CHILDREN

This investigation is too abstract for young children in its full form. But if the exploratory problem is presented as a hand–eye coordination activity, young students will enjoy it.

INVESTIGATION: *YOUR SENSE OF TOUCH*

What can you tell about an object by touch? What are some small objects you might know just by touching them?

EXPLORATORY PROBLEM

What objects can you match just by touch?

NEEDED

cloth blindfold
open cardboard box (with a hand-sized hole cut in each side)
matched pairs of small objects
partner

TRY THIS

1. Put a blindfold on your partner. Or, your partner's eyes should be closed. He should not see what you are doing.
2. Put two small, unlike objects inside the box, which should be upside down.
3. Place another small object outside the box. It should match one of the objects inside. Let your blindfolded partner feel it.
4. Next, have your partner feel the objects inside the box. Can he tell which one matches the outside object?
5. Take turns with your partner in playing this game. Use different objects each time. Later use as many objects each time as you can.

DISCOVERY PROBLEMS

observing and inferring   **A.** Which objects are hard to tell apart? Which are easy? What makes them easy or hard to tell apart?

classifying   **B.** Can you use touch to put objects in order by size? by roughness? Which objects?

experimenting   **C.** Is it easier to tell what an inside object is if you can see the outside objects? How can you find out?

experimenting   **D.** Is it easier to tell what an inside object is with two hands than with one? How can you find out?

TEACHING COMMENT

PREPARATION AND BACKGROUND

Many small objects around the classroom and home may be used in this activity. Among objects easily paired are these: chalk, pencils, leaves, erasers, crayons, nails, coins, washers, rubber bands, cloth of various sizes and textures, paper, foil, and toy figures.

Size, texture, shape, hardness, and, to a minor extent, weight will be the properties used by children to identify objects by touch.

GENERALIZATION

Several properties of an object can be discovered by touch.

SAMPLE PERFORMANCE OBJECTIVES

Process: The child infers the identities of objects and matches them by touch.
Knowledge: The child describes the properties that can be used to identify an object.

FOR OLDER CHILDREN

Try a challenging variation that stresses communication skills. One child holds an object behind her and describes its properties to a partner. The partner touches the several objects inside the box and selects one that matches the description. The described and selected objects are then compared to see if they are identical.

To make the task harder, make the differences among the objects less obvious. Also, put more objects inside the box.

INVESTIGATION: *THE SENSITIVITY OF YOUR SKIN*

Suppose you could not tell if something was touching your skin. How might this change your life?

EXPLORATORY PROBLEM

How can you find out how sensitive your skin is to touch?

NEEDED

ruler
paper and pencil
partner
paper clip

TRY THIS

1. Open up and then bend a paper clip into a U shape.
2. Push the two points together so they meet.
3. Touch the points lightly to the palm of your partner's hand. Eyes should be closed.

4. Ask your partner if he feels two points or one.

5. Separate the two points a short distance. Ask again if he feels two points or one (Figure 9-8).

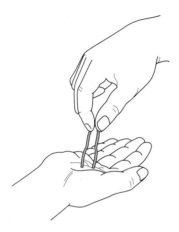

Figure 9-8

6. Keep repeating this action. Each time, move the two points farther apart until your partner feels two points. Then measure the distance between the two points with a ruler.

7. Switch with your partner so you can have your skin tested.

DISCOVERY PROBLEMS

observing, measuring, and communicating   **A.** Where on your skin can you feel the two points soonest? Let your partner measure and make a record such as this one:

BODY PART   DISTANCE BETWEEN THE POINTS

Finger tip

Palm of hand

Back of hand

Back of neck

Lips

inferring and classifying   Look carefully at your completed record. Which seems to be the most sensitive place measured? In what order should the places go if arranged from least to most sensitive?

inferring

B. How does your record compare to those of other people? Are some people more sensitive than others? If so, which people? Are certain places on people's skin more sensitive than others? If so, which places?

TEACHING COMMENT

PREPARATION AND BACKGROUND

Many of our nerve ends are found near the skin surface and are distributed unevenly. Typically, our fingertips are more sensitive to touch than other body parts. This is because a high concentration of nerve endings is located there.

It is important that children who are being tested keep their eyes closed. Otherwise, their perception of touch may be altered by what they see. *Caution:* Supervise closely to ensure that the paper clip points are touched *lightly* to the skin.

GENERALIZATION

Some places on our skin are more sensitive to touch than other places; also, some people are more sensitive to touch than others.

SAMPLE PERFORMANCE OBJECTIVES

Process: The child can measure and compare skin sensitivity at several places on the body.

Knowledge: The child can predict which places on a person's skin are more likely to be sensitive to touch.

FOR YOUNGER CHILDREN

Most primary students should be able to do the exploratory section of this investigation and contrast the sensitivity of a fingertip with the palm of the hand.

INVESTIGATION: *YOUR SENSITIVITY TO TEMPERATURE*

Suppose you have two containers of water. One is slightly warmer than another. Could you tell by touch a temperature difference in the water? Does it depend on how much of a difference there is?

EXPLORATORY PROBLEM

How can you find out the smallest temperature difference you can feel?

NEEDED

two cups half-filled with water (one water sample should be warm)
paper and pencil
partner
thermometer (one you can get wet)

TRY THIS

1. Dip a finger into each cup. It is probably easy now for you to tell which cup of water is cooler and which is warmer (Figure 9-9).

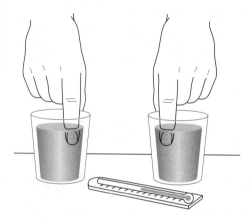

Figure 9-9

2. Let your partner pour a little of the cooler water into the warmer water. You can probably still easily feel the temperature difference.

3. Have your partner continue to reduce the temperature difference between the two cups. She can do this by pouring a little water back and forth between the cups. Keep feeling the water in both cups each time.

4. Stop when you can just barely tell there is a temperature difference. Make sure you are not just imagining this. Close your eyes and let your partner switch around the cups a few times. Tell your partner which cup is cooler or warmer each time. Always keep your eyes closed when the cups are switched.

5. Put the thermometer into each cup for at least half a minute. What is the difference between the two readings?

DISCOVERY PROBLEMS

experimenting   **A.** What is the smallest temperature difference your partner can feel? Get some more warm and cool water and find out.

experimenting **B.** Are some people more sensitive than others? Are people with thin fingers more sensitive than those with thicker fingers? Are toes more sensitive than fingers?

hypothesizing **C.** What questions would you like to investigate?

TEACHING COMMENT

PREPARATION AND BACKGROUND

The beginning temperature difference between the two water samples should be obvious. But it need not be a wide one. If you do not have access to a hot-water tap, warm some water on a hot plate. Or draw two half-cups of tap water and slip an ice cube into one for several minutes.

Children will need the ability to read thermometers to do this investigation. The average child can detect a temperature difference as little as 1.5°C (3°F). Some students will detect an even smaller difference. Eyes are closed for each test.

GENERALIZATION

People differ in their sensitivity to temperature.

SAMPLE PERFORMANCE OBJECTIVES

Process: The child can measure and compare the abilities of different people to detect small differences in water temperature.

Knowledge: The child can state the approximate range of children's differences in detecting water temperature.

CIRCULATORY AND RESPIRATORY SYSTEM EXPERIENCES
(Concepts p. 296)

INVESTIGATION: PEOPLE'S PULSE BEATS

Your heart pumps blood through long tubes in your body called arteries. Your arteries are very elastic. They stretch then shrink slightly each time the heart pumps more blood through them. These tiny movements are called *pulse* beats. You can tell how fast your heart pumps by feeling your pulse beats.

EXPLORATORY PROBLEM

How can you feel and measure how fast your pulse beats?

NEEDED

watch or clock with second hand
paper and pencil

TRY THIS

1. Press on the inside part of your wrist with four fingers. (See Figure 9-10.)

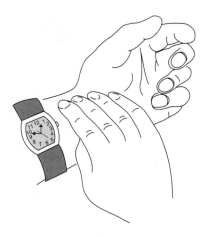

Figure 9-10

2. Find where you can best feel your pulse.

3. Count how often your pulse beats in one minute while sitting. The number of pulse beats in one minute is your "resting" pulse rate (this would differ when exercising).

4. Record your pulse rate on paper.

DISCOVERY PROBLEMS

experimenting **A.** How does what you do change your pulse rate? For example, how does standing affect it? lying down? exercise?

experimenting **B.** How do your pulse rates compare before and after eating?

observing **C.** Where else on your body can you feel your pulse? Is the pulse rate there the same as at the wrist?

experimenting **D.** How do the pulse rates of different people compare? For example, how do the pulse rates of boys and girls compare? How do adults and children compare? How do young and old adults compare? Does how tall a person is make a difference in pulse rate? Does how heavy a person is make a difference?

hypothesizing **E.** What else do you notice about people, or what they do, that might affect pulse rates?

observing F. How do you think the pulse rates of dogs, cats, and other animals compare with those of humans? How can you find out?

TEACHING COMMENT

PREPARATION AND BACKGROUND

The pulse may also be felt quite easily on each side of the throat just under the chin.

The pulse rate usually slows with age and size. Also, boys have slightly slower rates than girls. Seven-year-olds average around 90 beats per minute, which is almost twice the rate for the very aged. Athletic training also reduces the rate because it develops a larger, stronger heart. These factors similarly influence animal pulse rates, particularly size. An elephant, for example, has a very slow pulse rate.

There are several opportunities to make useful graphs in this investigation. For example, how long does it take for the pulse to return to a resting rate after exercise? What is the effect of eating on the rate? Also, watch for chances to control variables and make operational definitions: What is a tall, young, old, heavy, or tired person? If we are testing for age, how can we control height and weight?

GENERALIZATION

One's pulse rate is a measure of how fast the heart beats in one minute. A variety of conditions may affect it.

SAMPLE PERFORMANCE OBJECTIVES

Process: The child can accurately measure his pulse rate.
Knowledge: The child can describe several conditions that influence the pulse rate.

INVESTIGATION: THE VOLUME OF AIR YOU BREATHE

How much air do you breathe in a single breath? How big a container do you think you would need to hold it?

EXPLORATORY PROBLEM

How can you find out how much air you breathe?

NEEDED

large bowl or pail, placed in a sink
masking tape
plastic or glass bottle with cap (1 gallon or 4 liter)
string
rubber tube

ruler
paper sheet
partner
pencil

TRY THIS

1. Stick a strip of tape down the side of the bottle.
2. Mark the strip into 10 equal parts.
3. Partly fill a large bowl or pail with water.
4. Fill the bottle with water and cap it.
5. Put the bottle, upside down, into the bowl.
6. Remove the cap while the bottleneck is underwater.
7. Put one end of the tube into the bottle. (You may have to tip the bottle a little. Have someone hold the bottle so it does not go far over.)
8. Wrap some paper around the other end of the tube (Figure 9-11).

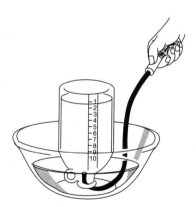

Figure 9-11

9. Take a regular breath. Then blow out the air through the tube. Quickly pinch the tube shut when you finish blowing. Observe how much water is forced out of the bottle. This tells you how much air you blow out.
10. Refill the bottle each time you try a breath test.

DISCOVERY PROBLEMS

measuring

A. By what tape mark is the water level for a regular breath? Make a record, so you can compare it to other marks.

measuring

B. How much more air can you hold when you breathe deeply? Take a deep breath. Blow out all the air you can. Compare the new and old marks.

measuring

C. How much air can other persons blow out in one breath? (Wrap a fresh paper around the tube end each time someone new blows through it.)

communicating

D. Make a graph of your findings. Use each person's chest size, or height, or weight for one part of your graph. Use their water level mark for the other part, as in Figure 9-12.

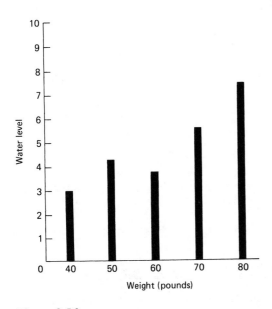

Figure 9-12

predicting

E. Can you use your graph to predict more findings? For example, will two persons who weigh the same get the same results? Will two people with the same height or chest size get the same results?

hypothesizing and communicating

F. What else do you notice about people that might affect how much air they can hold? For example, do athletes have more lung space than others? What is an "athlete"?

TEACHING COMMENT

PREPARATION AND BACKGROUND

A child can measure chest sizes with string. For good hygiene, a fresh, small slip of paper should be wrapped around the tube end each time it is used.

A typical plastic one-gallon container has curved sides and some space for the bottle neck. Therefore, to divide it accurately into 10 parts requires more mathematics than is presently suggested. Students can use a measuring cup to calculate the total number of ounces (or milliliters) in the bottle, and divide by 10. Then they can fill the bottle a tenth at a time to make each mark.

GENERALIZATION

The volume of water displaced by "lung" air is a rough measure of lung capacity. People's lungs vary greatly in air capacity.

SAMPLE PERFORMANCE OBJECTIVES

Process: The child can construct a graph that shows the relationship of weight (or other measurable property) to lung capacity.

Knowledge: The child can explain how the volume of the displaced water is associated with lung capacity.

FOR YOUNGER CHILDREN

Younger students will enjoy and profit from making rough comparisons of their lung capacities.

INVESTIGATION: *HOW FAST PEOPLE BREATHE*

How many breaths do you take each minute? Does everyone breathe equally fast? What conditions may affect how fast people breathe?

EXPLORATORY PROBLEM

How can you find out how many breaths you take each minute?

NEEDED

watch or clock with second hand
pencil and paper

TRY THIS

1. Count one breath each time you breathe *out* while sitting.

2. Observe the time on a clock. Count the number of times you breathe out in one minute (Figure 9-13).

3. Record the number on a piece of paper.

Figure 9-13

DISCOVERY PROBLEMS

measuring

A. How fast do you breathe after exercise? Bend and touch your toes or do some other easy exercise for one minute. Then count your breaths for one minute.

measuring and communicating

B. How fast do other people breathe while sitting? Compare people who are different in weight, height, and sex. Tell them how to count their breaths. Keep time for one minute. Record each person's name and how fast each breathes.

measuring

C. How fast do other people breathe after exercise? Record your findings.

predicting

D. Can you predict how fast some people will breathe? Study your records and observe the people. What are the people like who are slow breathers? faster breathers? Perhaps other people who are like them will also be fast or slow. Pick a few people you have not tested before and find out.

hypothesizing

E. What else about people, or what they do, might affect how fast they breathe?

TEACHING COMMENT

PREPARATION AND BACKGROUND

The main purpose of this investigation is to help children record and think about data. Children will discover a variety of breathing rates, but reasons for these differences will be inconclusive at their level of understanding. You might mention that there is no single proper breathing rate for everyone. What is natural for one person may not be for another.

GENERALIZATION

People have different breathing rates; exercise affects one's breathing rate.

SAMPLE PERFORMANCE OBJECTIVES

Process: The child can compare two sets of breathing data and note likenesses and differences.

Knowledge: The child can predict the approximate average breathing rate of several classmates who are in sitting positions.

DIGESTIVE SYSTEM EXPERIENCES
(Concepts page 298)

ACTIVITY: *HOW DOES CHANGING STARCH INTO SUGAR HELP THE BODY?*

NEEDED

two small jars or glasses
teaspoon
starch
sugarless soda
cracker
sugar
water

TRY THIS

1. Bite off a piece of sugarless cracker and chew it for at least one minute.

   a. How does the taste of the cracker change as you chew it? A soda cracker is made up mostly of starch. The saliva in your mouth starts changing the starch into a sugar. It is changed the rest of the way in your small intestine. Before food can be used by your body cells, it must be in a *dissolved* form. Does changing a starch into a sugar help it to dissolve? Find out for yourself.

2. Half-fill two small jars with water.

3. Put a teaspoon of sugar in one jar and one of starch in the other. Mix each for a minute.

   b. Which food dissolves? Will more stirring make the undissolved food dissolve?

TEACHING COMMENT

Students will need to know that when a material dissolves it is no longer visible. The solution looks clear.

FOOD AND NUTRITION EXPERIENCES
(Concepts p. 299)

ACTIVITY: *WHICH FOODS HAVE STARCH?*

NEEDED

iodine
piece of white chalk
medicine dropper
cornstarch
tiny pieces of foods (such as white bread, rice, macaroni, cheese, potato, cereals)
teaspoon
waxed paper

TRY THIS

1. Place a bit of cornstarch on waxed paper. Crush a small piece of white chalk next to it with a spoon.

2. Put one drop of iodine on each. Notice how the cornstarch turns purple-black. The chalk should look red-brown. When a food turns purple-black, it has starch.

3. Test your food samples with the iodine. Crush each sample first with the spoon. Wash it off each time.

   a. Which samples seem to have starch? Which do not?

4. Try the starch test on part of an unripe banana. Then test part of a very ripe banana. Taste a little of each.

   b. What difference do you notice? When does a banana seem to have more starch? When does it seem to have more sugar?

ACTIVITY: *WHICH FOODS HAVE FATS?*

NEEDED

brown paper bag
drop of oil
small pieces of different foods (such as bacon, olive, margarine, bread, apple, cheese)
drop of water

TRY THIS

1. Spread a drop of oil on the brown paper. Fat is mostly oil.
2. Spread a drop of water alongside it. Allow it to dry.
3. Hold up the paper to the light. Notice the difference in the two spots. Fat shows as a shiny, oily spot.
    a. Which foods do you think have fat?
4. Make a list and then test the foods you can. Rub each small piece into the brown paper.
    b. Which made an oily stain? How do your findings compare with what you thought?

INVESTIGATION: *SOME PROPERTIES OF POWDERED FOODS*

You eat many different white powders. Cake is made with baking powder. White bread is made with white flour. Cornstarch helps to make gravy. You can even make milk by mixing powdered milk with water.

If you take a quick look at most white powders, they seem alike. But each is really different in several ways.

EXPLORATORY PROBLEM

How can you tell one white powder from another? *Caution:* Do not use taste for this investigation.

NEEDED

white powders (such as baking powder, baking soda, white flour, powdered sugar, cornstarch, powdered milk)
small jar of water
three medicine droppers
teaspoon

small jar of iodine solution
paper towel
small jar of white vinegar
magnifier

TRY THIS

1. Put less than a quarter-teaspoon of one powder on a paper towel. Only a little is needed (Figure 9-14).

Figure 9-14

2. Observe it carefully through a magnifier. How does it look?
3. Feel the powder with your fingers. How does it feel?
4. Put a drop of water on the powder. What happens?
5. Put a drop of iodine solution on the powder. What happens?
6. Put a drop of vinegar on the powder. What happens?

DISCOVERY PROBLEMS

observing and communicating **A.** How does this powder compare to other powders? Test a few more powders. Record what you observe on a chart such as this:

Powder Tested	How It Looks Magnified	How It Feels	Reaction to Water	Reaction to Iodine	Reaction to Vinegar
Cornstarch					
Flour					
Baking soda					

inferring

B. Which test or tests seem most useful to tell the powders apart? least useful?

inferring

C. Can you identify an unknown powder? Ask someone to put a quarter-teaspoon of powder on a fresh paper towel. You should not know what powder it is, but it should be one recorded on your chart. Make some tests and use your chart to identify it.

inferring

D. Can you identify two unknown powders mixed together? Have someone choose two chart powders and mix them. Do the rest as in Problem C.

hypothesizing

E. What other ways can you test white powders? What other powders can you test?

TEACHING COMMENT

PREPARATION AND BACKGROUND

Any material has certain physical properties that may be used to identify it. By performing certain tests, children may learn some of the different properties of similar-looking powdered foods as well as other powders.

Small baby food jars make excellent containers for the powders and test liquids. For the iodine solution, mix two full medicine droppers of iodine in a half-full baby food jar of water.

Children may try additional tests such as heating the powders and mixing them with water. A small cup can be formed from kitchen foil and held over a candle flame with a spring clothespin. *Caution:* Supervise closely for safety. Only a tiny amount of powder need be heated. A powder may also be mixed in water in a clear glass jar and then compared with other water-powder mixtures.

Caution: Students should not taste powders. Explain that some powders they should not eat may get mixed with some powdered foods in this investigation. For example, some nonfoods they may want to test are powdered detergent, white tempera paint powder, crushed white chalk, talcum powder, alum, scouring powder, tooth powder, and plaster of paris.

GENERALIZATION

A material may be identified by tests to reveal its physical properties.

SAMPLE PERFORMANCE OBJECTIVES

Process: The child can infer the identity of several powders by interpreting recorded data.

Knowledge: The child can describe several different physical properties of at least two common powdered foods.

FOR YOUNGER CHILDREN

Younger students can do this activity well with fewer tests and powders. For example, have them observe two powders and make perhaps two tests, such as how they look magnified and how they feel. They can then receive an "unknown" powder and try to match it with one of the two powders tested.

REFERENCES

American Association for the Advancement of Science. (1993). *Benchmarks for science literacy.* New York: Oxford University Press.

Mintzes, J. J. (1984). Naive theories in biology: Children's concepts of the human body. *School Science and Mathematics, 84* (7), 548–55.

National Research Council. (1996). *National science education standards.* Washington, DC: National Academy Press.

SELECTED TRADE BOOKS: HUMAN BODY AND NUTRITION

For Younger Children

Adler, D. A. (1991). *You breathe in, you breathe out.* Watts.

Berger, M. (1983). *Why I cough, sneeze, shiver, hiccup, and yawn.* Harper & Row.

Bishop, P. R. (1991). *Exploring your skeleton.* Watts.

Cole, J. (1989). *The magic school bus inside the human body.* Scholastic.

Hoover, R., & Murphy, B. (1981). *Learning about our five senses.* Good Apple.

Hvass, U. (1986). *How my body moves.* Viking.

Kindersley, D. (1991). *What's inside my body?* Peter Lang.

Parker, S. (1991). *Eating a meal: How you eat, drink and digest.* Watts.

Penn, L. (1986). *The human body.* Good Apple.

Sattler, H. R. (1982). *Noses are special.* Abingdon.

Showers, P. (1982). *You can't make a move without your muscles.* Crowell.

Sproule, A. (1987). *Body watch: Know your insides.* Facts on File.

For Older Children

Allison, L. (1976). *Blood and guts: A working guide to your own little insides.* Little, Brown.

Behm, B. (1987). *Ask about my body.* Raintree.

De Bruin, J. (1983). *Young scientists explore the five senses.* Good Apple.

Gabb, M. (1991). *The human body.* Watts.

Galperin, A. (1991). *Nutrition.* Chelsea House.

Harlow, R., & Morgan, G. (1991). *Energy and growth.* Watts.

Hausherr, R. (1989). *Children and the AIDS virus: A book for children, parents, and teachers.* Clarion.

Klein, A. E. (1977). *You and your body.* Doubleday.

Parker, S. (1991). *Nerves to senses: Projects with biology.* Watts.

Rayner, C. (1980). *The body book.* Barron.

Rutland, J. (1977). *Human body.* Watts.

Simon, S. (1979). *About the foods you eat.* McGraw-Hill.

Taylor, R. (1982). *How the body works.* EMC Publications.

Walpole, B. (1987). *The human body.* Messner.

Ward, B. R. (1991). *Diet and health.* Watts.

Wilson, R. (1979). *How the body works.* Larousse.

Wolf, D., & Wolf, M. L. (Eds.). (1982). *The human body.* Putnam.

Wong, O. (1986). *Your body and how it works.* Children's Press.

Zim, H. S. (1979). *Your skin.* Morrow.

Resource Books

Butzow, C. M., & Butzow, J. W. (1989). *Science through children's literature. An integrated approach* (nutrition topics, pp. 107–111). Teachers Ideas Press.

Fredricks, A. D., Meinbach, A. M., & Rothlein, L. (1993). *Thematic units: An integrated approach to teaching science and social studies* (health topics, pp. 140–145; body system topics, pp. 189–194). HarperCollins.

Shaw, D. G., & Dybdahl, C. S. (1996). *Integrating science and language arts. A sourcebook for K–6 teachers* (circulatory system topic, pp. 65–67). Allyn and Bacon.

CHAPTER 10

THE EARTH'S CHANGING SURFACE

Building Up of
the Land

How Rocks Are
Formed

Earth's Changing Surface
Benchmarks and Standards

Magma and
Volcanoes

Rock Cycle

Fossils

Faults and
Earthquakes

Plate Tectonics

Sedimentary,
Igneous, and
Metamorphic

Weathering and
Erosion

Wind and Water
Erosion

Soil and Its
Makeup

Conservation
Practices

THE EARTH'S
CHANGING
SURFACE

Plant Action

Chemical
Weathering

Humus, Loam,
Sand, Silt, and
Clay

Shifting sand dunes, eroding hillsides, weeds growing on an asphalt playground, and muddy water running in gutters are all evidence that the earth's surface is changing.

This chapter examines some of the forces that wear down and build up the earth and their rock and soil products. Four sections include weathering and erosion, soil and its makeup, the building up of the land, and how rocks are formed.

WEATHERING AND EROSION CONCEPTS
(Experiences p. 345)

Perhaps the only permanent feature about the earth's surface is the continuous process of change it reveals. The forces that weather and erode the land are powerful and ceaseless.

Strictly speaking, *weathering* refers to the breaking down of rocks into smaller parts through the action of agents such as plants, chemicals, frost, and changes of temperature. *Erosion* includes weathering plus the process of transporting weathered material from one location to another, as in the action of running water, wind, and glaciers.

Plant Actions

It is hard for some children to realize at first that plants break down rocks. After all, rocks are "hard" and plants are "soft," they reason. But plants weather rocks in several ways.

Growing roots may wedge deeply into a cracked rock and force it apart. As dry plant seeds absorb water, they swell with surprising force and may perform a similar wedging function. Tiny flat plants called *lichens* grow on bare rock (Figure 10-1). Acids released by these plants decompose and soften the rock. Larger plants may then follow in a long succession, each contributing to the rock's destruction.

Figure 10-1
Lichens play a part in weathering rock.

Chemical Weathering

Oxygen and water in the air combine with rock surfaces to produce "rust." Reddish soils, for example, usually contain oxidized iron compounds.

Falling rain picks up a small amount of carbon dioxide in the air and forms carbonic acid. Although it is well diluted, this substance slowly wears down limestone. Older limestone buildings and statuary have a soft, worn look from the dissolving effect of acidic rainwater. This is especially noticeable in England and in several areas in the northeastern United States, where coal burning has been prevalent. Abnormal quantities of sulfur dioxide released into the air increase the acidic content of rain and hasten weathering. (We will consider acid rain again in the next chapter.)

Rainwater that percolates into the ground may encounter a limestone formation and dissolve some of it, so forming a cave. This is how the Carlsbad Caverns of New Mexico, Luray Caverns of Virginia, and Mammoth Caves of Kentucky were formed. Because the surface appearance of a rock is somewhat altered by chemical weathering, we must often chip or break it to note its natural color.

Expansion–Contraction

Frozen water also contributes to weathering. Many rocks are relatively porous. Water, you may remember, is one of the few substances that expands in freezing. As absorbed water expands, bits of rock are broken off. In addition, ice may wedge apart cracked rocks.

Stones placed around campfires are sometimes cracked because rocks conduct heat poorly. The difference between a hot surface and cooler interior may produce strains that cause parts to flake off. But some of this *exfoliation,* as it is called, may be from expansion due to release of pressure. Rocks formed underground are subjected to great pressures. When they finally appear on the surface, because of erosion or other means, there may be a tendency for these rocks to "unsqueeze" slightly, thus starting some cracks.

Running Water

Moving water is no doubt the most erosive force on earth. Abrasive, waterborne rocks and particles have gradually formed the Grand Canyon over millions of years. Millions of tons of soil daily wash from banks and hills over the world into streams and are eventually carried into the ocean. Ocean waves ceaselessly pound huge cliffs and boulders into sand.

Water running down hills usually forms gullies. As the slope angle increases, water moves more swiftly, so hastening erosion. Rain splashing on near-level fields has a different erosive effect. Broad sheets of soil wash off into lower places without obvious gullying.

Wind Erosion

The effect of wind erosion became dramatically apparent to millions of Americans in the Dust Bowl years of 1934–1935. Prairie lands originally covered by a grassy sod had been broken up for agriculture. A combination of dry weather and marginal farming practices resulted in the most destructive dust storms ever seen in the United States.

Glacial Erosion

Glaciers also contribute to land erosion. Huge snow deposits build up when snowfall exceeds the melting rate. Gradually, some of the underlying snow compacts into ice and the glacier flows slowly downhill, as in the case of mountain valley glaciers.

Continental glaciers are much larger, ranging to thousands of square miles in size. At one time, a large part of North America was buried under snow and ice. Today, much of Greenland and Antarctica are covered by such glaciers. Gravity forces these glaciers to spread out as more and more snow piles on top.

When glaciers move, they scour the land under their tremendous weight, scooping out basins and leveling hills. As they melt, huge deposits of soil and rocks are left at the sides and leading edge. Effects of glaciation may be seen in many parts of our country, particularly in New England and the north central states (Figure 10-2).

Soil and Its Makeup Concepts
(Experiences p. 355)

Many children understand that weathering and erosion can wear underlying rock into small particles. But they often do not realize that there is more to productive soil than just rock

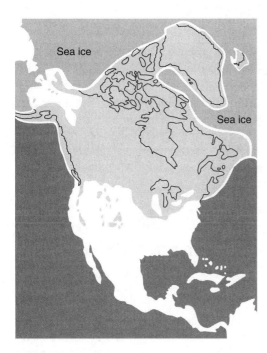

Figure 10-2
About 11,000 years ago, glaciers advanced deeply into what is now the northern United States.

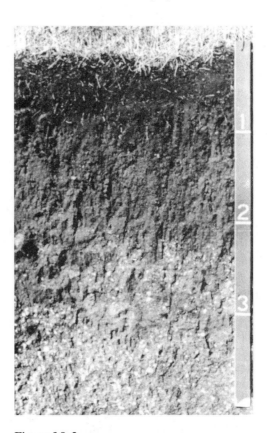

Figure 10-3
A soil profile, or cross section, 3 feet (0.9 meters) deep. Subsoil becomes coarser and contains less humus with depth.

particles. It is not until decomposed plant and animal matter is added (or manufactured chemicals applied) that the soil becomes productive enough to support agriculture (Figure 10-3).

Humus, as this organic matter is called, supplies plants with nitrogen, phosphorus, potassium, and other essential elements. The decomposition of organic material is done by soil bacteria. Acids released in decomposition also dissolve other minerals in the soil particles. Humus retains water well and so keeps soil from drying out rapidly. The darkish color of humus-laden soil absorbs sunlight efficiently, and so it is warmer than light-colored soil. This speeds up plant growth and reduces seed failure.

Earthworms, you may recall, are important to soil for several reasons. They help break up the soil, which permits air, as well as water, to reach the plant roots. Root cells die unless they

absorb sufficient oxygen. And, as earthworms eat through soil, they mix it and leave castings that contain rich fertilizing ingredients. ■

Soil Makeup

The composition of soil is easily studied if you mix some earth in a water-filled jar and allow the jar to stand several hours. Gravity causes the several materials to settle in order. Heavier, coarser particles like pebbles settle first, followed by sand, silt, and clay. Any humus present floats on the water surface.

The best soil for most plants is *loam,* composed of sand (30 to 50 percent), silt (30 to 50 percent), clay (up to 20 percent), and abundant humus. Silt and clay have small particles that retain water well. Having been eroded from rocks rich in certain minerals, they contain elements plants need for healthy growth. Coarser sand particles make soil porous, enabling air and water to reach plant roots. A soil composed of sand or clay alone lacks the moderate degree of porosity that seems best for watering plant roots.

Soils differ greatly in their degree of acidity and alkalinity. Strawberry plants thrive in acidic soil. Many grasses grow well in alkaline or basic soils. Clover does best in soil that is neither basic nor acidic, but neutral.

Soil Conservation

One of the reasons erosion is a fearsome enemy of the farmer is the time required for good soil to form. It may take up to 500 years for a single inch of good topsoil to be produced by natural means. With a rapidly multiplying world population, topsoil conservation is a serious concern.

Some of the things farmers do to preserve topsoil are shown in Figure 10-4. Each is directed toward a specific problem. *Contour plowing,* for example, is used when plowing hilly land. Plowing straight up or down a hill will cause gullies to form during rain or irrigation. Plowing around the hill reduces gully erosion. *Strip cropping* alternates a row crop that has much bare soil exposed, such as corn, with a ground cover crop, such as clover. This reduces wind erosion. A tree *windbreak* will also help if the field is located where a strong wind usually blows from one direction. *Terracing* may be used to prepare relatively flat areas for growing crops on steep slopes. *Check dams* of stones or logs may be used to slow down water in a stream or prevent a gully from widening.

Perhaps the greatest advance of this century in conserving farm topsoil is a recently adopted practice called *residue management,* which does away with the plow. Even the best plowing practices bare soil to water and wind erosion. Now, many farmers leave the residue or stubble from harvested crops in place to hold soil and moisture. Tractor-pulled machines gouge places for seeds, which then sprout and grow through the decomposing residue. Besides minimizing erosion, the method actually rebuilds the precious topsoil.

BUILDING UP OF THE LAND CONCEPTS
(Experiences p. 359)

Careful geological studies show that the powerful forces of weathering and erosion should have long ago worn down the earth's surface to a low-lying plain. Then why are there mountains? Part of the answer is seen in volcanic activity.

Magma

Fiery molten rock from deep underground, called *magma,* thrusts up through weak spots and cracks in the earth's crust. When this material reaches the surface, it is called *lava.*

Sometimes the accumulation of magma and high-pressure gases is so great that the molten rock shoots up to the surface in a spectacular eruption. This can happen under the ocean, as well as on land. The Hawaiian Islands are the eroded tops of volcanoes, as are the Azores in the Atlantic Ocean.

Sometimes magma may quietly ooze up through great cracks in the crust and spread out over the ground. Large parts of the Pacific Northwest are covered with hardened lava beds to depths of thousands of feet. Similar lava flows have occurred in Iceland.

Figure 10-4
Some ways of preventing erosion: *(a)* **contour plowing,** *(b)* **strip crops,** *(c)* **terraces,**
(d) **check dam,** *(e)* **tree windbreak.**

Several types of magmatic activity are not directly visible until erosion has worn away parts of the crust. Magma may stop flowing and cool before it reaches the surface, or it may push up part of the crust, forming a dome, or *laccolith*. Erosion of the surrounding crust makes the dome more prominent (Figure 10-5).

Where does heat energy for volcanoes originate? There are several theories, one of which we will look at now. Some scientists think that radioactive rocks are responsible in some places.

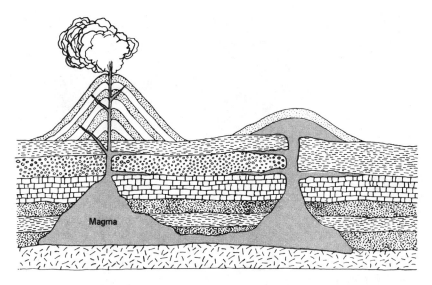

Figure 10-5
A volcano and a laccolith.

One radioactive element is uranium, which continually shoots off helium atoms and changes to lead. In the process, a tiny amount of heat energy is generated. If many rocks of this type become concentrated, it is conceivable that they could bring about enough heat energy to melt rocks. (The known rate of decay of uranium into lead is useful in finding the age of rocks. Since the rate apparently never changes, scientists can figure age by noting the ratio of remaining uranium to lead.)

Earthquakes and Faults

Earthquakes happen when the crust breaks under the strain of its deforming forces. Parts of the crust may move horizontally, diagonally, or vertically along a huge crack, or *fault*. Over a long time, *block mountains* may develop through tilted or vertical movements along a fault line. This seems to be how the Sierra Nevada range was formed.

Other mountains seem to be made through *folding*. Immense forces push parts of the crust into giant wrinkles. The Appalachians are an example.

Plate Theory

How does modern science explain such major changes in the earth's crust? When we look at a world map, certain land masses of the earth, while far apart, seem to fit together like pieces of a jigsaw puzzle. The east coast of South America and the west coast of Africa are examples. Could it be that these and other continents were once joined?

Many modern earth scientists infer this. They think that the earth's thin crust was once solid, but now is fragmented into six to eight immense "plates" and several smaller ones that fit in between. The plates drift on the earth's fiery mantle of molten rock some 100 kilometers (60 miles) or so below. The continents float on the plates like passengers on rafts. Plate edges do not necessarily coincide with the edges of continents. According to *plate tectonics theory*, the plates continually pull apart, collide, grind edges, or partially slide under each other.

Ocean floors, for example, form when two plates drift apart. Magma pushes up from the mantle and fills the ever-widening gap between the plates. When one plate pushes into or under another, folded mountains and block mountains may be formed. A plate edge that thrusts downward under another melts into the fiery mantle below. Some of the magma that results thrusts up through weak spots in the solid crust to form volcanoes. Earthquakes may happen as plates slide past each other in opposite directions. The great friction between the two massive plates may cause the movements to temporarily stop. However, stresses build up until the crust suddenly fractures and the plates grind onward.

Plate movements are surprisingly fast, up to 20 centimeters (8 inches) a year in some locations, given the approximate 5-billion-year age of the earth. Apparently, the force needed to move the rigid plates comes from convection currents in the molten mantle below.

Note the correlation between regions of earthquake and volcanic activity in Figure 10-6. Many scientists infer that these active regions reveal some boundaries of the huge, drifting plates. A Cakequake (Hardy & Tolman, 1991)—which introduces plate tectonics through types of plate movements—makes learning these concepts a fun activity.

How Rocks Are Formed Concepts
(Experiences p. 360)

"What are rocks made of?" children often ask. Rocks are made up of *minerals* which are natural inorganic materials that make up most of the earth's crust. Some minerals are composed of a single element, such as copper or carbon. A beautiful diamond is an example of almost pure carbon formed under enormous pressure underground. Other minerals are compounds of two or more minerals, such as mica or quartz. The chemical makeup of a mineral is the same anywhere it is found on earth. A pure copper or quartz sample is as recognizable in Asia as in North America.

Geologists have developed many ways of identifying minerals. These may include observing its color, hardness, luster, how it splits along a plane, how it breaks, its density, its crystal structure, and how it reacts to chemicals.

Just as a word may be made up of one or more letters of the alphabet, rocks may be composed of one or more minerals. But there are far more known minerals than letters of the alphabet (about 2,000). Most are seldom seen. Fewer than 100 minerals make up the bulk of the earth's crust.

Usually, rocks are given the same name when they contain essentially the same minerals, like granite. Some samples, though, may contain a greater proportion of one or more of the minerals than other samples. So not all granite samples look alike, nor do many other rock samples given a certain name. Although there are many minerals, rocks are formed in just three ways.

Sedimentary Rocks

Sediments from eroded rocks are the raw materials for new sedimentary rocks. The sediments are usually moved and deposited by rivers into coastal trenches and basins. Some rivers deposit sediments into large lakes. Sand, clay, silt, pebbles, and stones are common sedimentary materials. Sediments gradually collect layer upon layer where they are deposited, which makes the layers press harder and harder on the lower sediments. The enormous pressure, plus chemicals dissolved in the water, cement the sediments together. Sand particles

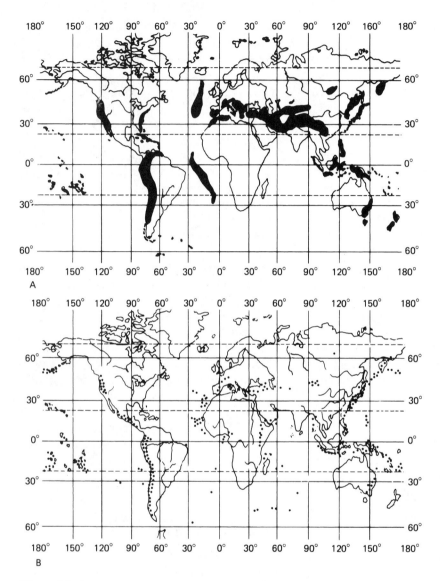

Figure 10-6
Earthquake (A) and volcano (B) regions of the world.

become sandstone, mud or clay becomes shale, and pebbles and rocks and sand combine to form conglomerate.

Not all sediments come from eroded materials. Limestone and chalk are examples of rock formed on the ocean floor from the compressed skeletons and shells of billions of ocean animals, including clams, mussels, and corals. Some sedimentary rock may also form from previously dissolved chemicals that deposit out of solution when the water can no longer hold them.

Igneous Rocks

A second way rocks are formed is through the cooling of magma or lava. These are igneous rocks (the word *igneous* means "formed from fire"). A common example of igneous formation happens in domes, or laccoliths. Magma squeezes under a surface rock layer, slowly cools, and becomes solid. When the surface rocks erode away, the underlying rock is exposed. Granite is the most frequently found rock of this kind. Its large crystals reveal that it cooled slowly.

Lava that is blown from a volcano or that flows out of cracks in the crust cools quickly. So it has small crystals or no visible crystals. The light, spongy rock called pumice and the black, glassy rock called obsidian are examples.

Metamorphic Rocks

Sedimentary and igneous rocks may undergo severe pressure and heat as parts of the crust move, fold, thrust deeper under the ground, or are buried under lava flows. This may cause physical and chemical changes in the rocks, making them metamorphic rocks (the word *metamorphic* means "changed in form"). Sedimentary rocks such as limestone become marble, sandstone may become quartzite, and shale becomes slate. Igneous rock such as granite changes to gniess (pronounced "nice") or soft coal changes to hard coal.

Metamorphic rocks are harder than the original rock material. They often have compression bands of different colors. Usually, crystals are small. Still, it is easy to confuse metamorphic rocks with igneous rocks.

Table 10-1 shows 12 kinds of rocks children can use to become acquainted with the three basic types. They are fairly distinctive and easy to obtain. Some, and perhaps all, of these rocks may be included in specimens students bring to school. If not, they may be acquired from local rock collectors, museums, and science supply companies.

Fossils

The remains, or signs, of animals or plants in rock are called fossils. The most likely rocks in which fossils are found are sedimentary. Occasionally, fossils are found in partly metamorphosed sedimentary rocks, but pressure and heat usually destroy fossils.

Fossils are formed in different ways. When some animals died, they were covered by sediments. The soft body parts decomposed, but teeth and skeletons remained, preserved by hardened layers of sediment. In other cases, even the skeletons disintegrated, but before they did, mineral-laden water infiltrated into the bones and replaced bone with minerals. This left a perfect cast replica of the skeleton in many cases. Some trees have left casts in a similar way. This is how specimens of the Petrified Forest in Arizona were formed. Additional fossils have been discovered frozen in ice, found in tar pits, and other places.

The so-called *fossil fuels*—coal, oil, and natural gas—were formed from the remains of plants and animals millions of years ago. Huge masses of organic matter in swampy forests were covered by mud, silt, and other sediments. Gradually, the sediments formed into stony layers. Pressure and heat from immense crustal movements caused physical and chemical changes in the buried organic matter. Some formed into seams of coal trapped between shale and slate. Some deposits changed into thick, black oil and natural gas, often trapped between layers of folded rock.

Rock Cycle

The same processes that formed rocks in the past continue today. Over many thousands of years, rocks change their forms. Even so, there is much evidence that the same mineral materials are

Table 10-1
Igneous, sedimentary, and metamorphic rocks

Igneous Rocks	Description	How Formed
Pumice	Grayish, fine pores, glassy, frothy, light, floats on water.	From rapid cooling of frothy, surface lava containing gases.
Volcanic Breccia	Consolidated fragments of volcanic ash, such as glass, pumice, quartz.	From being exploded high into the air from a volcano and settling.
Obsidian	Black, glassy, no crystals.	From very rapid surface cooling of lava.
Basalt	Dark, greenish-gray, very small crystals, may have some holes.	From rapid cooling of lava close to the surface. Escaping gases form holes.

Table 10-1
Igneous, sedimentary, and metamorphic rocks *(continued)*

Igneous Rocks	Description	How Formed
Granite	Coarse crystals, white to gray, sometimes pinkish.	From slow, below-surface cooling of molten rock (magma), as when domes are formed.

Sedimentary Rocks	Description	How Formed
Conglomerate	Rounded pebbles, stones, and sand cemented together.	From loose materials compacted by pressure of overlying sediments and bound by natural cement.
Sandstone	Sand grains clearly visible, gray, yellow, red.	From sand compacted by pressure of sediment, bound by natural cement.

Table 10-1
Igneous, sedimentary, and metamorphic rocks *(continued)*

Sedimentary Rocks	Description	How Formed
 Shale	Soft, smells like clay, fine particles, green, black, yellow, red, gray.	From compacted mud bound by natural cement.
 Limestone	Fairly soft, white, gray, red, forms carbon dioxide gas bubbles when touched with acids.	From dead organisms that used calcium carbonate in sea water in making body parts; from evaporation of sea water containing calcium carbonate.

Metamorphic Rocks	Description	How Formed
 Marble	Different, mixed colors, may have colored bands, medium to coarse crystals, fizzes if touched with acids.	Formed when pure limestone is subjected to intense heat and pressure.

Table 10-1
Igneous, sedimentary, and metamorphic rocks *(continued)*

Metamorphic Rocks	Description	How Formed
Slate	Greenish-gray, black, red, splits in thin layers, harder than shale.	Formed when shale is subjected to intense heat and pressure.
Quartzite	Very hard, white, gray, pink, indistinct grains, somewhat glassy.	Formed when sandstone is subjected to intense heat and pressure.

used over and over in a kind of rock cycle. Figure 10-7 shows what seems to happen.

All three kinds of rocks erode when exposed on the earth's surface. The resulting sediments, under pressure, form into rock cemented with water-borne chemicals. When these rocks undergo further pressure, torsion, and heat, they metamorphose. The metamorphic rocks turn into magma when heated further. When the magma cools and hardens, it becomes igneous rock. Some of it may metamorphose if folded or twisted or heated again. Some erodes. The cycle continues.

EARTH'S CHANGING SURFACE BENCHMARKS AND STANDARDS

Most children have explored with soil, rocks, and play sand or seen pictures or movies which include volcanoes and earthquakes. Activities in the elementary school should further refine these explorations and discover additional properties about the Earth. Sample Benchmarks and Standards include:

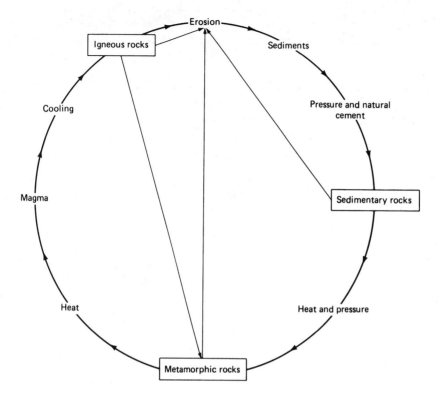

Figure 10-7
The rock cycle.

SAMPLE BENCHMARKS (AAAS, 1993).

■ Chunks of rocks come in many sizes and shapes, from boulders to grains of sand and even smaller (by Grades K–2, p. 72).

■ Waves, wind, water, and ice shape and reshape the Earth's land surface by eroding rock and soil in some areas and depositing them in other areas, sometimes in seasonal layers (by Grades 3–5, p. 72).

SAMPLE STANDARDS, (NRC, 1996).

■ Soils have properties of color and texture, capacity to retain water, and ability to support the growth of many kinds of plants, including those in our food supply (by Grades K–4, p. 134).

■ Some changes in the solid earth can be described as the "rock cycle." (by Grades 5–8, p. 160).

INVESTIGATIONS AND ACTIVITIES

WEATHERING AND EROSION EXPERIENCES
(Concepts p. 331)

ACTIVITY: *HOW CAN SEEDS BREAK UP ROCKS?*

NEEDED

two small topless milk or juice cartons
moist soil
plaster of paris
stick
bean seeds

TRY THIS

1. Soak some bean seeds in water overnight.
2. Plant them in a small carton half-filled with moist soil.
3. Mix some plaster of paris and water in a second carton. Make the mixture like a thick milk shake.
4. Pour the plaster mixture lightly over the soil. Make the cover about 0.5 centimeter (¼ inch) thick.
   a. Will the growing seeds be strong enough to break through the hard cover? If so, how long do you think it will take?
   b. If the seeds do break through, how thick a plaster cover will beans go through?
   c. What examples can you find of plants breaking up rocks and other hard materials? Look for plants growing in cracks in rocks, sidewalks, asphalt, and other paved surfaces.

INVESTIGATION: *HOW WEATHERING BREAKS DOWN MINERALS*

Over time, gases in the air can cause a chemical change in many different minerals in rocks. The process is called chemical *weathering*. A rock that is chemically weathered becomes loose and easily crumbled. Something like this happens when iron or steel breaks down as it rusts. You can learn more about chemical weathering by making things rust.

EXPLORATORY PROBLEM

How can you make an iron nail rust?

NEEDED

plain iron nails
container of dry soil
container of wet soil
steel wool

TRY THIS

1. Rub the nail with steel wool for a few seconds. This will take off any chemical that may have been put on to prevent rusting.

2. Get a container of wet soil. Bury the nail just under the surface. Dig up the nail each day to see if, or how much, it is rusting. Put the nail back in the same way each time. Keep the soil damp (Figure 10-8).

Figure 10-8

DISCOVERY PROBLEMS

observing **A.** When does rust first appear? How quickly is the whole nail covered with rust?

hypothesizing **B.** Will a nail rust more quickly on the wet soil's surface than below it? What do you think?

hypothesizing **C.** What would happen if you put a nail in water?

hypothesizing **D.** What would happen if you buried a nail in dry soil?

hypothesizing **E.** Will a piece of steel wool rust faster than a nail?

experimenting **F.** What are some other materials that might rust? In what other ways can you get them to rust? How can you prevent materials from rusting?

TEACHING COMMENT

PREPARATION AND BACKGROUND

Make sure that any steel wool used is the soapless variety. Plastic margarine or cottage cheese containers are handy to hold soil for this activity. Soil may be dried, if needed, by spreading it on a newspaper and exposing it to sunlight.

Oxygen chemically combines directly with many minerals, as in the rusting process. Carbon dioxide also produces chemical weathering, but indirectly. It dissolves in rainwater to form a weak acid called carbonic acid. This attacks limestone and cementing materials that hold minerals together in some rocks.

GENERALIZATION

Gases in the air may cause chemical weathering in rocks. Rust is an example of chemical weathering.

SAMPLE PERFORMANCE OBJECTIVES

Process: The child can experiment and determine which among several variables are likely to produce rust.

Knowledge: The child can identify several conditions that are likely to produce chemical weathering.

FOR YOUNGER CHILDREN

Younger children should be able to do Try This, Discovery Problem A, and the first question in Discovery Problem F.

ACTIVITY: *HOW DO MINERAL DEPOSITS FORM IN CAVES?*

NEEDED

Epsom salt
two small paper cups
thick, soft string
large paper cup
spoon
two small stones
thick wash cloth or piece of towel

TRY THIS

1. Fill a large paper cup three-fourths full with water. Dissolve as much Epsom salt in it as you can.

2. Pour the solution into the two small paper cups.

3. Tie a small stone to each string end to weigh them down. Put one string end into each small paper cup. Have the string sag between cups.

4. Place the cups on top of the wash cloth. Leave at least 4 centimeters (1½ inches) between the cloth and string. Allow a few days for mineral deposits to form on the string and cloth (Figure 10-9).

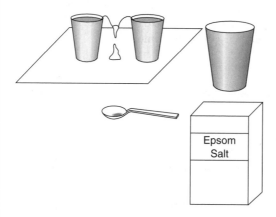

Figure 10-9

In a real cave, water with dissolved minerals in it drips from the cave ceiling to the floor. The water leaves minerals behind as it evaporates at both places. Little by little, the mineral deposits build up to look like "icicles" of stone. Those that hang down are called *stalactites*. Those that point up are *stalagmites*. (To remember them, think of *C* for ceiling and *G* for ground.)

a. In your model where is the stalactite? stalagmite?

b. How does your model work compared to the real thing?

ACTIVITY: *HOW DOES FREEZING WATER BREAK UP ROCKS?*

NEEDED

several porous or cracked rocks
freezer bag

TRY THIS

1. Leave some rocks in water for several hours. Use cracked rocks and those that soak up water. Sandstone and limestone are good to use.

2. Put the rocks in a bag. Place the bag in a freezer overnight. Examine the rocks the next day.

   a. What, if anything, happened to the rocks?

   b. How can you explain your results?

   c. If some rocks broke, maybe the cold alone did it. How can you experiment to be more sure that freezing water broke the rocks in this case?

TEACHING COMMENT

Porous rocks may be detected by placing some rocks in water and looking for those on which bubbles form. Students can be more sure that freezing water cracked their rocks by placing in the freezer another bag that contains similar, unsoaked rocks.

ACTIVITY: *HOW DOES WEATHERING CHANGE A ROCK?*

NEEDED

several different weathered rocks
thick paper bag
soft paper towel or facial tissue
hand lens
empty egg carton
hammer

TRY THIS

1. For safety, to break open a rock, put it into a thick paper bag. Hold the bag against a cement curb or sidewalk. Hit the rock a few times with a hammer through the bag.

2. Look at the weathered and fresh rock surfaces with a hand lens. How are they different? alike?

3. Make a weathered rock display. Take two of the larger pieces of the rock. Wrap one piece in tissue or a soft towel so only the weathered part shows. Wrap the other so only the fresh surface shows. Place them in opposite spaces in an egg carton. Do this with other broken rocks, also, until you fill the carton. What will happen if you shift the rocks around so the samples are not opposite one another? How many of the rocks will your friends be able to match? If someone shifts them for you, how many will *you* be able to match?

INVESTIGATION: *SOIL EROSION*

After a rain have you noticed how water has carried away, or *eroded*, soil? Splashing raindrops and running water are responsible for much soil erosion. But not all places with soil erode, and some places erode much more than others.

EXPLORATORY PROBLEM

How can you test to see what affects soil erosion?

NEEDED

two throw-away pie pans
soil
plastic sauce dishes (two matched)
juice cans (two small matched)
measuring cups
meter stick or yardstick
a small- and a medium-sized nail
hammer

TRY THIS

1. Punch 10 holes in the bottom of 1 juice can with a small nail. Use a medium-sized nail to punch 10 holes in the second can. Both cans should be open at the top.

2. Fill a sauce dish level and to the brim with soil. Put the dish into a pie pan to catch any spilled material.

3. Place a meter stick or yardstick upright behind the dish. Hold the small-hole can 60 centimeters (24 inches) above the dish.

4. Have someone pour a half-cup of water into the juice can. When the can stops "raining," observe the soil and pie pan (Figure 10-10).

DISCOVERY PROBLEMS

observing **A.** What, if any, signs of erosion can you observe?

observing **B.** How will a heavier "rain" affect erosion? Fill a second saucer with soil. Use the medium-hole can for rain. Compare the results with the first trial.

observing **C.** How will loose soil erode compared to tightly packed soil? Prepare two saucers and find out. (Use only one can for the "rain" in Problems C through E.)

observing **D.** How will tilted soil erode compared to level soil?

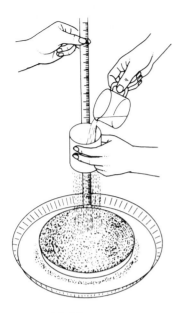

Figure 10-10

observing   **E.** How will covered soil erode compared to bare soil? Cover the soil in one dish with several leaves.

inferring   **F.** What are some conditions that seem to reduce soil erosion? That seem to increase soil erosion? What examples can you find outdoors that show some or all of these conditions?

TEACHING COMMENT

PREPARATION AND BACKGROUND

All of the preceding conditions are important in affecting soil erosion. But all are not easy to produce reliably with small-scale soil testing. Finding actual samples of erosion, as in Discovery Problem F, is important to achieving full understanding.

GENERALIZATION

Rainfall, soil cover, degree of incline, and compactness affect soil erosion.

SAMPLE PERFORMANCE OBJECTIVES

Process: The child can locate several outdoor examples of soil erosion and infer the conditions that influenced the examples.

Knowledge: The child can state several conditions that affect soil erosion.

INVESTIGATION: *WIND EROSION*

What happens to loose soil on a windy day? The moving of soil or rocks from one place to another is *erosion*. Soil erosion by wind is a big problem in some places.

EXPLORATORY PROBLEM

How can you find out about wind erosion around you?

NEEDED

two rulers
sticky tape
crayon
scissors
empty milk carton (small)
open, unpaved area outdoors
sand or soil
large sprinkling can
windy day

TRY THIS

1. Make a wind erosion recorder. Cut two narrow slots on top of a small milk carton. (See Figure 10-11.)
2. Stick two rulers through the slots.
3. Fill the carton with sand or soil to make it heavy.
4. Cut two 45-centimeter (18-inch) strips of sticky tape.
5. Put one strip evenly over the top of each ruler, *sticky side out*. Fasten the strip ends to each ruler with tape.
6. Draw an arrow on the carton top with crayon.
7. Place your recorder (Figure 10-11) where the wind is blowing loose soil. Point the arrow north. Leave the recorder for 30 minutes. Notice how bits of wind-blown soil collect on the sticky tape.

DISCOVERY PROBLEMS

observing and inferring

A. Examine the sticky tape on all four sides. Which side has the most soil? From which direction did the wind blow most?

hypothesizing

B. Where do you think there is the most wind erosion around the school? the least wind erosion? Make more recorders. Put one in each place and find out. What reasons can you give for what you find?

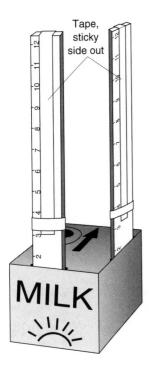

Tape, sticky side out

MILK

Figure 10-11

experimenting

C. What difference in wind erosion is there between grass-covered and bare soil? How can you find out?

experimenting

D. What difference in wind erosion is there between dry and damp soil? How can you find out?

classifying and inferring

E. Collect windblown soil bits each day for a week with your recorder. Change the sticky tape each day. Can you arrange the strips in order from most to fewest soil bits? On what day was there the most wind erosion? the least erosion? Can you tell from which main direction the wind blew each day?

hypothesizing

F. When during the day is there the most wind erosion where you live? How can you find out? What else can you discover with your recorder?

TEACHING COMMENT

PREPARATION AND BACKGROUND

Some children may not realize at first that some variables need to be controlled in this investigation. If two areas are to be tested, two identical recorders must be exposed to wind within equal areas at the same time. When possible, let students discover this for themselves.

GENERALIZATION

Soil erosion by wind depends on how hard the wind blows and how the soil is protected from the wind.

SAMPLE PERFORMANCE OBJECTIVES

Process: The child can place in order, from most to fewest soil particles, tape strips collected during a given time for one week.

Knowledge: The child can state several soil conditions that contribute to wind erosion.

ACTIVITY: *HOW DO GLACIERS CHANGE THE LAND?*

NEEDED

throw-away aluminum pie pan
freezer
stones and pebbles
place with bare soil

TRY THIS

1. Put some rocks and pebbles in a pie pan. Spread them about halfway around the pan's inside edge as shown in Figure 10-12.
2. Put some water into the pan, but let the tops of the rocks stick out of the water.
3. Leave the pan in a freezer overnight.
4. Remove your frozen glacier model from the pan. Turn it over so the rocks sticking out are underneath.

Figure 10-12

5. Place the model flat on some bare dirt. Push it so the stones are forward. Press down at the same time. Push it in a straight line for about 60 centimeters (2 feet).

6. Let your model stay and melt at the end of that distance. Come back to this place several hours later after it has melted. Observe carefully everything that has been left behind.

   a. How can you tell the direction in which the "glacier" moved?

   b. How can you tell how wide it was?

   c. How can you tell where the forward part of the glacier stopped and melted?

SOIL AND ITS MAKEUP EXPERIENCES
(Concepts p. 332)

INVESTIGATION: *THE MAKEUP OF SOILS*

What are some things you eat that grow in soil? How is soil important in your life? What do you think makes up soil?

EXPLORATORY PROBLEM

How can you find out what makes up soil?

NEEDED

fresh soils (two different types)
spoon
three glass jars with caps
newspaper
water
three sheets of white paper
magnifying glass
paper cup

TRY THIS

1. Spread newspaper on a table or desk. Put a sheet of white paper on top.

2. Pour some soil from one bag onto the white paper. What is the color of the soil? (See Figure 10-13.)

3. Spread out the soil with a spoon. Use a magnifier to see better. What animals or animal parts do you see? (Put live animals in a paper cup.) What plant or plant parts do you see? Animal and plant materials in soil are called humus.

4. Feel the soil between your fingers. Rough soil has more large-sized rock bits or particles than smooth soil. Use a magnifier. Can you find three sizes of rock particles? Which size makes up most rock particles in your sample?

Figure 10-13

5. Sort the different humus and rock materials into layers. Here is how. Fill a glass jar half full with the soil you are observing. Fill the rest of the jar with water. Shake the jar and then let it settle for an hour. Where does the humus settle? How much is there? In what order do the different-sized rock particles settle? How much is there of each size?

DISCOVERY PROBLEMS

observing and inferring   **A.** How good a soil detective are you? Can you tell which two soil samples are from the same place? Have a partner pour some soil into three white sheets. Two soil samples should come from one bag and one soil sample from the other bag. (Do not look while this is done.) Try to identify the two soil samples from the same bag. Observe color, humus, and rock particles. Do the shake test, also, if needed.

observing and inferring   **B.** What is the makeup of soil from different places? Get samples of different soils around school and home. How are the soil samples alike and different? How does deeper soil compare with surface soil from the same place? How many soil samples can you match as in Discovery Problem A?

TEACHING COMMENT

PREPARATION AND BACKGROUND

The two bags of soil in the first activity should come from two very different locations. Make sure the materials in each bag of soil are fairly evenly distributed. Otherwise, it will be hard to match soil samples that come from the same bag.

GENERALIZATION

Soil is made up of humus and rock particles; different soils may be identified by the kinds and amounts of these materials.

SAMPLE PERFORMANCE OBJECTIVES

Process: When shown three samples, two of which are the same, the child can observe similarities and differences and match the proper pair.

Knowledge: The child can describe the materials that make up soil and can explain that soils look different because these materials vary in kind and amount.

FOR YOUNGER CHILDREN

Primary students may be less systematic than older students in how they observe soil materials and may need more help in locating soil samples.

INVESTIGATION: *HOW WATER SINKS INTO DIFFERENT SOILS*

Some of the rain that falls on soil runs off it into streams. Some rain also soaks into the ground. This water can help crops grow. If water sinks deep below the surface, it may be pumped to the surface for many uses. How fast water soaks into soil depends on several conditions. You can find out some for yourself.

EXPLORATORY PROBLEM

What can you do to test how fast water sinks into soils?

NEEDED

two matched cans (one with both ends removed)
watch with second hand
water
different outdoor places with soil

TRY THIS

1. One can should be open at both ends. Scratch a mark sideways on the can's side 2.5 centimeters (1 inch) from one end.

2. Go to a place with soil outdoors. Use your foot to press the can into the soil up to the mark.

3. Have the second can filled with water. Pour the water into the first can without spilling any (Figure 10-14). With a watch, check how long it takes for all the water to sink in.

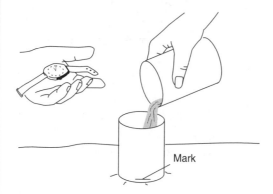

Figure 10-14

DISCOVERY PROBLEMS

measuring **A.** How much time is needed for the water to sink into the soil?

measuring **B.** Compare the sink times of different soils. How will soil with grass compare to the same kind of soil without grass?

measuring **C.** How will sandy soil compare with sticky soil?

measuring **D.** How will hard-packed soil compare with loose soil?

measuring **E.** How will soil that is usually in the sun compare with soil that is usually in the shade?

measuring **F.** How will soil on a hill compare with soil that is on a flat surface?

inferring **G.** What are some things about soil that seem to make water sink in quickly? slowly?

Teaching Comment

PREPARATION AND BACKGROUND

A steel can is likely to hold up better than an aluminum can for this activity. Some hard soils may require an adult's weight to push the can down to the mark.

GENERALIZATION

Permeable soils tend to be loosely packed and composed of coarse mineral particles with little or no humus.

SAMPLE PERFORMANCE OBJECTIVES

Process: The child can measure and compare the permeability of several different kinds of soils.

Knowledge: The child can explain the conditions that are likely to be found in highly permeable soils.

FOR OLDER CHILDREN

To make this investigation into an experiment for older students, start with Discovery Problem G. Then, after discussing hypotheses, ask, "How can we find out?"

BUILDING UP OF THE LAND EXPERIENCES
(Concepts p. 334)

ACTIVITY: *FORCES ACTING ON THE EARTH'S CRUST*

NEEDED

box lid or tray
round balloon (large)
sand or dry soil
three chocolate sheet cakes (unfrosted)

INTRODUCTION

When rocks melt underground, they form a thick fiery-hot liquid called *magma*. Hot gases and steam, released when the rocks melt, mix with the magma and build up great pressure. This forces the magma to squeeze into cracks or weak places under the earth's crust. Magma may push up and bend rock layers above without coming to the surface. This can make a *dome mountain*. You can make a model of one.

Earthquakes may also change the Earth's surface. There are three types of earthquakes where the crust moves horizontally, diagonally, or vertically.

TRY THIS

1. Spread a thin layer of sand or soil in a box lid or tray.
2. Lay a balloon on the sand. Let its neck stick out over the lid's side.
3. Cover the balloon with about 5 centimeters (2 inches) of sand or soil. Make the "land" surface level.
4. Slowly blow air into the balloon so it is partly filled.
   a. What happens to the land surface?
   b. What in the model is like the magma?
   c. What is like the layers of rock above the magma?
5. Now, holding the first of the 3 cakes with one hand on each side, push the cake together until a "fault" develops in the cake. (This is a fault.)
6. Hold the second cake with both hands on its sides and gently pull the cake apart until a "fault" forms a trench.
7. The final cake is held as above but the left hand pulls toward the body and the right hand pulls away from the body, producing a strike slip fault.

a. Compare and contrast each of the three faults.

b. Look on a raised surface (relief) globe and compare the faults produced to areas of the Earth where similar faults may have occurred.

TEACHING COMMENT

A large, round balloon is recommended. Small balloons are hard to inflate, and the weight of the soil will make this even harder to do. A small plastic bag may also be easily inflated if its opening is tightly wrapped around the end of a drinking straw and fastened with sticky tape.

Thin layers of alternating chocolate and vanilla simulate rock layers when performing the earthquake activity.

HOW ROCKS ARE FORMED EXPERIENCES
(Concepts p. 337)

INVESTIGATION: *THE PROPERTIES OF ROCKS*

Have you ever heard the saying, "It's as hard as a rock"? Does this mean all rocks are equally hard? What do you think?

EXPLORATORY PROBLEM A

How can you find out the hardness of different rocks?

NEEDED

penny
six different rocks
large iron nail
partner
glass baby food jar
pencil and paper

TRY THIS

1. Study this hardness scale. It can help you to group your rocks.

HARDNESS SCALE	ROCK TEST
Very soft	Can be scratched with your fingernail
Soft	A new penny will scratch it. A fingernail will not.
Medium	A nail will scratch it. A penny will not.
Hard	It will scratch glass. A nail will not scratch it.

2. Test each rock according to this scale.

3. Keep a record of how hard each rock is. One way is to label each rock with a different letter. Write the letter on a slip of paper. Then put the rock on the slip (Figure 10-15). Record each rock's letter and hardness on a sheet of paper.

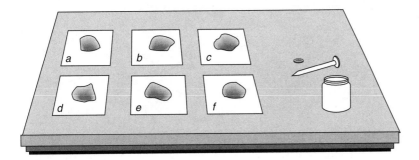

Figure 10-15

DISCOVERY PROBLEMS

observing and classifying **A.** Will someone else who tests your rock agree with you? Let your partner test your rocks. They should be on the lettered paper slips. Have her record each rock's letter and hardness. How much is this record like yours? Are there differences? Why?

classifying **B.** How can you put your six rocks in order from softest to hardest? (*Hint:* How can scratching one rock with another help?)

observing and classifying **C.** What other rocks can you test for hardness? How much will someone else agree with you if they test the same rocks?

EXPLORATORY PROBLEM B

What other properties of rocks can you observe and describe?

NEEDED

same materials as in Exploratory Problem A
vinegar
piece of white tile
new partner
paper cup

TRY THIS

1. *Color:* What is the color of the rock? Some rocks have several mixed colors. The best way to decide color is with a streak test. Rub the rock on the rough side of some tile. What color is the streak? (Figure 10-16.)

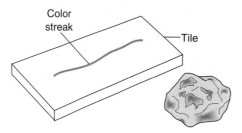

Figure 10-16

2. *Feel:* How does the rock feel to you? Is it rough? smooth? soapy? What else?
3. *Layers:* Does the rock seem to be made up of flat layers pressed together?
4. *Holes:* Does the rock have many small holes in it?
5. *Fizz:* If the rock is placed in a small cup of vinegar, do many tiny bubbles appear?
6. *Fossils:* Can you see tiny parts of sea shells or other such materials?
7. *Heaviness or Density:* How heavy does the rock seem for its size? light? medium? heavy?
8. *Other Properties:* What other properties of your rocks can you observe?

DISCOVERY PROBLEMS

classifying

A. Play a game with a partner. Sort some of your rocks into two groups according to one property (use color, or feel, etc.). Can a partner tell which property you used to sort them?

observing and communicating

B. Play the "I'm-Thinking-of-a-Rock" game with a partner. Place four or more rocks in a row. Think of just one rock and some of its properties. Can your partner find out what rock you have in mind? He must ask you only questions that can be answered by yes or no. Example: "Is it a rough rock?" (Yes.) "Does it have holes?" (No.)

communicating

C. How well can you describe your rocks? Can you make a chart that your partner can use to identify them? Make a chart of all properties you observe about your rocks. Label your rocks and try to remember which rock is which.

Rock	Hardness	Color	Feel	Layers	Holes
A	Medium	Gray	Smooth	No	Yes
B					
C					
D					

Give your completed chart and rocks to your partner. The rocks should be out of order, so he must study your chart to tell which rock is A, B, C, and so on.

inferring

D. Which chart descriptions were helpful? Which confused your partner? How could these be made clearer?

TEACHING COMMENT

PREPARATION AND BACKGROUND

Only about 30 minerals make up most common rocks. So you will observe some of the same minerals many times in different rocks.

GENERALIZATION

Rocks vary in hardness, color, texture, and other properties.

SAMPLE PERFORMANCE OBJECTIVES

Process: The child can classify rocks on the basis of hardness by using a simple hardness scale.

Knowledge: The child can state several properties by which rocks can be described.

FOR YOUNGER CHILDREN

Most younger students should be able to sort rocks by color and by either/or categories: smooth/rough, heavy/light, and holes/no holes.

INVESTIGATION: *CRYSTALS AND HOW THEY GROW*

It is interesting to see the crystals that make up some rocks. Most crystals are formed underground when melted minerals collect and grow in size as they cool. You can learn more about crystals and how they "grow" by making some yourself.

EXPLORATORY PROBLEM

How can you grow crystals?

NEEDED

glass or ceramic saucer
string
hand lens
hot water
table salt
cup
alum (potash)
spoon
borax

TRY THIS

1. Stir as much salt into a half-cup of hot water as will dissolve.

2. Pour the salt solution into a saucer. Put a small string in the solution. Leave part of it outside so you can pick up the string later (Figure 10-17). Put the saucer where it will not be disturbed.

3. Wait several days until most of the salt solution has evaporated. Carefully pour off what is left. Then give the crystals forming on the saucer bottom and string a day to dry.

4. Examine the dry crystals with a hand lens.

DISCOVERY PROBLEMS

observing   **A.** How do the salt crystals look? Study their shape, size, and how they stick together.

Figure 10-17

observing **B.** What do alum and borax crystals look like? Prepare crystals from these materials as you did from salt. Study the crystals carefully with a hand lens.

inferring **C.** Have someone place before you strings of crystals prepared from salt, alum, and borax. Can you tell which is which without being told?

observing **D.** How, if at all, does quickness of cooling affect crystal size? Prepare two solutions of alum in separate saucers. Put one in a refrigerator so it will cool fast. Put the other where it will cool slowly. Examine each solution the next day.

TEACHING COMMENT

PREPARATION AND BACKGROUND

Alum (potash) is sold in drugstores, rather than in grocery stores. Sugar is another substance from which a solution may be prepared for crystal growing. All solutions should be very heavy or saturated for good crystals to form.

A solution that cools quickly forms small crystals. This is like molten rock that cools relatively quickly at or near the earth's surface. A solution that cools more slowly has time to form larger, coarser crystals. This is like molten rock that cools slowly deep underground.

GENERALIZATION

Crystals may form from molten rock or may be grown from mineral solutions. The size of crystals depends on how fast the molten rock and solutions cool.

SAMPLE PERFORMANCE OBJECTIVES

Process: Through observing, the child can determine enough properties of three common minerals to identify them when they are unlabeled.

Knowledge: The child can explain that crystal size depends on the cooling rate of either molten rock or a mineral solution.

REFERENCES

American Association for the Advancement of Science. (1993). *Benchmarks for science literacy.* New York: Oxford University Press.

Hardy, G. R., & Tolman, M. N. (1991). Cakequake! An earthshaking experience. *Science and Children,* 29(1), 18–21.

National Research Council. (1996). *National science education standards.* Washington, DC: National Academy Press.

SELECTED TRADE BOOKS: THE EARTH'S CHANGING SURFACE
For Younger Children

Booth, E. (1985). *Under the ground.* Raintree.

Branley, F. M. (1991). *Earthquakes.* Crowell.

Butler, D. (1991). *First look under the ground.* Gareth Stevens.

Cole, J. (1988). *The magic schoolbus inside the earth.* Scholastic.

Harris, S. (1979). *Volcanoes.* Watts.

Ingoglia, G. (1991). *Look inside the earth.* Putnam.

Leutscher, A. (1983). *Earth.* Dial.

McNulty, F. (1979). *How to dig a hole to the other side of the world.* Harper.

Podendorf, I. (1982). *Rocks and minerals.* Children's Press.

Roberts, A. (1983). *Fossils.* Children's Press.

Schwartz, L. (1991). *My earth book.* Learning Works.

Sipier, P. (1986). *I can be a geologist.* Children's Press.

Williams, L. (1986). *The changing earth.* Wright Group.

Wyler, R. (1987). *Science fun with dirt and mud.* Messner.

For Older Children

Bramwell, M. (1987). *Planet earth.* Watts.

Challand, H. (1983). *Volcanoes.* Children's Press.

Fordor, R. V. (1978). *Earth in motion: The concept of plate tectonics.* Morrow.

Fordor, R. V. (1983). *Chiseling the earth: How erosion shapes the land.* Enslow.

Gallant, R. A. (1986). *Our restless earth.* Watts.

Lampton, C. (1991). *Earthquake.* Millbrook Press.

Lauber, P. (1991). *Volcanoes and earthquakes.* Scholastic.

Levine, S., & Grafton, A. (1992). *Projects for a healthy planet.* Wiley.

Lye, K. (1991). *The earth.* Millbrook Press.

Marcus, E. (1984). *All about mountains and volcanoes.* Troll Associates.

Nixon, H. H., & Nixon, J. L. (1980). *Glaciers: Nature's frozen rivers.* Dodd.

Rickard, G. (1991). *Geothermal energy.* Gareth Stevens.

Ruthland, J. (1987). *The violent earth.* Random House.

Rydell, W. (1984). *Discovering fossils.* Troll Associates.

Selden, P. (1982). *Face of the earth.* Children's Press.

Williamson, T. (1985). *Understanding the earth.* Silver Burdett.

Winner, P. (1986). *Earthquakes.* Silver Burdett.

Resource Books

Butzow, C. M., & Butzow, J. W. (1989). *Science through children's literature. An integrated approach* (volcano, rock, and soil topics, pp. 123–138). Teachers Ideas Press.

Butzow, C. M., & Butzow, J. W. (1994). *Intermediate science through children's literature: over land and sea* (geological topics, pp. 62–88). Teachers Ideas Press.

Fredericks, A. D., Meinbach, A. M., & Rothlein, L. (1993). *Thematic units: An integrated approach to teaching science and social studies* (the changing earth topics, pp. 202–209). HarperCollins.

Shaw, D. G., & Dybdahl, C. S. (1996). *Integrating science and language arts. A sourcebook for K–6 teachers* (rock cycle topic, pp. 78–82; rock topics, pp. 111–130). Allyn and Bacon.

WATER, AIR, AND WEATHER

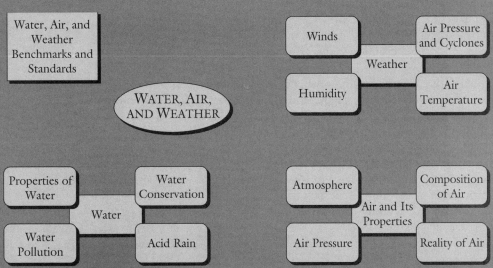

Water, Air, and Weather Benchmarks and Standards

WATER, AIR, AND WEATHER

Winds

Air Pressure and Cyclones

Weather

Humidity

Air Temperature

Properties of Water

Water Conservation

Water

Water Pollution

Acid Rain

Atmosphere

Composition of Air

Air and Its Properties

Air Pressure

Reality of Air

It's easy to take clean air and water for granted. And why not? For most of us, all we need do is breathe easily and turn on a faucet. But experiences of recent years with pollution and water shortages are making people lose their complacency.

In this chapter, we examine some properties of water and air, the importance of a clean supply of both, and some concepts basic to understanding weather, organized under three headings: water, air and its properties, and weather.

WATER CONCEPTS
(Experiences p. 382)

Our need for water commands our attention in both direct and indirect ways. Water is vital to life. You saw in another chapter how water transports chemicals to cells, removes waste materials, and performs other vital functions. Although humans may survive for weeks without food, water is needed within a few days. Bathing, cooking, and recreational activities also require water.

Agriculture consumes enormous volumes of water for irrigating plants in rain-poor regions. Industry, too, is a huge user of water. The manufacture of paper, steel, rubber, chemicals, and other products continually requires more water.

Even our future energy resources depend, in part, on having adequate water. For example, coal in the western United States would be most efficiently transported if crushed and sent through pipes after being mixed with water. The extraction of oil from shale rock also requires much water. But there is not enough water in the right places to meet all such needs.

Because water has so many uses, it is important to understand its properties. Let's look at some now.

Some Properties of Water

Water is an excellent solvent. In fact, more substances dissolve in water than in any other common liquid. Some other properties of water basic to our discussion are its molecular attraction, how it exerts pressure, and how it flows.

MOLECULES AND WATER. You may recall from Chapter 2, "Heat Energy," that there is an attractive force between molecules called cohesion. In a solid, the spaces between molecules are relatively small. So a solid material sticks together, or coheres, well enough to maintain its own shape. Molecules of a liquid are farther apart. Their weaker cohesion causes them to slide about and assume the shape of a container. The cohesion of gas molecules is weaker still since these molecules are even farther apart.

Cohesion of water molecules is central to the process of evaporation. Heat energy must overcome water's cohesive force, as well as the force of air pressing down. If this could not happen, evaporation could not take place. The sun, of course, is the chief source of heat energy. When we spread out a water puddle to make it dry faster, the sun's energy overcomes the cohesive force of more water molecules at one time. So the rate of evaporation increases.

PRESSURE. The weight of water gives it pressure. The deeper the water, the more pressure. This is one reason a dam is built with a thicker base than top. At any depth, the pressure is exerted in all directions and planes.

Pressure is also involved when something floats. For an object to float, opposing balanced forces work against each other. Gravity pulls down on the object, and the water pushes it up. The key to floating is the object's size relative to its weight. If it is light for its size, it has relatively high volume. That is, it presents a large surface area for the water to push against. This is why a ship made of steel floats. The water displaced by an object that is light for its size pushes up as forcefully as gravity pulls the object down.

An object floats higher in the ocean than in fresh water because ocean water has more minerals dissolved in it, especially salt. Therefore, a cup of ocean water weighs more than a cup of fresh water. Having more weight, it pushes back with greater force on any object that displaces it. This allows a ship to carry a heavier cargo in salt water than fresh water.

WATER FLOW. Gravity is the force that moves water in nature. Water cannot flow higher than its source unless some other force is more powerful. To store their water supply, some towns and small cities pump water into a large tank mounted on a tower. Water then flows by gravity through all pipes connected to the town tank. In some places, buildings are constructed that are taller than the tower. Pumps are installed in the buildings for water to reach the higher floors.

Clean, Adequate Water

Will there be enough water for enough people in enough places in the foreseeable future? A dependable answer to this question seems impossible now. But we can survey what it takes to get a clean and adequate supply of water, beginning with some sources of water.

SOURCES. A look at a globe tells us there is no shortage of water. About 71 percent of the earth's crust is covered with it. Most, though, is in the oceans and is too salty for either land plants or animals. So our immediate sources of fresh water are found elsewhere, in lakes, rivers, reservoirs, and beneath the land surface as groundwater.

Groundwater comes from rainwater that is absorbed into the soil and porous rock. It continues to sink until it reaches a layer of solid, nonporous rock. As more rainwater soaks into

the ground, more of the below-surface section becomes saturated. The upper limit of the saturated section is called the *water table*. The table profile often corresponds roughly to that of the surface. When the surface dips below the water table, we see a lake or spring. Groundwater in a location does not always come from rainwater sinking from directly above. Groundwater may percolate through ground and porous rock diagonally or horizontally for some distance before it stops.

To construct a water well, a hole is drilled or dug to some depth below the water table. This helps to ensure a steady supply of water should the water table lower during dry spells.

Ocean water is the main source of evaporating water on earth. So the oceans are the basic source for fresh water. When salt water evaporates, the salt is left behind. Air currents carry the water vapor far inland. There it condenses and falls as rain, hail, or snow.

Over the long run, the water cycle gives what should be a steady supply of groundwater and other water. But several factors today make it hard to find usable fresh water in many places. Increased uses for water, as mentioned earlier, is one reason. Another is pollution.

POLLUTION. Many cities continue to dump partly treated or raw sewage into nearby rivers or lakes, from which drinking water is often drawn. As a result, purification of water is getting harder and more expensive. Factories, too, often discharge wastes into accessible waters. Another major source of pollution is agriculture. Chemical fertilizers and pesticides wash off the land into streams and bays.

An overload of fertilizers or sewage in a lake or other body of water causes an abnormally large population of algae to grow. The algae block sunlight from reaching aquatic plants under the water's surface; so the plants, as well as the animals that feed on them, die. Dead material piles up on the lake bottom. The overcrowded algae also die in time, and the decomposers take over. Eventually, the oxygen supply in the water is largely depleted and the decomposers die, too. They are replaced by bacteria that can live without oxygen. What was once a source of clean water and a complex community of living things is a silted, near-dead, putrescent swamp. A reversal can occur through natural changes of the land surface and a gradual succession of ever-higher forms of life, but this may take centuries or longer.

In recent years, much publicity has been given to a particularly ominous threat to the nation's water supply, hazardous waste dumps. At such sites, poisonous chemicals may leak from storage containers and percolate down through the ground, contaminating groundwater, nearby streams, and lakes. Drinking or swimming in the water, and eating fish whose organs have accumulated the poisons, have been linked to severe health problems, including brain damage, cancer, and birth defects in children.

ACID RAIN. Many waste products are discharged into the air as well as on the ground and into bodies of water. These, also, may end up polluting our water and other natural resources. The burning of fossil fuels in factories, power plants, and automobiles releases sulfur and nitrogen oxides into the atmosphere. When water vapor is present, these gases are converted into sulfuric acid and nitric acid. The rain that falls from a polluted region can be as acidic as vinegar.

Acid rain, including acid sleet, hail, and snow, is contaminating water supplies, killing trees and fish stocks, and corroding water systems. Its effects are easily noticeable where there are large concentrations of coal-burning power plants, heavy industry, and automobiles. But even more damage may result far beyond these places. Winds aloft, especially the prevailing westerlies in our country, sweep the pollutants into large, distant regions. The northeastern United States and adjacent Canadian area have been most affected.

Some progress has been made in reducing the pollutants through the use of chemical filters in industry and pollution control devices for automobile exhaust systems. But large-scale improvements in industrial pollution bear a daunting price tag. Especially nettlesome is the answer to the question: Who pays? When suspected sources of pollution are hundreds of miles away, and thousands of jobs or millions of utility bills are affected, an acceptable answer becomes highly complicated.

CONSERVATION. It seems inevitable that people will need to change certain water-use habits. Many habits were fostered when regional populations were small, pollution was less severe, water uses were fewer, and resources were more abundant. Conservation, or wise use, of water resources is becoming more common because more persons now are aware of the consequences if it is not practiced.

Stricter laws to protect water supplies are continually enacted. More attention is being given to the recycling of industrial wastes and the safe storage of long-lasting, harmful chemicals. Bare slopes are being planted to protect watersheds. Fertilizers and pesticides are being used under more controlled conditions in agriculture. People are learning to use less water in more situations without wasting it. An important by-product of water conservation is energy conservation. A significant amount of the nation's energy is used in pumping water and heating it.

FUTURE WATER SUPPLY. It's possible that even increased conservation measures will fail to meet future needs for water. Where will more usable water come from? Just as some scientists are looking for ways to directly tap the sun's energy, others are investigating methods for directly converting ocean water to fresh water.

One way to remove salt from ocean water is to distill it. The water is heated, changed to a vapor, and condensed, much like in the water cycle. Another method freezes ocean water. The ice that forms at the surface is mostly fresh water. It is removed and melted. There are many other methods now being used and explored. At present, all are too expensive for widespread use. If more economical means can be found, the direct conversion of ocean water to fresh water could bring major changes in many dry regions of the world and in the world's food supply.

AIR AND ITS PROPERTIES CONCEPTS
(Experiences p. 391)

Air has many of the properties of water and may contain much water in gaseous form. However, air also has some unique properties. To better understand some of its specific features, let's first take an overall look at where our immediate air supply comes from: the atmosphere.

The Atmosphere

Space exploration has made us more aware of how dependent we are on our atmospheric environment. Without an air supply, humans cannot survive for more than minutes. Although we may travel in comfort thousands of kilometers across the earth's surface, an ascent of only 5 kilometers into the sky may require special oxygen apparatus.

How far out does the atmosphere extend? No one knows exactly, but meteorologists have identified four roughly separable layers of differing properties: the troposphere, stratosphere, ionosphere, and exosphere (Figure 11-1).

TROPOSPHERE. The troposphere extends to a height ranging from 8 kilometers (5 miles) at

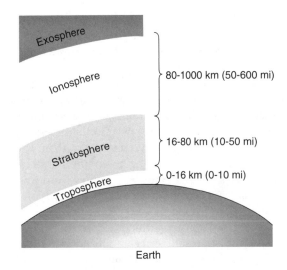

Figure 11-1
The atmosphere has several layers.

the poles to about 16 kilometers (10 miles) at the equator. This is the region where practically all weather conditions take place.

Why the difference in altitudes? Tropospheric air is coldest at the poles and so weighs more per unit than warmer, equatorial air. Also, the earth spins on its axis. The fastest speed of rotation, about 1,600 kilometers (1,000 miles) per hour, is at the equator. This offsets the earth's gravitational pull to some extent. The speed of rotation decreases as distance to the poles decreases, just as a person who runs on an inside track can slowly jog along, while someone on an outside track must run swiftly just to keep abreast. As the rotational speed slows, gravity has an increasing effect. In the troposphere, stable air temperature steadily decreases with altitude.

STRATOSPHERE. Just above the troposphere is the stratosphere, which reaches to about 80 kilometers (50 miles). This is the layer airlines use on some routes for long-range cruising. The cold, thin air is remarkably smooth and clear because vertical movements of warmed air and atmospheric dust particles are largely confined to the layer below. Air travelers may note some pale clouds of ice crystals above cruising altitude, but these are infrequent.

Between the lower reaches of the stratosphere and the troposphere are found winds that vary greatly in force and direction. Most interesting are the *jet streams,* rivers of high-velocity air several kilometers high and more than 150 kilometers wide. They range to thousands of kilometers in length and tend to flow from west to east. A pilot may increase the speed of a plane several hundred kilometers per hour by locating and staying within a jet stream.

In the stratosphere, at an altitude of 16 to 48 kilometers (10 to 30 miles), is a layer of *ozone* that absorbs much of the sun's harmful ultraviolet radiation. The layer is largely composed of molecules that have three atoms of oxygen, rather than the usual two. Certain chemicals released into the atmosphere, called *chlorofluorocarbons* (CFCs), collect unevenly in the ozone layer and destroy the ozone molecules. This greatly reduces the layer's capacity to block ultraviolet rays and so more get through to the earth's surface at various places.

Excess radiation increases the risk of skin cancer, eye damage, and immune system impairment. It can also reduce crop yields and disrupt ocean food chains. International agreements in force require the phasing out of CFCs, widely used in refrigerants, air conditioners, industrial cleaning solvents, and manufacture of some plastics. They are being replaced by less harmful but more expensive chemicals.

IONOSPHERE. Beyond a height of about 80 kilometers (50 miles), the stratosphere gradually blends into the ionosphere. In this region are ions, or electrically charged particles formed when air molecules are hit by high-energy solar and cosmic rays. These harmful rays are largely absorbed at and below this level. Auroras are sometimes visible. Meteors burn to ashes from friction as they strike scattered air molecules.

The ionosphere is an invaluable aid to radio communication on earth. The earth's surface is curved, but radio waves travel in straight lines. One way of overcoming this problem has been to transmit radio waves to the ionosphere, where they are reflected downward to other points on earth. Since solar "storms" frequently disturb the ionosphere and disrupt communication, this has not proved to be a completely satisfactory solution. Radio and television signals reflected from communications satellites are helping to solve this problem.

EXOSPHERE. The exosphere begins at about 1,000 kilometers (600 miles) and extends to an undetermined distance. A few air molecules have been detected beyond where the ionosphere adjoins the exosphere and it is probable that others are scattered thousands of kilometers beyond. For practical purposes, this region may be considered the beginning of interplanetary space.

Although scientists estimate the entire weight of our atmosphere at an enormous 4.5 quadrillion metric tons, more than half of all air molecules are concentrated below a height of 5.6 kilometers (3.5 miles). The combination of this enormous pressure and the unimaginably small size of air molecules results in the presence of air in practically everything on or near the earth's surface. Air is found in most soils, water, and even in some rocks. Consider now more effects of this pressure.

Air Pressure

Because the average weight of air is about 1 kilogram per square centimeter, or 14.7 pounds per square inch, at sea level, there are tons of air pressing against the human body. Why, then, are we not crushed? There are two basic reasons. Like water, air at a given level presses with equal force in all directions. Because there is a counteractive force for every force, the pressure is neutralized. Counteractive pressure also takes place in our bodies. Air molecules are so tiny that they dissolve in the blood stream, besides occupying space in our lungs and other body cavities.

Unlike free air, the air in our bodies lags somewhat in building up or reducing counteractive back pressure as atmospheric pressure changes. Have you noticed your ears "pop" while rising quickly in an elevator of a tall building? This happens because air pressure in the inner ear tends to remain the same while the outside air pressure decreases with increased altitude. The result is an uncomfortable outward pushing sensation behind the eardrums. A slow elevator gives more opportunity for inner ear pressure to be adjusted through the Eustachian tube, which connects the inner ear to the nasal passages and mouth.

A similar but much more dangerous situation is faced by deep-sea divers. As they descend into the water, air is pumped under increasing pressure into the diving helmet and suit to counteract increasing water pressure. After working for 20 to 30 minutes, the diver's circulatory system contains an abnormal amount of air. If the diver ascends rapidly to the surface, a region of much lower air pressure, air in the blood may expand and form bubbles. This causes a very painful and possibly fatal condition known as "the bends."

The lag in adjusting to outside atmospheric pressure may also be why some persons complain of aches and pains just before rainy weather. Outside air pressure usually lessens before a storm. If the body's blood pressure remains the same, the blood will now press outward a little more forcibly than usual against body joints and tissues. It is possible that the slight extra pressure may cause discomfort.

Makeup of Air

There are so many references to the earth's "ocean of air" that it is easy for us to get the impression that pure air is a uniform compound, such as pure water. Actually, the air we breathe is a mixture of several separate and distinct gases, of which the three most important to survival are oxygen, nitrogen, and carbon dioxide.

Oxygen makes up about 21 percent of the air, and nitrogen 78 percent. Oxygen is essential to us because it combines readily with sugars in our body cells and releases heat energy. Oxygen is also essential to burning.

Nitrogen is essential to survival because it is necessary for plant growth. It also dilutes the oxygen we breathe. Continual breathing of pure oxygen speeds up metabolic processes to the point where the body cannot get rid of waste products fast enough to survive. The small amount of carbon dioxide in the air, about $3/100$ of 1 percent, is needed for photosynthesis in green plants. Besides these gases, there is less than 1 percent of such gases as argon, krypton, helium, neon, radon, and xenon. All these atmospheric gases are remarkably well mixed by winds up to a height of 8 to 10 kilometers, or 5 to 6 miles.

But this is not all we breathe. As hay-fever sufferers know, there are other substances mixed in the air. Besides the troublesome pollens, there are dust, smoke, salt particles, water vapor, chemicals, spores, bacteria, and viruses.

The Reality of Air

Because pure air has no taste, color, or odor, its study for children, especially primary level students, has an elusive quality not present in many other areas. So it is usually good to begin with activities that bring out the tangibility of air.

Like other material objects such as automobiles, houses, books, and people, air is a real thing. Children can feel it and see it move things in the form of wind. A blown-up balloon or a soap bubble shows that air takes up space. A slowly falling parachute demonstrates that air resists motion. A can that is crushed when some inside air is removed shows that air has weight.

Sipping liquid through a straw shows this, too. Since many children are confused about how a straw works, consider it for a moment.

When we sip some air out of a straw, the air pressure in the straw is reduced. Since the atmosphere now has more relative pressure, it presses down on the liquid's surface and pushes it up inside the straw's space once occupied by the air.

If you are skeptical, try the following experiments. Place two straws in your mouth, but leave one *outside* the pop bottle or glass. You will find it is now practically impossible to drink the liquid. Why? Air traveling inward through the outside straw restores the pressure in your mouth and drinking straw to normal. For the second experiment, fill a flask with water and seal it tightly with a one-hole stopper containing a glass tube. No matter how hard you sip, no water goes up the tube. There is no air pressing down on the water. With a *two*-hole stopper, though, normal drinking is possible. Air pressure is exerted through the second hole.

As with drinking straws, the events we associate with "suction" are really due to removing or reducing air pressure from one part of a device. Air pressure on all other parts then pushes and performs the work. In vacuum cleaners, for example, the motor whirls a reversed fan that reduces air pressure at the cleaning nozzle. The surrounding air then *pushes* dirt particles into the nozzle. A "suction" cup works in a similar way. By pressing down on the pliable rubber cup, most of the air inside is forced out. Air from all other sides pushes against the cup's exterior and holds it fast to whatever surface it has been pressed.

WEATHER CONCEPTS
(Experiences p. 404)

Weather is the condition of the lower atmosphere at a given time and place. If you have been rained on while expecting a sunny afternoon, you know how quickly it can change. Weather changes happen because changes in temperature, moisture, pressure, and other variables alter the way air "behaves." We'll examine some of these variables next, one at a time.

Causes of Winds

At early morning off an African coast, hundreds of fishing boats point out to sea as a fresh land breeze fills their colorful lateen sails. The boats return in the afternoon with sails taut from a sea breeze blowing in the opposite direction. You have probably experienced a similar shift of winds at the seashore or by a large lake. How does this happen? (See Figure 11-2.)

TEMPERATURE DIFFERENCES. You may recall from the heat energy chapter that warmed air expands and is pushed up by denser, colder air that rushes in and replaces it. Winds are caused by the unequal heating and cooling of the earth's surface. During the day, solar radiation is absorbed by the sea and land. The land heats up much faster. One reason is that sunlight penetrates only a short distance below the land's surface, but penetrates more deeply into water. Another reason is the higher heat capacity of water.

After a short period of sunlight, air immediately above the earth is heated by the ground and begins expanding. Cooler, heavier air from the sea rushes in and pushes the lighter air upward. The reverse occurs at night and until the following morning. During this period, the land cools quickly and stays cool, while the sea remains relatively warmer. As air warmed by contact with the water expands, it is pushed upward by cooler air rushing in from the cooler land.

These air movements are not confined to land and sea settings. The same basic air movements take place between any surfaces that have a temperature difference. As temperature differ-

Day   Night

Figure 11-2
Winds are caused by unequal heating and cooling of the earth's surface.

ences increase, the resulting wind force increases. This is one reason why a large fire is so destructive. It creates a powerful, localized wind that fans and spreads the flames.

PREVAILING WINDS. The world's prevailing winds are caused by the same unequal heating of the earth's surface on a grand scale. But the earth's rotation adds a factor. If the earth did not rotate, heavy, cold air at the poles would simply flow due south and north, and push up warmed, expanding equatorial air. The rotation (named the *Coriolis effect*) results in a wind deflection to the *right* in the northern hemisphere. A deflection to the *left* occurs in the southern hemisphere.

You can see why this happens with a globe and some chalk. Rotate the globe from west to east. While it is moving, draw a line from the North Pole due south toward the equator. Note that the line curves to the right. Draw a line from the South Pole and the curve is reversed. (We will return to the Coriolis effect in a later section.)

WINDS ALOFT. Detailed understanding of wind patterns requires much more background than can be given here. For example, we have briefly discussed jet streams. There are, however, other winds aloft. It is possible for an airplane pilot to meet a wind blowing from one direction at one altitude and another blowing from another direction higher up. You will not want to explore this subject in detail at the elementary level. Still, it will be worthwhile to help students learn that wind direction aloft may differ from surface wind direction.

To calculate winds aloft, meteorologists use measuring instruments to observe small, helium-filled balloons as they rise to various altitudes. A cruder method is to observe cloud movements with a *nephoscope,* a circular mirror marked with the points of a compass. Properly aligned, this instrument can show children the direction of cloud movement as the cloud reflection moves across the mirror.

Air Temperature

In parts of Southern California and Mexico, it is sometimes possible in winter to observe snowy mountain peaks while lying on a warm, sunny beach. Children are curious about conditions like this ("Aren't the mountain peaks closer to the sun?"). Most adults know that air is colder at higher altitudes. But why?

TEMPERATURE AND ALTITUDE. One reason air is colder at higher altitudes is the varying distance of air molecules from the earth's surface. Air molecules closest to the earth are warmed more easily by conduction and heat waves radiated from the earth's surface than those farther away.

Second, as we get closer to sea level, more and more molecules are piled up. This increased weight compresses the air. With reduced space for movement, there is more energy exchange among molecules as they collide. So the heat energy in the denser molecule "population" is concentrated into a relatively low, dense layer.

There is also a third reason. As warmed air is pushed up, it expands and cools as it meets lower air pressure with the increased altitude. Whatever heat energy is contained in the original air parcel is dissipated throughout an ever-larger volume.

The combined effect of these causes makes pushed-up air cool about 2°C for each 300 meters, or 3.5°F for each 1,000 feet. As pushed-down air is compressed, the opposite happens.

TEMPERATURE AND POLLUTION. As you saw, the atmosphere is a gigantic greenhouse that slows the loss of heat received from solar radiation. Fortunately, the earth loses and gains about the same amount of heat each day. A narrow temperature range enables life to continue. Since the Industrial Revolution, though, conditions have been developing that may upset this delicate balance.

Most scientists think the lower atmosphere is gradually becoming slightly warmer through increased carbon dioxide from the burning of fuels such as coal and oil. As light waves from the sun warm the earth's surface, heat waves going from the surface into the atmosphere are partly blocked by carbon dioxide. Some of the heat energy cannot escape into space. This causes the atmosphere to lose slightly less heat than it gains from solar radiation. Recent data seem to support a global warming trend.

Yet a few scientists say it is also possible that the trend may be reversing. To them, the data suggest that the earth's atmosphere is cooling very gradually. In recent years, there has been a large increase in air pollution throughout the world. The greater number of suspended pollutants in the air may be causing more and more sunlight to be reflected away from the earth *before* it reaches the earth's surface. If true, this could overcome the effect of the increased carbon dioxide.

Although not everyone agrees about what is happening to the air temperature, a definite trend in either direction could bring trouble. An average increase of a few degrees could turn huge, fertile land areas into semi-deserts, and an average temperature drop of 4° to 5°C could launch another ice age.

Evaporation and Humidity

Many students understand in a limited way the concepts of evaporation and humidity, but may not understand how the two are related. This section can help deal with these concepts.

EVAPORATION. In an earlier chapter, you saw that heat and atmospheric pressure affect an evaporating liquid. Increased heat energy increases the speed of molecules. Additional speed enables molecules to overcome the cohesive forces of nearby molecules, and greater numbers leave the liquid's surface than before. Any decrease of atmospheric pressure also affects evaporation because it tends to "take the lid off." The counterforce of air molecules pressing down on the surface of an evaporating liquid becomes weaker, and more evaporation takes place. This is a reason mountain climbers must be so careful with dehydration.

It is easy to see why increasing a liquid's surface area increases the rate of evaporation. There is greater exposure to the air above and a higher probability of more molecules escaping. This is why you have to add water more often to a rectangular aquarium than to a fish bowl of equal volume.

The wind, too, speeds up evaporation. When air just above the surface of an evaporating fluid becomes quickly saturated, the wind blows it away and replaces it with drier air.

HUMIDITY. Another factor influencing evaporation is *humidity* which is the amount of moisture already present in the air. On humid days, we feel sticky and uncomfortable because our perspiration evaporates very slowly. We may turn on an electric fan to feel more comfortable. Moving air from a fan cools us because it speeds up evaporation of perspiration from the skin.

Without an evaporating liquid, *a fan has no cooling effect at all.* You can see this by putting a thermometer in front of a whirling electric fan. There is no difference in the before and after readings. But dampen some cotton and stick it to the thermometer bulb. The rapidly evaporating water will now cause a noticeable drop in temperature.

The moisture content of air changes considerably from time to time. The capacity of air to hold moisture depends on its temperature, so warm air holds more moisture than cooler air. The percentage of moisture in air at a certain temperature, compared to all it could hold at that temperature, is called its *relative humidity*. During a period of low relative humidity, our skin moisture evaporates more quickly than it can be effectively replaced. This results in dry, chapped skin.

One reason we have more colds in winter may be directly related to the relative humidity of air in our homes. The cool air of winter holds comparatively little moisture. As it is warmed by heaters, it expands and becomes even drier. Unless the home heating system is equipped to give additional moisture, the air becomes increasingly dry. The protective mucous film that coats the delicate nasal membrane evaporates, and we become more open to infections.

Relative humidity is often measured with a wet-and-dry bulb thermometer apparatus called a *hygrometer*. Two identical thermometers are placed next to each other. The bulb of one instrument is enclosed in a wet cotton wick that is immersed in water. The wet-bulb thermometer is fanned rapidly until its reading steadies at some lower point. As water evaporates from the wick, it is continually replaced by water traveling upward through the wick by capillary action. Any difference in thermometer readings is translated into the percentage of relative humidity by consulting a reference table.

Condensation

DEW. Many mornings we see dew drops glistening on lawns, parked automobiles, spider webs, and other surfaces. When the ground cools during the night, its temperature may fall below that of the surrounding air. As the surrounding air loses some heat energy, its molecules slow down. Water vapor molecules in the air slow enough to be attracted to, and condense on, a cool nearby surface. The same thing happens when water droplets form on a cold pop bottle or cold water pipe.

Remember, relative humidity varies with air temperature. Any parcel of air containing some water vapor becomes saturated if cooled enough. The loss of heat energy slows down molecular speed and reduces the range of molecular movement. The attractions of water molecules for one another now draw them together into visible drops.

DEW POINT. The temperature at which condensation takes place is called the *dew point*. In very humid air, as in a steamy shower room, water vapor condenses on walls and mirrors although they may be only several degrees cooler than the air. Comparatively dry desert air may have to be cooled much more before reaching its dew point.

FOG. We may see fog when the surface temperature is low enough to cool air that is a short distance above the ground to its dew point. In this case, water vapor condenses on tiny specks of airborne dust and remains suspended.

Sometimes fog results from the unequal cooling of land and water. Such fog is common over a lake in summer. Cool air from the land flows over warm, moist air just above the lake. As the warmer air cools to its dew point, condensation occurs and we see fog. Fog can be considered a low cloud.

CLOUDS AND CLOUD TYPES. Clouds at higher altitudes are formed in several ways, but all involve a parcel of air that is cooled to its saturation, or dew, point. In one method, wind may blow moist air up a mountain slope. As the air rises, it expands because of decreasing air pressure, cools, and condenses on airborne dust particles. If the dew point is below freezing, tiny ice crystals may form.

Sometimes air is pushed aloft when two huge air masses merge. The cooler, heavier air mass will push under the warmer, lighter mass. Again, expansion, cooling, and condensation take place.

A third method of cloud formation happens when heat from the ground develops convection currents. The affected air near the ground is heated and is pushed up by heavier, cooler surrounding air. The rising air finally cools and its moisture condenses.

When enough moisture is present, the tiny, constantly moving droplets within a cloud collide from time to time and form larger drops. These may fall as rain. In freezing temperatures, ice crystals collect and fall as snow.

Knowing the air temperature and its dew point can enable you or upper-grade students to roughly calculate cloud heights. Here is how it is done. Suppose the outdoor air temperature is now 88°F. Stir a thermometer around in a metal can of ice water. At the exact instant water droplets occur on the can, read the temperature of the immersed thermometer. This is the dew point. Say it reads 74°F, which makes a difference of 14°F between the two figures. Rising air cools at about 3.5°F for each 1,000 feet of altitude. Dividing 14 by 3.5 gives a quotient of 4. Multiply this figure by 1,000. The bases of nearby clouds should be about 4,000 feet above you. (With metric measures, use 2°C for 3.5°F and 300 meters for 1,000 feet.)

Although experts have invented more than 200 cloud classifications, young children can be taught to recognize three basic cloud forms. *Cirrus* clouds are high, wispy formations of ice crystals. *Cumulus* clouds are white, fluffy, and usually associated with clear visibility and fair weather. *Stratus* clouds are lower, darker formations that appear as a dense layer. These clouds may blanket the entire sky and precipitate rain within a short time. (See Figure 11-3.)

WATER CYCLE. You can see that condensation is the opposite of evaporation. Together, they form the water cycle. Powered by the sun, an immense but finite volume of water over the earth constantly evaporates, condenses, and falls without apparent end.

Air Masses and Cyclones

At one time, it was thought that air pressure over any one point was always the same. We now know otherwise. Huge masses of air are continually on the move over the earth, bringing changes in pressure and weather.

AIR MASSES. An air mass is a huge volume of air that picks up distinctive temperature and humidity conditions from the surface underneath. These conditions are fairly uniform throughout the mass, which may cover thousands of square kilometers or miles.

An ocean air mass is typically moist. Air over land is drier. Air near the polar regions is cold, while that near the equator is warm. So four different kinds of air masses are possible: cold

Figure 11-3
Three basic cloud forms: *(a)* **cirrus,** *(b)* **cumulus,** *(c)* **stratus.**

and dry, cold and moist, warm and dry, and warm and moist. Figure 11-4 shows the origins of four kinds of air masses that often move into the continental United States.

Cold air is heavier than warm air. Dry air is heavier than moist air. Just as water flows from a high point to a lower one, air flows from a region of relatively high pressure to one of lower pressure. But because of the earth's rotation, the flow is not in a straight line.

CYCLONES AND ANTICYCLONES. The Coriolis effect causes air masses and the general circulation of air to move in gigantic spirals called *cyclones* and *anticyclones.* (Cyclones should not be confused with tornadoes, which are small, violent, twisting air currents that come from a mixture of super-heated and cold air.) A cyclone is a larger area of relative lower pressure with the point of lowest pressure in the center; it is also called a *low.* An *anticyclone* is a large area of relatively high pressure with the highest pressure in the center; it is also called a high.

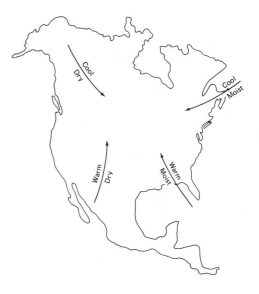

Figure 11-4
Four common air masses.

In the northern hemisphere, air movements spiral counterclockwise toward the center of a low. In a high, they spiral clockwise away from the center of highest pressure. These movements are reversed in the southern hemisphere. Highs and lows may move hundreds of kilometers a day. A typical pattern of movement in the United States is from west to east.

Lows often bring bad weather. This is because cold or dry heavier air moves in and pushes up warm or moist lighter air. The moisture condenses when the air rises to its dew-point altitude and falls as rain or snow.

Highs usually bring more pleasant weather. As cool or dry heavier air spirals downward from the center of a high, it warms about 2°C (3.5°F) for each 300 meters (1,000 feet) loss of altitude. As it warms, the mass of air is able to hold more and more moisture without it condensing. The result is usually clear, sunny weather.

Measuring Pressure

Highs and lows are detected by noting changes in cloud, temperature, and wind patterns. However, the most important changes observed are those in air pressure. An instrument used for measuring air pressure is the *barometer*. There are two kinds.

In a *mercurial* barometer, a glass tube about 90 centimeters (36 inches) long and closed at one end is filled with mercury and inverted into a dish of mercury. While some of the liquid runs out, a column of about 76 centimeters (30 inches) remains. This tells the force of air pressing on the liquid's surface. As air pressure increases, the column rises higher into the vacuum above. The reverse takes place with reduced pressure.

Since mercurial barometers are easily broken and cumbersome, most weather observers use the *aneroid* barometer (Figure 11-5). This consists of a thin, flexible, metal box from which air has been largely removed. As air pressure presses on it with varying degrees of force, the

Figure 11-5
Aneroid barometer.

box moves in and out accordingly. A cleverly linked leverage system transfers these movements to a movable needle on a dial.

Because air pressure also changes with altitude, aneroid barometers are used in many airplanes to indicate altitude. This is done by merely changing the dial to read in a unit of height rather than one of pressure. Such a barometer is called an altimeter.

WATER, AIR, AND WEATHER BENCHMARKS AND STANDARDS

Weather, water, and air are popular topics in the elementary grades. Students frequently complete daily weather logs and journal descriptions of the changing weather patterns, often including pictures of what they see. Representative Benchmarks and Standards related to water, air, and weather include:

SAMPLE BENCHMARKS (AAAS, 1993).

■ Water left in an open container disappears, but water in a closed container does not disappear (by Grades K–2, p. 67).

■ Some events in nature have a repeating pattern. The weather changes day to day, but things such as temperature and rain (or snow) tend to be high, low, or medium in the same months every year (by Grades K–2, p. 67).

SAMPLE STANDARDS (NRC, 1996).

■ Weather changes from day to day and over the seasons. Weather can be described in measurable quantities such as temperature, wind direction and speed, and precipitation (by Grades K–4, p. 134).

■ The atmosphere is a mixture of nitrogen, oxygen, and trace gasses that include water vapor (by Grades 5–8, p. 160).

INVESTIGATIONS AND ACTIVITIES

WATER EXPERIENCES
(Concepts p. 368)

INVESTIGATION: *HOW WATER AND OTHER LIQUIDS STICK TOGETHER*

Suppose you fill a glass with water to the very top. What do you think will happen if you add more water?

EXPLORATORY PROBLEM

How high can you fill a container of water before it spills?

NEEDED

three small plastic vials
spoon
two matched medicine droppers
newspaper
water
liquid soap or detergent
paper clips
rubbing alcohol
paper cup
meter stick or yardstick

TRY THIS

1. Fill a small container to the top with water.

2. Gently drop paper clips into the container one at a time. (See Figure 11-6.)

3. Watch how the water "heaps" higher in the container. Count the number of clips it takes for the water to spill. Make a record.

DISCOVERY PROBLEMS

observing   **A.** How high can you heap other liquids? Try soapy water and alcohol. How do these liquids compare with water? Put the three containers side by side and see. How many paper clips does it take for soapy water and alcohol to spill?

observing   **B.** How large are the drops of different liquids? Take up water in one medicine dropper and alcohol in another. Hold up the droppers

Figure 11-6

side by side. Slowly squeeze each bulb until a drop forms at each open end. How do the drop sizes compare? Try soapy water also.

observing

C. Which liquid—water, soapy water, or alcohol—has the largest drops? the smallest drops? Here is another way to find out. Put 100 drops of each liquid into separate, matched, small containers. Compare how high each liquid is inside.

observing

D. What kinds of drop prints do different liquids make on newspaper? (See Figure 11-7.) Hold a meter stick or yardstick upright over newspaper. Squeeze a drop of water from a medicine dropper held near and about halfway up the stick. What does the drop print look like on the newspaper? How large is it? Let a drop fall from the top of the stick. How does the print look now? Try drops of soapy water and alcohol, too.

inferring

E. Can you match up a liquid with its drop print? Can you tell from how high each drop fell? Ask a partner to make drop prints as you did. Do not watch as the prints are made.

hypothesizing

F. What other liquids can you test? How do you think they will compare with your first liquids?

TEACHING COMMENT

PREPARATION AND BACKGROUND

Any liquid has the property of cohesion, which is the tendency for its molecules to stick together. The cohesion of water is strong compared with some other liquids. This is why water forms a bulge that rises above the rim of an overly full glass. Soap weakens the cohesive power of water, so the bulge of slightly soapy water is noticeably lower. That of alcohol is lower still; its cohesion is relatively weak. This is one reason it evaporates so fast.

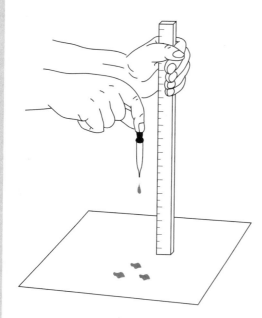

Figure 11-7

GENERALIZATION

Some liquids seem to stick together more strongly than others.

SAMPLE PERFORMANCE OBJECTIVES

Process: The child can observe and compare the relative sizes of drops of water, soapy water, and alcohol.

Knowledge: The child can predict the relative sizes of drops of two liquids after first observing how high each bulges in the filled container.

FOR YOUNGER CHILDREN

Most younger students are successful in manipulating the materials and making observations.

INVESTIGATION: *How to Measure Volume with Water*

Rocks and other solid objects have many different shapes. Sometimes it is hard to tell which of two different-shaped objects is larger; that is, takes up more space. (The amount of space an object takes up is its volume.)

EXPLORATORY PROBLEM

How can you compare the volumes of small solid objects?

NEEDED

five different-shaped rocks (small)
ruler
oil-base modeling clay
large jar with straight sides
small lead fishing sinker
water
masking tape and pencil
fork or spoon

TRY THIS

1. Fasten a strip of masking tape on a jar the long way.
2. Half-fill the jar with water.
3. Put one rock into the jar. Mark the water level on the tape with a pencil.
4. Remove the rock with a fork or spoon.
5. Put a second rock into the jar. Compare the new water level with the pencil mark (Figure 11-8).

DISCOVERY PROBLEMS

classifying

A. How can you put the rocks in order from smallest to largest?

Figure 11-8

inferring   **B.** Make a clay ball the size of some rock. Where will the water level be if you put it into the jar? Mark the tape to show your estimate, then test your hypothesis.

inferring   **C.** Suppose you form the same clay ball into another shape. Where do you think the water level will be? Try many different shapes.

inferring and observing   **D.** Suppose you break the same clay piece into two parts. Where do you think the water level will be? What happens to the water level when you break the clay into more than two parts?

inferring   **E.** Will a heavy clay ball make the water level rise higher than a lighter one? Make two clay balls the same size, but have a lead weight in the middle of one ball. Try each ball and find out.

measuring   **F.** How much larger is one rock compared to another? With a ruler and pencil, make evenly spaced marks on the jar's tape strip. Call each pencil mark one "unit." Compare the difference in water-level units before and after a rock is put in the jar. How much difference in units is there between your smallest and largest rock?

predicting   **G.** Get other small objects. How well can you predict the volume of each in units?

TEACHING COMMENT

PREPARATION AND BACKGROUND

This investigation may help some of your students learn to conserve volume as measured by displaced water. That is, the space an object takes up is determined by its overall surface, rather than shape, weight, or number of parts.

GENERALIZATION

The volumes of different-shaped solid objects may be compared by the water each displaces.

SAMPLE PERFORMANCE OBJECTIVES

Process: The child can measure the difference in volume between two rocks by using "water-level units."

Knowledge: The child can explain that the volume of water an object displaces is determined by the volume of space the object occupies.

FOR YOUNGER CHILDREN

The Exploratory Problem and Problems A through D may be used as readiness experiences.

INVESTIGATION: *THINGS THAT FLOAT IN WATER*

Can you tell, just by looking at an object, whether it will float in water? What kinds of objects float? What kinds of objects sink?

EXPLORATORY PROBLEM

How can you find out which small objects will float?

NEEDED

plastic bowl
salt
bag of small objects to test
ruler
oil-base modeling clay
spoon
large washers
paper towels
kitchen foil (15 centimeters or 6 inches square)

TRY THIS

1. Half-fill a plastic bowl with water.
2. Empty the bag of small objects on your desk. Put those you think will float into one group. Put those you think will sink in another group.
3. Place all the objects from one group into the water. Observe what happens, then remove the objects. Do the same thing with the other group of objects.

DISCOVERY PROBLEMS

inferring	**A.**	How many objects did what you thought? What are the objects like that floated? sank?
experimenting	**B.**	What can you do to sink the objects that floated?
experimenting	**C.**	What can you do to float the objects that sank?
experimenting	**D.**	In what ways can you get a piece of foil to float? sink?
experimenting	**E.**	How can you make a foil boat?
experimenting	**F.**	How many washers can your foil boat carry? What can you do to make it carry more washers?
experimenting	**G.**	How can you get a piece of clay to float?
inferring	**H.**	Make a clay boat the same size as your foil boat. Which do you think will carry more washers?

measuring   **I.** Can you make two foil boats that will carry, from the first try, exactly the same weight? two clay boats that will carry the same weight from the first try?

experimenting   **J.** What can you get to float in salt water that cannot float in fresh water?

inferring   **K.** Can you find anything that will float in fresh water and sink in salt water?

TEACHING COMMENT

PREPARATION AND BACKGROUND

Children can develop some understanding in this investigation about the buoyancy of different objects in water and how the density of water affects buoyancy. You might also want children to explore liquids other than water.

A bag of small objects to test for floating might include a wooden checker, pencil, key, marble, plastic objects, pieces of leather, rubber eraser, and small toy figures. The children can bring in many more.

Uniform objects other than large washers may be used to measure the weight-carrying capacity of children's boats. Identical marbles, pennies, or small pieces of ceramic tile work well. To avoid rust, be sure all steel washers are dried before they are stored.

GENERALIZATION

Objects that are light for their size float; adding salt to water makes floating easier.

SAMPLE PERFORMANCE OBJECTIVES

Process: Through measuring, the child can construct two near-identical boats with near-identical weight capacities.

Knowledge: When shown some new objects, the child can predict which will float.

FOR YOUNGER CHILDREN

Activities A through G have been done successfully by primary students. The other activities that involve careful measuring and counting may be difficult and are not recommended.

ACTIVITY: WHAT HAPPENS TO WATER PRESSURE WITH DEPTH?

NEEDED

empty milk carton (tall)
nail (or sharp pencil)
sink
water

TRY THIS

1. Punch a nail hole in the carton's side, halfway up, from the inside out.
2. Punch another hole above it and a third hole below it, from the inside out.
3. Cover all three holes tightly with three fingers. Fill the carton with water. Keep it in the sink.

   a. If you take away your fingers, what do you think will happen?

4. Remove your fingers quickly from the three holes.

   b. What happened? In what part of the carton was the water pressure the greatest?

TEACHING COMMENT

Sometimes the torn edges of the holes will impede the flow of water. Punching the holes from the inside out makes this less likely.

ACTIVITY: HOW HIGH CAN WATER FLOW COMPARED TO ITS ORIGIN?

NEEDED

rubber tube (1 meter or 1 yard long)
container of water
funnel that fits the tube
sink

TRY THIS

1. Stick the funnel end tightly into a tube end. Do this activity in a sink.
2. Hold up the funnel. Have someone pour water into it.
3. When water comes out of the tube, pinch it off.
4. Have someone fill the funnel with water. Keep the tube end pinched off. How high will you be able to hold the tube end and still have water come out? Higher than the funnel? as high? lower?
5. Let go of the tube end. Try holding it at different heights. What did you find?

INVESTIGATION: THE FILTERING OF POLLUTED WATER

Most cities have water treatment plants to clean, or *purify,* their drinking water. The unclean water is first pumped to a large settling tank, where it stays for a while. Some of the dirt and other polluting particles in the water settle to the bottom. The cleaner water on top then goes into a filtering tank, which has thick layers of sand and gravel. Sometimes there is a layer of charcoal between these layers. As the water filters through, still more polluting materials are left behind.

It's not easy to clean polluted water, even by filtering. You can find out more about this yourself.

EXPLORATORY PROBLEM

How can you clean polluted water by filtering?

NEEDED

cut-off pint milk carton
clean sand
charcoal briquette
cotton
small glass jar
nail
jar of soil water
small paper bag

TRY THIS

1. Punch some holes with a nail in the bottom of a cutoff milk carton.
2. Spread some cotton inside on the carton bottom. Add some clean sand.
3. Put crushed charcoal on top of the sand. (To crush charcoal, put a briquette into a small bag. Pound it with a rock.) Then add another layer of sand.
4. Place the filter on top of a small glass jar.
5. Pour some *clean tap water* into your filter. (This will pack the materials more tightly together.)
6. Prepare a jar of soil water. Put a handful of soil into a jar of water and mix. Let the water settle for a half hour.
7. Pour some soil water from the top of the jar into the filter. Watch the filtered water trickle into the small jar (Figure 11-9).

DISCOVERY PROBLEMS

observing   **A.** How clean is the filtered water compared to the soil water?

observing   **B.** How clean would the water get with fewer filtering materials? with just one filtering material?

observing   **C.** Will your filter remove ink or food coloring?

observing   **D.** Does the order in which you have your filter materials matter?

experimenting   **E.** Would more or other materials work better? How else could you improve your filter?

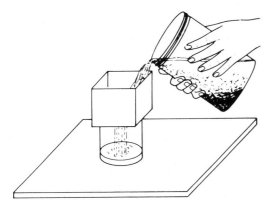

Figure 11-9

TEACHING COMMENT

PREPARATION AND BACKGROUND

Caution students not to drink their filtered water. They should know that a chemical is added to filtered water in city water plants to kill germs that survive filtering.

Your students may enjoy having a contest to determine the best filter. They may need to be reminded that everyone should filter samples of the same polluted water.

GENERALIZATION

Some water pollutants may be removed by filtering the water through layers of different permeable materials.

SAMPLE PERFORMANCE OBJECTIVES

Process: The child can experiment to find ways to improve the efficiency of a simple water filter.

Knowledge: The child can make a water filter with simple materials that removes larger particles from polluted water.

AIR AND ITS PROPERTIES EXPERIENCES
(Concepts page 371)

INVESTIGATION: WHERE AIR CAN BE

Air is found everywhere on the earth. Air can go into tiny places. But can air get inside everything? What things do you think have some air inside? do not have air inside?

EXPLORATORY PROBLEM

How can you find out what things have some air inside?

NEEDED

plastic bowl (half-filled with water)
orange peel
sand
coin
stone
cracker
piece of brick
leather
soft wood
several kinds of fabrics

TRY THIS

1. Put a piece of brick into a bowl of water (Figure 11-10).

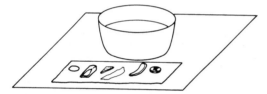

Figure 11-10

2. Watch for tiny bubbles on the brick. These are air bubbles. This shows there was some air inside the brick.
3. Put a coin into the water. You will probably see no bubbles. This shows the coin probably had no air inside.

DISCOVERY PROBLEMS

observing   **A.** Does a piece of cloth have air in it? Do some kinds of cloth have more air in them than others?

observing   **B.** Does leather have air in it? Can a soft piece of wood have air in it?

observing   **C.** Does a cracker have air in it? does an orange peel?

observing   **D.** Can a stone have air in it? Try several different kinds.

experimenting   **E.** Does sand have air in it? How can you find out?

inferring   **F.** What else do you think might have air in it? What else might not have air in it?

TEACHING COMMENT

PREPARATION AND BACKGROUND

Some soft materials show dramatically that they contain air if squeezed under water. Soft pine, balsa wood, and leather are examples. Pliers or tongs may serve as squeezers, if needed.

The spaces between sand or soil particles commonly contain much air. Surface air bubbles may easily be seen if water is poured into a small jar with sand inside. (While water also usually contains air, the volume is small compared to that found in the spaces between sand particles.)

GENERALIZATION

Air can be found almost everywhere. Most porous materials contain some air.

SAMPLE PERFORMANCE OBJECTIVES

Process: The child can infer which objects are likely to contain air by observing their physical properties.

Knowledge: The child can describe the properties of objects that contain or do not contain some air.

FOR OLDER CHILDREN

Older children can be challenged to detect if water contains air. They may look for bubbles in the water that rise to the surface and break. This can be seen in standing water, but is more quickly observable as water becomes heated.

Also, let them boil some aquarium water in a teakettle to remove most of the air. After the boiled water cools again to the aquarium temperature, a goldfish may be placed in the water. Have them compare the more rapid gill movements of the fish with those observed before in the aquarium. Return the fish to the aquarium after several minutes to avoid harming it.

INVESTIGATION: *SOAP BUBBLES*

Have you ever blown soap bubbles? If so, how big was your biggest bubble? how small was your smallest bubble?

EXPLORATORY PROBLEM

How can you blow soap bubbles? What is it like inside a bubble?

NEEDED

paper cup of bubble liquid
soda can with ends removed

bendable plastic straw
paper cup half full of water
small piece of cardboard
liquid detergent or soap
scissors
glycerin
thin wire (6 inches)
spoon
child's plastic swimming pool
hula-hoop
small wooden box or stool

TRY THIS

1. Cut the straw end into four parts. Use the end that bends.
2. Push back the four parts as shown in the drawing (Figure 11-11).
3. Bend the straw into a **J** shape.
4. Dip the cut end into the bubble liquid.
5. Put the other straw end into your mouth and blow gently.
6. Place a mixture of dish soap (32–64 ounces), glycerine (10 tablespoons), and water in a child's plastic pool. Set a small wooden box or stool in the center (above the water line).
7. Place a student on the stool and then quickly pick the hula-hoop straight up from the bottom of the pool to above the student's head. A bubble will form

Figure 11-11

and surround the child. Larger amounts of glycerin and/or dish soap will make longer-lasting bubbles.

DISCOVERY PROBLEMS

observing **A.** What different kinds of bubbles can you blow? How big a bubble can you make? how small?

observing **B.** How many bubbles can you blow with one dip of your pipe? How few?

observing **C.** What do you see when you look at a bubble? when you look through the large bubble around you?

predicting **D.** What will happen if you catch a bubble in your hand? What will happen if your hand is soapy?

experimenting **E.** How can you make a bubble floating in air stay up? Move to your left? right? up? (*Hint:* How might a piece of cardboard help you?)

experimenting **F.** Bend pieces of wire into loops and other shapes. Dip them into the liquid and blow. What kinds of bubbles do they make?

experimenting **G.** Make extra-large bubbles. Take a soda can that has no top or bottom. Dip one end into bubble liquid. How big a bubble can you make?

experimenting **H.** Can you make a better bubble liquid? Mix a capful of liquid detergent or soap in a half-cup of water. How does it work? Will adding some glycerin make bigger bubbles? How much works best?

TEACHING COMMENT

PREPARATION AND BACKGROUND

Use either a commercial bubble-blowing liquid or prepare your own from liquid detergent. Many teachers have gotten excellent results from Dawn™ or Joy™ liquid detergent. Both products contain a high glycerin content. A 1-part detergent to 16-parts water mix works well. Add some glycerin (sold at drugstores) for even bigger bubbles. Mix thoroughly.

This investigation is done best outdoors. However, when students try to steer their bubbles in a certain direction by waving a piece of cardboard, a near-windless condition is needed. On a windy day this activity can be done indoors in a more limited way. Students can discover that a bubble stays up best if the cardboard or hand is waved rapidly from side to side *over* the bubble. This decreases the air pressure over the bubble and so the surrounding air rushes in, holding up the bubble. Likewise, for lateral motion, a bubble will "follow" a waved cardboard.

GENERALIZATION

A soap bubble is made up of air inside and soap outside; big bubbles have more air inside than small ones. Moving air can make soap bubbles move.

SAMPLE PERFORMANCE OBJECTIVES

Process: When given the materials, the child can vary the mixture of a bubble liquid to produce larger bubbles.

Knowledge: The child can explain that a large bubble contains more air than a smaller one.

FOR OLDER CHILDREN

Older students enjoy and profit from an experimental approach to this investigation. Have them test the relative effectiveness of several commercial preparations or their own bubble preparations: Which one makes the biggest bubbles? Which one makes bubbles last the longest? Let them change the proportions of your prepared mixture or substitute other ingredients. For example, adding glycerin to bubble mix makes giant, long-lasting bubbles.

Invite them to compare several kinds of commercial bubble pipes and plastic rings ("wands") for making bubbles. Or, encourage them to invent their own devices. Challenge them to land soap bubbles inside a designed target area outdoors. To do so, they will have to consider wind velocity, the height from which they release bubbles, and bubble sizes.

INVESTIGATION: *PARACHUTES*

How does a parachute help someone who jumps from an airplane? What makes a parachute fall slowly? You can learn more about real parachutes by making small ones.

EXPLORATORY PROBLEM

How can you make a small parachute?

NEEDED

thin plastic (clothes covers from dry cleaners)
sticky tape
thin cloth (scrap cotton)
scissors
string
modeling clay

TRY THIS

1. Cut a square the size of a handkerchief from thin plastic.
2. Cut a small hole in the center of the plastic.
3. Cut four strings the same size.

4. Tie one string end to each corner of the plastic.

5. Tie the other string ends together in a knot.

6. Shape a small ball of clay around the knot (Figure 11-12).

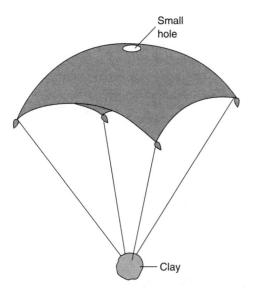

Figure 11-12

DISCOVERY PROBLEMS

observing **A.** Try out your parachute on the playground. Drop it from the top of the play slide. Then roll it up loosely and throw it into the air. Does rolling make it work better?

hypothesizing **B.** Suppose you cover the hole with sticky tape. What difference might this make?

hypothesizing **C.** Suppose you make the hole larger. What difference might this make?

hypothesizing **D.** Suppose you add more clay to the ball. What difference might this make?

experimenting **E.** How can you make a parachute that will fall slower than the one you have now?

experimenting **F.** How can you get a small and large parachute to fall equally fast?

experimenting **G.** What is the smallest parachute you can make that will work correctly?

experimenting **H.** What other materials can you use to make parachutes?

TEACHING COMMENT

PREPARATION AND BACKGROUND

Learning about parachutes allows children to thoughtfully manipulate several variables. In doing so, they learn to think of air as a tangible, material substance.

The thin plastic clothes bags dry cleaners use are excellent material for chutes. *Caution:* Remind students that a plastic bag should never be placed over the head.

GENERALIZATION

A parachute is built to catch the air as it falls; it can be changed to fall faster or slower.

SAMPLE PERFORMANCE OBJECTIVES

Process: When comparing the performance of two model parachutes, the child drops them from the same height at the same time.

Knowledge: The child can describe how to make a model parachute fall faster or slower.

FOR OLDER CHILDREN

Older students can construct parachutes with improved performance. In addition, they may invent rubber-band launchers (slingshot type, for example) to zip a rolled-up parachute into the air. Ask them to predict the effect of wind drift on their parachutes. Some may be able to predict direction and distance well enough to hit a named target area.

ACTIVITY: HOW CAN YOU SHOW THAT AIR TAKES UP SPACE?

NEEDED

deep glass bowl (large)
water
two small glasses
paper towels

TRY THIS

1. Fill the bowl three-fourths full with water.
2. Hold a glass with the open end down. Push it straight down into the water.
3. Put a second glass in the water sideways, so it fills with water.

4. Now tip the first glass. Try to "pour" the air up from the first glass into the second glass (Figure 11-13).

    a. What happens to the water in the higher glass?

    b. What happens in the lower glass?

    c. How can you get the air back into the first glass?

    d. Suppose you put a crushed paper towel in the bottom of a glass. How could you put the open glass underwater without getting the towel wet?

Figure 11-13

Teaching Comment

If no air bubbles are lost in the process, the air may be transferred from one glass to the next indefinitely. Because air is lighter than water, the air-filled glass will always need to be below the water-filled glass during the transfer.

Activity: *How Can You Tell If Air in a Balloon Weighs Anything?*

NEEDED

two matched balloons
meter stick or yardstick
scissors
sticky tape
string

TRY THIS

1. Hang a meter stick evenly from a doorway or other place. Use a string and tape.
2. Attach a string loosely to each of the two deflated balloons.

3. Tape each string to an *end* of the stick. Be sure the stick is level after the balloons are hung. If not, place a partly open paper clip on the stick where needed to balance it (Figure 11-14).

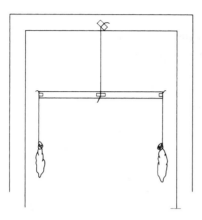

Figure 11-14

    a. What will happen if you blow up one balloon and rehang it?

    b. In what ways can you make the stick level again? The strings must stay at the ends of the stick.

TEACHING COMMENT

Be sure the balloon strings are always affixed to the stick *ends* to help assure balance. In **b,** the deflated balloon can be blown up like the inflated one. Or the inflated balloon may be slowly deflated by puncturing it at the neck with a pin.

INVESTIGATION: *AIR NEEDED FOR BURNING*

What are some ways you can stop a candle from burning? How important is air for a candle to keep burning?

EXPLORATORY PROBLEM

How long do you think a candle will burn inside a closed jar?

NEEDED

small candles
matches

modeling clay
four different-sized wide-mouth glass jars
clock or watch with second hand
metal pie pan
pencil and paper
paper towels
graph paper
measuring cup

TRY THIS

1. Stick some clay to the middle of a pie pan.
2. Stand a candle upright in the clay.
3. Light the candle. Put the used match in the pan.
4. Pick up your next-to-smallest jar. Put it upside down over the candle (Figure 11-15).

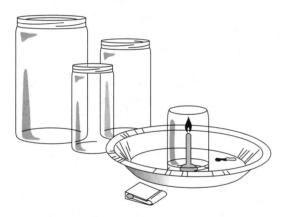

Figure 11-15

5. Look at a clock that has a second hand. How long does it take for the candle to go out? Record this time.
6. Remove the jar. Move a wad of several paper towels in and out of the jar a few times. This will clear out the bad air inside.

DISCOVERY PROBLEMS

measuring and communicating **A.** How long will the candle burn a second time? a third time? Be sure to remove the bad air after each trial. Record the trial times and the average time like this:

Jar Size	Time for Each			Average Time	Predicted Time
Smallest					
Next Smallest	30	34	32	32	—
Next to Largest					
Largest					

measuring and predicting

B. How long do you think the candle will burn in the smallest jar? in the next-to-largest jar? Write your predicted times on the chart. Use three trials for each jar. Record the trial times and the average times on your chart. Compare the average and predicted times.

observing and predicting

C. How much larger than the other jars is your largest jar? Compare your jars and then study your chart. How long do you think the candle will burn in the largest jar?

communicating

D. You can make better predictions. Get different jars. Use a measuring cup to discover how much water each jar holds. Find out burning times for the smallest and largest jars. Then make a graph. Mark the average burning times of the smallest and largest jars. Draw a light line in between.

predicting

E. How closely can you predict the burning times for other jars? Find the jar size column on the bottom of the graph. Follow the column up until you reach the drawn line. Then, look straight across to the left at the burning time. (See Figure 11-16.) How will recording more jar times make it easier to predict more accurately?

hypothesizing

F. What difference will it make in burning times if you change the candle? For example: Does candle size make a difference? Does the flame's closeness to the jar top make a difference? Will two candles die out twice as fast as one?

observing

G. Does the shape of the jar make a difference in burning times? Compare pairs of matched jars with different shapes and find out.

experimenting

H. How can you make a candle burn longer in a *small* jar than in a larger jar? Can you think of several ways?

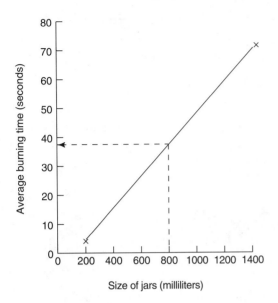

Candle burning experiments

Figure 11-16

TEACHING COMMENT

PREPARATION AND BACKGROUND

A candle flame dies out in a closed container after it uses a certain percentage of the oxygen in the air. The flame burns longer in a large jar than in a smaller one because of the larger oxygen supply.

Provide at least four different-sized, wide-mouth glass jars with straight sides for the investigation. You might try half-pint, pint, quart, and half-gallon sizes, or 200-, 400-, 800-, and 1,600-milliliter sizes. These exact capacities are not critical.

If you wish to stress the graphing activity in Problem D, you might begin with it and continue through the sequence. If you believe your students are not ready for it, omit this activity. If many points are plotted on this graph, the line drawn between them will resemble a curve rather than a straight line. Use this finding to demonstrate that using more data allows more accurate predictions. More than four jars will be needed to do Problem D.

Caution: Some schools restrict the use of matches or an open flame to responsible adults. In any event, it is wise to closely supervise their use.

GENERALIZATION

A flame needs air to burn; how long a flame burns depends, in part, on how much air it has.

SAMPLE PERFORMANCE OBJECTIVES

Process: When given minimal data, the child can construct a graph to predict the burning times of candles in different-sized containers.

Knowledge: The child can explain why a candle will burn longer in a large closed container than in a smaller one.

FOR YOUNGER CHILDREN

Supervise this investigation closely and omit the measuring and graphing activities. It is simpler to compare pairs or sets of jars in each activity than it is to time each candle-burning event. When done this way, most of the activities should be interesting and understandable. Only you should handle burning materials.

WEATHER EXPERIENCES
(Concepts p. 374)

ACTIVITY: *HOW FAST DOES SOIL HEAT AND COOL COMPARED TO WATER?*

NEEDED

two matched glass jars
sunshine
soil
water

TRY THIS

1. Fill one jar with soil and the other with water.
2. Leave the jars in a shady place for an hour.
3. Touch the soil and water surfaces to see if both are about the same temperature. If not, wait a while. If they are, then put both jars in the sun for an hour.
4. Touch both surfaces again.
   a. Which feels warmer, the soil or water surface?
   b. Which will cool faster if you put both back in the shade?

TEACHING COMMENT

This activity is useful when teaching how the unequal heating of the earth's surface causes winds.

INVESTIGATION: *EVAPORATION*

Many persons hang wet clothes on a clothesline. After a while, the clothes are dry. What do you think happens to the water? When water disappears into the air, we say it *evaporated*. You can find out more about evaporation by drying wet paper towels.

EXPLORATORY PROBLEM

How can you get a paper towel to dry? How long will it take?

NEEDED

plastic bowl of water
piece of cardboard
paper towels
two aluminum pie plates

TRY THIS

1. Put a paper towel underwater to soak it.
2. Bunch the wet towel in your fist. Squeeze out all the water you can.
3. Open the towel and lay it on a pie plate (Figure 11-17).
4. Leave the plate on your desk. Check the time.
5. Every so often feel the towel to see if it is dry. Check the time again when it is all dry.

DISCOVERY PROBLEMS

predicting
A. Suppose you put one wet towel where it is shady and cool, and another where it is sunny and warmer. Which wet towel do you think will dry first?

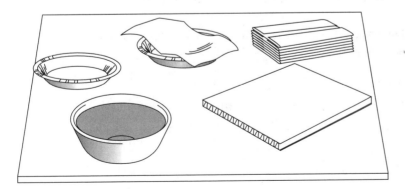

Figure 11-17

communicating **B.** What can you do to show that a dried-out towel is completely "dry"? How many others agree with you?

predicting **C.** Suppose that, to make it windy, you fan one wet towel with cardboard. You do not fan a second wet towel. Which towel do you think will dry first?

predicting **D.** Suppose you spread out one wet towel and leave another bunched like a ball. Which towel do you think will dry first?

predicting **E.** Suppose you leave one wet towel on top of a plate. You leave a second wet towel under another plate. Which towel do you think will dry first?

experimenting **F.** Play a game with a friend. Who can dry a wet paper towel faster? How can you make the game fair?

experimenting **G.** What is the longest you can keep a wet paper towel from drying?

TEACHING COMMENT

PREPARATION AND BACKGROUND

The foregoing sequence gives several chances for children to manipulate conditions that affect the evaporation rate of water. The last two activities encourage them to manipulate these conditions creatively. Discovery Problem C calls for fanning one wet towel with cardboard to simulate a windy condition. Clipping the towel to the pie plate with several paper clips will keep it from blowing off the plate.

GENERALIZATION

Wind, heat, and an uncovered and spread-out condition all help to make a wet paper towel dry faster.

SAMPLE PERFORMANCE OBJECTIVES

Process: The child can vary and control at least one condition to increase the drying rate of a wet paper towel.

Knowledge: The child can state at least one condition that will change the drying rate of a wet paper towel.

FOR OLDER CHILDREN

Invite older children to do the activities with more precision. For example, they might attempt to predict the drying times in each of the activities.

Have them calculate the drying *rate* of a wet towel or sponge by using a beam balance. Let them suspend a wet towel from one end of the beam, and clay or another object on the other end to achieve a balance. Then, as the towel dries and lightens, the beam will begin to tilt up. Students can add water to the towel with an eyedropper, one drop at a time, to keep the beam level.

Ask questions such as: "How many drops evaporate in one minute?"; "Does spreading out the drops you add make a difference in the evaporation rate?"; and "Will half of a wet towel have half the evaporation rate of a whole towel?" If you do not have a beam balance, just suspend a meter stick or dowel from a string. Your students will be delighted at the dramatic effect of the evaporation rate. It takes only a few minutes, under usual conditions, for it to be noticeable.

INVESTIGATION: *RELATIVE HUMIDITY*

Can you remember times when the air has felt very dry? very moist, or *humid*? The amount of moisture, or water vapor, in the air often changes. Warm air can hold more moisture without raining than cold air. The percent of moisture now in the air compared to what it can hold at the present temperature is the *relative humidity*. You can make an instrument to measure the relative humidity. It is called a hygrometer.

EXPLORATORY PROBLEM

How can you make a hygrometer?

NEEDED

two matched Fahrenheit thermometers
cardboard
narrow cotton strip or thick cotton shoelace
two rubber bands
quart milk carton
paper clip

TRY THIS

1. Fasten two thermometers to the sides of an empty milk carton. Use rubber bands to hold them in place.
2. Use a pencil to punch a hole in the carton under one thermometer.
3. Put about 2.5 centimeters (1 inch) of water into the carton. Close the top with a paper clip. This will keep the water from evaporating quickly.
4. Wet a strip of cotton with water.
5. Stick one end of the strip through the punched hole into the water inside. Fasten the other end to the bulb of the thermometer above (Figure 11-18).
6. To use your hygrometer, fan the thermometers with some cardboard for three minutes in a shady place. Read the temperatures of each thermometer.
7. Use the relative humidity table (Figure 11-19) to find the percent of moisture in the air. At the left, mark the wet bulb temperature lightly with pencil. At the top,

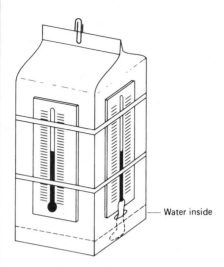

Water inside

Figure 11-18

lightly mark the dry bulb temperature. Move one finger across the row and another down the column from the marked spots. Notice the percent of relative humidity where your two fingers meet.

DISCOVERY PROBLEMS

measuring **A.** What is the relative humidity now?

hypothesizing **B.** How, if at all, might relative humidity change from day to day? How, if at all, does it change?

observing **C.** How well can you use your senses to tell if the air is drier or moister from day to day? Use your hygrometer to check how well you do.

measuring **D.** How does the relative humidity outdoors compare to that indoors?

hypothesizing **E.** What would you expect the relative humidity to be outdoors on a rainy day? Measure it in some partly sheltered place and see.

inferring **F.** How do your relative humidity measurements compare with those of the local weather bureau?

TEACHING COMMENT

PREPARATION AND BACKGROUND

When no difference appears between the wet and dry bulb temperatures, the relative humidity is 100 percent. This condition is unlikely to be recorded outdoors unless there is dense fog or rain.

Dry bulb temperature (°F)

Wet bulb (°F)	56	58	60	62	64	66	68	70	71	72	73	74	75	76	77	78	79	80	82	84
38	7	2																		
40	15	11	7																	
42	25	19	14	9	7															
44	34	29	22	17	13	8	4													
46	45	38	30	24	18	14	10	6	4	3	1									
48	55	47	40	33	26	21	16	12	10	9	7	5	4	3	1					
50	66	56	48	41	34	29	23	19	17	15	13	11	9	8	6	5	4	3		
52	77	67	57	50	43	36	31	25	23	21	19	17	15	13	12	10	9	7	5	3
54	88	78	68	59	51	44	38	33	30	28	25	23	21	19	17	16	14	12	10	7
56		89	79	68	60	53	46	40	37	34	32	29	27	25	23	21	19	18	14	12
58			89	79	70	61	54	48	45	42	39	36	34	31	29	27	25	23	20	16
60				90	79	71	62	55	52	49	46	43	40	38	35	33	31	29	25	21
62					90	80	71	64	60	57	53	50	47	44	42	39	37	35	30	26
64						90	80	72	68	65	61	58	54	51	48	46	43	41	36	32
66							90	81	77	73	69	65	62	59	56	53	50	47	42	37
68								90	86	82	78	74	70	66	63	60	57	54	48	43
70									95	91	86	82	78	74	71	67	64	61	55	49
72											95	91	86	82	79	75	71	68	61	56
74													96	91	87	83	79	75	69	62
76															96	91	87	83	76	69
78																	96	91	84	76
80																			92	84
82																				92

Percent of relative humidity

Figure 11-19

Students may notice a marked difference between indoor and outdoor readings. This is most likely in winter. As the room is heated, the air is able to hold more moisture, so the relative humidity goes down.

GENERALIZATION

A hygrometer can be used to measure the relative humidity. This is the percent of moisture that air holds compared to what it can hold at a given temperature.

SAMPLE PERFORMANCE OBJECTIVES

Process: The child can measure the relative humidity by using a hygrometer and consulting a table.

Knowledge: The child can describe conditions when high and low humidity are likely.

ACTIVITY: HOW CAN YOU "COLLECT" AND SEE WATER VAPOR IN THE AIR?

NEEDED

shiny can (clean)
thermometer
ice cubes

TRY THIS

1. Half-fill the can with water. Add five or six ice cubes.
2. Put a thermometer inside the can of ice water.
3. Watch for tiny drops on the can's sides. When they first appear, record the water temperature. (This is called the *dew point*. It tells the temperature at which water vapor will change from a gas to a liquid and *condense* on objects.)
   a. At what temperature was the dew point?
   b. Will the dew-point temperature be different in a smaller or larger container?
   c. Can an ice-water mixture get colder than the dew point?
   d. How, if at all, will the dew-point temperature change from day to day?

Activity: *How Can You Measure Changes in Air Pressure?*

NEEDED

glass jar
balloon
rubber band
scissors
straw
file card
glue

TRY THIS

1. Make a *barometer.* Cut out a large part of a balloon. Stretch it tightly over the jar opening. Use a rubber band to hold it fast.
2. Pinch one straw end flat. Cut a point with scissors at this end.
3. Glue the straw's other end to the center of the stretched balloon.
4. Fasten a file card to a wall. Place the barometer by it. Have the straw pointer centered on the card and almost touching.
5. Make a mark on the card where the straw points each day for a week (Figure 11-20).
   a. On what day was the air pressure the highest? lowest?
   b. When, if at all, was there no change in air pressure?

Teaching Comment

Increased air pressure pushes down harder on the balloon diaphragm. This makes the straw pointer go up. Decreased air pressure causes the higher pressure inside the

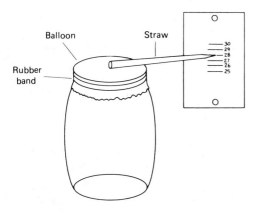

Figure 11-20

jar to push up on the diaphragm, so the pointer goes down. The movement can be increased a bit by gluing a piece of matchstick under the straw at the jar rim. You might challenge students to calibrate their barometers. They can note the daily barometric pressure in the newspaper or phone the weather bureau. After a week or so of recording the official pressure next to their own recordings, they may be able to predict roughly the official pressure from their own barometers. Place this kind of barometer where it will have the least change of temperature. Otherwise, the air in the jar may expand and contract so much that the effects of changing air pressure will be obscured.

References

American Association for the Advancement of Science. (1993). *Benchmarks for science literacy.* New York: Oxford University Press.

National Research Council. (1996). *National science education standards.* Washington, DC: National Academy Press.

Selected Trade Books: Water, Air, and Weather

For Younger Children

Ardley, N. (1983). *Working with water.* Watts.

Branley, F. M. (1987). *Air is all around you.* Harper & Row.

Carle, E. (1996). *Little Cloud.* Philomel.

Cole, J. (1986). *The magic schoolbus at the waterworks.* Scholastic.

Eden, M. (1982). *Weather.* Merrimack.

Gibbons, G. (1987). *Weather forecasting.* Macmillan.

Greene, C. (1991a). *Caring for our air.* Enslow.

Greene, C. (1991b). *Caring for our water.* Enslow.

Kalan, R. (1991). *Rain.* Morrow.

Kirkpatrick, R. K. (1985). *Look at weather.* Raintree.

Leutscher, A. (1983). *Water.* Dutton.

Llewellyn, C. (1991). *First look in the air.* Gareth Stevens.

Lloyd, D. (1983). *Air.* Dial Books.

Maki, C. (1993). *Snowflakes, sugar, and salt.* Lerner.

Martin, C. (1987). *I can be a weather forecaster.* Children's Press.

Otto, C. (1992). *That sky, that rain.* Harper.

Palazzo, J. (1982). *What makes the weather?* Troll Associates.

Pluckrose, H. (1987). *Think about floating and sinking.* Watts.

Seixas, J. S. (1987). *Water—what it is, what it does.* Greenwillow.

Smeltzer, P., & Smeltzer, V. (1983). *Thank you for a drink of water.* Winston.

Swallow, S. (1991). *Air.* Watts.

Taylor, K. (1992). *Flying start science series: Water; light; action; structure.* Wiley.

Webb, A. (1987). *Water.* Watts.

Webster, V. (1982). *Weather experiments.* Children's Press.

For Older Children

Arnov, B. (1980). *Water: Experiments to understand it.* Lothrop.

Branley, F. M. (1982). *Water for the world.* Harper & Row.

Bright, M. (1991). *Polluting the oceans.* Watts.

Cosner, S. (1982). *Be your own weather forecaster.* Messner.

De Bruin, J. (1983). *Young scientists explore the weather.* Good Apple.

Dickinson, J. (1983). *Wonders of water.* Troll Associates.

Flint, D. (1991). *Weather and climate.* Watts.

Ford, A. (1982). *Weather watch.* Lothrop.

Frevert, P. (1981). *Why does the weather change?* Creative Education.

Gallant, R. A. (1987). *Rainbows, mirages, and sundogs.* Macmillan.

Jeffries, L. (1983). *Air, air, air.* Troll Associates.

Kiefer, I. (1981). *Poisoned land: The problem of hazardous waste.* Atheneum.

Miller, C., & Berry, L. (1987). *Acid rain.* Messner.

Murata, M. (1993). *Science is all around you: Water and light.* Lerner.

Pollard, M. (1987). *Air, water, and weather.* Facts on File.

Riley, P. D. (1986). *Air and gases.* David & Charles.

Seymour, P. (1985). *How the weather works.* Macmillan.

Smith, H. (1983). *Amazing air.* Lothrop.

Snodgrass, M. E. (1991). *Environmental awareness: Water pollution.* BSP Publications.

Steele, P. (1991). *Wind: Causes and effects.* Watts.

Walpole, B. (1987). *Water.* Watts.

Ward, A. (1986). *Experimenting with surface tension and bubbles.* David & Charles.

Wu, N. (1991). *Planet earth: Life in the oceans.* Little, Brown.

Resource Books

Butzow, C. M., & Butzow, J. W. (1989). *Science through children's literature. An integrated approach* (water topics, pp. 150–157; weather topics, pp. 200–205). Teachers Ideas Press.

Butzow, C. M., & Butzow, J. W. (1994). *Intermediate science through children's literature: over land and sea* (weather topics, pp. 24–36; ocean and lake topics, pp. 131–169). Teachers Ideas Press.

Fredericks, A. D., Meinbach, A. M., & Rothlein, L. (1993). *Thematic units: An integrated approach to teaching science and social studies* (weather topics, pp. 153–160). HarperCollins.

LeCroy, B., & Holder, B. (1994). *Bookwebs: A brainstorm of ideas for the primary classroom* (air activities pp. 97–98). Teachers Ideas Press.

Shaw, D. G., & Dybdahl, C. S. (1996). *Integrating science and language arts. A sourcebook for K–6 teachers* (water cycle topic, pp. 73–78). Allyn and Bacon.

CHAPTER

12

THE EARTH IN SPACE

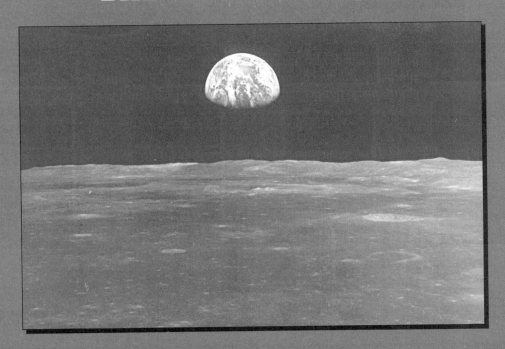

THE EARTH IN
SPACE

The Earth in Space
Benchmarks and Standards

Time and the Seasons	Moon, Earth, and Sun Interaction	Solar System and Beyond	Gravity and the Laws of Motion
Rotation of the Earth	Moon Phases	Planets	Causes of Orbits
Time Zones	Tides	Comets and Meteors	Zero Gravity
The Earth's Axis and Seasons	Eclipses	Stars	Rockets and Space Travel

The sky's the limit.

What goes up must come down.

Even tricycle riders today smile at these clichés. Television, magazines, and space missions have given children a beyond-the-earth outlook unknown to most previous generations.

But outside of school, few children learn the basic ideas and physical laws that give meaning to the motions of objects in space. We'll concentrate on several of these ideas and laws in this chapter as we examine how the earth's motions in space cause time and seasonal changes; how the relative motions of sun, earth, and moon bring about moon phases, eclipses, and tides; how to measure size and distance in the solar system and beyond; and how gravity and the laws of motion affect the movements of planets, satellites, and rockets.

TIME AND THE SEASONS CONCEPTS
(Experiences p. 428)

Because the earth is so large compared to the size of a person, it is hard at first to visualize the earth's motions in space. One remedy is to make the earth small compared to a person. That is what a globe model of the earth does.

Globe and Shadows

If you put a globe in the sun, the sunlight shines on one-half of the globe, as it does on one-half of the earth. If you position your town or city so it is upright, and north on the globe faces north, the globe will face the sun as the earth does.

How will you know this is so? You can test it. Stick a small nail through a piece of sticky tape and fasten the nail head down to your town on the globe. Be sure the nail is vertical.

(You may have to prop up the globe base with a book or two.) Then look at the nail's shadow. You'll find it identical in direction and proportional to shadows of other objects around you. Leave the globe in place during the day, and the nail shadow will move and change length like the other shadows do as the earth rotates. Or, if you want a preview of what shadows the earth objects will make, you can rotate the globe and watch the nail's shadow.

Rotation and Time

Most upper-grade children know the earth rotates, but few can tell in which direction. The sun rises in a generally eastern direction and sets in a generally western direction, with opposite shadows. Therefore it is a west-to-east rotation.

Figure 12-1 shows how persons on the east coast of the United States move into the sunlight. To them, it looks as though the sun is rising from the horizon and climbing higher as time goes by. Six hours from the time they first

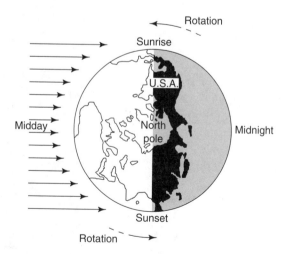

Figure 12-1
The apparent motion of the sun is caused by the earth's rotation.

observe "sunrise," the sun is closest to being directly overhead. This is midday, or the exact middle of the daylight period. Gradually, they continue to rotate counterclockwise. Shadows grow longer. Around 6:00 p.m., it is almost twilight, and the sun appears to sink into the western horizon. The next 12 hours they spend in darkness, until once again the sun appears to rise. A complete rotation takes 24 hours, or one complete day. Of course, most of the time people in New York (or elsewhere) do not have equal parts of daylight and darkness. You know that summer days are longer than winter days, for example. We shall discuss why shortly.

Expect some trouble with the term *day* because it has two meanings: the hours during which it is light, and the time for one complete rotation. You might use the terms *complete day* and *daylight* to separate the two.

Time Zones

It would be extremely inconvenient to judge time by where the sun is overhead. Every location a few kilometers east or west of another location would have a different noon time as the sun reached its midday position, for example. Though this was not a problem in the days of slow-moving transportation, it became intolerable when railroads were established.

The problem was solved in 1833 by creating four standard time zones in the United States.

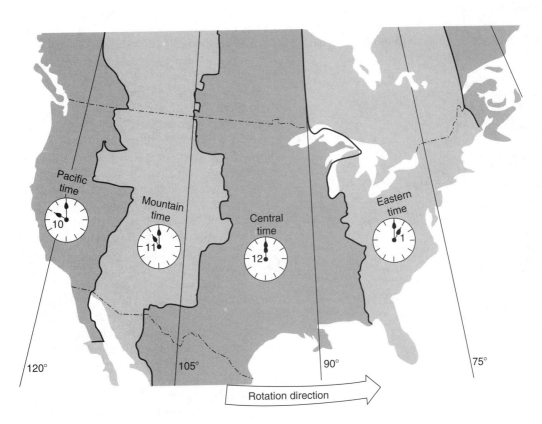

Figure 12-2
The continental United States has four time zones.

Figure 12-2 shows those in use today in the continental United States. We set our watches ahead going eastward and back going westward. The entire globe is now divided into 24 time zones, 15° apart. (The 15° separations came from dividing 360° by 24 hours, since the earth is a near sphere.)

The practical effect of having the same time zone for three cities hundreds of kilometers or miles apart is shown in Figure 12-3. Notice that only one city can experience midday at a given moment, although it is noon at all three cities.

Seasons

Persons in New York on December 21st experience about 9 hours of daylight and 15 hours of darkness. Six months later, the reverse happens. An even greater difference is found at a higher

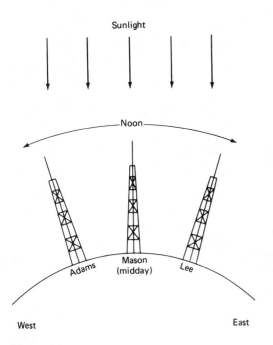

Figure 12-3
Midday at one city and noon at three cities in the same time zone. (Not to scale.)

latitude, such as near Seattle, Washington (50th parallel). To see why, first examine Figure 12-4. Notice that the earth's axis is tilted 23° from the plane of the earth's orbit around the sun. As the earth revolves about the sun, its axis continues to point in the same direction—toward the north star. Check the winter position. Because of the tilt, the northern hemisphere is in darkness longer than it is in daylight. You can see this by checking the length of the parallels of latitude shown. In the summer position, you see the reverse. Now the same latitude is exposed to sunlight for a much longer period. At the "in between" periods of spring and fall, day and night periods are more nearly equal.

Also observe that the southern hemisphere has opposite conditions to those in the northern hemisphere. While New York shivers in December, the beaches in sunny Rio de Janeiro are crowded with swimmers and sun bathers enjoying their summer.

However, besides the increased length of the days, there is another reason why summers are warmer than winters. The sun's rays are more nearly overhead during summer than at other times. Note the words *more nearly overhead*. Because the earth's axis is tilted, at noon the sun can never be completely vertical (at a 90° angle) north of the Tropic of Cancer or south of the Tropic of Capricorn.

If you ask students to explain why it is warmer in summer than it is in winter, don't be surprised if one replies, "The earth is closer to the sun." This is entirely logical, even though it is wrong. In fact, the opposite is true. The earth's path (orbit) around the sun is a slightly elongated circle, or ellipse, as are nearly all the orbits of celestial bodies. In winter, we are almost 5 million kilometers (3 million miles) closer to the sun than in summer. But because this distance is small compared to the average distance, about 150 million kilometers (93 million miles), the effect is negligible.

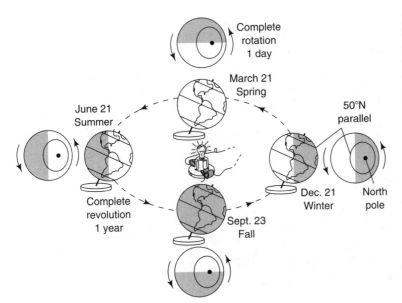

Figure 12-4
The seasons. Outside figures as viewed from above. Note the unequal periods of daylight at the 50th parallel except on March 21 (spring equinox) and September 23 (fall equinox).

MOON, EARTH, AND SUN INTERACTION CONCEPTS
(Experiences p. 435)

Why does the moon seem to change its shape? Why does the ocean have tides? What causes eclipses? Children are curious about these things. This section presents some ways the sun, earth, and moon interact. We'll consider moon phases first.

Moon Phases

You know that the moon, like our earth, receives and reflects light from the hot, glowing sun. Also, the moon revolves around the earth in about 28 days. Study Figure 12-5 for a moment. The drawings on the right show the earth and moon as seen from far out in space. The drawings of the moon on the left show how it looks to us when the moon is in each of eight different positions.

Imagine standing on the earth in the center of this illustration. Look at Position 1. This is the *new moon* position. The moon's face is now dark to us. Slowly, the moon moves on in its orbit. At Position 2, we see a *new crescent moon;* at Position 3, a *first-quarter moon.* At Position 4, we see a *new gibbous moon;* one side is now almost fully illuminated. At Position 5, there is a *full moon.* The other positions reverse the sequence of phases from old gibbous, last quarter, old crescent, to new moon.

As the moon moves from the new to full positions, more and more of it appears to be shining; it is said to be *waxing.* But from full to new moon positions, less and less of its lighted part is visible from earth, so it is said to be *waning.* Try the moon phase investigation on pages 435-437. Compare the phases you see with those in Figure 12-5.

Tides

The interaction of sun, moon, and earth also results in tides. How do they happen? The law

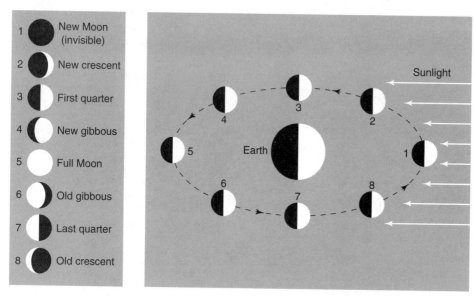

Figure 12-5
Moon phases as seen from the earth (left).

of universal gravitation, first formed by the great eighteenth-century philosopher and scientist, Sir Isaac Newton, provides much of the answer. Briefly stated, *every object in the universe attracts each other; the force of this attraction depends on the mass of each object and the distance between them.* ("Mass" is the amount of matter that makes up the object.)

As shown in the Figure 12-6, the mutual attraction between earth and moon causes the ocean to bulge at Position 1. This is a *direct high tide.* An *indirect high tide* appears at Position 3 because it is most distant from the moon, so gravitational attraction is weakest here. (We will add a refinement to this statement shortly.) Also, the land surface is pulled slightly away from this region. Positions 2 and 4 have low tides because these are areas of weak attraction that furnish the extra water making up the high tides.

What causes the tide to rise and fall? Put yourself in Position 1. As you rotate on the earth toward Position 2, the tide will seem to ebb, or fall. You experience a low tide. Moving

from Position 2 into 3, you gradually come into the bulge. It seems as though the tide is "coming in." You experience a high tide. Rotating onward, you have another low tide before once again arriving at the direct high-tide area. In other words, the oceans tend to bulge continually in the moon's direction and opposite point, as the earth rotates. The continual bulges create the illusion that the tides are moving in and out independently.

Since the earth's rotation takes about 24 hours, high tides happen about every 12 hours. (Remember, there is one direct and one indirect high tide simultaneously.) Six hours elapse between low and high tides. Actually, these times are a little longer because the moon itself moves some distance in its orbit while the earth rotates. Because the tidal bulge moves in alignment with the moon as it advances, the earth must rotate an extra 52 minutes each 24 hours before it is again in the direct high-tide zone.

Twice monthly, unusually high and low tidal ranges occur called *spring* tides. High tides are

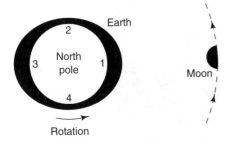

Figure 12-6
Mutual attraction between earth and moon causes ocean tides.

very high and low tides are very low. (Incidentally, there is no connection between *spring* tides and the season. Perhaps the name arose because these tides appear to "spring up" so fast.) A week later, there is much less variation from high to low tides. Tides during this period are called *neap* tides.

Figure 12-7 shows how these tides take place. When the sun and moon are aligned *(a)*, the sun's added gravitational attraction causes very high spring tides. This happens when the moon is in either the full or new moon phase. Because the sun is so far away, its tremendous mass adds only one-third to the force of gravitational attraction. When the sun and moon pull at right angles *(b)*, we have neap tides. This happens when the moon is in its first- and last-quarter phases.

Interestingly, besides water tides, there are also huge atmospheric tides and tiny land tides. All happen through the same interaction of sun, moon, and earth. Accurate measurements show that some land portions of the earth rise and fall more than 30 centimeters (one foot) with the tides.

Eclipses

Causes of eclipses are seen in Figure 12-8. Both earth and moon cast conelike shadows. When the moon is in Position 1, the tip of its shadow barely reaches the earth. Persons in this small, shadowy area see a *solar eclipse*. A total eclipse is never more than 272 kilometers (170 miles) across. Sunlight is cut off except for a whitish halo, called the *corona*. The shadow moves quickly over the ground, because both the earth and moon are in motion. Sunlight is never blocked for more than eight minutes.

In Position 2, the moon is eclipsed when it revolves into the earth's large shadow. Practically everyone on the earth's dark side can see a *lunar eclipse*, which may last for two hours before the moon revolves out of the earth's shadow. There are several partial lunar and solar eclipses each year.

Notice that eclipses happen in the full and new moon positions. Why, then, don't they occur every few weeks? The reason is that the

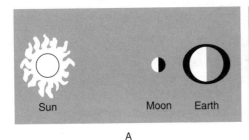

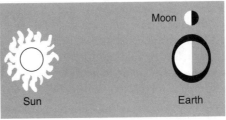

Figure 12-7
The sun also affects tidal flows.

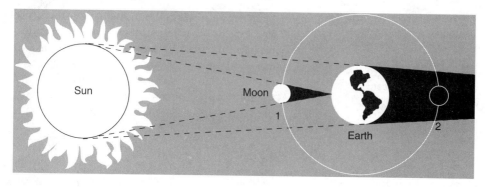

Figure 12-8
Causes of solar (1) and lunar (2) eclipses.

moon's plane of orbit is tilted about 5° from the earth's orbital plane around the sun. This usually causes the moon to pass above and below positions required for eclipses.

A 5° tilt would be only a minor deviation from the earth's orbital plane in Figure 12-8, hardly enough to make a difference. But in proper scale, this small deviation is quite significant. With a scale of 2.5 centimeters to 1,600 kilometers (1 inch to 1,000 miles), the earth's diameter is 20 centimeters (8 inches), and the moon's is 5 centimeters (2 inches). Their distance apart is 6 meters (20 feet). The sun's diameter and distance at this scale are even more surprising. Imagine a sun model 22 meters (72 feet) across, 2.4 kilometers (1½ miles) away!

The Earth–Moon System

We normally think of the moon revolving around the earth, but strictly speaking, this is not quite the case. The gravitational attraction of these two objects is such that they are locked together in a revolving system that has a common center of mass (barycenter). To see why this is so, look at Figure 12-9. The large ball of clay represents the earth, and the small one is the moon. A short wire joins the two to simulate their gravitational attraction. If you suspend System A from the middle with a string, the much

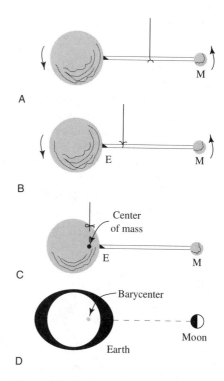

Figure 12-9
The earth–moon system has a common point of balance, or center of mass, called the barycenter. (Distance not to scale.)

heavier earth goes down and the moon goes up. The same thing would happen if a heavy adult and a small child got on a seesaw with the fulcrum in the middle. In System B, the balance is improved but much the same thing happens. In System C, though, a balance is found. If you spin each model system with a twisted string, System A and B will wobble and sway unevenly; but System C revolves uniformly and simulates the motion of the earth–moon system.

Now for the refinement on the cause of indirect tides, as promised earlier. In any spinning system such as this, there is a tendency for the two objects to fly apart. The gravitational attraction between the two prevents this from happening. In System D, the side of the earth facing the moon is strongly attracted to the moon. The water moves more easily than the solid earth, so it flows strongly toward the near side and becomes a high tide. The earth's opposite side is attracted less because it is farther away. So the tendency of this far side of the spinning system to fly apart is countered only weakly by the weakened gravitational pull. The result is an indirect high tide.

Our model is imperfect in several ways. The earth's mass is about 80 times greater than the moon's. Also, the distance scale is wrong. If we were to use the proper scale, our short wire connector would need to be at least several feet long.

The Moon's Orbit

From an earth reference position, it is natural to regard the moon as revolving in a circular path around the earth (or, more accurately, the barycenter). But motion is relative to the observer. If we could see the moon's path from far out in space, it would not look circular. Instead, it would weave in and out in a shallow, alternating pattern along the earth's orbit. (See Figure 12-10.) Since the sun is in motion, a similar pathway is woven by the earth. Is it wrong, then, to say the moon *revolves* around the earth and the earth around the sun? Not at all. It is just another way of looking at the same set of facts.

SOLAR SYSTEM AND BEYOND CONCEPTS
(Experiences p. 441)

Planets

The earth is one of nine planets revolving around a medium-sized star, the sun. How did the solar system begin? Scientists are not sure. One prominent theory holds that the sun and planets may have been formed from an enormous swirling cloud of dust and gases. Slowly, gravitational attraction caused these materials to come closer together. The speed of rotation increased more and more. As rotating dust and gas particles rubbed together, much friction and heat developed. A large mass in the center became so hot that it formed into the sun. Gradually, most of the remaining materials spread out as a result of their spinning and began revolving around the

Figure 12-10
The earth and moon orbits drawn to scale.

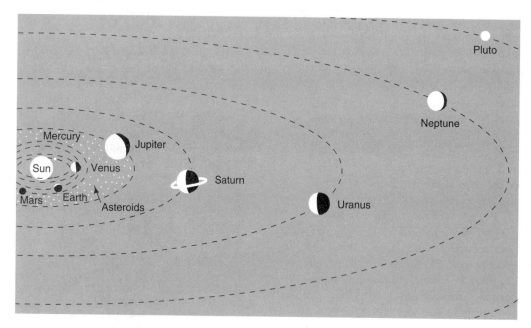

Figure 12-11
The solar system. (Not to scale.)

sun. They slowly shrank and cooled into nine separate masses, which became planets (see Figure 12-11).

Mercury is the closest planet to the sun. It rotates very slowly, only two-thirds around to one complete revolution around the sun, which takes only 88 days. Its small mass results in a surface gravity too weak to retain an atmosphere.

Venus, next in order from the sun, is enveloped in a dense atmosphere of mostly carbon dioxide. This reflects sunlight so well that, except for the sun and moon, Venus is the brightest object in the sky. Its surface temperature, too, is very high.

After the earth is *Mars.* It has an unusual reddish appearance and polar ice caps that advance and recede with the seasons. It is more like the earth than the other planets, but its very thin atmosphere and severe weather make it unlikely that living things are on this planet. In 1976, two remotely controlled space vehicles landed on Mars, but their instruments detected no forms of life. Two tiny natural satellites, or moons, revolve speedily around Mars.

Between Mars and the next planet, *Jupiter,* is an unusually large gap containing several thousand irregularly shaped chunks of stone and metal called *asteroids* (tiny "stars"). Some astronomers think these may be the remains of a planet that came too close to huge Jupiter and disintegrated under its powerful gravitational attraction. Ranging from about 1.6 to 800 kilometers (1 to 500 miles) in diameter, they are invisible to the unaided eye.

Jupiter and *Saturn* are by far the largest *outer planets.* Jupiter's diameter is 11 times greater than that of the earth. Saturn is conspicuous because of its many rings, believed to be composed of ice particles. *Uranus* and *Neptune* are nearly the same size, about three and one-half times the earth's diameter. *Pluto* is so small and distant that it was not discovered until 1930. Its orbital plane is tilted sharply from those of other planets, and its orbit is so elliptical that at times the planet is closer to the sun than Neptune.

Ancient sky-watchers were so puzzled by the changing appearance of the planets that they named them "wanderers." Long ago all such objects were thought to be stars, which ordinarily seem fixed in space. We realize now that their differences in brightness and position from time to time occur because they revolve at different distances and speeds in their orbits around the sun.

Today, astronomers are finding new planets and discovering more about distant bodies through the use of the Hubble Space telescope and other space probes. For an up-to-date account of new findings, students should be encouraged to log onto NASA's web pages on the Internet (http://spacelink.msfc.nasa.gov/).

Comets and Meteors

Comets are huge, unstable bodies apparently composed of gases, dust, ice, and small rocks. A few are briefly visible as they occasionally sweep near the sun and far out again in immense, highly elliptical orbits. They have so little mass that the pressure of sunlight causes a long streamer, or "tail," to flow from the comet head always in a direction opposite the sun. Like the planets, comets may have originated from the gases and dust of the solar nebula over 4 billion years ago.

Most children have seen "shooting stars." These are fragments of rock and metal, probably from broken-up asteroids and parts of comets, that hurtle through interplanetary space at high speeds. Although most are no larger than a grain of sand, some weigh tons. It is estimated that billions of such *meteors,* as they are called, plunge daily into the earth's atmosphere and burn into extinction from the heat of air friction. The few that do penetrate to the earth in solid form other than dust are called meteorites.

Is there any danger of being struck by a meteorite? Not much. There are only a few instances of anyone ever being injured. One such event happened in 1954. An Alabama woman was grazed by a 10-pound meteorite that crashed through her roof. In 1982, a 6-pound meteorite smashed through the roof of a home in Connecticut. No one was injured.

Size and Distances

By far the most difficult ideas in astronomy for children to grasp are the distances and sizes of objects in space. It would be helpful to their thinking if a large section of the playground could be used for scaled distance activities. Yet even a very large area can be inadequate to demonstrate both distance and size on the same scale. At 2.54 centimeters to 12,000 kilometers (1 inch to 8,000 miles), for example, Pluto would need to be located about 11 kilometers (7 miles) away!

Distances are even more astounding as we move beyond the solar system. Now, the kilometer or mile is too tiny as a unit of measurement for practical purposes. You will want to acquaint students with the light-year, defined as the distance a beam of light travels in one year. At 300,000 kilometers (186,000 miles) per second, this is almost 9.5 trillion kilometers (6 trillion miles).

The Stars

When we view the stars, some seem to group into a pattern, or constellation. People commonly think such stars are about the same in size and distance from the earth. But the only thing stars in a constellation typically share is a common direction. If we could view constellations from other angles (we can, very slightly, as the earth orbits the sun), most constellation patterns would disappear.

The light from the nearest star, the sun, takes about eight minutes to reach the earth. In contrast, a distance of 4.3 *light-years* separates us from the next nearest star, *Proxima Centauri*. These stars have over a hundred billion companions clustered in an immense aggregation of stars and filmy clouds of gas and dust called the *Milky Way galaxy*. The shape of our galaxy is like a pocket watch, with a thickened center, standing on end (Figure 12-12). It is thought to be about 100,000 light-years long and 12,000 light-years thick. The galaxy seems to be slowly rotating about its center, where the stars are most thickly concentrated.

Our galaxy is but one of millions more strewn throughout space at incomprehensible distances, containing further stars beyond reliable calculation.

GRAVITY AND THE LAWS OF MOTION CONCEPTS
(Experiences p. 445)

Nobody knows what caused the planets to begin moving, but the reason they keep moving is readily understandable: There is almost nothing in space to stop them. But why do they circle the sun? You have already been introduced to Newton's law of gravitation. Equally important to understand is Newton's law of *inertia*. Briefly stated, *any object at rest or in motion remains at rest or continues in motion in a straight line unless acted on by some outside force.*

Anyone who has ever tried to push a heavy, stalled automobile knows how hard it is to move a heavy body at rest. It has much inertia. Anyone who has ever tried to stop a heavy, rolling automobile by pushing against it knows how difficult *this* is. A body in motion has the inertia of motion (momentum). The more momentum it has, the harder it is to stop it.

Causes of Orbits

Figure 12-13 shows how the laws of gravitation and inertia combine to keep objects in orbit. Although a natural satellite, the moon, is shown in this case, the same laws operate with all bodies that orbit other bodies in space.

If the moon were unaffected by our earth's powerful gravitational force, it would follow a straight path owing to its inertial momentum.

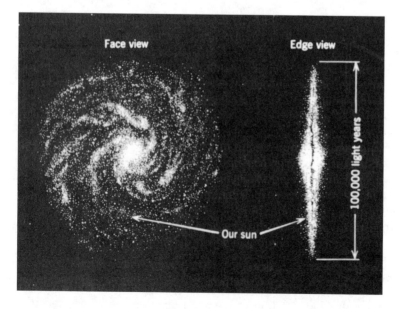

Figure 12-12
The Milky Way galaxy.

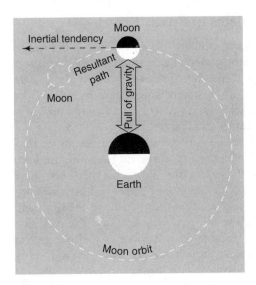

Figure 12-13
A balance between gravity and inertia keeps a satellite in orbit.

Because it is affected, the moon follows a path that is a result of each factor countering the other.

A common example of this countering effect happens when a ball rolls swiftly off a table. Instead of falling straight down, the ball's inertia of momentum keeps it going nearly sideways for an instant until gravity forces it to the floor. The resultant path of its fall is an arc.

In our illustration, gravity and inertia are equally powerful. If this were not so, the moon would either be drawn into the earth or pull away from it. This is what happens to an artificial satellite that moves too slowly or too fast. Clearly, getting a space satellite into a sustained orbit is tricky business. Its velocity and angle of entry into orbit must be calculated closely. Since perfection in these matters is nearly impossible, most orbits are markedly elongated (elliptical).

Because gravity weakens with distance, the speed of the orbiting body must be slower as the distance from its parent body increases.

This is necessary in order to maintain balance of the two forces. At 35,680 kilometers (22,300 miles) from the earth, for example, the proper orbital speed for a satellite results in one complete orbit each 24 hours. Because this is the period of the earth's rotation, a satellite positioned above the equator always stays in the same relative position. With several of these satellites properly spaced, television and radio signals are relayed to any place on earth.

Zero Gravity

When astronauts circle the earth in a satellite, they have no sensation of weight. This is because the pull of gravity is balanced exactly by the counteracting inertia of motion. We sometimes experience this *weightless,* or *zero gravity,* condition on earth for an instant when an elevator starts rapidly downward or an automobile goes too fast over the crown of a steep hill.

In one science lesson not long ago, a bright child asked her teacher an astute question: "If we would be weightless in an orbiting satellite, why wouldn't we be weightless on the moon?" The teacher had her reconsider the law of gravitation, especially the part that says ". . . this attraction depends on the *mass* of each object and the distance between them."

Because the moon has a much smaller mass than the earth, its surface gravity is only about one-sixth that of the earth's. An 81-kilogram (180-pound) astronaut weighs a mere 13.5 kilograms (30 pounds) on the moon. However, the moon's mass is almost infinitely greater than that of a space vehicle. The tiny mass of a space vehicle has practically no gravity at all.

Since prolonged periods of weightlessness seem detrimental to astronauts' health, attempts are being made to design space vehicles that create a gravity-like condition. This may be done by rotating the vehicle at a carefully calculated speed. The astronauts' inertia gives them a feeling of gravity as they are slightly pressed against the spaceship's interior. An analogy is the small ball that remains stationary on the rim of a roulette wheel until it stops turning.

Rockets

Through the ages, people have always yearned to explore what mysteries lie beyond the earth. But until recently, our technology has not been as advanced as our ambitions. Early devices and inventions designed for space travel included hitching a flock of geese to a wicker basket, hand-cranking propellers attached to hot-air balloons, and festooning a box with crude rockets containing gunpowder. Occasionally, such contraptions were personally occupied by their daring inventors—and some did depart from this earth, although not in the manner intended.

Because space is a near vacuum, no engine that draws oxygen from the air to burn its fuel can serve in a propulsion system. Instead, rocket engines are used; these carry their own oxygen supply. Rockets work because *for every action there is an equal and opposite reaction* (another law of motion by Newton). When a rocket pushes hot gases out of its combustion chamber (action), the gases push back (reaction) and thrust the rocket ahead.

Most rockets today are composed of multiple stages fastened together in a cluster or a tandem arrangement. The main rocket propels all the stages to a point where the rocket's fuel is expended and then it drops off. The remaining stages reach even higher velocities as the process continues, lightening the load each time. The speed of the last stage represents the accumulated sum of speeds attained by each stage. Perhaps future rockets will be efficient enough to reduce or eliminate the necessity for present cumbersome staging techniques.

Problems in Space Travel

Although modern rocketry provides the means to reach beyond the earth, travel for astronauts poses some difficult problems. As the rocket blasts off in a terrifying surge of power, the rapid acceleration pins the astronauts' bodies to the seats with crushing force.

Once beyond the earth's atmosphere, they need oxygen and sufficient pressure to keep their bodies working normally. They need some means of temperature control. Without air conduction of heat energy, the side of the spaceship facing the sun gets very hot, and the dark side grows freezing cold. Because of their weightless condition, the astronauts may eat and drink from plastic squeeze bottles.

To prevent the space vehicle from being burned to a cinder as it enters the atmosphere, the angle and speed of reentry must be exactly right. These are only some of the problems of space travel.

With so many difficulties, why do people venture into space? Although our curiosity is one answer, of course, there are many advantages to be gained from continued space efforts. Some benefits are improved communications, surveys of earth resources, long-range weather forecasting and possible weather control, astronomers' observation posts beyond the annoying interference of the earth's atmosphere, possible answers to how the universe was formed, and improved mapping and navigation. All these benefits may help us understand and solve problems here on Earth.

Eventually, there will be the most important reason of all. Someday, perhaps three to five billion years from now, the sun's nuclear fuel will be largely depleted. The sun should gradually expand and engulf the inner planets in an unimaginable inferno of extinction before it finally collapses and dies out. Perhaps by then our descendants will have found a comfortable haven among the stars.

THE EARTH IN SPACE BENCHMARKS AND STANDARDS

Students who observe the sun, moon, stars, and planets will begin to find patterns in their behavior. Seasons, tides, phases of the moon, and day and night are all relevant topics as indicated below in the sample Standards and Benchmarks.

SAMPLE BENCHMARKS (AAAS, 1993).

■ Like all planets, the earth is approximately spherical in shape. The rotation of the earth on its axis every 24 hours produces the night-and-day cycle (by Grades 3–5, p. 68).

■ We live on a relatively small planet, the third from the sun (by Grades 6–8, p. 68).

SAMPLE STANDARDS (NRC, 1996).

■ Objects in the sky have patterns of movement. The sun, for example, appears to move across the sky in the same way every day, but its path changes slowly over the seasons (by Grades K–4, p. 134).

■ Most objects in the solar system are in regular and predictable motion. Those motions explain such phenomena as the day, the year, phases of the moon, and eclipses (by Grades 5–8, p. 160).

INVESTIGATIONS AND ACTIVITIES

TIME AND THE SEASONS EXPERIENCES

(Concepts p. 414)

INVESTIGATION: *THE WAY THE EARTH ROTATES*

Each day, the sun seems to follow a pattern in the sky. It seems to rise in one direction, move across the sky, and then set in the opposite direction. But the sun is relatively still. We know that it only seems to move because the earth rotates. In which direction does the earth rotate? You can find out for yourself by using a globe and then the earth itself.

EXPLORATORY PROBLEM

How can you find out the direction in which the earth rotates?

NEEDED

globe
sunshine
small nail with large head
hammer
sticky tape
stick (1 meter or 1 yard long)

TRY THIS

1. Get a small nail. Push the nail point through the sticky side of a small piece of tape. Fasten the nail head down to the place on the globe where you live.
2. Take the globe, hammer, and stick out in the sunshine. Pound the stick upright into the ground.
3. Notice the shadow made by the stick. Position the globe so the nail is upright and makes a shadow exactly in the same direction. (You may have to slip a book under the globe's base to keep the nail upright.)
4. Rotate the globe from west to east as shown in Figure 12-14.

DISCOVERY PROBLEMS

observing **A.** What happens to the nail shadow if you rotate the globe a little from west to east? Make a record of the direction and length of the shadow.

observing **B.** What happens to the nail shadow if you rotate the globe a little from east to west? Make a record.

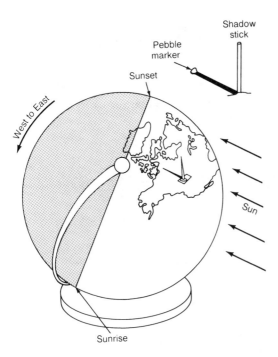

Figure 12-14

observing **C.** Put a pebble marker at the tip of your stick's shadow. Look at the shadow again 5 minutes later. In which direction did the shadow move?

inferring **D.** In which direction does the earth rotate?

inferring **E.** Notice other shadows around you. How does their direction compare to the direction of the stick's shadow? How does that help you with Problem D? Where will their shadows be in an hour? in 3 hours?

TEACHING COMMENT

PREPARATION AND BACKGROUND

Some students may need to be shown directions outdoors and on the globe. You might help them to understand that north always runs from where they are to the north pole and the south runs from there to the south pole.

For the best shadow, the stick needs to be reasonably upright. A plumb bob, made of string tied to a piece of chalk, can help students align the stick if needed. You may substitute a tetherball pole for the stick. The nail, also, should be upright. If needed, something can be slipped under the globe base to make the nail vertical.

Perhaps you can borrow briefly some globes from other teachers. If so, you might want to do this activity with your entire class divided into small groups.

GENERALIZATION

Daily shadows on earth move from west to east; this shows that the earth rotates the same way.

SAMPLE PERFORMANCE OBJECTIVES

Process: The child can infer from globe and shadow data the direction of the earth's rotation.

Knowledge: The child can explain why the sun seems to rise in the east and set in the west.

INVESTIGATION: *A Shadow Clock*

Before people had clocks, one way they told time was by watching shadows on sunny days. You can do that, too. But now you can use a clock to check how well you can keep time using shadows.

EXPLORATORY PROBLEM

How can you keep time with shadows?

NEEDED

blank file card (large)
pencil
nail
clock or watch
sunny day

TRY THIS

1. Lay the card in a sunny place. Put the nail, pointing up, in the center of the card. Trace a small circle around the nail head. If the nail falls over, be sure to replace it inside the circle.
2. Each hour you can, trace the nail shadow with a pencil, and then check a clock. Record the hour by the tip of the pencil tracing (Figure 12-15). It is all right to carry your shadow clock back and forth, but always put it back in the same way and place.
3. Plan to check your shadow clock on the next sunny day.

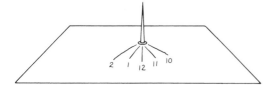

Figure 12-15

DISCOVERY PROBLEMS

observing **A.** Check the shadow clock each hour, or when you can. Notice where the shadow is. How well can you keep time by the hour?

observing **B.** Can you tell the right time on the half hour? Can you tell when it is 15 minutes before the hour? 15 minutes after the hour?

observing **C.** How long will your shadow clock keep the right time? a week? longer than a week?

observing **D.** Do the nail shadows slowly change? If so, how?

inferring **E.** Compare a regular clock with a shadow clock. What are some advantages and disadvantages of each?

TEACHING COMMENT

PREPARATION AND BACKGROUND

It is essential that students align their shadow clocks exactly the same way each time. Otherwise, their pencil recording may not coincide with additional shadows. A chalk outline or piece of tape to align an edge can be a helpful reminder.

Within a week, or sooner, children will detect a difference in the shadow alignments. This happens because the tilted earth continues to move around the sun. The same event is responsible for changes of seasons.

GENERALIZATION

It is possible to keep track of the time in a general way with a shadow clock. It gets less accurate as time goes on.

SAMPLE PERFORMANCE OBJECTIVES

Process: Within several days the child observes discrepancies between the first shadow and following shadows made by a shadow clock.

Knowledge: The child is able to make and estimate the approximate time with a shadow clock.

FOR YOUNGER CHILDREN

Try the basic activity. But have younger children record shadows for only one or two times: "How can the shadow clock tell us when it's time for lunch?" "Time to go home?" (Taping paper over the classroom clock will add interest.)

ACTIVITY: *HOW WARM IS SLANTED VERSUS DIRECT SUNSHINE?*

NEEDED

cardboard
two matched thermometers
black paper
stapler
scissors
books

TRY THIS

1. Cut two same-sized pieces of cardboard.
2. Staple black paper to each piece. Staple a pocket for each thermometer as shown in Figure 12-16. Slip a thermometer in each pocket.
3. Lay one thermometer flat in the sun. It will get slanted sunshine. Prop up the other thermometer with some books so the sun strikes it directly.
4. Look at each thermometer carefully. Be sure neither thermometer rises so high that it breaks. After a few minutes, take out the thermometers and check the temperatures.

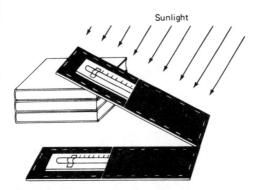

Figure 12-16

a. Which has the higher temperature?

b. Which seems to give more heat, slanted or direct sunshine?

TEACHING COMMENT

Your students may be unsure about how high they must prop up the direct-sunlight thermometer. You might have them tape a nail head down to the cardboard. They then can tilt the cardboard until the nail no longer makes a shadow, indicating relatively vertical sunlight.

INVESTIGATION: WHY WE HAVE SEASONS

Suppose you could see the earth from outer space as it circles the sun each year. This would help you to understand why we have seasons. But you might have to wait a long time to do that. You can use a globe and light to find out now.

EXPLORATORY PROBLEM

How can a model earth (globe) and sun (lighted bulb) be used to show seasons?

NEEDED

tilted globe
unshaded table lamp
small nail with large head
pencil and paper
sticky tape
ruler

TRY THIS

1. Get a tilted globe. The earth rotates on a make-believe pole. The pole's north end always points toward the North Star as the earth circles the sun. (That is why globes are tilted.)

2. Label one wall "north." (You will need to keep the globe tilted toward that wall.)

3. Tape a nail head down to the place on the globe where you live.

4. Set up the globe and lamp as you see in Figure 12-17. Darken the room.

5. Begin at the summer position. Center the nail in the "sunshine" and point the north pole toward north. Look at the nail shadow where you live. Measure and record how long it is. Notice how much daylight there is east and west of where you live.

6. Repeat Step 5 at each of the other three positions.

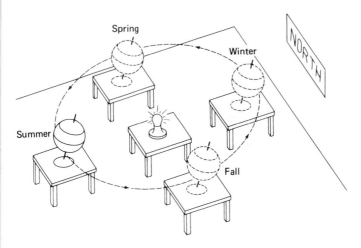

Figure 12-17

DISCOVERY PROBLEMS

observing **A.** During what season do you see the shortest shadow where you live? the longest shadow where you live? (A short shadow shows strong, direct sunshine. A long shadow shows weak, slanted sunshine.)

inferring **B.** When is the longest period of sunshine where you live? When is the shortest period of sunshine? (The longer the sun shines, the warmer it gets where you live.)

inferring **C.** During which seasons will the periods of daylight and darkness be about the same?

inferring **D.** Where and when north of you is it possible to have 24 hours of darkness? 24 hours of daylight? When and where can this happen south of you?

TEACHING COMMENT

PREPARATION AND BACKGROUND

If four globes are available, all four can be set up and used at the same time with four groups of students. Each group can rotate to a new position after a few minutes for observation and measurement. The best place from which to observe the amount of daylight and darkness at one's latitude is just above the globe's north pole.

GENERALIZATION

The earth's tilted axis and revolution about the sun cause seasonal changes.

SAMPLE PERFORMANCE OBJECTIVES

Process: The child can measure and compare shadow lengths and contrasting areas of daylight and darkness on the globe.

Knowledge: The child can explain that without a tilted axis and the earth's revolution around the sun there would be no seasons.

MOON, EARTH, AND SUN INTERACTION EXPERIENCES
(Concepts p. 417)

INVESTIGATION: *MOON PHASES*

Have you ever watched the moon over one or two weeks? If so, you know its shape seems to go through changes, or *phases*. You can predict what phase will show when you understand why the moon's appearance changes. Working with a *moon model* can help. A ball can be the moon, and your head can be the earth. Light from a bright window can be the sun.

EXPLORATORY PROBLEM

How can a model be used to show moon phases?

NEEDED

white ball (tennis or volleyball)
bright window
daytime moon

TRY THIS

1. Draw all the classroom shades except for one bright window.
2. Hold the ball above eye level and face the window (Figure 12-18). See the dark or shadowy side of the model. This is a *new moon*. (A real new moon cannot be seen from the earth.)
3. Turn the model moon to the left. Stop when you are sideways to the window. This is a *first-quarter* moon. The moon has gone a quarter, or one-fourth, of the way around the earth.
4. Make another quarter turn to the left. Stop when your back is to the window. Now all of the moon facing you is lighted by the sun. This is a *full* moon.
5. Move a quarter turn left until you are sideways to the window. This is a *last-quarter* moon. Compare it to the first-quarter moon. Notice that the opposite part shines now.

Figure 12-18

6. Move the last quarter turn to your left. This is the new moon again. From one new moon to the next takes about four weeks.

DISCOVERY PROBLEMS

inferring

A. Figure 12-19 shows eight moon phases out of order. Using your moon model, can you figure out the correct order? Start with the new moon.

observing

B. Go outside in the sun. Point your model toward the real moon. Notice where the sun shines on the real moon. Notice where it shines on the model. How does the real-moon phase compare to the model phase?

experimenting

C. How can you move your model in the sun to make other phases? (*Caution:* Never look at the sun. It may harm your eyes.)

predicting

D. Observe the moon now and then for a few days. Notice how its appearance changes. Keep a record. Can you predict what it will look like in a week? two weeks? Draw what you think and then find out.

Figure 12-19

TEACHING COMMENT

PREPARATION AND BACKGROUND

If a bright window is unavailable, use the light from a filmstrip projector in a dark room. To do Problem B, a daytime moon must be visible. Consult the detailed weather section of your local newspaper for moonrise and moonset times during a period when a daytime moon is visible.

GENERALIZATION

Moon phases appear because one-half of the moon is lighted by sunshine as it revolves around the earth.

SAMPLE PERFORMANCE OBJECTIVES

Process: The child can predict an upcoming sequence of moon phases after observing the moon for a week.

Knowledge: The child can demonstrate with a ball and sunshine how moon phases occur.

INVESTIGATION: *AN EARTH–MOON MODEL*

Astronauts have now walked on the moon several times, so it is easy to think that the moon is close to earth. However, the moon is far away. One way to show its distance is to make a scale model.

EXPLORATORY PROBLEM

How can you make a scale model of the earth and moon?

NEEDED

basketball
string
tennis ball
ruler
scissors
clay

TRY THIS

1. You will need a large ball for the earth and a smaller one for the moon. The earth is about four times as wide as the moon. Measure the width of a ball by putting it between two books. Use a ruler to find the distance between the books. A basketball is about four times wider than a tennis ball.

2. The moon is about 30 earth widths away, or 10 times farther away than the distance around the earth. Wrap a string 10 times around the basketball. Cut off what is left.

3. Stretch the string between the "earth" and "moon" (Figure 12-20). This scale model shows sizes and distance compared to the real earth.

Figure 12-20

DISCOVERY PROBLEMS

measuring **A.** How can you make a scale model that is half this size?

measuring **B.** Suppose you had a ball 10 centimeters (4 inches) wide to use as the earth. How large would the moon need to be? How far apart should the earth and moon be? (*Hint:* Check Steps 1 and 2 again.)

measuring **C.** Suppose you had a ball 5 centimeters (2 inches) wide to use as the moon. How large would the earth need to be? How far apart should the earth and moon be?

measuring **D.** Suppose you wanted your whole model to be no longer than a meter stick or yardstick. How large would you make your earth and moon? How far apart would you place them?

TEACHING COMMENT

PREPARATION AND BACKGROUND

The sequence is designed to help children gain an understanding of proportion without the mathematics of proportion. After these experiences, most students should have a realistically scaled view of the earth–moon system. If you want to, you might proceed directly with figures they can scale: earth diameter 12,800 kilometers (8,000 miles), moon diameter 3,200 kilometers (2,000 miles), and average distance between them 384,000 kilometers (240,000 miles).

GENERALIZATION

Relative sizes and distance in the earth–moon system may be shown in a scale model.

SAMPLE PERFORMANCE OBJECTIVES

Process: Given one measure, the child can derive the two other measures needed to make a scale model of the earth–moon system.

Knowledge: The child can make a scale model of the earth–moon system.

INVESTIGATION: *ECLIPSES OF THE SUN AND MOON*

Sometimes the earth, moon, and sun are in a straight line in space. Then, something interesting may happen: The moon may block off, or eclipse, the sunlight, or the earth may block, or eclipse, the moon. You can learn how eclipses work with a model of the sun, moon, and earth.

EXPLORATORY PROBLEM

How can you use a volleyball, a tennis ball, and a projector to show eclipses?

NEEDED

volleyball or basketball
filmstrip projector
tennis ball
sticky tape
string

TRY THIS

1. Set up the materials as shown in Figure 12-21. Put a basketball or volleyball on a table. This will be the "earth."
2. Fasten a short string to a tennis ball with sticky tape. This will be the "moon."
3. Darken the room. Turn on the projector "sun." Point it toward the earth.
4. Holding the string, move the moon around the earth. Notice the shadows made by the moon and the earth.

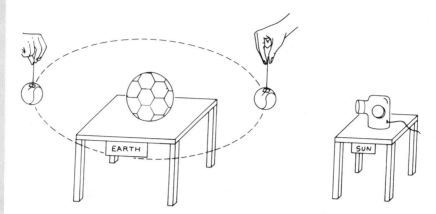

Figure 12-21

DISCOVERY PROBLEMS

observing **A.** At what position does the moon make a shadow on the earth? (This is an eclipse of the sun.)

observing **B.** How much of the earth is covered by the moon's shadow?

observing **C.** At what position does the earth make a shadow on the moon? (This is an eclipse of the moon.)

observing **D.** How much of the moon is covered by the earth's shadow?

inferring **E.** Would more people on earth be able to see a sun eclipse or a moon eclipse? Why?

inferring **F.** Move the moon around the earth again, but now have it go just above or below the earth. Do you see eclipses now? Why or why not?

TEACHING COMMENT

PREPARATION AND BACKGROUND

Some students may wonder why there are not a solar eclipse and a lunar eclipse every month. You might use Problem F to help them understand that the plane of the moon's orbit around the earth is somewhat tilted. Also, the two bodies are relatively much farther apart than in the model, so usually the moon's shadow misses the earth, and the earth's shadow misses the moon. The distance between the two bodies also means that the moon's shadow on earth in solar eclipses is much smaller than found in Problem B.

Caution: Children (or adults) should never look at the sun during a solar eclipse. The sun can quickly injure eyes.

GENERALIZATION

A lunar eclipse happens when the earth's shadow falls on the moon. A solar eclipse happens when the moon's shadow falls on the earth.

SAMPLE PERFORMANCE OBJECTIVES

Process: The child can infer from observing a model whether a solar or lunar eclipse is more likely to be viewed from the earth.

Knowledge: The child can describe the relative positions of the sun, moon, and earth during a lunar eclipse and solar eclipse.

SOLAR SYSTEM AND BEYOND EXPERIENCES
(Concepts p. 421)

INVESTIGATION: SIZE AND DISTANCE IN THE SOLAR SYSTEM

The solar system is huge. You cannot make a model that shows both size and distance at the same time. It would be too big to fit in the classroom or playground.

But you can make a scale model of part of the system—the sun and earth. It can help you to understand more about distance and size in the solar system.

EXPLORATORY PROBLEM

How can you make a scale model of the sun and earth?

NEEDED

yellow construction paper
clay
meter stick or yardstick
straight pin
sticky tape
playground
scissors

TRY THIS

1. Make a clay ball 1 centimeter (⅜ inch) wide for the earth.
2. The sun is 108 times wider than the earth, so cut out a circle 108 centimeters (43 inches) wide from yellow construction paper. (You may need to tape some sheets together.)
3. The sun is about 150 million kilometers (93 million miles) from the earth, so the 2 models will need to be about 116 meters (383 feet) apart.

4. Practice taking giant steps. Try to make each step a meter (or yard) long. Then step off the sun–earth distance on the playground (Figure 12-22).
5. Have someone hold up the model sun at one end. Hold up your tiny model earth, stuck on a pin, at the other end. Notice how far away the sun is?

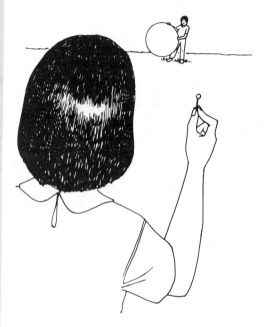

Figure 12-22

DISCOVERY PROBLEMS

measuring **A.** The planet Jupiter is five times farther away from the sun than the earth. How far away (meters or feet) would Jupiter be with your model?

measuring **B.** Uranus is almost 18 times farther from the sun than the earth. How far away would Uranus be with your model?

measuring **C.** Pluto, the farthest planet, is more than 39 times farther away. How far would Pluto be with your model?

measuring **D.** The largest of the solar system's nine planets is Jupiter. It is 11 times wider than the earth. How large would Jupiter be with your model?

measuring **E.** The smallest planet is Pluto. It is only about one-third as wide as the earth. How large would it be with your model?

TEACHING COMMENT

PREPARATION AND BACKGROUND

A large circle may be drawn with a pencil tied to a string. Its radius with the present sun model would be 54 centimeters (21 inches).

Many students will enjoy being challenged to extend their solar system model on a local map. Pluto will need to be placed several kilometers or miles away!

GENERALIZATION

The large distances among planets in the solar system make it difficult to scale planet sizes and distances together in a model.

SAMPLE PERFORMANCE OBJECTIVES

Process: The child can measure and calculate size and distance in constructing a model of the solar system.

Knowledge: The child states that either size or distance may be scaled in a partial solar system model, but not both, if the model is to fit into a classroom.

INVESTIGATION: *CONSTELLATIONS*

Most people have seen the group, or *constellation*, of stars called the Big Dipper. The stars make a pattern that looks like an old-fashioned water dipper. There are many more constellations of stars. But while they seem to make a pattern, they may be very different in size and millions of kilometers from each other. Seen from another angle, they may not look at all like constellations. You can find out more about what constellations are like by making a model.

EXPLORATORY PROBLEM

How can you make a model of a constellation?

NEEDED

cardboard box
aluminum foil
scissors
black thread
black paint or paper
sticky tape

TRY THIS

1. Cut off the top and one side of a cardboard box.
2. Cover the side and back inside with black paint or paper.
3. Snip different-sized pieces of black thread to hold your "stars."
4. Make different-sized stars from pieces of foil. Wrap each piece around a thread end. Squeeze each into a ball shape.
5. Ask someone to use tape and hang your stars in some pattern different from the one shown in Figure 12-23. (Notice that in the front view, this constellation looks like a *W*, but from the side it looks like an upside-down *V*. If the box's side was as long as the playground, you could put the stars even farther apart. Then you would see no pattern at all from the side.)

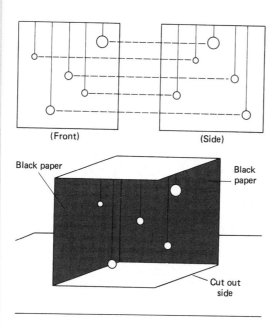

Figure 12-23

DISCOVERY PROBLEMS

observing   **A.** Look at the constellation your partner has made from the front view from 15 steps away. Can you draw its shape?

observing   **B.** At what distances from you are the stars? Which is closest, or next closest? Record what you think from left to right.

inferring   **C.** What do you think the constellation looks like from the side? Draw what you think.

observing   **D.** Ask your partner to twist the box around very slightly. How, if at all, does this help you to tell distances and the side pattern? How much more must the box be twisted around to tell?

inferring   **E.** Play a game with your partner. Each person hangs a different constellation. How many stars can you order properly by distance from you? How many side patterns can you tell from front patterns?

Teaching Comment

PREPARATION AND BACKGROUND

It is essential that students first view the constellation model directly from the front and from some distance. Otherwise, the activity may be less effective. The foil balls may quickly be suspended, and shifted as needed, by affixing each thread end to the box top inside with a bit of tape.

GENERALIZATION

Stars of a constellation share a common direction, but they may vary greatly in size and distance from each other.

SAMPLE PERFORMANCE OBJECTIVES

Process: The child can infer a "side" pattern of stars by observing the constellation from a slight angle. (The degree of skill is related to the size of the angle needed to make a correct inference.)

Knowledge: The child states that the pattern of a constellation depends on the position of the observer in space.

GRAVITY AND THE LAWS OF MOTION EXPERIENCES
(Concepts p. 424)

ACTIVITY: *WHY DOESN'T THE SUN'S GRAVITY PULL IN THE NEAR PLANETS?*

NEEDED

strong string (2 meters or 6 feet long)
partner
rubber ball
watch with second hand
sewing thread spool
outdoor place

TRY THIS

1. Tie one end of the string tightly to the ball. Slide the other end through the hole of a sewing spool.

2. You will be the "sun." The ball "planet" will revolve around you on the string. Hold the spool in one hand. Whirl the planet by moving the spool around. Hold the string with your other hand to keep it from slipping through the spool (Figure 12-24). (You could mark the string below the spool to easily see any slip.)

3. Feel how the ball pulls on the string. Have someone count the number of times your planet circles the sun in 15 seconds. Try to keep the string length above the spool the same.

4. Try it a second time. Keep the string length the same as before, but now pull harder on the string below the spool. This increases the pull of "gravity" on your planet. If the planet is to stay at the same distance, what must happen to its speed?

5. Have someone count again the number of orbits your planet makes in 15 seconds. How do the first and second counts compare? What do you think makes it possible for the closer planets not to be pulled into the sun?

Figure 12-24

ACTIVITY: *WHAT MAKES A ROCKET WORK?*

NEEDED

sausage-shaped balloon
sticky tape

string (6 meters or 20 feet long)
paper clip
soda straw
five pennies

TRY THIS

1. Thread one end of the string through a straw. Fasten that end low on a table leg. Fasten the other end high on a wall. The string should be tight.
2. Blow up the balloon. Fold over the small, open end and fasten it with a paper clip.
3. Fasten the balloon to the straw with tape (Figure 12-25).

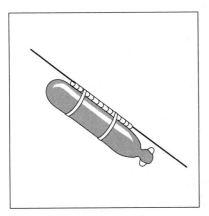

Figure 12-25

4. Hold the balloon near the floor end of the string. Quickly remove the paper clip and let go. What happens to the balloon? How can you explain what happens?
5. Have a contest with teams of classmates to see whose balloon rocket can lift the most weight to a "space station." Tie one end of each string to a light fixture or other high place. Fasten pennyweights to each balloon with sticky tape. Make some fair rules: The lower end of each string and rocket must touch the floor when the rocket is released. Each team gets two turns; the first is for practice. Observe carefully what the best rockets look like during the first trial. Use this information to prepare for the second trial. No team can change its rocket once the second trials begin. To win, here are some things to think about.

   ■ How much air should be in the balloon? (If it breaks, you're out of the contest.)
   ■ How long should the straw be? How should it be attached to the balloon?

■ Should the string be upright or at a slant? What kind of string is best?

■ How many pennies should be stuck on the balloon? Where is it best to put them for balance?

TEACHING COMMENT

When air rushes out of the balloon, there is an equal and opposite push inside, so the balloon moves. In a rocket engine, burned fuel forms hot gases that push out the open back of the engine. An equal and opposite push inside moves the rocket forward.

REFERENCES

American Association for the Advancement of Science. (1993). *Benchmarks for science literacy*. New York: Oxford University Press.

National Research Council. (1996). *National science education standards*. Washington, DC: National Academy Press.

SELECTED TRADE BOOKS: THE EARTH IN SPACE

For Younger Children

Bendick, J. (1991a). *Artificial satellites: Helpers in space*. Millbrook Press.

Bendick, J. (1991b). *Comets and meteors: Visitors from space*. Millbrook Press.

Branley, F. M. (1986). *What makes day and night*. Harper & Row.

Branley, F. M. (1987a). *The moon seems to change*. Harper & Row.

Branley, F. M. (1987b). *The planets in our solar system*. Harper & Row.

Branley, F. M. (1987c). *Rockets and satellites*. Harper & Row.

Branley, F. M. (1988). *The sun, our nearest star*. Crowell.

Branley, F. M. (1991). *The big dipper*. Harper Collins.

Calmenson, S. (1982). *My book of the seasons*. Golden Press.

Cole, J. (1990). *The magic school bus lost in the solar system*. Scholastic.

Fradin, D. (1984). *Spacelab*. Children's Press.

Friskey, M. (1982). *Space shuttles*. Children's Press.

Gorey, E., & Neumeyer, P. (1982). *Why we have day and night*. Capra Press.

Hamer, M. (1983). *Night sky*. Watts.

Jackson, K. (1985). *The planets*. Troll Associates.

Jay, M. (1987). *Planets*. Watts.

Weimer, T. E. (1993). *Space songs for children*. Pearce–Evetts.

For Older Children

Adams, R. (1983). *Our wonderful solar system*. Troll Associates.

Adler, I. (1980). *The stars: Decoding their messages*. Crowell.

Alexander, K. (1990). *The kid's book of space flight*. Running Press.

Asimov, I. (1990). *Projects in astronomy*. Gareth Stevens.

Asimov, I. (1991). *Ancient astronomy*. Dell.

Bendick, J. (1982). *Space travel*. Watts.

Berger, M. (1983). *Bright stars, red giants and white dwarfs*. Putnam.

Branley, F. M. (1987). *Star guide*. Harper & Row.

Cabellero, J. A. (1987). *Aerospace projects for young children*. Humanics.

Couper, H., & Henbest, N. (1987). *The moon*. Watts.

Fichter, G. S. (1982). *Comets and meteors*. Watts.

Furniss, T. (1987). *Let's look at outer space*. Watts.

Gallant, R. A. (1983). *Once around the galaxy*. Watts.

Gardner, R. (1988). *Projects in space science*. Messner.

Harris, A., & Weissman, P. (1990). *The great voyager adventure: A guided tour through the solar system*. Messner.

Kelch, J. (1990). *Small worlds: Exploring the 60 moons of our solar system*. Messner.

Lauber, P. (1982). *Journey to the planets*. Crown.

Lewellen, J. (1981). *Moon, sun and stars*. Children's Press.

Myring, L. (1982). *Sun, moon and planets*. EDC Press.

Richard, G. (1987). *Spacecraft*. Watts.

Ridpath, I. (1991). *Space*. Watts.

Riley, P. D. (1986). *The earth and space*. David & Charles.

Simon, S. (1982). *The long journey from space*. Crown.

Simon, S. (1984). *The moon*. Four Winds.

Vogt, G. (1982). *Mars and the inner planets*. Watts.

Vogt, G. (1987). *Space laboratories*. Watts.

Wood, R. (1991). *Thirty-nine easy astronomy experiments*. Tab Books.

Resource Books

Butzow, C. M., & Butzow, J. W. (1989). *Science through children's literature: An integrated approach* (astronomy and outer space topics, pp. 158–168). Teachers Ideas Press.

Fredericks, A. D., Meinbach, A. M., & Rothlein, L. (1993). *Thematic units: An integrated approach to teaching science and social studies* (earth, sun, and moon topics, pp. 161–167; space exploration, pp. 210–217). HarperCollins.

Shaw, D. G., & Dybdahl, C. S. (1996). *Integrating science and language arts. A sourcebook for K–6 teachers* (rocket and space travel topics, pp. 213–230). Allyn and Bacon.

PROFESSIONAL BIBLIOGRAPHY

GENERAL SOURCES OF ACTIVITIES

Bybee, R., Peterson, R., Bowyer, J., & Butts, D. (1984). Activities for teaching about science and society. Upper Saddle River, NJ: Merrill/Prentice Hall. (Activities that relate to social needs and problems.)

DeVito, A., & Krockover, G. H. (1991). *Creative sciencing: Ideas and activities for teachers and children*. Glenview, IL: Scott, Foresman (Good Year). (About 160 activities designed to stimulate creativity.)

Freidl, A. E. (1997). *Teaching science to children, an inquiry approach*. New York: Random House. (A large array of hands-on activities for children, including many discrepant events.)

Lowery, L. F., & Verbeeck, C. (1987). *Explorations* (3 volumes: *earth science, physical science, life science*). Carthage, IL: Fearon. (48 process-oriented activities for grades 1–3.)

Strongin, H. (1991). *Science on a shoestring*. Reading, MA: Addison-Wesley. (Easy-to-do investigations with readily found, inexpensive materials.)

Van Cleave, J. P. (1989–1991). *Science for Every Kid* (5 volumes: *biology, chemistry, earth, astronomy, physics*). New York: Wiley. (Each volume has 101 activities for grade three and beyond, many of which are suitable for science fair projects.)

TEACHER PERIODICALS

Discover, Time, Inc., 3435 Wilshire Blvd., Los Angeles, CA 90010. (Monthly. Interesting, up-to-date information about developments in science.)

Frontiers, National Science Foundation, 4201 Wilson Blvd., Arlington, VA 22230. (Newsletter of the National Science Foundation).

Journal of Elementary Science Education, contact Joseph Peters, Editor, The University of West Florida, 11000 University Parkway, Pensacola, FL 32514. (Practical and theoretical articles related to elementary science teaching and learning.)

Journal of Research in Science Teaching, contact Arthur White, National Association for Research in Science Teaching Executive Secretary, The Ohio State University, 1929 Kenny Rd., Columbus, OH 43210-1015. (Scholarly articles on research and practice.)

Journal of Science Teacher Education, contact Joseph Peters, Association for the Education of Teachers in Science Executive Secretary, The University of West Florida, 11000 University Parkway, Pensacola, FL 32514. (Practical and scholarly articles related to teacher preservice, teacher inservice, and science teaching.)

Natural History, American Museum of Natural History, Central Park West at 79th St., New York, NY 10024. (Monthly, 10 issues a year. Interesting articles on a variety of natural subjects, including ecology.)

School Science and Mathematics, contact Donald Pratt, School Science and Mathematics Association Executive Secretary, Curriculum and Foundations, Bloomsburgh University, Bloomsburgh, PA 17815-1301. (Monthly, nine issues a year. Includes articles on methods and research.)

Science, American Association for the Advancement of Science, 1515 Massachusetts Ave., N.W., Washington, DC 20005. (Monthly, except bimonthly Jan./Feb. and July/Aug. Accurate, up-to-date nontechnical information about developments in science.)

Science Activities, Science Activities Publishing Company, Skokie, IL 60076. (Ten issues a year. Useful activities for teachers of the upper grades and beyond.)

Science and Children, National Science Teachers Association, 1840 Wilson Blvd., Arlington, VA 22201-3000. (Monthly, eight issues a year. Articles of interest and practical value to elementary school teachers.)

Science Education, John Wiley and Sons, Inc., 605 Third Ave., New York, NY 10158. For individual subscriptions contact Joseph Peters, Association for the Education of Teachers in Science Executive Secretary, The University of West Florida, 11000 University Parkway, Pensacola, FL 32514. (Reports of research and essays on the teaching of elementary and secondary school science.)

Science News, Science Service, 1719 N Street, N.W., Washington, DC. (Weekly. Brief, easy-to-read reports on current findings of scientific research.)

CHILDREN'S PERIODICALS

Digit, P.O. Box 29996, San Francisco, CA 94129. (Six issues a year. Computer games, ideas, challenges. Upper elementary.)

Enter, One Disk Drive, P.O. Box 2686, Boulder, CO 80322. (Ten issues a year. Computer games, ideas, challenges from the producers of the Children's Television Workshop. Upper elementary.)

National Geographic World, National Geographic Society, Department 00481, 17th and M Streets, N.W., Washington, DC 20036. (Monthly. Articles on environmental features of interest to children.)

Odyssey, AstroMedia Corp., 625 E. St. Paul Ave., P.O. Box 92788, Milwaukee, WI 53202. (Bimonthly. Full-color astronomy and space magazine for children 7 to 13.)

Ranger Rick's Nature Magazine, National Wildlife Federation, 1412 Sixteenth St., N.W., Washington, DC 20036. (Monthly, for children of elementary school age. Interesting stories and pictures on natural subjects, including ecology. *Your Big Backyard,* also 10 issues, is for preschool and primary-level children.)

Scienceland, 501 Fifth Ave., Suite 2102, New York, NY 10017. (Monthly, eight softcover booklets issued a year. Well-received magazine for children, preschool to third grade.)

Science Weekly, P.O. Box 70154, Washington, DC 20088. (Twenty issues a year. Current science developments for children in grades one through six.)

3–2–1 Contact, Children's Television Workshop, P.O. Box 2933, Boulder, CO 80322. (Ten issues a year. Experiments, puzzles, projects, and articles for children 8 to 14.)

PROFESSIONAL TEXTS

Abruscato, J. (1996). *Teaching children science.* Englewood Cliffs, NJ: Allyn & Bacon. (Methods, activities, and content for elementary school science.)

Barba, R. H. (1995). *Science in the multicultural classroom: A guide to teaching and learning.* Needham Heights, MA: Allyn & Bacon. (Elementary science methods.)

Blough, G. O., & Schwartz, J. (1990). *Elementary school science and how to teach it.* New York: Holt, Rinehart and Winston. (Methods and comprehensive coverage of subject matter content.)

Cain, S. E., & Evans, J. M. (1990). *Sciencing: An involvement approach to elementary science methods.* Upper Saddle River, NJ: Merrill/Prentice Hall. (A methods text organized into six broad units to develop teaching competencies.)

Carin, Arthur A. (1997). *Teaching science through discovery.* Upper Saddle River, NJ: Merrill/Prentice Hall. (Methods and activities, with emphasis on discovery teaching.)

Esler, W. K., & Esler, M. K. (1996). *Teaching elementary science.* Belmont, CA: Wadsworth. (Methods and subject matter. Exemplifies and applies three kinds of lessons.)

Gabel, D. (1993). *Introductory science skills.* Prospect Heights, IL: Waveland Press. (A laboratory approach to learning science and mathematics skills, and basic chemistry.)

Good, R. G. (1977). *How children learn science.* New York: Macmillan. (Research on children's mental development and recommendations for teaching science.)

Harlan, J. (1992). *Science experiences for the early childhood years.* Upper Saddle River, NJ: Merrill/Prentice Hall. (Everyday science activities for younger children.)

Howe, A. C., & Jones, L. (1993). *Engaging children in science.* Upper Saddle River, NJ: Merrill/Prentice Hall. (Elementary science methods.)

Jacobson, W. J., & Bergman, A. B. (1991). *Science for children.* Upper Saddle River, NJ: Prentice Hall. (Methods and content of elementary-school science.)

Lind, K. K. (1996). *Exploring science in early childhood: A developmental approach.* Albany, NY: Delmar Publishers. (Elementary science methods.)

Martin, D. J. (1997). *Elementary science methods: A constructivist approach.* Albany, NY: Delmar Publishers. (Elementary science methods.)

Martin, R. E., Jr., Sexton, C., Wagner, K., & Gerlovich, J. (1994). *Teaching science for all children.* Needham Heights, MA: Allyn & Bacon. (Methods and content of elementary school science.)

Peterson, R., Bowyer, J., Butts, D., & Bybee, R. (1984). *Science and society: A source book for elementary and junior high school teachers.* Upper Saddle River, NJ: Merrill/Prentice Hall. (Content and comprehensive methods. Emphasizes science's impact on society.)

Renner, J. W., & Marek, E. A. (1988). *The learning cycle and elementary school science teaching.* Portsmouth, NH: Heinemann. (Emphasizes methods that match children's cognitive processes for successful science teaching.)

Sprague, C., Fiel, R. L., & Funk, H. J. (1995). *Learning and assessing science process skills.* Dubuque, IA: Kendall Hunt. (Process skill development and assessment.)

Tolman, M. N., & Hardy, G. R. (1995). *Discovering elementary science: Method, content, and problem-solving activities.* Needham Heights, MA: Allyn & Bacon. (Elementary science methods and content.)

Victor, E., & Kellough, R. (1997). *Science for the elementary and middle school.* New York: Macmillan. (Methods, content, and activities. Features an extensive scope of subject matter in outline form.)

Wassermann, S., & Ivany, J. W. G. (1988). *Teaching elementary science.* New York: Harper & Row. (Stresses informal, inquiry-type science experiences for children.)

AGENCIES AND SOCIETIES[1]

Association for the Education of Teachers in Science, 11000 University Parkway, Pensacola, FL 32514, email:jpeters@uwf.edu, http: // science.coe.uwf.edu/aets/aets.html

Computer Learning Foundation, P.O. Box 60007, Palo Alto, CA 94306-0007, http://www.thejournal.com/clf/support.html/

ERIC Clearinghouse for Science, Mathematics, and Environmental Education (ERIC/CSMEE), 1929 Kenny Rd., Columbus, OH 43210-1080., http://www.erisce.org/

ERIC Clearinghouse on Disabilities and Gifted Education, The Council for Exceptional Children, 1920 Association Dr., Reston, VA 22091-1589, (703) 264-9474, fax (703) 264-9494.

ERIC Clearinghouse on Elementary and Early Childhood Education (ERIC/EECE), University of Illinois at Urbana–Champaign, 805 W. Pennsylvania Ave., Urbana, IL 61801-4897.

Foundation for Science and Disability, E.C. Keller, Jr., Treasurer, 236 Grand St., Morgantown, WV 26505-7509.

Franklin Institute Science Activity Kits for Grades 1–4, Science Kit & Boreal Laboratories, Elementary Science Division, 777 East Park Dr., Tonawanda, NY 14150-6784, 1-800-828-7777.

International Council of Associations for Science Education (ICASE), Jack B. Holbrook, Executive Secretary, ICASE, P.O. Box 6138, Limassol, Cyprus.

International Council of Associations for Science Education (ICASE), Stepping Into Science Project, Homerton College, Cambridge, CB2 2PH, England, http://sunsite.anu.edu.au/icase/

National Audubon Society, A Teacher's Resource Manual, 700 Broadway, New York, NY 10003-9562, (212) 979-3000, fax: (212) 979-3188.

National Energy Foundation, 5225 Wiley Post Way, Suite 170, Salt Lake City, Utah 84116.

National Science Foundation, 4201 Wilson Blvd., Arlington, VA 22230, http://stis.nsf.gov/

National Weather Service, 1325 East West Highway, Silver Spring, MD 20910, http://tgsvs.nws.naaa.gov/

---

[1]For an updated list of agencies and their electronic addresses, see http://science.coe.uwf.edu/.

Office of Indian Education Programs, Bureau of Indian Affairs, U.S. Dept. of the Interior, 1951 Constitution Ave., N.W., Washington, DC 20240.

Society for Advancement of Chicanos and Native Americans in Science (SACNAS), University of California, 1156 High St., Santa Cruz, CA 95064, 408-459-4272, fax (408) 459-3156, email:sacnas@cats.ucsc.edu

TERC, 2067 Massachusetts Ave., Cambridge MA 02140, (617) 547-0430, fax (617) 349-3535, http://www.terc.edu/

U.S. Environmental Protection Agency, Headquarters Service Branch, Public Information Center, 401 M. St., S.W. (3406), Washington, DC 20460, (202) 260-2080, fax: (202) 260-7762, public-access@epamail.epa.gov.

U.S. Geological Survey, Information Services, P.O. Box 25286, Denver, CO 80225-9916., http://www.usgs.gov/

APPENDIX

B

SCIENCE CURRICULUM PROJECTS

ACTIVITIES FOR INTEGRATING MATHEMATICS AND SCIENCE (AIMS)

Grades K–8. This program, developed at Fresno (California) Pacific College, was originally funded by the National Science Foundation to train a group of teachers in the rationale and methods for integrating science and mathematics in Grades 5–8. The classroom testing of written materials produced such positive results that a full-fledged writing project was launched to develop additional teaching booklets. Materials are now available for K–8. The rationale for AIMS includes these points: (1) Math and science are integrated outside the classroom and so should also be integrated inside it; (2) as in the real world, a whole series of math skills and science processes should be interwoven in a single activity to create a continuum of experience; (3) the materials should present questions that relate to the student's world and arouse their curiosity; (4) the materials should change students from observers to participants in the learning process; (5) the investigations should be enjoyable because learning is more effective when the process is enjoyed.

For more information, write to AIMS Education Foundation, P.O. Box 8120, Fresno, CA 93747-8120. http://www.AIMSedu.org/

EDUCATION DEVELOPMENT CENTER INSIGHTS

Grades K–6. The Education Development Center is in Newton, MA. The program con-
tains 17 activity-based modules that can be used separately within another science curriculum or as a full curriculum within the life, earth, and physical science areas. Each module is organized around four phases of instruction: Getting Started, Exploring and Discovering, Organizing and Processing for Meaning, and Applying and Extending Ideas. Six major science themes are incorporated into the program: systems, change, structure and function, diversity, cause and effect, and energy. Content and process skills are balanced across the curriculum. Material from other school subjects is integrated into many activities to give an overall understanding of how they normally relate.

The activities, often open-ended, focus on experiences that draw on the urban environment. Playground apparatus, toys, and the students themselves may serve as resources for learning science concepts. Instructional materials are designed for both the inexperienced teacher and the veteran who seeks innovative strategies to develop critical and creative thinking in students.

An advisory group of teachers from seven major urban areas continually gave feedback to program developers about the quality of learning and assessment activities.

The commercial distributor is Improving Urban Elementary Science Project, Education Development Center, Inc. 55 Chapel St., Newton, Massachusetts 02158; phone: 617-969-7100, extension 2430.

454

Elementary Science Study (ESS)

Grades K–6. ESS was begun in the 1960s as a curriculum improvement project of the Education Development Center, a nonprofit organization devoted to generating new ideas for education.

The program consists of 56 units of instruction that cover a wide range of science subjects. Each unit has a teacher's manual, and most units have an accompanying kit of materials. No fixed master plan exists for scope and sequence. The developers felt that each school district was best qualified to assemble its own curriculum from the units to meet local conditions.

ESS is intentionally child centered. Activities are designed to reflect the wonder, curiosity, and natural play of childhood. While the teacher guide for each unit suggests an overall structure, the students help determine the direction the activities take and how much time is spent on each activity. Most classroom procedures are exploratory and open-ended. ESS believes that learning happens best when children are free to use their own styles without over-structuring and premature closing from adults.

Materials are available from Delta Education, Inc., P.O. Box 915, Hudson, NH 03051. http://www.delta-ed.com/

Full Option Science System (FOSS)

Grades K–6. This program is designed to serve both regular and most special education students in a wide cross-section of schools. Developed at the Lawrence Hall of Science, Berkeley, California, the program features several modules at each grade level that include science lesson plans in the earth, life, and physical sciences, and extension activities in language, computer, and mathematics applications.

The laboratory equipment includes several package options, from complete kits to individual items. Materials assembly directions show how teacher and students can gather and construct equipment for many activities. A correlation table tells how to integrate activities with other programs and state department of education guidelines for science.

Much care is taken to have a suitable match between activities and students' ability to think at different ages. Further work has been done to make the program easy to instruct and manage. Provisions for preparation time, ease of giving out and retrieving materials, cleanup, storage, and resupply have continually guided program developers.

The commercial distributor of FOSS is the Encyclopedia Britannica Educational Corporation, 310 South Michigan Avenue, Chicago, IL 60604.

Great Explorations in Math and Science (GEMS)

Grades Preschool–9. GEMS is a growing resource for activity-based science and mathematics. Developed at the University of California at Berkeley's Lawrence Hall of Science and tested in thousands of classrooms nationwide, over 50 GEMS Teacher's Guides and Handbooks offer a wide spectrum of learning opportunities from preschool and kindergarten through tenth grade. GEMS guides can be integrated into your curriculum or stand on their own as a stimulating way to involve students.

The GEMS series interweaves a number of educational ideas and goals. GEMS guides encompass important learning objectives summarized on the front page of each guide, under the headings of skills, concepts, science themes, mathematics strands, and the nature of science and mathematics. Taken together, these headings help summarize the objectives of the unit. These objectives can be directly and flexibly related to science and mathematics curricula, local and district guidelines, state frameworks, benchmarks, and the national standards. For more on flexible ways to build your own curricula using GEMS, contact the University of California, GEMS, Lawrence Hall of Science, Berkeley, CA 94720-5200.

NATIONAL GEOGRAPHIC KIDS NETWORK

Grades 4–6. The National Geographic Kids Network is a program that has children gather data on real science problems and then use a computer network to share their data with a scientist and children in other locations. The developer is the Technical Education Resource Center (TERC) in partnership with the National Geographic Society, which publishes and distributes the program.

Each of the instructional units is six weeks long and focuses on a central science problem. Children learn to ask questions and gather data in scientifically acceptable ways. The data are transmitted to an interested scientist who analyzes the data, answers children's questions, and then sends back an overview of all the collected information from cooperating schools.

Curriculum materials include children's handbooks that have background information on the topic of study, teacher guides, and computer software. The software is made up of a word-processing program, data charts, and a computer map of North America, all of which are used to ready and transmit data.

For details, write National Geographic Society Educational Services, 17th & M Streets, Washington, DC 20036.

NUFFIELD SCIENCE 5–13

Grades K–8. Science 5–13 is a series of reference and resource publications for the teacher that suggests an open-ended, child-centered approach to elementary science. ("5–13" signifies the age span of the children served.) This program was begun as a curriculum project at the Nuffield Education Foundation of Great Britain.

The basic set of teaching units is composed of 20 volumes. Some unit titles are: "Working with Wood"; "Science, Models, and Toys"; "Structure and Forces"; "Children and Plastics"; "Trees"; and "Ourselves." An additional set of six titles in environmental education complements the basic program.

A major contribution of Science 5–13 is how it takes children's beginning experiences with everyday things and freely extends them in many directions. All the while, children's intellectual development is carefully considered. In the United States, the distributor is Macdonald-Raintree, Inc., 205 W. Highland Ave., Milwaukee, WI 53203.

OUTDOOR BIOLOGY INSTRUCTIONAL STRATEGIES (OBIS)

Ages 10–15. Developed at the Lawrence Hall of Science, University of California (Berkeley), OBIS is designed for use with community youth organizations and schools that want to offer outdoor laboratory experiences. Four activity packets offer a broad selection of interesting, firsthand activities for studying ecological relationships in different environments: desert, seashore, forest, pond and stream, city lots, and local parks.

Each activity card consists of background information for the leader, description of materials needed and any advance preparation required, a lesson plan, and several follow-up suggestions. Each activity can be used alone or as part of a developmental sequence. The commercial distributor is: Delta Education, Box 915, Hudson, NH 03051.

SCIENCE FOR LIFE AND LIVING

Grades K–6. The full name for this curriculum is "Science for Living: Integrating Science, Technology, and Health." The developer is the BSCS Group, a nonprofit foundation for science education.

After readiness activities at the kindergarten level, these concepts and skills form the main curriculum structure: order and organization (Grade 1); change and measurement (Grade 2); patterns and prediction (Grade 3); systems and analysis (Grade 4); energy and investigation (Grade 5); and balance and decisions (Grade 6). Children build their own understanding of an integrated world of science, technology, and health as they work through activities that bring out the concepts and skills.

Each complete lesson contains five consecutive phases: (1) An *engagement* activity begins the lesson. Children connect what they know to the present material and reveal their prior knowledge, including misconceptions. (2) *Exploration* follows, in which students explore the materials or environment and form a common base of experience. (3) Next, an *explanation* phase gives students a chance to describe what they are learning, and the teacher is given an opportunity to state the intended learning. (4) *Elaboration* then provides activities that extend understandings and give further chances to practice skills. (5) The last phase, *evaluation*, allows students and teacher to assess what has been learned.

Published materials are available from the Kendall/Hunt Publishing Company, 2460 Kerper Blvd., Dubuque, IA 52001.

SCIENCE AND TECHNOLOGY FOR CHILDREN (STC)

Grades 1–6. The developer of this curriculum project is the National Science Resources Center, established in 1985 by the National Academy of Sciences and the Smithsonian Institution to improve the teaching of science and mathematics in the nation's schools. The project's mission is to significantly increase the number of schools that offer hands-on science programs to children, and to interest more females and minority members in science.

Teaching units include such titles as *Weather and Me* (Grade 1), *The Life Cycle of Butterflies* (2), *Plant Growth and Development* (3), *Electric Circuits* (4), *Microworlds* (5), and *Magnets and Motors* (6). They are designed to focus on easy-to-use materials and integrate science with other areas of the curriculum. Each unit includes a teacher's guide; pupil activity booklet; a description of needed materials; and annotated lists of recommended trade books, computer software, and audiovisual materials.

The developers sought to make the management of materials and activities as practical as possible. In the field testing of units, evaluation procedures monitored how well the units worked under a wide variety of classroom conditions.

For details, contact the National Science Resources Center, Arts and Industries Building, Room 1201, Smithsonian Institution, Washington, DC 20560.

SCIENCE—A PROCESS APPROACH (SAPA)

Grades K–6. SAPA has a unique structure. It uses process skills rather than subject-matter content as the base for its scope and sequence. Subject matter is used mainly as an aid to developing the skills, although much content is presented.

Eight "basic" processes are taught in Grades K–3: observing, using space/time relationships, using numbers, measuring, classifying, communicating, predicting, and inferring. In Grades 4–6, five "integrated" processes are taught that build on and extend the basic processes: formulating hypotheses, controlling variables, interpreting data, defining operationally, and experimenting. The method used to organize the development of the skills was to identify the process behaviors of scientists, and then to logically break down the behaviors into sequences through which they could be learned by children.

SAPA II, a more recent version of this program, has a more flexible structure than the first edition. Alternate procedures have been provided to allow the teacher more leeway in meeting students' individual differences and organizing teaching.

The commercial supplier is Delta Education, Inc., P.O. Box 915, Hudson, NH 03051.

SCIENCE CURRICULUM IMPROVEMENT STUDY (SCIS)

Grades K–6. SCIS is organized on a base of powerful and modern science concepts. Each of 12 instructional units features a central concept, with supporting subconcepts and process skills integrated into the activities.

Lessons have three parts: exploration, invention, and discovery. In the exploratory part, children are given objects to observe or manipulate. At times these observations are guided by the teacher; otherwise, the children observe and manipulate the objects as they wish.

Explorations allow firsthand contact with the material under study and provide a basis for children to use language. At the same time, the need arises for an explanation to make sense out of what has been observed. This is taken up in the second part of the lesson sequence. After discussion, the teacher gives a definition and a word for the new concept.

This "invention" of a concept sets up the third part of the lesson. Now, the children are given a variety of further experiences within which they discover many applications of the concept. These extend and reinforce their knowledge and skills.

An updated version of this program, *SCIS3*, is available from Delta Education, Inc., P.O. Box 915, Hudson, NH 03051.

SCIENCE IN A NUTSHELL

Grades K–8. Real fun with real science. Discover how exciting real science can be with Delta's new Science in a Nutshell mini-kit series. Introduce or enhance specific science content areas in the classroom, at home, in a resource room, or in an after-school program. Clearly written, hands-on activities challenge young scientists aged 6–12 to investigate their world. Mini-kits are suitable for use with individuals or with small groups of two to three. Contact Delta Education, P.O. Box 3000, Nashua, NH 03061, 1-800-442-5444, fax 1-800-282-9560.

UNIFIED SCIENCES AND MATHEMATICS (USMES)

Grades K–8. The Unified Sciences and Mathematics for Elementary Schools project was funded by the National Science Foundation to develop and try out interdisciplinary units of instruction involving science, mathematics, social sciences, and language arts. The units are centered on long-range investigations of real and practical problems geared to the local environment. The units, 26 in all, may be used by local school planners to design different curricula to meet their needs and reflect a problem-solving approach.

Several kinds of materials are provided for planners and teachers: an introductory guide to USMES, a teacher resource book for each major problem, background papers, a design lab manual (that tells how to set up and make needed apparatus), and a curriculum correlation guide.

More information may be obtained from ERIC Clearinghouse for Science, Mathematics, and Environmental Education (ERIC/CSMEE), 1929 Kenny Rd., Columbus, OH 43210–1080.

WONDERSCIENCE

Wonderscience offers hands-on science activities for elementary school teachers and students. Wonderscience is published monthly from October through May as a joint effort of the American Chemical Society, 1155 Sixteenth St., NW, Washington, DC 20036, and the American Institute of Physics, One Physics Ellipse, College Park, MD 20740. The single-copy subscription price is $6.00/eight issues plus $3.50 handling for each address. For subscription information call toll-free 1-800-333-9511 or write to Wonderscience at the ACS address.

COMMERCIAL SCIENCE SUPPLIERS

The following classifications of suppliers may not be entirely accurate, because suppliers often change offerings with business conditions. A current catalog should reveal the full scope of materials for sale in each case. Use school stationery when requesting free elementary-level catalogs. An annual, comprehensive listing of suppliers accompanies each January issue of *Science and Children*.

GENERAL SUPPLIES

Carolina Biological Supply Company
2700 York Road
Burlington, NC 27215
http://www.carosci.com/

Connecticut Valley Biological Supply
    Company
Valley Road
Southampton, MA 01073

Delta Education, Inc.
P.O. Box 915
Hudson, NH 03051
http://www.delta-ed.com/

Edmund Scientific Company
101 E. Gloucester Pike
Barrington, NJ 08007

Frey Scientific Company
905 Hickory Lane
Mansfield, OH 44905

Learning Things, Inc.
68A Broadway
Arlington, MA 02174

Ward's Natural Science Establishment
5100 West Henrietta Road
P.O. Box 92912
Rochester, NY 14692

BOTTLE BIOLOGY

Wisconsin Fast Plants
University of Wisconsin-Madison
College of Agricultural and Life Sciences
Dept. of Plant Pathology
1630 Linden Dr.
Madison, WI 53706
1-800-462-7417
fastplants@calshp.cals.wisc.edu
http://fastplants.cals.wisc.edu

BALANCES

Ohaus Scale Corporation
29 Hanover Road
Florham Park, NJ 07932

MICROSCOPES AND MICROPROJECTORS

American Optical Corporation
Eggert and Sugar Roads
Buffalo, NY 14215

Bausch & Lomb, Inc.
1400 North Goodman Street
Rochester, NY 14602

Brock Optical
414 Lake Howell Road
Maitland, FL 32751-5907

Ken-A-Vision Manufacturing Company
5615 Raytown Road
Raytown, MO 64133

Swift Instruments, Inc.
P.O. Box 95016
San Jose, CA 95016

AQUARIA, TERRARIA, CAGES

Carolina Biological Supply Company
2700 York Road
Burlington, NC 27215

Jewel Aquarium Company
5005 West Armitage Avenue
Chicago, IL 60639

Science Kit, Inc.
777 E. Park Drive
Tonawanda, NY 14150

KITS AND MODELS

Delta Education, Inc.
P.O. Box 915
Hudson, NH 03051

Denoyer-Geppert Company
5235 N. Ravenswood Avenue
Chicago, IL 60640

NASCO Company
901 Janesville Avenue
Fort Atkinson, WI 53538

Science Kit, Inc.
777 E. Park Drive
Tonawanda, NY 14150

SOFTWARE

Scholastic Software & Multimedia
2931 East McCarty St.
Jefferson City, MO 65101
1-800-724-6527

Sunburst Educational Software
Dept. EG53, 101 Castleton St.
P.O. Box 100
Pleasantville, NY 10570
1-800-321-7511
http://www.nysunburst.com

APPENDIX

D

ENVIRONMENTS AND NUTRITION FOR CLASSROOM ANIMALS[1]

Animal	Environment	Nutrition[2]
Ants	Glass terrarium or large jar with dirt (covered with black paper)	Small food scraps or dead insects
Birds	Bird cage (ensure cage is large enough for bird to move freely)	Birdseed (nutritional mix from pet store—not wild bird seed)
Butterflies & Moths	Butterfly "tent" (sold in kits) or large jar with wire screen on top with small branches	Sugar water solution
Caterpillars	Medium-sized jar with holes in lid; include a small branch	Leaves (preferably near to where they were found)
Chameleons & Lizards	Aquarium with screened top; dirt, stones, and branches on bottom	Mealworms or live insects
Fish	Aquarium with gravel and filter (dechlorinate water before use)	Fish food from pet store (do not overfeed); brine shrimp
Frogs & Toads	Aquarium with shallow water and rocks to climb out of the water	Mealworms, small caterpillars, or live insects
Fruit Flies	Small jars with fine mesh covering	A small amount of overly ripe fruit
Guinea Pigs & Rats	Large animal cage with secure openings and an exercise wheel	Guinea pig food; small amounts of fresh fruit and vegetables
Hamsters, Gerbils, & Mice	Medium or large animal cage with secure openings and an exercise wheel	Hamster or gerbil food; small amounts of fresh fruit and vegetables

(continues on next page)

[1]Contact the National Science Teachers Association (1840 Wilson Blvd., Arlington, VA 22201-3000) for the Guidelines for Responsible Use of Animals in the Classroom.

[2]All animals require plenty of fresh water. To remove the chlorine from water, leave it standing overnight.

(continued)

Mealworms	Wide jar or plastic bucket with screen or mesh cover	Oatmeal and small slices of fresh apple
Newts & Salamanders	Aquarium with shallow water and rocks rising above water line	Mealworms and live insects
Rabbits	Large animal cage (rabbits will chew on cage, so avoid wood)	Rabbit pellets, fresh vegetables (avoid too much lettuce)
Snakes	Terrarium with secure openings; heating device (contact pet shop)	Live mice or insects (contact pet shop for specifics)
Spiders	Glass jar covered with screen	Live insects
Tadpoles	Aquarium ¼ filled with water and rocks above the water line	Small insects or finely chopped meat
Turtles (land)	Terrarium with non-poisonous plants and water pool	Mealworms, insects, earthworms; finely chopped vegetables
Turtles (aquatic)	Aquarium which is mostly water-covered, but with small land area	Mealworms, insects, earthworms; finely chopped vegetables

SUMMARY OF CHILDREN'S THINKING[3]

Thought Process	Intuitive Thought[4]	Concrete Operations	Formal Operations
Cause and Effect	Logic often contradictory, unpredictable. Events may occur by magic or for human convenience.	Contradictions avoided. Physical objects are linked to show cause and effect. Common-sense explanations may be wrong but logical.	Can separate logic from content. Systematic control of variables possible, as well as hypothetical "thought experiments," to test ideas.
Relative Thinking	Egocentric perceptions and language. Little grasp of how variables interrelate. Physical properties viewed in absolute, not relative, ways.	Perceptions of position and objects more objective. Aware of others' views. Some understanding of interrelated variables, when connected to concrete objects and pictures.	Understand relative position and motion. Can define and explain abstract concepts with other concepts or analogies. May temporarily show some egocentricity in propositions.
Classifying and Ordering	Sort one property at a time. Little or no class inclusion. Trial-and-error ordering in early part of stage.	Understand class inclusion principle. More consistent seriation with diverse objects. Can follow successive steps, less discrete thinking.	Can recombine groups into fewer, more abstract categories. Can form hierarchical systems.
Conservative Thinking	Mostly do not conserve. Perceptions dominate thinking. Center attention on one variable and do not compensate. Little or no reverse thinking.	Can reverse thinking, consider several variables and compensate. Conserve most of the Piagetian test concepts.	Conserve all of the Piagetian test concepts, with displaced and solid volume usually last.

---

[3]Based on a format suggested by Robert Mele.
[4]Intuitive thought is the last period of the preoperational stage.

STATE EDUCATION AGENCIES

Alabama
Alabama State Dept. of Education
Gordon Persons Bldg.
Montgomery, AL 36130

Alaska
State of Alaska
Dept. of Education
801 W. 10th St., Ste. 200
Juneau, AK 99801-1894

Arizona
Arizona Dept. of Education
1535 West Jefferson St.
Phoenix, AZ 85007

Arkansas
Arkansas Dept. of Education
4 State Capitol Mall
Little Rock, AR 72201

Bureau of Indian Affairs
Dept. of Interior, BIA
1849 C Street, NW
Mail Stop 3525, Code 521
MIB
Washington, DC 20240

California
State Dept. of Education
721 Capitol Mall, 3rd Floor
Sacramento, CA 95814

Colorado
Colorado Dept. of Education
201 East Colfax Ave.
Denver, CO 80203

Connecticut
State Dept. of Education
P.O. Box 2219, Rm. 369
Hartford, CN 06145

Delaware
State Dept. of Public Instruction
Townsend Bldg.
P.O. Box 1402
Dover, DE 19903

District of Columbia
Education Program
D.C. Public Schools
415 12th St., NW, Rm. 1004
Washington, DC 20004

Florida
Florida Dept. of Education
Florida Education Center, Ste. 522
Tallahassee, FL 32399

Georgia
Georgia Dept. of Education
1862 Twin Towers East
Atlanta, GA 30334

Hawaii
Education Program
189 Lunalilo Home Rd., 2nd Floor
Honolulu, HI 96825

Idaho
LaRon Smith, Mathematics and Science
Coordinator
Idaho State Dept. of Education
650 W. State St.
P.O. Box 83720
Boise, ID 83720-0027
(208) 332-6943
lsmith@sde.state.id.us

Illinois
Illinois State Board of Education
100 North First St.
Springfield, IL 62777-0001

Indiana
Indiana Dept. of Education
Rm. 229 State House
Indianapolis, IN 46204-2798

Iowa
W. Tony Heiting, Ph.D.
Consultant, Science Education
Bureau of Instructional Services
State of Iowa
Department of Education
Grimes State Office Building
Des Moines, IA 50319-0146
(515) 281-3249

Kansas
Kansas Dept. of Education
120 East 10th St.
Topeka, KS 66612-1103

Kentucky
Kentucky Dept. of Education
Capitol Plaza Tower, 500 Mero St.
Frankfort, KY 40601

Louisiana
State Dept. of Education
P.O. Box 94064
Baton Rouge, LA 70804-9064

Maine
Maine State Dept. of Education
State House Station #23
Augusta, ME 04333

Maryland
Maryland State Dept. of Education
200 West Baltimore St.
Baltimore, MD 21201-2595

Massachusetts
Massachusetts Dept. of Education
350 Main St.
Malden, MA 02148-5023
(617) 388-3300

Michigan
Michigan Dept. of Education
P.O. Box 30008
Lansing, MI 48909

Minnesota
Minnesota Dept. of Education
Capitol Square Bldg., Rm. 922
St. Paul, MN 55101

Mississippi
State Dept. of Education
Walter Sillers Bldg., Ste. 501
P.O. Box 771
Jackson, MS 39205-0771

Missouri
Missouri Dept. of Education
Dept. of Elementary & Secondary Education
P.O. Box 480
Jefferson, MO 65102

Montana
Office of Public Instruction
State Capitol Bldg.
Helena, MT 59620

Nebraska
Nebraska Dept. of Education
301 Centennial Mall South
P.O. Box 84987
Lincoln, NE 68509-4987

Nevada
Nevada Dept. of Education
Capitol Complex
Carson City, NV 89710

New Hampshire
New Hampshire Dept. of Education
1010 Pleasant St.
Concord, NH 03301

New Jersey
New Jersey Dept. of Education
Division of Standards and Assessment
CN 500
Trenton, NJ 08625-0500

New Mexico
State of New Mexico
Dept. of Education
300 Don Gaspar
Santa Fe, NM 87501-2786
(505) 827-6516

New York
New York State Education Dept.
Bureau of Professional Career
Opportunity Programs
Empire State Plaza
Cultural Education Center
Rm. 5C64
Albany, NY 12230

North Carolina
Dept. of Public Instruction
116 West Edenton St.
Raleigh, NC 27603-1712

North Dakota
Dept. of Public Instruction
State Capitol
Bismark, ND 58505

Ohio
Ohio Dept. of Education
65 South Front St.
Columbus, OH 43266-0208

Oklahoma
State Dept. of Education
Sandy Garrett
State Superintendent of Public Instruction
2500 North Lincoln Blvd.
Oklahoma City, OK 73105-4599
(405) 521-3301
fax: (405) 521-6205

Oregon
Oregon Dept. of Education
700 Pringle Parkway, S.S.
Salem, OR 97310

Pennsylvania
G. Kip Bollinger, Ed.D.
Science Education Adviser
Division of Arts and Science
Bureau of Curriculum and Instruction
Pennsylvania Department of Education
8th Floor, 333 Market Street
Harrisburg, PA 17126-0333
(717) 783-6598
TDD (717) 783-8445
pa@panet.mste.org

Puerto Rico
Office of Education
Office 809
Dept. of Education
Hato Rey, PR 00919

Rhode Island
Dr. Dennis Cheek
Coordinator of Mathematics,
Science & Technology
Rhode Island Department of Education
255 Westminster Street
Providence, RI 02902-3400
(401) 277-4600

South Carolina
South Carolina Dept. of Education
Curriculum Section
801 Rutledge Bldg.
Columbia, SC 29201

South Dakota
Paula L. Lind
Administrative Assistant
Department of Education
and Cultural Affairs
700 Governors Drive
Pierre, SD 57501-2291
(605) 773-3426
FAX: (605) 773-6139

Tennessee
Tennessee Dept. of Education
4th Floor Northwing
Cordell Hull Bldg.
Nashville, TN 37243-0388

Texas
J. W. Collins
Director of Science
Texas Education Agency
1701 N. Congress
Austin, Texas 78701

Utah
Utah Dept. of Education
250 East 500 South
Salt Lake City, UT 84111

Vermont
Vermont State Dept. of Education
120 State St.
Montpelier, VT 05602

Virginia
James Firebaugh, Jr.
Science Specialist
Virginia Dept. of Education
P.O. Box 2120
Richmond, VA 23218-2120
(804) 225-2651
fax (804) 786-1703
jfirebau@pen.k12.va.us

Washington
David Kennedy
Program Supervisor for Science
Office of Superintendent of Public Instruction
P.O. Box 47200
Olympia, WA 98504-7200

West Virginia
West Virginia Dept. of Education
1900 Kanawha Blvd., East, Rm. B-252
Charleston, WV 25305

Wisconsin
Dept. of Public Education
125 South Webster St.
P.O. Box 7841
Madison, WI 53707-7841

Wyoming
State Dept. of Education
241 Hathaway Bldg.
Cheyenne, WY 82002-0050

INDEX